Applied Multiple Regression/Correlation Analysis for the Behavioral Sciences

Third Edition

Applied Multiple Regression/Correlation Analysis for the Behavioral Sciences

Third Edition

Jacob Cohen
(deceased)
New York University

Patricia Cohen
New York State Psychiatric Institute
and
Columbia University College of Physicians and Surgeons

Stephen G. West
Arizona State University

Leona S. Aiken
Arizona State University

Routledge
Taylor & Francis Group

NEW YORK AND LONDON

Published 2015 by Routledge
605 Third Avenue, New York, NY 10017
2 Park Square, Milton Park, Abingdon, Oxon OX14 4RN

Routledge is an imprint of the Taylor & Francis Group, an informa business

ISBN 13: 978-0-8058-2223-6 (hbk)

Cover design by Kathryn Houghtaling Lacey

Library of Congress Cataloging-in-Publication Data

Applied multiple regression/correlation analysis for the behavioral sciences.—3rd ed. Jacob Cohen...[et al]
    Rev. ed. of: Applied multiple regression /correlation analysis for the behavioral sciences / Jacob Cohen,
Patricia Cohen. 2nd ed. 1983.
        p. cm.
    Includes bibliographical references and index.
    ISBN 0-8058-2223-2 (hard cover: alk. paper)
    1. Regression analysis. 2. Correlation (Statistics) 3. Social sciences—Statisical methods. I. Cohen, Jacob,
    1923—Applied multiple regression/correlation analysis for the behavioral sciences.
    HA31.3 .A67   2003
    519.5'36—dc21   2002072068

To **Gideon**, whose revisions continue
under the auspices of his own children
J.C. and P.C.

To **Jack**
S.G.W. and L.S.A.

Contents

Preface   **xxv**

Chapter 1:   Introduction   **1**

1.1   Multiple Regression/Correlation
      as a General Data-Analytic System   1
      1.1.1   Overview   1
      1.1.2   Testing Hypotheses Using Multiple
              Regression/Correlation: Some Examples   2
      1.1.3   Multiple Regression/Correlation in Prediction
              Models   3
1.2   A Comparison of Multiple Regression/Correlation
      and Analysis of Variance Approaches   4
      1.2.1   Historical Background   4
      1.2.2   Hypothesis Testing and Effect Sizes   5
1.3   Multiple Regression/Correlation
      and the Complexity of Behavioral Science   6
      1.3.1   Multiplicity of Influences   6
      1.3.2   Correlation Among Research Factors and Partialing   6
      1.3.3   Form of Information   7
      1.3.4   Shape of Relationship   8
      1.3.5   General and Conditional Relationships   9
1.4   Orientation of the Book   10
      1.4.1   Nonmathematical   11
      1.4.2   Applied   11
      1.4.3   Data-Analytic   12
      1.4.4   Inference Orientation and Specification Error   13
1.5   Computation, the Computer, and Numerical Results   14
      1.5.1   Computation   14

1.5.2   Numerical Results: Reporting and Rounding   14
1.5.3   Significance Tests, Confidence Intervals,
            and Appendix Tables   15
1.6   The Spectrum of Behavioral Science   16
1.7   Plan for the Book   16
1.7.1   Content   16
1.7.2   Structure: Numbering of Sections, Tables,
            and Equations   17
1.8   Summary   18

Chapter 2:   Bivariate Correlation and Regression   19

2.1   Tabular and Graphic Representations of Relationships   19
2.2   The Index of Linear Correlation Between Two Variables:
        The Pearson Product Moment Correlation Coefficient   23
2.2.1   Standard Scores: Making Units Comparable   23
2.2.2   The Product Moment Correlation as a Function of
            Differences Between z Scores   26
2.3   Alternative Formulas for the Product Moment
        Correlation Coefficient   28
2.3.1 r as the Average Product of z Scores   28
2.3.2   Raw Score Formulas for r 29
2.3.3   Point Biserial r 29
2.3.4   Phi (ϕ) Coefficient   30
2.3.5   Rank Correlation   31
2.4   Regression Coefficients: Estimating Y From X 32
2.5   Regression Toward the Mean   36
2.6   The Standard Error of Estimate and Measures of the Strength
        of Association   37
2.7   Summary of Definitions and Interpretations   41
2.8   Statistical Inference With Regression and Correlation Coefficients   41
2.8.1   Assumptions Underlying Statistical Inference With B_{YX},
            B_0, $\hat{Y}_i$, and r_{XY} 41
2.8.2   Estimation With Confidence Intervals   42
2.8.3   Null Hypothesis Significance Tests (NHSTs)   47
2.8.4   Confidence Limits and Null Hypothesis
            Significance Testing   50
2.9   Precision and Power   50
2.9.1   Precision of Estimation   50
2.9.2   Power of Null Hypothesis Significance Tests   51
2.10   Factors Affecting the Size of r 53
2.10.1   The Distributions of X and Y 53
2.10.2   The Reliability of the Variables   55
2.10.3   Restriction of Range   57
2.10.4   Part-Whole Correlations   59
2.10.5   Ratio or Index Variables   60
2.10.6   Curvilinear Relationships   62
2.11   Summary   62

Chapter 3:   Multiple Regression/Correlation With Two or More Independent Variables   **64**

3.1   Introduction: Regression and Causal Models   64
    3.1.1   What Is a Cause?   64
    3.1.2   Diagrammatic Representation of Causal Models   65
3.2   Regression With Two Independent Variables   66
3.3   Measures of Association With Two Independent Variables   69
    3.3.1   Multiple R and R^2 69
    3.3.2   Semipartial Correlation Coefficients and Increments to R^2 72
    3.3.3   Partial Correlation Coefficients   74
3.4   Patterns of Association Between Y and Two Independent Variables   75
    3.4.1   Direct and Indirect Effects   75
    3.4.2   Partial Redundancy   76
    3.4.3   Suppression in Regression Models   77
    3.4.4   Spurious Effects and Entirely Indirect Effects   78
3.5   Multiple Regression/Correlation With k Independent Variables   79
    3.5.1   Introduction: Components of the Prediction Equation   79
    3.5.2   Partial Regression Coefficients   80
    3.5.3 R, R^2, and Shrunken R^2 82
    3.5.4 sr and sr^2 84
    3.5.5 pr and pr^2 85
    3.5.6   Example of Interpretation of Partial Coefficients   85
3.6   Statistical Inference With k Independent Variables   86
    3.6.1   Standard Errors and Confidence Intervals for B and β 86
    3.6.2   Confidence Intervals for R^2 88
    3.6.3   Confidence Intervals for Differences Between Independent R^2s   88
    3.6.4   Statistical Tests on Multiple and Partial Coefficients   88
3.7   Statistical Precision and Power Analysis   90
    3.7.1   Introduction: Research Goals and the Null Hypothesis   90
    3.7.2   The Precision and Power of R^2 91
    3.7.3   Precision and Power Analysis for Partial Coefficients   93
3.8   Using Multiple Regression Equations in Prediction   95
    3.8.1   Prediction of Y for a New Observation   95
    3.8.2   Correlation of Individual Variables With Predicted Values   96
    3.8.3   Cross-Validation and Unit Weighting   97
    3.8.4   Multicollinearity   98
3.9   Summary   99

**Chapter 4:   Data Visualization, Exploration, and Assumption
                Checking: Diagnosing and Solving
                Regression Problems I**   **101**

4.1   Introduction   101
4.2   Some Useful Graphical Displays of the Original Data   102
      4.2.1   Univariate Displays   103
      4.2.2   Bivariate Displays   110
      4.2.3   Correlation and Scatterplot Matrices   115
4.3   Assumptions and Ordinary Least Squares Regression   117
      4.3.1   Assumptions Underlying Multiple Linear
               Regression   117
      4.3.2   Ordinary Least Squares Estimation   124
4.4   Detecting Violations of Assumptions   125
      4.4.1   Form of the Relationship   125
      4.4.2   Omitted Independent Variables   127
      4.4.3   Measurement Error   129
      4.4.4   Homoscedasticity of Residuals   130
      4.4.5   Nonindependence of Residuals   134
      4.4.6   Normality of Residuals   137
4.5   Remedies: Alternative Approaches When Problems Are Detected   141
      4.5.1   Form of the Relationship   141
      4.5.2   Inclusion of All Relevant Independent Variables   143
      4.5.3   Measurement Error in the Independent Variables   144
      4.5.4   Nonconstant Variance   145
      4.5.5   Nonindependence of Residuals   147
4.6   Summary   150

**Chapter 5:   Data-Analytic Strategies Using Multiple
                Regression/Correlation**   **151**

5.1   Research Questions Answered by Correlations and Their Squares   151
      5.1.1   Net Contribution to Prediction   152
      5.1.2   Indices of Differential Validity   152
      5.1.3   Comparisons of Predictive Utility   152
      5.1.4   Attribution of a Fraction of the XY Relationship to a
               Third Variable   153
      5.1.5   Which of Two Variables Accounts for More of the XY
               Relationship?   153
      5.1.6   Are the Various Squared Correlations in One Population
               Different From Those in Another Given the Same
               Variables?   154
5.2   Research Questions Answered by B Or β 154
      5.2.1   Regression Coefficients as Reflections of Causal
               Effects   154
      5.2.2   Alternative Approaches to Making B_{YX} Substantively
               Meaningful   154
      5.2.3   Are the Effects of a Set of Independent Variables on Two
               Different Outcomes in a Sample Different?   157

5.2.4 What Are the Reciprocal Effects of Two Variables on One Another? 157

5.3 Hierarchical Analysis Variables in Multiple Regression/Correlation 158
    5.3.1 Causal Priority and the Removal of Confounding Variables 158
    5.3.2 Research Relevance 160
    5.3.3 Examination of Alternative Hierarchical Sequences of Independent Variable Sets 160
    5.3.4 Stepwise Regression 161

5.4 The Analysis of Sets of Independent Variables 162
    5.4.1 Types of Sets 162
    5.4.2 The Simultaneous and Hierarchical Analyses of Sets 164
    5.4.3 Variance Proportions for Sets and the Ballantine Again 166
    5.4.4 B and β Coefficients for Variables Within Sets 169

5.5 Significance Testing for Sets 171
    5.5.1 Application in Hierarchical Analysis 172
    5.5.2 Application in Simultaneous Analysis 173
    5.5.3 Using Computer Output to Determine Statistical Significance 174
    5.5.4 An Alternative F Test: Using Model 2 Error Estimate From the Final Model 174

5.6 Power Analysis for Sets 176
    5.6.1 Determining n^* for the F Test of sR_B^2 with Model 1 or Model 2 Error 177
    5.6.2 Estimating the Population sR^2 Values 179
    5.6.3 Setting Power for n^* 180
    5.6.4 Reconciling Different n^*s 180
    5.6.5 Power as a Function of n 181
    5.6.6 Tactics of Power Analysis 182

5.7 Statistical Inference Strategy in Multiple Regression/Correlation 182
    5.7.1 Controlling and Balancing Type I and Type II Errors in Inference 182
    5.7.2 Less Is More 185
    5.7.3 Least Is Last 186
    5.7.4 Adaptation of Fisher's Protected t Test 187
    5.7.5 Statistical Inference and the Stage of Scientific Investigations 190

5.8 Summary 190

Chapter 6: Quantitative Scales, Curvilinear Relationships, and Transformations

193

6.1 Introduction 193
    6.1.1 What Do We Mean by Linear Regression? 193

6.1.2   Linearity in the Variables and Linear Multiple
Regression   194

6.1.3   Four Approaches to Examining Nonlinear Relationships
in Multiple Regression   195

6.2   Power Polynomials   196

6.2.1   Method   196

6.2.2   An Example: Quadratic Fit   198

6.2.3   Centering Predictors in Polynomial Equations   201

6.2.4   Relationship of Test of Significance of Highest Order
Coefficient and Gain in Prediction   204

6.2.5   Interpreting Polynomial Regression Results   205

6.2.6   Another Example: A Cubic Fit   207

6.2.7   Strategy and Limitations   209

6.2.8   More Complex Equations   213

6.3   Orthogonal Polynomials   214

6.3.1   The Cubic Example Revisited   216

6.3.2   Unequal n and Unequal Intervals   219

6.3.3   Applications and Discussion   220

6.4   Nonlinear Transformations   221

6.4.1   Purposes of Transformation and the Nature
of Transformations   221

6.4.2   The Conceptual Basis of Transformations and Model
Checking Before and After Transformation—Is It Always
Ideal to Transform?   223

6.4.3   Logarithms and Exponents; Additive and Proportional
Relationships   223

6.4.4   Linearizing Relationships   225

6.4.5   Linearizing Relationships Based on Strong Theoretical
Models   227

6.4.6   Linearizing Relationships Based on Weak Theoretical
Models   232

6.4.7   Empirically Driven Transformations in the Absence
of Strong or Weak Models   233

6.4.8   Empirically Driven Transformation for Linearization:
The Ladder of Re-expression and the
Bulging Rule   233

6.4.9   Empirically Driven Transformation for Linearization in
the Absence of Models: Box-Cox Family of Power
Transformations on Y 236

6.4.10   Empirically Driven Transformation for Linearization in
the Absence of Models: Box-Tidwell Family of Power
Transformations on X 239

6.4.11   Linearization of Relationships With Correlations: Fisher
z' Transform of r 240

6.4.12   Transformations That Linearize Relationships for Counts
and Proportions   240

6.4.13   Variance Stabilizing Transformations and Alternatives for
Treatment of Heteroscedasticity   244

6.4.14   Transformations to Normalize Variables   246

6.4.15   Diagnostics Following Transformation   247

6.4.16   Measuring and Comparing Model Fit   248
6.4.17   Second-Order Polynomial Numerical Example
          Revisited   248
6.4.18   When to Transform and the Choice of
          Transformation   249
6.5   Nonlinear Regression   251
6.6   Nonparametric Regression   252
6.7   Summary   253

Chapter 7:   Interactions Among Continuous Variables   255

7.1   Introduction   255
       7.1.1   Interactions Versus Additive Effects   256
       7.1.2   Conditional First-Order Effects in Equations Containing
                Interactions   259
7.2   Centering Predictors and the Interpretation of Regression Coefficients
       in Equations Containing Interactions   261
       7.2.1   Regression with Centered Predictors   261
       7.2.2   Relationship Between Regression Coefficients in the
                Uncentered and Centered Equations   262
       7.2.3   Centered Equations With No Interaction   262
       7.2.4   Essential Versus Nonessential Multicollinearity   264
       7.2.5   Centered Equations With Interactions   264
       7.2.6   The Highest Order Interaction in the Centered Versus
                Uncentered Equation   266
       7.2.7   Do Not Center Y 266
       7.2.8   A Recommendation for Centering   266
7.3   Simple Regression Equations and Simple Slopes   267
       7.3.1   Plotting Interactions   269
       7.3.2   Moderator Variables   269
       7.3.3   Simple Regression Equations   269
       7.3.4   Overall Regression Coefficient and Simple Slope at the
                Mean   270
       7.3.5   Simple Slopes From Uncentered Versus Centered
                Equations Are Identical   271
       7.3.6   Linear by Linear Interactions   271
       7.3.7   Interpreting Interactions in Multiple Regression and
                Analysis of Variance   272
7.4   Post Hoc Probing of Interactions   272
       7.4.1   Standard Error of Simple Slopes   272
       7.4.2   Equation Dependence of Simple Slopes and Their
                Standard Errors   273
       7.4.3   Tests of Significance of Simple Slopes   273
       7.4.4   Confidence Intervals Around Simple Slopes   274
       7.4.5   A Numerical Example   275
       7.4.6   The Uncentered Regression Equation Revisited   281
       7.4.7   First-Order Coefficients in Equations Without and With
                Interactions   281
       7.4.8   Interpretation and the Range of Data   282

7.5   Standardized Estimates for Equations Containing Interactions   282
7.6   Interactions as Partialed Effects: Building Regression Equations
       With Interactions   284
7.7   Patterns of First-Order and Interactive Effects   285
       7.7.1   Three Theoretically Meaningful Patterns of First-Order
                and Interaction Effects   285
       7.7.2   Ordinal Versus Disordinal Interactions   286
7.8   Three-Predictor Interactions in Multiple Regression   290
7.9   Curvilinear by Linear Interactions   292
7.10   Interactions Among Sets of Variables   295
7.11   Issues in the Detection of Interactions: Reliability, Predictor
       Distributions, Model Specification   297
       7.11.1   Variable Reliability and Power to Detect
                Interactions   297
       7.11.2   Sampling Designs to Enhance Power to Detect
                Interactions—Optimal Design   298
       7.11.3   Difficulty in Distinguishing Interactions Versus
                Curvilinear Effects   299
7.12   Summary   300

Chapter 8:   Categorical or Nominal Independent Variables   302

8.1   Introduction   302
       8.1.1   Categories as a Set of Independent Variables   302
       8.1.2   The Representation of Categories or Nominal
                Scales   302
8.2   Dummy-Variable Coding   303
       8.2.1   Coding the Groups   303
       8.2.2   Pearson Correlations of Dummy Variables
                With Y 308
       8.2.3   Correlations Among Dummy-Coded Variables   311
       8.2.4   Multiple Correlation of the Dummy-Variable Set
                With Y 311
       8.2.5   Regression Coefficients for Dummy Variables   312
       8.2.6   Partial and Semipartial Correlations for Dummy
                Variables   316
       8.2.7   Dummy-Variable Multiple Regression/Correlation
                and One-Way Analysis of Variance   317
       8.2.8   A Cautionary Note: Dummy-Variable-Like Coding
                Systems   319
       8.2.9   Dummy-Variable Coding When Groups Are Not
                Mutually Exclusive   320
8.3   Unweighted Effects Coding   320
       8.3.1   Introduction: Unweighted and Weighted Effects
                Coding   320
       8.3.2   Constructing Unweighted Effects Codes   321
       8.3.3   The R^2 and the r_{Yi}s for Unweighted Effects Codes   324
       8.3.4   Regression Coefficients and Other Partial Effects in
                Unweighted Code Sets   325

8.4   Weighted Effects Coding   328
 8.4.1   Selection Considerations for Weighted Effects Coding   328
 8.4.2   Constructing Weighted Effects   328
 8.4.3   The R^2 and $\tilde{R}^2$ for Weighted Effects Codes   330
 8.4.4   Interpretation and Testing of B With Unweighted Codes   331
8.5   Contrast Coding   332
 8.5.1   Considerations in the Selection of a Contrast Coding Scheme   332
 8.5.2   Constructing Contrast Codes   333
 8.5.3   The R^2 and $\tilde{R}^2$ 337
 8.5.4   Partial Regression Coefficients   337
 8.5.5   Statistical Power and the Choice of Contrast Codes   340
8.6   Nonsense Coding   341
8.7   Coding Schemes in the Context of Other Independent Variables   342
 8.7.1   Combining Nominal and Continuous Independent Variables   342
 8.7.2   Calculating Adjusted Means for Nominal Independent Variables   343
 8.7.3   Adjusted Means for Combinations of Nominal and Quantitative Independent Variables   344
 8.7.4   Adjusted Means for More Than Two Groups and Alternative Coding Methods   348
 8.7.5   Multiple Regression/Correlation With Nominal Independent Variables and the Analysis of Covariance   350
8.8   Summary   351

Chapter 9:   Interactions With Categorical Variables   354

9.1   Nominal Scale by Nominal Scale Interactions   354
 9.1.1   The 2 by 2 Design   354
 9.1.2   Regression Analyses of Multiple Sets of Nominal Variables With More Than Two Categories   361
9.2   Interactions Involving More Than Two Nominal Scales   366
 9.2.1   An Example of Three Nominal Scales Coded by Alternative Methods   367
 9.2.2   Interactions Among Nominal Scales in Which Not All Combinations Are Considered   372
 9.2.3   What If the Categories for One or More Nominal "Scales" Are Not Mutually Exclusive?   373
 9.2.4   Consideration of pr, β, and Variance Proportions for Nominal Scale Interaction Variables   374
 9.2.5   Summary of Issues and Recommendations for Interactions Among Nominal Scales   374
9.3   Nominal Scale by Continuous Variable Interactions   375
 9.3.1   A Reminder on Centering   375

9.3.2   Interactions of a Continuous Variable With
Dummy-Variable Coded Groups   375
9.3.3   Interactions Using Weighted or Unweighted Effects
Codes   378
9.3.4   Interactions With a Contrast-Coded Nominal
Scale   379
9.3.5   Interactions Coded to Estimate Simple Slopes
of Groups   380
9.3.6   Categorical Variable Interactions With Nonlinear Effects
of Scaled Independent Variables   383
9.3.7   Interactions of a Scale With Two or More Categorical
Variables   386
9.4   Summary   388

**Chapter 10: Outliers and Multicollinearity: Diagnosing
and Solving Regression Problems II   390**

10.1   Introduction   390
10.2   Outliers: Introduction and Illustration   391
10.3   Detecting Outliers: Regression Diagnostics   394
10.3.1   Extremity on the Independent Variables:
Leverage   394
10.3.2   Extremity on Y: Discrepancy   398
10.3.3   Influence on the Regression Estimates   402
10.3.4   Location of Outlying Points and Diagnostic
Statistics   406
10.3.5   Summary and Suggestions   409
10.4   Sources of Outliers and Possible Remedial Actions   411
10.4.1   Sources of Outliers   411
10.4.2   Remedial Actions   415
10.5   Multicollinearity   419
10.5.1   Exact Collinearity   419
10.5.2   Multicollinearity: A Numerical Illustration   420
10.5.3   Measures of the Degree of Multicollinearity   422
10.6   Remedies for Multicollinearity   425
10.6.1   Model Respecification   426
10.6.2   Collection of Additional Data   427
10.6.3   Ridge Regression   427
10.6.4   Principal Components Regression   428
10.6.5   Summary of Multicollinearity Considerations   429
10.7   Summary   430

Chapter 11: Missing Data   431

11.1   Basic Issues in Handling Missing Data   431
11.1.1   Minimize Missing Data   431
11.1.2   Types of Missing Data   432
11.1.3   Traditional Approaches to Missing Data   433

11.2   Missing Data in Nominal Scales   435
    11.2.1   Coding Nominal Scale X for Missing Data   435
    11.2.2   Missing Data on Two Dichotomies   439
    11.2.3   Estimation Using the EM Algorithm   440
11.3   Missing Data in Quantitative Scales   442
    11.3.1   Available Alternatives   442
    11.3.2   Imputation of Values for Missing Cases   444
    11.3.3   Modeling Solutions to Missing Data in Scaled Variables   447
    11.3.4   An Illustrative Comparison of Alternative Methods   447
    11.3.5   Rules of Thumb   450
11.4   Summary   450

Chapter 12: Multiple Regression/Correlation and Causal Models   452

12.1   Introduction   452
    12.1.1   Limits on the Current Discussion and the Relationship Between Causal Analysis and Analysis of Covariance   452
    12.1.2   Theories and Multiple Regression/Correlation Models That Estimate and Test Them   454
    12.1.3   Kinds of Variables in Causal Models   457
    12.1.4   Regression Models as Causal Models   459
12.2   Models Without Reciprocal Causation   460
    12.2.1   Direct and Indirect Effects   460
    12.2.2   Path Analysis and Path Coefficients   464
    12.2.3   Hierarchical Analysis and Reduced Form Equations   465
    12.2.4   Partial Causal Models and the Hierarchical Analysis of Sets   466
    12.2.5   Testing Model Elements   467
12.3   Models With Reciprocal Causation   467
12.4   Identification and Overidentification   468
    12.4.1   Just Identified Models   468
    12.4.2   Overidentification   468
    12.4.3   Underidentification   469
12.5   Latent Variable Models   469
    12.5.1   An Example of a Latent Variable Model   469
    12.5.2   How Latent Variables Are Estimated   471
    12.5.3   Fixed and Free Estimates in Latent Variable Models   472
    12.5.4   Goodness-of-Fit Tests of Latent Variable Models   472
    12.5.5   Latent Variable Models and the Correction for Attenuation   473
    12.5.6   Characteristics of Data Sets That Make Latent Variable Analysis the Method of Choice   474
12.6   A Review of Causal Model and Statistical Assumptions   475

12.6.1   Specification Error   475
12.6.2   Identification Error   475
12.7   Comparisons of Causal Models   476
12.7.1   Nested Models   476
12.7.2   Longitudinal Data in Causal Models   476
12.8   Summary   477

Chapter 13: Alternative Regression Models: Logistic, Poisson Regression, and the Generalized Linear Model   479

13.1   Ordinary Least Squares Regression Revisited   479
13.1.1   Three Characteristics of Ordinary Least Squares Regression   480
13.1.2   The Generalized Linear Model   480
13.1.3   Relationship of Dichotomous and Count Dependent Variables Y to a Predictor   481
13.2   Dichotomous Outcomes and Logistic Regression   482
13.2.1   Extending Linear Regression: The Linear Probability Model and Discriminant Analysis   483
13.2.2   The Nonlinear Transformation From Predictor to Predicted Scores: Probit and Logistic Transformation   485
13.2.3   The Logistic Regression Equation   486
13.2.4   Numerical Example: Three Forms of the Logistic Regression Equation   487
13.2.5   Understanding the Coefficients for the Predictor in Logistic Regression   492
13.2.6   Multiple Logistic Regression   493
13.2.7   Numerical Example   494
13.2.8   Confidence Intervals on Regression Coefficients and Odds Ratios   497
13.2.9   Estimation of the Regression Model: Maximum Likelihood   498
13.2.10 Deviances: Indices of Overall Fit of the Logistic Regression Model   499
13.2.11 Multiple R^2 Analogs in Logistic Regression   502
13.2.12 Testing Significance of Overall Model Fit: The Likelihood Ratio Test and the Test of Model Deviance   504
13.2.13 χ^2 Test for the Significance of a Single Predictor in a Multiple Logistic Regression Equation   507
13.2.14 Hierarchical Logistic Regression: Likelihood Ratio χ^2 Test for the Significance of a Set of Predictors Above and Beyond Another Set   508
13.2.15 Akaike's Information Criterion and the Bayesian Information Criterion for Model Comparison   509
13.2.16 Some Treachery in Variable Scaling and Interpretation of the Odds Ratio   509

13.2.17   Regression Diagnostics in Logistic Regression   512

13.2.18   Sparseness of Data   516

13.2.19   Classification of Cases   516

13.3   Extensions of Logistic Regression to Multiple Response Categories:
Polytomous Logistic Regression and Ordinal Logistic Regression   519

13.3.1   Polytomous Logistic Regression   519

13.3.2   Nested Dichotomies   520

13.3.3   Ordinal Logistic Regression   522

13.4   Models for Count Data: Poisson Regression and Alternatives   525

13.4.1   Linear Regression Applied to Count Data   525

13.4.2   Poisson Probability Distribution   526

13.4.3   Poisson Regression Analysis   528

13.4.4   Overdispersion and Alternative Models   530

13.4.5   Independence of Observations   532

13.4.6   Sources on Poisson Regression   532

13.5   Full Circle: Parallels Between Logistic and Poisson Regression,
and the Generalized Linear Model   532

13.5.1   Parallels Between Poisson and Logistic
Regression   532

13.5.2   The Generalized Linear Model Revisited   534

13.6   Summary   535

Chapter 14: Random Coefficient Regression and Multilevel Models   536

14.1   Clustering Within Data Sets   536

14.1.1   Clustering, Alpha Inflation, and the Intraclass
Correlation   537

14.1.2   Estimating the Intraclass Correlation   538

14.2   Analysis of Clustered Data With Ordinary Least Squares Approaches   539

14.2.1   Numerical Example, Analysis of Clustered Data With
Ordinary Least Squares Regression   541

14.3   The Random Coefficient Regression Model   543

14.4   Random Coefficient Regression Model and Multilevel Data Structure   544

14.4.1   Ordinary Least Squares (Fixed Effects) Regression
Revisited   544

14.4.2   Fixed and Random Variables   544

14.4.3   Clustering and Hierarchically Structured Data   545

14.4.4   Structure of the Random Coefficient Regression
Model   545

14.4.5   Level 1 Equations   546

14.4.6   Level 2 Equations   547

14.4.7   Mixed Model Equation for Random Coefficient
Regression   548

14.4.8   Variance Components—New Parameters in the
Multilevel Model   548

14.4.9   Variance Components and Random Coefficient Versus
Ordinary Least Squares (Fixed Effects)
Regression   549

14.4.10   Parameters of the Random Coefficient Regression Model: Fixed and Random Effects   550

14.5   Numerical Example: Analysis of Clustered Data With Random Coefficient Regression   550

14.5.1   Unconditional Cell Means Model and the Intraclass Correlation   551

14.5.2   Testing the Fixed and Random Parts of the Random Coefficient Regression Model   552

14.6   Clustering as a Meaningful Aspect of the Data   553

14.7   Multilevel Modeling With a Predictor at Level 2   553

14.7.1   Level 1 Equations   553

14.7.2   Revised Level 2 Equations   554

14.7.3   Mixed Model Equation With Level 1 Predictor and Level 2 Predictor of Intercept and Slope and the Cross-Level Interaction   554

14.8   An Experimental Design as a Multilevel Data Structure: Combining Experimental Manipulation With Individual Differences   555

14.9   Numerical Example: Multilevel Analysis   556

14.10   Estimation of the Multilevel Model Parameters: Fixed Effects, Variance Components, and Level 1 Equations   560

14.10.1   Fixed Effects and Variance Components   560

14.10.2   An Equation for Each Group: Empirical Bayes Estimates of Level 1 Coefficients   560

14.11   Statistical Tests in Multilevel Models   563

14.11.1   Fixed Effects   563

14.11.2   Variance Components   563

14.12   Some Model Specification Issues   564

14.12.1   The Same Variable at Two Levels   564

14.12.2   Centering in Multilevel Models   564

14.13   Statistical Power of Multilevel Models   565

14.14   Choosing Between the Fixed Effects Model and the Random Coefficient Model   565

14.15   Sources on Multilevel Modeling   566

14.16   Multilevel Models Applied to Repeated Measures Data   566

14.17   Summary   567

Chapter 15: Longitudinal Regression Methods   568

15.1   Introduction   568

15.1.1   Chapter Goals   568

15.1.2   Purposes of Gathering Data on Multiple Occasions   569

15.2   Analyses of Two-Time-Point Data   569

15.2.1   Change or Regressed Change?   570

15.2.2   Alternative Regression Models for Effects Over a Single Unit of Time   571

15.2.3   Three- or Four-Time-Point Data   573

15.3   Repeated Measure Analysis of Variance   573

15.3.1   Multiple Error Terms in Repeated Measure Analysis of Variance   574

15.3.2   Trend Analysis in Analysis of Variance   575

15.3.3   Repeated Measure Analysis of Variance in Which Time Is Not the Issue   576

15.4   Multilevel Regression of Individual Changes Over Time   578

15.4.1   Patterns of Individual Change Over Time   578

15.4.2   Adding Other Fixed Predictors to the Model   582

15.4.3   Individual Differences in Variation Around Individual Slopes   583

15.4.4   Alternative Developmental Models and Error Structures   584

15.4.5   Alternative Link Functions for Predicting Y From Time   586

15.4.6   Unbalanced Data: Variable Timing and Missing Data   587

15.5   Latent Growth Models: Structural Equation Model Representation of Multilevel Data   588

15.5.1   Estimation of Changes in True Scores   589

15.5.2   Representation of Latent Growth Models in Structural Equation Model Diagrams   589

15.5.3   Comparison of Multilevel Regression and Structural Equation Model Analysis of Change   594

15.6   Time Varying Independent Variables   595

15.7   Survival Analysis   596

15.7.1   Regression Analysis of Time Until Outcome and the Problem of Censoring   596

15.7.2   Extension to Time-Varying Independent Variables   599

15.7.3   Extension to Multiple Episode Data   599

15.7.4   Extension to a Categorical Outcome: Event-History Analysis   600

15.8   Time Series Analysis   600

15.8.1   Units of Observation in Time Series Analyses   601

15.8.2   Time Series Analyses Applications   601

15.8.3   Time Effects in Time Series   602

15.8.4   Extension of Time Series Analyses to Multiple Units or Subjects   602

15.9   Dynamic System Analysis   602

15.10   Statistical Inference and Power Analysis in Longitudinal Analyses   604

15.11   Summary   605

Chapter 16: Multiple Dependent Variables: Set Correlation   608

16.1   Introduction to Ordinary Least Squares Treatment of Multiple Dependent Variables   608

16.1.1   Set Correlation Analysis   608

16.1.2 Canonical Analysis 609

16.1.3 Elements of Set Correlation 610

16.2 Measures of Multivariate Association 610

16.2.1 $R_{Y,X}^2$, the Proportion of Generalized Variance 610

16.2.2 $T_{Y,X}^2$ and $P_{Y,X}^2$, Proportions of Additive Variance 611

16.3 Partialing in Set Correlation 613

16.3.1 Frequent Reasons for Partialing Variable Sets From the Basic Sets 613

16.3.2 The Five Types of Association Between Basic Y and X Sets 614

16.4 Tests of Statistical Significance and Statistical Power 615

16.4.1 Testing the Null Hypothesis 615

16.4.2 Estimators of the Population $R_{Y,X}^2$, $T_{Y,X}^2$, and $P_{Y,X}^2$ 616

16.4.3 Guarding Against Type I Error Inflation 617

16.5 Statistical Power Analysis in Set Correlation 617

16.6 Comparison of Set Correlation With Multiple Analysis of Variance 619

16.7 New Analytic Possibilities With Set Correlation 620

16.8 Illustrative Examples 621

16.8.1 A Simple Whole Association 621

16.8.2 A Multivariate Analysis of Partial Variance 622

16.8.3 A Hierarchical Analysis of a Quantitative Set and Its Unique Components 623

16.8.4 Bipartial Association Among Three Sets 625

16.9 Summary 627

APPENDICES

Appendix 1: The Mathematical Basis for Multiple Regression/Correlation and Identification of the Inverse Matrix Elements

631

A1.1 Alternative Matrix Methods 634

A1.2 Determinants 634

Appendix 2: Determination of the Inverse Matrix and Applications Thereof

636

A2.1 Hand Calculation of the Multiple Regression/Correlation Problem 636

A2.2 Testing the Difference Between Partial βs and Bs From the Same Sample 640

A2.3 Testing the Difference Between βs for Different Dependent Variables From a Single Sample 642

Appendix Tables   643

Table A t Values for $\alpha = .01, .05$ (Two Tailed)   643
Table B z' Transformation of r 644
Table C Normal Distribution   645
Table D F Values for $\alpha = .01, .05$ 646
Table E L Values for $\alpha = .01, .05$ 650
Table F Power of Significance Test of r at $\alpha = .01, .05$
         (Two Tailed)   652
Table G n^* to Detect r by t Test at $\alpha = .01, .05$
         (Two Tailed)   654

References   655
Glossary   671
Statistical Symbols and Abbreviations   683
Author Index   687
Subject Index   691

Preface

Origins and Background

This book had its origin over 30 years ago, when it became apparent to Jack Cohen that there were relationships between multiple regression and correlation (MRC) on the one hand and the analysis of variance (ANOVA) on the other which were undreamed of (or at least did not appear) in the standard textbooks with which he was familiar. On the contrary, the texts of the era treated MRC and ANOVA as wholly distinct systems of data analysis intended for types of research that differed fundamentally in design, goals, and types of variables. Some research, both statistical and bibliographic, confirmed the relationships noted and revealed yet others. These relationships served to enrich both systems in many ways, but it also became clear that multiple regression/correlation was potentially a very general system for analyzing data in the behavioral sciences, one that could incorporate the analysis of variance and covariance as special cases. An article outlining these possibilities was published in the quantitative methods section of *Psychological Bulletin* (J. Cohen, 1968),[1] and it has gone on to become one of the most cited articles in the *Bulletin's* history (Sternberg, 1992).[2] The volume and sources of early reprint requests and requests to reprint the article suggested that a responsive chord had been struck among behavioral scientists in diverse areas. It was also obvious that a book-length treatment was needed for adequacy of both systematic coverage and expository detail.

In 1969 Jack and Pat were married and began a happy collaboration, one of whose chief products is this book. (Another has been saluted on the dedication page of each edition.) During the preparation of the first edition of the book, the ideas of the 1968 paper were expanded, further systematized, tried out on data, and hardened in the crucible of our teaching, research, and consulting. We find this system, which has now attained broad usage in the behavioral sciences, to be surprisingly easy to teach and learn. The first edition of this book was published in 1975 and, following further development and revision of the ideas, the second edition was published in 1983.

Despite the continuing popularity of the second edition of this text, by the early 1990s Jack and Pat were very aware of the need to update and extend its coverage of new methods, options,

---

[1]Cohen, J. (1968). Multiple regression as a general data-analytic system. *Psychological Bulletin*, 70, 426–443.

[2]Sternberg, R. J. (1992). Psychological Bulletin's top 10 "hit parade". *Psychological Bulletin*, 112, 387–388.

and graphics in the regression field. The methods that Jack had done so much to promote were becoming so familiar to scientists in the field that they no longer needed an extensive elaboration of their virtues. New improved methods of regression diagnostics and graphics, multilevel analyses, logistic and other nominal dependent variable methods of regression, and treatment of longitudinal data made updating seem critical. New generations of computer software for multiple regression analysis had been developed, including "point and click" computer programs that now reside on the desktop computer of every researcher and student. These new programs have combined the wonderful virtues of flexibility and ease of use that have made multiple regression analysis even more accessible. However, this increased accessibility has also increased the risk that multiple regression may be used in a mindless manner by those unfamiliar with its basic concepts. This development made the need for continued clear coverage of the basic concepts of multiple regression even more apparent.

Because Jack and Pat were aware of the magnitude of the revisions that should be made, and because they wanted statistical experts who were working in fields central to psychological research, they invited Drs. Leona Aiken and Stephen West, another "multivariate couple," to collaborate on the revision. Jack and Pat particularly admired Aiken and West's book *Multiple Regression: Testing and Interpreting Interactions* and its extensive use of graphical presentations. Not surprisingly, when we all started to work together, we found that the revisions that Jack and Pat had originally envisioned were not sufficient to cover all the changes that we collectively thought to be important.

Jack's death in 1998 has made this revision much more difficult for the remaining three of us and, in some ways, more important. The four of us had planned the changes together, divided the tasks, and were well started, but there was still a lot of work to be done. We wanted to decrease the emphasis on significance tests and increase the recommendations for confidence intervals and effect size measures, which Jack was so active in promoting. Some of his last writing could be incorporated, but in other cases we needed to work these ideas in without his help.

The Audience for the Book

To describe the primary audience for whom this book is intended requires two dimensions. Substantively, this book is addressed to behavioral and social scientists. These terms have no sharply defined reference, but we intend them in the most inclusive sense to include the academic sciences of psychology, sociology, economics, branches of biology, political science, anthropology, and social epidemiology, as well as to those in business, health sciences, communication and other applied fields of behavioral research.

The other dimension of our intended audience, amount of background in statistics and research, covers an equally broad span. We are very pleased that the book serves both as a textbook for students and as a handbook for researchers. One particular feature of this book will be appreciated by many in both groups of readers: Its orientation is nonmathematical, applied, and data-analytic. This orientation is discussed in the introductory chapter, and will not be belabored here. Our experience has been that with few exceptions, both students and substantive researchers in the behavioral and social sciences often approach statistics with considerable wariness, and profit most from a verbal-conceptual exposition, rich in redundancy and concrete examples. This we have sought to supply.

As a textbook, whether used in a course at the graduate or advanced undergraduate level, it is assumed that students have already had a semester's introductory statistics course. Roughly the first half of the book can be used as the foundation of a solid one semester regression course. We anticipate that two full semesters would be necessary to cover the entire book. As a manual, the researcher's specific interests may dictate the sequence of reference to the chapters that follow. As much as possible, we attempted to write the book in a manner that minimizes the need to refer to previous chapters.

The Third Edition: Old and New

The text of this revision remains very much in the spirit of the previous editions: that is, in the words of one of us, "multiple regression in the service of the ego" (J. Cohen, 1964).[3] We are delighted that the behavioral and social sciences have increasingly moved away from the use of statistical tests as a kind of mathematical blessing on an investigation, and toward a data-analytic point of view that focuses on answering the questions that motivated the investigation. While we have tried to keep the overall conceptual tone of previous editions of the book, we have felt it necessary to make many modifications to reflect the current and developing practices in the field. These have included an increased emphasis on graphical presentations throughout. We have somewhat down-played the comparison of MRC to ANOVA, feeling that the battle between these methods is as close to being resolved as it will ever be, and that MRC is now clearly recognized as the more general method (as well as sometimes being supplanted by other methods that better address failure of its assumptions). In addition, we recognize that although ANOVA may still hold sway in some experimental fields, many of our readers in other behavioral sciences will not be very familiar with these statistical models. We also believe that the behavioral sciences have developed to the point where it is appropriate to begin emphasizing the reporting of regression results in meaningful units rather than relying heavily on correlational statistics.

Because of the widely positive response to our presentation of the basic regression ideas, Chapters 1 through 3 are only moderately modified. Chapter 1 begins with an outline of the general system of data analysis made possible by multiple regression/correlation methods. Beginning students may benefit from rereading Chapter 1 after they gain greater familiarity with the specifics of this system through their reading of later chapters. Chapter 2 begins "from scratch" with bivariate correlation and regression, and reviews elementary statistical concepts and terminology. Chapter 2 is not really intended to be a thorough, basic exposition, but rather its purpose is to refresh the reader's memory, and to affix the basic meanings of regression and correlation so firmly in the reader's mind that later exposition will be readily understood. Chapter 3 extends this basic understanding to models with multiple independent variables. Chapter 4, new to this edition, considers the assumptions of multiple regression and outlines alternative procedures that may be taken when they are not met. We have organized old and new issues of data-analytic strategy into an independent Chapter 5. The chapters on curvilinear relationships and transformations (Chapter 6) and interactions between continuous variables (Chapter 7) have been substantially rewritten to reflect a variety of new developments in these areas. Chapter 8 on nominal (group) variables has been moderately rewritten and Chapter 9 on group by continuous variable interactions has been extensively rewritten to reflect new developments. Chapter 10, new to this edition, considers the potential problems of outliers and multicollinearity and their remedies. Chapter 11 on missing data now incorporates the full armamentarium of new methods that have been developed to cope with this common problem. Chapter 12 on causal analysis is updated. Chapter 13, new to this edition, covers a variety of techniques including logistic regression and Poisson regression that are useful

---

[3]Cohen, J. (1964). Lecture given at the New York Academy of Medicine. Published as J. Cohen (1968). Prognostic factors in functional psychosis: A study in multivariate methodology. *Transactions of the New York Academy of Sciences*, 30(6), 833–840.

in addressing data sets in which the dependent variables are binary, ordered categories, or counts. Chapter 14, also new to this edition, provides an introduction to multilevel models for clustered data. Another new Chapter (15) introduces the reader to the many methods of answering research questions using longitudinal data. Finally, Jack's Chapter 16 on set correlation analysis of multiple dependent variables has been revised based on his presentation in the Keren and Lewis (1993) volume.[4]

We have many to thank for help in this revision, including Dorothy Castille who suggested and created the first entry list for the technical glossary, Henian Chen who programmed the multilevel longitudinal examples, Tom Crawford who matched the SEM models of longitudinal data with the multilevel models and assisted on other path models, Larkin McReynold who volunteered with the SPSS programming of many examples. Steven C. Pitts developed many of the key numerical examples in Chapters 2, 3, 7, and 10 as well as graphical displays used in Chapters 6, 7, 10, 13, and 14, and Kathy Gordon did these jobs for other examples in Chapters 2, 3, 5, 9, 11, 12, and 15. Jennifer L. Krull developed the multilevel example in Chapter 14. Oi-Man Kwok and Jonathan Butner wrote the computer syntax for examples in a number of chapters. Technical production help was also provided by Jonathan Butner, Kathy Gordon, Steven C. Pitts, and Justin McKenzie. We are thankful for the substantial guidance on each new or rewritten chapter that we were able to get from experts, many of whom were drawn from our friends and colleagues in the Society for Multivariate Experimental Psychology. Thanks are due to the following colleagues who reviewed some of the chapters for us, including (in alphabetical order) Jeremy Biesanz, Barbara Byrne, Dianne Chambless, Patrick Curran, Mindy Erchull, John W. Graham, Fumiaki Hamagami, Siek-Toon Khoo, Bruce Levin, William Mason, John J. McArdle, Roger Millsap, John Nesselroade, Jason Newsom, Abigail Panter, Mark Reiser, David Rindskopf, Patrick Shrout, and Aaron Taylor. We give special thanks to William F. Chaplin, Daniel W. King, Lynda A. King, Harry Reis, Steven Reise, and Leland Wilkinson, who provided insightful and informative reviews of the entire volume. Of course, the errors that may remain are entirely our own.

JACOB COHEN
PATRICIA COHEN
STEPHEN G. WEST
LEONA S. AIKEN

---

[4]Keren, G., and Lewis, C. (Eds.). (1993). *A handbook for data analysis in the behavioral sciences: Statistical issues*. Hillsdale, NJ: Erlbaum.

Applied Multiple Regression/Correlation Analysis for the Behavioral Sciences

Third Edition

1

Introduction

1.1 MULTIPLE REGRESSION/CORRELATION AS A GENERAL DATA-ANALYTIC SYSTEM

1.1.1 Overview

Multiple regression/correlation analysis (MRC) is a highly general and therefore very flexible data analytic system. Basic MRC may be used whenever a quantitative variable, the dependent variable (Y), is to be studied as a function of, or in relationship to, any factors of interest, the independent variables (IVs).[1] The broad sweep of this statement is quite intentional.

    1. The form of the relationship is not constrained: it may be simple or complex, for example, straight line or curvilinear, general or conditional, or combinations of these possibilities.

    2. The nature of the research factors expressed as independent variables is also not constrained. They may be quantitative or qualitative, main effects or interactions in the analysis of variance (ANOVA) sense, or covariates in the analysis of covariance (ANCOVA) sense. They may be correlated with each other or uncorrelated as in balanced factorial designs in ANOVA commonly found in laboratory experiments. They may be naturally occurring ("organismic" variables) like sex, diagnosis, IQ, extroversion, or years of education, or they may be planned experimental manipulations (treatment conditions). In short, virtually any information whose bearing on the dependent variable is of interest may be expressed as research factors.

    3. The nature of the dependent variable is also not constrained. Although MRC was originally developed for scaled dependent variables, extensions of the basic model now permit appropriate analysis of the full range of dependent variables including those that are of the form of categories (e.g., ill vs. not ill) or ordered categories.

    4. Like all statistical analyses, the basic MRC model makes assumptions about the nature of the data that are being analyzed and is most confidently conducted with "well-behaved" data that meet the underlying assumptions of the basic model. Statistical and graphical methods now part of many statistical packages make it easy for the researcher to determine whether

---

[1] In this book we typically employ Y to indicate a dependent variable and IV to represent an independent variable to indicate their role in the statistical analysis without any *necessary* implication of the existence or direction of causal relationship between them.

1

estimates generated by the basic MRC model are likely to be misleading and to take appropriate actions. Extensions of the basic MRC model include appropriate techniques for handling "badly behaved" or missing data and other data problems encountered by researchers.

The MRC system presented in this book has other properties that make it a powerful analytic tool. It yields measures of the magnitude of the total effect of a factor on the dependent variable as well as of its partial (unique, net) relationship, that is, its relationship over and above that of other research factors. It also comes fully equipped with the necessary apparatus for statistical hypothesis testing, estimation, construction of confidence intervals, and power analysis. Graphical techniques allow clear depictions of the data and of the analytic results. Last, but certainly not least, MRC is a major tool in the methods of causal (path, structural equation) analysis. Thus, MRC is a versatile, all-purpose system of analyzing the data over a wide range of sciences and technologies.

1.1.2 Testing Hypotheses Using Multiple Regression/Correlation: Some Examples

Multiple regression analysis is broadly applicable to hypotheses generated by researchers in the behavioral sciences, health sciences, education, and business. These hypotheses may come from formal theory, previous research, or simply scientific hunches. Consider the following hypotheses chosen from a variety of research areas:

1. In health sciences, Rahe, Mahan, and Arthur (1970) hypothesized that the amount of major life stress experienced by an individual is positively related to the number of days of illness that person will experience during the following 6 months.

2. In sociology, England, Farkas, Kilbourne, and Dou (1988) predicted that the size of the positive relationship between the number of years of job experience and workers' salaries would depend on the percentage of female workers in the occupation. Occupations with a higher percentage of female workers were expected to have smaller increases in workers' salaries than occupations with a smaller percentage of female workers.

3. In educational policy, there is strong interest in comparing the achievement of students who attend public vs. private schools (Coleman, Hoffer, & Kilgore, 1982; Lee & Bryk, 1989). In comparing these two "treatments" it is important to control statistically for a number of background characteristics of the students such as prior academic achievement, IQ, race, and family income.

4. In experimental psychology, Yerkes and Dodson (1908) proposed a classic "law" that performance has an inverted U-shaped relationship to physiological arousal. The point at which maximum performance occurs is determined by the difficulty of the task.

5. In health sciences, Aiken, West, Woodward, and Reno (1994) developed a predictive model of women's compliance versus noncompliance (a binary outcome) with recommendations for screening mammography. They were interested in the ability of a set of health beliefs (perceived severity of breast cancer, perceived susceptibility to breast cancer, perceived benefits of mammography, perceived barriers to mammography) to predict compliance over and above several other sets of variables: demographics, family medical history, medical input, and prior knowledge.

Each of these hypotheses proposes some form of relationship between one or more factors of interest (independent variables) and an outcome (dependent) variable. There are usually other variables whose effects also need to be considered, for reasons we will be discussing in this text. This book strongly emphasizes the critical role of theory in planning MRC analyses. The researcher's task is to develop a statistical model that will accurately estimate the relationships among the variables. Then the power of MRC analysis can be brought to bear to test the hypotheses and provide estimations of the size of the effects. However, this task cannot be carried out well if the actual data are not evaluated with regard to the assumptions of the statistical model.

1.1.3 Multiple Regression/Correlation in Prediction Models

Other applications of MRC exist as well. MRC can be used in practical prediction problems where the goal is to forecast an outcome based on data that were collected earlier. For example, a college admissions committee might be interested in predicting college GPA based on high school grades, college entrance examination (SAT or ACT) scores, and ratings of students by high school teachers. In the absence of prior research or theory, MRC can be used in a purely exploratory fashion to identify a collection of variables that strongly predict an outcome variable. For example, coding of the court records for a large city could identify a number of characteristics of felony court cases (e.g., crime characteristics, defendant demographics, drug involvement, crime location, nature of legal representation) that might predict the length of sentence. MRC can be used to identify a minimum set of variables that yield the best prediction of the criterion for the data that have been collected (A. J. Miller, 1990). Of course, because this method will inevitably capitalize on chance relationships in the original data set, replication in a new sample will be critical. Although we will address purely predictive applications of MRC in this book, our focus will be on the MRC techniques that are most useful in the testing of scientific hypotheses.

In this chapter, we initially consider several issues that are associated with the application of MRC in the behavioral sciences. Some disciplines within the behavioral sciences (e.g., experimental psychology) have had a misperception that MRC is only suitable for nonexperimental research. We consider how this misperception arose historically, note that MRC yields identical statistical tests to those provided by ANOVA yet additionally provides several useful measures of the size of the effect. We also note some of the persisting differences in data-analytic philosophy that are associated with researchers using MRC rather than ANOVA. We then consider how the MRC model nicely matches the complexity and variety of relationships commonly observed in the behavioral sciences. Several independent variables may be expected to influence the dependent variable, the independent variables themselves may be related, the independent variables may take different forms (e.g., rating scales or categorical judgments), and the form of the relationship between the independent and dependent variables may also be complex. Each of these complexities is nicely addressed by the MRC model. Finally, we consider the meaning of causality in the behavioral sciences and the meanings of control. Included in this section is a discussion of how MRC and related techniques can help rule out at least some explanations of the observed relationships. We encourage readers to consider these issues at the beginning of their study of the MRC approach and then to reconsider them at the end.

We then describe the orientation and contents of the book. It is oriented toward practical data analysis problems and so is generally nonmathematical and applied. We strongly encourage readers to work through the solved problems, to take full advantage of the programs for three major computer packages and data sets included with the book, and, most important, to learn MRC by applying these techniques to their own data. Finally, we provide a brief overview of the content of the book, outlining the central questions that are the focus of each chapter.

1.2 A COMPARISON OF MULTIPLE REGRESSION/CORRELATION AND ANALYSIS OF VARIANCE APPROACHES

MRC, ANOVA, and ANCOVA are each special cases of the *general linear model* in mathematical statistics.[2] The description of MRC in this book includes extensions of conventional MRC analysis to the point where it is essentially equivalent to the general linear model. It thus follows that any data analyzable by ANOVA/ANCOVA may be analyzed by MRC, whereas the reverse is not the case. For example, research designs that study how a scaled characteristic of participants (e.g., IQ) and an experimental manipulation (e.g., structured vs. unstructured tasks) jointly influence the subjects' responses (e.g., task performance) cannot readily be fit into the ANOVA framework. Even experiments with factorial designs with unequal cell sample sizes present complexities for ANOVA approaches because of the nonindependence of the factors, and standard computer programs now use a regression approach to estimate effects in such cases. The latter chapters of the book will extend the basic MRC model still further to include alternative statistical methods of estimating relationships.

1.2.1 Historical Background

Historically, MRC arose in the biological and behavioral sciences around 1900 in the study of the natural covariation of observed characteristics of samples of subjects, including Galton's studies of the relationship between the heights of fathers and sons and Pearson's and Yule's work on educational issues (Yule, 1911). Somewhat later, ANOVA/ANCOVA grew out of the analysis of agricultural data produced by the controlled variation of treatment conditions in manipulative experiments. It is noteworthy that Fisher's initial statistical work in this area emphasized the multiple regression framework because of its generality (see Tatsuoka, 1993). However, multiple regression was often computationally intractable in the precomputer era: computations that take milliseconds by computer required weeks or even months to do by hand. This led Fisher to develop the computationally simpler, equal (or proportional) sample size ANOVA/ANCOVA model, which is particularly applicable to planned experiments. Thus multiple regression and ANOVA/ANCOVA approaches developed in parallel and, from the perspective of the substantive researchers who used them, largely independently. Indeed, in certain disciplines such as psychology and education, the association of MRC with nonexperimental, observational, and survey research led some scientists to perceive MRC to be less scientifically respectable than ANOVA/ANCOVA, which was associated with experiments.

Close examination suggests that this guilt (or virtue) by association is unwarranted—the result of the confusion of data-analytic method with the logical considerations that govern the inference of causality. Experiments in which different treatments are applied to randomly assigned groups of subjects and there is no loss (attrition) of subjects permit unambiguous inference of causality; the observation of associations among variables in a group of randomly selected subjects does not. Thus, interpretation of a finding of superior early school achievement of children who participate in Head Start programs compared to nonparticipating children depends on the design of the investigation (Shadish, Cook, & Campbell, 2002; West, Biesanz, & Pitts, 2000). For the investigator who randomly assigns children to Head Start versus Control programs, attribution of the effect to program content is straightforward. For the investigator who simply observes whether children whose parents select Head Start programs have higher school achievement than those who do not, causal inference becomes less certain. Many other possible differences (e.g., child IQ; parent education) may exist between

---

[2]For the technically minded, our primary focus will be on the "fixed" version of these models, representing the most common usage of the general linear model in the behavioral sciences.

the two groups of children that could potentially account for any findings. But each of the investigative teams may analyze their data using either ANOVA (or equivalently a t test of the mean difference in school achievement) or MRC (a simple one-predictor regression analysis of school achievement as a function of Head Start attendance with its identical t test). The logical status of causal inference is a function of how the data were produced, not how they were analyzed (see further discussion in several chapters, especially in Chapter 12).

1.2.2 Hypothesis Testing and Effect Sizes

Any relationship we observe, whether between independent variables (treatments) and an outcome in an experiment or between independent variables and a "dependent" variable in an observational study, can be characterized in terms of the strength of the relationship or its effect size (ES). We can ask how much of the total variation in the dependent variable is produced by or associated with the independent variables we are studying. One of the most attractive features of MRC is its automatic provision of regression coefficients, proportion of variance, and correlational measures of various kinds, all of which are kinds of ES measures. We venture the assertion that, despite the preoccupation of the behavioral sciences, the health sciences, education, and business with quantitative methods, the level of consciousness in many areas about strength of observed relationships is at a surprisingly low level. This is because concern about the statistical significance of effects has tended to pre-empt attention to their magnitude (Harlow, Mulaik, & Steiger, 1997). Statistical significance only provides information about whether the relationship exists at all, often a question of trivial scientific interest, as has been pointed out in several commentaries (e.g., J. Cohen, 1994; Meehl, 1967). The level of statistical significance reflects the sample size, incidental features of the design, the sampling of cases, and the nature of the measurement of the dependent variable; it provides only a very pale reflection of the effect size. Yet many research reports, at least implicitly, confuse the issues of effect size and level of statistical significance, using the latter as if it meant the former (Gigerenzer, 1993).

Part of the reason for this unfortunate tendency is that traditional ANOVA/ANCOVA yields readily interpretable F and t ratios for significance testing and differences between cell means for interpretation of the direction of the effect, but no standardized index of effect size. When the dependent measure is in commonly understood units, such as yield of cotton per acre in agricultural research or dollars of income in economic research, the difference in means provides an informative measure. In the social sciences mean differences may also be informative, providing that some method of establishing meaningful measurement units has been accomplished. However, such unit establishment is often not the case, a problem discussed further in Section 5.2. In such a case standardized measures of effect size provided by the MRC analysis often permit more straightforward interpretation. Indeed, researchers in the ANOVA/ANCOVA tradition have become aware of standardized measures of effect size because of the rise of meta-analytic approaches that provide quantitative summaries of entire research literatures (e.g., Rosenthal, 1991). Some journal editors have also begun to encourage or even require inclusion of standardized effect size measures in articles published in their journals.

In addition to effect size measures in original (raw) and standardized units, the MRC system routinely provides several measures of the proportion of variance accounted for (the squares of simple, multiple, partial, and semipartial correlation coefficients). These measures of effect size are unit free and are easily understood and communicated. Each of the measures comes with its significance test value for the null hypothesis (F or t) so that no confusion between the two issues of *whether* and *how much* need arise.

1.3 MULTIPLE REGRESSION/CORRELATION
AND THE COMPLEXITY OF BEHAVIORAL SCIENCE

The greatest virtue of the MRC system is its capacity to represent, with high fidelity, the types and the complexity of relationships that characterize the behavioral sciences. The word *complexity* is itself used here in a complex sense to cover several issues.

1.3.1 Multiplicity of Influences

The behavioral sciences inherited from older branches of empirical inquiry the simple experimental paradigm: Vary a single presumed causal factor (C) and observe its effects on the dependent variable (Y) while holding constant other potential factors. Thus, $Y = f(C)$; that is, to some degree, variation in Y is a function of controlled variation in C. This model has been, and continues to be, an effective tool of inquiry in the physical sciences, engineering, and in some areas of the behavioral sciences. A number of areas within the physical sciences and engineering typically deal with a few distinct causal factors, each measured in a clear-cut way, and each in principle independent of others.

However, as one moves to the broad spectrum of the basic and applied behavioral sciences ranging from physiological psychology to cultural anthropology to evaluation of educational programs, the number of potential causal factors increases, their representation in measures becomes increasingly uncertain, and weak theories abound and compete. Consider the following set of dependent variables from selected areas of the behavioral sciences, health sciences, education, and business: number of presidential vetoes (political science), extent of women's participation in the labor force (sociology), distance from home to work (geography), reaction time (experimental psychology), migration rate (demography), depression (clinical psychology), kinship system (anthropology), new business startups (economics), compliance with medical regime (health sciences), school achievement (education), and personnel turnover (business). A few moment's reflection about the context in which each of these is embedded suggests the multiplicity of both the potential causal factors and the forms of their relationships to the dependent variables. Given several research factors, C, D, E, etc., to be studied, one might use the single-factor paradigm repeatedly in a program of research: $Y = f(C)$, then $Y = f(D)$, then $Y = f(E)$, etc. But MRC permits the far more efficient simultaneous examination of the influences of multiple factors; that is, $Y = f(C, D, E,$ etc.). Moreover, techniques such as structural equation analysis use interlocking regression equations to estimate formal models of causal processes derived from complex substantive theories.

1.3.2 Correlation Among Research Factors and Partialing

A far more important type of complexity than the sheer multiplicity of research factors lies in the effect of relationships among them. The simplest condition is that in which the factors $C, D, E, \ldots$ are statistically unrelated (orthogonal) to each other, as is the case in experiments in which the subject's level on each factor is under the experimenter's control and equal (or proportional) numbers of subjects are represented at each combination of factors. The overall importance of each factor in the experiment can be unambiguously determined because its independence of the other factors assures that its effects on Y cannot overlap with the effects of the others. Consider an experiment in which the apparent age (30 vs. 40) and sex (male, female) of a communicator are manipulated and their separate and joint effects on attitude change of male subjects is observed. The orthogonality of the factors is assured by having equal numbers of subjects in each of the four cells defined by the possible combinations of gender and age of the communicator (30-year-old male, 30-year-old female, 40-year-old male, 40-year-old female). No part of the difference in overall Y means for the two communicator ages can be attributed to their gender, nor can any part of the difference in the overall Y means for the two sexes be attributed to their ages.

Complexity arises when one departs from equal or proportional numbers of subjects in different conditions, because the independent variables are no longer independent. If in an experiment, the majority of the 40-year-olds were male and the majority of the 30-year-olds were female, then any difference between male and female communicators in the overall Y means would be confounded with (correlated with) communicator age. The age and sex effects would no longer be additive. Many issues in the behavioral sciences are simply inaccessible to true experiments and can only be addressed by the systematic observation of phenomena as they occur in their natural context. In nature, factors that influence Y are generally correlated with one another. Thus, if attitudes toward abortion (Y) are studied in a sample of survey respondents as a function of political party (C), religious background (D), and socioeconomic status (E), it is likely that C, D, and E will be correlated with each other. Relationships with Y, taken singly, will not accurately represent their separate influences, because of correlations among the factors (see Section 3.4). This is the familiar phenomenon of redundancy among correlated independent variables with regard to what they explain. The Y relationship with each of the independent variables overlaps to some degree with their relationships with other variables in the statistical model. This, in turn, requires a concept of the unique ("partialed") relationship of each variable with Y, in the context of the other variables in the model. This picture is often sharply different from that provided by looking at each factor singly. For example, it might be argued that the apparent influence of political party on attitudes toward abortion is entirely attributable to the relationship of party affiliation to religious preference or socioeconomic status. Such a pattern of results suggests that the apparent influence of political party on attitudes when appraised by itself may be "spurious"; that is, within subgroups that are homogeneous with regard to religious background and socioeconomic status, there is no difference on the average between members of one party and members of the other. Detailed attention to the relationships *among* potentially causal independent variables and how these bear on Y is the hallmark of causal analysis, and may be accomplished by MRC.

MRC's capability for assessing unique or partial relationships is perhaps its most important feature. Even a small number of research factors define many alternative causal systems. Some of these causal systems will be implausible because of considerations of prior research findings, logic, or research design (e.g., in a longitudinal design variables that occur later in time may be ruled out as potential causes of earlier variables). However, selection among the remaining causal systems is greatly facilitated by the ability, using MRC, of assessing the unique effect of a research factor, statistically controlling for (partialing) the effects of any desired set of other factors. Correlation does not prove causation; however, the absence of correlation implies the *absence* of the existence of a causal relationship. Thus, the skillful use of MRC can invalidate causal alternatives, assist researchers in choosing between competing theories, and help disentangle multiple influences through its partialing feature.

1.3.3 Form of Information

Variables employed in MRC may represent several different levels of measurement, of which it is often useful to distinguish the following (S. S. Stevens, 1951, 1958):

1. *Ratio scales.*   These are equal interval scales with a true zero point, a point at which there is none of whatever the scale is measuring. Only such scales make statements such as "John weighs twice as much as Jim" or "Mary earns two-thirds as much as Jane" sensible.

Some examples of ratio scale measures include inches, pounds, seconds, size of group, dollars, distance from hospital, years in prison, and literacy rate.

2. *Interval scales.*   These scales have equal intervals but are measured from an arbitrary point. For example, the Fahrenheit temperature scale uses the temperature at which a certain concentration of salt water freezes to represent 0. Values on the scale of less than 0 can and do occur. Many psychological and sociological indices are at this level, for example, scores on tests of intelligence, special abilities, achievement, personality, temperament, vocational interest, and social attitude. Such scales may not have a meaningful zero value at all.

3. *Ordinal scales.*   Only the relative positions within a specific collection are signified by the values of ordinal scales. These scales do not have either equal intervals or a true zero point. Examples of ordinal scales include simple rankings of subjects in a sample as well as re-expressions of such rankings into percentiles, deciles, and quartiles.

4. *Nominal scales.*   Nominal (categorical) scales involve simple classification of subjects into categories. The categories of nominal scales represent distinguishable qualities without a natural order or other quantitative properties. Examples include ethnic group, experimental treatment condition, place of birth, religion, marital status, psychiatric diagnosis, type of family structure, political party, public versus private sector, and gender. The set of categories are usually mutually exclusive and exhaustive. Thus, nominal scales are sets of groups that differ on some qualitative attribute.

This classification scheme is not exhaustive of quantitative scales, and others have been proposed. For example, psychological test scores are unlikely to measure with exactly equal intervals and it may be argued that they fall between interval and ordinal scales. Also, some rating scales frequently used in psychological research are not covered by Stevens' conception of levels of measurement. For example, scales like "0 = never, 1 = seldom, 2 = sometimes, 3 = often, and 4 = always" have a defined zero point, but intervals of dubious equality, although for most purposes they are treated as if they are approximately equal.

Basic MRC analysis can potentially consider information at any single level or any mixture of these levels of measurement. Ratio- and interval-level independent variables can be directly included in MRC models. Nominal variables can be expressed as coded variables (e.g., male = 0; female = 1), as will be discussed in Chapters 2, 8, and 9. Ordinal IVs may be treated as if they were interval variables in MRC models, and the results of the analyses may often be satisfactory. However, such an employment of these variables requires special caution, as is discussed further in Chapter 4. On the dependent variable side, Y may be measured at any of the levels of measurement, but the basic MRC model will usually work best if the data are interval or ratio. Some types of dependent variables may lead to violations of basic assumptions of the MRC model. In such cases, generalizations of the basic MRC model (the generalized linear model) can lead to improvements in the accuracy of the results over the basic MRC model (discussed in Chapter 13). This capacity of MRC and its generalizations to use information in almost any form, and to mix forms as necessary, is an important part of its adaptive flexibility.

1.3.4 Shape of Relationship

Consider the relationship $Y = f(C)$, where Y is a measure of poor health such as number of days of illness per year. For some factors the relationship may be well described by a straight line on the usual graph, for example, if C is daily cigarette consumption. Or, adequate description may require that the line be curved; for example, if C is age in years, the very young and the elderly are more often sick than young and middle-aged adults. Or, the shape may not be definable, as when C is a nominal variable like sex, ethnic background, or religion. When multiple research factors are being studied simultaneously, each may relate to Y (and each other) in any of these ways. Thus, when we write $Y = f(C, D, E, ...)$, f (as a function of) potentially covers a variety of complex functions that are readily brought under the sway of MRC.

How so? Many readers will know that MRC is often (and properly) referred to as *linear* MRC and may well be under the impression that correlation and regression are restricted to the study of straight-line relationships. This mistaken impression is abetted by the common usage of *linear* to mean "rectilinear" (straight line) and *nonlinear* to mean "curvilinear" (curved line). What is meant by *linear* in the MRC framework is any relationship of the form

$$(1.1.1) \qquad\qquad Y = a + bU + cV + dW + eX + \cdots$$

where the lowercase letters are constants (either positive or negative) and the capital letters are variables. Y is said to be "linear in the variables U, V, etc." because it may be estimated by taking certain amounts (b, c, etc.) of each variable, and the constant a, and simply adding them together. In the fixed regression model framework in which we operate, there is no constraint on the nature of the IVs.[3] To illustrate this, consider substituting other variables for specific variables in the equation. For example, we could replace U and V in Eq. (1.1.1) with U and V^2, resulting in $Y = a + bU + cV^2$. Or, we could replace W with the logarithm of Z, resulting in $Y = a + d\log(Z)$. Or, we could replace X with a code variable representing sex (S, which takes values $0 =$ male and $1 =$ female), $Y = a + eS$. As our substitutions illustrate, the variables may be chosen to define relationships of *any* shape, rectilinear or curvilinear, or of no shape at all for unordered nominal independent variables, as well as all the complex combinations of these which multiple factors can produce.

Multiple regression equations are, indeed, linear; they are exactly of the form of Eq. (1.1.1). Yet they can be used to describe such a complex relationship as the length of psychiatric hospital stay as a function of ratings of patient symptoms on admission, diagnosis, age, sex, and average length of prior hospitalizations. This complex relationship is patently not rectilinear (straight line), yet it is readily described by a linear multiple regression equation.

To be sure, most relationships studied in the behavioral sciences are not of this order of complexity. But, the critical point is the capacity of MRC to represent any degree or type of shape—complexity is yet another of the important features which make it truly a *general* data-analytic system.

1.3.5 General and Conditional Relationships

Some relationships between Y and some factor C remain the same in regard to both degree and form despite variation in other factors D, E, F. In the MRC context, we will call such relationships *general* or *unconditional*: Readers familiar with ANOVA will know them as *main effects*. For example, suppose Y is a measure of visual acuity and C is age. In our example, both the form and degree of the relationship between visual acuity and age may remain the same under varying conditions of education level (D), ethnic group (E), and sex (F). The relationship between Y and C can then be said to be general insofar as the other specific factors are concerned. Note that this generality holds regardless of the form and degree of relationship between Y (visual acuity) and D, E, and F, between C (age) and D, E, and F, or among

---

[3]As we will note in Section 3.3, the "fixed" model we use throughout much of this book implies that we have generated or preselected the values of the IVs to which we wish to generalize.

D, E, and F. The Y–C relationship can thus be considered unconditional with regard to, or independent of, D, E, and F.

Now consider the same research factors, but with Y as a measure of attitudes toward abortion. The form and/or degree of relationship of age to Y is now almost certain to vary as a function of one or more of the other factors: it may be stronger or shaped differently at lower educational levels than higher (D), and/or in one ethnic group or another (E), and/or for men compared to women (F). The relationship of Y to C is now said to be conditional on D and/or E and/or F. In ANOVA contexts, such relationships are called *interactions*. For example, if the C–Y relationship is not constant over different values of D, there is said to be a $C \times D$ (age by educational level) interaction. Greater complexity is also possible: The C–Y relationship may be constant over levels of D taken by themselves, and over levels of E taken by themselves, yet may be conditional on the *combination* of D and E levels. Such a circumstance would define a "three-way" interaction, represented as $C \times D \times E$. Interactions of even higher order, and thus even more complex forms of conditionality, are theoretically possible, although rarely reliably found because of the very large sample size typically required to detect them.

Some behavioral science disciplines have found it useful to discriminate two types of conditional relationships.[4] *Moderation* indicates that the strength of the relationship between C and Y is *reduced* as the value of D increases. For example, researchers interested in the relationship between stress and illness report that social support moderates (weakens or buffers) this relationship. In contrast, *augmentation* or synergy means that the strength of the relationship between C and Y is *increased* as the value of D increases. Thus, moderation and augmentation describe particular forms of conditional relationships.

One facet of the complexity of the behavioral sciences is the frequency with which such conditional relationships are encountered. Relationships among variables often change with changes in experimental conditions (treatments, instructions, even experimental assistants), age, sex, social class, ethnicity, diagnosis, religion, personality traits, geographic area, etc. As essential as is the scientific task of estimating relationships between independent and dependent variables, it is also necessary to identify the conditions under which these estimates hold or change.

In summary, the generality of the MRC system of data analysis appropriately complements the complexity of the behavioral sciences, which complexity includes multiplicity and correlation among potential causal influences, a variety of forms in which information is couched, and variations in the shape and conditionality of relationships. Multiple regression/correlation also provides a full yield of measures of effect size with which to quantify various aspects of the strength of relationships (proportions of variance and correlation and regression coefficients). Finally, these measures are subject to statistical hypothesis testing, estimation, construction of confidence intervals, and power-analytic procedures.

1.4 ORIENTATION OF THE BOOK

This book was written to serve as a textbook and manual in the application of the MRC system for data analysis by students and practitioners in diverse areas of inquiry in the behavioral sciences, health sciences, education, and business. As its authors, we had to make many

---

[4]Elsewhere moderation may be used to describe both forms of conditional relationship. Whether a relationship may be considered to be moderated or augmented in the sense used here is entirely dependent on the (often arbitrary) direction of scoring of the IVs involved.

decisions about its level, breadth, emphasis, tone, and style of exposition. Readers may find it useful, at the outset, to have our orientation and the basis for these decisions set forth.

1.4.1 Nonmathematical

Our presentation of MRC is generally as conceptually oriented and nonmathematical as we could make it. Of course, MRC is itself a product of mathematical statistics, based on matrix algebra, calculus, and probability theory. There is little question that such a background makes possible a level of insight otherwise difficult to achieve. However, it is also our experience that some mathematically sophisticated scientists may lack the conceptual frame that links the mathematical procedures to the substantive scientific task in a particular case. When new mathematical procedures are introduced, we attempt to convey an intuitive conceptual rather than a rigorous mathematical understanding of the procedure. We have included a glossary at the end of the book in which the technical terms employed repeatedly in the book are given a brief conceptual definition. We hope that this aid will enable readers who have forgotten the meaning of a term introduced earlier to refresh their memories. Of course, most of these same terms also appear in the index with notation on the many times they may have been used. A separate table at the end of the book reviews the abbreviations used for the statistical terms in the book.

We thus abjure mathematical proofs, as well as unnecessary offhand references to mathematical concepts and methods not likely to be understood by the bulk of our audience. In their place, we heavily emphasize detailed and deliberately redundant verbal exposition of concrete examples. Our experience in teaching and consulting convinces us that our audience is richly endowed in the verbal, logical, intuitive kind of intelligence that makes it possible to understand how the MRC system works, and thus use it effectively (Dorothy Parker said, "Flattery will get you anywhere.") This kind of understanding is eminently satisfactory (as well as satisfying), because it makes possible effective use of the system. We note that to drive a car, one does not need to be a physicist, nor an automotive engineer, nor even a highly skilled auto mechanic, although some of the latter's skills are useful when one is stuck on the highway. That is the level we aim for.

We seek to make up for the absence of mathematical proofs by providing demonstrations instead. For example, the regression coefficient for a dichotomous or binary (e.g., male–female) independent variable that is scored 0–1 equals the difference between the two groups' Y means. Instead of offering the six or seven lines of algebra that would constitute a mathematical proof, we demonstrate that it holds using a small set of data. True, this proves nothing, because the result may be accidental, but curious readers can check it out using their own or our data (and we urge that such checks be made throughout). Whether it is checked or not, we believe that most of our audience will profit more from the demonstration than the proof. If the absence of formal proof bothers some readers from Missouri (the "show me" state), all we can do is pledge our good faith.

1.4.2 Applied

The first word in this book's title is *applied*. Our heavy stress on illustrations serves not only the function of clarifying and demonstrating the abstract principles being taught, but also that of exemplifying the kinds of applications possible. We attend to statistical theory only insofar as sound application makes it necessary. The emphasis is on "how to do it." This opens us to the charge of writing a "cookbook," a charge we deny because we do not neglect the whys and wherefores. If the charge is nevertheless pressed, we can only add the observation that in the kitchen, cookbooks are likely to be more useful than textbooks in organic chemistry.

1.4.3 Data-Analytic

Mathematical statisticians proceed from exactly specified premises such as independent random sampling, normality of distributions, and homogeneity of variance. Through the exercise of ingenuity and appropriate mathematical theory, they arrive at exact and necessary consequences (e.g., the F distribution, statistical power functions). They are, of course, fully aware that no set of real data will exactly conform to the formal premises from which they start, but this is not properly their responsibility. As all mathematicians do, they work with abstractions to produce formal models whose "truth" lies in their self-consistency. Borrowing their language, we might say that inequalities are symmetrical: Just as behavioral scientists are not mathematicians, mathematicians are not behavioral scientists.

The behavioral scientist relies very heavily on the fruits of the labors of theoretical statisticians. Taken together with contributions from substantive theory and previous empirical research, statistical models provide guides for teasing out meaning from data, setting limits on inference, and imposing discipline on speculation (Abelson, 1995). Unfortunately, in the textbooks addressed to behavioral scientists, statistical methods have often been presented more as harsh straightjackets or Procrustean beds than as benign reference frameworks. Typically, a method is presented with some emphasis on its formal assumptions. Readers are advised that the failure of a set of data to meet these assumptions renders the method invalid. Alternative analytic strategies may not be offered. Presumably, the offending data are to be thrown away.

Now, this is, of course, a perfectly ridiculous idea from the point of view of working scientists. Their task is to contrive situations that yield information about substantive scientific issues—*they must and will analyze their data*. In doing so, they will bring to bear, in addition to the tools of statistical analysis and graphical display of the data, their knowledge of theory, past experience with similar data, hunches, and good sense, both common and uncommon (Krantz, 1999). They attempt to apply the statistical model that best matches their data; however, they would rather risk analyzing their data using a less than perfect model than not at all. For them, data analysis is not an end in itself, but the next-to-last step in a scientific process that culminates in providing information about the phenomenon. This is by no means to say that they need not be painstaking in their efforts to generate and perform analyses of the data. They need to develop statistical models to test their preferred scientific hypothesis, to rule out as many competing explanations for the results as they can, and to detect new relationships that may be present in the data. But, at the end they must translate these efforts into substantive information.

Most happily, the distinction between data analysis and statistical analysis has been made and given both rationale and respectability by one of our foremost mathematical statisticians, John Tukey. In his seminal *The Future of Data Analysis* (1962), Tukey describes data analysis as the special province of scientists with substantial interest in methodology. Data analysts employ statistical analysis as the most important tool in their craft, but they employ it together with other tools, and in a spirit quite different from that which has come to be associated with it from its origins in mathematical statistics. Data analysis accepts "inadequate" data, and is thus prepared to settle for "indications" rather than conclusions. It risks a greater frequency of errors in the interest of a greater frequency of occasions when the right answer is "suggested." It compensates for cutting some statistical corners by using scientific as well as mathematical judgment, and by relying upon self-consistency and repetition of results. Data analysis operates like a detective searching for clues that implicate or exonerate likely suspects (plausible hypotheses) rather than seeking to prove out a balance. In describing data analysis, Tukey has provided insight and rationale into the way good scientists have always related to data.

The spirit of this book is strongly data-analytic, in exactly this sense. We offer a variety of statistical models and graphical tools that are appropriate for common research questions in the behavioral sciences. We offer straightforward methods of examining whether the assumptions of the basic fixed-model MRC are met, and provide introductions to alternative analytic approaches that may be more appropriate when they are not. At the same time, we are aware that some data sets will fail to satisfy the assumptions of any standard statistical model, and that even when identified there may be little that the data analyst can do to bring the data "into line." We recognize the limits on inference in such cases but are disposed to treat the limits as broad rather than narrow. We justify this by mustering whatever technical evidence there is in the statistical literature (especially evidence of the "robustness" of statistical tests), and by drawing upon our own and others' practical experience, even upon our intuition, all in the interest of getting on with the task of making data yield their meaning. If we risk error, we are more than compensated by having a system of data analysis that is general, sensitive, and fully capable of reflecting the complexity of the behavioral sciences and thus of meeting the needs of behavioral scientists. And we will reiterate the injunction that no conclusions from a given set of data can be considered definitive: Replication is essential to scientific progress.

1.4.4 Inference Orientation and Specification Error

As noted earlier, perhaps the single most important reason for the broad adoption of MRC as a data-analytic tool is the possibility that it provides for taking into account—"controlling statistically or partialing"—variables that may get in the way of inferences about the influence of other variables on our dependent variable Y. These operations allow us to do statistically what we often cannot do in real life—separate the influences of variables that often, or even usually, occur together. This is often critically important in circumstances in which it is impossible or unethical to actually control one or more of these related variables. However, the centrality of this operation makes it critically important that users of these techniques have a basic, sound understanding of what partialing influences does and does not entail.

In emphasizing the extraction of meaning from data we will typically focus primarily on potential problems of "specification error" in the estimates produced in our analyses. Specification errors are errors of inference that we make because of the way we analyze our data. They include the assumption that the relationship between the dependent variable Y and each of the independent variables (IVs) is linear (constant over the range of the independent variables) when it is not, and that the relationships of some IVs to Y do not vary as a function of other IVs, when they do. When we attempt to make causal inferences on the basis of the relationships expressed in our MRC analyses, we may also make other kinds of specification errors, including assuming that Y is dependent on the IVs when some of the IVs are dependent on Y, or that the relationship between Y and certain IVs is causal when these relationships reflect the influence of common causes or confounders. Or assuming that the estimated relationship reflects the relationship between Y and the theoretically implicated ("true") IV when it only reflects the relationship between Y and an imperfectly measured representative of the theoretically implicated IV. More technically, specification errors may include the conclusion that some relationship we seem to have uncovered in our sample data generalizes to the population, when our statistical analyses are biased by distributional or nonindependence problems in the data.

1.5 COMPUTATION, THE COMPUTER,
AND NUMERICAL RESULTS

1.5.1 Computation

Like all mathematical procedures, MRC makes computational demands. The amount of computation increases with the size of the problem. Indeed, Darlington and Boyce (1982) estimate that computation time increases roughly with k^5, where k is the number of IVs. Early in the book, in our exposition of bivariate correlation and regression and MRC with two independent variables, we give the necessary details with small worked examples for calculation by hand calculator. This is done because the intimate association with the arithmetic details makes plain to the reader the nature of the process: *exactly* what is being done, with what purpose, and with what result. With one to three independent variables, where the computation is easy, not only can one see the fundamentals, but a basis is laid down for generalization to many variables.

With most real problems, MRC requires the use of a computer. An important reason for the rapid increase in the use of MRC during the past three decades is the computer revolution. Widely available computers conduct analyses in milliseconds that would have taken months or even years in Fisher's time. Statistical software has become increasingly user friendly, with versions that allow either simple programming or "point and click" analysis. Graphical routines that permit insightful displays of the data and the results of statistical analyses have become increasingly available. These advances have had the beneficial effect of making the use of MRC analysis far faster and easier than in the past.

We have deliberately placed the extensive calculational details of the early chapters outside the body of the text to keep them from distracting attention from our central emphasis: understanding how the MRC system works. We strongly encourage readers to work through the details of the many worked illustrations using both a hand calculator and a statistical package. These can help provide a basic understanding of the MRC system and the statistical package.

But readers should then apply the methods of each chapter to *data of their own* or data with which they are otherwise familiar. The highest order of understanding is achieved from the powerful synergism of the application of unfamiliar methods to familiar data.

Finally, we caution readers about an unintended by-product of the ease of use of current statistical packages: Users can now easily produce misleading results. Some simple commonsense checks can often help avoid errors. Careful initial examination of simple statistics (means; correlations; number of cases) and graphical displays can often provide a good sense of the data, providing a baseline against which the results of more complicated analyses can be compared. We encourage readers using new software to try out the analysis first on a previously analyzed data set, and we include such data sets for the worked examples in the book, for which analyses have been carried out on the large SAS, SPSS, and SYSTAT statistical programs. Achieving a basic understanding of the MRC system and the statistical packages as well as careful checking of one's results is an important prerequisite to publication. There is no guarantee that the peer review process in journals will detect incorrect analyses.

1.5.2 Numerical Results: Reporting and Rounding

Statistical packages print out numerical results to several decimal places. For comparison purposes, we follow the general practice in this book of reporting computed correlation and regression coefficients rounded to two places (or significant digits) and squared coefficients rounded to three. When working with a hand calculator, the reader should be aware that small rounding errors will occur. Checks that agree within a few points in the third decimal may thus be taken as correct.

Following Ehrenberg (1977), we encourage readers to be conservative in the number of significant digits that are reported in their research articles. Despite the many digits of accuracy that characterize modern statistical programs, this level of accuracy only applies to the sample data. Estimates of population parameters are far less accurate because of sampling error. For the sample correlation (r) to provide an estimate of the population correlation (ρ) that is accurate to *two* decimal places would require as many as 34,000 cases (J. Cohen, 1990).

1.5.3 Significance Tests, Confidence Intervals, and Appendix Tables

Most behavioral scientists employ a hybrid of classical Fisherian and Neyman-Pearson null hypothesis testing (see Gigerenzer, 1993; Harlow, Mulaik, & Steiger, 1997), in which the probability of the sample result given that the null hypothesis is true, p, is compared to a prespecified significance criterion, α. If $p <$ (is less than) α, the null hypothesis is rejected and the sample result is deemed statistically significant at the α level of significance. The null hypothesis as typically specified is that the value of the parameter corresponding to the sample result is 0; other values can be specified based on prior research.

A more informative way of testing hypotheses in many applications is through the use of confidence intervals. Here an interval is developed around the sample result that would theoretically include the population value $(1 - \alpha)\%$ of the time in repeated samples. Used in conjunction with MRC procedures, the center of the confidence interval provides an estimate of the strength of the relationship and the width of the confidence interval provides information about the accuracy of that estimate. The lower and upper limits of the confidence interval show explicitly just how small and how large the effect size in the population (be it a regression coefficient, multiple R^2, or partial r) might be. Incidentally, if the population value specified by the null hypothesis is not contained in the confidence interval, the null hypothesis is rejected.

The probability of the sample result given that the null hypothesis is true, p, is based on either the t or F distribution in basic MRC. Nearly all statistical packages now routinely compute exact values of p for each significance test. We also provide tables of F and t for $\alpha = .05$ and $\alpha = .01$. These values are useful for the construction of confidence intervals and for simple problems which can be solved with a hand calculator. The $\alpha = .05$ criterion is widely used as a standard in the behavioral sciences. The $\alpha = .01$ criterion is sometimes used by researchers as a matter of taste or tradition in their research area. We support this tradition when there are large costs of falsely rejecting the null hypothesis; however, all too frequently researchers adopt the $\alpha = .01$ level because they erroneously believe that this decision will necessarily make their findings stronger and more meaningful. The $\alpha = .01$ level is often used as a partial control on the incidence of spuriously significant results when a large number of hypothesis tests are being conducted. The choice of α also depends importantly on considerations of statistical power (the probability of rejecting the null hypothesis), which is discussed in several places, particularly in Section 4.5. We present tables for statistical power analysis in the Appendix; several programs are commercially available for conducting statistical power analyses on personal computers (e.g., Borenstein, Cohen, & Rothstein, 2001).

The statistical tables in the Appendix were largely abridged from Owen (1962) and from J. Cohen (1988). The entry values were selected so as to be optimally useful over a wide range of MRC applications. In rare cases in which the needed values are not provided, linear interpolation is sufficiently accurate for almost all purposes. Should more extensive tables be required, Owen (1962) and Pearson and Hartley (1970) are recommended. Some statistical packages will also compute exact p values for any specified df for common statistical distributions such as t, F, and χ^2.

1.6 THE SPECTRUM OF BEHAVIORAL SCIENCE

When we address behavioral scientists, we are faced with an exceedingly heterogeneous audience. They range in level from student to experienced investigator and possess from modest to fairly advanced knowledge of statistical methods. With this in mind, we assume a minimum background for the basic exposition of the MRC system. When we must make assumptions about background that may not hold for some of our readers, we try hard to keep everyone on board. In some cases we use boxes in the text to present more technical information, which provides a greater understanding of the material. The boxes can be skipped on first reading without loss of continuity.

But it is with regard to substantive interests and investigative methods and materials that our audience is of truly mind boggling diversity. Behavioral science itself covers areas of "social", "human", and even "life" sciences—everything from the physiology of behavior to cultural anthropology, in both their "basic science" and "applied science" aspects. Add in health sciences, education, and business, and the substantive range becomes immense. Were it not for the fact that the methodology of science is inherently more general than its substance, a book of this kind would not be possible. This permits us to address substantive researchers whose primary interests lie in a bewildering variety of fields.

We have sought to accommodate to this diversity, even to capitalize upon it. Our illustrative examples are drawn from different areas, assuring the comfort of familiarity for most of our readers at least some of the time. Their content is presented at a level that makes them intellectually accessible to nonspecialists. We try to use the nontechnical discussion of the examples in a way that may promote some methodological cross-fertilization between fields of inquiry. Our hope is that this discussion may introduce better approaches to fields where data have been analyzed using traditional rather than more optimal procedures.

1.7 PLAN FOR THE BOOK

1.7.1 Content

Following this introductory chapter, we continue by introducing the origins and meanings of the coefficients that represent the relationship between two variables (Chapter 2). Chapter 3 extends these concepts and measures first to two independent variables and then to any larger number of independent variables. Chapter 4 expands on the graphical depiction of data, and particularly on the identification of data problems, and methods designed to improve the fit of the data to the assumptions of the statistical model. Chapter 5 describes the strategies that a researcher may use in applying MRC analyses to complex substantive questions, including selecting the appropriate statistical coefficients and significance tests. It continues by describing two widely useful techniques, hierarchical (sequential) analyses of data and the analysis of independent variables grouped into structural or functional sets.

Chapters 6 and 7 describe and illustrate the methods of identifying nonlinear and conditional relationships between independent variables and Y, beginning with methods for representing curvilinearity in linear equations. This chapter is followed by detailed presentations of the treatment and graphic display of interactions between scaled variables in their relationship with Y. Chapter 8 continues with the consideration of sets of independent variables representing mutually exclusive categories or groups. Relationships between scaled measures and Y may vary between sample subgroups; techniques for assessing and describing these interactions are reviewed in Chapter 9.

Chapter 10 presents the problem of multicollinearity among predictors and methods of controlling its extent. Chapter 11 details the full range of methods for coping with missing data in MRC, and the considerations appropriate for choosing among them.

Chapter 12 expands on the discussion of MRC applications to causal hypotheses that is found in earlier chapters and introduces the reader to some of the more complex methods of estimating such models and issues relevant to their employment.

Chapter 13 describes uses of the generalized linear model to analyze dependent variables that are dichotomous, ordered categories, or counts of rare phenomena. Chapter 14 introduces the reader to the multilevel analysis of data clusters arising from nonindependent sampling or treatment of participants.

Chapter 15 provides an introduction to a whole range of methods of analyzing data characterized by multiple observations of units over time. Beginning with simple repeated measure ANOVA and two time-point MRC, the chapter presents an overview of how the substantive questions and the structure of the data combine to suggest a choice among available sophisticated data analytic procedures.

The final chapter presents a multivariate method called set correlation that generalizes MRC to include sets (or partialed sets) of dependent variables and in so doing, generalizes multivariate methods and yields novel data-analytic forms.

For a more detailed synopsis of the book's contents, the reader is referred to the summaries at the ends of the chapters. The data for almost all examples in the book are also provided on the accompanying CD-ROM, along with the command codes for each of the major statistical packages that will yield the tabular and other findings presented in the chapters.

A note on notation. We have tried to keep the notation simultaneously consistent with the previous editions of this book and with accepted practice, insofar as possible. In general, we employ Greek letters for population estimates, but this convention falls down in two places. First, β is used conventionally both for the standardized regression coefficient and for the power: We have followed these conventions. Second, the maximum likelihood estimations methods discussed in Chapters 13 and 14 use a range of symbols, including Greek letters, designed to be distinct from those in use in OLS. We also use P and Q $(= P - 1.0)$ to indicate proportions of samples, to distinguish this symbol from $p =$ probability.

We have attempted to help the reader keep the major concepts in mind in two ways. We have included a glossary of technical terms at the end of the book, so that readers of later chapters may refresh their recall of terms introduced earlier in the book. We have also included a listing of the abbreviations of statistical terms, tests, and functions. In addition there are two technical appendices, as well as the appendix Tables.

One more difference between this edition and previous editions may be noted. In the introductory Chapter 2 we originally introduced equations using the sample standard deviation, with n in the denominator. This forced us into repeated explanations when later statistics required a shift to the sample-based population estimate with $n - 1$ in the denominator. The advantage was simplicity in the early equations. The serious disadvantage is that every statistical program determines sd with $n - 1$ in the denominator, and so students trying to check sds, z scores and other statistics against their computer output will be confused. In this edition we employ the population estimate sd consistently and adjust early equations as necessary.

1.7.2 Structure: Numbering of Sections, Tables, and Equations

Each chapter is divided into major sections, identified by the chapter and section numbers, for example, Section 5.4.3 ("Variance Proportions for Sets and the Ballantine Again") is the third subsection of Section 5.4. Further subdivisions are not numbered, but titled with an italicized heading.

Tables, figures, and equations within the body of the text are numbered consecutively within major sections. Thus, for example, Figure 5.4.1 is the first figure in Section 5.4, and Eq. (2.6.5) is the fifth equation in Section 2.6. We follow the usual convention of giving equation numbers in parentheses. A similar plan is followed in the two appendices. The reference statistical tables make up a separate appendix and are designated as Appendix Tables A through G.

On the accompanying data disk each chapter has a folder; within that folder each example for which we provide data and syntax/command files in SAS, SPSS, and SYSTAT has a folder.

1.8 SUMMARY

This introductory chapter begins with an overview of MRC as a data-analytic system, emphasizing its generality and superordinate relationship to the analysis of variance/covariance (Section 1.1). MRC is shown to be peculiarly appropriate for the behavioral sciences in its capacity to accommodate the various types of complexity that characterize them: the multiplicity and correlation among causal influences, the varieties of form of information and shape of relationship, and the frequent incidence of conditional (interactive) relationships. The special relevance of MRC to the formal analysis of causal models in described (Section 1.2).

The book's exposition of MRC is nonmathematical, and stresses informed application to scientific and technological problems in the behavioral sciences. Its orientation is "data analytic" rather than statistical analytic, an important distinction that is discussed. Concrete illustrative examples are heavily relied upon (Section 1.3).

The popularity of MRC in the analysis of nonexperimental data for which manipulation of variables is impossible or unethical hinges on the possibility of statistical control or partialing. The centrality of this procedure, and the various kinds of errors of inferences that can be made when the equations include specification error are discussed (Section 1.4).

The means of coping with the computational demands of MRC are briefly described and largely left to the computer, with details relegated to appendices so as not to distract the reader's attention from the conceptual issues (Section 1.5). We acknowledge the heterogeneity of background and substantive interests of our intended audience, and discuss how we try to accommodate to it and even exploit it to pedagogical advantage (Section 1.6).

The chapter ends with a brief outline of the book and the scheme by which sections, tables, figures, and equations are numbered.

2

Bivariate Correlation and Regression

One of the most general meanings of the concept of a relationship between a pair of variables is that knowledge with regard to one of the variables carries information about the other. Information about the height of a child in elementary school has implications for the probable age of the child, and information about the occupation of an adult can lead to more accurate guesses about her income level than could be made in the absence of that information.

2.1 TABULAR AND GRAPHIC REPRESENTATIONS OF RELATIONSHIPS

Whenever data have been gathered on two quantitative variables for a set of subjects or other units, the relationship between the variables may be displayed graphically by means of a scatterplot.

For example, suppose we have scores on a vocabulary test and a digit-symbol substitution task for 15 children (see Table 2.1.1). If these data are plotted by representing each child as a point on a graph with vocabulary scores on the horizontal axis and the number of digit symbols on the vertical axis, we would obtain the scatterplot seen in Fig. 2.1.1. The circled dot, for example, represents Child 1, who obtained a score of 5 on the vocabulary test and completed 12 digit-symbol substitutions.

When we inspect this plot, it becomes apparent that the children with higher vocabulary scores tended to complete more digit symbols (d-s) and those low on vocabulary (v) scores were usually low on d-s as well. This can be seen by looking at the average of the d-s scores, M_{d_v}, corresponding to each v score given at the top of the figure. The child receiving the lowest v score, 5, received a d-s score of 12; the children with the next lowest v score, 6, obtained an average d-s score of 14.67, and so onto the highest v scorers, who obtained an average of 19.5 on the d-s test. A parallel tendency for vocabulary scores to increase is observed for increases in d-s scores. The form of this relationship is said to be positive, because high values on one variable tend to go with high values on the other variable and low with low values. It may also be called linear because the tendency for a unit increase in one variable to be accompanied by a constant increase in the other variable is (fairly) constant throughout the scales. That is, if we

TABLE 2.1.1
Illustrative Set of Data on Vocabulary
and Digit-Symbol Tests

Child (no.)	Vocabulary	Digit-symbol
1	5	12
2	8	15
3	7	14
4	9	18
5	10	19
6	8	18
7	6	14
8	6	17
9	10	20
10	9	17
11	7	15
12	7	16
13	9	16
14	6	13
15	8	16

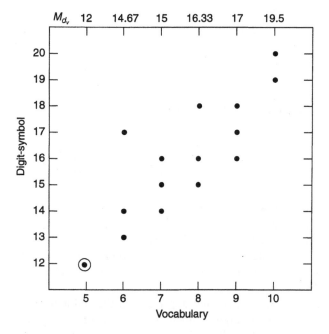

FIGURE 2.1.1   A strong, positive linear relationship.

were to draw the straight line that best fits the average of the d-s values at each v score (from the lower left-hand corner to the upper right-hand corner) we would be describing the trend or shape of the relationship quite well.

Figure 2.1.2 displays a similar scatterplot for age and the number of seconds needed to complete the digit-symbol task. In this case, low scores on age tended to go with high test time in seconds and low test times were more common in older children. This relationship may be

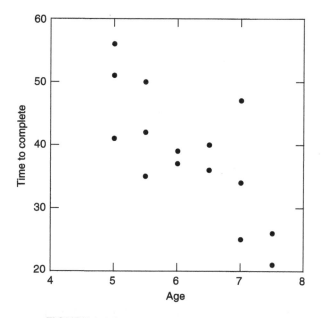

FIGURE 2.1.2 A negative linear relationship.

said to be negative and linear. It should also be clear at this point that whether a relationship between two variables is positive or negative is a direct consequence of the direction in which the two variables have been scored. If, for example, the vocabulary scores from the first example were taken from a 12-item test, and instead of scoring the number correct a count was made of the number wrong, the relationship with d-s scores would be negative. Because such scoring decisions in many cases may be essentially arbitrary, it should be kept in mind that any positive relationship becomes negative when either (but not both) of the variables is reversed, and vice versa. Thus, for example, a negative relationship between age of oldest child and income for a group of 30-year-old mothers implies a positive relationship between age of first becoming a mother and income.[1]

Figure 2.1.3 gives the plot of a measure of motivational level and score on a difficult d-s task. It is apparent that the way motivation was associated with performance score depends on whether the motivational level was at the lower end of its scale or near the upper end. Thus, the relationship between these variables is curvilinear. Finally, Fig. 2.1.4 presents a scatterplot for age and number of substitution errors. This plot demonstrates a general tendency for higher scores on age to go with fewer errors, indicating that there is, in part, a negative linear relationship. However, it also shows that the decrease in errors that goes with a unit increase in age was greater at the lower end of the age scale than it was at the upper end, a finding that indicates that although a straight line provides some kind of fit, clearly it is not optimal.

Thus, scatterplots allow visual inspection of the form of the relationship between two variables. These relationships may be well described by a straight line, indicating a rectilinear (negative or positive) relationship, or they may be better described by a line with one or more curves. Because approximately linear relationships are very common in all sorts of data, we will concentrate on these in the current discussion, and will present methods of analyzing nonlinear relationships in Chapter 6.

---

[1] Here we follow the convention of naming a variable for the upper end of the scale. Thus, a variable called *income* means that high numbers indicate high income, whereas a variable called *poverty* would mean that high numbers indicate much poverty and therefore low income.

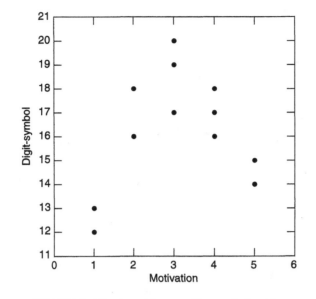

FIGURE 2.1.3 A positive curvilinear relationship.

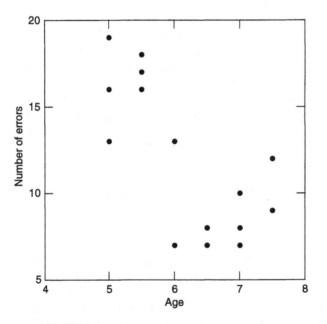

FIGURE 2.1.4 A negative curvilinear relationship.

Now suppose that Fig. 2.1.1 is compared with Fig. 2.1.5. In both cases the relationship between the variables is linear and positive; however, it would appear that vocabulary provided better information with regard to d-s completion than did chronological age. That is, the degree of the relationship with performance seems to be greater for vocabulary than for age because one could make more accurate estimates of d-s scores using information about vocabulary than using age. To compare these two relationships to determine which is greater, we need an index of the degree or strength of the relationship between two variables that will be comparable from one pair of variables to another. Looking at the relationship between v and d-s scores,

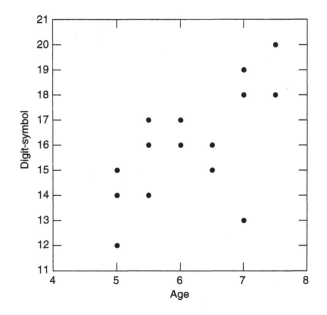

FIGURE 2.1.5   A weak, positive linear relationship.

other questions come to mind: Should this be considered a strong or weak association? On the whole, how great an increase in digit-symbol score is found for a given increase in vocabulary score in this group? If d-s is estimated from v in such a way as to minimize the differences between our estimations and the actual d-s scores, how much error will, nevertheless, be made? If this is a random sample of subjects from a larger population, how much confidence can we have that v and d-s are linearly related in the entire population? These and other questions are answered by correlation and regression methods. In the use and interpretation of these methods the two variables are generally treated as interval scales; that is, constant differences between scale points on each variable are assumed to represent equal "amounts" of the construct being measured. Although for many or even most scales in the behavioral sciences this assumption is not literally true, empirical work (Baker, Hardyck, & Petrinovich, 1966) indicates that small to moderate inequalities in interval size produce little if any distortion in the validity of conclusions based on the analysis. This issue is discussed further in Chapter 6.

2.2 THE INDEX OF LINEAR CORRELATION
BETWEEN TWO VARIABLES: THE PEARSON PRODUCT
MOMENT CORRELATION COEFFICIENT

2.2.1 Standard Scores: Making Units Comparable

One of the first problems to be solved by an index of the degree of association between two variables is that of measurement unit. Because the two variables are typically expressed in different units, we need some means of converting the scores to comparable measurement units. It can be readily perceived that any index that would change with an arbitrary change in measurement unit—from inches to centimeters or age in months to age in weeks, for example— could hardly be useful as a general description of the strength of the relationship between height and age, one that could be compared with other such indices.

TABLE 2.2.1
Income and Major Household Appliances in Original Units,
Deviation Units, and z Units

House-hold	Income	Appliances	$I - M_I$ $= i$	$A - M_A$ $= a$	i^2	a^2	Rank I	Rank A
1	24,000	3	−3,500	−1.75	12,250,000	3.0625	1	1
2	29,000	7	+1,500	+2.25	2,250,000	5.0625	3	4
3	27,000	4	−500	−.75	250,000	.5625	2	2
4	30,000	5	+2,500	+.25	6,250,000	.0625	4	3
Sum (Σ)	110,000	19	0	0	21,000,000	8.75		

Mean   27,500   4.75
$sd_I^2 = \Sigma i^2 / (n-1) = 7,000,000;$ $2.92 = sd_A^2$
$sd_I = \sqrt{\Sigma i^2 / (n-1)} = 2,645.75;$ $1.71 = sd_A$

	$i/sd_I = z_I$	$a/sd_A = z_A$	z_I^2	z_A^2
1	−1.323	−1.025	1.750	1.050
2	+0.567	+1.317	0.321	1.736
3	−0.189	−0.439	0.036	0.193
4	+0.945	+0.146	0.893	0.021
Σ	0	0	3.00	3.00

CH02EX01

To illustrate this problem, suppose information has been gathered on the annual income and the number of major household appliances of four households (Table 2.2.1).[2] In the effort to measure the degree of relationship between income (I) and the number of appliances (A), we will need to cope with the differences in the nature and size of the units in which the two variables are measured. Although Households 1 and 3 are both below the mean on both variables and Households 2 and 4 are above the mean on both (see i and a, scores expressed as deviations from their means, with the means symbolized as M_I and M_A, respectively), we are still at a loss to assess the correspondence between a difference of $3500 from the mean income and a difference of 1.5 appliances from the mean number of appliances. We may attempt to resolve the difference in units by ranking the households on the two variables—1, 3, 2, 4 and 1, 4, 2, 3, respectively—and noting that there seems to be some correspondence between the two ranks. In so doing we have, however, made the differences between Households 1 and 3 ($3000) equal to the difference between Households 2 and 4 ($1000); two ranks in each case.

To make the scores comparable, we clearly need some way of taking the different variability of the two original sets of scores into account. Because the standard deviation (sd) is an index of variability of scores, we may measure the discrepancy of each score from its mean (x) relative to the variability of all the scores by dividing by the sd:

(2.2.1)
$$sd_X = \sqrt{\frac{\sum x^2}{n-1}},$$

---

[2]In this example, as in all examples that follow, the number of cases (n) is kept very small in order to facilitate the reader's following of the computations. In almost any serious research, the n must, of course, be very much larger (Section 2.9).

where Σx^2 means "the sum of the squared deviations from the mean."[3] The scores thus created are in standard deviation units and are called *standard* or z scores:

$$(2.2.2) \qquad z_X = \frac{X - M_X}{sd_X} = \frac{x}{sd_X}.$$

In Table 2.2.1 the z score for income for Household 1 is -1.323, which indicates that its value ($24,000) falls about $1\frac{1}{3}$ income standard deviations ($2646) *below* the income mean ($27,500). Although income statistics are expressed in dollar units, the z score is a pure number; that is, it is unit-free. Similarly, Household 1 has a z score for number of appliances of -1.025, which indicates that its number of appliances (3) is about 1 standard deviation (1.71) below the mean number of appliances (4.75). Note again that -1.025 is not expressed in number of appliances, but is also a pure number. Instead of having to compare $24,000 and 3 appliances for Household 1, we can now make a meaningful comparison of -1.323 (z_I) and -1.025 (z_A), and note incidentally the similarity of the two values for Household 1. This gives us a way of systematically approaching the question of whether a household is as relatively wealthy as it is relatively "applianced."

It should be noted that the rank of the z scores is the same as that of the original scores and that scores that were above or below the mean on the original variable retain this characteristic in their z scores. In addition, we note that the difference between the incomes of Households 2 and 3 $(I_2 - I_3 = \$2000)$ is twice as large, and of opposite direction to the difference between Households 2 and 4 $(I_2 - I_4 = -\$1000)$. When we look at the z scores for these same households, we find that $z_{I2} - z_{I3} = .567 - (-.189) = .756$ is twice as large and of opposite direction to the difference $z_{I2} - z_{I4} = .567 - .945 = -.378$ (i.e., $.756/-.378 = -2$). Such proportionality of differences or distances between scores,

$$(2.2.3) \qquad \frac{X_i - X_j}{X_m - X_n} = \frac{z_{X_i} - z_{X_j}}{z_{X_m} - z_{X_n}}$$

is the essential element in what is meant by retaining the original relationship between the scores. This can be seen more concretely in Fig. 2.2.1, in which we have plotted the pairs of scores. Whether we plot z scores or raw scores, the points in the scatterplot have the same relationship to each other.

The z transformation of scores is one example of a linear transformation. A linear transformation is one in which every score is changed by multiplying or dividing by a constant or adding or subtracting a constant or both. Changes from inches to centimeters, dollars to francs, and Fahrenheit to Celsius degrees are examples of linear transformations. Such transformations will, of course, change the means and sds of the variables upon which they are performed. However, because the sd will change by exactly the same factor as the original scores (that is, by the constant by which scores have been multiplied or divided) and because z scores are created by subtracting scores from their mean, all linear transformations of scores will yield the same set of z scores. (If the multiplier is negative, the signs of the z scores will simply be reversed.)

Because the properties of z scores form the foundation necessary for understanding correlation coefficients, they will be briefly reviewed:

---

[3] As noted earlier, this edition employs the population estimate of sd with $n - 1$ in the denominator throughout to conform with computer program output, in contrast to earlier editions, which employed the sample sd with n in the denominator in earlier equations in the book and moved to the population estimate when inferences to the population involving standard errors were considered, and thereafter.

Also note that the summation sign, Σ, is used to indicate summation over all n cases here and elsewhere, unless otherwise specified.

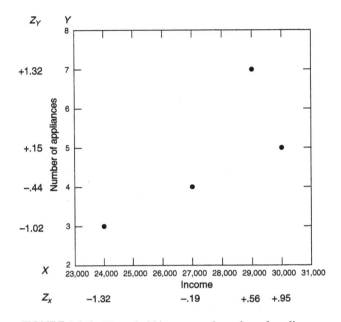

FIGURE 2.2.1   Household income and number of appliances.

1. The sum of a set of z scores (Σz) (and therefore also the mean) equals 0.
2. The variance (sd^2) of the set of z scores equals 1, as does the standard deviation (sd).
3. Neither the shape of the distribution of X nor its absolute correlation with any other variable is affected by transforming it to z (or any other linear transformation).

2.2.2 The Product Moment Correlation as a Function of Differences Between z Scores

We may now define a perfect (positive) relationship between two variables (X and Y) as existing when all z_X and z_Y pairs of scores consist of two exactly equal values. Furthermore, the degree of relationship will be a function of the departure from this "perfect" state, that is, a function of the differences between pairs of z_X and z_Y scores. Because the average difference between paired z_X and z_Y and is necessarily zero (because $M_{z_Y} = M_{z_X} = 0$), the relationship may be indexed by finding the average[4] of the squared discrepancies between z scores, $\Sigma(z_X - z_Y)^2/n$.

For example, suppose that an investigator of academic life obtained the (fictitious) data shown in Table 2.2.2. The subjects were 15 randomly selected members of a large university department, and the data include the time in years that had elapsed since the faculty member's Ph.D. was awarded and the number of publications in professional journals.

Several things should be noted in this table. Deviation scores ($x = X - M_X$ and $y = Y - M_Y$) sum to zero. So do z_X and z_Y. The standard deviations, sd_{z_X} and sd_{z_Y}, are both 1, M_{z_X} and M_{z_Y} are both 0 (all of which are mathematical necessities), and these equalities reflect the equal footing on which we have placed the two variables.

We find that the squared differences (Σsquared) between z scores sums to 9.614, which when divided by the number of paired observations equals .641. How large is this relationship? We have stated that if the two variables were perfectly (positively) related, all z score differences

---

[4]Because we have employed the sample-based estimate of the population sd, with a divisor of $n-1$, when z scores have been based on this sd this equation should also use $n-1$.

TABLE 2.2.2
z Scores, z Score Differences, and z Score Products on Data Example

Case	X Time since Ph.D.	Y No. of publications	$\dfrac{X_i - M_X}{sd_X} = z_{X_i}$	$\dfrac{Y_i - M_Y}{sd_Y} = z_{Y_i}$	$z_X - z_Y$	$z_X z_Y$
1	3	18	−1.020	−.140	−.880	.142
2	6	3	−.364	−1.225	.861	.446
3	3	2	−1.020	−1.297	.278	1.322
4	8	17	.073	−.212	.285	−.015
5	9	11	.291	−.646	.938	−.188
6	6	6	−.364	−1.008	.644	.367
7	16	38	1.821	1.307	.514	2.380
8	10	48	.510	2.030	−1.520	1.035
9	2	9	−1.238	−.791	−.447	1.035
10	5	22	−.583	.150	−.732	−.087
11	5	30	−.583	.728	−1.311	−.424
12	6	21	−.364	.077	−.441	−.028
13	7	10	−.146	−.719	.573	.105
14	11	27	.728	.511	.217	.372
15	18	37	2.257	1.235	1.023	2.787
Σ	115	299	0	0	0	
Σ squared	1235	8635	14	14	9.614	
M	7.67	19.93			.641	.613
sd^2	19.55	178.33	1	1		
sd	4.42	13.35	1	1		

would equal zero and necessarily their sum and mean would also be zero. A perfect negative relationship, on the other hand, may be defined as one in which the z scores in each pair are equal in absolute value but opposite in sign. Under the latter circumstances, it is demonstrable that the average of the squared discrepancies times $n/(n-1)$ always equals 4. It can also be proved that under circumstances in which the pairs of z scores are on the average equally likely to be consistent with a negative relationship as with a positive relationship, the average squared difference times $n/(n-1)$ will always equal 2, which is midway between 0 and 4. Under these circumstances, we may say that there is no linear relationship between X and Y.[5]

Although it is clear that this index, ranging from 0 (for a perfect positive linear relationship) through 2 (for no linear relationship) to 4 (for a perfect negative one), does reflect the relationship between the variables in an intuitively meaningful way, it is useful to transform the scale linearly to make its interpretation even more clear. Let us reorient the index so that it runs from −1 for a perfect negative relationship to +1 for a perfect positive relationship. If we divide the sum of the squared discrepancies by $2(n-1)$ and subtract the result from 1, we have

(2.2.4)
$$r = 1 - \left(\frac{\sum (z_X - z_Y)^2}{2(n-1)} \right),$$

---

[5]Note that this equation is slightly different from that in earlier editions. The $n/(n-1)$ term is necessary because the sd used here is the sample estimate of the population sd rather than the sample sd which uses n in the denominator.

which for the data of Table 2.2.2 gives

$$r = r = 1 - \left(\frac{9.614}{28}\right) = .657.$$

r is the product moment correlation coefficient, invented by Karl Pearson in 1895.[6] This coefficient is the standard measure of the linear relationship between two variables and has the following properties:

1. It is a pure number and independent of the units of measurement.
2. Its value varies between zero, when the variables have no linear relationship, and $+1.00$ or -1.00, when each variable is perfectly estimated by the other. The absolute value thus gives the degree of relationship.
3. Its sign indicates the direction of the relationship. A positive sign indicates a tendency for high values of one variable to occur with high values of the other, and low values to occur with low. A negative sign indicates a tendency for high values of one variable to be associated with low values of the other. Reversing the direction of measurement of one of the variables will produce a coefficient of the same absolute value but of opposite sign. Coefficients of equal value but opposite sign (e.g., $+.50$ and $-.50$) thus indicate equally strong linear relationships, but in opposite directions.

2.3 ALTERNATIVE FORMULAS FOR THE PRODUCT MOMENT CORRELATION COEFFICIENT

The formula given in Eq. (2.2.4) for the product moment correlation coefficient as a function of squared differences between paired z scores is only one of a number of mathematically equivalent formulas. Some of the other versions provide additional insight into the nature of r; others facilitate computation. Still other formulas apply to particular kinds of variables, such as variables for which only two values are possible, or variables that consist of rankings.

2.3.1 *r* as the Average Product of *z* Scores

It follows from algebraic manipulation of Eq. (2.2.4) that

(2.3.1)
$$r_{XY} = \frac{\sum z_X z_Y}{n-1}.$$

The product moment correlation is therefore seen to be the mean of the products of the paired z scores.[7] In the case of a perfect positive correlation, because $z_X = z_Y$,

$$r_{XY} = \frac{\sum z_X z_Y}{n-1} = \frac{\sum z^2}{n-1} = 1.$$

For the data presented in Table 2.2.1, these products have been computed and $r_{XY} = 9.193/14 = .657$, necessarily as before.

---

[6]The term *product moment* refers to the fact that the correlation is a function of the product of the *first moments*, of X and Y, respectively. See the next sections.

[7]If we used zs based on the *sample sd* which divides by n, this *average* would also divide by n.

2.3.2 Raw Score Formulas for *r*

Because z scores can be readily reconverted to the original units, a formula for the correlation coefficient can be written in raw score terms. There are many mathematically equivalent versions of this formula, of which the following is a convenient one for computation by computer or calculator:

$$(2.3.2) \qquad r_{XY} = \frac{n \sum XY - \sum X \sum Y}{\sqrt{\left[n \sum X^2 - (\sum X)^2\right]\left[n \sum Y^2 - (\sum Y)^2\right]}}.$$

When the numerator and denominator are divided by n^2, Eq. (2.3.2) becomes an expression of r in terms of the means of each variable, of each squared variable, and of the XY product:

$$(2.3.3) \qquad r_{XY} = \frac{M_{XY} - M_X M_Y}{\sqrt{(M_X^2 - M_{X^2})(M_Y^2 - M_{Y^2})}}.$$

It is useful for hand computation to recognize that the denominator is the product of the variables' standard deviations, thus an alternative equivalent is

$$(2.3.4) \qquad r_{XY} = \frac{\sum xy/(n-1)}{sd_X sd_Y}$$

This numerator, based on the product of the *deviation* scores is called the *covariance* and is an index of the tendency for the two variables to *covary* or go together that is expressed in deviations measured in the original units in which X and Y are measured (e.g., income in *dollars* and *number* of appliances). Thus, we can see that r is an expression of the covariance between standardized variables, because if we replace the *deviation* scores with *standardized* scores, Eq. (2.3.4) reduces to Eq. (2.3.1).

It should be noted that r inherently is *not* a function of the number of observations and that the $n - 1$ in the various formulas serves only to cancel it out of other terms where it is hidden (for example, in the *sd*). By multiplying Eq. (2.3.4) by $(n - 1)/(n - 1)$ it can be completely canceled out to produce a formula for r that does not contain any vestige of n:

$$(2.3.5) \qquad r_{XY} = \frac{\sum xy}{\sqrt{\sum x^2 \sum y^2}}.$$

2.3.3 Point Biserial *r*

When one of the variables to be correlated is a dichotomy (it can take on only two values), the computation of r simplifies. There are many dichotomous variables in the behavioral sciences, such as yes or no responses, left- or right-handedness, and the presence or absence of a trait or attribute. For example, although the variable "gender of subject" does not seem to be a quantitative variable, it may be looked upon as the presence or absence of the characteristics of being female (or of being male). As such, we may decide, arbitrarily, to score all females as 1 and all males as 0. Under these circumstances, the *sd* of the gender variable is determined by the proportion of the total n in each of the two groups; $sd = \sqrt{PQ}$, where P is the proportion in one group and $Q = 1 - P$, the proportion in the other group.[8] Because r indicates a relationship between two standardized variables, it does not matter whether we choose 0 and 1 as the two values or any other pair of different values, because any pair will yield the same absolute z scores.

---

[8]Note that here the *sd* is the sample *sd* (divided by n) rather than the sample-based estimate of the population σ. As noted earlier, because the ns in the equation for r cancel, this difference is immaterial here.

TABLE 2.3.1
Correlation Between a Dichotomous and a Scaled Variable

Subject no.	Stimulus condition (X)	Task score (Y)	X_A	X_B	z_Y	z_A	z_B	$z_Y z_A$	$z_Y z_B$
1	NONE	67	0	50	−0.41	−.802	.802	0.329	−0.329
2	NONE	72	0	50	1.63	−.802	.802	−1.307	1.307
3	NONE	70	0	50	0.81	−.802	.802	−0.650	0.650
4	NONE	69	0	50	0.41	−.802	.802	−0.329	0.329
5	STIM	66	1	20	−0.81	1.069	−1.069	−0.866	0.866
6	STIM	64	1	20	−1.63	1.069	−1.069	−1.742	1.742
7	STIM	68	1	20	0	1.069	−1.069	0	0
Sum		476	3	260	0	0	0	−4.565	4.565
Mean		68	.429	37.14	0	0	0		
sd in sample			2.45	.495	14.9		M_Y NONE = 69.5	M_Y STIM = 66.0	

CH02EX02

For example, Table 2.3.1 presents data on the effects of an interfering stimulus on task performance for a group of seven experimental subjects. As can be seen, the absolute value of the correlation remains the same whether we choose (X_A) 0 and 1 as the values to represent the absence or presence of an interfering stimulus or choose (X_B) 50 and 20 as the values to represent the same dichotomy. The sign of r, however, depends on whether the group with the higher mean on the other (Y) variable, in this case the no-stimulus group, has been assigned the higher or lower of the two values. The reader is invited to try other values and observe the constancy of r.

Because the z scores of a dichotomy are a function of the proportion of the total in each of the two groups, the product moment correlation formula simplifies to

$$(2.3.6) \qquad r_{pb} = \frac{(M_{Y_1} - M_{Y_0})\sqrt{PQ}}{sd_Y},$$

where M_{Y_1} and M_{Y_0} are the Y means of the two groups of the dichotomy and the sd_Y is the sample value, which is divided by n rather than $n - 1$. The simplified formula is called the point biserial r to take note of the fact that it involves one variable (X) whose values are all at one of two points and one continuous variable (Y). In the present example,

$$(2.3.7) \qquad r_{pb} = \frac{(66.0 - 69.5)\sqrt{(.429)(.571)}}{2.45} = -.707.$$

The point biserial formula for the product moment r displays an interesting and useful property. When the two groups of the dichotomy are of equal size, $p = q = .5$, so $\sqrt{PQ} = .5$. The r_{pb} then equals half the difference between the means of the z scores for Y, and so $2r_{pb}$ equals the difference between the means of the standardized variable.

2.3.4 Phi (φ) Coefficient

CH02EX03

When both X and Y are dichotomous, the computation of the product moment correlation is even further simplified. The data may be represented by a fourfold table and the correlation computed directly from the frequencies and marginals. For example, suppose a study investigated the

TABLE 2.3.2
Fourfold Frequencies for Candidate Preference
and Homeowning Status

	Candidate U	Candidate V	Total
Homeowners	A 19	B 54	$73 = A + B$
Nonhomeowners	C 60	D 52	$112 = C + D$
Total	$79 = A + C$	$106 = B + D$	$185 = n$

difference in preference of homeowners and nonhomeowners for the two candidates in a local election, and the data are as presented in Table 2.3.2. The formula for r here simplifies to the difference between the product of the diagonals of a fourfold table of frequencies divided by the square root of the product of the four marginal sums:

(2.3.8)
$$r_\phi = \frac{BC - AD}{\sqrt{(A+B)(C+D)(A+C)(B+D)}}$$
$$= \frac{(54)(60) - (19)(52)}{\sqrt{(73)(112)(79)(106)}} = -.272$$

Once again it may be noted that this is a computing alternative to the z score formula, and therefore it does not matter what two values are assigned to the dichotomy because the standard scores, and hence the absolute value of r_ϕ will remain the same. It also follows that unless the division of the group is the same for the two dichotomies ($P_Y = P_X$ or Q_X), their z scores cannot have the same values and r_ϕ cannot equal 1 or -1. A further discussion of this limit is found in Section 2.10.1.

2.3.5 Rank Correlation

Yet another simplification in the product moment correlation formula occurs when the data being correlated consist of two sets of ranks. Such data indicate only the ordinal position of the subjects on each variable; that is, they are at the ordinal level of measurement. This version of r is called the Spearman rank correlation (r_S). Because the sd of a complete set of ranks is a function only of the number of objects being ranked (assuming no ties), some algebraic manipulation yields

CH02EX04

(2.3.9)
$$r_S = 1 - \frac{6 \sum d^2}{n(n^2 - 1)},$$

where d is the difference in the ranks of the pair for an object or individual. In Table 2.3.3 a set of 5 ranks is presented with their deviations and differences. Using one of the general formulas (2.3.4) for r,

$$r = \frac{\sum xy}{\sqrt{\sum x^2}\sqrt{\sum y^2}}$$
$$= \frac{-3}{\sqrt{10}\sqrt{10}} = -.300$$

TABLE 2.3.3
Correlation Between Two Sets of Ranks

I.D.	X	Y	x	x^2	y	y^2	xy	d	d^2
1	4	2	1	1	−1	1	−1	2	4
2	2	1	−1	1	−2	4	2	1	1
3	3	4	0	0	1	1	0	−1	1
4	5	3	2	4	0	0	0	2	4
5	1	5	−2	4	2	4	−4	−4	16
Sum	15	15	0	10	0	10	−3	0	26

TABLE 2.3.4
Product Moment Correlation Coefficients
for Special Kinds of Data

Data type	Coefficient
A scaled variable and a dichotomous variable	Point biserial r (r_{pb})
Two dichotomous variables	ϕ or r_{ϕ}
Two ranked variables	Spearman rank order r (r_S)

The rank order formula (2.3.9) with far less computation yields

$$r_S = 1 - \frac{6(26)}{5(24)}$$

$$= 1 - \frac{156}{120} = -.300,$$

which agrees with the result from Eq. (2.3.4).

We wish to stress the fact that the formulas for r_{pb}, r_{ϕ}, and r_S are simply computational equivalents of the previously given general formulas for r that result from the mathematical simplicity of dichotomous or rank data (Table 2.3.4). They are of use when computation is done by hand or calculator. They are of no significance when computers are used, because whatever formula for r the computer uses will work when variables are scored 0–1 (or any other two values) or are ranks without ties. It is obviously not worth the trouble to use special programs to produce these special-case versions of r when a formula such as Eq. (2.3.2) will produce them.

2.4 REGRESSION COEFFICIENTS: ESTIMATING Y FROM X

Thus far we have treated the two variables as if they were of equal status. It is, however, often the case that variables are treated asymmetrically, one being thought of as a dependent variable or criterion and the other as the independent variable or predictor. These labels reflect the reasons why the relationship between two variables may be under investigation. There are two reasons for such investigation; one scientific and one technological. The primary or scientific question looks upon one variable as potentially causally dependent on the other, that is, as in part an effect of or influenced by the other. The second or technological question has for its goal forecasting, as for example, when high school grades are used to predict college grades with no implication that the latter are actually caused by the former. In either case the measure of this effect will, in general, be expressed as the number of units of change in the *Y* variable per unit change in the *X* variable.

To return to our academic example of 15 faculty members presented in Table 2.2.2, we wish to obtain an estimate of *Y*, for which we use the notation $\hat{Y}$, which summarizes the average amount of change in the number of publications for each year since Ph.D. To find this number, we will need some preliminaries. Obviously, if the relationship between publications and years were perfect and positive, we could provide the number of publications corresponding to any given number of years since Ph.D. simply by adjusting for differences in scale of the two variables. Because, when $r_{XY} = 1$, for any individual *j*, the estimated $\hat{z}_{Y_j}$ simply equals z_{X_j}, then

$$\frac{\hat{Y}_j - M_Y}{sd_Y} = \frac{X_j - M_X}{sd_X},$$

and solving for *j*'s estimated value of *Y*,

$$\hat{Y}_j = \frac{sd_Y(X_j - M_X)}{sd_X} + M_Y,$$

and because M_X, M_Y, and sd_Y are known, it remains only to specify X_j and then $\hat{Y}_j$ may be computed.

When, however, the relationship is not perfect, we may nevertheless wish to show the estimated $\hat{Y}$ that we would obtain by using the best possible "average" conversion or prediction rule from *X* in the sense that the computed values will be as close to the actual *Y* values as is possible with a linear conversion formula. Larger absolute differences between the actual and estimated scores $(Y_j - \hat{Y}_j)$ are indicative of larger errors. The average error $\Sigma(Y - \hat{Y})/N$ will equal zero whenever the overestimation of some scores is balanced by an equal underestimation of other scores. That there be no consistent over- or underestimation is a desirable property, but it may be accomplished by an infinite number of conversion rules. We therefore define *as close as possible* to correspond to the least squares criterion so common in statistical work—we shall choose a conversion rule such that not only are the errors balanced (they sum to zero), but also the sum of the squared discrepancies between the actual *Y* and estimated $\hat{Y}$ will be minimized, that is, will be as small as the data permit.

It can be proven that the linear conversion rule which is optimal for converting z_X to an estimate of $\hat{z}_Y$ is

(2.4.1) $$\hat{z}_Y = r_{XY}z_X.$$

To convert to raw scores, we substitute for $\hat{z}_Y = (\hat{Y} - M_Y)/sd_Y$ and for $\hat{z}_X = (\hat{X} - M_X)/sd_X$.
Solving for $\hat{Y}$ gives

(2.4.2) $$\hat{Y} = r_{XY}sd_Y \frac{(X - M_X)}{sd_X} + M_Y.$$

It is useful to simplify and separate the elements of this formula in the following way. Let

(2.4.3) $$B_{YX} = r_{XY} \frac{sd_Y}{sd_X},$$

and

(2.4.4) $$B_0 = M_Y - B_{YX}M_X,$$

from which we may write the regression equation for estimating Y from X as

(2.4.5) $$\hat{Y} = B_{YX}X + B_0.$$

Alternatively, we may write this equation in terms of the original Y variable by including an "error" term e, representing the difference between the predicted and observed score for each observation:

(2.4.6) $$Y = B_{YX}X + B_0 + e$$

These equations describe the regression of Y on X. B_{YX} is the regression coefficient for estimating Y from X and represents the rate of change in Y units per unit change in X, the constant by which you multiply each X observation to estimate Y. B_0 is called the regression constant or Y intercept and serves to make appropriate adjustments for differences in size between X and Y units. When the line representing the best linear estimation equation (the Y on X regression equation) is drawn on the scatterplot of the data in the original X and Y units, B_{YX} indicates the slope of the line and B_0 represents the point at which the regression line crosses the Y axis, which is the estimated $\hat{Y}$ when $X = 0$. (Note that B_0 is sometimes represented as A or A_{YX} in publications or computer output.)

For some purposes it is convenient to *center* variables by subtracting the mean value from each score.[9] Following such subtraction the mean value will equal 0. It can be seen by Eq. (2.4.4) that when both the dependent and independent variables have been centered so that both means $= 0$, the $B_0 = 0$. This manipulation also demonstrates that the predicted score on Y for observations at the mean of X must equal the mean of Y. When only the IV is centered, the B_0 will necessarily equal M_Y. For problems in which X does not have a meaningful zero point, centering X may simplify interpretation of the results (Wainer, 2000). The slope B_{YX} is unaffected by centering.

The slope of a regression line is the measure of its steepness, the ratio of how much Y rises (or, when negative, falls) to any given amount of increase along the horizontal X axis. Because the "rise over the run" is a constant for a straight line, our interpretation of it as the number of units of change in Y per unit change in X meets this definition.

Now we can deal with our example of 15 faculty members with a mean of 7.67 and a sd of 4.58 years since Ph.D. (Time) and a mean of 19.93 and a sd of 13.82 publications (Table 2.2.2). The correlation between time and publications was found to be .657, so

$$B_{YX} = .657(13.82/4.58) = 1.98,$$
$$B_0 = 19.93 - 1.98(7.67) = 4.73.$$

The regression coefficient, B_{YX}, indicates that for each unit of increase in Time (X), we estimate a change of $+1.98$ units (publications) in Y (i.e., about two publications per year), and that using this rule we will minimize our errors (in the least squares sense). The B_0 term gives us a point for starting this estimation—the point for a zero value of X, which is, of course, out of the range for the present set of scores. The equation $\hat{Y}_X = B_{YX}X + B_0$ may be used to determine the predicted value of Y for each value of X, and graphed as the $\hat{Y}X$ line in a scatterplot, as illustrated for these data in Fig. 2.4.1.

We could, of course, estimate X from Y by interchanging X and Y in Eqs. (2.4.3) and (2.2.2). However, the logic of regression analysis dictates that the variables are not of equal status, and estimating an independent or predictor variable from the dependent or criterion variable

---

[9]As will be seen in Chapters 6, 7, and 9, centering on X can greatly simplify interpretations of equations when relationships are curvilinear or interactive.

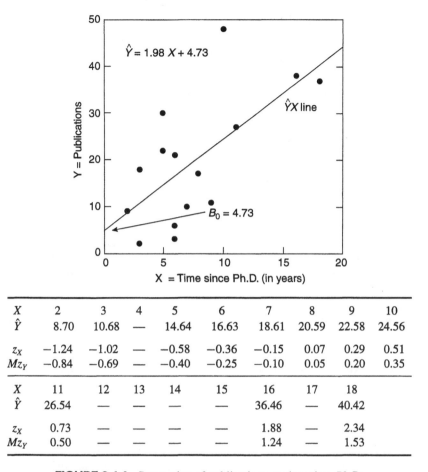

FIGURE 2.4.1   Regression of publications on time since Ph.D.

X	2	3	4	5	6	7	8	9	10
$\hat{Y}$	8.70	10.68	—	14.64	16.63	18.61	20.59	22.58	24.56
z_X	−1.24	−1.02	—	−0.58	−0.36	−0.15	0.07	0.29	0.51
Mz_Y	−0.84	−0.69	—	−0.40	−0.25	−0.10	0.05	0.20	0.35

X	11	12	13	14	15	16	17	18
$\hat{Y}$	26.54	—	—	—	—	36.46	—	40.42
z_X	0.73	—	—	—	—	1.88	—	2.34
Mz_Y	0.50	—	—	—	—	1.24	—	1.53

makes no sense. Suffice it to say that were we to do so, the line estimating X from Y (the X on Y regression) would not be the same as the line estimating Y from X (the Y on X regression). Neither its slope nor its intercept would be the same.

The meaning of the regression coefficient may be seen quite well in the case in which the independent variable is a dichotomy.[10] If we return to the example from Table 2.3.1 where the point biserial $r = -.707$ and calculate

$$B_{YX} = -.707\left(\frac{2.45}{.495}\right) = -3.5,$$

we note that this is exactly the difference between the two group means on Y, $66 - 69.5$. Calculating the intercept, we get

$$B_0 = 68 - (-3.5)(.428) = 69.5,$$

which is equal to the mean of the group coded 0 (the no-stimulus condition). This must be the case because the best (least squares) estimate of Y for each group *is* its own mean, and the

---

[10]Chapter 8 is devoted to the topic of categorical IVs, for which we provide only a brief introduction here.

regression equation for the members of the group represented by the 0 point of the dichotomy is solved as

$$\hat{Y} = B_{YX}(0) + B_0 = B_0 = M_Y.$$

2.5 REGRESSION TOWARD THE MEAN

A certain amount of confusion exists in the literature regarding the phenomenon of regression toward the mean. It is sometimes implied that this is an artifact attributable to regression as an analytic procedure. On the contrary, it is a mathematical necessity that whenever two variables correlate less than perfectly, cases that are at one extreme on one of the variables will, on the average, be less extreme on the other. There are many examples in the literature where investigators mistakenly claim that some procedure results in a beneficial result when only the regression effect is operating (Campbell & Kenny, 1999). Consider a research project in which a neuroticism questionnaire is administered to an entering class and the students with the poorest scores are given psychotherapy, retested, and found to improve greatly. The "artifact" is the investigator's claim of efficacy for the treatment when, unless the scores remained exactly the same so that the correlation between pretest and posttest was 1.0, they were certain to have scores closer to the mean than previously.

Although the number of cases in a small data set may be too small to show this phenomenon reliably at each data point, examination of the z_X and z_Y values in Fig. 2.4.1 will illustrate the point. The median of time since Ph.D. for the 15 professors is 6 years. If we take the 7 cases above the median, we find that their mean z score is $+.82$, whereas the mean z score for the 5 professors below the median is $-.92$. Now, the mean z score for *number of publications* for the older professors is only .52 and the mean z score for publications for the younger professors is $-.28$. The cases high and low in years since Ph.D. (X) are distinctly less so on publications (Y); that is, they have "regressed" toward the mean. The degree of regression toward the mean in any given case will vary with the way we define *high* and *low*. That is, if we defined high time since Ph.D. as more than 12 years, we would expect an even greater difference between their mean z on time and the mean z on publications. The same principle will hold in the other direction: Those who are extreme on number of publications will be less extreme on years since Ph.D. As can be seen from these or any other bivariate data that are not perfectly linearly related, this is in no sense an artifact, but a necessary corollary of less than perfect correlation.

A further implication of this regression phenomenon is evident when one examines the consequences of selecting extreme cases for study. In the preceding paragraph, we found that those whose Ph.D.s were no more than 5 years old had a mean z score for years since Ph.D. of $-.92$, but a mean z score for number of publication of $-.28$. An investigator might well be tempted to attribute the fact that these new Ph.D.s are so much closer to the mean on number of publications than they are on years since Ph.D. to their motivation to catch up in the well-documented academic rat race. However, recognition that a less than perfect correlation is a necessary and sufficient condition to produce the observed regression toward the mean makes it clear that any specific substantive interpretation is not justified. (There is a delicious irony here: the lower the correlation, the greater the degree of regression toward the mean, and the more to "interpret," spuriously, of course.)

Because regression toward the mean *always* occurs in the presence of an imperfect linear relationship, it is also observed when the variables consist of the same measure taken at two points in time. In this circumstance, unless the correlation is perfect, the extreme cases at Time 1 will be less extreme at Time 2. If the means and *sd*s are stable, this inevitably means that low scores improve and high scores deteriorate. Thus, on the average over time, overweight people lose weight, low IQ children become brighter, and rich people become poorer. To ask why these examples of regression to the mean occur is equivalent to asking why correlations between time points for weight, IQ, and income are not equal to $+1.00$. Of course, measurement error is one reason why a variable will show a lower correlation with itself over time, or with any other variables. However, regression to the mean is not solely dependent on measurement error, but on any mechanism whatsoever that makes the correlation less than perfect. Campbell and Kenny (1999) devote an entire volume to the many ways in which regression to the mean can lead to complexities in understanding change.

The necessity for regression toward the mean is not readily accessible to intuition but does respond to a simple demonstration. Expressed in standard scores, the regression equation is simply $\hat{z}_Y = r_{XY}z_X$ (Eq. 2.4.1). Because an r of $+1$ or -1 never occurs in practice, $\hat{z}_Y$ will necessarily be absolutely smaller than z_X, because r is less than 1. Concretely, when $r = .40$, whatever the value of z_X, $\hat{z}_Y$ must be .4 as large (see a comparable set of values below Fig. 2.4.1). Although for a single individual the actual value of z_Y may be larger or smaller than z_X, the expected or average value of the z_Ys that occur with z_X, that is, the value of $\hat{z}_y$, will be .4 of the z_X value (i.e., it is "regressed toward the mean"). The equation holds not only for the expected value of z_Y for a single individual's z_X, but also for the expected value of the mean z_Y for the mean z_X of a group of individuals. Of course, this holds true even when Y is the same variable measured at a later time than X. Unless the correlation over time is perfect, indicating no change, or the population mean and sd increase, *on the average*, the fat grow thinner, the dull brighter, the rich poorer, and vice versa.

2.6 THE STANDARD ERROR OF ESTIMATE AND MEASURES OF THE STRENGTH OF ASSOCIATION

In applying the regression equation $\hat{Y} = B_{YX}X + B_0$, we have of course only approximately matched the original Y values. How close is the correspondence between the information provided about Y by X (i.e., $\hat{Y}$), and the actual Y values? Or, to put it differently, to what extent is Y associated with X as opposed to being independent of X? How much do the values of Y, as they vary, coincide with their paired X values, as they vary: equivalently, how big is e in Eq. (2.4.6)?

As we have noted, variability is indexed in statistical work by the sd or its square, the variance. Because variances are additive, whereas standard deviations are not, it will be more convenient to work with sd_Y^2. What we wish to do is to partition the variance of Y into a portion associated with X, which will be equal to the variance of the estimated scores, $sd_{\hat{Y}}^2$, and a remainder not associated with X, $sd_{Y-\hat{Y}}^2$, the variance of the discrepancies between the actual and the estimated Y scores (e). (Those readers familiar with ANOVA procedures may find themselves in a familiar framework here.) $sd_{\hat{Y}}^2$ and $sd_{Y-\hat{Y}}^2$ will sum to sd_Y^2, provided that $\hat{Y}$ and $Y - \hat{Y}$ are uncorrelated. Intuitively it seems appropriate that they should be uncorrelated because $\hat{Y}$ is computed from X by the optimal (OLS[11]) rule. Because $\hat{Y} = B_{YX}X +$ (a constant), it is just a linear transformation of X and thus necessarily correlates perfectly with X. Nonzero correlation between $\hat{Y}$ and $Y - \hat{Y}$ would indicate correlation between X (which completely determines $\hat{Y}$) and $Y - \hat{Y}$, and would indicate that our original rule was not optimal. A simple algebraic proof confirms this intuition; therefore:

(2.6.1)
$$sd_Y^2 = sd_{\hat{Y}}^2 + sd_{Y-\hat{Y}}^2 = sd_{\hat{Y}}^2 + sd_e^2,$$

---

[11] We introduce the term ordinary least squares (OLS) here, to represent the model that we have described, in which simple weights of predictor variable(s) are used to estimate Y values that collectively minimize the squared discrepancies of the predicted from the observed Ys, so that any other weights would result in larger average discrepancy.

and we have partitioned the variance of Y into a portion determined by X and a residual portion not linearly related to X. If no linear correlation exists between X and Y, the optimal rule has us ignore X because $B_{YX} = 0$, and minimize our errors of estimation by using M_Y as the best guess for every case. Thus we would be choosing that point about which the squared errors are a minimum and $sd^2_{Y-\hat{Y}} = sd^2_Y$. More generally we may see that because (by Eq. 2.4.1) $\hat{z}_Y = r_{XY}z_X$,

$$sd^2_{z_{\hat{Y}}} = \frac{\sum (r_{XY}z_X)^2}{n-1} = r^2_{XY}\frac{\sum z^2_X}{n-1} = r^2_{XY},$$

and because $sd^2_{z_Y} = 1$, and

(2.6.2) $$sd^2_{z_Y} = r^2_{XY} + sd^2_{z_Y-\hat{z}_Y},$$

then r^2_{XY} is the proportion of the variance of Y linearly associated with X, and $1 - r^2_{XY}$ is the proportion of the variance of Y *not* linearly associated with X.

It is often helpful to visualize a relationship by representing each variable as a circle.[12] The area enclosed by the circle represents its variance, and because we have standardized each variable to a variance of 1, we will make the two circles of equal size (see Fig. 2.6.1). The degree of linear relationship between the two variables may be represented by the degree of overlap between the circles (the shaded area). Its proportion of either circle's area equals r^2, and $1 - r^2$ equals the area of the nonoverlapping part of either circle. Again, it is useful to note the equality of the variance of the variables once they are standardized: the size of the overlapping and nonoverlapping areas, r^2, and $1 - r^2$, respectively, must be the same for each. If one wishes to think in terms of the variance of the original X and Y, one may define the circles as representing 100% of the variance and the overlap as representing the proportion of each variable's variance associated with the other variable. We can also see that it does not matter in this form of expression whether the correlation is positive or negative because r^2 must be positive.

We will obtain the variance of the residual (nonpredicted) portion when we return to the original units by multiplying by sd^2_Y to obtain

(2.6.3) $$sd^2_{Y-\hat{Y}} = sd^2_Y(1 - r^2).$$

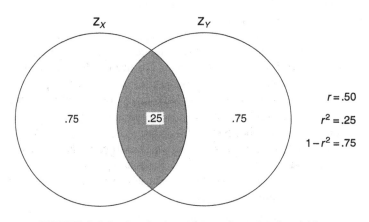

FIGURE 2.6.1   Overlap in variance of correlated variables.

---

[12]Such figures are called Venn diagrams in mathematical statistics. Here we call them "ballantines," a name taken from a logo for a now-defunct beer company, because we use them illustratively only, and do not wish to imply the mathematical precision that should accompany a Venn diagram.

The standard deviation of the residuals e, that is, of that portion of Y not associated with X is therefore given by

(2.6.4)
$$sd_{Y-\hat{Y}} = sd_Y\sqrt{1-r^2}.$$

For example, when $r = .50$, the proportion of shared variance $= r^2 = .25$, and $.75$ of sd_Y^2 is not linearly related to X. If the portion of Y linearly associated with X is removed by subtracting $B_{YX}X + B_0$ ($= \hat{Y}$) from Y, the sd of the residual is reduced compared to the original sd_Y to $sd_{Y-\hat{Y}} = sd_Y\sqrt{.75} = .866\, sd_Y$.

We see that, in this case, although $r = .50$, only 25% of the variance in Y is associated with X, and when the part of Y which is linearly associated with X is removed, the standard deviation of what remains is $.866$ as large as the original SD_Y.

To make the foregoing more concrete, let us return to our academic example. The regression coefficient B_{YX} was found to be 1.98, the intercept B_0 was 4.73, and r_{XY} was .657. Table 2.6.1 gives the Y, X, and z_Y values and estimated $\hat{Y}$ and $\hat{z}$ from the regression equations (2.4.5) and (2.4.1), which for these values are:

CH02EX05

$$\hat{Y} = 1.98\,X_0 + 4.73 \quad \text{and}$$

$$\hat{z}_Y = .657\,z_X.$$

The $Y - \hat{Y}$ values are the residuals for Y estimated from X or the errors of estimate in the sample. Because $\hat{Y}$ is a linear transformation of X, $r_{Y\hat{Y}}$ must equal r_{XY} ($= .657$). The correlations between $Y - \hat{Y}$ and $\hat{Y}$ must, as we have seen, equal zero. Parallel entries are given for the standardized $\hat{z}_Y$ values where the same relationships hold.

Turning our attention to the variances of the variables, we see that

$$\frac{sd_{\hat{Y}}^2}{sd_Y^2} = \frac{sd_{\hat{z}_Y}^2}{1} = r^2$$

(2.6.5)
$$= .657^2 = .4312.$$

The ratio $sd_{Y-\hat{Y}}/sd_Y = \sqrt{1-r^2} = .754$, which is called the coefficient of alienation, is the part of sd_Y that remains when that part of Y associated with X has been removed. It can also be thought of as the coefficient of noncorrelation, because r is the coefficient of correlation. The standard deviation of the residual scores is given by Eq. (2.6.4) as $sd_{Y-\hat{Y}} = sd_Y\sqrt{1-r^2} = 13.35(.754) = 10.07$, as shown in Table 2.6.1. For the bivariate case, the population variance error of estimate or residual variance has $df = n - 2$ and is given by

(2.6.6)
$$SE_{Y-\hat{Y}}^2 = \frac{\sum(Y-\hat{Y})^2}{n-2} = \frac{(1-r_{XY}^2)\sum(Y-M_Y)^2}{n-2}.$$

For the two summations, Table 2.6.1 gives in its $\Sigma\sqrt{x^2}$ row, 1521.51 for the $Y - \hat{Y}$ column and 2674.93 for the Y column. Substituting, we get

$$SE_{Y-\hat{Y}}^2 = \frac{1521.51}{15-2} = \frac{(1-.657^2)2674.93}{15-2},$$

and both equations give 117.04. When we take square roots, we obtain the standard error of estimate:

(2.6.7)
$$SE_{Y-\hat{Y}} = \sqrt{\frac{\sum(Y-\hat{Y})^2}{n-2}} = \sqrt{\frac{(1-r_{XY}^2)\sum(Y-M_Y)^2}{n-2}},$$

which equals 10.82. Here, too, $df = n - 2$.

TABLE 2.6.1
Estimated and Residual Scores for Academic Example

X Time since Ph.D.	Y No. of publications	$\hat{Y}$	$Y - \hat{Y}$	$\hat{z}_Y$	$z_Y - \hat{z}_Y$	$\hat{Y}_W$	$Y - \hat{Y}_W$	$\hat{Y}_V$	$Y - \hat{Y}_V = e$
3	18	10.68	7.32	−.67	.53	10.60	7.40	11.07	6.93
6	3	16.63	−13.63	−.24	−.99	16.60	−13.60	16.77	−13.77
3	2	10.68	−8.68	−.67	−.63	10.60	−8.60	11.07	−9.07
8	17	20.59	−3.59	.05	−.26	20.60	−3.60	20.57	−3.57
9	11	22.58	−11.58	.19	−.84	22.60	−11.60	22.47	−11.47
6	6	16.63	−10.63	−.24	−.77	16.60	−10.60	16.77	−10.77
16	38	36.46	1.54	1.20	.11	36.60	1.40	35.77	2.23
10	48	24.56	23.44	.33	1.70	24.60	23.40	24.37	23.63
2	9	8.70	0.30	−.81	.02	8.60	.40	9.17	−.17
5	22	14.65	7.36	−.38	.53	14.60	7.40	14.87	7.13
5	30	14.65	15.36	−.38	1.11	14.60	15.40	14.87	15.13
6	21	16.63	4.37	−.24	.32	16.60	4.40	16.77	4.23
7	10	18.61	−8.61	−.10	−.62	18.60	8.60	18.67	8.67
11	27	26.54	0.46	.48	.03	26.60	.40	26.27	73
18	37	40.42	−3.42	1.48	−.25	40.60	3.60	39.57	2.57
M 7.67	19.93	19.93	0	0	0	19.93	0	19.93	0
sd 4.577	13.82	8.77	10.07	.657	.754		10.072	8.40	10.07
sd^2 19.56	178.3	76.98	101.42	.431	.569		101.44	70.60	101.57
$\Sigma|x_i|$			120.29				116.40		120.07
$\Sigma\sqrt{x_i^2}$	2674.93		1521.51						

$$r_{Xz_X} = r_{Yz_Y} = r_{X\hat{Y}} = r_{z_X\hat{z}_Y} = r_{\hat{Y}X} = 1.$$

$$r_{XY} = r_{z_X z_Y} = r_{Y\hat{Y}} = .657$$

$$r^2_{Y(Y-\hat{Y})} = .5689; r_{(Y-\hat{Y})\hat{Y}} = r_{(Y-\hat{Y})X} = 0.$$

Finally, $\hat{Y}_W$ and $\hat{Y}_V$ in Table 2.6.1 have been computed to demonstrate what happens when any other regression coefficient or weight is used. The values $B_{WX} = 2.0$ and $B_{VX} = 1.9$ were chosen to contrast with $B_{YX} = 1.98$ (the regression constants have been adjusted to keep the estimated values centered on Y). The resulting sd^2 for the sample residuals was larger in each case, 101.44 and 101.57, respectively as compared to 101.42 for the least squares estimate. The reader is invited to try any other value to determine that the squared residuals will in fact always be larger than with 1.98, the computed value of B_{YX}.

Examination of the residuals will reveal another interesting phenomenon. If one determines the *absolute* values of the residuals from the true regression estimates and from the $\hat{Y}_W$, it can be seen that their sum is smaller for both $Y - \hat{Y}_W$ (116.40) and $Y - \hat{Y}_V$ (120.07) than it is for the true regression residuals (120.29). Whenever residuals are not exactly symmetrically distributed about the regression line there exists an absolute residual minimizing weight different from B_{YX}. To reiterate, B_{YX} is the weight that minimizes the squared residuals, not their absolute value. This is a useful reminder that ordinary least squares (OLS), although very useful, is only one way of defining discrepancies from estimation, or error.[13]

---

[13]Chapter 4 will introduce alternative methods, which are further presented in later chapters.

2.7 SUMMARY OF DEFINITIONS AND INTERPRETATIONS

The product moment r_{XY} is the rate of linear increase in z_Y per unit increase or decrease in z_X (and vice versa) that best fits the data in the sense of minimizing the sum of the squared differences between the estimated and observed scores.

r^2 is the proportion of variance in Y associated with X (and vice versa).

B_{YX} is the regression coefficient of Y on X. Using the original raw units, it is the rate of linear change in Y per unit change in X, again best fitting in the least squares sense.

B_0 is the regression intercept that serves to adjust for differences in means, giving the predicted value of the dependent variable when the independent variable's value is zero.

The coefficient of alienation, $\sqrt{1 - r^2}$, is the proportion of sd_Y remaining when that part of Y associated with X has been subtracted; that is, $sd_{Y-\hat{Y}}/sd_Y$.

The standard error of estimate, $SE_{Y-\hat{Y}}$, is the estimated population standard deviation (σ) of the residuals or errors of estimating Y from X.

2.8 STATISTICAL INFERENCE WITH REGRESSION AND CORRELATION COEFFICIENTS

In most circumstances in which regression and correlation coefficients are determined, the intention of the investigator is to provide valid inferences from the sample data at hand to some larger universe of potential data—from the statistics obtained for a sample to the parameters of the population from which it is drawn. Because random samples from a population cannot be expected to yield sample values that exactly equal the population values, statistical methods have been developed to determine the confidence with which such inferences can be drawn. There are two major methods of statistical inference, estimation using confidence intervals and null hypothesis significance testing. In Section 2.8.1, we consider the formal model assumptions involved. In Section 2.8.2, we describe confidence intervals for B_{YX}, B_0, r_{XY}, for differences between independent sample values of these statistics. In Section 2.8.3, we present the null hypothesis tests for simple regression and correlation statistics. Section 2.8.4 critiques null hypothesis testing and contrasts it with the approach of confidence limits.

2.8.1 Assumptions Underlying Statistical Inference with B_{YX}, B_0, $\hat{Y}_i$, and r_{XY}

It is clear that no assumptions are necessary for the computation of correlation, regression, and other associated coefficients or their interpretation when they are used to describe the available sample data. However, the most useful applications occur when they are statistics calculated on a sample from some population in which we are interested. As in most circumstances in which statistics are used inferentially, the addition of certain assumptions about the characteristics of the population substantially increases the useful inferences that can be drawn. Fortunately, these statistics are *robust*; that is, moderate departure from these assumptions will usually result in little error of inference.

Probably the most generally useful set of assumptions are those that form what has been called the *fixed linear regression model*. This model assumes that the two variables have been distinguished as an independent variable X and a dependent variable Y. Values of X are treated as "fixed" in the analysis of variance sense, that is, as selected by the investigator rather than sampled from some population of X values.[14] Values of Y are assumed to be randomly sampled for each of the selected values of X. The residuals ("errors") from the mean value of Y for each value of X are assumed to be normally distributed in the population, with equal variances across the full range of X values. It should be noted that no assumptions about the shape of the distribution of X and the total distribution of Y per se are necessary, and that, of course, the assumptions are made about the population and not about the sample. This model, extended to multiple regression, is used throughout the book.

2.8.2 Estimation With Confidence Intervals

A *sampling* distribution is a distribution of the values of a sample *statistic* that would occur in repeated random sampling of a given size, n, drawn from what is conceived as an infinite population. Statistical theory makes possible the estimation of the shape and variability of such sampling distributions. We estimate the population value (*parameter*) of the sample statistic we obtained by placing it within a *confidence interval* (*CI*) to provide an estimate of the margin of error (*me*), based on these distributions.

Confidence Interval for B_{YX}

We have seen that B_{YX} is a regression coefficient that gives the slope of the straight line that estimates Y from X. We will see that, depending on the context, it can take on many meanings in data analysis in MRC, including the size of a difference between two means (Section 2.4), the degree of curvature of a regression line (Chapter 6), or the effect of a datum being missing (Chapter 11).

Continuing our academic example, we found in Section 2.4 that for this sample the least squares estimate of $B_{YX} = 1.98$, indicating that for each additional year since Ph.D. we estimate an increase of 1.98 publications, that is, an increase of about two publications. If we were to draw many random samples of that size from the population, we would get *many* values of B_{YX} in the vicinity of $+1.98$. These values constitute the *sampling distribution* of B_{YX} and would be approximately normally distributed. The size of the vicinity is indicated by the standard deviation of this distribution, which is the *standard error* (SE) of B_{YX}:

(2.8.1)
$$\text{SE}_{B_{YX}} = \frac{sd_Y}{sd_X} \sqrt{\frac{1 - r_{YX}^2}{n - 2}}$$

Substituting,

$$\text{SE}_{B_{YX}} = \frac{13.82}{4.58} \sqrt{\frac{1 - .657^2}{15 - 2}} = .632.$$

Because this is a very small sample, we will need to use the t distribution to determine the multiplier of this *SE* that will yield estimates of the width of this interval. Like the normal distribution, the t distribution is a symmetrical distribution but with a relatively higher peak in the middle and higher tails. The t model is a family of distributions, each for a different number of *degrees of freedom* (df). As the df increase from 1 toward infinity, the t distribution becomes progressively less peaked and approaches the shape of the normal distribution. Looking in

---

[14]In the "multilevel" models discussed in Chapters 14 and 15 this assumption is not made for all independent variables.

Appendix Table A, we find that the necessary *t* at the two-tailed 5% level for 13 *df* is 2.16. Multiplying .632 by 2.16 gives 1.36, the 95% *margin of error* (*me*). Then, the 95% *confidence limits* (CLs) are given as $1.98 \pm 1.36 = +.62$ as its lower limit and $+3.34$ as its upper limit. If 1.98 is so much smaller than the population value of B_{YX} that only 2.5% of the possible sample B_{YX} values are smaller still, then the population value is 1.36 publications *above* 1.98, that is, 3.34 (see Fig. 2.8.1), and if 1.98 is so much larger that only 2.5% of the possible sample B_{YX} values are larger still, then the population value is 1.36 publications *below* 1.98, that is, .62 (see Fig. 2.8.2). Thus, the 95% CI is $+.62$ to $+3.34$. This CI indicates our 95% certainty that the population value falls between $+.62$ and $+3.34$. Note for future reference the fact that the CI for B_{XY} in this sample does *not* include 0 (see Section 2.8.3).

Although the *single most likely* value for the change in number of publications per year since Ph.D. is the sample value 1.98, or about 2 publications per year, we are 95% confident that the true change falls between .62 and 3.34 publications per year since Ph.D. This may be too large an interval to be of much use, as we should have expected when we examined so

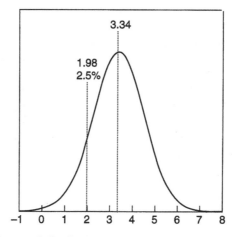

FIGURE 2.8.1 Expected distribution of *B*s from samples of 15 subjects when the population $B = 3.34$.

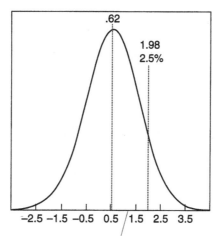

FIGURE 2.8.2 Expected distribution of *B*s from samples of 15 subjects when the population $B = 0.62$.

small a sample. Were we to have found the same sample value of 1.98 on a sample as large as 62, the standard error of B_{YX} would go down to .294 (Eq. 2.8.1). When $n = 62$, the df for $SE_{B_{YX}}$ is $n - 2 = 60$, so t for the 95% $CI = 2.00$ (Appendix Table A). The me (margin of error) is now 2.00 (.294) = .588, less than half as large as before, so the 95% CI is now $1.98 \pm (.588) = 1.40$ to 2.56, from about 1.5 to 2.5 publications per year since Ph.D., distinctly narrower and thus more useful.

Although 95% CIs are the most frequently used, other degrees of confidence, greater or smaller, may be preferred. A multiplier of 2.6 will give an approximate 99% CI, and 1.3 an approximate 80% interval for all but the smallest samples. Since standard errors are always reported in computer output, and should always be reported in research reports, one can easily approximate a CI that includes 68% (about ⅔) of the cases in the sampling distribution by taking the me for the sample B_{YX} value to equal its SE, so the approximate 68% CI is $B_{YX} \pm SE_{B_{YX}}$. The odds are then approximately 2 to 1 that the population B_{YX} value falls between those limits.

Confidence Interval for B_0

B_0 is the regression coefficient that gives the Y intercept, the value of $\hat{Y}$ when the $\hat{Y}X$ regression line that estimates Y from X is at $X = 0$. Although in many behavioral science applications this coefficient is ignored, because the means of the variables are essentially on an arbitrary scale, there are applications in which it is of interest. When zero on the X scale has a useful meaning, and is within the range of the observations, it tells us what the expected value of Y is for $X = 0$. In Section 2.4, we found using Eq. (2.4.4) that for our running example the intercept $B_0 = M_Y - B_{YX}M_X = 19.93 - 1.98 (7.67) = 4.73$, indicating a predicted value of 4.73 publications when years since Ph.D. equals 0, that is, the individual has just obtained a Ph.D. Of course, such a predicted value is not to be trusted under the circumstances in which it falls outside the observed data, as it does here.

The standard error of B_0 is given by

(2.8.2)
$$SE_{B_0} = SE_{Y-\hat{Y}} \sqrt{\frac{1}{n} + \frac{M_X^2}{(n-1)\,sd_X^2}}.$$

We found from Eq. (2.6.7) that for this example, $SE_{Y-\hat{Y}} = 10.82$. Substituting from Table 2.6.1 for $n = 15$, $M_X = 7.67$, and $sd^2 = 4.58^2 = 20.95$.

$$SE_{B_0} = 10.82 \sqrt{\frac{1}{15} + \frac{7.67^2}{(14)(20.95)}} = 5.59.$$

We generate CIs for B_0 as before, using the t distribution for $n - 2 = 13$ df. For the 95% CI, Appendix Table A gives $t = 2.16$, so the $me = 2.16(5.59) = 12.07$ and the 95% CI = $4.73 \pm 12.07 = -7.34$ to 16.80. The table gives for 13 df, $t = 1.35$ for the 80% CI, so $me = 1.35(5.59) = 7.55$, and the 80% $CI = 4.73 \pm 7.55$, -2.82 to 12.28. These large CIs, with their negative lower limits, mean that with such a small sample we cannot even confidently say whether, on the average, faculty members had published before they got their degrees!

Confidence Interval for an Estimated $\hat{Y}_i$ Value

When we employ the regression equation

(2.4.5)
$$\hat{Y} = B_{YX}X + B_0$$

to estimate a particular $\hat{Y}_i$ from a particular value of X_i, what we find is the Y coordinate of the point on the $\hat{Y}X$ regression line for that value of X. In the sample data, the Y values are scattered above and below the regression line and their distances from the line are the *residuals* or *errors*. The *standard error of estimate* (Eq. 2.6.7) estimates their variability in the population. In our running example estimating number of publications from number of years since Ph.D., we found $SE_{Y-\hat{Y}}$ to equal 10.82. Let's write the regression equation to estimate $\hat{Y}_i$, the number of publications estimated for a specific faculty member with 9 years since Ph.D. The equation for these values was found as $\hat{Y}_i = 1.98X + 4.73$. Substituting $X_i = 9$, we find $\hat{Y}_i = 22.58$.

It is useful to realize that, whatever sampling error was made by using the sample B_{YX} ($= 1.98$) instead of the (unavailable) population regression coefficient, it will have more serious consequences for X values that are more distant from the X mean than for those near it. For the sake of simplicity, let us assume that both X and Y are z scores with means of 0 and standard deviations of 1. Suppose that $B_{YX} = .20$ for our sample, whereas the actual population value is .25. For new cases that come to our attention with $X_i = .1$, we will estimate $\hat{Y}_i$ at .02 when the actual mean value of Y for all $X_i = .1$ is .025, a relatively small error of .005. On the other hand, new values of $X_i = 1.0$ will yield estimated $\hat{Y}_i$ values of .20 when the actual mean value of Y for all $X_i = 1$ is .25, the error (.05) being 10 times as large.

When a newly observed X_i is to be used to estimate $\hat{Y}_i$ we may determine the standard error and thus confidence limits for this $\hat{Y}_i$. The standard error of $\hat{Y}_i$ is given by

$$(2.8.3) \qquad SE_{\hat{Y}_i} = SE_{Y-Y_i} \sqrt{\frac{1}{n} + \frac{(X_i - M_X)^2}{(n-1)sd_X^2}},$$

where SE_{Y-Y_i} (Eq. 2.6.7) is the standard error of estimate and is based on $n - 2df$. We found from the regression equation that for $X_i = 9$ years since Ph.D., we estimate $\hat{Y}_i = 22.58$ publications. We find its standard error by substituting in Eq. (2.8.3),

$$SE_{\hat{Y}_i} = 10.82 \sqrt{\frac{1}{15} + \frac{(9 - 7.67)^2}{(14)(20.95)}} = 2.92$$

For the 95% *CI*, Appendix Table A gives $t = 2.16$ for 13 *df*, so the *me* is 2.16 (2.92) $= 6.30$ and the 95% *CI* $= 22.58 \pm 6.30 = 16.3$ to 28.9 publications (rounding). For the 80% *CI*, the table gives $t = 1.35$ for 13 *df*, so the *me* $= 1.35$ (2.92) $= 3.94$ and the *CI* is $22.58 \pm 3.94 = 18.6$ to 26.5 publications (rounding). These *CI*s are uselessly large because of the large SE_{Y_0}, due mostly in turn to the smallness of the sample.

Confidence Interval for r_{XY}

The approach we used in generating *CI*s for B_{YX} and B_0 will not work for r_{XY} because the sampling distribution for r_{XY} is not symmetrical except when ρ_{YX} (the population r_{XY}) equals 0. That is, the lower and upper limits for a *CI* for r_{XY} do not fall at equal distances from the obtained sample value. The reason for this is that, unlike $SE_{B_{YX}}$, the SE_r varies with ρ_{YX}, which is, of course, unknown. To solve this problem, R. A. Fisher developed the z prime (z') transformation of r:

$$(2.8.4) \qquad z' = \tfrac{1}{2}[\ln(1+r) - \ln(1-r)],$$

where ln is the natural (base e) logarithm.

The sampling distribution of z' depends only on the sample size and is nearly normal even for relatively small values of n. The standard error of a sample z' is given by

$$(2.8.5) \qquad SE_{z'} = \frac{1}{\sqrt{n-3}}$$

Appendix Table B gives the r to z' transformation directly, with no need for computation.

To find the *CI* for a sample *r*, transform the *r* to z' and, using the $SE_{z'}$ and the appropriate multiplier for the size of the *CI* desired, find the *me* and then the lower and upper limits of the *CI* for z'. Then transform them back to *r*. For our academic example, we found the *r* between years since Ph.D. and number of publications to be .657. In Appendix Table B we find the z' transformation to be approximately $z' = .79$. With $n = 15$, we find from (2.8.4) that

$$SE_{z'} = \frac{1}{\sqrt{15 - 3}} = .289.$$

Then, using the multiplier 1.96 from the *normal distribution* for the 95% limits (Appendix Table C), we find 1.96(.289) = .57 as the *me* for z', so .79 ± .57 gives the 95% limits for z' as .22 and 1.36. But what we want are the 95% limits for *r*, so using Appendix Table B we transform these z' values back to *r* and obtain $r = .22$ (from .22) and .88 (from 1.36). Thus, we can expect with 95% confidence that the population *r* is included in the approximate *CI* .22 to .88. Note that these limits are not symmetrical about the sample *r* of .657.

The 95% *CI* for *r* in this example, .22 to .88, is very wide, as are all the *CIs* for this small sample of $n = 15$.[15] The odds of inclusion here are 95 : 5 (that is, 19 to 1). For narrower and thus less definitive limits, the 80% *CI* gives 80 : 20 (4 to 1) odds of inclusion. To find it, we proceed as before, using the normal curve multiplier for an 80% *CI* of 1.28 (Appendix Table C). We first find the confidence limits for z' by subtracting and adding the *me* = 1.28 (.29) = .38 to the sample z' of .79, obtaining .41 and 1.17. From Appendix Table B we convert z' to *r* to find the approximate 80% *CI* for *r* to be .39 (from .41) to .82 (from 1.17). This is yet another object lesson in precision (or, rather, its lack) with small samples. For most purposes, limits as wide as this would not be of much use.

Confidence Interval for the Difference Between Regression Coefficients: $B_{XY_V} - B_{XY_W}$

Given the many uses to which regression coefficients are put, the size of the difference between a pair of B_{YX} sample values coming from different groups is often a matter of research interest. The *SE* of the difference between two independent B_{YX} values is a function of their standard errors, whose formula we repeat here for convenience:

(2.8.1)
$$SE_{B_{YX}} = \frac{sd_Y}{sd_X} \sqrt{\frac{1 - r_{YX}^2}{n - 2}}.$$

Assume that the sample in Section 2.4 in which we found the regression coefficient describing the relationship between time since Ph.D. and number of publications, 1.98, was drawn from University V and numbered 62 cases. Substituting the sample values found in Section 2.4 in Eq. (2.8.1), we find its standard error to be .294. Now assume that in a random sample of 143 cases from University W, we find $sd_{Y_W} = 13.64, sd_{X_W} = 3.45$, and $r_W = .430$. Substituting these values in Eq. (2.4.3), we find $B_W = 1.70$, and in Eq. (2.8.1) we find $SE_{B_W} = .301$. Now, the difference between B_V and B_W is $1.98 - 1.70 = .28$. The standard error of the difference between the two coefficients is

(2.8.6)
$$SE_{B_V - B_W} = \sqrt{(SE_{B_V})^2 + (SE_{B_W})^2}$$

Substituting, we find

$$SE_{B_V - B_W} = \sqrt{(.294)^2 + (.301)^2} = .42$$

---

[15]Indeed, it would be foolish to place any serious faith in the adequacy of the estimate based on such a small sample, which is employed here only for illustrative purposes.

Using the multiplier 2 (a reasonable approximation of 1.96) for the 95% *CI*, we find the *me* for the difference between the *B* values, 2 (.42) = .84, and obtain the approximate 95% *CI* for $B_V - B_W$ as .28 ± .84 = −.56 to +1.12. This means that the confidence limits go from University V's slope being .56 (about ½ of a publication) *smaller* per year since Ph.D. to being 1.12 (about 1) publication larger. Take particular note of the fact that the 95% *CI* includes 0. Thus, we cannot conclude that there is *any* difference between the universities in the number of publications change per year since Ph.D. at this level of confidence.

Equation (2.8.6) gives the standard error of the difference between regression coefficients coming from different populations as the square root of the sum of their squared standard errors. This property is not unique to regression coefficients but holds for *any* statistic—means, standard deviations, and, as we see in the next section, correlation coefficients as well.

Confidence Interval for $r_{XY_V} - r_{XY_W}$

We cannot approach setting confidence limits for differences between *rs* using the *z'* transformation because of the nonlinear relationship between them—equal distances along the *r* scale do not yield equal distances along the *z'* scale (which can be seen in Appendix Table B).

Recent work by Olkin and Finn (1995) has provided relatively simple means for setting confidence intervals for various functions of correlation coefficients. For *large* samples, the difference between r_{YX} in two independent samples, V and W, is normally distributed and is given approximately by

$$(2.8.7) \qquad SE_{r_V - r_W} = \sqrt{\frac{1 - r_V^2}{n_V} + \frac{1 + r_W^2}{n_W}}.$$

Returning to the example in which we compared the regression coefficients for our running problem, we can estimate confidence intervals for the difference between the correlations of .657 for University V ($n_V = 62$) and .430 for University W ($n_W = 143$). Substituting in Eq. (2.8.7),

$$SE_{r_V - r_W} = \sqrt{\frac{1 - .657^2}{62} + \frac{1 - .430^2}{143}} = .122$$

The difference between the *rs* is .657 − .430 = .277. Assuming normality, the 95% *CI* uses 1.96 as the multiplier, so the 95% *me* is 1.96 (.122) = .239. Then the approximate 95% *CI* is .277 ± .239 = +.04 to +.52. We interpret this to mean that we can be 95% confident that the ρ_{YX} of time since Ph.D with number of publications for University V is .04 to .52 *larger* than that for University W. Note here that the confidence interval of the difference between the *rs* of the two universities does not include 0, but the *CI* of the difference between their regression coefficients does. This demonstrates that correlation and regression coefficients are different measures of the degree of linear relationship between two variables. Later, we will argue that regression coefficients are often more stable across populations, in contrast to *rs* that reflect population differences in variability of *X*. In the preceding example, we saw $sd_X = 4.58$ in the original University V and $sd_X = 3.45$ in the comparison University W. The smaller *r* in University W is apparently attributable to their faculty's constricted range of years since Ph.D.

2.8.3 Null Hypothesis Significance Tests (NHSTs)

In its most general meaning, a null hypothesis (H_0) is a hypothesis that a population effect size (ES) or other parameter has some value specified by the investigator. The term "null" arises from R. A. Fisher's statistical strategy of formulating a proposition that the research data may be able to *nullify* or reject. By far, the most popular null hypothesis that is tested is the one that posits that a population effect size, such as a correlation coefficient or a difference between means, is *zero*, and the adjective "null" takes on the additional meaning of no relationship or no effect. We prefer to use the term "nil" hypothesis to characterize such propositions for reasons that will become clear later (J. Cohen, 1994).

The Nil Hypothesis Test for B_{YX}

In our running example of the 15 faculty members, we found that the regression coefficient for the number of publications on number of years since Ph.D. was 1.98 ($= B_{YX}$), which means that, on the average in this sample, each additional year since Ph.D. was associated with about two publications. The standard error of the coefficient ($SE_{B_{YX}}$) from Eq. (2.8.1) was .632. Let's perform a t test of the nil hypothesis that in the population, each additional year since Ph.D. is associated on the average with *no* additional publications, that is, that there is no linear relationship between years since Ph.D. and publications. We will perform this test at the $p < .05$ ($= \alpha$) significance level. The general form of the t test is

$$(2.8.8) \qquad t = \frac{\text{sample value} - \text{null-hypothetical value}}{\text{standard error}}$$

which, for regression coefficients, is

$$(2.8.9) \qquad t = \frac{B_{YX} - H_0}{SE_{B_{YX}}}.$$

Substituting,

$$t = \frac{1.98 - 0}{.632} = 3.14,$$

which, for $df = n - 2 = 13$ readily meets the $\alpha = .05$ significance criterion of $t = 2.16$ (Appendix Table A). We accordingly reject H_0 and conclude that there is a greater than zero relationship between years since Ph.D. and number of publications in the population. Note, however, that neither the size nor the statistical significance of the t value provides information about the *magnitude* of the relationship. Recall, however, that when we first encountered the $SE_{B_{YX}}$ at the beginning of Section 2.8.2, we found the 95% CI for B_{YX} to be +.62 to +3.34, which *does* provide a magnitude estimate. Moreover, note that the 95% CI *does not include 0*. After we have determined a CI for B_{YX}, a t test of the nil hypothesis for B_{YX} is unnecessary— once we have a CI that does not include 0, we know that the nil hypothesis can be rejected at that significance level (here, $\alpha = .05$). However, if the only relevant information about a population difference is whether it has some specified value, or whether it exists at all, and there are circumstances when that is the case, then CIs are unnecessary and a null hypothesis test is in order.

For example, assume that we wish to test the proposition as a non-nil null hypothesis that the population regression coefficient is 2.5 publications per year since Ph.D.: H_0: population $B_{YX} = 2.5$. We can proceed as before with Eq. (2.8.9) to find $t = (1.98 - 2.5)/.632 = .82$, which is not significant at $\alpha = .05$, and we can conclude that our results are consistent with the possibility that the population value is 2.5. But since the 95% CI (+.62 to +3.34) contains the null-hypothetical value of 2.5, we can draw the same conclusion. However, by obtaining the 95% CI we have the *range* of B_{YX} values for which the H_0 cannot be rejected at $\alpha = .05$. Not only 2.5 or 0, but *any value* in that range cannot be rejected as a H_0. Therefore, one may think of a CI as a range of values within which the H_0 *cannot* be rejected and outside of which H_0 *can* be rejected on the basis of this estimate. The CI yields more information than the NHST.

The Null Hypothesis Test for B_0

In the previous section, we found the Y intercept for our running example $B_0 = 4.73$ and, using its standard error (Eq. 2.8.2), found $SE_{B_0} = 5.59$. We can perform a t test for 13 df of the H_0 that the population intercept equals 0 in the usual fashion. Using Eq. (2.8.7) for B_0 and substituting in Eq. (2.8.7), we find

$$t = \frac{4.73 - 0}{5.59} = .85,$$

which fails to meet conventional significance criteria. (In Section 2.8.2 we found 95% and 80% CIs, both of which included 0.)

The Null Hypothesis Test for r_{XY}

When ρ_{XY} (the population r_{XY}) $= 0$, the use of the Fisher z' transformation is unnecessary. The t test of the *nil* hypothesis for r_{XY}, H_0: $\rho_{XY} = 0$, is

(2.8.10)
$$t = \frac{r_{XY}\sqrt{n - 2}}{\sqrt{1 - r_{XY}^2}} \quad \text{with} \quad df = n - 2.$$

Returning to our running example, the r_{XY} between years since Ph.D. and publications for the sample of 15 faculty members was .657. Substituting,

$$t = \frac{.657\sqrt{15 - 2}}{\sqrt{1 - .657^2}} = 3.14.$$

The $\alpha = .05$ significance criterion for t with 13 df is 2.16, readily exceeded by 3.14. We conclude that $\rho_{XY} \neq 0$. (The 95% CI was found via the Fisher z' transformation in the previous section to be .22 to .88.)

The Null Hypothesis Test for the Difference Between Two Correlations with Y: $r_{XY_V} - r_{XY_W}$

In Section 2.8.2 we presented a method for setting approximate confidence intervals for differences between independent rs suitable for large samples. For an approximate nil hypothesis test, suitable for samples of any size, we again resort to the Fisher z' transformation. The relevant data for the two universities are

University	N	r_{XY}	z'_{XY}
V	62	.657	.79
W	143	.430	.46

To test the H_0 that the difference between the population correlations: $\rho_V - \rho_W = 0$, we test the equivalent $H_0 : z'_V - z'_W = 0$ by computing the normal curve deviate

(2.8.11)
$$z = \frac{z'_V - z'_W}{\sqrt{1/(n_V - 3) + 1/(n_W - 3)}}.$$

Substituting,

$$z = \frac{.79 - .46}{\sqrt{1/(62 - 3) + 1/(143 - 3)}} = 2.13,$$

which exceeds 1.96, the two-tailed $\alpha = .05$ significance criterion for the normal distribution (see Appendix Table C), and we can conclude that University V's ρ_{XY} is probably larger than University W's. The reason that we can test for z's and conclude about ρs is that there is a one-to-one correspondence between z' and ρ so that when the z's are not equal, the ρs are necessarily also not equal. (The 95% *CI* for the difference between the *r*s was previously found to be $+.04$ to $+.52$.)

2.8.4 Confidence Limits and Null Hypothesis Significance Testing

For more than half a century, NHST has dominated statistical inference in its application in the social, biological, and medical sciences, and for just as long, it has been subject to severe criticism by methodologists including Berkson (1946), Yates (1951), Rozeboom (1960), Meehl (1967), Lykken (1968), and Tukey (1969), among others. More recently, many methodologists, including J. Cohen (1990, 1994) and a committee of the American Psychological Association (Wilkinson of the APA Task Force on Statistical Inference, 1999), among others, have inveighed against the excessive use and abuse of NHST.

We have seen repeatedly that when confidence intervals on statistics or effect sizes are available, they include the information provided by null hypothesis tests. However, there may be a useful role for NHST in cases where the direction of systematic differences is of much more interest than their magnitude and the information provided by confidence intervals may simply be distracting (Harlow, Mulaik, & Steiger, 1997). In addition, as we will see in subsequent chapters, significance tests are useful guides to the decision as to whether certain variables are or are not needed for the explanation of Y. Abelson (1995) notes the usefulness of NHST in making categorical claims that add to the background substantive scientific lore in a field under study.

2.9 PRECISION AND POWER

For research results to be useful, they must be accurate or, at least, their degree of accuracy must be determinable. In the preceding material, we have seen how to estimate regression parameters and test null hypothesis after the sample data have been collected. However, we can plan to determine the degree of precision of the estimation of parameters or of the probability of null hypothesis rejection that we shall be able to achieve.

2.9.1 Precision of Estimation

The *point estimate* of a population parameter such as a population B or ρ is the value of the statistic (B, r) in the sample. The margin of error in estimation is the product of the standard error and its multiplier for the degree of inclusion (95%, 80%) of the confidence interval. The standard error is a function of the sample size, n. We show how to estimate $n*$, the sample size necessary to achieve the desired degree of precision of the statistics covered in Section 2.8.2.

We begin by drawing a trial sample of the data for whose statistics we wish to determine *CI*s. The sample of $n = 15$ cases we have been working with is much too small to use as a trial sample, so let's assume that it had 50 rather than 15 cases so that we can use the same statistics as before: $M_X = 7.67$, $sd_X = 4.58$, $sd_Y = 13.82$, $r_{XY} = .657$, $B_{YX} = 1.98$, $B_0 = 4.73$, and $SE_{Y-\hat{Y}} = 10.82$.

We use the approximate multipliers (t, z) of the standard errors to determine the inclusion of the confidence limits: 99%, 2.6; 95%, 2; 80%, 1.3; and 68%, 1. The standard errors for the regression/correlation statistics of our $n = 50$ sample are as follows:

Estimated B$_{YX}$

Eq. (2.8.1)
$$SE_{B_{YX}} = \frac{13.82}{4.58}\sqrt{\frac{1-.657^2}{50-2}} = .329$$

Estimated intercept

Eq. (2.8.2)
$$SE_{B_0} = 10.82\sqrt{\frac{1}{50} + \frac{7.67^2}{(50-1)(20.95)}} = .301$$

Estimated value of $\hat{Y}$ for a case where X = 9

Eq. (2.8.3)
$$S\hat{E}_{\hat{Y}_i} = 10.82\sqrt{\frac{1}{50} + \frac{(9-7.67)^2}{(50-1)(20.95)}} = 1.59.$$

Estimated r$_{YX}$

Eq. (2.8.5)
$$SE_{z'} = \frac{1}{\sqrt{50-3}} = .146$$

Estimated difference between B in two populations

Eq. (2.8.6)
$$SE_{B_V - B_W} = \sqrt{.329^2 + .329^2} = \sqrt{.2165} = .465.$$

Estimated difference between r's in two large samples from different populations

Eq. (2.8.7)
$$SE_{r_V - r_W} = \sqrt{\frac{1-.657^2}{50} + \frac{1-.430^2}{50}} = \sqrt{.01136 + .01630} = .166.$$

The *SE* is inversely proportional to $\sqrt{n}$ to a sufficient approximation when *n* is not small. Quadrupling *n* cuts *SE* approximately in half. To make a standard error *x* times as large as that for *n* = 50, compute *n*∗ = n/x²*, where *n*∗ is the necessary sample size to attain *x* times the *SE*. For example, we found $SE_{B_{YX}}$ = .329 for our sample of *n* = 50 cases. To make it half (.5) as large, we would need *n*∗ = 50/.5² = 200*.

To change a standard error from *SE* to *SE*∗, find *n*∗ = n(SE/SE∗)²*. For example, to change the $SE_{B_{YX}}$ from .329 (for *n* = 50) to *SE*∗ = .20, we would need *n*∗ = 50 (.329/.20)² = 135* cases.

For differences between *B*s and *r*s, use their statistics from the trials to determine the desired changes in the *SE*s for the two samples and compute the anticipated *SE* of the difference (Eqs. 2.8.6 and 2.8.7). Adjust the *n*s as necessary.

2.9.2 Power of Null Hypothesis Significance Tests

In Section 2.8.3, we presented methods of appraising sample data in regard to α, the risk of mistakenly rejecting the null hypothesis when it is true, that is, drawing a spuriously positive conclusion (Type I error). We now turn our attention to methods of determining β,[16] the probability of *failing* to reject the null hypothesis when it is false (Type II error), and ways in which it can be controlled in research planning.

---

[16]We have been using β to represent the standardized regression coefficient. It is used here with a different meaning for consistency with the literature.

Any given test of a null hypothesis is a complex relationship among the following four parameters:

1. The power of the test, the probability of rejecting H_0, defined as $1 - \beta$.
2. The region of rejection of H_0 as determined by the α level and whether the test is one-tailed or two-tailed. As α increases, for example from .01 to .05, power increases.
3. The sample size n. As n increases, power increases.
4. The magnitude of the effect in the population, or the degree of departure from H_0. The larger this is, the greater the power.

These four parameters are so related that when any three of them are fixed, the fourth is completely determined. Thus, when an investigator decides for a given research plan the significance criterion α and n, the power of the test is determined. However, the investigator does not know what this power is without also knowing the magnitude of the effect size (ES) in the population, the estimation of which is the whole purpose of the study. The methods presented here focus on the standardized effect size, r in the present case.

There are three general strategies for estimating the size of the standardized population effect a researcher is trying to detect as "statistically significant":

1. To the extent that studies have been carried out by the current investigator or others which are closely similar to the present investigation, the ESs found in these studies reflect the magnitude that can be expected. Thus, if a review of the relevant literature reveals rs ranging from .32 to .43, the population ES in the current study may be expected to be somewhere in the vicinity of these values. Investigators who wish to be conservative may determine the power to detect a population ρ of .25 or .30.

2. In some research areas an investigator may posit some minimum population effect size that would have either practical or theoretical significance. An investigator may determine that unless $\rho = .05$, the importance of the relationship is insufficient to warrant a change in the policy or operations of the relevant institution. Another investigator may decide that a population correlation of .10 would have a material import for the adequacy of the theory within which the experiment has been designed, and thus would wish to plan the experiment so as to detect such an ES. Or a magnitude of B_{YX} that would be substantively important may be determined and other parameters estimated from other sources to translate B_{YX} into ρ.

3. A third strategy in deciding what ES values to use in determining the power of a study is to use certain suggested conventional definitions of *small*, *medium*, and *large* effects as population $\rho = .10$, .30, and .50, respectively (J. Cohen, 1988). These conventional ESs, derived from the average values in published studies in the social sciences, may be used either by choosing one of these values (for example, the conventional medium ES of .30) or by determining power for all three populations. If the latter strategy is chosen, the investigator would then revise the research plan according to an estimation of the relevance of the various ESs to the substantive problem. This option should be looked upon as the default option only if the earlier noted strategies are not feasible.

The point of doing a power analysis of a given research plan is that when the power turns out to be insufficient the investigator may decide to revise these plans, or even drop the investigation entirely if such revision is impossible. Obviously, because little or nothing can be done after the investigation is completed, determination of statistical power is of primary value as a preinvestigation procedure. If power is found to be insufficient, the research plan may be revised in ways that will increase it, primarily by increasing n, or increasing the number of levels or variability of the independent variable, or possibly by increasing α. A more complete general discussion of the concepts and strategy of power analysis may be found in J. Cohen (1965, 1988). It is particularly useful to use a computerized program for calculating the statistical power of a proposed research plan, because such a program will provide a graphic depiction of the effect of each of the parameters (*ES*, *n*, α) on the resulting power to reject a false null hypothesis.

2.10 FACTORS AFFECTING THE SIZE OF *r*

2.10.1 The Distributions of *X* and *Y*

Because $r = 1.00$ only when each $z_X = z_Y$, it can only occur when the shapes of the frequency distributions for X and Y are exactly the same (or exactly opposite for $r = -1.00$). The greater the departure from distribution similarity, the more severe will the restriction be on the maximum possible r. In addition, as such distribution discrepancy increases, departure from homoscedasticity—equal error for different predicted values—must also necessarily increase. The decrease in the maximum possible value of (positive) r is especially noticeable under circumstances in which the two variables are skewed in opposite directions. One such common circumstance occurs when the two variables being correlated are each dichotomies: With very discrepant proportions, it is not possible to obtain a large positive correlation.

For example, suppose that a group of subjects has been classified into "risk takers" and "safe players" on the basis of behavior in an experiment, resulting in 90 risk takers and 10 safe players. A correlation is computed between this dichotomous variable and self classification as "conservative" versus "liberal" in a political sense, with 60 of the 100 subjects identifying themselves as conservative (Table 2.10.1). Even if all political liberals were also risk takers in the experimental situation, the correlation will be only (by Eq. 2.3.6):

$$r_\phi = \frac{400 - 0}{\sqrt{90 \cdot 10 \cdot 40 \cdot 60}} = .272.$$

It is useful to divide the issue of the distribution of variables into two components, those due to differences in the distribution of the underlying constructs and those due to the scales on which we have happened to measure our variables. Constraints on correlations associated with differences in distribution inherent in the constructs are not artifacts, but have real interpretive meaning. For example, gender and height for American adults are not perfectly correlated, but we need have no concern about an artificial upper limit on r attributable to this distribution difference. If gender completely determined height, there would only be two heights, one for men and one for women, and r would be 1.00.

TABLE 2.10.1
Bivariate Distribution of Experimental and Self-Reported
Conservative Tendency

		Experimental		
		Risk takers	Safe players	Total:
Self-report	Liberal	40	0	40
	Conservative	50	10	60
	Total:	90	10	100

Similarly the observed correlation between smoking and lung cancer is about .10 (estimated from figures provided by Doll & Peto, 1981). There is no artifact of distribution here; even though the risk of cancer is about 11 times as high for smokers, the vast majority of both smokers and nonsmokers alike will not contract lung cancer, and the relationship is low because of the nonassociation in these many cases.

Whenever the concept underlying the measure is logically continuous or quantitative[17]—as in the preceding example of risk taking and liberal versus conservative—it is highly desirable to measure the variables on a many-valued scale. One effect of this will be to increase the opportunity for reliable and valid discrimination of individual differences (see Section 2.10.2). To the extent that the measures are similarly distributed, the risk of underestimating the relationship between the conceptual variables will be reduced (see Chapter 4). However, the constraints on r due to unreliability are likely to be much more serious than those due to distribution differences on multivalued scales.

The Biserial r

When the only available measure of some construct X is a dichotomy, d_X, an investigator may wish to know what the correlation would be between the underlying construct and some other quantitative variable, Y. For example, X may be ability to learn algebra, which we measure by d_X, pass–fail. If one can assume that the "underlying" continuous variable X is normally distributed, and that the relationship with Y is linear, an estimate of the correlation between X and Y can be made, even though only d_X and Y are available. This correlation is estimated as

(2.10.1)
$$r_b = \frac{(M_{Y_P} - M_{Y_Q})PQ}{h(sd_Y)} = r_{pb}\frac{\sqrt{PQ}}{h},$$

where M_{Y_P} and M_{Y_Q} are the Y means for the two points of the dichotomy, P and $Q \,(= 1 - P)$ are the proportions of the sample at these two points, and h is the ordinate (height) of the standard unit normal curve at the point at which its area is divided into P and Q portions (see Appendix Table C).

For example, we will return to the data presented in Table 2.3.1, where r_{pb} was found to be $-.707$. We now take the dichotomy to represent not the presence or absence of an experimentally determined stimulus but rather gross (1) versus minor (0) naturally occurring interfering stimuli as described by the subjects. This dichotomy is assumed to represent a continuous, normally distributed variable. The biserial r between stimulus and task score will be

$$r_b = \frac{(66 - 69.5)(.428)(.572)}{.392(2.45)} = -.893$$

where .392 is the height of the ordinate at the .428, .572 break, found by linear interpolation in Appendix Table C and $r_{pb} = -.707$.

The biserial r of $-.893$ may be taken to be an estimate of the product moment correlation that would have been obtained had X been a normally distributed continuous measure. It will always be larger than the corresponding point biserial r and, in fact, may even nonsensically exceed 1.0 when the Y variable is not normally distributed. When there is no overlap between the Y scores of the two groups, the r_b will be at least 1.0. It will be approximately 25% larger than the corresponding r_{pb} when the break on X is $.50 - .50$. The ratio of r_b/r_{pb} will increase

---

[17]*Continuous* implies a variable on which infinitely small distinctions can be made; *quantitative* or *scaled* is more closely aligned to real measurement practice in the behavioral sciences, implying an ordered variable of many, or at least several, possible values. Theoretical constructs may be taken as continuous, but their measures will be quantitative in this sense.

as the break on X is more extreme; for example with a break of $.90 - .10$, r_b will be about two-thirds larger than r_{pb}.

Confidence limits are best established on r_{pb} or, equivalently, on the difference between the Y means corresponding to the two points of d_X.

Tetrachoric r

As we have seen, when the relationship between two dichotomies is investigated, the restriction on the maximum value of r_ϕ when their breaks are very different can be very severe. Once again, we can make an estimate of what the linear correlation would be if the two variables were continuous and normally distributed. Such an estimate is called the tetrachoric correlation. Because the formula for the tetrachoric correlation involves an infinite series and even a good approximation is a laborious operation, tetrachoric rs are obtained by means of computer programs. Tetrachoric r will be larger than the corresponding phi coefficient and the issues governing their interpretation and use are the same as for r_b and r_{pb}.

Caution should be exercised in the use of biserial and tetrachoric correlations, particularly in multivariate analyses. Remember that they are not observed correlations in the data, but rather hypothetical ones depending on the normality of the distributions underlying the dichotomies. Nor will standard errors for the estimated coefficients be the same as those for the product moment coefficients presented here.

2.10.2 The Reliability of the Variables

In most research in the behavioral sciences, the concepts that are of ultimate interest and that form the theoretical foundation for the study are only indirectly and imperfectly measured in practice. Thus, typically, interpretations of the correlations between variables as measured should be carefully distinguished from the relationship between the constructs or conceptual variables found in the theory.

The reliability of a variable (r_{XX}) may be defined as the correlation between the variable as measured and another equivalent measure of the same variable. In standard psychometric theory, the square root of the reliability coefficient $\sqrt{r_{XX}}$ may be interpreted as the correlation between the variable as measured by the instrument or test at hand and the "true" (error-free) score. Because true scores are not themselves observable, a series of techniques has been developed to estimate the correlation between the obtained scores and these (hypothetical) true scores. These techniques may be based on correlations among items, between items and the total score, between other subdivisions of the measuring instrument, or between alternative forms. They yield a reliability coefficient that is an estimate (based on a sample) of the population reliability coefficient.[18] This coefficient may be interpreted as an index of how well the test or measurement procedure measures whatever it is that it measures. This issue should be distinguished from the question of the test's *validity*, that is, the question of whether *what* it measures is what the investigator intends that it measure.

The discrepancy between an obtained reliability coefficient and a perfect reliability of 1.00 is an index of the relative amount of measurement error. Each observed score may be thought of as composed of some true value plus a certain amount of error:

$$(2.10.2) \qquad X = X_t + X_e.$$

---

[18]Because this is a whole field of study in its own right, no effort will be made here to describe any of its techniques, or even the theory behind the techniques, in any detail. Excellent sources of such information include McDonald (1999) and Nunnally & Bernstein (1993).

These error components are assumed to have a mean of zero and to correlate zero with the true scores and with true or error scores on other measures. Measurement errors may come from a variety of sources, such as errors in sampling the domain of content, errors in recording or coding, errors introduced by grouping or an insufficiently fine system of measurement, errors associated with uncontrolled aspects of the conditions under which the test was given, errors due to short- or long-term fluctuation in individuals' true scores, errors due to the (idiosyncratic) influence of other variables on the individuals' responses, etc.

For the entire set of scores, the reliability coefficient equals the proportion of the observed score variable that is true score variance

(2.10.3)
$$r_{XX} = \frac{sd^2_{X_t}}{sd^2_X}$$

Because, as we have stated, error scores are assumed not to correlate with anything, r_{XX} may also be interpreted as that proportion of the measure's variance that is available to correlate with other measures. Therefore, the correlation between the observed scores (X and Y) for any two variables will be numerically smaller than the correlation between their respective unobservable true scores (X_t and Y_t). Specifically,

(2.10.4)
$$r_{XY} = r_{X_t Y_t} \sqrt{r_{XX} r_{YY}}.$$

Researchers sometimes wish to estimate the correlations between two theoretical constructs from the correlations obtained between the imperfect observed measures of these constructs. To do so, one corrects for attenuation (unreliability) by dividing r_{XY} by the square root of the product of the reliabilities (the maximum possible correlation between the imperfect measures). From Eq. (2.10.4),

(2.10.5)
$$r_{X_t Y_t} = \frac{r_{XY}}{\sqrt{r_{XX} r_{YY}}}.$$

Thus, if two variables, each with a reliability of .80, were found to correlate .44,

$$r_{X_t Y_t} = \frac{.44}{\sqrt{(.80)(.80)}} = .55.$$

Although correlations are subject to attenuation due to unreliability in either or both variables, bivariate regression coefficients are not affected by unreliability in Y. This can be seen from the following, where we consider unreliability only in Y. The regression coefficient expressed as the relationship between the perfectly reliable variables [by Eq. (2.4.3)] is

(2.10.6)
$$B_{Y_t X_t} = r_{X_t Y_t} \left(\frac{sd_{Y_t}}{sd_{X_t}} \right)$$

By Eq. (2.10.5), when $r_{XX} = 1.0$, $r_{XY} = r_{XY_t}\sqrt{r_{YY}}$. By Eq. (2.10.3),

$$r_{YY} = \frac{sd^2_{Y_t}}{sd^2_{Y_t} + sd^2_{Y_e}} \quad \text{and} \quad sd_Y = \sqrt{sd^2_{Y_t} + sd^2_{Y_e}}$$

so

$$r_{XY_t} = \frac{r_{XY}}{\sqrt{sd^2_{Y_t}/(sd^2_{Y_t} + sd^2_{Y_e})}} \quad \text{and} \quad r_{XY} = r_{XY_t} \frac{sd_{Y_t}}{\sqrt{sd^2_{Y_t} + sd^2_{Y_e}}}.$$

Therefore, using Eq. (2.4.3) where $B_{YX} = r_{XY}(sd_Y/sd_X)$, substituting:

$$B_{YX} = r_{XY_t} \left(\frac{sd_{Y_t}}{\sqrt{sd_{Y_t}^2 + sd_{Y_e}^2}} \right) \left(\frac{\sqrt{sd_{Y_t}^2 + sd_{Y_e}^2}}{sd_X} \right)$$

and canceling

$$= r_{XY_t} \left(\frac{sd_{Y_t}}{sd_X} \right) = B_{Y_tX}$$

As is generally true for coefficients based on a series of estimates, caution must be used in interpreting attenuation-corrected coefficients, because each of the coefficients used in the equation is subject to sampling error (as well as model assumption failure). Indeed, it is even possible to obtain attenuation-corrected correlations larger than 1.0 when the reliabilities come from different populations than r_{XY}, are underestimated, or when the assumption of uncorrelated error is false. Obviously, because the disattenuated r is hypothetical rather than based on real data, its confidence limits are likely to be very large.[19]

To reiterate, unreliability in variables as classically defined is a sufficient reason for low correlations; it *cannot* cause correlations to be spuriously high. Spuriously high correlations may, of course, be found when sources of *bias* are shared by variables, as can happen when observations are not "blind," when subtle selection factors are operating to determine which cases can and cannot appear in the sample studied, and for yet other reasons.

2.10.3 Restriction of Range

A problem related to the question of reliability occurs under conditions when the range of one or both variables is restricted by the sampling procedure. For example, suppose that in the data presented in Table 2.2.2 and analyzed in Table 2.6.1 we had restricted ourselves to the study of faculty members who were less extreme with regard to years since Ph.D., occupying the restricted range of 5 to 11 years rather than the full range of 3 to 18 years. If the relationship is well described by a straight line and homoscedastic, we shall find that the variance of the Y scores about the regression line, $sd_{Y-\hat{Y}}^2$, remains about the same. Because when $r \neq 0$, sd_Y^2 will be decreased as an incidental result of the reduction of sd_X^2, and because $sd_Y^2 = sd_{\hat{Y}}^2 + sd_{Y-\hat{Y}}^2$, the proportion of sd_Y^2 associated with X, namely, $sd_{\hat{Y}}^2$, will necessarily be smaller, and therefore, $r^2 (= sd_{\hat{Y}}^2/sd_Y^2)$ and r will be smaller. In the current example, r decreases from .657 to .388, and r^2, the proportion of variance, from .432 to .151. (See Table 2.10.2.) When the relationship is completely linear, the regression coefficient, B_{YX}, will remain constant because the decrease in r will be perfectly offset by the increase in the ratio sd_Y/sd_X. It is 2.456 here, compared to 1.983 before. (It increased slightly in this example, but could just as readily have decreased slightly.) The fact that regression coefficients tend to remain constant over changes in the variability of X (providing the relationship is fully linear and the sample size sufficiently large to produce reasonable estimates) is an important property of regression coefficients. It is shown later how this makes them more useful as measures of relationship than correlation coefficients in some analytic contexts (Chapter 5).

CH02EX06

---

[19]Current practice is most likely to test "disattenuated" coefficients via latent variable models (described in Section 12.5.4), although the definition and estimation is somewhat different from the reasoning presented here.

TABLE 2.10.2

Correlation and Regression of Number of Publications
on a Restricted Range of Time Since Ph.D.

	Publications	Time since Ph.D.	
	Y	X	
	3	6	
	17	8	
	11	9	
	6	6	$r_{XY} = .388\ (.657)^a$
	48	10	
	22	5	$r_{XY}^2 = .150\ (.431)$
	30	5	
	21	6	$sd_{Y-\hat{Y}} = 11.10\ (10.42)$
	10	7	
	27	11	$B_{YX} = 2.456\ (1.983)$
M	19.50	7.30	
sd	12.04	1.31	
sd^2	144.94	1.71	

^{a}Parenthetic values are those for the original (i.e., unrestricted) sample.

Suppose that an estimate of the correlation that would be obtained from the full range is desired, when the available data have a curtailed or restricted range for X. If we know the sd_Y of the unrestricted X distribution as well as the sd_{X_C} for the curtailed sample and the correlation between Y and X in the curtailed sample ($r_{X_C Y}$), we may estimate r_{XY} by

(2.10.7)
$$\tilde{r}_{YX} = \frac{r_{YX_C}(sd_X/sd_{X_C})}{\sqrt{1 + r_{YX_C}^2\left(\left(sd_X^2/sd_{X_C}^2\right) - 1\right)}}$$

For example, $r = .25$ is obtained on a sample for which $sd_{X_C} = 5$ whereas the sd_X of the population in which the investigator is interested is estimated to be 12. Situations like this occur, for example, when some selection procedure such as an aptitude test has been used to select personnel and those selected are later assessed on a criterion measure. If the finding on the restricted (employed) sample is projected to the whole group originally tested, $\tilde{r}_{XY}$ would be estimated to be

$$\tilde{r}_{XY} = \frac{.25(12/5)}{\sqrt{1 + .25^2[(12/5)^2 - 1]}} = \frac{.60}{\sqrt{1.2975}} = .53$$

It should be emphasized that .53 is an estimate and assumes that the relationship is linear and homoscedastic, which might not be the case. There are no appropriate confidence limits on this estimate.

It is quite possible that restriction of range in either X or Y, or both, may occur as an incidental by-product of the sampling procedure. Therefore, it is important in any study to report the sds of the variables used. Because under conditions of homoscedasticity and linearity regression coefficients are not affected by range restriction, comparisons of different samples using the same variables should usually be done on the regression coefficients rather than on the correlation coefficients when sds differ. Investigators should be aware, however, that the questions answered by these comparisons are not the same. Comparisons of correlations answer the question, Does X account for as much of the variance in Y in group E and in Group F? Comparisons of regression coefficients answer the question, Does a change in X make the same amount of score difference in Y in group E as it does in group F?

Although the previous discussion has been cast in terms of restriction in range, an investigator may be interested in the reverse—the sample in hand has a range of X values that is large relative to the population of interest. This could happen, for example, if the sampling procedure was such as to include disproportionately more high- and low-X cases and fewer middle values. Equation (2.10.7) can be employed to estimate the correlation in the population of interest (whose range in X is less) by reinterpreting the subscript C in the equation to mean changed (including increased) rather than curtailed. Thus, r_{YX_C} and sd_{X_C} are the "too large" values in the sample, sd_Y is the (smaller) sd of the population of interest, and the estimated r in that population will be smaller. Note that the ratio sd_Y/sd_{X_C}, which before was greater than one, is now smaller than one. Because the correlation (the ES) will be higher in a sample with a larger sd, sampling in order to produce a larger sd, as in studies in which the number of "cases" is larger than in a random sample of the general population, is a major strategy for increasing the statistical power of a study.

2.10.4 Part-Whole Correlations

Occasionally we will find that a correlation has been computed between some variable J and another variable W, which is the sum of scores on a set of variables including J. Under these circumstances a positive correlation can be expected between J and W due to the fact that W includes J, even when there is no correlation between J and $W - J$. For example, if k test items of equal sd and zero r with each other are added together, each of the items will correlate exactly $1/\sqrt{k}$ with the total score. For the two-item case, therefore, each item would correlate .707 with their sum, W, when neither correlates with the other. On the same assumptions of zero correlation between the variables but with unequal sds, the variables are effectively weighted by their differing sd_i and the correlation of J with W will be equal to $sd_J/\sqrt{\Sigma sd_i^2}$, where sds are summed over the items. Obviously, under these circumstances $r_{J(W-J)} = 0$. In the more common case where the variables or items are correlated, the correlation of J with $W - J$ may be obtained by

$$(2.10.8) \qquad r_{J(W-J)} = \frac{r_{JW} sd_W - sd_J}{\sqrt{sd_W^2 + sd_J^2 - 2 r_{JW} sd_W sd_J}}$$

This is not an estimate and may be tested via the usual t test for the significance of r.

Given these often substantial spurious correlations between elements and totals including the elements, it behooves the investigator to determine $r_{J(W-J)}$, or at the very least determine the expected value when the elements are uncorrelated before interpreting r_{JW}. Such a circumstance often occurs when the interest is in the correlation of a single item with a composite that includes that item, as is carried out in psychometric analysis.

Change Scores

It is not necessary that the parts be literally added in order to produce such spurious correlation. If a subscore is subtracted, a spurious negative component in the correlation will also be produced. One common use of such difference scores in the social sciences in the use of postminus pretreatment (change) scores. If such change scores are correlated with the pre- and posttreatment scores from which they have been obtained, we will typically find that subjects initially low on X will have larger gains than those initially high on X, and that those with the highest final scores will have made greater gains than those with lower final scores. Again, if $sd_{pre} = sd_{post}$ and $r_{pre\ post} = 0$, the $r_{pre\ change} = -.707$ and $r_{post\ change} = +.707$. Although in general, we would expect the correlation between pre- and posttreatment scores to be some positive value, it will be limited by their respective reliabilities (Section 2.10.2) as well as by individual differences in true change.

If the post- minus pretreatment variable has been created in order to control for differences in pretreatment scores, the resulting negative correlations between pretreatment and change scores may be taken as a failure to remove all influence of pretreatment scores from posttreatment scores. This reflects the regression to the mean phenomenon discussed in Section 2.5 and the consequent interpretive risks. The optimal methods of handling this and related problems are the subject of a whole literature (Collins & Horn, 1993) and cannot be readily summarized. However, the appropriate analysis, as always, depends on the underlying causal model. (See Chapters 5, 12, and 15 for further discussion of this problem.)

2.10.5 Ratio or Index Variables

Ratio (index or rate) scores are those constructed by dividing one variable by another. When a ratio score is correlated with another variable or with another ratio score, the resulting correlation depends as much on the denominator of the score as it does on the numerator. Because it is usually the investigator's intent to "take the denominator into account" it may not be immediately obvious that the correlations obtained between ratio scores may be spurious—that is, may be a consequence of mathematical necessities that have no valid interpretive use. Ratio correlations depend, in part, upon the correlations between all numerator and denominator terms, so that $r_{(Y/Z)X}$ is a function of r_{YZ} and r_{XZ} as well as of r_{YX}, and $r_{(Y/Z)(X/W)}$ depends on r_{YW} and r_{XZ} as well as on the other four correlations. These correlations also involve the coefficients of variation

$$(2.10.9) \qquad\qquad v_X = \frac{sd_X}{M_X}$$

of each of the variables. Although the following formula is only a fair approximation of the correlation between ratio scores (requiring normal distributions and homoscedasticity and dropping all terms involving powers of v greater than v^2), it serves to demonstrate the dependence of correlations between ratios on all vs and on rs between all variable pairs:

$$(2.10.10) \qquad r\,(Y/Z)\,(X/W) = \frac{r_{YX}v_Y v_X - r_{YW}v_Y v_W - r_{XZ}v_X v_Z - r_{ZW}v_Z v_W}{\sqrt{v_Y^2 + v_Z^2 - 2r_{YZ}v_Y v_Z}\sqrt{v_X^2 + v_W^2 - 2r_{XW}v_X v_W}}$$

When the two ratios being correlated have a common denominator, the possibility of spurious correlations becomes apparent. Under these circumstances, the approximate formula for the correlation simplifies, because $Z = W$. If all coefficients of variation are equal when all three variables are uncorrelated we will find $r_{(Y/Z)(X/Z)} \approx .50$.

Because the coefficient of variation depends on the value of the mean, it is clear that whenever this value is arbitrary, as it is for many psychological scores, the calculated r is also arbitrary. Thus, ratios should not be correlated unless each variable is measured on a ratio scale, a scale for which a zero value means literally none of the variable (see Chapters 5 and 12). Measures with ratio scale properties are most commonly found in the social sciences in the form of counts or frequencies.

At this point it may be useful to distinguish between rates and other ratio variables. Rates may be defined as variables constructed by dividing the number of instances of some phenomenon by the total number of opportunities for the phenomenon to occur; thus, they are literally proportions. Rates or proportions are frequently used in ecological or epidemiological studies where the units of analysis are aggregates of people or areas such as counties or census tracts. In such studies, the numerator represents the incidence or prevalence of some phenomenon and the denominator represents the population at risk. For example, a delinquency rate may be calculated by dividing the number of delinquent boys ages 14–16 in a county by the total number of boys ages 14–16 in the county. This variable may be correlated across the counties in a region with the proportion of families whose incomes are below the poverty level, another rate. Because, in general, the denominators of these two rates will reflect the populations of the counties, which may vary greatly, they can be expected to be substantially correlated. In other cases the denominators may actually be the same—as, for example, in an investigation of the relationship between delinquency rates and school dropout rates for a given age-gender group. The investigator will typically find that these rates have characteristics that minimize the problem of spurious correlation. In most real data, the coefficients of variation of the numerators will be substantially larger than the coefficients of variation of the denominators, and thus the correlation between rates will be determined substantially by the correlation between the numerators. Even in such data, however, the resulting proportions may not be optimal for the purpose of linear correlation. Chapter 6 discusses some nonlinear transformations of proportions, which may be more appropriate for analysis than the raw proportions or rates themselves.

Experimentally produced rates may be more subject to problems of spurious correlation, especially when there are logically alternative denominators. The investigator should determine that the correlation between the numerator and denominator is very high (and positive), because in general the absence of such a correlation suggests a faulty logic in the study. In the absence of a large correlation, the coefficients of variation of the numerator should be substantially larger than that of the denominator if the problem of spurious correlation is to be minimized.

Other Ratio Scores

When the numerator does not represent some subclass of the denominator class, the risks involved in using ratios are even more serious, because the likelihood of small or zero correlations between numerators and denominators and relatively similar values of v is greater. If the variables do not have true zeros and equal intervals, correlations involving ratios should probably be avoided altogether, and an alternative method for removing the influence of Z from X or Y should be chosen, as presented in Chapters 3 and 12.

The difficulties that may be encountered in correlations involving rates and ratios may be illustrated by the following example. An investigator wishes to determine the relationship between visual scanning and errors on a digit-symbol (d-s) task. All subjects are given 4 minutes to work on the task. Because subjects who complete more d-s substitutions have a greater opportunity to make errors, the experimenter decides, reasonably enough, to determine the error rate by dividing the number of errors by the number of d-s substitutions completed. Table 2.10.3 displays the data for 10 subjects. Contrary to expectation, subjects who completed more d-s tasks did not tend to produce more errors ($r_{ZX} = -.105$), nor did they scan notably more than did low scorers ($r_{ZY} = .023$). Nevertheless, when the two ratio scores are computed, they show a substantial positive correlation (.427) in spite of the fact that the numerators showed slight negative correlation ($-.149$), nor is there any tendency for scanning and errors to be correlated for any given level of d-s task completion. Thus, because $r_{ZZ} = 1$, the $r_{(X/Z)(Y/Z)}$ may here be seen to be an example of spurious correlation.[20]

---

[20] An alternative method of taking into account the number completed in considering the relationship between errors and number of scans might be to partial Z (see subsequent chapters).

TABLE 2.10.3
An Example of Spurious Correlation Between Ratios

Subject	No. completed d-s tasks (Z)	No. errors (X)	No. scans (Y)	Error rate (X/Z)	Scan rate (Y/Z)
1	25	5	24	.20	.96
2	29	3	30	.10	1.03
3	30	3	27	.10	.90
4	32	4	30	.12	.94
5	37	3	18	.08	.49
6	41	2	33	.05	.80
7	41	3	27	.07	.66
8	42	5	21	.12	.50
9	43	3	24	.07	.56
10	43	5	33	.12	.77

$$r_{ZX} = -.105, \quad r_{ZY} = .106, \quad r_{XY} = -.149$$

$$r_{(X/Z)(Y/Z)} = .427$$

2.10.6 Curvilinear Relationships

When the relationship between the two variables is only moderately well fitted by a straight line, the correlation coefficient that indicates the degree of linear relationship will understate the predictability from one variable to the other. Frequently the relationship, although curvilinear, is monotonic; that is, increases in Z are accompanied by increases (or decreases) in Y, although not at a constant rate. Under these circumstances, some (nonlinear) monotonic transformation of X or Y or both may straighten out the regression line and provide a better indication of the size of the relationship between the two variables (an absolutely larger r). Because there are several alternative ways of detecting and handling curvilinear relationships, the reader is referred to Chapters 4 and 6 for a detailed treatment of the issues.

2.11 SUMMARY

A linear relationship exists between two quantitative variables when there is an overall tendency for increases in the value of one variable to be accompanied by increases in the other variable (a positive relationship), or for increases in the first to be accompanied by decreases in the second (a negative relationship); (Section 2.1). Efforts to index the degree of linear relationship between two variables must cope with the problem of the different units in which variables are measured. Standard (z) scores are a conversion of scores into distances from their own means, in standard deviation units, and they render different scores comparable. The Pearson product moment correlation coefficient, r, is a measure of the degree of relationship between two variables, X and Y, based on the discrepancies of the subjects' paired z scores, $z_X - z_Y$. r varies between -1 and $+1$, which represent perfect negative and perfect positive linear relationships, respectively. When $r = 0$, there is no linear correlation between the variables (Section 2.2).

r can be written as a function of z score products, a function of variances and covariance, or in terms of the original units. Special simplified formulas are available for r when one variable is a dichotomy (point biserial r), when both variables are dichotomies (r_ϕ), or when the data are two sets of complete ranks (Spearman rank order correlation); (Section 2.3).

The regression coefficient, B_{YX}, gives the optimal rule for a linear estimate of Y from X, and is the change in Y units per unit change in X, that is, the slope of the regression line. The intercept, B_0, gives the predicted value of Y for a zero value of X. B_{YX} and B_0 are optimal in the sense that they provide the smallest squared discrepancies between Y and estimated $\hat{Y}$. r is the regression coefficient for the standardized variables. When X is centered, $B_0 = M_Y$ (Section 2.4). Unless $r = 1$, it is a mathematical necessity that the average score for a variable being estimated (e.g., $\hat{Y}$) will be relatively closer to M_Y than the value from which it is being estimated (e.g., X) will be to its mean (M_X) when both are measured in sd units (Section 2.5).

When Y is estimated from X the sd of the difference between observed scores and the estimated scores (the sample standard error of estimate) can be computed from r and sd_Y. The coefficient of alienation represents the error as a proportion of the original sd_Y. r^2 equals the proportion of the variance (sd^2) of each of the variables that is shared with or can be estimated from the other (Sections 2.6 and 2.7).

The two major methods of statistical inference are estimation and null hypothesis testing. The formal model assumptions are presented (Section 2.8.1), confidence intervals are given for B_{YX}, B_{Y0}, r_{XY}, for differences between independent sample values of these statistics, and for the estimated $\hat{Y}_i$ (Section 2.8.2). Given α, confidence intervals provide the range of values within which the corresponding population values can be expected to fall. In Section 2.8.3, we present the null hypothesis tests for simple regression and correlation statistics. Section 2.8.4 critiques null hypothesis testing and contrasts it with the use of confidence intervals.

The degree of accuracy (precision) in the estimation of parameters is reflected in the statistic's confidence interval. The probability of null hypothesis rejection (statistical power) can be assessed before the research sample is collected (Section 2.9). Methods of finding the sample size to produce a margin of error for a given degree of inclusion in the confidence interval (95%, 80%) are presented (Section 2.9.1) and methods are given for determining the sample size needed for the desired statistical power, that is, the probability of rejecting the null hypothesis (Section 2.9.2).

A number of characteristics of the X and Y variables will affect the size of the correlation between them. Among these are differences in the distribution of the X and Y variables (Section 2.10.1), unreliability in one or both variables (Section 2.10.2), and restriction of the range of one or both variables (Section 2.10.3). When one variable is included as a part of the other variable, the correlation between them will reflect this overlap (Section 2.10.4). Scores obtained by dividing one variable by another will produce spurious correlation with other variables under some conditions (Section 2.10.5). The r between two variables will be an underestimate of the magnitude of their relationship when a curved rather than a straight line best fits the bivariate distribution (Section 2.10.6). Under such circumstances, transformation of one or both variables or multiple representation of one variable will provide a better picture of the relationship between the variables.

3

Multiple Regression/ Correlation With Two or More Independent Variables

3.1 INTRODUCTION: REGRESSION AND CAUSAL MODELS

In Chapter 2 we examined the index of linear correlation between two variables, the Pearson product moment correlation r and the regression equation for estimating Y from X. Because of the simplicity of the two-variable problems, we did not need to go into detail regarding the interpretive use of these coefficients to draw substantive inferences. The inferences were limited to the unbiased estimation of their magnitudes in the population; the assertion, in the case of the regression coefficient, that one variable was, in part, related to or dependent on the other; and the demonstration of the significance of the departure of the coefficients from zero. When we move to the situation with more than one independent variable, however, the inferential possibilities increase more or less exponentially. Therefore, it always behooves the investigator to make the underlying theoretical rationale and goals of the analysis as explicit as possible. Fortunately, an apparatus for doing so has been developed in the form of the analysis of causal models. Because the authors advocate the employment of these models in virtually all investigations conducted for the purpose of understanding phenomena (as opposed to simple prediction), this chapter begins with an introduction to the use of causal models. A more complete presentation is found in Chapter 12.

3.1.1 What Is a Cause?

Conceptions of causality and definitions of cause and effect have differed among proponents of causal analysis, some offering no explicit definitions at all. Causal analysis as a working method apparently requires no more elaborate a conception of causality than that of common usage. In our framework, to say that X is a cause of Y carries with it four requirements:

1. X precedes Y in time (temporal precedence).
2. Some mechanism whereby this causal effect operates can be posited (causal mechanism).
3. A change in the value of X is accompanied by a change in the value of Y on the average (association or correlation).
4. The effects of X on Y can be isolated from the effects of other potential variables on Y (non-spuriousness or lack of confounders).

When X or Y is a quantitative variable (e.g., dollars, score points, minutes, millimeters, percentile ranks), the meaning of value is obvious. When X is a categorical scale (i.e., a collection of two or more qualitative states or groups), a change in value means a change from one state to another (e.g., from Protestant to Catholic or Protestant to non-Protestant, from depressed to not depressed, or from one diagnosis to another). When Y is a dichotomy (schizophrenia-nonschizophrenia), a change in value on the average means a change in proportion (e.g., from 10% schizophrenia for some low value of X to 25% schizophrenia for some higher value).

The third proposition should not be simplified to mean, If you change X, Y will change. This may, of course, be true, but it need not be. First, it may not be possible to manipulate X. For example, boys have a higher incidence of reading disability than girls; here sex (X) causes reading disability (Y), but it is meaningless to think in terms of changing girls into boys. Second, even when X can be manipulated, the way it is manipulated may determine whether and how Y changes, because the nature of the manipulation may defeat or alter the normal causal mechanism whereby X operates.

The models that we are employing have their roots in the path-analytic diagrams developed by the geneticist Sewell Wright (1921) for untangling genetic and nongenetic influences. These are often currently referred to as structural models or structural equation models. The purpose of the models is to make explicit exactly what the investigator has in mind about the variables and the meaning of their interrelationships. As such, they contribute to the clarity and internal consistency of the investigation. It should be recognized at the outset, however, that a causal model may never be established as proven by a given analysis; all that may be said is that the data are to some extent consistent with a given model or that they are not. Thus, the value of a given model is determined as much by the logic underlying its structure as by the empirical demonstrations of the fit of a given set of data to the model.[1]

3.1.2 Diagrammatic Representation of Causal Models

The basic rules for representing a causal model are quite simple.[2] Causal effects are represented by arrows going from the cause to the effect (the "dependent" variable). Usually, by convention, the causal flow is portrayed as going from left to right. In a simple model the independent variables are considered *exogenous* or predetermined variables. These variables are taken as given, and the model requires no explanation of the causal relationships among them. The relationships among these variables are represented by curved double-headed arrows connecting each pair.

To illustrate the use of a causal diagram, let us expand the academic example employed in Chapter 2. The investigator has collected the data on number of publications and time (expressed in number of years) since Ph.D. to determine the influence of productivity (as indexed by publications) and seniority (time since Ph.D.) on academic salaries. The resulting causal diagram is shown in Fig. 3.1.1. In this simple model we assert that academic salary is in part determined by time since Ph.D. and in part by publications. These latter two variables may be correlated with each other, but no causal explanation is offered for any relationship between them. However, salary is assumed not to cause changes in numbers of publications nor in time since Ph.D.

---

[1] The logical frame and historical development of causal models are discussed further in Section 12.1.

[2] This initial discussion is limited to elementary models and omits consideration of the effects of unmeasured causes and the assumptions underlying the models, for which see Chapter 12.

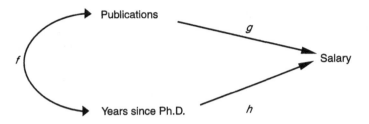

FIGURE 3.1.1 Causal model of academic salary example.

3.2 REGRESSION WITH TWO INDEPENDENT VARIABLES

To provide the estimates of effects required by our causal model we need a weight for each of our exogenous variables whose application will account for as much of the variance of our dependent variable as possible. Recalling that the regression equation, $Y = B_X + B_0$, was designed to be such an estimate for a single independent variable, we may anticipate that a similar procedure may produce the appropriate weights for two independent variables.

CH03EX01

For example, suppose we have gathered the data in Table 3.2.1 to estimate the model for academic salaries presented in Fig. 3.1.1.[3] The correlation between salary (Y) and time since Ph.D. (X_1) is .710 and B_{Y1} is therefore .710($7889.77/4.577$) = \$1224 per year. The correlation between salary and number of publications (X_2) is .588, and its regression coefficient is therefore .588($7889.77/13.823$) = \$336 per publication (Table 3.2.1). If X_1 and X_2 were uncorrelated, we could simply use B_{Y1} and B_{Y2} together to estimate Y. However, as might be expected, we find a tendency for those faculty members who have had their degrees longer to have more publications than those who more recently completed their education ($r_{12} = .657$). Thus, X_1 and X_2 are to some extent redundant, and necessarily their respective estimates, $\hat{Y}_1$ and $\hat{Y}_2$ will also be redundant. What we need to estimate Y optimally from both X_1 and X_2 is an equation in which their redundancy (or more generally the relationship between X_1 and X_2) is taken into account. The regression coefficients in such an equation are called *partial regression coefficients* to indicate that they are optimal linear estimates of the dependent variable (Y) when used in combination with specified other independent variables.[4] Thus, $B_{Y1.2}$ is the partial regression coefficient for Y on X_1 when X_2 is also in the equation, and $B_{Y2.1}$ is the partial regression coefficient for Y on X_2 when X_1 is also in the equation. The full equation is

$$(3.2.1) \qquad \hat{Y} = B_{Y1.2}X_1 + B_{Y2.1}X_2 + B_{0Y.12}$$

The partial regression coefficients or B weights in this equation, as well as the regression constant B_0, are determined in such a way that the sum of the squared differences between (actual) Y and (estimated) $\hat{Y}$ is a minimum. Thus, the multiple regression equation is defined by the same ordinary least squares criterion as was the regression equation for a single independent variable. Because the equation *as a whole* satisfies this mathematical criterion, the term *partial regression coefficient* is used to make clear that it is the weight to be applied to an independent

---

[3] Again, the number of cases has been kept small to enable the reader to follow computations with ease. No advocacy of such small samples is intended (see sections on precision and power). We also present population estimates of variance and *sd*, rather than sample values, in conformity with computer statistical packages.

In this and the remaining chapters the dependent variable is identified as Y and the individual independent variables as X with a numerical subscript, that is X_1, X_2, etc. This makes it possible to represent independent variables by their subscripts only, for example B_{YX_3} becomes B_{Y3}.

[4] Hereafter we may refer to bivariate statistics such as correlations or regression coefficients as "zero-order" coefficients, in contrast to partial coefficients when other IVs are in the equation.

TABLE 3.2.1
Seniority, Publication, and Salary Data on 15 Faculty Members

Time since Ph.D. (X_1)	No. of Publications (X_2)	Salary (Y)	
3	18	$51,876	
6	3	54,511	
3	2	53,425	$r_{Y1} = .710$ ($r_{Y1}^2 = .505$)
8	17	61,863	$r_{Y2} = .588$ ($r_{Y2}^2 = .346$)
9	11	52,926	$r_{12} = .657$
6	6	47,034	
16	38	66,432	$\hat{Y}_1 = \$1{,}224X_1 + \$43{,}659$
10	48	61,100	
2	9	41,934	$\hat{Y}_2 = \$336X_2 + \$46{,}357$
5	22	47,454	
5	30	49,832	
6	21	47,047	
7	10	39,115	
11	27	59,677	
18	37	61,458	
M 7.67	19.93	$53,046	
sd 4.58	13.82	$8,166	

variable (IV) when one or more specified other IVs are also in the equation. Thus $B_{Y1.2}$ indicates the weight to be given X_1 when X_2 is also in the equation, $B_{Y2.13}$ is the X_2 weight when X_1 and X_3 are in the equation, $B_{Y4.123}$ is the X_4 weight when X_1, X_2, and X_3 are also used in the equation for Y, and so on. The weights for the IVs taken together with B_0 constitute the necessary constants for the linear regression equation.

When the regression equation is applied to the IV values for any given observation, the result will be an estimated value of the dependent variable ($\hat{Y}$). For any given set of data on which such an equation is determined, the resulting set of $\hat{Y}$ values will be as close to the observed Y values as possible, given a single weight for each IV. "As close as possible" is defined by the least squares principle.

For our example of estimating salary (Y) from time since Ph.D. (X_1) and number of publications (X_2), the full regression equation is

$$(3.2.2) \qquad \hat{Y}_{12} = \$983X_1 + \$122X_2 + \$43{,}082,$$

where $983 is the partial regression coefficient $B_{Y1.2}$ for X_1 and $122 is the partial regression coefficient $B_{Y2.1}$ for X_2. The redundancy of information about Y carried by these two variables is reflected in the fact that the partial regression coefficients ($983 and $122) are each smaller in magnitude than their separate zero-order Bs ($1,224 and $336). We may interpret $B_{Y2.1} = \$122$ directly by stating that, for any given time since Ph.D. (X_1), on the average each additional publication is associated with an increase in salary of only $122 rather than the $336 that was found when time since Ph.D. were ignored. The $B_{Y1.2} = \$983$ may be similarly interpreted as indicating that, for faculty members with a given number of publications (X_2), on the average each additional year since Ph.D. is associated with an increase in salary of $983 rather than the $1224 that was found when number of publications was ignored. From a purely statistical point of view, these changes are a consequence of the redundancy of the two causal variables (i.e., the tendency for faculty who have had their Ph.D.s longer to have more publications ($r_{12} = .657$); the partialing process controls for this tendency.[5] Viewed through the lens of causal analysis we see (particularly in the case of number of publications) how seriously we can be misled about the causal impact of a variable when we fail to include in our model other important causes. This, then, is an instance in which we have failed to consider the need to *isolate* the effects of a presumably causal variable from other correlated potential causes (Bollen, 1989).

Thus far, we have simply asserted that the regression equation for two or more IVs takes the same form as did the single IV case without demonstrating how the coefficients are obtained. As in the case of presenting correlation and regression with one IV, we initially standardize the variables to eliminate the effects of noncomparable raw (original) units. The regression equation for standardized variables[6] is

$$\hat{z}_Y = \beta_{Y1.2} z_1 + \beta_{Y2.1} z_2 \tag{3.2.3}$$

Just as r_{YX} is the standardized regression coefficient for estimating z_Y from z_X, $\beta_{Y1.2}$ and $\beta_{Y2.1}$ are the standardized partial regression coefficients for estimating z_Y from z_1 and z_2 with minimum squared error.

The equations for $\beta_{Y1.2}$ and $\beta_{Y2.1}$ can be proved via differential calculus to be

$$
\begin{aligned}
\beta_{Y1.2} &= \frac{r_{Y1} - r_{Y2} r_{12}}{1 - r_{12}^2} \\
\beta_{Y2.1} &= \frac{r_{Y2} - r_{Y1} r_{12}}{1 - r_{12}^2}.
\end{aligned}
\tag{3.2.4}
$$

A separation of the elements of this formula may aid understanding: r_{Y1} and r_{Y2} are "validity" coefficients, that is, the zero-order (simple) correlations of the IVs with the dependent variable. r_{12}^2 represents the variance in each IV shared with the other IV and reflects their redundancy. Thus, $\beta_{Y1.2}$ and $\beta_{Y2.1}$ are partial coefficients because each has been adjusted to allow for the correlation between X_1 and X_2.

To return to our academic example, the correlations between the variables are $r_{Y1} = .710$, $r_{Y2} = .588$, and $r_{12} = .657$. We determine by Eq. (3.2.4) that

$$\beta_{Y1.2} = \frac{.710 - (.588)(.657)}{1 - .657^2} = .570,$$

$$\beta_{Y2.1} = \frac{.588 - (.710)(.657)}{1 - .657^2} = .213,$$

and that the full regression equation for the standardized variables is therefore

$$\hat{z}_Y = .570 z_1 + .213 z_2.$$

---

[5]The terms *holding constant* or *controlling for*, *partialing the effects of*, or *residualizing* some other variables(s) indicate a mathematical procedure, of course, rather than an experimental one. Such terms are statisticians' shorthand for describing the average effect of a particular variable for any given values of the other variables.

[6]We employ the greek symbol β for the standardized coefficient in order to be consistent with the literature and with the earlier edition. It should not be confused with the other use of this symbol to indicate Type II errors of inference.

Once $\beta_{Y1.2}$ and $\beta_{Y2.1}$ have been determined, conversion to the original units is readily accomplished by

(3.2.5)
$$B_{Y1.2} = \beta_{Y1.2} \frac{sd_Y}{sd_1}$$
$$B_{Y2.1} = \beta_{Y2.1} \frac{sd_Y}{sd_2}.$$

Substituting the values for our running example (Table 3.2.1), we find

$$B_{Y1.2} = .570 \left(\frac{\$7622}{4.42} \right) = \$983$$

$$B_{Y2.1} = .213 \left(\frac{\$7622}{13.35} \right) = \$122.$$

Because we are again using the original units, we need a constant B_0 that serves to adjust for differences in means. This is calculated in the same way as with a single IV:

(3.2.6)
$$B_0 = M_Y - B_{Y1.2} M_1 - B_{Y2.1} M_2$$
$$= \$53,046 - \$983(7.67) - \$122(19.93)$$
$$= \$43,082.$$

The full (raw score) regression equation for estimating academic salary is therefore

$$\hat{Y}_{12} = \$983 X_1 + \$122 X_2 + \$43,082,$$

and the resulting values are provided in the third column of Table 3.3.1 later in this chapter.

The partial regression coefficients, $B_{Y1.2} = \$983$ and $B_{Y2.1} = \$122$, are the empirical estimates, respectively, of h and g, the causal effects of our independent variables accompanying the arrows in the causal diagram (Fig. 3.1.1).

3.3 MEASURES OF ASSOCIATION WITH TWO INDEPENDENT VARIABLES

Just as there are partial regression coefficients for multiple regression equations (equations for predicting Y from more than one IV), so are there partial and multiple correlation coefficients that answer the same questions answered by the simple product moment correlation coefficient in the single IV case. These questions include the following:

1. How well does this group of IVs together estimate Y?
2. How much does any single variable add to the estimation of Y already accomplished by other variables?
3. When all other variables are held constant statistically, how much of Y does a given variable account for?

3.3.1 Multiple R and R^2

Just as r is the measure of association between two variables, so the multiple R is the measure of association between a dependent variable and an optimally weighted combination of two or more IVs. Similarly, r^2 is the proportion of each variable's variance shared with the other, and R^2 is the proportion of the dependent variable's variance (sd_Y^2) shared with the optimally weighted IVs. Unlike r, however, R takes on only values between 0 and 1, with the former indicating no relationship with the IVs and the latter indicating a perfect relationship. (The reason that Rs are always positive becomes clear shortly.) The formula for the multiple correlation coefficient for two IVs as a function of the original rs is

(3.3.1)
$$R_{Y.12} = \sqrt{\frac{r_{Y1}^2 + r_{Y2}^2 - 2r_{Y1}r_{Y2}r_{12}}{1 - r_{12}^2}}.$$

A similarity between the structure of this formula and the formula for β coefficients may lead the reader to suspect that R may be written as a function of these coefficients. This is indeed the case; an alternative formula is

(3.3.2)
$$R_{Y.12} = \sqrt{\beta_{Y1.2}r_{Y1} + \beta_{Y2.1}r_{Y2}}.$$

For the example illustrated in Table 3.1.1 the multiple correlation is thus, by Eq. (3.3.1),

$$R_{Y.12} = \sqrt{\frac{.5047 + .3455 - 2(.710)(.588)(.657)}{1 - .4313}},$$
$$= \sqrt{.5300} = .728$$

or by Eq. (3.3.2),

$$R_{Y.12} = \sqrt{.570(.710) + .213(.588)},$$
$$= \sqrt{.5300} = .728.$$

(We again remind the reader who checks the previous arithmetic and finds it "wrong" of our warning in Section 1.2.2 about rounding errors.)

We saw in Chapter 2 that the absolute value of the correlation between two variables $|r_{YX}|$ is equal to the correlation between Y and $\hat{Y}_X$. The multiple correlation is actually definable by this property. Thus, with two IVs,

(3.3.3)
$$R_{Y.12} = r_{Y\hat{Y}_{12}},$$

and taking the example values in Table 3.3.1 we see that indeed $r_{Y\hat{Y}_{12}} = .728 = R_{Y.12}$. That $r_{Y\hat{Y}_{12}}$ and hence $R_{Y.12}$ cannot be negative can be seen from the fact that by the least squares criterion $\hat{Y}$ is as close as possible to Y.

The reader will again recall that r_{XY}^2 is the proportion of variance of Y shared with X. In exact parallel, $R_{Y.12}^2$ is the proportion of sd_Y^2 shared with the optimally weighted composite of X_1 and X_2. These optimal weights are, of course, those provided by the regression equation used to estimate Y. Thus,

(3.3.4)
$$R_{Y.12}^2 = \frac{sd_{\hat{Y}.12}^2}{sd_Y^2}$$
$$= \frac{5549^2}{7622^2} = .5300;$$

TABLE 3.3.1
Actual, Estimated, and Residual Salaries

1 Y	2 $\hat{Y}_1$	3 $\hat{Y}_{12}$	4 $Y - \hat{Y}_{12}$	5 $\hat{X}_{2.1}$	6 $X_2 - \hat{X}_{2.1}$	7 $Y - \hat{Y}_1$
$51,876	$47,332	$48,223	$3,653	10.68	7.32	$4,544
54,511	51,005	49,345	5,166	16.63	−13.63	3,506
53,425	47,332	46,275	7,150	10.68	−8.68	6,093
61,863	53,454	53,016	8,847	20.59	−3.59	8,409
52,926	54,678	53,268	−342	22.58	−11.58	−1,752
47,034	51,005	49,710	−2,676	16.63	−10.63	−3,971
66,432	63,249	63,437	2,995	36.46	1.54	3,183
61,100	55,903	58,757	2,343	24.56	23.44	5,197
41,934	46,107	46,144	−4,210	8.70	.30	−4,173
47,454	49,781	50,676	−3,222	14.64	7.36	−2,327
49,832	49,781	51,651	−1,819	14.64	15.36	51
47,047	51,005	51,537	−4,490	16.63	4.37	−3,958
39,115	52,229	51,180	−12,065	18.61	−8.61	−13,114
59,677	57,127	57,183	2,494	26.54	.46	2,550
61,458	65,698	65,281	−3,823	40.42	−3.42	−4,240
M $53,046	$53,046	$53,046	$0	19.93	0	$0
sd $7,622	$5,415	$5,552	$5,227	8.77	10.07	$5,365

Correlations

	$\hat{Y}_1$	$\hat{Y}_{12}$	$X_2 - \hat{X}_{2.1}$
Y	$.710 = r_1$	$.728 = R_{Y.12}$	$.161 = sr_2$
$Y - \hat{Y}_1$	$0 = r_{(Y.1)1}$	.051	$.228 = pr_2$

that is, some 53% of the variance in salary (Y) is linearly accounted for by number of years since doctorate (X_1) and number of publications (X_2) in this sample.

Again in parallel with simple correlation and regression the variance of the residual, $Y - \hat{Y}_{12}$, is that portion of sd_Y^2 not linearly associated with X_1 and X_2. Therefore (and necessarily),

(3.3.5)
$$r_{\hat{Y}(Y-\hat{Y})} = 0,$$

and since such variances are additive,

(3.3.6)
$$sd_Y^2 = sd_{\hat{Y}_{12}}^2 + sd_{Y-\hat{Y}_{12}}^2.$$

It should also be apparent at this point that a multiple R can never be smaller than the absolute value of the largest correlation of Y with the IVs and must be almost invariably larger. The optimal estimation of $\hat{Y}_{12}$ under circumstances in which X_2 adds nothing to X_1's estimation of $\hat{Y}$ would involve a 0 weight for X_2 and thus $R_{Y.12}$ would equal $|r_{Y1}|$, the absolute value of r_{Y1}. Any slight departure of X_2 values from this rare circumstance necessarily leads to some (perhaps trivial) increase in $R_{Y.12}$ over $|r_{Y1}|$.

As with bivariate correlation the square root of the proportion of Y variance *not* associated with the IVs is called the *coefficient of* (multiple) *alienation*. This value is $\sqrt{1 - R^2} = \sqrt{1 - .5300} = .686$ for these data.

3.3.2 Semipartial Correlation Coefficients and Increments to R^2

One of the important problems that arises in MRC is that of defining the contribution of each IV in the multiple correlation. We shall see that the solution to this problem is not so straightforward as in the case of a single IV, the choice of coefficient depending on the substantive reasoning underlying the exact formulation of the research questions. One answer is provided by the semipartial correlation coefficient sr and its square, sr^2. To understand the meaning of these coefficients, it is useful to consider the "ballantine." Recall that in the diagrammatic representation of Fig. 2.6.1 the variance of each variable was represented by a circle of unit area. The overlapping area of two circles represents their relationship as r^2. With Y and two IVs represented in this way, the total area of Y covered by the X_1 and X_2 circles represents the proportion of Y's variance accounted for by the two IVs, $R^2_{Y.12}$.

Figure 3.3.1 shows that this area is equal to the sum of areas designated a, b, and c. The areas a and b represent those portions of Y overlapped uniquely by IVs X_1 and X_2, respectively, whereas area c represents their simultaneous overlap with Y. The "unique" areas, expressed as proportions of Y variance, are squared semipartial correlation coefficients, and each equals the increase in the squared multiple correlation that occurs when the variable is added to the other IV.[7] Thus

(3.3.7)
$$a = sr_1^2 = R^2_{Y.12} - r^2_{Y2},$$
$$b = sr_2^2 = R^2_{Y.12} - r^2_{Y1}.$$

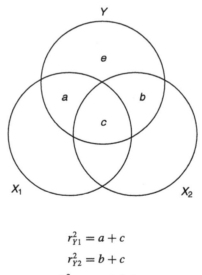

$$r^2_{Y1} = a + c$$
$$r^2_{Y2} = b + c$$
$$R^2_{Y.12} = a + b + c$$

FIGURE 3.3.1   The ballantine for X_1 and X_2 with Y.

---

[7]Throughout the remainder of the book, whenever possible without ambiguity, partial coefficients are subscripted by the relevant independent variable only, it being understood that Y is the dependent variable and that all other IVs have been partialed. In this expression (i) indicates that X_i is not included in the variables X_1 to X_k that are being partialed. Thus, $sr_i = r_{Y(i.12...(i)...k)}$, the correlation between Y and X_i from which all other IVs in the set under consideration have been partialed. Similarly, R without subscript refers to $R_{Y.12...k}$.

A formula for sr for the two IV case may be given as a function of zero-order rs as

$$sr_1 = \frac{r_{Y1} - r_{Y2}r_{12}}{\sqrt{1 - r_{12}^2}}$$

(3.3.8)   and

$$sr_2 = \frac{r_{Y2} - r_{Y1}r_{12}}{\sqrt{1 - r_{12}^2}}.$$

For our running example (Table 3.2.1), these values are

$$sr_1 = \frac{.710 - .588(.657)}{\sqrt{1 - .657^2}} = .430,$$

$$sr_1^2 = .1850$$

or, by Eq. (3.3.7)

$$sr_1^2 = .5305 - .3455 = .1850.$$

For X_2,

$$sr_2 = \frac{.588 - .710(.657)}{\sqrt{1 - .657^2}} = .161$$

$$sr_2^2 = .0258,$$

or, by Eq. (3.3.7),

$$sr_2^2 = .5305 - .5047 = .0258.$$

The semipartial correlation sr_1 is the correlation between all of Y and X_1 from which X_2 has been partialed. It is a *semi*partial correlation because the effects of X_2 have been removed from X_1 but not from Y. Recalling that in this system "removing the effect" is equivalent to subtracting from X_1 the X_1 values estimated from X_2, that is, to be working with $X_1 - \hat{X}_{1.2}$, we see that another way to write this relationship is

(3.3.9) $$sr_1 = r_{Y(X_1 - \hat{X}_{1.2})}.$$

Another notational form of sr_1 used is $r_{Y(1.2)}$, the 1.2 being a shorthand way of expressing "X_1 from which X_2 has been partialed," or $X_1 - \hat{X}_{1.2}$. It is a convenience to use this dot notation to identify which is being partialed from what, particularly in subscripts, and it is employed whenever necessary to avoid ambiguity. Thus $i \cdot j$ means i *from which j is partialed*. Note also that in the literature the term *part* correlation is sometimes used to denote semipartial correlation.

In Table 3.3.1 we present the $X_2 - \hat{X}_{2.1}$ (residual) values for each case in the example in which salary was estimated from publications and time since Ph.D. The correlation between these residual values and Y is seen to equal .4301, which is sr_1; and $.4301^2 = .1850 = sr_1^2$, as before.

To return to the ballantine (Fig. 3.3.1) we see that for our example, area $a = .1850$, $b = .0258$, and $a + b + c = R_{Y.12}^2 = .5305$. It is tempting to calculate c (by $c = R_{Y.12}^2 - sr_1^2 - sr_2^2$) and interpret it as the proportion of Y variance estimated jointly or redundantly by X_1 and X_2. However, any such interpretation runs into a serious catch—there is nothing in the mathematics that prevents c from being a negative value, and a negative proportion of variance hardly makes sense. Because c is not necessarily positive, we forgo interpreting it as a proportion of variance. A discussion of the circumstances in which c is negative is found in Section 3.4. On the other hand, a and b can never be negative and are appropriately considered proportions of variance; each represents the increase in the proportion of Y variance accounted for by the addition of the corresponding variable to the equation estimating Y.

3.3.3 Partial Correlation Coefficients

Another kind of solution to the problem of describing each IV's participation in determining R is given by the *partial* correlation coefficient pr_1, and its square, pr_1^2. The squared partial correlation may be understood best as that proportion of sd_Y^2 *not* associated with X_2 that *is* associated with X_1. Returning to the ballantine (Fig. 3.3.1), we see that

(3.3.10)
$$pr_1^2 = \frac{a}{a+e} = \frac{R_{Y.12}^2 - r_{Y2}^2}{1 - r_{Y2}^2}$$

$$pr_2^2 = \frac{b}{b+e} = \frac{R_{Y.12}^2 - r_{Y1}^2}{1 - r_{Y1}^2}.$$

The a area or numerator for pr_1^2 is the squared semipartial correlation coefficient sr_1^2; however, the base includes not all the variance of Y as in sr_1^2 but only that portion of Y variance that is not associated with X_2, that is, $1 - r_{Y2}^2$. Thus, this squared partial r answers the question, How much of the Y variance that is not estimated by the other IVs in the equation is estimated by this variable? Interchanging X_1 and X_2 (and areas a and b), we similarly interpret pr_2^2. In our faculty salary example, we see that by Eqs. (3.3.10)

$$pr_1^2 = \frac{.5305 - .3455}{1 - .3455} = \frac{.1850}{.6545} = .2826$$

$$pr_2^2 = \frac{.5305 - .5046}{1 - .4312} = \frac{.0259}{.5688} = .0455$$

Obviously, because the denominator cannot be greater than 1, partial correlations will be larger than semipartial correlations, except in the limiting case when other IVs are correlated 0 with Y, in which case $sr = pr$.

pr may be found more directly as a function of zero-order correlations by

(3.3.11)
$$pr_1 = \frac{r_{Y1} - r_{Y2}r_{12}}{\sqrt{1 - r_{Y2}^2}\sqrt{1 - r_{12}^2}}$$

$$pr_2 = \frac{r_{Y2} - r_{Y1}r_{12}}{\sqrt{1 - r_{Y1}^2}\sqrt{1 - r_{12}^2}}.$$

For our example

$$pr_1 = \frac{.710 - .588(.657)}{\sqrt{1 - .3455}\sqrt{1 - .4312}} = .5316$$

and $pr_1^2 = .5316^2 = .2826$, as before;

$$pr_2 = \frac{.588 - .710(.657)}{\sqrt{1 - .5047}\sqrt{1 - .4312}} = .2133$$

and $pr_2^2 = .2133^2 = .0455$, again as before.

In Table 3.3.1 we demonstrate that pr_2 is literally the correlation between X_2 from which X_1 has been partialed (i.e., $X_2 - \hat{X}_{2.1}$) and Y from which X_1 has also been partialed (i.e., $Y - \hat{Y}_1$). Column 6 presents the partialed X_2 values, the residuals from $\hat{X}_{2.1}$. Column 7 presents the residuals from Y_1 (given in column 2). The simple correlation between the residuals in columns 6 and 7 is $.2133 = pr_2$ (the computation is left to the reader, as an exercise). We thus see that the partial correlation for X_2 is literally the correlation between Y and X_2, each similarly residualized from X_1. A frequently employed form of notation to express the partial r is $r_{Y2.1}$, which conveys that X_1 is being partialed from both Y and X_2 (i.e., $r_{(Y.1)(2.1)}$), in contrast to the semipartial r, which is represented as $r_{Y(2.1)}$.

Before leaving Table 3.3.1, the other correlations at the bottom are worth noting. The r of Y with $\hat{Y}_1$ of .710 is identically r_{Y1} and necessarily so, since $\hat{Y}_1$ is a linear transformation of X_1 and therefore must correlate exactly as X_1 does. Similarly, the r of Y with $\hat{Y}_{12}$ of .728 is identically $R_{Y.12}$ and necessarily so, by definition in Eq. (3.3.3). Also, $Y - \hat{Y}_1$ (that is, $Y \cdot X_1$) correlates zero with $\hat{Y}_1$, because when a variable (here X_1) is partialed from another (here Y), the residual will correlate zero with any linear transformation of the partialed variables. Here, $\hat{Y}_1$ is a linear transformation of X_1 (i.e., $\hat{Y}_1 = B_1X_1 + B_0$).

Summarizing the results for the running example, we found $sr_1^2 = .1850$, $pr_1^2 = .2826$ and $sr_2^2 = .0258$, $pr_2^2 = .0522$. Whichever base we use, it is clear that number of publications (X_2) has virtually no *unique* relationship to salary, that is, no relationship beyond what can be accounted for by time since doctorate (X_1). On the other hand, time since doctorate (X_1) is uniquely related to salary (sr_1) and to salary holding publications constant (pr_1) to a quite substantial degree. The reader is reminded that this example is fictitious, and any resemblance to real academic departments, living or dead, is mostly coincidental.

3.4 PATTERNS OF ASSOCIATION BETWEEN Y AND TWO INDEPENDENT VARIABLES

A solid grasp of the implications of all possible relationships among one dependent variable and two independent variables is fundamental to understanding and interpreting the various multiple and partial coefficients encountered in MRC. This section is devoted to an exposition of each of these patterns and its distinctive substantive interpretation in actual research.

3.4.1 Direct and Indirect Effects

As we have stated, the regression coefficients $B_{Y1.2}$ and $B_{Y2.1}$ estimate the causal effects of X_1 and X_2 on Y in the causal model given in Fig. 3.4.1, Model A. These coefficients, labeled f and g in the diagram, are actually estimates of the *direct effects* of X_1 and X_2, respectively. Direct effects are exactly what the name implies—causal effects that are not mediated by any other variables in the model. All causes, of course, are mediated by some intervening mechanisms. If such an intervening variable is included, we have Model B shown in Fig. 3.4.1. In this diagram X_1 is shown as having a causal effect on X_2. Both variables have direct effects on Y. However, X_1 also has an *indirect* effect on Y via X_2. Note that the difference between Models A and B is not in the mathematics of the regression coefficients but in the understanding of the substantive causal process.

The advantage of Model B, if it is valid, is that in addition to determining the *direct* effects of X_1 and X_2 on Y, one may estimate the *indirect* effects of X_1 on Y as well as the effect of X_1 on X_2. This latter (h) in Model B is, of course, estimated by the regression coefficient of X_2 on X_1, namely B_{21}. The direct effects, f and g, are the same in both Models A and B and

Partial redundancy:

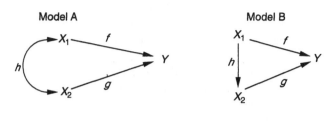

Full redundancy:

Model C: Spurious relationships

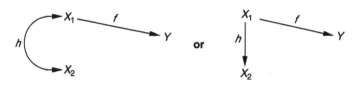

Model D: Indirect effect

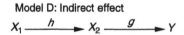

FIGURE 3.4.1   Representation of relationships between Y and two IVs.

are estimated by the sample regression coefficients for X_1 and X_2 from the equation for Y. The relationship between two exogenous variables, h in Model A, is conventionally represented by the correlation between the variables. The magnitude of the indirect effect of X_1 on Y in Model B may also be estimated by a method described in Chapter 11.

3.4.2 Partial Redundancy

We have included Models A and B under the rubric *partial redundancy* because this is by far the most common pattern of relationship in nonexperimental research in the behavioral sciences. It occurs whenever $r_{Y1} > r_{Y2}r_{12}$ and $r_{Y2} > r_{Y1}r_{12}$ [see Eqs. (3.2.4), (3.3.8), and (3.3.11)], once the variables have been oriented so as to produce positive correlations with Y. The sr_i and β_i for each IV will be smaller than its r_{Yi} (and will have the same sign) and thus reflect the fact of redundancy. Each IV is at least partly carrying information about Y that is also being supplied by the other. This is the same model shown by the ballantine in Fig. 3.3.1. We consider another situation in which r_{Y2} is negative in the next section.

Examples of Model A two-variable redundancy come easily to mind. It occurs when one relates school achievement (Y) to parental income (X_1) and education (X_2), or delinquency (Y) to IQ (X_1) and school achievement (X_2), or psychiatric prognosis (Y) to rated symptom severity (X_1) and functional impairment (X_2), or—but the reader can supply many examples of his or her own. Indeed, redundancy among explanatory variables is the plague of our efforts to understand the causal structure that underlies observations in the behavioral and social sciences.

Model B two-variable redundancy is also a very common phenomenon. Some substantive examples are given in Fig. 3.4.2. Here we see that age is expected to produce differences in

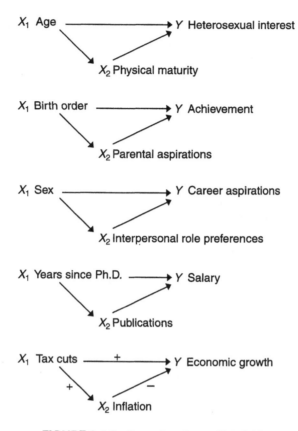

FIGURE 3.4.2   Examples of causal Model B.

physical maturity in a sample of school children and that each is expected to cause differences in heterosexual interest. The presence of an arrow from age to heterosexual interest implies that physical maturity is not the only reason why heterosexual interest increases with age. Birth order of offspring is expected to produce differences in parental aspirations and both are causally related to achievement. We might expect sex differences in interpersonal role preferences and that both of these variables will produce differences in career aspirations. Also, for our running example, we expect the passage of time since Ph.D. to produce increases in the number of publications and increases in both of these variables to produce increases in salary.

3.4.3 Suppression in Regression Models

In each of the causal circumstances we have discussed, we expect the *direct* effects of the variables to be smaller than the zero-order (unpartialed) effects. In addition, we anticipate an *indirect* effect of our X_1 variables to take place via the X_2 variables. Although partial redundancy is the most commonly observed pattern for causal Models A and B, it is not the only possible model. *Suppression* is present when either r_{Y1} or r_{Y2} is less than the product of the other with r_{12}, or when r_{12} is negative (assuming, as throughout, positive r_{Y1} and r_{Y2}). In this case the partialed coefficients of X_1 and X_2 will be larger in value than the zero-order coefficients and one of the partialed (direct effect) coefficients may become negative.

The term *suppression* can be understood to indicate that the relationship between the independent or causal variables is hiding or suppressing their real relationships with Y, which would be larger or possibly of opposite sign were they not correlated. In the classic psychometric literature on personnel selection, the term suppression was used to describe a variable (such as verbal ability) X_2 that, although not correlated with the criterion Y (e.g., job performance), is correlated with the available measure of the predictor X_1 (e.g., a paper and pencil test of job skills) and thus adds irrelevant variance to it and reduces its relationship with Y. The inclusion of the suppressor in the regression equation removes (suppresses) the unwanted variance in X_1, in effect, and enhances the relationship between X_1 and Y by means of $B_{Y1.2}$. This topic is discussed again in Chapter 12.

For a substantive example, suppose a researcher is interested in the roles of social assertiveness and record-keeping skills in producing success as a salesperson. Measures of these two characteristics are devised and administered to a sample of employees. The correlation between the measure of social assertiveness (X_1) and sales success (Y) is found to be $+.403$, the correlation between record keeping (X_2) and $Y = +.127$ and $r_{12} = -.305$, indicating an overall tendency for those high on social assertiveness to be relatively low on record keeping, although each is a desirable trait for sales success. Because $-.305 < (.403)(.127)$ we know that the situation is one of suppression and we may expect the direct effects (the regression and associated standardized coefficients) to be larger than the zero-order effects. Indeed, the reader may confirm that the β coefficients are .487 for social assertiveness and .275 for record keeping, both larger than their respective correlations with Y, .403 and .127. The coefficients may be considered to reflect appropriately the causal effects, the zero-order effects being misleadingly small because of the negative relationship between the variables.

A Model B example of suppression may be found in the (overly simple) economic model shown in Fig. 3.4.2, in which tax cuts are expected to produce increases in economic growth but also inflation. Because inflation is expected to have negative effects on economic growth, one can only hope that the direct positive effects of the tax cuts on economic growth will exceed the indirect negative effect attributable to the effect on inflation.

Suppression is a plausible model for many homeostatic mechanisms, both biological and social, in which force and counterforce tend to occur together and have counteractive effects. The fact that suppression is rarely identified in simple models may be due to the difficulty in finding appropriate time points for measuring X_1, X_2, and Y. Suppression effects of modest magnitude are more common in complex models. Material suppression effects are likely to be found in analyses of aggregate data, when the variables are sums or averages of many observations and R^2s are likely to approach 1 because of the small error variance that results in these conditions. Tzelgov and Henik (1991) provide an extensive discussion of conditions under which suppression occurs.

3.4.4 Spurious Effects and Entirely Indirect Effects

Model C in Fig. 3.4.1 describes the special case in which $r_{Y2} = r_{Y1}r_{12}$. This model is of considerable interest because it means that the information with regard to Y carried by X_2 is *completely* redundant with that carried by X_1. This occurs whenever the B, sr, and pr coefficients for X_2 are approximately zero. This occurs when their numerators are approximately zero (i.e., when $r_{Y2} \approx r_{12}r_{Y1}$). For the causal model the appropriate conclusion is that X_2 is not a cause of Y at all but merely associated (correlated) with Y because of its association with X_1. In some fields such as epidemiology, X_1 is referred to as a *confounder* of the relationship between X_2 and Y. (But note the appropriate considerations before drawing such a conclusion from sample results, as discussed in Section 3.7.) A great many analyses are carried out precisely to determine this issue—whether some variable has a demonstrable effect on Y when correlated variables are held constant or, alternatively, whether the variable's relationship to Y is (or may be) spurious. Thus, for example, a number of investigations have been carried out to determine whether there is a family size (X_2) influence on intelligence (Y) independent of parental social class (X_1), whether maternal nutrition (X_2) has an effect on infant behavior (Y) independent of maternal substance use (X_1), whether the status of women (X_2) in various countries has an effect on fertility rate (Y) independent of economic development (X_1), or indeed whether any of the X_2 effects on Y shown in Fig. 3.4.2 are nil. Generally, the question to be answered is the "nothing but" challenge. Is the relationship between Y and X_2 nothing but a manifestation of the causal effects of X_1?

Complete redundancy, however, does not always imply a spurious relationship. In Fig. 3.4.1, Model D we see a situation in which the partial coefficients for X_1 approach zero, indicating correctly that there is no *direct* effect of X_1 on Y. There is, however, an *indirect* effect that, according to the model, takes place entirely via X_2; that is, the effect of X_1 is mediated by X_2.

Many investigations are designed to answer questions about intervening mechanisms—for example, is the higher female (X_1) prevalence of depression (Y) entirely attributable to lower female income/opportunity structure (X_2)? Are ethnic (X_1) differences in achievement (Y) entirely due to economic deprivation (X_2)? Is the demonstrable effect of poor parent marital relationship (X_1) on delinquency (Y) entirely attributable to poor parent-child relationships (X_2)? In these cases the relationships between X_1 and Y cannot be said to be spurious but are nevertheless likely to have different theoretical implications and policy import when they are entirely redundant than when they are not.

As in the case of the comparison of Models A and B, the difference between Models C and D lie not in the coefficients but in one's understanding of the causal processes that gave rise to the coefficients. Again, one can only demonstrate consistency of sample data with a model rather than prove the model's correctness.

3.5 MULTIPLE REGRESSION/CORRELATION WITH k INDEPENDENT VARIABLES

3.5.1 Introduction: Components of the Prediction Equation

When more than two IVs are related to Y, the computation and interpretations of multiple and partial coefficients proceed by direct extension of the two-IV case. The goal is again to produce a regression equation for the k IVs of the (raw score) form

$$(3.5.1) \quad \hat{Y} = B_{Y1.23...k}X_1 + B_{Y2.13...k}X_2 + B_{Y3.12...k}X_3 + \ldots + B_{Yk.123...k-1}X_k + B_{Y0.123...k},$$

or, expressed in simpler subscript notation,

$$\hat{Y} = B_1X_1 + B_2X_2 + B_3X_3 + \ldots + B_k + B_0,$$

or, as in the simple two variable equation, expressed in terms of the original Y plus the errors of prediction e:

$$Y = B_1X_1 + B_2X_2 + B_3X_3 + \ldots + B_kX_k + B_0 + e.$$

When this equation is applied to the data, it yields a set of $\hat{Y}$ values (one for each of the n cases) for which the sum of the $(Y - \hat{Y})^2$ values over all n cases will (again) be a minimum. Obtaining these raw-score partial regression weights, the B_i, involves solving a set of k simultaneous equations in k unknowns, a task best left to a computer program, although

Appendix 2 provides the method of hand calculation for MRC.) The purpose of the present section is to lay down a foundation for understanding the various types of coefficients produced by MRC for the general case of k independent variables, and their relationship to various MRC strategies appropriate to the investigator's research goals.

3.5.2 Partial Regression Coefficients

By direct extension of the one- and two-IV cases, the raw score partial regression coefficient B_i $(=B_{Yi.123...(i)...k})$ is the constant weight by which each value of the variable X_i is to be multiplied in the multiple regression equation that includes all k IVs. Thus, B_i is the average or expected change in Y for each unit increase in X_i when the value of each of the $k-1$ other IVs is held constant. β_i is the partial regression coefficient when all variables have been standardized. Such standardized coefficients are of interpretive interest when the analysis concerns test scores or indices whose scaling is arbitrary, or when the magnitudes of effects of variables in different units are to be compared.

CH03EX02

For example, let us return to the study in which we seek to account for differences in salary in a university department by means of characteristics of the faculty members. The two IVs used thus far were the number of years since each faculty member had received a doctoral degree (X_1) and the number of publications (X_2). We now wish to consider two additional independent variables, the gender of the professor and the number of citations of his or her work in the scientific literature. These data are presented in Table 3.5.1, where sex (X_3) is coded (scored) 1 for female and 0 for male, and the sample size has been increased to 62 as a more reasonable size for analysis. The correlation matrix shows that sex is negatively correlated with salary $(r_{Y3} = -.210)$, women having lower salaries on the average than men. The number of citations (X_4) is positively associated with salary $(r_{Y4} = .550)$, as well as with the other IVs. Sex correlates very little with the other IVs, except for a tendency in these data for women to be more recent Ph.D.s than men $(r_{13} = -.201)$.

The (raw-score) multiple regression equation for estimating academic salary from these four IVs may be obtained from computer output or by the matrix inversion method of Appendix 2 (where this problem is used illustratively). It is $\hat{Y} = \$857X_1$ (time) $+ \$92.8$ (publications) $-$ $\$918X_3$ (female) $+ \$202X_4$ (citations) $+ \$39,587$. These partial B_i coefficients indicate that for any given values of the other IVs, an increase of one in the number of citations is associated with a salary increase of $\$202$ $(=B_4)$; an increase of one unit in X_3, and hence the average difference in salary (holding constant the other IVs) is $-\$918$ (favoring men); and the effects of an additional year since degree (X_1) and an increase of one publication (X_2) are $\$857$ and $\$93$, respectively. Note also that $B_0 = \$39,587$ is the estimated salary of a hypothetical male professor fresh from his doctorate with no publications or citations, that is, all $X_i = 0$.

In this problem, the salary estimated by the four IVs for the first faculty member (Table 3.5.1) is

$$\hat{Y} = \$857(3) + \$92.8(18) - \$918(1) + \$202(50) + \$39,587$$
$$= \$2,571 + \$1,670 - \$918 + \$10,100 + \$39,587$$
$$= \$53,007.[8]$$

The remaining estimated values are given in the last column of Table 3.5.1.

---

[8] Within rounding error.

TABLE 3.5.1
Illustrative Data With Four Independent Variables

I.D.	Time since Ph.D. (X_1)	No. of publications (X_2)	Sex (X_3)	No. of citations (X_4)	Salary (Y)	Estimated Salary
01	3	18	1	50	$51,876	$53,007
02	6	3	1	26	54,511	49,340
03	3	2	1	50	53,425	51,523
04	8	17	0	34	61,863	54,886
05	9	11	1	41	52,926	55,682
06	6	6	0	37	47,034	52,757
07	16	38	0	48	66,432	66,517
08	10	48	0	56	61,100	63,917
09	2	9	0	19	41,934	45,973
10	5	22	0	29	47,454	51,769
11	5	30	1	28	49,832	51,391
12	6	21	0	31	47,047	52,937
13	7	10	1	25	39,115	50,644
14	11	27	0	40	59,677	59,596
15	18	37	0	61	61,458	70,763
16	6	8	0	32	54,528	51,933
17	9	13	1	36	60,327	54,858
18	7	6	0	69	56,600	60,076
19	7	12	1	47	52,542	55,272
20	3	29	1	29	50,455	49,786
21	7	29	1	35	51,647	54,426
22	5	7	0	35	62,895	51,589
23	7	6	0	18	53,740	49,778
24	13	69	0	90	75,822	75,302
25	5	11	0	60	56,596	57,008
26	8	9	1	30	55,682	52,418
27	8	20	1	27	62,091	52,833
28	7	41	1	35	42,162	55,539
29	2	3	1	14	52,646	43,489
30	13	27	0	56	74,199	64,541
31	5	14	0	50	50,729	55,267
32	3	23	0	25	70,011	49,340
33	1	1	0	35	37,939	47,605
34	3	7	0	1	39,652	43,010
35	9	19	0	69	68,987	62,996
36	3	11	0	69	55,579	57,112
37	9	31	0	27	54,671	55,628
38	3	9	0	50	57,704	53,090
39	4	12	1	32	44,045	49,672
40	10	32	0	33	51,122	57,789
41	1	26	0	45	47,082	51,943
42	11	12	0	54	60,009	61,032
43	5	9	0	47	58,632	54,198
44	1	6	0	29	38,340	46,857
45	21	39	0	69	71,219	75,135
46	7	16	1	47	53,712	55,643
47	5	12	1	43	54,782	52,751
48	16	50	0	55	83,503	69,043

TABLE 3.5.1 (continued)

I.D.	Time since Ph.D. (X_1)	No. of publications (X_2)	Sex (X_3)	No. of citations (X_4)	Salary (Y)	Estimated Salary
49	5	18	0	33	47,212	52,206
50	4	16	1	28	52,840	49,236
51	5	5	0	42	53,650	52,817
52	11	20	0	24	50,931	55,716
53	16	50	1	31	66,784	63,279
54	3	6	1	27	49,751	47,249
55	4	19	1	83	74,343	60,620
56	4	11	1	49	57,710	53,012
57	5	13	0	14	52,676	47,905
58	6	3	1	36	41,195	51,359
59	4	8	1	34	45,662	49,705
60	8	11	1	70	47,606	60,681
61	3	25	1	27	44,301	49,011
62	4	4	1	28	58,582	48,123
M	6.79	18.18	.56	40.23	\$54,816	\$54,816
sd	4.28	14.00	.50	17.17	\$9,706	\$6,840

Correlation Matrix

	Time since Ph.D. (X_1)	No. of publications (X_2)	Sex (X_3)	No. of citations (X_4)	Salary (Y)
Time since Ph.D.	1.000	.651	−.210	.373	.608
No. of publications	.651	1.000	−.159	.333	.506
Sex	−.210	−.159	1.000	−.149	−.201
No. of citations	.373	.333	−.149	1.000	.550
Salary	.608	.506	−.201	.550	1.000

Standardized Partial Regression Coefficients

The regression equation may be written in terms of standardized variables and β coefficients as

$$\hat{z}_Y = .378z_1 + .134z_2 - .047z_3 + .357z_4.$$

The β values may always be found from B values by inverting Eq. (3.2.5):

(3.5.2)
$$\beta_i = B_i \frac{sd_i}{sd_Y}.$$

for example, $\beta_4 = .202(17.17/9706) = .357$. As always, with standardized Y and IVs the intercept β_0 is necessarily zero, and thus may be omitted.

3.5.3 R, R^2 and Shrunken R^2

Multiple R and R^2

Application of the regression equation to the IVs yields a set of estimated $\hat{Y}$ values. The simple product moment correlation of Y with $\hat{Y}$ equals the multiple correlation; in this example,

$r_{Y\hat{Y}} = R = .709$. As with the one- or two-IV case, R^2 is the proportion of Y variance accounted for and $R^2 = sd_{\hat{Y}}^2/sd_Y^2 = (6885)^2/(9706)^2 = .5032$.

R^2 may also be written as a function of the original correlations with Y and the β coefficients by extension of Eq. (3.3.2):

(3.5.3) $$R_{Y.12...k}^2 = \sum \beta_i r_{Yi},$$

where the summation is over the k IVs. Thus in the current example,

$$R_{Y.1234}^2 = .378(.608) + .134(.506) - .047(.201) + .357(.550) = .5032,$$

as before.

Lest the reader think that this represents a way of apportioning the Y variance accounted for among the IVs (that is, that X_i's proportion is its $\beta_i r_{Yi}$), it is important to recall that β_i and r_{Yi} may be of opposite sign (under conditions of suppression). Thus, the suppressor variable on this interpretation would appear to account for a negative proportion of the Y variance, clearly a conceptual impossibility. The fact that $\beta_i r_{Yi}$ is not necessarily positive is sufficient to preclude the use of Eq. (3.5.3) as a variance partitioning procedure.

R^2 may also be obtained as a function of the β coefficients and the associations between the IVs as

(3.5.4) $$R^2 = \sum (\beta_i^2) + 2 \sum (\beta_i \beta_j r_{ij})$$

where the first summation is over the k IVs, and the second over the $k(k-1)/2$ distinct pairs of IVs. In the current problem,

$$\begin{aligned} R_{Y.1234}^2 = {}& .378^2 + .134^2 + .047^2 + .357^2 + 2[(.378)(.134)(.651) \\ &+ (.378)(.047)(.210) + (.378)(.357)(.373) + (.134)(.047)(.159) \\ &+ (.134)(.357)(.333) + (.047)(.357)(.150)] = .5032 \end{aligned}$$

This formula appears to partition R^2 into portions accounted for by each variable uniquely and portions accounted for jointly by pairs of variables, and some authors so treat it. However, we again note that any of the $k(k-1)/2$ terms $\beta_i \beta_j r_i$ may be negative. Therefore, neither Eq. (3.5.4) nor Eq. (3.5.3) can serve as variance partitioning schemes. This equation does, however, make clear what happens when all correlations between pairs of IVs equal 0. The triple-product terms will all contain $r_{ij} = 0$ and hence drop out, and $R^2 = \Sigma\beta_i^2 = \Sigma r_{Yi}^2$, as was seen for the two-IV case (Section 3.4.2).

Shrunken or Adjusted R²: Estimating the Population ρ²

The R^2 that we obtain from a given sample is not an unbiased estimate of the population squared multiple correlation, ρ^2. To gain an intuitive understanding of part of the reason for this, imagine the case in which one or more of the IVs account for no Y variance in the population, that is, $r_{Yi}^2 = 0$ in the population for one or more X_i. Because of random sampling fluctuations we would expect that only very rarely would its r^2 with Y in a sample be exactly zero; it will virtually always have some positive value. (Note that although r can be negative, neither r^2 nor R^2 can be.). Thus, in most samples it would make some (possibly trivial) contribution to R^2. The smaller the sample size, the larger these positive variations from zero will be, on the average, and thus the greater the inflation of the sample R^2. Similarly, the more IVs we have, the more opportunity for the sample R^2 to be larger than the true population ρ^2. It is often desirable to have an estimate of the population ρ^2 and we naturally prefer one that is more accurate than the positively biased sample R^2. Such a realistic estimate of the population ρ^2 (for the fixed model) is given by

$$(3.5.5) \qquad \tilde{R}_Y^2 = 1 - (1 - R_Y^2)\frac{n-1}{n-k-1}$$

This estimate is necessarily (and appropriately) smaller than the sample R^2 and is thus often referred to as the "shrunken" R^2. The magnitude of the "shrinkage" will be larger for small values of R^2 than for larger values, other things being equal. Shrinkage will also be larger as the ratio of the number of IVs to the number of subjects increases. As an example, consider the shrinkage in R^2 when $n = 200$ and cases where $k = 5$, 10, and 20 IVs, thus yielding k/n ratios of 1/40, 1/20, and 1/10, respectively. When $R^2 = .20$, the shrunken values will equal, respectively, .1794, .1577, and .1106, the last being a shrinkage of almost one-half. When $R^2 = .40$, the comparable values are, respectively, .3845, .3683, and .3330, smaller shrinkage either as differences from or proportions of R^2. For large ratios of k/n and small R^2, these shrunken values may be negative; for example, for $R^2 = .10$, $k = 11$, $n = 100$, Eq. (3.6.3) gives $-.0125$. In such cases, by convention, the shrunken R^2 is reported as zero.

It should be clear from this discussion that whenever a subset of IVs has been selected post hoc from a larger set of potential variables on the basis of their relationships with Y, not only R^2, but even the shrunken R^2 computed by taking as k the number of IVs selected, will be too large. This is true whether the computer capitalizes on chance by performing a stepwise regression, or the experimenter does so by selecting IVs with relatively larger r_{Yi}s. A more realistic estimate of shrinkage is obtained by substituting for k in Eq. (3.6.3) the *total* number of IVs from which the selection was made.

3.5.4 *sr* and *sr*^{2}

The semipartial correlation coefficient sr and its square sr^2 in the general case of k IVs may be interpreted by direct extension of the two IV case. Thus sr_i^2 equals that proportion of the Y variance accounted for by X_i beyond that accounted for by the other $k - 1$ IVs, and

$$(3.5.6) \qquad sr_i^2 = R_{Y.12...i...k}^2 - R_{Y.12...(i)...k}^2,$$

(the parenthetical i signifying its omission from the second R^2), or the increase in the squared multiple correlations when X_i is included over the R^2 that includes the other $k - 1$ IVs, but excludes X_i. This may be thought of as the unique contribution of X_i to R^2 in the context of the remaining $k - 1$ IVs. As in the two-IV case, the semipartial r equals the correlation between that portion of X_i that is uncorrelated with the remaining IVs and Y:

$$(3.5.7) \qquad sr_i = r_{Y(i.12...(i)...k)}$$

$$= r_{Y(X-\hat{X}_i.12...(i)...k)}.$$

As might be expected, sr_i may also be written as a function of the multiple correlation of the other IVs with X_i,

$$(3.5.8) \qquad sr_i = \beta_i \sqrt{1 - R_{i.12...(i)...k}^2}.$$

Neither sr_i nor sr_i^2 is provided as default output by most MRC computer programs; however, the term $1 - R_{i.12...(i)...k}^2$ is often provided. This term, called the variable's *tolerance*, alerts the data analyst to the level of redundancy of this variable with other predictors.[9] Occasionally sr_i^2 values are provided, possibly labeled as the "unique" contribution to R^2. When pr_i is available, sr_i^2 is readily determined by

$$(3.5.9) \qquad sr_i^2 = \frac{pr_i^2}{1 - pr_i^2} (1 - R_{Y.123...k}^2).$$

3.5.5 *pr* and *pr²*

The partial correlation coefficient pr_i, we recall from the two-IV case, is the correlation between that portion of Y that is independent of the remaining variables, $Y - \hat{Y}_{12...(i)...k}$, and that portion of X_i that is independent of the (same) remaining variables, $X_i - \hat{X}_{i.12...(i)...k}$, that is,

$$(3.5.10) \qquad pr_i = r_{Yi.12...(i)...k}$$
$$= r_{(Y - \hat{Y}_{12...(i)...k})(X_i - \hat{X}_{i.12...(i)...k})}.$$

pr^2 is thus interpretable as the proportion of that part of the Y variance that is independent of the remaining IVs (i.e., of $1 - R_{Y.12...(i)...k}^2$) accounted for *uniquely* by X_i:

$$(3.5.11) \qquad pr_i^2 = \frac{sr_i^2}{1 - R_{Y.12...(i)...k}^2}$$

It can be seen that pr_i^2 will virtually always be larger than and can never be smaller than sr_i^2, because sr_i^2 is the unique contribution of X_i expressed as a proportion of the *total* Y variance whereas pr_i^2 expresses the same unique contribution of X_i as a proportion of that *part* of the Y variance not accounted for by the other IVs.

3.5.6 Example of Interpretation of Partial Coefficients

Table 3.5.2 presents the semipartial and partial correlations and their squares for the salary example. We see that publications (X_2) accounts for 26% (r_{Y2}^2) of the salary variance, it accounts uniquely for only 1% of the salary variance ($sr_2^2 = .01$), and only 2% of the salary variance not accounted for by the other three variables ($pr_2^2 = .02$). Notice that in this example the partial coefficients of the four IVs are ordered differently from the zero-order correlations. Although time since Ph.D. taken by itself accounts for .37 (r_{Y1}^2) of the variance in salary, it uniquely

TABLE 3.5.2
Correlations of Predictors With *Y*

Predictor	r_{Yi}	r_{Yi}^2	sr_i	sr_i^2	pr_i	pr_i^2
X_1, Time since Ph.D.	.608	.370	.278	.077	.367	.135
X_2, No. of publications	.506	.256	.101	.010	.142	.020
X_3, Sex	−.201	.040	−.046	.002	−.065	.004
X_4, No. of citations	.550	.302	.328	.107	.422	.178

[9]Chapter 10 deals with this and other indices of IV intercorrelation in more detail.

accounts for only 8% of this variance, whereas citations, which alone accounts for 30% of the salary variance, accounts uniquely for 11%. The reason for this is the much greater redundancy of time since Ph.D. with other predictors (46%) as compared with citations (16%); (see next section).

3.6 STATISTICAL INFERENCE WITH k INDEPENDENT VARIABLES

3.6.1 Standard Errors and Confidence Intervals for B and β

In Section 2.8.2 of Chapter 2 we showed how to determine standard errors and confidence intervals for r and B in the two-variable case, provided that certain distributional assumptions are made. Similarly, one may determine standard errors for partial regression coefficients; that is, one may estimate the sampling variability of partial coefficients from one random sample to another, using the data from the single sample at hand.

The equation for estimating the standard error of B is particularly enlightening because it shows very clearly what conditions lead to large expected sampling variation in the size of B and hence in the accuracy one can attribute to any given sample B value. A convenient form of the equation for the standard error of B for any X_i is

$$(3.6.1) \qquad SE_{B_i} = \frac{sd_Y}{sd_i} \sqrt{\frac{1}{1 - R_i^2}} \sqrt{\frac{1 - R_Y^2}{n - k - 1}}$$

where R_Y^2 is literally $R_{Y.12\ldots k}^2$, and R_i^2 is literally $R_{i.12\ldots(i)\ldots k}^2$. The ratio of the sds, as always, simply adjusts for the scaling of the units in which X_i and Y are measured. Aside from this, we see from the third term that the size of the SE_B will decrease as the error variance proportion $(1 - R_Y^2)$ decreases and its $df (= n - k - 1)$ increase. (On reflection, this should be obvious.) Note that this term will be constant for all variables in a given regression equation. The second term reveals an especially important characteristic of SE_B, namely, that it increases as a function of the squared multiple correlation of the remaining IVs with X_i, R_i^2. Here we encounter a manifestation of the general problem of multicollinearity, that is, of substantial correlation among IVs. Under conditions of multicollinearity there will be relatively large values for at least some of the SE_Bs, so that any given sample may yield relatively poor estimates of some of the population regression coefficients, that is, of those whose R_i^2s are large. (See Chapter 10 for further discussion of this issue.)

In order to show the relationship given in Eq. (3.6.1) more clearly it is useful to work with variables in standard score form. B_i expressed as a function of standard scores is β_i. The standard error of β_i drops the first term from (3.6.1) because it equals unity, so that

$$(3.6.2) \qquad SE_{\beta_i} = \sqrt{\frac{1 - R_Y^2}{n - k - 1}} \sqrt{\frac{1}{1 - R_i^2}}$$

To illustrate the effects of differences in the relationships of a given X_i, with the remaining IVs, we return to our running example presented in Tables 3.5.1 and 3.5.2. In this example, number of publications and number of citations had very similar zero-order correlations with salary, .506 and .550, respectively. Their correlations with other IVs, especially time since Ph.D. differed substantially, however, with publications correlating .651 and number of citations correlating .373 with time. The squared multiple correlation with other IVs is .4330 for number of publications and .1581 for number of citations. Substituting these values into Eq. (3.6.2) we find

$$SE_{\beta_{Publications}} = \sqrt{\frac{1 - .5032}{57}} \sqrt{\frac{1}{1 - .4330}}$$
$$= .0934(1.3280) = .124,$$

$$SE_{\beta_{Citations}} = \sqrt{\frac{1 - .5032}{57}} \sqrt{\frac{1}{1 - .1581}}$$
$$= .0934(1.0899) = .102.$$

Thus we can see that the redundancy with other variables has not only reduced the β for publications (to .134 from $r_{Y.Publications} = .506$) as compared to citations (to .357 from $r_{Y.Citations} = .550$), it also has made it a less reliable estimate of the population value. In contrast, the β for sex, although smaller in size than that for citations, .047 versus .357, has a slightly smaller SE, .096 versus .102. Sex shared 5% of its variance with the other IVs, whereas citations shared 16% of its variance with the other IVs.

Converting from these back to the SE_B we find

$$SE_{B_{Publications}} = 9706/14.0(.124) = 85.9$$
$$SE_{B_{Citations}} = 9706/17.17(.102) = 57.5$$

In Section 2.8.2 of Chapter 2, we showed how to compute and interpret confidence intervals in simple bivariate correlation and regression. For MRC, we proceed in the same way, using our faculty salary example. For the regression coefficients, the B_i, we found the standard errors for publications and citations to be, respectively, 85.9 and 57.5. The *margin of error* (*me*) for B_i is $t_c(SE_{Bi})$, where t_c is the multiplier for a given confidence interval for the error *df*. Most frequently 95% confidence intervals are reported in the literature. However, 80% *CI* may provide a more realistic feeling for the likely population value in some cases.

See the regression equation in Section 3.5.2 for the B values (93 and 202) in what follows. Using the approximate critical value of t for $\alpha = .20$, $t_c = 1.3$ as the multiplier, the 80% *me* for publications $= 1.3(85.9) = 112$, so the 80% *CI* $= 93 \pm 112$, from -19 to 205. For citations, the 80% *me* $= 1.3(57.5) = 74.6$, so the 80% *CI* $= 202 \pm 74.6$, from 127 to 277. Using $t_c = 2$ as the multiplier, the 95% *me* for B for publications is $2(85.9) = 172$, so the 95% *CI* is $93 \pm 172 = -79$ to 265. For citations, the 95% *me* is $2(57.5) = 115$ and the 95% *CI* for B for citations is $202 \pm 115, = 87$ to 317.

One may use the SE to determine the bounds within which we can assert with a chosen level of confidence that the population β falls much as we did in Chapter 2 for its zero-order analog, r. There, in Section 2.8.2, we initially used the exact t values for the available degrees of freedom. Using that method, for the 95% confidence interval, the *margin of error*, $me_\beta = t(SE_\beta)$, where, for $df = n - k - 1 = 62 - 4 - 1 = 57$, $t = 2.002$ (Appendix Table A). The *me* for a β_i is 2.002 $(SE_{\beta i})$. The standard errors for publications and citations are, respectively, .124 and .102, and the *margins of error* are .248 and .204, so the 95% confidence interval for β for publications is $.134 \pm .248$, from $-.11$ to .38, and the 95% confidence interval for β for citations is $.357 \pm .204$, from .15 to .56.

3.6.2 Confidence Intervals for R^2

The *CI*s that follow for R^2 and differences between independent R^2s are from Olkin and Finn (1995). They are based on large-sample theory and will yield adequate approximations for $df > 60$.

We have found that for our sample of 62 faculty members, our four IVs yield an R^2 of .5032. The variance error of R^2 is given by

$$\text{(3.6.3)} \qquad SE_{R^2}^2 = \frac{4R^2(1 - R^2)^2(n - k - 1)^2}{(n^2 - 1)(n + 3)}.$$

Substituting,

$$SE_{R^2}^2 = \frac{4(.5032)(.4968^2)(57^2)}{(62^2 - 1)(65)} = .006461.$$

Therefore the standard error, $SE_{R^2} = \sqrt{.00646} = .080$.

95% confidence intervals using exact t values are routinely reported in the literature. Alternatively, one may opt to use some other probability, such as 80%, as providing reasonable bounds for the purposes of the study. In recognition of the fairly rough approximation provided by any of these limits, one may use the approximate constant multipliers (t_c) of the *SE*s for the desired degree of inclusion of Section 2.8.2:

CI	99%	95%	80%	2/3
t_c	2.6	2	1.3	1

The 80% *me* for $R^2 = 1.3\,(.0804) = .1045$, so the approximate 80% *CI* is $.503 \pm .104$, from .40 to .61. (The 95% *me* $= 2\,(.0804) = .161$, so the approximate 95% *CI* for R^2 is $.503 \pm .161$, from .34 to .66.)

3.6.3 Confidence Intervals for Differences Between Independent R^2s

For our running example of 62 cases (University V), we found the $R_V^2 = .5032$ for the $k = 4$ IVs. For the same IVs in University W, where $n = 143$, assume that $R_W^2 = .2108$. The difference is $.5032 - .2108 = .2924$. Since these are different groups that were independently sampled, we can find *CI*s and perform null hypothesis significance tests on this difference, using the *SE* of the difference. As we have seen for other statistics, this is simply the square root of the sum of the SE^2s of the two R^2s. We found the SE^2 for V to be .006461 in the previous section, and assume we find the SE^2 for W to be .003350. Substituting,

$$\text{(3.6.4)} \qquad SE_{R_V^2 - R_W^2} = \sqrt{SE_{R_V^2}^2 + SE_{R_W^2}^2}$$

$$= \sqrt{.006461 + .003350} = \sqrt{.006811} = .0825.$$

The approximate 95% *me* $= 2(.0825) = .1650$, so the approximate 95% *CI* for a *nil* hypothesis significance test $= .2924 \pm .1650$, from .13 to .46. Since the 95% *CI* does not include 0, the difference between the universities' R^2s is significant at the $\alpha = .05$ level.

3.6.4 Statistical Tests on Multiple and Partial Coefficients

In Chapter 2 we presented statistical inference methods for the statistics of simple regression and correlation analysis, that is, when only two variables are involved. As we have seen, the test of the null hypothesis that R^2 is zero in the population can be accomplished by examination of the lower confidence limit for the desired alpha level (e.g., the 95% two-tailed CI). Equivalently, the statistic F may be determined as

(3.6.5)
$$F = \frac{R^2(n - k - 1)}{(1 - R^2)k}$$

with $df = k$ and $n - k - 1$.

F may also be computed (or provided as computer output) as a function of raw scores in the classic analysis of variance format. As we saw in the one-IV case, the total sample variance of Y may be divided into a portion accounted for by the IV, which is equal to the variance of the estimated $\hat{Y}$ values, $sd_{\hat{Y}}^2$, and a portion not associated with the IV, the "residual" or "error" variance, $sd_{Y-\hat{Y}}^2$. Similarly, the sum of the squared deviations about the mean of Y may be divided into a sum of squares (SS) due to the regression on the set of IVs, and a residual sum of squares. When these two portions of the total are divided by their respective df, we have the mean square (MS) values necessary for determining the F values, thus

(3.6.6)
$$\text{regression MS} = \frac{\text{regression SS}}{k} = \frac{R^2 \sum y^2}{k},$$
$$\text{residual or error MS} = \frac{\text{residual SS}}{n - k - 1} = \frac{(1 - R^2) \sum y^2}{n - k - 1}.$$

When F is expressed as the ratio of these two mean squares, we obtain

(3.6.7)
$$F = \frac{\text{regression MS}}{\text{residual MS}} = \frac{R^2 \sum y^2 / k}{(1 - R^2)\left(\sum y^2\right)/(n - k - 1)}.$$

Canceling the $\sum y^2$ term from the numerator and denominator and simplifying, we obtain Eq. (3.6.5).

Let us return to our running example of academic salaries. The four independent variables produced $R^2 = .5032$. Because there were 62 faculty members, by Eq. (3.6.5),

$$F = \frac{.5032\,(62 - 4 - 1)}{(1 - .5032)\,4} = 14.43$$

for $df = 4, 57$.

Turning to the tabled F values for $\alpha = .01$ (Appendix Table D.2), we find an F value (by interpolation) of 3.67 is necessary for significance. Because the obtained F value exceeds this value, we conclude that the linear relationship between these four IVs and salary is not likely to be zero in the population.

As previously noted, sr_i, pr_i, and β_i differ only with regard to their denominators. Thus none can equal zero unless the others are also zero, so it is not surprising that they must yield the same t_i value for the statistical significance of their departure from zero. It should also be clear that because B_i is the product of β and the ratio of standard deviations, it also can equal zero only when the standardized coefficients do. Thus, a single equation provides a test for the significance of departures of all the partial coefficients of X_i from zero. They either are, or are not, all significantly different from zero, and to exactly the same degree.

(3.6.8)
$$t_i = sr_i \sqrt{\frac{n - k - 1}{1 - R^2}},$$

t_i will carry the same sign as sr_i and all the other partial coefficients for that variable.

For example, let us return to the running example where the obtained R^2 of .5032 was found to be significant for $k = 4$ and $n = 62$. The sr_is for the four IVs were, respectively, .278, .101, −.046, and .328.

Determining their t values we find

$$t_{Time} = .278 \sqrt{\frac{62 - 4 - 1}{1 - .5032}} = 2.98$$

$$t_{Publications} = .101 \sqrt{\frac{62 - 4 - 1}{1 - .5032}} = 1.08$$

$$t_{Sex} = -.046 \sqrt{\frac{62 - 4 - 1}{1 - .5032}} = -.49$$

$$t_{Citations} = .328 \sqrt{\frac{62 - 4 - 1}{1 - .5032}} = 3.51.$$

Looking these values up in the t table (Appendix Table A) for 57 df, we find that time since Ph.D. and number of citations are significant at the .01 level but publications and sex are not significant at the .05 level. We conclude that time and citations both make unique (direct) contributions to estimating salary. We may *not* reject the nil hypothesis that sex and publications have no unique (direct) relationship to salary in the population once the effects of time and citations are taken into account.

It is quite possible to find examples where R^2 is statistically significant but none of the tests of significance on the individual IVs reaches the significance criterion for rejecting the nil hypothesis. This finding occurs when the variables that correlate with Y are so substantially redundant (intercorrelated) that none of the unique effects (βs) is large enough to meet the statistical criterion (see Chapter 10 for a more extensive discussion of this problem). On the other hand, it may also happen that one or more of the t tests on individual variables does reach the criterion for significance although the overall R^2 is not significant. The variance estimate for the regression based on k IVs is divided by k to form the numerator of the F test for R^2, making of it an average contribution per IV. Therefore, if most variables do not account for more than a trivial amount of Y variance they may lower this average (the mean square for the regression) to the point of making the overall F not significant in spite of the apparent significance of the separate contributions of one or more individual IVs. In such circumstances, we recommend that such IVs *not* be accepted as significant. The reason for this is to avoid spuriously significant results, the probability of whose occurrence is controlled by the requirement that the F for a set of IVs be significant before its constituent IVs are t tested. This, the "protected t test," is part of the strategy for statistical inference that is considered in detail in Chapter 5.

3.7 STATISTICAL PRECISION AND POWER ANALYSIS

3.7.1 Introduction: Research Goals and the Null Hypothesis

Almost every research effort is an attempt to estimate some parameter in some population. In the analyses described in this book, the parameters in question are represented by multiple and partial regression and correlation coefficients. Traditionally the behavioral sciences have focused almost entirely on the issue of the simple presence and direction of a partial regression coefficient, or the confidence that there is some correlation between a dependent variable and a set of independent variables in the population. Thus the statistical tests have generally been focused on the null (nil) hypothesis that the population coefficient is zero. Although this is sometimes a useful question and thus an appropriate research goal, its limitations in advancing the progress of science have been recognized in articles as well as in an organized effort to change the focus of research reports (Wilkinson & the APA Task Force on Statistical Inference, 1999).

The precision of any statistic is identified by its standard error and the associated confidence interval. Its statistical power is the probability of rejecting the null hypothesis when it is false. Both are determined as a function of three elements, the size of the effect in the population, the *df* which are determined primarily by the sample size, and the chosen margin of error or alpha level. Thus, it is appropriate to view statistical power as a special case of the more general issue of the precision of our estimates.

In this section we extend consideration of these issues, which were introduced in Chapter 2, to the multiple independent variable case. Although we review the steps necessary for the hand computation of power and precision, and provide the necessary Appendix tables, we recommend the use of a contemporary user-friendly computer program such as Sample Power (SPSS) or Power and Precision (Borenstein, Cohen, and Rothstein, 2001), which will facilitate the user's appreciation of the interaction among the determinants of statistical power. The emphasis of this presentation is an understanding of the influences that contribute to the precision and power of any study, so that each investigator can make appropriate choices of such parameters in planning or evaluating research.

3.7.2 The Precision and Power of R^2

As noted earlier, both precision and power are determined as a function of the effect size, the sample size, and the selected probability parameter. For simplicity let us begin with the assumption that we will be using 95% *CI* or, equivalently for the special case of the nil hypothesis, the .05 significance criterion. As we plan our study, the question is what precision and power will we have for a given proposed *n*, or for each of a set of alternative *n*s. The effect size that is relevant is the population R^2.

Precision

Suppose that we anticipate that the population R^2 as estimated by a set of six IVs is about .2. The sample size that we have budgeted for is 120 cases. Application of Eq. (3.6.3) gives us the SE_{R^2} and tells us that an empirical estimate of this population value (which would average .24 in a sample of this size; see the section on shrinkage) would have an 80% *CI* of .16 – .32. Our substantive theory will be needed to guide us in the judgment as to whether this *CI* is so large that it fails to contribute an increment to our knowledge about these phenomena. If it is judged that it is too large, there are two possible remedies. The simple, but often expensive and sometimes infeasible one is to increase the sample size. If this is possible the precision can be recomputed with a new *n*.

An alternative method of increasing the *df* for precision (and power) is to reduce the number of IVs from the proposed six to a smaller number, if that will result in no material loss of effect size or critical information. The effective *n* in these equations is not the actual sample size but rather the *df*, which is $n - k - 1$. If some of the variables are substantially correlated it may be that they can be usefully consolidated. If the loss to R^2 is small enough, a recomputation of the *CI* may demonstrate adequate precision.

The selected *me* can also be altered. As we argued earlier, it is often the case that an 80% *CI*, or even a *CI* that yields 2 to 1 odds of including the parameter, may be adequate for the scientific purposes of the investigation.

For an illustration, let us return to our academic salary example. Suppose that we were interested in examining another university department for the same issues. This department has 34 current faculty members. We anticipate that this department is a member of the same population, and that the population R^2 will be about the same as it was in the department represented by our current data, where we found $R^2 = .503$ (80% $CI = .40 - .61$, Section 3.6.2). We find that in the proposed department the 80% CI, given a .5 R^2 in the population, would be on average $.38 - .74$. If this is too large to be informative, and we do not feel that using the 2/1 odds rule to generate narrower CI would serve our purpose, there is little point in carrying out the study. Once again, this SE was developed for large samples, so caution must be used in applying it to small samples.

Power Analysis

As we noted earlier, statistical power analysis is concerned with the special case of determining the probability that the sample value will be significantly different from some hypothesized value, typically one of no effect such as a zero R^2. This is a special case because when the CI does not include this null value the statistical criterion has been met (at the α criterion used to determine the CI). Again, one employs the appendix tables (or more conveniently a computer program) by selecting the expected population R^2, the proposed sample n, the number of predictor variables, and the significance criterion, and determining (or reading out) the probability that the sample CI will not include the null value. Although more complete tables for this purpose are provided in J. Cohen (1988), this can also be accomplished by following these steps:

1. Set the significance criterion to be used, α. Provision is made in the appendix for $\alpha = .01$ and $\alpha = .05$ in the L tables (Appendix Tables E.1 and E.2).
2. Determine the population effect size ES for $R^2 =$

$$(3.7.1) \qquad f^2 = \frac{R^2}{1 - R^2}.$$

3. Determine L by

$$(3.7.2) \qquad L = f^2(n - k - 1)$$

4. Determine the power by finding the row corresponding to the df in the selected appendix table, locating an L as close as possible to the computed value, and looking up the column to determine the estimated power.

For example, in the case noted earlier of the new department with 34 faculty members, if the population value is similar to our computed one (.50), the ES $= .503/1 - .503 = 1.012$, and $L = 1.012(34 - 3 - 1) = 30.36$. Looking in Appendix Table E.1 at $k_B = df = 3$, we find that the computed L is larger than the value in the last column and thus the probability of finding the sample R^2 to be greater than zero with $\alpha = .01$ is at least $\beta = .99$. On the other hand, the reader may confirm that if the relationship were more in the range that is typical of many behavioral studies—for example, a population R^2 of .2—even using the less conservative $\alpha = .05$, our chances of finding the sample value to be statistically significant are only slightly better than 50-50.

When the expected power is unacceptably low it may be increased by increasing the df (mainly by increasing n) or by lowering the selected value of α. The first two steps used to determine the $n*$ required for a desired power and R^2 are as shown earlier. L is located for the row corresponding to the df and column corresponding to the desired power. Then $n*$ is determined by

(3.7.1)
$$n* = \frac{L}{f^2} + k + 1.$$

In the proposed example of population $R^2 = .20$, so $ES = f^2 = R^2/(1-R^2) = .2/(1-.2) = .25$, if we desire power $= .80$ we will need $L = 10.90$ (Appendix Table E.2, with 3 df) so that $n* = (10.90/.25) + 3 + 1 = 48$.

Sometimes the effect size can be increased by changes in the sampling strategy (for example, by selecting more extreme subjects), by improvement of measures (increases in their reliability and validity), or by altering the experimental protocol to produce a stronger experimental manipulation. These methods of enhancing power are likely to be especially positive for the scientific payoff of a study, and thus may often be recommended as the first alterations to be considered.

Although it is much to be preferred that the substantive theory and prior research determine the expected population value of R^2, some rules of thumb have been suggested for the use of researchers who are unable to provide more appropriate values. Values of .02, .13, and .26 have been proposed as potentially useful estimates of small, medium, and large effect sizes for the population R^2. These values should probably be adjusted upward by the researcher who intends to use more than a few IVs.

3.7.3 Precision and Power Analysis for Partial Coefficients

Precision

As noted earlier, partial coefficients for a given IV share the same numerator, the exception being the raw unit regression coefficient for which the ratio of standard deviations of Y and that IV also appears. When the units employed for B are meaningful, the CI for B will provide the most useful information about the precision of the expected sample values. (See Chapter 5 for a discussion of methods of improving the utility of measure units.) When the units are not meaningful, precision is usually referenced to β as a function of its SE.[10]

For example, again using our academic salary illustration, we are interested in the value of the gender difference in salary in departments from some other academic field than that represented by our current data. We would like to be able to assess the sex difference with a me of $1000. The researcher may know that about 30% of the faculty members in these departments are women; thus the sd of sex will be about $\sqrt{.30(.70)} = .458$ in the proposed study. The sd of faculty salaries may be determined from administration records or estimated from the current study as about $8000. Using Eq. (3.6.1), rearranging, and solving for $SE_B = me/2 = \$500$, we find

$$(n - k - 1)(\$500)^2 = \frac{\$8000^2(1 - .40)}{.21(1 - .10)}$$

$$n - k - 1 = 948,$$

so that we will need nearly a thousand cases. If, on the other hand, we were content with a me representing about 2/1 odds of including the population value (so that we could tolerate a SE_B of $1000), a sample of about 230 would suffice.

---

[10]We do not provide CIs for sr or sr^2, which are asymmetrical and complex.

Suppose, however, that for the research that we are planning we have no reasonable precedent for estimating B, previous research having used different measures of this construct than the one we are planning to employ. In this case we may use the β obtained in these studies to estimate the value expected in the planned study, and appropriately adjust for correlations with other IVs.

Statistical Power of Partial Coefficients

As we have noted, partial coefficients have a common test of statistical significance. Therefore they also have in common the statistical power to reject a false null (nil) hypothesis that the population value is zero. In the case of statistical power, however, it is convenient to define the effect size as the increment in R^2 attributable to a given IV, that is, its sr^2. As we noted earlier in the chapter, sr differs from β by the square root of its tolerance, the proportion of its variance that is independent of other predictors. As noted previously and discussed in Chapter 10, other things being equal, the SEs of the partial effects of an IV, and thus imprecision in their estimates, are generally increased by increases in correlation with other IVs.

In order to calculate the power of the proposed study to reject the null hypothesis that the partial coefficients are nonzero, one enters the first row of the power tables (or, preferably, a computer program) for the selected significance criterion with the L determined from the proposed n and the estimated proportion of Y variance that is uniquely accounted for by the IV in question. If it should happen that the investigator can more readily estimate B or β, these coefficients can be converted to sr^2 providing that the multiple correlation of the IV in question with the other IVs and, in the case of B, S_Y, and S_i or their ratio, can be estimated.

To illustrate, suppose that we want to have 90% power to detect a sex difference in salary under the same assumptions as in the previous example. Using Eq. (3.5.8) to convert from B to sr, we estimate

$$sr = \$3000 \left(\frac{\sqrt{.21}}{\$8000} \right) \left(\sqrt{1 - .3} \right) = .144,$$

and $sr^2 = .02$. These parameters may be looked up in the computer program. Alternatively, we may compute the $ES =$

(3.7.2)
$$f^2 = \frac{sr^2}{1 - R^2}.$$

If $R^2 = .20$ the $ES = .02/.80 = .025$. Looking up L in Appendix Table E.2 for row $k_B = 1$ and column $\beta = .90$ we find that $L = 10.51$, and applying this to Eq. (3.7.1), we find that we will need 422 cases to have a 90% chance of rejecting the null hypothesis at $\alpha = .05$. Further calculation will show that we will need $n* = 510$ if we wish to reject the null hypothesis at the .01 level. If this number is too large, we may reconsider whether we can be content with 80% power.[11]

In general it is likely to be more practically and theoretically useful to examine the consistency of the new data against some non-nil value. For example, it might be decided that any discrepancy as large as $1000 in annual salary (net of the effects attributable to other causes) would be unmistakably material to the people involved. In such a case the difference between our estimated population value ($3000) and this value is only $2000, so we re-enter the equation with this value.

---

[11]One reason we like computer programs for determining power and needed sample sizes is that they quickly train the researcher to appreciate how statistical power is closely linked to α, ES, df, and n, which may lead to improvements in judgments and strategy on these issues.

Once again, for those investigators who absolutely cannot come up with a more substantively or theoretically based estimate of the population effect size, some rules of thumb are sometimes useful. These values are usually expressed in terms of the proportion of the Y variance that is not explained by other variables that is explained by X_i. Small effects may be defined as 2% of the unexplained variance, medium effects as 15% of the unexplained variance, and large effects as 35%. As we will see in Chapter 5, these values are relatively large when we are talking about a single IV, and it may be at least as appropriate to use the values of r given in Chapter 2 as small, medium, and large, when one is examining a single sr_i.

Several other topics in power analysis are presented in Chapter 5, following the exposition of power analysis when multiple sets of IVs are used. Among the issues discussed there are determination of power for a given n, reconciling different $n*$s for different hypotheses in a single analysis, and some tactical and other considerations involved in setting effect size and power values.

3.8 USING MULTIPLE REGRESSION EQUATIONS IN PREDICTION

One use of MRC is for prediction, literally forecasting, with only incidental attention to explanation. Although we have emphasized the analytic use of MRC to achieve the scientific goal of explanation, MRC plays an important role in several behavioral technologies, including personnel and educational selection, vocational counseling, and psychodiagnosis. In this section we address ourselves to the accuracy of prediction in multiple regression and some of its problems.

3.8.1 Prediction of Y for a New Observation

The standard error of estimate, $SE_{Y-\hat{Y}}$, as we have seen, provides us with an estimate of the magnitude of error that we can expect in estimating $\hat{Y}$ values over sets of future $X_1, X_2, \ldots, X_k$ values that correspond to those of the present sample. Suppose, however, we wish to determine the standard error and confidence intervals of a *single* estimated $\hat{Y}_O$ from a new set of observed values $X_{1O}, X_{2O}, \ldots, X_{kO}$. In Section 2.8.2 we saw that the expected magnitude of error increases as the X_i values depart from their respective means. The reason for this should be clear from the fact that any discrepancy between the sample estimated regression coefficients and the population regression coefficients will result in larger errors in $\hat{Y}_O$ when X_i values are far from their means than when they are close.

Estimates of the standard error and confidence intervals for $\hat{Y}_O$ predicted from known *values* $X_{1i}, X_{2i}, \ldots, X_{ki}$ is given by

(3.8.1)
$$sd_{Y_O-\hat{Y}_O} = \frac{SE_{Y-\hat{Y}}}{\sqrt{n}}\sqrt{n+1+\sum \frac{z_{iO}^2}{1-R_i^2} - 2\sum \frac{\beta_{ij}z_{iO}z_{jO}}{1-R_i^2}},$$

where the first summation is over the k IVs, the second over the $k(k-1)/2$ pairs of IVs (i.e., $i < j$) expressed as standard scores, β_{ij} is the β for estimating X_i from X_j, holding constant the remaining $k-2$ IVs, and R_i^2 is literally $R_{i.12...(i)...k}^2$. Although at first glance this formula appears formidable, a closer examination will make clear what elements affect the size of this error. The $SE_{Y-\hat{Y}}$ is the standard error of estimate, and as in the case of a single IV, we see that increases in it and/or in the absolute value of the IV (z_{iO}) will be associated with larger error. The terms that appear in the multiple IV case that did not appear in the Eq. (2.8.3) for the single variable case (β_{ij} and R_i^2) are functions of the relationships among the independent variables. When all independent variables are uncorrelated (hence all β_{ij} and all R_i^2 equal zero), we see that the formula simplifies and $sd_{Y_o - \hat{Y}_o}$ is minimized (for constant $SE_{Y - \hat{Y}}$, n, and z_{iO} values).

It is worth emphasizing the distinction between the validity of the significance tests performed on partial coefficients and the accuracy of such coefficients when used in prediction. In analytic uses of MRC, including formal causal analysis, given the current level of theoretical development in the behavioral and social sciences, the information most typically called upon is the significance of the departure of partial coefficients from zero and the sign of such coefficients. The significance tests are relatively robust to assumption failure, particularly so when n is not small. Using the regression equation for prediction, on the other hand, requires applying these coefficients to particular individual variable values for which the consequence of assumption failure is likely to be much more serious.

As an illustration, let us examine the scatterplot matrix (SPLOM)[12] for our running example of academic salaries. Figure 3.8.1 provides the scatterplot for each pair of variables, including the predicted salary and the residual. As can be seen, the original distributions of years and publications are not as symmetrical as is the distribution of salary. Probably as a consequence, the residuals above the mean $\hat{Y}$ appear to have a somewhat higher variance than those below the mean (the reader may check to determine that this is indeed the case). The variance of the residuals otherwise looks passably normal (as indeed they should, because this example was generated to meet these assumptions in the population). Failure of the homoscedasticity assumption may not be serious enough to invalidate tests of statistical significance, but it still could invalidate actual prediction if based on the assumption of equal error throughout the distribution.

3.8.2 Correlation of Individual Variables With Predicted Values

Further insight may be gained by noting that regardless of the sign, magnitude, or significance of its partial regression coefficient, the correlation between X_i and the $\hat{Y}$ determined from the entire regression equation is

(3.8.2)
$$r_{\hat{Y}i} = \frac{r_{Yi}}{R_{Y.123...k}}.$$

Thus it is invariably of the same sign and of larger magnitude than its zero-order r with Y. (See values at the bottom of Fig. 3.8.1 for reflection of this in our running example.) Reflection on this fact may help the researcher to avoid errors in interpreting data analyses in which variables that correlate materially with Y have partial coefficients that approach zero or are of opposite sign. When partial coefficients of the X_i approximate zero, whatever linear relationship exists between X_i and Y is accounted for by the remaining independent variables. Because neither its zero-order correlation with Y nor its (larger) correlations with $\hat{Y}$ is thereby denied, the interpretation of this finding is highly dependent on the substantive theory being examined. Even without a full causal model, a weak theoretical model may be employed to sort out the probable meaning of such a finding. One theoretical context may lead to the conclusion that the true causal effect of X_i on Y operates fully through the other IVs in the equation. Similarly, when the B_{Yi} and r_{Yi} are of opposite sign, X_i and one or more of the remaining IVs are in a suppressor relationship. Although it is legitimate and useful to interpret the partialed relationship, it is also important to keep in mind the zero-order correlations of X_i with Y (and hence with $\hat{Y}$).

---

[12]The fact that we have not previously introduced this graphical aid should not be taken to deny an assertion that such a matrix is probably the first step in analyzing a data set that should be taken by a competent data analyst (see Chapter 4). The figures along the diagonal reflect the distribution of each variable.

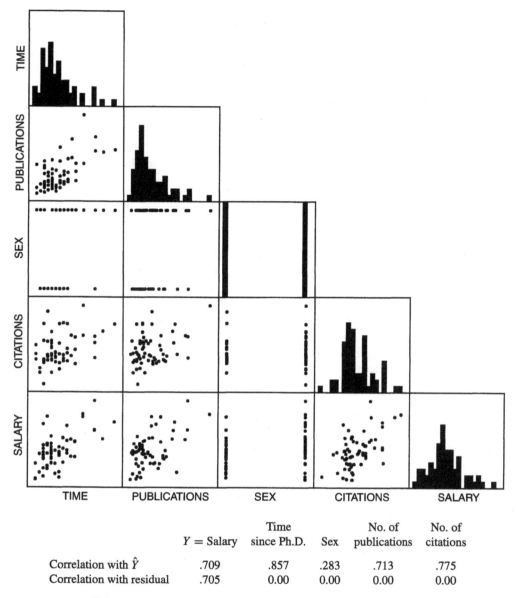

	Y = Salary	Time since Ph.D.	Sex	No. of publications	No. of citations
Correlation with $\hat{Y}$	.709	.857	.283	.713	.775
Correlation with residual	.705	0.00	0.00	0.00	0.00

FIGURE 3.8.1 Scatterplot matrix for the academic salary example.

3.8.3 Cross-Validation and Unit Weighting

Several alternatives to regression coefficients for forming weighted composites in prediction have been proposed (Darlington, 1978; Dawes, 1979; Green, 1977; Wainer, 1976). Although β weights are guaranteed to produce composites that are most highly correlated with z_Y (or Y) in the sample on which they are determined, other weights produce composites (call them u_Y) that are almost as highly correlated in that sample. "Unit weighting", the assignment of the weights of +1 to positively related, −1 to negatively related, and 0 to poorly related IVs are popular candidates—they are simple, require no computation, and are not subject to sampling error (Green, 1977; Mosteller & Tukey, 1977; Wainer, 1976). For our running example on academic salary, we simply add (that is, we use weights of $+1.0$) the z scores of each subject for time since Ph.D., publications, and citations, and subtract (that is, use weights of -1.0) each score for female to produce the composite u_Y for each subject. We find that u_Y correlates .944 with the β-weighted $\hat{z}_Y$ (or $\hat{Y}$), and therefore (not surprisingly) .670 with z_Y (or Y), only modestly lower than the .709 ($= R_Y$) of $\hat{z}_Y$ with z_Y (or Y).

However, the real question in prediction is not how well the regression equation determined for a sample works on that sample, but rather how well it works in the population or on other samples from the population. Note that this is *not* the estimate of the population $\hat{\rho}_Y^2$, (i.e., the "shrunken" value given in Eq. 3.5.5), but rather an estimate of the "cross-validated" $r_{Y\hat{Y}}^2$ for each sample's β applied to the other sample, which is even more shrunken and which may be estimated by

$$(3.8.3) \qquad \hat{R}^2 = 1 - (1 - R^2)\frac{(n+k)}{(n-k)}$$

(Rozeboom, 1979). $\hat{R}^2$ answers the relevant question, "If I were to apply the *sample* regression weights to the population, or to another sample from the population, for what proportion of the Y variance would my thus-predicted Y values account?"

For our running example with $n = 62$, our sample regression equation yields $\hat{R}^2 = 1 - (1 - .5032)(62 + 4)/(62 - 4) = .4347$, so $\hat{R} = .659$. We found earlier, however, that the unit-weighted composite for the cases we have yielded an $r = .670$, greater than $\hat{R}$. Now this value is subject to sampling error (so is $\hat{R}$), but *not* to shrinkage, because it does not depend on unstable regression coefficients. As far as we can tell, unit weights would do as well or better in prediction for these data than the sample's standardized regression weights based on only 62 cases.

Unit weights have their critics (Pruzek & Fredericks, 1978; Rozeboom, 1979). For certain patterns of correlation (suppression is one) or a quite large $n:k$ ratio (say more than 20 or 30), unit weights may not work as well in a new sample as the original regression coefficients will. An investigator who may be in such a circumstance is advised to compute $\hat{R}$ and compare it with the results of unit weighting in the sample at hand.

3.8.4 Multicollinearity

The existence of substantial correlation among a set of IVs creates difficulties usually referred to as the problem of multicollinearity. Actually, there are two distinct problems—the substantive interpretation of partial coefficients and their sampling stability.

Interpretation

We have already seen in Section 3.4 that the partial coefficients of highly correlated IVs analyzed simultaneously are reduced. Because the IVs involved lay claim to largely the same portion of the Y variance by definition, they cannot make much by way of unique contributions. Interpretation of the partial coefficients of IVs from the results of a simultaneous regression of such a set of variables that ignores their multicollinearity will necessarily be misleading.

Attention to the R_i^2 of the variables may help, but a superior solution requires that the investigator formulate some causal hypotheses about the origin of the multicollinearity. If it is thought that the shared variance is attributable to a single central property, trait, or *latent variable*, it may be most appropriate to combine the variables into a single index or drop the more peripheral ones (Sections 4.5 and 5.7), or even to turn to a latent variable causal model (see Chapter 12). If, on the other hand, the investigator is truly interested in each of the variables in its own right, analysis by a hierarchical procedure may be employed (Section 5.3). To be sure, the validity of the interpretation depends on the appropriateness of the hierarchical sequence, but this is preferable to the complete anarchy of the simultaneous analysis in which everything is partialed from everything else indiscriminately.

Sampling Stability

The structure of the formulas for SE_{B_i} (Eq. 3.6.1) and SE_{β_i} (Eq. 3.6.2) makes plain that they are directly proportional to $\sqrt{1/(1 - R_i^2)}$. A serious consequence of multicollinearity, therefore, is highly unstable partial coefficients for those IVs that are highly correlated with the others.[13] Concomitantly, the trustworthiness of individually predicted $\hat{Y}_O$ is lessened as the R_i^2s for a set of IVs increase, as is evident from the structure of Eq. (3.6.1). Large standard errors mean both wide confidence intervals and a lessened probability of rejecting a null hypothesis (see Section 3.7). Chapter 10 discusses issues of multicollinearity in more detail.

3.9 SUMMARY

This chapter begins with the representation of the theoretical rationale for analysis of multiple independent variables by means of causal models. The employment of an explicit theoretical model as a working hypothesis is advocated for all investigations except those intended for simple prediction. After the meaning of the term cause is briefly discussed (Section 3.1.1) rules for diagrammatic representation of a causal model are presented (Section 3.1.2).

Bivariate linear regression analysis is extended to the case in which two or more independent variables (IVs), designated $X_i (i = 1, 2, \ldots, k)$ are linearly related to a dependent variable Y. As with a single IV, the multiple regression equation that produces the estimated $\hat{Y}$ is that linear function of the k IVs for which the sum over the n cases of the squared discrepancies of $\hat{Y}$ from Y, $\Sigma(Y - \hat{Y})^2$, is a minimum.

The regression equation in both raw and standardized form for two IVs is presented and interpreted. The standardized partial regression coefficients, β_i, are shown to be a function of the correlations among the variables; β_i may be converted to the raw score B_i by multiplying each by sd_Y/sd_i (Section 3.2).

The measures of correlation in MRC analysis include:

1. R, which expresses the correlation between Y and the best (least squared errors) linear function of the k IVs ($\hat{Y}$), and R^2, which is interpretable as the proportion of Y variance accounted for by this function (Section 3.3.1).

2. Semipartial correlations, sr_i, which express the correlation of X_i from which the other IVs have been partialed with Y. sr_i^2 is thus the proportion of variance in Y uniquely associated with X_i, that is, the increase in R^2 when X_i is added to the other IVs. The ballantine is introduced to provide graphical representation of the overlapping of variance with Y of X_1 and X_2 (Section 3.3.2).

3. Partial correlations, pr_i, which give the correlation between that portion of Y not linearly associated with the other IVs and that portion of X_i that is not linearly associated with the other IVs. In contrast with sr_i, pr_i partials the other IVs from both X_i and Y. pr_i^2 is the proportion of Y variance not associated with the other IVs that is associated with X_i (Section 3.3.3).

Each of these coefficients is exemplified, and shown to be a function of the zero-order correlation coefficients. The reader is cautioned that none of these coefficients provides a basis for a satisfactory Y variance partitioning scheme when the IVs are mutually correlated.

---

[13]This is the focus of the discussion in Section 4.5.

The alternative causal models possible for Y and two IVs are discussed, exemplified, and illustrated. The distinction between direct and indirect effects is explained, and models consistent with partial redundancy between the IVs are illustrated. Mutual suppression of causal effects will occur when any of the three zero-order correlations is less than the product of the other two (Section 3.4.1). Spurious effects and entirely indirect effects can be distinguished when the causal sequence of the IVs is known (Section 3.4.2).

The case of two IVs is generalized to the case of k IVs in Section 3.5. The use of the various coefficients in the interpretation of research findings is discussed and illustrated with concrete examples. The relationships among the coefficients are given.

Statistical inference with k IVs, including SEs and CIs for standardized and raw unit regression coefficients and R^2 are presented in Section 3.6. CIs for the difference between independent R^2s are shown as well as a series of statistical tests on multiple and partial coefficients.

Determination of the precision of expected findings from proposed investigations is described and illustrated. Statistical power analysis is shown to be a special case when the question is limited to a non-nil value of a multiple or partial coefficient (Section 3.7).

A range of prediction situations are described in Section 3.8, including the prediction of a value of Y for a newly observed case. Correlations among the predictors will affect the adequacy of the estimation of the individual coefficients and the stability of the model. It is shown that least squares estimation may not yield optimal prediction for future studies or cases.

4

Data Visualization, Exploration, and Assumption Checking: Diagnosing and Solving Regression Problems I

4.1 INTRODUCTION

In Chapters 2 and 3 we focused on understanding the basic linear regression model. We considered fundamental issues such as how to specify a regression equation with one, two, or more independent variables, how to interpret the coefficients, and how to construct confidence intervals and conduct significance tests for both the regression coefficients and the overall prediction. In this chapter, we begin our exploration of a number of issues that can potentially arise in the analysis of actual data sets. In practice, not all data sets are "textbook" cases. The purpose of the present chapter is to provide researchers with a set of tools with which to understand their data and to identify many of the potential problems that may arise. We will also introduce a number of remedies for these problems, many of which will be developed in more detail in subsequent chapters. We believe that careful inspection of the data and the results of the regression model using the tools presented in this chapter helps provide substantially increased confidence in the results of regression analyses. Such checking is a fundamental part of good data analysis.

We begin this chapter with a review of some simple graphical displays that researchers can use to visualize various aspects of their data. These displays can point to interesting features of the data or to problems in the data or in the regression model under consideration when it is applied to the current data. Indeed, Tukey (1977) noted that a graphical display has its greatest value "when it *forces* us to notice **what we never expected to see**" (p. v, italics and bold in original.) Historically, labor-intensive analyses performed by hand or with calculators served the function of providing researchers with considerable familiarity with their data. However, the simplicity of "point and click" analyses in the current generation of statistical packages has made it easy to produce results without any understanding of the underlying data or regression analyses. Modern graphical methods have replaced this function, producing displays that help researchers quickly gain an in-depth familiarity with their data. These displays are also very useful in comparing one's current data with other similar data collected in previous studies.

Second, we examine the assumptions of multiple regression. All statistical procedures including multiple regression make certain assumptions that should be met for their proper use. In the case of multiple regression, violations of these assumptions *may* raise concerns as to whether the estimates of regression coefficients and their standard errors are correct. These concerns, in turn, may raise questions about the conclusions that are reached about independent variables based on confidence intervals or significance tests. But, even more important, violations of assumptions can point to problems in the specification of the regression model and provide valuable clues that can lead to a revision of the model, yielding an even greater understanding of the data. In other cases, violations of assumptions may point to complexities in the data that require alternative approaches to estimating the original regression model. We present a number of graphical and statistical approaches that help diagnose violations of assumptions and introduce potential remedies for these problems.

The themes of data exploration/visualization coupled with careful checking of assumptions are familiar ones in statistics. Yet, diffusion of these themes to the behavioral sciences has been uneven, with some areas embracing and some areas neglecting them. Some areas have primarily emphasized hypothesis testing, confirmatory data analysis. Yet, as Tukey (1977) emphasized, **"Today, exploratory and confirmatory can—and should—proceed side by side"** (p. vii, bold in original). Some areas such as econometrics and some areas of sociology have emphasized careful checking of assumptions, whereas some areas of psychology have been more willing to believe that their results were largely immune to violations of assumptions. The increasing availability of both simple methods for detecting violations and statistical methods for addressing violations of assumptions decreases the force of this latter belief. Proper attention to the assumptions of regression analysis leads to benefits. Occasionally, gross errors in the conclusions of the analysis can be avoided. More frequently, more precise estimates of the effects of interest can be provided. And often, proper analyses are associated with greater statistical power, helping researchers detect their hypothesized effects (e.g., Wilcox, 1998). We hope to encourage researchers in those areas of the behavioral sciences that have overlooked these powerful themes of data exploration/visualization and assumption checking to begin implementing them in their everyday data analysis.

We defer until later in the book consideration of two other issues that arise in multiple regression with real data sets. First is the existence of *outliers*, unusual cases that are far from the rest of the data. In some cases, the existence of a few outliers, even one, can seriously jeopardize the results and conclusions of the regression analysis. Second is multicollinearity, the problem of high redundancy between the IVs first introduced in Section 3.8.4. Multicollinearity leads to imprecise estimates of regression coefficients and increased difficulty in interpreting the results of the analysis. Both of these issues receive detailed consideration in Chapter 10.

Boxed Material in the Text

Finally, the structure of Chapter 4 adds a new feature. We adopt a strategy of putting some material into boxes to ease the presentation. The material in the boxes typically contains technical details that will be of primary interest to the more advanced reader. The boxes provide supplementation to the text; readers who are new to regression analysis can skip over the boxed material without any loss of continuity. Boxed material is set apart by bold lines; boxes appear in the section in which the boxed material is referenced. Readers not interested in the technical details may simply skip the boxed material.

4.2 SOME USEFUL GRAPHICAL DISPLAYS
OF THE ORIGINAL DATA

In regression analysis, the analyst should normally wish to take a careful look at both the original data and the residuals. In this section, we present graphical tools that are particularly useful in examining the original data. Reflecting the ease of producing graphical displays on modern personal computers, our focus here is on using graphical tools as a fundamental part of the data-analysis process. These tools help display features of the distributions of each of the variables as well as their joint distributions, providing initial clues about the likely outcomes and potential problems of the regression analysis. Graphical displays can provide a more complete and more easily understandable portrayal of the data than typically reported summary statistics. Graphical displays also do not depend on assumptions about the form of the distribution or the nature of the relationship between the independent and dependent variables. These themes will be further considered in Section 4.4, where we introduce graphical tools for the examination of the residuals.

We begin Section 4.2 with univariate displays that describe single variables, then consider the scatterplot, which shows the relationship between two variables, and finally the scatterplot matrix, which simultaneously displays each possible pair of relationships between three or more variables. The basics of several of these graphical displays will be familiar to many readers from introductory statistics courses and Chapters 2 and 3 of this book. What will be new are several enhancements that can increase the information available from the plot. We will also use many of these displays as building blocks for graphical examination of data in later sections of this chapter.

4.2.1 Univariate Displays

Univariate displays present a visual representation of aspects of the distribution of a single variable. Data are typically portrayed in textbooks as having a normal or bell-shaped distribution. However, real data can be skewed, have multiple modes, have gaps in which no cases appear, or have *outliers*—atypical observations that do not fit with the rest of the data. Because each of the univariate displays portrays different aspects of the data (Fox, 1990; Lee & Tu, 1997), it is often helpful to examine more than one display to achieve a more complete understanding of one's data.

Frequency Histograms

Perhaps the most commonly used univariate display is the frequency histogram. In the frequency histogram, the scores on the variable are plotted on the x axis. The range of the scores is broken down into a number of intervals of equal width called *bins*. The number of scores in each interval, the frequency, is represented above the interval. Frequency histograms provide a rough notion of the central tendency, variability, range, and shape of the distribution of each separate variable. They also have some ability to identify outliers.

Figure 4.2.1 presents two different histograms of the variable years since Ph.D. for the faculty salaries data set ($n = 62$) originally presented in Table 3.5.1. Panel (A) uses 5 bins. This histogram depicts a single mode around 2.5 years since the Ph.D. (the midpoint of the interval) with a right skewed distribution. Panel (B) uses 20 bins. Here, the distribution still appears to be right skewed, but this histogram suggests that there may be two modes at about 2.5 years and 6 years post Ph.D., and that there may be an outlier at about 21 years post Ph.D. The shape of the distribution is a bit less apparent and gaps in the distribution (scores with a frequency of 0) are now more apparent.

The comparison of the two panels illustrates that histograms derived from the same data can give different impressions with respect to the distribution of the underlying data and the presence of outliers in the data set. The exact shape of the distribution will depend on two decisions made by the analyst or the statistical package generating the histogram: (1) The number of *bins*, which are intervals of equal width (e.g., 0–4, 5–9, 10–14, etc.), and (2) the range of the data represented by the histogram. With respect to (2), some histograms represent

(A) Five bins.

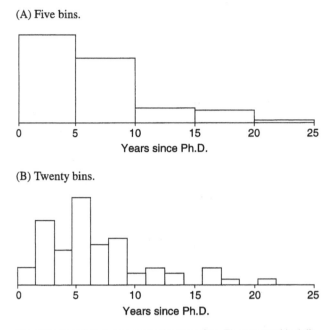

(B) Twenty bins.

Note: The two histograms portray the same data. The two graphical displays give somewhat different impressions of the underlying distribution. The gaps and outlying values in the data are distinct with 20 bins.

FIGURE 4.2.1 Histograms of years since Ph.D.

the range of possible scores, some represent the actual range of data, and some represent a convenient range (e.g., 0–25 years in the present case rather than the actual range of the data, 1–21 years). Statistical packages use one of several algorithms[1] to calculate the number of bins to be displayed, none of which assure that the frequency histogram will optimally represent all of the features of the distribution. With complicated distributions, it can often be useful to vary the number of bins and to examine more than one histogram based on the data. A large number of bins should be used to identify outliers. Some statistical packages now permit the analyst to easily vary the number of bins using a simple visual scale (a "slider") with the histogram being continuously redisplayed as the number of bins is changed.

Stem and Leaf Displays

Closely related to the histogram is the stem and leaf display. This display is of particular value in data sets ranging from about 20 to 200 cases. The stem and leaf display is the *only* graphical display that retains the values of the original scores so that the original data can be precisely reconstructed. Otherwise, the strengths and limitations of the stem and leaf display closely parallel those of the histogram presented above (see also Fox, 1990, pp. 92–93 for a more detailed discussion).

---

[1]One popular algorithm is Sturgis' rule—the number of bins is $1 + \log_2(N)$. For example, for $N = 62$, $1 + \log_2(62) = 1 + 5.95 \approx 7$ bins would be used. The interval width is chosen as the (maximum−minimum score + 1)/(number of bins). If for the 62 cases the highest score were 21 and the lowest score were 1, Sturgis' rule produces an interval width of $(21 - 2 + 1)/7 = 2.86$. When graphs are constructed by hand, easily interpretable interval widths are often chosen (e.g., interval width = 1, 2, 5, 10). For example, if interval width = 5 were chosen, the intervals would be 0–4, 5–9, 10–14, 15–19, and 20–24.

Stem	Leaves
0–4	11122333333333444444
5–9	5555555555566666667777777788889999
10–14	0011133
15–19	6668
20–24	1

Note: Each stem represents the interval. Leaves represent the last digit of values of the observations within the interval. The number of times the digit is repeated corresponds to the frequency of the observation.

FIGURE 4.2.2 Stem and leaf display of years since Ph.D.

To illustrate, Fig. 4.2.2 presents a stem and leaf display for the years since Ph.D. data ($n = 62$) presented in Table 3.5.1. To construct this display, an interval width is initially chosen. We have chosen an interval width of 5 so that the display will be similar to the histogram with 5 bins presented in Fig. 4.2.1, Panel (A). The stem indicates the range of scores that fall in the interval.[2] The lowest interval (0–4) includes scores from 0 to 4 and the second from the highest interval (15–19) includes scores from 15 to 19. *Leaves* provide information about the exact values that fall in each interval. The frequency of occurrence of each score is indicated by repeating the value. For example, the lowest interval indicates no scores with a value of 0, three scores with a value of 1, two scores with a value of 2, nine scores with a value of 3, and six scores with a value of 4. The second to highest interval (15–19) has no scores with a value of 15, three scores with a value of 16, no scores with a value of 17, one score with a value of 18, and no scores with a value of 19.

Stem and leaf displays must be presented using a fixed-width typefont (e.g., Courier). The leading digit of the leaves (for example, 1 for 10–14 and 2 for 20–24) is dropped so that each number is represented as the same size in the display. If the stem and leaf display is rotated 90° counterclockwise so that the numbers form vertical columns, then the display depicts the same distribution as a histogram with the same number of bins. However, stem and leaf displays have the advantage of also representing the exact numerical values of each of the data points.

Smoothing: Kernel Density Estimates

A technique known as smoothing provides the foundation for an excellent visual depiction of a variable's underlying general frequency distribution. Often in the behavioral sciences the size of our samples is not large enough to provide a good depiction of distribution in the full population. If we were to take several samples from the same population and construct histograms or stem and leaf displays, there would be considerable variation in the shape of the distribution from sample to sample. This variation can be reduced by averaging adjacent data points prior to constructing the distribution. This general approach is called *smoothing*.

The simplest method of smoothing is the *running average* in which the frequencies are averaged over several adjacent scores. To illustrate, Table 4.2.1 presents the subset of data from Table 3.5.1 for the six faculty members who have values between 12 and 20 years

---

[2]The apparent limits of the interval are shown (e.g., 0–4 for first interval). Recall from introductory statistics that when the data can be measured precisely, values as low as −0.5 or up to 4.50 could fall in the first interval. These values are known as the real limits of the interval.

TABLE 4.2.1
Weights Based on the Bisquare Distribution for $X = 16$

X_i	f	$\left(\dfrac{X_i - X_C}{d}\right)$	W_i	f	$\left(\dfrac{X_i - X_C}{d}\right)$	W_i
		(A) $d = 4$			(B) $d = 3$	
20	0	1.0	0.00	0	1.33	0.00
19	0	0.75	0.19	0	1.00	0.00
18	1	0.50	0.56	1	0.67	0.31
17	0	0.25	0.88	0	0.33	0.79
16*	3	0.00	1.00	3	0.00	1.00
15	0	−0.25	0.88	0	−0.33	0.79
14	0	−0.50	0.56	0	−0.67	0.31
13	2	−0.75	0.19	2	−1.00	0.00
12	0	−1.00	0.00	0	−1.33	0.00

Note: X_i is the score, f is the frequency of the score, X_C is the location of the center of the smoothing window, d is the bandwidth distance, and W_i is the weight given to a score of X_i. W_i is calculated from the bisquare distribution. (A) provides the weights when the bandwidth distance $= 4$; (B) provides the weights when the bandwidth distance $= 3$. X_C is a score of 16 in this example, which is marked by an asterisk.

since the Ph.D. We identify a smoothing window over which the averaging should occur. The *smoothing window* is a symmetric range of values around a specified value of the variable. We identify a score of interest which establishes the center of the smoothing window, X_C. We then identify a bandwidth distance, d, which represents the distance from the center to each edge of the smoothing window. The width of the smoothing window is then $2d$. For our illustration of the calculation of a running average, we arbitrarily choose $X_C = 16$ and $d = 2$. The running average is calculated using all scores that fall in the smoothing window between $X_C - d$ and $X_C + d$. In our example the smoothing window only includes the scores from 14 to 18, so the width of the smoothing window is 4. For $X_C = 16$, the score marked by an asterisk in Table 4.2.1, we would average the frequencies for scores of 14, 15, 16, 17, and 18, so for $X_C = 16, f_{avg} = (0 + 0 + 3 + 0 + 1)/5 = 0.8$. For $X_C = 17$, we would average the frequencies for frequencies 15, 16, 17, 18, and 19, so for $X_C = 17, f_{avg} = (0 + 3 + 0 + 1 + 0) = 0.8$. Running averages are calculated in a similar fashion for each possible score in the distribution—we simply let X_C in turn equal the value of each possible score.

In practice, a more complex smoothing method known as the *kernel density estimate* is typically used because this method provides an even more accurate estimate of the distribution in the population. The kernel density estimate is based on a *weighted* average of the data. Within the smoothing window, the scores that lie close to X_C, the center of the smoothing window, are given a relatively high weight. Scores that are further from X_C characterize the smoothing window less well and are given a lower weight. Scores that lie outside the smoothing window are given a weight of 0. This method of smoothing results in a density curve, a continuous function whose height at any point estimates the relative frequency of that value of X_C in the population. The height of the density curve at any point is scaled so that the total area under the curve will be 1.0. Unlike the previous topics we have considered in this book, kernel density estimation requires very intensive calculation and is consequently only performed on a computer. Box 4.2.1 shows the details of the calculation for interested readers.

BOX 4.2.1
Inside the Black Box: How Kernel Density Estimates
Are Calculated

To illustrate how a kernel density estimate is created at a single point, consider $X_C = 16$ in our distribution of years since Ph.D. in Table 4.2.1. We arbitrarily choose the bandwidth distance $d = 4$ so that the width of the smoothing window $= 8$. Recall that we wish to give scores at the center of the smoothing window a high weight and scores further from the center of the interval lower weights. Several different weight functions will achieve this goal; the bisquare weight function presented in Eq. (4.2.1) is commonly used.

$$(4.2.1) \qquad \text{Bisquare} \quad W_i = \left[1 - \left(\frac{X_i - X_C}{d}\right)^2\right]^2 \quad \text{when} \quad |X_i - X_C| \le d.$$

$$W_i = 0 \qquad \text{when} \quad |X_i - X_C| > d.$$

Table 4.2.1 presents the values used in the calculation of the weights and shows the desired pattern of high weights at the center of the smoothing window and lower weights for scores further from the center of the smoothing window. For example, for $X_i = 17$,

$$W_i = \left[1 - \left(\frac{17 - 16}{4}\right)^2\right]^2 = \left[1 - (0.25)^2\right]^2 = (1 - 0.0625)^2 = 0.88.$$

Returning to our kernel density estimate, we can calculate its height at any value of X_C using the following equation:

$$(4.2.2) \qquad \text{height at } X_C = \frac{1}{nd} \sum_{i=1}^{n} f W_i.$$

In Eq. (4.2.2), the height of the density curve is calculated at our chosen value of X_C, here 16, n is the number of cases in the *full* sample (here, 62 cases), d is bandwidth distance, and f is the frequency of cases at X_i. W_i is the weight given to each observation at X_i. The weight for X_1 is determined by the value of the bisquare function applied to $(X_i - X_C)/d$.

Let us apply Eq. (4.2.2) to the data in Table 4.2.1A for $d = 4$. The score is given in column 1, the frequency in column 2, $(X_i - X_C)/d$ in column 3, and the weight from the bisquare weight function (Eq. 4.2.1) in column 4. Beginning at $X = 12$ and continuing to $X = 20$, we get

$$\text{height} = \frac{1}{(62)(4)}[(0)(.00) + (2)(.19) + 0(.56) + 0(.88)$$
$$+ 3(1.0) + 0(.88) + 1(.56) + 0(.19) + (0)(.00)] = .03.$$

In practice, the statistical package calculates the value of the height for *every* possible value of X_C over the full range of X, here $X = 1$ to $X = 21$, and produces the kernel density estimate, which is a smooth curve that estimates the distribution of X in the population.

In Table 4.2.1B, we also provide the values of W_i if we choose a smaller bandwidth, here $d = 3$. As can be seen, the weight given to each observed score declines more quickly as we move away from the X_C of interest. For example, when $d = 3$, the weight for a score of 18 is 0.31, whereas when $d = 4$ the weight for a score of 18 is 0.56. The analyst controls the amount of smoothing by selecting the bandwidth d, with larger values of d producing more smoothing.

The central problem for the analyst is to decide how big the width of the smoothing window should be. Some modern statistical packages allow the analyst to change the size of the smoothing window using a visual scale (slider), with the resulting kernel density estimate being continuously redisplayed on the computer screen. Simple visual judgments by the analyst are normally sufficient to choose a reasonable window size that provides a good estimate of the shape of the distribution in the population. Figure 4.2.3 provides an illustration of the effect of choosing different bandwidth distances for the full years since Ph.D. data ($n = 62$) originally presented in Table 3.5.1. Figure 4.2.3(A) depicts bandwidth = 10, in which oversmoothing has occurred and features of the data are lost (e.g., the mode near the score of 5 is not distinct). Figure 4.2.3(B) depicts bandwidth = 1.5, in which too little smoothing has occurred and the distribution is "lumpy." Figure 4.2.3(C), with bandwidth = 4, provides a smooth curve that appears to depict the major features of the data. Good kernel density plots include enough detail to capture the major features of the data, but not to the extent of becoming "lumpy." Figure 4.2.3(D) shows a kernel density estimate as an overlay over a histogram so that both depictions of the same data set are available.

The great strength of kernel density plots is their ability to depict the underlying distribution of the data in the population. However, kernel density estimates do not reproduce the information about the data in the original sample and do not clearly portray unusual observations or gaps in the distribution over which the scores have a frequency of 0.

Boxplots

Another commonly used univariate display is the boxplot, also known as the "box and whiskers plot." Figure 4.2.4 displays a boxplot of the years since Ph.D. data. Note that the values of the scores, here years since Ph.D., are represented on the y axis. The center line of the box at a value of 6 is the median of the distribution. The upper edge of the box at a value of about 8.5 is the third quartile, Q_3 (75% of the cases fall at or below this value); the lower edge of the box at a value of about 4 is the first quartile, Q_1 (25% of the cases fall at or below this value). The semi-interquartile range, $SIQR$, is $(Q_3 - Q_1)/2 = (8.5 - 4)/2 = 2.25$, or half the distance between the upper and lower edges of the box. The $SIQR$ is a measure of the variability of the distribution that is useful when the distribution is skewed. When there are no outlying observations, the two vertical lines (termed whiskers) extending from the box represent the distance from Q_1 to the lowest score (here, 1) and Q_3 to the highest score in the distribution. Values of any outlying scores are displayed separately when they fall below $Q_1 - 3SIQR$ or above $Q_3 + 3SIQR$. If the distribution were normal, these scores would correspond to the most extreme 0.35% of the cases. In Fig. 4.2.4 the value of the horizontal line corresponding to the end of the top whisker is $Q_3 + 3SIQR$ (here, about 14). The open circles above this line corresponding to 16, 18, and 21 years are outlying cases. If one whisker is long relative to the other or there are outlying values on only one side of the distribution, the distribution will be skewed in that direction. Figure 4.2.4 depicts a positively skewed distribution.

The boxplot provides a good depiction of the skewness of the distribution and clearly identifies the existence, but not the frequency, of outlying observations in the data set. When multiple cases occur at a single outlying score (here at $X = 16$, $f = 3$), a problem known as *overplotting* occurs. Standard computer programs plot one case on top of the other, and the multiple cases cannot be discerned. The boxplot also provides clear information about the range and the median of the data in the sample. However, the boxplot does not portray the existence of more than one mode or gaps in the distribution over which the scores have a frequency of 0.

(A) Width = 10: too much smoothing.

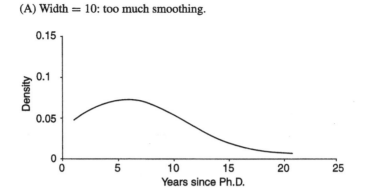

(B) Width = 1.5: too little smoothing.

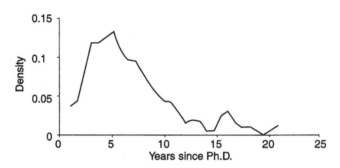

(C) Width = 4: appropriate smoothing.

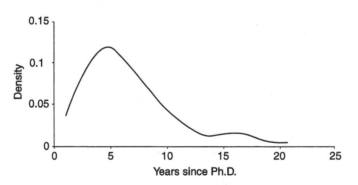

(D) Histogram with kernel density superimposed (combines Fig. 4.2.1B with Fig. 4.2.3C).

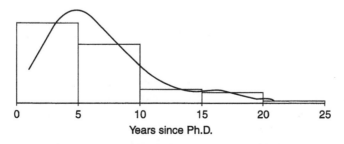

FIGURE 4.2.3   Kernel density estimates: years since Ph.D.

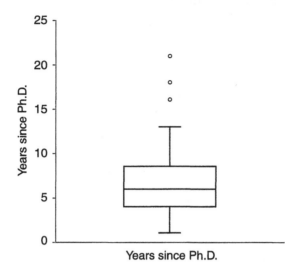

Note: From bottom to top, the first four horizontal lines in the figure represent the lowest score (year $= 1$), the first quartile (years $= 4$), the median (years $= 6$), and the third quartile (Q_3, years $= 8.5$). Because there are high outliers in the data set, the top line represents $Q_3 + 3SIQR$ (years $= 14$). The outlying cases are plotted as separate points (here, at years $= 16$, 18, and 21).

FIGURE 4.2.4   Boxplot of years since Ph.D.

Comparisons With the Normal Distribution

Researchers may wish to compare the univariate distribution of their sample data with a normal distribution. The regression model that we emphasize in this volume makes no assumption about the distribution of the independent or dependent variables. However, as we will present in Section 4.3, this model does make the assumption that the residuals are normally distributed. Normal curve overlays and normal q-q plots permitting comparison of the residuals with the normal distribution are presented in Section 4.4.6. These plots can be applied to the original data as well. For example, these plots can be particularly useful in the context of structural equation modeling with latent variables (see Chapter 12), a technique which assumes that each measured variable has a normal distribution.

4.2.2 Bivariate Displays

We will often wish to examine the relationship between two variables. These can be two independent variables, X_1 and X_2, or one of the independent variables and the dependent variables, for example, X_1 and Y. As we have already seen in Chapters 2 and 3, scatterplots present an excellent way of doing this. In a scatterplot, variable 1 is plotted on the x axis and variable 2 is plotted on the y axis. Note that scatterplots are not symmetric: Unless $sd_Y = sd_X$, the scatterplot of variable 2 (on the y axis) versus variable 2 (on the x axis) will have a different appearance than the scatterplot of variable 1 (on the y axis) versus variable 2 (on the x axis). Recall from Chapter 2 that the regression of Y on X and the regression of X on Y are different unless the standard deviations of X and Y are equal.

Figure 4.2.5(A) presents a scatterplot of years since Ph.D. versus salary. In this figure the salaries are large numbers, so they are printed in scientific notation, a useful method of compactly representing large numbers.[3] The minimum value on the y axis is $2e+04 = 2 \times 10^4 = \$20,000$. The maximum value is $1e+05 = 1 \times 10^5 = 1 \times 100,000 = \$100,000$. Scatterplots help us detect whether the relationship between each X and Y is linear or takes some other form.

One special problem in interpreting scatterplots occurs when one of the variables is categorical. For example, we may wish to compare the years since Ph.D. of male and female faculty members in our sample. This relationship is depicted in Fig. 4.2.5(B), where males and females are represented by values of 0 and 1, respectively. A problem arises with the graph because cases having the same value on Y, here years since Ph.D., are plotted on top of each other and cannot be discerned—another instance of overplotting.[4] This problem can be reduced by adding a small random value to each case's score on X, which helps spread out the points, a technique known as *jittering*. Figure 4.2.5(C) presents the same data after the points have been jittered. Note that points at the same value of Y have been spread out, making it much easier to get a sense of the distribution of cases within each group.

Our understanding of the $X–Y$ relationship can be improved by superimposing lines on the scatterplot. Figure 4.2.5(D) returns to the data depicted in Fig. 4.2.5(A) and superimposes the best fitting regression line, $\hat{Y} = 1379X + 45,450$. This plot suggests that a straight line provides a good characterization of the data. Figure 4.2.5(E) superimposes a *lowess* fit line[5] representing the best nonparametric fit of the $X–Y$ relationship. Lowess is a method of producing a smooth line that represents the relationship between X and Y in a scatterplot. The lowess method makes no assumptions about the form of the relationship between X and Y. It follows the trend in the data instead of superimposing a line representing a linear or some other specified mathematical relationship. If this relationship is linear in the population, the lowess line should look like a very rough approximation of a straight line. Perhaps an apt metaphor is that it will look like a young child's freehand drawing of a straight line. To provide a contrast, Fig. 4.2.5(F) illustrates a case in which a straight line does not characterize the data (we will consider nonlinear relationships in Chapter 6). Lowess is very computer intensive and is calculated only using a computer. For interested readers we have presented the details of how lowess is calculated in Box 4.2.2.

As with kernel density estimates, the central problem for the analyst is to choose an appropriate value of the smoothing parameter α. This parameter represents the proportion of the data that is included in the smoothing window. Higher values of α produce more smoothing. Good lowess lines include enough detail to capture the major features of the data, but not to the extent of becoming "lumpy." Simple visual judgments by the analyst are normally sufficient to choose a reasonable value of α that provides a good estimate of the relationship between X and Y. Figure 4.2.5(F), (G), and (H) provide an illustration of the effect of choosing different values of α depicting three different lowess fits to the nonlinear data that will be presented in Chapter 6. Figure 4.2.5(G), with $\alpha = .05$, does not provide enough smoothing, and the $X–Y$ relationship appears "lumpy." Figure 4.2.5(H), with $\alpha = .95$, provides too much smoothing such that the lowess line exceeds the observed values of Y for the lowest values of X. In contrast, Fig. 4.2.5(F)

---

[3]Another useful method for the present example would be to divide each person's salary by 1,000. The values then represent salary in thousands of dollars.

[4]Some programs (e.g., SPSS) print different symbols (e.g., 1, 2, 3) representing the number of cases that are overplotted.

[5]Lowess has become an acronym for *lo*cally *we*ighted *s*catterplot *s*moother. In his original writings describing the technique, Cleveland (1979) used the term *loess*.

(A) Basic scatterplot: salary vs. years since Ph.D.

(B) Basic scatterplot: years since Ph.D. vs. female.

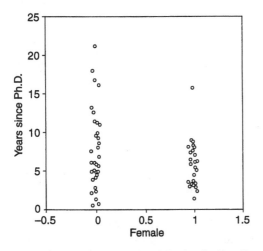

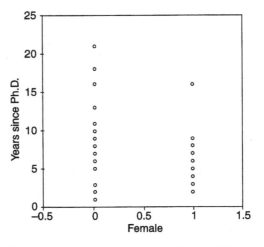

Note: Each point represents one case ($n = 62$). Salary is presented in scientific notation (e.g., $2e + 04 = \$20,000$).

Note: $0 =$ male; $1 =$ female. Some points are overplotted.

(C) Jittered scatterplot: years since Ph.D. vs. female.

(D) Salary vs. years since Ph.D. superimposed regression line.

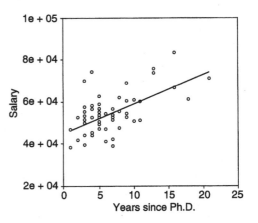

Note: Regression line is $\hat{Y} = 1379X + 45{,}450$.

Note: Each case is now distinct following jittering. In jittering a small random value is added to or subtracted from each case's score on the categorical variable (here, 0 or 1).

FIGURE 4.2.5 Scatterplots and enhanced scatterplots.

with $\alpha = .60$ produces a smooth line that appears to adequately represent the X–Y relationship.

Analysts normally choose values of α that range between about 0.25 and 0.90. Some modern computer programs are beginning to allow the analyst to vary the value of α using a slider, with the original data and the lowess line being continuously redisplayed on the computer screen. Other programs (e.g., SPSS 10) require the analyst to specify a series of different

(E) Superimposed lowess fit: salary vs. years since Ph.D.

(F) Superimposed lowess fit $\alpha = 0.6$: nonlinear relationship.

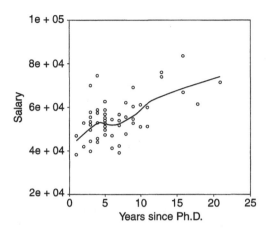

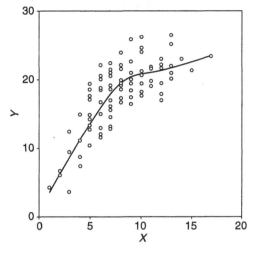

(G) Lowess fit $\alpha = .05$: too little smoothing.

(H) Lowess fit $\alpha = .95$: too much smoothing.

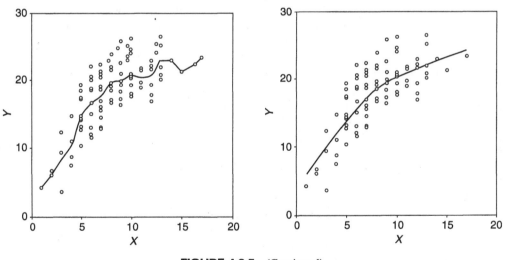

FIGURE 4.2.5   (Continued)

values of α and compare the results. Smaller values of α can be chosen as sample size increases because more cases will be included in each window that is used in the calculation of the lowess line. In addition, a smaller value of α should be chosen if the relationship between X and Y has many peaks and valleys. The lowess line provides a good overall summary of the relationship between X and Y. However, the lowess estimates at the ends of the distribution of X (where the data are often sparse) may be far less precise than in the center.

BOX 4.2.2
Inside the Black Box: How Lowess Lines Are Computed

As an illustration of the computation of lowess, consider again the data for the 62 cases originally presented in Table 3.5.1. We wish to plot a lowess curve for the relationship between years since Ph.D. on the x axis and salary on the y axis. We illustrate the calculation of the predicted lowess value using only one value of X. In practice, the computer calculates the values for hundreds of different possible values of X within the actual range of the data.

Suppose we wished to compute the predicted lowess value of Y corresponding to an arbitrarily chosen value of time since Ph.D. of 16. We must first define a symmetric smoothing window centered around our central score $X_C = 16$. Rather than using a fixed bandwidth, lowess defines its smoothing window so that there is a constant number of cases in the smoothing window, n_{window}. The smoothing parameter α specifies the proportion of cases that are to be used, $n_{window} = \alpha n$. The smoothing window becomes narrower in regions where there are many cases and wider in regions where data are sparse.

We will arbitrarily[6] choose a value of $\alpha = .1$, which leads to $(62)(.1) = 6$ cases being included in the smoothing window. We identify those 6 cases that are closest to $X_C = 16$ regardless of whether they are higher or lower in value. In Table 4.2.1, we see that a symmetrical smoothing window from $X = 13$ to $X = 19$ contains 6 cases. For this smoothing window, $d = 3$. We then calculate the bisquare function weights for these cases using Eq. (4.2.1). The resulting bisquare weights are shown in column 7 of Table 4.2.1 for $d = 3$. Once again, scores at the center of the window ($X_C = 16$) are given a weight of 1, whereas scores further from the center of the window have a lower weight.

Lowess now estimates a regression equation $\hat{Y} = B_1 X + B_0$ for the six cases in the smoothing window. The bisquare function weights are used in determining the fit of the regression line. A method known as weighted least squares regression (to be presented in Section 4.5) is used, which gives cases further from the center of the smoothing window less importance in determining the fit of the regression line. Once the regression equation for the six cases in the smoothing window is determined, the value of $\hat{Y}$ for the lowess line is calculated by substituting the value of the center point, here $X_C = 16$, into the equation. The computer program then calculates the value of $\hat{Y}$ for a large number of different values over the full range of X, here $X = 1$ to $X = 21$. That is, the window is moved along X and a large number (e.g., 100–200) of values of X serve in turn as X_C. For each value of X_C, those six cases that fall closest to X_C are used to define the width of the smoothing window and to compute each separate local regression equation. The value of X_C is then substituted into the local regression equation, giving the lowess value of $\hat{Y}$ corresponding to the value of X_C. The $\hat{Y}$ values are connected to produce the lowess line.

Other, more complicated variants of lowess fitting may be used when the relationship between X and Y is very complicated (e.g., there are sharp peaks and valleys in the X–Y relationship) or when there are extreme outlying observations on Y. Accessible introductions to these more advanced lowess techniques[7] can be found in Cleveland (1993) and Fox (2000a).

---

[6]This value is chosen only to simplify our presentation of the computations. In practice, a much larger value of α (e.g., .6 to .8) would be chosen for these data.

[7]Alternatives to lowess such as cubic splines and kernel smoothers (Fox, 2000a; Silverman, 1986) exist that can also be used to produce lines representing good nonparametric fits of the X–Y relationship.

4.2.3 Correlation and Scatterplot Matrices

Correlation matrices present a convenient method of summarizing the correlations between each pair of predictors as well as the correlation between each predictor and the dependent variable, thus providing considerable information on the direction and magnitude of the *linear* relationships among the variables. Table 4.2.2 presents the correlation matrix for the five variables in our faculty salary example presented in Section 3.5. To illustrate, row 2, column 1, presents the correlation between publications and years since Ph.D. ($r = .65$) and row 4, column 5 presents the correlation between citations and salary ($r = .55$). We see from the correlation matrix that, although years, publications, and citations are all strongly related to salary, some of the independent variables are themselves highly intercorrelated so that they may not provide substantial unique prediction of salary over and above that of the other independent variables.

An improvement on the correlation matrix is the scatterplot matrix, which provides a graphical display of the scatterplot for each pair of variables. The scatterplot matrix corresponding to the faculty salary data is presented in Fig. 4.2.6. Each row and column of the scatterplot matrix forms a cell. Within each cell is a scatterplot depicting the relationship between two of the variables. The variable identified in the row is depicted on Y and the variable identified in the column is depicted on X. For example, row 1, column 1 depicts the regression of salary on the y axis on years since Ph.D. on the x axis. This cell is identical to the scatterplot presented in Fig. 4.2.5(A). Row 1, column 4 depicts the regression of salary on the y axis on number of citations on the x axis. Row 2, column 3 depicts the regression of number of citations on the y axis on female (male = 0; female = 1) on the x axis. The present illustration identifies each of the variables and its range on the minor diagonal of the matrix going from the lower left to upper right corner. Some versions of scatterplot matrices present a histogram of each variable on the diagonal (e.g., SYSTAT, which terms this graphical display a SPLOM, Tukey's term for *scatterplot matrix*).

The scatterplot matrix provides a compact visual summary of the information about the relationship between each pair of variables. First, the analyst can make visual judgments about the nature of the relationship between each pair of variables. Unlike the correlation matrix, which only represents the direction and magnitude of the linear relationship, the scatterplot matrix helps the analyst visualize possible nonlinear relationships between two variables. Strong nonlinear relationships between either two independent variables or an independent and a dependent variable suggest that the linear regression model discussed in previous chapters may not be appropriate. In addition, cases in which the variance of Y is not constant but changes as a function of the value of X can also be observed. Any of these problems would lead the analyst to consider some of the remedies considered later in Section 4.5. Second, the panels of the scatterplot matrix can be linked in some personal computer–based statistical packages.

TABLE 4.2.2
Correlation Matrix for Faculty Salary Example

	Years	Publications	Sex	Citations	Salary
Years	1.00	0.65	0.21	0.37	0.61
Publications	0.65	1.00	0.16	0.33	0.51
Sex	0.21	0.16	1.00	0.15	0.20
Citations	0.37	0.33	0.15	1.00	0.55
Salary	0.61	0.51	0.20	0.55	1.00

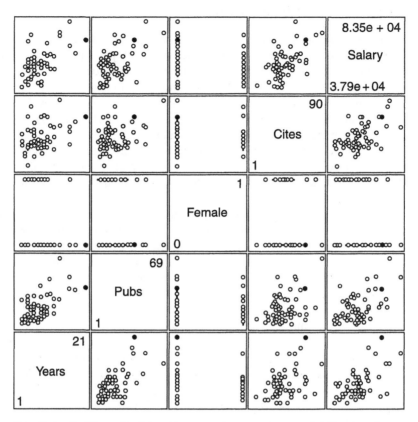

Note: Each cell of the scatterplot matrix represents a separate scatterplot. For example, row 4, column 1 has years since Ph.D. on the *x* axis and number of publications on the *y* axis. The dark point that appears in each cell of the scatterplot matrix is the case with the highest value on time since Ph.D. (years = 21).

FIGURE 4.2.6   Faculty salary example: scatterplot matrix.

Individual cases can then be selected and highlighted in *all* panels of the matrix. This feature is particularly important in the examination of outlying cases. For example, in Fig. 4.2.6, we have highlighted the faculty member (the dark filled circle) who has completed the largest number of years of service—21 years since the Ph.D. From the other panels of the scatterplot, we see that this person is a male who has a relatively high number of publications and a high number of citations. This feature of being able to link single or multiple cases across different panels of a scatterplot matrix can be very useful in understanding data sets involving several variables[8] (Cleveland, 1993).

CH04EX01

---

[8]Computer code is only provided for the base system for each computer package. Not all of the features described in this chapter are presently available in each of the packages. The graphical capabilities of each of the packages is changing rapidly, with new features coming on line every few months. SAS users may wish to investigate the additional capabilities of SAS/INSIGHT. ARC, an outstanding freeware regression and interactive graphics package, is described in Cook and Weisberg (1999) and is downloadable from the School of Statistics, University of Minnesota, Twin Cities: http://stat.umn.edu/arc/

4.3 ASSUMPTIONS AND ORDINARY LEAST SQUARES REGRESSION

All statistical procedures including multiple regression require that assumptions be made for their mathematical development. In this section we introduce the assumptions underlying the linear regression models presented in the previous chapters. Of importance, violation of an assumption may potentially lead to one of two problems. First and more serious, the estimate of the regression coefficients may be biased. *Bias* means that the estimate based on the sample will not on average equal the true value of the regression coefficient in the population. In such cases, the estimates of the regression coefficients, R^2, significance tests, and confidence intervals may all be incorrect. Second, only the estimate of the standard error of the regression coefficients may be biased. In such cases, the estimated value of the regression coefficients is correct, but hypothesis tests and confidence intervals may not be correct.

Violations of assumptions may result from problems in the data set, the use of an incorrect regression model, or both. Many of the assumptions focus on the residuals; consequently, careful examination of the residuals can often help identify problems with regression models. In Section 4.4, we present both graphical displays and statistical tests for detecting whether each of the assumptions is met. We particularly focus on graphical displays because they can detect a wider variety of problems than statistical tests. We then provide an introduction in Section 4.5 to some remedial methods that can produce improved estimates of the regression coefficients and their standard errors when the assumptions underlying multiple regression are violated.

4.3.1 Assumptions Underlying Multiple Linear Regression

We focus on the basic multiple linear regression equation with k predictors originally presented in Chapter 3,

$$(4.3.1) \qquad Y = B_1X_1 + B_2X_2 + B_3X_3 + \cdots + B_kX_k + B_0 + e.$$

The assumptions presented here and their effects on estimates of regression coefficients and their standard errors also apply to most of the more complex regression models discussed in later chapters.

Correct Specification of the Form of the Relationship Between IVs and DVs

An important assumption of multiple regression is that we have properly specified the *form* or mathematical shape of the relationship between Y and each of the IVs in the population. In Chapters 2 and 3 we have consistently assumed that all relationships are linear (straight line). To illustrate the meaning of this assumption in the one IV case, imagine we could identify the set of all cases in the population with a specific value of X_1, for example $X_1 = 5$, and compute the mean of their Y scores. This mean is called the *conditional mean* of Y given X_1, $\mu_{Y|X_1}$. If the assumption of linearity is correct, then each of $\mu_{Y|X_1}$ values that resulted as X_1 took on different values would fall precisely on a straight line, $\hat{Y} = B_1X_1 + B_0$. The slope B_1 of the straight line will be constant across the full range of X_1.

These same ideas apply to regression equations with more than one IV. Figure 4.3.1 provides an illustration of the regression plane when there are two independent variables. We imagine selecting all cases in the population with a specified value of X_1 and a specified value of X_2. We calculate the conditional mean value of Y given the specified values of X_1 and X_2, $\mu_{Y|X_1,X_2}$. The conditional mean in the population must fall exactly on the regression plane

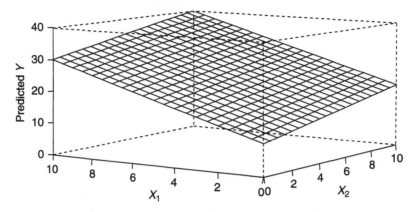

Note: The equation for the linear regression plane is $Y = B_0 + 2X_1 + 1X_2$. B_1 has the same value (here, $B_1 = 2$) regardless of the value of X_2. B_2 has the same value (here $B_2 = 1$) regardless of the value of X_1.

FIGURE 4.3.1   Linear regression plane with two IVs.

$\hat{Y} = B_1X_1 + B_2X_2 + B_0$ for all possible values of X_1 and X_2 if the regression model is properly specified.

To understand the meaning of the regression plane, look at Fig. 4.3.1. The intercept, $B_0 = 10$, is located at the front corner of the plane and represents the predicted value of Y when $X_1 = 0$ and $X_2 = 0$. The line representing $B_{Y1.2}$ is the edge of the plane above the axis labeled X_1. This line goes from $\hat{Y} = 10$ when $X_1 = 0$ to $\hat{Y} = 30$ when $X_2 = 10$. Recall that $B_{Y1.2}$ represents the predicted change in Y for a 1 unit change in X_1 when X_2 is held constant (here, $X_2 = 0$), so $B_{Y1.2} = 2$. The other lines in the plane that are parallel to this edge line represent the regression lines that result when X_2 takes on different values between 0 and 10 $(0, 0.5, 1.0, \ldots, 9.5, 10)$. Each of these lines has the identical slope, $B_{Y1.2} = 2$. Now look at the edge of the regression plane above the axis labeled X_2. The line representing $B_{Y2.1}$ is the edge of the plane where $X_1 = 0$. This line goes from $\hat{Y} = 10$ when $X_2 = 0$ to $\hat{Y} = 20$ when $X_2 = 10$. The slope of this regression line is $B_{Y2.1} = 1$. The other lines in the plane that are parallel to this edge line represent the regression lines that result as X_1 takes on different values between 0 and 10. Each of these lines has the same identical slope, $B_{Y2.1} = 1$. The condition illustrated here of having linear relationships between each of the IVs and the DV is known as *linearity in the variables*.

Not all IVs have linear relationships to the DV. Beginning with Chapter 6, we will consider regression models that specify a variety of nonlinear relationships between the IVs and DV. For example, if we have a curvilinear (quadratic) relationship in which Y is low at low values of X, high at moderate values of X, and low at high values of X, the relationship between Y and X cannot be properly represented with a linear regression equation. The slope of the curve will change as the value of X changes. Chapter 6 will consider how to build terms into the regression so that they properly specify the relationship between Y and each of the IVs.

When the form of the relationship between the IVs and the DV in the population is not properly specified, severe problems may result. The estimates of both the regression coefficients and standard errors may be biased, resulting in incorrect significance tests and incorrect confidence intervals. This conclusion applies to regression models that are linear in the variables that we have discussed in Chapters 2 and 3. It also applies to regression models specifying nonlinear relationships between the IVs and DV that we will consider in later chapters.

Correct Specification of the Independent Variables in the Regression Model

The second assumption is related to the first but focuses on the IVs in the regression model. If we presume that the theory we are testing is correct, then correct specification implies that all variables identified by the theory are included in the model, that they are properly measured (see next section on measurement error), and that the form of the relationship between each IV and DV has been properly specified. If these conditions are met, then each of the IVs and the residuals will be independent in the population and the estimates of regression coefficients will be unbiased. Of course, if any of these assumptions is not correct, then the IVs and the residuals will not be independent and the estimates of the regression coefficients and standard errors may be biased. This result also implies that significance tests and confidence intervals will not be correct. We consider these issues in more detail in our discussion of specification error in Section 4.4.

No Measurement Error in the Independent Variable (Perfect Reliability)

A third closely related assumption is that each independent variable in the regression equation is assumed to be measured without error. Recall from Section 2.10.2 that reliability is defined as the correlation between a variable as measured and another equivalent measure of the same variable. When there is no error of measurement in X, the reliability $r_{XX} = 1.0$. In practice, measures in the behavioral sciences differ in the magnitude of their reliabilities. Measures of some demographic variables such as age and gender typically have very close to perfect reliabilities, measures of adult abilities such as IQ typically have reliabilities in the range of about .80 to .95, and measures of attitudes and personality traits typically have reliabilities in the range of about .70 to .90.

When the assumption of no measurement error in the independent variable (perfect reliability) is violated, we saw in Section 2.10.2 that the estimate of r_{YX} will be biased. When there is only one IV in the regression equation, all of the indices of partial relationship between X and Y including B, standardized β, sr, and pr will be attenuated (too close to 0 regardless of the sign). Otherwise stated, the strength of prediction, R^2, will always be underestimated. When there are two or more IVs that are not perfectly reliable, the value of each measure of partial relationship including B, standardized β, sr, and pr will most commonly be attenuated. However, there is no guarantee of attenuation given measurement error—the value of a specific measure of partial relationship may be too low, too high, or even on rare occasions just right. Thus, measurement error commonly leads to bias in the estimate of the regression coefficients and their standard errors as well as incorrect significance tests and confidence intervals. We include a more detailed presentation of the effects of unreliability in multiple regression in Box 4.3.1.

Constant Variance of Residuals (Homoscedasticity)

For any value of the independent variable X, the *conditional variance* of the residuals around the regression line in the population is assumed to be constant. Conditional variances represent the variability of the residuals around the predicted value for a specified value of X. Imagine we could select the set of cases that have a specified value of X in the population (e.g., $X = 5$). Each of these cases has a residual from the predicted value corresponding to the specified value of X, $e_i = Y_i - \hat{Y}_i$. The variance of the set of residuals is the conditional variance given that X_i equals the specified value. These conditional variances are assumed to be constant across all values of X in the population. Otherwise stated, the variance of the residuals around the regression line is assumed to be constant regardless of the value of X. When the assumption of constant variance of the residuals regardless of the value of X is met,[9] this condition is termed *homoscedasticity*. When the variance changes as the value of X changes, this condition is termed *heteroscedasticity*. When there is heteroscedasticity, the estimates of the regression coefficients remain unbiased, but the standard errors and hence significance tests and confidence intervals will be incorrect. In practice, the significance tests and confidence intervals will be very close to the correct values unless the degree of nonconstant variance is large. A rule of thumb for identifying a large degree of nonconstant variance is that the ratio of the conditional variances at different values of X exceeds 10.

Independence of Residuals

The residuals of the observations must be independent of one another. Otherwise stated, there must be no relationship among the residuals for any subset of cases in the analysis. This assumption will be met in any random sample from a population. However, if data are clustered or temporally linked, then the residuals may not be independent. *Clustering* occurs when data are collected from groups. For example, suppose a set of groups such as university residence halls, high schools, families, communities, hospitals, or organizations are first selected, then a random sample is taken from each group. In such cases, the responses of any two people selected from within the same group (e.g., fraternity A) are likely to be more similar than when the two people are selected from two different groups (e.g., fraternity A; honors dorm B). Similarly, in designs that repeatedly measure the same person or group of persons over time, responses that are collected from the same person at adjacent points in time tend to be more similar than responses that are collected from the same person at more distant points in time. This issue commonly occurs in studies of single individuals (single-subject designs) or in panel studies in which a group of participants is measured on the independent and dependent variables at several time points. For example, if we measure stressful events and mood in a sample of college students each day for two months, the similarity of mood from one day to the next will be greater than the similarity of mood from one day to a day two weeks later. Nonindependence of the residuals does *not* affect the estimates of the regression coefficients, but it does affect the standard errors. This problem leads to significance tests and standard errors which are incorrect.

Normality of Residuals

Finally, for any value of the independent variable X, the residuals around the regression line are assumed to have a normal distribution. Violations of the normality assumption do not lead to bias in estimates of the regression coefficients. The effect of violation of the normality assumption on significance tests and confidence intervals depends on the sample size, with problems occurring in small samples. In large samples, nonnormality of the residuals does not lead to serious problems with the interpretation of either significance tests or confidence intervals. However, nonnormal residuals are often an important signal of other problems in the regression model (e.g., *misspecification*–using an incorrect regression model) and can help guide appropriate remedial actions.

---

[9] In the multiple IV case, the variance of the residuals should not be related to any of the IVs or to $\hat{Y}$.

BOX 4.3.1
The Effects of Measurement Error in Two-Predictor Regression

Measurement error is a common and important problem in regression analysis. To understand more fully the potential effects of measurement error on the results of multiple regression analysis, it is very informative to study what happens when one of the variables is unreliable in the two-IV case. We focus initially on the partial correlation because its relation to the standardized effect size makes it useful in many applications.

Recall from Chapter 3 that we can calculate the partial correlation between Y and X_2 holding X_1 constant from the simple correlations using Eq. (3.3.11):

$$(3.3.11) \qquad pr_2 = r_{Y2 \cdot 1} = \frac{r_{Y2} - r_{Y1}r_{12}}{\sqrt{(1 - r_{Y1}^2)(1 - r_{12}^2)}}.$$

Note in Eq. (3.3.11) that X_1 is the IV that is being partialed. As it will turn out, the reliability of the IV being partialed is of particular importance.

To illustrate the use of Eq. (3.3.11), we can calculate $r_{Y2 \cdot 1}$ if $r_{12} = .3, r_{Y2} = .4$, and $r_{Y1} = .5$,

$$r_{Y2 \cdot 1} = \frac{.4 - (.5)(.3)}{\sqrt{(1 - .5^2)(1 - .3^2)}} = .30$$

We define $r_{Y,X2_t \cdot X1_t}$ as the partial correlation of the true score Y_t with the true score X_{2_t} with the true score[10] X_{1_t} partialed out. If all of the variables have perfect reliability, $r_{Y2 \cdot 1}$ will be identical to $r_{Y,X2_t \cdot X1_t}$.

Now suppose that one of the variables is measured with error. What would the partial correlation have been if the one fallible variable had been measured with perfect reliability? In Chapter 2 we showed that we can express a correlation between the true scores X_t and Y_t in terms of the reliabilities of X and Y and the correlation between measured variables X and Y,

$$(2.10.5) \qquad r_{X_t Y_t} = \frac{r_{XY}}{\sqrt{r_{XX}r_{YY}}}.$$

If measurement error occurs only in X, Eq. (2.10.5) simplifies to

$$(4.3.2a) \qquad r_{X_t Y_t} = \frac{r_{XY}}{\sqrt{r_{XX}}};$$

if measurement error occurs only in Y, Eq. (2.10.5) simplifies to

$$(4.3.2b) \qquad r_{X_t Y_t} = \frac{r_{XY}}{\sqrt{r_{YY}}}.$$

Consider first the effect of only having unreliability in X_2 on $r_{Y2 \cdot 1}$. Based on Eq. (4.3.2a) we know that $r_{Y,X2_t} = r_{Y2}/\sqrt{r_{22}}$ and $r_{X1,X2_t} = r_{12}/\sqrt{r_{22}}$. When we substitute these values into Eq. (3.3.11) and algebraically simplify the resulting expression, we find

$$(4.3.3) \qquad r_{YX2_t \cdot X1} = \frac{r_{Y2} - r_{Y1}r_{12}}{\sqrt{(1 - r_{Y1}^2)(r_{22} - r_{12}^2)}}.$$

(Continued)

---

[10]Recall from Section 2.10.2 that a true score is a hypothetical error-free score. True scores represent the mean score each individual would receive if he or she could be measured an infinite number of times.

Comparing Eq. (3.3.11) to Eq. (4.3.3), we see that the numerator does not change. However, the second term in the denominator changes from $(1 - r_{12}^2)$ to $(r_{22} - r_{12}^2)$. Because r_{22} is less than 1.0, if there is unreliability in X_2, the value of the denominator will always decrease. Thus, $r_{YX2_t \cdot X1}$ (after correction for measurement error) will always be larger in magnitude than $r_{Y2 \cdot 1}$ if there is unreliability in X_2. To illustrate, using the values $r_{12} = .3, r_{Y2} = .4$, and $r_{Y1} = .5$ from our previous numerical example, but now setting $r_{22} = .7$, we find

$$r_{YX2_t \cdot X1} = \frac{.4 - (.5)(.3)}{\sqrt{(1 - .5^2)(.7 - .3^2)}} = .37$$

as compared to $r_{Y2.1} = .30$.

Following the same procedures, we can draw on Eq. (4.3.2b) to study the effect of unreliability only in Y on the partial correlation for the case in which X_1 and X_2 are both perfectly reliable. Paralleling the results observed for X_2, $r_{Y2.1}$ will be attenuated relative to $r_{Y_t X2_t \cdot 1}$. Correcting for measurement error in X_2, Y, or both invariably leads to increases in the absolute value of the partial correlation.

Now we turn to unreliability only in X_1, the IV being partialed in the present example, and find a far more complex set of results. Following the same procedures, the partial correlation corrected for unreliability only in X_1 is

(4.3.4)
$$r_{Y2 \cdot 1_t} = \frac{r_{11} r_{Y2} - r_{Y1} r_{12}}{\sqrt{(r_{11} - r_{Y1}^2)(r_{11} - r_{12}^2)}}.$$

Unlike in our previous equations, both the numerator and the denominator are changed from Eq. (3.3.11). The same general finding of change in both the numerator and denominator also occurs when there is unreliability in X_1, X_2 and Y,

(4.3.5)
$$r_{Y_t 2_t \cdot 1_t} = \frac{r_{11} r_{Y2} - r_{Y1} r_{12}}{\sqrt{(r_{11} r_{YY} - r_{Y1}^2)(r_{11} r_{22} - r_{12}^2)}}.$$

The change in both the numerator and denominator in Eqs. (4.3.4) and (4.3.5) means that the effect of correcting for unreliability only in X_1 will depend on the specific values of r_{11}, r_{Y1}, r_{Y2}, and r_{12} in the research problem.

We illustrate in Table 4.3.1 the range of effects that unreliability in X_1, the variable being partialed, can have on measures of partial relationship presented in Section 3.2. In addition to partial correlations, we also report standardized regression coefficients. Recall that the standardized regression coefficient $\beta_{Y2.1}$ for the relation between Y and X_2 controlling for X_1 is

(3.2.4)
$$\beta_{Y2.1} = \frac{r_{Y2} - r_{Y1} r_{12}}{1 - r_{12}^2}.$$

Again using the strategy of substituting Eq. (4.3.2a) into Eq. (3.2.4) and algebraically simplifying the results, we find that the standardized regression coefficient corrected for measurement error in X_1 is

(4.3.6)
$$\beta_{YX2 \cdot X1_t} = \frac{r_{Y2} r_{11} - r_{Y1} r_{12}}{r_{11} - r_{12}^2}$$

TABLE 4.3.1
Effects of Unreliability of a Partialed Variable (X_1)

Example	r_{Y2}	r_{Y1}	r_{12}	$r_{Y2 \cdot 1}$ (Eq. 3.3.11)	$r_{Y2 \cdot 1_t}$ (Eq. 4.3.4)	$\beta_{Y2 \cdot 1}$ (Eq. 3.2.4)	$\beta_{Y2 \cdot X1_t}$ (Eq. 4.3.6)
1	.3	.5	.6	.00	−.23	.00	−.26
2	.5	.7	.5	.24	.00	.20	.00
3	.5	.7	.6	.14	−.26	.13	−.21
4	.5	.3	.6	.42	.37	.50	.50
5	.5	.3	.8	.45	.58	.72	1.83

Note: In each example, the reliabilities are $r_{11} = 0.70, r_{22} = 1.00, r_{YY} = 1.00$.

Once again, r_{11} appears in both the numerator and denominator of Eq. (4.3.6), meaning that measurement error in X_1 will have complex effects on the standardized regression coefficient. The effect of measurement error on standardized regression coefficients is an important issue in structural equation (path) models, which are considered in Chapter 12 and in O. D. Duncan (1975, chapter 9) and Kenny (1979, chapter 5).

Table 4.3.1 explores the effect of varying r_{11}, r_{Y1}, r_{Y2} on the partial correlation and standardized regression coefficients. In each case, there is only unreliability in X_1, with the value of r_{11} being set at .70, a value that is commonly cited as a minimum value for "acceptable" reliability of a measure. The value of $r_{Y2 \cdot 1}$ is computed using Eq. (3.3.11) and the value of $r_{Y2 \cdot 1_t}$ (corrected for measurement error) is computed using Eq. (4.3.4). The value of $\beta_{Y2 \cdot 1}$ is calculated using Eq. (3.2.4) and the value of $\beta_{Y2 \cdot 1_t}$ is calculated using Eq. (4.3.8).

We focus on the results for the partial correlation in Table 4.3.1 (columns 5 and 6). In Example 1, measurement error in X_1 results in an observed partial r of 0, whereas the true partialed relationship ($r_{Y2 \cdot 1_t}$) is −.23. Thus, a real partial relationship is wiped out by measurement error in X_1, the variable being partialed. In Example 2, the converse occurs: An observed partial correlation, $r_{Y2 \cdot 1} = .24$, is actually 0 when the unreliability of the partialed IV is taken into account. Example 3 has the most dangerous implications. Here, an apparently positive partial correlation, $r_{Y2 \cdot 1} = .14$, turns out to be negative (and of larger magnitude) when corrected for measurement error. This result is not merely a mathematical curiosity of only academic interest. For example, Campbell and Erlebacher (1970) have strongly argued that incorrect conclusions were drawn about the effectiveness of the Head Start program because circumstances like those in Example 3 obtained. Example 4 illustrates for the partial correlation the most frequent outcome: Correction for measurement error in X_1 will lead to a decrease in the magnitude of the partial correlation. Finally, Example 5 illustrates a case in which the value of the partial correlation is increased after correction for measurement error. Note also in Example 5 the value of the standardized regression coefficient after correction for measurement error, $\beta_{YX2 \cdot X1_t} = 1.83$ (see Table 4.3.1, column 8). The magnitude of the standardized regression coefficient substantially exceeds 1.0, indicating a potential problem. Note that in Example 5, $r_{12} = .8, r_{11} = .7$, and $r_{22} = 1.0$ so that from Eq. (4.3.2a) the value of $X1_t X2_t$ (corrected for measurement error) is .96. Such a result may mean that X_1 and X_2 are so highly related that their influence cannot be adequately distinguished (see Section 10.5 on multicollinearity for a discussion of this issue). Alternatively, the estimated value of $r_{11} = .70$ based on the sample data may be lower than the true value

(Continued)

of the reliability in the population. The results of Example 5 emphasize that the results of correction for unreliability must be undertaken cautiously, a point to which we will return in our presentation of remedies for measurement error in Section 4.5.3.

We have shown that measurement error in the dependent variable leads to bias in all standardized measures of partial relationship including sr, pr, and standardized $\beta_{Y2 \cdot 1}$. Of importance, unlike measurement error in the independent variables, it does *not* lead to bias in the values of the *unstandardized* regression coefficients. Measurement error in the dependent variable does not affect the slope of the regression line, but rather only leads to increased variability of the residuals around the regression line (see, e.g., O. D. Duncan, 1975). This increase in the variability of the residuals means that confidence intervals will increase in size and the power to reject a false null hypothesis will be decreased.

4.3.2 Ordinary Least Squares Estimation

In the simplest case of one-predictor linear regression, we fit a straight line to the data. Our goal is to choose the best values of the intercept B_0 and the slope B_1 so that the discrepancy between the straight line and the data will be as small as possible. Carefully drawing a straight line through the data by hand can do a pretty good job of achieving this in the one-predictor case. However, we would like to have a more objective mathematical method of identifying the regression coefficients that would yield the best fitting straight line. The "obvious" method of doing this, examining the sum of the differences between the observed and predicted values of Y, $\Sigma(Y_i - \hat{Y}_i) = \Sigma e_i$, does not work because the sum of the residuals will always be 0 regardless of the values of B_0 and B_1 that are chosen. Several different mathematical methods could be used, but by far the most commonly used method is *ordinary least squares* (*OLS*). OLS seeks to minimize the sum of the squared differences between the observed and predicted squares of Y. That is, in the one-predictor case B_1 and B_0 are chosen so that

$$\sum e_i^2 = \sum (Y_i - \hat{Y}_i)^2 = \sum (Y_i - B_1 X_i - B_0)^2$$

is the smallest possible value. In the multiple predictor case, $B_0, B_1, \ldots, B_k$ are chosen so that $\Sigma(Y_i - \hat{Y}_i)^2$ is the smallest possible value. All equations we have considered so far in this book are based on the OLS method. A formal mathematical derivation of OLS estimation is given in Appendix 1.

In the previous section, the assumptions we presented were those associated with OLS estimation. When these assumptions are met, the OLS estimates of the population regression coefficients have a number of important and desirable properties.

1. They are unbiased estimates of each true regression coefficient in the population. If many samples were selected, the mean of the sample regression coefficients for B_0 and B_1 would equal the values of the corresponding regression coefficients in the population. The expected value of B_j, $E(B_j)$, will equal the corresponding regression coefficient β_j in the population.

2. They are consistent. The standard errors of each regression coefficient will get smaller and smaller as sample size increases.

3. They are efficient. No other method of estimating the regression coefficients will produce a smaller standard error. Small standard errors yield more powerful tests of hypotheses.

Taking these properties together, OLS is described as the *Best Linear Unbiased Estimator* (BLUE). However, when the assumptions of OLS regression are not met, these properties may not always not hold. When there are violations of assumptions, the values of the regression coefficients, their standard errors, or both may be biased. For example, as we will show in our consideration of outliers (unusual observations) in Chapter 10, one very extreme data point for which the squared difference between the observed and predicted scores, $(Y_i - \hat{Y}_i)^2$, is very large may be too influential in the computation of the values of the regression coefficients.

In cases in which the assumptions of OLS regression are violated, we may need to use alternative approaches to the analysis. Three different general approaches may be taken. First, the analyst may build terms into the OLS regression model so that the form of the relationship between each IV and DV more adequately represents the data. Second, the analyst may be able to improve the data by deleting outlying observations or by transforming the data so that the assumptions of OLS regression are not so severely violated. Third, the analyst may consider using an alternative to OLS estimation that is more robust to the specific problem that has been identified. After considering methods for detecting violations of assumptions in Section 4.4, we will see examples of each of these approaches in subsequent sections of this chapter and Chapter 10.

4.4 DETECTING VIOLATIONS OF ASSUMPTIONS

A goal in regression analysis is that the model under consideration will account for all of the meaningful systematic variation in the dependent variable Y. Residuals ("errors") represent the portion of each case's score on Y that cannot be accounted for by the regression model, $e_i = Y_i - \hat{Y}_i$ for case i. If substantial *systematic* variation remains in the residuals, this suggests that the regression model under consideration has been misspecified in some way. Residuals magnify the amount of remaining systematic variation so that careful use of graphical displays of residuals can be very informative in detecting problems with regression models. We will also briefly present some formal statistical tests, but we will emphasize graphical displays because they make minimal assumptions about the nature of the problem.

4.4.1 Form of the Relationship

In current practice, most regression models specify a linear relationship between the IVs and the DV. Unless there is strong theory that hypothesizes a particular form of nonlinear relationship, most researchers begin by specifying linear regression models like those we considered in Chapters 2 and 3. However, there is no guarantee that the form of the relationship will in fact be linear. Consequently, it is important to examine graphical displays to determine if a linear relationship adequately characterizes the data.

As we saw in Section 4.2, we can construct a separate scatterplot for the dependent variable (Y) against each independent variable (X) and superimpose linear and lowess curves to see if the relationship is linear. Even more revealing, we can plot the residuals on the y axis separately against each IV ($X_1, X_2, \ldots, X_k$) and against the predicted variable ($\hat{Y}$). The residuals will magnify any deviation from linearity so that nonlinear relationships will become even more apparent.

Returning to the salary data presented in Table 3.5.1, recall that the regression model using all four independent variables years, number of publications, gender, and number of citations was

$$\hat{Y} = 857 \text{ years} + 93 \text{ publications} - 918 \text{ female} + 202 \text{ citations} + 39{,}587.$$

We plot the residuals against each measured independent variable and against the predicted values, and look for evidence of nonlinearity.

Figure 4.4.1(A) is a scatterplot of the residuals from the regression equation against one of the IVs, years since Ph.D. The horizontal line identifies the point where the residuals are

(A) Residuals vs. years since Ph.D.   (B) Residuals vs. predicted values $(\hat{Y})$

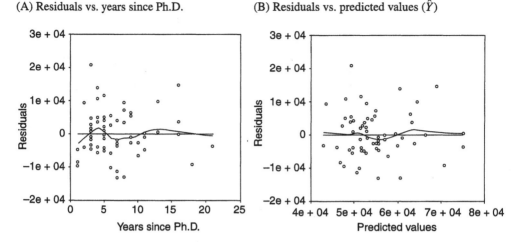

Note: The horizontal line corresponds to a value of 0 for the residuals (0-line). The lowess line is also shown. No systematic relationship between the residuals and either years or $\hat{Y}$ is indicated.

FIGURE 4.4.1   Scatterplots of salary data.

0 (i.e., *0-line*), where the predicted and observed values of Y are identical. If the form of the relationship is properly specified, then the mean of the residuals should be 0 regardless of the value of the IV. The curved line is the lowess fit. Recall that the lowess fit line follows the general trend of the data. If the form of the relationship is properly specified, then the lowess fit line should not exhibit any large or systematic deviations from the 0-line. In the present example, the lowess line generally follows the 0-line, suggesting that the relationship between X_1 (years since Ph.D.) and Y (salary) approximates linearity. Plots of the residuals against number of publications and of the residuals against number of citations (not depicted) also do not show any evidence of deviations from linear relationships. Plots of the residuals against female (gender) will not be informative about linearity because female is a nominal (qualitative) variable. Finally, Fig. 4.4.1(B) shows the scatterplot of the residuals against the predicted values $(\hat{Y})$ with superimposed zero and lowess fit lines. These scatterplots support the specified linear relationship between each of the independent variables and the outcome variable.

In contrast, consider the data originally presented in Fig. 4.2.5(F). These data were generated to have a nonlinear relationship between X and Y. The lowess curve for the original (raw) data indicated that the relationship is nonlinear. Suppose a researcher mistakenly specified a linear regression model to account for these data. The resulting regression equation, $\hat{Y} = 1.14X + 8.72$, appears to nicely account for these data: $R^2 = .56$; test of $B_1, t(98) = 11.2$, $p < .001$. Figure 4.4.2 plots the residuals from this regression equation against X. The lowess fit does not follow the 0-line. It clearly indicates that there is a relatively large and systematic nonlinear component in these data. By comparing Fig. 4.2.5(F) for the original data with Fig. 4.4.2 for the residuals, we see how the plot of residuals magnifies and more clearly depicts the nonlinear component of the X–Y relationship.

The graphical methods presented here are particularly powerful. The true relationship between the IVs and DVs may take many different mathematical forms. Graphical methods can detect a very wide range of types of misspecification of the form of the relationship. In contrast, statistical tests in polynomial regression presented in Section 6.2 are much more focused, contrasting only the fit of two different model specifications chosen by the analyst.

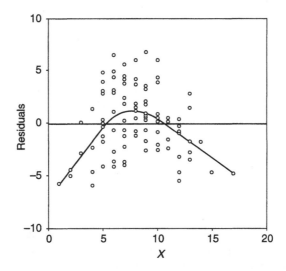

Note: The horizontal line corresponds to a value of 0 for the residuals (0-line). The lowess line is also shown. The clear curvilinear form of the lowess line indicates a nonlinear relationship between the residuals and X.

FIGURE 4.4.2   Scatterplot of residuals vs. X: nonlinear relationship.

4.4.2 Omitted Independent Variables

In specifying the regression model, we include all IVs specified by our hypothesis. Theory and prior empirical research will often provide strong guidelines for the variables that should be included. However, in some cases, the analyst will be unsure whether or not certain variables should be included in the regression equation. The analyst may believe that a theory has omitted important variables or that theory and prior empirical research may be unclear or contradictory about the importance of certain IVs. In such cases, the analyst can explore the effects of including additional variables in the regression equation.

The simplest method of approaching this issue is to construct a series of scatterplots. The analyst first runs a regression analysis in which the originally hypothesized model is specified and saves the residuals. Then, a series of scatterplots are constructed in which the value of the residuals is represented on the y axis and an additional candidate variable (omitted from the regression equation) is represented on the x axis. If the original regression model is correct and a lowess line is fitted to these data, the lowess line should ideally be very close to the 0-line (horizontal line where residuals $= 0$). In contrast, if the lowess curve suggests either a linear or nonlinear relationship, the omitted variable should receive further investigation.

An improvement over this basic scatterplot is the *added variable plot* (AVP, also known as the *partial regression leverage plot*). The AVP allows the analyst to directly visualize the effect of adding a candidate IV to the base regression model. To understand conceptually how the added variable plot is constructed, assume we have specified a base regression equation with three independent variables,

$$(4.4.1) \qquad \hat{Y} = B_1 X_1 + B_2 X_2 + B_3 X_3 + B_0.$$

We wish to investigate whether another candidate variable, X_4, should have also been included in the regression equation as an independent variable.

In constructing the added variable plot, the statistical package first estimates the regression equation predicting the candidate variable, X_4, from the other three IVs,

$$(4.4.2) \qquad \hat{X}_4 = B'_1 X_1 + B'_2 X_2 + B'_3 X_3 + B'_0.$$

In Eq. (4.4.2) B'_0 through B'_3 are used to represent the unstandardized regression coefficients, as they will typically take on different values than those in Eq. (4.4.1). The residual $e'_i = X_4 - \hat{X}_4$ is calculated for each case. This residual represents the unique part of X_4 that remains after X_1, X_2, and X_3 have been accounted for. Using the predicted value from Eq. (4.4.1), the residual, $e_i = Y - \hat{Y}$, is computed. This residual represents the part of Y that is not accounted for by X_1, X_2, and X_3. Then the added variable plot is constructed; this is a scatterplot with the residuals e'_i from Eq. (4.4.2) on the x axis and the residuals e_i from Eq. (4.4.1) on the y axis. A straight line and lowess curve can be superimposed to the added variable plot to help elucidate the relationship of X_4 to Y, partialing out X_1, X_2, and X_3.

To illustrate, suppose in our example of faculty salaries that we had hypothesized a model with salary as the dependent variable and years since Ph.D. (X_1), number of publications (X_2), and female (X_3) as the independent variables. Using the 62 cases presented in Table 3.5.1, this regression equation is

$$\hat{Y} = 1066 \text{ years} + 131 \text{ publications} - 1408 \text{ female} + 45{,}810.$$

The 62 residuals $Y - \hat{Y}$ are calculated using Eq. (4.4.1). Suppose some literature suggests that number of citations (X_4) is also an important IV, so we are concerned that we have incorrectly omitted X_4 from the regression model. A second regression equation with number of citations as the dependent variable and years since Ph.D., number of publications, and female as the independent variables is estimated,

$$\hat{X}_4 = 1.03 \text{ years} + 0.19 \text{ publications} - 2.43 \text{ female} + 30.81.$$

The 62 residuals $X_4 - \hat{X}_4$ are calculated. Plotting $Y - \hat{Y}$ on the y axis and $X_4 - \hat{X}_4$ on the x axis produces the added variable plot shown in Fig. 4.4.3. The positive slope of the straight line suggests there is a positive linear relationship between the candidate variable X_4 and Y, controlling for X_1, X_2, X_3. Indeed, the exact value of the slope of the straight line for the regression of $(Y - \hat{Y})$ on $(X_4 - \hat{X}_4)$ will equal the numerical value of B_4 in the regression equation including the candidate variable, $\hat{Y} = B_1 X_1 + B_2 X_2 + B_3 X_3 + B_4 X_4 + B_0$. In the present case, the lowess fit does not deviate substantially or systematically from the straight line, suggesting that the relationship between X_4 and Y does not have a curvilinear component. Taken together, these results suggest that X_4 should be included in the specification of the linear regression equation as we did in our original analysis presented in Section 3.5.

Interpreting the results of added variable plots is straightforward. If the slope of the best fitting regression line produced by the added variable is 0, the independent variable has no unique relation to Y. If the slope is positive, the added variable will have a positive relationship to Y; if the slope is negative it will have a negative relationship to Y. If the lowess line indicates some form of systematic curvature, then the relationship of X and Y will be nonlinear. Added variable plots can be used to study the effects of adding a candidate independent variable to base regression equations involving one or more independent variables and with more complex base regression models involving interactions (Chapter 7) and nonlinear effects represented by power polynomials (Chapter 6). They can also be used to visualize and identify outlying data points that strongly influence the estimate of the regression coefficient associated with the

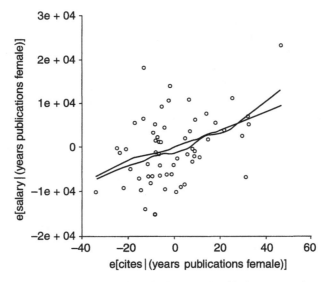

Note: The straight line depicts the linear relationship between number of citations and salary controlling for the independent years (X_1), publications (X_2), and female (X_3). The slope of this line $= B_4$ in the full regression model, $\hat{Y} = B_1X_1 + B_2X_2 + B_3X_3 + B_4X_4 + B_0$. The curved line represent the lowess fit. Values on the y axis are residuals, $Y - \hat{Y}$ and values on the x axis are residuals, $X_4 - \hat{X}_4$. The value 0 occurs on each axis when the observed value of X_4 and Y equal their respective predicted values.

FIGURE 4.4.3   Added variable plot.

added variable.[11] However, the analyst must remember that the added variable plot provides information relative to the base regression model that has been specified. If the base model has not been properly specified (e.g., the relationship between X_1 and Y is in fact nonlinear), the added variable plot can give misleading results.

4.4.3 Measurement Error

Measurement error is easily detected with a measure of reliability. One common type of measure is a scale in which the participants' scores are based on the sum (or mean) of their responses to a set of items. In cross-sectional studies in which the measures are collected on a single occasion, the most commonly used measure of reliability (internal consistency) is *coefficient alpha* (Cronbach, 1951). Imagine that we have a 10-item scale. We can split the scale into two halves and correlate the subjects' scores on the two halves to get a measure of reliability. Coefficient alpha represents the mean of the correlations between all of the different possible splits of the scale into two halves. Another common form of reliability known as *test-retest reliability* is the correlation between subjects' scores on the scale measured at two different times. When two judges rate the subjects' score on the variable, *interrater reliability* is the

[11]If there is a single outlying point, the AVP corresponds to a visualization of $DFBETAS_{ij}$ presented in Chapter 10. However, the AVP also allows analysts to identify clumps of outliers that influence the regression coefficient for the candidate IV.

correlation between scores given by the two judges. With these correlation-based measures of reliability, scores close to 1.0 indicate high levels of reliability.

Measurement is a large and important area of study in its own right (see Crocker & Algina, 1986; Nunnally & Bernstein, 1993) so we cannot provide a full treatment here. Readers should keep in mind three points when they encounter measures of reliability with which they are unfamiliar. First, not all indices of reliability are based on correlations, so different criteria for judging the reliability of the measure will be needed for some indices. Values near 1.0 are not expected for all measures of reliability. Second, the best measure of reliability will depend on the design of the study and the nature of the construct being studied. For example, some constructs, such as adult personality traits, are expected to be very stable over time whereas other constructs, such as moods, are expected to change very quickly. Measures of test-retest reliability are unlikely to be appropriate for mood measures. Finally, some newer approaches to measurement such as item response theory do not yield traditional measures of reliability. However, some of the newer methods can help researchers attain interval level measurement scales that are nearly free of measurement error (Embretson & Reise, 2000).

4.4.4 Homoscedasticity of Residuals

If the variance of the residuals $sd^2_{Y-\hat{Y}}$ is not constant, but is related to any of the IVs or to $\hat{Y}$, the standard methods of developing confidence intervals and conducting significance tests presented in Chapters 2 and 3 may potentially become compromised. A simple graphical method of detecting this problem is to construct a set of scatterplots, plotting the residuals in turn against each of the independent variables $X_1, X_2, \ldots, X_k$ and the predicted value, $\hat{Y}$. Figure 4.4.4(A) plots the residuals against years since Ph.D. for the faculty salary data ($n = 62$) using the full regression equation, $\hat{Y} = 857$ years $+ 93$ publications $- 918$ female $+ 202$ citations $+ 39,587$, originally presented in Section 3.5. Figure 4.4.4(B) plots the residuals against the predicted values, $\hat{Y}$. These plots do not suggest that there is a relationship between the variability of the residuals and either years since Ph.D. or the predicted value.

Some statistical packages allow the analyst to plot lowess fit lines at the mean of the residuals (0-line), 1 standard deviation above the mean, and 1 standard deviation below the mean of the residuals. Figure 4.4.4(C) replots the residuals against years since Ph.D. adding these lowess lines. The middle line corresponds to the lowess line described in Section 4.2.2. The other two lines are created using the lowess procedure to estimate values 1 standard deviation above and 1 standard deviation below the lowess line. In the present case, the two lines remain roughly parallel to the lowess line, consistent with the interpretation that the variance of the residuals does not change as a function of X. Examination of plots of the residuals against number of publications and against number of citations (not depicted) also do not suggest any relationship.

What do these scatterplots look like when there is a relationship between the variance of the residuals and X or $\hat{Y}$? Figure 4.4.5 displays three relatively common patterns using data sets with 400 cases. Figure 4.4.5(A) again shows the relationship when the data are homoscedastic. In Fig. 4.4.5(B), the variance in the residuals increases in magnitude as the value of X increases, often termed a right-opening megaphone. For example, such a pattern can occur in experimental psychology in such tasks as people's judgments of distances or the number of identical objects in a standard container—low values are judged more accurately. In contrast, Fig. 4.4.5(C) shows a pattern in which the residuals are highest for middle values of X and become smaller as X becomes smaller or larger. Such patterns are found for some

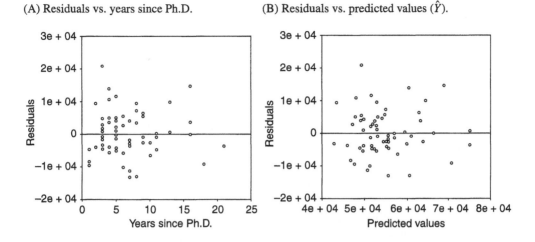

(A) Residuals vs. years since Ph.D.   (B) Residuals vs. predicted values ($\hat{Y}$).

(C) Residuals vs. years since Ph.D. (lowess fit added).

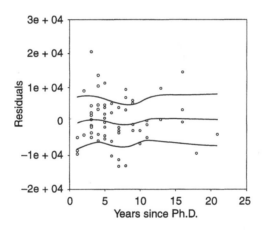

Note: Lowess fit values have been added. The middle line is the lowess fit. The upper line is the lowess fit $+1$ *sd*. The lower line is the lowess fit -1 *sd*. The set of lowess lines do not suggest any evidence of a substantial departure from linearity or heteroscedasticity.

FIGURE 4.4.4   Plots of residuals.

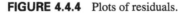

personality tests where people who are extremely high or low on the personality trait are more accurately measured. In each panel lowess fit lines have been added at the mean, 1 standard deviation above the mean, and 1 standard deviation below the mean of the residuals so that these patterns can be more easily discerned.

Formal statistical tests of nonconstant variance have also been developed. Most of these tests focus on detecting a specific pattern of heteroscedasticity. Interested readers can find an introduction to some of these tests in Box 4.4.1.

(A) Homoscedasticity: constant variance across values of X.

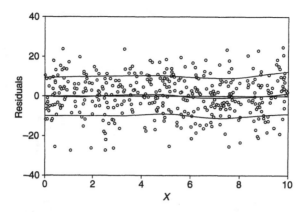

(B) Heteroscedasticity: variance increases with X (right-opening megaphone).

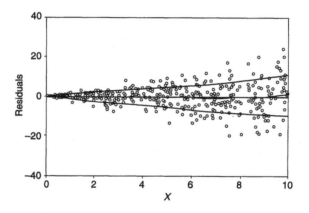

(C) Heteroscedasticity: curvilinear relationship between X and variance of residuals.

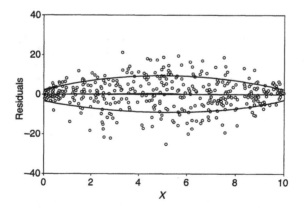

Note: $n = 400$ cases. The 0-line, the lowess line for the mean, the lowess lines for the mean $+ 1$ sd, and the lowess line for the mean $- 1$ sd are superimposed.

FIGURE 4.4.5 Plots of residuals versus X. Illustrations of homoscedasticity and heteroscedasticity.

BOX 4.4.1
Statistical Tests of Nonconstant Variance

The *modified Levene test* provides a formal statistical test of the pattern depicted in Fig. 4.4.5(B) in which the variance of the residuals appears to increase (or decrease) as a function of the IV. The residuals are initially divided into two groups, one containing the cases that are high and one containing the cases that are low relative to a threshold value on the independent variable that is chosen by the analyst. For example, in our salary example ($n = 62$), an analyst might choose to examine whether the residuals are related to years since Ph.D. Using the 62 cases presented in Table 3.5.1, she would pick a threshold value—for example a score of 6 years, which is near the median of the distribution—and classify the $n_L = 30$ scores < 6 as low and $n_H = 32$ scores ≥ 6 as high. She would then calculate the median value for the residuals in each group: In the low group, the 30 residuals have a median value of -408.49; in the high group, the 32 residuals have a median value of -1634. She would then calculate the absolute deviation (ignoring sign) of the residuals in each group from the corresponding group median.

$$d_{\text{low}} = |e_{i_{\text{low}}} - mdn_{e_{\text{low}}}| \qquad d_{\text{high}} = |e_{i_{\text{high}}} - mdn_{e_{\text{high}}}|$$

The variance of the absolute deviations is

$$s^2 = \frac{\sum_1^{n_{\text{low}}} (d_{i_{\text{low}}} - M_{d_{\text{low}}})^2 + \sum_1^{n_{\text{high}}} (d_{i_{\text{high}}} - M_{d_{\text{high}}})^2}{n_{\text{low}} + n_{\text{high}} - 2}$$

where $M_{d_{\text{low}}}$ is the mean of the absolute residuals corresponding to the low values on and $M_{d_{\text{high}}}$ is the mean of the absolute residuals corresponding to the high values on X. Finally, she would calculate Levene's t^*

$$\text{Levene's } t^* = \frac{M_{d_{\text{low}}} - M_{d_{\text{high}}}}{\sqrt{s^2\left(\frac{1}{n_{\text{low}}} + \frac{1}{n_{\text{high}}}\right)}}.$$

The result of the Levene's t^* test is compared to the critical values of the t distribution from Appendix Table A with $df = n_{\text{low}} + n_{\text{high}} - 2$. Failure to reject the null hypothesis is nearly always the desired outcome—it is consistent with the use of standard OLS regression models, which consider the residuals to be homoscedastic.

Several other tests have also been proposed to test for various forms of homoscedasticity. R. D. Cook and Weisberg (1983) and Breusch and Pagan (1979) independently developed an alternative test that detects increases or decreases in the variance of the residuals. This test performs very well in large samples when the residuals have a normal distribution. This test can also be modified to test for other specified relationships (e.g., quadratic) between X or $\hat{Y}$ and the variance of the residuals (see Weisberg, 1985). White (1980) has developed a general test that can potentially detect all forms of hetereoscedasticity. This test requires large sample size, has relatively low statistical power, and can yield misleading results if there are other problems in the regression model (e.g., the regression model is misspecified). A discussion of advantages and disadvantages of several of the tests of heterogeneity of variance of residuals can be found in Greene (1997).

4.4.5 Nonindependence of Residuals

Multiple regression assumes that the residuals are independent. Index plots (also termed case-wise plots) provide a simple method for exploring whether the residuals are related to some systematic feature of the manner in which the data were collected. In the present context, index plots are simply scatterplots in which the value of the residual is presented on the y axis and an ordered numerical value is presented on the x axis. Statistics and graphical displays that are more sensitive to specific forms of nonindependence can also be used.

One form of dependency in the residuals occurs when there is a systematic change over time in the nature of the participants or in the research procedures. To illustrate, patients with more severe diagnoses may be recruited in the later phase of a clinical study, or less conscientious students in introductory psychology classes may delay their participation in experiments until late in the semester, or the delivery of an experimental treatment may improve over time, yielding greater improvement on the dependent variable. In such cases, plots of the residuals against the order of participation (i.e., first $= 1$, second $= 2, \ldots$) can potentially show systematic relationships. Adding a lowess line to the plot can be useful in revealing the form of the relationship. Joiner (1981) presents several illustrative examples in which the use of plots of residuals against variables related to order of participation have helped uncover what he terms "lurking variables" in the data.

A second form of dependence of residuals, known as clustering, occurs when the data are collected in groups or other clusters. In this case the residuals may be more similar within clusters than between clusters. Figure 4.4.6(A) illustrates 100 residuals from a random sample in which the residuals are independent. Figure 4.4.6(B) and Fig. 4.4.6(C) present two different ways of depicting residuals from a data set in which observations are collected from each of 10 clusters—observations 1–10 are from cluster 1, 11–20 are from cluster 2, and so on. Figure 4.4.6(B) presents an index plot of the residuals using different plotting symbols to represent each cluster. Note that the residuals within clusters tend to bunch together more than the residuals in Fig. 4.4.6(A). For example, in Fig. 4.4.6(B) residuals in cluster 3 (case numbers 21–30, represented by the symbol ×) tend to bunch together below the 0-line, whereas residuals in cluster 7 (case numbers 61–70, represented by the symbol ○) tend to bunch together above the 0-line. Figure 4.4.6(C) presents a series of 10 side-by-side boxplots of the same data with each boxplot in turn representing a different cluster. The median value, depicted by the horizontal line in each box, suggests that there is substantial variability in the typical (median) value of each cluster.

A more precise statistical estimate of the amount of clustering will be presented in Section 14.1.2 when we consider the intraclass correlation coefficient. Briefly the intraclass correlation can theoretically range[12] from 0 to 1. To the extent the intraclass correlation exceeds 0, the standard errors of the regression coefficients will be too small. This problem is further exacerbated as the number of cases in each cluster increases (Barcikowski, 1981). Significance tests of regression coefficients will be too liberal, meaning that the null hypothesis will be rejected when it is true at rates far exceeding the stated value (e.g., $\alpha = .05$). The width of confidence intervals will typically be smaller than the true value.

Finally, if the data are repeatedly collected from a single individual or the same sample of individuals over time, then the residuals will often show *serial dependency*. Figure 4.4.6(D) presents an illustration of residuals that exhibit serial dependency. Note that temporally adjacent observations tend to have more similar values than in Fig. 4.4.6(A). For example, the last 15 residuals of the series all have positive values. A more precise statistical measure of serial

---

[12] In practice, the intraclass correlation coefficient can take on small negative values due to sampling error. In such cases, it is assigned a value of 0.

(A) Independent residuals from a random sample.

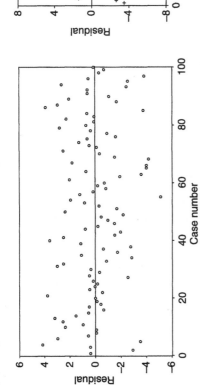

(B) Residuals from clustered data (10 cases per cluster).

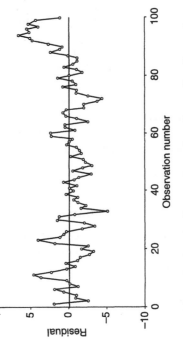

Note: Each cluster of 10 cases (1–10; 11–20; . . . ; 91–100) is represented by a different symbol.

(C) Side by side boxplots of the 10 clusters.

Note: Each boxplot represents a different cluster of 10 cases. The horizontal line in each box represents the median of the cluster. The medians of the 10 clusters show more variation than would be expected by chance.

(D) Autocorrelated residuals ($\rho_1 = .7$).

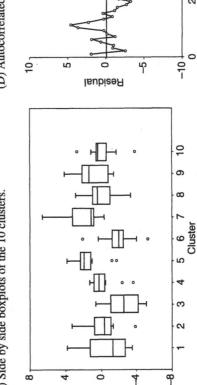

Note: Observations are equally spaced over time. Temporally adjacent observations are connected by straight lines.

FIGURE 4.4.6 Index plots of residuals.

dependency is provided by a measure known as *autocorrelation*. Autocorrelation assesses the correlation of the temporal series with itself after the series has been shifted forward a specified number of time periods. The number of time periods the series is shifted forward is termed the lag. In most applications of multiple regression using temporal data, only the lag 1 autocorrelation is investigated. Like Pearson rs, autocorrelations may theoretically range in value from -1 to $+1$. An autocorrelation of 0 indicates that there is no relationship between the original and shifted series. A positive lag 1 autocorrelation indicates that the residual at time $t - 1$ is positively related to the residual at time t. For example, yesterday's mood level will tend to be positively related to today's mood. A negative lag 1 autocorrelation indicates that the residual at time $t - 1$ is negatively related to the residual at time t. Negative lag 1 autocorrelations can arise when there is a homeostatic process. For example, regular cigarette smokers are likely to smoke at lower than normal rates the hour after they have consumed a larger than normal number of cigarettes. Both positive and negative autocorrelations can lead to incorrect standard errors and consequently incorrect hypothesis tests and confidence intervals. Interested readers will find an illustration of the calculation and test of significance of lag 1 autocorrelation in Box 4.4.2.

BOX 4.4.2
Calculating Autocorrelation and the Durbin-Watson Test

We illustrate here the calculation of the lag 1 autocorrelation. Imagine we have recorded the number of cigarettes smoked for eight consecutive 2-hour periods. After we fit a regression equation, we have the eight residuals listed here and wish to calculate the lag 1 autocorrelation. In this example, the residuals are presented in order by time period in row 2, but are shifted 1 period forward in time in row 3.

Time period (t)	1	2	3	4	5	6	7	8	
Residual	4	-3	-2	3	-1	3	2	-1	
Residual (shifted)		4	-3	-2	3	-1	3	2	-1

The lag 1 autocorrelation can then be calculated between the residual series and the shifted residual series using Eq. (4.4.3),

(4.4.3)
$$r_1 = \frac{\sum_{t=2}^{T}(e_t)(e_{t-1})/(T - 1)}{\sum_{t=1}^{T}(e_t)^2/(T)},$$

where e_t is the value of the residual at time t, and e_{t-1} is the value of the residual at time $t - 1$, T is the number of equally spaced observations in the original temporal series (here, $T = 8$), and r_1 is the value of the autocorrelation at lag 1. To form the product in the numerator of Eq. (4.4.3), we start with second residual in the original series and multiply it by the shifted residual immediately below, continuing to do this until we get to the final original residual, here $t = 8$. Note that there are now $T - 1$ pairs, here 7, in the residual and shifted residual series. In this example,

$$r_1 = \frac{[(-3)(4) + (-2)(-3) + (3)(-2) + \cdots + (-1)(2)]/7}{[(4)^2 + (-3)^2 + (-2)^2 + \cdots + (-1)^2]/8} = -0.30$$

Standard statistical packages will calculate the lag 1 autocorrelation. In long time series with say 100 observations, autocorrelations can also be calculated at lags 2, 3, 4, etc. using the time series routines within the statistical packages; however, in most applications serial dependency is investigated by only examining the autocorrelation at lag 1.

The Durbin-Watson test is used to test the null hypothesis that the lag 1 autocorrelation is 0 in the population. As a focused test, the Durbin-Watson D test does not address autocorrelation of lag 2 or higher. The expression for the Durbin-Watson D is shown in Eq. (4.4.4),

$$(4.4.4) \qquad D = \frac{\sum_{t=2}^{T}(e_t - e_{t-1})^2}{\sum_{t=1}^{T} e_t^2}.$$

Given that $D \approx 2(1 - r_1)$, values close to $D = 2$ will lead to retention of the null hypothesis of no lag 1 autocorrelation in the population. The exact critical value of the Durbin-Watson statistic is difficult to calculate. Consequently, the value of D is compared with both upper bound (D_U) and lower bound (D_L) critical values. The null hypothesis that the lag 1 autocorrelation in the population $\rho_1 = 0$ is rejected if $D < D_L$ for positive autocorrelations or $D > 4 - D_L$ for negative autocorrelations. The null hypothesis that $\rho_1 = 0$ in the population is retained if $D > D_U$ for positive autocorrelations or $D < 4 - D_U$ for negative autocorrelations. When D falls between D_L and D_U or between $4 - D_L$ and $4 - D_U$, most analysts consider the results of the Durbin-Watson test to be inconclusive since the exact critical value of the Durbin-Watson statistic is unknown. The regression modules of SAS, SPSS, and SYSTAT all calculate the Durbin-Watson statistic.

4.4.6 Normality of Residuals

Two different graphical methods can provide an indication of whether the residuals follow a normal distribution. In the first, more straightforward, but less accurate method, the analyst plots a histogram of the residuals and then overlays a normal curve with the same mean and standard deviation as the data. If the distribution is normal, then the histogram and the normal curve should be similar. Figure 4.4.7(A) depicts a histogram of the residuals and a normal curve for the 62 residuals from the salary example with four independent variables: $\hat{Y} = 857$ years $+ 93$ publications $- 918$ female $+ 202$ citations $+ 39,587$. The histogram of the residuals does not appear to be obviously discrepant from the normal curve overlay, although these judgments are often very difficult in small samples. Most standard statistical packages will now generate normal curve distribution overlays for histograms.

The second method known as a *normal q-q plot* takes advantage of the great accuracy of humans in the perception of straight lines. Many standard statistical packages[13] including SAS and SYSTAT construct the normal q-q plot, and the analyst has only to judge whether the plot approximates a straight line. This judgment task is far easier than with the normal curve overlay.

Figure 4.4.7(B) displays a normal q-q plot for the 62 residuals from the salary data set. As can be seen, the residuals do appear to be close to the straight line which is superimposed. Figure 4.4.7(C) presents the same plot but overlays an approximate 95% confidence interval[14] around the values expected from the normal curve. Nearly all of the residuals from the actual sample fall inside the approximate confidence interval, supporting the interpretation that the residuals have close to a normal distribution. As illustrated in Fig. 4.4.7(C), the 95% confidence

---

[13]Both SAS and SYSTAT can produce normal q-q plots.

[14]A computer intensive method (Atkinson, 1985) is used to construct this confidence interval. The computer program draws a large number (e.g., 1000) of samples from a normally distributed population. All samples are the same size as the sample being studied, here $n = 62$. These simulated data are then used to construct the empirical distributions for upper 2.5% and the lower 2.5% of the residuals.

(A) Histogram of residuals with normal curve overlay.

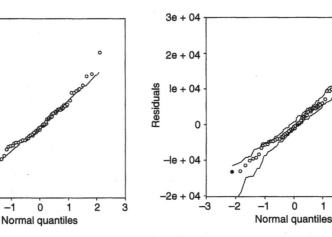

Note: The mean ($M = 0$) and standard deviation of the normal curve are set equal to the mean and standard deviation of the residuals ($n = 62$).

(B) Normal q-q plot of residuals with superimposed straight line.

(C) Normal q-q plot of residuals with an approximate 95% confidence interval.

Note: The points do not exhibit substantial discrepancy from the superimposed straight line. Thus, the residuals appear to be approximately normally distributed. The darkened point is the most negative residual (discussed in the text).

Note: The lines represent an approximate 95% confidence interval for a normal distribution. The points represent the actual values of the residuals. The residuals appear to follow a normal distribution.

FIGURE 4.4.7   Plots to assess normality of the residuals.

interval for the residuals is narrower (more precise) near the center than near the ends of the distribution of residuals.

Although the normal q-q plot provides an excellent method of determining whether the data follow a normal distribution, interpreting the meaning of a substantial deviation from normality in a q-q plot can be difficult at first. Many analysts supplement normal q-q plots with histograms or kernel density plots of the residuals to provide a more familiar display of

(A) Normal.

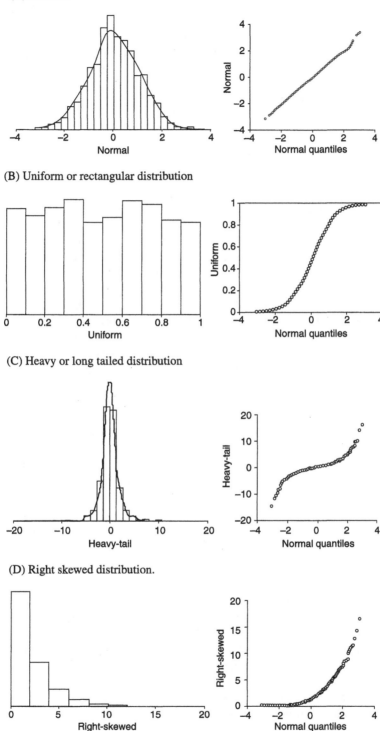

(B) Uniform or rectangular distribution

(C) Heavy or long tailed distribution

(D) Right skewed distribution.

Note: The histogram are on the left and corresponding q-q plots are on the right in each panel. Kernel density estimates are superimposed on the histograms in (A) and (C). Data sets represent random samples of $n = 1000$ from the following population distributions: (A) normal, (B) uniform, (C) *t*-distribution, $df = 2$, and (D) chi-square distribution, $df = 2$.

FIGURE 4.4.8 Histograms and q-q plots illustrating some common distributions. 139

BOX 4.4.3

Inside the Black Box: How Normal q-q Plots Are Constructed

The construction of the normal q-q plot starts by putting the cases in rank order $(1, 2, 3, \ldots, n)$ according to the values of their residuals. The smallest (most negative) residual receives rank 1 and the case with the largest (most positive) residual receives rank n. For a case with rank i, we first calculate $f(i)$, the approximate fraction of the data that falls at or below this rank:

$$f(i) = \frac{(i - .5)}{n}.$$

For our salary example with $n = 62$, $f(i = 1)$ for the lowest case would correspond to $(1 - 0.5)/62 = .0089$ and $f(2)$ for the second lowest case would correspond to $(2 - 0.5)/62 = .0242$. These values represent the proportion of the area under the normal curve that falls at or below rank i. Looking in the normal curve table (Appendix Table C gives an abbreviated normal curve table), we find the z score that most closely corresponds to $f(i)$ for each of the cases in the data set. For $f(1) = .0089$, we look in the column labeled P and find the closest value, .009, which corresponds to a z score of -2.35. For $f(2) = .0242$, $z = -2.00$. z scores corresponding to the normal distribution are calculated in this manner for each of the cases in the data set from 1 to n. These z scores are termed normal quantiles. The original values of the residuals are then plotted on the y axis and the quantiles (z scores) corresponding to the normal curve are plotted on the x axis. For example, in Fig. 4.4.7(B), the darkened point at the lower left represents case 28, the most negative residual. The value of this residual $= -13,376.8$ is represented on the y axis; the quantile $= -2.35$ corresponding to its rank $i = 1$ of 62 cases is plotted on the x axis. The data are scaled so that the physical length of the y axis is equal to the physical length of the x axis (e.g., 3 inches by 3 inches). The result of this scaling is that the q-q plot of the residuals against the quantiles will result in a straight line at a 45° angle if the residuals precisely follow a normal distribution. The task of the analyst then is simply to judge the extent to which the actual q-q plot matches a straight line.

---

the distribution of residuals. Some analysts also compare the obtained q-q plot to examples depicting common alternative distributions. For example, Fig. 4.4.8(A) to (D) presents side by side plots of several common distributions. In each panel a histogram of the distribution is plotted on the left (in some cases with a kernel density plot overlayed) and a q-q plot of the same distribution against the normal distribution is presented on the right. Figure 4.4.8(A) portrays a normal distribution, (B) a uniform or rectangular distribution, (C) a heavy or long-tailed distribution, and (D) a right skewed distribution. Only in the case of the normal distribution does the q-q plot follow a straight line. Box 4.4.3 presents the details of the calculation of q-q plots for interested readers.

CH04EX02

Several formal statistical tests of normality have also been proposed. For example, using a method similar to the idea underlying the normal q-q plot, Looney and Gulledge (1985; see also Shapiro & Wilk, 1965) compute the correlation between the value of each residual in order from lowest to highest and the value of the residual that would expected based on a normal distribution. The obtained correlation is then tested against a population value of 1. Another approach (D'Agostino, 1986) performs a joint test of whether skewness and excess kurtosis[15] of the residuals both equal 0 in the population. Recall, however, that the primary value of examining the normality of the residuals in multiple regression is to help identify problems in the specification of the regression model. Consequently, we have stressed the graphical examination of the distribution of the residuals. Such graphical examination helps reveal the magnitude and nature of any non-normality in the residuals, information that is nearly always far more useful than the significance or nonsignificance of a formal statistical test.

4.5 REMEDIES: ALTERNATIVE APPROACHES WHEN PROBLEMS ARE DETECTED

The diagnostic procedures discussed in Section 4.4 are useful in identifying a variety of potential problems that result from violations of the assumptions of regression analysis. As is the case with routine medical tests, these diagnostic procedures will often indicate that no important problems have occurred. When no problems are detected, standard OLS regression with linear relations specified between the independent and dependent variables will provide the best approach to the analysis. However, researchers cannot know that this will be the case without examining their own data. Problems stemming from violations of the assumptions of linear regression do occur with some regularity in analyses in all areas of the behavioral sciences. These problems raise questions about the conclusions that are reached based on standard linear regression analyses. When problems are diagnosed, then potential remedial actions should be explored. In this section, we identify several common problems that may occur in regression analysis and outline potential remedies. Several of these remedies will be developed in greater detail in later chapters in this book.

4.5.1 Form of the Relationship

When the form of the relationship between X and Y is not properly specified, the estimate of the regression coefficient and its standard error will both be biased. Chapters 2 and 3 have focused on linear relationships between independent and dependent variables. However, a variety of forms of nonlinear relationships may exist between X and Y. In some cases these relationships may be specified by theory or prior research. In other cases, a linear relationship may be initially specified, but the fit of the lowess curve will strongly indicate that the relationship between X and Y is nonlinear. When nonlinear relationships are specified or detected, an alternative approach that accounts for the nonlinear relationship will need to be taken. Chapter 6 considers these approaches in detail.

Four questions should be posed as a basis for choosing among methods for restructuring the regression equation to properly capture the form of the relationship.

1. Is there a theory that predicts a specific form of nonlinear relationship? To cite two examples, the Yerkes-Dodson law predicts there will be an inverted-U (quadratic) relationship between motivation (X) and performance (Y) in which moderate levels of motivation lead to the highest levels of performance. Many learning theories predict that performance on a new task will follow an exponential form in which it initially increases rapidly and then increases more slowly up to a maximum level of performance (asymptote).

2. What is the observed relationship between each pair of IVs? OLS regression only controls for linear relationships among the IVs. If a scatterplot shows a strong nonlinear relationship between two IVs, then these IVs should be re-expressed to make their relationship more linear.

---

[15]Excess kurtosis = kurtosis − 3. This index rescales the value so that it will be 0 when the distribution is normal.

3. What is the shape of the lowess curve of the original data? The lowess curve portrays the best estimate of the X–Y relationship in the sample. What is the shape of the curve? Does it need to bend in one direction or have multiple bends? Does the curve appear to have an asymptote in which it approaches a maximum or minimum level? Identifying the general shape of the lowess curve is very helpful in trying to identify a mathematical function that can represent the data.

4. Does the variance of the residuals remain constant or does it increase or decrease systematically? This question can be addressed through plots of the residuals against each IV and $\hat{Y}$, particularly when enhanced with lines 1 sd above and below the lowess line (see Fig. 4.4.5).

The diagnostic tools we have considered in this chapter help provide answers to questions 2, 3, and 4. The answers help guide the analyst toward the approach to representing nonlinearity that is most likely to prove fruitful. We provide brief guidelines here, and Chapter 6 discusses approaches to nonlinearity in detail.

Theoretically Predicted Relationship

The analyst should specify a regression equation that conforms to theoretically specified mathematical relationship. The test of the Yerkes-Dobson law involves specifying a quadratic relationship between X and Y; The test of the learning theory prediction involves specifying an exponential relationship between X and Y.

Nonlinear Relationship Between Independent Variables and Nonlinear Relationship of Independent Variables to the Dependent Variable

The analyst should consider transforming the IVs involved in the nonlinear relationships. In transformation, the original variable is replaced by a mathematical function of the original variable. As one example, X_1 and X_2 might be replaced by their logs so that the new regression equation would be $\hat{Y} = B_1 \log X_1 + B_2 \log X_2 + B_0$. Ideally, the proper choice of transformation will yield a linear relationship between the pair of IVs and between each of the IVs and the DV. Residuals that are homoscedastic in lowess plots remain homoscedastic following transformation of the IVs. Section 6.4 presents rules for choosing transformations.

Nonlinear Relationship Between Independent Variables and the Dependent Variable and Homoscedasticity

The most common approach to this situation is to include power polynomial terms in the regression equation. Power polynomials are power functions of the original IV such as X_1^2 and X_1^3. For example, the regression equation $\hat{Y} = B_1 X_1 + B_2 X_1^2 + B_0$ can represent any form of quadratic relationship including U-shaped, inverted U-shaped, and relationships in which the strength of the relationship between X and Y increases or decreases as X gets larger. Residuals that are homoscedastic in lowess plots will also remain homoscedastic if the proper polynomial regression model is specified. In some cases simple polynomial functions may not be adequate, so more complicated nonparametric functions may be needed to represent the relationship between the IVs and DVs. Sections 6.2 and 6.3 give a full presentation of multiple regression including power polynomials; Section 6.6 gives an introduction to nonparametric regression.

Nonlinear Relationship Between Independent Variables and the Dependent Variable and Heteroscedasticity

Proper choice of a transformations of Y can potentially simultaneously address problems of nonlinearity, heteroscedasticity, and non-normal residuals in the original linear regression model.[16] Here, the dependent variable is replaced by a nonlinear mathematical function of Y such as $\log Y$ or $\sqrt{Y}$ and the Xs are not changed. As one example, we could replace Y with $\log Y$ so that the new regression equation would be $\log Y = B_1 X_1 + B_2 X_2 + B_0 + e$. In this transformed regression equation, the residuals are now equal to the observed value of $\log Y$ minus the predicted value of $\log Y$. This means that the relationship between the variance of the residuals and the IVs will be different than was observed with the original data. Ideally, heteroscedasticity can be minimized with the proper choice of transformation of Y. Section 6.4 provides a thorough discussion of methods of transformation of Y.

4.5.2 Inclusion of All Relevant Independent Variables

When a theory or prior research states that a set of Xs (e.g., X_1, X_2, X_3, X_4) should be included in the regression model, omission of any of the independent variables (e.g., X_4) leads to *potential* bias in the estimates of the remaining regression coefficients and their standard errors. Similarly, when there is theoretical reason to believe that a candidate independent variable should be added to the model and the added variable plot supports its inclusion, then it is nearly always a good idea to estimate a new regression model with this variable included. These are the clear-cut cases.

In contrast, other cases may be less clear-cut. We can gain insight into these more difficult situations by considering the various possible relationships between the candidate IV, the other IVs, in the equation, and the DV.

Consider a situation in which X_1 and X_2 are important independent variables, but the candidate IV X_3 has no relevance to the actual process generating the dependent variable in the population. If the irrelevant variable X_3 is not related to either the other independent variables or the dependent variable, then the regression coefficients for the other variables, B_1 and B_2, will be unbiased estimates of the true values in the population. The primary cost of including X_3 in the regression model is a small increase in the standard errors of the B_1 and B_2 coefficients. This increase in the standard errors implies that confidence intervals will be slightly too large and the statistical power of the tests of B_1 and B_2 will be slightly reduced.

Now consider a situation in which X_3 is related to the DV but is unrelated to the IVs. This situation commonly occurs in randomized experiments in which the two IVs are experimental treatments and X_3 is an individual difference characteristic (e.g., IQ, an attitude, or a personality trait). Once again, the regression coefficients for X_1 and X_2 will be unbiased estimates of the true values in the population. There are two potential costs of failing to include X_3 in the regression equation. First, to the extent that the researchers are interested in individual differences, they have omitted an important predictor of behavior, particularly if there is a good theoretical rationale for inclusion of the candidate variable. Second, the standard errors of B_1 and B_2 will be larger if X_3 is not included in the regression model so that the confidence intervals for B_1 and B_2 will be larger and the corresponding significance tests will be lower in power. We will further consider this second issue in Section 8.7 in our discussion of analysis of covariance.

---

[16]Researchers who predict specific forms of nonlinear relationships between X and Y or interactions between IVs should be very cautious in the use of transformations of either X or Y. Transformations change the form of the relationship between the new variables potentially eliminating the predicted X–Y relationship when it exists in the original data.

Finally, the most difficult situation occurs when X_3 is related to X_1 and X_2 as well as Y. Here, the correct answer depends on knowing the actual process that determines Y in the population. If the analyst omits X_3 from the regression equation when it should be included, the estimates of B_1 and B_2 will be biased. If the analyst includes X_3 when it should be omitted, the estimates of B_1 and B_2 will be biased. In practice, the analyst can never know for sure which regression model is correct. Careful thought about candidate variables often provides the best solution to the omitted variable problem. Analysts should never simply "throw independent variables into a regression equation." Careful consideration of whether the addition of the candidate variable makes conceptual sense in the substantive area of research is required.[17] In Chapter 5 we will consider two statistical approaches to this dilemma. Hierarchical regression adds a set of candidate variables to the regression equation to determine how much the set of candidate variables adds to the prediction of Y over and above the contribution of the previously included independent variables (Sections 5.3–5.5). Sensitivity analysis involves estimating regression models that include and do not include the candidate variables and comparing the results. If the effect of an independent variable (e.g., X_1) that is included in all of the analyses does not change appreciably, then the analyst can claim that the effect of this variable appears to be robust regardless of which model is estimated. Other more advanced statistical methods of probing the effects of omitted variables can be found in Maddala (1988) and Mauro (1990).

Beginning analysts are advised to be very clear about which variables are included in their originally hypothesized regression model. The originally hypothesized model has a special status in statistical inference because it has been developed independently of the current data. When model modifications are made based on the current data set, then all findings become exploratory. Analysts cannot know for certain whether they have discovered an important new relationship that holds in general or whether they have detected a relationship that is peculiar to this one particular sample. Exploratory findings are potentially important and should not be ignored. However, they should be clearly labeled as exploratory in any report or publication, and their interpretation should be very tentative. Exploratory findings should be replicated in a fresh data set before any strong conclusions are reached (see Diaconis, 1985, for a fuller discussion of inferential issues in exploratory data analysis).

4.5.3 Measurement Error in the Independent Variables

When one or more independent variables has been measured with less than perfect reliability, the estimates of the regression coefficients and their standard errors for each independent variable will be biased. Methods of correcting for measurement error in the one-IV and two-IV cases were introduced in Section 4.5. A general strategy with more than two IVs is to correct each separate correlation in the full correlation matrix including all independent variables and the dependent variable for measurement error. A simple method is to apply Eq. (2.10.5) (reproduced here) to each pair of variables in the correlation matrix:

(2.10.5)
$$r_{X_t Y_t} = \frac{r_{XY}}{\sqrt{r_{XX} r_{YY}}}.$$

The corrected correlation matrix can then be used as input to standard statistical packages such as SAS, SPSS, and SYSTAT, and the desired measures of partial relationship can be

---

[17]Recall that the addition of IVs also changes the meaning of the regression coefficients. In the equation $\hat{Y} = B_1 X_1 + B_0, B_1$ represents the linear relationship between X_1 and Y. In the equation, $\hat{Y} = B_1 X_1 + B_2 X_2 + B_0, B_1$ represents the conditional linear relationship between X_1 and Y given that X_2 is held constant.

computed. A particular value of this method is that it produces estimates of the unstandardized and standardized regression coefficients that are corrected for measurement error. The analyst can compare these results to the corresponding results based on the uncorrected data to get an idea of the extent to which the direction and magnitude of the relationships may be affected by measurement error.

The central drawback of this simple approach to correction for unreliability is that the standard errors of the corrected regression coefficients, and hence significance tests and confidence intervals, will not be accurate. Proper estimation of the standard errors of corrected regression coefficients can be obtained from structural equation modeling programs (see, e.g., Bryne, 1998, for details of reliability correction using the LISREL program). Chapter 12 introduces the basic concepts of path analysis and structural equation modeling.

Correction for measurement error may involve difficult issues. The correction procedures assume that we have a very good estimate of the reliability for each variable. And *all* independent variables in the regression equation must be corrected for unreliability or the estimates of the regression coefficients will be biased (Won, 1982). Precise estimates of reliability are typically only available for tests that report reliabilities for large standardization samples or when the researchers' own work with the measures has involved very large samples. Estimates of reliability based on small samples will often be too high or too low, and may produce estimates of correlations between true scores that are grossly inaccurate.

Another problem that may occur when inaccurate estimates of reliability are used is that the corrected correlation matrix may no longer have the standard mathematical properties that define correlation matrices.[18] For example, correlations between true scores are sometimes found that are greater than 1.0 in magnitude, or the correlation between two variables may be higher or lower than is mathematically possible given their pattern of correlations with other variables. In such cases, more advanced techniques of correcting for measurement error may be needed (Fuller, 1987).

Although these correction methods can lead to improved estimates of the regression coefficients, the best strategy is to confront measurement error before the study is designed. Choosing the most reliable available measure of each construct will minimize the bias due to measurement error. Using multiple measures of each construct and analyzing the data using multiple indicator, structural equation models (see Chapter 12; Bollen, 1989) also leads to regression coefficients and standard errors that are corrected for measurement error. Implementing one of these procedures at the design stage helps avoid the potential problems with the reliability correction methods that occur when one or more of the reliabilities is inaccurate or if other conditions for the application of the correction procedure are not met.

4.5.4 Nonconstant Variance

We now consider situations in which our graphical examination of the residuals suggests that the form of the regression model was properly specified, but that the variance of the residuals is not constant (heteroscedasticy). Recall from Section 4.4 that estimates of the regression coefficients are unbiased in this situation, but that the standard errors may be inaccurate. Section 4.4 also presented graphical displays and statistical tests of the residuals against each IV and $\hat{Y}$. These approaches are useful in detecting whether nonconstant variance exists. However, in deciding whether or not corrective action is needed, it is more important to get an

---

[18]For each pair of variables, no observed correlation r_{12} can exceed the product of the square root of the reliabilities, $\sqrt{r_{11}r_{22}}$, of X_1 and X_2. For each triplet of variables, r_{12} has mathematical upper and lower limits of $r_{13}r_{23} \pm \sqrt{(1 - r_{13}^2)(1 - r_{23}^2)}$. Correlation matrices that do not have these properties are described as ill conditioned. Mathematically, correlation and covariance matrices are ill conditioned if they have at least one negative eigenvalue.

estimate of the magnitude of the nonconstant variance problem. Recall that heteroscedasticity does not have a material effect on the results of the regression analysis until the magnitude of the problem becomes "large."

One simple method of determining the magnitude of the nonconstant variance problem is to order the cases from lowest to highest according to their values on X and then to divide them into a number of sets with approximately an equal number of cases in each set. Each of these sets is termed a *slice*. The number of slices chosen reflects a compromise between having a relatively stable estimate of the variance in each slice versus having the ability to examine different portions of the data.

For example, with 200 cases, the analyst might divide the data into five sets by putting the 40 cases with the smallest values of X in set 1, the next lowest 40 cases in set 2, and so on, yielding 5 sets. The analyst calculates the variance of the residuals around the regression line within each slice separately,

$$sd^2_{Y-\hat{Y}|slice} = \sum_{i=1}^{n_{slice}} \frac{(Y - \hat{Y})^2}{(n_{slice} - 2)}.$$

In this equation, n_{slice} is the number of cases in the slice and $sd^2_{Y-\hat{Y}|slice}$ represents the conditional variance of the residuals within the slice. If the ratio of the largest to the smallest conditional variance for the slices exceeds 10 or the conditional variance changes in a regular and systematic way as the IV increases in value, the analyst may wish to consider the remedial procedure of weighted least squares regression.

Weighted least squares (WLS) regression is the most commonly used remedial procedure for heteroscedasticity. Recall from Section 4.3 that in OLS estimation each case is given the same weight ($w_i = 1$) in calculating the regression coefficients. The values of B_0 and B_1 are chosen so as to minimize the value of sum of the squared residuals. With one independent variable, this expression is

$$\min \left(\sum e_i^2 \right) = \min \sum (Y_i - B_1 X_i - B_0)^2.$$

In contrast, in WLS each case is given a weight, w_i, depending on the precision of the observation of Y for that case. For observations for which the variance of the residuals around the regression line is high, the case is given a low weight. For observations for which the variance of the residuals around the regression line is low, the case is given a high weight. In the regression equation the values of B_0 and B_1 are chosen so as to minimize the sum of the weighted squared residuals,

(4.5.1) $$\min \left(\sum w_i e_i^2 \right) = \min \sum w_i (Y_i - B_1 X_i - B_0)^2.$$

When there is heteroscedasticity, WLS produces regression coefficients with the smallest possible standard errors when w_i is the inverse of the conditional variance of the residuals in the population corresponding to the specified value of X,

$$w_i = \frac{1}{\sigma^2_{Y-\hat{Y}|X}}.$$

The notation $\sigma^2_{Y-\hat{Y}|X}$ represents the variance of the residuals in the population conditional on the specified value of X. In practice, $\sigma^2_{Y-\hat{Y}|X}$ will not usually be known and must be estimated from the data. Interested readers will find an illustration of how weights are estimated in Box 4.5.1.

BOX 4.5.1
An Example of Estimating Weights for Weighted Least Squares

WLS regression is often used when the variance of the residuals has an increasing or decreasing linear relationship with X. In this case, the two-step process may be used to estimate the weights. We illustrate this process in the one predictor case.

1. We estimate the usual OLS regression equation, $Y = B_1 X + B_0 + e$. The residuals are saved for each case in the sample.

2. The residual for each case is squared. The squared residuals are regressed on X in a second regression equation,

$$\hat{e}_i^2 = B_1' X + B_0'.$$

In this equation, $\hat{e}_i^2$ is the predicted value of the squared residual for case i, B_0' is the intercept, and B_1' is the slope. Note that B_0 and B_1 in the regression equation from step 1 will not typically equal B_0' and B_1' in the regression equation from step 2. To estimate w_i for case i, the value of X for case i is substituted in Eq. (4.5.1), and the weight is the inverse of the predicted value of the squared residual, $w_i = 1/\hat{e}_i^2$. Once the weights are calculated, they are typically added to the data set as a new variable with a value for each case.[19] Standard statistical packages will then perform weighted least squares regression.

Two observations about WLS regression are in order. First, the primary difficulty in using WLS regression is choosing the proper value of the weight for each case. To the degree that the weights are not accurately estimated, WLS will not give optimal performance. Consequently WLS will show the best performance when there is a large sample size or when there are multiple cases (replicates) for each fixed value of X, as occurs in a designed experiment. If the WLS weights have been properly estimated in a sample, the regression coefficients from OLS, in which each case receives an equal weight, and WLS, in which each case is weighted according to the precision of the observation, should be very similar. Because of the imprecision in estimating the weights, OLS regression will often perform nearly as well as (or sometimes even better than) WLS regression when the sample size is small, the degree to which the variance of the residuals varies as a function of X is not large, or both. Second, WLS regression involves one important cost relative to OLS regression. In WLS the measures of standardized effect size, such as R^2 and pr^2, do not have a straightforward meaning as they do in OLS. Although standard computer programs include these measures in their output, they should not normally be presented when WLS regression is used. Taken together, these two observations suggest that OLS regression will be preferable to WLS regression except in cases where the sample size is large or there is a very serious problem of nonconstant variance.

4.5.5 Nonindependence of Residuals

Nonindependence of the residuals arises from two different sources, clustering and serial dependency. We consider the remedies for each of these problems in turn.

---

[19]When there are a few unusually large positive or negative values of the raw residuals, e_i, that are highly discrepant from the rest of the residuals (i.e., outlying values, see Section 10.2), the weights will be very poorly estimated. When there are outlying values, regressing $|e_i|$ on X and then using $w_i = 1/(|\hat{e}_i|)^2$ will yield improved estimates of the weights (Davidian & Carroll, 1987). $(|\hat{e}_i|)^2$ is the square of the predicted value of the absolute value (ignoring sign) of the residual.

Clustering

When data are collected from groups or other clusters, the estimates of the regression coefficients are unbiased, but the standard errors will typically be too small. Although historically a number of approaches were proposed to remedy this problem, two different general approaches appear to be the most promising.

In the first approach, a set of dichotomous variables known as dummy variables is used to indicate group membership. Coding schemes for representing group membership are initially presented in Chapter 8 and then are applied to the specific problem of clustering in Section 14.2.1 (disaggregated analysis with dummy coded groups). This approach removes the effects of mean differences among the groups on the results of the regression analysis. The results are easy to interpret, and the analysis does not require assumptions beyond those of OLS regression. However, the dummy-variable approach does not permit generalization of the results beyond the specific set of g groups that have been studied.[20] This approach also excludes the study of many interesting research questions that involve group-level variables such as the influence of group-level variables (e.g., total amount of interaction among family members) on individual-level variables (e.g., individual happiness).

The second approach is known variously by the terms *multilevel models* or hierarchical linear models. A form of regression analysis know as *random coefficient regression* is utilized. Conceptually, this approach may be thought of as specifying two levels of regression equations. At level 1, a separate regression equation is used to specify the intercept and slope of relationships within each of the groups. At level 2, regression equations specify the relationships between group-level variables and the slope and intercept obtained within each group from the level 1 analyses. For example, an educational researcher might study whether the income of the neighborhood in which schools are located is related to the overall level (intercept) of math achievement in each school and also to the relationship (slope) between student IQ and math achievement within each school.

Random coefficient regression models represent an important extension of multiple regression analysis that have opened up important new lines of inquiry in several substantive areas. At the same time, these models use more complex estimation procedures than OLS. These estimation procedures have several statistical advantages over OLS, but they come at a cost of requiring more stringent assumptions than OLS regression. Chapter 14 provides an extensive introduction to both approaches to the analysis of clustered data. Raudenbush and Bryk (2002), Kreft and de Leeuw (1998), and Snijders and Bosker (1999) provide more advanced treatments.

Serial Dependency

Analyses of temporal data that include substantial serial dependency lead to regression coefficients that are unbiased, but that have standard errors that are incorrect. A data transformation procedure is used to remedy the problem, here with the goal of removing the serial dependency. Successful transformation yields transformed values of each observation that are independent. Regression analyses may then be performed on the transformed values. For interested readers Box 4.5.2 provides an illustration of the transformation procedure when the residuals show a lag 1 autocorrelation.

---

[20]In some applications generalization is not an issue because the entire population of clusters is included in the sample. For example, a political scientist studying samples of voters selected from each of the 50 states in the United States would not wish to generalize beyond this set of states. However, in most research contexts, researchers wish to make inferences about a population of groups rather than a specific set of groups.

BOX 4.5.2
Transformation of Data with Lag 1 Autocorrelation

The transformation strategy illustrated here involves separately removing the part of Y that relates to the previous observation in the series:

(4.5.2) $$Y_t^* = Y_t - r_1 Y_{t-1}.$$

In Eq. 4.5.2, Y_t^* is the transformed value of Y at time t, Y_t is the observed value of Y at time t, and Y_{t-1} is the observed value of Y at time $t-1$. r_1 is the lag 1 autocorrelation. The regression analysis is then conducted on the transformed data,

(4.5.3) $$\hat{Y}_t^* = B_1^* X_t + B_0^*$$

where $\hat{Y}_t^*$ is the predicted value of transformed Y, B_1^* is the slope for the transformed data, and B_0^* is the intercept for the transformed data.

How do the results of the regression analysis performed on the transformed Y_t^* data using Eq. 4.5.3 compare with the results of the regression analysis, $\hat{Y}_t = B_1 X_t + B_0$, performed on the original data? The transformation has no effect on the slope: $B_1^* = B_1$. We can use the results of the analysis of the transformed data directly and report the estimate of B_1, its standard error, and the significance test and confidence interval. However, $B_0^* = (1 - r_1)B_0$. To recover the original (untransformed) intercept B_0 with its corrected standard error SE_{B_0}, an adjustment of the results of the analysis of the transformed data is necessary. The adjusted values of B_0, SE_{B_0}, and the t test of B_0 are calculated as follows:

$$\text{Adjusted } B_0 = \frac{B_0^*}{1 - r_1}$$

$$\text{Adjusted } SE_{B_0} = \frac{SE_{B_0^*}}{1 - r_1}$$

$$t = \frac{\text{Adjusted } B_0}{\text{Adjusted } SE_{B_0}}$$

The transformation procedure described here assumes that r_1 is a very good estimate of the value of the lag 1 autocorrelation ρ_1 in the population. Econometric texts (e.g., Greene, 1997) present more advanced analysis procedures that simultaneously estimate the values of the regression coefficients and the autocorrelation parameter. When more complicated forms of serial dependency than lag 1 autocorrelation are detected or there are several independent variables, statistical procedures known as time series analysis are used. These procedures include specialized methods for detecting complex forms of serial dependency and for transforming each series so that unbiased estimates of the regression coefficients and their standard errors can be obtained. Section 15.8 presents an introduction to time series analysis and other approaches to temporal data. McCleary and Hay (1980) provide a comprehensive introduction to time series analysis for behavioral science researchers. Box, Jenkins, and Reinsel (1994) and Chatfield (1996) provide more advanced treatments.

4.6 SUMMARY

Chapter 4 considers the full variety of problems that may arise in multiple regression analysis and offers remedies for those problems. A key feature of good statistical analysis is becoming very familiar with one's data. We present a variety of graphical tools that can quickly provide this familiarity and help detect a number of potential problems in multiple regression analysis.

Univariate displays include the frequency histogram, stem and leaf displays, kernel density estimates, and boxplots. Scatterplots are useful in seeing both linear and nonlinear relationships between two variables, particularly when enhanced with superimposed straight lines or lowess lines. Scatterplot matrices make it possible to examine all possible pairwise relationships between the IVs and the DV (Section 4.2).

The assumptions underlying multiple regression and ordinary least squares estimation are then considered. Violations of some of the assumptions can lead to biased estimates of regression coefficients and incorrect standard errors (Section 4.3). Violations of other assumptions lead to incorrect standard errors. Serious violations of the assumptions potentially lead to incorrect significance tests and confidence intervals. Graphical and statistical methods of detecting violations of several of the assumptions including incorrect specification of the form of the regression model, omitted variables, heteroscedasticity of residuals, clustering and serial dependency, and non-normality of residuals are then presented (Section 4.5). A variety of remedies that are useful when the assumptions of regression analysis are violated are then introduced. Some of the remedies address various issues in the specification of the regression model including the form of the IV-DV relationship, omitted IVs, and measurement error in the IVs. Other remedies address nonconstant variance of the residuals, clustering, and serial dependency. A fuller presentation of some of the remedies is deferred to later chapters, where the problems receive a more in-depth treatment.

5

Data-Analytic Strategies Using Multiple Regression/Correlation

5.1 RESEARCH QUESTIONS ANSWERED BY CORRELATIONS AND THEIR SQUARES

Until this point we have presented regression/correlation analysis as if the typical investigation proceeded by selecting a single set of IVs and producing a single regression equation that is then used to summarize the findings. Life, however, is seldom so simple for the researcher. The coefficient or set of coefficients that provide the answers depend critically on the questions being asked. There is a wealth of information about the interrelationships among the variables not extractable from a single equation. It is, perhaps, the skill with which other pertinent information can be ferreted out that distinguishes the expert data analyst from the novice. In this chapter we address five major issues of strategy that should be considered in using MRC analysis. The first examines the fit between the research questions and the coefficients that answer them. The second examines some options and considerations for making regression coefficients more substantively interpretable. The third strategic consideration is the use of sequential or hierarchical analysis to wrest the best available answers from the data. The fourth is the employment of sets of independent variables in hierarchical analyses. The final section discusses strategies for controlling and balancing Type I and Type II errors of inference in MRC.

It is often the case that regression coefficients provide the most informative answers to scientific questions. However, there are a number of questions that are best answered by correlation coefficients and their comparisons. Indeed, it is sometimes hard to avoid the suspicion that correlation coefficients and squared correlations of various kinds are not reported or not focused on, even when most relevant, because they are typically so small. There is something rather discouraging about a major effort to study a variable that turns out to account uniquely for 1 or 2 percent of the dependent variable variance. We have tried to indicate that such a small value may still represent a material effect (see Section 2.10.1), but there is no getting around the more customary disparagement of effects of this magnitude.

Different questions are answered by different coefficients and comparisons among them. Standard statistical programs in MRC produce both regression and correlation coefficients for the use of scientists in interpreting their findings. All coefficients, but especially correlation coefficients, need a definable population to which to generalize, of which one has a random, or at least representative or unbiased sample. Without a population framework some coefficients may be meaningless, and this is especially true of coefficients based (standardized) on the variance of the current sample. Researchers often make the untested assumption that the sample being examined is representative of some larger population. Assumptions about the stability and generalizability of model estimates from the sample at hand to the population of interest are probably more serious sources of bias than many other more familiar or researched statistical problems, such as variable distribution problems.

What kinds of hypotheses and research situations are best examined by comparisons of correlations, partial correlations, and semipartial correlations? The fundamental difference between questions involving correlations and those involving regression coefficients has often been overlooked because they share certain significance tests. Thus, the unique contribution to the prediction of Y, the squared semipartial correlation, shares the t test of statistical significance with the partial regression coefficients, both standardized and in raw units. Nevertheless, a focus on the magnitude and confidence intervals of these different coefficients will be informative to different research questions.

5.1.1 Net Contribution to Prediction

How much does X_i Increment $R^2(sr^2)$? How much improvement in prediction of Y is associated with the addition of X_i to other predictors? Here our interest is in the value of the squared semipartial correlation. Note that this is fundamentally a prediction question, rather than one of causal inference. For example, how much more predictable is academic success when we add health history to prior achievement and IQ? This is a question of utility rather than of causality. The latter would focus on the regression coefficient.

In addition to applied research that is designed to select variables on the basis of utility, correlation coefficients of various kinds may also answer scientific questions. We have indicated that questions about causal impact are generally best answered with regression coefficients. However, there are a number of scientific questions that are not causal in nature.

5.1.2 Indices of Differential Validity

Is measure A better than measure B? Perhaps some of the most frequently asked questions that are better answered by correlation functions than by regression coefficients involve evaluation of whether some measure or index is a better measure of a common construct than is an alternative, when the two measures are not measured in comparable units. For example, a study attempting to answer the question of whether child or parent is a better informant with regard to parental conflict by correlating scales appropriate to each informant with some criterion is best answered with correlations. Similarly, the question of which of two scales is better with regard to some criterion or outcome is better indexed by a comparison of correlations than by comparison of regression coefficients. For such questions the difference between correlations bounded by the confidence interval on this difference provides the best answer. Although the exact test is a complicated function of the average squared validity and the correlation between the predictors, in general, the standard error of this difference, expressed in Fisher's z', is less than $\sqrt{2/(n-3)}$ when all correlations are positive and the correlation between the predictors is comparable to their average validities (Meng, Rosenthal, & Rubin, 1992).

5.1.3 Comparisons of Predictive Utility

Is X_1 a better predictor than X_2? A question similar to that posed in the previous section may be answered by a comparison of semipartial correlations from a single sample: Which of two predictors is more related to Y net of other influences? For example, is maternal education or paternal occupational status a better indicator of social class and thus more predictive of academic success, net of IQ? If the predictors were in the same units as, for example, a comparison of the influence of maternal education and paternal education, we might wish to compare Bs to answer the question of whether an additional year of mother's education or of father's education had a higher "payoff" in terms of offspring academic success. However, when the predictors to be compared are in different units, such Bs are not directly comparable. An alternative index would be a comparison of βs; methods for comparing which are described in Appendix 2.

5.1.4 Attribution of a Fraction of the *XY* Relationship to a Third Variable

How much of the XY relationship is accounted for by W? This question may be answered by comparing the zero-order r_{XY}^2 with the semipartial $r_{YX \cdot W}^2$. Among other questions, this may represent a test of the mediation of the effect of X by W. This question is not the same as the one answered by a comparison of the zero-order B_{YX} with the partial $B_{YX \cdot W}$. The answer to the first question tells us how much of the prediction of Y by X is accounted for or attributable to W. The second asks whether, for constant values of W—that is, averaged over the values of W—changes in X have the same consequences for Y that they appeared to have when W was ignored. It is quite possible for W to account for a substantial fraction of the XY correlation and still have B_{YX} unchanged when W is partialed. For example, if $r_{XY} = .6$, $r_{YW} = .5$ and $r_{XW} = .83$, the unique contribution of X to the prediction of Y is [by Eq. (3.3.8) squared]

$$sr_{YX \cdot W}^2 = \left(\frac{r_{YX} - r_{YW}r_{XW}}{\sqrt{1 - r_{XW}^2}} \right)^2 = \left(\frac{.6 - .5(.83)}{\sqrt{1 - .83^2}} \right)^2 = .11$$

as compared to .36 for the zero-order r_{YX}^2. In contrast,

$$\beta_{YX \cdot W} = \frac{r_{YX} - r_{YW}r_{XW}}{1 - r_{XW}^2} = \frac{.6 - .5(.83)}{1 - .83^2} = .6$$

Since B is equivalent to β with adjustment for standard deviations [Eq. (3.2.5)], it too will remain constant in this situation. Naturally confidence intervals and statistical power for all coefficients will be much affected by the r_{XW}.

5.1.5 Which of Two Variables Accounts for More of the *XY* Relationship?

Olkin and Finn (1995) present an example in which the question of interest is whether change in Y (adolescent drug use) over time $(=Y_2 \cdot Y_1)$ is better explained by peer (V) or family (W) variables. Other examples might be whether family member differences are better explained by genetic closeness or period of time they lived together, or whether intergenerational differences on some variable are better explained by socioeconomic status or other differential experiences. Again, the question is posed in terms of variance proportions, and the answer is given by comparing the partial correlation of X with Y_2, partialing Y_1 to the partial correlation of W with Y_2, partialing Y_1.

5.1.6 Are the Various Squared Correlations in One Population Different From Those in Another Given the Same Variables?

This is a sort of popular "bottom line" question, that ignores (for the moment) the theoretically relevant details. Such questions can be asked with regard to zero-order r^2, partial or semipartial r^2, or R^2. Are social values as reflective of mental health in New Zealand as in American adolescents? Can we predict equally well in men and women, old persons and middle aged persons? Note that our overall prediction as assessed by R^2 can be equally good in two populations, although entirely different predictors in the set may be operative, or predictors may have quite different Bs.

5.2 RESEARCH QUESTIONS ANSWERED BY B OR β

5.2.1 Regression Coefficients as Reflections of Causal Effects

The (partial) regression coefficient B, as we have indicated, is often viewed as the premier causal indicator because it informs us about the estimated effect on the dependent variable of a change in the value of a putative cause.[1] Nevertheless, B coefficients as frequently presented have limitations, especially those associated with measurement units that are unfamiliar or that lack intrinsic meaning. These limitations are separable from the problems of equality of scale units, that is, whether the measures being employed can be considered to have the properties of interval scales. (See Cliff, 1982, for a discussion of methods of determining scale qualities and the inseparability of measurement from the scientific enterprise in general.)

As a consequence of a lack of consensus on measures, it is often easier to interpret β than B. β, as we have seen, essentially rescales the effects in terms of the standard deviations of the sample at hand. This is particularly useful when our research question has to do with comparing different variables for their (partialed) effects on Y in a given population represented by this sample. It is also often a necessary convenience when comparing effects of a given (conceptual) X_i on Y across studies, which may differ on the chosen measures of X_i and Y, and may even differ with regard to the population from which the sample was drawn. For example, we may measure depression with different scales in two studies, but wish to determine how similar their relationships are to some common Y. Consequently, it is generally recommended that β be reported, along with its SE in any research report.

5.2.2 Alternative Approaches to Making B_{YX} Substantively Meaningful

Clear interpretation of a (raw unit) B is often absent because the units of our measures are essentially arbitrary or are unfamiliar. Variable scores in the behavioral sciences often consist of simple sums of items, and statistics based on these scores will often be hard to interpret because of reader unfamiliarity with the number of items, the number of response options per item, and the numbers assigned to those response options in a given study. In such cases, even when major concerns about scale quality are absent, it is often difficult to determine anything useful about the meaning of a particular B other than, perhaps, the confidence that it differs

---

[1]Of course, use of B for these purposes does not, as such, imply that the researcher has provided the necessary theoretical argument that justifies such an interpretation.

from zero in a given direction. However, it is possible to provide data in ways that will enhance the interpretation and utility of the analyses.[2]

Units With Conventionally Shared Meaning

Some units are intrinsically meaningful (e.g., bushels, dollars, inches, years, and degrees, for which our familiarity with the units provides a framework that makes them generally understood). There are a few such cases in the behavioral sciences, in which long familiarity with a scale, and, usually, substantial standardization data has made relatively familiar units out of measures of abstract constructs. In psychology we have become familiar enough with the IQ unit to convey a sense of what are meaningful differences, even though the methods used to assess and calculate IQ vary. A long clinical tradition with the Hamilton Depression Scale has led to some consensus about the meaning and clinical significance of a difference or change of, for example, 5 units. The running example that we have used in this text was selected partly because its variables have such intrinsic meaning—dollars, years, publications, citations, and sex.

The fact that the units are agreed upon does not necessarily mean that a definition of a material difference is clear; rather the meaning is defined in context. Thus, for example, a difference of 4° Fahrenheit may be immaterial when one is cooking, of modest importance when one is deciding whether to go to the beach, and of considerable impact when one is measuring human body temperature (if within a certain range of values in the vicinity of 99°). The difficulty in accomplishing a conversion to centigrade (Celsius) measures of degrees in the United States is testimony to the importance of familiarity in context for ordinary interpretation of temperature units.

When the units (of both dependent and independent variable) are familiar in the context in which they are being used, the B is intrinsically useful. Thus, for example, if we say that the presence of some illness is associated with temperature increases of 5°, we understand its significance (although we would want to know its variability and duration as well as its mean).

Scales With a True Zero: None is None

Perhaps the typical scores that can be said to have true zeros are counts of events or objects. However, when such counts are meant to represent a more abstract construct or lack a familiar context that supplies meaning (e.g., the number of lever pecks a pigeon will complete as a function of the rate of reinforcement), the fact that they are counts is not enough to supply a useful meaning. No doubt experimenters who work in a given specialty area often develop a kind of consensus as to what are "material" effects, just as those working with biological assays do; however, those outside the area are likely to have to take their word for it, having no framework for understanding what is a lot and what is a little.

Under the circumstances in which both independent and dependent variables have true zeros, a useful conversion of B is to a measure of elasticity (E), used by economists to describe the percent change on a variable for which there is an available count (like dollars) but no upper limit (e.g., Goldberger, 1998). Elasticity is the percent change at the mean of Y for each 1% change in X.[3] Thus $B_{YX} = 1.36$ in our running example of faculty salary meant 1.36 publications per year since Ph.D., in relationship to an overall average of 19.93 publications, so there would be a $1.36/19.93 = 7\%$ increase at the mean in publications per year since Ph.D. The average faculty member is 6.79 years post Ph.D., so an increase in one year is a 1/6.79 or

---

[2]A more detailed presentation of these considerations and options can be found in P. Cohen, J. Cohen, Aiken, and West, 1999.

[3]The coefficient E is defined at the mean of the distribution; the regression is carried out on the raw variables.

14.7% increase. Dividing the 7% by 14.7% gives an elasticity of .476, or nearly a half percent increase in publications per 1% increase in time since Ph.D. (evaluated at the mean). Note that an advantage of this measure is that no upper limit is placed on the magnitude of either measure; an established range is not necessary to produce a meaningful effect size.

Scores for Which Both Zero and a Maximum Are Defined by the Measure

With many novel measures, a convenient unit is the percent of the maximum possible (POMP) score. School grades are often presented in this format, and conventions have developed that tend to lend differences in these units an intrinsic meaning (although again context matters, as one can easily see by comparing the meaning of a score of 80% in high school and in graduate school). The school grades example is also instructive because it makes it clear that the end points of the test do not necessarily define states of zero and complete knowledge of the subject matter. Furthermore, different instructors may devise tests of the same material that are seen as inappropriately easy, difficult, or appropriately discriminating among students.

There is nothing intrinsic about the percent reflecting "correctness," that is, it can equally be the percent of items endorsed in the scored direction regardless of the construct being scaled. Thus, if we have 20 true-false items measuring extroversion, each item endorsed in the extroversion direction would be worth 5 percentage points. Just as in educational tests of subject matter knowledge, a given test may be "hard" or "easy," and may allow for a range of scores that covers the potential range of the construct well or may restrict the range (qualities that may be inferred in part by the distribution of observed scores on the measure). These are qualities that are, in theory, as important as the reliability of the test. The reliability, of course, restricts both the correlation with other measures and the range of the observed scores (as can be seen by the fact that an individual with a true maximum or minimum score would have an observed score closer to the mean due to unreliability).

POMP scores need not be restricted to the number of dichotomous items endorsed in the scored direction. One may extend this procedure to use the full possible range of scores to define the zero and 100% points. For example, for a 10-item scale on which there are four Likert-scaled response options each, scored 0, 1, 2, 3, the potential range is from 0 to 30. A score of 12 would be 12/30 or 40%.

Using Item Response Alternatives as a Scale

An alternative when all item responses are on a Likert scale expressing degree of agreement or frequency is to use the average item score (with items reversed as necessary to conform to the scored direction). Then a unit is the difference between an average score of, for example, "disagree a little" and "agree a little," or "disagree a little" and "disagree a lot." This method is widely used in some research areas but rarely used in others.

When both the IV of interest and Y are treated in this manner, and they have been measured with the same number of response options, the B resulting from this transform will be exactly the same as that resulting from a percentaging of the same scores (POMP scores).

Using the Sample's Standard Deviation as a Scale; z Scores

The most common current method of placing scores in a more familiar unit is to subtract the score from the mean and divide by the standard deviation, thus creating z scores. As we have seen in Chapter 2, this method of scoring X and Y yields a bivariate B_{YX} that is equivalent to r_{XY}. This equivalence also holds between partial B and partial β when both Y and the IV in question have been z scored. Either this method of scoring or the use of partial β have the considerable advantage of making the units on different variables comparable in one particular, useful sense. They enable us to say, for example, that X_1 had more influence on Y than X_2. However, as noted earlier, standardized measures and statistics are not without potential problems. In addition to potential disadvantages of failure to attend to a measure's units for the advancement of the scientific field, there is the problem that the *sd* unit will typically vary across populations as well as in different samples from a given population. Nevertheless, as things currently stand, β is often the most useful coefficient for answering questions about the influence of one variable on another, with or without other variables in the equation.

5.2.3 Are the Effects of a Set of Independent Variables on Two Different Outcomes in a Sample Different?

There are times when the issue at hand is whether the same IVs have essentially the same influence on two different dependent variables in the same sample. A "net regression" method of testing this issue, both as a single overall question and with regard to individual coefficients is presented in Appendix 2.[4] This method takes advantage of the fact that the predicted value of Y is the sum of the B-weighted IVs. Therefore one can test the difference between these weights, considered simultaneously, by using this $\hat{Y}$ value. Assuming that dependent variables W and Y are in the same units, or creating unit "equivalence" by standardizing them, we begin by estimating either (or each) from the set of IVs. We continue by subtracting $\hat{Y}$ from W and determining the relationship of the (same) IVs to this new $W - \hat{Y}$ variable as a dependent variable. If this equation is statistically significant, we have shown that the IVs are related significantly differently to dependent variable W than they are related to dependent variable Y. In addition, each regression coefficient in this new equation is tested by its *SE*, which indicates whether the influence (weight or B_i) of X_i on W is greater (positive) or less than (negative) its influence on Y. (The symmetrical analysis can be carried out on $Y - \hat{W}$, but the coefficients will simply be reversed in sign.)

5.2.4 What Are the Reciprocal Effects of Two Variables on One Another?

As noted earlier, we are usually forced to assume that Y does not cause X when we test our theories with cross-sectional (one-time-point) data. Unfortunately, in the social sciences this is quite often patently unlikely to hold true. For example, we may wish to examine the effect of stressful life events on adaptive function, but we are aware that poor adaptive function is likely to put one at risk of more stressful life events. Or we know that achievement is likely to be hampered by poor student attachment to the school but worry that such attachment may also be lowered by poor achievement.

A classic strategy for estimating such reciprocal effects from data collected at two points in time is called cross-lagged analysis.[5] In these analyses we require each of the two variables, W and Y, to be measured at two points in time. Then W measured at time 1 (W_1) is used to predict Y_2 in an equation that includes Y_1 as an IV, and Y_1 is used to predict W_2 in an equation that includes W_1 as an IV. Other control variables may be included as well, as appropriate to the substantive research issues. The resulting estimates are of the effect of each variable on (regressed) change in the other variable. As will be discussed in Chapter 12, the appropriateness of such estimates are highly dependent on the correct selection of a time between the two measurement occasions.

---

[4]An alternative method employing SEM is described in Chapter 12.

[5]An alternative approach that can sometimes be employed with cross-sectional data is described in Chapter 12.

5.3 HIERARCHICAL ANALYSIS VARIABLES IN MULTIPLE REGRESSION/CORRELATION

A sequential or hierarchical analysis of a set of independent variables may often produce the coefficients necessary to answer the scientific questions at hand.[6] In its simplest form, the k IVs are entered cumulatively in a prespecified sequence and the R^2 and partial regression and correlation coefficients are determined as each IV joins the others. A full hierarchical procedure for k IVs consists of a series of k regression analyses, each with one more variable than its predecessor. (In a subsequent section we see that one may proceed hierarchically with sets of variables rather than single variables.) The choice of a particular cumulative sequence of IVs is made in advance (in contrast with the *stepwise* regression procedures discussed in Section 5.3.3), dictated by the purpose and logic of the research. Some of the basic principles underlying the hierarchical order for entry are causal priority and the removal of confounding or spurious relationships, research relevance, and structural properties of the research factors being studied. As we will see in subsequent chapters, there are also circumstances in which a "tear down" procedure, in which one begins with the full set of variables and removes them selectively if they do not contribute to R^2, may be more in keeping with one's goals than the hierarchical "build up" procedure that we feature here.

5.3.1 Causal Priority and the Removal of Confounding Variables

As seen earlier (Section 3.4), the relationship between any variable and Y may be partly or entirely spurious, that is, due to one or more variables that are a cause of both. Thus, each variable in the investigation should be entered only after other variables that may be a source of spurious relationship have been entered. This leads to an ordering of the variables that reflects their presumed causal priority—no IV entering later should be a presumptive cause of an IV that has been entered earlier.[7]

One advantage of the hierarchical analysis of data is that once the order of the IVs has been specified, a unique partitioning of the total Y variance accounted for by the k IVs, $R^2_{Y.123...k}$, may be made. Indeed, this is the *only* basis on which variance partitioning can proceed with correlated IVs. Because the sr_i^2 at each stage is the increase in R^2 associated with X_i, when all (and only) previously entered variables have been partialed, an *ordered* variance partitioning procedure is made possible by

$$\text{(5.3.1)} \qquad R^2_{Y.123...k} = r^2_{Y1} + r^2_{Y2 \cdot 1} + r^2_{Y3 \cdot 12} + r^2_{Y4 \cdot 123} + \cdots + r^2_{Yk \cdot 123...(k-1)}$$
$$= r^2_{Y1} + sr^2_{2 \cdot 1} + sr^2_{3 \cdot 12} + sr^2_{4 \cdot 123} + \cdots + sr^2_{k \cdot 123...(k-1)}.$$

Each of the k terms is found from a simultaneous analysis of IVs in the equation at that point in the hierarchy; each gives the increase in Y variance accounted for by the IV entering at that point beyond what has been accounted for by the previously entered IVs. r^2_{Y1} may be thought of as the increment from zero due to the first variable in the hierarchy, an sr^2 with nothing

---

[6]We regret the confusion that sometimes occurs between this older reference to variables entered in a hierarchical sequence with a more recent development of hierarchical linear models (HLM) or hierarchical regression, which refers to a structure of the data in which subject scores are nested within occasions or within some other grouping (e.g., classrooms or families) that tends to prevent independence of observations. The latter procedure is discussed in Chapters 14 and 15.

[7]When a variable X_j that may be an effect of X_i is entered prior to or simultaneously with X_i we have the circumstance referred to by epidemiologists as *overcontrol*, that is, removal from the estimated effect of X_i on Y of some fraction that is mediated or indirect by way of X_j.

partialed. Summing the terms up to a given stage in the hierarchy gives the cumulative R^2 at that stage; for example, $r_{Y1}^2 + sr_{2\cdot1}^2 + sr_{3\cdot12}^2 = R_{Y.123}^2$.

The reader is reminded that the increment attributable to any IV may change considerably if one changes its position in the hierarchy, because this will change what has and what has not been partialed from it. This is indeed why one wishes the IVs to be ordered in terms of the specific questions to be answered by the research, such as causal priority. Otherwise part of the variance in Y due to some cause X_1 is instead attributed to an IV that is another effect of this cause. This stolen (spurious) variance will then mislead the investigator about the relative importance to Y of the cause and its effect.

Of course, it will frequently not be possible to posit a single sequence that is uncontroversially in exact order of causal priority.[8] In such circumstances more than one order may be entertained and the results then considered together. They may not differ with regard to the issue under investigation, but if they do, the resulting ambiguity must be acknowledged.

When the variables can be fully sequenced—that is, when a full causal model can be specified that does not include any effect of Y on IVs or unmeasured common causes, the hierarchical procedure becomes a tool for estimating the effects associated with each cause. Formal causal models use regression coefficients rather than variance proportions to indicate the magnitude of causal effects, as discussed earlier. Because Chapter 12 is devoted to an exposition of the techniques associated with this and other types of causal models, we do not describe them here.

To illustrate a hierarchical analysis, organized in terms of causal priority, we turn again to the academic salary data (from Table 3.5.1). The order of assumed priority is sex (X_3), time (years) since Ph.D. (X_1), number of publications (X_2), and number of citations (X_4) (but note the further discussion of this sequence in Section 12.1). Note that no variable can be affected by one that appears after it; whatever causality occurs among IVs is assumed to be from earlier to later in the sequence. We entered these variables in the specified order and determined the R^2 after each addition. We found $r_{Y3} = .201$, and therefore $R_{Y.3}^2 (= r_{Y3}^2) = .040$, that is, 4% of the academic salary variance was accounted for by sex. When time since Ph.D. (X_1) was added to sex, we found that $R_{Y.31}^2 = .375$ and we may say that the increment in predicted Y variance of time since Ph.D. over sex, or for time partialing or taking into account the difference in time since Ph.D. between male and female faculty, was $sr_{1\cdot3}^2 = R_{Y.13}^2 - r_{Y3}^2 = .375 - .040 = .335$. Next we added publications (X_2) and found $R_{Y.312}^2 = .396$, a very small increment: $sr_{2\cdot31}^2 = R_{Y.123}^2 - R_{Y.31}^2 = .396 - .375 = .021$. Finally, when citations (X_4) was added, we have the R^2 we found in Section 3.5. $R_{Y.3124}^2 = .503$, so the increment for X_4 or $sr_{4\cdot123}^2 = .503 - .396 = .107$. The final R^2 for the four IVs is necessarily the sum of these increments, by Eq. (3.8.1):

$$.503 = .040 + .335 + .021 + .107.$$

Of course, a different ordering would result in different increments (which would also sum to .503), but to the extent that they violated the direction of causal flow, the findings might be subject to misinterpretation. For example, if entered first, publications would have all of the salary variance associated with its r^2 credited to it, but only on the unlikely premise that time since Ph.D. (or the forces associated with time) did not contribute causally to the number of publications. The causal priority ordering makes it clear that (in these fictitious data) the strong relationship between salary and publications merely reflects the operation of the passage of time.

---

[8]Not infrequently one can identify one or more variables that are thought of as "controls," meaning that although their causal role is not certain, removal of their potential influence will strengthen the inferences that can be made about the role of one or more IVs that will be entered later in the sequence. See *Functional Sets* in Section 5.4.1.

The increments here are sr^2 values, but they are different from those determined previously (Section 3.5.4) and given in Table 3.5.2. For the latter, all the other $k-1(=3)$ IVs were partialed from each, whereas here only those preceding each IV in the hierarchy were partialed. They therefore agree only for the variable entering last. When the significance test of Eq. (3.6.8) is employed for these cumulative sr^2 values (for $n = 62$), it is found that all are significant except the sr^2 for number of publications.[9]

A special case of the hierarchical model is employed in the analysis of change. Under circumstances in which pre- and postscore values are available on some variable and the researcher wishes to determine whether and to what extent treatment or other variables are associated with change, the postscore may be used as the dependent variable, with prescore entered as the first IV in the hierarchy. Unlike the alternative method involving differences (postscores minus prescores), when subsequent IVs are entered into the equation their partial correlations will reflect their relationship with postscores from which prescore influence has been removed. Note that this method effectively removes from consideration any influence that earlier values of the DV may have had on other IVs.[10]

5.3.2 Research Relevance

Not infrequently an investigator gathers data on a number of variables in addition to those IVs that reflect the major goals of the research. Thus, X_1 and X_2 may carry the primary focus of the study but X_3, X_4, and X_5 are also available. The additional IVs may be secondary because they are viewed as having lesser relevance to the dependent variable than do X_1 and X_2, or because hypotheses about their relationships are weak or exploratory. Under these circumstances, X_1 and X_2 may be entered into the equation first (perhaps ordered on the basis of a causal model) and then X_3, X_4, and X_5 may follow, ordered on the basis of their presumed relevance and/or priority. Aside from the clarity in interpretations of the influence of X_1 and X_2 that is likely to result from this approach (because the secondary X_3, X_4, and X_5 variables are not partialed from X_1 and X_2), the statistical power of the test of the major hypothesis is likely to be maximal because the df are not deflated by these less important variables. Under these circumstances, the additional steps answer the question of whether these variables add anything to the prediction of Y.

5.3.3 Examination of Alternative Hierarchical Sequences of Independent Variable Sets

Sometimes the appropriate sequencing of some variable sets is theoretically ambiguous. Although one usually begins with the more distal causes and gradually adds the more proximal causes that may mediate those distal causes, there are times when theory is inadequate to determine such a sequence, when it is likely that there are effects of these IV sets on each other, or when sets are alternative mediators of an unmeasured more distal cause. Such a circumstance might occur, for example, if one set of IVs involved a set of physiological measures and another set consisted of a set of motivational variables, and the study was examining the impact of each on behavior. In such cases the addition of each set to the prediction of Y, over and above the prediction of the other set, would be of interest, and both sequences would usually be reported.

---

[9] An alternative test of significance, in which "Model 2" error is employed, is discussed in Section 5.5.4 in the context of significance tests for sets of IVs entered hierarchically.

[10] This procedure is discussed in greater detail in Chapter 15, where analyses of longitudinal data are more thoroughly reviewed.

5.3.4 Stepwise Regression

There are dangers in letting a computer program sequence the variables for you as happens when one uses the stepwise option, in which variables are selected on the basis of their contribution to R^2. Although stepwise regression has certain surface similarities with hierarchical MRC (and hierarchical MRC and stepwise regression are the same thing when the investigator "forces" the sequencing of the IVs), it is considered separately, primarily because it differs in its underlying philosophy. Stepwise programs are designed to select from a group of IVs the one variable at each stage that has the largest sr^2 and hence makes the largest contribution to R^2. Such programs typically stop admitting IVs into the equation when no IV makes a contribution that is statistically significant at a level specified by the program user.[11] Thus, the stepwise procedure defines an a posteriori order based solely on the relative uniqueness of the variables in the sample at hand.

When an investigator has a large pool of potential IVs and very little theory to guide selection among them, these programs are a sore temptation. If the computer selects the variables, the investigator is relieved of the responsibility of making decisions about their logical or causal priority or relevance before the analysis, although interpretation of the findings may not be made easier. We take a dim view of the routine use of stepwise regression in explanatory research for various reasons (see the following), but mostly because we feel that more orderly advance in the behavioral sciences is likely to occur when researchers armed with theories provide an a priori ordering that reflects causal hypotheses rather than when computers order IVs post and ad hoc for a given sample.

An option that is available on some computer programs allows for the a priori specification ("forcing") of a hierarchy among groups of IVs. An investigator may be clear that some groups of variables are logically, causally, or structurally prior to others, and yet not have a basis for ordering variables within such groups. Under such conditions, variables may be labeled for entering in the equation as one of the first, second, or up to hth group of variables. The sequence of variables within each group is determined by the computer in the usual stepwise manner. This type of analysis is likely to be primarily hierarchical (between classes of IVs) and only incidentally stepwise (within classes), and computer programs so organized may be effectively used to accomplish hierarchical MRC analysis by sets of IVs as described in Section 5.4.4.

Probably the most serious problem in the use of stepwise regression programs arises when a relatively large number of IVs is used. Because the significance tests of each IV's contribution to R^2 and associated confidence intervals proceed in ignorance of the large number of other competing IVs, there can be very serious capitalization on chance and underestimation of confidence intervals. A related problem with the free use of stepwise regression is that in many research problems the ad hoc order produced from a set of IVs in one sample is likely not to be found in other samples from the same population. When among the variables competing for entry at any given step there are trivial differences among their partial relationships with Y, the computer will dutifully choose the largest for addition at that step. In other samples and, more important, in the population, such differences may well be reversed. When the competing IVs are substantially correlated with each other, the problem is likely to be compounded, because the losers in the competition may not make a sufficiently large unique contribution to be entered at any subsequent step before the problem is terminated by the absence of a variable making a statistically significant addition.

---

[11] Some stepwise programs operate backward, that is, by elimination. All k IVs are entered simultaneously and the one making the smallest contribution is dropped. Then the $k - 1$ remaining variables are regressed on Y, and again the one making the smallest contribution is dropped, and so on. The output is given in reverse order of elimination. This order need not agree with that of the forward or accretion method described here.

Although, in general, stepwise programs are designed to approach the maximum R^2 with a minimum number of IVs for the sample at hand, they may not succeed very well in practice. Sometimes, with a large number of IVs, variables that were entered into the equation early no longer have nontrivial relationships after other variables have been added. Some programs provide for the removal of such variables, but others do not. Also, although it is admittedly not a common phenomenon in practice, when there is suppression between two variables, neither may reach the criterion for entrance to the equation, although if both were entered they would make a useful contribution to R^2.

However, our distrust of stepwise regression is not absolute, and decreases to the extent that the following conditions obtain:

1. The research goal is entirely or primarily predictive (technological) and not at all, or only secondarily, explanatory (scientific). The substantive interpretation of stepwise results is made particularly difficult by the problems described earlier.
2. n is very large, and the original k (that is, before stepwise selection) is not too large; a k/n ratio of 1 to at least 40 is prudent.
3. Particularly if the results are to be substantively interpreted, a cross-validation of the stepwise analysis in a new sample should be undertaken and only those conclusions that hold for both samples should be drawn. Alternatively, the original (large) sample may be randomly divided in half and the two half-samples treated in this manner.

5.4 THE ANALYSIS OF SETS OF INDEPENDENT VARIABLES

A set of variables is a group classified as belonging together for some reason. As we will describe them, the grouping of variables into sets may be motivated by structural or formal properties of the variables that the sets include or the sets may have a common functional role in the substantive logic of the research. The basic concepts of proportion of variance accounted for and of correlation (simple, partial, semipartial, multiple) developed in Chapter 3 for single IVs hold as well for sets of IVs. This use of sets as units of analysis in MRC is a powerful tool for the exploitation of data.

5.4.1 Types of Sets

Structural Sets

We use the term *research factor* to identify an influence operating on Y or, more generally, an entity whose relationship to Y is under study. The word *factor* is used here to imply a single construct that may require two or more variables for its complete representation. Such will be the case when the construct consists of multiple independent or overlapping categories, or when more than one variable is required to express the shape of the relationship between a quantitative scale and the dependent variable. Examples of categorical variables are experimental treatment, religion, diagnosis, ethnicity, kinship system, and geographic area. In general it will require $g - 1$ variables to represent g groups or categories (see Chapter 8). When they are not mutually exclusive, g variables will generally be required. Thus, in a laboratory experiment in which subjects are randomly assigned to three different experimental groups and two different control groups (hence, $g = 5$), the research factor G of treatment group requires exactly $g - 1 = 4$ IVs to fully represent the aspects of G, that is, the distinctions among the 5 treatment groups. The several different methods for accomplishing this representation are the subject of Chapter 8, but in each case $g - 1$ variables are required to fully represent G.

Quantitative scales, such as scores of psychological tests, rating scales, or sociological indices, may also require multiple variables to fully represent them. When one needs to take into account the possibility that a research factor such as age may be related curvilinearly to Y (or to other research factors), other aspects of age must be considered. Age as such represents only one aspect of the A research factor, its linear aspect. Other aspects, which provide for various kinds of nonlinearity in the relationship of A to Y, may be represented by other IVs such as age squared and age cubed. Considerations and methods of representing aspects of scaled research factors are the subject of Chapter 6.

The preceding implies that if we are determining the proportion of variance in a dependent variable Y due to a single research factor, we will (in general) be finding a squared *multiple* correlation, because the latter will require a set of two or more IVs.

Functional Sets

Quite apart from structural considerations, IVs are grouped into sets for reasons of their substantive content and the function they play in the logic of the research. Thus, if you are studying the relationship between the psychological variable field dependence (Y) and personality (P) and ability (A) characteristics, P may contain a set of k_P scales from a personality questionnaire and A a set of k_A subtests from an intelligence scale. The question of the relative importance of personality and ability (as represented by these variables) in accounting for Y would be assessed by determining R^2_{YP}, the squared multiple correlation of Y with the k_P IVs of P, and R^2_{YA}, the squared multiple correlation of Y with k_A IVs of A, and then comparing them. Similarly, research that is investigating (among other things) the socioeconomic status (S) of school children might represent S by occupational status of head of household, family income, mother's education, and father's education, a substantive set of four ($= k_S$) IVs. For simplicity, these illustrations have been of sets of single research factors, but a functional set can be made up of research factors that are themselves sets. For example, a demographic set (D) may be made up of structural sets to represent ethnicity, marital status, and age. A group of sets is itself a set and requires no special treatment.

It is often the nature of research that in order to determine the effect of some research factor(s) of interest (a set B), it is necessary to statistically control for (partial out) the Y variance due to causally antecedent variables in the cases under study. A group of variables deemed antecedent either temporally or logically in terms of the purpose of the research could be treated as a functional set for the purpose of partialing out of Y's total variance the portion of the variance due to these antecedent conditions. Thus, in a comparative evaluation of compensatory early education programs (B), with school achievement as Y, the set to be partialed might include such factors as family socioeconomic status, ethnicity, number of older siblings, and pre-experimental reading readiness. This large and diverse group of IVs functions as a single covariate set A in the research described. In research with other goals these IVs might have different functions and be treated separately or in other combinations.

An admonitory word is in order. Because it is possible to do so, the temptation exists to assure coverage of a theoretical construct by measuring it in many ways, with the resulting large number of IVs then constituted as a set. Such practice is to be strongly discouraged, because it tends to result in reduced statistical power and precision for the sets and an increase in spuriously "significant" single-IV results, and generally bespeaks muddy thinking. It is far better to sharply reduce the size of such a set, and by almost any means.[12] One way is

---

[12] See the discussion of multicollinearity in Section 3.8 and in later chapters, especially Chapter 10.

through a tightened conceptualization of the construct, a priori. In other situations, the large array of measures is understood to cover only a few behavioral dimensions, in which case their reduction to scores on one or more factors by means of factor analysis or latent variable modeling (Chapter 12) is likely to be most salutary for the investigation, with little risk of losing Y-relevant information. Note that such analyses are performed completely independent of the sample values of the r_{Yi} correlations.

It is worth noting here that the organization of IVs into sets of whatever kind bears on the interpretation of MRC results but has no effect on the basic computation. For any Y and k IVs $(X_1, X_2, \ldots, X_k)$ in a given analysis, each X_i's coefficients (sr_i, pr_i, B_i, β_i) and their associated confidence intervals and significance tests are determined as described in Chapter 3.

5.4.2 The Simultaneous and Hierarchical Analyses of Sets

We saw in Chapter 3 that, given k IVs, we can regress Y on all of them simultaneously and obtain $R^2_{Y.12\ldots k}$ as well as partial statistics for each X_i. We will generally write these partial statistics in shorthand notation (i.e., β_i, B_i, sr_i, pr_i), where it is understood that all the other IVs are being partialed. This immediately generalizes to sets of IVs: when sets U, V, W are simultaneously regressed on Y, there are a total of $k_U + k_V + k_W = k$ IVs that together determine $R^2_{Y.UVW}$. The partial statistics for each IV in the set U has *all* the remaining $k - 1$ IVs partialed: both those from V and W (numbering k_V and k_W) and also the remaining IVs from its own set. It can be shown that, for example, the adjusted Y means of ANCOVA (analysis of covariance) are functions of the regression coefficients when a covariate set and a set of groups are simultaneously regressed on Y.

In Section 5.3 we saw that each of the k IVs can be entered cumulatively in some specified hierarchy, at each stage of which an R^2 is determined. The R^2 for all k variables can thus be analyzed into cumulative increments in the proportion of Y variance due to the addition of each IV to those higher in the hierarchy. These increments in R^2 were noted to be squared semipartial correlation coefficients, and the formula for the hierarchical procedure for single IVs was given as

$$(5.3.1) \qquad R^2_{Y.12\ldots k} = r^2_{Y1} + r^2_{Y2\cdot 1} + r^2_{Y3\cdot 12} + r^2_{Y4\cdot 123} + \cdots + r_{Yk\cdot 123\ldots(k-1)}$$

The hierarchical procedure is directly generalizable from single IVs to sets of IVs. Replacing k single IVs by h sets of IVs, we can state that these h sets can be entered cumulatively in a specified hierarchical order, and upon the addition of each new set an R^2 is determined. The R^2 for all h sets can thus be analyzed into increments in the proportion of Y variance due to the addition of each new set of IVs to those higher in the hierarchy. These increments in R^2 are, in fact, squared *multiple* semipartial correlation coefficients, and a general hierarchical equation for sets analogous to Eq. (5.3.1) may be written. To avoid awkwardness of notation, we write it for four ($= h$) sets in alphabetical hierarchical order and use the full dot notation; its generalization to any number of sets is intuitively obvious:

$$(5.4.1) \qquad R^2_{Y.TUVW} = R^2_{YT} + R^2_{Y(U\cdot T)} + R^2_{Y(V\cdot TU)} + R^2_{Y(W\cdot TUV)}.$$

We defer a detailed discussion of the multiple semipartial R^2 to the next section. Here it is sufficient to note merely that it is an increment to the proportion of Y variance accounted for by a given set of IVs (of whatever nature) beyond what has already been accounted for by prior sets, that is, sets previously entered in the hierarchy. Further, the amount of the increment in Y variance accounted for by that set cannot be influenced by Y variance associated with subsequent sets; that is, those which are later in the hierarchy.

Consider an investigation of length of hospital stay (Y) of $n = 500$ randomly selected psychiatric admissions to eight mental hospitals in a state system for a given period. Assume that data are gathered and organized to make up the following sets of IVs:

1. Set D—Demographic characteristics of patients: age, sex, socioeconomic status, ethnicity.   Note that this is a substantive set, and may be thought of as a set of control variables, meaning that they are not themselves of major interest but are there to make sure that effects attributed to later sets are not really due to demographic differences with which they are correlated. Assume $k_D = 9$.

2. Set I—Patient illness scores on nine of the scales of the Minnesota Multiphasic Personality Inventory.   This set is also substantive, and $k_I = 9$. This set is placed prior to the information on which hospital the patient has been treated in because it is known that patient illness enters into the decision about which hospital will treat them.

3. Set H—Hospitals.   The hospital to which each patient is admitted is a nominally scaled research factor. With eight hospitals contributing data, we will require a (structural) set of $k_H = 7$ IVs to represent fully the hospital group membership of the patients (see Chapter 8).

Although there are 25 ($k_D + k_I + k_H = k$) IVs, our analysis may proceed in terms of the three ($= h$) sets hierarchically ordered in the assumed causal priority of accounting for variance in length of hospital stay as D, I, H.

Suppose that we find that $R^2_{YD} = .20$, indicating that the demographic set, made up of nine IVs accounts for 20% of the Y variance. Note that this ignores any association with illness scores (I) or effects of hospital differences (H). When we add the IVs of the I set, we find that $R^2_{Y.DI} = .22$; hence, the increment due to I over and above D, or with D partialed, is $R^2_{Y(I \cdot D)} = .02$. Thus, an additional 2% of the Y variance is accounted for by illness beyond the demographic set. Finally, the addition of the seven IVs for hospitals (set H) produces an $R^2_{Y.DIH} = .33$, an increment over $R^2_{Y.DI}$ of .11, which equals $R^2_{Y(H \cdot DI)}$. Thus, we can say that which hospital patients enter accounts for 11% of the variance in length of stay, after we partial out (or statistically control, or adjust for, or hold constant) the effect of differences in patients' demographic and illness characteristics. We have, in fact, performed by MRC an analysis of covariance (ANCOVA) for the research factor "hospitals," using sets D and I as covariates.[13] Of course, one's substantive interest is likely to focus on the actual B_{Yi} coefficients as each new set is entered. To the extent to which one is interested in the final "adjusted" mean differences in LOS between hospitals, the answer will lie in the final regression coefficients. However, much can also be learned by examination of the extent to which these coefficients differ from those obtained when set H is entered *without* the "covariate" sets D and I. For example, it may be that some initially large differences between hospitals were entirely attributable to demographic and symptom differences between patients. This could be concluded when certain B_{Yi} coefficients from the equation with only set H were what could be considered large in the context (and had acceptably narrow confidence limits), but declined substantially in value when the covariate set D, or sets D and I, were added.

There is much to be said about the hierarchical procedure and, indeed, it is said in the next section and throughout the book. For example, as pointed out in regard to single variables, the increment due to a set may depend critically upon where it appears in the hierarchy; that is, what has been partialed from it, which, in turn, depends on the investigator's theory about the mechanisms that have generated the associations between the variables. As we will see, not all theories permit unambiguous sequencing.

---

[13] Omitting the significance test; see subsequent section. Also, a valid ANCOVA requires that there be no interaction between H and the aggregate I, D covariate set (see Chapter 9).

5.4.3 Variance Proportions for Sets and the Ballantine Again

We again employ the ballantine to illustrate the structure of relationships of sets of IVs to a dependent variable Y. It was presented in Fig. 3.3.1 for single IVs X_1 and X_2, and we present it as Fig. 5.4.1 here for sets A and B. It is changed in no essential regard, and we show how the relationships of sets of IVs to Y, expressed as proportions of Y variance, are directly analogous to similarly expressed relationships of single IVs.

A circle in a ballantine represents the total variance of a variable, and the overlap of two such circles represents shared variance or squared correlation. This seems reasonable enough for single variables, but what does it mean when we attach the set designation A to such a circle? What does the variance of a set of multiple variables mean? Although each of the k_A variables has its own variance, remember that a multiple $R^2_{Y.12...k}$ is in fact a simple r^2 between Y and $\hat{Y}$, the latter optimally estimated from the regression equation of the k_A IVs that make up set A (and similarly for set B—i.e., $\hat{Y}_B$—or any other set of IVs). Thus, by treating a set in terms of how it bears on Y, we effectively reduce it to a single variable. This lies at the core of the generalizability of the ballantine from single IVs to sets of IVs.

The ballantine in Fig. 5.4.1 presents the general case: A and B share variance with Y, but also with each other.[14] This is, of course, the critical distinction between MRC and the standard

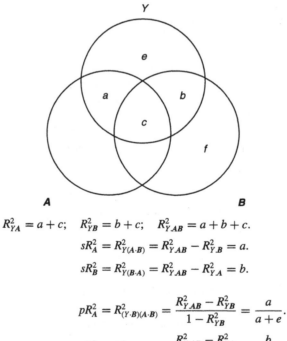

$$R^2_{YA} = a + c; \quad R^2_{YB} = b + c; \quad R^2_{Y.AB} = a + b + c.$$

$$sR^2_A = R^2_{Y(A \cdot B)} = R^2_{Y.AB} - R^2_{Y.B} = a.$$

$$sR^2_B = R^2_{Y(B \cdot A)} = R^2_{Y.AB} - R^2_{Y.A} = b.$$

$$pR^2_A = R^2_{(Y \cdot B)(A \cdot B)} = \frac{R^2_{Y.AB} - R^2_{YB}}{1 - R^2_{YB}} = \frac{a}{a + e}.$$

$$pR^2_B = R^2_{(Y \cdot A)(B \cdot A)} = \frac{R^2_{Y.AB} - R^2_{YA}}{1 - R^2_{YA}} = \frac{b}{b + e}.$$

FIGURE 5.4.1   The ballantine for sets A and B.

---

[14]It can be proved that the correlation between A and B, where each is scored by using the equation that predicts Y from the variables within that set, is given by

(5.4.2)
$$r_{\hat{Y}_A \hat{Y}_B} = \frac{\sum \beta_i \beta_j r_{ij}}{R_{YA} R_{YB}}$$

where i indexes an X_i in set A, j indexes an X_j in set B, and the summation is taken over all i, j pairs (of which there are $k_A k_B$).

orthogonal analysis of variance. In an $A \times B$ factorial design ANOVA, the requirement of proportional cell frequencies makes A and B (specifically $\hat{Y}_A$ and $\hat{Y}_B$) uncorrelated with each other; therefore the A and B circles do not overlap each other, and each accounts for a separate and distinguishable (that is, additive) portion of the Y variance. This is also what makes the computation simpler in ANOVA than in MRC.

The ballantine allows proportions of variance (i.e., squared correlations of various kinds) to be represented as ratios of the corresponding areas of the circle to the whole area of Y, as we saw in Section 3.3. The total variance of Y is taken to equal unity (or 100%) and the Y circle is divided into four distinct areas identified by the letters a, b, c, and e. Because overlap represents shared variance or squared correlation, we can see immediately from Fig. 5.4.1 that set A overlaps Y in areas a and c; hence

$$(5.4.3) \qquad R^2_{YA} = \frac{YA \text{ overlap}}{sd^2_Y} = \frac{a+c}{1} = a+c.$$

The c area arises inevitably from the AB overlap, just as it did in the single IV ballantine in Section 3.3, and is conceptually identical with it. It designates the part of the Y circle jointly overlapped by A and B, because

$$(5.4.4) \qquad R^2_{YB} = \frac{YB \text{ overlap}}{sd^2_Y} = \frac{b+c}{1} = b+c.$$

Because the c area is part of both A's and B's overlap with Y, for sets, as for single IVs, it is clear that (for the general case, where $\hat{Y}_A$ and $\hat{Y}_B$ are correlated) the proportion of Y variance accounted for by sets A and B together is not simply the sum of their separate contributions, because area c would then be counted twice, but rather

$$(5.4.5) \qquad R^2_{Y.AB} = \frac{a+b+c}{1} = a+b+c.$$

Thus, the areas a and b represent the proportions of Y variance uniquely accounted for respectively by set A and set B. By uniquely we mean relative to the other set, thus area b is Y variance not accounted for by set A, but only by set B; the reverse is true for area a.

This idea of unique variance in Y for a set is directly analogous to the unique variance of a single IV discussed in Chapter 3. There we saw that for X_i, the unique variance in Y is the squared semipartial correlation of Y with X_i, which in abbreviated notation we called sr^2_i. It was shown literally to be the r^2 between that part of X_i that could not be estimated from the other IVs and all of Y, the complete cumbersome notation for which is $r^2_{Y(i \cdot 12...(i)...k)}$, the inner parentheses signifying omission. For a set B, we similarly define its unique variance in Y to be the squared *multiple* semipartial correlation of B with the part of Y that is not estimable from A, or $1 - \hat{Y}_A$. Its literal notation would be $R^2_{Y(B \cdot A)}$, or, even more simply, sR^2_B. In the latter notation, Y is understood, as is the other set (or sets) being partialed. (Obviously, all the above holds when A and B are interchanged.)

The Semipartial R^2

The ballantine may again make this visually clear. "That part of B which is not estimable from A" is represented by the part of the B circle not overlapped by the A circle, that is, the combined area made up of b and f. That area overlaps with the (complete) Y circle only in area b, therefore the proportion of the total Y variance accounted for uniquely by set B is

$$(5.4.6) \qquad sR^2_B = R^2_{Y(B \cdot A)} = \frac{b}{1} = b.$$

and, by symmetry, the proportion of Y variance accounted for uniquely by set A is

(5.4.7)
$$sR_A^2 = R_{Y(A \cdot B)}^2 = \frac{a}{1} = a.$$

The ballantine shows how these quantities can be computed. If $R_{Y \cdot AB}^2$ is area $a + b + c$ (Eq. 5.4.5) and $R_{Y \cdot A}^2$ is area $a + c$ (Eq. 5.4.3), then patently

$$b = (a + b + c) - (a + c),$$
(5.4.8)
$$sR_B^2 = R_{Y \cdot AB}^2 - R_{YB}^2.$$

The sR^2 can readily be found by subtracting from the R^2 for both sets the R^2 for the set to be partialed.

It is not necessary to provide for the case of more than two sets of IVs in the ballantine,[15] or, indeed, in the preceding equations. Because the result of the aggregation of any number of sets is itself a set, these equations are self-generalizing. Thus, if the unique variance in Y for set B among a group of sets is of interest, we can simply designate the sets other than B collectively as set A, and find sR_B^2 from Eq. (5.4.8). This principle is applied successively as each set is added in the hierarchical analysis, each added set being designated B relative to the aggregate of prior sets, designated A. We shall see that this framework neatly accommodates both significance testing and power analysis.

We offer one more bit of notation, which, although not strictly necessary, will be found convenient later on in various applications of hierarchical analysis. In the latter, the addition of a new set B (or single IV X_i) results in an increase in R^2 (strictly, a nondecrease). These increases are, of course, the sR_B^2 (or sr_i^2), as already noted. It is a nuisance in presenting such statistics, particularly in tables, to always specify all the prior sets or single IVs that are partialed. Because in hierarchical MRC the hierarchy of sets (or single IVs) is explicit, we will have occasion to identify such sR_B^2 (or sr_i^2) as increments to Y variance at the stage of the hierarchy where B (or X_i) enters.

The Partial R^2

We have already identified the overlap of that part of a set circle that is unique (e.g., areas $b + f$ of set B) with the total Y circle as a squared multiple *semi*partial correlation (e.g., $sR_B^2 = R_{Y(B \cdot A)}^2$ = area b). With sets as with single IVs, it is a *semi*partial because we have related the partialed $B \cdot A$ with all of Y. We wrote it as $b/1$ in Eq. (5.4.6) to make it explicit that we were assessing the unique variance b as a proportion of the *total* Y variance of 1. We can however also relate the partialed $B \cdot A$ with the *partialed* Y, that is, we can assess the unique b variance as a proportion not of the total Y variance, but of that part of the Y variance not estimable by set A, actually $Y - \hat{Y}_A$. The result is that we have defined the squared multiple partial correlation as

(5.4.9)
$$pR_B^2 = R_{(Y \cdot A)(B \cdot A)}^2 = \frac{b}{b + e}$$

and symmetrically for set A as

(5.4.10)
$$pR_A^2 = R_{(Y \cdot B)(A \cdot B)}^2 = \frac{a}{a + e}.$$

---

[15] A fortunate circumstance, because the complete representation of three sets would require a three-dimensional ballantine and, generally, the representation of h sets, an h-dimensional ballantine.

Thus, sR^2 and pR^2 (as sr^2 and pr^2) differ in the base to which they relate the unique variance as a proportion: sR^2 takes as its base the total Y variance whereas pR^2 takes as its base that proportion of the Y variance not accounted for by the other set(s). Inevitably, with its base smaller than (or at most equal to) 1, pR^2 will be larger than (or at least equal to) sR^2 for any given set.

It is easy enough to compute the pR^2. We have seen how, for example, the b area is found by [Eq. (5.4.8)]; the combined areas $b + e$ constitute the Y variance not accounted for by set A, hence $1 - R^2_{Y.A}$. Substituting in Eq. (5.4.9),

(5.4.11)
$$pR^2_B = \frac{b}{b + e} = \frac{R^2_{Y.AB} - R^2_{YA}}{1 - R^2_{YA}},$$

and, symmetrically,

(5.4.12)
$$pR^2_A = \frac{a}{a + e} = \frac{R^2_{Y.AB} - R^2_{YB}}{1 - R^2_{YB}}.$$

To illustrate the distinction between sR^2 and pR^2, we refer to the example of the hierarchy of sets of demographics (D), illness (I), and hospitals (H) in relationship to length of hospital stay (Y) of Section 5.3.2. $R^2_{Y.D} = .20$, and when I is added, $R^2_{Y.DI} = .22$. The increment was .02; hence, $sR^2_I = .02$, that is, 2% of the *total* Y variance is uniquely (relative to D) accounted for by I. But if we ask "what proportion of the variance of Y not accounted for by D is uniquely accounted for by I?" our base is not the total Y variance, but only $1 - R^2_{YD} = 1 - .20 = .80$ of it, and the answer is $pR^2_I = .02/.80 = .025$. Letting $D = A$ and $I = B$, we have simply substituted in Eqs. (5.4.7) and (5.4.11).

It was also found that the further addition of H resulted in $R^2_{Y.DIH} = .33$. Thus, H accounted for an additional .11 of the *total* Y variance, hence $sR^2_H = .11$. If we shift our base from total Y variance to Y variance not already accounted for by D and I, the relevant proportion is $.11/(1 - .22) = .141$ (i.e., pR^2_H). Now letting sets $D + I = A$, and $H = B$, we again have simply substituted in Eqs. (5.4.7) and (5.4.11). Any desired combination of sets can be created: If we wished to combine I and H into set B, with $D = A$, we could determine that $sR^2_{IH} = .13$, and $pR^2_{IH} = .13/(1 - .20) = .162$, by the same equations.

It is worth noting that the pR^2 is rather in the spirit of ANCOVA. In ANCOVA, the variance due to the covariates is removed from Y and the effects of research factors are assessed with regard to this adjusted (partialed) Y variance. Thus, in the latter example, D and I may be considered to be covariates whose function is to "equate" the hospitals, so that they may be compared for length of stay, free of any possible hospital differences in the D and I of their patients. In that spirit, we are interested only in the $1 - R^2_{Y.DI}$ portion of the Y variance, and the pR^2_H takes as its base the .78 of the Y variance *not* associated with D and I; hence, $pR^2_H = .11/.78 = .141$ of this adjusted (or partialed, or residual) variance is the quantity of interest.

5.4.4 *B* and β Coefficients for Variables Within Sets

As we have noted, the strongest scientific inferences are likely to come from an examination of raw or standardized regression coefficients. When variables are treated in sets, attention to these coefficients is still indicated. To understand these issues, let us first attend to the influence of other variables in the same set on B and β. We will assume that a functional set is being examined, that is, that there is some theoretical role shared by the variables in the set, such as control for spurious effects, or representation of a set of related concepts. Effects of other variables in a categorical set are discussed in Chapters 9 and 10.

It is usually the case that members of functional sets are at least somewhat correlated. Thus, the fundamental principal that regression coefficients reflect the influence of a variable net of the influence (controlling for or ceteris paribus) of all other variables in the equation, applies equally to other IVs in the same set and those in other sets. When the correlations among the variables in a set are relatively large, it can happen that no individual variable is significantly related to Y even when the set as a whole accounts for a large and statistically significant proportion of the Y variance. In such a case we will find large SEs on at least some Bs and βs, relative to zero-order SEs on the bivariate r_{Yi} or B_{yi}.[16] We will discuss this problem at the end of this chapter in a section on balancing Type I and Type II errors (Section 5.7.1). In the present discussion it will suffice for the reader to keep firmly in mind that each of these coefficients is indicating the effect of the individual variables net of others in the set (as well as any variables in other sets that are also in the equation).

As noted earlier, sometimes the causal hierarchical ordering of functional sets cannot be unambiguously asserted. It is not infrequent that variable sets are created to represent domains of influence on Y that may best be thought of as also influencing one another. For example, a previous illustration presented an analysis of the influence of demographic and person-ality differences of patients in different hospitals on length of hospital stay. Suppose we wanted to add to this analysis a set of variables representing the functional impairment of patients (e.g., competence in activities of daily living, reliability and tenure in occupational settings, ability to relate to and care for others). We may now feel ourselves to be in the all-too-frequent position of ambiguity as to whether the personality (symptom) set or the impairment set should be considered causally prior, and thus added to the equation at an earlier point.

A common practice in such a situation is to examine differences in the estimated regression coefficients (as well as sR^2) when the hierarchical ordering is altered. Again, it is also useful to attend to changes in the SEs for these individual partial coefficients, because, as was shown in Eq. (3.6.1), they are enlarged by the multiple correlation of the variable in question with other variables in the equation.

Area c

Finally, returning once more to the ballantine for sets (Fig. 5.4.1), we call the reader's attention to area c, the double overlap of sets A and B in Y. It is conceptually the same as the area c in the ballantine for single IVs (Fig. 3.3.1) and shares its problems. Although in the ballantine it occupies an area, unlike the areas a, b, and e it *cannot* be understood to be a proportion of Y variance, because, unlike these other areas, it may take on a negative value as discussed in Section 3.3. Note that it is never properly interpreted as a proportion of variance, whether or not in any given application it is found to be positive, because we cannot alter the fundamental conception of what a statistic means as a function of its algebraic sign in a particular problem. Because variance is sd^2, a negative quantity leads to sd being an imaginary number, for example, $\sqrt{-.10}$, a circumstance we simply cannot tolerate. Better to let area c stand as a useful metaphor that reflects the fact that $R^2_{Y.AB}$ is not equal in general to $R^2_{YA} + R^2_{YB}$, but may be either smaller (positive c) or larger (negative c) than the sum. When area c is negative for sets A and B, we have exactly the same relationship of suppression between the two sets as was described for pairs of single IVs in Section 3.4.

---

[16]Note, too, the discussion of this issue in Section 4.5.3.

5.5 SIGNIFICANCE TESTING FOR SETS

We have seen that the addition of a set of variables B to a set A results in an increment in the Y variance accounted for by $R^2_{Y.AB} - R^2_{YA}(= sR^2_B)$, represented by the area b in the ballantine (Fig. 5.4.1). This quantity is properly called an increment because it is not mathematically possible for it to be negative, because $R^2_{Y.AB}$ cannot be smaller than R^2_{YA}.[17]

Our interest, of course, is not in the characteristics of the sample for which these values are determined as such but rather in those of the population from which it comes. Our mechanism of statistical inference posits the null (nil) hypothesis to the effect that in the population, there is literally no increment in Y variance accounted for when B is added to A, that is, that $R^2_{Y.AB} - R^2_{YA} = 0$ in the population. When this null hypothesis is rejected, we conclude that set B does account for Y variance beyond that accounted for by set A in the population. This null hypothesis may be tested by means of

$$(5.5.1) \qquad F = \frac{(R^2_{Y.AB} - R^2_{YA})/k_B}{(1 - R^2_{Y.AB})/(n - k_A - k_B - 1)}$$

for the source (numerator) $df = k_B$, the error (denominator) $df = n - k_A - k_B - 1$, and referred to the F tables in the appendices (Appendix Tables D.1 and D.2).

This formula is applied repeatedly in varying contexts throughout this book, and its structure is worth some comment. Both the numerator and denominator are proportions of Y variance divided by their respective df; thus both are "normalized" mean squares. The numerator is the normalized mean square for unique B variance (area b of the ballantine) and the denominator is the normalized mean square for a particular estimate of error (i.e., $1 - R^2_{Y.AB}$), that represents Y variation accounted for by neither A nor B (area e of the ballantine). F is the ratio of these mean squares and, when the null hypothesis is true, has an expected value of about one. When F is sufficiently large to meet the significance criterion, as determined by reference to Appendix Tables D.1 and D.2, the null hypothesis is rejected.[18]

For computational purposes Eq. (5.5.1) can be somewhat simplified:

$$(5.5.2A) \qquad F = \frac{R^2_{Y.AB} - R^2_{YA}}{1 - R^2_{Y.AB}} \times \frac{n - k_A - k_B - 1}{k_B}$$

(for $df = k_B, n - k_A - k_B - 1$, as before). F may equivalently be determined by means of the regression sums of squares (SS) and mean squares usually provided by the computer output. The numerator for F for the increment equals the difference between the regression SS for the equation including A and B and the regression SS for the equation including only A, divided by the df for B. The denominator equals the residual MS for the equation with both A and B. Thus:

$$(5.5.2B) \qquad F = \frac{(\text{Regression SS}_{AB} - \text{Regression SS}_A)/df_B}{\text{Residual MS}_{AB}}$$

When there are additional IV sets to be considered this method is referred to as employing Model 1 error. An alternative strategy is to use the residual MS from the equation that includes all sets, with error df equal to the df for that term. Such a strategy may be considered to employ Model 2 error in the significance tests.

---

[17]This proposition does not hold for R^2 corrected for shrinkage, that is, $\tilde{R}^2_{Y.AB} - \tilde{R}^2_{Y.A}$ may be negative. This will occur whenever the F of Eq. (5.5.1) is less than one.

[18]Readers who know ANOVA will find this all familiar. But the reasoning and structure are not merely analogous but rather mathematically identical, because ANOVA and MRC are applications of the OLS model.

5.5.1 Application in Hierarchical Analysis

To illustrate the application of this formula, let us return to the study presented in the previous sections on the length of stay of 500 hospital admissions, using demographic ($D, k_D = 9$), illness ($I, k_I = 10$), and hospital ($H, k_H = 7$) sets in that hierarchical order. We let A be the set(s) to be partialed and B the set(s) whose unique variance in Y is posited as zero by the null hypothesis. Table 5.5.1 organizes the ingredients of the computation to facilitate the exposition.

The null hypothesis that with D partialed (holding demographic characteristics constant) I accounts for no Y variance in the population is appraised as follows (Table 5.5.1, Example 1). It was given that $R^2_{YD} = .20$ and $R^2_{Y.DI} = .22$, an increase of .02. To use Eq. (5.5.2), call I set B and D set A. For $n = 500, k_B = 10, k_A = 9$, we find

$$F = \frac{.22 - .02}{1 - .22} \times \frac{500 - 9 - 10 - 1}{10} = 1.231,$$

which for df of 10 ($= k_B$) and 480 ($= n - k_A - k_B - 1$) fails to be significant at the $\alpha = .05$ level (the criterion value for $df = 10, 400$ is 1.85, Appendix Table D.2). The increase of .02 of the Y variance accounted for by I over D in the sample is thus consistent with there being no increase in the population.

In Example 2 of Table 5.5.1, we test the null hypothesis that the addition of H (which we will now call set B, so $k_B = 7$) to the sets D and I (which together we will call set A, so $k_A = 9 + 10 = 19$) results in no increase in Y variance in the population. Because $R^2_{Y.DIH} = .33$ and $R^2_{Y.DI} = .22$ (and hence $sR^2_H = .11$), substituting the values for sets A and B as redefined we find

$$F = \frac{.33 - .22}{1 - .33} \times \frac{500 - 19 - 7 - 1}{7} = 11.094,$$

TABLE 5.5.1
Illustrative F Tests Using Model 1 Error

$R^2_{YD} = .20; R^2_{Y.IH} = .18; R^2_{YI} = .03; R^2_{Y.DI} = .22; R^2_{Y.DH} = .32; R^2_{YH} = .17; R^2_{Y.DIH} = .33.$

Example	Set B	k_B	Set A	k_A	$R^2_{Y.AB}$	$R^2_{Y.A}$	$R^2_{Y(B \cdot A)}$ $= sR^2_B$	Error $1 - R^2_{Y.AB}$	Source df	Error df	F
1	I	10	D	9	.22	.20	.02	.78	10	480	1.23
2	H	7	D,I	19	.33	.22	.11	.67	7	473	11.09
3	I,H	17	D	9	.33	.20	.13	.67	17	473	5.40
4	D	9	I,H	17	.33	.18	.15	.67	9	473	11.77
5	I	10	D,H	16	.33	.32	.01	.67	10	473	.71
6	D	9	I	10	.22	.03	.19	.78	9	480	12.99
7	D	9	H	7	.32	.17	.15	.68	9	483	11.84
8	H	7	D	9	.32	.20	.12	.68	7	483	12.18
9	I	10	H	7	.18	.17	.01	.82	10	482	.59
10	H	7	I	10	.18	.03	.15	.82	7	482	12.60
11	D	9	—	0	.20	0	.20	.80	9	490	13.61
12	I	10	—	0	.03	0	.03	.97	10	489	1.51
13	H	7	—	0	.17	0	.17	.83	7	492	14.40

$$F = \frac{R^2_{Y.AB} - R^2_{Y.A}}{R^2_{Y.AB}} \times \frac{n - k_A - k_B - 1}{k_B},$$

with source (numerator) $df = k_B$, error I (denominator) $df = n - k_A - k_B - 1$.

which for $df = 7,473$ is highly significant, because the criterion F at $\alpha = .01$ for $df\ 7,400$ is 2.69 (Appendix Table D.1).

It was pointed out in Section 5.4.4 that our appraisal of this .11 increment by H over D and I constitutes the equivalent of an ANCOVA with the 19 IVs of the combined D and I sets as covariates. Indeed, hierarchical MRC may be viewed as equivalent to a series of ANCOVAs, at each stage of which all prior sets are covariates (because they are partialed), whereas the set just entered is the research factor whose effects are under scrutiny. The set just entered may itself be an aggregate of sets. Although it would not likely be of substantive interest in this research, Example 3 of Table 5.5.1 illustrates the F test for the aggregate of I and H (as set B) with D (as set A) partialed.

5.5.2 Application in Simultaneous Analysis

The F test of Eqs. (5.5.1) and (5.5.2) is also applicable in simultaneous analysis. The latter simply means that, given h sets, we are interested in appraising the variance of one of them with all the remaining $h-1$ sets partialed. Whereas in the hierarchical model only higher-order (prior) sets are partialed, in the absence of a clear rationale for such a hierarchy it is all other sets that are partialed. For this application of the F test we designate B as the unique source of variance under scrutiny and aggregate the remaining sets that are to be partialed into set A.

Let us reconsider the running example of length of stay (Y) as a function of D, I, and H, but now propose that our interest is one of appraising the unique Y variance accounted for by each set. No hierarchy is intended, so by "unique" to a set we mean relative to all (here, both) other sets (i.e., D relative to I and H, I relative to D and H, and H relative to D and I). To proceed, we need some additional R^2 values not previously given in this problem: $R^2_{Y.IH} = .18$ and $R^2_{Y.DH} = .32$.

To determine the unique contribution of D relative to I and H, one simply finds $R^2_{Y.DIH} - R^2_{Y.IH} = .33 - .18 = .15 = R^2_{Y(D.IH)}$, the sR^2_D with both I and H partialed. This quantity might be of focal interest to a sociologist in that it represents the proportion of variance in length of stay of patients associated with differences in their demographic (D) characteristics, the latter freed of any illness differences (I) and differences in admitting hospitals (H) associated with D. This .15 is a sample quantity, and Example 4 (Table 5.5.1) treats D as set B and aggregates I and H as set A for substitution in Eq. (5.5.2):

$$F = \frac{.33 - .18}{1 - .33} \times \frac{500 - 17 - 9 - 1}{9} = 11.766,$$

which is statistically significant because the criterion F at $\alpha = .01$ for $df = 9,400$ is 2.45 (Appendix Table D.1). Note, incidentally, that this example simply reverses the roles of D and I, H of Example 3.

The unique variance contribution of I relative to D and H is tested without further elaboration as Example 5. This might be of particular interest to a clinical psychologist or personality measurement specialist interested in controlling demographic variables and systematic differences between hospitals in assessing the relationship of illness to length of stay. The last of this series, the Y variance associated with $H \cdot DI$, has already been presented and discussed as Example 2.

Thus, the investigator's choice of what to partial from what is determined by the logic and purpose of the inquiry. For specificity, assume that the h sets are partitioned into three groups of sets as follows: the groups whose unique source is under scrutiny is, as before, designated set B, the covariate group to be partialed from B (again as before) constitutes set A, but now the remaining set(s) constitute a group to be ignored, which we designate set C. All we are doing with this scheme is making explicit the obvious fact that not all sets of IVs on which there are data in an investigation need to be active participants in each phase of the analysis. Indeed, the (fully) hierarchical analysis with h sets is simply a predefined sequence of simultaneous analyses in the first of which a prespecified $h - 1$ sets are ignored, in the second a prespecified $h - 2$ sets are ignored, and, generally, in the jth of which a prespecified $h - j$ sets are ignored until finally, in the last of which, none is ignored. The analysis at each stage is simultaneous—all IVs in the equation at that stage are being partialed from each other. Thus, a single simultaneous analysis with all other sets partialed and a strictly hierarchical progression of analyses may be viewed as end points of a continuum of analytic possibilities. A flexible application of MRC permits the selection of some intermediate possibilities when they are dictated by the causal theory and logic of the given research investigation.

5.5.3 Using Computer Output to Determine Statistical Significance

Of course, current data analysts are likely to accept the statistical tests presented by the computer output. In some programs it is possible to specify a set of variables the contribution of which to R^2 is to be evaluated. If such an option is not available, the computer-provided output for various sets and combinations of sets of variables may be employed in Eq. (5.5.2A or B).

In Chapter 3 we saw that the partialed statistics of a single IV, X_i (i.e., sr_i, pr_i, B_i, and β_i) all shared equivalent null (nil) hypotheses and hence the same t test for the same $df = n - k - 1$. Conceptually, this can be explained as due to the fact that when any one of these coefficients equals zero, they all must necessarily equal zero.

For any set B, the same identity in significance tests holds for sR_B^2 and pR_B^2 (hence for sR_B and pR_B). Recall that these are both unique proportions of Y variance, the first to the base unity and the second to the base $1 - R_{Y.A}^2$. In terms of areas of the ballantine for sets (Fig. 5.5.1), $sR_B^2 = b$, and $pR_B^2 = b/(b + e)$. But the null hypothesis posits that area b is zero, hence $pR_B^2 = 0$. Whether one reports sR_B^2 as was done in Table 5.5.1, or divides it by $1 - R_{Y.A}^2$ and reports pR_B^2, or reports both, the F test of Eq. (5.5.2) tests statistical significance of both sR_B^2 and pR_B^2 because the null hypothesis is the same.

One highly desired test is a comparison of the utility of two different sets of variables in predicting the same Y. Because determination of the standard errors of these coefficients and their difference is extremely complicated, involving the covariance among all predictor sets, it is not possible to calculate from the output ordinarily provided to the users of standard statistical programs. Olkin and Finn (1995) provide the test for the special case in which each of the sets consists of a single variable, which is itself complex. It is hoped that a solution to this problem will be found for variable sets and programmed in the next few years.

5.5.4 An Alternative F Test: Using Model 2 Error Estimate From the Final Model

An F test is a ratio of two mean square or variance estimates, the numerator associated with a source of Y variance being tested, and the denominator providing a reference amount in the form of an estimate of error or residual variance. In the previous section, identifying A and B as sets or set aggregates, the numerator source was $B \cdot A$, and the denominator contained $1 - R_{Y.AB}^2$ (area e of the ballantine; Fig. 5.4.1) thus treating all Y variance not accounted for by A and B as error in the F test of Eqs. (5.5.1) and (5.5.2). We later introduced the idea of a third set (or set of sets) C, whose modest purpose was "to be ignored." Not only was it ignored in that it was not partialed from B in defining $B \cdot A$ as the source for the numerator, but it was ignored in that whatever Y variance it might uniquely contribute was not included in $R^2_{Y.AB}$ and therefore was part of the error, $1 - R^2_{Y.AB}$.

These two ways of ignoring C are conceptually quite distinct and may be considered independently. We obviously have the option of not partialing whatever we do not wish to partial from B. Presumably the source of variance in the numerator is precisely what the theory and logic of the investigation dictates it to be (i.e., $B \cdot A$ and not $B \cdot AC$). We may either choose or not choose to ignore C in defining the error term. The first choice, Model 1 error uses $1 - R^2_{Y.AB}$ in the F test of Eqs. (5.5.1) and (5.5.2) and thus ignores C. The alternative, Model 2 error, defines an F ratio for $B \cdot A$ that removes whatever additional unique Y variance can be accounted for by C from the error term, resulting in the following error term and associated df, expressed here both in terms of the various R^2 values (proportions of variance) and in terms of the SS and error MS from various equations:

$$(5.5.3) \qquad F = \frac{(R^2_{Y.AB} - R^2_{YA})/k_B}{(1 - R^2_{Y.ABC})/(n - k - 1)} = \frac{(SS_{Y.AB} - SS_{YA})/k_B}{\text{error } MS_{ABC}/(n - k - 1)}$$

where k is the total number of IVs in all sets, that is, $k = k_A + k_B + k_C$ or equivalently,

$$(5.5.4) \qquad F = \frac{(R^2_{Y.AB} - R^2_{YA})}{(1 - R^2_{Y.ABC})} \times \frac{n - k - 1}{k_B},$$

with numerator $df = k_B$, and error $df = n - k - 1$. Note that, as with the F that considers only the sets already entered, this tests both sR^2_B and pR^2_B. The standard F tables (Appendix Tables D.1 and D.2) are used. Of course, although we have discussed Model 2 error in the context of the hierarchical analysis of sets of IVs, any set may consist of a single variable, and the procedure may thus be employed equally appropriately in the case of the determination of statistical significance for a single IV.

Which model to choose? One view notes that because the removal of additional Y variance associated uniquely with C serves to produce a smaller and "purer" error term, one should generally prefer Model 2 error. But although $1 - R^2_{Y.ABC}$ will always be smaller (strictly, not larger) than $1 - R^2_{Y.AB}$ and hence operate so as to increase F, one must pay the price of the reduction of the error df by k_C, that is from $n - k_A - k_B - 1$ of Eq. (5.5.2) to $n - k_A - k_B - k_C - 1$ of Eq. (5.5.4), which clearly operates to decrease F. In addition, as error df diminish, the criterion F ratio for significance increases and sample estimates become less stable, seriously so when the diminished error df are absolutely small. The competing factors of reducing proportion of error variance and reducing error df, depending on their magnitudes, may either increase or decrease the F using Model 2 error relative to the F using Model 1 error.

We can illustrate both possibilities with the running example (Table 5.5.1), comparing Model 1 F (Eq. 5.5.2) with Model 2 F (Eq. 5.5.4). If, in testing $I \cdot D$ in Example 1, instead of using Model 1 error, $1 - R^2_{Y.DM} = .78$ with 480 ($= 500 - 9 - 10 - 1$) df, we use Model 2 error, $1 - R^2_{Y.DMH} = .67$ with 473 ($= 500 = 9 - 10 - 7 - 1$) df, F increases to 1.412 from 1.231 (neither significant). On the other hand, shifting to Model 2 error in testing $D \cdot H$ in Example 7 brings F down from 11.838 to 11.766 (both significant at $p < .01$).

In Table 5.5.1 the F ratios of the two models differ little and nowhere lead to different decisions about the null hypothesis. But before one jumps to the conclusion that the choice makes little or no difference in general, certain characteristics of this example should be noted and discussed, particularly the relatively large n, the fact that there are only three sets, and that two of these (D and H) account uniquely for relatively large proportions of variance. If n were much smaller, the differences of k_C loss in error df in Model 2 could substantially reduce the size and significance of F, particularly in the case where we let I be set C: the addition of I to D and H results in only a quite small decrease in error variance, specifically from $1 - R^2_{Y.DH} = .68$ to $1 - R^2_{Y.DHM} = .67$. If n were 100, the drop in error df from Model 1 to Model 2 would be from 83 to 73. Example 7, which tests $D \cdot H$ would yield a significant Model 1 $F = 2.034$ ($df = 9, 83, p < .05$), but a nonsignificant Model 2 $F = 1.816$ ($df = 9, 73$).

Further, consider the consequence of Model 2 error when the number of sets, and therefore the number of sets in C and, particularly, k_C is large. Many behavioral science investigations can easily involve upward of a dozen sets, so that collectively C may include many IVs and thus df. The optimal strategy in such circumstances may be to order the sets from those judged a priori to be most important to those judged to contribute least, or least confidently judged to account for Y variance, and use Model 1 error. Using the latter successively at each level of the hierarchy, the lower-order sets are ignored and, although their (likely small) contribution to reducing the proportion of error variance is given up, their large contribution to the error df is retained.

On the other hand, if sets are few and powerful in accounting uniquely for Y variance, Model 1 error will contain important sources of variance due to the ignored C, and may well sharply negatively bias (reduce) F at a relatively small gain in error df. No simple advice can be offered on the choice between error models in hierarchical analysis of MRC. In general, large n, few sets, small k, and sets whose sR^2 are large move us toward a preference for Model 2 error. One is understandably uneasy with the prospect of not removing from the Model 1 error the variability due to a set suspected a priori of having a large sR^2 (e.g., Examples 9 through 13) during the planning of an investigation, which ideally is when it should be made. Unfortunately, because most computer programs do not offer Model 2 error as an option, the data analyst who relies completely on the program-produced tests of statistical significance will necessarily be using Model 1 error.

5.6 POWER ANALYSIS FOR SETS

In Chapters 2 and 3 we focused on the precision of estimates and the statistical power for detecting differences from various null hypotheses for the relationship, zero-order or partial, between a single IV and Y. In determining the power against the null hypothesis of no contribution to the Y variance in the population for a set of variables, we will again generally use a computer program to determine:

1. The power of the F test of significance for partialed sets, given the sample size (n), k, the significance criterion (α), and the effect size (ES), an alternative to the null (nil) hypothetical value for the population. This ES is a ratio of two variances, that due to the predictor(s) being considered (sR^2_B), and the error variance ($1 - R^2_Y$).
2. The necessary sample size (n^*) for the significance test of a set involving k variables, given the desired power, α, and the alternate hypothetical value for the contribution to R^2, relative to the null hypothesis of no population effect.

Assume that an investigation is being planned in which at some point the proportion of Y variance accounted for by a set B, over and above that accounted for by a set A, will be determined. We have seen that this critically important quantity is $R^2_{Y.AB} - R^2_{YA}$ and has variously and equivalently been identified as the increment due to B, the squared multiple semipartial correlations for B (sR^2_B or $R^2_{Y(B \cdot A)}$) and as area b in the ballantine for sets (Fig. 5.4.1). This sample quantity will then be tested for significance, that is, the status of the null hypothesis that its value in the population is zero will be determined by means of an F test.

5.6.1 Determining n^* for the F Test of sR_B^2 with Model 1 or Model 2 Error

As was the case for determining n^* for an F test on $R_{Y.12...k}^2$ (Section 3.7), the procedure for determining n^* for an F test on $sR_B^2 = R_{Y.AB}^2 - R_{YA}^2$ proceeds with the following steps:

1. Set the significance criterion to be used, α.
2. Set desired power for the F test.
3. Identify the number of IVs to be included in Set A, in Set B, and, if Model 2 error is to be used, in Set C.
4. Identify the alternate hypothetical ES in the population for which n^* is to be determined, that is, the population sR_B^2.
5. Identify the anticipated error variance, that is, $(1 - R_{Y.AB}^2)$ for Model 1 or $(1 - R_{Y.ABC}^2)$ for Model 2 error.

If a computer power analysis program is used to determine n^*, these values are entered into the program and the necessary n^* is read out. If the computation is done by hand, the next step is to look up the value of L for the given k_B (row) and desired power (column) in a table for the selected α (Appendix Table E.1 or E.2). One then determines the ES index f^2, which is the ratio of the variances determined in steps 4 and 5. In determining n^* to test $R_{Y.AB}^2 - R_{YA}^2$ using Model 1 error,

$$(5.6.1) \qquad f^2 = \frac{R_{Y.AB}^2 - R_{YA}^2}{1 - R_{Y.AB}^2},$$

or, using Model 2 error,

$$(5.6.2) \qquad f^2 = \frac{R_{Y.AB}^2 - R_{Y.A}^2}{1 - R_{Y.ABC}^2}.$$

We remind the reader that these R^2s are alternate hypothetical values referring to the population, *not* sample values. When the same ratio for *sample* values is combined with the *df*, the formulas are equivalent to those for F [Eqs. (5.5.1) and (5.5.3)]. This occurs after there *is* a sample, whereas in the planning taking place *before* the investigation the formulation is "*if* f^2 is thus and such in the population, given α and the desired probability of rejecting the null, what n^* do I need?" To estimate this one draws on past experience in the research area, theory, intuition, or conventional values to answer the questions "What additional proportion of Y variance do I expect B to account for beyond A? (the numerator), and "What proportion of Y variance will no be accounted for by A or B, or not by A or B or C"? (the denominators for Model 1 and Model 2 error, respectively). The values from these steps are then substituted in

$$(5.6.3) \qquad n^* = \frac{L}{f^2} + k_A + k_B + 1$$

for Model 1 error, or

$$(5.6.4) \qquad n^* = \frac{L}{f^2} + k_A + k_B + k_C + 1$$

for Model 2 error. The result is the number of cases necessary to have the specified probability of rejecting the null hypothesis (power) at the α level of significance when f^2 in the population is as posited.

For illustration, we return to the running example, where length of stay of psychiatric admissions (Y) is studied as a function of sets of variables representing their demographic characteristics (D), their illness scores (I), and the hospitals where they were admitted (H) as described originally in Section 5.4.4. To this point this example has been discussed after the fact—results from a sample of 500 cases were presented and used to illustrate significance testing. Now we shift our perspective backward in time to illustrate the power analysis associated with the planning of this research.

In planning this investigation we know that we will eventually be testing the null hypothesis (among others) that I will account for no variance in Y beyond what is accounted for by D. Thus, I is the set B and D is the set that is partialed from B, set A, and this null hypothesis is that $R^2_{Y.DI} - R^2_{YD} = R^2_{Y.AB} - R^2_{YA} = 0$, to be tested with Model 1 error, $1 - R^2_{Y.DI} = 1 - R^2_{Y.AB}$ (that is, the test eventually performed as Example 1, Table 5.5.1). Assume that we intend to use as significance criterion $\alpha = .05$ (step 1) and that we wish the probability of rejecting this hypothesis (the power of the test) to be .90 (step 2). There are 9 variables in set D and 10 IVs in set I, so $k_B = 10$ (step 3). We estimate the actual population value for $sR^2_I = R^2_{Y.DI} - R^2_{YD} = .03$ and $R^2_{Y.DI} = .18$ (and hence, necessarily, $R^2_{YD} = .15$). If determining the necessary n^* by computer program, these values are entered and $n^* = 580$ is read out. For hand calculation from Eq. (5.6.1),

$$f^2 = \frac{.03}{1 - .18} = \frac{.03}{.82} = .0366$$

(step 4). Looking up the value for L in Appendix Table E.2 for $\alpha = .05$, in row $k_B = 10$, column power $= .90$, we find $L = 20.53$, and, solving Eq. (5.6.1) for

$$n^* = \frac{20.53}{.0366} + 9 + 10 + 1 = 581,$$

approximately the same value provided by the program.[19] Thus, if the unique Y variance of $I \cdot D$ in the population (sR^2_I) is .03, and Model 1 error is $1 - .18 = .82$, then in order to have a .90 probability of rejecting the null hypothesis at $\alpha = .05$, the sample should contain 581 cases. As was the case for single variables, lowering α, the desired power, or the number of variables will reduce the estimated number of cases required, whereas lowering the estimate of the population effect size, or the proportion of Y variance accounted for by other sets will increase the number of cases required.

What if we had decided to use Model 2 error? In this case we add an estimate of the (net) effect of differences among the hospitals on Y, length of stay, that is, estimate $R^2_{Y.DIH}$. Suppose we posit this value to be .25 so that Model 2 error is $1 - .25 = .75$. Therefore,

$$f^2 = \frac{.03}{1 - .25} = \frac{.03}{.75} = .04$$

from Eq. (5.6.2), which, of course, cannot be smaller than the f^2 for Model 1, which was .0366. Again, we either enter these values in the computer program or go on to look up L in the relevant Appendix Table E. We find $L = 20.53$, as it was for the Model 1 calculations. Solving Eq. (5.6.4), we find

$$n^* = \frac{20.53}{.04} + 9 + 10 + 7 + 1 = 540$$

[19]Hand calculation inevitably involves the use of tabled approximations, whereas the computer provides a more nearly exact value. Of course the degree of precision is adequate in either, as one can see by the crude approximation of the population ES that is necessary for these estimates.

for Model 2, compared with 581 for Model 1. In this case we found that n^* was smaller for Model 2 than for Model 1 for the same specifications. However, this case should not be overgeneralized, as we have already argued. The relative size of the n^* of the two models depends on how much reduction in the (alternate hypothetical) proportion of error variance occurs relative to the cost of df due to the addition of the k_C IVs of set C. Model 2 will require smaller n^* than Model 1 when sR_C^2 is large relative to k_C, but larger n^* than Model 1 when sR_C^2 is small relative to k_C. If, for example, we had posited $R_{Y \cdot DIH}^2$ to be .19, so that the Model 2 $f^2 = .03/(1 - .19) = .0370$. Solving Eq. (5.6.4), we find

$$n^* = \frac{20.53}{.037} + 9 + 10 + 7 + 1 = 582$$

as compared to 581 for Model 1. (The exact values provided by the computer program actually finds n^* to be equivalent in the two cases.) It is interesting to note that even when we posited that the differences between the eight hospitals uniquely accounted for only 1% of the Y variance, the Model 2 n^* was very close to the Model 1 n^*.

5.6.2 Estimating the Population sR^2 Values

The key decision required in the power analysis necessary for research planning in MRC, and generally the most difficult, is estimating the population ESs. One obviously cannot *know* the various population R^2 values, or the research would be unnecessary. Nevertheless, unless some estimates are made in advance, there is no rational basis for planning. Furthermore, unless they bear some reasonable resemblance to the true state of affairs in the population, sample sizes will be too large or (more often) too small, or, when sample sizes are not under the control of the researcher, the power of the research will be under- or (more often) overestimated.

The best way to proceed is to muster all one's resources of empirical knowledge, both hard and soft, about the substantive field of study and apply them, together with some insight into how magnitudes of phenomena are translated into proportions of variance, in order to make the estimates of the population R^2 values that are required. Some guidance may be obtained from a handbook of power analysis (J. Cohen, 1988), which proposed operational definitions or conventions that link qualitative adjectives to amounts of correlation broadly appropriate to the behavioral sciences. Translated into proportion of variance terms (r^2 or sr^2), these are "small," .01; "medium," .09; and "large," .25. The rationale for these quantities and cautions about their use are given by J. Cohen (1962, 1988).

One may think of f^2 as the approximate percentage of the Y variance *not* accounted for by the other variables (in the error term) that *is* accounted for by the set (**B**) under consideration. With some hesitation, we offer the following as a frame of reference: "small" = .02, "medium" = .15, and "large" = .35. Our hesitation arises from the following considerations. First, there is the general consideration of obvious diversity of the areas of study covered by the rubric "behavioral and social sciences." For example, what is large for a personality psychologist may well be small for a sociologist. The conventional values offered can only strike a rough average. Second, because we are required to estimate two or three distinct quantities (proportions of Y variance), their confection into a single quantity offers opportunities for judgment to go astray. Thus, what might be thought of as a medium-sized expected sR_B^2 (numerator) may well result in either a large or quite modest variance ratio, depending on whether the expected contributions to R^2 of sets A and C are small or large. Furthermore, 15% may be appropriately thought of as a "medium" ES in the context of 5 or 10 IVs in a set but seems too small when $k = 15$ or more, indicating that, on the average, these variables account for, at most $(.15/15 =) .01$ of the Y variance. Nevertheless, conventions have their uses, and the ones modestly offered here should serve to give the reader *some* sense of the ES to attach to these verbal formulations, particularly when it is hard to cope with estimating the population values themselves. The latter is, as we have said, the preferred route to determining power and sample size. For further discussion of this issue, see J. Cohen (1988, Chapters 8 and 9).

5.6.3 Setting Power for n^*

In the form of power analysis discussed thus far, we find the necessary sample size n^* for a given desired power (given also α and f^2). What power do we desire? If we follow our natural inclinations and set it quite large (say at .95 or .99), we quickly discover that except for very large f^2, n^* gets to be very large, often beyond our resources. (For example, in the first example of Section 5.6.1, the test of I, for $\alpha = .05$ and power $= .99$, n^* works out to be 905, about double what is required at power $= .80$) If we set power at a low value (say at .50 or .60), n^* is relatively small (for this example, at power $= .50$, $n^* = 271$), but we are not likely to be content to have only a 50-50 chance of rejecting the null hypothesis (when it is as false as we expect it to be).

The decision as to what power to set is a complex one. It depends upon the result of weighing the costs of failing to reject the null hypothesis (Type II error in statistical inference) against the costs of gathering and processing research data. The latter are usually not hard to estimate objectively, whereas the former include the costs of such imponderables as failing to advance knowledge, losing face, and editorial rejections, and of such painful ponderables as not getting continued research support from funding agencies. This weighing of costs is obviously unique to each investigation or even to each null hypothesis to be tested. This having been carefully done, the investigator can then formulate the power value desired.

Although there will be exceptions in special circumstances, most investigators choose some value in the .70 to .90 range. A value in the lower part of this range may seem reasonable when the dollar cost per case is large or when the more intangible cost of a Type II error in inference is not great (i.e., when rejecting the null hypothesis in question is of relatively small importance). Conversely, a value at or near the upper end of this range would be chosen when the additional cost of collecting and processing cases is not large, or when the hypothesis is an important one.

It has been proposed, in the absence of some preference to the contrary, that power be set at .80 (J. Cohen, 1965, 1988). This value falls in the middle of the .70 to .90 range and is a reasonable one to use as a convention when such is needed.

5.6.4 Reconciling Different n^*s

When more than one hypothesis is to be tested in a given investigation, the application of the methods described earlier will result in multiple n^*s. Because a single investigation will have a single n, these different n^*s will require reconciliation.

For concreteness, assume plans to test three null hypotheses (H_i) whose specifications have resulted in $n_1^* = 100, n_2^* = 300$, and $n_3^* = 400$. If we decide to use $n = 400$ in the study, we will meet the specifications of H_3 and have much more power than specified for H_1 and more for H_2. This if fine if, in assessing our resources and weighing them against the importance of H_3, we deem it worthwhile. Alternatively, if we proceed with $n = 100$ we will meet the specification of H_1 but fall short of the power desires for H_2 and H_3. Finally, if we strike an average of these n^*s and proceed with $n = 267$, we shall have more power than specified for H_1, slightly less for H_2, and much less for H_3.

There is of course no way to have a single n that will simultaneously meet the n^* specifications of multiple hypotheses. No problem arises when resources are sufficient to proceed with the largest n^*; obviously there is no harm in exceeding the desired power for the other hypotheses and improving the precision of those estimates. But such is not the usual case, and difficult choices may be posed for the investigator. Some help is afforded if one can determine exactly how much power drops from the desired value when n is to be less than n^* for some given hypothesis. Stated more generally, it is useful to be able to estimate the power of a test given some specified n, the inverse of the problem of determining n^* given some specified desired power. The next section is devoted to the solution of this problem.

5.6.5 Power as a Function of n

Thus far, we have been pursuing that particular form of statistical power analysis wherein n^* is determined for a specified desired power value (for given α and f^2). Although this is probably the most frequently useful form of power analysis, we have just seen the utility of inverting n and power, that is, determining the power that would result for some specified n (for given α and f^2). The latter is not only useful in the reconciliation of different n_i^*, but in other circumstances, such as when the n available for study is fixed or when a power analysis is done on a hypothesis post hoc as in a power survey (J. Cohen, 1962). To find power as a function of n, we enter the computer program with n, α, and f^2, and read out the power.

If this calculation is to be done by hand, one needs to use the L tables (J. Cohen, 1988) backward. Enter the table for the significance criterion α to be used in the row for k_B, and read across to find where the obtained L^* falls. Then read off at the column heading the power values that bracket it.[20]

To illustrate: In Section 5.6.1 we considered a test of $R^2_{Y.DI} - R^2_{YD}$ using Model 1 error at $\alpha = .05$, where $k_I = k_B = 10$, $k_D = k_A = 9$, and $f^2 = .0366$. Instead of positing desired power (e.g., .80) and determining $n^*(= 581)$, let us instead assume that (for whatever reason) we will be using $n = 350$ cases. Enter these values into the computer program to determine the power or alternatively, use hand calculation to find

$$(5.6.5) \qquad\qquad L^* = f^2(n - k - 1),$$

where k is the number of variables contributing to the R^2 in the denominator of f^2 (the error term), whether one is using Model 1 or Model 2 error. In our illustration $L^* = .0366 (350 - 9 - 10 - 1) = 12.07$.

Recall that L is itself a function of k_B, α, and power. To find power one simply uses the L tables backward. Enter Appendix E Table E.1 or E.2 for the significance criterion α to be used in the row for k_B, and read across to find where the obtained L^* falls. Then read off at the column heading the power values that bracket it. We find that for this example, $L^* = 12.07$ falls between $L = 11.15$ at power $= .60$ and $L = 13.40$ at power $= .70$. Thus, with $n = 350$ for these specifications, power is between .60 and .70. (Linear interpolation gives us an approximate value of .64, which agrees closely with the computer program value of .65). Power may similarly be found for the other hypotheses to be tested in this data set, with a specified n of 350.

A major advantage of computer programs such as those cited here is the possibility of plotting the power as a function of n and in general obtaining a clearer picture of the consequences for each of the parameters in the equation as a function of changes in other parameters.

---

[20]It is for such applications that the tables provide for low power values (.10 to .60). When a specified n results in low power, it is useful to have some idea of what the power actually is.

5.6.6 Tactics of Power Analysis

We noted earlier that power analysis concerns relationships among four parameters: power, n, α, and ES (indexed by f^2 in these applications). Mathematically, any one of these parameters is determined by the other three. We have considered the cases where n and power are each functions of three others. It may also be useful to exploit the other two possibilities. For example, if one specifies desired power, n, and α for a hypothesis, the computer program will provide the detectable ES, that is, the population f^2 one can expect to detect using this α, with probability given by the specified power desired in a sample of n cases. One can also determine what α one should use, given the ES, desired power, and a sample of size n.

It must be understood that these mathematical relationships among the four parameters should serve as tools in the service of the behavioral scientist turned applied statistician, not as formalisms for their own sake. We have in the interest of expository simplicity implicitly assumed that when we seek to determine n^*, there is only one possible α, one possible value for desired power, and one possible ES. Similarly, in seeking to determine power, we have largely operated as if only one value each for α, ES, and n is to be considered. But the realities of research planning often are such that more than one value for one of these parameters can and indeed must be entertained. Thus, if one finds that for a hypothesis for which $\alpha = .01$, power $=$ .80, and $f^2 = .04$, the resulting n^* is 600, and this number far exceeds our resources, it is sensible to see what n^* results when we change α to .05. If that is also too large, we can invert the problem, specify the largest n we can manage, and see what power results for this n at $\alpha = .05$. If this is too low, we might examine our conscience and see if it is reasonable to entertain the possibility that f^2 is larger, perhaps .05 instead of .04. If so, what does that do for power at that given n? At the end of the line of such reasoning, the investigator either has found a combination of parameters that makes sense in the substantive context or has decided to abandon the research, at least as originally planned. Many examples of such reasoning among a priori alternatives are given in J. Cohen (1988).

With the multiple hypotheses that generally characterize MRC analysis, the need for exploring such alternatives among combinations of parameters is likely to increase. If H_1 requires $n^* = 300$ for desired power of .80, and 300 cases give power of .50 for H_2 and .60 for H_3, etc., only a consideration of alternate parameters for one or more of these hypotheses may result in a research plan that is worth undertaking.

To conclude this section with an optimistic note, we should point out that we do not always work in an economy of scarcity. It sometimes occurs that an initial set of specifications results in n^* much smaller than our resources permit. Then we may find that when the parameters are made quite conservative (for example, $\alpha = .01$, desired power $= .95$, f^2 at the lower end of our range of reasonable expectation), we still find n^* smaller than our resources permit. We might then use the power analysis to avoid "overkill," and perhaps use our additional resources for obtaining better data, for testing additional hypotheses, or even for additional investigations.

5.7 STATISTICAL INFERENCE STRATEGY IN MULTIPLE REGRESSION/CORRELATION

5.7.1 Controlling and Balancing Type I and Type II Errors in Inference

In the preceding sections we have set forth in some detail the methods of hypothesis testing and power analysis for sets. Testing for significance is the procedure of applying criteria designed to control at some rate α, the making of a Type I error in inference, that is, the error of rejecting true null hypotheses or, less formally, finding things that are not there. Power analysis focuses on the other side of the coin of statistical inference, and seeks to control the making of a Type II error, the error of failing to reject false null hypotheses and failing to find things that *are* there. Of course current thinking (e.g., Harlow, Mulaik, & Steiger, 1997) notes that it is likely very rare that an effect in a population will be *precisely* zero, and that failing to find an effect to be significantly different from zero should *never* be so interpreted. However, the making of provisional judgments about the presence in the population of an effect of practical or material magnitude is, in many cases, aided by the use of tests of statistical significance (Abelson, 1995, 1997). Thus, one fundamental demand of an effective strategy of statistical inference is the balancing of Type I and Type II errors in a manner consistent with the substantive issues of the research. In practice, this takes the form of seeking to maintain a reasonably low rate of Type I errors while not allowing the rate of Type II errors to become unduly large or, equivalently, maintaining good power for realistic alternatives to the null hypothesis.

For any discrete null hypothesis, given the usual statistical assumptions and the requisite specification, the procedures for significance testing and power analysis are relatively simple, as we have seen. When one must deal with multiple hypotheses, however, statistical inference becomes exceedingly complex. One dimension of this complexity has to do with whether the Type I error rate is calculated per hypothesis, per group of related hypotheses ("experiment-wise"), or for even larger units ("investigation-wise"). Another is whether α is held constant over the multiple hypotheses or is varied. Still another is whether the hypotheses are planned in advance or stated after the data have been examined (post hoc) the latter being sometimes referred to as "data snooping." And there are yet others. Each of the possible combinations of these alternatives has one or more specific procedures for testing the multiple hypotheses, and each procedure has its own set of implications to the statistical power of the tests it performs.

An example may help clarify the preceding. Assume an investigator is concerned with hypotheses about the means of a dependent variable across levels of a research factor, *G*, made up of 6 $(= g)$ groups. Any of the following kinds of multiple hypotheses may be of interest, and each has its own procedure(s):

1. *All simple comparisons between means.* There are $g(g-1)/2 = 15$ different pairs of means and 15 simple comparisons and their null hypotheses. Assume each is *t* tested at $\alpha = .05$; thus the Type I error rate *per hypothesis* is controlled at .05. But if, in fact, the population means are all equal, it is intuitively evident that the probability that *at least one* comparison will be "significant" (i.e., the experiment-wise error rate) is greater than .05. The actual rate for $g = 6$ is approximately .40.[21] Thus, the separate α's escalate in this case to .40. This error rate may well be unacceptable to the investigator, and almost certainly so to scientific peers. But each *t* test at $\alpha = .05$ will be relatively powerful.

There is a large collection of statistical methods designed to cope with the problem of making all simple comparisons among *g* means. These vary in their definition of the problem, particularly in their conceptualization of Type I error, and they therefore vary in power and in their results. For example, the Tukey HSD test (Winer, 1971, pp. 197–198) controls the experiment-wise error rate at α. The Newman-Keuls test and the Duncan test both approach Type I error via "protection levels" that are functions of α, but the per-hypothesis Type I error risks for the former are constant and for the latter vary systematically (Winer, 1971, pp. 196–198). Bonferroni tests employ the principle of dividing an overall α into as many (usually equal) parts as there are hypotheses, and then setting the per-hypothesis significance criterion accordingly;

---

[21] The calculation requires special tables and the result depends somewhat on sample size. Some other experimentwise error rates for these conditions are (approximately) for $g = 10$, .60 and for $g = 20$, .90. Even for $g = 3$ it is .13. Only for $g = 2$ is it .05.

thus, for $\alpha = .05$, each of the 15 comparisons would be tested with significance criterion set at $\alpha = .05/15 = .0033$ (R. G. Miller, 1966, pp. 67–70). The preceding tests of all pairs of means are the most frequently employed, and by no means exhaustive (Games, 1971).

One of the oldest and simplest procedures for all pairs of g means is Fisher's "protected t" (or *LSD*) test (Carmer & Swanson, 1973). First, an ordinary (ANOVA) overall F test is performed on the set of g means ($df = g - 1, n - g$). If F is not significant, no pair-wise comparisons are made. Only if F is significant at the α criterion level are the means compared; this being done by an ordinary t test. The t tests are protected from large experiment-wise Type I error by the requirement that the preliminary F test must meet the α criterion. As we will see, this procedure is readily adapted for general use in MRC analysis.

Note that each of these tests approaches the control of Type I errors differently, and that therefore each carries different implications to the rate of Type II errors and hence to the test's power.

2. *Some simple comparisons between means.*   With g means, only differences between some pairs may be of interest. A frequent instance of this case occurs when $g - 1$ of the groups are to be compared with a single control or reference group, which thus calls for $g - 1$ hypotheses that are simple comparisons. In this special case the Dunnett test, whose α is controlled experiment-wise, applies (Winer, 1971, pp. 201–204). For the more general case where not all pair-wise hypotheses are to be tested, protected t and Bonferroni tests (and others) may be used. Again these different tests, with their different strategies of Type I error control have different power characteristics.

3. *Orthogonal comparisons.*   With g groups, it is possible to test up to $g - 1$ null hypotheses on comparisons (linear contrasts) that are orthogonal (i.e., independent of each other). These may be simple or complex. A complex comparison is one that involves more than two means, for example, M_1 versus the mean of M_3, M_4, M_5, or the mean of M_1 and M_2 versus the mean of M_3 and M_5. These two complex "mean of means" comparisons are, however, not orthogonal. (The criterion for orthogonality of contrasts and some examples are given in Chapter 8.) When the maximum possible number of orthogonal contrasts, $g - 1$, are each tested at α, the experiment-wise Type I error rate is larger, specifically, it is approximately $1 - (1 - \alpha)^{g-1} = .226$. It is common practice, however, not to reduce the per-contrast rate α below its customary value in order to reduce the experiment-wise rate when orthogonal contrasts are used (Games, 1971).

Planned (a priori) orthogonal comparisons are generally considered the most elegant multiple comparison procedure and have good power characteristics, but alas, they can only infrequently be employed in behavioral science investigations because the questions to be put to the data are simply not usually independent (e.g., those described in paragraphs 1 and 2 previously discussed and in the next paragraph).

4. *Nonorthogonal, many, and post hoc comparisons.*   Although only $g - 1$ orthogonal contrasts are mathematically possible, the total number of different mean of means contrasts is large, and the total number of different contrasts of all kinds is infinite for $g > 2$. An investigator may wish to make more than $g - 1$ (and therefore necessarily nonorthogonal) comparisons, or may wish to make comparisons that were not contemplated in advance of data collection, but rather suggested post hoc by the sample means found in the research. Such "data snooping" is an important part of the research process, but unless Type I error is controlled in accordance with this practice, the experiment-wise rate of spuriously "significant" t values on comparisons becomes unacceptably high. The Scheffé test (Edwards, 1972; Games, 1971; R. G. Miller, 1966) is designed for these circumstances. It permits *all possible* comparisons, orthogonal or nonorthogonal, planned or post hoc, to be made subject to a controlled experiment-wise Type I error rate. Because it is so permissive, however, in most applications it results in very conservative tests, i.e., in tests of relatively low power (Games, 1971).

The reasons for presenting this brief survey are twofold. The first is to alert the reader to the fact that for specific and well defined circumstances of hypothesis formulation and Type I error definition, there exist specific statistical test procedures. But even for the simple case of a single nominally scaled research factor G made up of g groups, the basis for choice among the alternatives is complex. Indeed, an entire book addressed to mathematical statisticians has been written in this area (R. G. Miller, 1966).

The second reason for presenting this survey is to emphasize the fact that given the variety of approaches to the conception of Type I errors, there are differential consequences to the rate of Type II errors and thus to the statistical power of the tests. Conventional statistical inference is effectively employed only to the extent that Type I and Type II error risks are appropriately balanced. The investigator can neither afford to make spurious positive claims (Type I) nor fail to find important relationships (Type II). Since, all other things equal, these two types of errors are inversely related, some balance is needed. Yet the complexity that we encountered earlier when confronted only with the special case of a single nominal scale makes it clear that any effort to treat this problem in comprehensive detail is far outside the bounds of practicality and not in keeping with this book's purpose and data-analytic philosophy, nor with the needs of its intended audience.

What is required instead are some general principles and simple methods that, over the wide range of circumstances in research in the behavioral and social sciences, will serve to provide a practical basis for keeping both types of errors acceptably low and in reasonable balance. The major elements of this approach include parsimony in the number of variables employed, the use of a hierarchical strategy, and the adaptation of the Fisher protected t test to MRC.

5.7.2 Less Is More

A frequent dilemma of the investigator in behavioral science arises in regard to the number of variables she will employ in a given investigation. On the one hand is the need to make sure that the substantive issues are well covered and nothing is overlooked, and on the other is the need to keep in bounds the cost in time, money, and increased complexity that is incurred with an increase in variables. Unfortunately, the dilemma very often is resolved in favor of having more variables to assure coverage.

In addition to the time and money costs of more variables (which are frequently negligible, hence easily incurred), there are more important costs to the validity of statistical inference that are very often overlooked. The more variables, dependent or independent, there are in an investigation, the more hypotheses are tested (either formally or implicitly). The more hypotheses are tested, the greater the probability of occurrence of spurious significance (investigation-wise Type I error). Thus, with 5 dependent and 12 independent variables analyzed by 5 MRC analyses (one per dependent variable), there are a total of 60 potential t tests on null hypotheses for partial coefficients alone. At $\alpha = .05$ per hypothesis, if all these null hypotheses were true, the probability that one or more ts would be found "significant" approaches unity. Even at $\alpha = .01$ per hypothesis, the investigation-wise rate would be in the vicinity of .50.[22] It is rare in research reports to find their results appraised from this perspective, and many investigations are not reported in sufficient detail to make it possible for a reader to do so—variables that "don't work" may never surface in the final report of a research.

One might think that profligacy in the number of variables would at least increase the probability of finding true effects when they are present in the population, even at the risk of

---

[22]Because the 60 tests are not independent, exact investigation-wise error rates cannot be given. If they were independent, the two investigation-wise Type I error rates would be $(1 - .95)^{60} = .954$ (for $\alpha = .05$) and $(1 - .99)^{60} = .453$ (for $\alpha = .01$).

finding spurious ones. But another consideration arises. In each MRC, the greater the number of IVs ($= k$), the lower the power of the test on each IV (or set of IVs). We have seen this in several ways. First, for any given n, the error $df = n - k - 1$ and are thus diminished as k increases. Second, a glance at the L tables (Appendix Tables E.1 and E.2) quickly reveals that all other things being equal, as k_B increases, L increases, and therefore power decreases for any given f^2, α, and n. Also, it is likely that as k increases, the R_is among the IVs increase, which in turn increases the standard errors of partial coefficients (e.g., SE_{Bi}s) and reduces the t_is and hence the power. Thus, having more variables when fewer are possible increases the risks of both finding things that are not so and failing to find things that are. These are serious costs, indeed.

Note that a large n does not solve the difficulties in inference that accompany large numbers of variables. True, the error df will be large, which, taken by itself, increases power. The investigation-wise Type I error rate depends, however, on the number of hypotheses and not on n. And even potentially high power conferred by large n may be dissipated by large k, and by the large R_is (low tolerances) that large k may produce.

Within the goals of a research study, the investigator usually has considerable leeway in the number of variables to include, and too frequently the choice is made for more rather than fewer. The probability of this increases with the "softness" of the research area and the degree to which the investigation is exploratory in character, but no area is immune. When a theoretical construct is to be represented in data, a large number of variables may be used to represent it in the interest of "thoroughness" and "just to make sure" that the construct is covered. It is almost always the case, however, that the large number is unnecessary. It may be that a few (or even one) of the variables are really central to the construct and the remainder peripheral and largely redundant. The latter are better excluded. Or, the variables may all be about equally related to the construct and define a common factor in the factor-analytic sense, in which case they should be combined into an index, factor score, or sum (or treated in a latent variable model, see Chapter 12). The latter not only will represent the construct with greater reliability and validity, but will do so with a single variable (recall in this connection the lessons of unit weighting in Section 3.8.3). Perhaps more than one common factor is required, but this is still far more effective than a large number of single variables designed to cover (actually smother) the construct. These remarks obtain for constructs in both dependent and independent variables.

Other problems in research inference are attendant upon using many variables in the representation of a construct. When used as successive dependent variables, they frequently lead to inconsistent results that, as they stand, are difficult to interpret. When used as a set of IVs, the partialing process highlights their uniqueness, tends to dissipate whatever common factor they share, may produce paradoxical suppression effects, and is thus also likely to create severe difficulties in interpretation.

5.7.3 Least Is Last

The hierarchical model with Model 1 error can be an important element in an effective strategy of inference. We have already commented briefly on its use when IVs may be classified into levels of research relevance (Section 5.3.2). This type of application is appropriate in investigations that are designed to test a small number of central hypotheses but may have data on some additional research factors that are of exploratory interest, and also in studies that are largely or wholly exploratory in character. In such circumstances, the IVs can be grouped into two or more classes and the classes ordered with regard to their status in centrality or relevance. Each class is made up of one or more research factors, which are generally sets of IVs. Thus, for example, the first group of IVs may represent the research factors whose effects the research was designed to appraise, the second some research factors of distinctly secondary interest, and the third those of the "I wonder if" or "just in case" variety. Depending on the investigator's interest and the internal structure of the research, the levels of the hierarchy may simply be the priority classes or one or more of these may also be internally ordered by research factors or single IVs.

The use of the hierarchical model, particularly when used with Model 1 error at each priority class level, then prevents variables of lower priority, which are likely to account uniquely for little Y variance, from reducing the power of the tests on those of higher priority by stealing some of their variance, increasing the standard errors of their partial coefficients, and reducing the *df* for error. In using this stratagem, it is also a good idea to lend less credence to significant results for research factors of low priority, particularly so when many IVs are involved, because the investigation-wise Type I error rate over their IVs is likely to be large. We thus avoid diluting the significance of the high priority research factors. This is in keeping with the sound research philosophy that holds that what is properly obtained from exploratory research are not conclusions, but hypotheses to be tested in subsequent investigations.

When hierarchical MRC is used for relevance ordering, it is recommended that Model 1 error be used at each level of relevance, that is, the first class (U) made up of the centrally relevant research factors uses $1 - R_{YU}^2$ (with $df = n - k_U - 1$) as the error term for its F and t tests, the second class (V) made up of more peripheral research factors used $1 - R_{Y.UV}^2$ (with $df = n - k_U - k_V - 1$), and so on. This tends to make it probable that the tests at each level have minimum error variance per *df* and thus maximal power. Of course, it is always possible that a test using Model 1 error is negatively biased by an important source of variance remaining in its error term, but the declining gradient of unique relevance in this type of application makes this rather unlikely. It is, in fact, in analyses of this kind that Model 1 error has its major justification and use.

We summarize this principle, then, as "least is last"—when research factors can be ordered as to their centrality, those of least relevance are appraised last in the hierarchy and their results taken as indicative rather than conclusive.

5.7.4 Adaptation of Fisher's Protected *t* Test

The preceding sections of the chapter have been devoted to the use of sets of IVs as units of analysis in MRC. We have seen how Y variance associated with a set or partialed set can be determined, tested for significance, and power analyzed. The chapters that follow show how research factors can be represented as sets of IVs. It should thus not come as a surprise that in formulating a general strategy of statistical inference in MRC, we accord the set a central role.

In Section 5.7.1, in our brief review of alternative schemes of testing multiple hypotheses for the special case where the research factor is a nominal scale G, we noted that among the methods available for the comparison of pairs of groups' means was a method attributed to R. A. Fisher: The usual ANOVA overall F test over the set of g means is first performed, and if it proves to be significant at the α level specified, the investigator may go on to test any or all pairs at the same α level, using the ordinary t test for this purpose, and interpret results in the usual way. If F fails to be significant, no t tests are performed—all g population means are taken to be potentially equivalent, based on the evidence, so that no difference between means (or any other linear contrast function of them) can be asserted, whatever value it may yield. This two-stage procedure combines the good power characteristics of the individual t tests at a conventional level of α with the protection against large experiment-wise Type I error afforded by the requirement that the overall F also meet the α significance criterion. For example, in Section 5.7.1, we saw that when all 15 pair-wise comparisons among 6 means are performed by t tests using $\alpha = .05$ per comparison, the probability that one or more will be found "significant" when all 6 population means are equal (i.e., the experiment-wise Type I error rate) is about .40. But if these tests are performed only if the overall F meets the .05 criterion, the latter prevents us from comparing the sample means 95% of the time when the overall null hypothesis is true. Thus, the t tests are protected from the mounting up of small per-comparison α to large experiment-wise error rates.

The virtues of simplicity and practicality of the protected t test procedure are evident. What is surprising is how effective it is in keeping Type I errors low while affording good power. In an extensive investigation of 10 pair-wise procedures for means compared empirically over a wide variety of conditions, it was unexcelled in its general performance characteristics (Carmer & Swanson, 1973).

To adapt and generalize the protected t test to the MRC system, we use the framework of sets as developed in this chapter and used throughout the book. We discussed in Section 5.4.1 the principle that information on research factors of all kinds can be organized into sets of IVs for structural and functional reasons and in the ensuing sections illustrated how these sets may then serve as the primary units of MRC analysis. Now, the protected t test described previously covers only one type of set—a research factor defined by a nominal scale (i.e., a collection of g groups). We generalize the protected t procedure, applying it to the functional sets that organize an MRC analysis, whatever their nature. Specifically,

1. The MRC analysis proceeds by sets, using whatever analytic structure (hierarchical, simultaneous, or intermediate) is appropriate.

2. The contribution to Y variance of each set (or partialed set) is tested for significance at the α level by the appropriate standard F test of Eqs. (5.6.2), (5.6.6), or their variants.

3. If the F for a given set is significant, the individual IVs (aspects) that make it up are each tested for significance at α by means of a standard t test (or its equivalent $t^2 = F$ for numerator $df = 1$). It is the partial contribution of each X_i that is t tested, and any of the equivalent tests for its sr_i, pr_i, or B_i may be used [Eq. (3.6.8)]. All standard MRC computer programs provide this significance test, usually for B_i.

4. If the setwise F is not significant, no tests on the set's constituent IVs are permitted. (The computer program will do them automatically, but the t_is, no matter how large, are ignored.) Overriding this rule removes the protection against large setwise Type I error rates, which is the whole point of the procedure.

This procedure is effective in statistical inference in MRC for several reasons. Because the number of sets is typically small, the investigation-wise Type I error rate does not mount up to anywhere nearly as large a value over the tests for sets as it would over the tests for the frequently large total number of IVs. Then, the tests of single IVs are protected against inflated setwise Type I error rates by the requirement that their set's F meet the α significance criterion. Further, with Type I errors under control, both the F and t tests are relatively powerful (for any given n and f^2). Thus, both types of errors in inference are kept relatively low and in good balance.

To illustrate this procedure, we return to the running example of this chapter: length of hospital stay (Y) for $n = 500$ psychiatric patients was regressed hierarchically on three sets of IVs, demographic ($D, k_D = 9$), illness ($I, k_I = 10$), and a nominal scale of 8) hospitals ($H, k_H = 7$), in that order. Using F tests with Model 1 error and $\alpha = .05$ as the criterion for significance, it was found that set D was significant. Note that the primary focus on sets helps control the investigation-wise Type I error risk. Even for $\alpha = .05$. The latter is in the vicinity of .14; the more conservative $\alpha = .01$ for significance per set would put the investigation-wise Type I error rate in the vicinity of .03.[23]

---

[23] Again, because the tests are not independent, exact rates cannot be determined. The rates given are "ballpark" estimates computed on the assumption of independence, that is, $1 - .95^3$ and $1 - .99^3$, respectively.

Because set D was found to be significant, one may perform a t test (at $\alpha = .05$) on each of the nine IVs that represent unique aspects of patient demography.[24] Because these t tests are protected by the significance of F, the mounting up of set-wise Type I error is prevented. Without this protection, the set-wise error rate for nine t tests, each at $\alpha = .05$, would be in the vicinity of $(1 - .95)^9 = .37$.

Set I's increment (over D) to R^2 was found to be nonsignificant, so no t tests on the unique (within I and D) contributions of its 10 IVs are admissible. It would come as no surprise if the computer output showed that 1 of these 10 t values exceeded the nominal $\alpha = .05$ level. With 10 tests each at $\alpha = .05$, the set-wise Type I error rate would be large. Although the tests are not independent, the "ballpark" estimate of the error rate computed with an assumption of independence is $(1 - .95)^{10} = .40$. In the protected t strategy, the failure of F for the set to be significant is treated so as to mean that all IVs in the set have zero population partial coefficients, a conclusion that cannot be reversed by their individual ts.

Finally, the increment of set H (over D and I) to R^2 was found to be significant, and its constituent $k_H = g - 1 = 7$ IVs were t tested, and the significant ones interpreted. These seven aspects of hospital-group membership may include simple (pair-wise) or complex (involving more than two hospitals) comparisons among the eight hospital Y means, depending on which of several different methods of representing group membership was employed. (The latter is the subject matter of Chapter 8). The method used in this example was presumably chosen so that the seven partialed IVs would represent those comparisons (aspects) of central interest to the investigator and their protected ts test these aspects. Thus far, we have proceeded as with any other set. However, because H is a nominal scale and is thus made up of g groups, we admit under the protection of the F test any comparisons of interest in addition to the 7 ($= g - 1$) carried by the IVs. Thus, in full compliance with both the letter and spirit of Fisher's original protected t test, one could t test any of the $(8 \times 7)/2 = 28$ pair-wise simple comparisons (not already tested) that may be of substantive interest.[25]

We reiterate the generality of our adaptation of the protected t test to MRC. Whether one is dealing with one set or several, whether they are related to Y hierarchically or simultaneously, whether error Model 1 or 2 is used, and whatever the substantive nature of the set(s), the same procedure is used: The first order of inference is with regard to the set(s), and only when a set's significance is established by its F test are its contents further scrutinized for significance.

In using the protected t procedure, it may happen that after a set's F is found to be significant, none of its IVs yields a significant t. This is apparently an inconsistency, because the significant F's message is that at least one of the IVs has a nonzero population partial coefficient, yet each t finds its null hypothesis tenable. A technically correct interpretation is that collectively (set-wise) there is sufficient evidence that there is something there, but individually, not enough evidence to identify what it is. A risky but not unreasonable resolution of this dilemma is to tentatively interpret as significant any IV whose t is almost large enough to meet the significance criterion; whatever is lost by the inflation of the Type I error is likely to be compensated by the reduction of Type II error and the resolution of the apparent inconsistency. It is also very prudent to examine the tolerance for each variable ($= 1 - R^2_{i.123...(i)..k}$) to try to identify high levels of correlations that may have greatly increased the standard errors for some variables that have apparent high levels of influence as suggested by β. Fortunately, the occurrence of this anomaly is rare, and virtually nonexistent when error df are not very small.

---

[24] A refinement of this procedure would be to test the sR^2s for subsets (for example, the nominal scale for ethnicity) by F and then perform t tests on the subset's IVs only if F is significant. This gives added protection to the t tests, which is probably a good idea when k for the set is large, as it is here.

[25] In compliance at least with the spirit of Fisher's procedure, one could also test any complex comparisons of interest, but there would usually be few, if any, that had not been included as IVs.

Another difficulty that may arise with the protected t test is best described by a hypothetical example. Assume, for a set made up of many IVs, that one or two of them have large population partial coefficients and that the remainder all have population partial coefficients equal to zero. Now when we draw a random sample of reasonable size from this population, we will likely find that the F for the set is statistically significant. This result is quite valid, because this F tests the composite hypothesis that all the IVs in the set have zero population coefficient, and we have posited that this is not true. But using the protected t test, the significance of F confers upon us the right to t test *all* the IVs, including those for which the null hypothesis *is* approximately true. For that large group of IVs, the subset-wise Type I error rate will obviously mount up and be high. Of course, we do not know the state of affairs in the population when we analyze the sample. We cannot distinguish between an IV whose t is large because its null hypothesis is false from one (of many t values) that is large because of chance. Obviously, in circumstances such as these our t tests are not as protected as we should like.

Fortunately, a means of coping with this problem is available to us: We invoke the principle of Section 5.7.2—"less is more." By having few rather than many IVs in a set, a significant F protects fewer ts for IVs whose null hypotheses may be true and inhibits the mounting up of Type I error. Moreover, if the investigator's substantive knowledge is used to carefully select or construct these few IVs, fewer still of the ts are likely to be testing true null hypotheses. In this connection, we must acknowledge the possibility that sets D and I in our running example are larger than they need have been; the former may be benefited from reduction by a priori selection and the latter by either selection or factor-analytic reduction.

5.7.5 Statistical Inference and the Stage of Scientific Investigations

Some of the problems of statistical inference can be seen in better perspective when the stage or level of information already available about the phenomena under investigation is taken into account. In early studies, tests of statistical inference will be useful in establishing the direction of effect and in aiding decisions about the probable approximate magnitude of effects in certain populations. These estimates will then be useful in planning future studies. As we will see in subsequent chapters, such significance tests on individual variables or variable sets can be very useful in aiding decisions about whether certain covariate sets will be needed in current or future studies, whether nonlinear functions of variables contribute materially to the prediction of Y, and whether important interactive effects among IVs are present. All such significance tests have to be treated as providing very tentative answers to our questions, that is, answers badly in need of confirmation by replication. (However, the unwary researcher is warned about the problems associated with modest power in "replicating" studies).

Having established the presence and direction of effects, latter stage investigations may be devoted to improving the precision of estimated effects and determining the limits of generalizations across populations and changes in methods, measures, or controlled variables. When this sequence is followed it is likely that problems associated with Type I errors will fade. Problems associated with inadequate statistical power should also be minimized once it is determined what population ES is likely, providing that such estimates can be and are used in the planning of subsequent studies.

5.8 SUMMARY

This chapter introduces five of the major strategic considerations for the employment of MRC analyses to answer research questions. Sections 5.1 and 5.2 discuss considerations in selecting the coefficients that will best answer particular research questions. Section 5.2 also discusses methods of making regression coefficients maximally informative. Sections 5.3 and 5.4 present the hierarchical analyses of individual IVs and of sets of IVs as a strategic aid to answering research questions. Section 5.4 presents the utility of considering IVs in sets, and multiple partial correlation coefficients (the ballantine again). Sections 5.5 and 5.6 present significance testing and power analysis for sets of variables. The final section considers strategies for controlling and balancing Type I and Type II errors in making inferences from findings.

There are a number of different correlation and regression coefficients produced by MRC analyses, and each of them is optimal for particular kinds of research questions. The squared semipartial correlation tells us how much of the variance in Y is uniquely attributable to that IV, a figure that is particularly useful in situations in which the predictive utility or a comparison of predictive utility is at issue. A comparison of a zero-order r_{YX}^2 with $sr_{X \cdot W}^2$ tells us how much the prediction of Y by X is attributable to W. In contrast, a comparison of $B_{Y.X}$ with $B_{YX \cdot W}$ tells us whether averaged over the values of W, changes in X had the same consequences for Y that they had when W was ignored. Some investigations may target the question of differential partialed correlations of two different predictors with Y. A series of questions about differences between populations in squared zero-order, partial, or semipartial correlations of variance proportions may be appropriate targets of research studies (Section 5.1).

In order for zero-order and partialed B to provide useful answers to research questions they must reflect meaningful units of Y and the IV in question. When meaningful units are used, B is the premier causal indicator. Meaningful units may come from long familiarity and established conventions. When units represent counts in both Y and X, an alternative to B is elasticity (E), the percent change on Y per percent change in X, measured at the mean. When measures are novel, there are several options to be preferred to the simple sum that is frequently used. These include POMP scores (percent of the maximum possible score) and item averages (when all items have the same response options). Often the sample's sd may be used as a scale; if both X and Y are so standardized zero-order and partial $B = \beta$ (Section 5.2).

The choice of the analytic model will determine the amount of information extracted from a data set. Hierarchical analysis allows appropriate consideration of causal priorities and removal of confounding variables. It may also be used to reflect the research relevance or structural properties of variables. An alternative strategy, "step-wise" MRC, in which IVs are entered in a sequence determined by the size of their increment to R^2 is also discussed. Use of this strategy is generally discouraged because of the necessarily post hoc nature of interpretation of the findings and the substantial probability of capitalizing on chance (Section 5.3).

Sets of IVs may be treated as units or fundamental entities in the analysis of data. From this perspective, the single IVs and single group of k IVs treated in Chapter 3 are special cases. Two types of sets are described: sets that come about because of the *structure* of the research factors they represent (for example, religion is represented as a set of IVs because it is a categorical variable), and sets that have a specific *function* in the logic of the research, such as a set of control variables that must be adjusted for, or a set of variables that collectively represent "demographic characteristics"). Groups of sets are also described, and such set aggregates are treated simply as sets (Section 5.4.1).

The simultaneous and hierarchical procedures of MRC are shown to apply to sets as units of analysis, and it is shown that Y variance associated with set A may be partialed from that associated with set B, just as with single IVs. For h sets, the simultaneous procedure appraises Y variance for a given set with the remaining $h - 1$ sets partialed. The hierarchical procedure orders the sets into an a priori hierarchy and proceeds sequentially: For each set in hierarchical order of succession, all higher level sets (and no lower level sets) are partialed. The chief quantities of interest are the increments of Y variance accounted for by each set uniquely, relative to sets of higher order of priority (Section 5.4.2).

The ballantine for sets is presented as a device for visualizing proportions of Y variance associated with sets (A, B) and with partialed sets, analogously with those for single IVs. The increments referred to above are squared multiple semipartial correlations and represent the proportion of total Y variance associated with $B \cdot A$. Similarly, we define the squared multiple partial correlation of B as the proportion of Y variance not accounted for by A that is associated with $B \cdot A$. These two statistics are compared and exemplified. As with single IVs, the troublesome area of overlap of sets A and B with Y, area c, cannot be interpreted as a proportion of variance because it may be negative, in which case we have an instance of suppression between sets (Section 5.4.3).

A general test of statistical significance for the Y variance due to a partialed set $B \cdot A$ is presented. Two error models for this test are described. Model 1 error is $1 - R^2_{Y \cdot AB}$, with sets other than A or B (collectively, set C) ignored. Model 2 error is $1 - R^2_{Y \cdot ABC}$, so the Y variance unique to C (together with its df) is additionally excluded from error in the significance test of $B \cdot A$s Y variance. The applicability of the two error models to the hierarchical and simultaneous procedures of MRC is described and exemplified (Section 5.5).

Methods of statistical power analysis for partialed sets, necessary for research planning and assessment, together with the use of a computer program or hand calculations are presented. The determination of n^*, the necessary sample size to attain a desired degree of power to reject the null hypothesis at the α level of significance for a given population effect size (ES), is given for both error models, as well as the means of estimating power that results from a specified n, α, and ES. The section concludes with a discussion of the tactics of power analysis in research planning, particularly those of specifying alternative combinations of parameters and studying their implications (Section 5.6).

Finally, the issue of a general strategy of statistical inference in MRC is addressed. One element of such a strategy involves minimizing the number of IVs used in representing research factor constructs by judicious selection and the use of composites. Another exploits the hierarchical procedure of MRC and the use of Model 1 error in significance testing. A generalization of the protected t test is offered as a simple but effective means of coping with the multiplicity of null hypotheses in MRC. This procedure prevents the rapid inflation of set-wise and investigation-wise Type I error that would occur if the individual ts were not so protected and at the same time enjoys the good power characteristics of the t test. When an investigation is placed in a sequence of scientific research, problems associated with both Type I and Type II errors should be minimized. Early analyses and replications may establish the presence, direction, and estimated magnitude of effects. Subsequent research can be planned with realistic levels of statistical power. This work can then improve the precision of estimates and their variability across changes in methods, measures, and populations (Section 5.7).

6

Quantitative Scales, Curvilinear Relationships, and Transformations

6.1 INTRODUCTION

In Chapter 6 we continue our treatment of quantitative scales; that is, scales that can take on a continuous range of values. We include ordinal, interval, and ratio scales (Section 1.3.3), and note that they share the minimum property that the scale numbers assigned to the objects order the objects with regard to the measured attribute. Ordinal (rank-order) scales have only this property, interval scales add the property of equal units (intervals), and ratio scales have both equal intervals and equal ratios, hence a true scale zero. Despite these differences in the amount of information they yield, we find it convenient to treat them together. To this point we have treated quantitative variables as if they have only a *linear* relationship to the criterion. We would argue that in some research problems there may be other *nonlinear* aspects that should be used in addition to, or in place of, this linear aspect. This chapter thus addresses itself to the question of how nonlinear relationships can be detected, represented, and studied within the confines of *linear* MRC, by the use of multiple and/or nonlinear aspects of research variables.

6.1.1 What Do We Mean by Linear Regression?

Linear regression refers to regression models that take the form we have used throughout the book:

(6.1.1) $$\hat{Y} = B_1 X_1 + B_2 X_2 + \cdots + B_k X_k + B_0.$$

More formally, regression equations of the form of Eq. (6.1.1) are said to be *linear in the parameters* (or linear in the coefficients), where the parameters refer to the coefficients $B_0, B_1, \ldots, B_k$. If a regression equation is linear in the parameters, then the predicted score is a *linear combination* of the predictors: Each predictor is simply multiplied by the regression coefficient and the products are added to produce the predicted score. Any relationship between a set of predictors and a criterion that can be expressed in the form of Eq. (6.1.1) can be handled in linear MR. The actual relationship between a predictor and the criterion need not be a linear (straight line) relationship in order to use linear MR to analyze the relationship.

193

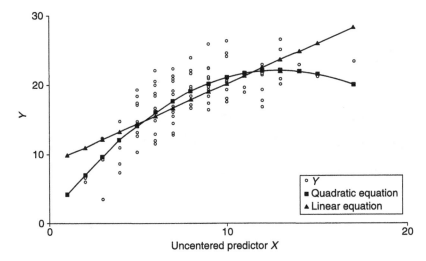

FIGURE 6.1.1 Quadratic relationship between X (number of credits taken in minor subject) and Y (interest in further course work in the minor). The triangles characterize the best fit linear regression of Y on X; the squares, the best fit quadratic regression of Y on X.

Theories in the social sciences sometimes predict a curvilinear relationship between two variables, such as that illustrated in Fig. 6.1.1. In Fig. 6.1.1, the outcome Y increases as X increases up to some maximum value; thereafter, as X increases, Y remains the same or even declines. For example, Janis (1967) hypothesized that one could motivate people to engage in health protective behaviors (e.g., to quit smoking, exercise) through fear communication (i.e., through strong threats about disease) but only up to a point. If the fear induced became too great, then people would deny the existence of the threat and health protective behavior would decline, rather than continue to rise with increasing fear. We will be able to capture this curvilinear relationship between X and Y with *polynomial regression*, a special case of linear MR, which we develop in Sections 6.2 and 6.3. The point here is that any regression model of the form of Eq. (6.1.1) can be analyzed in linear MR, even if the relationship of the predictor to the criterion is not linear.

6.1.2 Linearity in the Variables and Linear Multiple Regression

It is worth reviewing what we mean by a *linear relationship,* that is, a relationship of X to Y best summarized by a straight line (as apart from linear regression). The conditional means of Y, that is, the means of Y at each value of X, $\mu_{Y|X}$, lie on a straight line (see Section 4.3.1). More formally, *linearity in the variables* of a relationship means that the regression of Y on X is constant across all values of X; that is, a one-unit increase in X is associated with a constant magnitude of increase in Y (namely, B_{YX}), regardless of where in the X scale it occurs. If we use linear MR to characterize a predictor-criterion relationship, we are forcing this constant regression of Y on X across the range of X.

Of course, linearity is a special case of relationship; there are a variety of nonlinear relationships that can occur between predictors and a dependent variable. For example, we say that the cost of college tuition has "risen exponentially over the years"; what we mean is that the cost of college tuition has been rising at an ever increasing rate over the years. Obviously, the relationship of time (X) to tuition (Y) fails to meet the definition of linearity in the variables, which would require a constant increase in tuition with each year.

In Fig. 6.1.1 linearity in the variables does not hold, since the slope of the regression of Y on X changes over the range of X. If we predict Y from X in Fig. 6.1.1 with linear regression equation $\hat{Y} = B_1 X + B_0$, the best fit straight line, shown in Fig. 6.1.1 with the triangles, does not capture the curvilinearity. The linear regression suggests that Y continues to increase as X increases; the leveling off and then declining of Y at high levels of X is not captured. To anticipate our discussion of polynomial regression, the curvilinear relationship of variable X to Y in Fig. 6.1.1 can be handled within linear MR through a regression equation in which a single research variable X is entered both as a linear predictor X, and as a curvilinear (second-order) predictor such as X^2. The second-order predictor is simply X^2, and together the two predictors X and X^2 represent the relationship of the variable to the criterion:

$$\text{(6.1.2)} \qquad\qquad \hat{Y} = B_{1.2} X + B_{2.1} X^2 + B_0.$$

This equation is *linear in the parameters*; by this we mean that predictors are simply multiplied by the regression coefficients and the products summed to form the predicted score, rather than being in some more complex form, for example, $X^{1/B}$. Note that Eq. (6.1.2) is linear in the parameters, even though it is not linear in the variables, since X^2 is a predictor. So long as an equation is linear in the parameters, it can be analyzed with MR. The characterization of the relationship of the variables to the criterion in Eq. (6.1.2) is novel in that it requires two distinct predictors to capture the relationship: X representing a linear aspect and X^2 or some other transform, representing a curvilinear aspect.

6.1.3 Four Approaches to Examining Nonlinear Relationships in Multiple Regression

There are four broad classes of approaches to examining nonlinear relationships in MR. Of traditional and common use in the behavioral sciences is *polynomial regression*, explored here in depth. Power polynomials are a convenient method of fitting curves of almost any shape, although other functions such as a log function will often work as well. Second is the use of *monotonic nonlinear transformations* (i.e., transformations that shrink or stretch portions of the scale differentially). That is, these transformations change the relative spacing between adjacent points on the scale (i.e., the nonlinearity) but maintain the rank order of the scores (i.e., the monotonicity). We choose the particular transformation in order to create rescaled variable(s) after transformation that bear a close to linear relationship to one another so that they may be treated in linear MR. The choice of transformation may be either theory driven or empirically driven by the data. Transformations are treated in Section 6.4. Third is *nonlinear regression*, a distinctly different class of analysis in which the central point of the analysis is estimation of complex (nonlinear) relationships among variables that may be implied by theory. We introduce nonlinear regression here in Section 6.5 and devote much of Chapter 13 to two common forms of nonlinear regression: logistic regression and Poisson regression. Fourth are *nonparametric regression approaches* (Hastie & Tibshirani, 1990), introduced briefly in Section 6.6.

Our presentation is a mix of approaches already familiar in the behavioral sciences and approaches that have not heretofore been much used in the behavioral sciences, though they are standardly used in related fields. We hope that the presentation of the unfamiliar approaches may lead to innovation in the analysis of behavioral science data.

For our treatment of curvilinear relationships we must distinguish between a variable X, and the predictors that carry the various aspects of the relationship of that variable to the criterion (e.g., X and X^2 of Eq. 6.1.2). The variable will be represented in bold italics (here X), and its aspects will be characterized by the same letter, in regular type, with the particular function, $X, X^2, \log X$ specifically indicated. Capital letters will represent raw scores X, squares of raw scores X^2, etc. Lowercase letters will represent deviation (centered) scores of the form $x = (X - M_X)$; $x^2 = (X - M_X)^2$, as in earlier chapters.

Boxed Material in the Text

In this chapter we adopt a strategy initiated in Chapter 4 of putting some material into boxes, typically material of interest to the more mathematically inclined reader. The boxes provide supplementation to the text; the text can be read without the boxes. Boxes appear within the section in which the boxed material is relevant. Readers not interested in boxed material should simply skip to the beginning of the next numbered section.

6.2 POWER POLYNOMIALS

6.2.1 Method

It is a most useful mathematical fact that in a graph of n data points relating Y to X (where the values of X are all different), an equation of the following form will define a function that fits these points *exactly*:

$$(6.2.1) \qquad \hat{Y} = BX + CX^2 + DX^3 + \cdots + QX^{n-1} + A.$$

This *polynomial equation* relates the one variable X to Y by using $(n-1)$ aspects of X to the criterion Y. Each term X, X^2, etc., is said to have *order* equal to its exponent,[1] (e.g., X^2 is of order 2). The order of the polynomial equation is the order of the highest term, here $(n-1)$. The term with the highest exponent is referred to as the *highest order term* (here X^{n-1}) and all other terms are referred to as *lower order terms*. The relationship of variable X to Y is nonlinear, and several powers of the linear X term serve as predictors in addition to the linear term. Put another way, the regression equation includes stand-in variables (X^2, X^3, etc.) that possess a known nonlinear relationship to the original variables. Yet the regression equation is linear in the parameters and can be analyzed with MR. By structuring nonlinear relationships in this way, we make it possible to determine *whether* and specifically *how* a relationship is nonlinear and to write an equation that *describes* this relationship. The higher order terms X^2, X^3, etc. in the polynomial equation are nonlinear transformations of the original X; thus polynomial regression falls within the general strategy of creating nonlinear transformations of variables that can be handled in linear MR.

The linear, quadratic, and cubic polynomials follow. The highest order term in a polynomial equation determines the *overall shape* of the regression function within the range between $-\infty$ and $+\infty$, that is, the number of bends in the function. The $B_{2.1}X^2$ term in the quadratic Eq. (6.2.3) causes the regression line to be a parabola (one bend), as in Fig. 6.1.1. The $B_{3.12}X^3$ term in the cubic Eq. (6.2.4) produces an S-shaped function (two bends), as in Fig. 6.2.1. There are $(q-1)$ bends in a polynomial of order q.

$$(6.2.2) \qquad \text{Linear}: \quad \hat{Y} = B_1 X + B_0 \qquad \text{with no bends;}$$

$$(6.2.3) \qquad \text{Quadratic}: \quad \hat{Y} = B_{1.2} X + B_{2.1} X^2 + B_0 \qquad \text{with one bend;}$$

$$(6.2.4) \qquad \text{Cubic}: \quad \hat{Y} = B_{1.23} X + B_{2.13} X^2 + B_{3.12} X^3 + B_0 \qquad \text{with two bends.}$$

In reality, a bend may occur outside the range of the observed values of the predictor.

---

[1] In more complex terms considered in Chapter 7, the order is equal to the sum of the exponents (e.g., X^2Z is of order 3).

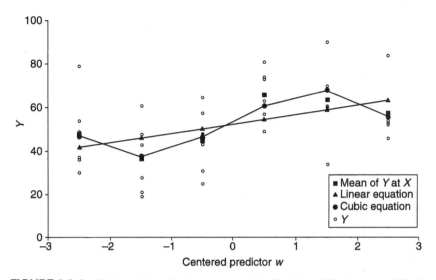

FIGURE 6.2.1 Cubic relationship between w and Y. Predictor W is in centered (deviation) form, $w = (W - M_w)$. The triangles characterize the best fit linear regression of Y on w; the solid circles, the best fit cubic regression of Y on w. The conditional dependent variable means at each value of w are represented by squares. Note that the cubic equation does not track the conditional means with complete accuracy.

The signs (positive, negative) of the highest order terms in polynomial regressions determine the direction of the curvature. In the quadratic equation, positive B_2 indicates a curve that is U-shaped (concave upward, as a smile); negative B_2 indicates a curve that is inverted U-shaped (concave downward, as a frown), as in Fig. 6.1.1. In the cubic equation, negative B_3 indicates a curve that is first concave upward and then concave downward as X increases, as in Fig. 6.2.1; positive B_3 yields the opposite pattern, concave downward followed by concave upward.

What Order Polynomial to Estimate?

From a mathematical perspective, we may fit up to a polynomial of order $(q - 1)$ for a variable whose scale contains q distinct values (e.g., a 19th-order polynomial for a 20-point scale). From a research perspective, we have neither theoretical rationale nor practical benefit from fitting a polynomial of high order that captures every random jiggle in the data. Our nonlinear curve fitting with power polynomials should make substantive sense. We argue that theory should guide the choice and that for the most part theory in the social sciences predicts quadratic, and at most cubic, relationships. For example, opponent process theories predict phenomena that are properly cubic (i.e., a reaction in one direction followed by a compensatory over-response in the opposite direction, followed by a return to baseline, as in physiological responses to stressors). The quality of data must also be considered: social science data typically do not support explorations above the cubic level. Finally, coefficients of higher order polynomials (above cubic) are difficult to interpret (Neter, Kutner, Nachtsheim, & Wasserman, 1996). In this presentation we focus on quadratic and cubic equations.

We realize that theorizing may be weak and that there may be an exploratory character to the analysis. In the behavioral sciences, the prediction is often that the relationship is "nonlinear" absent the specific form of the nonlinearity. One may suspect that behavior will approach a peak (asymptote) and then remain essentially level, or will decline and then level off at some minimal level. A quadratic equation can be used to represent either of these relationships. We caution that *polynomial equations may be only approximations* to nonlinear relationships. Finally, we must distinguish nonlinear relationships from relationships that exhibit cyclic variation over time (e.g., activity levels of people over 24-hour cycles, or mood levels over 7 days of the week); here time series analysis is appropriate (see Section 15.8).

Detecting Curvilinear Relationships Through Graphical Displays

In the absence of specific predictions concerning nonlinearity, the detection of nonlinearities begins with *scatterplots* of predictors against the criterion (see Section 4.2.2). These plots should be augmented with superimposed curves for better visualization of the data, for example, a curve connecting the means of the criterion Y at specific values of X. A *lowess* (or, equivalently, *loess*) curve, a nonparametric curve that follows the data and traces the X–Y relationship (Section 4.2.2), will help to visualize nonlinearity; in Fig. 6.2.2(A), the data of Fig. 6.1.1 are plotted with a lowess curve. *Residual scatterplots* (Section 4.4.1) are even more useful. The residual scatterplot in Fig. 6.2.2(B) is generated from the data in Fig. 6.1.1 by predicting the criterion from only the linear aspect of X: $\hat{Y} = B_1 X + B_0$, and plotting the residuals from this analysis against the predictor. Once the strong linear increasing trend in the data has been removed, the curvilinearity is clearly apparent. The residuals are systematically related to the value of X: below zero for low and high values of X, and above zero for moderate values of X. The detection of curvilinearity in a residual scatterplot is also enhanced with a lowess line. Should nonlinearity be suspected, a polynomial regression equation is specified. Higher order predictor(s) are created simply by squaring (and perhaps cubing) the original linear variable X. Multiple regression is applied to the polynomial equation.

6.2.2 An Example: Quadratic Fit

Consider again the gestalt of the 100 points in Fig. 6.1.1, which suggests that Y reaches a maximum and then declines slightly as variable X increases. As an example, we might think of variable X as the number of elective credits undergraduate students have taken in a particular minor subject and Y as their expressed interest in taking further electives in this minor. We hypothesize that interest in course work in a minor will increase as students take more courses in the minor, but only up to a point. After several courses, students then will shift their interest to electives in other topics and interest in the particular minor will begin to decline.

The linear correlation between variable X and Y is substantial, $r = .75$, and reflects the strong positive relationship between variable X and Y. However, this linear correlation does not capture the onset of decline in interest above about 12 credits (four 3-credit courses). In Table 6.2.1 we summarize a series of polynomial regressions fitted to these data, the linear, quadratic, and cubic polynomials of Eqs. (6.2.2), (6.2.3), and (6.2.4), respectively. We present the regression equations, tests of significance of each of the individual regression coefficients, and 95% confidence intervals on the regression coefficients. The triangles in Fig. 6.1.1 are predicted scores from the linear regression equation $\hat{Y} = 1.15X_1 + 8.72$. The linear regression coefficient B_1 in the linear equation is significant, due to the strong increasing trend in the data, $B_1 = 1.15$, confidence interval (*CI*): [.95, 1.35], $t(98) = 11.19$, $p < .01$. This coefficient only signifies the generally increasing trend in the data and does not test our curvilinear prediction.

In Fig. 6.1.1 the squares are predicted scores from the quadratic regression equation $\hat{Y}_2 = 3.27X - .13X^2 + 1.00$. The $B_{2.1}$ coefficient is negative, $B_{2.1} = -.13$, the 95% confidence interval does not include zero, *CI*: $[-.17, -.08]$, and $t(97) = -5.75$, $p < .01$. Negative $B_{2.1}$ reflects the hypothesized initial rise followed by decline in interest in taking further courses as number of credits in the minor accumulates.

(A) Scatterplot of data from Fig. 6.1.1 with best fit linear regression of Y on X and lowess curve superimposed. The lowess curve is useful in visual detection of the curvilinear relationship of X to Y.

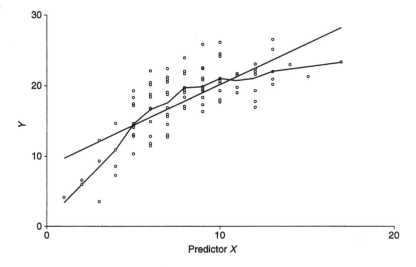

(B) Residual scatterplot of data from Fig. 6.1.1 following prediction from linear equation $\hat{Y} = B_1 X + B_0$. The increasing linear trend shown in Fig. 6.2.2(A) has been removed and the residuals exhibit the remaining curvilinearity. A lowess curve is superimposed to highlight the remaining curvilinearity.

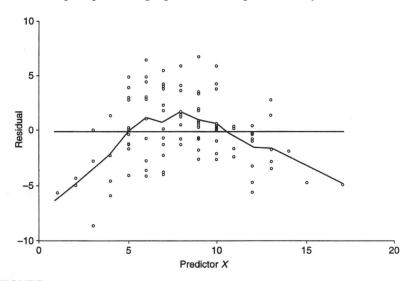

FIGURE 6.2.2 Exploration of data to detect the presence of curvilinearity. The data are the same as in Fig. 6.1.1.

We might wonder whether the students' interest once again rises among those students who take many credits in the minor (say after 15 credits or five 3-credit courses); hence we examine the cubic equation. In the cubic equation, the confidence interval for the $B_{3.12}$ coefficient includes zero, CI: $[-.0007, .02]$. There is no evidence of a cubic relationship in the data, that is, after decline in student interest above about 12 credits, interest does not increase again with higher credits.

TABLE 6.2.1

Polynomial Multiple Regression Analysis of Regression of Y on X
with Uncentered Data

	Mean	sd		Y	X	X^2	X^3
						Uncentered correlation matrix	
Y	18.11	4.75	Y	1.000	.749	.650	.554
X	8.17	3.10	X	.749	1.000	.972	.911
X^2	76.23	53.45	X^2	.650	.972	1.000	.981
X^3	781.99	806.44	X^3	.554	.911	.981	1.000

Regression Equations

Linear: $\hat{Y}_{linear} =$ 1.15X   +8.72
95% CI: [.95, 1.35]
t_{B_i} (98):   11.19

Quadratic: $\hat{Y}_{quadratic} =$ 3.27X $-.13X^2$ +1.00
95% CI: [2.52, 4.03]   [−.17, −.08]
t_{B_i} (97):   8.62   −5.75

Cubic: $\hat{Y}_{cubic} =$ 4.94 X $-.34X^2$ $+.01X^3$ −2.58
95% CI: [2.99, 6.89]   [−.58, −.10]   [−.0007, .02]
t_{B_i} (96):   5.03   −2.86   1.83

Hierarchical Model

Equation	IVs	R^2	F	df	I	F_I	df
Linear	X_1	.56	125.14**	1, 98	.56	125.14**	1, 98
Quadratic	X_1 X_2	.67	99.62**	2, 97	.11	33.11**	1, 97
Cubic	X_1 X_2 X_3	.68	69.15**	3, 96	.01	3.35	1, 96

$**p < .01$
Note: I is the increment in R^2.

Structuring Polynomial Equations: Include all Lower Order Terms

Each polynomial equation in Table 6.2.1 contains all lower order terms, (i.e., the quadratic equation contains the linear term; the cubic equation, the linear and quadratic terms). In order that higher order terms have meaning, all lower order terms must be included, since higher order terms are reflective of the specific level of curvature they represent only if all lower order terms are partialed out. For example, in Table 6.2.1, had we not included the linear term in the quadratic equation, the regression coefficient for X^2 would have confounded linear and quadratic variance.

Conditional Effects: Interpretation of Lower Order Coefficients in Higher Order Equations Based on Uncentered Variables

In equations containing linear predictors and powers of these predictors, the actual slope of the regression of Y on X differs for each value of X. In Fig. 6.1.1, one can imagine drawing a tangent line to each of the darkened squares representing the quadratic relationship. The tangent line summarizes the linear regression of Y on X *at that particular value of X* as characterized in the quadratic equation. The actual slope of each tangent line[2] at a particular value of X for the quadratic equation (Eq. 6.2.3) is given by the expression $(B_{1.2} + 2B_{2.1}X)$. The value of this expression depends on X, i.e., is different for every value of X. This expression equals $B_{1.2}$ only at $X = 0$. Hence the $B_{1.2}$ coefficient in the quadratic equation represents the linear regression of Y on X at only the point $X = 0$, as characterized by the quadratic equation. The conditional nature of the $B_{1.2}$ coefficient makes sense when we consider that the slope of the linear regression of Y on X is different for every value of X if the relationship is curvilinear. In our example, the $B_{1.2}$ coefficient in the quadratic equation ($B_{1.2} = 3.27$) represents the linear regression of Y on X at $X = 0$. A glance at Fig. 6.1.1 tells us that this is not a meaningful value, since there are no data points in which $X = 0$; all students under consideration have taken at least one credit in the subject area; that is, observed scores on the predictor range from 1 through 17. To understand what the $B_{1.2}$ coefficient represents, imagine projecting the quadratic curve (the squares) downward to $X = 0$. The slope of the regression of Y on X at the point $X = 0$ would be steeply positive; the large positive $B_{1.2} = 3.27$ is this slope. That is, if we extrapolate our quadratic relationship to students who have never taken even a one-credit course in the subject in question, we would predict a rapid rise in their interest in the subject. We warn the reader not to report this $B_{1.2}$ coefficient or test of significance of this coefficient unless (a) zero is a meaningful value that occurs in the data set, (b) one wishes to consider the linear trend in the data only at the value zero, and (c) the meaning of the coefficient is carefully explained, since these coefficients are little understood and will be grossly misinterpreted.

6.2.3 Centering Predictors in Polynomial Equations

Lower order coefficients in higher order regression equations (regression equations containing terms of higher than order unity) only have meaningful interpretation if the variable with which we are working has a meaningful zero. There is a simple solution to making the value zero meaningful on any quantitative scale. We *center* the linear predictor, that is we convert X to deviation form:

$$\text{centered linear predictor } x: \qquad x = (X - M_X).$$

With centered variables, the mean M_X is, of course, zero. Thus the regression of Y on x at $x = 0$ becomes meaningful: it is the linear regression of Y on Z at the mean of the variable X. Once we have centered the linear predictor, we then form the higher order predictors from centered x:

$$\text{centered quadratic predictor } x^2: \qquad x^2 = (X - M_X)^2,$$

and

$$\text{centered cubic predictor } x^3: \qquad x^3 = (X - M_X)^3.$$

We use these predictors in our polynomial regression equations. For example, the cubic equation becomes

$$\hat{Y} = B_{1.23}(X - M_X) + B_{2.13}(X - M_X)^2 + B_{3.12}(X - M_X)^3 + B_0$$
$$= B_{1.23}x \qquad\quad + B_{2.13}x^2 \qquad\quad + B_{3.12}x^3 \qquad\quad + B_0.$$

To gain the benefits of interpretation of lower order terms, we do not need to center the criterion Y; we leave it in raw score form so that predicted scores will be in the metric of the observed criterion.

---

[2]The expression $(B_{1.2} + 2B_{2.1}X)$ is actually the first derivative of Eq. (6.2.3).

TABLE 6.2.2

Polynomial Multiple Regression Analysis of Regression of Y on X
with Centered Data

| | Mean | sd | | Centered correlation matrix | | | |
				Y	x	x^2	x^3
Y	18.11	4.75	Y 1.000		.749	−.250	.586
x	0.00	3.10	x .749	1.000		.110	.787
x^2	9.48	12.62	x^2 −.250	.110	1.000		.279
x^3	4.27	102.70	x^3 .586	.787	.279	1.000	

Regression Equations

Linear:	$\hat{Y}_{linear} =$	1.15x	+18.10		
95% CI:		[.95, 1.35]			
$t_{B_i}(98)$:		11.19			
Quadratic:	$\hat{Y}_{quadratic} =$	1.21x	$-13x^2$	+19.30	
95% CI:		[1.03, 1.38]	[−.17, −.08]		
$t_{B_i}(97)$:		13.45	−5.75		
Cubic:	$\hat{Y}_{cubic} =$	1.00x	$-.14x^2$	$+.01x^3$	+19.39
95% CI:		[.70, 1.28]	[−.19, −.09]	[−.0007, .02]	
$t_{B_i}(96)$:		6.86	−6.10	1.83	

Hierarchical Model

Equation	IVs	R^2	F	df	I	F_I	df
Linear	x_1	.56	125.14**	1, 98	.56	125.14**	1, 98
Quardratic	x_1, x_2	.67	99.62**	2, 97	.11	33.11**	1, 97
Cubic	x_1, x_2, x_3	.68	69.15**	3, 96	.01	3.35	1, 96

**$p < .01$

Note: I is the increment in R^2.

CH06EX01

Table 6.2.2 provides a reanalysis of the data of Fig. 6.1.1, following centering of X. To prepare the table, the original X variable with $M_X = 8.17$ was centered by subtracting the mean from each value of X, yielding predictor x with $M_X = 0$. Figure 6.2.3 shows the data set and the linear and quadratic regression functions based on centered x; $x = 0$ is approximately at the middle of the x axis. Note that Figs. 6.1.1 and 6.2.3 are identical in form. The shapes of the regression functions do not change on centering X; only the scaling of the x axis changes.

Essential Versus Nonessential Multicollinearity

There are substantial differences, however, between the results presented in Table 6.2.1 for uncentered X versus Table 6.2.2 for centered x. The means of the three predictors have changed, as have the standard deviations of all but the linear term. Dramatic changes have occurred in the correlation matrix. Consider first the correlation between X and X^2. In the uncentered case (Table 6.2.1), this correlation is .972. However, in the centered case (Table 6.2.2), the corresponding correlation is only .110. Whenever we take an uncentered predictor X (a predictor with a nonzero mean) and compute powers of the predictor (X^2, X^3, etc.), these powers will be highly correlated with the original linear predictor X. There are two sources of correlation between a predictor and an even power of the predictor, say between X and X^2 (Marquardt,

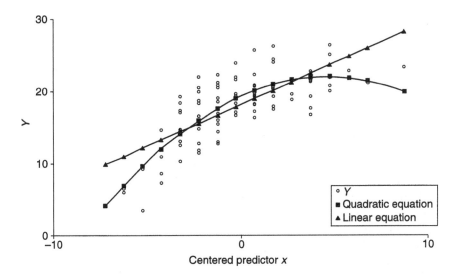

FIGURE 6.2.3 Data of Fig. 6.1.1 with predictor X in centered (deviation) form $x = (X - M_X)$. The triangles characterize the best fit linear regression of Y on x; the squares, the best fit quadratic regression of Y on X.

1980). First is *nonessential multicollinearity* that exists merely due to the scaling (nonzero mean) of X. If we set the mean of X to zero, then all nonessential multicollinearity is removed. This accounts for the drop in correlation from .972 to .110. Second is *essential multicollinearity*, correlation that exists because of any nonsymmetry in the distribution of the original X variable. For a perfectly symmetric predictor X, if we center it, producing x, and then square the centered x, producing x^2, x and x^2 will be completely uncorrelated. In fact, this will also be so for the correlation of x with all even powers of x (i.e., x^2, x^4, x^6, etc.). The correlation between x and x^2 in our example of .110 is attributable to the very slight asymmetry of X. Centering leads to computational advantages because very high correlations between predictors may cause computational difficulties. The correlation between X and X^3 is .911 in the uncentered case and .787 in the centered case. Correlations between a predictor and odd powers (i.e., x^3, x^5, x^7, etc.) of the predictors will not drop dramatically when we center.

Now consider the correlations of each predictor with the criterion Y. The linear transformation of X to x leaves the correlation with Y unchanged, $r = .749$. However, the correlation of the X^2 term with Y changes dramatically, from .650 in the uncentered case to $-.250$ in the centered case. We know from Figs. 6.1.1 and 6.2.3 that the shape of the relationships in the data has changed *not at all* on centering. Consistent with our consideration of MR with correlated predictors, the examination of hypotheses about the effects of individual predictors is considered in the context of all other predictors. We interpret partial effects of individual predictors with all other predictors held constant. The polynomial regression case is no exception. The zero-order correlations of the linear, quadratic, and cubic predictors with the criterion should not be interpreted in examining hypotheses about fit. Interpretation of the overall shape of the regression function should be based on the *partial regression coefficient for the highest order predictor in the context of the full polynomial equation*, that is, the regression equation containing all lower order terms. Again, if we omit lower order terms, then the variance attributed to higher order terms will be confounded with variance attributable to the omitted lower order terms. Finally, we would not look at effects in reverse order, for example, asking whether the linear term contributes over and above the quadratic term, even if the quadratic relationship were expected.

Regression Coefficients in Centered Versus Uncentered Polynomial Regressions

Although the regression functions in Figs. 6.1.1 and 6.2.3 are identical, there is a striking difference between the coefficients of the regression equations. First, the intercepts differ because they reflect the scaling of the means of the variables. For the uncentered predictor, zero represents no previous credit hours, whereas for the centered predictor, 0 represents the mean hours of credit ($M_X = 8.17$). In addition, the lower order terms differ. Consider the centered quadratic equation: $\hat{Y}_2 = 1.21X - .13X^2 + 19.30$. Examine Fig. 6.2.3. The $B_{1.2} = 1.21$ coemcient gives the linear regression of Y on x at the point $x = 0$, now the mean of x. That this coefficient is positive tells us that at the mean of x, the criterion Y is still increasing. In terms of our numerical example, at the mean number of credits taken in the minor (raw $M_X = 8.17$), interest in the minor is still increasing. Note that the centered $B_{1.2}$ of 1.21 is much smaller than the uncentered $B_{1.2}$ of 3.27. Recall that uncentered $B_{1.2}$ of 3.27 represented the slope of Y on X if the regression curve for uncentered X in Fig. 6.1.1 were extended downward to $X = 0$, a very steep portion of the curve.

The $B_{1.2}$ coefficient in the centered quadratic regression equation also has another useful interpretation; it is the average linear slope of the regression of Y on X *in the quadratic equation*. That $B_{1.2} = 1.21$ tells us that the overall linear trend in the data is positive. It is important to note that we can use both coefficients of the *centered* quadratic equation for interpretation. Both the linear and quadratic terms in the quadratic equation are meaningful once we have centered predictor X.

The $B_{1.2} = 1.21$ coefficient from the centered quadratic equation is not identical to that from the centered linear equation ($B_1 = 1.15$). In the quadratic equation, the $B_{1.2}$ coefficient is that for x with x^2 partialed out; in the linear equation, the B_1 coefficient has no terms partialed from it.

The $B_{2.1}$ coefficient ($B_{2.1} = -.13$) in the quadratic equation is constant over additive transformations (adding, subtracting a constant) and thus does not change from the uncentered to centered equation. In a polynomial regression equation of any order the regression coefficient for the highest order term is identical in the uncentered and centered solutions, but all lower order coefficients are different.

Predictors in Polynomial Regression Equations Should Be Centered

Centering renders all the regression coefficients in a polynomial regression equation meaningful as reflecting the regression function at the mean of the predictor. Centering also eliminates the extreme multicollinearity associated with using powers of predictors in a single equation. We therefore strongly recommend the use and reporting of centered polynomial equations. Although lower order terms have interpretations in uncentered equations, these interpretations often are not meaningful in terms of the range of the data and are guaranteed to be misleading to the naive consumer of polynomial regression equations. Only in cases in which X is measured on a ratio scale with a true 0 point is the use of polynomial equations with the raw data likely to lead to easily interpretable results.

6.2.4 Relationship of Test of Significance of Highest Order Coefficient and Gain in Prediction

The tests of the highest order coefficients in polynomial equations are actually tests of whether these aspects of the relationship of variable X to Y contribute to overall prediction above and beyond all lower order terms. The hierarchical tests reported in Tables 6.2.1 and 6.2.2 are the now familiar F tests of the contribution of a set B of predictors to an equation containing set A (see Section 5.5). Consider the centered analysis in Table 6.2.2. The squared multiple correlation R^2_{linear} for the linear equation is .56, for the quadratic equation, $R^2_{\text{quadratic}} = .67$. This represents an increment of .11 (an 11% gain in total prediction) from the addition of the quadratic term to the linear term. This increment I is the squared semipartial correlation sr^2_2 of the quadratic term with the criterion, over and above the linear term (for x^2 with x partialed). In general the F test for this increment in any order polynomial is computed by treating the highest order term as set B and all other lower terms as Set A, as in Section 5.5, Eq. (5.5.2A):

$$(5.5.2A) \qquad F = \frac{R^2_{Y.AB} - R^2_{Y.A}}{1 - R^2_{Y.AB}} \times \frac{n - k_A - k_B - 1}{k_B} \qquad (df = k_B, n - k_A - k_B - 1).$$

For the quadratic term,

$$F = \frac{.67257 - .56082}{1 - .67257} \times \frac{97}{1} = 33.11 \qquad (df = 1, 97).$$

Actually, the F test for the gain in prediction by the addition of the quadratic term is the square of the t test for the significance of the quadratic term[3] in the quadratic equation, $t(97) = -5.75$.

Our emphasis on the increment in prediction by the quadratic term over and above the linear term should highlight once again that it is not the X^2 term per se that carries the quadratic component of the relationship of variable X to Y. Hence inspection of the correlation of the X^2 term with the criterion does not reflect the curvilinear nature of the data, as we warned in Section 6.2.3. Rather it is the *partialed* $X^2_{2.1}$, that is, X^2 with linear X partialed out, that represents the pure quadratic variable (Cohen, 1978).

6.2.5 Interpreting Polynomial Regression Results

Plots of Curvilinear Relationships

Plotting curvilinear relationships has now been made easy with the graphics contained in widely available statistical software, but plotting by hand can be accomplished by substituting values of X into the regression equation and generating the predicted scores. This must be done for a number of points to capture the shape of the curve. Be certain that if you are using the centered regression equation, you substitute centered values of X. Further, be certain that you use the highest order regression equation you have selected, *not* the linear term from the linear equation, the quadratic term from the quadratic equation, etc. The graph of the quadratic function in Fig. 6.2.3 is generated from centered equation $\hat{Y} = 1.21x - .13x^2 + 19.30$. For example, for centered $x = 0, \hat{Y} = 1.21(0) - .13(0^2) + 19.30 = 19.30$. For centered $x = 5, \hat{Y} = 1.20(5) - .13(5^2) = 19.30 = 22.05$. It is straightforward to translate the values of centered x into the original scale. Centered $x = 0$ corresponds to $M_X = 8.17$; centered $x = 5$ corresponds to $X = 5 + 8.17 = 13.17$.

Maxima and Minima

The polynomial of Eq. (6.2.1) defines a function that contains powers of X up to (let us say) the kth, with $k - 1$ bends. We may be interested in identifying the value of X at which each of the bends occurs,[4] for example, after what number of credits taken does interest in taking further courses begin to decline. Box 6.2.1 shows the computation of this value for the one bend in the quadratic polynomial equation.

---

[3]Note that this equation is equivalent to that of the test for sr_i (Eq. 3.6.8).

[4]In the quadratic equation, Eq. (6.2.3), the first derivative $B_{1.2} + 2B_{2.1}X$ is set to zero to solve for the value of X at which the function reaches a maximum or minimum.

BOX 6.2.1
Maximum and Minimum for a Quadratic Equation

For the quadratic, Eq. (6.2.3), there is one bend at the value X_M,

$$(6.2.5) \qquad X_M = \frac{-B_{1.2}}{2B_{2.1}}.$$

In the centered quadratic equation of Table 6.2.2, $X_M = -1.21/2(-.13) = 4.65$. Recall that the mean of X was 8.17. The value 4.65 is the number of points above the mean after centering, which is equivalent to $8.17 + 4.65 = 12.82$ in raw score units. Students' interest in further course work in a minor subject is estimated to peak at just under 13 credits of course work in the minor and to decline thereafter. We know from inspection of Fig. 6.2.3 that the value 4.65 is the value of centered x at which $\hat{Y}$ is maximum. In a quadratic equation with a negative $B_{2.1}$ coefficient, the value of $\hat{Y}$ is a maximum because the overall shape of the curve is concave downward; with $B_{2.1}$ positive, the value of $\hat{Y}$ is a minimum, since the overall shape of the curve is concave upward. Note that although X_M falls within the range of the observed data in this example, it need not. It may be that we are fitting a quadratic equation to data that rise to some point and then level off (reach asymptote). The maximum of a quadratic equation may fall outside the meaningful range of the data (e.g., be higher than the highest value of predictor X) and will be expected to do so if the data being fitted are asymptotic in the observed range.

The value of $\hat{Y}$ at its maximum or minimum value (here at centered $x = 4.65$) can be found by substituting Eq. (6.2.5) into the quadratic regression equation, which yields

$$(6.2.6) \qquad \hat{Y}_M = \frac{4\,(B_{2.1})(B_0) - B_{1.2}^2}{4\,(B_{2.1})}$$

For the quadratic numerical example in Table 6.2.2, this value is 22.12 on the 30-point scale of interest. Note that because we did not center Y, all predicted values for Y, including the predicted maximum, are in the original scale of the criterion.

Maxima and minima of polynomial regression equations are of interest in some applications, but they need not be routinely determined. They also require some caution in interpretation, since they are subject to sampling error, like other statistics, and hence are only approximations of the corresponding population values. The values of X_M identified by Eq. (6.2.5) are themselves sample estimates and exhibit sampling variability. For large samples, approximate standard errors of these sample X_M values can be estimated (see Neter, Wasserman, & Kutner, 1989, p. 337, Eq. 9.22).

Simple Slopes: Regression of Y on X at Specific Values of X

Once again refer to Fig. 6.2.3, and focus on the quadratic equation, identified with the squares. Imagine that we place a tangent line to the curve at each square, which represents the linear regression of Y on X at the particular value of X represented by the square. Recall from Section 6.2.2 that we can actually calculate the value of the linear regression of Y on X for each value of X using the expression

$$(6.2.7) \qquad B_{1.2} + 2B_{2.1}X.$$

These values are referred to as *simple slopes* (Aiken & West, 1991). In polynomial equations, the simple slopes represent the linear regression of Y on X at a particular value of X; each is the slope of a tangent line to the polynomial curve at a particular value of X. These values are useful in describing the polynomial regression function. For the centered quadratic regression equation in Table 6.2.2, the simple slope is $B_{1.2} + 2B_{2.1}x = 1.21 + 2(-.13)x$. For a case with centered $x = -3.10$ (one standard deviation below the mean of centered x), for example, the simple slope $= 1.21 + 2(-.13)(-3.10) = 2.02$. For centered $x = 0$, the simple slope is $1.21 + 2(-.13)(0.00) = 1.21$, the value of B_1. For centered $x = 3.10$ (one standard deviation above the mean of centered x), the simple slope $= 1.21 + 2(-.13)(3.10) = .40$. Finally, for centered $x = 6.20$ (two standard deviations above the mean of centered x), the simple slope becomes negative, $1.21 + 2(-.13)(6.20) = -.40$. Considered together, these four values of the simple slope confirm that interest rises strongly as students accumulate a few credits in a subject, then begins to level off, and finally diminishes after they have taken a relatively high number of credits in the subject.

As has been illustrated here, a series of these simple slopes is useful in describing the nature of the relationship of X to Y across the range of X (or another predictor). In fact, the simple slopes may be tested for significance of difference from zero in the population (see Aiken & West, 1991, p. 78). For example, we might examine whether interest is still rising significantly after three 3-credit courses (or 9 credit hours). The reader is warned that the algebraic expression for the simple slope changes as the order of the polynomial changes.

A Warning About Polynomial Regression Results

The quadratic polynomial regression equation plotted in Fig. 6.2.3 shows a relatively strong downward trend in the data at high values of predictor X. On the other hand, the lowess curve in Fig. 6.2.2(A) does not. (Recall from Section 4.2.2 that the lowess curve is a nonparametric curve that is completely driven by the data—no model is imposed.) The question is how to interpret the outcome of the polynomial regression. The data at hand are very, very sparse at high values of X. There is insufficient information to make a judgment about whether Y drops at very high values of X; hence judgment must be suspended. Both lowess curves and polynomial regression are uninformative at extreme values if data at these extreme values are sparse. In Section 6.2.7 we suggest a strategy of sampling heavily from extreme values on X to ameliorate this problem. It is always important to examine the actual data against both the polynomial regression and some nonparametric curve such as lowess with graphs that show both the fitted curves and the data points, as in Figs. 6.1.1, 6.2.1, 6.2.2, and 6.2.3. One must ask whether the data support the interpretation at the extremes of the predictors.

A Warning About Extrapolation

Extrapolation of a polynomial regression function beyond the extremes of observed X is particularly dangerous. Polynomial regression functions may be very steep and/or change directions at the extremes of the data. If we fit a second order polynomial to an asymptotic relationship that levels off but does not decline at high values of observed X and we project that function to even higher values of X, the function will eventually reverse direction. If we were to extrapolate beyond the highest observed X to predict the criterion, we would make incorrect predictions of scores that differed from the observed asymptote.

6.2.6 Another Example: A Cubic Fit

We offer another example of polynomial regression to demonstrate its operation for a more complex relationship and to further exemplify the general method. The variable W is of a different nature than X; it has only 6 integer values (1, 2, 3, 4, 5, 6 in uncentered form), they are equally spaced, and for each of these values there is the same number of points, 6 per value

CH06EX02

TABLE 6.2.3

Polynomial Multiple Regression Analysis of Regression of Y on W
with Centered Data

	Mean	sd	Centered correlation matrix			
				Y	w	w^2	w^3
Y	52.75	18.09	Y 1.000	.415	−.052	.251
w	0.00	1.73	w .415	1.000	.000	.934
w^2	2.92	2.53	w^2 −.052	.000	1.000	.000
w^3	0.00	9.36	w^3 .251	.934	.000	1.000

Regression Equations

Linear:	$\hat{Y}_{\text{linear}} =$	4.34w	+52.75
95% CI:		[1.03, 7.65]	
$t_{B_i}(34)$:		2.66	

Quadratic:	$\hat{Y}_{\text{quadratic}} =$	4.34w	−.38w^2	+53.84
95% CI:		[.98, 7.70]	[−2.67, 1.92]	
$t_{B_i}(33)$:		2.63	−.33	

Cubic:	$\hat{Y}_{\text{cubic}} =$	14.89w	−.38w^2	−2.09w^3	+53.84
95% CI:		[6.20, 23.58]	[−2.49, 1.74]	[−3.70, −.48]	
$t_{B_i}(32)$:		3.49	−.36	−2.65	

Hierarchical Model

Equation	IVs	R^2	F	df	I	F_I	df
Linear	w_1	.17	7.09**	1, 34	.173	7.09**	1, 34
Quadratic	w_1, w_2	.18	3.51*	2, 33	.003	.11	1, 33
Cubic	w_1, w_2, w_3	.32	5.10**	3, 32	.148	7.01**	1, 32

**$p < .01$

Note: I is the increment in R^2.

of W. These features suggest that W is a variable produced by experimental manipulation (e.g., number of exposures to a stimulus, or drug dosage level) and that the data structure is the product of a laboratory experiment rather than a field study. These features are important to substantive interpretation of the results but are not relevant to the present analysis; we would proceed as we do here with data at unequal intervals and/or unequal ns at each level of W (see Section 6.3.3). The mean of W is 3.5, and we center W, yielding w (−2.5, −1.5, −.5, .5, 1.5, 2.5) in centered form. Consider the plot of points in Fig. 6.2.1, relating Y to centered w and the analysis in Table 6.2.3 for the centered data.

The correlations among the centered predictors are instructive. The centered linear predictor w is perfectly symmetric. Its correlation with the centered quadratic predictor w^2 is 0.00. (Recall that in the previous example the correlation between centered x and x^2 was only .110, with this very small correlation due to minor asymmetry in x.) However, the correlation between w and w^3, the centered cubic predictor, is .934. Even with centering, all odd powers of the linear predictor (w, w^3, w^5, etc.) will be highly intercorrelated; similarly, all even powers will be highly intercorrelated (w^2, w^4, w^6, etc.). Even with these high interpredictor correlations, the analysis can proceed.

The correlation of Y with w (the centered linear aspect of W) is found to be .415, so that 17.2% of the Y variance can be accounted for by w, corresponding to a moderate to large effect size (Cohen, 1988). Again we caution the reader that this only means that in the population (as well as in the sample) a straight line accounts for some variance and not necessarily that it provides an optimal fit. The equation for this line is given in the middle of Table 6.2.3; the confidence interval for B_1, CI: [1.03, 7.65], does not include zero and reflects the strong positive trend in the data, with $t(34) = 2.66, p < .05$, or, equivalently, $F(1, 34)$ for prediction from the linear prediction equation $= 7.07, p < .05$, where $t = \sqrt{F}$. The linear equation is plotted in Fig. 6.2.1, noted by triangles. Since this data set is structured to have replications at each value of w (i.e., 6 cases at each value of w), we can examine the arithmetic mean observed Y score at each value of w, represented by the squares in Fig. 6.2.1. Although the straight line accounts for substantial variance in Y, we note the S-shaped function of these means; they decrease from $w = -2.5$ to $w = -1.5$, then rise to $w = 1.5$, and then drop again, a two-bend pattern.

When the quadratic term w^2 is added into the equation, R^2 increases by only .003, and the confidence interval CI: [−2.67, 1.92] for the $B_{2.1}$ coefficient ($B_{2.1} = -.38$) in the quadratic equation includes zero. The data do not support the relevance of the quadratic aspect of W to Y. Note that it is not curvilinearity that is being rejected, but quadratic curvilinearity, that is, a tendency for a parabolic arc to be at least partially descriptive of the regression; a higher order, necessarily curvilinear, aspect of W may characterize the overall form of the relationship of W to Y.

The addition of the cubic term w^3, in contrast, does make a substantial difference, with an increment in R^2 over the quadratic R^2 of .15, a moderate effect size (J. Cohen, 1988). The confidence interval for the cubic coefficient, CI: [−3.70, −.48] does not include zero, $t(32) = -2.65, p < .05$. Table 6.2.3 gives the cubic equation, which is also plotted in Fig. 6.2.1 (noted by filled circles). The cubic always gives a two-bend function (although the bends need not appear within the part of the range of the independent variable under study—see Section 6.2.5), and the fit of the cubic equation to the data is visibly improved; the cubic equation better tracks the means of Y at each value of w, though the match is not perfect. We conclude that this regression equation is curvilinear and, more particularly, that it is cubic. By this we mean that the cubic aspect of W relates to Y, and also that the best fitting equation utilizing w, w^2, and w^3 will account for more Y variance in the population than one that has only w and w^2, or (necessarily) only w.

Since we have centered W, the coefficients for the w and w^2 terms in the cubic equations have meaning, though the utility of these terms seems less clear than for the quadratic equation. The $B_{1.23}$ coefficient is the slope of a tangent line to the cubic function at the value $w = 0$. Note in Fig. 6.2.3 that the slope of the cubic function is much steeper at this point than the slope of the linear function, and the $B_{1.23}$ coefficient from the cubic equation is substantially larger (14.89) than the $B_{1.2}$ coefficient in the quadratic equation (Eq. 4.34). The $B_{2.13}$ coefficient indicates the curvature (concave upward, concave downward) at the value $w = 0$. Once again we caution that if one reports these coefficients, their meaning should be explained, because they are little understood.

The cubic function has both a maximum and a minimum; values of the independent variable W at these points may be useful in interpretation. Simple slopes can also be calculated for a cubic function and can be used to describe the function. Computations are given in Box 6.2.2.

6.2.7 Strategy and Limitations

What Order Polynomial, Revisited

In Section 6.2.1 we argued that theory should drive the choice of the order polynomial to be estimated. Yet there may be some exploratory aspect to the analysis. In the quadratic example of student interest in academic minor subjects, we hypothesized a quadratic relationship of

---

BOX 6.2.2
Maximum, Minimum, and Simple Slopes for a Cubic Equation

In the case of the quadratic equation there is either a minimum or maximum point; in the full cubic equation (Eq. 6.2.4), there are both a minimum and a maximum value. The values of W at which the minimum and maximum occur are given as the two solutions to Eq. (6.2.8).

(6.2.8)
$$W_M = \frac{-B_{2.13} \pm \sqrt{B_{2.13}^2 - 3B_{1.23}B_{3.21}}}{3B_{3.21}}$$

For the cubic numerical example in Table 6.2.3, the two solutions to W_M are -1.60 and 1.48, on the centered X scale. These values correspond to uncentered .90 and 3.98 respectively on the original 1 to 6 point X scale. The corresponding values of $\hat{Y} = 37.60$ (the minimum) and $\hat{Y} = 68.28$ (the maximum), respectively.

The *simple slope* of the regression of Y on W in the cubic equation[5] is given as

(6.2.9)
$$B_{1.2} + 2B_{2.1}W + 3B_{3.12}W^2.$$

Once again, the simple slope indicates the slope of Y on W at a particular value of W in the polynomial equation. For centered $w = -1.5$, just above the value of w at which $\hat{Y}$ attains a minimum, the simple slope is $14.89 + 2(-.38)(-1.5) + 3(-2.09)(-1.5)^2 = 1.92$ (i.e., the function is rising). For centered $w = 1.5$, just above the value of w at which $\hat{Y}$ attains a maximum, the simple slope is $14.89 + 2(-.38)(1.5) + 3(-2.09)(1.5)^2 = -.36$ (i.e., the function has begun to fall below the maximum).

---

rising followed by falling interest. We also had some curiosity about whether interest returned among students who had taken a large number of credits, as would be detected with a cubic polynomial. We thus examined the quadratic and cubic relationships. We recommend that the application of polynomial regression begin with setting out the theoretical rationale that might be provided for each polynomial examined. It makes little sense to fit a series of increasingly higher order polynomials and to identify a high-order polynomial term as significant when there is no rationale for the meaning of this term. We also caution that vagaries of the data, particularly outliers in Y with X values at the ends of the range of observed values, may dramatically alter the order of the polynomial that is detected.

Two approaches to exploring polynomial equations exist. First is a *build-up* procedure in which one examines first the linear equation, then the quadratic equation, and so forth; each equation examined includes all lower order terms. A *tear-down* procedure reverses the process, beginning with the highest order equation of interest and simplifying by working down to lower order equations. First, the highest order term in the complete highest order equation also containing all lower order terms is examined by some criterion (traditional significance level, effect size, confidence interval). If the term accounts for a proportion of variance deemed material by the researcher, then the polynomial at this level is retained. If not, then the highest order term is eliminated from the equation, the next lower order equation is estimated, and the highest order term in this equation is examined.

---

[5]In the cubic equation, Eq. (6.2.4), the first derivative is $B_{1.23} + 2B_{2.13}W + 3B_{3.12}W^2$. This derivative is set to zero to determine the minimum and maximum of the cubic function, given in Eq. (6.2.5).

Each of these approaches has its advantages and its limitations. The difficulty in the build-up procedure is in deciding when to stop in adding terms. Consider the cubic numerical example of Table 6.2.3, in which the linear term is significant in the linear equation and accounts for 17% of the criterion variance: The quadratic term is not significant in the quadratic equation, accounting for less than 1% of variance over and above the linear term, but the cubic term is significant in the cubic equation, accounting for an additional 15% of the variance in the criterion. A rule that indicates we should stop adding terms at the point at which there is no longer a gain in predictability (measured in terms of significance or effect size) would lead us, in the cubic example, to stop with the linear equation. The quadratic term does not contribute material accounted for variance over and above the linear effect. But the relationship is cubic; by build-up cutoff rules we would not reach the cubic equation.

The tear-down procedure has the advantage of insuring a test of the highest order term of interest. In the cubic numerical example, the tear-down procedure would begin with a test of the cubic term in the cubic equation (assuming we had some hypothesis of a cubic relationship). Having found the cubic term to be significant (or to have a large effect size), we would stop the exploration; that is, we would retain the cubic equation and not test terms from lower order equations. Of course, we would still miss any higher order terms that might have been statistically significant although unanticipated.

Must one pick one of the two strategies and rigidly adhere to it in deciding upon the order of the polynomial? Absolutely not. One can first target the theoretically predicted equation (e.g., the quadratic equation in our earlier example of taking further credits in one's minor, depicted in Fig. 6.1.1.) If there is some reason to suspect a higher order trend in the data (e.g., the cubic term), we may then examine the cubic equation. There are no rigid rules for identifying the appropriate equation. Consider a cubic example. Suppose we identified the cubic equation as appropriate in a large sample based on the highest order term but in plotting the equation we saw that the curvature was slight compared to the strong linear trend and that the cubic equation very closely approximated the linear equation plotted on the same graph. We could estimate the linear equation to determine the percentage of variance accounted for by only the linear trend. We might even decide, based on effect size (additional variance accounted for) that we would not retain the cubic equation but would use the linear equation, particularly if there were not a strong theoretical rationale for the higher order term.

There are no hard and fast rules for the inclusion of higher order terms in polynomial equations. An aspect of selecting the final equation is the behavior of residuals, as illustrated in Fig. 6.2.2(B). Model checking (described in Section 4.4) will be informative and is advised. For example, an added variable plot for a higher order term may help clarify the role of this higher order term. To decide between two equations of adjacent order, one of several criteria may be employed:

1. *Statistical significance.*   We would examine the loss (or gain) in prediction attributable to the highest order term in a tear-down (or build-up) procedure, employing some conventional level of significance.

2. *Change in R^2.*   The difference in R^2 between two adjacent polynomial equations is closely related to the measure of effect size for change in prediction specified by J. Cohen (1988, pp. 412–413). The change from $R^2_{Y.A}$ to $R^2_{Y.AB}$ is the squared semipartial correlation of B with the criterion, over and above A. The squared partial correlation is given as Eq. (5.4.11):

(5.4.11)
$$R^2_{YB \cdot A} = \frac{R^2_{Y.AB} - R^2_{Y.A}}{1 - R^2_{Y.A}}.$$

Cohen (1988) suggested that squared partial correlations of .02, .13, and .26 were reflective of small, moderate, and large effect sizes, respectively.

3. *Change in* $\tilde{R}^2$. Thus far in this chapter, we have been concerned only with the observed R^2 and changes in R^2. However, we know that the addition of any independent variable to a set, even a random, nonpredictive variable, will result in an increase in R^2—a decrease is mathematically impossible and an increment of exactly zero is exceedingly rare. It can be instructive to track the change in the shrunken $\tilde{R}^2$, the estimated proportion of variance in Y accounted for in the population by a polynomial of that order (see Section 3.5.3). Unlike the increment in the R^2 observed, this increment may be positive or negative. A reasonable criterion for deciding between two equations is that the change in $\tilde{R}^2$ between the equations is some arbitrary minimum constant, say between .02 and .05.

The overriding preference in using polynomial equations is that the order of the polynomial be small. Relatively weak data quality in the social sciences (i.e., the presence of substantial measurement error), mitigates against fitting high order equations. Our theories do not predict higher order terms. We gain no benefit in interpretation from fitting an equation of high order. We do not advocate a curve fitting approach in which higher order terms are added merely because they increase the R^2 by small amounts. The likelihood of replication is low indeed. Finally, the polynomial terms may be included in more complex equations. The variable represented by a polynomial may be hypothesized to interact with other variables. As we will see in Chapter 7, each interaction requires predictors involving all the terms in the polynomial equation.

Impact of Outliers and Sampling to Increase Stability

Polynomial equations may be highly unstable and can be grossly affected by individual outliers. Examine Fig. 6.1.1 for the quadratic polynomial. Note that at the highest value of $X, X = 17$, there is only one data point. Its Y value ($Y = 23.38$) lies between the linear and quadratic equations. Changing the value of Y for this point to the highest scale value ($Y = 30.00$, or an increment of 6.62 points) produces substantial changes in the regression equation. In the original analysis, summarized in Table 6.2.2, the increments in prediction were .56, .11, and .01 for the linear, quadratic, and cubic terms, respectively; the cubic term was not significant. In the analysis with the one modified data point, the corresponding increments are .59, .07, and .03. The cubic term is significant, $B_{3.12} = .01$, CI: [.01, .02], $t(96) = 3.22, p < .01$. One data point out of 100 cases has produced the cubic effect.

Sparseness of the data points at the ends of the X distribution contributes to the instability. We may sample cases systematically to increase both the stability of regression equations and the power to detect effects (McClelland & Judd, 1993; Pitts & West, 2001). The X variable in the quadratic example is normally distributed, with relatively few cases in the two tails. If X were rectangularly (uniformly) distributed, with an approximately equal number of data points at each value of X, then there would be many more points in the tails, on average just under 6 data points for each of the 17 observed values of X (see Fig. 6.2.4). In a simulation in which 100 values of X were rectangularly distributed, and the same population regression equation was employed, there were 6 points with $X = 17$. Of these 6 points, the point with the highest Y value, initially 30.93, was modified by increasing the Y value the same amount as was done in the normally distributed case, 6.62 points, to 37.55. Before modifying the point the increments in prediction were .63, .24, and .00, for linear, quadratic, and cubic, respectively. After modifying the point, these increments were .64, .22, and .00, respectively. The cubic term accounted for essentially no variance either before or after the modification of the single point.

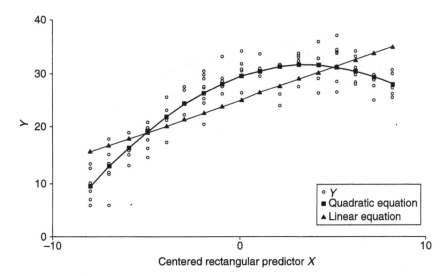

FIGURE 6.2.4   Quadratic relationship with predictor X sampled to have a rectangular distribution. The population regression equation for the quadratic regression equation is identical to that generating the data of Figure 6.1.1 (or centered data of Fig. 6.2.3). The triangles characterize the best fit linear regression of Y on x; the squares, the best fit quadratic regression of Y on x. Note that the density of points in the extremes of the distribution is much greater here than with normally distributed predictor X in Fig. 6.2.3.

There are other more complex rules for sampling X than simple rectangular sampling. These rules arise from an area of statistics termed *optimal design*; McClelland and Judd (1993) and Pitts and West (2001) provide easily accessible introductions to the topic. See Atkinson and Donev (1992) for a complete development.

6.2.8 More Complex Equations

Polynomial equations may also include other predictors. Recall that Janis (1967) predicted that compliance with medical recommendations (Y) would first increase and then decrease as fear of a health threat (X) increases. Medical compliance also increases with the belief that health can be controlled by medical practitioners (W) (Wallston, Wallston, & DeVellis, 1978). We would specify these predictions in the equation $\hat{Y} = B_{1.23}X + B_{2.13}X^2 + B_{3.12}W + B_0$. A simulated data set that follows these predictions is illustrated in Fig. 6.2.5. Instead of the usual flat regression plane generated by two predictors that bear linear relationships to the criterion, we have a curved regression surface. The curve is produced by predictor X that follows the Janis (1967) prediction. A strategy for examining this equation is first to estimate the full equation containing X, X^2 and W as predictors, as well as an equation containing only the linear X and linear W terms. The difference in prediction between these two equations is used to gauge whether the curvilinear term is required. Once this is decided, the effect of the W predictor should be considered in the presence of the X terms retained. Note that in this strategy, the test of curvilinearity of the relationship of X to Y is carried out in the presence of W. The test of W is carried out in the presence of X in the form in which it apparently relates to the criterion. Since predictors X and/or X^2 may be correlated with W, it is appropriate to treat each variable in the presence of the others, as is usual in multiple regression with correlated predictors. The relationship between predictors X and W may not be linear. Darlington (1991)

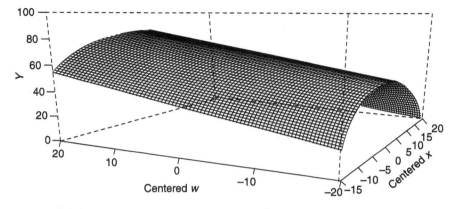

FIGURE 6.2.5   Regression surface for equation $\hat{Y} = .06x - .12x^2 + .86w + 66.08$. Predictor variables X and W produce a regression surface. The quadratic relationship of variable X to Y produces the concave downward shape of the surface. The positive linear relationship of W to Y produces the tilt of the plane. Note that the front right hand corner of the figure represents the lowest values of centered predictors x and w.

warns that difficulties are introduced when there are nonlinear relationships between predictors. In this case, nonlinear relationships of the predictor to the criterion may be obscured in residual scatterplots.

6.3 ORTHOGONAL POLYNOMIALS

In instances in which the values of a variable W form ordered categories, as in the cubic numerical example, it is possible to examine nonlinearity with a special class of variables, *orthogonal polynomials*. Orthogonal polynomials are unique variables that are structured to capture specific curve components—linear, quadratic, cubic, etc. Orthogonal polynomials exist in sets (one linear, one quadratic, one cubic, etc.). For a variable W with u categories, there are $(u - 1)$ orthogonal polynomials in the complete set; for the cubic example with $u = 6$, there are $(u - 1) = 5$ orthogonal polynomials (linear, quadratic, cubic, quartic, quintic). The orthogonal polynomials are used as predictors in a regression equation to represent the variable W. The members of a set of orthogonal polynomials have the special property of being mutually orthogonal, that is, they are uncorrelated with one another. Thus they account for independent portions of variance in a criterion when W represents a complete set of categories ($X = 1, 2, 3, \ldots, u$, with no skipped categories) and there are equal ns at each value of W.

Each orthogonal polynomial is a series of integer coefficients or weights; the weights for each orthogonal polynomial sum to zero. Orthogonal polynomials have two defining properties: mutually orthogonal codes that sum to zero.[6] The specific integer weights of an orthogonal polynomial depend upon the number of values (ordered categories) of the predictors. Table 6.3.1 provides sets of orthogonal polynomials for the linear, quadratic and cubic terms of predictors

---

[6]Orthogonal polynomials are a special case of code variables called *contrast codes*, which have the properties of being mutually orthogonal and summing to zero. In general, code variables are structured variables specifically designed to be applied to categorical predictors. Chapter 8 is devoted to code variables; contrast codes are presented in Section 8.5.

TABLE 6.3.1

Orthogonal Polynomial Coding for u-Point Scales; First-, Second-, and Third-Order Polynomials for $u = 3$ to 12^a

$u = 3$		$u = 4$			$u = 5$			$u = 6$			$u = 7$		
X_1	X_2	X_1	X_2	X_3	X_1	X_2	X_3	X_1	X_2	X_3	X_1	X_2	X_3
1	1	-3	1	-1	-2	2	-1	-5	5	-5	-3	5	-1
0	-2	-1	-1	3	-1	-1	2	-3	-1	7	-2	0	1
-1	1	1	-1	-3	0	-2	0	-1	-4	4	-1	-3	1
		3	1	1	1	-1	-2	1	-4	-4	0	-4	0
					2	2	1	3	-1	-7	1	-3	-1
								5	5	5	2	0	-1
											3	5	1

$u = 8$			$u = 9$			$u = 10$			$u = 11$			$u = 12$		
X_1	X_2	X_3	X_1	X_2	X_3	X_1	X_2	X_3	X_1	X_2	X_3	X_1	X_2	X_3
-7	7	-7	-4	28	-14	-9	6	-42	-5	15	-30	-11	55	-33
-5	1	5	-3	7	7	-7	2	14	-4	6	6	-9	25	3
-3	-3	7	-2	-8	13	-5	-1	35	-3	-1	22	-7	1	21
-1	-5	3	-1	-17	9	-3	-3	31	-2	-6	23	-5	-17	25
1	-5	-3	0	-20	0	-1	-4	12	-1	-9	14	-3	-29	19
3	-3	-7	1	-17	-9	1	-4	-12	0	-10	0	-1	-35	7
5	1	-5	2	-8	-13	3	-3	-31	1	-9	-14	1	-35	-7
7	7	7	3	7	-7	5	-1	-35	2	-6	-23	3	-29	-19
			4	28	14	7	2	-14	3	-1	-22	5	-17	-25
						9	6	42	4	6	-6	7	1	-21
									5	15	30	9	25	-3
												11	55	33

^{a} This table is abridged from Table 20.1 in Owen (1962). (Courtesy of the U.S. AEC.)

with from $u = 3$ to 12 categories.[7] Although for u ordered categories there exist a set of $u - 1$ codes, those above cubic are not likely to be useful for reasons we have discussed (Section 6.2.7). Note that within any set for $u = k$ categories, the sum of the products of corresponding weights for any pair of polynomials is zero, for example for the quadratic and cubic terms for $u = 5$: $(2)(-1) + (-1)(2) + (-2)(0) + (-1)(-2) + (2)(1) = 0$; this is the orthogonality property. Finally, each column of coefficients in Table 6.3.1, when plotted against an equal interval scale from low to high has the distinctive shape of its order (e.g., the quadratic coefficients for X_2 form a concave upward parabola).

Orthogonal polynomials are applied to *ordered categories* which are assumed to be *equally spaced* along some underlying continuum. For example, if the continuum were a drug dosage continuum, the categories should result from equal increments in dosages across the continuum. There are two further requirements for the use of orthogonal polynomials to produce orthogonal portions of variance accounted for by individual curve components. First, the ordered values of the original predictor must be a *full set of numerically equally spaced categories*; that is, if

---

[7]High-order polynomials and larger numbers of points are available elsewhere. The most extensive are those of Anderson and Houseman (1942), which go up to the fifth order and to $u = 104$. Pearson and Hartley (1954) give up to the sixth order and to $u = 52$. Kleinbaum, Kupper, and Muller (1988) provide all $(u - 1)$ polynomial coefficients for $u = 3, \ldots, 10$ categories.

there are six categories, all six categories must be represented in the data set. Second, there must be *equal numbers of cases* in each ordered category.[8] These conditions for the use of orthogonal polynomials are most likely to be met in laboratory experiments, as in the example of dose responses to drugs.

The polynomials we have used as predictors to this point are *natural polynomials*, generated from the linear predictor by centering and then powering the linear predictor. Natural polynomials are typically correlated so that effects (linear, quadratic, etc.) are necessarily partialed effects. Orthogonal polynomials eliminate this complexity by eliminating the correlation among polynomials. With correlated natural polynomials, we examined increments of variance accounted for by individual polynomial terms. Since, given equal ns, the orthogonal polynomials are uncorrelated with each other, the square of the correlation of each orthogonal polynomial with the criterion r_{Yi}^2 indicates the proportion of variation accounted for by that curve component in the regression equation containing the set of orthogonal polynomials. This squared correlation is exactly equal to the increment in prediction of the criterion by the inclusion of the particular polynomial. In other words, since the orthogonal polynomials are mutually uncorrelated (with equal ns) and there is thus nothing to partial, the correlations r_{Yi} will equal the semipartial correlations sr_{Yi}. These correlations r_{Yi} will also equal the standardized regression coefficients for the orthogonal polynomials β_i.

6.3.1 The Cubic Example Revisited

To accomplish polynomial regression, the natural polynomials are replaced as predictors in the regression equation by the orthogonal polynomials. The linear orthogonal polynomial $X_{\text{linear}} = -5, -3, -1, 1, 3, 5$ replaces w; the quadratic polynomial $X_{\text{quadratic}} = 5, -1, -4, -4, -1, 5$ replaces w^2; similarly, X_{cubic} replaces w^3.

Results of a simultaneous MR analysis are given in Table 6.3.2. Note first that the correlations among the predictors $X_{\text{linear}}, X_{\text{quadratic}}$, and X_{cubic} are all zero. This occurs because the data set contains an equal number of cases at each value of W. Were this not the case, then despite the orthogonality of the polynomial coefficients, the predictors created from substituting the coefficients of the orthogonal polynomials would be correlated. Since the predictors are uncorrelated, the squared correlation of each predictor with the criterion is the proportion of variation accounted for by that curve component. These are *identical* to the respective increments I for the individual curve components in Table 6.2.3. The partialing out of lower order terms for correlated natural polynomials in Table 6.2.3 is replaced in Table 6.3.2 by the use of orthogonal predictors, thus rendering partialing unnecessary. Because the orthogonal polynomial predictors are uncorrelated, $R_{Y.123}^2$ is simply the sum of the three r_{Yi}^2: $R_{Y.123}^2 = .172 + .003 + .148 = .323$, as in the original cubic example. The unstandardized regression coefficients for $X_{\text{linear}}, X_{\text{quadratic}}$, and X_{cubic} in Table 6.3.2 do not equal the corresponding coefficients for w, w^2 and w^3 in Table 6.2.3. Nonetheless, the two equations generate identical predicted scores; that is, the same cubic function is generated by both equations.

Tests of Significance and Confidence Intervals for Curve Components

We describe three approaches to testing the significance of coefficients in orthogonal polynomials. These approaches are all special cases of the general strategy for testing sets of

---

[8]The derivation of orthogonal polynomials for unequal ns is given in Gaito (1965) and in Appendix C of Kirk (1995).

TABLE 6.3.2

Simultaneous Orthogonal Polynomial Multiple Regression Analysis of Regression of *Y* on *W* (same data as Table 6.2.3).

	Mean	sd				Uncentered correlation matrix				
					Y	linear	quadratic	cubic	$r_{r_i}^2$	t_{r_t}
Y	52.75	18.09	Y	1.000	.415	−.052	−.385		
linear	.00	3.46	linear	.415	1.000	.000	.000	.172	2.663*
quadratic	.00	3.80	quadratic	−.052	.000	1.000	.000	.003	−.306
cubic	.00	5.56	cubic	−.385	.000	.000	1.000	.148	2.433*

Regression Equation

Cubic: $\hat{Y}_{cubic} =$ 2.17 linear   −.25 quadratic   −1.25 cubic   +52.75
95% CI: [.62, 3.72]   [−1.66, 1.16]   [−2.22, 2.89]
t_{B_i} (32):   2.86*   −.36   −2.65*

R^2 (linear, quadratic, cubic) = .32356 with 3, 32 df.

Analysis of Variance of Trend Components

Source	SS	df	MS	F
Treatment	4020.9167	5		
Linear	1976.0024	1	1976.0024	7.97*
Quadratic	31.5000	1	31.5000	.12
Cubic	1697.5148	1	1697.5148	6.85*
Higher order	315.8995	2	157.9497	.64
Error (within)	7429.8333	30	247.6611	
Total	11450.7500			

R^2 (linear, quadratic, cubic, quartic, quintic) = .35115 with 5, 30 df.

* *p* < .05.

predictors in Section 5.5, in which there is a set **B** of predictor(s) that is tested while another set **A** is partialed out, the Model 1 approach. What varies from approach to approach is the specific terms partialed out, (i.e., set **A**).

1. The first strategy involves specifying a single polynomial equation at the highest order trend level of interest and testing each regression coefficient in the equation against the $MS_{residual}$ from that highest order regression equation. Tests of terms in the cubic equation in Table 6.2.3 exemplify this strategy. The $MS_{residual}$ is a Model 1 error in that the particular term being tested constitutes set **B**, and all other terms in the equation, all of which are partialed, constitute set **A**. In the cubic equation of Table 6.2.3, the test of the quadratic coeffcient (set **B**) is carried out with both the linear and cubic terms (set **A**) partialed out.

2. The second strategy is a hierarchical strategy, as described in Section 6.2.4, in which one tests the linear term in the linear equation, the quadratic term in the quadratic equation, and so forth. The $MS_{residual}$ for each test comes from a different regression equation. Again this is a form of the Model 1 strategy; the particular term being tested constitutes set **B**; all *lower order* terms constitute set **A**. In this strategy, the quadratic term (set **B**) is tested in the quadratic equation, with the linear term (set **A**) partialed out.

3. The third strategy is one that we have not heretofore encountered. In this strategy, all $(u - 1)$ possible trend components are included in a single regression equation. The coefficient for each trend component is tested against $MS_{residual}$ from the complete equation. This is again a form of Model 1 testing, in which the term being tested constitutes set B and all other terms, both lower and higher order, constitute set A. For the cubic example, with $(u - 1) = 5$ orthogonal polynomials, the test of the quadratic term (set B) would be carried out with the linear, cubic, quartic, and quintic terms (set B) partialed out.

Coefficients in different equations.   With orthogonal polynomials and equal ns, since the predictors are uncorrelated, each coefficient in the equation containing one set of curve components equals the corresponding coefficient in an equation with fewer or more curve components. For the cubic example, the linear, quadratic, and cubic equations are as follows: linear, $\hat{Y} = 2.17$ linear $+ 52.75$; quadratic: $\hat{Y} = 2.17$ linear $-.25$ quadratic $+ 52.75$; cubic: $\hat{Y} = 2.17$ linear $- .25$ quadratic $- 1.25$ cubic $+ 52.75$.

Residual variance in different equations and resulting statistical power. Although the three approaches will yield the same regression coefficients for corresponding polynomial components, these approaches differ in the specific sources of variance included in $MS_{residual}$, as we have seen for the test of the quadratic term in each strategy described earlier. Thus they yield different values of $MS_{residual}$ with different associated degrees of freedom, and thus different tests of significance of individual coefficients and different confidence intervals on the coefficients. The relative statistical power of the three approaches depends on the magnitude of trend components other than the specific individual trend being tested and whether these other trends are included as predictors in the model or are pooled into $MS_{residual}$.

Table 6.3.3 shows the t tests for the linear coefficient in the data from Table 6.3.2 according to the three testing approaches. There is a general principle that emerges: If one includes in the model extra terms that do not account for material amounts of variance (e.g., the quartic and quintic terms), one reduces power. In contrast, including a term that accounts for a material amount of variance (here the cubic term), increases power for the tests of other effects.

TABLE 6.3.3
t Tests of Alternative Models for Testing Orthogonal Polynomials
Under Three Approaches to Testing

		Approach					
		(1) Simultaneous subset		(2) Hierarchical buildup		(3) Simultaneous full set	
Aspect of W	Increment	t	df	t	df	t	df
Linear	.173	2.857	32	2.663	34	2.825	30
Quadratic	.003	−.361	32	−.332	33	−.357	30
Cubic	.148	−2.648	32	−2.648	32	−2.618	30
Quartic						.755	30
Quintic						.840	30

Note: Approach (1): each term tested in a model contained the same subset of all possible trend components (linear, quadratic, and cubic); approach (2): each term tested in a model in which all lower order terms are included; approach (3); each term tested in a model containing all possible trend components (linear, quadratic, cubic, quartic, and quintic).

Choosing Among the Three Approaches

The choice among the three approaches requires resolution of the competing demands of maximizing statistical power, minimizing the risk of having negatively biased statistical tests (i.e., tests that underestimate statistical signficance), and obtaining confidence intervals that are as narrow as possible.

Approach 1 requires that a particular level of polynomial be specified in advance, hopefully driven by theory. It is recommended when k is small (e.g., 3) and n is large. We expect that k chosen based on theorizing in the behavioral sciences will, in fact, be small—at most cubic. It is generally sensible to exclude from error the k terms in which one is seriously interested, and when n is sizable, the df for $MS_{residual}$, $n - k - 1$ df, are sufficient to maintain power.

Approach 2 in the build-up mode is very much exploratory. If there are substantial higher order components, then tests of lower order components are negatively biased, as in the cubic numerical example. When there are clear hypotheses about the order of the appropriate equation, approach 1 is preferred.

Approach 3 is safe in its avoidance of underestimating tests of significance because all trend components are included. It requires that $n - u$ be large enough to achieve adequate power for the effect size expected for the critical term. It should be used if the test of gain in prediction from the higher order terms (e.g., the quartic and quintic test in our cubic example) is of substantial effect size (i.e., accounting for more than a few percent of variance). In such a case, the approach 1 tests would be negatively biased.

*Trend Analysis in Analysis of Variance
and Orthogonal Polynomial Regression*

The third approach to testing orthogonal polynomials in MR is isomorphic with trend analysis in a one factor non-repeated measures ANOVA applied to a factor consisting of ordered categories. In trend analysis, $SS_{between\ cell}$ from the overall design is partitioned into $(u - 1)$ trend components (linear, quadratic, etc.) for the u levels of the factor. $MS_{residual}$ from the regression analysis with all trend components is identical to $MS_{within\ cell}$ from the one factor ANOVA. The bottom section of Table 6.3.2 presents a trend analysis of the cubic data set from Table 6.3.2, showing the partition of $SS_{treatment}$ into trend components. The ratio of the SS for each component (linear, quadratic, etc.) to SS_{total} yields the squared correlation of each trend component with the criterion. The F tests for the individual components, each with $(1, 30)$ df are the squares of the t tests reported in Table 6.3.3, approach 3. The overall $R^2 = SS_{treatment}/SS_{total} = .35$ with the five components included represents the maximum predictability possible from a full set of trend components. Here trend analysis is applied to non-repeated measures data, with different subjects in each ordered category of predictor W. Trend analysis may also be applied to repeated measures data, in which the same individuals appear at each level of the repeated measured factor (see Section 15.3.2).

6.3.2 Unequal *n* and Unequal Intervals

The previous example had equal ns at each of the u points of variable W. This property is required in order that the curve components of variable W account for orthogonal portions of variance in the criterion Y. When the ns are not equal, the correlations r_{ij} among the aspects of W are generally not zero, because the orthogonal polynomial coefficients are unequally weighted. With the curve components not independent, equality among r_{Yi}^2s and sr_{Yi}^2s in the simultaneous model is lost and r_{Yi}^2 no longer equals the amount of variance accounted for purely by the ith trend component, I_i. This, however, constitutes no problem in analyzing the data—we simply revert to strategies involving the exploration of partialed effects, as discussed in Section 6.2.4.

Another circumstance that defeats the simplicity of the use of orthogonal polynomials but can be handled in MR is inequality of the given intervals in the variable W. A scale with unequal given intervals can be conceived as one with equal intervals some of whose scale points have no data. For example, on a $u = 9$-point scale (e.g., an experiment with potentially 9 equally spaced drug dosages) data may have been obtained for only $q = 5$ values of W: 1, 2, 4, 6, 9. We can code these as if we had a 9-point scale, using coefficients under $u = 9$ in Table 6.3.1, but, of course, omitting the coded values for points 3, 5, 7, and 8. The effect on the r_{ij} among the trend components is as before: They take on generally nonzero values, and the analysis proceeds by examining partialed effects. With q different observed values of variable W, in all only $(q - 1)$ trend components are required to perfectly fit the q means of the criterion, computed for each value of W.

Finally, using orthogonal polynomial coefficients and partialed contributions of individual trend components, we can analyze problems in which neither the given intervals nor the numbers of observations per scale are equal, by simply proceeding as in the preceding paragraph (J. Cohen, 1980).

6.3.3 Applications and Discussion

A number of circumstances in research may seem to invite the use of orthogonal polynomials. However, alternative approaches, discussed here, may be more appropriate.

Experiments

The greatest simplicity in the application of orthogonal polynomials occurs under equal n, and u equally spaced points of a variable V. Such data are produced by experiments where V is some manipulated variable (number of rewards, level of illumination, size of discussion group) and Y is causally dependent on this input. Typically, such data sets are characterized by relatively small number of observations per condition. These are the circumstances in which testing approach 1 would be preferred if there are few trends of interest, approach 2 if there are a large number of trends of interest. Note that throughout this chapter, the n observations at each of the u points of predictor X are taken to be independent. The frequently occurring case where n subjects or matched sets of subjects yield observations for each of the conditions is not analyzed as described previously. Chapter 15 addresses the analysis of repeated measures data.

Sampling from a Continuum

In some research applications cases are sampled at specific values or small subranges across a continuum. For example, in a developmental study, cases may be sampled in discrete age ranges (e.g., 3–3.5 years of age, 4–4.5 years, etc.). If so, then these discrete categories may be considered as points on a continuum, as in experiments, and orthogonal polynomials applied to the series of ordered age categories. There is argument in favor of treating the ages continuously in MR with polynomial regression applied to the actual ages. Statistical power is higher with MR applied to actual ages than to data sampled with coarse categories (Pitts & West, 2001).

Sometimes, as in surveys, continua are broken into response categories, as in age: under 20, 20–30, 30–40, . . . , over 70. Such variables may be treated provisionally as if they represented equal intervals, even if the two extreme categories are "open." The end intervals produce lateral displacements of the true curve. If the true relationship is (or is assumed to be) smooth, distortion due to inequality of the end intervals may be detected by the polynomial.

Serial Data Without Replication

Thus far we have been assuming that at each of the u points of a variable V, there are multiple Y observations or "replications," the means of which define the function to be fitted. We now consider instances in which a single individual is observed repeatedly over time, for example, ratings by a psychotherapist of each of a series of 50 consecutive weekly sessions; thus $n = u = 50$. The purpose of analysis might be to test propositions about the nature of the trend over time of Y for this patient. Observations on a single case collected repeated over time are referred to as *time series* data and are appropriately treated in *time series analysis*, discussed in Section 15.8. Time series analysis takes into account the autocorrelation among successive observations on the individual (see Sections 4.4 and 4.5 for discussions of autocorrelation).

6.4 NONLINEAR TRANSFORMATIONS

Thus far in this chapter, we have sought to assure the proper representation of a quantitatively expressed research factor X, by coding it as a set of k IVs, each representing a single aspect of X: as a set of integer powers $X, X^2, \ldots, X^k$ in *polynomial regression* (Section 6.2) or as a set of orthogonal polynomials (Section 6.3). In these treatments of the IV, we left the scale of the dependent variable Y intact. The purpose of our treatments of the IVs as polynomials or orthogonal polynomials was to permit the use of linear MR to characterize a nonlinear relationship of the IV to Y.

6.4.1 Purposes of Transformation and the Nature of Transformations

In this section we consider a wide variety of transformations that can be made on predictors X or the dependent variable Y. By transformations we mean changes in the scale or units of a variable, for example, from X to $\log X$ or to $\sqrt{X}$. From a statistical perspective there are three overarching goals for carrying out transformations.

1. *Simplify the relationship.* First, transformations are employed to simplify the relationship between X and Y. Nonlinear transformations always change the form of the relationship between X and Y. The primary goal is to select a transformation that leads to the simplest possible X–Y relationship—nearly always a linear relationship. This first goal, of simplifying the relationship, often is not merely to create a mathematical condition (linearity) but rather to create more conceptually meaningful units. For example, when economists use $\log(\text{dollars})$ as their unit of analysis, it is partly because this function better reflects the utility of money; the use of the decibel scale for loudness and the Richter scale for earthquake intensity provide other examples (Hoaglin, 1988).

2. *Eliminate heteroscedasticity.* Transformations of Y also serve to change the structure of the variance of the residuals around the best fitting regression function. The second goal of transformations is to eliminate problems of heteroscedasticity (unequal conditional variances of residuals, see Sections 4.3.1 and 4.4.4).

3. *Normalize residuals.* Finally, nonlinear transformations serve to change the distribution of both the original variable and the residuals. The third goal of transformations is to make the distribution of the residuals closer to normal in form.

In many cases, particularly when data are highly skewed and the range of variables is wide, transformations simultaneously achieve all three goals, greatly simplifying the interpretation of the results and meeting the assumptions in linear MR. Yet this result is not inevitable. Nonlinear transformations operate simultaneously on the form of the relationship, the variance of the residuals, and the distribution of the residuals. Occasionally, transformations may improve the regression with respect to one goal while degrading it with respect to others.

The effect of a *linear transformation* of a variable (multiplying or dividing by a constant, adding or subtracting a constant) is to stretch or contract the variable *uniformly* and/or to shift it up or down the numerical scale. Because of the nature of the product-moment correlation, particularly its standardization of the variables, linear transformation of X or Y has no effect on correlation coefficients of any order or on the proportions of variance that their squares yield. The POMP scores described in Section 5.2.2 are a linear transformation of an original scale.

The transformations we will encounter here, in contrast, are *nonlinear* transformations, such as $\log X$, or a^X, or $2 \arcsin \sqrt{X}$. These transformations stretch or contract X nonuniformly. However, they are also strictly *monotonic*, that is, as X increases, the transformed value either steadily increases or steadily decreases.

Linearizing Relationships

When the analyst is seeking to simplify the relationship between X and Y and a constant additive change in X is associated with other than a constant additive change in Y, the need for nonlinear transformations may arise. Certain kinds of variables and certain circumstances are prone to monotonic nonlinearity. For example, in learning experiments, increases in the number of trials do not generally produce uniform (linear) increases in the amount learned. As another example, it is a fundamental law of psychophysics that constant increases in the size of a physical stimulus are not associated with constant increases in the subjective sensation. As children mature, the rate of development slows down. As total length of prior hospitalization of psychiatric patients increases, scores of psychological tests and rating scales do not generally change linearly. Certain variables are more prone to give rise to nonlinear relationships than others: time-based variables such as age, length of exposure, response latency; money-based variables such as annual income, savings; variables based on counts, such as number of errors, size of family, number of hospital beds; and proportions of all kinds.

The application of nonlinear transformations arises from the utilization of a simple mathematical trick. If Y is a logarithmic function of X, then, being nonlinear, the Y–X relationship is not optimally fitted by linear correlation and regression. However, the relationship between Y and $\log X$ is linear. Similarly, if Y and X are reciprocally and hence nonlinearly related, Y and $1/X$ are linearly related. Thus, by taking nonlinear functions of X or Y that represent specific nonlinear aspects, we can *linearize* some relationships and bring them into our MR system.

Assumptions of Homoscedasticity and Normality of Residuals

In addition to the linearization of relationships, nonlinear transformation is of importance in connection with the formal statistical assumptions of regression analysis—that residuals be normally distributed and of constant variance (homoscedastic) over sets of values of the IVs (see Section 4.3.1). If data exhibit heteroscedasticity, the standard errors of regression coefficients are biased, as they are if residuals are non-normal, thus leading to less accurate inferences. If heteroscedasticity and nonnormality of residuals obtain in MR, it may be possible to find a nonlinear transformation of Y that not only linearizes the X-Y relationship but simultaneously transforms the residuals from MR predicting the transformed Y to be closer to meeting the conditions of homoscedasticity and normality.

In the remainder of Section 6.4 we consider, in turn, the linearizing of relationships and transforming to achieve homoscedasticity and normality of residuals. We also address issues in the use of transformations. Some of what we present is familiar in the behavioral sciences.

Yet other approaches to transformations presented here have rarely been employed in the behavioral sciences, although they are standardly used in statistics and other social sciences—for example, economics. We believe that part of the reason they have not been employed in the behavioral sciences is that researchers in the behavioral sciences have paid less attention to the assumptions of MR and the negative impact of violation of these assumptions on accuracy of inference.

6.4.2 The Conceptual Basis of Transformations and Model Checking Before and After Transformation—Is It Always Ideal to Transform?

It is very important to consider the conceptual basis of transformations. In many disciplines, certain transformations are considered standard procedure, arising out of long experience. Transformations should always be conducted with cognizance of other researchers' experience with similar variables. In fact, there are times when it may be unwise to carry out (or not) a transformation on a particular data set, when the circumstances of that data set suggest something other than what is standard in a research area. On the other hand, slavish adherence to historical precedents may be problematic, if an area has failed in the past to consider important aspects of the data (e.g., heteroscedasticity) that may suggest the need for transformation.

Diagnostic plots, described in Sections 4.2 and 4.4, are useful for examining whether relationships are linear and for checking assumptions on residuals. These plots may signal the need for transformation. Kernel density plots of individual variables are useful for detecting skewness (see Fig. 4.2.3). Scatterplots of residuals against predicted scores with lowess fit lines highlight nonlinearity of relationship. If plots include lowess lines one standard deviation above and below the lowess fit line, heteroscedasticity is also highlighted, as illustrated in Fig. 4.4.5. Before undertaking transformations, it is also important to use regression diagnostics to ask whether one or few influential data points are producing the nonlinearity or violations of assumptions, as in the example in Section 6.2.7, in which a single outlying case produced a cubic trend. If justified, the removal of the case may eliminate the need for transformation.

Model checking after transformation is also important, because transformation to remedy one aspect of a regression situation (e.g., nonlinearity) may lead to problems in other aspects of the regression situation. For example, in a situation in which Y is transformed to achieve linearity, there may be no outliers in the original analysis with Y as the dependent variable. However, in the revised analysis in which transformed dependent variable Y' is employed, outliers may have been produced by the transformation. Or, it is possible that in the original regression equation with Y, the residuals were approximately homoscedastic and normal; after transformation, they may not be, so that it may be more desirable to stay with the original nonlinear regression. The issue of when to transform is discussed in more detail in Section 6.4.18.

6.4.3 Logarithms and Exponents; Additive and Proportional Relationships

The transformations we employ often involve logarithms and exponents (or powers). A quick review of their workings is in order. Regression equations we estimate after variable transformation often involve combinations of variables in original form and variables transformed into logarithms; the meaning of relationships in these equations is also explored here.

A logarithm of a value X to the base m is the exponent to which the value m must be raised in order to produce the original number. We are probably most familiar with *base 10* logarithms, noted $\log_{10}$, where $m = 10$. For example, $\log_{10} 1000 = 3$, since $10^3 = 1000$.

TABLE 6.4.1

Exponents, Logarithms, and Their Relationships

A. Some rules for exponents
   (1) $X^a X^b = X^{(a+b)}$
   (2) $X^a / X^b = X^{(a-b)}$
   (3) $X^{-n} = 1/X^n$
   (4) $X^{1/2} = \sqrt{X}$
   (5) $X^0 = 1$

B. Some rules for logarithms
   (6) $\log(bX) = \log b + \log X$
   (7) $\log(b/X) = \log b - \log X$
   (8) $\log(X^b) = b \log X$

C. Relationship between exponents and logarithms
   (9) $\log_m m^x = X$, so $\log_{10} 10^X = X$ for base 10 logs
       and $\ln_e e^X = X$ for natural (base e) logs

Note: This presentation is drawn from presentations by Hagle (1995) and Hamilton (1992).

Many presentations of transformations use *natural logarithms*, noted *ln*, with a base (specially noted e instead of m) of $e = 2.71878$ (approximately). For example, $\ln 1000 = 6.907755279$, since $2.71878^{6.907755279} = 1000$. A third form of logarithms are base 2 logarithms, for example, $\log_2 8 = 3$, since $2^3 = 8$.

The computations for base 10 and natural logarithms can be accomplished on a simple statistical calculator that has the following functions: log, ln, 10^X, and e^X. Enter 1000, press **log** to get $\log_{10} 1000$. Enter 3, press $\mathbf{10^X}$ to get $10^3 = 1000$. Enter 1000, press **ln**, to get $\ln 1000 = 6.907755279$. Enter 6.907755279, press e^X to get $2.71878^{6.907755279} = 1000$. From the perspective of transforming variables using logarithms, it actually does not matter whether $\log_{10}$ or ln is used—the two logarithms are linearly related to one another. In fact, $2.302585 \ln = \log_{10}$. We will use the general notation "log" throughout this section, to indicate that either ln or $\log_{10}$ can be employed.

In the numerical examples, we first took the logarithm of the number 1000. Then we took the result and raised the base of the logarithm to the log (e.g. 10^3); the latter manipulation is called taking the *antilog* of a logarithm. Having found the logarithm of a number, taking the antilog returns the original number. In general, raising any number to a power is called *exponentiation*, and the power to which a number is raised is called the *exponent*. Logarithms and exponents are inverse functions of one another. In Table 6.4.1, we present rules for exponents, for logarithms, and for the relationship between exponents and logarithms.

Logarithms and Proportional Change

When, as X changes by a constant proportion, Y changes by a constant additive amount, then Y is a logarithmic function of X; hence Y is a linear function of $\log X$. Following are a series of values of X in which each value is 1.5 times the prior value, a *constant proportionate increase*; for example, $12 = 1.5(8)$. In the corresponding series of Y, each value of Y is 3 points higher than the prior value (e.g., $8 = 5 + 3$); Y exhibits *constant additive increase*. When a variable like X increases by a proportionate amount, $\log X$ (either $\log_{10}$ or ln) increases by a constant additive amount. Within rounding error, $\log_{10} X$ increases by .18 through the series; $\ln X$ increases by .40 through the series; $\log_2 X$ increases by .585 through the series. The increases in $\log X$ are constant additive increases, as with Y. Thus, the relationship between $\log X$ and Y is linear and can be estimated in linear OLS regression, as in Eq. (6.4.7).

X	8	12	18	27	40.5	where $X_{(i+1)} = 1.5 X_i$
$\log_{10} X$	.90	1.08	1.26	1.43	1.61	
$\ln X$	2.08	2.48	2.89	3.29	3.70	
$\log_2 X$	3	3.58	4.17	4.75	5.34	
Y	5	8	11	14	17	where $Y_{(i+1)} = Y_i + 3$

Conversely, if constant additive changes in X are associated with proportional changes in Y, then $\log Y$ is a linear function of X, and again the linear regression model correctly represents the relationship.

In some circumstances, we may transform Y rather than X. When only Y is log transformed, our basic regression equation for transformed Y becomes $\hat{Y}' = \log Y = B_1 X + B_0$. In this equation, B_1 is the amount of change that occurs in Y' given a 1-unit change in X. Note that now the change in Y is in $\log Y$ units. A 1-unit increase in $\log_{10} Y$ is associated with a 10-fold increase in raw Y; a 2-unit increase in $\log_{10} Y$ is associated with a 100-fold increase in raw Y. Similarly a 1-unit increase in $\log_2 Y$ is associated with a twofold increase (doubling of raw Y), and a 2-unit increase in $\log_2 Y$ is associated with a fourfold increase in raw Y.

Finally, proportionate changes in X may be associated with proportionate changes in Y, for example:

X	8	12	18	27	40.5	where $X_{(i+1)} = 1.5 X_i$
Y	2	4	8	16	32	where $Y_{(i+1)} = 2 Y_i$

If logarithms of both variables are taken, then

$\log_{10} X$	.90	1.08	1.26	1.43	1.61
$\log_{10} Y$	.30	.60	.90	1.20	1.51

Each proceeds by constant additive changes and again $\log Y$ is a linear function of $\log X$, this time after logarithmic transformation of both X and Y, as in Eq. (6.4.11) below.

6.4.4 Linearizing Relationships

Given that some nonlinear relationship exists, how does one determine which, if any, of a number of transformations is appropriate to linearize the relationship? For some relationships—for example, psychophysical relationships between stimulus intensity and subjective magnitude—there are strong theoretical models underlying the data that specify the form of the relationship; the task is one of transforming the variables into a form amenable to linear MRC analysis. Weaker models imply certain features or aspects of variables that are likely to linearize relationships. In the absence of any model to guide selection of a transformation, empirically driven approaches, based on the data themselves, suggest appropriate transformation. These include procedures presented here, including the ladder of re-expression and bulge rules of Tukey (1977) and Mosteller and Tukey (1977), and more formal mathematical approaches like the Box-Cox and Box-Tidwell procedures.

Intrinsically Linear Versus Intrinsically Nonlinear Relationships

Whether a strong theoretical model can be linearized for treatment in linear MR depends upon the way that random error is built into the model, as a familiar *additive* function or as a *multiplicative* function. Multiplicative error in a model signifies that the amount of error in the dependent variable Y increases as the value of Y increases. Suppose we have a multiplicative theoretical model with multiplicative error.

$$(6.4.1) \qquad\qquad Y = B_0 X_1^{B_1} X_2^{B_2} e^\varepsilon,$$

where ε refers to random error, and e is the base of the natural logarithm.

This form of regression equation, with regression coefficients as exponents, is not the familiar form of an OLS regression; it signals a nonlinear relationship of the predictors to Y.[9] The question before us is whether we can somehow transform the equation into an equation that can be analyzed with OLS regression.

Using rule (8) from Table 6.4.1, we take the logarithms of both sides of the equation. This yields a transformed equation that is linear in the coefficients (Section 6.1) and that thus can be analyzed using OLS regression:

$$(6.4.2) \qquad\qquad \log Y = \log B_0 + B_1 \log X_1 + B_2 \log X_2 + \varepsilon$$

Eq. (6.4.1) has been linearized by taking the logarithms of both sides. As shown in Eq. (6.4.2) the regression coefficients B_1 and B_2 can be estimated by regressing $\log Y$ on $\log X_1$ and $\log X_2$; the resulting B_1 and B_2 values are the values of B_1 and B_2 in Eq. (6.4.1). The value of B_0 in Eq. (6.4.1) can be found by taking the antilog of the resulting regression constant from Eq. (6.4.2). In other words, we started with a nonlinear equation (Eq. 6.4.1), transformed the equation into an equation (Eq. 6.4.2) that could be solved through OLS regression, and were able to recover the regression coefficients of the original nonlinear equation (Eq. 6.4.1). The errors are assumed to be normally distributed with constant variance in the *transformed* equation (Eq. 6.4.2). Because Eq. (6.4.1) can be linearized into a form that can be analyzed in OLS regression, it is said to be *intrinsically linearizable*. In Section 6.4.5 we illustrate four nonlinear models used in psychology and other social and biological sciences. All four are intrinsically linearizable; we show how the linearization can be accomplished.

Now we modify the equation slightly to

$$(6.4.3) \qquad\qquad Y = \beta_0 X_1^{\beta_1} X_2^{\beta_2} + \varepsilon,$$

where the error ε is additive, not multiplicative; that is, the variance due to error in predicting Y is constant across the range of the predictors in the form of regression equation Eq. (6.4.3). Additive error is our standard assumption in linear MR. If we try to linearize Eq. (6.4.3) by taking the logarithms of both sides, we discover that in the resulting expression the error variance is a function of the value of Y. Heteroscedasticity would be introduced by the logarithmic transformation of the equation (see Myers, 1986, for a complete demonstration). The equation is *intrinsically nonlinear*. *Nonlinear regression*, introduced in Section 6.5, must be employed.

Whether we specify a model with multiplicative or additive error is a matter for theory. As Draper and Smith (1998) point out, a strategy that is often used is to begin with transformation of variable(s) to linearize the relationship (implicitly assuming that the error is multiplicative in the original scale); OLS (ordinary least squares) regression is then employed on the transformed variables. Then the residuals from the OLS regression with the transformed variable(s) are examined to see if they approximately meet the assumptions of homoscedasticity and normality. If not, then a nonlinear regression approach may be considered. (From now on, we will refer to linear MR as OLS regression in order to clearly distinguish this model from alternative regression models.)

---

[9]Logistic regression, covered in Chapter 13, is a form of nonlinear regression with regression coefficients as exponents.

Equation (6.4.2) illustrates that transformations to linearize relationships may involve both the predictors $X_1, X_2, \ldots, X_k$ and the dependent variable Y. As indicated later, the choice of transformation of both X and Y may be driven by strong theory.

6.4.5 Linearizing Relationships Based on Strong Theoretical Models

In such fields as mathematical biology, psychology and sociology, neuropsychology, and econometrics, relatively strong theories have been developed that result in postulation of (generally nonlinear) relationships between dependent and independent variables. The adequacy of these models is assessed by observing how well the equations specifying the relationships fit suitably gathered data. We emphasize that the equations are not arbitrary but are hypothetically descriptive of "how things work." The independent and dependent variables are observables, the form of the equation is a statement about a process, and the values of the constants of the equation are estimates of parameters that are constrained or even predicted by the model. In our presentations of models, we assume *multiplicative error* in the nonlinearized form, omit the error term, and show the expression with the predicted score $\hat{Y}$ in place of the observed Y. (We discuss the treatment of the same models but with additive error assumed in Section 6.5 on nonlinear regression.) Here we illustrate four different nonlinear relationships that appear as *formal models* in the biological or social sciences, including psychology and economics.

Logarithmic Relationships

Psychophysics is a branch of perceptual psychology that addresses the growth of subjective magnitude of sensation (e.g., how bright, how loud a stimulus seems) as a function of the physical intensity of a stimulus. A common psychophysical model of the relationship of energy X of a physical stimulus to the perceived magnitude Y of the stimulus is given in Eq. (6.4.4),

$$\text{(6.4.4)} \qquad c^{\hat{Y}} = dX_1,$$

where c and d are constants. The equation asserts that changes in stimulus strength X are associated with changes in subjective response Y as a power of a constant. The relationship between X and Y is clearly nonlinear. Figure 6.4.1(A) illustrates an example of this relationship for the specific equation $8^Y = 6X$, where $c = 8$ and $d = 6$. Suppose we wish to analyze data that are proposed to follow the model in Eq. (6.4.5) and to estimate the coefficients c and d. We transform Eq. (6.4.5) into a form that can be analyzed in OLS regression. We take logarithms of both sides of the equation, yielding

$$\text{(6.4.5)} \qquad \hat{Y} \log c = \log d + \log X_1,$$

Solving for Y we find

$$\text{(6.4.6)} \qquad \hat{Y} = \frac{\log d}{\log c} + \frac{1}{\log c} \log X_1.$$

If we let $(\log d)/(\log c) = B_0$ and $1/(\log c) = B_1$, we see that the psychophysical model in Eq. (6.4.4) postulates a logarithmic relationship between stimulus strength (X), and subjective response (Y), which is, in fact, a form of Fechner's psychophysical law (Fechner, 1860), given in Eq. (6.4.7).

$$\text{(6.4.7)} \qquad \hat{Y} = B_1 \log X_1 + B_0.$$

We can apply Eq. (6.4.7) to suitably generated data using OLS regression by regressing Y (e.g., judgments of brightness of lights) on $\log X_1$ (e.g., the logarithm of a measure of light intensity). This yields estimates of B_1 and B_0. From these estimates, we solve for the constant c in Eq. (6.4.4) from the relationship $1/(\log c) = B_1$, or the reciprocal, yielding $\log c = 1/B_1$. Then

(6.4.8)
$$c = \text{antilog}\, \frac{1}{B_1}.$$

To solve for the constant d, we use $(\log d)/(\log c) = B_0$, which yields

(6.4.9)
$$d = \text{antilog}\, \frac{B_0}{B_1}.$$

The values of c and d will be of interest because they estimate parameters in the process being modeled (e.g., the relationship of light intensity to perceived brightness), as will R^2 as a measure of the fit of the model (see Section 6.4.16). Finally, the shape of the function in Fig. 6.4.1(A) is typical of logarithmic relationships between X and Y in which Y varies linearly as a function of $\log X$.

Power Relationships

Now consider an alternative formulation of the psychophysical relationship of stimulus to subjective magnitude expressed by the equation

(6.4.10)
$$\hat{Y} = cX^d$$

where c and d are constants, and Y is a power function of X, such that proportional growth in Y relates to proportional growth in X. This theoretical model has been offered by Stevens (1961) as the psychophysical law that relates X, the energy of the physical stimulus, to the perceived magnitude of sensation Y. In Stevens' model, the exponent or power d estimates a parameter that characterizes the specific sensory function and is not dependent on the units of measurement, whereas c does depend on the units in which X and Y are measured. We stress that Stevens' law is not merely one of finding an equation that fits data—it is rather an attempt at a parsimonious description of how human discrimination proceeds. It challenges Fechner's law, which posits a different fundamental equation, one of the form of Eq. (6.4.4), in which proportional growth in X relates to additive growth in Y. Two specific examples of Eq. (6.4.5) are given in Fig. 6.4.1(B). The left hand panel of Fig. 6.4.1(B) illustrates a power function with an exponent $d > 1$, specifically $Y = .07X^{1.7}$, where $c = .07$ and $d = 1.7$. The right-hand panel of Fig. 6.4.1(B) illustrates a power function with $d < 1$, specifically $Y = .07X^{.2}$, where $c = .07$ and $d = .20$. Values of d are a critical component of Stevens' law applied to different sensory continua. For example, the exponent d for perceived brightness of short duration lights is $d = .33$; for perceived saltiness of sips of sodium chloride (salt) solution, $d = 1.3$ (Marks, 1974).

To linearize the relationship in Eq. (6.4.10), we take the logarithms of both sides, yielding

(6.4.11) $\log \hat{Y} = d \log X + \log c$ or $\log \hat{Y} = B_1 \log X_1 + B_0.$

To analyze the relationship between X and Y in Eq. (6.4.10) using OLS regression, we would compute the logarithms of X and Y and predict $\log Y$ from $\log X$. In Eq. (6.4.11) $B_0 = \log c$, so that

(6.4.12) $c = \text{antilog}\, B_0.$

(6.4.13) $d = B_1.$

(A) Logarithmic relationship.

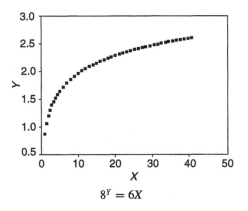

$$8^Y = 6X$$

(B) Power relationships.

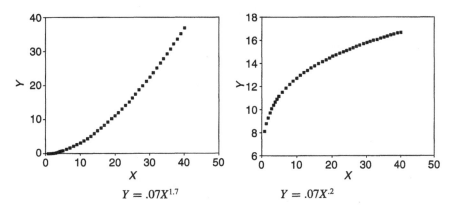

$$Y = .07X^{1.7} \qquad\qquad Y = .07X^{.2}$$

FIGURE 6.4.1 Some functions used to characterize the relationship of X to Y in theoretical models.

Note that Eq. (6.4.11) informs us that the predicted scores will be in the log metric; to convert the predicted scores to the raw metric, we would take the antilog of each predicted score in the log metric, that is, antilog $\hat{Y}_{\log} = \hat{Y}_{\text{original units}}$.

Exponential Growth Model Relationships

There is great interest in psychology in the trajectories of growth of various phenomena over time (e.g., drug use, learning, intellectual growth and decline). An exponential relationship between X and Y used to model growth or decay of Y as a function of X is given by

(6.4.14) $$\hat{Y} = ce^{dX}.$$

In this model, the change in Y at any point depends on the level of Y. If $d > 0$, Y grows from a starting value of c when $X = 0$, with Y rising in ever increasing amounts, for example, as in college tuition over time, referred to as *exponential growth*. Exponential growth is illustrated in

(C) Exponential growth relationships.

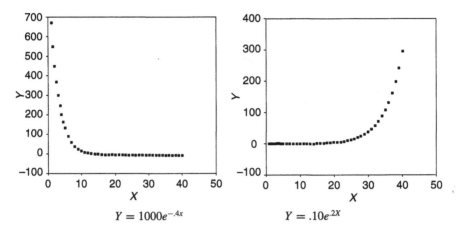

$$Y = 1000e^{-.4x} \qquad\qquad Y = .10e^{.2X}$$

(D) Hyperbolic (inverse polynomial) relationships.

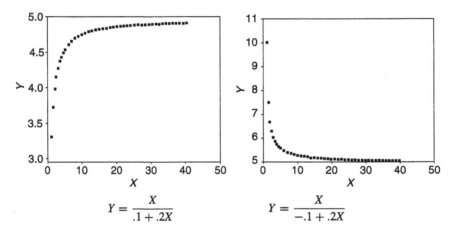

$$Y = \frac{X}{.1 + .2X} \qquad\qquad Y = \frac{X}{-.1 + .2X}$$

Note: The scaling of the y-axis changes from panel to panel.

FIGURE 6.4.1   Continued.

the right-hand panel of Fig. 6.4.1(C), specifically in the equation $Y = .10e^{.2X}$, where $c = .10$ and $d = .2$. If $d < 0$, we have *exponential decay*. Y declines from an initial value of c when $X = 0$, illustrated in the left-hand panel of Fig. 6.4.1(C), specifically in the equation $Y = 1000e^{-.4X}$, where $c = 1000$ and $d = -.4$. If c were the amount of knowledge of statistics one had on the day of a statistics final exam, and the amount one forgot each day following the exam were proportional to the amount retained by the early morning of the day, we would have *exponential decay*. Eq. (6.4.14) is linearized by taking the logarithms of both sides, yielding

(6.4.15) $\log \hat{Y} = dX + \log c \quad \text{or} \quad \log \hat{Y} = B_1 X_1 + B_0$

so that

(6.4.16) $B_0 = \log c$

and

(6.4.17) $B_1 = d.$

If the model $\hat{Y} = ce^{dX}$ is expanded to include an asymptote a, as in the expression $\hat{Y} = a + ce^{dX}$, and the coefficients c and d are negative, then the resulting form of the equation will be a curve that rises and levels off at the value a—as, for example, the additional amount of statistics learned for each additional hour of studying before an exam, up to an asymptote representing all the material in the statistics course. If the model is applied in an experiment with a treated and a control group, another dichotomous predictor can be added to code the groups; the result will be curves of different elevations with the difference in height representing the effect of treatment (Neter, Kutner, Nachtsheim, & Wasserman, 1996, Chapter 13).

Hyperbolic Relationship (Inverse Polynomial Model)

A second form of growth model used in economics and biology (Myers, 1986) is a *diminishing returns model*, which characterizes growth to some asymptote (upper limit or lower limit). This is the hyperbolic (inverse polynomial) function:

(6.4.18) $$\hat{Y} = \frac{X}{c + dX}.$$

In this model the value $1/d$ is the asymptote; the increase in Y is inversely related to distance from the asymptote, hence the term *diminishing return*. Figure 6.4.1(D) illlustrates two such curves. The left hand panel shows the equation $Y = X/(.1 + .2X)$, where $c = .1$ and $d = .2$; it rises to an asymptote of 5, since $d = .2$, and $1/d = 5$. The right-hand figure shows the equation $Y = X/(-.1 + .2X)$, where $c = -.1$ and $d = .2$; it falls to an asymptote of 5, again because $d = .2$.

Unlike the use of logarithms to linearize the previous equations, linearizing Eq. (6.4.18) involves the use of reciprocals. By algebraic manipulation, Eq. (6.4.18) can be written as a linear function of the reciprocals of X and Y:

(6.4.19) $\dfrac{1}{\hat{Y}} = c\dfrac{1}{X} + d$ or $\dfrac{1}{\hat{Y}} = B_1\dfrac{1}{X} + B_0.$

To estimate this equation using OLS regression, we would predict the reciprocal of Y from the reciprocal of X. The coefficient B_1 from the OLS regression equals c from Eq. (6.4.18), and $B_0 = d$.

Assessing Model Fit

Even when we accomplish the transformation to linear form, as has been shown for four different theoretical models, a problem exists that is worth mentioning. When the dependent variable analyzed in the transformed equation is not itself Y, but is rather some function of Y—for example, $\log Y$ or $1/Y$—the B_0 and B_1 coefficients from the transformed equation are the coefficients that minimize the sum of squared residuals (the least squares estimates) for predicting the transformed Y. They are not the least squares estimates that would result if the untransformed Y were predicted. There is no direct function for converting the coefficients from the transformed equation to corresponding coefficients from the untransformed equation. The issue arises as to whether there is better fit in a variance accounted for sense (R_Y^2) in the transformed over the untransformed equation. The R^2s associated with models predicting different forms of Y (e.g., $Y, \log Y, \sqrt{Y}$) are not directly comparable. *In general, one cannot directly compare the fit of two models with different dependent variables.* Comparing fit across models employing different transformations is explored in Section 6.4.16.

6.4.6 Linearizing Relationships Based on Weak Theoretical Models

We may employ the same transformations from strong theoretical models in linearizing relationships between variables that are well below the level of exact mathematical specification of the strong theoretical models discussed previously. However, our present "weak theory" framework is more modest; we are here not generally interested in estimating model parameters c and d, as we are in Section 6.4.5, because we do not have a theory that generated the equations in the first place.

Logarithmic Transformations

Logarithmic transformations often prove useful in biological, psychological, social science, and economics applications. All we might have, for example, is a notion that when we measure a certain construct X by means of a scale X, it changes proportionally in association with additive changes in other variables. As we discussed earlier, if we expect that proportionate changes in X are associated with additive changes in Y, we might well transform X to $\log X$. If we expect proportionate changes in Y to be associated with proportionate changes in X, we might well transform Y to $\log Y$ and X to $\log X$. Variables such as age or time-related ordinal predictors such as learning trials or blocks of trials are frequently effectively log-transformed to linearize relationships. This is also frequently the case for physical variables, as for example energy (intensity) measures of light, sound, chemical concentration of stimuli in psychophysical or neuropsychological studies, or physical measures of biological response. At the other end of the behavioral science spectrum, variables such as family size and counts of populations as occur in vital statistics or census data are frequently made more tractable by taking logarithms. So, often, are variables expressed in units of money, for example, annual income or gross national product.

By logarithmic transformation, we intend to convey not only $\log X$ but such functions as $\log (X - K)$ or $\log (K - X)$, where K is a nonarbitrary constant. Note that such functions are not linearly related to $\log X$, so that when they are appropriate, $\log X$ will not be. K, for example, may be a sensory threshold or some asymptotic value. (In Section 6.4.8 we discuss the use of small arbitrary additive constants for handling the transformation of Y scores of zero, yielding *started logs and powers*.)

Reciprocal Transformation

Reciprocals arise quite naturally in the consideration of rate data. Imagine a perceptual-motor or learning task presented in time limit form—all subjects are given a constant amount of time (T), during which they complete a varying number of units (u). One might express the scores in the form of rates at u/T, but because T is a constant, we may ignore T and simply use u as the score. Now, consider the same task, but presented in work limit form—subjects are given a constant number of units to complete (U) and are scored as to the varying amounts of time (t) they take. Now if we express their performance as *rates*, it is U/t and, if we ignore the constant U, we are left with $1/t$, not t. If rate is linearly related to some other variable X, then for the time limit task, X will be linearly related to u, but for the work limit task, X will be linearly related not to t, but to $1/t$. There are other advantages to working with $1/t$. Often, as a practical matter in a work limit task, a time cutoff is used that a few subjects reach without completing the task. Their exact t scores are not known, but they are known to be very large. This embarrassment is avoided by taking reciprocals, because the reciprocals of very large numbers are all very close to zero and the variance due to the error of using the cutoff $1/t$ rather than the unknown true value of $1/t$ is negligible relative to the total variance of the observations.

6.4.7 Empirically Driven Transformations in the Absence of Strong or Weak Models

Suppose that through our use of diagnostic approaches suggested in Chapter 4, we discover in our data characteristics that suggest the need for transformation. Graphical displays of X–Y relationships (e.g., lowess plots, Section 4.2.2) may suggest nonlinear relationships. Scatterplots of residuals around the lowess line (Section 4.4.4 and Fig. 4.4.5) may suggest heteroscedasticity. Quantile-quantile (q-q, Section 4.4.6) plots of residuals against a normal variate may uncover their nonnormality.

Suppose, however, that we have neither strong nor weak models to suggest specific transformations to ameliorate these conditions in our data. We can nonetheless draw on a rich collection of strategies for linearizing relationships and for improving the characteristics of residuals. Sections 6.4.8 through 6.4.14 describe these strategies. Our use of these strategies is empirically driven by our data rather than by theory. This approach is usual in statistics but to date has had less impact in the behavioral sciences. The approach is certainly appropriate and potentially useful for behavioral science data. The purpose of undertaking empirically driven transformations is to produce a regression equation that both characterizes the data and meets the conditions required for accurate statistical inference. Section 4.5 provides a discussion of the form of relationships and conditions in the data that lead to particular strategies for transformation.

6.4.8 Empirically Driven Transformation for Linearization: The Ladder of Re-expression and the Bulging Rule

Let us assume that a lowess plot of Y against X has revealed a curvilinear relationship that is monotonic with one bend, as in all the illustrations of Fig. 6.4.1. Also assume that we have no theoretical rationale for declaring that a particular mathematical function generated the curve. How should we approach linearizing (straightening) the relationship? Both informal (by inspection) and formal (numerical) approaches have been developed to guide transformation for linearization. If the relationship we observe is monotonic and has a single bend, one strong possibility for transformation is the use of *power transformations*, in which a variable is transformed by raising it to some power. In general, the power function is

$$(6.4.20) \qquad\qquad Y' = Y^{\lambda},$$

where Y is the original variable, Y' is the transformed variable, and λ is the exponent, (i.e., the power to which Y is raised). The transformed variable then replaces the original variable in regression analysis.

The Ladder of Re-expression

Actually, we have already encountered and will continue to encounter examples of power transformations, which include reciprocals, logarithms, powers in polynomial regression, square roots, and other roots. In their classic work, Mosteller and Tukey (1977) described a *ladder of re-expression* (*re-expression* is another term for *transformation*) that organizes these seemingly disparate transformations under a single umbrella. This ladder of re-expression was proposed to guide the selection of transformations of X and Y to linearize relationships. The ladder can also be used to transform skewed variables prior to analysis.

The ladder is a series of *power functions* of the form $Y' = Y^\lambda$, which transform Y into Y' (or, equivalently, X into X'). Again, power functions are useful for straightening a relationship between X and Y that is monotonic and has a single bend; hence power functions are characterized as *one-bend transformations*.

The problem is to find an appropriate value of λ to use in transforming a variable that makes its distribution more normal or that eliminates nonlinearity of relationship between that variable and another variable. Some values of λ, shown below, lead to familiar transformations (Neter, Kutner, Nachtsheim, & Wasserman, 1996, p. 132), though many values of λ other than those given here are possible.

In general	$Y' = Y^\lambda$.
Square	$Y' = Y^2; \lambda = 2$.
Square root	$Y' = Y^{1/2} = Y^{.5} = \sqrt{Y}; \lambda = .5$.
Logarithm	$Y' = \ln Y; \lambda = 0$ (a special case).[10]
Reciprocal	$Y' = \dfrac{1}{Y}; \lambda = -1$.

Transforming Individual Variables Using the Ladder of Re-expression and Changes in Skew

Transforming individual variables to be more symmetric is not our focus here (linearizing relationships through appropriate selection of a λ is), but it is useful to understand how the various powers on the ladder change the distribution of individual variables. These changes are the basis of straightening out nonlinear relationships. Values of $\lambda > 1$ compress the lower tail of a distribution and stretch out the upper tail; a negatively skewed (i.e., long, low tail) variable becomes less skewed when a transformation with $\lambda > 1$ is applied. Values of $\lambda < 1$ stretch the lower tail of a distribution and compress the upper tail; a positively skewed (i.e., long, high tail) variable becomes less skewed when a transformation with $\lambda < 1$ is applied. The farther from 1 on either side is the value of λ, the more extreme is the compression and stretching. This allows us to compare the familiar logarithmic and square root transformations: $\log X$ (associated with $\lambda = 0$) and $\sqrt{X}$ (where $\lambda = \frac{1}{2}$). The logarithmic transformation is stronger; that is, it compresses the upper tail and stretches the lower tail of a distribution more than does the square root transformation.

The Bulging Rule

In addressing the problem of how to select a value of λ to apply to X or Y so as to linearize a relationship, Mosteller and Tukey (1977) proposed a simple graphical bulging rule. To use the bulging rule, one examines one's data in a scatterplot of Y against X, imposes a lowess curve to suggest the nature of the curvature in the data, and selects a transformation based on the shape of the curve. Suppose the curve in the data follows the curve in Figure 6.4.1(A), that is, Y rises rapidly for low values of X and then the curve flattens out for high values of X. There are two options for transforming that will straighten the relationship between X and Y. One option is to transform Y by moving up the ladder above $\lambda = 1$; this means applying a power transformation to Y with an exponent greater than 1, (e.g., $Y^{1.5}, Y^2$). This will stretch up the high end of Y (pulling the high values of Y even higher), straightening the relationship. Alternatively, one may transform X by moving down the ladder below $\lambda = 1$

---

[10]The logarithm bears special comment. In fact, the expression Y^0 transforms all values of Y to 1.0, since $Y^0 = 1$. However, as $\lambda \to 0$, the expression $(Y^\lambda - 1)/\lambda \to \ln Y$, leading to the use of the natural logarithm as the transformation when $\lambda = 0$.

(e.g., $X^{.5} = \sqrt{X}, \log X$). This will stretch the low end of X (to the left), again straightening out the relationship. Suppose one finds in one's data that Y increases as X increases, but with but with the shape of the curvature as in Fig. 6.4.1(B, left-hand panel), that is, a slow initial rise in Y as a function of X for low values of X and a rapid rise at high values of X. We may straighten the relationshhip by moving up the ladder for X (e.g., to X^2) or down the ladder for Y (e.g., $Y^{.5} = \sqrt{Y}, \log Y$). For a shape like that in Fig. 6.4.1 (C, left-hand panel) one could either move down the ladder for X or down the ladder for Y. One may try a range of values of λ applied to either X or Y, typically between -2 and $+2$. Mosteller and Tukey (1977) present a simple numerical method for deciding if straightening has been successful. Modern graphical computer packages[11] make this work easy by providing a "slider" representing values of λ that can be moved up and down with a mouse. As the slider is moved, the value of λ is changed; the data are graphically displayed in a scatterplot of Y against X with a lowess function superimposed, and one can visually select the value of λ that straightens the X–Y relationship. Sections 6.4.9 and 6.4.10 describe quantitative approaches to selecting value of λ to transfrom Y and X, respectively.

Should X or Y Be Transformed?

The bulging rule makes it clear that for linearizing a one-bend nonlinear relationship, we may transform either X or Y. The choice between X and Y is dictated by the nature of the residuals when untransformed Y is regressed on untransformed X. If the residuals are well behaved with the untransformed data, then transformation of Y will lead to heteroscedasticity; one should transform X. If, on the other hand, the residuals are problematic (heteroscedastic, non-normal) with the untransformed data, then transforming Y may improve the distribution of residuals, as well as linearize the relationship. Figure 6.4.2, discussed in Section 6.4.17, illustrates transformation of Y versus X.

What to Do with Zeros in the Raw Data: Started Logs and Powers

Use of the family of power functions assumes that the variables to be transformed have zero as their lowest value. Logarithms, a frequently used transformation from the power function family, are undefined for numbers less or equal to zero. Mosteller and Tukey (1977) proposed a remedy for distributions containing scores equal to zero—add a very small constant c to all the scores in the distribution and apply the logarithmic transformation to $\log(Y + c)$. For negative values of λ the same approach is used; one transforms $(Y + c)^{\lambda}$. These transformations are referred to as *started logs* and *started powers*.

Variable Range and Power Transformations

Power transformations assume that all values of the variable being transformed are positive and without bound at the upper end. Power functions are most effective when the ratio of the highest to lowest value on a variable is large, at least 10 (e.g., Draper & Smith, 1998). If the ratio is small, then power transformations are likely to be ineffective, because for very small ratios, the power transformations are nearly linear with the original scores.

---

[11] The ARC software developed by R. D. Cook and Weisberg (1999) provides this technology, and much other technology useful for regression graphics and transformations. ARC is freeware accessible from the School of Statistics, University of Minnesota: www.stat.umn.edu/arc/.

(A) The regression of $Y^{1.73}$ on X.

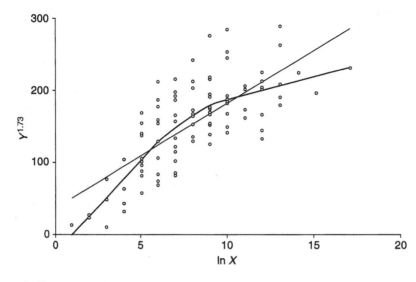

(B) The regression of Y on $\ln(X)$.

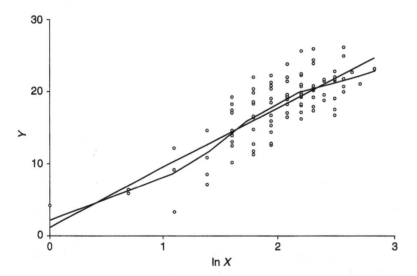

FIGURE 6.4.2   Power transformation of Y versus logarithmic transformation of X to linearize a relationship. The data are the same data as in Fig. 6.1.1 and Table 6.2.1.

6.4.9 Empirically Driven Transformation for Linearization in the Absence of Models: Box-Cox Family of Power Transformations on Y

Again suppose we find a one-bend monotonic relationship in our data and also observe problems with the residuals from an OLS regression. In lieu of a trial and error approach to selecting λ to transform Y, Box and Cox (1964) provided a numerical procedure for selecting a value of λ to be applied the dependent variable Y (but not X). The goal of the Box-Cox procedure is to select λ to achieve a linear relationship with residuals that exhibit normality and homoscedasticity. Both linearization and improved behavior of residuals drive the choice of λ. Box-Cox is a standard approach in statistics; although it has not been much used in some areas of behavioral science, Box-Cox transformation may be usefully applied to behavioral science data.

The mathematical details of the Box-Cox transformation are given in Box 6.4.1 for the interested reader. Maximum likelihood estimation (described in Section 13.2.9) is used to estimate λ in statistical software. Box 6.4.1 also provides a strategy for comparing the fit of regression models that use different transformations. Suppose we wished to try two transformations of Y, say $\sqrt{Y}$ and $\log Y$. One cannot simply fit two regression equations, one with $Y' = \sqrt{Y}$ as the DV and one with $Y' = \log Y$ as the DV and compare the fit of these models directly, because the dependent variables are on different scales (see also Section 6.4.16 for model comparison across transformations). Finally, Box 6.4.1 describes an approach to a diagnostic test whether a transformation is required; this approach also provides a preliminary estimate of λ. The approach can be implemented with OLS regression software; no specialized software is required. The value of λ produced by Box-Cox is often used to suggest the choice of a familiar transformation. For example, if $\hat{\lambda}$ from Box-Cox is .43, we might well choose a square root transformation, where $\lambda = .5$.

BOX 6.4.1
Achieving Linearization with the Box-Cox Transformation of Y

The Box-Cox transformation in its non-normalized form (Atkinson, 1985; Draper & Smith, 1998, p. 280) is given as

(6.4.22a)
$$Y_i^{(\lambda)} = \frac{Y_i^{\lambda} - 1}{\lambda} \quad \text{for} \quad \lambda \neq 0$$

and

(6.4.22b)
$$Y_i^{(\lambda)} = \ln Y_i \quad \text{for} \quad \lambda = 0.$$

The notation $Y^{(\lambda)}$, used by Ryan (1997), distinguishes the full Box-Cox transformation from simply raising Y to the power λ, written as Y^{λ}. Division by λ in Eq. (6.4.22a) preserves the direction of ordering from low to high after transformation of Y to $Y^{(\lambda)}$ when $\lambda < 0$ (Fox, 1997).

Expressions (6.4.22a) and (6.4.22b) are non-normalized, which means that we cannot try different values of λ, fit regression models, and compare the results directly to see which value of λ produces the best fit. Instead, we use the normalized transformation, which allows comparison across models of the same data using different values of λ (Draper & Smith, 1998, p. 280):

(6.4.23a)
$$Z_i^{(\lambda)} = \frac{Y_i^{\lambda} - 1}{\lambda (Y_G)^{\lambda - 1}} \quad \text{for} \quad \lambda \neq 0$$

and

(6.4.23b)
$$Z_i^{(\lambda)} = Y_G \ln Y_i \quad \text{for} \quad \lambda = 0$$

The term Y_G is the geometric mean of the Y scores in the untransformed metric and is computed as follows:

(6.4.24)
$$Y_G = (Y_1 Y_2 Y_3 \cdots Y_n)^{1/n}$$

The geometric mean of a set of Y scores is easily calculated in two steps, following the transformation of each Y score into $\ln Y$. First, compute the arithmetic mean of the

$\ln Y$ scores:

$$\frac{\sum \ln(Y_i)}{n}$$

Then exponentiate this value to find the geometric mean

(6.4.25)
$$Y_G = e^{\sum \ln(Y_i)/n}$$

The use of the geometric mean preserves scaling as Y is transformed to $Z^{(\lambda)}$. This, in turn, means that values of $SS_{residual}$ as a measure of lack of model fit may be compared across equations using different values of λ.

There are three ways to proceed in using Box-Cox to select a value of λ. One may try a series of values of λ to transform Y for a single data set (Draper & Smith, 1998). For each value of λ one would compute the values of $Z^{(\lambda)}$ according to normalized Eqs. (6.4.23a) and (6.4.23b), and predict $Z^{(\lambda)}$ in an OLS regression, retaining the value of residual sums of squares for that equation $SS_{residual:Z_i^{(\lambda)}}$. Then one would plot the values of $SS_{residual:Z_i^{(\lambda)}}$ against λ and select a value of λ that appeared to bring $SS_{residual:Z_i^{(\lambda)}}$ close to a minimum. A range of λ from about -2 to $+2$ might be tried, perhaps in increments of $\frac{1}{2}$: $-2, -1.5, -1.0, \ldots, 2$ (Draper & Smith, 1998).

Second, a form of statistical estimation (a method of selecting estimates of parameters) called *maximum likelihood estimation*[12] can be used mathematically to estimate the value of λ and simultaneously to estimate the values of the regression coefficients for $X_1, X_2, \ldots, X_K$ for predicting $Z^{(\lambda)}$ in the regression equation $\hat{Z}^{(\lambda)} = B_0 + B_1 X_1 + B_2 X_2 + \cdots + B_k X_k$. The value of λ selected by the method of maximum likelihood is referred to as the *maximum likelihood estimate* of λ. In addition, a confidence interval can be computed around the maximum likelihood estimate of λ. If the confidence interval includes the value $\lambda = 1$, this suggests that there is no need for transformation, since any score raised to the power 1 is simply the score itself.

Constructed variables and a diagnostic test of the need for transformation. A third method for estimating λ derives from a statistical test of whether a transformation of the dependent variable Y would improve prediction, suggested by Atkinson (1985) and described in detail in Fox (1997, p. 323). The null hypothesis is H_0: $\lambda = 1$, i.e., that no power transformation is needed. To operationalize the test, we create a *constructed variable* of the form:

(6.4.26)
$$W_i = Y_i \left(\ln \frac{Y_i}{Y_G} - 1 \right)$$

where Y_G is the geometric mean given in Eq. (6.4.25).

This constructed variable is included as an additional predictor in an OLS regression predicting Y in its original untransformed scale from the set of predictors $X_1, X_2, \ldots, X_k$:

(6.4.27)
$$\hat{Y} = B_0 + B_1 X_1 + B_2 X_2 + \cdots + B_k X_k + \theta W_i$$

If the θ coefficient is significant, this supports the need for transformation. The value $(1 - \hat{\theta}) = \hat{\lambda}$ provides a preliminary estimate of λ for use in transformation. The question then arises as to how we apply the estimated value of λ to generate a transformed Y score. We can use Eqs. (6.4.22a) and (6.4.22b) to generate transformed $Y^{(\lambda)}$. Alternatively, when $\lambda = 0$, we can simply compute Y^λ, using log Y.

---

[12]Maximum likelihood estimation for λ in Box-Cox is implemented in the ARC software of R. D. Cook and Weisberg (1999). The likelihood function to be maximized in selecting λ is monotonically related to $SS_{residual}$: $Z_i^{(\lambda)}$

6.4.10 Empirically Driven Transformation for Linearization in the Absence of Models: Box-Tidwell Family of Power Transformations on X

Suppose we observe a one-bend nonlinear relationship, but the residuals are well behaved (i.e., are homoscedastic and normal in form). To linearize the relationship we should transform X; transforming Y may introduce heteroscedasticity and/or non-normality of residuals. Again, we confront the question of how to choose the value of λ. Paralleling the Box-Cox procedure for transforming Y, Box and Tidwell (1962) provided a numerical strategy for the choice of transformations on predictors. The Box-Tidwell procedure may be simultaneously applied to several predictors, each with a different power transformation. Box 6.4.2 presents the procedure for a single predictor X. Atkinson (1985), Fox (1997), and Ryan (1997) present the multiple-predictor case in detail. As with Box-Cox, a test is provided for whether transformation of the predictor is required; the strategy also yields a preliminary estimate of λ and requires only OLS regression software. Again, this is a standard procedure in statistics that may well be useful for behavioral science data.

BOX 6.4.2
Achieving Linearization With the
Box-Tidwell Transformation of X

The expressions for transformed X in Box-Tidwell closely resemble those in Eqs. (6.4.22a) and (6.4.22b) for Box-Cox:

(6.4.28a)
$$X_i^{(\lambda)} = X_i^\lambda \quad \text{for} \quad \lambda \neq 0,$$

(6.4.28b)
$$X_i^{(\lambda)} = \ln X \quad \text{for} \quad \lambda = 0.$$

Unlike Box-Cox, there is no need for normalization of the transformed scores in order to compare models using different values of λ, since the dependent variable Y is identical across equations being compared.

One may use a constructed variable strategy to provide a test of the need for transformation and a preliminary estimate of λ. For a single predictor X, the constructed variable is given as

(6.4.29)
$$V_i = X_i \ln X_i.$$

In a series of steps provided by Box and Tidwell (1962) and described in detail in Fox (1997 p. 325), one can test whether a transformation of X will provide improved prediction of Y; again, H_0: $\lambda = 1$ (no transformation is required). One can also estimate the value of λ in Eqs. (6.4.28a) and (6.4.28b).

1. First, predict Y from untransformed X in the equation $\hat{Y}_i = B_0 + B_1 X_i$.
2. Then, predict Y from untransformed X plus constructed variable V from Eq. (6.4.29) in the following equation:

(6.4.30)
$$\hat{Y} = B_0' + B_1'X + \phi V_i = B_0' + B_1'X + \phi X_i \ln X_i.$$

If the ϕ coefficient is significant, this supports the need for transformation.

3. An estimate of λ is given as follows:

(6.4.31)
$$\hat{\lambda} = \frac{\phi}{B_1} + 1,$$

where B_1 is taken from step 1, and ϕ is taken from step 2.

A second iteration of the same three steps, but using $X_i^{\hat{\lambda}}$ in place of X throughout, (i.e., in the regression equations in steps 1 and 2, and in the computation of $V_i = X_i \ln X_i$ for step 2 where $\hat{\lambda}$ is taken from the first pass of step 3), yields a better estimate of the maximum likelihood estimate of λ. These iterations continue until the estimates of λ change by only tiny amounts.

6.4.11 Linearization of Relationships With Correlations: Fisher z' Transform of r

Sometimes a variable is measured and expressed in terms of the Pearson product moment correlation r. Two examples arise from personality psychology. First, measures of consistency of judgments of personality by the same person over time are cast as correlations. Second, in the Q-sort technique for assessing personality, items are sorted into rating categories of prescribed size (usually defining a quasi-normal distribution) so as to describe a complex phenomenon such as personality. The similarity of two such Q-sort descriptions, for example, actual self and ideal self, is then indexed by the r between ratings over the set of items. The sampling distribution of r is skewed; the Fisher z' transformation described in Section 2.8.2 functions to normalize the distribution of r. The Fisher z' transformations of correlations are more likely to relate linearly to other variables than are the correlations themselves. The Fisher z' transformation has its greatest effect as the magnitude of r approaches 1.0. The z' transformation of r is given in Appendix Table B.

6.4.12 Transformations That Linearize Relationships for Counts and Proportions

In our presentation of transformations to linearize relationships, we have not mentioned dependent variables with special characteristics, such as counts of the number of events that occur in a given time period, or proportions. Counts have the special property that they are bounded at (cannot be lower than) zero and are positively skewed for rare events. Proportions are bounded at zero at the low end of the scale and at one at the high end of the scale. The fact that both counts and proportions are bounded means that they may not be linearly related to other continuous variables.

Arcsine, Logit, and Probit Transformations of Proportions

Since proportions are bounded at zero and one, the plot of a DV in the form of proportions against a continuous predictor may be S-shaped, as illustrated in Fig. 13.1.1(B), with values of Y compressed (flattened out) for low and high values of X. We note that there are two bends in the S-shaped curve. Therefore a simple power transformation will not straighten the function. Three transformations are commonly employed to transform dependent variables in the form of proportions; the arcsine, logit, and probit transformations. All three transformations linearize relationships by stretching out the tails of the distribution of proportions, eliminating the two bends of the S-shape. Hence, they are referred to as *two-bend transformations*. Of the three, *only the arcsine transformation* stabilizes variances, as well a straightening out the relationship. Here we illustrate how these transformations can be calculated by hand to facilitate reader insight. In practice, standard statistical packages are used to calculate these transformations.

Arcsine transformation.   The arcsine transformation is given as follows:

$$(6.4.32) \qquad\qquad A = 2 \arcsin \sqrt{P},$$

that is, twice the angle (measured in radians) whose trigonometric sine equals the square root of the proportion being transformed. Use of this transformation assumes that the number of scores on which the proportions in a data set are based is constant across cases (e.g., when the proportion of correct responses as a DV is taken as the proportion correct on a 40-item scale completed by all participants).

Table 6.4.2 gives the A values for proportions P up to .50. For A values for $P > .50$, let $P' = (1 - P)$, find A_P from the table, and then compute

$$(6.4.33) \qquad\qquad A_{P'} = 3.14 - A_P.$$

For example, for the arcsine transformation of .64, find A for .36 ($= 1 - .64$), which equals 1.29, then find $3.14 - 1.29 = 1.85$. Table 6.4.2 will be sufficient for almost all purposes. The transformation is easily calculated on a statistical calculator . First, set the calculator mode to Radians. Enter the value of the proportion, take the square root, hit $\sin^{-1}$, and multiply the result by 2. Statistical packages also provide this transformation.[13] See also Owen (1962, pp. 293–303) for extensive tables of the arcsine transformation.

The amount of tail stretching effected by a transformation may be indexed by the ratio of the length of the scale on the transformation of the P interval from .01 to .11 to that of the interval from .40 to .50, that is, two equal intervals, one at the end and one at the middle of the distribution, respectively. For A, this index is 2.4 (compared with 4.0 for the probit and 6.2 for the logit).

Probit transformation.   This transformation is variously called *probit*, *normit*, or, most descriptively, *normalizing transformation of proportions*, a specific instance of the general normalizing transformation. We use the term *probit* in recognition of its wide use in bioassay, where it is so designated.

Its rationale is straightforward. Consider P to be the cumulative proportion of a unit normal curve (that is, a normal curve "percentile"), determine its baseline value, z_P, which is expressed in *sd* departures from a mean of zero, and add 5 to assure that the value is positive. The probit (PR) is

$$(6.4.34) \qquad\qquad PR = z_P + 5.$$

Table 6.4.2 gives PR as a function of P for the lower half of the scale. When $P = 0$ and 1, PR is at minus and plus infinity, respectively, something of an embarrassment for numerical calculation. We recommend that for $P = 0$ and 1, they be revised to

$$(6.4.35) \qquad\qquad P_0 = \frac{1}{2v}$$

and

$$(6.4.36) \qquad\qquad P_1 = \frac{2v - 1}{2v},$$

---

[13]Most statistical software provides the arcsine transformation: in SPSS, within the COMPUTE statement; in SAS, as a statement in PROC TRANSREG; in SYSTAT, in DATA(LET-ACS).

TABLE 6.4.2

Arcsine (*A*), Probit (*PR*), and Logit (*L*) Transformations
for Proportions (*P*)

P	A	PR	L	P	A	PR	L
.000	.00	—[b]	—[b]	.16	.82	4.01	−.83
.002	.09	2.12	−3.11	.17	.85	4.05	−.79
.004	.13	2.35	−2.76	.18	.88	4.08	−.76
.006	.16	2.49	−2.56	.19	.90	4.12	−.72
.008	.18	2.59	−2.41	.20	.93	4.16	−.69
.010	.20	2.67	−2.30	.21	.95	4.19	−.66
.012	.22	2.74	−2.21	.22	.98	4.23	−.63
.014	.24	2.80	−2.13	.23	1.00	4.26	−.60
.016	.25	2.86	−2.06	.24	1.02	4.29	−.58
.018	.27	2.90	−2.00	.25	1.05	4.33	−.55
.020	.28	2.95	−1.96	.26	1.07	4.36	−.52
.022	.30	2.99	−1.90	.27	1.09	4.39	−.50
.024	.31	3.02	−1.85	.28	1.12	4.42	−.47
.026	.32	3.06	−1.81	.29	1.14	4.45	−.45
.028	.34	3.09	−1.77	.30	1.16	4.48	−.42
.030	.35	3.12	−1.74	.31	1.18	4.50	−.40
.035	.38	3.19	−1.66	.32	1.20	4.53	−.38
.040	.40	3.25	−1.59	.33	1.22	4.56	−.35
.045	.43	3.30	−1.53	.34	1.25	4.59	−.33
.050	.45	3.36	−1.47	.35	1.27	4.61	−.31
.055	.47	3.40	−1.42	.36	1.29	4.64	−.29
.060	.49	3.45	−1.38	.37	1.31	4.67	−.27
.065	.52	3.49	−1.33	.38	1.33	4.69	−.24
.070	.54	3.52	−1.29	.39	1.35	4.72	−.22
.075	.55	3.56	−1.26	.40	1.37	4.75	−.20
.080	.57	3.59	−1.22	.41	1.39	4.77	−.18
.085	.59	3.63	−1.19	.42	1.41	4.80	−.16
.090	.61	3.66	−1.16	.43	1.43	4.82	−.14
.095	.63	3.69	−1.13	.44	1.45	4.85	−.12
.100	.64	3.72	−1.00	.45	1.47	4.87	−.10
.11	.68	3.77	−1.05	.46	1.49	4.90	−.08
.12	.71	3.83	−1.00	.47	1.51	4.92	−.06
.13	.74	3.87	−.95	.48	1.53	4.95	−.04
.14	.77	3.92	−.91	.49	1.55	4.97	−.02
.15	.80	3.96	−.87	.50[a]	1.57	5.00	.00

[a] See text for values when *p* > .50.

[b] See text for transformation when *P* = 0 or 1.

where v is the denominator of the counted fraction. This is arbitrary, but usually reasonable. If in such circumstances this transformation makes a critical difference, prudence suggests that this transformation be avoided.

For *PR* values for *P* > .50, as before, let $P' = 1 - P$, find PR_P from Table 6.4.2, and then find

(6.4.37)
$$PR_{P'} = 10 - PR_P.$$

For example, the PR for $P = .83$ is found by looking up P for $.17 = (1 - .83)$ which equals 4.05, and then finding $10 - 4.05 = 5.95$. For a denser argument for probits, which maybe desirable in the tails, see Fisher and Yates (1963, pp. 68–71), but any good table of the inverse of the normal probability distribution will provide the necessary z_P values (Owen, 1962, p.12). Statistical computing packages also provide inverse distribution functions.[14]

Logit transformation. This transformation is related to the logistic curve, which is similar in shape to the normal curve but generally more mathematically tractable. The logistic distribution is discussed in more detail in Section 13.2.4 in the presentation of logistic regression. The logit transform is

$$(6.4.38) \qquad L = \frac{1}{2} \ln \frac{P}{1 - P}$$

where ln is, as before, the natural logarithm (base e); the ½ is not a necessary part of the definition of the logit and is here included by convention. The relationship of values of L to P is illustrated in Fig. 13.2.1; the manner in which the logit stretches both tails of the distribution of proportions is clearly illustrated. As with probits, the logits for $P = 0$ and 1 are at minus and plus infinity, and the same device for coping with this problem (Eqs. 6.4.35 and 6.4.36) is recommended: replace $P = 0$ by $P = 1/(2v)$ and $P = 1$ by $(2v - 1)/(2v)$ and find the logits of the revised values. As before, Table 6.4.2 gives the L for P up to .50; for $P > .50$, let $P' = 1 - P$, find L_P and change its sign to positive for $L_{P'}$, that is,

$$(6.4.39) \qquad L_{P'} = -L_P$$

For $P = .98$, for example, find L for .02 ($= 1 - .98$), which equals -1.96, and change its sign, thus L for .98 is $+1.96$.

The logit stretches the tails of the P distribution the most of the three transformations. The tail-stretching index (described previously) for the logit is 6.2, compared with 4.0 for the probit and 2.4 for the arcsine.

The quantity $P/(1 - P)$ is the odds related to P (e.g., when $P = .75$, the odds are .75/.25 or simply 3). The logit, then, is simply half the natural logarithm of the odds. Therefore logits have the property that for equal intervals on the logit scale, the odds are changed by a constant multiple; for example, an increase of .35 on the logit scale represents a doubling of the odds, because .35 is ½ ln 2, where the odds are 2. The relationship of the logit to odds and their role in logistic regression is explained in detail in Section 13.2.4.

We also note the close relationship between the logit transformation of P and Fisher's z' transformation of the product-moment r (see Section 2.8.2 and Appendix Table B). If we let $r = 2P - 1$, then the z' transformation of r is the logit of P. Logit transformations are easily calculated with a statistical calculator: divide P by $(1 - P)$ and hit the ln key. Or, the computation is easily programmed within standard statistical software (see, for example, the SPSS code in Table 13.2.1).

Note that all three transformations are given in the form most frequently used or more conveniently tabled. They may be further transformed linearly if it is found convenient by the user to do so. For example, if the use of negative values is awkward, one can add a constant to L of 5, as is done for the same purpose in probits. Neither the 2 in the arcsine transformation in Eq. (6.4.32) nor the ½ in the logit transformation in Eq. (6.4.38) is necessary for purposes of correlation, but they do no harm and are tabled with these constants as part of them in accordance with their conventional definitions.

---

[14]The inverse normal function is also provided in SPSS, with the function IDF.NORMAL within the COMPUTE syntax.

The choice among the arcsine, probit, and logit transformations to achieve linearity may be guided by examining a scatterplot of each of the three transformations of the proportion against the variable with which it exhibited a nonlinear relationship in the untransformed state. A lowess line plus a linear regression line superimposed on the scatterplot will aid in discerning how well the linearization has been achieved by each transformation. Once again, the reader is warned that if the transformed proportion variable is the DV, then the fit of the regression equations with the three different transformed variables cannot be directly compared (see Section 6.4.16).

6.4.13 Variance Stabilizing Transformations and Alternatives for Treatment of Heteroscedasticity

Although we assume homoscedasticity in OLS regression, there are numerous data structures in which the predicted score $\hat{Y}_i$ is related to the variance of the residuals $sd^2_{Y|\hat{Y}}$ among individuals with that particular predicted score $\hat{Y}_i$. Often the variance increases as the predicted score increases; this is so for variables that have a lower bound of zero but no upper bound. Consider again "count" variables (e.g., the count of number of sneezes in an hour during cold season). If we take people with an average of 1 sneeze per hour, the variance in their number of sneezes over hours will be quite small. If we take people with an average of 20 sneezes per hour, the variance in number of sneezes over hours can be much larger. If we predict number of sneezes per hour in an OLS regression, we may well encounter heteroscedasticity of residuals. Now consider a measure of proportion (e.g., the proportion of days during winter flu season on which a person takes "flu" remedies). Here the variance does not simply increase as the mean proportion increases; rather, the variance increases as the mean proportion increases from 0 to .5, and then declines as the mean proportion increases further from .5 to 1.0.

Approaches to Variance Stabilization: Transformation, Weighted Least Squares, the Generalized Linear Model

Dependent variables that exhibit heteroscedasticity (nonconstant variance of the residuals) pose difficulties for OLS regression. Several approaches are taken to address the problem of heteroscedasticity. The first is transformation of the DV. Second is use of *weighted least squares regression*, presented in Section 4.5.4. Third and newest is the application of a class of regression methods subsumed under the name *generalized linear model*; this class of methods is composed of particular regression models that address specific forms of heterogeneity that commonly arise in certain data structures, such as dichotomous (binary) or count DVs. Most of Chapter 13 is devoted to two such methods: *logistic regression* for analysis of dichotomous and ordered categorical dependent variables, and *Poisson regression* for the analysis of count data. The availability of these three approaches reflects the evolution of statistical methodology. It is recommended that the reader carefully consider the developments in Chapter 13 before selecting among the solutions to the variance heterogeneity problem. Where the choice is available to transform data or to employ an appropriate form of the generalized linear model, current recommendations lean to the use of the generalized linear model.

Variance Stabilizing Transformations

The choice of variance stabilizing transformation depends on the relationship between the value of the predicted score $\hat{Y}_i$ in a regression analysis and the variance of the residuals $sd^2_{Y|\hat{Y}}$ among individuals with that particular predicted score. We discuss the use of four variance stabilizing transformations: square roots, logarithms, reciprocals, and the arcsine transformation.

The first three are one-bend transformations from the power family that we also employ to linearize relationships. The fourth is a *two-bend transformation*. That we encounter the same transformations for linearization and for variance stabilization illustrates that one transformation may, in fact, ameliorate more than one difficulty with data. We again warn, however, that a transformation that fixes one problem in the data (e.g., variance heterogeneity), may introduce another problem (e.g., nonlinearity).

We first present the three one-bend transformations from the power family Y^λ, the square root transformation ($\lambda = \frac{1}{2}$), the logarithmic transformation ($\lambda = 0$), and the reciprocal transformation ($\lambda = -1$). We then suggest approaches for selecting an approximate value of λ for variance stabilization.

Square Root Transformation ($\lambda = \frac{1}{2}$) and Count Variables

The most likely use of a square root transformation occurs for count variables that follow a Poisson probability distribution, a positively skewed distribution of counts of rare events that occur in a specific time period, for example, counts of bizarre behaviors exhibited by individuals in a one-hour public gathering (see Section 13.4.2 for further description of the Poisson distribution). In a Poisson distribution of residuals, which may arise from a count DV, the variance of the residual scores $sd^2_{Y|\hat{Y}}$ around a particular predicted score $\hat{Y}_i$ is proportional to the predicted score $\hat{Y}_i$. Count data are handled by taking $\sqrt{Y}$. This will likely operate so as to equalize the variance, reduce the skew, and linearize relationships to other variables. A refinement of this transformation, $\sqrt{Y} + \sqrt{Y+1}$ suggested by Freeman and Tukey (1950) provides more homogeneous variances when the mean of the count variable across the data set is very low (i.e., the event being counted is very rare). Poisson regression, developed in Section 13.4, is a more appropriate approach to count dependent variables, when treatment of Y with a square root transformation fails to produce homoscedasticity.

Logarithmic Transformation ($\lambda = 0$)

The logarithmic transformation is most often employed to linearize relationships. If the variance of the residuals $sd^2_{Y|\hat{Y}}$ is proportional to the *square* of the predicted score $\hat{Y}_i^2$, the logarithmic transformation will also stabilize variances. Cook and Weisberg (1999) suggest the use of logarithmic transformations to stabilize variance when residuals are a percentage of the score on the criterion Y.

Reciprocal Transformation ($\lambda = -1$)

We encountered the reciprocal transformation in our consideration of linearizing relationships. If the residuals arise from a distribution in which the predicted score $\hat{Y}_i$ is proportional to the square of the variance of the residuals $(sd^2_{Y|\hat{Y}})^2$, the reciprocal transformation will stabilize variances.

An Estimate of λ for Variance Stabilization:
The Family of Power Transformations Revisited

The choice among the square root ($\lambda = \frac{1}{2}$); log($\lambda = 0$), or reciprocal ($\lambda = -1$) as a variance stabilizing transformation depends on the relationship between the predicted score $\hat{Y}_i$ and the variance of residuals $sd^2_{Y|\hat{Y}}$. An approach for selecting an appropriate λ for variance stabilization is described in Box 6.4.3. An alternative to this approach is to transform Y with each of the three transformations, carry out the regression analysis with each transformed DV, and examine the residuals from each analysis. The transformation that leads to the best behaved residuals is selected. Again, the reader is warned that measures of fit cannot be directly compared across

---

BOX 6.4.3
What Value of λ: Selecting a Variance Stabilizing Transformation
From Among the Family of Power Transformations

To solve for a value of λ for variance stabilization, we find an estimate of δ that relates predicted score $\hat{Y}_i$ to the standard deviation of the residuals $sd_{Y|\hat{Y}}$, according to the expression $sd_{Y|\hat{Y}}$ is proportional to $\hat{Y}^\delta$ or, equivalently, $\ln sd_{Y|\hat{Y}} = \delta_0 + \delta \ln \hat{Y}$. Draper and Smith (1998) suggest that one regress untransformed Y on untransformed X, then select several vaues of the predicted score $\hat{Y}_i$, and for each of these values of $\hat{Y}_i$, find the band width (range) of the residuals (a procedure that requires a number of scores with essentially the same value of $\hat{Y}$). One then assumes that this range is approximately $4\, sd_i$, where sd_i is the standard deviation of the residuals for the value $\hat{Y}_i$, and plots $\ln sd_i$ as a function of $\ln \hat{Y}_i$ to estimate the slope δ. To stabilize the variance of Y, we use $\lambda = (1 - \delta)$ to transform Y.

---

the regression equations because the dependent variables are on different scales. Strategies for model comparison across power transformations of the DV are discussed in Section 6.4.16 and in Box 6.4.1, with a complete numerical example provided in Section 6.4.17.

Box-Cox Transformation Revisited and Variance Stabilization

We introduced the Box-Cox approach to selection of λ in the context of linearization of relationships. The Box-Cox approach aims to simultaneously achieve linearization, homoscedasticity, and normality of residuals, and is applicable to the problem of variance stabilization.

Variance Stabilization of Proportions

Suppose our dependent variable were a proportion (e.g., the proportion of correct responses on a test comprised of a fixed number of items). The variance of a proportion is greatest when the proportion $P = .50$, and diminishes as P approaches either 0 or 1; specifically, $\sigma_P^2 = P(1 - P)$. The arcsine transformation introduced in Section 6.4.12 stabilizes variances.

Weighted Least Squares Regression for Variance Stabilization

Weighted least squares regression provides an alternative approach to the analysis of data that exhibit heteroscedasticity of residuals. This approach was described in detail in Section 4.5.4.

6.4.14 Transformations to Normalize Variables

We undertake transformations to normalize variables in several circumstances. One is that we have skewed Xs and/or Y. Another is that we are dealing with variables that are inherently not normally distributed, for example ranks.

Transformations to Eliminate Skew

Recall that inference in OLS regression assumes that *residuals* are normally distributed. If we analyze a data set with OLS regression and find that residuals are not normally distributed, for example, by examining a q-q plot of residuals against a normal variate (Section 4.3), then transformation of Y may be in order. Skew in the dependent variable may well be the source of the skewed residuals. Our approach, then, is to transform the DV in the hopes of achieving more normal residuals.

We can transform Y to be more normally distributed following the rules from the ladder of re-expression, that values of $\lambda > 1$ decrease negative skew, and values of $\lambda < 1$ decrease positive skew in the distribution of the transformed variable (see Section 6.4.8). Several values of λ can be tried, the transformed variable plotted as a histogram with a normal distribution overlayed or in a q-q plot against a normal variate (see Section 4.4.6). Modern statistical graphics packages provide a slider for values of λ and display the distribution of the variable as λ changes continuously. Alternatively, we may employ Box-Cox transformation of Y, which attempts to achieve more normally distributed residuals, as well as linearity and homoscedasticity.

Normalization of Ranks

A normalization strategy based on percentiles of the normal curve may be useful when data consist of *ranks*. When a third-grade teacher characterizes the aggressiveness of her 30 pupils by ranking them from 1 to 30, the resulting 30 values may occasion difficulties when they are treated numerically as measures. Ranks are necessarily rectangularly distributed; that is, there is one score of 1, one score of 2, ..., one score of 30. If, as is likely, the difference in aggressiveness between the most and next-most (or the least and next-least) aggressive child is greater than between two adjacent children in the middle (e.g., those ranked 14 and 15), then the scale provided by the ranks is not likely to produce linear relationships with other variables. The need to stretch the tails is the same phenomenon encountered with proportions; it presupposes that the distribution of the construct to be represented has tails, that is, is bell shaped or normal. Because individual differences for many well-measured biological and behavioral phenomena seem to approximate this distribution, in the face of ranked data it is a reasonable transformation to apply in the absence of specific notions to the contrary. Even if the normalized scale is not optimal, it is likely to be superior to the original ranks.

The method for accomplishing this is simple. Following the procedure described in elementary statistics textbooks for finding centiles (percentiles), express the ranks as cumulative proportions, and refer these to a unit normal curve (Appendix Table C) to read off z_P, or use the *PR* column of Table 6.4.2, where 5 has been added to z_P to yield probits. Mosteller and Tukey (1977) suggest an alternative approach for transforming ranks, but with the same goal of normalization in mind. Other methods of addressing ordinal data are presented by Cliff (1996).

6.4.15 Diagnostics Following Transformation

We reiterate the admonition about transformation made in Section 6.4.2, that it is imperative to recheck the regression model that results from use of the transformed variable(s). Transformation may fix one difficulty and produce another. Examining whether relationships have been linearized, checking for outliers *produced by* transformation, and examining residuals are all as important after transformation as before. If difficulties are produced by transformation (e.g., heteroscedasticity of residuals), the decision may be made not to transform.[15]

---

[15]The constructed variable strategy described for Box-Cox transformation in Box 6.4.1, and Box-Tidwell in Box 6.4.2 provides an opportunity for the use of regression diagnostics to determine whether the apparent need for transformation signaled by the test of θ in Eq. (6.4.27), or of ϕ in Eq. (6.4.30) is being produced by a few outliers. An added variable plot (partial regression residual plot) is created in which the part of Y which is independent of untransformed X is plotted against the part of W in Eq. (6.4.26) for Box-Cox or V in Eq. (6.4.29) for Box-Tidwell, which is independent of untransformed X; the plot is inspected for outliers that may be producing the apparent need for transformation.

6.4.16 Measuring and Comparing Model Fit

We transform variables in part in the hope that our overall model will improve with transformation. In selecting transformations, we need to compare model fit among regression equations employing the same data but different transformations. We warn that when different nonlinear transformations of Y are employed, the R^2 values generated for the different models are not directly comparable. In other words, one cannot compare the R_Y^2 resulting from predicting untransformed Y versus $R_{\sqrt{Y}}^2$ from predicting transformed $Y' = \sqrt{Y}$, versus $R_{\log Y}^2$ from predicting transformed $Y'' = \log Y$. Each dependent variable is on a different scale; the R^2s are not comparable (Kvålseth, 1985). Very misleading results with regard to the fit of models in the raw versus transformed metric may be reached by comparing the R^2 values that are reported in statistical software for these models (Alastair & Wild, 1991). To assess model fit after transformation, the predicted scores should be converted back to raw score units by reversing the transformation. For example, for $Y'' = \log Y$, the predicted scores $\hat{Y}_{\text{transformed}}$ are in logarithmic units. The antilog (Section 6.4.3) of each predicted score should be computed, yielding predicted scores in the original metric arising from the prediction of $Y' = \log Y$, that is, $e^{\hat{Y}_{\text{transformed}}} = \hat{Y}_{\text{original units}}$. (If the square root transformation were used, then we would square each predicted score to return to a predicted score in raw units.) Then two options are available for measuring fit. We may compute an index of fit as follows (Kvålseth, 1985):

$$(6.4.40) \qquad R_1^2 = 1 - \frac{\sum (Y_i - \hat{Y}_{\text{original units}})^2}{\sum (Y_i - M_Y)^2}.$$

Alternatively, we may compute the correlation between the observed Y scores and $\hat{Y}_{\text{original units}}$ (Ryan, 1997), $R^2_{Y_i, \hat{Y}_{\text{original units}_i}}$, and compare these values across models. Ryan (1997) warns that both approaches may yield difficulties. First, if predicted scores are negative, then they cannot be transformed back to original units for many values of λ. Second, if $\hat{Y}_{\text{transformed}}$ is very close to zero, then the corresponding $\hat{Y}_{\text{original units}}$ may be a huge number, causing Eq. (6.4.40) to be negative. Ryan (1997) recommends use of $R^2_{Y_i, \hat{Y}_{\text{original units}_i}}$, with cases yielding negative predicted scores discarded.

6.4.17 Second-Order Polynomial Numerical Example Revisited

The data presented in Figs. 6.1.1 and 6.2.3 were actually simulated to follow a second-order polynomial with additive homoscedastic, normally distributed error. The second-order polynomial in Table 6.2.1 provides a well-fitting model with $R^2_{\text{second-order polynomial}} = .67$. In real life, we would not know the true form of the regression equation in the population that led to the observed data. We might try several transformations. What happens if we try a power transformation of Y to linearize the relationship? The bulge in the data follows Fig. 6.4.1(A), suggesting that we either transform X with $\lambda < 1.0$ or transform Y with $\lambda > 1.0$. Using Box-Cox transformation, the maximum likelihood estimate of λ is 1.73, derived from an iterative solution. We compute $Y_{\text{Box-Cox}} = Y^{1.73}$ and predict $Y_{\text{Box-Cox}}$ from untransformed X. The data, resulting linear regression line, $\hat{Y}_{\text{Box-Cox}} = 14.82X + 35.56$, plus a lowess line are shown in Fig. 6.4.2(A) (p. 236). From inspection of the lowess lines in Fig. 6.2.2(A) for untransformed Y versus Fig. 6.4.2(A) for transformed Y, the X-Y relationship appears more linear in Fig. 6.4.2(A), a result of transforming Y. However, the lowess curve in Fig. 6.4.2(A) tells us that we have not completely transformed away the curvilinear relationship in the data. Moreover, the transformation of Y has produced heteroscedasticity in Y: The spread of the Y

scores increases as X increases. As we have warned, transformation to fix one problem (here, nonlinearity) has produced another problem (nonconstant variance). We compare the fit of the polynomial model to that of the Box-Cox transformed Y model. Following Ryan (1997), we compute the predicted scores from $\hat{Y}_{\text{Box-Cox}} = 14.82X + 35.56$, which are in the transformed metric. We then convert the $\hat{Y}_{\text{Box-Cox}}$ predicted scores back to the original metric by computing $\hat{Y}_{\text{original units}} = (\hat{Y}_{\text{Box-Cox}})^{1/1.73}$. For example, for a single case $X = 7$, and observed $Y = 16.08$, $\hat{Y}_{\text{Box-Cox}} = Y^{1.73} = 16.08^{1.73} = 122.11$. The predicted score from the regression equation $\hat{Y}_{\text{Box-Cox}} = 14.82X + 35.56 = 139.29$. Finally $\hat{Y}_{\text{original units}} = (\hat{Y}_{\text{Box-Cox}})^{1/1.73} = 139.29^{1/1.73} = 17.35$. We then compute $R^2_{Y_i, \hat{Y}_{\text{original units}_i}} = .60$, the squared correlation between observed Y in its original units and the predicted score from the Box-Cox equation transformed back into original units. The Box-Cox transformation leads to a slightly less well fitting model than does the original polynomial equation. It also adds the woes of heteroscedasticity.

Suppose we focus on transforming X. The bulge rule suggests a value of $\lambda < 1$. With the left bulge, a logarithmic relationship is often helpful; we compute $\ln X$ and predict Y from $\ln X$. The resulting data, the regression equation $\hat{Y} = 8.34 \ln X + 1.34$, and a lowess curve are given in Fig. 6.4.2(B). The lowess line tells us that the logarithmic transformation succeeded in linearizing the relationship. The data look quite homoscedastic (though sparse at the low end). Because we have left Y in its original metric, the predicted scores are in the original metric as well. We do not have to transform the predicted scores before examining model fit; we may use the squared multiple correlation resulting from the regression equation $\hat{Y} = 8.34 \ln X + 1.34$, which is $R^2_{Y, \log X} = .67$, the same fit as from the second-order polynomial. With the data of Fig. 6.2.1, the second order polynomial and the logarithmic transformation are indistinguishable. The real difference between the logarithmic transformation and the quadratic polynomial is that the quadratic polynomial turns downward at the high end, as in Figure 6.1.1, but the logarithmic transformation, a one-bend transformation from the power family, does not. The data are too sparse at the high end to distinguish the polynomial equation from the logarithmic transformation. The lowess curve is not informative in this regard, due to the weakness of lowess at the ends of the X continuum. In contrast, the rectangularly distributed data in Fig. 6.2.4, with a number of cases with high values of X, would distinguish the polynomial versus logarithmic transformation; the downward turn in the data is obvious.

6.4.18 When to Transform and the Choice of Transformation

The choice between an untransformed versus a transformed analysis must take into consideration a number of factors: (a) whether strong theory, (as in psychophysics) dictates the use of transformation for estimation of critical model parameters, (b) whether the equation in the transformed metric provides a better explanation of the phenomenon under investigation than in the raw metric, for example, in the use of log dollars to reflect the utility of money, (c) whether overall fit is substantially improved by virtue of transformation, and (d) whether transformation introduces new difficulties into the model. In the behavioral sciences our focus is often on regression coefficients of particular predictors of strong theoretical interest, above and beyond an interest in overall level of prediction.

There are certainly examples of cases in which transformation yields new findings not detected in the original metric. For example, R. E. Millsap (personal communication, February 23, 2000) found evidence of salary discrimination in one of two demographic groups relative to another when salary as Y was transformed using a log metric, but not when salary was treated in the raw metric. When critical results like this differ across transformations, the researcher is pressed to develop an explanation of why the results in the transformed metric are more appropriate.

The opposite possibility exists, that is, that an important effect may be transformed away. There are instances in which we may predict a curvilinear relationship (e.g., a rise in performance as X increases to an asymptote) or an interaction between two variables (Chapter 7 is devoted to interactions). Transformation may remove the very effect we have proposed. In that case, we would obviously stay in the original metric, having once assured ourselves that the curvilinearity or interaction was not due to one or a few outliers. If the data in the original metric posed other problems (e.g., heteroscedasticity), we could retain the data in the original metric but use a more appropriate regression model, here weighted least squares regression instead of OLS regression.

In many instances, transformation may have little effect, particularly if scores contain substantial measurement error. In addition, if scores have a small range, the family of power transformations will have little effect. If data are in the form of proportions and most proportions fall between .3 and .7, or even .2 and .8, then the arcsine, logit, and probit transformation will have little effect; it is when events are very rare or very frequent (P close to 0 or 1) that transformations will make a difference. Reflection on these conditions leads us to expect that in a substantial number of cases in psychological research, (e.g., when our dependent variables are rating scales with small range), transformations will have little effect. In contrast, in areas where the DVs are physical measurements covering a large range, transformations will often be of considerable value.

An easy approach to examining whether a variable distribution (e.g., extreme skew in a predictor or the dependent variable) is producing an effect is to convert the variable to ranks[16] and repeat the analysis replacing the variable itself by its associated ranks. If the results remain the same, particularly whether theoretically important variables do or do not have an effect, then we have some confidence that the results in the raw metric are appropriate.

The choice among transformations, say the log versus square root for highly positively skewed data, will be guided by which transformation provides the better fit, given that there is no strong theoretical rationale for the choice of either. The choice will also be guided by the extent to which transformation leads to residuals that have constant variance and are normally distributed. However, the similarity of curves that are generated by different transformation equations (as illustrated in Fig. 6.4.1) coupled with random error in data mean that we may well not be able to distinguish among the transformations that may be applied to an individual data set. An interesting choice arises between polynomial regression, relatively often employed in psychology, and other transformations of the same data that lead to approximately the same fit (e.g., the use of a quadratic polynomial versus a logarithmic transformation of X). If one finds that with both transformations, the assumptions on residuals are similarly met, then interpretability in relationship to theory dictates choice. If the nonlinear relationship of X to Y is nonmonotonic, then polynomial regression must be employed; the family of power transformations handles only monotonic relationships. Finally, even when data properties point to a particular transformation, researchers should not act without simultaneously considering theoretical appropriateness.

Transformations should be tried when both violations of assumptions and evidence of nonlinearity exist and the researcher wishes to use OLS regression. The researcher should consider whether a form of the generalized linear model is more appropriate (Chapter 13). This may well be the case (e.g., the use of Poisson regression for counts of rare events).

Two alternatives exist to the use of either polynomial regression or the transformations described in Section 6.4: nonlinear least squares regression when an intrinsically nonlinear

---

[16]The Rank Cases procedure in SPSS ranks scores, as does rank transformation in SAS PROC TRANSREG and the rank option in the SYSTAT data module.

relationship is to be fitted, and nonparametric regression, in which no assumptions are made concerning the form of relationship of X to Y.

Sources on Transformation in Regression

The legacy of the ladder of re-expression and the bulge rule and much practical wisdom about transformation are found in Mosteller and Tukey (1977). Draper and Smith (1998) and Fox (1997) are useful starting points for further reading. Cook and Weisberg (1999) show the integration of the use of graphics and graphical software into transformation. Classic sources from mathematical statistics on transformation in regression include Atkinson (1985) and Carroll and Ruppert (1988).

6.5 NONLINEAR REGRESSION

Nonlinear regression (NR) is a form of regression analysis in which one estimates the coefficients of a nonlinear regression model that is *intrinsically nonlinear*, that is, cannot be linearized by suitable transformation (Section 6.4.4). Recall that whether an equation is intrinsically linear versus intrinsically nonlinear depends on whether the errors are assumed to be *multiplicative* versus *additive*, respectively. The nonlinear equations presented in Section 6.4.5 were all shown to be linearizable, but if and only if we assumed that the errors were multiplicative in the original metric, as was the assumption for all the models presented in Section 6.4.5. For example, when we assumed multiplicative error underlying the exponential growth model in Eq. (6.4.14), that is $Y = c(e^{dx})\varepsilon_i$, where ε represents error, the equation could be linearized to Eq. (6.4.15), $\log \hat{Y} = B_1 X_1 + B_0$. If, on the other hand, we were to have assumed additive error, such that $Y = c(e^{dx}) + \varepsilon_i$, we would have needed to estimate the coefficients c and d using NR.

The use of NR begins with choice of a nonlinear model, either due to strong theory or some weaker evidence of the appropriateness of the model. The user of NR regression software must specify the particular nonlinear equation to be estimated. This is, of course, unlike the use of OLS regression or variants like WLS regression, which always employ a linear model. Ratkowsky (1990) provides graphical representations of relationships that can be useful in selecting a nonlinear model. The criterion for the choice of weights in NR is the same as in OLS regression, the least squares criterion (Section 4.3.2). However, there is not an analytic solution in the form of a set of equations (the normal equations) that we use to solve directly for the regression coefficients, as there are in OLS regression. The coefficients in NR must be found by trial and error, in an *iterative solution*. (Iterative solutions are explained in Section 13.2.9.) Iterative solutions require initial estimates of the coefficients, termed *start values* (e.g., initial estimates of the c and d coefficients in the equation $\hat{Y} = ce^{dx}$), in order that the iterative search for estimates of coefficients be successful. The values of coefficients obtained from using OLS regression to estimate the *corresponding* linearized equation (for example, the coefficients from fitting $\log \hat{Y} = B_1 X_1 + B_0$) may serve as start values for NR on the same data. The regression coefficients from NR may be tested for significance under assumptions that the coefficients are asymptotically approximately normally distributed and that their variances are asymptotically approximately distributed as chi square; large sample sizes are required to approach these asymptotic conditions. An overall goodness of fit measure for the model follows the same approach as for transformed variables, given in Eq. (6.4.40).

Sources on Nonlinear Regression

In Chapter 13, we present logistic regression, a form of nonlinear regression, in some detail and also introduce another form of nonlinear regression, Poisson regression. Matters of statistical inference, diagnostics, model fit are all explored for the logistic model and are applicable more generally to NR. Rawlings (1988) provides a highly readable introduction to nonlinear regression, and characterizes commonly used nonlinear models. Neter, Kutner, Nachtsheim and Wasserman (1996) provide an example of relevance to psychologists of fitting a common learning curve in two groups with an exponential growth model expanded to include an asymptote plus a variable representing group membership. Neter, Kutner, Nachtsheim and Wasserman (1996), Ryan (1997), and Draper and Smith (1998) provide useful practical advice and examples. Seber and Wild (1989) present a more advanced treatment.

6.6 NONPARAMETRIC REGRESSION

Nonparametric regression is an approach to discerning the pattern of the relationship of a predictor X (or set of predictors) to a dependent variable Y without first specifying a regression model, such as the familiar OLS regression model $\hat{Y} = B_0 + B_1X_1 + B_2X_2 + \cdots + B_kX_k + B_0$. In nonparametric regression we discover the form of the relationship between X and Y by developing a smooth function relating X to Y *driven solely by the data themselves* absent any assumption about the form of the relationship. The nonparametric regression line (or curve) follows the trends in the data; the curve is smoothed by generating each point on the curve from a number of neighboring data points. The *lowess* (or *loess*) methodology explained in Chapter 4 and utilized in Fig. 6.2.2(A) is a central methodology in nonparametric regression. (See Section 4.2.1 for a discussion of smoothing and Section 4.2.2 for a discussion of lowess). Fox (2000a) provides a highly accessible introduction to nonparametric simple (one-predictor) regression; an accompanying volume (Fox, 2000b) extends to nonparametric multiple regression.

The lowess curve in Fig. 6.2.2(A) is a regression function. However, we note that it is not accompanied by a regression equation (i.e., there is no regression coefficient or regression constant). Yet we gain a great deal of information from the curve—that the relationship of X to Y is curvilinear, that there is one clearly discernable bend at low values of X, and that the relationship "bulges" to the upper left in the Mosteller and Tukey (1977) sense, illustrated in Fig. 6.4.2. We used the lowess curve in Fig. 6.2.2(A) to argue that quadratic polynomial regression was warranted to characterize the relationship. We could have gleaned further inferential information from the lowess analysis. The lowess curve in Fig. 6.2.2(A) provides a predicted score for each value of X on the lowess line: $\hat{Y}_{lowess}$. Thus it is possible to generate a measure of residual variation $SS_{residual} = \Sigma(Y_i - \hat{Y}_{lowess\ i})^2$, which leads to an F test of the null hypothesis that there is no relationship between X and Y. Further, since the linear regression line shown in Fig. 6.2.2(A) is nested in the more general lowess regression curve, we could have tested whether the lowess curve contributed significantly more predictability than the linear regression.

Nonparametric regression represents a new way of thinking about fitting functions to data, one that has been hardly exploited in the behavioral sciences at the time of this writing. How might we use nonparametric regression when considering the relation of X to Y? First, the lowess regression curve might be graphically presented, along with the statistical tests of relationship and nonlinearity, and the relationship described simply by the lowess curve. Second, the appearance of the lowess curve could guide the choice of transformation, either polynomial regression or one of the transformations reviewed in Section 6.4, or the selection of a function for nonlinear regression.

Nonparametric regression can be extended to multiple predictors. In the *additive nonpara-metric model*, a separate nonparametric regression function is fitted to each predictor (e.g., a lowess curve for each predictor). Overall fit can be tested, as can the partial contribution of each predictor to prediction over and above the other predictors. Illustrating the shape of the regression function for two predictors as a two-dimensional irregular mountain rising from the regression plane is straightforward with modern graphical packages. Difficulty in visualizing the relationship arises with more than two predictors. Further, large sample sizes are required for multiple nonparametric regression in order to have sufficient cases at various combinations of values on all the predictors to generate the predicted scores for nonparametric regression (i.e., to develop the shape of the nonparametric regression surface). Nonetheless, nonparametric regression holds promise for highly informative exploration of relationships of predictors to a dependent variable. A classic reference in multiple nonparametric regression is Hastie and Tibshirani (1990).

6.7 SUMMARY

Multiple regression analysis may be employed to study the shape of the relationship between independent and dependent variables when these variables are measured on ordinal, interval, or ratio scales. Polynomial regression methods capture and represent the curvilinear relationship of one or more predictors to the dependent variable. Alternatively, transformations of variables in MR are undertaken to achieve linear relationships, and to eliminate heteroscedasticity and nonnormality of residuals as well so that data may be analyzed with linear MR. Nonlinear regression and nonparametric regression are also employed when data exhibit nonlinearity.

1. *Power polynomials.* The multiple representation of a research factor X by a series of predictors, X, X^2, X^3, etc., makes possible the fitting of regression functions of Y on X of any shape. Hierarchical MR makes possible the assessment of the size and significance of linear, quadratic, cubic (etc.), aspects of the regression function, and the multiple regression equation may be used for plotting nonlinear regression of Y on X (Section 6.2).

2. *Orthogonal polynomials.* For some purposes (for example, laboratory experiments where the number of observed values of X is not large), it is advantageous to code X so that the X_i not only carry information about the different curve components (linear, quadratic, etc.) but are orthogonal to each other as well. Some interpretive and computational advantages and alternate error models are discussed (Section 6.3).

3. *Nonlinear transformations.* Nonlinear transformations are one-to-one mathematical relationships that change the relative spacing of scores on a scale (e.g., the numbers 1, 10, 100 versus their base$_{10}$ logs 0, 1, 2). Nonlinear transformations of predictors X and/or the dependent variable Y are carried out for three reasons. First, they are employed to simplify relationships between predictors and the DV; simplification most often means linearization of the relationship so that the relationship can be examined in linear MR. Second, they are employed to stabilize the variances of the residuals, that is, to eliminate heteroscedasticity of residuals. Third, they are used to normalize residuals. Homoscedasticity and normality of residuals are required for inference in linear MR. The circumstances in which logarithmic, square root, and reciprocal transformations are likely to be effective for linearization are described. Such transformations arise frequently in conjunction with formal mathematical models that are expressed in nonlinear equations, for example in exponential growth models. More generally, a full family of power transformations are employed for linearization. To select among transformations, graphical and statistical methods are employed; these include the ladder of re-expression and the bulging rule, plus the Box-Cox and Box-Tidwell methodologies. Tail-stretching transformations of proportions are also employed; they include the arcsine, probit, and logit transformations. Transformations also serve to render residuals homoscedastic and normal, so that data are amenable to treatment in linear MR (Section 6.4).

4. *Nonlinear regression* (NR).   Nonlinear regression is a form of regression analysis in which one estimates the coefficients of a nonlinear regression model that is *intrinsically nonlinear*, that is, cannot be linearized by suitable transformation (Section 6.5).

5. *Nonparametric regression.*   Nonparametric regression is an approach to discerning the pattern of the relationship of a predictor X (or set of predictors) to a dependent variable Y without first specifying a regression model. In nonparametric regression the form of the relationship between X and Y is discerned by developing a smooth function relating X to Y driven solely by the data themselves absent any assumption about the form of the relationship (Section 6.6).

7

Interactions Among Continuous Variables

7.1 INTRODUCTION

In this chapter we extend MR analysis to interactions among continuous predictors. By *interactions* we mean an interplay among predictors that produces an effect on the outcome Y that is different from the sum of the effects of the individual predictors. Many theories in the social sciences hypothesize that two or more continuous variables interact; it is safe to say that the testing of interactions is at the very heart of theory testing in the social sciences. Consider as an example how ability (X) and motivation (Z) impact achievement in graduate school (Y). One possibility is that their effects are additive. The combined impact of ability and motivation on achievement equals the sum of their separate effects; there is no interaction between X and Z. We might say that the whole equals the sum of the parts. A second alternative is that ability and motivation may interact synergistically, such that graduate students with both high ability and high motivation achieve much more in graduate school than would be expected from the simple sum of the separate effects of ability and motivation. Graduate students with both high ability and high motivation become "superstars"; we would say that the whole is greater than the sum of the parts. A third alternative is that ability and motivation compensate for one another. For those students who are extremely high in ability, motivation is less important to achievement, whereas for students highest in motivation, sheer native ability has less impact. Here we would say that the whole is less than the sum of the parts; there is some partial trade-off between ability and motivation in the prediction of achievement. The second and third alternatives exemplify interactions between predictors, that is, combined effects of predictors that differ from the sum of their separate effects.

When two predictors in regression analysis interact with one another, the regression of Y on one of those predictors *depends on* or is *conditional on* the value of the other predictor. In the second alternative, a *synergistic interaction* between ability X and motivation Z, the regression coefficient for the regression of achievement Y on ability X increases as motivation Z increases. Under the synergistic model, when motivation is very low, ability has little effect because the student is hardly engaged in the graduate school enterprise. When motivation is higher, then more able students exhibit greater achievement.

Continuous variable interactions such as those portrayed in alternatives two and three can be tested in MR analysis, treating both the original variables and their interaction as continuous

255

predictors. In this chapter we explore how to specify interactions between continuous variables in multiple regression equations, how to test for the statistical signficance of interactions, how to plot them, and how to interpret them through post hoc probing.

We suspect that some readers are familiar with the testing, plotting, post hoc probing, and interpretation of interactions between categorical variables in the analysis of variance (ANOVA) context. Historically, continuous variable interactions have often been analyzed by breaking the continuous variables into categories, so that interactions between them can be examined in ANOVA. For example, an analyst might perform median splits on ability and motivation to create four combinations (hi-hi, hi-lo, lo-hi, and lo-lo) of ability and motivation that could be examined in a 2×2 ANOVA. *This dichotomization strategy is ill-advised, and we strongly recommend against it.* The strategy evolved because methods were fully developed for probing interactions in ANOVA long before they were fully developed in MR. Dichotomization is problematic first because it decreases measured relationships between variables. For example, dichotomization at the median of a single continuous normally distributed predictor X reduces its squared correlation with a normally distributed dependent variable Y to .64 of the original correlation (Cohen, 1983). Dichotomization of a single predictor is equivalent to throwing out over a third of the cases in the data set. Dichotomization of two continuous variables X and Z so that their interaction can be examined in ANOVA lowers the power for detecting a true nonzero interaction between the two continuous predictors. As Maxwell and Delaney (1993) point out, if loss of power were the only impact of dichotomization and researchers found significance nonetheless after dichotomization, the practice might not seem so undesirable from a theoretical standpoint. But Maxwell and Delaney (1993) show much more deleterious effects from a validity standpoint. Carrying out median splits on two continuous predictors X and Z can produce spurious main effects, that is, effects of the individual predictors that are "significant" when the dichotomized data are analyzed, although the effects do not, in fact, exist in the population. Moreover, in one special circumstance in which there is no true interaction between two continuous predictors X and Z, a spurious interaction may be produced between the dichotomized predictors. This can happen if one of the predictors X or Z has a quadratic relationship to Y.

In this chapter we provide prescriptions for specifying, plotting, testing, post hoc probing, and interpretating interactions among continuous variables. In Chapter 8, we introduce the implementation of true categorical predictors (e.g., gender, ethnicity) in MR. In Chapter 9, we extend MR to interactions among categorical variables and between categorical and continuous variables.

7.1.1 Interactions Versus Additive Effects

Regression equations that contain as IVs only predictors taken separately signify that the effects of continuous variables such as X and Z are *additive* in their impact on the criterion, that is,

$$(7.1.1) \qquad\qquad \hat{Y} = B_1 X + B_2 Z + B_0.$$

Note that Eq. (7.1.1) is the same equation as Eq. (3.2.1), except that the notation X and Z has been substituted for X_1 and X_2, respectively.

For a specific instance, consider the following numerical example:

$$\hat{Y} = .2X + .6Z + 2.$$

The estimated DV increases .2 points for each 1-point increase in X and another .6 points for each 1-point increase in Z. (Strictly speaking, this is correct only if X and Z are uncorrelated. If they are correlated, these effects hold only when the two IVs are used together to estimate Y.) The effects of X and Z are additive. By *additivity* is meant that the regression of the criterion on one predictor, say predictor X, is constant over all values of the other predictor Z.

Interactions as Joint Effects

In Eq. (7.1.2) we add a predictor XZ to carry an interaction between X and Z:

(7.1.2) $$\hat{Y} = B_1X + B_2Z + B_3XZ + B_0.$$

Literally, the predictor is the product of scores on predictors X and Z, calculated for each case. While the interaction is carried by the XZ product term, the interaction itself is actually that part of XZ that is independent of X and Z, from which X and Z have been partialed (more about this in Section 7.6).

Consider our numerical example, but with the product term added:

$$\hat{Y} = .2X + .6Z + .4XZ + 2.$$

If X and Z are uncorrelated, the criterion Y increases .2 points for each 1-point increase in X and an additional .6 points for each 1-point increase in Z. Moreover, the criterion Y increases an additional .4 points for a 1-point increment in the part of the cross-product XZ that is independent of X and Z. The partialed component of the cross-product represents a unique combined effect of the two variables working together, above and beyond their separate effects; here a *synergistic* effect, as in the example of ability X and motivation Z as predictors of graduate school achievement Y. Thus two variables X and Z are said to interact in their accounting for variance in Y when *over and above* any additive combination of their separate effects, they have a *joint effect*.

We can compare the joint or interactive effect of X and Z with the simple additive effects of X and Z in three-dimensional graphs. For data, we plot 36 cases for which we have scores on predictors X and Z (see Table 7.1.1A). Both X and Z take on the values 0, 2, 4, 6, 8, and 10; the 36 cases were created by forming every possible combination of one X value and one Z value. This method of creating cases makes X and Z uniformly distributed, that is, produces an equal number of scores at each value of X and Z. The method also assures that X and Z are uncorrelated. These special properties facilitate the example but are not at all necessary or typical for the inclusion of interactions in MR equations. The means and standard deviations of X and Z, as well as their correlations with Y, are given in Table 7.1.1B.

Figure 7.1.1(A) illustrates the additive effects (absent any interaction) of X and Z from the equation $\hat{Y} = .2X + .6Z + 2$. Predictors X and Z form the axes on the floor of the graph; all 36 cases (i.e., points representing combinations of values of the predictors) lie on the floor. Predicted $\hat{Y}$s for each case (unique combinations of X and Z) were generated from the regression equation. The *regression plane*, the tilted plane above the floor, represents the location of $\hat{Y}$ for every possible combination of values of X and Z. Note that the regression plane is a flat surface. Regardless of the particular combination of values of X and Z, the $\hat{Y}$ is incremented (geometrically raised off the floor) by a constant value relative to the values of X and Z, that is, by the value $(.2X + .6Z)$.

The regression plane in Fig. 7.1.1(B) illustrates the additive effects of X and Z plus the interaction between X and Z in the equation $\hat{Y} = .2X + .6Z + .4XZ + 2$. The same 36 combinations of X and Z were used again. However, $\hat{Y}$s were generated from the equation containing the interaction. Table 7.1.1B gives the mean and standard deviation of the product term that carries the interaction, and its correlation with the criterion Y. In Fig. 7.1.1(B) the regression plane is now a stretched surface, pulled up in the corner above the height of the

TABLE 7.1.1
Multiple Regression Equations Containing Interactions:
Uncentered Versus Centered Predictors

A. Thirty-six cases generated from every possible combination of scores on predictors X and Z.

$$X\ (0, 2, 4, 6, 8, 10)$$
$$Z\ (0, 2, 4, 6, 8, 10)$$

Cases (X, Z combinations)

$$(0, 0), (0, 2), \ldots, (4, 6), \ldots, (6, 8), \ldots, (10, 10)$$

B. Summary Statistics for X, Z, and XZ (uncentered, in raw score form).

Means and standard deviations			Correlation matrix			
	M	$sd^{\bullet}$		X	Z	XZ	Y
X	5.000	3.464	X	1.00	0.00	.637	.600
Z	5.000	3.464	Z		1.00	.637	.709
XZ	25.000	27.203	XZ			1.00	.995

C. Unstandardized regression equations: prediction of Y from X and Z, and from X, Z, and XZ (uncentered, in raw score form).

1. Uncentered regression equation, no interaction:

$$\hat{Y} = .2X + .6Z + 2$$

2. Uncentered regression equation, with interaction:

$$\hat{Y} = .2X + .6Z + .4XZ + 2$$

D. Simple regression equations for Y on X at values of Z with uncentered predictors and criterion.

$$\text{At } Z_{\text{high}}: \quad \hat{Y} = 3.4X + 6.8$$
$$\text{At } Z_{\text{mean}}: \quad \hat{Y} = 2.2X + 5.0$$
$$\text{At } Z_{\text{low}}: \quad \hat{Y} = 1.0X + 3.2$$

E. Summary statistics for x, z and xz (centered, in deviation form).

Means and standard deviations			Correlation matrix			
	M	sd		x	z	xz	Y
x	0.000	3.464	x	1.00	.000	.000	.600
z	0.000	3.464	z		1.00	.000	.709
xz	0.000	11.832	xz			1.00	.372

F. Unstandardized regression equations: prediction of Y from x and z, and from x, z, and xz (centered, in deviation form).

1. Centered regression equation, no interaction:

$$\hat{Y} = .2x + .6z + 6$$

2. Centered regression equation, with interaction:

$$\hat{Y} = 2.2x + 2.6z + .4xz + 16$$

G. Simple regression equations for Y on x at values of z with centered predictors and criterion.

$$\text{At } z_{\text{high}}: \quad \hat{Y} = 3.4x + 23.8$$
$$\text{At } z_{\text{mean}}: \quad \hat{Y} = 2.2x + 16.0$$
$$\text{At } z_{\text{low}}: \quad \hat{Y} = 1.0x + 8.2$$

(A) Regression surface: $\hat{Y} = .2X + .6Z + 2$

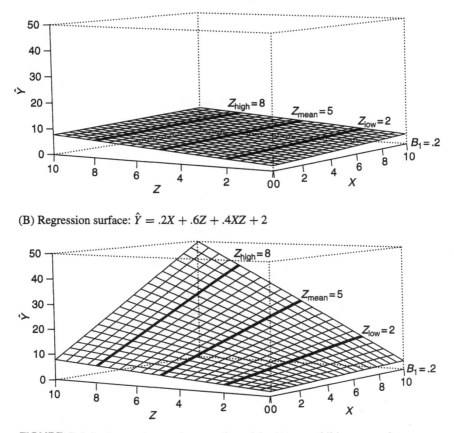

(B) Regression surface: $\hat{Y} = .2X + .6Z + .4XZ + 2$

FIGURE 7.1.1 Regression surface predicated in (A) an additive regression equation containing no interaction and (B) a regression equation containing an interaction. Predictors and criterion are in raw score (uncentered) form.

flat regression plane in Fig. 7.1.1(A). The amount by which the stretched surface is lifted above the flat regression plane represents unique variance due to the interaction of X and Z, over and above the individual additive effects of X and Z. What is the source of the upward stretching? The stretching occurs because the increment in Y depends not only on additive values of X and Z but also on their product XZ, and the product XZ increases in a curvilinear fashion as X and Z increase linearly. Note the dramatic rise in the product XZ relative to the sum $X + Z$:

X	0	2	4	6	8	10
Z	0	2	4	6	8	10
$X + Z$	0	4	8	12	16	20
XZ	0	4	16	36	64	100

7.1.2 Conditional First-Order Effects in Equations Containing Interactions

As in polynomial regression explained in Chapter 6, we make the distinction between *first-order effects* and *higher order effects* in regression equations containing interactions. First-order effects refer to the effects of the individual predictors on the criterion. Higher order effects refer to the partialed effects of multiplicative functions of the individual predictors, for example the XZ term with X and Z partialed out in Eq. (7.1.2).

When the effects of individual predictors are purely additive, as in Eq. (7.1.1), the first-order regression coefficient for each predictor is constant over all values of the other predictor (again, this is the definition of *additivity*). The constancy is illustrated in Fig. 7.1.1(A). In Fig. 7.1.1(A), three lines on the regression plane defined by $\hat{Y} = .2X + .6Z + 2$ are darkened: at $Z = 2, Z = 5$ (i.e., the mean of Z, M_Z) and $Z = 8$. These lines show the regression of Y on X at each of these three values of Z: Z_{low}, Z_{mean}, and Z_{high}, respectively. These three regression lines are parallel, signifying that the regression of Y on X is constant over values of Z. Thus the regression coefficient for the X predictor applies equally across the range of Z. The only characteristic that varies across the three regression lines is the overall height of the regression line (distance from the floor of the graph). The displacement upward of the lines as Z increases signifies that as Z increases, the criterion Y increases as well (a first-order effect). On average, values of Y are higher for higher values of Z.

Figure 7.1.1(B) represents the regression equation $\hat{Y} = .2X + .6Z + .4XZ + 2$. Regression lines for the regression of Y on X are drawn at the same three values of Z as in Fig. 7.1.1(A): $Z = 2, 5, 8$. We see immediately that the regression line for Y on X becomes steeper as Z increases. The regression of Y on X is not constant over all values of Z but depends specifically on the particular value of Z at which the regression of Y on X is taken. Predictors X and Z are no longer additive in their effects on Y; they are interactive. The regression of Y on X is *conditional upon* (i.e., depends upon) the value of Z. In regression equations containing interactions, the *first-order effects* of variables are conditional on (depend upon, or are *moderated by*) the values of the other predictors with which they interact.

We have cast this discussion of *conditional effects* in terms of the regression of Y on X at values of Z. However, the interaction between X and Z is symmetric. We could examine the regression of Y on Z at values of X. The result would be the same: the regression of Y on Z would differ as a function of X; that is, the regression of Y on Z is again conditional upon the value of X.

Now we focus on the angle formed between the regression plane and the floor of Fig. 7.1.1(A). This angle is best seen at the right edge of Fig. 7.1.1(A) (predictor X), where $Z = 0$. In Fig. 7.1.1(A), with no interaction, the slope of the regression of Y on X equals .2 at $Z = 0$. Recall that .2 is the regression coefficient for Y on X in Eq. (7.1.1). This same angle is maintained across the range of Z, which is another way of saying that the regression of Y on X is constant across all values of Z, meeting the definition of additivity.

Examine the right edge of Fig. 7.1.1(B) (predictor X), where $Z = 0$. The regression of Y on X also equals .2 at $Z = 0$ in Fig. 7.1.1(B), and the regression coefficient B_1 for Y on X in our numerical example containing an interaction is .2. However, in Fig. 7.1.1(B), the slope of the regression of Y on X is only .2 at $Z = 0$. As Z increases, the slope of Y on X also increases. Thus the numerical value of the regression coefficient $B_1 = .2$ is only an accurate representation of the regression of Y on X at one point on the regression plane. In general, in a regression equation containing an interaction, the first-order regression coefficient for each predictor involved in the interaction represents the regression of Y on that predictor, *only at the value of zero on all other individual predictors with which the predictor interacts*. The first-order coefficients have different meanings depending on whether the regression equation does or does not include interactions. To reiterate, without an interaction term the B_1 coefficient for X represents the overall effect of X on Y across the full range of Z. However, in Eq. (7.1.2), the B_1 coefficient for X represents the effect of X on the criterion only at $Z = 0$.

7.2 CENTERING PREDICTORS AND THE INTERPRETATION OF REGRESSION COEFFICIENTS IN EQUATIONS CONTAINING INTERACTIONS

The interpretation of the first-order coefficients B_1 and B_2 in the presence of interactions is usually problematic in typical social science data. The B_1 coefficient represents the regression of Y on X at $Z = 0$, and the B_2 coefficient represents the regression of Y on Z at $X = 0$. Only rarely in the social sciences is zero a meaningful point on a scale. For example, suppose, in a developmental psychology study, we predict a level of language development (Y) of children aged 2 to 6 years from mother's language development (D), child's age (A), and the interaction of mother's language development and child's age, carried by the DA term. In the regression equation $\hat{Y} = B_1D + B_2A + B_3DA + B_0$, the regression coefficient B_1 of child's language development on mother's language development D is at child's age $A = 0$, not a useful value in that all children in the study fall between ages 2 and 6. To interpret this B_1 coefficient, we would have to extrapolate from our sample to newborns in whom the process of language development has not yet begun. (Our comments about the dangers of extrapolation in Section 6.2.5 apply here as well.)

7.2.1 Regression With Centered Predictors

We can make a simple linear transformation of the age predictor that renders zero on the age scale meaningful. Simply, we *center* age, that is, put age in deviation form by subtracting M_A from each observed age (i.e., $a = A - M_A$). If age were symmetrically distributed over the values 2, 3, 4, 5, and 6 years, $M_A = 4$ years, and the centered age variable a would take on the values $-2, -1, 0, 1, 2$. The mean of the centered age variable a necessarily would be zero. When a is used in the regression equation $\hat{Y} = B_1D + B_2a + B_3Da + B_0$, the B_1 coefficient represents the regression of child's language development on mother's language development at the mean age of the children in the sample. This strategy of centering to make the regression coefficients of first-order terms meaningful is identical to the use of centering in polynomial regression (Section 6.2.3.).

The symmetry in interactions applies to centering predictors. If we center mother's language development into variable $d = D - M_D$ and estimate the regression equation $\hat{Y} = B_1d + B_2A + B_3dA + B_0$, then the B_2 coefficient represents the regression of child's language development on child's age at the mean of mother's language development in the sample.

Finally, suppose we wish to assess the interaction between age and mother's language development. We center both predictors and form the product of the centered variables da to carry the interaction and estimate the regression equation $\hat{Y} = B_1d + B_2a + B_3da + B_0$. Both the B_1 and B_2 coefficients represent the first-order relationships at the *centroid* (mean on both predictors) of the sample. The regression equation characterizes the typical case. In sum, if all the predictors in a regression equation containing interactions are centered, then each first-order coefficient has an interpretation that is meaningful in terms of the variables under investigation: the regression of the criterion on the predictor at the sample means of all other variables in the equation.

With centered predictors, each first-order regression coefficient has yet a second meaningful interpretation, as the *average regression* of the criterion on the predictor across the range of the other predictors. In the developmental study, if the d by a interaction were nonzero, then the regression of child's language development on mother's language development would differ at each age. Assume that there were an equal number of children at each age. Imagine computing the regression coefficient B_1 of child's language development on mother's language development separately at each age and then averaging all these B_1 coefficients. The B_1 coefficient for the impact of mother's language development in the overall centered regression equation containing all ages would equal the average of the individual B_1 coefficients at each child's age. If there were an unequal number of children at each age, then the overall B_1 coefficient would equal the weighted average of the individual B_1 coefficients, where the weights were the number of children at each age. In sum, when predictors are centered, then each first-order coefficient in a regression equation containing interactions is the *average regression of the criterion on a predictor* across the range of the other predictors in the equation.

7.2.2 Relationship Between Regression Coefficients in the Uncentered and Centered Equations

As noted in Chapter 2, correlational properties of variables do not change under linear transformation of variables. Linear transformations include adding or subtracting constants, and multiplying and dividing by constants. If we correlate height in inches with weight in pounds, we obtain the same value as if we correlate height in inches with weight in ounces or kilograms. *Centering*, or putting predictors in deviation score form by subtracting the mean of the predictor from each score on the predictor, is a linear transformation. *Thus our first intuition might be that if predictors were centered before they were entered into a regression equation, the resulting regression coefficients would equal those from the uncentered equation. This intuition is correct only for regression equations that contain no interactions.*

As we have seen, centering predictors provides tremendous interpretational advantages in regression equations containing interactions, but centering produces a very puzzling effect. When predictors are centered and entered into regression equations containing interactions, the regression coefficients for the first-order effects B_1 and B_2 are different numerically from those we obtain performing a regression analysis on the same data in raw score or *uncentered* form. We encountered an analogous phenomenon in Chapter 6 in polynomial regression; when we centered the predictor X, the regression coefficient for all but the highest order polynomial term changed (see Section 6.2.3). The explanation of this phenomenon is straightforward and is easily grasped from three-dimensional representations of interactions such as Fig. 7.1.1(B). An understanding of the phenomenon provides insight into the meaning of regression coefficients in regression equations containing interactions.

7.2.3 Centered Equations With No Interaction

We return to the numerical example in Table 7.1.1 and Fig. 7.1.1. The means of both predictors X and Z equal 5.00. Uncentered and centered X and Z would be as follows:

$X_{\text{uncentered}}$	0	2	4	6	8	10
x_{centered}	−5	−3	−1	1	3	5

and

$Z_{\text{uncentered}}$	0	2	4	6	8	10
z_{centered}	−5	−3	−1	1	3	5

Now, assume that we keep the criterion Y in its original uncentered metric, but we use x and z, and re-estimate the regression equation without an interaction. The resulting regression equation is

$$\hat{Y} = .2x + .6z + 6.$$

The regression coefficients for x and z equal those for uncentered X and Z. Only the regression intercept has changed. From Chapter 3, Eq. (3.2.6), the intercept is given as

$B_0 = M_Y - B_1 M_X - B_2 M_Z$. Centering X and Z changed their means from 5.00 to 0.00, leading to the change in B_0. In fact, there is a simple algebraic relationship between B_0 in the centered versus uncentered equations. For the uncentered regression equation $\hat{Y} = B_1 X + B_2 Z + B_0$ versus the centered regression equation $\hat{Y} = B_1 x + B_2 z + B_0$,

(7.2.1) $B_{0,\text{centered}} = B_{0,\text{uncentered}} + B_{1,\text{uncentered}} M_{X,\text{uncentered}} + B_{2,\text{uncentered}} M_{Z,\text{uncentered}}$

For our example, this is

$$B_{0,\text{centered}} = 2 + .2(5.00) + .6(5.00) = 6.$$

The centered regression equation is plotted in Fig. 7.2.1(A). The only difference between Fig. 7.1.1(A) and Fig. 7.2.1(A) is that the scales of the X and Z axes in Fig. 7.2.1(A) have been changed from those in Fig. 7.1.1(A) to reflect centering. Note that $x = 0$ and $z = 0$ in Fig. 7.2.1(A) are now in the *middle of the axes*, rather than at one end of the axes, as in Fig. 7.1.1(A). Note also that the criterion Y is left uncentered.

Figure 7.2.1(A) confirms the numerical result that the regression coefficients B_1 and B_2 do not change when we center predictors in regression equations containing no interactions.

(A) Regression surface from centered regression equation: $\hat{Y} = .2x + .6z + 6$

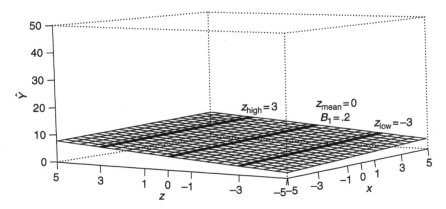

(B) Regression surface from centered regression equation: $\hat{Y} = 2.2x + 2.6z + .4xz + 16$

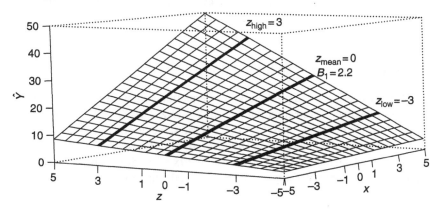

FIGURE 7.2.1 Regression surface predicted in (A) an additive regression equation containing no interaction and (B) a regression equation containing an interaction. Predictors are in centered (deviation) form.

Consider B_1; the slope of Y on X at $Z = 0$ in Fig. 7.1.1(A) is the same as that for Y on x at $z = 0$ in Figure 7.2.1(A), though the location of $Z = 0$ differs across the figures.

A comparison of Figures 7.1.1(A) and 7.2.1(A) also confirms the change in intercept. The intercept is the height of the regression plane from the floor at the point $X = 0, Z = 0$. In Fig. 7.1.1(A) for the uncentered equation, this point is in the lower right-hand corner of the plane; here the plane is only two units from the floor, so $B_0 = 2$. As pointed out earlier, in Fig. 7.2.1(A) for the centered equation, the point $x = 0, z = 0$ is now in the center of the regression plane. (When all predictors have been centered, the value 0, 0 is the *centroid* of the predictor space.) The overall elevation of the plane is farther from the floor at this point, specifically six units from the floor, so $B_0 = 6$. The change in the location of the point $X = 0, Z = 0$ produced by centering also produces the change in the intercept.

7.2.4 Essential Versus Nonessential Multicollinearity

The correlation matrix among the centered predictors, including xz, and of the centered predictors with the criterion is given in Table 7.1.1E. This correlation matrix should be compared with that in Table 7.1.1B for the uncentered predictors. There is one dramatic change when predictors are uncentered versus centered. The correlations of the X and Z terms with XZ ($r = .637$ in each case) are substantial in the uncentered case but fall to zero in the centered case. This drop is another example of *essential* versus *nonessential multicollinearity* (Marquardt, 1980), also encountered in our work with polynomial regression equations (Section 6.2.3).

Algebraically, the covariance (numerator of the correlation coefficient) between X and XZ is in part a function of the arithmetic means of X and Z. If X and Z are each completely symmetrical, as in our numerical example, then the covariance (cov) between X and XZ is as follows (Aiken & West, 1991, p. 180, eq. A.15):

$$\text{cov}(XZ, X) = sd_X^2 M_Z + \text{cov}(X, Z)M_X$$

If X and Z are centered, then M_X and M_Z are both zero, and the covariance between x and xz is zero as well. Thus the correlation between x and xz is also zero. The same holds for the correlation between z and xz. The amount of correlation that is produced between X and XZ or Z and XZ by the nonzero means of X and Z, respectively, is referred to as *nonessential multicollinearity* (Marquardt, 1980). This nonessential multicollinearity is due purely to scaling—when variables are centered, it disappears. The amount of correlation between X and XZ that is due to skew in X cannot be removed by centering. This source of correlation between X and XZ is termed *essential multicollinearity*. The same is true for the correlation between Z and XZ.

7.2.5 Centered Equations With Interactions

Now consider the use of centered predictors in an equation containing an interaction. How do the coefficients of the uncentered equation $\hat{Y} = B_1 X + B_2 Z + B_3 XZ + B_0$ relate to those in the centered equation $\hat{Y} = B_1 x + B_2 z + B_3 xz + B_0$? For the same reason as in the equation without an interaction, the intercept changes here. However, B_1 and B_2 also change, often dramatically, in association with the changes in the correlation matrix of predictors just described.

In the numerical example of Table 7.1.1, the centered equation is

$$\hat{Y} = 2.2x + 2.6z + .4xz + 16.$$

This equation was found by retaining the criterion Y in raw score form, centering X and Z into x and z, respectively, forming the cross-product of centered X and Z (i.e., xz), and predicting

Y from x, z, and xz. Note that the intercept B_0 has changed from $B_0 = 2$ in the uncentered regression equation to 16 in the centered equation. Coefficients B_1 and B_2 have changed from .2 and .6, respectively, to 2.2 and 2.6, respectively. As we will see, these changes do not mean that the relationships of X and Z to the criterion Y have somehow changed with centering.

The centered regression equation containing an interaction is plotted in Fig. 7.2.1(B). As noted earlier, the value $x = 0, z = 0$ has moved from the lower right-hand corner of the regression plane in Fig. 7.1.1(B) to the middle of the regression plane in Fig. 7.2.1(B) due to centering.

A comparison of Fig. 7.1.1(B) with Fig. 7.2.1(B) gives insight into the source of the change in regression coefficients. In the uncentered equation, the B_1 coefficient represented the regression of Y on X at $Z = 0$, at the far right edge of Fig. 7.1.1(B). For higher values of Z (moving left along Fig. 7.1.1(B)), the regression of Y on X became increasingly steep. With centered z, in Fig. 7.2.1(B), the value $z = 0$ is no longer at the right edge of the figure; it is halfway up the regression plane. At $z_{mean} = 0$ the regression of Y on x has risen to 2.2, the value of B_1 in the centered regression equation.

In general, centering predictors moves the value of zero on the predictors along the regression surface. If the regression surface is a flat plane (i.e., the regression equation contains no interaction), then the regression of Y on X is constant at all locations on the plane. Moving the value of zero by linear transformation has no effect on the regression coefficient for the predictor. If the regression surface is not flat (i.e., the regression equation contains an interaction), then the regression of Y on X varies across locations on the plane. The value of the B_1 regression coefficient will always be the slope of Y on X at $Z = 0$ on the plane, but the location of $Z = 0$ on the plane will change with centering.

What about the interpretation of B_1 as the *average* regression slope of Y on x across all values of z in the centered regression equation, $\hat{Y} = B_1 x + B_2 z + B_3 xz + B_0$? A closer examination of Fig. 7.2.1(B) confirms this interpretation. In Fig. 7.2.1, the far right-hand edge now is at $z = -5$; at this point the regression of Y on X is .2. At the far left edge, $z = 5$ and the slope of the regression of Y on X is 4.2. The distribution of Z is uniform, so the average slope across all cases represented in the observed regression plane is $(.2 + 4.2)/2 = 2.2$; this is the value of the B_1 coefficient. Thus B_1 is the average slope of the regression of Y on X across all values of centered predictor Z.

There are straightforward algebraic relationships between the B_0, B_1, and B_2 coefficients in the uncentered versus centered regression equation containing the interactions:

(7.2.2)
$$B_{1,centered} = B_{1,uncentered} + B_{3,uncentered} M_{Z,uncentered};$$
$$B_{2,centered} = B_{2,uncentered} + B_{3,uncentered} M_{X,uncentered}.$$

For our numerical example,

$$B_{1,centered} = .2 + .4(5.00) = 2.20, \quad \text{and} \quad B_{2,centered} = .6 + .4(5.00) = 2.60.$$

Note that if there is no interaction (i.e., $B_3 = 0$), then the B_1 and B_2 coefficients would remain the same if X and Z were centered versus uncentered. This confirms what we know—*only if there is an interaction does rescaling a variable by a linear transformation change the first order regression coefficients.*

For the relationship of the intercept $B_{0,centered}$ to $B_{0,uncentered}$, we have

(7.2.3)
$$B_{0,centered} = B_{0,uncentered} + B_{1,uncentered} M_{X,uncentered} + B_{2,uncentered} M_{Z,uncentered}$$
$$+ B_3 M_{X,uncentered} M_{Z,uncentered}.$$

For our numerical example

$$B_{0,\text{centered}} = 2 + .2(5.00) + .6(5.00) + .4(5.00)(5.00) = 16.$$

Equations (7.2.1), (7.2.2), and (7.2.3) pertain only to Eq. (7.1.1). These relationships differ for every form of regression equation containing at least one interaction term; they would be different for more complex equations, for example, Eqs. (7.6.1) and (7.9.2) given below. Aiken and West (1991, Appendix B) provide an extensive mapping of uncentered to centered regression equations.

7.2.6 The Highest Order Interaction in the Centered Versus Uncentered Equation

By inspection the shapes of the regression surfaces in Fig. 7.1.1(B) for uncentered data and Fig. 7.2.1(B) for centered data are identical. Consistent with this, there is no effect of centering predictors on the value of regression coefficient B_3 in Eq. (7.1.2). The B_3 coefficient is for the highest order effect in the equation; that is, there are no three-way or higher order interactions. The interaction, carried by the XZ term, reflects the shape of the regression surface, specifically how this shape differs from the flat regression plane associated with regression equations having only first-order terms. This shape does not change when variables are centered. In general, *centering predictors has no effect on the value of the regression coefficient for the highest order term* in the regression equation. For Eq. (7.1.2) we have

(7.2.4) $B_{3,\text{centered}} = B_{3,\text{uncentered}}.$

7.2.7 Do Not Center Y

In computing the centered regression equations and in displaying the regression surfaces in Figs. 7.1.1 and 7.2.1, Y has been left in uncentered form. There is no need to center Y because when it is in its original scale, predicted scores will also be in the units of the original scale and will have the same arithmetic mean as the observed criterion scores.

7.2.8 A Recommendation for Centering

We recommend that continuous predictors be centered before being entered into regression analyses containing interactions. Doing so has no effect on the estimate of the highest order interaction in the regression equation. Doing so yields two straightforward, meaningful interpretations of each first-order regression coefficient of predictors entered into the regression equation: (1) effects of the individual predictors at the mean of the sample, and (2) average effects of each individual predictors across the range of the other variables. Doing so also eliminates nonessential multicollinearity between first-order predictors and predictors that carry their interaction with other predictors.[1]

There is one exception to this recommendation: If a predictor has a meaningful zero point, then one may wish to keep the predictor in uncentered form. Let us return to the example of language development. Suppose we keep the predictor of child's age (A). Our second predictor

---

[1]The issue of centering is not confined to continuous variables; it also comes into play in the coding of categorical variables that interact with other categorical variables or with continuous variables in MR analysis, a topic developed in Chapter 9.

is number of siblings (S). Following our previous argument, we center age. However, zero siblings is a meaningful number of siblings; we decide to retain number of siblings S in its uncentered form. We expect age and number of siblings to interact; we form the cross-product aS of centered a with uncentered S and estimate the following regression equation:

$$\hat{Y} = B_1a + B_2S + B_3aS + B_0.$$

The interpretation of the two first-order effects differs. The effect of number of siblings is at $a = 0$; since a is centered, B_2 is the regression of language development on number of siblings at the mean age of children in the sample. The effect of child's age is at $S = 0$, where $S = 0$ stands for zero siblings. Hence B_1 is the regression of language development on age *for children with no siblings*. If this is a meaningful coefficient from the perspective of data summarization or theory testing, then centering is not advised. But even if the variable has a meaningful zero point, it may be centered for interpretational reasons. If number of siblings had been centered, then B_1 would be interpreted as the regression of language development on age at mean number of siblings. Finally, B_3 is not affected by predictor scaling and provides an estimate of the interaction between the predictors regardless of predictor scaling.

Our discussion of centering predictors has been confined to those predictors that are included in the interaction. But it is entirely possible that we include a predictor that is not part of any interaction in a regression equation that contains interactions among other variables. Suppose in the example of language development, we wish to control for mother's education level (E) while studying the interaction between child's age and number of siblings in predicting child's language development. Assume we wish to center number of siblings for interpretational reasons. We estimate the following regression equation:

$$\hat{Y} = B_1a + B_2s + B_3as + B_4E + B_0.$$

It is not necessary to center E. The B_1, B_2, and B_3 coefficients will not be affected by the scaling of E because E does not interact with any other predictors in the equation. In addition, since E does not interact with the other predictors, the B_4 coefficient will be completely unaffected by changes in scaling of age and number of siblings. In fact, the only effect of centering E is on the intercept B_0. However, we recommend that for simplicity, if one is centering the variables entering the interaction, one should also center the remaining variables in the equation.

To reiterate our position on centering, *we strongly recommend the centering of all predictors* that enter into higher order interactions in MR prior to analysis. The cross-product terms that carry the interactions should be formed from the centered predictors (i.e., center each predictor first and then form the cross-products). Centering all predictors has interpretational advantages and eliminates confusing nonessential multicollinearity.

There is only one exception to this recommendation to center. If a predictor has a meaningful zero point, then one may wish to have regression coefficients in the overall regression equation refer to the regression of the criterion on predictors at this zero point. For the remainder of this chapter, we will assume that all predictors in regression equations containing an interaction have been centered, unless otherwise specified.

7.3 SIMPLE REGRESSION EQUATIONS AND SIMPLE SLOPES

If an interaction is found to exist in a regression equation, the issue becomes one of interpretation of the interaction. The approach we take harkens back to the idea of conditional effects in MR with interactions: When X and Z interact, the regression of each predictor depends on the value of the other predictor. To characterize interactions, we examine the regression of the criterion Y on one predictor X at each of several values of the other predictor Z, as when we examine the regression of Y on x at z_{low}, z_{mean}, and z_{high} in Fig. 7.2.1(B). Following Aiken and West (1991), we call the regression line of Y on X at one value of Z a *simple regression line*. Hence, Figs. 7.2.1(A) and 7.2.1(B) each contain three simple regression lines.

In Fig. 7.3.1, we plot the centered simple regression lines of Fig. 7.2.1 in more familiar two-dimension representations. In Fig. 7.3.1(A), the regression lines of Y on x at z_{low}, z_{mean}, and z_{high} are reproduced from Fig. 7.2.1(A). Similarly, the three regression lines of Y on x in Fig. 7.3.1(B) are those from Fig. 7.2.1(B). Each line in Figs. 7.3.1(A) and 7.3.1(B) is the regression of Y on x at one value of the other predictor z, a *simple regression line*. The rule for discerning the presence of an interaction is straightforward. If the lines are parallel, there is no interaction, since the regression of Y on X is constant across all values of Z. If the lines are not parallel, there is an interaction, since the regression of Y on X is changing as a function of Z.

(A) Simple regression lines and equations based on Eq. (7.1.1), no interaction. Simple regression lines correspond to those in Fig. 7.2.1(A).

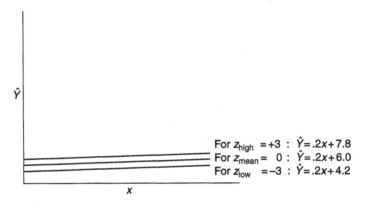

(B) Simple regression lines and equations based on Eq. (7.1.2), with interaction. Simple regression lines correspond to those in Fig. 7.2.1(B).

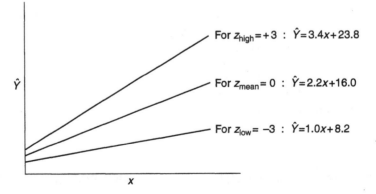

FIGURE 7.3.1   Simple regression lines and equations for Y on centered x at three values of centered z. The simple regression lines correspond directly to the simple regression lines in Fig. 7.2.1.

7.3.1 Plotting Interactions

Plotting interactions is the first step to their interpretation. We recommend plotting the regression of Y on X at three values of Z: the mean of Z plus a low and a high value of Z. Often a convenient set of values to choose are the mean of Z (Z_{mean}), one standard deviation below the mean of Z (Z_{low}), and one standard deviation above the mean of Z (Z_{high}). However, there may be specific meaningful values of Z—for example, clinical cutoffs for diagnostic levels of illness, or the income in dollars defined as the poverty level for a family of four. The symmetry of interactions means that the choice of plotting Y on X at values of Z as compared to Y on Z at values of X will depend on the theoretically more meaningful characterization of the data.

7.3.2 Moderator Variables

Psychological theories often hypothesize that a relationship between two variables will depend on a third variable. The third variable is referred to as a *moderator* (Baron & Kenny, 1986). These third variables may be organismic (e.g., gender, ethnicity, personality traits, abilities) or situational (e.g., controllable versus uncontrollable stressful events). They may be merely observed or manipulated. Of course, they are characterized statistically in terms of interactions. If a theory predicts that a variable M will moderate the relationship of another variable X to the criterion, then it is appropriate to plot regression of Y on X at meaningful values of the *moderator M*.

7.3.3 Simple Regression Equations

We can write a *simple regression equation* for each of the simple regression lines of Figs. 7.3.1(A) and 7.3.1(B). The use of simple regression equations is the key to the interpretation of interactions in MR analysis. *A simple regression equation* is the equation for the regression of the criterion on one predictor at a specific value of the other predictor(s), here Y on x at specific values of z.

For Figs. 7.2.1(A) and 7.3.1(A) with centered x and z, we place brackets in the regression equation with no interaction, $\hat{Y} = .2x + .6z + 6$, to show the regression of Y on x at values of z, in the form of a *simple regression equation*:

$$\hat{Y} = .2x + [.6z + 6].$$

Here the intercept of the simple regression equation $[.6z + 6]$ depends on the value of z; the slope of .2 does not. For each of the three values of z, we generate a simple regression equation. Recall that centered z takes on the values $(-5, -3, -1, 1, 3, 5)$, with $z_{mean} = 0$. We choose $z_{low} = -3$, and $z_{high} = 3$.

$$\text{For } z_{low} = -3: \quad \hat{Y} = .2x + [.6(-3) + 6] = .2x + 4.2;$$
$$\text{For } z_{mean} = 0: \quad \hat{Y} = .2x + [.6(0) + 6] = .2x + 6.0;$$
$$\text{For } z_{high} = 3: \quad \hat{Y} = .2x + [.6(3) + 6] = .2x + 7.8.$$

We note that in all three equations the regression coefficient for x has the constant value .2. The intercept increases from 4.2 to 6.0 to 7.8, as z increases from -3 to 0 to 3.

To plot a simple regression line, we follow standard practice for plotting lines: we substitute into the equation two values of x, and find $\hat{Y}$ corresponding to those two values, giving us two points for plotting. For example, for z_{high}, where $\hat{Y} = .2x + 7.8$, if $x = -3$, then $\hat{Y} = 7.2$; if $x = 3, \hat{Y} = 8.4$. To plot the simple regression line for z_{high} in Fig. 7.3.1(A), we used the points $(-3, 7.2)$ and $(3, 8.4)$.

The numerical result corresponds completely with the graphical results in Figs. 7.2.1(A) and 7.3.1(A). The *simple slopes* of the simple regression lines (i.e., the regression coefficients for Y on x in the simple regression equations) are constant at .2. The *simple intercepts*, that is, the regression constants in the simple regression equations (values of Y at $x = 0$ for specific values of z), increase with increasing values of z.

For Figs. 7.2.1(B) and 7.3.1(B), we first rearrange the regression equation containing the interaction, $\hat{Y} = 2.2x + 2.6z + .4xz + 16$, placing the terms involving x at the beginning of the equation:

$$\hat{Y} = 2.2x + .4xz + 2.6z + 16$$

We then factor out x and include some brackets to show the regression of Y on x at z in the form of a simple regression equation:

$$\hat{Y} = [2.2 + .4z]x + [2.6z + 16]$$

The expression $[2.2 + .4z]$ is the simple slope of the regression of Y on x at a particular value of z; $[2.6z + 16]$ is the simple intercept. In an equation with an xz interaction, both the simple slope and simple intercept for the regression of Y on x depend on the value of z.

For each of the three values of z, we generate a simple regression equation:

For $z_{\text{low}} = -3$: $\hat{Y} = [2.2 + .4(-3)]x + [2.6(-3) + 16] = 1.0x + 8.2$;
For $z_{\text{mean}} = 0$: $\hat{Y} = [2.2 + .4(0)]x + [2.6(0) + 16] = 2.2x + 16.0$;
For $z_{\text{high}} = -3$: $\hat{Y} = [2.2 + .4(3)]x + [2.6(3) + 16] = 3.4x + 23.8$.

The numerical result is the same as the graphical results in Fig. 7.2.1(B) and 7.3.1(B): The simple slopes of the simple regression lines increase from 1.0 to 2.2 to 3.4 as z increases; the simple intercepts (values of Y at $x = 0$), increase from 8.2 to 16.0 to 23.8 as z increases. To plot a simple regression we follow the same approach as described earlier, that is, to substitute two values of x and solve for $\hat{Y}$. For z_{low}, where $\hat{Y} = 1.0x + 8.2$, if $x = -3$, then $\hat{Y} = 5.2$; if $x = 3$, then $\hat{Y} = 11.2$. To plot the regression line for z_{low} in Fig 7.3.1(B), we used the points $(-3, 5.2)$ and $(3, 11.2)$.

7.3.4 Overall Regression Coefficient and Simple Slope at the Mean

The overall regression coefficient B_1 for the regression of Y on x in the centered regression equation containing the interaction is 2.2 and represents the regression of Y on x at $z = 0$. The simple regression coefficient for Y on centered x at $z_{\text{mean}} = 0$ is also 2.2. This equality of coefficients is expected, since both coefficients represent the regression of Y on x at $z = 0$. In general, the simple regression coefficient for the regression of Y on x at the mean of z will equal the overall regression coefficient of Y on x in the centered regression equation.

We may cast simple regression equations in a general form. First, we have the overall regression equation containing predictors X and Z and their interaction:

(7.1.2) $$\hat{Y} = B_1 X + B_2 Z + B_3 XZ + B_0,$$

where B_3 is the regression coefficient for the interaction. We rearrange Eq. (7.1.2) to show the regression of Y on X at values of Z:

(7.3.1)
$$\hat{Y} = [B_1 X + B_3 XZ] + [B_2 Z + B_0]$$
$$\hat{Y} = [B_1 + B_3 Z]X + [B_2 Z + B_0],$$

the simple regression equation for the regression of Y on X at specific values of Z. The coefficient $[B_1 + B_3 Z]$ for X in Eq. (7.3.1) is the simple slope, an expression for the slopes of simple regression lines such as those in Fig. 7.3.1(B). If B_3 is nonzero, meaning that there is an interaction between X and Z, then the value of this simple slope $[B_1 + B_3 Z]$ will differ for every value of Z. If B_3 is zero, signifying that there is no interaction between X and Z, then the simple slope will always equal B_1, the coefficient for predictor X, regardless of the value of Z.

We stated earlier that the interaction between X and Z is symmetric. Thus we can also rearrange Eq. (7.1.2) to show the regression of Y on Z at values of X:

(7.3.2)
$$\hat{Y} = [B_2 Z + B_3 XZ] + [B_1 X + B_0]$$
$$\hat{Y} = [B_2 + B_3 X]Z + [B_1 X + B_0].$$

The simple slope $[B_2 + B_3 X]$ for the regression of Y on Z shows that if B_3 is nonzero, the regression of Y on Z will differ for each value of X. If B_3 is zero, meaning that there is no interaction, the regression of Y on Z is constant for all values of X. The symmetry is complete. It should also be noted that the expressions for simple slopes depend completely on the regression equation for the entire sample, including both main effects and interactions.

7.3.5 Simple Slopes From Uncentered Versus Centered Equations Are Identical

We learned in Section (7.2.6) that the regression coefficient B_3 for the highest order interaction term XZ in Eq. (7.1.2) remains invariant when predictors are centered; this is so because the shape of the regression surface is unchanged by centering. Simple slopes are regressions of Y on a predictor, say X, at particular points on that surface, defined by the other predictor, here Z. If simple regression equations are computed at analogous values of Z in the centered and uncentered case, then the slopes of these simple regression lines will be identical in the centered versus uncentered case; only the intercepts will differ. This point cannot be overemphasized. The interpretation of the interaction remains identical across the centered versus the uncentered form of a regression equation. This is why we can move between the uncentered and centered forms of an equation without jeopardizing interpretation.

In our example, uncentered Z has the values $(0, 2, 4, 6, 8, 10)$ and the corresponding values of centered z are $(-5, -3, -1, 1, 3, 5)$. Uncentered $Z = 2$, for example, corresponds to centered $z = -3$. We rearrange the uncentered equation $\hat{Y} = .2X + .4XZ + .6Z + 2$ into the simple regression equation $\hat{Y} = (.2 + .4Z)X + (.6Z + 2)$ and substitute $Z = 2$, yielding $\hat{Y} = (.2 + .4(2))X + (.6(2) + 2)$, or $\hat{Y} = 1.0X + 3.2$. The simple regression of Y on x at $z = -3$ in the centered equation $\hat{Y} = 2.2x + 2.6z + .4xz + 16$ is $\hat{Y} = 1.0x + 8.2$. The simple slopes are identical; only the intercept has changed. Simple slopes from the uncentered and centered regression equations are given in Table 7.1.1D and G, respectively.

7.3.6 Linear by Linear Interactions

The interaction between X and Z in Eq. (7.1.2) is a *linear by linear interaction*. This means that the regression of Y on X is linear at every value of Z or, equivalently, that the regression coefficient of Y on X changes at a constant rate as a function of changes in Z. Thus we find the symmetric fanning of simple regression lines illustrated in Fig. 7.3.1(B). All the simple regression equations characterize straight lines; they change slope at a constant rate as Z increases. This linearity is symmetric: The regression of Y on Z is linear at every value of X; the regression of Y on Z changes at a constant rate as a function of changes in X.

Chapter 6 explored the treatment of curvilinear relationships of individual variables through polynomial regression. Interactions of curvilinear functions of one predictor with linear or curvilinear components of another predictor are possible. In Section 7.9 we will take up more complex interactions that include curvilinear relationships.

7.3.7 Interpreting Interactions in Multiple Regression and Analysis of Variance

The reader familiar with ANOVA will note the similarity of the proposed strategy to the well-developed strategy used in ANOVA for the interpretation of interactions. In ANOVA with factors A and B interacting, the approach involves examining the effect of one factor A involved in the interaction at each of the several levels of the other factor B involved in the interaction. The purpose of the analysis is to determine the levels of factor B at which factor A manifests an effect. In ANOVA, the effect of a factor on the outcome, confined to one level of another factor, is termed a *simple main effect* (e.g., Kirk, 1995; Winer, Brown, & Michels, 1991). The format of Fig. 7.3.1 is highly similar to that typically used in ANOVA to illustrate the effects of two factors simultaneously. In ANOVA we have plots of means of one factor at specific levels of another factor. In MR, we have plots of simple regression lines of the criterion on one predictor at specific values of another predictor. In Section 7.4 we present a method for post hoc probing of simple slopes of simple regression lines in MR that parallels post hoc probing of simple main effects in ANOVA.

7.4 POST HOC PROBING OF INTERACTIONS

Plotting interactions provides substantial information about their nature. In addition to inspecting simple slopes to describe the specific nature of interactions, we may also create confidence intervals around simple slopes. Further we may test whether a specific simple slope, computed at one value of the other predictor(s), differs from zero (or from some other value).

7.4.1 Standard Error of Simple Slopes

In Chapter 3 (Section 3.6.1), we introduced the *standard error of a partial regression coefficient*, SE_{B_i}, a measure of the expected instability of a partial regression coefficient from one random sample to another. The square of the standard error is the *variance of the regression coefficient*.

We also may measure the *standard error of a simple slope*, that is, of the simple regression coefficient for the regression of Y on X at a particular value of Z. For example, if Z were a 7-point attitude scale ranging from 1 to 7, $M_Z = 4$, and we centered Z into z, ranging from -3 to $+3$, we might examine the simple slope of Y on x at values of z across the centered attitude scale, say at the values $[-3 \quad -1 \quad 1 \quad 3]$. The numerical value of the standard error of the simple slope of Y on x is different at each value of z.

In Eq. (7.3.1) for the regression of Y on X at values of z, the simple slope is $[B_1 + B_3 Z]$. The standard error of the simple slope depends upon the variances of both B_1 and B_3. It also varies as a function of the covariance between the estimates of B_1 and B_3. This is a new concept—that regression coefficients from the same equation may be more or less related to one another. Some intuition can be gained if one imagines carrying out the same regression analysis on repeated random samples and making note of the values of B_1 and B_3 in each sample. Having carried out the analysis many times, we could measure the covariance between the B_1 and B_3 coefficients across the many samples; this is the covariance we seek.

For Eq. (7.1.2), the variances of B_1, B_2, and B_3 and their covariances are organized into a matrix called the *covariance matrix of the regression coefficients*; it appears as follows:

$$
\begin{array}{c}
\qquad\qquad B_1 \qquad\quad B_2 \qquad\quad B_3 \\
\textbf{(7.4.1)} \qquad \mathbf{S}_B =
\begin{array}{c} B_1 \\ B_2 \\ B_3 \end{array}
\left[
\begin{array}{ccc}
SE^2_{B_{11}} & \mathrm{cov}_{B_{12}} & \mathrm{cov}_{B_{13}} \\
\mathrm{cov}_{B_{21}} & SE^2_{B_{22}} & \mathrm{cov}_{B_{23}} \\
\mathrm{cov}_{B_{31}} & \mathrm{cov}_{B_{32}} & SE^2_{B_{33}}
\end{array}
\right]
\end{array}
$$

where $SE^2_{B_{ii}}$ is the variance of regression coefficient B_i and $\mathrm{cov}_{B_{ij}}$ is the covariance between regression coefficients B_i and B_j. This matrix is provided by standard programs for multiple regression, including SAS, SPSS, and SYSTAT.

The standard error of the simple slope for the regression of Y on X at a particular value of Z is given as follows:

(7.4.2) $$SE_{B \text{ at } Z} = [SE^2_{B_{11}} + 2Z\mathrm{cov}_{B_{13}} + Z^2 SE^2_{B_{33}}]^{1/2}.$$

Specific values are taken from the covariance matrix in Eq. (7.4.1) and from the predictor Z itself. This equation applies whether centered or uncentered variables are used. However, the values in the $\mathbf{S}_B$ matrix will differ depending on predictor scaling, just as do the values in the correlation matrix of the predictors themselves.

Each standard error of a simple slope only applies to a particular regression coefficient in a particular regression equation. For the regression of Y on Z at values of X, the standard error is

(7.4.3) $$SE_{B \text{ at } X} = [SE^2_{B_{22}} + 2X\mathrm{cov}_{B_{23}} + X^2 SE^2_{B_{33}}]^{1/2}.$$

7.4.2 Equation Dependence of Simple Slopes and Their Standard Errors

As was stated earlier, the expressions for both the simple slopes depend on the particular regression equation for the full sample. This is also the case for the standard errors of simple slopes. The simple slopes determined by Eqs. (7.3.1) and (7.3.2), and their respective standard errors in Eqs. (7.4.2) and (7.4.3), apply *only* to equations with two-variable linear interactions such as Eq. (7.1.2). *These expressions are not appropriate for more complex equations with higher order terms or interactions involving quadratic terms*, such as Eqs. (7.6.1) and (7.9.2). Aiken and West (1991, pp. 60 and 64) provide expressions for both the simple slopes and the standard errors of simple slopes for a variety of regression equations.

7.4.3 Tests of Significance of Simple Slopes

Tests of significance of individual predictors in a multiple regression equation are given in Chapter 3 (Section 3.6.4). These tests generalize directly to tests of significance of simple slopes. Suppose we wish to test the hypothesis that the simple slope of Y on X is zero at some particular value of Z. The t test for this hypothesis is

(7.4.4) $$t_{B \text{ at } Z} = (B_1 + B_3 Z)/SE_{B \text{ at } Z} \quad \text{with} \quad (n - k - 1)\, df,$$

where k is the number of predictors. For the significance of difference from zero of the regression of Y on Z at values of X, the appropriate t test is

(7.4.5) $$t_{B \text{ at } X} = (B_2 + B_3 X)/SE_{B \text{ at } X} \quad \text{with} \quad (n - k - 1)\, df.$$

7.4.4 Confidence Intervals Around Simple Slopes

The structure of the confidence interval for a simple slope follows that described in Section 2.8.2 for the confidence interval on the predictor in a one-predictor equation and in Section 3.6.1 for the confidence interval on a regression coefficient in a multiple prediction equation. For a two-tailed confidence interval for the regression of Y on X at a specific level of confidence $(1 - \alpha)$ the *margin of error (me)* is given as follows:

$$(7.4.6) \qquad me = t_{1-\alpha/2} SE_{B \text{ at } Z},$$

where $t_{1-\alpha/2}$ refers to a two-tailed critical value of t for specified α, with $(n - k - 1) \, df$. The critical value of t is the same value as for the t test for the significance of each regression coefficient in the overall regression analysis and for the significance of the simple slope.

The confidence interval is given as

$$(7.4.7) \qquad CI = [(B_1 + B_3 Z) - me \leq \beta^*_{Y \text{ on } X \text{ at } Z} \leq (B_1 + B_3 Z) + me],$$

where $\beta^*_{Y \text{ on } X \text{ at } Z}$ is the value of the simple slope in the population. For the regression of Y on Z at values of X, the margin of error and confidence interval are as follows:

$$(7.4.8) \qquad me = t_{1-\alpha/2} SE_{B \text{ at } X},$$

where $t_{1-\alpha/2}$ is as in Eq. (7.4.6).

The confidence interval on the simple slope is

$$(7.4.9) \qquad CI = [(B_2 + B_3 X) - me \leq \beta^*_{Y \text{ on } Z \text{ at } X} \leq (B_2 + B_3 X) + me],$$

where $\beta^*_{Y \text{ on } Z \text{ at } X}$ is the value of the simple slope in the population.

The interpretation of the *CI* for a simple slope follows that for a regression coefficient. For example, for level of confidence 95%, we can be 95% confident that the true simple slope $\beta^*_{Y \text{ on } X \text{ at } Z}$ falls within the interval we have calculated from our observed data. An alternative frequentist interpretation is that if we were to draw a large number of random samples from the same population, carry out the regression analysis, and compute the confidence interval of Y on X at one specific value of Z, 95% of those intervals would be expected to contain the value $\beta^*_{Y \text{ on } X \text{ at } Z}$. Of course, the *CI* on the simple slope provides all the information provided by the null hypothesis significance tests given in Eq. (7.4.4) when the α selected in determining the *me* is equivalent. If the confidence interval on the simple slope includes zero, we do not reject the null hypothesis that the simple slope differs from zero.

Some caution in our thinking is required here. Consider once again the developmental example of the prediction of child's language development (Y) from child's age (A) as a function of number of siblings (S). In each of a large number of samples of children from the same population, we might construct the 95% confidence interval for the regression of Y on A for $S = 1$ sibling. Our frequentist interpretation would be that across a large number of samples, 95% of the confidence intervals would include the true population value of the slope for the regression of child's language development on child's age for children with only one sibling. Suppose, however, we computed the regression of Y on A for the mean number of siblings in each sample; that is, we would not pick a specific number of siblings, but would rather use the mean number of siblings in a particular sample as the value of S for examining the regression of Y on age (A) at S. The mean number of siblings varies across samples. Thus the *CI* on the simple slope would be for a different value of S in each sample. We could not strictly use the frequentist interpretation of the *CI* calculated at the mean of any particular sample. Put another way, in comparing the simple regression of Y on X at a value of Z across different samples, the value of Z must be held constant (fixed) across the samples.

7.4.5 A Numerical Example

In Table 7.4.1 and Fig. 7.4.1 we present an example in which physical endurance (Y) of $n = 245$
adults is predicted from their age (X) and the number of years of vigorous physical exercise
(Z) in which they have engaged. In the sample, the mean age is 49.18 $(sd = 10.11$, range 20   CH07EX01
to 82), and the mean number of years of vigorous physical exercise is 10.67 $(sd = 4.78$, range
0 to 26 years). Physical endurance is measured as the number of minutes of sustained jogging
on a treadmill. The mean number of minutes of sustained performance is 26.53 $(sd = 10.82$,
range 0 to 55 minutes, a sample with noteworthy stamina).

Centered and Uncentered Scale in Plots

In Fig. 7.4.1 we have adopted a convention of plotting on the x axis both the original raw
score scale of the predictor and the centered scale in which data are being analyzed. This
strategy is useful for conceptually retaining the meaning of the original scale units of the
predictor during analysis and interpretation. Since the criterion is not centered for analysis, it
is shown only in raw score form in the graph. We plot the range of the variable on the x axis
from one standard deviation below the mean (age = 39.07 years) to one standard deviation
above the mean (age = 59.29 years). This range is smaller than the full range of the X variable
of 20 to 82 years.

In the overall centered regression of endurance (Y) on centered age (x) and centered years
of exercise (z), $\hat{Y} = -.262x + .973z + .047xz + 25.888$. Endurance, not surprisingly, declines
with age. Since the predictors are centered, the amount of decline with age signified by the
regression coefficient $(B_1 = -.26)$ is a loss in endurance of .26 minutes on the treadmill test
for a one-year increase in age for people at the mean level of years of exercise in the sample
(uncentered $M_Z = 10.67$ years). Endurance, in contrast, increases with exercise $(B_2 = .97)$,
with the amount of increase of .97 minutes on the endurance test for each year of vigorous
exercise, applicable to people at the mean age of the sample (uncentered $M_X = 49.18$ years).

The XZ interaction signifies that the decline in endurance with age depends on a history of
exercise, as illustrated in Fig. 7.4.1(A); the regression of endurance (Y) on age (x) is plotted at
three values of exercise (z). In fact, the decline in endurance with age is buffered by a history of
exercise; that is, the more vigorous is exercise across the life span, the less dramatic the decline
in endurance with age. In general, if one variable weakens the impact of another variable on
the criterion, that variable is said to *buffer* the effect of the other variable. One can intuit the
numerical workings of the interaction by considering some cross-product values of centered x
and z. If a person is above the mean age and above the mean exercise, then the cross-product is
positive and increases predicted endurance; that is, the person's predicted endurance is higher
than would be expected from his/her age alone. If the person is above the mean age but below
the mean exercise, the cross-product is negative and decreases predicted endurance below that
expected for people of that age at the average exercise level in the sample.

A comment is in order about the magnitude of the interaction. As shown in Table 7.4.1B,
R^2 with only x and z but without the interaction as predictors is .17; inclusion of the interaction
increases R^2 to .21. Thus the interaction accounts for 4% of the variance in the criterion, over
and above the main effects, $F_{\text{gain}}(1, 241) = 12.08, p < .01$. This may seem to be a small
amount, but it is of the order of magnitude typically found in behavioral research (Chaplin,
1991; Champoux & Peters, 1987; Jaccard & Wan, 1995). While this is "only" 4% of the
variance accounted for, the buffering effect is strong indeed, as shown in Fig. 7.4.1(A). With a
short history of exercise, there is a decline of .49 minutes in treadmill performance per year of
age; yet with a long history of exercise, there is essentially no decline in treadmill performance
(a bit of wishful thinking on the part of the creator of this example).

TABLE 7.4.1
Regression Analysis of Physical Endurance (Y) as a Function of Age (X) and Years of Vigorous Exercise (Z), $n = 245$

A. Summary Statistics for centered x and z and cross-product xz.

	Means and standard deviations			Correlation matrix			
	M	sd		x	z	xz	Y
x	0.00	10.11	x	1.00	.28	.01	−.13
z	0.00	4.78	z		1.00	−.12	.34
xz	13.59	46.01	xz			1.00	.15
Y	26.53	10.82	Y				1.00

B. Centered regression equations:
   1. Prediction of Y from centered x and z:
$$\hat{Y} = -.257x^{**} + .916z^{**} + 26.530$$
$$R^2 = .17$$
   2. Prediction of Y from centered x and z, and xz:
$$\hat{Y} = -.262x^{**} + .973z^{**} + .047xz^{**} + 25.888$$
$$R^2 = .21$$

C. Covariance matrix of the regression coefficients in the centered regression equation containing interactions (Part B2):

	B_1	B_2	B_3
B_1	.00410	−.00248	−.00001806
B_2	−.00248	.01864	.0002207
B_3	−.00001806	.0002207	.0001848

D. Analysis of simple regression equations for regression of uncentered endurance (Y) on centered age (x) at three values of centered years of exercise (z):

Value of z	Simple regression equation	Standard error of simple slope	t test	95% CI
At $z_{low} = -4.78$	$\hat{Y} = -.487x + 21.24$	.092	−5.29**	[−.67, −.31]
At $z_{mean} = 0.00$	$\hat{Y} = -.262x + 25.89$	.064	−4.09**	[−.39, −.14]
At $z_{high} = +4.78$	$\hat{Y} = -.036x + 30.53$	.090	−.40**	[−.21, .14]

E. Analysis of simple regression equations for regression of uncentered endurance (Y) on centered years of exercise (z) at three values of centered age (x):

Value of x	Simple regression equation	Standard error of simple slope	t test	95% CI
At $x_{low} = -10.11$	$\hat{Y} = .495z + 28.53$	.182	2.72**	[.14, .85]
At $x_{mean} = 0.00$	$\hat{Y} = .973z + 25.89$	.137	7.12**	[.70, 1.24]
At $x_{high} = +10.11$	$\hat{Y} = 1.450z + 23.24$	.205	7.08**	[1.05, 1.85]

F. Regression equation with uncentered data ($M_x = 49.18; M_z = 10.67$)
$$\hat{Y} = -.766X^{**} - 1.35 Z^* + .047 XZ^{**} + 53.18$$
$$R^2 = .21$$

$^{**}p < .01; \, ^*p < .05.$

(A) Regression of endurance (Y) on age (x) at three levels of exercise (z). Simple regression equations are for centered data.

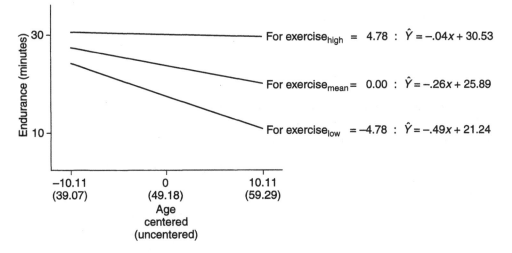

(B) Regression of endurance (Y) on exercise (z) at three levels of age (x). Simple regression equations are for centered data.

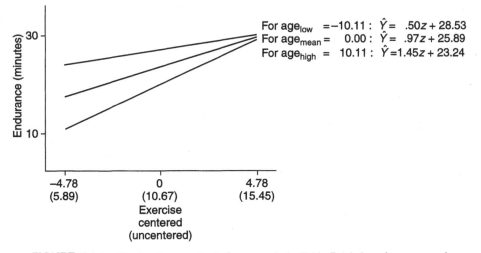

FIGURE 7.4.1   Simple slope analysis for example in Table 7.4.1, based on centered regression equation.

Tests of Significance of Simple Slopes

The analysis of simple slopes of endurance (Y) on centered age (x) at various years of centered exercise (z), given in Table 7.4.1D corroborates our inspection of Fig. 7.4.1(A). First, we rearrange the overall equation to show the regression of Y on x at values of z:

$$\hat{Y} = (-.262 + .047z)x + (.973z + 25.888).$$

Then we compute three simple regression equations, using the mean of z ($z_{mean} = 0$ for centered z), and the values one standard deviation above and below the mean of centered z ($sd = 4.78$).

These simple regression equations are given in Table 7.4.1D. For example, for $z_{high} = 4.78$, within rounding error we have

$$\hat{Y}_{at\ z_{high}} = (-.262 + .047(4.78))x + (.973(4.78) + 25.888)$$

$$\hat{Y}_{at\ z_{high}} = (-.262 + .224)x + (4.646 + 25.888)$$

$$\hat{Y}_{at\ z_{high}} = -.036x + 30.53$$

To test for the significance of difference of each simple slope from zero, we compute the standard error of the simple slope of Y on x at a particular value of z (Eq. 7.4.2). The covariance matrix of the predictors is given in Table 7.4.1C. We need the values

$$SE_{B_{11}}^2 = .00410, \ cov_{B_{13}} = -.00001806, \ and \ SE_{B_{33}}^2 = .0001848. \ Then \ at \ z_{high} = 4.78$$

$$SE_{B\ at\ z_{high}} = [SE_{B_{11}}^2 + 2Z cov_{B_{13}} + Z^2 SE_{B_{33}}^2]^{1/2}$$

$$SE_{B\ at\ z_{high}=4.78} = [.00410 + 2(4.78)(-.00001806) + (4.78)^2 .0001848]^{1/2}$$

$$= (.00410 - .000172 + .004221) = .008149^{1/2} = .090.$$

Finally, the t test is

$$t_{B\ at\ Z} = (B_1 + B_3 Z)/SE_{B\ at\ Z} = (-.262 + .047(4.78))/.090$$

$$= -.036/.090 = -.40.$$

With $(n - k - 1) = 245 - 3 - 1 = 241\ df$, at $\alpha = .05$, two tailed, $t_{critical} = 1.97$; there is no evidence of decline in endurance with age when there is a long history of exercise.

Confidence Intervals Around Simple Slopes

We may estimate a confidence interval on the simple slope at z_{high} for the decline in endurance (minutes on the treadmill) with age at one standard deviation above the mean on exercise. Using Eq. (7.4.6) for the margin of error (*me*) for $\alpha = .05$, we find

$$me = t_{1-\alpha/2} SE_{B\ at\ z_{high}=4.78} = 1.97\ (.090) = .177.$$

From (7.4.7) the 95% confidence interval is given as

$$CI = [(B_1 + B_3 Z) - me \leq \beta_{Y\ on\ x\ at\ z_{high}}^* \leq (B_1 + B_3 Z) + me]$$

$$CI = [(-.036) - .177 \leq \beta_{Y\ on\ x\ at\ z_{high}}^* \leq (-.036) + .177]$$

$$CI = [-.213 \leq \beta_{Y\ on\ x\ at\ z_{high}}^* \leq .141]$$

where $\beta_{Y\ on\ X\ at\ Z}^*$ is a population value of a simple slope.

The confidence interval includes zero, indicating a lack of statistical evidence for decline in endurance with increasing age for people with a substantial history of exercise (one *sd* above the mean), consistent with the outcome of the statistical test.

We need not confine ourselves to values of z like z_{high} or z_{low}. We might wish to estimate a confidence interval on the decline with age in endurance for people who have exercised a particular numbers of years. Here, as examples, we choose decline for people who have exercised not at all, in comparison to those who have exercised a full decade (10 years). The choice of 0 years and 10 years is arbitrary; researchers might pick other values on the basis of theory or because the values represent practical points of interest. Note that 0 years and 10 years are on the uncentered scale (in the original units of number of years of exercise). To center years of exercise, we subtracted $M_Z = 10.67$ from each score on raw years. Now we convert 0 and 10 raw years to the centered scale by subtracting 10.67 from each number of raw years:

Raw years of exercise (Z)   0   10
Centered years of exercise (z) -10.67 $-.67$

We form confidence intervals at each number of centered years. First we compute the simple slope for the regression of Y on x at $z = -10.67$, corresponding to 0 years of exercise:

$$(B_1 + B_3 z) = (-.262 + .047(-10.67)) = -.763.$$

Then we compute the standard errors at each number of centered years, using

(7.4.2) $$SE_{B \text{ at } z=i} = [SE_{B_{11}}^2 + 2z \text{ cov}_{B_{13}} + z^2 SE_{B_{33}}^2]^{1/2}$$

For zero years of exercise (equal to -10.67 years on the centered scale),

$$SE_{B \text{ at } Z=-10.67} = [.00410 + 2(-10.67)(-.00001806) + (-10.67)^2 .0001848]^{1/2}$$
$$= (.00410 + .0003854 + .0210392)^{1/2}$$
$$= .0255246^{1/2} = .160.$$

Then we compute the margin of error for $\alpha = .05$, using

$$me = t_{1-\alpha/2} SE_{B \text{ at } z=-10.67} = (1.97)(.160) = .315.$$

Finally, we compute the confidence interval using

$$CI = [(B_1 + B_3 z) - me \leq \beta_{Y \text{ on } X \text{ at } Z}^* \leq (B_1 + B_3 z) + me]$$
$$CI = [-.763 - .315 \leq \beta_{Y \text{ on } X \text{ at } Z}^* \leq -.763 + .315]$$
$$CI = [-1.078 \leq \beta_{Y \text{ on } X \text{ at } Z}^* \leq -.448]$$

This confidence interval indicates that we can be 95% certain that there is somewhere between a half minute ($-.448$) and full minute (-1.078) decline on the endurance test for each year of increasing age for individuals who have no history of exercise.

What is the decline for individuals who have a 10-year history of exercise? Ten raw-score years translates into $-.67$ years on the centered scale (since the mean years of exercise is 10.67).

The simple slope for the regression of Y on x at $z = -.67$ is

$$(B_1 + B_3 z) = (-.262 + .047(-.67)) = -.293.$$

The standard error of this simple slope is given as

$$SE_{B \text{ at } Z=-.67} = [.00410 + 2(-.67)(-.00001806) + (-.67)^2 .0001848]^{1/2}$$
$$= (.00410 + .0000242 + .0000829)^{1/2} = .004207^{1/2} = .065.$$

Then we compute the margin of error, $\alpha = .05$, using

$$me = t_{1-\alpha/2} SE_{B \text{ at } Z=-.67} = (1.97)(.065) = .128.$$

Finally, we compute the 95% confidence interval using

$$CI = [(B_1 + B_3z) - me \leq \beta^*_{Y \text{ on } X \text{ at } Z = -.67} \leq (B_1 + B_3z) + me]$$
$$CI = [-.293 - .128 \leq \beta^*_{Y \text{ on } X \text{ at } Z = -.67} \leq -.293 + .128]$$
$$CI = [-.421 \leq \beta^*_{Y \text{ on } X \text{ at } Z = -.67} \leq -.165].$$

This confidence interval indicates that we can be 95% certain that for individuals who have exercised for 10 years, the true decline is from about a sixth (i.e., $-.165$) of a minute to at most 4/10 (i.e., $-.421$) of a minute for each year of age. If we compare the two confidence intervals, that for zero versus 10 years of exercise, we see that the intervals do not overlap. Thus we may also conclude that there is materially less decline in endurance among people with a 10-year history of exercise than among those with no exercise.

No Tests of Significance of Difference Between Simple Slopes

We might be tempted to say that the simple slope for the decline of endurance with increasing age at 10 years of exercise ($-.293$) is "significantly less" than the decline of endurance with increasing age at 0 years of exercise ($-.763$). We cannot say this, however. There exists no test of significance of difference between simple slopes computed at single values (points) along a continuum (e.g., along the age continuum). The issue then comes down to a matter of meaningfulness. Here we would ask if the savings of almost a half minute in a measure of endurance with each year of exercise is meaningful (judging how long people live, a half a minute a year translates into a lot of endurance over the life span). We said there was a material difference in the two measures of decline in endurance since the *CI*s did not overlap. However, the *CI*s might overlap and the difference in simple slopes be material from a substantive perspective.

Regression of Y on z at Values of x

We also display the *XZ* interaction in Fig. 7.4.1(B), but now showing the regression of endurance (Y) on exercise (z) at three values of age (x). That is, instead of Y on x at values of z, we have Y on z at values of x. This display tells us about the impact of exercise on endurance as a function of age. We would expect exercise to have a more profound effect on endurance as age increases. The appearance of the interaction is quite different, but tells the same story in a different way. Figure 7.4.1(B) shows us that as age increases, the positive impact of exercise on endurance becomes more pronounced (i.e., a steeper positive slope, even though, overall, younger individuals have greater endurance than older individuals. The corresponding simple slope analysis is carried out in Table 7.4.1E. In fact, there is a significant gain in endurance with increased length of exercise history at the mean age ($M_X = 49.18$ years, which is equivalent to centered $M_x = 0.00$ years), at one *sd* below the mean age ($X_{\text{low}} = 39.07$ years, equivalent to centered $x_{\text{low}} = -10.11$ years) and at one *sd* above the mean age ($X_{\text{high}} = 59.29$ years, $x_{\text{high}} = 10.11$ years).

Simple Slope Analysis by Computer

The numerical example develops the analysis of simple slopes for Y on X at values of Z by hand computation for Eq. (7.1.2). The complete analysis of simple slopes can easily be carried out by computer using standard regression analysis software. Aiken and West (1991) explain the computer method and provide computer code for computing simple slopes, standard errors, and tests of significance of simple slopes.

7.4.6 The Uncentered Regression Equation Revisited

We strongly recommend working with centered data. We visit the uncentered regression equation briefly to show just how difficult it may be to interpret uncentered regression coefficients. Uncentered equations are primarily useful when there are true zeros on the predictor scales.

As shown in Table 7.4.1F, the regression equation based on uncentered data is

$$\hat{Y} = -.766X - 1.351Z + .047XZ + 53.18.$$

This equation is different from the centered equation in that now the regression of endurance on exercise (Z) is significantly *negative*: the more exercise, the less endurance. How can this be? A consideration of the regression of endurance on exercise at values of age (Y on uncentered Z at values of uncentered X) provides clarification. The simple regressions are computed from the overall uncentered regression equation by:

$$\hat{Y} = (-1.351 + .047X)Z + (-.766X + 53.18).$$

We choose meaningful values of age on the uncentered scale: $X_{\text{mean}} = 49.18$ years, $X_{\text{low}} = 39.07$ (one standard deviation below the mean age), and $X_{\text{high}} = 59.29$. (Again, these values correspond to centered ages of -10.11, 0, and 10.11, respectively in the simple slope analysis of Table 7.4.1E. For ages 39.07 to 59.29, the regression of endurance on exercise is positive, as we expect. At $X_{\text{low}} = 39.08$ years, $(B_2 + B_3Z) = [-1.351 + (.047)(39.08)] = .96$; at $X_{\text{high}} = 59.29$, $(B_2 + B_3Z) = 1.44$. As we already know, the slopes of the simple regression lines from the uncentered equation and those from the corresponding simple regression lines from the centered regression equation are the same. The interpretation of the interaction is unchanged by centering.

The significantly negative B_2 coefficient (-1.351) from the uncentered equation represents the regression of endurance (Y) on exercise (Z), for individuals at age zero (X = 0). At X = 0, the simple slope $(B_2 + B_3Z) = [-1.351 + (.047)(0)] = -1.351$. We know that this simple regression line for age zero with its negative slope is nonsensical, because it represents the number of years of exercise completed by people of age zero years (i.e., newborns). We may compute simple regression lines for regions of the regression plane that exist mathematically, since mathematically the regression plane extends to infinity in all directions. However, the simple regression equations only make sense in terms of the meaningful range of the data. It is reasonable, for example, that someone 29.01 years of age might have a 12-year history of strenuous exercise, if he played high school and college football or she ran in high school and college track. However, in this example, years of exercise is limited by age. Moreover, the age range studied is adults who have had an opportunity to exercise over a period of years.

In computing simple regression lines we must consider the *meaningful range of each variable* in the regression equation and limit our choice of simple regression lines to this meaningful range. This is why we caution about the uncentered regression equation once again—zero is often not a meaningful point on scales in the behavioral sciences. We do not mean to say that the use of uncentered variables produces incorrect results; rather, uncentered regression equations often produce interpretation difficulties for behavioral science data, difficulties that are eliminated by centering.

7.4.7 First-Order Coefficients in Equations Without and With Interactions

Suppose we have a data set that contains an interaction, as in the example of endurance, age, and exercise in Table 7.4.1. We compare the centered regression equation without the interaction versus with the interaction in Table 7.4.1B. We note that the B_1 coefficient for x is $-.257$ versus $-.262$ in the equation without versus with the interaction, respectively. The B_2 coefficient is $.916$ versus $.973$, respectively. Why do these coefficients change when the interaction term is added? These coefficients are partial regression coefficients, and x and z are both slightly correlated with the cross-product term xz, as shown in Table 7.4.1A. These very slight correlations reflect essential multicollinearity (Section 7.2.4) due to very slight nonsymmetry of X and Z. If X and Z were perfectly symmetric, then $r_{x,xz} = 0$ and $r_{z,xz} = 0$. In this latter case, the addition of the cross-product xz term would have no effect on the B_1 and B_2 coefficients.

The result of adding the interaction term in the uncentered equation is dramatically different. The uncentered equation containng the interaction is given in Table 7.4.1F. The uncentered equation without the interaction is $\hat{Y} = -.257X + .916Z + 29.395$. The large changes in B_1 and B_2 when the XZ term is added are due to the fact that the B_1 and B_2 coefficients in the uncentered equation without versus with the interaction represent different things. In the equation without the interaction they are overall effects; in the equation with the interaction, the B_1 and B_2 coefficients are conditional, at the value of zero on the other predictor. In the centered equation, the B_1 and B_2 coefficients are again conditional at zero on the other predictor. However, they also represent the average effect of a predictor across the range of the predictor, much more closely aligned with the meaning of the B_1 and B_2 coefficients in the overall centered equation without an interaction.

The reader is cautioned that this discussion pertains to predicting the same dependent variable from only first-order effects and then from first-order effects plus interactions, as in the age, exercise, and endurance example. The example in Section 7.2 is not structured in this manner, but rather is a special pedagogical case—the dependent variables are different for the equation without versus with interactions, so the principles articulated here do not apply.

7.4.8 Interpretation and the Range of Data

A principle is illustrated in our cautions about interpreting coefficients in the uncentered data—regression analyses should be interpreted only within the range of the observed data. This is so whether or not equations contain interactions, and whether or not variables are centered. In graphical characterizations of the nature of the interaction between age and years of exercise on endurance, we confined the range of the x and y axes in Figs. 7.4.1(A) and 7.4.1(B) to well within the range of the observed data. We certainly would not extrapolate findings beyond the youngest and beyond the oldest participant ages (20 years, 82 years). Beyond limiting our interpretations to the confines of the range of the observed data, we encounter the issue of sparseness (very few data points) near the extremes of the observed data, just as we did in polynomial regression (Section 6.2.5). The limitation that sparseness places on interpretation of regression results is further discussed in Section 7.7.1.

7.5 STANDARDIZED ESTIMATES FOR EQUATIONS CONTAINING INTERACTIONS

To create a standardized solution for regression equations containing interactions, we must take special steps. First, we must standardize X and Z into z_x and z_z. Then we must form the cross-product term $z_x z_z$ to carry the interaction. The appropriate standardized solution has as the cross-product term the *cross-product of the z-scores for the individual predictors entering the interaction*. What happens if we simply use the "standardized" solution that accompanies the centered solution in usual regression analysis output? This "standardized" solution is improper in the interaction term. The XZ term that purportedly carries the interaction in the "standardized" solution reported in standard statistical packages is formed from the XZ term standardizing subjects' scores on the XZ product *after* the product is formed. It is the z-score of the product XZ, rather than the correct product of the z-scores $z_X z_Z$. The "standardized" solution that accompanies regression analyses containing interactions should be ignored. Instead, X and Z should be standardized first, then the cross-product of the z-scores should be computed, and these predictors should be entered into a regression analysis. The *"raw" coefficients from the analysis based on z-scores* are the proper standardized solution (Friedrich, 1982; Jaccard, Turrisi, & Wan, 1990). The improper and proper standardized solutions are given in Table 7.5.1 for the endurance example. The improper solution is given in Table 7.5.1A, the proper solution in Table 7.5.1B. There are two differences between the two solutions. First, the value of the

TABLE 7.5.1
Standardized Solution for the Regression of Endurance on Age and
Years of Strenuous Exercise ($n = 245$)

A. Improper standardized solution taken from computer printout. The solution is the "standardized" solution that accompanies the centered regression analysis reported in Table 7.4.1.

$$\hat{Y} = -.244X + .429Z + .201XZ$$

Coefficient	SE	t test
$B_1 = -.244$	.060	−4.085
$B_2 = .429$	.060	7.124
$B_3 = .201$	.058	3.476
$B_0 = 0.00$		

B. Proper standardized solution. The solution is computed by forming z-scores from centered predictors and forming the cross-product of the z-scores.

1. Summary statistics for centered x and z and cross-product xz.

	Means and standard deviations			Correlation matrix			
	M	sd		x	z	xz	y
x	0.00	1.000	x	1.00	.28	.01	−.13
z	0.00	1.000	z		1.00	−.12	.34
xz	.28	.953	xz			1.00	.15
y	0.00	1.000	y				1.00

2. Proper standardized regression equation containing interaction:

$$\hat{Y} = -.244X + .429Z + .211XZ - .059.$$

Coefficient	SE	t test
$B_1 = -.244$	.060	−4.085
$B_2 = .429$	.060	7.124
$B_3 = .211$	.061	3.476
$B_0 = -.059$		

coefficient for the interaction B_3 changes slightly. The change, however slight in the present example, is important, because it affects the values of the simple slopes. In other circumstances, the difference may be more pronounced. Second, there is a nonzero intercept in the proper solution, since the $z_X z_Z$ term will have a nonzero mean to the extent that X and Z are correlated.

7.6 INTERACTIONS AS PARTIALED EFFECTS: BUILDING REGRESSION EQUATIONS WITH INTERACTIONS

In Eq. (7.1.2) the regression coefficient for the interaction, B_3, is a partial regression coefficient. It represents the effect of the interaction *if and only if* the two predictors comprising the interaction are included in the regression equation (Cohen, 1978). If only the XZ term were included in the regression equation and the X and Z terms were omitted, then the effect attributed to XZ would include any first order effects of X and Z that were correlated with the XZ term as well. Recall that in our numerical example X and Z each had an effect on the criterion, independent of their interaction. If X and Z had been omitted from regression Eq. (7.1.2), then any first-order effects of X and Z that were correlated with XZ would have been incorrectly attributed to the interaction. Only when X and Z have been linearly partialed from XZ does it, in general, become the interaction predictor we seek; thus,

$$X \text{ by } Z = XZ \cdot X, Z.$$

Interactions in MR analysis may be far more complex than the simple two-way interaction portrayed here. The next order of generalization we make is to more than two predictors. Whatever their nature, the predictors $X, Z,$ and W may form a three-way interaction in their relationship to Y; that is, they may operate jointly in accounting for Y variance *beyond* what is accounted for by $X, Z, W, XZ, XW,$ and ZW. This could mean, for example, that the nature of an interaction between X and Z differs as a function of the value of W. Put another way, the three-way interaction would signal that the Y on X regression varies with differing ZW *joint* values, or is conditional on the specific Z, W combination, being greater for some than others. The symmetry makes possible the valid interchange of $X, Z,$ and W. The X by Z by W interaction is carried by the XZW product, which requires refining by partialing of constituent variables and two-way products of variables; that is,

$$X \text{ by } Z \text{ by } W = XZW \cdot X, Z, W, XZ, XW, ZW.$$

The proper regression equation for assessing the three-way interaction is

$$(7.6.1) \qquad \hat{Y} = B_1 X + B_2 Z + B_3 W + B_4 XZ + B_5 XW + B_6 ZW + B_7 XZW + B_0.$$

All lower order terms must be included in the regression equation for the B_7 coefficient to represent the effect of the three-way interaction on Y. (Consistent with the discussion of centering predictors in Section 7.2, if we were to center predictors $X, Z,$ and W in Eq. 7.6.1, then only the value of the B_7 coefficient would remain constant across the centered versus uncentered equation, since now B_7 is the invariant highest order term.)

Higher order interactions follow the same pattern, both in interpretation and representation: a d-way interaction is represented by the d-way product from which the constituent main effect variables, the two-way, three-way, etc. up to $(d-1)$-way products have been partialed, most readily accomplished by including all these lower order terms in the same multiple regression equation with the highest order term.

The fact that the mathematics can rigorously support the analysis of interactions of high order, however, does not mean that they should necessarily be constructed and used. Interactions greater than three-way certainly may exist. The many variables that are controlled to create uniform laboratory environments in the biological, physical, and social sciences are all potential sources of higher order interactions. Nonetheless, our current designs (and theories, to some extent) make it unlikely that we will detect and understand these effects. Recall that in Chapter 6, a similar argument was made about polynomial terms above the cubic (X^3). The reader should recognize that a quadratic polynomial term (X^2) is of the same order as a two-way cross-product term, XZ; both are of order 2. The cubic (X^3) term and the XZW interaction terms are of order 3. Data quality may well not support the treatment of interactions among more than three variables.

7.7 PATTERNS OF FIRST-ORDER AND INTERACTIVE EFFECTS

Thus far, we have encountered two different patterns of first-order and interaction effects in the two numerical examples. In our first numerical example the increases in predictor Z strengthened the relationship of X to Y, as illustrated in Fig. 7.3.1(B). In the second example, illustrated in Fig. 7.4.1(A), the nature of the interaction was quite different, in that a history of exercise weakened the deleterious effect of increased age on endurance.

In fact, a variety of interaction patterns are possible, and are reflected in the possible combinations of values of regression coefficients B_1, B_2 and B_3 in Eq. (7.1.2). We may have any combination whatever of zero, positive, and negative regression coefficients of first-order effects (B_1 and B_2), coupled with positive and negative interactive effects (B_3). The appearance of the interaction will depend on the signs of all three coefficients. Moreover, the precise nature of the interactions will be determined by the relative magnitudes of these coefficients.

7.7.1 Three Theoretically Meaningful Patterns of First-Order and Interaction Effects

We characterize three theoretically meaningful and interesting interaction patterns between two predictors; each pattern depends on the values of B_1, B_2, and B_3 in Eq. (7.1.2). First are *synergistic or enhancing interactions* in which both predictors affect the criterion Y in the same direction, and together they produce a stronger than additive effect on the outcome. As already mentioned, the interaction in the first numerical example (Fig. 7.3.1B) is synergistic; all three regression coefficients in the centered equation are positive. When both the first-order and interactive effects are of the same sign, the interaction is synergistic or enhancing. If all three signs are negative, we have the same synergistic effect. Suppose life satisfaction (Y) is negatively related to job stress (X) and to level of marital problems (Z). Their interaction is negative, so that having both high job stress and high marital problems leads to even less life satisfaction than the sum of X and Z would predict.

A theoretically prominent pattern of first-order and interactive effects is the *buffering interaction*, already defined in Section 7.4.5. Here the two predictors have regression coefficients of opposite sign. In addition, one predictor weakens the effect of the other predictor; that is, as the impact of one predictor increases in value, the impact of the other predictor is diminished. Buffering interactions are discussed in both mental and physical health research in which one predictor may represent a *risk factor* for mental or physical illness while the other predictor represents a *protective factor* that mitigates the threat of the risk factor (e.g., Cleary & Kessler, 1982; Cohen & Wills, 1985; Krause, 1995) . In the second numerical example in this chapter, increasing age (X) is the risk factor for diminished endurance (Y) and vigorous exercise is the protective factor (Z); the negative impact of age on endurance is lessened by a history of vigorous exercise. In this example $B_1 < 0, B_2 > 0$, and $B_3 > 0$.

A third pattern of interaction is an *interference or antagonistic interaction* in which both predictors work on the criterion in the same direction, and the interaction is of opposite sign (Neter, Kutner, Nachtsheim, & Wasserman, 1996). Recall the example mentioned at the outset of Section 7.1, that perhaps ability and motivation have compensatory effects on graduate school achievement. Surely both ability and motivation are each positively related to achievement ($B_1 > 0$ and $B_2 > 0$). Yet the importance of exceptional ability may be lessened by exceptional motivation, and vice versa, a partially "either-or" pattern of influence of the two predictors on the criterion. If so, their interaction is negative ($B_3 < 0$), that is, of the opposite sign of the two first-order effects.

It is clear from these examples that it is not simply the sign of the B_3 regression coefficient for the interaction that determines whether an interaction is enhancing or buffering or antagonistic. Rather the pattern of signs and magnitudes of the coefficients for all three terms in Eq. (7.1.2) determine the form of the interaction.

All the interactions we have considered here are linear by linear (see Section 7.3.4); the simple slopes are all linear in form. Such patterns of interactions may be observed in more complex regression equations, for example, as components of three-way interactions, described in Section 7.8. The patterns of interactions are not confined to linear by linear interactions. These patterns generalize as well to more complex equations with curvilinear relationships as well, described in Section 7.9.

7.7.2 Ordinal Versus Disordinal Interactions

The interactions in both numerical examples [illustrated in Figs. 7.3.1(B) and 7.4.1(A)] are both *ordinal* interactions. Ordinal interactions are those interactions in which the rank order of the outcomes of one predictor is maintained across all levels of the other predictor *within the observed range of the second predictor*. These interactions are typical of interactions obtained in observational studies. In psychological research in which existing variables are measured (there is no manipulation), we most often observe *ordinal interactions*.

Figure 7.7.1 illustrates a *disordinal interaction* between level of problem solving training (X) and type of training (Z) on problem solving performance (Y). Here the rank order of factor Z in relation to the criterion Y changes as a function of the value of factor X (i.e., whether cases with high or low scores on variable Z have higher criterion scores varies with changing X).

What produces the noncrossing (ordinal) versus crossing (disordinal) appearance of Fig. 7.4.1(A) versus Fig. 7.7.1(A) is the strength of the first-order effects also portrayed in the figures. In Fig. 7.4.1(A), the large first-order effect of exercise on endurance forces the three regression lines apart; people with a long history of exercise have much greater endurance regardless of age than those with moderate exercise histories; the same is true for moderate versus low histories of exercise. Figure 7.4.1(A) actually portrays both the first-order effects of exercise and age and their interaction. If we subtracted out the effects of exercise and age, leaving a pure interaction plot, then the simple regression lines would cross. All the figures in this chapter include both first-order and interactive effects; they are not pure graphs of interactions only and so are better termed plots of simple regression lines than plots of interactions per se.

The more specific term *crossover interaction* is sometimes applied to interactions with effects in opposite directions; hence, Fig. 7.7.1(A) can also be termed a crossover interaction (see Section 9.1 for further discussion). Crossover interactions are often predicted in experimental settings. In a study of teaching methods (lecture versus seminar), we might predict that teaching method interacts with subject matter. For example, our prediction might be that lecture leads to better learning of statistical methods, whereas a seminar format leads to better

(A) Performance in an experiment on Type R versus Type S problems as a function of level of training (Low, High) received in the experiment.

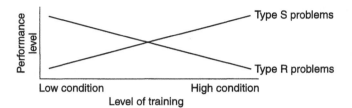

(B) Performance in an observational study as a function of training experienced by individuals prior to participation in the observational study.

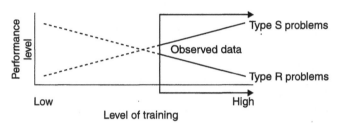

(C) Weak interaction with strong first-order effect of problem type.

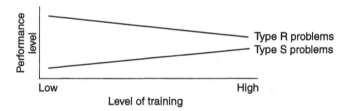

FIGURE 7.7.1 Forms of interactions as a function of sampled range of predictor variables and strength of first-order versus interaction effects.

learning of substantive material, a crossover prediction. We do not mean to imply that crossover interactions never obtain in observational research in which there is no manipulation—they are simply more rare.

The phrase *within the range of the observed data* adds a level of complexity in MR analysis applied to observational data rather than to data gathered in experimental settings. In experiments, the experimental conditions implemented define the range of the predictors (the conditions of experimental variables are translated into predictors in MR). In Fig. 7.7.1(A), suppose there is a crossover interaction between amount of training and performance on two types of problems, Types R and S. Extensive training on Type S facilitates performance but extensive training on Type R leads to boredom and performance deficits. The range of the *x* axis, amount of training, is fixed by the specific conditions implemented in the experiment. Now consider an observational study in which people are interviewed to assess their amount of previous training on a specific type of task (a continuous variable) and then their performance is assessed on tasks R and S. The study is observational because there is no experimental manipulation of training on the tasks. Instead of a fixed range of training having been manipulated in the experiment, the range of training is determined by the previous experience of the particular subjects sampled. Suppose all subjects have had moderate to extensive levels of training. The simple regression equations might appear as in the right-hand portion of Fig. 7.7.1(B), the portion of "observed data." Within the range of training represented on variable X in the sample, the simple regression lines do not cross. In fact, these simple regression lines would cross at lower levels of extent of training, not observed in the sample. This crossover is represented by the dashed portion of the regression lines in Fig. 7.7.1(B)—if we assume linear relationships across all levels of training. In sum, whether we observe ordinal or disordinal interactions in MR analysis may depend upon the range of values on particular predictors across the subjects of a sample. We say *may* here, because the simple regression lines may cross at some numerical point outside the meaningful range of the variable.

In the experimental setting, the researcher controls the range of manipulated variables such as training level by the nature of the particular conditions implemented. In fact, wise experimenters pilot test various forms of their manipulations until they find ones strong enough to produce effects they seek (this is not to say experimenters "cheat," but rather they structure their experiments to optimize the possibility of observing the predicted relationships.) Hence, an experimenter would wisely create dramatically different training levels in the two training conditions to optimize the possibility of observing the crossover (here, perhaps, by training people not at all or by training them to distraction). In an observational setting, the researcher may also control this range by systematic sampling of cases (Pitts & West, 2001) if there is prior knowledge of subjects' scores on variables of interest—here, level of previous experience. In our training example, if experience scores on a large pool of subjects had been available, then the researcher might have systematically sampled a very wide range of experience, thereby leading to the observation of the disordinal (crossover) interaction.

Crossing Point of Simple Regression Lines

The value of a predictor at which simple regression lines cross can be determined algebraically for any specific regression equation and predictor within that equation. For Eq. (7.1.2), the value of X at which the simple regressions of Y on X cross is

(7.7.1)
$$X_{\text{cross}} = -B_2/B_3$$

for the simple regressions of Y on X at values of Z.

For Eq. (7.1.2), the value of Z at which the simple regressions of Y on Z cross is

(7.7.2)
$$Z_{\text{cross}} = -B_1/B_3$$

for the simple regressions of Y on Z at values of X. Equation (7.7.1) and (7.7.2) are instructive in three ways.

1. First, the denominator in both cases is the regression coefficient B_3 for the interaction. If this interaction is zero, then the simple regression lines will not cross—the simple regression lines are parallel.

2. Second, the numerators of these expressions tell us that the crossing point also depends on the magnitude of the first-order effects relative to the interaction. In Eq. (7.3.1) for the regression of Y on X at values of Z, suppose B_2, the regression coefficient for Z, is very large, relative to the interaction (in ANOVA terms, a large main effect coupled with a small interaction). If so, then if B_3 is positive, the regression lines will cross somewhere near minus infinity for positive B_2 or plus infinity for negative B_2. This is illustrated in Fig. 7.7.1(C) versus Fig. 7.7.1(A). In Fig. 7.7.1(A), there is no first-order effect of type of task, $B_2 = 0$ (on average performance on Type R and Type S problems is equal). In Fig. 7.7.1(C), however, there is a large first-order effect of type of task coupled with a smaller interaction than in Fig. 7.7.1(A).

That Type R problems are so much better solved than are Type S problems in Fig. 7.7.1(C) means that regardless of the boredom level induced by training, performance on the Type R problems will not deteriorate to that on Type S problems.

3. Third, the crossing point of the lines depends on the pattern of signs (positive versus negative) of the first-order and interactive effects. First, consider the centered regression equation corresponding to the illustration of simple slopes in Fig. 7.3.1(B); that is, $\hat{Y} = 2.2x + 2.6z + .4xz + 16$. From Fig. 7.3.1(B) it appears as though the simple regression lines cross at a low numerical value outside the range of centered variable x. In fact, for this regression equation $x_{\text{cross}} = -B_2/B_3 = -2.6/4 = -6.5$, well outside the range of the variables illustrated in Fig. 7.3.1(B). Now consider the centered regression equation for the prediction of endurance as a function of age (x) and years of vigorous exercise (z), $\hat{Y} = -.26x + .97z + .05xz + 25.89$. Simple slopes for the regression of endurance on age as a function of exercise (Y on centered x at centered z) are given in Fig. 7.4.1(A). For this regression equation, $X_{\text{cross}} = -B_2/B_3 = -.97/.05 = -19.40$, or 19.40 years below the mean age of 49.18 years. This suggests that for people of age $49.18 - 19.40 = 30.4$ years of age, endurance does not vary as a function of level of vigorous exercise—all the simple slope lines converge. Note that this crossing point is almost two standard deviations below the mean age ($sd_{\text{age}} = 10.11$). Data would be expected to be very sparse at two sds below the M_{age}; in fact, there are only 7 cases of the 245 who are younger than 30. We would not wish to make generalizations about endurance and age in individuals under 30 with so few data points; there is no guarantee that the relationships are even linear at younger ages. This is an important point to note—in MR we may extend the simple regression lines graphically as far as we wish (as opposed to in an experiment where the experimental conditions set the limits); the issue becomes one of whether there are data points at the extremes. Now consider Fig. 7.4.1(B), which shows the regression of endurance on exercise as a function of age (Y on centered z as a function of centered x). For this representation of the data, $Z_{\text{cross}} = -B_1/B_3 = -(-.26)/.05 = 5.20$, or 5.20 years above the mean level of exercise. With a mean years of exercise of 10.67 this corresponds to $10.67 + 5.20 = 15.87$ years of exercise; the data thus suggest that for individuals who have exercised vigorously for 16 years, endurance is independent of age. Only 23 individuals of the 245 have exercised more than 16 years. Again we do not wish to make inferences beyond this point with so few cases, since the form of the regression equation might be quite different for very long-term exercisers.

It is mathematically true that so long as the interaction term is nonzero (even minuscule!) there is a point at which the simple regression lines will cross. In the case of both numerical examples, if we assume that the x axis as illustrated in Fig. 7.3.1 or the x and z axes in Fig. 7.4.1 represent the meaningful ranges of the variables, then there is no crossover within these meaningful ranges. Putting this all together, whether an interaction is ordinal or disordinal depends on the strength of the interaction relative to the strength of the first-order effects coupled with the presence of cases in the range of predictors where the cross occurs, if B_3 is nonzero. When main effects are very strong relative to interactions, crossing points are at extreme values, even beyond the meaningful range (or actual limits) of the scale on which they are measured, that is, the scale of predictor X in Eq. (7.7.1) or the scale of Z in Eq. (7.7.2). Whether we observe the crossing point of simple slopes depends on where it is relative to the distribution of scores on the predictor in the population being sampled and whether the sample contains any cases at the crossing point. The crossing point may have no real meaning—for example, if we were to find a crossing point at 120 years of age (for a sample of humans, not Galapagos tortoises). In contrast, a crossing point expected to occur at about 70 years of human age might be illuminated by systematically sampling cases in a range around 70 years of age, if the crossing point is of theoretical interest.

Crossing Points Are Equation Specific

There is an algebraic expression for the crossing with regard to each predictor in a regression equation containing higher order terms. This expression differs by equation; see Aiken and West (1991) for crossing-point expressions for more complex equations.

7.8 THREE-PREDICTOR INTERACTIONS IN MULTIPLE REGRESSION

Linear by linear interactions in multiple regression generalize beyond two-variable interactions. We provide a brief treatment of the three-way interaction Eq. (7.6.1):

(7.6.1) $\hat{Y} = B_1X + B_2Z + B_3W + B_4XZ + B_5XW + B_6ZW + B_7XZW + B_0.$

First, we reiterate that all lower order terms must be included in the regression equation containing the XZW variable. The X by Z by W interaction is carried by the XZW term but only represents the interaction when all lower order terms have been partialed.

In our example of endurance predicted from age (X) and exercise history (Z), suppose we add a third predictor W, a continuously measured index of healthy life style that includes having adequate sleep, maintaining appropriate weight, not smoking, and the like. We predict endurance from age (X), exercise history (Z), and healthy life style (W), using Eq. (7.6.1). We find that the three-variable interaction is significant and wish to interpret it.

Given three factors, we may break down the interaction into more interpretable form by considering the interaction of two of the factors at different values of the third factor. Suppose we consider the XZ interaction of age with strenuous exercise at two values of W, that is, for those people who have maintained a healthy life style versus not. We choose W_{low} and W_{high} to represent people whose life style practices are one standard deviation below and above the mean life style score. (In a more complete analysis of the XZW interaction, we also would have plotted the XZ interaction at the mean of W, i.e., at W_{mean}). Further, we could have chosen any combination of variables (e.g., the interaction of exercise Z with lifestyle W for different ages).

To plot the three-way interaction as the XZ interaction at values of W, we choose which variable of X and Z will form the x axis. Suppose we follow Fig. 7.4.1(B), which shows the regression of endurance on exercise (Z) at values of age (X). We will make two such graphs, for W_{low} and W_{high}, respectively. This amounts to characterizing the XZW interaction as a series of simple regression equations of Y on Z at values of X and W. We arrange Eq. (7.6.1) to show the regression of Y on Z at values of X and W, yielding the following simple slope expression:

(7.8.1) $\hat{Y} = (B_2 + B_4X + B_6W + B_7XW)Z + (B_1X + B_3W + B_5XW + B_0).$

Figure 7.8.1 provides a hypothetical outcome of the three-way interaction. The pattern of regression of Y (endurance) on Z (exercise) as a function of age (X) differs depending on the extent of a healthy life style (W), signaling the presence of a three-way XZW interaction. For individuals who have maintained a healthy life style (at W_{high}), endurance increases with length of exercise history. The amount of increase depends upon age: exercise has an increasingly salutary effect with increasing age. In statistical terms, there is an XZ interaction at W_{high}. We note that the interaction is ordinal in the range of the data (the three simple regression lines do not cross). If individuals older than those represented in Fig. 7.8.1 had been sampled, these simple regression lines would have been observed to cross, yielding a disordinal interaction within the range of the observed data. For individuals who have not maintained a healthy life style (at W_{low}), exercise does not have an increasingly salutary effect

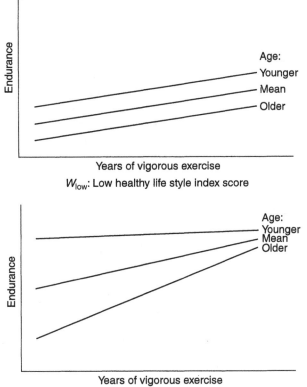

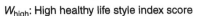

FIGURE 7.8.1 Display of simple slopes for a three-way continuous variable interaction. Regression of endurance (Y) on years of vigorous exercise (Z) is shown at three values of age (X) and at low versus high values of a healthy life style index.

with increasing age. Although endurance increases with increasing exercise, older individuals do not show a stronger benefit from exercise than do younger individuals. Apparently, the special benefit of exercise for older individuals is offset by lack of an otherwise healthy life style. In statistical terms, there is not a significant XZ interaction at W_{low}. We note that the regression lines at W_{low} are parallel; they never cross. ANOVA users will recognize the interactions XZ at W_{high} and XZ at W_{low} to be *simple interactions* (Kirk, 1995; Winer, Brown, & Michaels, 1991), interactions between two variables confined to one level (or value) of a third variable.

As an aid to interpretation of the three-way interaction, one may test each of the six simple slopes in Fig. 7.8.1 for significance. Aiken and West (1991, Chapter 4) provide a full development of post hoc probing of the three-way continuous variable interaction including standard errors and t tests for the simple slope in Eq. (7.8.1), a numerical example of probing a three-way interaction, and computer code for probing the three-way interaction with standard MR software. Beyond simple slopes, one may test for the significance of the interaction between X and Z at varying values of W, that is, the *simple interactions* illustrated in Figure 7.8.1 (Aiken & West, 2000).

7.9 CURVILINEAR BY LINEAR INTERACTIONS

All the interactions we have considered are linear by linear in form. However, curvilinear variables may interact with linear variables. Figure 7.9.1 provides an example of such an interaction. In this hypothetical example, we are predicting intentions to quit smoking from smokers' fear of the negative effects of smoking on health (X). According to theorizing on the impact of fear communication on behavior mentioned in Chapter 6 (Janis, 1967), fear should be curvilinearly related to intention to act. Intention should increase with increasing fear up to a point. Then as the fear becomes more intense, individuals should wish to avoid the whole issue or become so focused on managing the fear itself that intention to quit smoking is lowered. If we considered only the regression of intention on fear, we would have the polynomial regression equation given in Chapter 6:

$$(6.2.3) \qquad \hat{Y} = B_{1.2}X + B_{2.1}X^2 + B_0,$$

where the combination of predictors X and X^2 represents the total effect of variable X on Y.

A second predictor is now considered, the individual's self-efficacy for quitting smoking (Z), that is, the individual's belief that he or she can succeed at quitting smoking. Suppose that intentions to quit smoking rose in a constant fashion as self-efficacy increased, but that there was no interaction between fear (X) and self-efficacy (Z). The appropriate regression equation would be as follows:

$$(7.9.1) \qquad \hat{Y} = B_1X + B_2X^2 + B_3Z + B_0.$$

Two things would be true about the relationship of X to Y illustrated at different values of Z. First, the shape of the simple regressions of Y on X would be constant across values of Z; put another way, any curvilinearity of the relationship of X to Y represented by the $B_1X + B_2X^2$ terms would be constant over all values of Z. Second, the simple slope regression curves of Y on

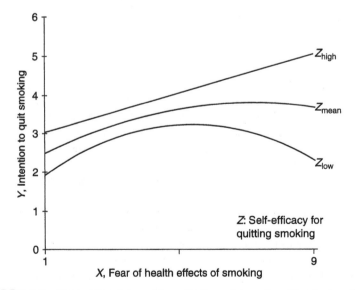

FIGURE 7.9.1 Illustration of a curvilinear by linear interaction. The degree of curvilinearity of the relationship of fear (X) to intention (Y) depends linearly upon the level of self-efficacy for quitting smoking (Z).

X would be parallel for all values of Z, as before. However, it is quite evident from Fig. 7.9.1 that neither of these conditions holds. First, the simple slope equations are not parallel, suggesting the presence of an XZ interaction. Second, the three simple regressions are not of the same shape; variable Z moderates the curvilinearity of the relationship of X to Y. When self-efficacy for quitting is low (at Z_{low}), the relationship of X to Y is strongly curvilinear. As self-efficacy for quitting increases, the relationship of X to Y becomes increasingly linear; high self-efficacy appears to overcome the decrease in intentions at high fear. We have a *curvilinear by linear interaction*; that is, the curvilinear relationship of X to Y changes as variable Z increases linearly. The appropriate regression equation to model this relationship is as follows:

$$(7.9.2) \qquad \hat{Y} = B_1 X + B_2 X^2 + B_3 Z + B_4 XZ + B_5 X^2 Z + B_0.$$

Here for the first time we encounter two interaction components of a single pair of variables, XZ and $X^2 Z$. These interaction terms are formed by crossing each of the terms in the "set" of variables that represent the impact of X on Y (i.e., X and X^2) with the predictor Z. Together XZ and $X^2 Z$ represent the interaction of X and Z in predicting Y, given that lower order predictors X, X^2, and Z are included in the equation. There are now two components of the interaction, the familiar XZ linear by linear component plus the curvilinear by linear component represented by $X^2 Z$. In Eq. (7.9.2) the highest order term is $X^2 Z$; for this term to represent the curvilinear by linear interaction, all lower order terms must be included. To see these terms clearly we can rewrite $X^2 Z$ as XXZ. The lower order terms are all the terms that can be constructed by taking one or two of the three letters of XXZ, that is, $X, Z, X^2 = XX$, and XZ. The equation is estimated by taking centered x and centered z and forming the higher order terms from them. The new term $x^2 z$ is formed by squaring centered x and multiplying the square by centered z. This term represents the curvilinear by linear interaction between x and z if and only if all the other terms in Eq. (7.9.2) are included in the model; these are all the lower order terms that can be created from x and z.

In centered Eq. (7.9.2) the role of each term can be separately characterized, given the presence of all other terms in the equation. From Fig. 7.9.1 on average, intention to quit smoking increases on average as fear increases; hence B_1 is positive. The overall relationship of X to Y is concave downward; hence B_2 is negative. Intention to quit increases as self-efficacy (Z) increases; therefore B_3 is positive. As indicated, the XZ term represents the linear by linear component of the XZ interaction. If we ignored the curvilinear relationship of X to Y and just found the best fitting straight line relating X to Y at each value of Z, these simple regression lines would not be parallel; we have the synergistic interaction that as both fear and self-efficacy increase, intentions increase by more than just their sum; thus the B_4 term is positive. Finally, the B_5 term is positive. It is juxtaposed against the negative B_2 term, which carries the curvilinearity of the X–Y relationship. The positive B_5 term in a sense "cancels out" the downward curvilinearity in the B_2 term as Z increases; that is, when Z is high, the curvilinearity in the prediction of Y by X disappears.

Rearranging Eq. (7.9.2) to show the regression of Y on X at values of Z provides further insight.

$$(7.9.3) \qquad \begin{aligned} \hat{Y} &= B_1 X + B_4 XZ + B_2 X^2 + B_5 X^2 Z + B_3 Z + B_0 \\ \hat{Y} &= (B_1 + B_4 Z)X + (B_2 + B_5 Z)X^2 + (B_3 Z + B_0). \end{aligned}$$

Equation (7.9.3) is in the form of a second-order polynomial of the regression of Y on X. However, it is more complex than Eq. (6.2.3). In Eq. (7.9.3) we see that the overall linear regression of Y on X, given in the coefficient $(B_1 + B_4 Z)$ depends on the value of Z, as do both the extent of curvilinearity of the regression of Y on X^2, given in the coefficient $(B_2 + B_5 Z)$, and the intercept $(B_3Z + B_0)$. The coefficients $(B_1 + B_4Z)$, $(B_2 + B_5Z)$, and $(B_3Z + B_0)$ give the global form of the regression of Y on X. These are not simple slope coefficients.

CH07EX02

Table 7.9.1 characterizes the data and summarizes the outcome of the regression analysis. In Table 7.9.1B, Eq. (7.9.1) containing no interaction is estimated. Interestingly, the B_2 coefficient for X^2 is not different from zero. Fitting the data with a regression equation that does not capture the appropriate interaction leads to failure to detect the curvilinearity that exists for some portion (but not all) of the regression surface. Including the two interaction terms in the regression equation, as given in Table 7.9.1C, leads to an increment in R^2 of .03. The full interaction carried by the combination of the XZ and X^2Z terms accounts for 3% of variance in the criterion over and above the X, X^2 and Z terms, $F_{gain}(2, 244) = 8.30$, $p < .001$.

Putting the full regression equation of Table 7.9.1C into the form of Eq. (7.9.3) quantifies the relationships of x to y at values of Z observed in Fig. 7.9.1. The rearranged equation is given in Table 7.9.1D. Now we see that the term $(B_2 + B_5Z) = (-.052 + .065z)$ becomes less and less negative as the numerical value of z increases, consonant with the decreasing downward curvilinearity in the relationship of X to Y as Z increases. With $sd_z = .76$, substituting the values of $z_{low} = -.76$, $z_{mean} = 0.0$, and $z_{high} = .76$ yields the three simple regression equations given in Table 7.9.1D. At z_{low}, there is a strong curvilinear relationship between X and Y. This curvilinear relationship diminishes as z increases. In contrast, the linear component of the impact of x on y is close to zero at z_{low} and increases as z increases. These simple equations show

TABLE 7.9.1
Regression Analysis of Intention to Quit Smoking (Y) as a Function of Centered Fear of Health Effects of Smoking (x) and Centered Self-Efficacy for Quitting Smoking (z) $(n = 250)$

A. Summary statistics for centered x, x^2, centered z, xz, and x^2z

	Means and standard deviations			Correlations					
	M	sd		x	x^2	z	xz	x^2z	Y
x	0.00	1.22	x	1.00	.19	.32	.10	.58	.49
x^2	1.47	2.04	x^2		1.00	.07	.51	.23	.08
z	0.00	.76	z			1.00	-.01	.62	.65
xz	.29	.91	xz				1.00	.07	.14
x^2z	.12	1.95	x^2z					1.00	.58
Y	3.63	.86	Y						1.00

B. Centered regression equation with no interaction $(R^2_{Y.123} = .51)$
$$\hat{Y} = .224x^{**} - .008x^2 + .620z^{**} + 3.642.$$

C. Centered regression equation with curvilinear by linear interaction $(R^2_{Y.12345} = .54)$
$$\hat{Y} = .178x^{**} - .052x^{2*} + .551z^{**} + .164xz^{**} + .065x^2z^* + 3.651.$$

D. Centered regression equation with curvilinear by linear interaction showing regression of Y on X.
$$\hat{Y} = (.178 + .164z)x + (-.052 + .065z)x^2 + (.551z + 3.561)$$

$$\text{For } z_{low} = -.76: \quad \hat{Y} = .053x - .101x^{2**} + 3.230$$
$$\text{For } z_{mean} = 0.00: \quad \hat{Y} = .178x^{**} - .052x^{2*} + 3.651$$
$$\text{For } z_{high} = .76: \quad \hat{Y} = .304x^{**} - .003x^2 + 4.072$$

$^{**}p < .01$; $^*p < .05$.
$R^2_{Y.12345}$ is the squared multiple correlation from all 5 predictors.

quantitatively what we observe in Fig. 7.9.1. Estimating curvilinear by linear interactions has been useful theoretically; for an example, see Krause (1995). Aiken and West (1991) provide a full treatment of the probing of curvilinear by linear interactions, along with computer code for use in standard regression software.

7.10 INTERACTIONS AMONG SETS OF VARIABLES

In the curvilinear by linear interaction, Eq. (7.9.2), the interaction was carried by a set of predictors that included XZ and X^2Z. This is but one example of a broad characterization of interactions. All the statements previously made about interactions among single variables x, z, and w also hold for *sets* of variables X, Z, and W (here we denote a set of variables in bold italics). Specifically, if X is a set of k IVs ($x_i; i = 1, 2, \ldots, k$), and Z a different set of j IVs ($z_j; j = 1, 2, \ldots, j$), then we can form an XZ product set of kj variables by multiplying each x_i by each z_j. The X by Z interaction is found in the same way as

$$X \text{ by } Z = XZ \cdot X, Z.$$

As in Eq. (7.9.2) the interaction is now carried by a set of cross-product terms. Generalizing further, suppose we had two predictors X_1 and X_2 in set X, and two predictors Z_1 and Z_2 in set Z. Then our regression equation is as follows:

(7.10.1) $\hat{Y} = B_1X_1 + B_2X_2 + B_3Z_1 + B_4Z_2 + B_5X_1Z_1 + B_6X_1Z_2 + B_7X_2Z_1 + B_8X_2Z_2 + B_0.$

The interaction between sets X and Z is carried by the set of terms $[B_5X_1Z_1 + B_6X_1Z_2 + B_7X_2Z_1 + B_8X_2Z_2]$. To assess the contribution of the X by Z interaction to the overall regression over and above the first-order effects of the four individual predictors, we must use a hierarchical approach. The contribution of the interaction to variance accounted for in the criterion is the difference between $R^2_{Y.12345678}$ and $R^2_{Y.1234}$.

Interpretively, an exactly analogous joint or conditional meaning obtains for interactions of sets X and Z: the regression coefficients that relate Y to the X_i of the X set are not all constant, but vary with the changes in the Z_i values of the Z set (and, too, when X and Z are interchanged in this statement). Stated in less abstract terms, this means that the nature and degree of relationship between Y and X varies, depending on Z. Note again that if only the first-order effects of set X and Z are included, whatever is found to be true about the relationship of Y with X alone is true across the full range of the Z set. However, when an X by Z interaction is present, the relationship of the X set to the criterion changes with (is conditional on) changes in the Z_j values of Z. (Again, symmetry permits interchanging X and X_i with Z and Z_j.)

The importance of this analytic strategy lies in the fact that some of the most interesting findings and research problems in behavioral and social science lie in conditional relationships. For example, the relationship between performance on a learning task (Y) and anxiety (X) may vary as a function of psychiatric diagnosis (Z). As another example, the relationship between income (Y) and education (X) may vary as a function of race (Z). As yet another example, in aggregate data where the units of analysis are urban neighborhoods, the relationship between incidence of prematurity at birth (Y) and the female age distribution (X) may depend on the distribution of female marital status (Z). The reader can easily supply other examples of possible interactions. The reason we represent these research factors as sets is that it may take more than one variable to represent each or, in the language of our system, each research factor may have been represented in more than one aspect of interest to us (as discussed in Chapter 5). As we saw in Chapter 6, and again in Section 7.9, if a research factor has a curvilinear relationship to the criterion, then more than one predictor is required to represent that relationship. (If anxiety bore an inverted U-shaped relationship to performance, we would require two predictors X_i and X_i^2 to represent the linear and quadratic aspects of anxiety in the prediction equation.) Non-normally distributed variables (say, of age distributions in census tracts) may be represented in terms of their first three moments ($X_1 = \text{mean}, X_2 = sd, X_3 = \text{skew}$), and any categorical variable of more than two levels requires for complete representation at least two terms (see Chapter 8 for categorical predictors).

A most important feature of the aforementioned procedure is the interpretability of each of the single product terms $X_i Z_j$. As noted, the multiplication of the k X predictors of the X set by the j Z predictors of the Z set results in a product set that contains kj IVs (for example, the four IVs in Eq. 7.10.1). Each X_i is a specifiable and interpretable aspect of X and each Z_j is a specifiable and interpretable aspect of Z. Thus when partialed, each of these kj IVs, X_i by Z_j represents an interpretable aspect of X by aspect of Z interaction, a *distinct* conditional or joint relationship, and like any other IV, its B, sr, pr, and their common t test are meaningful statements of regression, correlation, and significance status.

There are issues in working with interactions of sets of predictors that bear consideration. First, we note in Eq. (7.10.1) that multiple cross-product terms necessarily include the same variable (e.g., the $X_1 Z_1$ and $X_1 Z_2$ terms both include X_1). If the predictors are not centered, then cross-product terms that share a common predictor will be highly correlated, rendering separate interpretation of the individual components of the interaction difficult. Centering will eliminate much of this correlation. Hence our recommendations for centering apply here. Second, the issue of how Type I error is allocated in testing the interaction must be considered. The omnibus test of the complete interaction is the hierarchical test of gain in prediction from the inclusion of all the cross-product terms that comprise the interaction. In the hierarchical regression, we would assign a nominal Type I error rate, say $\alpha = .05$, to the overall multiple degree of freedom omnibus test of the interaction. However, in Eq. (7.10.1), for example, four terms comprise the single set X by set Z interaction. If these terms are tested in the usual manner in the MR context, then a nominal Type I error rate, say $\alpha = .05$, will be assigned to each of the four components of the interaction. The overall collective error rate for the test of the set X by set Z will exceed the nominal Type I error rate. The issue here is closely related to the issue of multiple contrasts in the ANOVA contrast (see Kirk, 1995, pp. 119–123 for an excellent discussion), where thinking about assignment of Type I error to multiple contrasts versus an omnibus test is well developed. If there is only a global hypothesis that set X and set Z interact, then it is appropriate to assign a nominal Type I error rate, say $\alpha = .05$, to the overall multiple degree of freedom omnibus test of the interaction, and to control the collective error on the set of tests of the individual interaction components that comprise the overall test. If, on the other hand, there are a priori hypotheses about individual components of the overall interaction, then following practice in ANOVA, one may assign a nominal Type I error rate to the individual contrast.

As discussed in Chapter 5, the concept of set is not constrained to represent aspects of a single research factor such as age, psychiatric diagnostic group, or marital status distribution. Sets may be formed that represent a functional class of research factors, for example, a set of variables collectively representing demographic status, or a set made up of the subscales of a personality questionnaire or intelligence scale, or, as a quite different example, one made up of potential common causes, that is, variables that one wishes to statistically control while studying the effects of others. However defined, the global X by Z interactions and their constituent $X_i Z_j$ single-interaction IVs are analyzed and interpreted as described previously.

7.11 ISSUES IN THE DETECTION OF INTERACTIONS: RELIABILITY, PREDICTOR DISTRIBUTIONS, MODEL SPECIFICATION

7.11.1 Variable Reliability and Power to Detect Interactions

The statistical power to detect interaction effects is a serious concern. We pointed out that interactions typically observed in psychological and other social science research often account for only a few percentage points of variance over and above first-order effects (i.e., squared semipartial or part correlations of .01 to .05 or so). J. Cohen (1988) defined squared partial correlations of .02, .13, and .26 of a term in MR with the criterion as representing small, moderate, and large effect sizes, respectively. Large effect size interactions are rarely found in observational studies in social science, business, and education; small to moderate effect size interactions predominate.

If predictors are measured without error (i.e., are perfectly reliable), then the sample size required to detect interactions in Eq. (7.1.2) are 26 for large effect size, 55 for moderate effect size, and 392 for small effect size interaction (J. Cohen, 1988). Even though fixed effects regression analysis assumes error-free predictors (see Chapter 4), in reality predictors are typically less than perfectly reliable. In fact, we are typically pleased if the reliabilities of our predictors reach .80.

The reliability of the XZ cross-product term in Eq. (7.1.2) is a function of the reliabilities of the individual variables. With population reliabilities ρ_{xx} and ρ_{zz} for X and Z, respectively, the reliability $\rho_{xz,xz}$ of the cross-product term of two *centered* predictors x and z with uncorrelated *true scores* (see Section 2.10.2) is the product of the reliabilities of the individual predictors (Bohrnstedt & Marwell, 1978; Busemeyer & Jones, 1983):

(7.11.1) $$\rho_{xz,xz} = \rho_{xx}\rho_{zz}$$

For example, if two uncorrelated predictors X and Z each have an acceptable reliability of .80, the estimate of reliability of their cross-product term according to Eq. (7.11.1) is quite a bit lower at $(.8)(.8) = .64$. The effect of unreliability of a variable is to reduce or *attenuate* its correlation with other variables (as discussed in Section 2.10.2). If a predictor is uncorrelated with other predictors in an equation, then the effect of unreliability of the predictor is to attenuate its relationship to the criterion, so its regression coefficient is underestimated relative to the true value of the regression coefficient in the population. With centered x and z in Eq. (7.1.2), we expect minimal correlation between the x and xz, and between the z and xz terms; the nonessential multicollinearity has been eliminated by centering (see Section 7.2.4). Thus, when individual predictors are less than perfectly reliable, the interaction term is even more unreliable, and we expect the power to detect the interaction term to be reduced, relative to the power to detect the first-order effects, even if they have equal effect sizes in the population. When predictors X and Z have reliability 1.0 and the true effect size of the interaction is moderate, 55 cases are required for power .80 to detect the interaction. When each predictor (X, Z) has reliability .88, the required sample size for power .80 to detect an interaction ranges from 100 to 150 or more, depending on the amount of variance accounted for by the main effects of X and Z. For a small effect size interaction, the required sample size for .80 power to detect an interaction may exceed 1000 cases when the reliabilities of the individual predictors are each .80! (See Aiken and West, 1991, Chapter 8, for an extensive treatment of reliability, effect sizes, and power to detect interactions between continuous variables.)

7.11.2 Sampling Designs to Enhance Power to Detect Interactions—Optimal Design

Reviews of observational studies indicate that interactional effects may be of only a small magnitude. In contrast, interactions with substantially larger effect sizes are often obtained in experiments. Moreover, the types of interactions in experiments are often disordinal interactions (Section 7.7.1). Such interactions are much easier to detect statistically than are the ordinal interactions typically found in observational studies. In experiments carried out in laboratory settings, the experimental conditions are likely to be implemented in a highly structured fashion, such that all cases in a condition receive a nearly identical treatment manipulation. This same control cannot be exercised in observational studies, where scores on IVs are merely gathered as they exist in the sample (though efforts can be made to have highly reliable measures).

To further compare experiments with observational studies, we need to make a translation from the levels of a treatment factor consisting of a treatment and a control condition to a predictor in MR. In fact, a binary variable (consisting of two values, here corresponding to treatment and control) can be entered as a predictor in MR. A code variable is created that equals $+1$ for all cases who are in the treatment condition and -1 for all cases who are in the control condition, referred to as an *effect code*. The conditions of an experiment are thus translated into a predictor in MR. Chapter 8 is devoted to the treatment of categorical variables in MR and the creation of such code variables.

A second and critical source of difference between experiments and observational studies with regard to detection of interactions is the distribution of the predictor variables. McClelland and Judd (1993) provide an exceptionally clear presentation of the impact of predictor distribution on power to detect interactions; highlights are summarized here. McClelland and Judd draw on *optimal design*, a branch of research design and statistics that characterizes designs that maximize statistical power to detect effects and provide the shortest confidence intervals (i.e., smallest standard errors) of parameter estimates. In experiments, predicting linear effects, the treatment conditions are implemented at the ends of a continuum, as characterized in Section 7.7.2. Again, the IVs corresponding to the coded variables are typically effects codes in which a two-level treatment factor is coded $(+1, -1)$. Thus the scores of all the subjects on the treatment predictor are at one or the other extreme of the continuum from -1 to $+1$; there are no scores in the middle. If there are two 2-level factors (a 2×2 design), the resulting treatment conditions represent *four corners* of a two-dimensional surface—that is, hi-hi $(+1, +1)$; hi-lo $(+1, -1)$; lo-hi $(-1, +1)$, and lo-lo $(-1, -1)$. All the cases fall at one of the four corners based on their scores on the treatment predictors corresponding to the two factors.

The distribution of two predictors X and Z in an observational study is quite another matter. If X and Z are bivariate normally distributed, then cases in the four corners are extremely rare. Instead, most cases pile up in the middle of the joint distribution of X and Z. Given the same population regression equation and the same reliability of predictors, if predictors X and Z are bivariate normally distributed, then about 20 times as many cases are required to achieve the same efficiency to detect the XZ interaction as in the four-corners design!

The reader is warned that dichotomizing continuous predictors is not a way to increase the efficiency of observational studies to detect interactions (Cohen, 1983). Dichotomizing normally distributed predictors merely introduces measurement error because all the cases coded as being at a single value of the artificial dichotomy actually have substantially different true scores (they represent half the range of the predictor's distribution).

A possible strategy for increasing power to detect interactions in observational studies is to oversample extreme cases, if one has prior information about the value of the cases on the predictors (Pitts & West, 2001). Merely randomly sampling more cases won't offer as much improvement, since the most typical cases are in the middle of the distribution. If one oversamples extreme cases, then the efficiency of the data set (the statistical power) for detecting interactions will be improved. A downside of oversampling extreme cases is that the standardized effect size for the interaction in the sample will exceed that in the population, so that sample weights will be needed to be used to generate estimates of the population effects.

This discussion merely opens the door to the area of optimal design applied in multiple regression. As regression models change, optimal designs change. Pitts and West (2001) present an extensive discussion of sampling of cases to optimize the power of tests of interactions in MR, as do McClelland and Judd (1993). This consideration is important in the design of both laboratory and observational studies that seek to examine high-order effects.

7.11.3 Difficulty in Distinguishing Interactions Versus Curvilinear Effects

In Chapter 4 we discussed specification errors, that is, errors of estimating a regression equation in the sample that incorrectly represents the true regression model in the population. One form of specification error is of particular concern when we are studying interactions in MR. This error occurs when we specify an interactive model when the true model in the population is quadratic in form. That is, we estimate the model of Eq. (7.1.2):

(7.1.2) $$\hat{Y} = B_1 X + B_2 Z + B_3 XZ + B_0$$

when the correct model is as follows (Lubinski & Humphreys, 1990; MacCallum & Mar, 1995):

(7.11.2) $$\hat{Y} = B_1 X + B_2 Z + B_3 X^2 + B_0$$

or

(7.11.3) $$\hat{Y} = B_1 X + B_2 Z + B_3 X^2 + B_4 Z^2 + B_0$$

or even as follows (Ganzach, 1997):

(7.11.4) $$\hat{Y} = B_1 X + B_2 Z + B_3 X^2 + B_4 Z^2 + B_5 XZ + B_0.$$

When the true regression model is curvilinear in nature, with no interaction existing in the population, if Eq. (7.1.2) is mistakenly estimated in the sample, a significant interaction can potentially be detected. This possibility arises from the correlation between predictors X and Z. In the common situation in which IVs are correlated, the X^2 and Z^2 terms will be correlated with XZ. Centering X and Z does not eliminate this essential multicollinearity. Table 7.9.1A provides a numerical illustration. The correlation between x and z is .32; between x^2 and xz, .51. Only if x and z are completely uncorrelated will the correlations of x^2 and z^2 with xz be zero. Compounding these inherent correlations is unreliability of X and Z. This unreliability results in unreliability of the terms constructed from X and Z, that is, X^2, Z^2, and XZ (Busemeyer & Jones, 1983). In fact, the reliability of the X^2 and the Z^2 terms will be lower than that of the XZ term, except in the instance in which X and Z are completely uncorrelated (MacCallum & Mar, 1995). This is so because the reliability of the XZ term increases as the correlation between X and Z increases.

Lubinski and Humphreys (1990) suggested that one might choose between X^2, Z^2, and XZ as appropriate terms by assessing which of these three predictors contributed most to prediction over and above the X and Z terms. MacCallum and Mar (1995) in an extensive simulation study showed that this procedure is biased in favor of choosing XZ over the squared terms and attributed this outcome primarily to the lower reliability of the squared terms than the cross-product term.

There is currently debate about whether one should examine regression Eq. (7.11.2) when the analyst's central interest is in the XZ term. To guard against spurious interactions (i.e., interactions detected in a sample that do not exist in the population, particularly in the face of true quadratic effects), Ganzach (1997) has argued in favor of using Eq. (7.11.4); he provides empirical examples of the utility of doing so. Both Aiken and West (1991) and MacCallum and Mar (1995) argue that terms included should be substantively justified and caution that the inclusion of multiple higher order terms in a single regression equation will introduce multicollinearity and instability of the regression equation.

7.12 SUMMARY

Interactions among continuous predictors in MR are examined. Such interactions are interpreted and illustrated as conditional relationships between Y and two or more variables or variable sets; for example, an X by Z interaction is interpreted as meaning that the regression (relationship) of Y to X is conditional on (depends on, varies with, is not uniform over) the status of Z. An interaction between two variable sets X and Z is represented by multiplication of their respective IVs and then linearly partialing out the X and Z sets from the product set. The contribution of the X by Z interaction is the increment to R^2 due to the XZ products over and above the X set and Z set.

The regression equation $\hat{Y} = B_1X + B_2Z + B_3XZ + B_0$ is first explored in depth. The geometric representation of the regression surface defined by this regression equation is provided. The first-order coefficients (B_1, B_2) for predictors X and Z, respectively, in an equation containing an XZ interaction represent the regression of Y on each predictor at the value of zero on the other predictor; thus B_1 represents the regression of Y on X at $Z = 0$. Zero is typically not meaningful on psychological scales. Centering predictors (i.e., putting them in deviation form, $(x = X - M_X), (z = Z - M_Z)$ so that $M_X = M_Z = 0$) renders the interpretation of the first-order coefficients of predictors entering an interaction meaningful: the regression of Y on each predictor at the arithmetic mean of the other predictor (Section 7.2).

Post hoc probing of interactions in MR involves examining simple regression equations. Simple regression equations are expressions of the regression of Y on one predictor at specific values of another predictor, as in the expression $\hat{Y} = [B_1 + B_3Z]X + [B_2Z + B_0]$ for the regression of Y on X at values of Z. Plotting these regression equations at several values across the range of Z provides insight into the nature of the interaction. The simple slope is the value of the regression coefficient for the regression of Y on one predictor at a particular value of the other predictor, here $[B_1 + B_3Z]$. The simple slope of Y on X at a specific value of Z may be tested for significance, and the confidence interval around the simple slope may be estimated (Sections 7.3 and 7.4).

Standardized solutions for equations containing interactions pose special complexities (Section 7.5). The structuring of regression equations containing interactions requires that all lower order terms be included for interaction effects to be accurately measured (Section 7.6).

Interactions in MR may take on a variety of forms. In interactions, predictors may work synergistically, one may buffer the effect of the other, or they may work in an interference pattern (i.e., in an "either-or" fashion). They may be ordinal (preserving rank order) or disordinal (changing rank order) within the meaningful range of the data (Section 7.7).

More complex equations containing interactions may involve three IVs (Section 7.8). They may also involve the interaction between a predictor that bears a curvilinear relationship to the criterion and one that bears a linear relationship to the criterion (Section 7.9). Further, interactions may occur between sets of predictors (Section 7.10).

Issues in the assessment of interactions in MR include the low statistical power for their detection, particularly in the face of predictor unreliability. The power to detect interactions also varies as a function of the distribution of predictors, particularly the extent to which there are scores at the extremes of the predictor distributions. It is difficult to distinguish between models containing an XZ interaction versus quadratic relationships X^2 or Z^2 except in experimental settings where X and Z are uncorrelated (Section 7.11).

8

Categorical or Nominal Independent Variables

8.1 INTRODUCTION

8.1.1 Categories as a Set of Independent Variables

In this chapter, we introduce the options for treating categorical variables (nominal or qualitative scales) as independent variables in MRC. These IVs, such as religion or experimental treatments, may be represented by sets of IVs known as code variables. Each code variable represents a different aspect of the nominal variable. Taken together, the set of code variables represents the full information available in the original categories. As we will see, several different methods of selecting code variables are available, with the best method being determined by the researchers' central questions.

Our presentation in this initial chapter on categorical IVs is limited to simple regression models that do not involve interactions or nonlinear relationships. However, the central idea of this chapter—the representation of nominal variables as a set of code variables—sets the stage for the consideration of more complex regression models that include nominal IVs. Chapter 9 then considers more complex models, including curvilinear relationships in experiments, interactions between nominal variables, and interactions between nominal and continuous variables. In each case, the basic ideas presented in the present chapter provide the foundation for the interpretation of unstandardized Bs in even the most complex regression models involving nominal variables.

8.1.2 The Representation of Categories or Nominal Scales

Nominal scales or categories are those that make qualitative distinctions among the objects they describe such as religion, treatment groups in experiments, region of country, ethnic group, occupation, diagnosis, or marital status. Each such research factor G categorizes the participants into one of g groups, where $g \geq 2$. The g groups are mutually exclusive and exhaustive: No participant is in more than one category, and all participants are categorized into one of the groups. Again, in the general case the g groups are not necessarily ordered from "lower" to "higher." To use nominal variables as IVs in MRC, it is necessary to represent them quantitatively, that is, as numbers. This problem can be summarized as "How do you score religion?"

There are several frequently used coding systems among the many possible systems used to accomplish this scoring. As we will see in this chapter, each system, *taken as a set*, produces identical results for the overall effect of the nominal variable (R, R^2, and the F test of significance of the IV). However, the regression coefficients produced for each of the variables in the set when considered simultaneously answer different questions, depending on the coding system. All coding systems use $g - 1$ different IVs (code variables) to represent the g groups, each representing *one* aspect of the distinctions among the g groups. As we will see, there are several different rationales for choosing the code variable set, because each of the alternatives will put the focus on different specific aspects of the differences among the groups. An important characteristic of alternative coding systems to be noted by the novice is that the numerical value and the interpretation of a regression coefficient for any given variable in the set may change as a function of the coding system that is chosen.

Taken as a set, the $g - 1$ code variables that comprise the coding system, however selected, represent all the information contained in the nominal scale or categories. Thus, if our nominal scale of religion is a classification into the $g = 4$ categories Catholic, Protestant, Jewish, and Other (in which we have decided to include "None" so that all respondents are categorized[1]), it will take $g - 1 = 3$ code variables [C_1, C_2, C_3] to fully represent the information in this classification. One might think that it would take $g = 4$ code variables [C_1, C_2, C_3, C_4] to do so, but in our MRC model, the C_4 variable would be fully redundant with (predictable from) the other three and thus C_4 provides no additional information beyond what is contained in the set [C_1, C_2, C_3]. This redundancy is most easily seen if we consider a nominal variable with $g = 2$ categories such as gender. Once we have a code variable to identify all females, anyone left over is a male; the distinction on sex has been completely made. A second code variable identifying males would provide no new information about the distinction on sex. Indeed, the gth code variable is not only unnecessary, but mathematically mischievous: Its redundancy renders the regression equation not (uniquely) solvable (see Section 10.5.1 on exact collinearity).

Given that religion can be represented by a set of three code variables, what are they? Among the more popular choices are dummy variables, unweighted effects, weighted effects, and planned contrasts. Each of these coding systems leads to a different interpretation of the meaning of the results for the individual code variables. Researchers should choose the coding system that provides information that most directly addresses their substantive research questions.

8.2 DUMMY-VARIABLE CODING

8.2.1 Coding the Groups

Consider the example of the four groups (Catholic, Protestant, Jewish, and Other) that comprise our nominal variable of religion. Table 8.2.1 presents alternative dummy-variable coding schemes that could be used for our numerical example. In dummy coding, one group (in Table 8.2.1B, Protestant) is designated as the reference group and is assigned a value of 0 for every code variable. The choice of the reference group is statistically but not substantively arbitrary. Hardy (1993) has suggested three practical considerations that should guide this choice. First, the reference group should serve as a useful comparison (e.g., a control group;

---

[1]This decision is substantive rather than statistical, possibly made because the numbers in both groups are too small to produce reliable estimates, and the expected differences from other groups too heterogeneous to investigate in either group.

TABLE 8.2.1
Illustration of Dummy-Variable Coding Systems:
Religious Groups

A. Catholic as reference group.				C. Jewish as reference group.			
	Code variables				Code variables		
Religion	C_1	C_2	C_3	Religion	C_1	C_2	C_3
Catholic	0	0	0	Catholic	1	0	0
Protestant	1	0	0	Protestant	0	1	0
Jewish	0	1	0	Jewish	0	0	0
Other	0	0	1	Other	0	0	1

B. Protestant as reference group (used in chapter).				D. Other as reference group			
	Code variables				Code variables		
Religion	C_1	C_2	C_3	Religion	C_1	C_2	C_3
Catholic	1	0	0	Catholic	1	0	0
Protestant	0	0	0	Protestant	0	1	0
Jewish	0	1	0	Jewish	0	0	1
Other	0	0	1	Other	0	0	0

the group expected to score highest or lowest on Y; a standard treatment). Second, for clarity of interpretation of the results, the reference group should be well defined and not a "wastebasket" category (e.g., "Other" for religion). Third, the reference group should *not* have a very small sample size relative to the other groups. This consideration enhances the likelihood of replication of individual effects in future research. We chose Protestant as the reference category for the example we will use in this chapter. Protestant is a well-defined category, and Protestants represent the largest religious group in the United States population. We also chose Protestants for a purely pedagogical reason (contrary to Hardy's first recommendation). Protestants are expected to have a mean somewhere in the middle of the scale for the DV in this (fictitious) example, attitude toward abortion (ATA). This choice permits us to illustrate the interpretation of outcomes in which other groups have higher as well as lower means than our reference group.

Having chosen Protestant as our reference group, each of the other groups is given a value of 1 on the dummy-coded variable that will contrast it with the reference group in the regression analysis and a value of 0 on the other dummy-coded variables. As is illustrated in Table 8.2.1B, C_1 contrasts Catholic with Protestant, C_2 contrasts Jewish with Protestant, and C_3 contrasts Other with Protestant in the regression equation. All $g - 1$ code variables (here, 3) must be included in the regression equation to represent the overall effect of religion. Each code variable contributes 1 df to the overall $g - 1$ df that comprise the nominal variable. If some of the code variables are omitted, the interpretation of each of the effects can dramatically change (see Serlin & Levin, 1985). Indeed, we will see later in this section that the interpretation of zero-order (simple Pearson) correlations or Bs of dummy variables with Y is strikingly different from the interpretation of regression coefficients.

The other sections in Table 8.2.1 show alternative dummy codes in which each of the categories of religion are taken as the reference group. Table 8.2.1A shows that coding system taking Catholic as the reference group, Table 8.2.1C shows the coding system taking Jewish as the reference group, and Table 8.2.1D shows the coding system taking Other as the reference group. In each case, the group whose row entries are coded [0 0 0] will be the reference group when the variables are considered as a set. The specific group being contrasted with the reference group in the regression analysis by the specific code variable (e.g., C_1) is represented by a 1.

Table 8.2.2 displays other examples of dummy coding of nominal variables. In Part A, four regions of the United States are represented by $g - 1 = 3$ dummy codes. In this example, South was chosen as the reference group. In Table 8.2.2B, three treatment conditions in a randomized experiment are represented by 2 dummy codes with Control as the reference group. In Table 8.2.2C, sex is represented by a single dummy code with male as the reference group. The coding systems presented in this chapter are completely general and can be applied to any nominal variable with 2 or more categories. Whether the nominal variable represents a natural category like religion or experimental treatment groups has no consequence for the analysis.

Table 8.2.3 presents hypothetical data for our example of the four religious groups for $n = 36$ cases. The sample sizes of these groups are Catholic ($n_1 = 9$), Protestant ($n_2 = 13$), Jewish ($n_3 = 6$), and Other ($n_4 = 8$). Throughout this chapter we will use these four groups and the dependent variable of attitude toward abortion (ATA) as our illustration. On this measure, higher scores represent more favorable attitudes. The sample sizes are deliberately unequal because this is the more general case. Where equal sample sizes simplify the interpretation of

TABLE 8.2.2
Other Illustrations of Dummy-Variable Coding

A. Dummy coding of regions of the United States ($g = 4$).

	Code variables		
Region	C_1	C_2	C_3
Northeast	1	0	0
Midwest	0	1	0
West	0	0	1
South	0	0	0

B. Dummy coding of experimental treatment groups ($g = 3$).

	Code variables	
Experimental group	C_1	C_2
Treatment 1	1	0
Treatment 2	0	1
Control	0	0

C. Dummy coding of sex ($g = 2$).

	Code variable
Sex	C_1
Female	1
Male	0

Note: The reference group for each dummy variable coding scheme is in boldface type.

CH08EX01

TABLE 8.2.3
Illustrative Data for Dummy-Variable Coding for
Religion and Attitude Toward Abortion ($g = 4$)

Case no.	Group	DV	C_1	C_2	C_3
1	C	61	1	0	0
2	O	78	0	0	1
3	P	47	0	0	0
4	C	65	1	0	0
5	C	45	1	0	0
6	O	106	0	0	1
7	P	120	0	0	0
8	C	49	1	0	0
9	O	45	0	0	1
10	O	62	0	0	1
11	C	79	1	0	0
12	O	54	0	0	1
13	P	140	0	0	0
14	C	52	1	0	0
15	P	88	0	0	0
16	C	70	1	0	0
17	C	56	1	0	0
18	J	124	0	1	0
19	O	98	0	0	1
20	C	69	1	0	0
21	P	56	0	0	0
22	J	135	0	1	0
23	P	64	0	0	0
24	P	130	0	0	0
25	J	74	0	1	0
26	O	58	0	0	1
27	P	116	0	0	0
28	O	60	0	0	1
29	J	84	0	1	0
30	P	68	0	0	0
31	P	90	0	0	0
32	P	112	0	0	0
33	J	94	0	1	0
34	P	80	0	0	0
35	J	110	0	1	0
36	P	102	0	0	0

Group means: $M_C = 60.67$; $M_P = 93.31$; $M_J = 103.50$; $M_O = 70.13$.

Note: DV is attitude toward abortion. Higher scores represent more favorable attitudes. For religious group, C = Catholic; P = Protestant; J = Jewish; O = Other.

the results, this will be pointed out. Table 8.2.3 also includes the set of dummy code variables C_1, C_2, and C_3 presented in the coding system in Part B of Table 8.3.1. Thus, cases 3, 7, 13, 15, and 21 (among others) are Protestant. As members of the reference group, their C_1, C_2, C_3 scores are [0 0 0]. Similarly, cases 1, 4, and 5 (among others) are Catholic and are scored [1 0 0]; cases 18, 22, and 25 (among others) are Jewish and are scored [0 1 0]; and Cases 2, 6 and 9 (among others) are members of other religions and are scored [0 0 1].

TABLE 8.2.4

Correlations, Means, and Standard Deviations of the Illustrative
Data for Dummy-Variable Coding

		r				r^2_{Yi}	$t_i (df = 34)$
		ATA	C_1	C_2	C_3		
ATA		1.000	−.442	.355	−.225	—	
Catholic	C_1	−.442	1.000	−.258	−.309	.1954	−3.214*
Jewish	C_2	.355	−.258	1.000	−.239	.1260	0.881
Other	C_3	−.225	−.309	−.239	1.000	.0506	−2.203*
	M	81.69	.250	.167	.222		
	sd	27.88	.439	.378	.422		

$R^2_{Y.123} = .3549$; $F = 5.869*$ $(df = 3,\ 32)$.
$\tilde{R}^2_{Y.123} = .2945$.

Note: C_1 is the dummy code for Catholic, C_2 is the dummy code for Jewish, and C_3 is the dummy code for Other religions (see Table 8.2.1B). C_1 represents Catholic vs. non-Catholic, C_2 represents Jewish vs. non-Jewish, and C_3 represents Other vs. non-Other, if each code variable is taken separately. ATA = attitude toward abortion. $*P < .05$.

Through the use of dummy codes, the categorical information has been rendered in quantitative form. We can now fully and meaningfully exploit the data in Table 8.2.3 through the use of MRC: Statistics on individual variables and combinations of variables can be computed, bounded by confidence limits, and tested for statistical significance to provide projections to the population. The MRC results for our illustrative example are given in Tables 8.2.4 and 8.2.5.

TABLE 8.2.5

Analysis of Illustrative Data: Attitude Toward Abortion

A. Dummy-variable coding: partial and semipartial correlations and regression coefficients.

C_i	pr_i	pr_i^2	sr_i	sr_i^2	β_i	B_i	SE_{B_i}	t_i
C_1	−.494	.2441	−.456	.2083	−.5141	−32.64	10.16	−3.214*
C_2	.154	.0237	.125	.0157	.1382	10.19	11.56	0.882
C_3	−.363	.1317	−.313	.0978	−.3506	−23.18	10.52	−2.203*

B. Predicted values in groups.

$$\hat{Y} = B_1 C_1 + B_2 C_2 + B_3 C_3 + B_0$$
$$= -32.64 C_1 + 10.19 C_2 - 23.18 C_3 + 93.31.$$

Catholic:	$\hat{Y}_1 = -32.64(1) + 10.19(0) - 23.18(0) + 93.31 = 60.67 = \hat{Y}_1$
Protestant:	$\hat{Y}_2 = -32.64(0) + 10.19(0) - 23.18(0) + 93.31 = 93.31 = \hat{Y}_2$
Jewish:	$\hat{Y}_3 = -32.64(0) + 10.19(1) - 23.18(0) + 93.31 = 103.50 = \hat{Y}_3$
Other:	$\hat{Y}_4 = -32.64(0) + 10.19(0) - 23.18(1) + 93.31 = 70.13 = \hat{Y}_4$

$$sd^2_{Y-\hat{Y}} = sd^2_Y(1 - R^2) \frac{n}{(n-k-1)} = 27.49^2(1 - .3549) \frac{36}{36-3-1} = 548.41.$$

Note: $df = 32$. $*P < .05$.

8.2.2 Pearson Correlations of Dummy Variables With Y

Each dummy-code variable C_i is a dichotomy that expresses one meaningful aspect of group membership. For example, when considered alone, C_1 represents Catholic versus non-Catholic. When we calculate the Pearson correlation between C_1 and ATA, we get the point-biserial correlation (see Section 2.3.3) between Catholic versus non-Catholic and ATA in this sample. These r_{Yi} values are given in the first column of Table 8.2.4. Thus, Catholic versus non-Catholic status in this sample correlates $-.442$ with ATA or equivalently accounts for $(-.442)^2 = .1954$ of the variance in ATA (column labeled r_{Yi}^2). Jewish versus non-Jewish status correlates $.355$ and accounts for $(.355)^2 = .1260$ of the ATA variance. Other versus non-Other (Catholic, Protestant, and Jewish combined) correlates $-.225$ with ATA and accounts for $(-.225)^2 = .0506$ of the ATA variance.

Table 8.2.4 displays the correlations for the code variables corresponding to Catholic, Jewish, and Other. However, no correlations or proportions of variance accounted for are given for the reference group, here Protestant. How do we get these values? There are two ways. First, we can rerun the analysis using any of the other dummy variable coding systems shown in Table 8.2.1 in which Protestant is *not* the reference group. For example, if we use the dummy codes in Part A of the table, we find that Protestant versus non-Protestant correlates $.318$ with ATA and the proportion of variance accounted for is $(.318)^2 = .1011$. The r_{Yi} values for Jewish and Other in this second analysis will be identical to those reported in Table 8.2.4. Alternatively, we can calculate r_{Yi} for the reference group from our knowledge of the proportion of subjects in the total sample in each group and the correlations of each of the dummy code variables with the dependent variable. When the proportion of subjects in each group is *not* equal,

(8.2.1)
$$r_{Yr} = \frac{\sum r_{Yi}\sqrt{P_i(1 - P_i)}}{\sqrt{P_r(1 - P_r)}}.$$

In this equation, r_{Yi} represents the correlations of each of the $g-1$ dummy codes with the dependent variable (ATA), r_{Yr} is the correlation of the reference group with the dependent variable, P_i is the proportion of the total sample in the group coded 1 on each dummy variable, and P_r is the proportion of the sample in the reference group. Applying this formula to our present example,

$$r_{Yr} = -\frac{-0.442\sqrt{(.25)(.75)} + .355\sqrt{(.167)(.833)} + (-.225)\sqrt{(.222)(.778)}}{\sqrt{(.361)(.639)}}$$

$$= .318.$$

When n_i is equal in each of the groups, Eq. (8.2.1) simplifies to $r_{Yr} = -\Sigma r_{Yi}$.

In interpreting the correlations, the sign of r_{Yi} indicates the direction of the relationship. If the group coded 1 has a higher mean than the mean of the other groups combined, then the sign is positive. For example, C_2 codes Jewish versus non-Jewish students. Since Jewish students had a higher mean ATA than non-Jewish students, the sign of r_{Y2} was positive. If the group coded 1 has a lower mean than the mean of the other groups combined, then the sign is negative (e.g., r_{Y1} for Catholic). The proportion of variance in Y accounted for is as described in Section 2.6, except that the source of the variance is group membership (for example, Catholic versus non-Catholic) rather than a continuous IV.

The interpretation of r_{Yi} and r_{Yi}^2 also requires careful attention to how cases were sampled. The magnitude of r_{Yi} will depend in part on the proportion of the sample that is composed of members of the group that is coded 1. We learned in Chapter 2 that rs increase directly with the variability of the variables being correlated. As noted, for dichotomies in which each case has a score of 0 or 1, the sample sd is $\sqrt{(P)(1-P)}$. Thus, the sd of a dummy variable depends solely on its proportion in the total sample. This value reaches its maximum when $P_i = .50$ for the group and becomes smaller as P_i either increases toward 1.0 or decreases toward 0.0. Because r_{Yi} varies with sd, the magnitude of a correlation with a dummy variable will change with the relative size of the group coded 1 in the total sample, reaching its maximum at $P_i = .50$. Therefore, the interpretation of any given r_{Yi} (or r_{Yi}^2) depends on the meaning of P_i in the sample.

To illustrate this point, let us revisit our example of religion and attitude toward abortion. If the 36 cases were randomly sampled from the population of students at a Midwestern university, then the r_{Yi} is a reasonable estimate of ρ_{Yi} in this population. This occurs because the proportion of each group in the sample reflects within sampling error the proportion of each group in this population. For the Catholic group (G_3), $P_i = 9/36 = .25$, $r_{Yi} = -.258$, and $r_{Yi}^2 = .0667$ in this Midwestern university sample. On the other hand, other university populations will have different proportions of Catholic students. If the random sample were now taken at another university in which the proportion of Catholic students were closer to .50 (i.e., $.25 < P_i < .75$), then r_{Yi}^2 would be larger, all other things being equal.

Another circumstance resulting in different r_{Yi}s is a sampling plan in which equal numbers of Catholics, Protestants, Jews, and Others are sampled from the population and their attitude toward abortion scores are measured. The equal Ps (.25) in the resulting data do not reflect the actual proportions of each group in the population. The resulting data will yield different r_{Yi}s from those obtained using random sampling. For our hypothetical Midwestern university population, we would expect no change in the correlation for Catholics (original $P_i = .250$), a smaller correlation for Protestants (original $P_i = .361$), a larger correlation for Jews (original $P_i = .167$), and a slightly larger correlation for Other (original $P_i = .222$) under this equal number sampling plan. In comparing the original correlations referenced on random sampling with the correlations referenced on equal sampling, the correlation for any group whose P_i was originally closer to .50 would be expected to decrease, whereas the correlation for any group whose P_i was originally further from .50 would be expected to increase. Once again, these changes in r_{Yi} occur with changes in the proportion of the group in the sample because the associated sds of the dummy variables correspondingly increase or decrease.

These examples illustrate the importance of carefully considering the population and the sampling method when interpreting correlations and squared correlations involving dummy variables. Correlations computed from random or other types of representative samples produce good estimates of the value of the correlation in that particular population. Correlations computed from samples containing an equal number of cases in each group permit generalization to a hypothetical population in which each group occurs in an equal proportion.[2] Such sampling plans are useful for two different reasons. First, there may be an interest in within-group effects in groups having a low proportion in the population. For example, researchers studying ethnic minority groups often oversample such groups in order to have sufficient numbers to study within group relationships with reasonable statistical power. Second, it may be that the theory generalizes not to a particular population but rather to abstract properties of subjects within a population, and subjects are therefore either selected or manipulated to allow a comparison of these properties with maximal statistical power (e.g., Pitts & West, 2001). The interpretation of the proportion of variance accounted for is then appropriate only for the hypothetical population with those relative group frequencies. In interpreting correlations,

---

[2]When the proportions of each group in the population are known and groups have been oversampled or undersampled relative to their respective population proportions, weighted regression techniques can be used to provide good estimates of the population values (Winship & Radbill, 1994). Weighted regression techniques were introduced in Section 4.5.4 in another context.

considerable care must be taken because of the effects of the population and the sampling plan on the obtained values.

Confidence Intervals and Significance Tests for Bivariate r

In Section 2.8.2, we considered the confidence interval for r. The calculation of a confidence interval (CI) for a correlation between a dichotomous (e.g., dummy-coded) and a continuous variable follows the identical procedure.

To briefly review, the upper and lower limits of the CI do not fall at equal distances from r. We use the Fisher z' transformation of r to bypass this problem. Values of the r to z' transform are given in Appendix Table B. For our Midwestern University example, $-.44$ (rounded down) is the correlation between the dummy code corresponding to Catholic and favorable attitude toward abortion. This r converts to a z' of .472. z' has an approximately normal distribution and a standard error as applied to Eq. (2.8.3) of

$$SE_{z'} = \frac{1}{\sqrt{n-3}} = \frac{1}{\sqrt{36-3}} = .174.$$

For the 95% confidence interval, we then find the upper and lower limits for z'. Recall that for the normal distribution, 1.96 is the multiplier for the standard error to construct the confidence limits (see Appendix Table C). Thus, the confidence interval is $.472 \pm (1.96)(.174)$. This gives the 95% limits for z' as .131 and .813. We then convert these values back to r, again using Appendix Table B, and restore the original negative sign for the correlation. This results in a 95% confidence interval for r from $-.13$ to $-.67$.

For researchers who prefer significance tests, we can alternatively test the obtained sample correlation against a population value of $\rho = 0$ as discussed in Section 2.8.3. We use Eq. (2.8.10) reproduced below:

(2.8.10) $$t = \frac{r\sqrt{n-2}}{\sqrt{1-r^2}} \quad \text{with} \quad df = n - 2.$$

For our Midwestern University example, $r = -.442$ for the correlation between Catholic and favorable attitude towards abortion referenced on our 36 cases. Substituting into the formula, we find

$$t = \frac{-.442\sqrt{36-2}}{\sqrt{1-(-.442)^2}} = -2.87.$$

For $df = n - 2 = 34$, this value of t (ignoring the negative sign) easily exceeds the $p < .05$ significance criterion of 2.032. We therefore reject H_0 and conclude there is a negative correlation in the Midwestern University population between being Catholic and having a favorable attitude toward abortion.

This is exactly the same t value we would obtain if we used the familiar t test for the means between two independent groups,

(8.2.2) $$t = \frac{M_{Y_1} - M_{Y_0}}{\sqrt{SD^2_{pooled}\left(\frac{1}{n_1} + \frac{1}{n_2}\right)}},$$

to test the difference between the means of ATA for Catholic and non-Catholic groups. The two significance tests represented by Eqs. (2.8.10) and (8.2.2) are algebraically identical when two groups are being compared.[3] The chief advantage of the use of the t test of r rather the t test of the

---

[3]Eq. (2.3.7), $r_{pb} = (M_{Y_1} - M_{Y_0})\sqrt{PQ}/sd_Y$, reminds us that the point biserial correlation can be expressed directly in terms of the mean difference.

mean difference between the two groups is that it gives us the proportion of variance accounted for (r^2) directly. The correlational context also helps remind us of the critical importance of the sampling plan in interpreting our results. The population and sampling issues discussed in the previous section are equally important in interpreting group differences in observational studies and in experiments, but these issues are often ignored.

8.2.3 Correlations Among Dummy-Coded Variables

The definition of nominal variables requires that each case be classified into one and only one group. For such mutually exclusive categories, the correlation between pairs of categories must be negative. If a person who is Protestant is necessarily non-Catholic, and if Catholic, necessarily non-Protestant. However, this correlation is never -1.00 when there are more than two categories: a person who is non-Protestant, may be either Catholic or non-Catholic, because there are other groups (Jewish, Other) as well. Because these correlations are between dichotomies (e.g., Catholic vs. non-Catholic; Jewish vs. non-Jewish), they are phi coefficients (see Section 2.3.4) and can be computed by hand or computer using the usual Pearson product-moment correlation formula. The correlation between two dummy codes (C_i, C_j) can be calculated using the following formula:

$$r_{ij} = -\sqrt{\frac{n_i n_j}{(n - n_i)(n - n_j)}} = -\sqrt{\frac{P_i P_j}{(1 - P_i)(1 - P_j)}}.$$

For example, the correlation between the dummy codes representing Catholic and Jewish in our running example is

$$r_{12} = -\sqrt{\frac{(.250)(.167)}{(1 - .250)(1 - .167)}} = -.259.$$

Thus, we conclude that dummy codes, which represent separate aspects of the nominal variable G, will necessarily be partly redundant (correlated with each other). This conclusion has two important implications that will be developed more fully in Sections 8.2.5 and 8.2.6. First, the unstandardized regression coefficients will usually be the focus of interpretation. They compare the unique effect of the group of interest (e.g., Catholic) with the effects of other groups that comprise the nominal variable G held constant. Second, we cannot find the proportion of variance in Y due to G simply by summing the separate r_{Yi}^2 for the $g - 1$ dummy variables. We must necessarily use the squared multiple correlation which takes into account the redundancy (correlation) between the set of dummy codes that comprise G. To see this, readers may compare the sum of the values in the r_{Yi}^2 column of Table 8.2.4 with the value of $R_{Y.123}^2$. The value of $R_{Y.123}^2$ is less than the sum of the r_{Yi}^2 values because of the partial redundancy among the dummy codes.

8.2.4 Multiple Correlation of the Dummy-Variable Set With Y

Returning to our running example of the effects of religion on ATA, we can write a regression equation that specifies the influence of the set of dummy-coded variables in the usual way,

(8.2.3) $$\hat{Y} = B_1 C_1 + B_2 C_2 + B_3 C_3 + B_0.$$

When we run an MRC analysis using this equation and the religion and attitude toward abortion data in Table 8.2.3, we find that $R_{Y.123}^2 = .3549$. Since the three dummy codes C_1, C_2, and

C_3 as a set comprise the group (here, religion), this also means that $R^2_{Y.G} = .3549$. As noted earlier, any of the dummy-variable coding systems shown in Table 8.2.1 will yield this same value for $R^2_{Y.G}$. We thus can state that 35.5% of the variance in ATA scores is associated with religion in this sample or that the R of ATA and religion is .596. Note that R^2 depends on the distribution of the n_i of the four groups; a change in the relative sizes holding the M_{Y_i}s constant would in general change R^2. This dependence on the P_i is characteristic of R, as it is of any kind of correlation, and must be kept in mind in interpreting the results.

We can construct a confidence interval for R^2 as shown in Section 3.6.2. In the present example, substituting into Eg. 3.6.2, we find

$$SE^2_{R^2} = \frac{4(.3549)(1 - .3549)(36 - 3 - 1)^2}{(36^2 - 1)(36 + 3)} = .0186.$$

The square root of this variance, SE_{R^2}, is the standard error of R^2, which is used in the calculation of the confidence interval, $SE_{R^2} = \sqrt{.0186} = .136$. From Appendix Table A, the critical value of t for $df = 32$ and $\alpha = .05$ is 2.037. The approximate 95% confidence interval is calculated as $R^2 \pm t(SE_{R^2}) = .3549 \pm (2.037)(.136)$. Thus, the 95% confidence interval for R^2 ranges from .0773 to .6325. This confidence interval is only approximate and should be interpreted cautiously given the relatively small n (see Olkin & Finn, 1995).

Alternatively, for researchers who prefer significance tests, we can use Eq. (3.6.5) (reproduced here) to test the significance of R^2 as compared to the null (nil) hypothesis:

(3.6.5) $$F = \frac{R^2(n - k - 1)}{(1 - R^2)k} = \frac{R^2(n - g)}{(1 - R^2)(g - 1)}.$$

Substituting in our present values, we find

$$F = \frac{.3549(36 - 4)}{(1 - .3549)(3)} = 5.869.$$

For $df = 3, 32$, the F required for significance at $\alpha = .05$ is 2.90 (see Appendix Table D.2), hence our obtained F is statistically significant. We reject the null hypothesis that religion accounts for no variance in ATA scores in the population that was sampled.

We may also wish to report the adjusted (or shrunken) R^2. We saw in Chapter 3 that R^2 provides an accurate value for the sample but overestimates the proportion of variance accounted for in the population. For a better estimate of the Y variance accounted for by religion in the population, we use Eq. (3.7.4) to estimate the shrunken R^2 as

$$\tilde{R}^2 = 1 - (1 - .3549)\frac{35}{32} = .2945.$$

Our best estimate of the proportion of ATA variance accounted for by religion in the population is 29.4%. Here again it is important to keep in mind how the sampling was carried out, because the population to which we may generalize is the one implicit in the sampling procedure.

8.2.5 Regression Coefficients for Dummy Variables

Let us consider the meaning of each of the unstandardized regression coefficients in the equation predicting Y in more depth. That equation (Eq. 8.2.3) as we have seen will be $\hat{Y} = B_1C_1 + B_2C_2 + B_3C_3 + B_0$. In our running example, $\hat{Y}$ is the predicted value of ATA, B_0 is the intercept, B_1 is unstandardized regression coefficient for the first dummy code, B_2 is the unstandardized regression coefficient for the second dummy code, and B_3 is the unstandardized regression coefficient for the third dummy code. If we use the dummy coding system presented in Table 8.2.1B in which Protestant is the reference group, then C_1 corresponds to Catholic, C_2 corresponds to Jewish, and C_3 corresponds to Other. Substituting the values of the dummy codes corresponding to each religion into the equation, we find

$$\text{Catholic:} \quad \hat{Y} = B_1(1) + B_2(0) + B_3(0) + B_0 = B_1 + B_0 = M_{\text{Catholic}};$$

$$\text{Protestant:} \quad \hat{Y} = B_1(0) + B_2(0) + B_3(0) + B_0 = B_0 = M_{\text{Protestant}} \text{ (reference group)};$$

$$\text{Jewish:} \quad \hat{Y} = B_1(0) + B_2(0) + B_3(0) + B_0 = B_2 + B_0 = M_{\text{Jewish}};$$

$$\text{Other:} \quad \hat{Y} = B_1(0) + B_2(0) + B_3(1) + B_0 = B_3 + B_0 = M_{\text{Other}}.$$

Thus, in Eq. (8.2.3) when $C_1 = 0$, $C_2 = 0$, and $C_3 = 0$ for the reference group (Protestant), the predicted value of Y equals B_0, the regression intercept, which also equals the mean of the reference group. The same value $\hat{Y} = B_0$ is predicted for all subjects in the reference group. A 1-unit change on C_1 (i.e., a change from $C_1 = 0$ to $C_1 = 1$) represents the difference in the value of the Group 1 (Catholic) mean from the reference group (Protestant) mean on the DV. A 1-unit change on C_2 represents the difference in the value of the Group 2 (Jewish) mean from the reference group mean on the DV. Finally, a 1-unit change in the value on C_3 represents the difference in the value of the Group 3 (Other) mean from the reference group mean on the DV. Thus, each regression coefficient and its significance test is a comparison of the mean of one of the groups with the mean of the reference group, here Protestant.

To illustrate these relationships for our numerical example,

$$\hat{Y} = -32.64C_1 + 10.19C_2 - 23.18C_3 + 93.31.$$

Table 8.2.5 shows the results of substituting the dummy codes corresponding to each religious group into this equation. For each group, $\hat{Y}$ is identical to the mean for the group shown in Table 8.2.3.

Graphical Depiction

Figure 8.2.1 depicts the results of the regression analysis graphically. Figure 8.2.1(A) shows the scatterplot of the raw data for the four religious groups, which have been numbered $1 =$ Catholic, $2 =$ Protestant, $3 =$ Jewish, and $4 =$ Other on the x axis. Over these values the plot displays the distribution of scores on ATA corresponding to each religious group.[4] Figure 8.2.1(B) shows the predicted values (group means) on ATA for each of the religious groups, again plotted over the numbers identifying each religious group. Figure 8.2.1(C) shows the residuals $Y_i - \hat{Y}_i$ from predicting each case's score on ATA. The values on the x axis are the predicted values, $\hat{Y}$, for each group. The residuals for each group are now displayed above their respective group means. Thus, the residuals for Catholic are displayed above 60.7 (the mean for the Catholic group; see Table 8.2.3), the residuals for Other are displayed above 70.1, the residuals for Protestant are displayed above 93.3, and the residuals for Jewish are displayed above 103.5. This plot allows us to examine whether the variability around the predicted values differs greatly across the groups (heteroscedasticity). Finally, Fig. 8.2.1(D) shows a q-q plot of

---

[4]In the present example, the simple scatterplot clearly presents the data because each person in a group has a different value on ATA. In larger data sets more than one person in the group (often many) may have the same value on the dependent variable. Each of these points will then be plotted on top of each other (overplotting) and cannot be distinguished. The graphical option of "jittering" points presented in Section 4.2.2 will help. Other graphs that allow for the comparisons of the distributions across the groups avoid these problems (see Cleveland, 1994).

(A) Scatterplot of raw data.   (B) Scatterplot of predicted ATA vs. group.

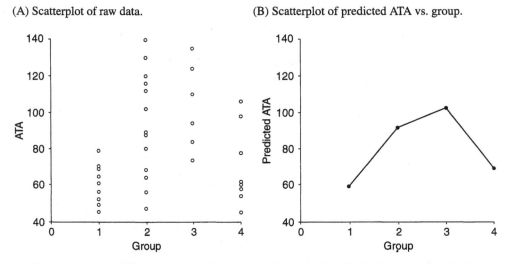

Note: In Parts (A) and (B), the values of religion are as follows: 1 = Catholic, 2 = Protestant, 3 = Jewish, 4 = Other. In Part (B) the predicted ATA values for each group are plotted over the group number. These predicted values equal the means for each group.

(C) Scatterplot of residuals vs. fit values.   (D) q-q plot of residuals against normal distribution.

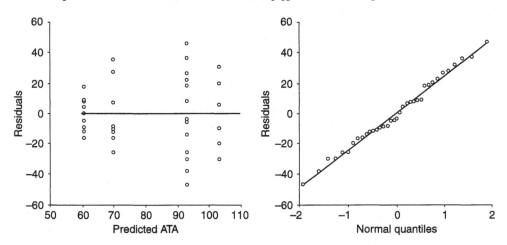

Note: In Part (C) the horizontal line indicates where the residuals = 0. In Part (D) the q-q plot of the residuals closely follows a straight line, indicating the residuals are normally distributed.

FIGURE 8.2.1   Results of regression analysis for religious groups and ATA.

the residuals against a normal distribution (see Section 4.4.6). The q-q plot indicates that the residuals approximate a straight line, so the assumption of normality of the residuals is met.

Confidence Intervals and Significance Tests for Regression Coefficients

Once again, we can directly use the methods for constructing confidence intervals and for performing significance tests for the unstandardized regression coefficients that were presented in Chapter 3. Each of the unstandardized regression coefficients has a t distribution with

$df = n - k - 1$, where k is the number of code variables ($= g - 1$). For our running example of religion, $df = 36 - 3 - 1 = 32$. Thus, to construct a confidence interval, we simply take $B_i \pm tSE_{B_i}$. In general, SE_{B_i} will differ for each dummy variable's regression coefficient.

To illustrate we construct 95% confidence intervals for each of the regression coefficients in our running example. For C_1, the dummy code for Catholic, $B_1 = -32.64$ and the corresponding SE is 10.15. From Appendix Table A, the critical value of t for $df = 32$ and $\alpha = .05$ is 2.037. Then the confidence interval (CI) is $-32.64 \pm (2.037)(10.15)$ which ranges from -53.31 to -11.96. The CI for each B is

$$B_1: \quad -32.64 \pm (2.037)(10.15) = -53.31 \quad \text{to} \quad -11.96;$$
$$B_2: \quad 10.19 \pm (2.037)(11.56) = -13.36 \quad \text{to} \quad 33.74;$$
$$B_3: \quad -23.18 \pm (2.037)(10.52) = -44.61 \quad \text{to} \quad -1.75;$$
$$B_0: \quad 93.31 \pm (2.037)(6.50) = 80.07 \quad \text{to} \quad 106.55.$$

indicating that we are 95% confident that the population difference between Protestants and Catholics on ATA is between -12 and -53, the difference between Protestants and Jews is between -13 and 34, the difference between Protestants and Others who are neither Catholics nor Jews is between -2 and -45, and the population mean for the reference group falls between 80 and 107. Of course, these estimates hold only for the population represented by the study sample (presumably students at a Midwestern University).

The significance tests of the null hypothesis that unstandardized regression coefficient $B_i = 0$ is similarly straightforward, t equaling the coefficient divided by its SE. In our running example, the null (nil) hypothesis significance test of the B_1 coefficient for Catholic is $t = -32.64/10.15 = -3.21$, which exceeds the magnitude of the critical $t = 2.037$ for $\alpha = .05$ and $df = 32$, leading us to the conclusion that the mean ATA is higher for Protestants than for Catholics. Researchers having a null hypothesis that the value of B_i is equal to some specific value c (e.g., $H_0: B_1 = -10$ in the population) can test this hypothesis by $t = (B_1 - c)/SE_{B_1}$ with $df = n - k - 1$. In this equation, c is the constant representing the new "null" hypothesis. In this case $[-32.64 - (-10)]/10.15 = 2.23$, which again exceeds the critical $t = 2.037$. Thus, the population mean for Protestants exceeds the population mean for Catholics by more than 10 points (a statement that might also have been based on the CI for this difference).

Finally, researchers may sometimes be interested in comparisons of two groups in which neither of these groups is the reference group. For example, the researcher may be interested in comparing the mean of the Catholic with the mean of the Jewish group. The easiest way to accomplish this is to rerun the analysis after the data have been recoded using another dummy coding system in which one of the groups being compared is the reference group. Rerunning the analysis with the dummy coding system from Table 8.2.1A, in which Catholic is the reference group, will yield $B_2 = 42.83$, indicating that the mean of ATA in the Jewish group is 42.83 larger than in the reference Catholic group. The analysis also produces $SE_{B_2} = 12.34$ and $t = 3.47$, $df = 32, p < .05$. Alternatively, this test may be performed by hand to compare B_i to B_j by

$$(8.2.4) \qquad t = \frac{B_i - B_j}{\sqrt{SE_{Y-\hat{Y}}\left(\frac{1}{n_i} + \frac{1}{n_j}\right)}},$$

where $SE_{Y-\hat{Y}}$ is the standard error of estimate available from the computer printout. Recall from Sections 2.6 and 3.6 that the standard error of estimate represents the standard deviation of the residuals about the regression line. Its square can also be expressed as

$$sd^2_{Y-\hat{Y}} = \frac{\sum(Y - \hat{Y})^2}{n - k - 1} = sd^2_Y(1 - R^2)\frac{n}{n - k - 1}$$

Applying this equation to the comparison of the Jewish (B_2) with the Catholic (B_1) groups, we find

$$t = \frac{10.19 - (-32.64)}{\sqrt{(23.42)^2 \left(\frac{1}{6} + \frac{1}{9}\right)}} = \frac{42.83}{12.34} = 3.47$$

which is significant at $p < .05$. Any other possible comparisons of group means not involving the reference group may also be carried out using these procedures.

At the same time, caution must be exercised in conducting such comparisons, particularly when there is not a strong a priori prediction that two specific groups will differ. Although it is possible to compare all pairs of group means, such procedures are not advisable because they increase the level of α for the study beyond the stated level, typically $\alpha = .05$. Kirk (1995, Chapter 4) and Toothaker (1991) present a full discussion of procedures for controlling the Type I error rate when multiple groups are compared.

Standardized Regression Coefficients

The standardized regression coefficient (β_i) is far less useful for nominal than for continuous variables. Unlike continuous variables, the variability of a dichotomy cannot be changed without also changing its mean (that is, the proportion of the sample coded 1). In the previous section we saw that unstandardized regression coefficients for dummy variables represent differences between means. These differences do not depend on the relative sizes of the groups. In general, the standardized β_i for coded nominal scales will vary with changes in the relative n_is, decreasing their general usefulness. When βs are reported, they must always be carefully interpreted in light of the population and sampling procedures, which will affect their magnitude. We have presented the standardized β_is in Table 8.2.5 for the sake of completeness.

8.2.6 Partial and Semipartial Correlations for Dummy Variables

Partial Correlation

The partial correlation is the correlation of X_i with that part of Y that is independent of the other IVs in the equation. In the specific context of dummy variables, holding the other IVs constant means retaining *only* the distinction between the ith group and the reference group. Concretely, pr_1 ($= -.494$; see Table 8.2.5) in our example is the correlation between ATA and Catholic versus non-Catholic, holding Jewish versus non-Jewish and Other versus non-Other constant. Consequently, $pr_1 = -.494$ is an expression in correlational terms of the difference between the Catholic group and Protestant group in ATA scores. Similarly, from Table 8.2.5, $pr_2 = .154$ relates ATA to Jewish versus Protestant (holding constant Catholic and Other) and $pr_3 = -.363$ relates ATA to Other versus Protestant (holding constant Catholic and Jewish). Otherwise stated, the pr_i can be viewed as a representation of B_i in a correlational rather than raw score metric. As with other measures of correlation, the interpretation of a given pr_i must take into account the population and sampling plan.

Semipartial Correlation

Recall that the squared semipartial correlation sr_i^2 is the amount by which $R_{Y.123...k}^2$ would be reduced if X_i were omitted from the IVs. That is, $sr_i^2 = R_{Y.123...k}^2 - R_{Y.123...(i)...k}^2$. Here, the ($i$) in the subscript symbolizes the omission of X_i. With dummy-variable coding, the omission of X_i is equivalent to collapsing group i in with the reference group. Consider what happens in our example if C_1 is omitted. Both Catholic and Protestant are coded $C_2 = 0$, $C_3 = 0$ and are therefore not distinguished. The result is that we have reduced our four original religious groups to three: Catholic/Protestant (combined), Jewish, and Other. We see in Table 8.2.5 that $sr_1^2 = .2083$. This means that the loss of the Catholic-Protestant distinction would result in the loss of 20.8% of the ATA variance accounted for by religion. Equivalently, our R^2 would drop from .3549 to .1468. Thus, sr_i^2 in dummy-variable regression provides a measure in terms of the proportion of total Y variance of the importance of distinguishing group i from the reference group. Thus, the Jewish-Protestant distinction (sr_2^2) accounts for only 1.6%, whereas the Other-Protestant distinction (sr_3^2) accounts for 9.8% of the ATA variance. We note again that these values, as all correlations involving dummy variables, are dependent on the proportions of the cases in each group.

In a previous section, we presented a significance test for the null (nil) hypothesis that $B_i = 0$ in the population. As noted in Chapter 3, t tests of partial coefficients including B_i, standardized β_i, pr_i, and sr_i for any given IV, including a dummy variable C_i will yield identical results. As we saw in Section 3.6, these equivalent t tests of the null (nil) hypothesis for partial relationships can be written in several different ways. One simple one in terms of the semipartial correlation and R^2 is given below:

$$t = sr_i \sqrt{\frac{n - k - 1}{1 - R^2}} \quad \text{with} \quad df = (n - k - 1).$$

Applying this equation to our example to test sr_1, we find

$$t = -.456 \sqrt{\frac{36 - 3 - 1}{1 - .3549}} = 3.214 \quad \text{with} \quad df = 32.$$

The results of this test are identical to the test of the unstandardized regression coefficient reported in Table 8.2.5. This value of $t = 3.214$ exceeds the required value of $t = 2.037$ for $\alpha = .05$, so we can reject the null hypothesis. The result of this test may be interpreted equivalently in terms of B_i, standardized β_i, pr_i, or sr_1^2. Interpreting the test for B_1, it shows that Catholics have a lower mean ATA score than Protestants (reference group). In terms of the partial correlation pr_1, if we consider only Catholics and Protestants in the population, there is a negative point-biserial correlation between this religious dichotomy and ATA. Finally, in terms of the squared semipartial correlation, sr_1^2, the test shows that if we dropped the distinction between Catholics and Protestants, R^2 would drop from its value obtained when religion is categorized into four groups.

8.2.7 Dummy-Variable Multiple Regression/Correlation and One-Way Analysis of Variance

Readers familiar with analysis of variance (ANOVA) may wonder about its relationship to MRC. Both are applications of the same general linear model, and when the independent variables are nominal scales they are identical. This equivalence has been obscured by differences in terminology between MRC and ANOVA, and divergent traditions that have linked observational designs with MRC and experimental designs with ANOVA (see Chapter 1; also Aiken & West, 1991, Chapter 9; Tatsuoka, 1975).

Viewed from the perspective of ANOVA, the problem addressed in this chapter is one way analysis of variance. We have considered g levels of a factor, with n_i observations on Y in each group. For the illustrative data of Table 8.2.3 we would assemble the Y values into the g-designated groups and proceed to find three sums of squares: total (SS_{TOTAL}), between groups (SS_{BG}), and within groups (SS_{WG}). These sums of squares are defined as follows:

$$SS_{TOTAL} = \sum (Y_j - M_G)^2 \qquad\qquad df_{TOTAL} = n - 1;$$
$$SS_{BG} = \sum n_i (M_i - M_G)^2 \qquad\qquad df_{BG} = g - 1;$$
$$SS_{WG} = SS_{TOTAL} - SS_{BG} \qquad\qquad df_{WG} = n - g.$$

In these equations Y_j is the score on Y for subject j, M_i is the mean of the ith group, n_i is the number of subjects in the ith group, M_G is the grand mean (the unweighted mean of the group means), g is the number of groups, and n is the total number of subjects in the entire sample. As is shown in Table 8.2.6 for our running example of attitude toward abortion, each SS is divided by its corresponding df, yielding three mean square (MS) values. The mean square between groups (MS_{BG}) is then divided by the mean square within groups (MS_{WG}) to yield an F statistic. This F statistic tests the null (nil) hypothesis that there are no differences among the means of the groups on Y in the population represented by the sample.

When we examine Table 8.2.6, we note that the F from the ANOVA is *identical* to the F computed earlier as a test of R^2 (see Table 8.2.4) using these data. This can be understood conceptually in that the null hypothesis of the ANOVA, equality of the g population means, is mathematically equivalent to the null hypothesis of the MRC analysis, which is that no variance in Y is accounted for by group membership. Clearly, if the population means are all equal, Y variance is not reduced by assigning to the members of the population their respective identical group means. These group means are necessarily also equal to the grand mean of the combined populations. Each null hypothesis implies the other; they differ only verbally.

The two F ratios are, in fact, algebraically identical:

$$SS_{BG} = R^2 SS_{TOTAL};$$
$$SS_{WG} = (1 - R^2) SS_{TOTAL}.$$

TABLE 8.2.6
Analysis of Variance of Attitude Toward Abortion Data

A. Analysis of variance summary table.

Source	SS	df	MS	F
Total	27,205.64	35	—	
Between groups	9,656.49	3	3,218.83	5.869
Within groups	17,549.15	32	548.41	

B. Cell means for attitude toward abortion.

	G_1	G_2	G_3	G_4
M_{Y_i}	60.67	93.31	103.50	70.13
n_i	9	13	6	8

Note: G_1 is Catholic; G_2 is Protestant; G_3 is Jewish; G_4 is Other.

C. Calculations.

$$F = \frac{SS_{BG}/(g-1)}{SS_{WG}/(n-g)} = \frac{MS_{BG}}{MS_{WG}} = \frac{R^2/(g-1)}{(1-R^2)(n-g)} = 5.869 \qquad df = 3, 32.$$

$$\eta^2 = \frac{SS_{BG}}{SS_{TOTAL}} = \frac{9,656.49}{27,205.64} = .3549 = R^2.$$

Substituting these in the ANOVA formula for F, we find

$$F = \frac{SS_{BG}/(g-1)}{SS_{WG}/(n-g)} = \frac{R^2 SS_{TOTAL}/(g-1)}{(1-R^2)SS_{TOTAL}/(n-g)} = \frac{R^2/(g-1)}{(1-R^2)/(n-g)}.$$

The final value is the F ratio for the significance test of R^2 in MRC.

Many modern ANOVA texts also present the formula for the proportion of variance in Y accounted for by the G factor. This statistic is known as η^2 (eta squared) and is written as follows:

(8.2.5)
$$\eta^2 = \frac{SS_{BG}}{SS_{TOTAL}}.$$

Note in Table 8.2.6 that the application of this formula to our running example gives $\eta^2 = .354944$, the same value as found for $R^2_{Y.123}$. In general, $\eta^2 = R^2_{Y.123...(g-1)}$.

Further, just as the shrunken (or adjusted) R^2 of Eq. (3.5.5) yields an improved estimate of the proportion of variance of Y accounted for in the population, the same improved estimate in ANOVA is known as ϵ^2 (epsilon squared), and it is readily proved that $\epsilon^2 = \tilde{R}^2_{Y.123...(g-1)}$. Thus, we see that the yield of an MRC analysis of coded nominal group membership includes the information that a one-way ANOVA yields. In addition, we also directly obtain various useful correlational measures such as simple, partial, semipartial, and multiple correlations. These measures are typically not reported in standard ANOVA statistical packages. In subsequent sections of this chapter we will see that other coding systems bring out still other identities between ANOVA and MRC. Later in this chapter we will see how analysis of covariance can be duplicated and extended by means of MRC. In Chapter 9, we will consider more complex fixed effects ANOVA models such as factorial ANOVA.

8.2.8 A Cautionary Note: Dummy-Variable-Like Coding Systems

Researchers sometimes use other dummy-variable-like coding systems in which a number other than 0 is assigned to the reference group and numbers other than 1 are used to represent group membership. As one example, some researchers use a coding system in which sex is coded female $= 1$ and male $= 2$. This coding system will yield the same results for the correlations and t tests of regression coefficients as were described here. However, recall that the intercept is the value of $\hat{Y}$ when C has a value $= 0$. Thus, the intercept will represent the mean of Y for the nonexistent case in which gender $= 0$ in this coding system. As a second example, a coding system in which female $= 2$ and male $= 0$ might be used. Here, the intercept will correctly equal the M_Y in the male reference group. However, B for the dummy variable will have a different meaning than is normally intended. Recall that the unstandardized regression coefficient represents the value of a 1-unit change in the variable. However, in this coding scheme there is a 2-unit difference between the male and female coded values. Because B provides the value of a 1-unit change, it will now equal *one-half* of the difference between the male and female means on Y.

These examples illustrate that the use of dummy-variable-like coding systems lead to complications in the interpretation of the results of the MRC analysis of a single nominal independent variable. The moral here is "keep it simple": use a standard zero-one dummy coding system. In more complex models, the use of nonstandard dummy-variable-like coding systems may not only change the meaning of certain regression coefficients, it may also lead to inappropriate confidence intervals and significance tests for these coefficients. If a data set is encountered with such a nonstandard coding scheme, researchers are advised to transform (recode) the data to permit analysis using conventional dummy codes.

8.2.9 Dummy-Variable Coding When Groups Are Not Mutually Exclusive

As indicated in the beginning of this chapter, dummy coding is intended for the situation in which each subject may belong to only one group in the set. When this is not the case—for example, if the nominal scale is intended to measure ethnicity in a circumstance in which an individual may claim more than one ethnic identity—the interpretation of the coefficients resulting from the inclusion of the $g-1$ variables in the equation predicting Y will necessarily change. The B coefficients will no longer readily reproduce the original Y means of the groups as in the analyses we have just reviewed. Instead, each B will represent the mean difference between the group coded 1 and the reference group *from each of which has been partialed the effects of the overlap in group membership*. Other coefficients such as partial and semipartial correlations will necessarily be similarly partialed for overlap among the groups. Interpretation of the variables in such cases needs to be done with *extreme care* to avoid erroneous conclusions.

8.3 UNWEIGHTED EFFECTS CODING

8.3.1 Introduction: Unweighted and Weighted Effects Coding

In Section 8.2 on dummy coding variables, we showed that all measures of the partial effect of a single code variable—the regression coefficients and the partial and semipartial correlation coefficients—are interpreted with respect to a reference group. Such interpretations are very often useful, which contributes to the popularity of dummy codes. However, situations arise in which such interpretations may *not* be optimal, as the following example adapted from Suits (1984) illustrates.

Imagine you have conducted a large study comparing the number of years of schooling attained by residents in different regions of the United States. Dummy-variable codes are used to represent residence in the four regions of the United States as shown in Table 8.2.2A, in which South is designated as the reference group. You are invited to present your findings to a Senate committee.

> If you explain in the usual language that you have "omitted the (code) variable for 'South'," a distinguished Southern senator might well demand indignantly, "Now just a minute here. Let me get this straight. You did what?"
> To straighten out the natural confusion, you might explain that you haven't really "left out" the South. On the contrary, you have "established the South as the reference group from which to measure the educational attainment in other regions as deviations." The resulting confusion and consternation among the rest of the committee can well be imagined (adapted with small changes from Suits, 1984, p. 178).

Problems such as those addressed by this educational research project are often better represented by other coding systems. For many research questions, the central issue is how the outcomes in each separate group differ from the average (mean) outcome for the entire sample. To answer such questions, we will use effects coding. In this coding system we again use $g-1$ codes to represent the g groups. However, as we will see, the B_is now represent the deviation of the outcome for each separate group from the mean of the groups rather than from a selected reference group.

When the sample sizes of the groups differ, we need to decide between two possible comparisons with the separate group means. One possibility is the unweighted mean, in which each of the groups count equally. The unweighted mean is represented in the case of four groups and in general as

$$(8.3.1) \qquad M_U = \frac{M_1 + M_2 + M_3 + M_4}{4} = \frac{\sum M_i}{g}.$$

Even if there are 100 cases in group 1, and only 10 cases in group 2, 20 cases in group 3, and 50 cases in group 4, the means of each separate group contribute equally to the overall unweighted mean. This unweighted coding system is particularly useful when the groups represent different experimental treatment groups and differences in sample size are the result of incidental factors such as the cost or difficulty of mounting each experimental treatment. For the example noted, this would mean we wished to compare the mean years of each region of the country to the mean education of the four regions (treated equally).

The second possibility is to use the weighted mean, in which the number of cases in each group are involved in the computation. In the case of four groups and in general, the weighted mean is represented as

$$(8.3.2) \qquad M_W = \frac{n_1 M_1 + n_2 M_2 + n_3 M_3 + n_4 M_4}{n_1 + n_2 + n_3 + n_4} = \frac{\sum n_i M_i}{\sum n_i}.$$

Of importance, $\Sigma n_i = n$, the total sample size, so that the weighted mean $M_W = \Sigma Y / n$, the usual sample mean when group membership is ignored. Weighted effects coding will be of particular importance when the relative size of each group in the sample is representative of its proportion in the population. For example, if we have taken a random sample and wish to generalize the results to the population, weighted effects coding would be the approach of choice. In our earlier example, this would imply the total population of the United States as the reference, complete with its unequal population size in the various regions.

To understand this difference more fully, consider a group of researchers who wish to study the average income of adult residents of the southwestern United States. If they select a random sample of adult residents in the four southwestern states of Arizona, California, Nevada, and New Mexico, the great majority of the people included in the sample would be from the state with the largest population, California. California residents also have a substantially higher mean income than the other states. The use of the weighted mean would permit generalization to the income of residents of the southwestern region, which in fact is dominated in both population and income by residents of California. In contrast, the use of the unweighted mean would permit generalization to a hypothetical southwestern population in which each of the states contributed equally, regardless of its population.

In this Section (8.3), we consider unweighted effects coding in which comparisons are made with the unweighted mean. As noted earlier, this is often the most useful choice for analyzing data from experiments. In the next Section (8.4), we consider weighted effects codes, which are most useful when cases have been sampled from some larger population using random or representative sampling. When the sample sizes (n_i) are equal in each group, weighted effects codes simplify and become identical to unweighted effects codes.

8.3.2 Constructing Unweighted Effects Codes

Table 8.3.1 presents four examples of unweighted effects codes. In each case, $g - 1$ code variables will be needed to represent the g groups that comprise the nominal variable. In the case of unweighted effects coding, one of the groups must be chosen as the base for the coding scheme and is assigned a value of -1 on all of the code variables. We will term this group the *base group*. In contrast to dummy-variable coding (Section 8.2.1), the base group is often

TABLE 8.3.1
Illustration of Unweighted Effects Coding

A. Catholic as base group.

Religion	C_1	C_2	C_3
Catholic	−1	−1	−1
Protestant	1	0	0
Jewish	0	1	0
Other	0	0	1

Code variables

C. Unweighted effects coding of experimental treatment groups ($g = 3$).

Experimental group	C_1	C_2
Treatment 1	1	0
Treatment 2	0	1
Control	−1	−1

Code variables

B. Protestant as base group (used in chapter).

Religion	C_1	C_2	C_3
Catholic	1	0	0
Protestant	−1	−1	−1
Jewish	0	1	0
Other	0	0	1

Code variables

D. Dummy coding of sex ($g = 2$).

Sex	C_1
Female	1
Male	−1

Code variable

selected to be the group for which comparisons with the mean are of *least* interest. This is because the MRC analyses do not *directly* inform us about this group. In unweighted effects coding the regression coefficients represent comparisons of the mean of each group, except the base group, with the unweighted mean.

Table 8.3.1A presents a set of unweighted effects codes using Catholic as the base group, and Table 8.3.1B presents a second set of unweighted effects codes using Protestant as the base group for our running example of four religious groups. The unweighted effects codes presented in Table 8.3.1B will be used throughout this section. Other unweighted effects coding schemes using Jewish or Other as the omitted group could also be constructed. Table 8.3.1C presents a set of unweighted effects codes for comparisons of three experimental treatment groups, and Table 8.3.1D presents the unweighted effect code for comparisons on sex.

To construct unweighted effects codes, we designate one group to serve as the "base group." In Table 8.3.1B, the Protestant group was chosen as the base group to facilitate direct comparison with the results of the dummy-coded analysis presented in Section 8.3. The base group is assigned a value of −1 for each code variable. Each of the other groups is assigned a value of 1 for one code variable and a value of 0 for all other code variables, paralleling the assignment of dummy codes. In Table 8.3.1B, Catholic is assigned [1 0 0], Jewish is assigned [0 1 0], and Other is assigned [0 0 1]. The critical difference between the dummy coding scheme of Table 8.2.1B and the present unweighted effects coding scheme is the set of codes for the Protestant base group [−1 −1 −1].

In this unweighted effects coding system, C_1 contrasts Catholic, C_2 contrasts Jewish, and C_3 contrasts Other with the unweighted mean of the four religious groups in the regression equation. The contrast of the base group with the unweighted mean is not given directly, but can be easily calculated. As with dummy variables, all $g - 1$ code variables

TABLE 8.3.2

Illustrative Data for Unweighted Effects Coding for Religion and
Attitude Toward Abortion ($g = 4$)

Case no.	Group	DV	C_1	C_2	C_3
1	1	61	1	0	0
2	4	78	0	0	1
3	2	47	−1	−1	−1
4	1	65	1	0	0
5	1	45	1	0	0
6	4	106	0	0	1
7	2	120	−1	−1	−1
8	1	49	1	0	0
9	4	45	0	0	1
10	4	62	0	0	1
11	1	79	1	0	0
12	4	54	0	0	1
13	2	140	−1	−1	−1
14	1	52	1	0	0
15	2	88	−1	−1	−1
16	1	70	1	0	0
17	1	56	1	0	0
18	3	124	0	1	0
19	4	98	0	0	1
20	1	69	1	0	0
21	2	56	−1	−1	−1
22	3	135	0	1	0
23	2	64	−1	−1	−1
24	2	130	−1	−1	−1
25	3	74	0	1	0
26	4	58	0	0	1
27	2	116	−1	−1	−1
28	4	60	0	0	1
29	3	84	0	1	0
30	2	68	−1	−1	−1
31	2	90	−1	−1	−1
32	2	112	−1	−1	−1
33	3	94	0	1	0
34	2	80	−1	−1	−1
35	3	110	0	1	0
36	2	102	−1	−1	−1

Group means: $M_1 = 60.67$; $M_2 = 93.31$; $M_3 = 103.50$; $M_4 = 70.13$.
$M_U = (60.67 + 93.31 + 103.50 + 70.13)/4 = 81.90 = B_0$.

Note: DV is attitude toward abortion. For religious group, $1 =$ Catholic, $2 =$ Protestant, $3 =$ Jewish, $4 =$ Other. M_U is unweighted mean of four groups.

(here, 3) must be included in the regression equation to represent the overall effect of religion. Each code variable contributes $1\,df$ to the $g - 1\,df$ that comprise religion. If any code variables are omitted, the interpretation of the results can dramatically change. Table 8.3.2 presents the data file that would be created using the unweighted effects codes from Table 8.3.1B, for our running example. Tables 8.3.3 and 8.3.4 present the results from the MRC analysis.

TABLE 8.3.3
Correlations, Means, and Standard Deviations of the
Illustrative Data for Unweighted Effects Coding

		r					
		ATA	C_1	C_2	C_3	r_{Yi}^2	t_i $(df = 34)$
ATA		1.000	−.444	−.029	−.328	—	—
Catholic	C_1	−.444	1.000	.629	.595	.1974	−2.892*
Jewish	C_2	−.029	.629	1.000	.636	.0008	−0.170
Other	C_3	−.328	.595	.636	1.000	.1074	−2.022
	M	81.69	−.111	−.194	−.139		
	SD	27.49	.807	.730	.783		

$R_{Y.123}^2 = .3549;$ $\quad F = 5.869*$ $(df = 3, 32).$

$\tilde{R}_{Y.123}^2 = .2944.$

Note: ATA = attitude toward abortion. *$p < .05$. M is the unweighted mean of the group means.

8.3.3 The R^2 and the r_{Yi}s for Unweighted Effects Codes

R^2 and $\tilde{R}^2$

We first note that $R^2 = .3549, F = 5.899$, and $\tilde{R}^2 = .2945$, the same values as were obtained by dummy-variable coding. We remind readers that the different coding systems are alternative ways of rendering the information as to group membership into quantitative form. Each of these coding systems *taken as a set* carries all the group information and represents the same nominal variable. Given the same Y data they must yield the same R^2 and hence the same

TABLE 8.3.4
Analysis of Illustrative Data: Attitude Toward Abortion

A. Unweighted effects coding: partial and semipartial correlations and regression coefficients.

C_i	pr_i	pr_i^2	sr_i	sr_i^2	β_i	B_i	SE_{B_i}	t_i
C_1	−.481	.2310	−.440	.1937	−.5977	−21.23	6.85	−3.10*
C_2	.436	.1900	.389	.1513	.5500	21.60	7.88	2.74*
C_3	−.281	.0787	−.235	.0551	−.3217	−11.77	7.12	−1.65

Note: $df = 32.$ *$p < .05$.

B. Predicted values in groups.

$$\hat{Y} = B_1 C_1 + B_2 C_2 + B_3 C_3 + B_0$$
$$= -21.23 C_1 + 21.60 C_2 - 11.77 C_3 + 81.90.$$

Catholic:	$\hat{Y}_1 = -21.23(1) + 21.60(0) - 11.77(0) + 81.90$	$= 60.67$	$= \hat{Y}_1.$
Protestant:	$\hat{Y}_2 = -21.23(-1) + 21.60(-1) - 11.77(-1) + 81.90$	$= 93.31$	$= \hat{Y}_2.$
Jewish:	$\hat{Y}_3 = -21.23(0) + 21.60(1) - 11.70(0) + 81.90$	$= 103.50$	$= \hat{Y}_3.$
Other:	$\hat{Y}_4 = -21.23(0) + 21.60(0) - 11.77(1) + 81.90$	$= 70.13$	$= \hat{Y}_4.$

Note: $B_0 = 81.90$ is unweighted mean of four groups means.

$SD_{Y-\hat{Y}}^2 = SD_Y^2(1 - R^2)\frac{n}{(n-k-1)} = 27.49^2(1 - .354944)\frac{36}{36-3-1} = 548.41.$

F statistic. In contrast, the results for the individual code variables (C_is) change with changes in the coding scheme.

Pearson Correlations

The interpretation of the simple Pearson correlations between each of the code variables with Y is less straightforward for unweighted effects coding than for dummy coding. For each code variable C_i there are now three possible values: $+1, 0, -1$. For example, in Table 8.3.1B, the code variable C_1 has the following values:

Group	C_1
Catholic	$+1$
Protestant	-1
Jewish	0
Other	0

For C_1 the Pearson correlation with Y, R_{Y_i}, reflects the contrast between the group coded 1 and the base group coded -1 with the effect of the other groups minimized.[5] If the sample sizes in the group coded $+1$ (here, Catholic, $n_1 = 9$) differs appreciably in size from the group coded -1 in the contrast (here, Protestant, $n_2 = 13$), it is prudent not to interpret the individual r_{Y_i}s from unweighted effects codes. In the special case in which the n_is of these two groups are equal, the r_{Y_i} for unweighted effects codes will have the same value and interpretation as sr_i from the dummy coding scheme when the reference group is the same as the base group.

As with dummy codes, unweighted effects codes are in general correlated with each other. This means that $R^2_{Y.123}$ will not equal the sum of the three $r^2_{Y_i}$s. When all groups are of the same size, r_{ij} between any two code variables will be .50 regardless of the number of groups. When the groups have unequal ns, intercorrelations will be larger or smaller than .50 depending on the relative sizes of the groups. In Table 8.4.3, the r_{ij}s range from .595 to .636.

8.3.4 Regression Coefficients and Other Partial Effects in Unweighted Code Sets

Once again, we can substitute into our standard regression equation to help understand the meaning of each of the unstandardized regression coefficients. Substituting values of the unweighted effects codes from Table 8.3.1B, we find

Catholic: $\quad \hat{Y} = B_1(+1) + B_2(0) + B_3(0) + B_0 = B_1 + B_0 = M_1;$

Protestant: $\quad \hat{Y} = B_1(-1) + B_2(-1) + B_3(-1) + B_0 = -B_1 - B_2 - B_3 + B_0 = M_2;$

Jewish: $\quad \hat{Y} = B_1(0) + B_2(+1) + B_3(0) + B_0 = B_2 + B_0 = M_3;$

Other: $\quad \hat{Y} = B_1(0) + B_2(0) + B_3(+1) + B_0 = B_3 + B_0 = M_4.$

In unweighted effects coding, B_0 is the unweighted mean of the four groups, $M_U = (M_1 + M_2 + M_3 + M_4)/4$. Each of the unstandardized regression coefficients represents the discrepancy of the corresponding group mean from the unweighted grand mean associated with a 1-unit change on C_i. Thus, B_1 represents the difference between the mean of the group coded 1 on C_1 (Catholic) and the unweighted grand mean of the four religious groups. B_2 represents the

---

[5]The word *minimized* is used to avoid lengthy discussion of a minor mathematical point. The minimum influence of the 0-coded groups on r_{Y_i} is literally nil whenever the n of the group coded $+1$ equals the n of the group coded -1.

difference between the mean of the group coded 1 on C_2 (Jewish) and the unweighted grand mean. And B_3 represents the difference between the group coded 1 on C_3 (Other) and the unweighted grand mean. The difference between the mean of the omitted group (Protestant) and the unweighted grand mean is obtained by subtraction:

$$M_2 = -B_1 - B_2 - B_3 + B_0.$$

To illustrate these relationships, we estimated our standard regression equation (Eq. 8.2.3), $\hat{Y} = B_1 C_1 + B_2 C_2 + B_3 C_3 + B_0$, using the unweighted effects codes shown in Table 8.3.1B with Protestant as the base group. The result is shown in Eq. (8.3.3):

(8.3.3) $$\hat{Y} = -21.23 C_1 + 21.60 C_2 - 11.77 C_3 + 81.90.$$

Table 8.3.4 shows the results of substituting the unweighted effect codes corresponding into our standard regression equation. For each group, $\hat{Y}$ is identical to the mean for the religious group shown in Table 8.3.2. The graphical depiction of the results for unweighted effects codes is identical to that for dummy codes.

Confidence Intervals and Significance Tests for B_i

Procedures for constructing confidence intervals and conducting significance tests for each of the unstandardized regression coefficients are identical to those presented in Section 8.2.3 for dummy variables. We simply take $B_i \pm t_{SE_{B_i}}$ where $df = n - k - 1$. As before, $df = 32$ and $t = 2.037$. Note that the values of each B_i and SE_i have changed (compare Table 8.2.5 with Table 8.3.4) so the actual values of the confidence intervals will change. Substituting in the current values for B_i and SE_{B_i}, we find

$$B_0: \quad 81.90 \pm (2.037)(4.55) \quad = 72.62 \quad \text{to} \quad 91.18;$$
$$B_1: \quad -21.23 \pm (2.037)(6.85) = -35.18 \quad \text{to} \quad -7.28;$$
$$B_2: \quad 21.60 \pm (2.037)(7.88) \quad = 5.55 \quad \text{to} \quad 37.65;$$
$$B_3: \quad -11.77 \pm (2.037)(7.12) = -26.27 \quad \text{to} \quad 2.73.$$

Significance tests for each of the unstandardized regression coefficients are presented in Table 8.3.4. Again, these values differ from those presented in Table 8.2.5 for the analysis of the dummy-coded variables. These changes reflect the change in the meaning and the value of the unstandardized regression coefficients between dummy coding and unweighted effects coding.

Two other significance tests may be of interest to researchers. First is the test of the difference between the mean of the base group and the unweighted grand mean. This test can be accomplished most simply by using another unweighted effects coding system with a different base group. For example, if we use the coding system depicted in Table 8.3.1A, in which Catholic is the base group, the test of B_1 provides a test of the difference between the mean of the Protestant group and the unweighted grand mean. Alternatively, this test can be performed using information from the original analysis with Protestant as the base group. The equation is as follows:

$$t_b = \frac{-g \sum B_i}{\sqrt{sd_{Y-\hat{Y}}^2 \left[\frac{(g-1)^2}{n_b} + \sum \frac{1}{n_i} \right]}} \qquad df = n - g - 1.$$

In this equation, g is the number of groups comprising the nominal variable, k is the number of code variables, i runs from 1 to $g - 1$ (i.e., not including the base group), and n_b is the number of subjects in the base group. Applying this formula to our running example using the results presented in Table 8.3.4, we find

$$t_b = \frac{-4(-21.23 + 21.60 - 11.77)}{\sqrt{548.41\left(\frac{(4-1)^2}{13} + \frac{1}{9} + \frac{1}{6} + \frac{1}{8}\right)}} = \frac{11.41}{6.13} = 1.862 \qquad df = 32.$$

Since the critical value of t with $df = 32$ and $\alpha = .05$ is 2.037, we conclude that the mean of the Protestant base group does not differ from the unweighted mean of the four groups in the population.

Finally, researchers may be interested in testing the difference between the means of two groups i and j in the population. Recall that the analysis using dummy codes directly tests the difference between each group mean and the reference group. Thus, this question can be directly answered by recoding the data so that dummy codes are used as the set of code variables. The reference group for the dummy codes should be chosen so that it is one of the two groups involved in the comparison. For example, if the researcher wished to compare the Protestant and Catholic groups, the test of C_1 using the dummy coding system presented in Table 8.3.1A provides a test of the hypothesis.

Alternatively, these tests may be computed by hand using the output from the unweighted effects codes analysis. If neither of the groups being compared is the base group, Eq. (8.2.4) for comparing two groups i and j (neither of which is the base group) is used. This equation is reproduced here:

$$t = \frac{B_i - B_j}{\sqrt{SD^2_{Y-\hat{Y}}\left(\frac{1}{n_i} + \frac{1}{n_j}\right)}}.$$

When the base group is included in the comparison, a different formula must be used since there is no regression coefficient directly available for the base group. This formula is as follows:

$$t = \frac{2B_i + \sum B_j}{\sqrt{SD^2_{Y-\hat{Y}}\left(\frac{1}{n_i} + \frac{1}{n_b}\right)}} \qquad (j \neq i) \qquad df = n - k - 1.$$

Note that the summation is over all of the B coefficients, except B_i, the regression coefficient for the group being compared with the base group. The numerator is a re-expression of $M_i - M_b$. Applying this formula to our running example for the comparison of Catholic and Protestant (omitted group),

$$t = \frac{2(-21.32) + (21.60 - 11.77)}{\sqrt{548.41\left(\frac{1}{9} + \frac{1}{13}\right)}} = -3.214.$$

This t value exceeds the critical value of $t = 2.037$ for $df = 32$ and $\alpha = .05$. Note that this is exactly the same value as the t for B_1 in the regression analysis using dummy codes presented in Table 8.2.5.

Once again, we encourage readers to exercise caution in conducting such comparisons, particularly when there is not a strong a priori prediction that two specific groups will differ. Multiple comparisons of group means increase the level of α for the study beyond the stated level, typically $\alpha = .05$, and special procedures described by Kirk (1995, Chapter 4) and Toothaker (1991) need to be taken.

Semipartial and Partial Correlations

As noted, the regression coefficients provide a contrast between a given group and the unweighted mean of all the groups. Because the mean of all the groups includes the group in question, this is functionally equivalent to contrasting this group with the remaining groups taken collectively. Thus, sr_i^2 is the proportion of Y variance accounted for by this contrast. Concretely, for our running example, sr_1^2 means that 19.4% of the variance in ATA scores is accounted for by the distinction between Catholic on one hand and equally weighted Protestant-Jewish-Other on the other hand. Thus, 19.4% of the ATA variance in the sample is accounted for by the "distinctiveness" of Catholics relative to the other groups.

The partial correlations relate the partialed effects-coded IV (e.g., $X_{1.23}$) with that part of Y left after the other variables have been removed. Thus, pr_1^2 gives

$$\frac{\text{ATA variance due to Catholic group distinctiveness}}{\text{ATA variance } not \text{ accounted for by remaining groups' distinctiveness}}.$$

Recall that the denominator of pr_i^2 is always equal to or smaller than the denominator of sr_i^2 (which is 1.0). Hence, pr_i^2 will typically be larger than sr_i^2.

8.4 WEIGHTED EFFECTS CODING

8.4.1 Selection Considerations for Weighted Effects Coding

Weighted effects coding is most appropriate when the proportion of cases in each group in the sample can be considered to represent the corresponding proportion of cases in the population. This situation will most commonly occur when random or representative samples have been selected from a population. In weighted effects coding it is the comparison of each group with the aggregate population mean that is at issue. As a metaphor, unweighted effects codes may be thought of as the "Senate" option—since every state in the United States has two Senators regardless of its population size—whereas weighted effects codes would be the "House" option, since the 435 U.S. Representatives are divided among the states in proportion to their population size.

Like the situation with unweighted effects coding, one of the groups must be designated as the base group in the coding scheme. Once again, the group for which comparisons with the mean are of least interest will normally be chosen to be the base group because the MRC information regarding that group will be less accessible than for the other groups.

8.4.2 Constructing Weighted Effects

Table 8.4.1 presents four examples of weighted effects codes. These examples parallel exactly those in Table 8.3.1, permitting direct comparison of weighted and unweighted effect codes. Table 8.4.1A presents a set of weighted effect codes for religion using Catholic as the base group; Table 8.4.1B presents the set of weighted effect codes for religion using Protestant as the base group.[6] Table 8.4.1C presents a set of weighted effects codes for comparisons of three experimental treatment groups and Table 8.4.1D presents the weighted effect code for sex. In Tables 8.4.1A and B, we have written a general expression and the specific codes given the

---

[6]In practice, the decimal value corresponding to the fraction would be used for each code variable. Thus, in the Protestant base group in our example, the actual values entered would be $-.6923076$ ($=-9/13$), $-.4615384$ ($=-6/13$), and $-.6153846$ ($=-8/13$) for C_1, C_2, and C_3, respectively.

TABLE 8.4.1
Illustration of Weighted Effects Coding Systems

A. Religious groups: Catholic as base group.

Religion		General case: code variables			Example: code variables		
		C_1	C_2	C_3	C_1	C_2	C_3
Catholic	($n_1 = 9$)	$-n_2/n_1$	$-n_3/n_1$	$-n_4/n_1$	$-13/9$	$-6/9$	$-8/9$
Protestant	($n_2 = 13$)	1	0	0	1	0	0
Jewish	($n_3 = 6$)	0	1	0	0	1	0
Other	($n_4 = 8$)	0	0	1	0	0	1

B. Religious groups: Protestant as base group (used in chapter).

Religion		General case: code variables			Example: code variables		
		C_1	C_2	C_3	C_1	C_2	C_3
Catholic	($n_1 = 9$)	1	0	0	1	0	0
Protestant	($n_2 = 13$)	$-n_1/n_2$	$-n_3/n_2$	$-n_4/n_2$	$-9/13$	$-6/13$	$-8/13$
Jewish	($n_3 = 6$)	0	1	0	0	1	0
Other	($n_4 = 8$)	0	0	1	0	0	1

C. Unweighted effects coding of experimental treatment groups ($g = 3$).

Experimental group	Code variables	
	C_1	C_2
Treatment 1	1	0
Treatment 2	0	1
Control	$-n_1/n_3$	$-n_2/n_3$

D. Dummy coding of sex ($g = 2$).

Sex	Code variable
	C_1
Female	1
Male	$-n_1/n_2$

stated sample sizes for the groups in the illustrative example. Whenever the sample size of the groups changes, the values of the unweighted effects codes for the base group change as well.

Once again, we arbitrarily designate one group to be the base group. Table 8.4.1B, which presents the coding scheme used in this section, designates Protestant as the base group. For the other groups, the coding exactly parallels that of unweighted effects codes. The critical difference between the unweighted effects coding system of Table 8.3.1 and the weighted effects coding system of Table 8.4.1 is in the set of codes assigned to the base group. The values of each code are weighted for the base group to reflect the different sample sizes of each of the groups. For each code variable, the base group receives the value of *minus* the ratio of the size of the group coded 1 and the size of the base group. Note that when sample sizes are equal across groups, $n_1 = n_2 = n_3 = n_4 = \cdots = n_g$, the codes for the base group simplify to $[-1 \quad -1 \quad -1 \quad -1 \quad \cdots \quad -1]$. Under these conditions, weighted effects codes are identical to unweighted effects codes.

In this coding system, C_1 contrasts Catholic, C_2 contrasts Jewish, and C_3 contrasts Other with the weighted mean of the four religious groups in the regression equation. Recall that the weighted mean is $\Sigma n_i M_i / \Sigma n_i = (\Sigma Y)/n$, where $n = \Sigma n_i$. This is the mean of the scores of all of the subjects on the dependent variable, ignoring group membership. Once again, each code variable contributes $1\ df$ to the $g - 1\ df$ that comprise religion. If any of the code variables are omitted, the interpretation of the results can dramatically change. Unlike the other coding systems for nominal variables we have considered thus far, weighted effects codes are centered. In our example (and in general), the means for C_1, C_2, and C_3 are each equal to 0 in the sample. The correlations between pairs of code variables are also smaller than for unweighted effect codes, ranging from .347 to .395.

8.4.3 The R^2 and $\tilde{R}^2$ for Weighted Effects Codes

Table 8.4.2 presents the results from the MRC analysis. Once again, we note that $R^2 = .3549$, $F = 5.899$, and $\tilde{R}^2 = .2945$, values identical to those we obtained using dummy coding and unweighted effects coding. Each coding system taken as a set is equivalent because it represents the same nominal variable.

TABLE 8.4.2
Analysis of Illustrative Data: Attitude Toward Abortion

A. Weighted effects coding: regression coefficients.

C_i	β_i	B_i	SE_{B_i}	t_i
C_1	−.4975	−21.03	6.76	−3.11*
C_2	.3915	21.81	8.72	2.50*
C_3	−.2522	−11.57	7.30	−1.58

$R^2_{Y.123} = .3549$ $\qquad$ $F = 5.869^*\ (df = 3, 32)$

$\tilde{R}^2_{Y.123} = .2945$

Note: $df = 32$. $^*p < .05$.

B. Predicted values in groups.

$$\hat{Y} = B_1 C_1 + B_2 C_2 + B_3 C_3 + B_0$$
$$= -21.03 C_1 + 21.81 C_2 - 11.57 C_3 + 81.69.$$

Catholic:	$\hat{Y}_1 = -21.03(1) + 21.81(0) - 11.57(0) + 81.69$	$= 60.67$	$= \hat{Y}_1$.
Protestant:	$\hat{Y}_2 = -21.03(-9/13) + 21.81(-6/13) - 11.57(-8/13) + 81.69$	$= 93.31$	$= \hat{Y}_2$.
Jewish:	$\hat{Y}_3 = -21.03(0) + 21.81(1) - 11.57(0) + 81.69$	$= 103.50$	$= \hat{Y}_3$.
Other:	$\hat{Y}_4 = -21.03(0) + 21.81(0) - 11.57(1) + 81.69$	$= 70.13$	$= \hat{Y}_4$.

Note: $B_0 = 81.69$ is unweighted mean of four group means.

$$SD^2_{Y-\hat{Y}} = SD^2_Y (1 - R^2)\frac{n}{(n-k-1)} = 27.49^2(1 - .354944)\frac{36}{36-3-1} = 548.41.$$

8.4.4 Interpretation and Testing of B with Weighted Codes

To understand the meaning of each of the regression coefficients, we can take the usual strategy of substituting the value of each code variable into our standard regression equation. Although this procedure leads to the correct answers, the algebra becomes very tedious (see the appendix of West, Aiken, & Krull, 1996 for the algebraic derivation). Fortunately, the *results* of the algebra are not complex; these results are presented here:

Catholic: $\hat{Y} = B_1 + B_0 = M_1;$

Protestant: $\hat{Y} = -(n_1/n_2)B_1 - (n_3/n_2)B_2 - (n_4/n_2)B_3 + B_0 = M_2;$

Jewish: $\hat{Y} = B_2 + B_0 = M_3;$

Other: $\hat{Y} = B_3 + B_0 = M_4.$

In weighted effects coding, B_0 is the *weighted* mean of the groups. Each of the regression coefficients represents the deviation of the corresponding group mean from the weighted mean of the entire sample. Thus B_1 represents the difference between the mean of the group coded 1 on C_1 (Catholic) and the weighted mean, B_2 represents the difference between the mean of the group coded 1 on C_2 (Jewish) and the weighted mean, and, B_3 represents the difference between the mean of the group coded 1 on C_3 and the weighted mean. The difference between the mean of the Protestant base group and the weighted mean may be obtained by subtraction:

$$M_2 = -(n_1/n_2)B_1 - (n_3/n_2)B_2 - (n_4/n_2)B_3 + B_0.$$

These interpretations of B_1, B_2, and B_3 using weighted effects codes parallel those of unweighted effects except that the mean of each group is contrasted with the weighted mean rather than the unweighted mean of the set of groups.

To illustrate these relationships, we estimated our standard regression equation, $\hat{Y} = B_1 C_1 + B_2 C_2 + B_3 C_3 + B_0$, using the weighted effects codes shown in Table 8.4.1B with Protestant as the base group. The result is

$$\hat{Y} = -21.03 C_1 + 21.81 C_2 - 11.60 C_3 + 81.69.$$

Table 8.4.2 shows the results of substituting the weighted effect codes into the standard regression equation. For each group, $\hat{Y}$ is again identical to the mean for the group.

Confidence Intervals and Significance Tests for B_i

Procedures for constructing confidence intervals and conducting significance tests for each of the unstandardized coefficients are identical to those presented in Sections 8.2.3 for dummy codes and 8.3.3 for unweighted effects codes. To construct confidence intervals, we take $B_i \pm tSE_{B_i}$, where $df = n - k - 1$. Substituting in the current values for B_i and SE_{B_i}, we find

B_0: $81.69 \pm (2.037)(3.90)$ $= 73.75$ to $89.63;$

B_1: $-21.03 \pm (2.037)(6.76) = -34.80$ to $-7.26;$

B_2: $21.81 \pm (2.037)(8.73)$ $= 4.03$ to $39.59;$

B_3: $-11.60 \pm (2.037)(7.30) = -26.47$ to $3.27.$

Significance tests divide each B_i by its corresponding $SE, t = B_i/SE_{B_i}$. These values are presented in Table 8.4.2. Note that these values differ from those presented in Table 8.2.5 for dummy codes and Table 8.3.4 for unweighted effects codes. These discrepancies reflect the differences in the meaning and the value of the mean comparisons reflected by the Bs in the three coding systems. Recall that in dummy coding, the Bs represent the comparison of each group mean with the reference group mean. In unweighted effects coding, the Bs represent the comparison of each group mean with the unweighted mean. And in weighted effects coding, the Bs represent the comparison of each group mean with the weighted mean. Analysts should decide in advance which coding scheme represents their research question of interest and report the corresponding results. In the present example, the discrepancy in the results for unweighted and weighted effects codes is not large because the ns did not differ greatly. Other data sets can produce larger (or smaller) differences between unweighted and weighted effects coding depending on the specific values of the n_is and the M_is in the groups.

Determining whether the mean of the base group differs from the weighted mean is most easily done by reanalyzing the data using a coding system that provides the answer directly.[7] In this case the use of another weighted effects coding system with a different omitted group will provide the answer. For example, using the coding system in Table 8.4.1A in which Catholic is the base group, the significance test of C_1 provides a test of the difference between the mean of the Protestant group and the unweighted mean. The significance of the difference between two group means can be tested through the use of dummy codes (see Section 8.2). A dummy coding scheme should be chosen in which the omitted group is one of the two groups of interest.

8.5 CONTRAST CODING

8.5.1 Considerations in the Selection of a Contrast Coding Scheme

Researchers often have specific research questions or formal hypotheses based on substantive theory that can be stated in terms of expected mean differences between groups or combinations of groups. For example, consider a team of drug abuse researchers who wish to evaluate the effectiveness of two new prevention programs. They have collected data on the amount of drug use (dependent variable) on three groups of children: (a) children who are exposed to the drug prevention program in their middle school classrooms (school-based-only program), (b) children who are exposed to the drug prevention in their middle school classrooms in addition to a home-based drug prevention program led by their parents (school-based plus home-based program), and (c) children not exposed to a prevention program (control group). The researchers have two explicit, a priori hypotheses:

1. Children in the two prevention groups ($a + b$) will have less drug use than children in the control group (c);
2. Children in the school-based plus home-based program (b) will have less drug use than children in the school-based-only program (a).

Contrast codes provide a method of testing such focused hypotheses. They are used when researchers have specific research questions or hypotheses, particularly those that involve comparison of means of combined groups. As we will see, the particular contrast codes

---

[7]Paralleling unweighted effects codes, algebraic expressions may be written for these significance tests for weighted effects codes. For comparisons involving the base group, the calculations quickly become very tedious as the number of groups increases. Using recode statements to develop a coding system that directly answers the questions of interest and then reanalyzing the data is a far simpler alternative. The exception is the test of the difference between two group means (not involving the base group), which is identical to the same test for dummy and unweighted effects codes (see Eq. 8.2.4).

selected depend on the researchers' hypotheses. Many methodologists (Abelson, 1995; Judd, McClelland, & Culhane, 1995; Rosenthal & Rosnow, 1985) strongly recommend the use of such contrasts in order to sharpen the interpretation of the results. The method allows the researcher to test the specific hypotheses of interest rather than some other hypothesis that is a consequence of simply using a default coding scheme such as dummy variables. The use of contrasts may increase the power of the statistical test to reject a false null hypotheses relative to less focused, omnibus tests. For readers familiar with ANOVA, contrast codes are the familiar a priori or planned comparisons discussed in traditional ANOVA texts (e.g., Kirk, 1995; Winer, Brown, & Michels, 1991). In the next section we initially focus on the mechanics of constructing contrast codes, returning later to the issue of choosing the set of contrast codes that best represents the researchers' hypotheses.

8.5.2 Constructing Contrast Codes

Overview and Illustration

To illustrate the use of code variables for contrasts, let us reconsider the three drug abuse prevention programs in the preceding example. The first hypothesis compares the unweighted mean of the two prevention groups with the mean of the control group. This hypothesis is represented in Table 8.5.1D by the C_1 code variable $[+\frac{1}{3} \quad +\frac{1}{3} \quad -\frac{2}{3}]$. The second hypothesis compares the mean of the school-based only program with the mean of the school-based plus home-based program. This hypothesis is represented in Table 8.5.1D by the C_2 code variable $[\frac{1}{2} \quad -\frac{1}{2} \quad 0]$. There are $g = 3$ groups in this example, so $g - 1 = 2$ code variables are necessary to represent the categorical IV of treatment group.

We use three rules to construct contrast codes. The first two rules are part of the formal statistical definition of a contrast. The third rule is not required, but it greatly simplifies the interpretation of the results.

Rule 1.   The sum of the weights across all groups for each code variable must equal zero. In the prevention program example, $\frac{1}{3} + \frac{1}{3} - \frac{2}{3} = 0$ for C_1 and $\frac{1}{2} - \frac{1}{2} + 0 = 0$ for C_2.

Rule 2.   The sum of the products of each pair of code variables, C_1C_2, must equal 0. In the example,

$$\text{group 1 (school-based only):} \quad (\tfrac{1}{3})(\tfrac{1}{2}) \quad\quad = \tfrac{1}{6};$$
$$\text{group 2 (school + home–based):} \quad (\tfrac{1}{3})(-\tfrac{1}{2}) = -\tfrac{1}{6};$$
$$\text{group 3 (control):} \quad (-\tfrac{2}{3})(0) \quad\quad = 0.$$

The sum of the products of the code variables $= \frac{1}{6} - \frac{1}{6} + 0 = 0$. When the group sizes are equal ($n_1 = n_2 = n_3 = \cdots = n_g$), this rule guarantees that the contrast codes will be orthogonal so they will share no overlapping variance.

Rule 3.   As will be discussed in detail in our more formal presentation, the difference between the value of the set of positive weights and the value of the set of negative weights should equal 1 for each code variable. In our example, $\frac{1}{3} - (-\frac{2}{3}) = 1$ for C_1 and $\frac{1}{2} - (-\frac{1}{2}) = 1$ for C_2. This rule ensures easy interpretation: Each unstandardized regression coefficient corresponds exactly to the difference between the unweighted means of the groups involved in the contrast.[8]

---

[8]If the present set of contrast codes are multiplied by a constant, the new set of codes also meets the formal definition of a contrast. Multiplying a set of contrast codes by a constant does not affect any standardized measure. The Pearson, partial, and semipartial correlations as well as the standardized regression coefficient are all unaffected by

More Formal Presentation

To facilitate a more formal presentation of contrast codes, we need to define each contrast weight in the table, C_{hi}. C_{hi} is the weight for the hth group (row) for the ith code variable (column). In our example (see Table 8.5.1D), $C_{31} = -\frac{2}{3}$ for control group, code variable 1; $C_{32} = 0$ for control group, code variable 2; and $C_{21} = +\frac{1}{3}$ for school-based plus home-based group, code variable 1. This notation allows us to refer to the specific weights corresponding to the value of the code variable for a specific group.

Let us first consider the construction of a code variable corresponding to a single contrast. A contrast for g sample means (or other statistics) is defined as any linear combination of them of the form

$$\text{Contrast} = C_{1i}M_1 + C_{2i}M_2 + \cdots + C_{gi}M_g$$

This equation represents the contrast produced by the ith code variable. The values corresponding to each group for the code variable must be chosen subject to the restriction stated earlier as Rule 1. Rule 1 is stated more formally below as Eq. (8.5.1), where h stands for group and i stands for code variable.

(8.5.1)
$$\sum_{h=1}^{h=g} C_{hi} = 0, \quad i.e., \ C_{1i} + C_{2i} + \cdots + C_{gi} = 0$$

To see how the form of Eq. (8.5.1) expresses a contrast, consider any set of g groups comprising a nominal variable G. We partition the g groups into three subsets: (1) a subset u, (2) a subset v that we wish to contrast with subset u, and (3) a subset w containing groups, if any, that we wish to exclude from the contrast. The contrast compares the unweighted mean of the groups in subset u with the unweighted mean of the groups in subset v.

As a concrete example, consider the responses to a question about respondent's occupation in a survey. Respondents are classified into one of nine occupational groups based on their responses to the survey question. The first 4 ($=u$) response options represent "white collar" occupations (e.g., educator; medical professional), the next 3 ($=v$) response options represent "blue collar" occupations (e.g., skilled laborer; unskilled laborer), and the final two ($=w$) response options represent other occupational categories (e.g., unemployed, did not answer). The researcher is interested in comparing the responses of white collar and blue collar workers to other survey items measuring their beliefs about equal pay for women. To accomplish this comparison, we assign the contrast code for each group in subset u as $-v/(u+v)$ and the contrast for each group in subset v as $+u/(u+v)$. In the present example comparing white collar and blue collar workers, $-v/(u+v) = -3/(4+3)$ and $+u/(u+v) = +4/(4+3)$, so that the contrast may be expressed as

$$\text{contrast} = -\frac{3}{7}M_{Y_1} - \frac{3}{7}M_{Y_2} - \frac{3}{7}M_{Y_3} - \frac{3}{7}M_{Y_4} + \frac{4}{7}M_{Y_5} + \frac{4}{7}M_{Y_6} + \frac{4}{7}M_{Y_7} + 0M_{Y_8} + 0M_{Y_9}.$$

Note that the set of C_{hi} coefficients that comprise the contrast satisfy the restriction in Eq. (8.5.1):

$$\sum_{h=1}^{h=g} C_{hi} = -\frac{3}{7} - \frac{3}{7} - \frac{3}{7} - \frac{3}{7} + \frac{4}{7} + \frac{4}{7} + \frac{4}{7} + 0 + 0 = \frac{-12}{7} + \frac{+12}{7} = 0.$$

Thus, we can state generally how the values of the code variables for each group are assigned for a specific contrast represented by code variable C_i. The values of C_{hi} for each of the u

___

such transformation. Rule 3 is emphasized here because it permits straightforward interpretation of the unstandardized regression coefficients. With other contrast coding schemes, the unstandardized regression coefficient will represent the mean difference of interest multiplied by a constant.

groups is $-v/u+v$; the value of C_{hi} for each of the v groups is $u/u + v$; and the value of C_{hi} is 0 for each of the w groups, if any. Once again, the choice of these values for the code variable allow us to interpret the unstandardized regression coefficient B_i corresponding to the code variable as the difference between the unweighted means of the groups in u and the groups in v. If the unweighted mean of the groups in u and the unweighted mean of the groups in v are precisely equal, then the value of B_i for the contrast will be 0.

Throughout this chapter we have seen that the full representation of the information entailed in membership in one of g groups requires a set of $g - 1$ code variables. The contrast described here is only one member of such a set. A total of $g - 1$ code variables must be specified to represent the full set of contrasts. For example, 8 code variables will be required to represent the 9 occupational groups in our example.[9]

In our overview presentation of contrast codes, we also stated Rule 2. Rule 2 establishes the part of the definition of contrast codes that each possible pair of code variables must be linearly independent. Formally, this condition can be written as

$$\sum_{h=1}^{h=g} C_{hi}C_{hi'} = 0, \quad i.e., \quad C_{1i}C_{1i'} + C_{2i}C_{2i'} + \cdots + C_{gi}C_{gi'} = 0,$$

where the C_{hi} represent the weights for code variable i of each of the groups and the $C_{hi'}$ represent the weights for code variable i' for each of the groups, where h identifies the group number from 1 to 9.

Three different sets of contrast codes for our example of religions and ATA are shown in Table 8.5.1A, B, and C. Applying the linear independence (Rule 2) condition to each of the three possible pairs of contrast codes (C_1C_2, C_1C_3, C_2C_3) in Part A, we find

$$C_1C_2: (\tfrac{1}{2})(\tfrac{1}{2}) + (\tfrac{1}{2})(-\tfrac{1}{2}) + (-\tfrac{1}{2})(0) + (-\tfrac{1}{2})(0) = 0;$$
$$C_1C_3: (\tfrac{1}{2})(0) + (\tfrac{1}{2})(0) + (-\tfrac{1}{2})(\tfrac{1}{2}) + (-\tfrac{1}{2})(-\tfrac{1}{2}) = 0;$$
$$C_2C_3: (\tfrac{1}{2})(0) + (-\tfrac{1}{2})(0) + (0)(\tfrac{1}{2}) + (0)(-\tfrac{1}{2}) = 0.$$

Rule 2 is met for all possible pairs of contrast codes. Note, however, that the set of contrasts will *not* be orthogonal (i.e., share no overlapping variance) unless all groups have equal sample sizes ($n_1 = n_2 = \cdots = n_g$). All of the sets of contrast codes displayed in each panel of Table 8.5.1 are independent.

Choosing Among Sets of Contrast Codes

A very large number of potential contrasts may be constructed. Indeed, the total number of different means of group means contrasts among g groups is $1 + [(3^g - 1)/2] - 2^g$. For $g = 4$, this number is 25; for $g = 6$, it is 301; and for $g = 10$, it is 28,501. However, relatively few of these contrasts will test hypotheses that are meaningful to the researcher. The goal in choosing contrast codes is to select a set of $g - 1$ codes that map neatly onto the researcher's hypotheses of interest.

Consider the set of contrast codes displayed in Table 8.5.1A. Code variable 1 contrasts the unweighted mean of Protestant and Catholic with the unweighted mean for Jewish and Other. Code variable 2 contrasts Protestant with Catholic. Code variable 3 contrasts Jewish with Other. Suppose a researcher hypothesized that members of minority religions (Jewish, Other)

---

[9]In the case where the group sizes are precisely equal, the contrasts will be independent and code variables can be dropped from the regression equation. However, even when there are equal ns, including all of the $g - 1$ contrasts provides an important check on model specification (see Sections 4.3.1 and 4.4.1). Abelson and Prentice (1997) strongly emphasize the importance of checking the fit of the contrast model.

TABLE 8.5.1

A. Contrast A: minority versus majority religions.

Religion	Code variables		
	C_1	C_2	C_3
Catholic	1/2	1/2	0
Protestant	1/2	−1/2	0
Jewish	−1/2	0	1/2
Other	−1/2	0	−1/2

C. Contrast C: religious groupings.

Religion	Code variables		
	C_1	C_2	C_3
Catholic	1/4	1/3	1/2
Protestant	1/4	1/3	−1/2
Jewish	1/4	−2/3	0
Other	−3/4	0	0

Note: C_1: Western religions vs. Other
C_2: Christian vs. Jewish
C_3: Catholic vs. Protestant

B. Contrast B: value on women's rights.

Religion	Code variables		
	C_1	C_2	C_3
Catholic	−1/2	0	−1/2
Protestant	1/2	−1/2	0
Jewish	1/2	1/2	0
Other	−1/2	0	1/2

D. Contrast coding of experimental treatment groups ($g = 3$).

Experimental group	Code variables	
	C_1	C_2
Treatment 1	1/3	1/2
Treatment 2	1/3	−1/2
Control	−2/3	0

are more opposed to restrictions on religious freedom than members of majority religions (Catholic, Protestant). If majority versus minority religious status is the only critical difference among the groups, the contrast associated with code variable 1 should show a large difference. However, the contrast associated with code variable 2, which compares the two majority religions, and the contrast associated with code variable 3, which compares the two minority religions, should not differ appreciably.

Table 8.5.1(B) presents a different set of contrast codes. Here, code variable 1 contrasts the unweighted mean of Protestant and Jewish with the unweighted mean of Catholic and Other. Code variable 2 contrasts Protestant with Jewish and code variable 3 contrasts Catholic with Other. Suppose the researcher has a theory that suggests that the Protestant and Jewish religions place a particularly high value on women's rights, whereas Catholic and Other religions place a lower value on women's rights. In this example, the contrast associated with code variable 1 would be expected to show a substantial difference, whereas the contrasts associated with code variables 2 and 3 should not differ appreciably. Table 8.5.1(C) provides yet another set of contrasts among the religious groups.

Each of the sets of contrast codes represents a different partitioning of the variance associated with the g groups. The strategy of contrast coding is to express the researcher's central hypotheses of interest in the form of $g - 1$ independent contrast codes. The MRC analysis then directly yields functions of the contrast values, confidence intervals, and significance tests.

Contrast codes are centered; however, the corresponding contrast = $C_{1i}M_1 + C_{2i}M_2 + \cdots + C_{gi}M_g$ may or may not be centered. The means for the contrasts corresponding to C_1, C_2, and C_3 will equal 0 only if the number of subjects in each group is equal. However, when there is one categorical IV, the correlations among the contrast code variables will typically be low to moderate. In our running example of religion and attitudes toward abortion, the correlations between the contrast variables range from $-.12$ to $+.11$ for the codes presented in Table 8.5.1A and from $-.26$ to $+.04$ for the codes presented in Table 8.5.1B.

8.5.3 R^2 and $\tilde{R}^2$

Tables 8.5.2 and 8.5.3 present the results from the two separate MRC analysis for the sets of contrast codes presented in Table 8.5.1A and B, respectively. We again note that $R^2 = .3549, F = 5.899$, and $\tilde{R}^2 = .2945$ for both analyses. These values are identical to those obtained for dummy, unweighted effects, and weighted effects coding.

8.5.4 Partial Regression Coefficients

The contrast codes recommended here lead to unstandardized regression coefficients that are directly interpretable. The unstandardized regression coefficients will equal the difference between the unweighted mean of the means of the groups contained in u and the unweighted mean of the means of the groups contained in v. To illustrate, consider the contrast coding scheme in Table 8.5.1A: C_1 represents the difference between majority religions (Catholic, Protestant) and minority religions (Jewish, Other). We see the value of B_1 is -9.82. We also see that the mean ATA are Catholic $= 60.67$, Protestant $= 93.31$, Jewish $= 103.50$, and Other $= 70.13$. The difference in the unweighted means between the two sets is

$$\frac{M_1 + M_2}{2} - \frac{M_3 + M_4}{2} = \frac{60.67 + 93.31}{2} - \frac{103.50 - 70.13}{2} = -9.83.$$

Similarly, the value of $B_2 = -32.64$, which is equal to the difference between the Catholic (60.67) and Protestant (93.31), means and the value of $B_3 = 33.38$ which is equal to the

TABLE 8.5.2
Analysis of Illustrative Data: Attitude Toward Abortion

A. Contrast coding: majority versus minority religions.

C_i	pr_i	pr_i^2	sr_i	sr_i^2	β_i	B_i	SE_{B_i}	t_i
C_1	$-.209$	.0437	$-.172$	.0296	$-.1742$	-9.82	8.11	-1.21
C_2	$-.494$	.2331	$-.456$	.2083	$-.4594$	-32.64	10.15	$-3.21*$
C_3	.423	.1789	.375	.1404	.3770	33.38	12.65	$2.64*$

$R^2_{Y.123} = .3549 \quad F = 5.869* \; (df = 3, 32)$

$\tilde{R}^2_{Y.123} = .2945$

Note: $*p < .05$.

B. Predicted values in groups.

$$\hat{Y} = B_1 C_1 + B_2 C_2 + B_3 C_3 + B_0$$
$$= -9.83 C_1 - 32.64 C_2 + 33.38 C_3 + 81.90$$

Catholic:	$\hat{Y}_1 = -9.83(.5) - 32.64(.5) + 33.38(0) + 81.90$	$= 60.67 \; = \hat{Y}_1$
Protestant:	$\hat{Y}_2 = -9.83 (.5) + 21.60(-.5) + 33.38(0) + 81.90 = 93.31 \; = \hat{Y}_2$	
Jewish:	$\hat{Y}_3 = -9.83 (-.5) + 21.60(0) + 33.38(.5) + 81.90 \; = 103.50 = \hat{Y}_3$	
Other:	$\hat{Y}_4 = -9.83(-.5) + 21.60(0) + 33.38(-.5) + 81.90 = 70.13 \; = \hat{Y}_4$	

$$SD^2_{Y-\hat{Y}} = SD^2_Y (1 - R^2)\frac{n}{(n-k-1)} = 27.49^2 (1 - .3549)\frac{36}{36-3-1} = 548.41.$$

Note: $B_0 = 81.90$ is unweighted mean of four group means. Decimal value of each contrast code value is used (e.g. $1/2 = .5$).

TABLE 8.5.3

Analysis of Illustrative Data: Attitude Toward Abortion

A. Contrast coding: pro- versus anti-women's rights religions.

C_i	pr_i	pr_i^2	sr_i	sr_i^2	β_i	B_i	SE_{B_i}	t_i
C_1	.584	.3411	.578	.3339	.599	33.01	8.11	4.07*
C_2	.154	.0237	.125	.0157	.130	10.19	11.56	.88
C_3	.145	.0120	.118	.0139	.118	9.46	11.38	.83

$$R^2_{Y.123} = .3549 \quad F = 5.869^* \ (df = 3, 32)$$
$$\tilde{R}^2_{Y.123} = .2945$$

Note: $^*p < .05.$

B. Predicted values in groups.

$$\hat{Y} = B_1 C_1 + B_2 C_2 + B_3 C_3 + B_0$$
$$= 33.01 C_1 + 10.19 C_2 + 9.46 C_3 + 81.90$$

Catholic: $\hat{Y}_1 = +33.01(-.5) + 10.19(0) + 9.46(.5) + 81.90 \quad = 60.67 \ = \hat{Y}_1$

Protestant: $\hat{Y}_2 = +33.01(.5) + 10.19(-.5) + 9.46(-.5) + 81.90 = 93.31 \ = \hat{Y}_2$

Jewish: $\hat{Y}_3 = +33.01(.5) + 10.19(.5) + 9.46(0) + 81.90 \quad = 103.50 = \hat{Y}_3$

Other: $\hat{Y}_4 = +33.01(-.5) + 10.10(0) + 9.46(0) + 81.90 \quad = 70.13 \ = \hat{Y}_4$

$$SD^2_{Y-\hat{Y}} = SD^2_Y (1 - R^2)\frac{n}{(n-k-1)} = 27.49^2(1 - .3549)\frac{36}{36-3-1} = 548.41.$$

Note: $B_0 = 81.90$ is unweighted mean of four group means. Decimal value of each contrast code value is used (e.g. $\frac{1}{2} = .5$).

difference between the Jewish (103.50) and Other (70.13) means. Finally, the intercept, $B_0 = 81.90$ equals the unweighted mean of the four group means, just as in unweighted effects coding.

Table 8.5.2 provides further insight into how contrast coding partitions the variance of the set of groups. When the contrast code values are substituted into the regression equation, the predicted value $\hat{Y}$ for each group is once again equal to the unweighted group mean. The contrast model yields the mean for a group by adding to the unweighted mean of the group means the effect provided by each group's role in the set of contrasts. For example, the Protestant mean M_2 comes about by adding the unweighted mean (81.90), one-half of the majority-minority contrast (C_1) $[\frac{1}{2}(-9.82)] = -4.91$, and minus one-half the value of the Protestant-Catholic contrast (C_2) $[(-\frac{1}{2})(-32.64)] = 16.32$, but none of the irrelevant Jewish versus Other contrast (C_3) $[(0)(33.38)] = 0$. Thus, for Protestants, $M = 81.90 - 4.91 + 16.32 + 0 = 93.31$.

Contrast-coded unstandardized B_i values are *not* affected by varying sample sizes. Because they are a function only of unweighted means, the expected value of each contrast is invariant over changes in relative group size.[10] Unfortunately, standardized β_i coefficients lack this property, rendering them of little use in many applications involving categorical IVs. This same property of invariance of unstandardized B_i regression coefficients and lack of invariance of standardized β_i coefficients also holds for dummy and unweighted effects codes.

---

[10]Contrast coding is most frequently used to test a priori hypotheses in experiments. In observational studies in which large random samples have been selected from a population, it may be useful to construct weighted contrast codes that take sample size into account. In weighted contrast codes, the intercept is the weighted mean of the group means and each contrast represents the weighted mean of the groups in set u versus the weighted mean of the groups in set v. Serlin and Levin (1985) outline methods of constructing weighted effect codes.

Confidence Intervals and Significance Tests for B_i

Procedures for constructing confidence intervals and conducting significance tests for each of the unstandardized regression coefficients are identical to those presented in Section 8.2.5 for dummy variables. Again, we simply take $B_i \pm tSE_{B_i}$, with $df = n - k - 1$, where k is the number of code variables ($= g - 1$). Substituting in the values for B_i and SE_{B_i} for the regression analysis presented in Table 8.5.2 corresponding to the contrast code variables in Table 8.5.1A, we find

$$B_0: \quad 81.90 \pm (2.037)(4.05) \quad = 73.65 \quad \text{to} \quad 90.15;$$

$$B_1: \quad -9.83 \pm (2.037)(8.11) \quad = -26.35 \quad \text{to} \quad 6.69;$$

$$B_2: \quad -32.64 \pm (2.037)(10.15) = -53.32 \quad \text{to} \quad -11.97;$$

$$B_3: \quad 33.38 \pm (2.037)(12.65) \quad = 7.59 \quad \text{to} \quad 59.17.$$

Null hypothesis t tests for each B_i are calculated by dividing the coefficient by its SE. These values are presented in Table 8.5.2A.

Semipartial and Partial Correlations

The squared semipartial correlation, sr_i^2, is the proportion of the total Y variance accounted for by contrast i in the sample. Thus, from Table 8.5.2, .0296 of the total ATA variance is accounted for by C_1, the majority-minority religion contrast. Each of the groups contributing to the contrast is unweighted; religions within the majority category count equally and religions within the minority category count equally. However, the relative sizes of the two categories being contrasted (e.g., majority vs. minority religion) is influential, with sr being maximal when the two categories have equal sample sizes. Similarly, $sr_2^2 = .2082$ is the proportion of the ATA variance accounted for by C_2, the Protestant-Catholic distinction, and $sr_3^2 = .1404$ is the proportion of the ATA variance accounted for by C_3, the Jewish-Other distinction. Note that the sum of the sr_i^2s does not equal $R_{Y.123}^2$ because the n_is are not equal, and, as we saw earlier, the correlations between the contrasts are not equal to 0.

The squared partial correlation, pr_i^2, is the proportion of that part of the Y variance *not accounted for by the other contrasts* that is accounted for by contrast i. Thus, $pr_2^2 = .2331$ indicates that C_2 (the Protestant-Catholic distinction) accounts for 23.3% of the Y variance remaining after the variance due to contrasts C_1 and C_3 have been removed. As usual, $pr_2^2 = .2331$ is larger than $sr_2^2 = .2083$. Recall that in MRC, $pr_i^2 \geq sr_i^2$, the equality holding when the other IVs account for no variance.

The choice between sr and pr depends, as always, on what seems to be more appropriate interpretive framework, the total Y variance or the residual Y variance after the effects of the other variables have been removed. With contrast codes, the source of the overlapping variance between the code variables is unequal sample sizes among groups. When participants have been randomly or representatively sampled and G represents a set of naturally occurring categories, the difference in sample sizes will reflect true differences in the proportion of each group in the population. But, when G represents a set of experimental manipulations, the difference in sample size will usually be due to nonmeaningful, incidental sources like difficulty (or cost) in mounting each of the treatment conditions or simply the randomization process itself.[11] Typically, sr_i which uses the total variance may be more meaningful for natural categories and pr_i which considers only the unique, nonoverlapping variance will be more meaningful for experiments.

---

[11]One additional source of unequal ns in missing data due to participant nonresponse or dropout. Missing data may require special analysis procedures (see Chapter 12, Little & Rubin, 1990, and Schafer & Graham, in press).

8.5.5 Statistical Power and the Choice of Contrast Codes

With one categorical IV, many hypotheses that give rise to contrast analysis are comprised of two parts. First, researchers propose a central theoretical distinction that they believe will lead to strong differences between two sets of groups. Second, the researcher proposes that there are only negligible differences among the groups *within* each set involved in the central theoretical distinction.

To illustrate this, let us consider the results of the analyses of two researchers who have different hypotheses about the critical determinant of religion's influence on ATA. Researcher A hypothesizes that minority vs. majority status is the critical determinant. The test of B_1 using the coding system in Table 8.5.1A provides the test of the first part of this hypothesis (see Table 8.5.2). Using either the confidence interval or significance testing approach, we see there is little evidence for this hypothesis. The confidence interval overlaps 0; the test of the null hypothesis is not significant. The second part of the hypothesis is that B_2 and B_3 should show negligible effects.[12] Otherwise stated, we expect no difference between the means of the groups involved in each contrast. Examination of the two tests that jointly comprise the second part of the hypothesis shows that these two confidence intervals do *not* overlap 0, contrary to prediction. Failure of either part of the test of the hypothesis suggests that minority versus majority status is not the critical determinant of religion's influence on ATA. Even if the first part of the hypothesis were supported, statistically significant effects for the second (no difference) part of the hypothesis would suggest that the contrast model is misspecified.

Researcher Z proposes that the central determinant of religion's influence on ATA is the religion's view of the general rights of women. Based on her theorizing, this researcher uses the contrast coding scheme presented in Table 8.5.1B to test her hypothesis (see Table 8.5.3). The test of B_1, representing the central theoretical distinction, shows considerable support for this part of the hypothesis, 95% $CI = 26.49$ to 49.53, $t(32) = 4.07$, $p < .05$. The tests of B_2, $CI = -13.36$ to 33.74, $t(32) = 0.88$, *ns*, and of B_3, $CI = -13.72$ to 32.64, $t(32) = 0.83$, *ns*, show no evidence of differences within the critical distinction of women's general rights. Such an outcome provides support for researcher Z's hypothesis.

Recall that for both of the coding systems, the overall influence of religion on ATA was substantial, $R^2 = .355$, $F(3, 32) = 5.86$, $p < .05$. The juxtaposition of the results of the two coding systems in Tables 8.5.2 and 8.5.3 makes clear that the use of contrast codes rather than an omnibus test can either raise or lower statistical power. To simplify the comparison, we can report F tests corresponding to the 1 df contrasts since $F = t^2$ for this case. The 1 df contrast associated with the majority vs. minority religion contrast, $F(1, 32) = 1.46$, *ns*, explained 8.3% of the overall effect of religion on ATA. This value is calculated as follows:

$$\frac{sr_i^2}{R^2} = \frac{.0296}{.3549} = .083.$$

In comparison, the 1 df contrast associated with general attitude toward women's rights, $F(1, 32) = 16.56$, $p < .001$, was significantly significant. Since sr_i^2 for this contrast is $.3339$, $.3339/.3539 = 94.1\%$ of the variance in ATA accounted for by religion is accounted for by the 1 df general attitude toward women's rights contrast. When the sample sizes in each of the groups are equal, this quantity can also be expressed as the squared correlation (r^2) between the contrast code values and the observed means for each of the groups. Otherwise stated, this

---

[12]A joint test of the two parts of the within category equivalence may be performed using techniques discussed in Chapter 5. The full regression equation includes all three contrast code variables. The reduced regression equation only includes the central contrast of theoretical interest, here C_1. The gain in prediction (R^2) from the reduced to the full equation is tested. This test corresponds to a joint test of within-category equivalence.

quantity can be taken as a measure of the degree to which the contrast codes mimic the true pattern of means.

In conclusion, researchers having hypotheses about the central distinctions between groups can often use contrast codes to provide sharp tests of the hypotheses. When the observed pattern of means closely follows the predicted pattern, researchers also gain an extra benefit in terms of enhanced statistical power to reject the null hypothesis associated with the central contrasts of interest. However, when hypotheses about the patterning of the means are not sharp, or when the pattern of observed means does not closely match the pattern of predicted means, the use of contrast coding is less likely to detect true mean differences among groups.

8.6 NONSENSE CODING

We have repeatedly stated that $g - 1$ code variables are needed to carry information of membership in one of the g groups. These code variables must be nonredundant: The R of each code variable with the remaining $g - 2$ code variables must *not* equal 1.00 (see the discussion of exact collinearity in Section 10.5.1). These conditions characterize dummy, unweighted effects, weighted effects, and contrast codes. In general, any set of $g - 1$ code variables that meets these conditions will yield exactly the same R^2, F, and regression equations that solve for the group means.

We can explore the limits of these conditions by creating a set of $g - 1$ nonsense codes: nonredundant code variables created in an arbitrary manner. We selected four random numbers between -9 and $+9$ for C_1, then squared and cubed them to produce nonredundant values for C_2 and C_3, respectively. These values are shown in Table 8.6.1A, along with two other arbitrary sets of nonredundant code variables in Parts B and C. Applying the values in Part A to our

TABLE 8.6.1
Illustration of Three Nonsense Coding Systems: Religious Groups

A. Nonsense codes I.

Religion	C_1	C_2	C_3
Catholic	5	25	125
Protestant	0	0	0
Jewish	-4	16	-64
Other	6	36	256

B. Nonsense codes II.

Religion	C_1	C_2	C_3
Catholic	1	-7	0
Protestant	-1	-1	0
Jewish	4	.5	24
Other	1	6	-1

C. Nonsense codes III.

Religion	C_1	C_2	C_3
Catholic	0	0	.71
Protestant	0	0	.04
Jewish	1	4	1
Other	2	108	2

D. Overall results for each nonsense coding scheme.

$R^2_{Y.123} = .3549$ $F = 5.869^*$ $(df = 3, 32)$

$\tilde{R}^2_{Y.123} = .2945$

Note: $^*p < .05$.

running example of religion and ATA, we find that $R^2 = .3549$ and $F = 5.869$, the exact values we have obtained with the previously discussed coding systems. The unstandardized regression equation is

$$\hat{Y} = 10.69C_1 + 2.60C_2 - .6867C_3 + 60.67.$$

When the values of the nonsense codes in Table 8.6.1A are substituted into the equation, it correctly yields the means for each of the four groups. But, here the results diverge sharply from those of all of the coding systems we have considered previously. The values for all individual effects—unstandardized and standardized regression coefficients, simple correlations, partial and semipartial correlations—are gibberish.

The point is that despite the nonsensical character of the coding, any full set of $g - 1$ nonredundant codes carries complete information about group membership. Any result that depends upon the set as a whole will yield correct and meaningful results: $R^2, \tilde{R}^2, F$, and the group means from the regression equation. In contrast, all results from single variables will be nonsensical.

8.7 CODING SCHEMES IN THE CONTEXT OF OTHER INDEPENDENT VARIABLES

8.7.1 Combining Nominal and Continuous Independent Variables

Most analyses involving nominal IVs carried out by means of MRC are likely to include additional nominal or quantitative IVs as well. As one example, a political scientist might wish to study the effect of ethnic group (black, hispanic, white), sex, and family income level on political attitudes. As a second example, an educational researcher might wish to compare the mathematics achievement of public versus private school students, with family income held constant. In these analyses the other nominal or quantitative IVs may be included because their influence on Y is also of interest, as in the first example where ethnic group, sex, and family income are all believed to influence political attitudes. Or, the IV may serve as a control for the effect of one or more IVs of interest as in the second example. The IVs involved in these multiple regression equations may be nominal, quantitative, or combinations of the two.

Consider the first example. The researcher would choose a coding scheme for the nominal variables that best represented her research questions. Suppose the researcher were interested in comparing the political attitudes of the two minority groups with the white group. One way to specify the regression equation would be to use two dummy codes for ethnic group, using white as the reference group, and one dummy code for gender, using male as the reference group. The regression equation would be

(8.7.1) $\hat{Y} = B_1C_1 + B_2C_2 + B_3 Female + B_4 Income + B_0$ (full model).

In this coding scheme, C_1 is a code variable that equals 1 if the participant is hispanic and 0 otherwise. C_2 is a code variable that equals 1 if the participant is black and 0 otherwise. Female is a code variable that equals 1 if the participant is female and 0 otherwise (male). Income is the participant's yearly income, and $\hat{Y}$ is the participant's predicted attitude.

Recall from Chapter 3 that the intercept is the predicted value of Y when all IVs are equal to 0. Thus, B_0 represents the predicted attitude of a white, male participant with \$0 income. B_1 represents the mean difference in attitude between the hispanic and white groups and B_2 represents the mean difference in attitude between the black and white groups when sex and income are held constant. B_3 represents the mean difference in attitude between females and males when ethnic group and income are held constant. And B_4 represents the change in attitude for each 1-unit ($1) increase in income when ethnic group and sex are held constant. Each of these effects is a partialed effect. For example, the estimated values of B_1 and B_2 from the regression equation,

$$(8.7.2) \qquad\qquad \hat{Y} = B_1 C_1 + B_2 C_2 + B_0,$$

would not in general equal those from Eq. (8.7.1). In Eq. (8.7.2), B_1 is the mean difference in attitude between hispanics and whites and B_2 is the mean difference in attitude between blacks and whites without controlling for sex or income. Only if income and sex are both unrelated to ethnic group will the regression coefficients B_1 and B_2 be equal in the two equations. When the same proportion of females are in each ethnic group, sex and ethnic group will be unrelated.

The interpretation we have presented holds only for the dummy coding scheme described here. As we have seen in this chapter, the interpretation of the individual partial regression coefficients depends on the coding scheme that is chosen. Dummy codes compare each group with a reference group. Unweighted effects codes compare each group with the unweighted mean of the groups, weighted effects codes compare each group with the weighted mean of the groups, and contrast codes compare the unweighted means of the two sets of groups that are involved in the contrast. The inclusion of additional quantitative or nominal IVs changes these from unconditional to conditional comparisons. Otherwise stated, in the comparison the effect of the additional IVs has been partialed out (held constant).

In Chapter 3 we learned about testing partialed effects. The procedures discussed there and earlier in this chapter can be used to construct confidence intervals and to conduct tests of significance for each B_i. In addition, the significance of nominal IVs with three or more groups can be tested using the gain in prediction formula presented in Section 5.5. For example, to test the effect of ethnic group, we would specify the full model, here represented by Eq. (8.7.1). We would then specify a reduced model that included all terms except for the nominal IV of interest (ethnic group), here represented by Eq. (8.7.3):

$$(8.7.3) \qquad \hat{Y} = \qquad B_3 Female + B_4 Income + B_0 \qquad (reduced\ model).$$

Applying the significance test for the gain in prediction, Eq. (5.5.1), we would have

$$F = \frac{(R^2_{full} - R^2_{reduced})/(g - 1)}{(1 - R^2_{full})/(n - k - 1)} \quad with \quad df = (g - 1, n - k - 1).$$

where R^2_{full} represents the full model (here, Eq. 8.7.1), $R^2_{reduced}$ represents the reduced model (here, Eq. 8.7.3), g is the number of groups comprising the nominal variable (here, $g = 3$), and k is the number of terms in the full model, here 4. As we have seen throughout this chapter, the result of the significance test of the nominal variable will be identical regardless of whether a dummy, unweighted or weighted effects, or contrast coding scheme is used.

8.7.2 Calculating Adjusted Means for Nominal Independent Variables

Beyond reporting significance tests or confidence intervals, it is sometimes desired to report the "adjusted means" that correspond to these comparisons. Adjusted means are the predicted means for each group involved in the regression equation. To illustrate the calculation of adjusted means in a regression equation with two nominal IVs, suppose we estimate a simplified version of Eq. (8.7.1) in which family income is not considered and obtain the following hypothetical results:

$$(8.7.4) \qquad\qquad \hat{Y} = 10C_1 + 5C_2 - 3Female + 50.$$

To calculate the adjusted means, we would simply substitute in the values of the code variables corresponding to each group. In our example, there are 3 ethnic groups by 2 genders, yielding 6 total adjusted group means. Using the dummy coding scheme described earlier in this section, we would have:

Group	C_1	C_2	Female	Adjusted mean
White Male	0	0	0	50
Hispanic Male	1	0	0	60
Black Male	0	1	0	55
White Female	0	0	1	47
Hispanic Female	1	0	1	57
Black Female	0	1	1	52

The calculation of the adjusted means for two of the groups is:

White Male: adjusted mean $= 10(0) + 5(0) - 3(0) + 50 = 50$;

Hispanic Female: adjusted mean $= 10(1) + 5(0) - 3(1) + 50 = 57$.

When there is more than one IV in the regression equation, these adjusted group means will not in general equal the original group means. The adjusted means are estimated based on a particular regression equation, here Eq. (8.7.4). If the regression equation is misspecified, then there may be substantial differences between the adjusted means and the actual means of the groups. In the present example, if there is a true interaction between ethnic group and sex in determining political attitudes, the original and the adjusted means will differ substantially because the interaction is not represented in Eq. (8.7.4). We will return to the topic of interactions between nominal variables in Chapter 9.

8.7.3 Adjusted Means for Combinations of Nominal and Quantitative Independent Variables

When quantitative IVs are included in the regression equation, the approach of substituting in the possible values of the IV to calculate adjusted means is no longer feasible. A simple way to calculate adjusted means is to use a regression equation in which all quantitative variables have been centered by subtracting their respective means. Given our focus on mean differences in this section, we will refer to the other IVs as covariates. If the nominal variable has been dummy coded, the intercept will now reflect the adjusted mean of the reference group. Each of the B_is will reflect the mean difference between the group coded 1 and the reference group, again adjusted for the group differences in the quantitative IVs.

Let us consider a fictitious investigation of background factors and altruism. The researchers have hypothesized that there are influences of population density on altruism, and have drawn samples of residents of a city and the surrounding area outside the city (noncity). As a first analysis, the researchers compared respondents living in the city (City $= 1$) with those not living in the city (City $= 0$), finding that city-dwellers were 18.37 points lower on the DV of altruism (see Table 8.7.1). However, the researchers are concerned that this difference may only reflect differences in neuroticism between city and noncity respondents. They therefore carry out a second regression analysis in which a dummy variable city and $Neurot_C$ are used as IVs, where centered Neuroticism, $Neurot_C =$ Neuroticism $-$ mean(Neuroticism). $Neurot_C$ correlates $-.247$ with altruism and .169 with city residence. The resulting regression equation is

(8.7.5) $\hat{Y} = -17.62\ City - .22\ Neurot_C + 52.88$

CH08EX02

TABLE 8.7.1
Original and Neuroticism-Partialed Scores
for Altruism and Residence

	n	$M_{\text{altruism}}(sd)$	$M_{\text{neuroticism}}(sd)$
Total sample	150	46.42 (14.48)	56.29 (9.72)
City residents	55	34.79 (10.92)	58.44 (10.44)
Noncity residents	95	53.16 (11.79)	55.04 (9.10)
Mean difference	$(t_{148\,df})$	18.37 (6.45) $p < .01$	3.40 (2.09) $p < .05$

Partial Data: First 10 Non–City Dwellers and Last 10 City Dwellers

	Altruism	City	Neuroticism	Altruism · Neurot$_C$	City · Neurot$_C$
1	69.13	0	61.01	70.86	−0.039
2	56.18	0	73.55	62.53	−0.145
3	65.57	0	41.15	60.00	0.128
4	65.85	0	55.93	65.72	0.003
5	63.08	0	46.41	59.44	0.084
6	50.61	0	58.21	51.31	−0.016
7	63.47	0	54.57	62.84	0.015
8	69.11	0	47.46	65.86	0.075
9	69.87	0	58.94	70.84	−0.022
10	49.05	0	49.05	46.39	0.061
⋮	⋮	⋮	⋮	⋮	⋮
141	32.18	1	61.35	34.04	0.958
142	40.47	1	34.21	32.34	1.186
143	15.21	1	66.48	18.96	0.914
144	27.23	1	52.31	25.76	1.034
145	48.44	1	34.32	40.36	1.185
146	26.52	1	71.87	32.25	0.870
147	39.36	1	55.73	39.15	1.005
148	54.30	1	35.44	46.63	1.176
149	33.77	1	63.78	36.52	0.937
150	40.15	1	65.39	43.50	0.924

In this equation the intercept $B_0 = 52.88$ is the adjusted mean level of altruism for those not living in the city and $-17.62 = B_{\text{City}}$ is the adjusted mean difference between those living in the city minus those not living in the city. The adjusted mean level of altruism for city residents is $52.88 - 17.62 = 35.26$. From Table 8.7.1, we see that the original means on altruism were 34.79 for city residents and 53.16 for noncity residents so that the difference is 18.37. The inclusion of Neurot$_C$ in the regression equation has slightly reduced the difference between city and noncity residents in altruism. The difference in the two results stems from the partialing process that is so central to MRC analysis.

It is useful here to review briefly the meaning of partialing. Partialing means that we are removing any variation that is associated with other IVs in the regression equation (see Sections 3.3 and 3.4). One way to do this is to follow the procedure used to construct added variable plots, presented in Section 4.4.2. Y is regressed on the other covariates (excluding the variable of interest, IV$_i$). Then IV$_i$ is regressed on the other covariates. In this present two-variable example, altruism and then city would be regressed on Neurot$_C$. For this sample, the regression equation predicting altruism is

(8.7.6) $$\hat{Y}_{\text{Altruism}} = -.368 \, Neurot_C + 67.13.$$

The regression equation predicting City is:

(8.7.7) $$\hat{Y}_{\text{City}} = .008 \, Neurot_C - .11.$$

We then save the residuals from each regression equation and add the original means back in for altruism and city, respectively, to return to the original scaling of each of the variables (recalling that residuals always have a mean of zero). The new variables Altruism · $Neurot_C$ and City · $Neurot_C$ represent the values of Altruism and City, respectively, with the linear effect of $Neurot_C$ partialed out.

In Table 8.7.1 we present data that illustrates the results of this procedure. We include the first ten of the noncity cases (1–10) and the last ten of the city cases (141–150) from this sample. Columns 1, 2, and 3 present the original scores on Altruism, City, and Neuroticism (not centered). Column 4 (Altruisum · $Neurot_C$) presents the Altruism score adjusted for level of $Neurot_C$ and Column 5 (City · $Neurot_C$) presents the City score, adjusted for $Neurot_C$. For example, case 1 was a noncity dweller with an Altruism score of 69.13 and a Neuroticism score of 61.01. Using Eq. 8.7.5, the predicted Altruism score is $(-.368)(61.01) + 67.13 = 44.68$. The residual is thus $69.13 - 44.68 = 24.45$, indicating that this respondent was more altruistic than his or her $Neurot_C$ score would have led one to expect. Adding the mean back gives $46.42 + 24.45 = 70.87$, which is the partialed score (within rounding error).

Carrying out the same operation for the city dichotomy using Eq. (8.7.6), we find this value to $= (.0084)(61.01) - .108 = .406$ for case 1. Our "observed" value for this noncity dweller was, of course, 0, so the residual is $-.406$. Adding in the mean for city of .367 (the proportion of the sample coded 1), the partialed score is $.367 - .406 = -.039$.

The critical point is what happens when partialed Altruism is regressed on partialed City. Exactly the same estimates for the intercept B_0 (the adjusted mean for the noncity dwellers) and the regression weight B_{City} (representing the adjusted mean difference between noncity and city) are obtained as in the equation in which the unpartialed variables were employed in combination with $Neurot_C$. Thus, the effect of partialing of $Neurot_C$, or any other covariate(s), can be seen to be equivalent whether it is accomplished by inclusion in a single prediction equation with IV_i or by prior removal of covariate influence using residuals from the separate equations for Y and IV_i. In addition, the standard errors in the significance tests will also be equal. And the adjusted means have exactly this meaning—means on partialed Y corresponding to scores of 0 and 1 on this partialed dichotomy.

Figure 8.7.1(A) and (B) presents two scatterplots of these same data. Figure 8.7.1(A) presents the original neuroticism covariate on the x axis; Figure 8.7.1 (B) presents the centered $Neurot_C$ covariate on the x axis. Both plots are identical except for the values represented by the scaling of the x axis. In both panels, non–city residents are indicated by open circles and city residents are indicated by ×. Two parallel lines have been fit to the data, the solid line for the non–city residents and the dashed line for the city residents. We see that the two lines are always the same distance apart (17.62, the distance between the adjusted city and noncity means) regardless of the value of the IV on the x axis. The specific value of the adjusted means is the value of $\hat{Y}$ for each group estimated at the mean of value of neuroticism ($=56.29$) or equivalently at the 0 value of $Neurot_C$. Substituting into Eq. 8.7.5, the adjusted means are

$$\hat{Y}_{\text{City}} = -(17.62)(1) - (.22)(0.0) + 52.88 = \text{adjusted } M_{\text{City}}$$

$$\hat{Y}_{\text{Noncity}} = -(17.62)(0) - (.22)(0.0) + 52.88 = \text{adjusted } M_{\text{Noncity}}$$

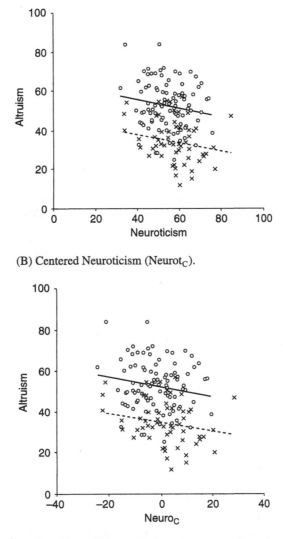

(A) Uncentered Neuroticism.

(B) Centered Neuroticism (Neurot$_C$).

Note: City residents are designated by ×; noncity residents are designated by o. The dashed line is the regression line for the city group; the solid line is the regression line for the noncity group. The regression equation including neuroticism is $\hat{Y} = -17.62\ City - 0.22\ Neurot_C + 65.24$. The regression equation including Neurot$_C$ is $\hat{Y} = -17.62\ City - 0.22\ Neurot_C + 52.88$.

FIGURE 8.7.1   Scatterplot of altruism versus neuroticism.

Figure 8.7.1(A) presents a plot of the data in which neuroticism has not been centered. When quantitative IVs have not been centered, the adjusted means in the equations that include them need to take the means of the other IVs into account by adding the products of their B coefficients times their means to the estimate. For our running example of altruism, the equation with the uncentered neuroticism is

$$\hat{Y} = -17.62\ \text{City} - .22\ \text{Neuroticism} + 65.24$$

for which we see that only the intercept B_0 is changed. As is illustrated in Fig. 8.7.1(A), the intercept now represents the predicted value of a noncity resident who has a score of 0 on neuroticism, a score that falls far outside the range of observed values of neuroticism in the sample. Estimating the adjusted mean now requires that the mean value of neuroticism ($= 56.29$) be entered into the equation:

$$\hat{Y}_{City} = (-17.62)(1) + (-.22)(56.29) + 65.24 = -17.62 - 12.39 + 65.24 = 35.26$$

$$\hat{Y}_{Noncity} = (-17.62)(0) + (-.22)(56.29) + 65.24 = 0 - 12.39 + 65.24 = 52.88.$$

8.7.4 Adjusted Means for More Than Two Groups and Alternative Coding Methods

The two principles just articulated generalize to any number of groups and any of the methods of coding group membership (the nominal or categorical variable) described in this chapter:

1. When covariates have been centered, their inclusion in the equation will produce adjusted means by the same methods used to produce unadjusted group means in their absence.
2. When covariates have not been centered one must add (or subtract) the products of their B coefficients in the equation times their full sample means—$\Sigma B_{cov_i} M_{cov_i}$—to the intercept in order for the methods described earlier for retrieving Y means to work.

To illustrate these principles, let us develop our running example in more detail. Suppose we had actually sampled altruism in three subpopulations: city, small town, and rural areas. (The last two subpopulations were combined into a single noncity group for our previous analysis). Our theory leads us to hypothesize that those living in small towns are more altruistic than those living in either rural areas or cities. In addition, previous research has suggested that neuroticism and socioeconomic status (SES) may also be related to altruism. Consequently, we are also worried that our findings may be contaminated by these two factors.

Because our theory suggests that the small town residents will be different from both city and rural respondents, we have used dummy codes in which town is the reference group. C_1 represents city residence and C_2 represents rural residence. Table 8.7.2A presents the mean Altruism, Neuroticism, and SES by residential area. Table 8.7.2B presents the correlation matrix including the two dummy codes. Of importance, some of the relationships between the dummy variables, (Rural, City), SES, and Neuroticism are statistically significant, suggesting the possibility that any differences between residence areas may be contaminated (in part) by the effects of Neuroticism and SES.

For pedagogical purposes, we estimate two regression equations. Equation (8.7.8) does not include the covariates:

(8.7.8)   Predicted *Altruism* $= -24.94$ *City* $- 11.15$ *Rural* $+ 59.73$.

Equation (8.7.9) now includes the two centered covariates, Neurot$_C$ and SES$_C$, to partial out any effects of these two variables.

(8.7.9)   Predicted *Altruism* $= -24.97$ *City* $- 10.21$ *Rural* $- 0.190$*Neurot*$_C$
$$+ 0.196\ SES_C + 59.39.$$

Comparing the results of Eq. (8.7.8) with Eq. (8.7.9), we note that the difference in mean Altruism between the City dwellers and those from small towns shows hardly any net effect of the partialing of the covariate ($B_{city} - 24.94$ versus -24.97). However, the magnitude of the difference in mean Altruism between rural and small towns decreases by about 1 unit

TABLE 8.7.2
Altruism and Three Types of Residential Area

A. Mean scores by area.

	Altruism	Neuroticism	SES
Rural ($n = 56$)	48.58	56.11	44.06
Small town ($n = 39$)	59.73	53.51	46.31
City ($n = 55$)	34.79	58.44	51.21
Total ($n = 150$)	46.42 ($sd = 14.48$)	56.29 ($sd = 9.72$)	47.27 ($sd = 10.72$)

B. Correlation matrix including dummy-variable coded area.

	Altruism	City	Rural	Neuroticism	SES
Altruism	1.0				
City	−.613	1.0			
Rural	.115	−.587	1.0		
Neuroticism	−.247	.169	−.014	1.0	
SES	−0.25	.281	−.231	.118	1.0

C. Regression equation without covariates.
$$Predicted\ Altruism = -29.94 City - 11.15 Rural + 59.73$$

D. Regression equation with centered covariates.
$$Predicted\ Altruism = -24.97 City - 10.21 Rural - 0.190 Neurot_C + 0.196 SES_C + 59.39$$

E. Regression equation with uncentered covariates.
$$Predicted\ Altrusim = -24.97 City - 10.21 Rural - 0.190 Neurotism + 0.196 SES + 60.83$$

Note: City residents are coded $C_1 = 1, C_2 = 0$. Small town residents are coded $C_1 = 0, C_2 = 0$ (reference group). Rural residents are coded $C_1 = 0, C_2 = 1$. C_1 is referred to as *City* and C_2 is referred to as *Rural* in the text.

(B_{rural}: -11.15 versus -10.21). This change is attributable to the influence of the Neuroticism and SES covariates. In general, the effect of including covariates on the group difference is indeterminate. The group difference may be the same, larger, smaller, or even reversed in sign, depending on the structure of the data.

To calculate the adjusted mean Altruism for the three groups in our example, we substitute the appropriate values into Eq. (8.7.9):

$$Adjusted\ M_{Y(Town)} = (B_{City})(0) + (B_{Rural})(0) + (B_{Neurot_C})(M_{Neurot_C}) + (B_{SES_C})(M_{SES_C}) + B_0$$
$$= 0 + 0 + 0 + 0 + B_0 = B_0 = 59.39;$$

$$Adjusted\ M_{Y(City)} = (B_{City})(1) + (B_{Rural})(0) + (B_{Neurot_C})(M_{Neurot_C}) + (B_{SES_C})(M_{SES_C}) + B_0$$
$$= -24.97 + 0 + 0 + 0 + 59.39 = 34.42;$$

$$Adjusted\ M_{Y(Rural)} = (B_{City})(0) + (B_{Rural})(1) + (B_{Neurot_C})(M_{Neurot_C}) + (B_{SES_C})(M_{SES_C}) + B_0$$
$$= 0 - 10.21 + 0 + 0 + 59.39 = 49.18.$$

If we had not centered the covariates, we would need to add in the product of their regression weights times their respective means, so

$$Adjusted\ M_{Y(Town)} = (B_{City})(0) + (B_{Rural})(0) + (B_{Neuroticism})(M_{Neuroticism}) + (B_{SES})(M_{SES}) + B_0$$
$$= 0 + 0 + (-0.190)(56.29) + (0.196)(47.27) + 60.83 = 59.39$$

$$\text{Adjusted } M_{Y(\text{City})} = (B_{\text{City}})(1) + (B_{\text{Rural}})(0) + (B_{\text{Neuroticism}})(M_{\text{Neuroticism}}) + (B_{\text{SES}})(M_{\text{SES}}) + B_0$$

$$= -24.97(1) + 0 + (-0.190)(56.29) + (0.196)(47.27) + 60.83 = 34.42$$

and

$$\text{Adjusted } M_{Y(\text{Rural})} = (B_{\text{City}})(0) + (B_{\text{Rural}})(1) + (B_{\text{Neuroticism}})(M_{\text{Neuroticism}}) + (B_{\text{SES}})(M_{\text{SES}}) + B_0$$

$$= 0 - 10.21(1) + (-0.190)(56.29) + (0.196)(47.27) + 60.83 = 49.18$$

as before.

CH08EX03   The analyst may use dummy codes, unweighted effect codes, weighted effect codes, or contrast codes to calculate adjusted means. When the covariates have been centered, the code values for the particular coding system are simply substituted into the corresponding regression equation. When the covariates have not been centered, the sum of the products of the covariates regression weights times their full sample means is added to the intercept term.[13]

Once again, we caution the reader that the adjusted means are estimated based on a specific regression equation, here Eq. (8.7.9). If the regression equation has been misspecified, then there may be substantial differences between the adjusted means and the true means in the population. Of particular importance, Eq. (8.7.9) assumes that possible interactions between the code variables representing the group and the covariates are 0. Methods of investigating interactions between nominal and quantitative variables are presented in Chapter 9.

8.7.5 Multiple Regression/Correlation with Nominal Independent Variables and the Analysis of Covariance

Analysis of Covariance (ANCOVA) is an analysis strategy typically applied to assess the impact of one (or more) group factors (e.g., treatment groups; gender) while statistically controlling for other IVs (called the covariates). ANCOVA is often treated as an extension of ANOVA that includes additional variables to be controlled. ANCOVA is treated in statistical packages (SAS, SPSS, SYSTAT) within the ANOVA framework. Readers familiar with ANCOVA may wonder about its relationship to MRC. Paralleling our observations in Section 8.2.7 about one-way ANOVA, they are identical. The F test for the Group effect in ANCOVA will be identical to the gain in prediction tests associated with the Group in MRC. The gain in R^2 associated with the Group ($R^2_{\text{full}} - R^2_{\text{reduced}}$) will equal η^2 from the ANCOVA. MRC analysis has the advantage relative to standard ANCOVA of allowing for the choice of a coding scheme that optimally represents the researchers' questions of interest.

The juxtaposition of MRC and ANCOVA also highlights several important issues in the interpretation of group differences in these analyses. As we have repeatedly emphasized, the use of the MRC approach assumes that the regression model has been properly specified. In Chapter 4, we considered five assumptions that we can apply in the present context.

1. The form of the relationship between each of the IVs and the DV is properly specified. In this chapter we have focused only on linear relationships. If there is a nonlinear relationship between one or more of the covariates and the DV, the model will be misspecified. Or, if there is a group × covariate interaction such that the regression of the DV on the covariate differs in each of the groups, the model will be misspecified. Regression models that include interactions between nominal IVs and between nominal and continuous IVs are considered in Chapter 9.

2. All relevant IVs are included in the model. MRC only adjusts for those covariates that are included in the regression equation.[14] Any other unmeasured covariates that (a) are

---

[13]The reader may wish to practice obtaining the desired contrasts with these data.

[14]In experiments, covariates are measured prior to treatment and mediators are measured following treatment.

associated with group status and (b) affect the DV lead to bias in the estimates of the group effect (see Section 4.5.2). One special exception occurs in the case of mediational analysis (see Section 12.2.1; Baron & Kenny, 1986) in which the group variable is presumed to cause changes in the mediator, which, in turn, causes changes in the DV (indirect effect).

3. All IVs are measured with perfect reliability. In the present context, group status (e.g., treatment versus control; city versus rural) is likely to be measured with near perfect reliability. With a single covariate, the effect of unreliability is to lead to too little adjustment of the mean difference for the covariate. With multiple unreliable covariates, the direction of bias is uncertain, although it will typically be toward underadjustment of mean differences.

4. The variance of the residuals within each group is equal (homoscedasticity). When large differences in the residual variances are obtained, the actual alpha level of significance tests may be too high or too low relative to the stated alpha level (typically, $\alpha = .05$, see Section 4.4.6).

5. The residuals from the regression equation should follow a normal distribution. Although this assumption is not critical in moderate or large n studies, non-normally distributed residuals may be a symptom of model misspecification.

In the context of MRC, these five are standard assumptions that should always be checked. In the context of ANCOVA, only some of these assumptions have received emphasis. In large part, this difference in emphasis stems from the application of ANCOVA to randomized experimental designs. In the context of randomized experiments, assumption 2 is automatically met because the treatment group will on average not be correlated with any of the covariates. Violation of assumption 3 (reliable covariates) can lead only to underestimation of the magnitude of the treatment effect (low power statistical test) but not to spurious results indicating a treatment effect exists when in fact it does not. Finally, violation of assumption 4 (equality of residual variances in each treatment group) does not typically occur—in practice relatively few treatments have large effects on the variance of the DV. Consequently, the emphasis in the traditional ANCOVA literature has been on the issues of possible nonlinear covariate-DV relationships and possible treatment × covariate interactions (assumption 1).

However, when MRC or ANCOVA is used to compare groups in nonexperimental contexts, it is important that each of the five assumptions be examined. Assumptions 1–4 are critical to inferring a treatment effect, and violation of assumption 5 can provide clues about model misspecification. Whether the groups are naturally existing groups (males and females; city, small town, rural residents) or are treatment groups in a quasi-experimental design (e.g., community 1 receives treatment; community 2 receives control), it cannot be definitely presumed that the groups are initially equivalent. Reichardt (1979); Shadish, Cook, and Campbell (2002); and West, Biesanz, and Pitts (2000) present full discussions of the conceptual and statistical issues associated with randomized and nonrandomized designs.

8.8 SUMMARY

A nominal independent variable G that partitions observations into g groups can be represented as $g - 1$ independent variables by various coding systems. All coding systems yield identical R^2, adjusted R^2, F for R^2, and, via the regression equations, group means on Y. All of these results are identical with those of analysis of variance. In contrast, the coding systems differ sharply in the meaning of the results for the individual code variables, C_i. Researchers should choose the coding system that provides the best answers to the specific research questions they are posing. Remaining questions that are not addressed by the coding system can typically be answered by using a second coding system that provides a direct answer to those questions. The various alternative coding methods facilitate the interpretation of the results for a

TABLE 8.8.1

Comparison of Coding Systems

Coding	r_{Yi}^2	B_0	B_i	sr_i^2	pr_i^2
Dummy	PV[a] due to i vs. non-i dichotomy	M_b (mean of reference group)	$M_i - M_b$ (difference between means of reference and ith groups)	PV due to i vs. non-i dichotomy	PV due to i vs. non-i dichotomy, excluding other effects
Unweighted effects	Ambiguous[b]	M_U (unweighted mean)	$M_i - M_u$ (difference between mean of ith group and unweighted mean)	PV due to i's effect	PV due to i's effect, excluding other effects
Weighted effects	Ambiguous	M_W (weighted mean)	$M_i - M_W$ (difference between mean of ith group and weighted mean)	—	—
Contrast	Ambiguous	M_U (unweighted mean)	varies	PV due to the i contrast	PV due to the i contrast, excluding other contrasts
Nonsense[c]	—	—	—	—	—

Note: [a]Proportion of variance. [b]Ambiguous interpretation unless sample sizes are equal in all groups. [c]All individual results are meaningless. For ease of presentation, we have assumed that the *i*th code variables also refers to the ith group.

single C_i for different frames of reference or desired comparisons. Table 8.8.1 provides a concise summary of the meaning of regression coefficients and simple, semipartial, and partial correlation coefficients for the different coding methods.

1. *Dummy-variable coding.*   One group is selected as the reference group. The intercept is the mean of the reference group, and each of the unstandardized regression coefficients is the difference between the mean of one of the groups and the mean of the reference group. This coding system is particularly appropriate for research in which one group is a control group and the others are to be compared with it (Section 8.2).

2. *Unweighted effects coding.*   The reference point here is the unweighted mean of all of the group means; this value is the intercept. The unstandardized regression coefficients represent the difference between each group's mean and the unweighted mean. This coding system is useful with experimental designs (Section 8.3).

3. *Weighted effects coding.*   The intercept is the weighted mean of the individual group means. The unstandardized regression coefficients represent the difference between each group's mean and the weighted mean. This coding system is particularly useful when the groups represent natural categories and a large random sample has been taken from the population (Section 8.4).

4. *Contrast coding.*   The $g - 1$ variables are constructed so as to provide a set of independent comparisons between means or unweighted means of means, selected in accordance with the researchers' specific research hypotheses. The intercept is the unweighted mean of the individual group means. The unstandardized regression coefficient provides the difference between the unweighted mean of the means of the groups in set u and the unweighted mean of the groups in set v, where u and v and the two sets of groups involved in the contrast. Contrast codes are particularly important when researchers have a priori hypotheses about the specific pattern of differences about the group means (Section 8.5).

5. *Nonsense coding.*   Here the coding values are arbitrary and individual results are meaningless, although those for the set as a whole are identical to those of the other coding systems. Nonsense codes were included because they illustrate how any set of $g - 1$ nonredundant code variables fully captures the information in a nominal IV (Section 8.6).

Finally, we noted that coding systems for nominal independent variables provide the foundation for understanding the meaning of more complex regression models including both categorical and continuous scale variables. Group means on the dependent variables adjusted for covariates are easily determined, especially when covariates have been centered. Any of the coding methods may be employed in these models combining groups and covariates. However, as always, the researcher is cautioned about the consequences of inadequate reliability in the covariates (Section 8.7).

9

Interactions With Categorical Variables

9.1 NOMINAL SCALE BY NOMINAL SCALE INTERACTIONS

In the last chapter we introduced four coding systems—dummy codes, unweighted effect codes, weighted effect codes, and contrast codes—that may be used to represent nominal (categorical) IVs. We also saw that regression equations could easily be specified that contain a mixture of nominal and quantitative IVs. However, the presentation in Chapter 8 was limited in two important ways. First, we did not consider any models that contained interactions between IVs. And second, we did not consider models in which the effect of the quantitative IV was nonlinear.

The purpose of this chapter is to address these more complex regression models that contain nominal IVs. We begin by considering a series of regression models that contain interactions between nominal variables. The progression of these models starts with the simplest case of the 2 by 2 design and then considers regression models of increasing complexity up to one that includes the interaction between three nominal variables. We then turn to regression models involving the interaction of quantitative and nominal IVs. Finally, we consider regression models that specify nonlinear interactions between nominal and quantitative variables. The material in this chapter builds not only on the foundation for the treatment of nominal IVs presented in Chapter 8, but also on the presentations in earlier chapters on the treatment of nonlinear effects (Chapter 6) and interactions (Chapter 7) of quantitative IVs in MRC.

9.1.1 The 2 by 2 Design

To provide a concrete illustration for our discussion of the 2 by 2 design, we present an example that we will use in the first part of this chapter. Imagine an experiment in which Y is the number of performance errors on a standard task made by each of a sample of rats. One factor in the design is surgery condition, in which the rats are divided into those receiving surgery that destroys a portion of the frontal lobes of their brains (the frontal group); and those whose surgery results in no brain destruction (the sham group). The second factor is drug condition: Within each of the two surgery groups, some rats receive an active drug (the active group), which is expected to minimize the effect of the frontal lobe destruction, and the remainder are given a placebo (the placebo group). Combining the two experimental factors, there are four treatment conditions:

Condition 1: Frontal, active
Condition 2: Sham, active
Condition 3: Frontal, placebo
Condition 4: Sham, placebo

The researcher is interested in answering three questions. First, is there an overall effect of the surgery condition: Do the rats receiving frontal lobe damage (frontal) make more errors on average than those without brain damage (sham)? Second, is there an overall effect of the active drug: Do the rats on active drug make fewer errors on average than rats receiving the placebo? Third, is the magnitude of the effect of frontal damage conditional on the drug condition? This third question asks whether there is a statistical interaction between the surgery and drug effects.

As we saw in Chapter 7, two variables are said to interact in their accounting for variance in Y when *over and above* any additive combination of their separate effects, they have a *joint* effect. In the case of two nominal IVs, novices often confuse the simple linear combination of two main effects with their joint effect, which is something quite different. Table 9.1.1 gives three 2 by 2 tables of means designed to illustrate this distinction. These data are hypothetical and are used to illustrate three different potential outcomes.

In each of the panels of Fig. 9.1.1 and as shown in Table 9.1.1, there is a nonzero "main" effect of both drug and surgery. A main effect is more properly referred to as an *average* effect, that is, it is the effect of a factor averaged over the levels of the other factor. In Table 9.1.1A, for example, rats in the active drug group have made an average effect of four fewer errors than those in the placebo group ($5 - 9 = -4$), and those with frontal lesion had an average of two more errors than those with the sham lesion ($8 - 6 = 2$). However, in the special case considered in Table 9.1.1A each of these average effects is *constant* over the levels of the other, for example, the effect of surgery under the active condition, $6 - 4 = 2$, is exactly the same as

TABLE 9.1.1
Y Means Illustrating No Interaction, Crossed Interaction, and Ordinal Interaction[a]

CH09EX01

	A. No interaction			B. Crossed interaction			C. Ordinal interaction		
	Frontal	Sham	Mean of means	Frontal	Sham	Mean of means	Frontal	Sham	Mean of means
Active	6	4	5	14	4	9	8	2	5
Placebo	10	8	9	10	12	11	12	10	11
Mean of means	8	6	7	12	8	10	10	6	8

$M_A - M_P = B_D$	$5 - 9 = -4$		$9 - 11 = -2$		$5 - 11 = -6$
$M_F - M_S = B_S$	$8 - 6 = 2$		$12 - 8 = 4$		$10 - 6 = 4$
$M_{AF} - M_{AS} = B_{(S)A}$	$6 - 4 = 2$		$14 - 4 = 10$		$8 - 2 = 6$
$M_{PF} - M_{PS} = B_{(S)P}$	$10 - 8 = 2$		$10 - 12 = -2$		$12 - 10 = 2$
$B_{(S)A} - B_{(S)P} = B_{S \times D}$	$2 - 2 = 0$		$10 - (-2) = 12$		$6 - 2 = 4$
B_0	7		10		8

[a]For simplicity, means are rounded to the nearest integer. For generality, the numbers in the cells all differ.

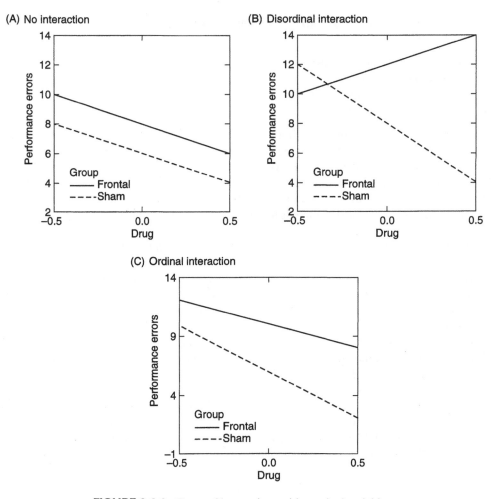

FIGURE 9.1.1   Types of interactions with nominal variables.

its effect under the placebo condition, $10 - 8 = 2$. Similarly, and necessarily, because there is only one *df* for the interaction in a 2 by 2 table, the average (main) effect for active versus placebo of -4 holds for both the frontal ($6 - 10 = -4$) and the sham groups ($4 - 8 = -4$). No interaction exists—each effect, whatever it may be, operates quite independently of the other or, equivalently, quite uniformly for each level of the other.

Consider, by way of contrast, Table 9.1.1B which presents a crossed (or disordinal) interaction. Here, the average mean for the frontal groups is 4 more errors than for sham, $12 - 8 = 4$. However, this is not uniform: for the animals given the active drug, the frontal cases average 10 *more* errors than sham ($14 - 4 = 10$), whereas for those receiving a placebo the frontal cases average 2 *fewer* errors ($10 - 12 = -2$). These two separate effects average out to the surgery main effect $(10 - 2)/2 = 4$, but are obviously quite different, and the fact of their differences constitutes the interaction. The interaction is said to be crossed or disordinal because the effects are of opposite sign ($+10$ and -2). Necessarily it is also crossed if one examines the separate drug effects for frontal ($14 - 10 = 4$) and for control ($4 - 12 = -8$) lesions.

The oppositeness of the signs of the differences is what makes the interaction crossed, but what reveals the interaction is the fact that the effects are different in magnitude. Table 9.1.1C illustrates an ordinal interaction where lines joining the means do not cross within the observed range of the data.[1] The difference between the means of the frontal and sham conditions for animals in the active condition is $8 - 2 = 6$, and for placebo $12 - 10 = 2$. These differences are of the same sign, hence ordinal. Although for both active and placebo groups the frontal lesion results in more errors, this occurs to different degrees, hence an interaction is present. Again, of course, the interaction is also apparent if one takes differences in means vertically instead of horizontally.

Table 9.1.1 should make clear what is meant by a joint effect. Only in Part A can one account for the means in terms of one constant effect for active drug versus placebo and a second constant effect for frontal versus control. In Parts B and C the two factors have an additional joint effect—the combination active drug-frontal and the combination placebo-control have a larger mean number of errors and the active drug-control and frontal-placebo combinations have a smaller mean number of errors than are accounted for by the average effect of drug and the average effect of surgery.

How would the researcher analyze the data corresponding to these 2 by 2 tables using MRC? As we saw in Chapter 8, $g - 1 = 3$ code variables are required to represent the four treatment conditions (cells). The central issue faced by the researcher would be to choose the best coding system to represent his research questions. As we saw in Chapter 8, there are a number of different choices—dummy codes, unweighted effect codes, weighted effect codes, and contrast codes. Recall that dummy codes contrast the mean of each of the other groups with the mean of a selected reference group, unweighted effect codes make comparisons with the unweighted mean of the groups, weighted effect codes make comparisons with the weighted mean of the groups, and contrast codes make a specific set of planned comparisons.

Earlier in this chapter, we noted that the researcher had three research questions corresponding to the average effect of drug, the average effect of surgery, and the conditionality of the surgery effect on the drug condition, the drug by surgery interaction. This set of hypotheses is best represented by a set of contrast codes. The researcher would code rats in the active drug condition $+.5$ and $-.5$ for those in the placebo condition for the first IV, C_D. The researcher would use $+.5$ for rats in the frontal lesion condition and $-.5$ for those in the sham condition for C_S, the surgery variable. Finally, the interaction is a function of the product of these codes on C_D and C_S, that is, $(C_D \times C_S = C_{S \times D})$.[2] When we analyze these data by MRC using these codes, we obtain the regression coefficients given below each 2 by 2 table. In full accord with what has been noted, the interaction $B_{S \times D}$ is 0 for Table 9.1.1, Part A, but takes on nonzero values for Parts B and C. This outcome reflects the requirement that over and above whatever average effects the two research factors have (reflected in B_D and B_S respectively), a third source of Y variation, namely their joint or interaction effect is operating in the latter two data sets. Note also that with contrast coding B_0 is the mean of all the cell means.

Providing that all of the $g - 1$ df are represented as code variables, any of the coding schemes presented in Chapter 8 will produce the same R^2 and significance test for the contribution of the set as a whole to the prediction of Y. Here there are four treatment groups, and any coding scheme that produces three less than perfectly correlated IVs will do. However, when the two dichotomous average effects of the 2 by 2 design and their product are coded by the method of contrast coding, not only R^2 and its F ratio are produced, but also meaningful values of B_i, sr_i, pr_i, the t test they share, and B_0 will also be produced. Here B_0 is the unweighted mean of means.

---

[1] Of course, all lines that are not parallel will cross at some point. In a disordinal crossed interaction they cross within the observed data.

[2] Note that these contrast codes satisfy the three criteria described in Section 8.5. Also note that these codes are perfectly correlated with unweighted effects codes for the two-group case—a desirability that will be discussed in the next section.

Contrast codes are particularly useful for interactions involving nominal scales because they are designed to be orthogonal and to represent meaningful differences between means of particular groups or combinations of groups. They allow the analyst to test the focal questions of interest whether there are two (or more) levels of each factor. These characteristics greatly facilitate the interpretation of interactions. However, other coding schemes may also be used, provided that the investigator keeps firmly in mind the meaning of both zero and a 1-unit change in each B_i in such sets.

To illustrate, suppose that the two research factors in Table 9.1.1 had been dummy-variable coded, with 0 assigned to the placebo and control conditions. In such a case X_3 the interaction, created as the product of the two main effects, would be coded 1 for the drug-frontal group ($X_1 = 1$ times $X_2 = 1$) and 0 for the other three groups. This results in the following set of code variables:

Treatment condition	X_D	X_S	X_{SxD}
Active drug, frontal	1	1	1
Active drug, sham	1	0	0
Placebo, frontal	0	1	0
Placebo, sham	0	0	0

As was shown for the interaction terms involving uncentered quantitative variables in Chapter 7, the results of this analysis may be interpreted. The significance test of the interaction term (X_{SxD}) and its partial correlation is not affected by the use of this dummy coding scheme. However, the absence of centering makes the average (first-order) effects awkward to interpret. The three data sets from Table 9.1.1 are shown analyzed using this dummy variable coding scheme in Table 9.1.2.

We can recreate the cell means by noting their representation in the three IVs and the intercept. The active drug-frontal group is coded 1 on all three variables—the dummy variable representing active drug, the dummy variable representing frontal lesion, and the product of these two variables—and we will need to add in the intercept in order to recreate its mean. Therefore $M_{DF} = B_1 + B_2 + B_3 + B_0$. The active drug-sham group is coded 1 on the drug dummy variable but 0 on the other IVs, so that its mean will $= B_2 + B_0$. The placebo-frontal group is coded 1 on the lesion dummy variable but 0 on the other IVs so that its mean

TABLE 9.1.2
Examples With No Interaction, Crossed Interaction, and Ordinal Interaction

	A. No interaction	B. Crossed interaction	C. Ordinal interaction
Dummy-variable analyses omitting the interaction:			
Frontal-sham difference $= B_1$	$8 - 6 = 2$	$12 - 8 = 4$	$10 - 6 = 4$
Active-placebo difference $= B_2$	$5 - 9 = -4$	$9 - 11 = -2$	$5 - 11 = -6$
B_0	8	10	9
Analyses including the dummy variable product:			
$M_{PF} - M_{PS} = B_1$	$10 - 8 = 2$	$10 - 12 = -2$	$12 - 10 = 2$
$M_{AS} - M_{PS} = B_2$	$4 - 8 = -4$	$4 - 12 = -8$	$2 - 10 = -8$
$M_{AF} - M_{AS} - M_{PF} + M_{PS} = B_3$	$6 - 4 - 10 + 8 = 0$	$14 - 4 - 10 + 12 = 12$	$8 - 2 - 12 + 10 = 4$
$B_0 = M_{PS}$	8	12	10

will $= B_1 + B_0$. And finally, the placebo-sham group is coded 0 on all IVs so that its mean will $= B_0$. Thus, the regression coefficients will have the interpretation given in Table 9.1.2B.[3] From this exercise we see that using dummy codes and taking the product to represent the interaction leads to regression estimates that, on the whole, are unlikely to represent the actual hypotheses for which the analyses were carried out. The proper interaction effect is preserved, but all average effects and the intercept differ from the researcher's hypotheses. For example, B_1 is now the difference between the means of the placebo-frontal and the placebo-sham (reference) groups rather than the average difference between the means of the active drug and placebo conditions. This example illustrates the importance of choosing the appropriate coding system to represent one's research hypotheses.

The Relationship of Coding Method to CI and Significance Tests for Nominal Scale Interactions

To carry our fictitious example yet further, we test the significance of the estimated coefficients in models using the two alternative coding schemes in Table 9.1.3. The first table of each pair tests the average effects and interaction using contrast codes, and the second tests the same data using dummy-variable codes.[4] As we have noted, the variables in the two models do not, in general, test the same effects. Nevertheless, two comparisons are particularly relevant to a full understanding of the differences. The first is the overall R for the equation estimating Y from the three predictors, which is precisely the same in the two representations of these nominal variables, as we saw in Chapter 8 for the general case of coding g groups with $g - 1$ variables.

The second thing to note in these comparisons of dummy-variable and contrast coding of nominal scales and their interaction is that the significance test (and thus, necessarily, the statistical significance of sr and pr, not shown) for the interaction term has precisely the same t value, and therefore our confidence in its departure from zero in the population is precisely equal in the two cases. It happens in this example that B_3 also takes on the same value, although this equivalence will not hold in general. This is, of course, another special case of the principle presented in Section 7.2.6, that the significance of interactions is invariant over linear transformations of the variables. When not provided by output from computer programs, sr may be determined by

(9.1.1)
$$sr_i = \frac{\beta_i}{\sqrt{1/\text{tolerance}}}.$$

A third thing to note in the comparison of the dummy variables and contrast-coded variables is the change in the tolerance of the variables depending on the coding scheme. The tolerance $(= 1 - R^2_{i.12...(i)...k})$ is the proportion of an IV's variance that is independent of the other IVs and thus a measure of collinearity, which we will consider in more detail in Section 10.5.3. When the tolerance is equal to 1.0 the variable is uncorrelated with the other IVs. As the tolerance decreases, there is increasing overlap between X_i and the other IVs, and thus increasing difficulty in interpreting the meaning of the coefficients. In this case, as usual, the dummy-variable codes are substantially intercorrelated, as shown by the tolerance. The contrast codes, however, are nearly independent, all nonessential collinearity having been eliminated. Only essential collinearity that is due to the unequal numbers of cases in the different cells of our example keeps this value from being equal to 1.0.

---

[3]The reader may carry out the calculations to see that these equations do in fact recreate the means given in Table 9.1.1.

[4]For these tables we have not rounded the estimates to integers, as we had done in the earlier tables.

TABLE 9.1.3
Statistical Tests of 2 by 2 Data With and Without Interactions
by Two Coding Methods

Effect	Value	SE_B	CI_B	Tolerance	t	p
(A) No interaction data: Contrast codes, $R = .913$						
B_0	7.01	.08	6.85–7.17	—	86.08	<.01
B_1	2.01	0.16	1.69–2.33	.99	12.34	<.01
B_2	−4.00	0.16	−3.68–(−4.32)	.95	−24.55	<.01
B_3	.03	0.33	−.30–(+.34)	.96	0.10	.92
No interaction data: Dummy-variable codes, $R = .913$						
B_0	8.01	0.138	7.74–8.28	—	58.05	<.01
B_1	1.99	0.23	1.54–2.45	.50	8.65	<.01
B_2	−4.01	0.21	−3.61–(−4.42)	.60	−19.52	<.01
B_3	.03	0.33	−.61–(+.68)	.36	0.10	.92
(B) Crossed interaction data: Contrast codes, $R = .970$						
B_0	10.01	0.08	9.85–10.17	—	122.94	<.01
B_1	4.01	0.16	3.69–4.33	.99	24.62	<.01
B_2	−2.00	0.16	−2.32–(−1.68)	.95	−12.27	<.01
B_3	12.03	−.33	5.70–6.34	.96	36.96	<.01
Crossed interaction data: Dummy-variable codes, $R = .970$						
B_0	12.01	0.14	11.74–12.28	—	87.03	<.01
B_1	−2.01	0.23	1.55–2.46	.50	−8.72	<.01
B_2	−8.01	0.21	−8.42–(−7.61)	.60	−38.98	<.01
B_3	12.03	0.33	11.39–12.68	.36	36.96	<.01
(C) Ordinal interaction data: Contrast codes, $R = .969$						
B_0	8.00	0.08	7.84–8.16	—	99.85	<.01
B_1	4.02	0.16	3.70–4.34	.99	25.07	<.01
B_2	−5.99	0.16	−6.39–(−5.67)	.95	−37.35	<.01
B_3	4.01	0.32	1.69–2.32	.96	12.52	<.01
Ordinal interaction data: Dummy-variable codes, $R = .969$						
B_0	9.99	0.14	9.72–10.26	—	73.53	<.01
B_1	2.01	0.23	1.56–2.46	.50	8.87	<.01
B_2	−7.99	0.20	−8.39–(−7.59)	.60	−39.49	<.01
B_3	4.01	0.32	3.38–4.65	.36	12.52	<.01

Lessons Learned from the 2 by 2 Example

From this simple example we may draw several conclusions that may be applied to more complex interactions involving nominal scales. They are:

1. Analysts should choose a coding scheme that most adequately represents their research questions. In experimental designs, this will typically be unweighted effects or contrast coding.

2. The significance tests on the total interaction effect for nominal scales,[5] as for continuous scales, will be invariant. In exploratory analyses, a hierarchical entering of IV sets into the regression equation can be used to test the contribution of the interaction set. This is likely to be an especially attractive option if one is merely checking the interactions to make sure that

---

[5]Taken collectively, as we shall see later. In this example there was only one interaction term.

they are not needed in the model, as in the ANCOVA model presented in Section 8.7. That is, if we have not expected or theorized an interaction, we may code the main effects in any way that makes most sense for the investigative purposes. We then use the products of these main effects collectively to test the significance of the interaction, expecting that the interaction terms will not add significantly to prediction and therefore can be omitted from the final equations to be reported. Note that the regression coefficients from the initial steps of the hierarchical analysis will differ from those in the final model. If the interaction term turns out to be significant, then the regression coefficients from the full model including the interaction should be reported. The analyst should also revisit whether the coding scheme continues to represent the research questions of interest in light of the changes in the interpretation of the lower order regression coefficients in the presence of an interaction.

3. Regardless of the coding scheme for nominal variable main effects and interactions, providing that they include $g - 1$ IVs, where g equals the number of groups (cells) in the design, and none of these $g - 1$ IVs is perfectly predictable from the others, the multiple R and R^2 will be invariant. In a two-factor design, g will equal the product of the number of levels of the first factor times the number of levels of the second factor. Such an invariance, in combination with the invariance of the interaction contribution to R^2, means that the contribution of the combined main effects is also invariant over alternative methods of coding.

4. The values of the regression coefficients for lower order terms that are part of higher order interactions may change dramatically when the coding scheme changes, and must be interpreted as the effect of each factor only at zero on the other factor(s).

9.1.2 Regression Analyses of Multiple Sets of Nominal Variables With More Than Two Categories

There are two distinct aspects of the analysis of k groups by k groups designs. The first is the determination of which research factors, including interactions, should be included in the full model. This decision is often made on the basis of the significant contribution of sets of variables to the overall prediction, as discussed in Chapter 5. Thus this analysis may determine whether certain sets of variables or interactions may be dropped from further consideration.

With equal ns in each condition of the design, the various main effect and interaction sets of independent variables are uncorrelated or orthogonal. When cell ns are proportional these sets are also orthogonal. By proportional, we mean that the number of cases in any cell can be exactly determined by multiplying the proportion of cases in that cell for each research factor by the proportion in that cell for every other research factor. Thus, if half the cases were in category 1 for research factor B and one fourth of the cases are in category 2 for research factor C, then the proportion of the full sample that is in cell $B_1 C_2$ should be $.50 \times .25 = .125$. In this case a χ^2 on the table of sample ns will equal 0. Such a design is said to be balanced.

When the study design is fully balanced, with equal or proportional ns in all cells so that research factors are uncorrelated, the analysis may proceed by hierarchically examining sets representing research factors and interactions coded by whatever system best reflects the major research hypotheses. When the cell ns are unequal, however, it will matter how these codes are assigned to groups: Significance tests will vary as a function of these codes.

Often this first step will be considered essential before proceeding with the second task that is selecting the optimal code system for the categorical variables to represent the major research questions in the analytic output.

Significance Tests of Research Factors and Interaction Sets: Type I, II, and III Regression Sums of Squares

We will present the three approaches to testing the significance of group differences by considering the situation in which research factor A (with, e.g., four groups) is represented by a set of three variables A, research factor B (with, e.g., three groups) is represented by a set of two variables B, and the interaction between these sets is represented in this case by six variables, set $A \times B$. Type I sum of squares uses a hierarchical build up approach to estimate the overall significance of each effect, as presented in Section 5.4. Assume that A is the effect of most interest. Then three hierarchical regression equations are estimated, using A in the first, A and B in the second, and A, B and $A \times B$ in the third. The test of A is taken from the first equation, the test of B uses the gain in R^2 (increase in regression SS) from the second equation, and the test of $A \times B$ uses the gain in prediction from the third over the second equation. Recall that the gain in prediction in a hierarchical regression model is tested using either Model 1 error [Eq. (5.5.1)] in which each effect is tested for significance when it is first entered, or Model 2 error, in which the MS for the error is taken from the final equation. With this method the test of A ignores any possible overlap of A with B or the interaction, and the test of B controls for the effect of A, but ignores the effect of the interaction. The decision about the sequence of A and B is made on the substantive grounds of most interest or presumed causal priority. The methods of coding A and B do not affect these tests. Even if the interaction were the effect of most interest, it would be tested at step 3: Interactions are partialed effects (see Chapter 7; J. Cohen, 1978).

Type II sum of squares uses a modified hierarchical approach. In addition to the hierarchical sequence used in Type I sum of squares we also estimate Y from an equation using only B. The effect of B is determined as before, by the gain in prediction from the equation using only A to the equation using both A and B. The effect of A is determined in a parallel manner, by the gain in prediction from the equation using only B to the equation using both A and B. The test of the interaction is as before, its contribution to R^2 above the main effects. Again, the Model 1 or Model 2 error term may be employed, usually depending on whether there is an a priori reason for expecting an interaction effect.

The Type III sum of squares approach compares the prediction of the full model to submodels in which only the effect of interest is eliminated. This model is that used by current ANOVA programs applied to unequal n designs, and it depends critically on using unweighted effects codes (Section 8.3) to represent research factors A and B and their products to represent their interaction. One begins by estimating the "full model" equation for Y from A, B and $A \times B$. Then an equation employing B and $A \times B$ is used to determine the difference in the regression SS between the full model and the model omitting A, and the resulting MS (dividing that difference by the *df* for A) is tested using the full equation residual MS, as in Eq. (5.5.2). A parallel set of procedures, starting with an equation employing A and $A \times B$ is used to test the independent contribution of B. Finally, the $A \times B$ effect is tested by determining the difference in regression SS between the combined A and B effects and the full model equation. This test is necessarily equivalent to the tests using either Type I or Type II SS approaches. The Type III sum of squares approach provides a test of the unique effect of each research factor with any contribution due to unequal cell ns partialed out. For this reason, it is viewed as the most conservative approach. It is the same approach used when we test the significance of each predictor in the full equation, providing that we have used unweighted effects codes.

As we saw in Chapter 5, researchers should choose the approach that best represents their central questions of interest. A critical prerequisite in making this choice is to consider whether a random or representative sample has been selected from a population. The Type I sum of squares approach implies the strong assumption that the differences in sample sizes represent differences in the proportion of cases in each of the conditions in the population. Thus, it is not appropriate for experimental studies in which investigators (and perhaps chance factors) determine cell sizes that the Type I SS be used. Differences in sample sizes across conditions almost always represent either procedural decisions by the experimenter (e.g., using fewer participants in a particularly difficult to implement or costly treatment condition), a failure of the randomization procedure to achieve equal allocation of the participants to treatment conditions, or missing data in one or more of the treatment conditions (see Chapter 11 for a discussion of missing data issues). For this reason, sources emphasizing the analysis of experiments discourage the use of the Type I sum of squares approach (e.g., Kirk, 1995).

Given a random or representative sample, there are a number of research contexts in which the Type I sum of squares approach provides the optimal approach. For example, imagine a sociologist is studying the effects of family socioeconomic status (low versus middle versus upper) and high school graduation (no versus yes) on lifetime income. The researcher may theorize that family socioeconomic status (SES) is a cause of successful high school graduation so that any overlapping variance between these two IVs should be assigned to SES. Howell and McConaughty (1982) offer several illustrations of contexts in which both theoretical and applied policy questions may be optimally answered using the Type I sum of squares approach.

The choice between the Type II and Type III sum of squares approaches is normally based on the researcher's assumption about the existence of the interaction term in the population. If the effect of the interaction set is assumed to be 0, then the Type II sum of squares approach provides a more powerful test of the main effects of A and B. However, if the $A \times B$ interaction is not 0 in the population, then the model is not correctly specified and the estimates of A and B will be biased. We previously considered this general issue of bias versus efficiency in model specification in Chapter 4. A reasonable approach in the absence of an expected interaction effect is to test the significance of the interaction effect and, if it is not significant, to delete it from the model. The usefulness of this approach will also depend on the power of the test of interaction—the interaction may exist in the population, but may not be detected in a small sample.

Designs involving more than two factors will involve straightforward extensions of these procedures. Maxwell and Delaney (1990, Chapters 7 and 8) present a full and balanced discussion of issues in the analysis of factorial designs with unequal sample sizes.

Selection of Group Coding Method and Significance Tests of Individual Variable Effects

Having determined the significance of the overall effect of each research factor and interactions among research factors, the next task is determination of the best coding system to represent the substantive issues in the full equation model. In a sense this is the payoff of analyzing the data using an MRC rather than an ANOVA approach, in addition to the flexibility of including other, noncategorical, variables as appropriate to the substantive issues. For these decisions we refer back to the options presented in Chapter 8. We also note that one may employ an unweighted effects code system in order to assess the unique contribution of a set, using Model III SS as above and yet switch to some other method of coding to provide the best possible answers to the substantive questions motivating the research.

Illustrative Example

Consider a study comparing the efficacy (Y) of three different treatment procedures (T), two experimental and one control. The researchers succeed in getting each of the four medical school hospitals in a large metropolitan area to participate. The three different procedures are employed on randomly assigned samples of suitably selected patients at each of the four medical school hospitals (H: H_1, H_2, H_3, H_4), thus making possible an appraisal of the uniformity of the treatment effects across the medical school hospitals. Since the four hospitals constitute the

CH09EX02

TABLE 9.1.4
Effects of Research Factors and Interaction
in an Experimental Study

	SS	df	MS	F
IV sets				
$H, T, H \times T$	75,209.071	11		
Residual$_{H,T,H \times T}$	30,891.422	96	321.79	
$H, H \times T$	52,193.908			
$T, H \times T$	71,077.543			
H, T	30,820.806			
Unique contribution				
H	75,209.071	3	1377.18	4.28
	−71,077.543			
	4,131.528			
T	75,209.071	2	11,007.58	34.21
	−53,193.908			
	22,015.163			
$H \times T$	75,209.071	6	7,398.04	22.99
	−30,820.806			
	44,388.265			

entire population of hospitals of interest, this is a 4 by 3 factorial design, with the interaction (H by T) directly addressing the issue of uniformity of effects.[6] Each of the 12 cells contains efficacy scores for the patients treated by one of the three procedures at one of the four hospitals, and in the interest of generality, there are a different number of cases in each of the 12 subgroups. The n for the entire study is 108.

Given the unequal ns in this example, and the fact that it includes an experimental component, our first task will be to test the overall contribution of between hospital differences, treatments, and their interaction by means of the Type III SS method. Thus we will code the three variables representing the four hospitals H and the two variables representing the three treatment conditions T by unweighted effects codes. For this purpose it is immaterial which group is selected as the contrast group, the estimated SS will remain the same. The regression SS for the full equation including H, T and $H \times T$ is 75209.071, and the residual MS from that equation = 321.79. To test each of the individual factor sets H, T and $H \times T$ we take the difference between the full equation regression SS and the regression SS for all other sets, as shown in Table 9.1.4. In this example all three sets are statistically significant ($p < .01$).

Having determined the importance of all three sets, we now turn to the task of optimal coding of the individual variables to represent our major research questions in the full equation. Presuming that we have no special interest in any single one of the hospitals our coding method should treat them all on an equal footing, so that any H involves comparisons among the four hospitals all on equal footing, and any comparison conveniently proceeds as being between the Y mean of any given hospital and the unweighted mean of means of all four hospitals. Because there are four hospitals and only three df, one hospital must be selected as the base group and coded consistently −1. Table 9.1.5 provides the effects codes for the four hospitals as X_1 to X_3.

---

[6]Technically, hospitals is a fixed effect in the present design because our conclusions are intended to apply only to these three treatments and these four hospitals. In cases in which many hospitals are randomly selected from a population of hospitals, multilevel modeling techniques described in Chapter 14 should be employed.

For the T factor, on the other hand, the presence of a control group to which each of the experimental groups is to be compared suggests the possible use of dummy-variable coding (Section 8.2). The three treatments are thus represented by two IVs (X_4 and X_5) with the control condition consistently assigned 0, as shown in Table 9.1.5. Thus, each patient is characterized on hospital of origin by three IVs and for treatment group by two IVs, which together produce the coding of X_1 through X_5 in Table 9.1.4.

The interaction set $H \times T$ is again created by multiplying each of the H set variables by each of the T set variables, creating $2 \times 3 = 6$ new IVs. The 11 IVs in the three sets exactly identify the $H_i T_j$ cell of each patient. We emphasized in Chapter 8 that to fully represent G, made up of g groups, $g - 1$ IVs are necessary, whatever the form of coding. This 4 by 3 design results in 12 groups, hence full representation requires 11 IVs. From the many optional methods of coding membership in one of 12 groups, the coding given in Table 9.1.5 represents these 12 groups as three effects-coded IVs for H, two dummy-coded IVs for T, and the six interaction-bearing IVs that result from their set by set multiplication. As we will see, designs in which two different coding systems are employed require special care to assure proper interpretation of the individual regression coefficients.

TABLE 9.1.5
Codes for the H by T (4 by 3) Factorial Design

	(A) H (unweighted-effects codes)			(B) T coding (dummy codes)		
	X_1	X_2	X_3		X_4	X_5
H_1	1	0	0	T_1	1	0
H_2	0	1	0	T_2	0	1
H_3	0	0	1	Control	0	0
H_4	−1	−1	1			

(C) Joint coding of the 12 cells of the H by T factorial design

	Hospitals			Treatments		Hospitals by treatment					
						$X_1 X_4$	$X_1 X_5$	$X_2 X_4$	$X_2 X_5$	$X_3 X_4$	$X_3 X_5$
Cell	X_1	X_2	X_3	X_4	X_5	X_6	X_7	X_8	X_9	X_{10}	X_{11}
$H_1 T_1$	1	0	0	1	0	1	0	0	0	0	0
$H_1 T_2$	1	0	0	0	1	0	1	0	0	0	0
$H_1 C$	1	0	0	0	0	0	0	0	0	0	0
$H_2 T_1$	0	1	0	1	0	0	0	1	0	0	0
$H_2 T_2$	0	1	0	0	1	0	0	0	1	0	0
$H_2 C$	0	1	0	0	0	0	0	0	0	0	0
$H_3 T_1$	0	0	1	1	0	0	0	0	0	1	0
$H_3 T_2$	0	0	1	0	1	0	0	0	0	0	1
$H_3 C$	0	0	1	0	0	0	0	0	0	0	0
$H_4 T_1$	−1	−1	−1	1	0	−1	0	−1	0	−1	0
$H_4 T_2$	−1	−1	−1	0	1	0	−1	0	−1	0	−1
$H_4 C$	−1	−1	−1	0	0	0	0	0	0	0	0

TABLE 9.1.6
M_Y and n_i in the 4 by 3 Nominal Scale Example

	T_1	T_2	T_3 = control	M_H	M_{mT}
H_1	47.8 (9)	123.9 (9)	86.6 (6)	86.0 (24)	86.1
H_2	71.2 (10)	134.5 (8)	59.5 (9)	86.1 (27)	88.4
H_3	54.7 (12)	95.5 (9)	97.9 (9)	79.9 (30)	82.7
H_4	93.9 (9)	53.9 (6)	68.0 (12)	73.5 (27)	71.7
M_T	66.1 (40)	105.4 (32)	76.4 (36)	81.2 (108)	
M_{mH}	66.7	102.0	78.0		82.2

Given the efficacy scores (Y) for the 108 patients, together with the representation of each patient as to hospital H and treatment group T membership using the 11 IVs of Table 9.1.5, the data matrix is completely defined.

The full equation with IV sets H, T and $H \times T$ is

$$\hat{Y} = 8.60X_1 - 19.55X_2 - 19.94X_3 - 11.29X_4 + 23.95X_5 - 27.49X_6 + 13.38X_7 + 22.99X_8$$
$$t\ 1.43 \quad -3.54 \quad 3.81 \quad -2.69 \quad 5.38 \quad -3.48 \quad 1.67 \quad 3.20$$
$$+ 51.05X_9 - 31.92X_{10} - 26.37X_{11} + 78.01$$
$$t\ 6.72 \quad -4.56 \quad -3.54$$

and the t tests for these effects are provided beneath each term. With 96 error df a $t \geq 2.63$ is significant with $\alpha = .05$. Each of these unstandardized coefficients represents a specific effect. B_1 represents the difference between the mean of hospital 1 and the unweighted mean of the four hospitals in the control condition. Table 9.1.6 provides the full means and ns for each cell in these data where it can be seen that this coefficient, 8.60, does in fact = 86.6 − 78.0. B_2 and B_3 represent similar comparisons for hospitals 2 and 3, respectively. B_4 represents the comparison of the mean for T_1 with the mean of the control group. The mean for T_1 is the unweighted mean of the T_1 groups across the four hospitals and the mean for the control is the unweighted mean of the control groups across the four hospitals. B_5 represents a similar comparison of the mean of T_2 with the mean of the control group. Each of the six interaction terms represents a specific facet of the nonuniformity of effects. Each of these IVs represents a specific effect aspect of H by dummy aspect of T, its B gives the size of this discrete interaction effect, and the accompanying t provides its significance test. Five of these six are significant in this fictitious example. The first is X_6, the interaction between the effect of hospital 1 (relative to the unweighted mean of the hospitals) and the treatment 1 comparison with the control. The T_1 versus control comparison in H_1 is 47.8 − 86.6 = −38.8. The T_1 versus control at the unweighted mean of hospitals is 66.7 − 78.0 = −11.3. The difference between these (the interaction) is −38.8 − (−11.3) = −27.5, the B for the first interaction term, X_6. The second interaction term tests the (nonsignificant) difference between T_2 and control in H_1 (again as compared to the mean of the hospital mean differences), and the third term X_8 compares the H_2T_1 versus control mean difference (71.2 − 59.5 = 11.7) with the same T_1 versus control difference at the unweighted mean of the hospitals = 11.7 − (−11.3) = 23. The remaining three terms can be similarly interpreted.

9.2 INTERACTIONS INVOLVING MORE THAN TWO NOMINAL SCALES

In Chapter 7 we saw that when the interaction among more than two continuous variables is being examined it is necessary to include in the equation all of the lower order interactions for the model to be hierarchically well specified (see Section 7.8; Peixoto, 1987). Otherwise, the interpretation of the terms in the regression equation will be confounded by any absence of lower order terms. Similarly, when nominal scales are each represented as a set of $k - 1$ code variables, where k is the number of categories (groups) that comprise the nominal variable, interactions involving more than two such nominal variables will require inclusion of the full set of code variables representing each possible lower order interaction and the original nominal variables. Thus, examination of the triple interaction between three categories of ethnicity E, three religious affiliations R, and three school grades S (e.g., 6th, 8th, and 10th) in predicting Y would require, in addition to $E_1, E_2, R_1, R_2, S_1, S_2$, and the triple interaction set of eight variables $E_1 \times R_1 \times S_1, E_1 \times R_2 \times S_1, E_1 \times R_1 \times S_2, E_1 \times R_2 \times S_2, E_2 \times R_1 \times S_1, E_2 \times R_2 \times S_1, E_2 \times R_1 \times S_2, E_2 \times R_2 \times S_2$, the three sets of two-way interactions collectively having another 12 variables, for a total of $6 + 12 + 8 = 26$ variables representing the 27 cells of this 3 by 3 by 3 design.[7] Necessarily such an investigation would require either a very large sample or very large expected effect sizes to detect such differences with reasonable power and confidence limits on estimates. Thus it is most frequent that researchers will investigate such interactions only when there is both a strong theoretical reason for interest and a large sample to assure adequate statistical power. The fact that several nominal variables exist in a data set and can be used to create a large number of different potential two-way, three-way, four-way, or higher way interactions does not necessarily mean that they are all to be investigated in the absence of compelling research questions.

As we have noted, when cell sizes are unequal the different group factors will be correlated. Thus, the first step will be to use an appropriate method of testing the contribution of group and interaction sets. In experimental studies this will most readily be accomplished by employing a standard ANOVA program, which will use unweighted effects codes to estimate these effects. Alternatively, effects codes can be created by the investigator and the Type III Regression SS method described earlier carried out. In other research designs the investigator may choose a Type I Regression SS method, using hierarchical sequences of main effect and interaction sets, or a Type II Regression SS method, using multiple hierarchical sequences of main effect and interaction sets.

Once the determination of the significance of sets and the level of interaction to be retained in the final model is made, the investigator proceeds to the decision regarding coding methods to employ in the full equation model.

9.2.1 An Example of Three Nominal Scales Coded by Alternative Methods

We present here a fictitious data set based in part on the theorizing and experimental findings of Carol Dweck (1999). The dependent variable of interest is the amount of effort the individual exerts in solving a set of problems in the *second* part of an experimental session. The manipulations take place in association with the participant's work on an experimental task given during the first part of the experimental session. The first factor is task difficulty (D)—the experimental task is either hard or easy. The second factor is feedback (F)—participants are told that they have either succeeded or failed on the experimental task. The final factor is attribution (A) with three levels. Participants are led to believe that the outcome of their performance was due to their effort (A_1) their ability (A_3), or they are given no basis for making an attribution about the cause of their performance (control group, A_2). Thus, we have a 2 (D) by 2 (F) by 3 (A) design in which each of the $2 \times 2 \times 3 = 12$ possible treatment conditions are represented.

---

[7]This exposition assumes no empty or nearly empty cells in the design. If there are empty cells some appropriate simplification is required. Typically, researchers consider collapsing categories within a nominal category that they do not expect to differ or dropping consideration of the three-way and possibly some of the two-way interactions from the model.

TABLE 9.2.1
Hierarchical Analysis of Effects-Coded Variables in a Three Factor Example

Predictor sets	SS	df	MS	R^2	F	p
Main effects	612.17	4	153.04	.350	15.47	<.01
Main effects + two-way interactions	890.60	9		.509		
Full model	909.50	11	82.68	.520	10.62	<.01
Residual	840.41	108	7.78			

A central tenet of Dweck's theorizing is that important consequences follow from viewing task successes and failures as resulting from a relatively fixed ability ("trait" attribution) or a function of the degree and kind of effort put into the task ("effort" attribution). The theory states that the effect of this *attribution* variable on effort (Y) will depend on the previous success or failure experience with a comparable task, with the "trait" group more likely to give up and put less effort into a task that is similar to a previously failed task, whereas the "effort" group is more likely to put more effort into such a task. Furthermore, this interaction may also depend on the difficulty of the task. Our fictitious example has unequal ns in the various cells, which makes it as general as possible.

We first determine the significance of main effects and interaction sets in the full model. Given the unequal ns and the experimental nature of this study, for this analysis we may either use an ANOVA computer program or, equivalently, code all sets by unweighted effects codes and their products and carry out a Type III Regression SS analysis.

CH09EX03

Carrying out these analyses by a "step-down" procedure, starting from the full model including attribution $= A$ with $k = 2$, difficulty $= D$ with $k = 1$, and failure $= F$ with $k = 1$; $A \times D, A \times F, D \times F$ two-way interactions with $k = 5$, and 2 three-way interaction variables, $A_1 \times D \times F$ and $A_2 \times D \times F$. Table 9.2.1 provides these analyses.

In the first analysis comparing the prediction for all 11 variables with the prediction omitting the three-way interaction terms, we see that these two variables added only $909.50 - 890.60 = 18.90$ to the regression SS above the two-way interactions. This contribution of only about 1% to the prediction was not statistically significant. We decide to omit the triple interaction from further consideration, and proceed to investigate the two-way interaction contribution. For that model we see that the addition of the five two-way interaction terms added 278.45 to the regression SS over the main effects. Dividing by the 5 $df = MS = 55.69$, and testing this by the new residual $MS = 849.31/110 = 7.72$ yields $F = 7.21$, which with 5 and 110 df indicates $p < .01$. Of course the existence of two-way interactions indicates the necessity of including the main effects, and this model is accepted for the analysis of the study.

Variable Coding for Analysis of the Full Model

A second consequence of the potentially large number of total variables when more than two-way interactions among sets representing nominal scales are investigated is the critical importance of the selection of the method of coding the variables. As we saw in the previous example, when interactions among nominal scales are being examined, as elsewhere, it is important that the meaning of the specific statistical tests being made is pertinent to the purposes of the investigation; otherwise the individual t tests may refer to comparisons that are not of any interest. Such a consideration is at least equally important when one is considering interactions among more than two nominal scales or, as we shall see subsequently, interactions between nominal and continuous scales. For pedagogical purposes, we will use each of the four major coding systems to code all three factors in the analyses presented here. However, as we saw in the earlier example investigating treatments at different hospitals, the investigator's hypotheses should determine which coding scheme is used for each of the nominal IVs. Such hypotheses may indicate different coding approaches to the different nominal scales in a single analysis.

Table 9.2.2 presents the details of the four coding schemes. The particular coding system that is employed is indicated by the addition of (D), (U), (W), or (C) to the subscript for each of the code variables. For example, $X_{1(D)}$ represents the first dummy code which involves the comparison of the effort attribution group with the control group. As an overview, the first system is dummy-variable coding, where we must select one of the groups for each nominal scale as the reference group against which the other groups will be compared. In this case we have selected A_2, the control group for attribution, as well as the difficult task condition (D_2), and the failure outcome condition (F_2). The second set of codes represent the unweighted effects codes, where we have chosen for the base group for each factor the same groups that were used as the reference groups for the dummy codes. Following the practice in unweighted effects codes, each base group is coded -1. The third coding scheme is unweighted effects coding which is included here only for illustrative purposes. As noted in Section 8.4, this coding scheme is almost never appropriate for experimental work because it looks upon the actual cell sizes as being representative of their proportion in some population. It uses the number of cases in the group that makes up each nominal category to determine to the values of the code variables for the base group. Dweck's theory would predict a specific pattern of means as a function of the attribution condition in the amount of effort the individual exerts in solving the problems in the second part of the experiment ($M_{A1} > M_{A2} > M_{A3}$). The difference in the means of the attribution groups would be expected to be greater in the failure than in the success group, yielding an attribution × outcome interaction. The strong form of this hypothesis suggests that the $M_{A1} - M_{A2}$ difference is equal to the $M_{A3} - M_{A2}$ difference within each of the outcome conditions. This hypothesis is represented by code variable $X_{1(C)}$ that has values of $-0.5, 0$, and $+0.5$ for the ability, no attribution, and effort conditions, respectively. The second code variable $X_{2(C)}$ for A has values of $-0.5, 1$, and -0.5, and represents the nonlinear (quadratic) component of the differences among the groups. In the context of the strong version of the hypothesis, it is expected to be nonsignificant and serves as a check that the linear effect of attribution adequately represents the pattern of means in this data set. Given the $G_A - 1 = 2\,df$ for A these two contrasts fully represent the nominal variable. The contrast

TABLE 9.2.2
Alternative Codes for Main Effects in a Three-Nominal-Scale Example

Method	Dummy codes		Unweighted effects		Weighted effects		Contrast	
	$X_{1(D)}$	$X_{2(D)}$	$X_{1(U)}$	$X_{2(U)}$	$X_{1(W)}$	$X_{2(W)}$	$X_{1(C)}$	$X_{2(C)}$
Attribution set								
Group A_1	1	0	1	0	1	0	.5	$-.5$
Group A_2	0	0	-1	-1	$-n_{A1}/n_{A2}$	$-n_{A3}/n_{A2}$	0	1
Group A_3	0	1	0	1	0	1	$-.5$	$-.5$
Difficulty set	$X_{3(D)}$		$X_{3(U)}$		$X_{3(W)}$		$X_{3(C)}$	
Group D_1	1		1		1		.5	
Group D_2	0		-1		$-n_{D1}/n_{D2}$		$-.5$	
Failure set	$X_{4(D)}$		$X_{4(U)}$		$X_{4(W)}$		$X_{4(C)}$	
Group F_1	1		1		1		.5	
Group F_2	0		-1		$-n_{F1}/n_{F2}$		$-.5$	

codes for the three nominal variables all meet the three rules for contrast codes (see Section 8.5). Values on each code variable sum to zero, the code variables are linearly independent across variables [equivalently, the products of the coefficients across each possible pair of the four code variables $(X_{1(C)}, X_{2(C)}, X_{3(C)}, X_{4(C)})$ sum to zero], and the difference between the values of the codes for the two groups or combinations of groups on each variable equals 1.

For each of the coding schemes, there are three first-order (average) effects for the factors represented by the four code variables X_1, X_2, X_3, and X_4. Interactions between nominal variables are represented as products of the code variables representing the factors. There are three two-way interactions, which are represented by five code variables: the products of the two variables in A with the single code variables in D and F and the product of the D and F code variables. These five two-way interactions are represented by five code variables X_5, X_6, X_7, X_8, X_9, and X_{10} in our example.

Table 9.2.3 provides the means and sample sizes for each of the cells in the design, as well as certain means of means. The coefficients produced by the alternative coding methods in this model are shown in Table 9.2.4. The first thing to notice is that the values, meaning, and significance tests for variables within sets are not equivalent across methods.

Taking these analyses in sequence, we note that the intercept B_0 for the full dummy-variable model must equal the mean of the group consistently coded 0 on all IVs, here the middle A group in the high difficulty and failure condition. In the model omitting the nonsignificant triple interactions, the intercept is only an approximation of that value. The meaning of other coefficients in the dummy-variable model is quite difficult to interpret because the high collinearity between the IVs thus coded requires consideration of most other coefficients in the interpretation of any one of them. In the full model tolerances for both main effects and interactions are less than 25%, and mostly less than 20%. Thus this method of coding is difficult to interpret, and the more so when sample sizes are unequal.[8]

The unweighted effects solution is the solution employed by ANOVA programs for unequal cell n, and is straightforward to interpret. B_0 in the full model equals the mean of all the cell means, and in the reduced model we have chosen is an approximation of this value.[9] The tolerances are much higher in this model, going little below 70%, indicating the greater simplicity of the model. As in ANOVA, the two-way interaction effects are tests of differences between differences. For example, the $X_{3(U)}$ by $X_{4(U)}$ interaction of .3 estimates the difference between the mean difference between easy and difficult conditions for the succeed condition $(11.9 - 11.2 = .7)$ and the mean difference between easy and difficult conditions for the fail condition $[10.9 - (-)11.0 = .1]$ be .3 times 2 (because the effects codes are 1 and -1) = .6.

TABLE 9.2.3
Cell Means and Numbers in the Three-Nominal-Scale Example

	Succeed = F_1		Fail = F_2			
	Easy = D_1	Difficult = D_2	Easy = D_1	Difficult = D_2	M_M	M_Y
Attribution$_1$ = Effort	13.04 (9)	12.57 (9)	14.80 (9)	16.70 (10)	14.28	14.34
Attribution$_2$ = None	11.23 (11)	10.43 (11)	12.28 (8)	10.14 (16)	11.01	10.84
Attribution$_3$ = Trait	11.49 (11)	9.60 (10)	6.54 (8)	6.07 (8)	8.43	8.74
M_M	11.92	10.87	11.21	10.97	11.24	11.27

---

[8]We have included on the disk a data file using approximately the same cell means but with equal cell sample sizes for the reader's examination. The dummy-variable solution is not really easier in this case, and tolerances are still less than .25.

[9]In the equal cell n condition, the estimated effects for main effects and interaction models do not change for the unweighted (or equivalent weighted) means solution because collinearity is only between IVs within sets.

TABLE 9.2.4

Table of B_i (SE), and t Values in Curtailed Model With Alternative
Coding Methods

$B_i(SE), t$	Dummy variable	Unweighted effects	Weighted effects	Contrast
B_0	10.5 (0.7)	11.2 (0.3)	11.2 (0.3)	11.2 (0.3)
B_{A1}	5.8 (1.0)	3.1 (0.4)	3.2 (0.4)	5.9 (0.7)
t	5.8**	8.3**	8.3**	9.0**
B_{A2}	−4.6 (1.1)	−2.8 (0.4)	−2.9 (0.4)	−0.3 (0.4)
t	4.3**	7.5**	7.4**	0.8
B_D	1.1 (1.0)	0.3 (0.3)	0.3 (0.3)	0.6 (0.5)
t	1.1	1.2	1.3	1.3
B_F	−0.6 (0.9)	0.2 (0.3)	0.2 (0.3)	0.4 (0.5)
t	0.6	0.7	0.6	0.7
$B_{A1 \times D}$	−2.2 (1.3)	−0.7 (0.4)	−0.7 (0.4)	−2.0 (1.3)
t	1.7	1.9	1.9	1.5
$B_{A2 \times D}$	−0.2 (1.3)	0.3 (0.4)	0.3 (0.4)	0.8 (0.7)
t	0.2*	0.8	0.7	1.1
$B_{A1 \times F}$	−2.8 (1.2)	−1.7 (0.4)	−1.8 (0.4)	−7.2 (1.3)
t	2.2**	4.5**	4.3**	5.5**
$B_{A2 \times F}$	4.4 (1.3)	1.9 (0.4)	2.1 (0.4)	−0.6 (0.7)
t	3.5**	5.2**	5.1**	0.8
$B_{D \times F}$	0.7 (1.0)	0.2 (0.3)	0.2 (0.3)	0.7 (1.0)
t	0.7	0.7	0.7	0.7

*The .05 α criteria has been met.
**The .01 α criteria has been met.

The weighted effects solution is intended to generalize to a population in which cell frequencies are not equal. The estimates are similar to the unweighted estimates to the extent that cell ns do not differ very substantially and, of course, are equivalent when they are equal. Because the cell ns within factors are not necessarily proportionate, it is generally not advisable to attempt to interpret a reduced model with this model, but the interpretation of the B_is is otherwise essentially comparable to those for the unweighted effects model, the difference lying in the population to which the generalization is desired.

The IVs in the contrast model are nearly orthogonal (exactly orthogonal in the equal cell n case), and thus both easier to interpret and more stable between the full and reduced models. We have designed them to emphasize the investigator's hypotheses. Once again, the intercept equals the mean of means. $X_{1(C)}$ gives us the mean difference in effort between the trait (A_1) and effort (A_3) groups across conditions (−5.8), $X_{2(C)}$ gives us the less interesting difference between the middle group (A_2) and the mean of the trait and effort groups. The interaction term B_5 contrasts the $A_1, D_1 + A_3, D_2$ means = 13.9 + 7.8 = 21.7 (averaged across F) with the $A_1, D_2 + A_3, D_1$ means = 14.6 + 9.0 = 23.6 (averaged across F) = 1.9 (in the full model, approximated by 2.0 in the model without triple interactions). Other effects can be similarly interpreted on the basis of the cell mean contrasts selected by the investigator.

The full set of cell means (or adjusted means if there are other variables in the model) can always be reproduced by summing across the B and code value products. For example, with dummy variables the means for the 12 cells estimated from the model without interactions are as shown in Table 9.2.5. The reproduced means omitting the triple interaction terms, as we have done here, are not exactly equal to the original means, although they clearly show the overall

TABLE 9.2.5
Recreating Adjusted Cell Means From the Regression Coefficients
Using Dummy Variables

Cell	B_{A_1} 5.8 Code	B_{A_2} −4.6 Code	B_D 1.1 Code	B_F −0.6 Code	$B_{A_1 \times D}$ −2.2 Code	$B_{A_2 \times D}$ −0.2 Code	$B_{A_1 \times F}$ −2.8 Code	$B_{A_2 \times F}$ 4.4 Code	$B_{D \times F}$ 0.7 Code	B_0 10.5 Code	$\sum B_i \times$ Code
$A_1D_1F_1$	1	0	1	1	1	0	1	0	1	1	12.5
$A_1D_2F_1$	1	0	0	1	0	0	1	0	0	1	12.9
$A_1D_1F_2$	1	0	1	0	1	0	0	0	0	1	15.2
$A_1D_2F_2$	1	0	0	0	0	0	0	0	0	1	16.3
$A_2D_1F_1$	0	0	1	1	0	0	0	0	1	1	11.8
$A_2D_2F_1$	0	0	0	1	0	0	0	0	0	1	9.9
$A_2D_1F_2$	0	0	1	0	0	0	0	0	0	1	11.6
$A_2D_2F_2$	0	0	0	0	0	0	0	0	0	1	10.5
$A_3D_1F_1$	0	1	1	1	0	1	0	1	1	1	11.3
$A_3D_2F_1$	0	1	0	1	0	0	0	1	0	1	9.7
$A_3D_1F_2$	0	1	1	0	0	1	0	0	0	1	6.8
$A_3D_2F_2$	0	1	0	0	0	0	0	0	0	1	5.9

pattern. The reader may use the accompanying file to determine that if all 11 terms had been included the original means will be reproduced by summing the regression coefficient–code value products.

9.2.2 Interactions Among Nominal Scales in Which Not All Combinations Are Considered

Of course, if one is simply trying to reproduce the ANOVA with unequal cell numbers unweighted effects coding is mathematically equivalent to the method employed by most computer packages. And, as noted, one can reproduce the original cell means from any of the other coding systems. But there are much easier ways to reproduce the original cell means, and ANOVA and multiple comparison methods are tailored to test mean differences and differences between differences for statistical significance. When sets of variables representing nominal scales are used in MRC analyses, they are generally used in quite different ways than in ANOVA and ANCOVA. One purpose of nominal scale variable sets is serving as control variables in regression equations in which the effects of one or more quantitative variables are of major interest. Under these conditions and in many other situations the investigator may not be interested in or may not expect many of the potential interactions between the nominal and quantitative variables to contribute significantly to the prediction of Y. Although our focus was on the nominal variable, Section 8.7 considered these models. Yet another situation, to be reviewed in Section 9.3, is when there may be interactions between quantitative and nominal IVs so that the effects of some continuous variables may vary as a function of the categories that comprise the nominal IV.

There are many cases in which it is reasonable to examine certain interactions among nominal variables, but not all of them, either for reasons of parsimony, or in the effort to conserve degrees of freedom where hypotheses are not compelling. Most frequently such circumstances will arise in observational research, where potential interactions may be very many and clear a priori hypotheses may not exist. Occasionally, such circumstances may also arise in experimental studies. For example, an additional treatment factor or nominal individual difference variable (e.g., sex, ethnic group) may be included in the design to explore the generality of the hypothesized treatment effects.

To illustrate this issue, consider an observational study in which male and female (S) participants from three ethnic groups (E) are included in the study of a DV. The design is a 2 by 3 factorial design, and the investigator has clear hypotheses about that there will be overall sex differences and a S by E interaction. He anticipates that ethnic groups 1 and 2 will show clear sex differences in their mean scores on Y, but ethnic group 3 will show no sex differences. He uses two contrast codes for ethnic group with $E_1 = +1/3, +1/3$, and $-2/3$, and $E_2 = -0.5, +0.5$, and 0. In principle, the $S \times E_2$ interaction term may be omitted as not hypothesized or of interest. However, in general the first reasonable check will be to make certain that this variable does not contribute significantly to the prediction. The candidate term is tested and if it is *not* statistically significant, it is dropped from the model. It is prudent in such tests of possible model respecification to use a higher than usual value of the Type I error, say $\alpha = .20$, to help minimize the possibility that effects that in fact exist in the population (but which are not detected because of low statistical power) are inappropriately dropped from the regression equation. A complex regression equation must be "trimmed" from the highest order term down; one would not retain a three-way interaction term such as $A \times B \times C$ but eliminate a two-way interaction term between included factors such as $A \times B$ because all lower order terms must be included in equations containing higher order terms. Aiken and West (1991, Chapter 6) discuss procedures for identifying the order in which terms may be trimmed in complex regression equations.[10]

In fact, many tests of interaction sets of all kinds are designed more as assumption checks or tests of the generality of one's findings of interest than as hypothesis tests. As considered in the previous example of treatments in medical school hospitals, it may be that the test of the hospital by treatment interaction was appropriately carried out only as a test of the assumption that such interactions were not needed. If the results had turned out that the interaction set as a whole did not contribute significantly to the prediction of Y, and the investigator had no a priori reason for thinking that it would, the terms representing the H by T interaction could be dropped from the regression model, although doing so would depart from the ANOVA model. Such tests of assumptions and of the generality of findings are typically briefly noted in research reports but are not fully presented.

If the investigator decides to leave out one or more of the highest order interactions between two or more nominal IVs, the choice of an appropriate coding system for the remaining variables will be quite critical. As we have noted throughout our presentation of nominal scale codes, it is not always intuitively obvious what the contrast will be when the regression model is modified. It follows, then, that it may also not be obvious what the consequences may be of omitting or adding one or more of a set of interaction variables. Because this will depend highly on the coding system, the most general advice is to beware of mistaken inferences drawn from incomplete sets. Each time the regression model is changed by adding or deleting interactions (or other higher order effects), the proper interpretation of each effect in the model needs to be revisited.

9.2.3 What If the Categories for One or More Nominal "Scales" Are Not Mutually Exclusive?

As noted briefly in Chapter 8, some categorical variables include some overlap among certain categories. Under such circumstances, the simplest alternative is to create additional categories that consist of combinations of overlapping categories to maintain the mutually exclusive

---

[10]Researchers should be cautious in their conclusions and clearly label any results as exploratory when post hoc model modifications have been made. Section 4.5.2 discusses this issue in another context (see also Diaconis, 1985, for full discussion of inference in exploratory data analysis).

nature of the categories comprising the nominal scale. In some cases there may be a basis in the substantive area for assigning the invididuals with overlapping categories to a single category involved in the overlap.

An illustration of this problem arose in the 2000 U.S. census data. For the first time participants could identify themselves as a member of more than one ethnic or racial group. Investigators of population-based associations using the census data need to decide how to treat these data. Depending on their purposes and the size and location of the sample they are investigating they may try to treat each group as if it were distinct, so that each effect will be estimated with partialing for the overlap of other group membership from the variable in question. Of course, under these conditions the coding schemes for interactions cannot be employed in a straightforward manner. Alternatively, if main effects or interactions with specific combinations of ethnicity or race are anticipated, separate variables will need to be created.

No general solution to this problem can be proposed; indeed, we believe that considerable development of statistical models that address overlapping categories is likely to take place during the coming decade. The purpose of the current discussion is to remind the researcher that such issues deserve thoughtful attention. The method of coping with this fairly common problem may make a substantive difference, and should be considered carefully in the context of the purpose of the analyses.

9.2.4 Consideration of pr, β, and Variance Proportions for Nominal Scale Interaction Variables

In this chapter we have emphasized the cell means and differences between mean differences as represented in the study's B_i. As always, it is also possible to examine the various standardized coefficients and the proportions of Y variance that are represented by their squared values. As we first saw in Chapter 8, these coefficients are as much affected by the proportion of the sample that is in the cell as by the mean differences compared in the coefficients. Consequently, such coefficients will not generally be of as central an interest as they often are for continuous scales.

βs are usually not a focus of attention for nominal scales because the standardization (creation of a unit variance) for variables created by any of the coding methods usually makes no particular sense. If the investigator wishes to determine the unique contribution of an individual variable, it will be convenient to do so by squaring the value computed from (Eq. 9.1.1), based on β, whenever such information is not part of the computer output.

9.2.5 Summary of Issues and Recommendations for Interactions Among Nominal Scales

Many of the details of interactions among nominal scales involve careful attention to alternative coding choices, cell sizes, and study purposes. These issues will necessarily need careful consideration once the context and purposes of the analysis are clearly before the investigator. However, it may be useful to recap some of the major points made in this presentation of interactions among nominal scales.

1. All methods of coding nominal scales will yield the same aggregate significance test values for interaction sets (and, necessarily, R^2 and increments to R^2), when a full model is compared to a reduced model.

2. The coding method that is equivalent to the method used for ANOVA or ANCOVA is unweighted effects coding that treats group means as equally important, regardless of cell n. Such programs also use the residual MS from the full model to test all effects.

3. Specific B_i in different coding systems, however, will not in general have the same values, test the same mean differences or differences between differences, or have equivalent statistical significance tests. The interpretation of the unstandardized regression coefficients depends on the coding system that is used for each nominal IV and the specific interaction (or other higher order) terms, if any, that are included in the model.

4. When interaction terms are created as products of nominal scale codes for certain coding methods, these products will produce B_is corresponding to each code variable with fairly straightforward interpretations. Dummy codes, unweighted effects codes, and contrast codes produce B_is that are not affected by the sample size in each group. In contrast, weighted effect codes produce B_is that are direct functions of the relative proportion of cases in each group. Interactions in weighted effects code models can become more difficult to interpret in studies in which cell ns are not proportional (see Section 9.1.2).

5. Once again, we caution that the dummy coding option that is so often considered the "default" will frequently not be the optimal coding scheme. The coding scheme selected for each nominal IV should be the one that most directly reflects the study's hypotheses. Indeed, this is the main advantage of using a regression analysis rather than an ANOVA approach when all study factors are categorical. These are often, but not always, created as contrast codes, which have two other advantages: They are typically easy to interpret and uncorrelated in the variables except for correlations due to unequal sample sizes in the cells.

9.3 NOMINAL SCALE BY CONTINUOUS VARIABLE INTERACTIONS

9.3.1 A Reminder on Centering

As noted in all previous presentations of interactions, we will generally find that the interpretation of equations involving product terms will be more readily accomplished if the continuous variables have been centered. In the sections that follow we will assume that this centering has been done but will also note the consequences of not having done so. There is still complexity of interpretation when the continuous variable is centered, but the categorical variable(s) are not. See Section 7.2.8 for an example of a regression with interactions in which some of the IVs are centered but others are not.

9.3.2 Interactions of a Continuous Variable With Dummy-Variable Coded Groups

As is the case with equations with interactions between continuous scales, interactions between continuous and nominal scales generally employ variables that are products of the original "main effect" variables. When the nominal scale has been coded with dummy variables, these product variables will constitute a set of $g - 1$ variables that are each equal to the continuous scale for one group and zero for the other groups. When entered simultaneously with the original variables these interaction variables each reflect and test the difference between the slope for the group with a nonzero value and the reference group. Thus, the interaction between a continuous variable Z and a nominal scale W consisting of five groups coded as four dummy variables will be fully represented by an interaction set $Z \times W$ consisting of the products of each of the four dummy variables with Z.

TABLE 9.3.1

Characteristics of Separate and Combined Departments
in the Academic Salary Example

Department	n	$M_{\text{Publications}}$	M_{Salary}	B_{SP}	SE_B
Psychology	60	19	$61,719	$1,373	$222
Sociology	44	15.2	66,523	258	481
History	46	11.2	64,937	412	400
Mean of means		15.1	64,393	681	211
Combined	150	15.5	64,115	926	179

As an illustration let us return to our fictitious example of academic salary. In the data presented in Table 9.3.1 we have drawn a new sample from three departments in our university: psychology, sociology, and history. The primary purpose of this investigation is to see whether publications have an equivalent influence on salary in these departments. We have decided that psychology will be the reference department and have created dummy variables accordingly. Our original investigation of the main effects of the study variables is given in Table 9.3.2. In this equation the intercept is the estimated mean for a faculty member in psychology with an average number of publications (where the average is computed across the entire sample $= 15.5$ publications). We note that across the three departments the average return per publication is $926. Although the observed mean salaries were not significantly different (psychology $-$ sociology $= -\$4,805$ and psychology $-$ history $= -\$3,219$, $t = -1.42$ and $-.90$ respectively) the department salaries adjusted for the number of publications were substantially and statistically significantly different. The estimated salary for a

TABLE 9.3.2

Dummy-Variable Interactions for the Academic Salary Example

	B	SE_B	Tolerance	t	p
Main effects					
B_0	$58,485	$2,168			
B_P	926	193	.81	4.78	<.01
B_{D_1}	8,282	3,249	.78	2.55	<.02
B_{D_2}	10,447	3,472	.66	3.01	<.01

Regression MS $= 215,311,000$; $F = 8.46$; $p < .01$; $R^2 = .148$.
Residual MS $= 25,453,100$.

	B	SE_B	Tolerance	t	p
Full model					
B_0	$56,922	$2,207			
B_P	1,373	252	.46	5.44	<.01
B_{D_1}	9,669	3,235	.76	2.99	<.01
B_{D_2}	9,793	3,616	.59	2.71	<.01
B_{PD_1}	−1,115	495	.74	2.25	<.05
B_{PD_2}	−961	466	.52	2.06	<.05

Regression MS $= 1,650,940,000$; $F = 6.72$; $p < .01$; $R^2 = .189$.
Residual MS $= 24,559,800$.

Increment to regression MS $= 89,768,000$; $F = 3.66_{2,144}$; Increment to $R^2 = .041$; $p < .05$.

psychologist with 15.5 publications is $58,485, the intercept. Sociologists earned $8,282 more than psychologists, considering the number of publications, and historians earned $10,447 more, after a comparable adjustment (that is, estimated at 15.5 publications). This increase in the mean differences should not surprise us, because we saw already in Table 9.3.1 that the psychologists published more than the other disciplines. This adjustment, however, presumes a comparable "reward" per publication in the three departments, and it is this presumption that our test of the publication by department interactions is designed to test.

In the next equation we have added the two interaction terms. Once again, our intercept is the estimated effect for a psychology faculty member with an average number of publications. However, in this case the interaction terms provide for the possibility of a different effect of publications in each department. Therefore, the intercept is now the estimated salary in the psychology department for a member with 15.5 publications, taking into consideration the reward per publication in the psychology department. The regression coefficient for the "main effect" of publications is the B for publications in the psychology department ($1,373, compare with Table 9.3.1). The B_is for the two dummy variables are the differences in salary between the psychology department and the other departments ($66,592 − $56,922 = $9,669, and $66,715 − $56,922 = $9,793). The regression coefficients for the two interaction terms are the differences between the publication slope (the increase in salary per publication) for each department and that for the psychology department ($258 − $1,373 = −$1,115 and $412 − $1,373 = −$961). Each of these differences is significant in the full model, as is the effect of publications in the psychology department. The slopes predicting salary from publications in each of the three departments are shown in Fig. 9.3.1.

Thus we see that the interaction effects for dummy variables contrast the other groups with the selected reference group with regard to both the means on the dependent variable and the slopes—the regression effects—of the continuous variable, and that the resulting coefficients are equivalent to those of the original separate groups. If other variables (U) are added to the equation without including their potential interaction effects with the nominal scale, the

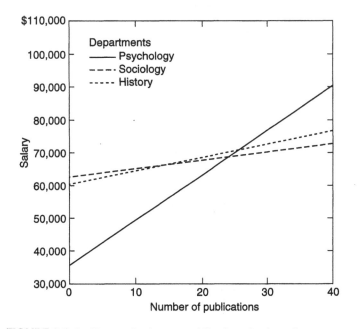

FIGURE 9.3.1   Slopes of salary on publications for three departments.

resulting B_is will vary somewhat from those that would have been obtained had the groups been analyzed separately. This is because the regression estimates treat the effects (slopes) of these other variables in every group as equivalent to those in the total group.[11]

If the continuous variable had not been centered prior to entrance into these equations, the intercept B_0 would no longer have represented the salary mean for the reference group, but rather the estimated salary for a member of that department with zero publications (which in this example is outside the range of the scores). The effects of the two dummy variables representing the other departments would similarly have represented the difference between the estimated difference between a member of each department with zero publications and a member of the psychology department also with zero publications. The interaction terms would have remained the same.

9.3.3 Interactions Using Weighted or Unweighted Effects Codes

Suppose we used effects codes to represent a nominal scale and its interaction with a continuous measure. As is equally true of the selection of the reference group in dummy variable coding, it can make a great deal of difference which group is selected to be the base group in effects codes. In this case our selection of this method of coding and of the psychology department as the base group suggests that our real interest lies in the comparison of the sociology and history departments with the "average" department. [The comparison of psychology with the average department is measured by the value $-(B_{E_1} + B_{E_2})$.]

The interpretation of B_0 in equations with effects codes is the unweighted mean of means when the continuous scales have been centered. Table 9.3.3 provides the regression analyses

TABLE 9.3.3
Effects-Coded Variable Interactions for the Academic Salary Example

	B	SE_B	Tolerance	t	p
Main effects					
B_0	$64,728	$1,316			
B_P	926	193	.81	4.78	<.01
B_{E_1}	2,038	1,912	.68	1.07	NS
B_{E_2}	4,204	2,039	.58	2.06	<.05

Regression MS = 215,311,000; $F = 8.46$; $R^2 = .148$.
Residual MS = 25,453,100.

Full model with interaction					
B_0	$63,410	$1,440			
B_P	681	210	.66	3.23	<.01
B_{E_1}	3,182	1,985	.61	1.60	NS
B_{E_2}	3,306	2,193	.49	1.51	NS
B_{PE_1}	423	324	.42	1.31	NS
B_{PE_2}	269	309	.43	.87	NS

Regression MS = 1,650,940,000; $F = 6.72$; $R^2 = .189$; $p < .01$.
Residual MS = 24,559,800.

Increment to regression MS = 89,768,000; $F = 3.66_{2,144}$; Increment to $R^2 = .041$; $p < .05$.

---

[11] The reader may explore the consequences for this fictitious example by including in equations the variable time since Ph.D., which is included in the data file.

for the main effects and full model for the academic salary example. Once again, the intercept provides our estimated adjusted mean of mean salaries. In the first equation this value is slightly higher than the observed mean of means ($64,393, see Table 9.3.1) because we have used a single combined estimate of the influence of publications, $926 per publication, as estimated in the dummy variable equation as well. We note also that the adjusted mean difference between the sociology department and the adjusted mean of department means is not statistically significant, but the history department is significantly different than the average department ($p < .05$). Nevertheless, as is always true of alternative methods of coding nominal scales (Section 6.1.2), the multiple R^2 and its significance test is precisely the same as for the equation employing the dummy variable coded set.

In the full model using the effects coded scale, the adjusted mean of means is now estimated at $63,410. The B for publication is the (unweighted) mean of the department Bs for the effects of publications. The Bs for the individual effects are the adjusted mean differences between the sociology and history departments, respectively, and the adjusted mean of mean salary. And the interaction variable effects reflect the differences between the effect of publications in each of these two departments and the mean of the department mean effect of publications; that is, $258 − $681 = −$423$, and $412 − $681 = 269, respectively.

Perhaps one of the most important things to note in this table is that none of the effects in the full model are statistically significant except the intercept and the mean of the mean effect of publications. *Nevertheless*, these variables fully represent the model, as can be seen by the fact that the R^2 and its significance test are identical with that of the dummy variable model for which the two interaction terms and their joint contribution added significantly. The reason for this apparent paradox may be viewed from either of two perspectives. First, we may note substantively that we decided to use the psychology department as the base department, and that this department was the most discrepant from the mean of means. Indeed, if we had used one of the other departments as the reference in the dummy-variable equation we would also have found some variables to predict less than required for statistical significance. Second, we may note that our terms in the effects coded model were less independent, that is, had lower tolerances. This lack of independence in the terms also reflects overlaps among the tests and is another way of understanding the lack of statistical significance for the individual tests in the full model.

Perhaps the most important lesson to be learned is that it is quite possible to have a *set* of variables add significantly to the prediction of a DV although none of the individual variables adds a significant unique effect. Thus, an investigator must beware of dismissing a set as of trivial importance and nonsignificant on the basis of the significance of the individual variables alone. Attention to the tolerance values usually included in the output will alert the investigator to potential problems with IV collinearity that may produce the problem we see here.[12]

9.3.4 Interactions With a Contrast-Coded Nominal Scale

Another method that is often useful for coding nominal scales is contrast coding. In this case the investigator selects orthogonal group contrasts that are of particular interest and codes them in accordance with the rules previously noted (Sections 8.5 and 9.1). Suppose our real interest was in whether the psychology department was different from the other departments either in its (adjusted) mean salary or in the influence of publications on salary. We therefore code the first nominal scale to reflect this interest (⅔ or .667 for the psychology department and −⅓ or .333 for each of the other two departments). We code the second nominal scale variable with orthogonal codes of 0 for the psychology department and .5 and −.5 for the other

---

[12]See further discussion of this issue in Chapter 10.

TABLE 9.3.4
Contrast-Coded Variable Interactions With a Continuous Scale
for the Academic Salary Example

	B	SE_B	Tolerance	t	p
Main effects					
B_0	$64,728	$1,317			
B_P	926	193	.81	4.78	<.01
B_{C_1}	−6,243	1,923	.85	3.25	<.01
B_{C_2}	2,165	3,455	.95	.63	NS

Regression MS = 215,311,000; $F = 8.46$; $R^2 = .148$; $p < .01$.
Residual MS = 25,453,100.

Full model with interaction					
B_0	$63,410	$1,440			
B_P	681	211	.66	3.23	<.01
B_{C_1}	−6,487	1,923	.82	3.37	<.01
B_{C_2}	124	3,714	.79	.03	NS
B_{PC_1}	1,038	256	.77	2.70	<.01
B_{PC_2}	154	579	.82	.27	NS

Regression MS = 1,650,940,000; $F = 6.72$; $R^2 = .189$; $p < .01$.
Residual MS = 24,559,800.

Increment to regression MS = 89,768,000; $F = 3.66_{2,144}$; Increment to $R^2 = .041$; $p < .05$.

two departments, respectively. The interaction terms are products of these two terms and the centered publication variable.

In Table 9.3.4 we see that in the main effects equation the intercept and B_P are the same as in the previous two models, and the effects for the contrast are the differences between the psychology department and the mean of the other two department means ($t = 3.2, p < .01$), and the difference in adjusted mean between the sociology and history departments (which also equals the difference between the two nominal scale Bs in each of the two previous main effects models using dummy or effects codes), not statistically significant. Of course, the full main effects model is precisely as large and statistically significant as it was with the previous two methods of coding.

When we move to the interaction of publications with the contrast-coded nominal scale we again find that the first contrast, comparing the psychology department with the mean of the other two departments, is statistically significant. Its value, $1,038, reflects the difference between the effect of publications in the psychology department, $1,373, and that of the mean of the other two [($258 + $412)/2 = 335]. The second contrast, between the effects of publications on salary in the sociology department as compared to the history department, is small (as we saw in the subgroup analyses reflected in Table 9.3.1) and not significant. In aggregate, again, the interaction set adds precisely the same contribution to R^2 for this coding as for any other.

9.3.5 Interactions Coded to Estimate Simple Slopes of Groups

It is not unusual for an investigator to be as interested in whether a particular variable is or is not a significant predictor of Y in each and every group. The answer to this question can be obtained in a number of ways, but perhaps the simplest one takes advantage of the fact that there are g

variables involved in the interactions: the continuous scale and the $g - 1$ variables representing the nominal scale.[13] In the previous coding methods we included the scaled variable Z and $g - 1$ main effect variables for the nominal scale and $g - 1$ interaction products. To obtain separate group slopes (simple slopes for groups) we now instead create g variables in which each group's Z values (preferably but not necessarily centered) are coded on a variable for which all other groups are coded 0. These variables are then entered simultaneously with any of the other methods of coding the $g - 1$ nominal scale variables (but with the "main effect" Z omitted). The B coefficients in this equation will be the slopes of Y on the continuous scale for each of the g groups with their appropriate standard errors and statistical significance tests.

For example, let us return to our academic department model. In Table 9.3.5 we reproduce the original dummy-variable main effects model. In the full model, however, we have removed the publications variable, and instead have included three variables representing the publications effect for each of the three departments. As noted, the first variable consists of the publications for each member of the psychology department and zero for each member of the other departments. The second variable consists of the publications for each member of the sociology department and zero for each member of the other departments. The third variable consists of the publications of each member of the history department, etc. When considered simultaneously these variables reflect precisely the slopes of the individual groups. Figure 9.3.1 presents the slopes of salary on publications for each of the three departments. The significance tests suggest that although publications have a powerful influence on salary in the psychology department, they have little or no impact on salary in the sociology or history departments.

TABLE 9.3.5
Interactions Coded for Individual Department Simple Slopes
of Salary on Publications

CH09EX05

	B	SE_B	Tolerance	t	p
Main effects					
B_0	$58,485	$2,168			
B_P	926	193	.81	4.78	<.01
B_{D_1}	8,282	3,249	.78	2.55	<.02
B_{D_2}	10,447	3,472	.66	3.01	<.01

Regression MS = 215,311,000; $F = 8.46$; $R^2 = .148$.
Residual MS = 25,453,100.

	B	SE_B	Tolerance	t	p
Full model with interaction					
B_0	$56,922	$2,207			
B_{D_1}	9,669	3,235	.76	2.99	<.01
B_{D_2}	9,793	3,616	.59	2.71	<.01
B_{SD_0}	1,373	252	.90	5.4	<.01
B_{SD_1}	258	426	1.00	.60	NS
B_{SD_2}	412	392	.73	1.05	NS

Regression MS = 1,650,940,000; $F = 6.72$; $R^2 = .189$; $p < .01$.
Residual MS = 24,559,800.

Increment to regression MS = 89,768,000; $F = 3.66_{2,144}$; Increment to $R^2 = .04$; $p < .05$.

---

[13] Aiken and West (1991) provide a method for hand calculation of individual slopes, and note that one can also alternate the reference group in a dummy variable model, since the coefficient for the continuous variable in that model and its significance test represent the simple slope for the reference group.

(The reader is reminded that any resemblance of these data to actual departments is purely coincidental.) These analyses may be repeated using contrast or effects codes to confirm that the slope estimates are not affected by the method of coding the main effects of the nominal scale.

Perhaps the most crucial thing for the reader to note is that all of these methods share precisely the same significance test values for the total contribution of the interaction set to the prediction of Y. However, as noted, depending on the coding selected, the individual variables may all be statistically significant or none of them may be individually statistically significant. Thus it is important to check on the contribution of the set as a whole, especially if one is concerned about the possible significance of the set as a check on the assumption of equal slopes. And it is also important to select a coding method that is consistent with the investigator's need to detect and estimate the most theoretically or practically important interactions.

We also note that although the equations we have examined here using any of the coding methods produced coefficients that were relatively simple functions of the raw coefficients in subgroups, that is by no means necessarily the case in practice. This is because typically the researcher will include one or more other variables in the equation for which interaction terms are not hypothesized and, often, not investigated. The slopes for these variables are thus assumed to be equivalent for subgroups, although they are hardly ever precisely so. The effects of these covariates on the adjusted estimates of group by continuous scale interactions will be based on the covariates' full sample average effects, and may well influence the Bs and significance tests of the interaction variables (West, Aiken, and Krull, 1996).

Examination of Group Differences at a Point Other Than the Mean of the Continuous Scale

It is sometimes of particular interest whether the group means are significantly different at a particular point on the continuous scale. For example, in our academic example a member of the sociology department counters the findings by saying that any departmental differences in rewards for publications do not have effects on the more accomplished (that is, published) members of the department. He defines this group as those with 20 publications.

To test this hypothesis we begin by noting that the comparison of Y means of the groups in the full model is at a score of zero on the continuous variable. This point equals the full sample continuous variable mean when the continuous scale has been centered. Thus, by simple extension we may subtract from our continuous scale scores any other constant in order to make zero the point of interest and proceed with the analysis, as before. Regression coefficients reflecting mean differences among cells will now reflect those Y differences *at the selected point*.

CH09EX06

Therefore, we rescore publications by subtracting from the original scores 20 rather than the mean. Running the full equation with dummy variables representing the comparison of the sociology and history departments with psychology, including interactions, we find the estimated effects as shown in Table 9.3.6.

In the first model we reproduce the equation estimates from the dummy-variable model using the centered publication variable. As noted earlier, the D_1 and D_2 variables show significant t values, indicating that both the sociology and history departments have a higher estimated salary for those members with the mean (aggregated across department) number of publications, taking into account the differences in the publication effects in the different departments.

The next column shows the equation estimates when the publications variable has been "re-centered" by subtracting 20 from each value, rather than the 15.49 publications subtracted

TABLE 9.3.6

Estimation of Department Salary Differences at Alternative
Levels of Publications

IV	Predictor: Publications centered at mean		Predictor: Publications − 20		Predictor: Publications − 10	
	B(SE)	t	B(SE)	t	B(SE)	t
Intercept	$56,922		$63,114		$49,385	
	($2,207)		($2,039)		($3,030)	
D_1	$9,669	2.99	$4,640	1.25	$15,790	3.55
	($3,235)		($3,726)		($4,448)	
D_2	$9,793	2.71	$5,458	1.18	$15,069	3.92
	($3,616)		($4,633)		($3,846)	
Publications	$1,373	5.44	$1,373	5.44	$1,373	5.44
	($252)		($252)		($252)	
$D_1 \times$ *Publications*	−$1,115	2.26	−$1,115	2.26	−$1,115	2.26
	($495)		($495)		($495)	
$D_2 \times$ *Publications*	−$961	2.06	−$961	2.06	−$961	2.06
	($466)		($466)		($466)	

when we centered in the usual way. It turns out that our sociologist was right (in this fictitious example), and the estimated differences between department salaries for members with 20 publications is not statistically significant. We note, however, that the interactive effects, reflecting the differences in the effect of publications on salary in the different departments remain unaltered.

"Aha!" counters a junior member of the psychology department. "That's all very well for senior members, but the situation is even worse for those of us who have not yet had time to publish. Look at members with 10 publications in each department."

In the final set of columns in Table 9.3.6 we present the same equation in which 10 is now subtracted from each person's publications. As suspected by our junior colleague, the estimated mean difference in department salary for those with 10 publications is over $15,000 (taking into account the differences in the effects of publications). Necessarily, in all of these equations the different linear transform of publications has not altered the estimates of the main effects or interactions of publications, since the slopes cannot be affected by subtracting a constant from a variable. Nor can there be any influence of this transform on the overall R^2 or its statistical significance.

9.3.6 Categorical Variable Interactions With Nonlinear Effects of Scaled Independent Variables

Just as nominal scale interactions with a continuous scale are readily accomplished, nominal scale interactions with additional functions or powers of a continuous scale are also entirely feasible. The constraints against routine inclusion of such interaction terms are more likely to come from an inadequacy of theory to predict their presence and meaning than any difficulties in computing their effects. And, as we noted in Chapter 6, any problems of unreliability will tend to diminish our power to detect curvilinearity in relationships even more than it does for linear relationships. When the effective sample size is cut by examination of the subgroups represented by a nominal scale, such statistical power considerations are even more restricting.

Thus, although we present these methods here, the investigator should reflect carefully on the theory that predicts such effects, on the expected size of the difference, and on the statistical power considerations that may restrict one's ability to detect differences in curve shapes in subgroups.

The method is a straightforward extension of the previously presented treatment of interactions with nominal scales. One may use any of the methods of coding the nominal scale, as appropriate to the researcher's purpose and hypotheses. Interaction terms with continuous scales, including power functions, are created as simple products of the main effect sets. Thus, with 4 groups and z (centered, of course) and z^2, there will be six interaction terms created by the product of the $g - 1 = 3$ nominal scale variables and the two z variables.

For example, suppose that in our academic department salary investigation we had a further hypothesis. This hypothesis posits that these departments had different policies with regard to the influence of seniority on salary. It is believed that the history department is inclined to value the perspective and prestige associated with long familiarity with and by the professional field, and thus salary increases may be enhanced by seniority, perhaps even more than linearly. In psychology, it is hypothesized, academics tend to forget research and theoretical contributions that are more than a few years old, and thus the influence of seniority on salary diminishes over time. No specific hypothesis is made about the effects of seniority in the sociology department.

CH09EX07

The analyses of these effects in our fictitious example are presented in Table 9.3.7 for each of the individual departments.[14] As can be seen, the linear effect of seniority is largest in the psychology department, but there is also a significant negative curvilinear effect, indicating an overall "frown" effect—a downturn from the linear trend at the upper end (as hypothesized).

TABLE 9.3.7
Differential Curvilinear Effects of Seniority in the Academic
Department Example: Individual Department Effects

	Coefficient value	SE	t (or F)
Psychology department			
B_0	$65,670	$2,548	25.8
$\text{Time}_c = B_1$	$2,424	$390	6.2; $df = 57$
$(\text{Time}_c)^2 = B_2$	−$143	$49	2.9; $df = 57$
Total R^2	.404		$F = 19.3$; $df = 2, 57$
Sociology department			
B_0	$63,319	$3,677	17.2; $df = 41$
$\text{Time}_c = B_1$	$930	$539	1.7; $df = 41$
$(\text{Time}_c)^2 = B_2$	$109	$105	1.0; $df = 41$
Total R^2	.112		$F = 2.58$; $df = 2, 41$
History department			
B_0	$64,535	$2,820	22.9; $df = 43$
$\text{Time}_c = B_1$	$1,606	$492	3.3; $df = 43$
$(\text{Time}_c)^2 = B_2$	−$61	$78	.8; $df = 43$
Total R^2	.210		$F = 5.72$; $df = 2, 43$

---

[14] In these analyses we have centered years at the combined department mean, which makes the intercepts somewhat different than they would be if each department's years were centered separately but also makes the findings more directly comparable with the combined analysis. Also note that the dependent variable salary is not the same one used in the previous section.

Neither the linear nor the quadratic trend is statistically significant in the sociology department. In the history department there is a statistically significant linear trend of $1,606 per additional year, but no significant quadratic trend.

Analyzing these three departments simultaneously in order to test the significance of the curvilinear component, we will use dummy-variable coding with the psychology department as the reference group. There will be eight IVs in these analyses, two variables representing the main effects for groups, centered years and centered years squared, the two products of the group variables with years, and the two products of the group variables with years squared. The hierarchical regression analyses are presented in Table 9.3.8, where we can see that there was a generally significant quadratic effect, and that the quadratic effect differed among the departments, although not precisely as anticipated. The quadratic term was $252 less negative in the sociology department than in the psychology department (noting that the first dummy variable compares the sociology department to the psychology department), and only $83 less negative (and not significantly so) in the history department. Note that these are precisely the differences that we noted in the analyses of the individual departments where the sociology = psychology difference = $109 − (−$143) = $252 and the history psychology difference = −$61 − (−$143) = $83 (within rounding error). Now we also know that the psychology department is more likely to show a decline in seniority effects on salary among its most senior members to a greater extent than is the sociology department (which in fact is hardly influenced by seniority at all).

Once again, we can usefully reconstruct the slopes of each department in our combined analyses by using our group slope coding method in which we omit the continuous variable(s) and include a set of variables in which each group's (centered) continuous variable is coded on

TABLE 9.3.8
Hierarchical Multiple Regression Analysis of Seniority Effects

Model	B(SE)		Tolerance	t	Increment to R^2, F, numerator df
Main effects					.236; 15.0; 3 df
Intercept	$60,370	($2,058)		29.3	
Department dummy 1	$5,487	($3,153)	.81	1.7	
Department dummy 2	$2,653	($3,152)	.79	0.8	
$Time_c$	$1,548	($251)	.96	6.2	
Main effects + $Time_c^2$					.016; 3.0; 1 df
$Time_c^2$	−$69	($40)	.84	1.7	
Main effects, $Time_c^2$ + $T \times D$					.015; 3.0; 2 df
$T \times Dept_1$	−$1,050	($612)	.60	1.7	
$T \times Dept_2$	−$545	($599)	.58	0.9	
Main effects, $T \times D, T^2 \times D$					.028; 7.6; 2 df
Intercept	$65,670	($2,689)		24.4	
$Dept_1$	$2,424	($412)	.34	5.9	
$Dept_2$	−$2,351	($4,239)	.43	.6	
$Time_c$	−$1,135	($4,022)	.46	.3	
$Time_c^2$	−$143	($52)	.49	2.8	
$Dept_1 \times Time_c$	−$1,494	($633)	.54	2.4	
$Dept_2 \times Time_c$	−$818	($665)	.46	1.2	
$Dept_1 \times Time_c^2$	$252	($107)	.43	2.4	
$Dept_2 \times Time_c^2$	$83	($97)	.37	.4	

TABLE 9.3.9
Quadratic Interaction Example Coded for Simple Quadratic Slopes

Predictor	B(SE)		Tolerance	t	Cumulative R^2; F; df
Intercept ($= M_M$)	$64,507	($1,730)		37.3	
$Psychology_{(vs.\ others)}$	$1,743	($3,486)	.54	.5	
$Sociology_{(vs.\ history)}$	−$1,216	($4,437)	.54	.3	.014; $F = 1.1$; 2, 147 df
$Time_{c(psychology)}$	$2,424	($412)	.80	5.9	
$Time_{c(sociology)}$	$930	($481)	.94	1.9	
$Time_{c(history)}$	$1,606	($522)	.74	3.1	.189; $F = 6.7$; 5,144 df
$Time^2_{c(psychology)}$	−$143	($52)	.63	2.8	
$Time^2_{c(sociology)}$	$109	($94)	.56	1.2	
$Time^2_{c(history)}$	−$61	($83)	.52	.7	.295; $F = 7.4$; 8,141 df

a variable on which the other groups are coded zero. When we wish to examine the quadratic effects of the individual groups in the simultaneous analysis, we simply square the group slope variables. As was true in the example presented in the previous section, the increments to R^2 will be the same as in the previous hierarchical analysis (except the quadratic term of the continuous variable will be included with the final step rather than earlier).

In Table 9.3.9 the final equation is presented for the academic salary example in which we have used contrast codes (contrasting psychology with the other two departments and sociology with history) for the group main effects.[15] These linear and quadratic slope components for the individual departments are precisely what we obtained in their separate analyses in Table 9.3.6, and the R^2 for the full equation is precisely what it was for the previous analysis using dummy codes in the interactions.

The standard errors of the Bs are not the same as in the individual department analyses, since they are based on the full combined sample n. We note that neither the linear nor the quadratic effect was statistically significant in the sociology department. As is always the case, these slopes should be graphed in order to make sure that the interpretation is correct. Figure 9.3.2 presents the quadratic slopes for the three departments. Here we see clearly that in the psychology department the linear effect of seniority is steepest, but also the "fall off" in salary at the upper end is greatest.

Of course, if one only needed to know the shape of the quadratic slopes for each of these groups one could just as well run the equations separately for the departments, as we did in Table 9.3.7. However, when there are other predictors in the model, for which one is either ready to assume that the effects are roughly equivalent across groups, the adjusted group linear and quadratic slopes can most readily be obtained in the combined sample.

9.3.7 Interactions of a Scale With Two or More Categorical Variables

Just as easily as one can accomplish an examination of possible group differences in the effects of a continuous variable with one nominal scale, one may include interactions with two or more such scales in one's equations. In fact, it is not at all unusual to do so when a scale has only two categories; e.g., sex, handedness, treatment, residence type, zygosity, and many demographic variables often appear as dichotomies in studies. Interactions with more than one

---

[15]The reader is reminded that it doesn't matter for any of the simple slope variables whether we use dummy, effects, or contrast codes for the main effects of groups.

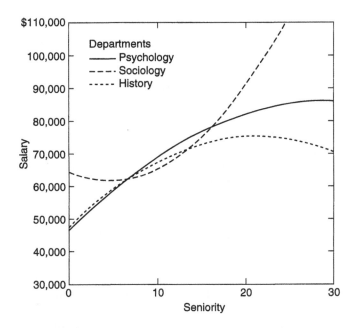

FIGURE 9.3.2 Quadratic slopes of salary on seniority.

such two-group variable are often plausible and of interest. When the sample is divided into more groups, however, the statistical power to detect multiple interactions is likely to quickly dissipate. Thus investigators are likely to need to exert considerable substantive and statistical judgment in the decisions as to which interactions to include.

Interactions involving continuous scales with multiple nominal scales also require consideration of whether the interaction terms *among the nominal scales* need to be included in the interactions with the continuous scales. As we noted in Section 9.2.1, with three nominal scales, even when two of these were dichotomies and the other only 3 groups, there are, in addition to four main effects, seven interaction terms. Thus, the full representation of the interactions of these groups with a continuous scale would require 11 interaction products of the nominal scale codes with the continuous scale. Unless the sample is huge, or the expected differences very large indeed, the power of the aggregate contribution to R^2 is likely to be small. As we have noted in Chapter 5, it is often a useful strategy to protect oneself against an excessive number of Type I errors ("findings" that are not characteristic of the population and thus will not replicate) by testing the contribution of a set of variables to R^2 for statistical significance before proceeding to examine the effects of individual variables. As always, such protection comes at a price, in terms of the risk of Type II errors (failure to detect effects that are actually present in the population). The investigator's goal must always be to balance these risks in ways that will further the scientific contribution of the study.

One possibility to be considered when the potential number of interaction terms in the equation mushrooms, is to examine only some of the potential group differences. For example, in the contrast-coded example of the effect of publication on salary presented in Section 9.3.4 our hypothesis and interest was in the comparison of the psychology department with the other two departments. The second contrast, that between the other two departments, was present only for completeness. This second term could have been omitted altogether (and its interaction term as well).

As we have noted repeatedly, beginning in Section 8.1.1, when a nominal scale is represented by $g - 1$ variables, these variables considered together may reflect different differences than they do when each is considered separately. In particular, although each variable in a dummy-coded set reflects a dichotomy between one group and all other groups, when considered simultaneously in a regression equation these individual effects are comparisons between that group and the group consistently coded zero, the reference group. This means that consideration of omitting some of the variables in a nominal scale set, whether in the main effects or in interaction terms involving the variable, needs to be done with great care to make sure that the remaining variables accurately reflect the comparison of interest. The easiest way to ensure selection appropriateness is by contrast coding for the desired effect.

For example, in the previous section we determined the difference in curvilinearity of the seniority effect on salary by interactions with the dummy-variable coded academic departments. However, as stated, our hypothesis had only to do with a difference in curvilinearity between the psychology and history departments, with no prediction made for the sociology department. For the dummy variable interaction we used four variables, the product of the two dummy variables reflecting the comparison of the sociology and history departments, respectively, with the linear and quadratic aspects of seniority (time since Ph.D.). However we might instead have contrast coded for the term that was actually of interest (1 for psychology, -1 for history, 0 for sociology). In computing the interaction effect then we could have omitted two of the interaction terms and thus increased our power to detect the remaining two, considered as a set.[16]

As noted at many points in the book, such strategic considerations are the hallmark of thoughtful research, and must be justified by the "principled argument" (Abelson, 1995) of the investigator.

9.4 SUMMARY

The chapter begins with a summary of how the interactions among nominal scales reflect differences between differences in cell means on Y. The 2 by 2 design is revisited, and cases with no interaction, crossed interaction, and uncrossed interaction are illustrated to reveal the meaning of a joint effect reflected in an interaction term. Alternative methods of coding nominal scales are reviewed. It is noted that when scales are coded by methods that produce correlations between main effects and interactions, it will generally be necessary to carry out hierarchical analyses to test the effects of the interaction set (Section 9.1.1). Analysis of k by k designs using different coding methods for the nominal scales is discussed (Section 9.1.2). Such an analysis begins by testing unequal n experimental studies using ANOVA-equivalent methods. Other research designs may employ variations of hierarchical MRC analyses to determine overall group effects and interactions. An illustrative example is presented.

In Section 9.2 interactions involving more than two nominal scales are discussed and illustrated with a 3 by 2 by 2 example. Subsections also discuss the possibilities of omitting some interaction terms and of having some overlap in the categories of one or more nominal scales. The utility of the various coefficients resulting from a regression analysis including interactions among nominal scales is reviewed (Section 9.2.4). Finally, a summary of strategic issues and recommendations for interactions among nominal scales is offered (Section 9.2.5).

Section 9.3 considers the interaction between continuous and nominal scales. After a reminder on the general utility of centering the continuous variable, an example is carried through the following section illustrating the consequences of coding with dummy variables,

---

[16]As it turned out, the significant difference was found with the sociology department, or with the combined sociology and history departments, rather than with the history department. If only the latter had been tested, this "finding" would not have emerged.

effects codes, and contrast codes. It is emphasized that the selection of the coding method should be closely linked to the investigator's hypotheses, and that the coefficients and significance tests of the individual variables are not at all equivalent across coding schemes. However, as is necessarily the case with alternative coding methods for nominal scale main effects (Chapter 8), all methods produce in aggregate the same contributions to R^2 of both main effects and interactions when analyzed hierarchically (Sections 9.3.2 to 9.3.4). Section 9.3.5 describes and illustrates an easy method of obtaining simple slopes, that is, the increase in Y per unit of the continuous variable, for the individual categories in a nominal scale. It also reviews a method for determining whether the Y means of subgroups are significantly different at a point on the continuous variable other than its mean.

Section 9.3.6 reviews the considerations that should operate when planning an analysis of the difference in curvilinearity of effect of a continuous variable for subgroups on a nominal scale. An illustration of such an analysis is provided. Finally, Section 9.3.7 discusses the interactions of a scaled variable with two or more nominal scales and reviews the considerations in determining whether and which such interactions should be included, and how codes should be selected when not all interaction terms are represented.

10

Outliers and Multicollinearity: Diagnosing and Solving Regression Problems II

10.1 INTRODUCTION

In Chapters 2, 3, and 5 through 9 we focused on presenting multiple regression/correlation analysis as a general data analytic system. We have illuminated the flexibility and power of this analytical tool to answer a wide variety of research questions of interest to behavioral scientists. Our presentation has progressed from simple to complex models, from linear to nonlinear and interactive relationships, and from quantitative to qualitative to combinations of quantitative and qualitative IVs. The sole exception to this progression was in Chapter 4. There we considered problems that arise from the violation of the assumptions underlying multiple regression analysis. We considered graphical and statistical methods of detecting such violations and methods of solving these problems when they are detected. These procedures help researchers gain a fuller understanding of their data so that they do not report misleading results. The present chapter continues this theme, considering two problems in regression analysis that were not considered in Chapter 4.

First is the problem of *outliers*—one or more atypical data points that do not fit with the rest of the data. Outliers may represent data that are contaminated in some way (e.g., a recording error; an error in the experimental procedure). Or, they may represent an accurate observation of a rare case (e.g., a 12-year-old college student). Whatever the source of the outliers, they can in some cases have a profound impact on the estimates of the regression coefficients and their standard errors, as well as on the estimate of the overall prediction, R^2. We present graphical and statistical methods of detecting outliers and remedial approaches that may be taken when outliers are discovered. These methods become particularly important as the number of variables in the data set increases. They help researchers avoid reporting misleading results when outliers are present in the data.

Second is the problem of *multicollinearity*. This problem occurs in data sets in which one (or more) of the IVs is highly correlated with the other IVs in the regression equation. The estimate of the regression coefficient B_i for this correlated predictor will be very unreliable because little unique information is available from which to estimate its value—the regression coefficient will have a *very* large standard error. Although the estimate of the value of the regression coefficient B_i will on average be equal to the value in the population, its confidence interval will be so large as to make the estimate of little or no value. The regression coefficient will also often become more difficult to interpret. We present methods of detecting multicollinearity and methods for addressing this problem when it does occur.

10.2 OUTLIERS: INTRODUCTION AND ILLUSTRATION

We turn first to the problem of outliers, one or more atypical data points that do not fit with the rest of the data. We begin with the presumption that the data being analyzed have been carefully entered. Ideally, the full data set has been entered a second time using a data entry program that cross checks the two sets of entries and identifies errors. Checks have been performed for out of range values (e.g., a score of 8 on a 1 to 5 scale) and logical inconsistencies (e.g., a person who reports no lifetime alcohol consumption who also reports he consumed five drinks during the past week). Yet, even under conditions in which the data set has been thoroughly cleaned and checked, errors, unusual cases, or both may be present. For example, Cleveland (1993) presents evidence indicating that there were serious undetected errors even in a classic data set that had been repeatedly analyzed (Immer, Hayes, & Powers, 1934; presented as an illustrative example, for example, by R. A. Fisher in his classic *Design of Experiments*, 1971). Hoaglin and Velleman (1995) present a case study showing that analytic teams that did not perform adequate checks for outliers overlooked errors in a large data set, produced incorrect regression results, and reached seriously flawed conclusions. On a more successful note, climatologists checking for outliers discovered an anomalous observation of too low a reading for ozone levels in the upper atmosphere over Antarctica. Further study of this outlier led to the discovery of the Antarctic ozone hole, which has raised world concerns about loss

TABLE 10.2.1
Years Since Ph.D. and Number of Publications: Data

CH10EX01

	A. Original data set		B. Data set containing outlier for case 6	
Case	X Years since Ph.D.	Y Number of publications	X Years since Ph.D.	Y Number of publications
1	3	18	3	18
2	6	3	6	3
3	3	2	3	2
4	8	17	8	17
5	9	11	9	11
6	6	6	**60**	6
7	16	38	16	38
8	10	48	10	48
9	2	9	2	9
10	5	22	5	22
11	5	30	5	30
12	6	21	6	21
13	7	10	7	10
14	11	27	11	27
15	18	37	18	37

Note: The data in A are from Table 2.2.2. The data in B are identical to those in A except that the observation on *X* for case 6 has been replaced by an outlier. The outlier in B is highlighted in boldface type.

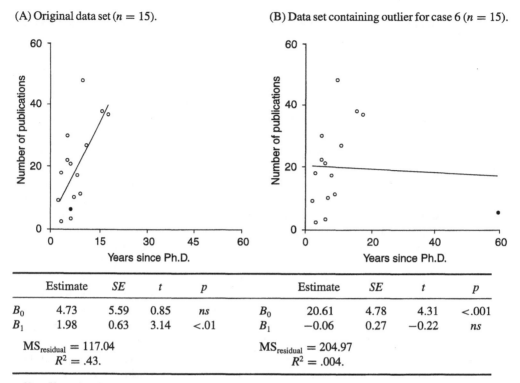

(A) Original data set ($n = 15$).

(B) Data set containing outlier for case 6 ($n = 15$).

	Estimate	SE	t	p		Estimate	SE	t	p
B_0	4.73	5.59	0.85	ns	B_0	20.61	4.78	4.31	<.001
B_1	1.98	0.63	3.14	<.01	B_1	−0.06	0.27	−0.22	ns

$MS_{residual} = 117.04$
$R^2 = .43.$

$MS_{residual} = 204.97$
$R^2 = .004.$

Note: Years since Ph.D. is shown on the abscissa (*x* axis). Number of publications is shown on the ordinate (*y* axis). Case 6 is denoted by a • in each plot. The best fitting linear regression line is superimposed in each plot. The results of the regression analysis are presented below each part.

FIGURE 10.2.1   Plot of years since Ph.D. vs. number of publications.

of ozone in the upper atmosphere.

To provide a basis for consideration of outliers, let us reconsider the faculty salary example originally presented in Chapter 2. Suppose we had found an observation that indicated that a faculty member received his Ph.D. 60 years ago! This observation may represent an error in the data (e.g., a transcription error in which 6 is mistakenly recorded as 60). Alternatively, such a data point might represent an accurate observation of a rare case—a faculty member in his 80s who is still holding a full-time position.[1] When outliers are present, regression analyses may produce results that strongly reflect a small number of atypical cases rather than the general relationship observed in the rest of the data. Even one outlier in a data set can produce a dramatic result (e.g., an interaction that disappears when the outlier is removed). Thus, a researcher may report exciting and unexpected "new results" only to discover later that they cannot be replicated because they were produced by an outlier. On the other hand, important predicted results may not be detected because they are masked by outliers. If the outliers are detected and appropriate remedial actions are taken, then the important predicted effect will emerge. The impact of outliers will typically decrease as sample size increases. However, under conditions in which there is substantial multicollinearity or the regression equation contains interactions or power polynomials, outliers may have dramatic effects even in moderate or large samples.

---

[1] In 2000, at least one major university had an active professor who was still teaching full time at the age of 100.

(C) Data set deleting case 6 ($n = 14$).

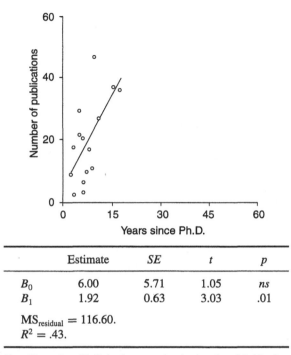

	Estimate	SE	t	p
B_0	6.00	5.71	1.05	ns
B_1	1.92	0.63	3.03	.01

$MS_{residual} = 116.60.$
$R^2 = .43.$

Note: Years since Ph.D. is shown on the abscissa (x axis). Number of publications is shown on the ordinate (y axis). Case 6 is deleted. The best fitting linear regression line is superimposed. The results of the regression analysis are presented for each part.

FIGURE 10.2.1   Continued.

Table 10.2.1A reproduces the original 15 cases of the faculty salary data set originally presented in Chapter 2. Corresponding to these data is Fig. 10.2.1(A), which depicts the regression line and the results of the regression analyses based on these 15 cases. The regression estimate is $\hat{Y} = 1.98X + 4.73$, where $\hat{Y}$ is the predicted number of publications and X is years since Ph.D. For simplicity in our initial presentation, we will presume that the original data set is correct and study what happens to the results of our regression analysis if one data point is replaced by an outlier.

Let us start with the case just presented. The original case with $X = 6$ is replaced by a single outlying case with $X = 60$ years. Table 10.2.1B illustrates this situation. All of the entries in the right panel are identical except that for subject 6, the number of years since the Ph.D. is 60 instead of 6 (in boldface type). How would this affect our results? Figure 10.2.1(B) shows the regression line and the results of the regression analysis based on this altered data set. The results change dramatically: The relationship between years and publications has disappeared, the R^2 dropping from .43 in the original data set to .00 in the data set containing the single outlier. For comparison purposes, Fig. 10.2.1(C) shows the results of another analysis, which we consider in Section 10.3. In this third analysis, outlying case 6 is dropped from the data set and the regression analysis is recomputed. The results are similar but not identical to the analysis presented in Fig. 10.2.1(A) with the original data. As this example dramatically illustrates, a single outlier can potentially have a major impact on the results of a regression analysis, especially with a small sample.

10.3 DETECTING OUTLIERS: REGRESSION DIAGNOSTICS

In the example presented in Fig. 10.2.1(B), the outlier (case 6) was easy to detect. The errant data point was far from the rest and could be detected by visual inspection of the raw data or the scatterplot of X (years) by Y (publications). Scatterplot matrices, presented in Section 4.2, can also be very useful in identifying outliers when there is more than one independent variable. In cases when there are more than one or two IVs, some outliers may be difficult to identify by such visual inspection. We encourage analysts to supplement such visual inspection with the use of specialized statistics known as regression diagnostics which can greatly aid in the detection of outliers. Regression diagnostics are *case statistics*, meaning there will be one value of each diagnostic statistic for each of the n cases in the data set. A sample of 150 cases will produce 150 values of each diagnostic statistic, one representing each case in the data set. Regression diagnostic statistics are used to examine three characteristics of potentially errant data points. The first is *leverage*: How unusual is the case in terms of its values on the IVs? The second is the *discrepancy* (or distance[2]) between the predicted and observed values on the outcome variable (Y). The third is *influence*, which reflects the amount that the regression coefficients would change if the outlier were removed from the data set. Conceptually, influence represents the product of leverage and discrepancy. Each of these characteristics should be examined, as they identify different aspects of errant data points.

In this section, we present definitions and simple worked examples to convey a conceptual understanding of the meaning of each major diagnostic statistic. We illustrate with the two data sets introduced in Section 10.2: (1) The original 15-case data set from Chapter 2 and (2) the same data set, in which 60 is used as the value for years since Ph.D. for case 6. The comparison of the results for the two data sets highlights how relatively extreme values of the diagnostic statistics may be obtained when there is an outlier in the data set, here case 6. For convenience in our initial presentation, the value of the outlier in data set (2) was chosen to produce extreme values on each of the measures of leverage, discrepancy, and influence. This need not be the case: Outliers may produce high values on leverage, but not discrepancy—or high values on discrepancy, but not leverage. We return to this issue and consider these possibilities at this end of this section. Each of the diagnostic statistics provides somewhat different information that is useful in identifying and understanding the effects of potentially errant points in the data. Remedial actions that may be taken when outliers are detected follow in Section 10.4.

10.3.1 Extremity on the Independant Variables: Leverage

Leverage reflects only the case's standing on the set of IVs. For each case, leverage tells us how far the observed values for the case are from the mean values on the set of IVs. When there is only one IV, leverage can be determined as

$$(10.3.1) \qquad \text{leverage} = h_{ii} = \frac{1}{n} + \frac{(X_i - M_X)^2}{\sum x^2},$$

where h_{ii} is the leverage for case i, n is the number of cases, X_i is the score for case i on the predictor variable, M_X is the mean of X, and Σx^2 is the sum over the n cases of the squared deviations of X_i from the mean. If case i has a score at the value of M_X, then the second term of equation 1 will be 0 and h_{ii} will have the minimum possible value of $1/n$. As case i's score on X gets further and further from M_X, h_{ii} increases in size. The maximum value of h_{ii} is 1.0.

---

[2]To avoid confusion, we use the term *discrepancy* to represent the difference between the observed and predicted value of Y for specified values on each of the predictors. The term *distance* is associated with indices of leverage, discrepancy, and influence in the regression diagnostics literature.

The mean value of leverage for the n cases in the sample is $M_{h_{ii}} = (k + 1)/n$, where k is the number of IVs.

To illustrate, let us return to the original 15 cases from Table 10.2.1A. Consider first case 4, with 8 years since Ph.D., a value very close to the mean of 7.67. The value of Σx^2 is 293.33. Substituting into Eq. (10.3.1), we find

$$h_{ii} = \frac{1}{15} + \frac{(8 - 7.67)^2}{293.33} = .0670,$$

which is very close to the minimum value of $1/n$ for h_{ii}, here $1/15 = .0667$. In contrast, consider case 15, with 18 years since Ph.D., the most extreme value of X in the original data set. Substituting case 15's value of 18 into Eq. (10.3.1) yields

$$h_{ii} = \frac{1}{15} + \frac{(18 - 7.67)^2}{293.33} = .43,$$

a considerably larger value. Not surprisingly, this value of leverage is larger than the mean leverage value for our sample, $M_{h_{ii}} = (1 + 1)/15 = .13$.

Figure 10.3.1 is an index plot that displays the values of leverage for each of the cases in the original data set. Index plots provide a convenient method of displaying the value of regression diagnostic statistics in small and moderate sized data sets by displaying the value of the diagnostic statistic on the ordinate (vertical or y axis) and the case number on the abscissa (horizontal or x axis). Index plots make it easy to identify those cases that have particularly extreme values of the diagnostic statistic. Figure 10.3.1(A) displays the leverage values for the original data set in which $X = 6$ for case 6. Figure 10.3.1(B) displays the leverage values for the data set that includes the outlier ($X = 60$ for case 6). The highest values of leverage for each data set are highlighted (•) in the figure.

(A) Original data set.   (B) Data set containing outlier for case 6.

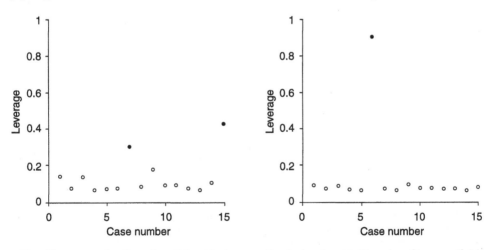

Note: The case number for each participant is shown on the abscissa (x axis). The value of leverage (h_{ii}) is shown on the ordinate (y axis). Cases with relatively high values of leverage are indicated by • in each panel. In Fig. 10.3.1(A), which contains the original data, cases 7 ($h_{ii} = .30$) and 15 ($h_{ii} = .43$) have somewhat higher leverage values than the other points since their years since Ph.D. are the most extreme in the data set (case 7, $X = 16$; case 15, $X = 18$). In Fig. 10.3.1(B), which contains the outlier, case 6 ($X = 60; h_{ii} = .90$) has an extremely high value for leverage that differs dramatically from the values for leverage of the other cases.

FIGURE 10.3.1   Index plot of leverage vs. case number.

Cases further from the mean of the single IV have a greater *potential* to influence the results of the regression equation. The leverage values identify these cases. Whether a particular case actually influences the regression coefficients or R^2 also depends on the discrepancy between the observed and predicted values of Y for that case, $Y_i - \hat{Y}_i$.

The basic idea of leverage generalizes directly to regression models in which there is more than one IV. We are now interested in how far case i's score on each of the k independent variables, $X_{i1}, X_{i2}, X_{i3}, \ldots, X_{ik}$, is from the centroid of the independent variables. Recall that the *centroid* is the point corresponding to the mean of the independent variables, $M_1, M_2, M_3, \ldots, M_k$. Conceptually, the sum of each case's squared deviations from the sample's means across the IVs is "adjusted" by the correlation between each pair of IVs. Because the algebraic expressions become complex,[3] statistical packages are used to compute the value of h_{ii} for each case in the sample.

As an illustration, consider the two-predictor regression equation presented in Section 3.2. Years since Ph.D. (X_1) and number of publications (X_2) are the independent variables, and salary (Y) is the dependent variable. The data for the 15 cases are presented in Chapter 3 in Table 3.2.1. Figure 10.3.2 presents a scatterplot of the two independent variables. In this scatterplot the centroid of the $X_1 X_2$ space, $M_{X_1} = 7.67, M_{X_2} = 19.93$, is indicated by the symbol ×. We have identified four of the cases in the scatterplot by case number. Note that case 4 $(X_1 = 8, X_2 = 17, h_{ii} = .08)$ and case 12 $(X_1 = 6, X_2 = 21, h_{ii} = .09)$ are located close to the centroid and have values of h_{ii} that are only slightly higher than the minimum leverage value $1/n = .07$. In contrast, case 8 $(X_1 = 10, X_2 = 48, h_{ii} = .45)$ and case 15 $(X_1 = 18, X_2 = 37, h_{ii} = .44)$ are located at a greater distance from the centroid as is indicated by the substantially higher leverage values. The standard statistical packages include options that compute h_{ii} for all cases in the data set. Note that leverage is based *only* on the IVs in the regression model. Changing only the DV in a regression equation will not affect the leverage values.

Centered Leverage Values

Caution must be employed in interpreting leverage values because some statistical packages[4] calculate a centered index of leverage which we will term h_{ii}^*. The centered index h_{ii}^* may be expressed in terms of the unstandardized index, h_{ii}, as

$$h_{ii}^* = h_{ii} - \frac{1}{n}.$$

The minimum possible value of h_{ii}^* is 0, and the maximum value is $1 - 1/n$. To illustrate, we calculated that $h_{ii} = .43$ for case 15 in Table 10.2.1A, so $h_{ii}^* = .43 - 1/15 = .43 - .07 = .36$.

---

[3]For readers familiar with matrix algebra, a simple matrix algebra expression is available to calculate leverage. The hat matrix is defined as $\mathbf{H} = \mathbf{X}(\mathbf{X'X})^{-1}\mathbf{X'}$. $\mathbf{H}$ is an $n \times n$ matrix and $\mathbf{X}$ is the $n \times (k + 1)$ augmented matrix of the predictor scores. This matrix has a 1 in the first column of the matrix for each case. The next k columns of the matrix contain each case's (participant's) scores on the k IVs (see Appendix 1 for an overview of matrix algebra). The main diagonal of $\mathbf{H}$ contains the leverage values. Thus, the leverage for case i, h_{ii}, is the value for the ith row and ith column of $\mathbf{H}$. It is this diagonal value that gives the leverage its identification as h_{ii}.

[4]SAS and SYSTAT programs report h_{ii} whereas SPSS reports the corresponding centered value h_{ii}^*. h_{ii} is labeled in SAS output as "Hat Diag H" and SYSTAT output as "leverage." h_{ii}^* is labeled in SPSS output as "lever." Conceptually, h_{ii} has a value of $1/n$ for a case at the centroid of the IVs because the case can still potentially affect the value of the intercept. h_{ii}^* excludes consideration of the cases potential effect on the intercept as would occur if both the IVs and DV were centered.

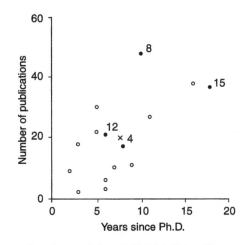

Note: Data set is from Table 3.2.1. Values of years since Ph.D. (X_1) are shown on the abscissa. Values of number of publications (X_2) are shown on the ordinate. The open and filled in circles depict the values of X_1 and X_2 for the 15 cases. × is the centroid $(M_{X_1} = 7.67; M_{Y_1} = 19.93)$ of the $X_1 X_2$ space. The four filled circles (with their case numbers) are the four cases presented in the text.

FIGURE 10.3.2   Scatterplot of time since Ph.D. vs. number of publications.

Guidelines for Identifying Cases With High Leverage Values

Two general approaches have been suggested for identifying cases with high leverage. The first approach is to plot the distribution of the h_{ii} values and to identify a very small number of cases with leverage values that are *substantially* higher than those of the other cases. Index plots are typically used in small or moderate sized samples; histograms with a large number of bins or stem and leaf displays are often used in large samples. Figure 10.3.1(B) presents an index plot of leverage by case number for the data set with the outlying case 6 ($X = 60$). The leverage of case 6 sharply stands out from the other cases.

The second approach is to examine leverage values that fall above rough rule of thumb cutoff values. Different authors have proposed different rule of thumb cutoff values. So that the cutoff values we present are consistent across the various regression diagnostic measures, we will present the guidelines of Belsley, Kuh, and Welsch (1980) that identify approximately the most extreme 5% of the cases when all of the predictors are normally distributed. For leverage, they proposed that values of h_{ii} greater than $2M_h = 2(k+1)/n$ be considered to have high leverage when both the number of predictors and the number of cases are large. For small samples, a more stringent cutoff of about $3M_h = 3(k+1)/n$ is sometimes recommended to avoid identifying too many points for examination. In the present small sample ($n = 15$) case, values greater than $(3)(.13) = .39$ might be selected for possible examination. For the centered measure of leverage, h_{ii}^*, the cutoffs will be lower. Since $h_{ii}^* = h_{ii} - (1/n)$, the corresponding cutoffs for the centered measure h_{ii}^* will be $2k/n$ in large samples and $3k/n$ in small samples.

Belsley, Kuh, and Welsch's guidelines identify a *minimum* threshold at which it may be worthwhile to identify cases for examination. In large samples, the use of the Belsley, Kuh, and Welsch guidelines will nearly always identify far too many cases. In practice, we encourage analysts to identify for examination only a *very small* number of cases that have the highest leverage values. In particular, those cases for which there is a *large* gap in the value of leverage from the remainder (i.e., unusual values) should be carefully checked for accuracy. When no cases exceed Belsley, Kuh, and Welsch's rule of thumb cutoffs, special checking of cases with relatively high leverage values is not indicated.[5] Chatterjee and Hadi (1988, Chapter 4) present a full discussion of possible cutoff values for leverage.

Mahalanobis Distance

A measure that is closely related to leverage is reported by some statistical packages (e.g., SPSS). This measure, known as Mahalanobis distance, is a measure of the distance between the specific case's values on the predictor variables and the centroid of the IVs. Weisberg (1985) points out that Mahalanobis distance can be expressed as $(n-1)h_{ii}^*$. Thus, Mahalanobis distance provides the same information as leverage, but will have different rule of thumb cutoffs. J. P. Stevens (1984) presents more information on Mahalanobis distance and conventional cutoff scores for the interpretation of this measure.

10.3.2 Extremity on Y: Discrepancy

A second set of statistics measures the *discrepancy* or distance between the predicted and observed values on Y. In Chapters 2 and 3, we saw that the raw residual for case i, $e_i = Y_i - \hat{Y}_i$, typically provides an excellent measure of this discrepancy. However, reconsider the regression lines and the data presented in Fig. 10.2.1(A) and (B). Figure 10.3.3(A) displays the raw residuals for the original data and Fig. 10.3.3(B) displays the residuals from the data containing the outlier. As can be seen, the discrepancy between case 6 (marked by •) and the regression line in Fig. 10.3.3(B) is smaller than the discrepancy for several of the other cases. In essence, the outlying point has pulled the regression line toward it to improve the overall fit. Other diagnostic statistics are needed that are less influenced by this problem. Two are commonly calculated by statistical packages, internally studentized residuals and externally studentized residuals. Externally studentized residuals will nearly always be the preferred measure of discrepancy.

Internally Studentized Residuals

Internally studentized residuals address one of two problems associated with raw residuals. As a case's scores on the predictor get further from the centroid, the estimate of the value of the residual for that case gets more precise (Behnken & Draper, 1972). The expected variance of the residual for case i can be expressed as:

$$(10.3.2) \qquad \text{variance}(e_i) = \text{MS}_{\text{residual}}(1 - h_{ii}).$$

---

[5]Whenever humans transcribe and key data into the computer, errors leading to incorrect values should be presumed to occur in a small proportion of the cases. As noted in Section 10.2, a variety of checks on the accuracy should always be performed on the data prior to any analysis. Examination of leverage values provides an important additional check because other procedures do not identify multivariate outliers.

(A) Original data set.   (B) Data set containing outlier for case 6.

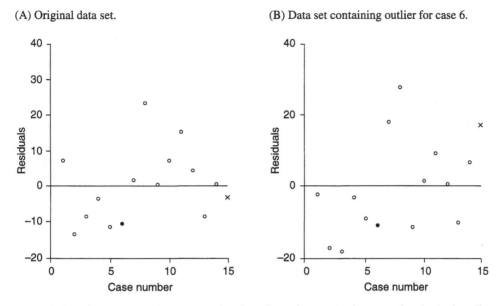

Note: Values of the raw residuals are presented on the ordinate. Case number is presented on the abscissa. The horizontal line in each panel represents a value of 0 for the raw residual. The highlighted point (•) is case 6. Note that the magnitude of this residual is not particularly large in either part because the outlying point in (B) pulls the regression line toward itself. In contrast, case 15 (years since Ph.D. = 18; number of publications = 37) is marked by × in each panel. In (A), this case has a small negative residual (−3.42). In (B), the regression line has been pulled away from this point by the outlier, so the residual is now positive and much larger in magnitude (+17.47).

FIGURE 10.3.3   Index plot of residuals vs. case number.

Recall from Section 3.6 that $MS_{residual}$ is the estimate of overall variance of the residuals around the regression line $= (1 - R^2)(\Sigma y^2)/(n - k - 1)$. h_{ii} is the leverage of case i. The standard deviation of the residual for case i is then

$$sd_{e_i} = \sqrt{MS_{residual}(1 - h_{ii})}.$$

The internally studentized residual takes the precision of the estimate of the residual into account. The internally studentized residual is the ratio of the size of the residual for case i to the standard deviation of the residual for case i,

(10.3.3) $$\text{internally studentized residual}_i = \frac{e_i}{sd_{e_i}}.$$

The magnitude of the internally studentized residual ranges between 0 and $\sqrt{n - k - 1}$ (Gray and Woodall, 1994). Unfortunately, internally studentized residuals do not follow a standard statistical distribution (the numerator and denominator in Eq. 10.3.3 are not independent), so they can *not* be interpreted using normal curve or t tables.

Externally Studentized Residuals

Externally studentized residuals directly address a second issue associated with outliers. Recall that the outlier can pull the regression line toward itself as we saw in Fig. 10.2.1(B). Externally studentized residuals address this issue by considering what would happen if the outlying case were deleted from the data set.

In Fig. 10.2.1(B) we saw that case 6 was an outlier. Suppose that we deleted case 6 from the data set and recalculated the regression equation based only on the other $n - 1 = 14$ cases. The results of this analysis are presented in Fig. 10.2.1(C). With case 6 deleted, the new regression equation is $\hat{Y}_{i(i)} = 1.92X_i + 6.00$. The notation $\hat{Y}_{i(i)}$ indicates that we are calculating the predicted value for case i, but with case i deleted from the data set. The outlier contributes substantially to the estimate of the variance of the residuals around the regression line, $MS_{residual}$. $MS_{residual(i)}$ for the new regression equation with case 6 deleted is 116.6, whereas $MS_{residual}$ for the full 15 cases (including the outlier, case 6) is 204.0.

Using the new regression equation with case 6 deleted, we calculate the predicted value for case 6 based on this new regression equation with case 6 deleted: $\hat{Y}_{i(i)} = 1.92(60) + 6.00 = 121.05$. We define the deleted residual d_i as the difference between the original Y observation for case i and the predicted value for case i based on the data set with case i deleted:

$$d_i = Y_i - \hat{Y}_{i(i)}.$$

In our present example, $d_i = 6 - 121.05 = -115.05$. For purposes of comparison, we calculated the raw residual based on all 15 cases in the data set, $e_i = Y_i - \hat{Y}_i = 6 - 17.00 = -11.00$. The greater magnitude of the deleted residual than of the raw residual helps highlight case 6 as an outlier. Case 6 can no longer hide itself by drawing the regression line toward itself.

The externally studentized residual draws on this idea of deletion of case i to remove its influence. The externally studentized residual for case i, t_i, is calculated as follows:

(10.3.4)
$$t_i = \frac{d_i}{SE_{d_i}}.$$

Paralleling the general form of Eq. (10.3.3) for the internally studentized residual, the numerator is now the *deleted* residual for case i, and the denominator is the standard error of the *deleted* residual for case i. Most sources attempt to simplify Eq. (10.3.4). The deleted residual d_i can also be computed from the raw residual e_i:

$$d_i = \frac{e_i}{1 - h_{ii}}.$$

The standard error of the deleted residual for case i can also be expressed as

$$SE_{d_i} = \sqrt{\frac{MS_{residual(i)}}{1 - h_{ii}}}.$$

If these values are substituted into Eq. (10.3.4) and the resulting expression is simplified, the internally studentized residual t_i can be expressed in terms of the following equation:

(10.3.5)
$$t_i = \frac{e_i}{\sqrt{MS_{residual(i)}(1 - h_{ii})}}.$$

Here, e_i is the raw residual, $MS_{residual(i)}$ is the mean square residual with case i deleted from the data, and h_{ii} is the leverage for case i. When years has a value of 60 for case 6:

$$t_i = \frac{-11.00}{\sqrt{116.60(1 - .90)}} = -3.29$$

Standard statistical packages will compute the externally studentized residual for all cases in the data set. In Fig. 10.3.4, we present index plots of the externally studentized residuals.

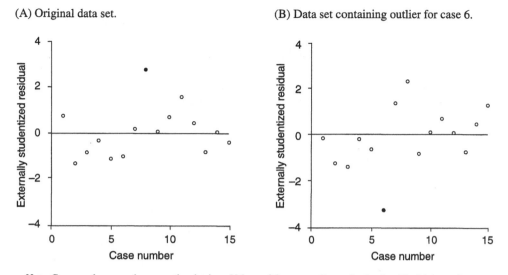

(A) Original data set.

(B) Data set containing outlier for case 6.

Note: Case numbers are shown on the abscissa. Values of the externally studentized residual (t_i) are shown on the ordinate. The horizontal line represents a value of 0 for t_i. In (A), the value of t_i for case 8 is larger in magnitude (2.80) than any of the other points. In (B) the value of t_i for case 6, the outlier, is larger in magnitude (-3.29) than any of the other points. The case with largest magnitude of t_i is identified with the symbol • in each panel.

FIGURE 10.3.4 Index plot of externally studentized residuals (t_i) vs. case number.

In Fig. 10.3.4(A) we present the plot of t_i for the original 15 cases in which $X = 6$ for case 6; in Fig. 10.3.4(B) we present the plot of t_i for the 15 cases including the outlier—case 6 has a value of $X = 60$. In Fig. 10.3.4(B), the magnitude of t_i for case 6 (denoted by •, $t_i = -3.29$) is the most extreme value for the cases in the data set.

Guidelines for Identifying Cases with High Discrepancy Values

The externally studentized residual is the preferred statistic to use to identify cases whose Y values are highly discrepant from their predicted values. As with h_{ii}, one good strategy is to use an index plot like that in Fig. 10.3.4 to identify a very small number of cases that have the most extreme values of t_i in the data set for examination. Outliers for which there are *large* gaps in the value of t_i (ignoring sign) from the remainder of the cases merit particular attention.

Alternatively, recommendations have been made for cutoff values for t_i. If the regression model fits the data, the externally studentized residuals will follow a t distribution with $df = n - k - 1$. About 5% of the cases are expected to be greater than about 2.0 in magnitude for moderate to large sample sizes. Therefore some authors recommend that a value of ±2.0 should be chosen as a cutoff for selecting cases to examine. However, once again the use of this cutoff can result in far too many cases that would need to be examined in large samples, even if there are no real outliers in the data. For example, if $n = 1000$, about 50 cases (5%) would be selected, a very large number for individual attention. Consequently, many data analysts use a higher cutoff score (e.g., ±3.0, ±3.5, ±4.0) in larger samples. Once again, both large positive and large negative values of externally studentized residuals indicate a point that is discrepant from the rest.

Beckman and Cook (1983) have suggested a procedure for testing the significance of the *largest* studentized residual. They propose that the Bonferroni procedure be used to adjust the level of α based on the number of cases in the sample (i.e., the number of cases that can potentially be tested). The value chosen should be α/n. For example, in the present sample of 15 cases with $\alpha = .05$, two tailed, $\alpha/n = .05/15 = .0033$. For $df = n - k - 1 = 13$, the critical two tailed value of t for $\alpha = .0033$ can be found using extensive statistical tables or computed using standard statistical packages. Here, the exact critical value of 3.23 is less than the magnitude of the $t_i = -3.29$ for the largest outlier, case 6, so we would conclude that the observed Y value for case 6 showed a statistically significant discrepancy from its predicted value. Note that the case with the highest discrepancy in the original data set is case 8 (see Fig. 10.3.4A). Its value of $t_i = 2.80$ does not exceed the Bonferroni adjusted critical value of 3.23.

A note on terminology.   Our terminology for the internally studentized and externally studentized residuals follows that of Cook and Weisberg (1982). However, considerable confusion is created in this area because authors have failed to use consistent terminology in referring to these statistics. The internally studentized residual has been given terms such as the standardized residual and studentized residual; the externally studentized residual has been given terms such as the studentized residual and the studentized deleted residual. The internally studentized residual is labeled "SRESID" in SPSS and "Student Residual" in SAS. The externally studentized residual is labeled "SDRESID" in SPSS, "RStudent" in SAS, and "Student" in SYSTAT output. When consulting other sources or referring to the output of other computer programs, researchers should take care to be sure they understand which statistic is being reported.

10.3.3 Influence on the Regression Estimates

Measures of influence combine information from measures of leverage and discrepancy to inform us about how the regression equation would change if case i were removed from the data set. Two types of measures of influence are commonly considered. First, global measures of influence (*DFFITS*, Cook's D) provide information about how case i affects overall characteristics of the regression equation. Second, specific measures of influence (*DFBETAS*) provide information about how case i affects each individual B. Generally, both global and specific measures of influence should be examined.

Global Measures of Influence

Standard statistical packages report one or both of two global measures of influence, $DFFITS_i$ (Belsley, Kuh, and Welsch, 1980) or Cook's D_i (Cook, 1977). Like the externally studentized residual, both are deletion statistics that compare aspects of the regression equations when case i is included versus is not included in the data set. The two global measures of influence are very closely related; analysts may use the measure they prefer as the two measures provide redundant information.

$DFFITS_i$.   The first global measure of influence is $DFFITS_i$, which is defined as

$$(10.3.6) \qquad DFFITS_i = \frac{\hat{Y}_i - \hat{Y}_{i(i)}}{\sqrt{MS_{residual(i)}h_{ii}}},$$

where $\hat{Y}_{i(i)}$ is the predicted value of Y if case i were deleted from the data set. The numerator of Eq. (10.3.6), sometimes termed *DFFIT*, tells us how much the predicted value for case i would change in the raw score units of Y if case i were deleted from the data set. The denominator serves to standardize this value so that $DFFITS_i$ estimates the number of standard deviations by which $\hat{Y}_i$, the predicted value for case i, would change if case i were deleted from the data set. *DFFITS* stands for "difference in fit, standardized."

To illustrate conceptually how $DFFITS_i$ is calculated, consider once again the data set with the outlier presented in Table 10.2.1B. As shown in Fig. 10.2.1(B), the regression equation with all 15 cases (including case 6) included is $\hat{Y}_i = -0.06X_i + 20.61$. For case 6, the predicted value is $\hat{Y}_i = -(0.06)(60) + 20.61 = 17.00$. As we saw in Section 10.2.2, when case 6 is dropped from the data set and the regression equation is computed based on the remaining 14 cases, the new regression equation is $\hat{Y}_{i(i)} = 1.92X + 6.00$, so $\hat{Y}_{i(i)} = 121.05$. Thus, the change in the predicted value of Y that results from deleting case i from the data set is $\hat{Y}_i - \hat{Y}_{i(i)} = -104.05$—an enormous difference in the predicted number of publications for this faculty member! Recall from Section 10.3.2 that with case 6 deleted $MS_{\text{residual}(i)} = 116.60$ and from Fig. 10.3.1(B) that h_{ii} for case 6 is .90. Substituting into Eq. (10.3.7), we find that for case 6,

$$DFFITS_i = \frac{17.00 - 121.05}{\sqrt{(116.60)(.90)}} = -10.13,$$

a change of over 10 standard deviations. In Fig. 10.3.5, we present an index plot of the values of $DFFITS_i$ for (a) the original data set and (b) the data set containing the outlying value for case 6. As can be seen, in Fig. 10.3.5(B), in which case 6 is an outlier, the value of $DFFITS_i$ for this case differs greatly from the values for the other cases.

Earlier we noted that measures of influence can be thought of as reflecting the product of leverage and discrepancy. Another expression for $DFFITS_i$ that is algebraically equivalent to Eq. (10.3.6) clearly shows this relationship:

(10.3.7) $$DFFITS_i = t_i \sqrt{\frac{h_{ii}}{1 - h_{ii}}}.$$

The first term in this equation is t_i, the externally studentized residual for case i. The second term is a function of the leverage for case i, h_{ii}. As values of t_i and h_{ii} both increase in magnitude, the magnitude of $DFFITS_i$ will also increase indicating the case has a larger influence on the results of the regression analysis. $DFFITS_i$ has its minimum magnitude of 0 when the deletion of case i has no effect on the predicted value of Y, $\hat{Y}_i$. $DFFITS_i = 0$ when case i falls exactly on the regression line so that $\hat{Y}_i$ will not change when case i is deleted. Cases at the centroid

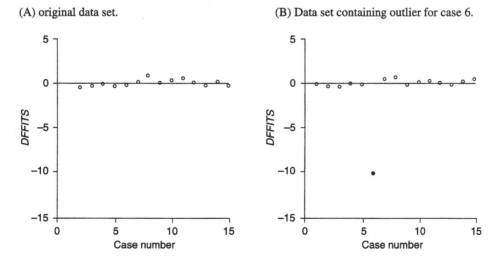

Note: Values of $DFFITS_i$ are presented on the ordinate. Case number is presented on the abscissa. The highlighted point in (B) corresponds to case 6, the outlier. The horizontal line in each panel represents a value of 0 for $DFFITS_i$.

FIGURE 10.3.5 Index plot of $DFFITS_i$ vs. case number.

of the sample can still have some influence[6] because the minimum value of h_{ii} is $1/n$. The sign of $DFFITS_i$ will be positive when $Y_i > \hat{Y}_{i(i)}$ and negative when $Y_i < \hat{Y}_{i(i)}$. Most standard statistical packages will compute $DFFITS_i$ for all cases in the data set.

Cook's D_i.   An alternative measure of the global influence of case i on the results of the regression equation known as Cook's D_i is also reported by statistical packages. Cook's D_i can be expressed as

$$\text{(10.3.8)} \qquad \text{Cook's } D_i = \frac{\sum (\hat{Y} - \hat{Y}_{(i)})^2}{(k+1)\text{MS}_{\text{residual}}}.$$

Thus, Cook's D_i compares the predicted value of Y with case i included and deleted for all cases in the data set. These differences are squared and then summed. The denominator serves to standardize the value. Cook's D_i ranges upward from its potential minimum value of 0 with higher numbers indicating the case has a larger influence on the results of the regression analysis. Unlike $DFFITS_i$, Cook's D_i will always be ≥ 0; it cannot be negative.

$DFFITS_i$ and Cook's D_i are closely related measures. Cook and Weisberg (1982) have shown that Cook's D_i and $DFFITS_i$ have the following mathematical relationship

$$\text{Cook's } D_i = \frac{(DFFITS)_i^2 \text{MS}_{\text{residual}(i)}}{(k+1)\text{MS}_{\text{residual}}}.$$

Since the values of $\text{MS}_{\text{residual}(i)}$ and $\text{MS}_{\text{residual}}$ will be very similar except in those small data sets in which case i has an extreme discrepancy relative to the other cases, this relationship can typically be approximated as

$$\text{Cook's } D_i \approx \frac{DFFITS_i^2}{(k+1)}.$$

Guidelines for Identifying Cases with High Global Influence

$DFFITS_i$ and Cook's D_i can be viewed as interchangeable statistics. Either measure can be used to provide information about the global influence of case i. Once again, one good strategy in small to moderate sized samples is to use an index plot—either $DFFITS_i$ or Cook's D_i is plotted against case number. The analyst identifies a very small number of cases that have the most extreme values as being potentially influential. Those cases that have large gaps in the value of $DFFITS_i$ or Cook's D_i relative to other cases deserve particular scrutiny.

Alternatively, rule of thumb cutoffs may be used. For $DFFITS_i$ a conventional cutoff is that cases with magnitudes (ignoring sign) of $DFFITS_i > 1$ in small or medium sized data sets or $> 2\sqrt{(k+1)/n}$ in large data sets be flagged as potentially influential observations. For Cook's D_i a value of 1.0 or the critical value of the F distribution at $\alpha = .50$ with $df = (k+1, n-k-1)$ is used. For example, in the present case with 1 IV, if Cook's D_i exceeded $F(2, 13) = 0.73$, the 50th percentile of the F distribution, the case would be flagged as influential. We will provide further discussion of guidelines following the next section.

A Measure of Influence on a Specific Regression Coefficient

$DFBETAS_{ij}$ is a second type of influence statistic that is very important when the researcher's interest focuses on specific regression coefficients within the equation. Once again, it is a deletion statistic that compares regression coefficients when case i is included versus not included in the sample.

---

[6]When cases fall at the centroid, they can still affect the regression intercept.

To provide a simple illustration of when $DFBETAS_{ij}$ would provide a useful measure, suppose a researcher is interested in the relationship between IQ and children's school performance. This researcher might also include parent's income in the regression equation, performance $= B_1 Income + B_2 IQ + B_0$. Here the researcher's interest is not in parents' income per se, but to control for the effects of parents' income in understanding the relationship between IQ and performance. $DFBETAS_{ij}$ provides information about the effect of case i on the specific regression coefficient(s) of interest, here B_2, that is, $DFBETAS_{i2}$.

$DFBETAS_{ij}$ for case i is defined for regression coefficient B_j as follows:

$$(10.3.9) \qquad DFBETAS_{ij} = \frac{B_j - B_{j(i)}}{SE_{B_{j(i)}}}.$$

We see in this equation that the numerator is the difference between the B_j calculated with all cases in the data set and the $B_{j(i)}$ calculated after case i is deleted. The denominator is the SE of $B_{j(i)}$, calculated after case i is deleted. The calculation of the standard error is complex when there is more than one predictor,[7] but this calculation is performed by standard statistical packages. The division serves to standardize $DFBETAS_{ij}$, facilitating a common interpretation of the influence of case i across each of the regression coefficients. Each *case* will have $(k+1)$ $DFBETAS_{ij}$ associated with it, one corresponding to each of the regression coefficients in the equation including the intercept.

To illustrate the interpretation of $DFBETAS_{ij}$, consider once again the data set containing the outlier presented in Table 10.2.1B. For case 6, which is the outlier, $DFBETAS_{ij} = 4.05$ for the intercept B_0, and $DFBETAS_{ij} = -9.75$ for the slope B_1. The sign of $DFBETAS_{ij}$ indicates whether the *inclusion* of case i leads to an increase or decrease in the corresponding regression coefficient. For case 6, we see that its inclusion leads to an increase in B_0, but a decrease in B_1. The magnitude of $DFBETAS_{ij}$ describes the magnitude of the change with higher values indicating greater change. Figure 10.3.6(A) and (B) provide an index plot of $DFBETAS_{ij}$ for the intercept, B_0. Figure 10.3.6(A) displays these values based on the original data for case 6 ($X = 6$); Fig. 10.3.6(B) displays the values for the data including the outlier for case 6 ($X = 60$). Figure 10.3.6(C) and (D) present index plots of $DFBETAS_{ij}$ for the slope. Figure 10.3.6(C) displays the values based on the original data; Fig. 10.3.6(D) displays the values for the data including the outlier for case 6. Case 6 is highlighted in each panel. As can be seen, no extreme values of $DFBETAS_{ij}$ are observed for the original data in either Fig. 10.3.6(A) for the intercept or Fig. 10.3.6(C) for the slope. In contrast, in Fig. 10.3.6(B) and Fig. 10.3.6(D) case 6 is far from the values of the other cases for both the intercept and the slope.

Guidelines for Identifying Cases With High Influence on Specific Regression Coefficients

For small to moderate sized samples, it is useful to construct a separate index plot for each regression coefficient of $DFBETAS_{ij}$ against the case number. Any cases that have large values of $DFBETAS_{ij}$ relative to the remaining cases have high influence on the regression coefficient B_j. Only those few cases with the most extreme values are studied. Histograms with a large number of bins or stem and leaf displays can be used with large samples.

For researchers who prefer rule of thumb guidelines, cases having $DFBETAS_{ij} > \pm 1$ for small or moderate sized data sets or $DFBETAS_{ij} > \pm 2/\sqrt{n}$ for large data sets are considered

---

[7]The standard error does not have a simple algebraic expression when there is more than one IV. The matrix formula is $SE_{B_{j(i)}} = \sqrt{MS_{residual(i)}(\mathbf{X'X})_{jj}^{-1}}$. For B_j, the term in the jth row and jth column (on the diagonal) of the inverse of the $(\mathbf{X'X})$ matrix is used as the value of $(\mathbf{X'X})_{jj}^{-1}$.

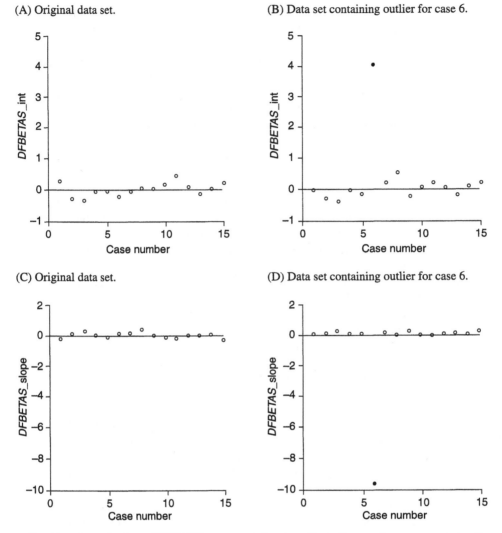

(A) Original data set.

(B) Data set containing outlier for case 6.

(C) Original data set.

(D) Data set containing outlier for case 6.

Note: In each panel, values of $DFBETAS_{ij}$ are presented on the ordinate. Case numbers are presented on the abscissa. The values of $DFBETAS_{ij}$ presented in Figs. 10.3.6(A) and (B) are for the intercept, B_0. The values of $DFBETAS_{ij}$ presented in Figs. 10.3.6(C) and (D) are for the slope, B_1. The highlighted points correspond to case 6, the outlier. The horizontal line represents a value of 0 for $DFBETAS_{ij}$ in each panel.

FIGURE 10.3.6   (A), (B): Index plot of $DFBETAS_{ij}$ vs. case number: intercept. (C), (D): Index plot of $DFBETAS_{ij}$ vs. case number: slope.

to be influential. In the present illustration involving a small sample ($n = 15$), the value of $DFBETAS_{ij}$ for the intercept B_0 and the slope B_1 both far exceed the rule of thumb cutoff of 1 for our outlying case 6.

10.3.4 Location of Outlying Points and Diagnostic Statistics

In the example using case 6 (with $X = 60$) and the outlying point that we have used throughout this section, the measures of leverage, discrepancy, and influence for case 6 were all extreme in value. However, leverage and discrepancy measure two distinct properties of outliers; they

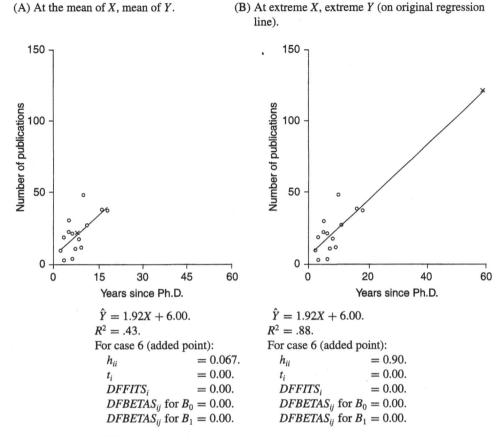

(A) At the mean of X, mean of Y.

(B) At extreme X, extreme Y (on original regression line).

$\hat{Y} = 1.92X + 6.00.$ $\hat{Y} = 1.92X + 6.00.$
$R^2 = .43.$ $R^2 = .88.$

For case 6 (added point):   For case 6 (added point):

h_{ii}	$= 0.067.$	h_{ii}	$= 0.90.$
t_i	$= 0.00.$	t_i	$= 0.00.$
$DFFITS_i$	$= 0.00.$	$DFFITS_i$	$= 0.00.$
$DFBETAS_{ij}$ for B_0	$= 0.00.$	$DFBETAS_{ij}$ for B_0	$= 0.00.$
$DFBETAS_{ij}$ for B_1	$= 0.00.$	$DFBETAS_{ij}$ for B_1	$= 0.00.$

FIGURE 10.3.7 Effect of adding a single data point at various locations.

are not necessarily related. Recall also that influence can be conceptually thought of as the product of leverage and discrepancy (see Eq. 10.3.7). Cases with high values of influence will typically have at least moderately high values of both leverage and discrepancy.

To illustrate these ideas, we will use the 14 cases presented in Fig. 10.2.1(C). These are the 14 cases included in the original data set with case 6 deleted. In Fig. 10.3.7 we try adding different values of a single case to this data set and observe what happens to the regression equation and the diagnostic statistics. For the 14 original cases, the regression equation is $\hat{Y} = 1.92X + 6.00, R^2 = .43, M_X = 7.79, M_Y = 20.93$.

Figure 10.3.7(A)

In Fig. 10.3.7(A), the new point has been added at the mean of X and mean of Y (case 6, $X = 7.79, Y = 20.93$). The new regression equation is identical to the original regression equation based on the 14 cases. For the new case (case 6) in the regression equation based on 15 cases, $h_{ii} = 0.0667$, which is equal to the minimum leverage value of $1/n$; t_i (the externally studentized residual, the measure of discrepancy) $= 0$; and Cook's D_i (the measure of overall influence) $= 0$.

Figure 10.3.7(B)

Figure 10.3.7(B) adds the new point at an extreme value of X and the corresponding value of Y that falls exactly on the original regression line. The point is added at $X = 60, Y = 121.07$.

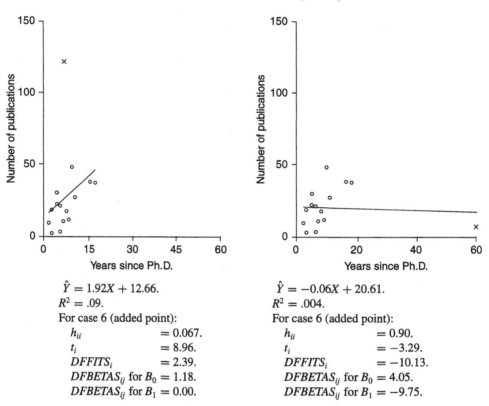

(C) At the mean of X, extreme value of Y.

(D) Extreme value of X, extreme value of Y (not on original regression line).

$\hat{Y} = 1.92X + 12.66.$
$R^2 = .09.$
For case 6 (added point):

h_{ii}	$= 0.067.$
t_i	$= 8.96.$
$DFFITS_i$	$= 2.39.$
$DFBETAS_{ij}$ for $B_0 = 1.18.$	
$DFBETAS_{ij}$ for $B_1 = 0.00.$	

$\hat{Y} = -0.06X + 20.61.$
$R^2 = .004.$
For case 6 (added point):

h_{ii}	$= 0.90.$
t_i	$= -3.29.$
$DFFITS_i$	$= -10.13.$
$DFBETAS_{ij}$ for $B_0 = 4.05.$	
$DFBETAS_{ij}$ for $B_1 = -9.75.$	

Note: Years since Ph.D. is shown on the abscissa. Number of publications is shown on the ordinate. The added case (case 6) in each Part is denoted by ×. The best fitting linear regression line is superimposed in each plot. The data presented in Fig. 10.3.7(D) were previously displayed in Fig. 10.2.1(B). The results of the regression analysis and diagnostic statistics are also presented for each panel.

FIGURE 10.3.7   Continued.

To calculate the value of Y, we substituted $X = 60$ into the original regression equation: $\hat{Y} = 1.92(60) + 6.00 = 121.07$. The new regression equation is $\hat{Y} = 1.92X + 6.00, R^2 = .88, M_X = 11.27, M_Y = 27.61$. Note that the new regression equation is identical to the original. The new R^2 has doubled—from .43 based on the original 14 cases to .88 in the new data set. This result indicates how selecting cases with extreme values on X can potentially increase the R^2 and the power of significance tests of the regression coefficients.[8] Extreme cases located on the regression line stabilize the regression line and decrease the SEs of both the slope and intercept. For the new case (case 6) in the regression equation based on 15 cases, $h_{ii} = .90, t_i = 0$, and $DFFITS_i = 0$. Only the measure of leverage reflects this outlying case.

Figure 10.3.7(C)

Figure 10.3.7(C) illustrates what happens when the new point is added at an extreme value of Y, but the value of X is at the mean ($M_X = 7.79$) of the original cases. For purposes of

---

[8]It may be useful to refer back to Section 2.11, where the discussion of the impact of the range of values on r is discussed.

comparison, we add the point at the same Y value ($Y = 121.07$) as in Fig. 10.3.7(B). As shown in Fig. 10.3.7(C), the slope of the new B_1 is identical to that of the original data set, but B_0 has increased from 6.00 to 12.66. The addition of a point far from the original regression line leads to a large decrease in R^2—from .43 for the original sample of 14 cases to .09 with the case added. For case 6 in this new regression equation based on 15 cases, $h_{ii} = .0667, t_i = 8.96$, and $DFFITS_i = 2.39$. Leverage is at the minimum possible value, but the externally studentized residual is very large, and the measure of global influence, $DFFITS_i$, has a large value. To understand the effect of case 6 on the global measure of influence, it is useful to consider the measures of specific influence, the values of $DFBETAS_{ij}$ for the slope and intercept. For case 6, the value of $DFBETAS_{ij}$ for B_0 is high, 1.18. In contrast, the value of $DFBETAS_{ij}$ for B_1 is 0. These values of $DFBETAS_{ij}$ indicate that all of the change was in the intercept; the slope has not changed.

Figure 10.3.7(D)

Finally, Fig. 10.3.7(D) reprises the example used throughout this section—an outlier is added that is extreme on both X and Y ($X = 60; Y = 6$). As we saw earlier, the regression equation changes dramatically from $\hat{Y} = 1.92X + 6.00$ to $\hat{Y} = -0.06X + 20.61$ with the addition of the outlier, case 6. Case 6 has high leverage ($h_{ii} = 0.90$), high discrepancy ($t_i = -3.29$), and high measures of both global ($DFFITS_i = -10.13$) and specific influence ($DFBETAS_{ij} = 4.05$ for intercept; $DFBETAS_{ij} = -9.75$ for slope).

10.3.5 Summary and Suggestions

In summary, each of the diagnostic statistics provides different information about the effect of an outlier on the regression equation. Leverage (h_{ii}) informs us about how far the point is from the centroid of the predictor space, and discrepancy (t_i = externally studentized residual) informs us about how far the point is from the regression line with case i deleted. The two measures of global influence, $DFFITS_i$ and Cook's D_i, provide interchangeable information about the overall influence of the single case on the regression equation, whereas $DFBETAS_{ij}$ informs us about how the single case i affects each regression coefficient. Each of these sources of information is useful in studying the effects of outliers. Table 10.3.1 summarizes the diagnostic statistics and provides rule of thumb cutoff values.

We present here some suggestions for looking at diagnostic statistics, deferring our consideration of possible remedial actions until the next section.

1. When the data are initially received, it is very useful to examine histograms with a large number of bins (or boxplots) of each variable to look for univariate outliers. Plots of leverage values can help identify multivariate outliers in initial data screening. For example, calculating leverage values for each participant based on the responses to each item of a 20-item scale can help identify any participants with unusual response patterns that may be problematic. Recall that leverage is based only on the IVs.[9] These statistics can be useful as a final step in the initial data checking and cleaning.

2. For any data analysis that may be reported, it is useful to examine diagnostic statistics. The extent of scrutiny of these statistics depends on the nature of the study. If the study is one of a series of replications, inspection of graphical displays for any obvious outliers is normally sufficient. Consistency of the findings across replications provides assurance that the presence

---

[9]Standard regression programs require that a regression equation be specified to calculate leverage. We recommend that a regression analysis be specified that includes all IVs of potential interest and an arbitrary numeric variable that is *complete* for all cases (e.g., case number) as the DV. Leverage is not affected by the DV that is chosen.

TABLE 10.3.1
Summary of Regression Diagnostics for Individual Cases

Diagnostic index	Measures	Proposed cutoff	Expected cases identified
Leverage (h_{ii})	Extremity on IVs	$2(k + 1)/n$ for large n $3(k + 1)/n$ for small n	5%
Centered leverage (h_{ii}^*)	Extremity on IVs	$2k/n$ for large n $3k/n$ for small n	5%
Externally studentized residuals (t_i)	Discrepancy of Y_i from regression line excluding the case	± 3.0 or ± 4.0 for large n ± 2.0 for small n	0.3%, 0.01% 5%
DFFITS	Influence: change in predicted Y if case omitted from estimate	$\pm 2\sqrt{\frac{k+1}{n}}$ for large n ± 1.0 for small n	5% —
Cook's D	Influence measured as aggregate change in set of B_is if case omitted from estimate	1.0 or F distribution value for $\alpha = .50$	—
DFBETAS	Influence measured as change in a specific B_i if case omitted from estimate	$\pm 2/\sqrt{n}$ for large n ± 1.0 for small n	5% —

Note: Some proposed minimum cutoffs for diagnostic statistics. Only a few of the most extreme cases that exceed minimum cutoffs merit examination.

of an outlier is not responsible for the results. On the other hand, if the data set is unique and unlikely to be replicated (e.g., a study of 40 individuals with a rare medical disorder), very careful scrutiny of the data is in order.

3. In large samples, visual inspection of index plots becomes difficult. Analysts may use boxplots or histograms with a large number of bins to identify outlying values, and then identify these cases in the data set. Alternatively, analysts may save the values of the diagnostic statistics, order them from lowest to highest, and plot only the highest values (e.g., top 50) on an index plot. Ideally, the most extreme values relative to the remainder should be apparent.

4. If the researchers' interest is in overall prediction or they have not made any prediction about specific regression coefficients, we encourage examination of influence statistics focused on $DFFITS_i$ or Cook's D_i. If the researchers have made a priori predictions about specific regression coefficients, then we encourage examination of the associated $DFBETAS_{ij}$ regardless of whether the measure of global influence is extreme. If the researchers find an unpredicted new result, we also encourage examination of the associated $DFBETAS_{ij}$ (and ideally replication in a new sample[10]) prior to reporting the result. This helps assure that "exciting new results" are indeed potentially exciting and not merely produced by an outlier. Note that measures of influence are associated with a specific regression equation; the values of these diagnostic statistics will change if the regression equation is modified.

---

[10]Maxwell (2000) provides a striking demonstration of the importance of replication in the interpretation of unpredicted findings in multiple regression.

5. In regression equations including power polynomial (e.g., X^2) or interaction (e.g., XZ) terms, outlying points can have profound effects on measures of both global and specific influence even in moderate and large samples. For example, Pillow, West, and Reich (1991) found that a single extreme outlier in a sample of over 300 cases produced an inexplicable three-way interaction and that the originally predicted results were obtained when this case was deleted. Even though a case may be only moderately extreme on X and on Z separately, the product of these values may yield an extreme point that has a substantial influence on the results of the regression analysis. Such outliers can create spurious effects or mask a priori predicted effects. Very careful screening for outliers is encouraged in such regression equations.

6. Cases that do not have high values of influence but that are extreme in terms of the externally standardized residual do not greatly alter the estimates of the regression coefficients (except for B_0). Nonetheless, they do affect the standard errors and hence the power of the statistical tests. Measures of discrepancy are associated with a specific regression equation; these diagnostic statistics will change if the regression equation is modified.

7. The values of the diagnostic statistics change whenever a case is removed. If a serious outlier is detected and removed, the effects of its removal should be studied. The diagnostic statistics for the new data set should be recomputed before any additional cases are considered for removal. If the removal of outlying cases continues to produce new outlying cases after a few repetitions of this process, other strategies of addressing the outlier (e.g., transformation) should be sought.

Other sources (Bollen & Jackman, 1990; Chatterjee & Hadi, 1988) present a fuller discussion of cutoff values for the diagnostic statistics and illustrations of the use of diagnostic statistics with real data sets.

10.4 SOURCES OF OUTLIERS AND POSSIBLE REMEDIAL ACTIONS

When outliers are discovered in data, the researcher needs to decide what remedial actions, if any, should be undertaken. This decision needs to be based on careful detective work using clues provided by the regression diagnostic statistics to try to understand the source of the outliers and their influence on the results of the regression analysis. However, good detective work also depends on a clear understanding of the substantive problem that is being studied, the methods through which the data were collected, the nature of the sample, and the population to which generalization is sought. In some cases, a clear understanding of the source of the outliers may not emerge even with the best detective work. In such cases, the choice of the optimal remedial action will be associated with considerable uncertainty. More than one remedial action may be investigated, or researchers may choose to employ the remedial action that is most commonly used in their substantive area.

10.4.1 Sources of Outliers

Outliers can arise from many sources. To help readers in thinking about this problem, we have grouped sources of outliers into two general classes: contaminated observations and rare cases.

Contaminated Observations

Outliers may occur because the data have been contaminated in some way. Here we present several of the possible sources of contamination in the behavioral sciences together with examples. Contaminated observations can and should be minimized by careful research procedure and data preparation. Nonetheless, contaminated observations will occur even for the most careful researchers.

1. *Error of execution of the research procedure.* An interviewer may misread some of the questions; an experimenter may deliver the wrong or an incomplete treatment.

2. *Inaccurate measurement of the dependent measure.* Equipment may fail so that measurement of the DV (e.g., response time) is not accurately recorded.

3. *Errors in recording or keying the data.* An interviewer may write down the participant's response incorrectly, or the data may not be keyed into the computer properly.

4. *Errors in calculation of the measures.* The researcher may incorrectly count up the number of responses or make a mistake in the calculation of a measure (e.g., percentage of correct responses).

5. *Nonattentive participants.* In certain cases, participants may be fatigued, ill, or drunk, and be unable to respond in their typical manner to the experimental materials.

Each of the diagnostic statistics (leverage, discrepancy, and influence) can potentially aid in detecting contaminated data. Whenever researchers detect outliers, they should first attempt to rule out the possibility that the outliers represent contaminated data. Data and calculations should be checked for accuracy; research notes should be checked for procedural anomalies that may explain the outlier.[11] If it can be verified that the outliers represent contaminated data, these data points should *not* be included in the data analysis. The researcher should replace the contaminated data with the correct data for the case if possible or delete the contaminated case from the data set. In other situations, it may be possible to make a second observation on the case and to replace the outlying value in the data set. To illustrate, in our example of faculty publications, it may be possible to check personnel records or to reinterview the faculty member in question (case 6) to determine the correct value for time since Ph.D. The corrected value should always be used in the data set.

Rare Cases

For other cases, the outlying observations may be correct (or alternatively, not show any detectable evidence of contamination). The outlying case may represent a valid, but extremely rare observation in the population. For example, imagine researchers are conducting a study of the relationship between year in college (freshman $= 1$; senior $= 4$) and sexual attitudes. Suppose that the sample contains a single 12-year-old freshman male. Although very rare, such individuals do exist in the U.S. college population. The results of the regression analysis could *potentially* be affected by this one outlying case if his sexual attitudes differed greatly from those of his classmates.

When outliers having high influence are detected that are not contaminants, how they should be treated in the data analysis can often be a serious issue that can be difficult to resolve. In general, there is a tension between two scientific goals. On one side, eliminating or minimizing the effect of the rare case can often lead to a regression equation that provides a more accurate description of the X-Y relationship in the population of interest. On the other side, the outlier may represent a subtle signal of an important phenomenon or the inadequacy of the specific regression model that was tested. Research attempting to understand rare cases has sometimes

---

[11] In complex experiments or interviews, many observations (including apparently valid observations) may be associated with anomalies in the procedure. The researcher should examine outliers as well as a random sample of other observations to be sure the two classes of observations can be distinguished on the basis of procedural problems.

led to important lines of scientific research. The discovery of the Antarctic ozone hole and the discovery of penicillin both depended on understanding the source of rare cases.

In some research situations, the decision may be relatively straightforward. The rare case may be thought of as a different kind of contaminant—the participant is from a different population than the one of interest. In such cases, researchers may conclude that they wish to restrict their generalization to a specific population and exclude the rare case(s) from the analysis. Returning to our example on college sexual attitudes, the researcher may decide to exclude all students from the analysis who began college at less than a minimum age (e.g., 16 years old). The result is that the regression equation will better characterize a population of normatively aged college students. The high potential for a small number of young (prepuberty) students to influence the results of the regression analysis if they have different sexual attitudes is eliminated. Now, however, generalization of the results is limited to students who were at least 16 years old when they began college.

Unfortunately, in practice the source of any rare cases will be difficult (or impossible) to determine. Rare cases can arise from many sources.

1. There may be an *undetected* (and perhaps unknowable) contaminant in the data. For example, an experimenter may fail to observe and record a procedural error in an experiment.

2. One or more of the predictor variables may have an unusual distribution that produces extreme values. For example, even though intelligence is usually thought of as having a normal distribution, there are a substantially larger than expected number of cases in the population with very low intelligence because of specific constitutional insults or anomalies. In some samples such cases may cause potential distortions of the relationship between variables.

3. The dependent variable may have properties that lead to a potential for occasional large residuals. For example, the distribution of the number of absences from work during a month in a group of typically very healthy workers may include rare high outliers associated with workers who experienced major illnesses such as a heart attack.

4. The regression model being studied may be incorrect. This issue is illustrated in Fig. 10.4.1 through a series of scatterplots based on a small artificial data set developed by Huber (1981). Note that in Fig. 10.4.1(A) and (B) there is one point marked by × which is an outlier. Figure 10.4.1(A) depicts the poor fit of a linear regression to the full set of 6 data points. Figure 10.4.1(B) illustrates that a regression equation including a quadratic term may fit the data extremely well and the case marked by an × is no longer an outlier.

Figure 10.4.1 nicely illustrates the dilemma created by outliers. In reality, researchers often do not know for sure that the point marked × has not in fact been contaminated by unknown influences. Nor will they always have prior theory or empirical work that would lead them to expect this form of curvilinear relationship between X and Y. Figure 10.4.1(C) illustrates what happens if we delete the outlier: The linear regression fits well, indicating a strong negative relationship between X and Y, $B_1 = -0.98, t(3) = -5.57, p = .01$. The proposal of a curvilinear relationship is based only on a single outlying data point; this is generally a very risky practice, as the odds of being able to replicate this unexpected curvilinear relationship in another sample are low. Indeed, $DFBETAS_{ij}$ for case 6 for the nonlinear (quadratic) term in the regression equation is -14.74, indicating the extraordinary degree to which the nonlinear function is dependent on the inclusion of this one case. At the same time, a decision to exclude the outlier in Fig. 10.4.1(C) may mean the researcher has discarded the basis for an important potential insight. Collecting a larger sample in which there are a sizeable number of cases at the higher values of X would enable the researcher to resolve this dilemma.

CH10EX02

Consider yet again our earlier example, in which very young students were excluded from the analysis to provide a better characterization of the relationship between year in college and sexual attitudes in "typical" college students. The distinctly different college experience

(A) Fit of linear model.   (B) Fit of quadratic model.

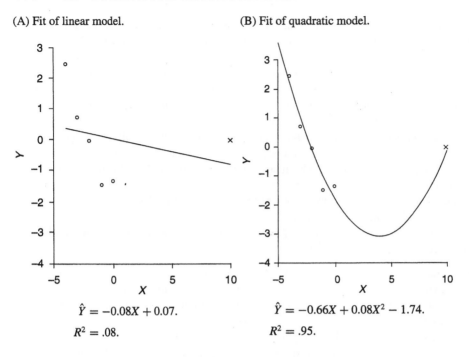

$\hat{Y} = -0.08X + 0.07.$ $\hat{Y} = -0.66X + 0.08X^2 - 1.74.$

$R^2 = .08.$ $R^2 = .95.$

(C) Fit of linear model with outlier deleted.

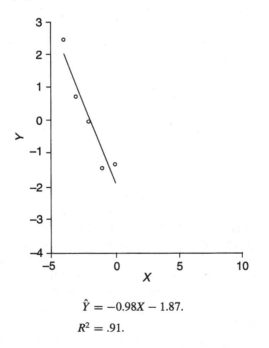

$\hat{Y} = -0.98X - 1.87.$

$R^2 = .91.$

Note: In Panels (A) and (B), the outlier is denoted by ×.

FIGURE 10.4.1   Scatterplot of Huber's (1981) example.

of very young students, especially with regard to their social and sexual attitudes and relationships, may be a very interesting focus of study in its own right. The outlying cases may be providing an important signal about differences between young and normatively aged college students. Other researchers might note the information about such outliers in published reports, perceive this possibility, and design a study in which a large number of very young students were included in the sample. More precise estimates of the effects of number of years of college attendance on sexual attitudes for both the older, normative population and this younger population could be obtained.

Given this tension between accurately characterizing relationships for the nonoutlying participants versus missing important information provided by the rare case(s), it is important to provide information about outliers in published research reports. Kruskal (1960) has emphatically argued that no matter the reason, apparent outliers should be reported.[12]

> I suggest that it is of great importance to preach the doctrine that apparent outliers should *always* be reported, even when one feels that their causes are known or rejects them for whatever good rule or reason. The immediate pressures of practical statistical analysis are almost uniformly in the direction of suppressing announcements that do not fit the pattern; we must maintain a strong sea-wall against these pressures (p. 158, italics in original).

10.4.2 Remedial Actions

As we have discussed, addressing data that are known to be contaminated is easy. The contaminated data point(s) are simply corrected, deleted, or replaced as is appropriate. In contrast, three different general approaches may be taken with outliers that represent rare cases. First, the data may be analyzed with the outliers deleted. Second, the regression model may be revised, adding terms that may account for outliers, or the data may be transformed so that the outliers are no longer present. Or third, alternative robust regression methods (to be described later) may be used that attempt to minimize the influence of outliers on the results of the regression equation.

Deletion of Outliers

The classic method of addressing outliers is to delete them and to reanalyze the remaining data (e.g., Chatterjee & Wiseman, 1983; Stevens, 1984). This is the simplest method and in many (but certainly not all) cases, it will provide estimates of the regression coefficients that are very similar to those produced by more complex robust regression procedures. Researchers will typically base their conclusions on the regression equation with outlying cases deleted. However, the nature of the outliers and the results of the original regression analysis with all cases included should normally be reported, at least in footnotes.

There are several potential problems with this approach. First, as noted in Section 10.3.5, analysis of the diagnostic statistics for the new data set (now with the original outliers deleted) may yield still other cases with extreme values on the diagnostic statistics. Second, the specific cases chosen for deletion will often depend on the subjective judgment of a particular researcher. Other researchers analyzing the same data set may come to different conclusions. Third, although diagnostic statistics do a good job of detecting single outliers, the presence of several outliers in close proximity (known as a "clump") can sometimes mask the problem.

Figure 10.4.2 illustrates this third problem with a scatterplot of years since Ph.D. versus publications. The 62 cases we considered in Chapter 3 are plotted as circles (one case to be discussed later is plotted as a solid circle). We add to this data set a clump of three outliers CH10EX3

---

[12]Journal space limitations preclude the provision of extensive information about outliers. Succinct information about the number and type of outliers and their effects on the regression analysis can typically be reported.

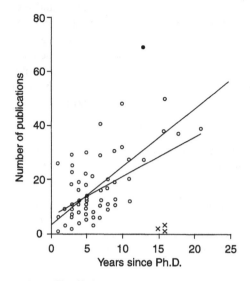

Note: The 62 data points denoted by circles (o) are the original 62 cases presented in Table 3.5.1. Three outliers denoted by × have been added to form a clump at the lower right of the plot. One data point with high discrepancy from the original data set has been darkened (•). The longer line that touches the *y* axis is the regression line for the original 62 cases. The shorter line is the regression line for all 65 cases including the clump of 3 outliers.

FIGURE 10.4.2   Illustration of a clump of outliers: Scatterplot of years since Ph.D. vs number of publications.

having 15–16 years since the Ph.D. and few publications; these cases are denoted with an ×. The first regression equation for the 62 original cases is $\hat{Y} = 2.13X + 3.72$, $R^2 = .42$. The second regression equation for the 65 cases (including the clump of 3 outliers) is $\hat{Y} = 1.46X + 6.88$, $R^2 = .23$. These regression lines are illustrated in Fig. 10.4.2.

The values of the diagnostic statistics corresponding to these three cases (case numbers 63, 64, 65 in data file) for the second regression equation would *not* be considered to be unusually extreme by most guidelines. Leverage values for the three cases are moderate ($h_{ii} = .06, .07, .07$, respectively, compared to a rule of thumb *minimum* cutoff value of $h_{ii} = .09$ for small samples (see Table 10.3.1). $DFFITS_i = -.58, -.71, -.66$; $DFBETAS_{ij} = .27, .36, .33$ for the intercept and $DFBETAS_{ij} = -.50, -.63, -.59$ for the slope, respectively. These values are not large relative to rule of thumb cutoffs of ± 1.0 that have been proposed for small samples. The values of the externally studentized residuals for the clump of outliers, $t_i = -2.29, -2.54, -2.34$, respectively, might draw some attention, but would likely be overshadowed by another data point from the original sample ($X = 13, Y = 69$; marked by •) that has a much higher externally studentized residual, $t_i = 3.89$. What makes the three outliers stand out is that they form a visually distinct clump with similar values on X and Y. In situations with multiple predictors, clumps of outliers can not always be easily detected by visual inspection of scatterplots.

Because the standard diagnostic statistics perform poorly in finding clumps of outliers, other methods need to be used. Promising methods of detecting clumps of outliers in complex data sets have recently been developed (e.g., Hadi, 1994; Hadi & Simonoff, 1993), but to date they have not yet become available in common statistical packages. Alternatively, robust regression approaches (to be discussed later) minimize the weight given to outlying cases in the calculation of regression coefficients. These approaches will produce improved estimates of the regression coefficients and the standard errors, even when there are clumps of outliers.

Respecification and Transformation

There is a second and often overlooked consideration when outliers are discovered. Outliers may result from misspecification of the regression model rather than any problems with the data. If the appropriate regression model is specified, the originally outlying cases may be well fit by the new model. The data set presented in Fig. 10.4.1 illustrated this idea: The original equation illustrated in Fig. 10.4.1(A) does not fit the data well and produces an extreme outlier with high influence. However, the nonlinear model illustrated in Fig. 10.4.1 fits all of the data very well—there is a high R^2 and all of the residuals are small. Consequently, it is very important to use the approaches presented in Section 4.4 to look for evidence of model misspecification before outliers are deleted. Models that specify curvilinear effects (see Chapter 6) or interactions between IVs (see Chapter 7) can sometimes address the problem of outliers.

Alternatively, a linear regression model may be used, but the individual variables may be transformed so that the data are more appropriate for a linear regression equation. Recall from Chapter 6 that transformation uses a mathematical expression to change the value of the IV, DV, or both for each case. For example, an outcome variable with a few cases with high values (i.e., a long upper tail) is sometimes more appropriately analyzed when the value of Y for each case replaced by a new value equal to the logarithm of the original value, i.e., $Y_{new}^* = \log(Y_{original})$. Chapter 6 presented a thorough discussion of transformations.

Robust Approaches

Robust approaches refer to a family of techniques that use alternatives to the ordinary least squares (OLS) method to estimate the regression coefficients. Robust approaches can be thought of as a kind of insurance policy (Anscombe, 1960). Ideally, robust approaches should perform better than OLS when there are outliers or the residuals have a non-normal distribution with many extreme residuals in the tails. And when the data are well behaved, robust approaches should perform *almost* as well as OLS. We should only pay a small cost in terms of lower statistical power when there are no outliers and the assumptions of OLS regression are fully met.

In Section 10.3 we showed that in OLS estimation the values of $B_0, B_1, \ldots, B_k$ are chosen so as to minimize the sum of the squared residuals. When an observed Y_i is far from the regression line of the other cases, it can strongly affect the values of the Bs that are chosen. As we have shown, cases that have both high leverage and high discrepancy (high influence) can greatly alter the values of the regression coefficients that are chosen. Under these circumstances, robust alternatives to OLS may be considered. Examples of four approaches to robust estimation are briefly presented next.

One alternative estimator is *least absolute deviation* (LAD; also called L^1). This method chooses values of the regression coefficients $B_0, \ldots, B_k$ so as to minimize the value of $\Sigma|Y - \hat{Y}|$, where $|Y - \hat{Y}|$ refers to the magnitude of the difference, ignoring its sign (absolute value). Because the difference between Y_i and $\hat{Y}_i$ is not squared, this estimator may provide better results than OLS when there are cases with high discrepancy (externally studentized residuals). However, the LAD estimator is potentially very sensitive to cases that are also extreme on X(high leverage). A single outlying case with high influence can have a greater impact on the regression results when LAD is used rather than OLS.

A second approach is the *least trimmed squares* (LTS) estimator. In LTS the squared residuals for each of the n cases $e_1^2, e_2^2, \ldots, e_n^2$ are ordered from lowest to highest. The analyst chooses a proportion of the cases (e.g., proportion $= .25$) with the highest value of e^2 to be "trimmed", that is, removed from the analysis producing the regression estimates. LTS chooses values of the regression coefficients $B_0, \ldots, B_k$ so as to minimize the value of $\Sigma_{i=1}^{n'}(Y - \hat{Y})^2$ where n is the number of squared residuals remaining after the largest residuals are trimmed. Rousseeuw, Van Aelst, and Hubert (1999) note that LTS generally performs well, but that it can on rare occasions mislead by providing highly inaccurate estimates when there is a clump of outliers.

A third approach is known as *M-estimation* (Huber, 1981). This approach uses a variant of weighted least squares regression (see Section 4.5.4) in which the function to be minimized is $\Sigma w_i e_i^2$, where w_i is the weight that is given to the ith case. In M-estimation the weight for each case is chosen by how far the residual is from the regression line. Huber suggested that residuals that fall on or near the regression line be given full weight so that $w_i = 1$ and that residuals that fall beyond a threshold be given weights that decrease as $|Y - \hat{Y}|$ becomes larger. Like the LAD estimator, M-estimation will provide better results than OLS when cases with high discrepancy, but it also shares the major liability of LAD—it can produce poor results relative to OLS when cases are also extreme on X, that is, that have high leverage as well as discrepancy (i.e., high influence).

Bounded influence estimators (also called generalized M-estimators or GM estimators) follow the same general logic as M-estimation, except that the weights are chosen based on consideration of both leverage and discrepancy. For example, Welsch (1980) proposed that cases having high values of the $DFFITS_i$ statistic be given less weight. The bounded influence estimators give very good performance in many situations but can provide poor estimates in some cases when there are clumps of outliers or when outliers on Y have low leverage.

In summary, the four estimators considered—LAD, LTS, M-estimates, and bounded influence estimates—represent examples of four of the general approaches to robust estimation that have been proposed. Each of these robust statistics can potentially produce greatly improved estimates relative to OLS when certain patterns of outliers are present in the data; however, rare conditions do exist under which each of the robust estimators can be badly misleading and produce very poor estimates relative to OLS. In addition, OLS will always produce accurate estimates of regression coefficients with the smallest possible standard errors when its assumptions are met.

There are currently few published applications of robust statistics in the behavioral sciences. Perhaps the primary reason for the lack of use to date is that many of the common statistical packages have been slow to incorporate robust regression procedures. Currently, many statistical packages do not include robust estimators, include them in another specialized module (e.g., SAS NLIN), or include only the earlier developed procedures such as LAD and M-estimation. Some of the procedures (e.g., LTS) are computer intensive and may require considerable computer time when applied to large data sets. Alternative procedures described in Staudte and Sheather (1990) should be used for significance testing and construction of confidence intervals for regression coefficients. And robust techniques must be used cautiously because they can hide problems associated with the use of a misspecifed regression model (Cook, Hawkins, & Weisberg, 1992).

Despite some limitations, robust approaches are a very valuable addition to our available tools for multiple regression when there are outliers present in the data. Researchers may usefully compare the results obtained using (a) OLS regression and (b) two robust approaches that are believed to have different strengths and weakness (e.g., LTS; M-estimation). When the different approaches lead to similar conclusions, we gain increased confidence in our results. When the results do not agree, information from these analyses, diagnostic statistics, and careful examination of scatterplot matrices can often be very helpful in understanding the source of the differences.

We have provided only a brief introduction to the complex topic of robust regression. Readers wishing to use robust regression techniques in their own research should consult recent chapters and texts (e.g., Draper & Smith, 1998, Chapter 25; Ryan, 1997, Chapter 11; and Wilcox, 1997, Chapter 8, for introductions; Rousseeuw, 1998; Rousseeuw & Leroy, 1987; Staudte & Sheather, 1990 for more advanced treatments).

10.5 MULTICOLLINEARITY

We now shift our attention from problems that may arise from specific cases in the data set to problems that may arise from specific IVs. In multiple regression, we assume that each IV can *potentially* add to the prediction of the dependent variable Y. However, as one of the independent variables, X_i, becomes increasingly correlated with the set of other IVs in the regression equation, X_i will have less and less unique information that it can potentially contribute to the prediction of Y. This causes a variety of problems when the multiple correlation of X_i with the set of other predictors, $R_{X_i.X_1X_2...(X_i)...X_k}$, becomes very high. The individual regression coefficients can change appreciably in magnitude and even in sign, making such coefficients difficult to interpret. As the predictors become increasingly correlated, the estimate of the individual regression coefficients also becomes more and more unreliable, a problem that is reflected in large standard errors. In the limiting case of *exact collinearity*, in which X_i is perfectly correlated with the other predictor variables (that is, when X_i can be perfectly predicted from the remaining IVs), the individual regression coefficients cannot even be properly computed. Short of exact collinearity, small changes in the data such as adding or deleting a few observations can lead to large changes in the results of the regression analysis. This set of problems that result from high correlations between some of the IVs is known as *multicollinearity*. Multicollinearity depends only on the set of IVs—regardless of the Y that is chosen, the degree of multicollinearity will be the same.

10.5.1 Exact Collinearity

Exact collinearity occurs when one IV has a correlation or multiple correlation of 1.0 with the other IVs. Exact collinearity indicates that a mistake was made in setting up the regression analysis. Consider the regression equation $\hat{Y} = B_1X_1 + B_2X_2 + B_0$. If X_1 and X_2 are the same or if one is a linear transformation of the other as when X_1 and X_2 represent the same variable expressed in different units (e.g., $X_1 = $ person's weight in pounds; $X_2 = $ person's weight in kilograms), neither variable conveys any *unique* information to the prediction of Y. Exact collinearity can also occur for more subtle reasons. For example, consider the regression equation $\hat{Y} = B_1X_1 + B_2X_2 + B_3D + B_0$, in which X_1 is the person's score at time 1, X_2 is the person's score at time 2, and D is the difference between the time 1 and time 2 scores, $D = X_1 - X_2$. Note that D contains no unique information that is not contained in X_1 and X_2 so that the multiple correlation of D with X_1 and X_2, $R_{D.X_1.X_2}$, will be 1.0. As another example, suppose a researcher asks students to explain their performance on their first statistics exam by dividing 100 points among four potential explanations. These explanations are $X_1 = $ ability in statistics, $X_2 = $ difficulty of the test, $X_3 = $ amount of effort studying the material, and $X_4 = $ luck. The researcher wishes to predict Y, the student's performance on the final exam. But, note that for each student $X_1 + X_2 + X_3 + X_4$ must equal a constant, here 100 points. This means that if for a particular student we know that the value of $X_1 = 20, X_2 = 10, X_3 = 20$, then we know that the value of X_4 must be 50, i.e., $100 - X_1 - X_2 - X_3$. Once again, X_4 adds no unique information that is not contained in X_1, X_2, and X_3, and the multiple correlation between any one of the IVs and the other three must be 1.0. These more subtle forms of exact collinearity typically occur when the sum of the predictors must equal a constant value or when composite scores and the original scores from which they are derived are included in the same regression equation.

When exact collinearity occurs, there is no mathematically unique solution for the regression coefficients. Major statistical packages perform an initial check to determine if one (or more) of the IVs is highly redundant with the other IVs in the regression equation.[13] When they detect this problem, some regression programs will not run. Other programs will attempt to "fix" the problem by arbitrarily dropping one (or more) IVs with exact collinearity from the regression model, perhaps even an IV in which the researcher has particular interest.

10.5.2 Multicollinearity: A Numerical Illustration

Multicollinearity occurs when highly related IVs are included in the same regression model. In cross-sectional research, serious multicollinearity most commonly occurs when multiple measures of the same or similar constructs (e.g., depression, anxiety) are used as the IVs in a regression equation. In longitudinal research, serious multicollinearity most commonly occurs when similar measures collected at several previous time points are used to predict the participants' score at a later time point (e.g., all four test scores in a statistics class are used as IVs in a regression equation predicting the final exam score). As with exact collinearity, highly related IVs can occur in more subtle ways as well. Some measures which purport to measure different constructs are based on overlapping sets of similar items so that they will be highly related. For example, some MMPI-based scales used in clinical psychology are based on partially overlapping sets of items.

As was introduced in Section 3.8, multicollinearity may lead to unstable regression coefficients that are associated with large standard errors. Multicollinearity can also lead to complexities in interpreting regression coefficients. We illustrate these ideas with two examples. In our first example we examine data with two IVs to explore what happens to the regression estimates as r_{12} takes on increasingly large values. In this example $r_{Y1} = .30$ and $r_{Y2} = .40$ are kept constant. These values represent a moderate and a moderate to large effect size, respectively, according to the normative values presented in Chapter 2. The variances are $sd_Y^2 = 5, sd_{X1}^2 = 3, sd_{X2}^2 = 4$; x_1 and x_2 are centered, M_Y is set equal to 20, and $n = 100$.

CH10EX4

Table 10.5.1 presents the results of several regression analyses based on this data set. First, consider Table 10.5.1A, which presents the results when $r_{12} = 0$. The intercept $B_0 = 20$ (the mean value of Y), $B_1 = .39, SE_{B_1} = .11, B_2 = .45, SE_{B_2} = .10$ (to two decimals). We can construct the 95% confidence interval for each B_1, $CI = B_i \pm t\, SE_{B_1}$. Thus, the 95% confidence interval for $B_1 = .16$ to .61 and the 95% confidence interval for $B_2 = .25$ to .64. Examining null hypothesis significance tests, for B_1, $t = 3.41$, $df = 97, p < .001$ and for $B_2, t = 4.55$, and again, $p < .001$. These results indicate that both x_1 and x_2 make independent contributions to the prediction of Y.

Now, let us consider what happens as we increase the value of r_{12}. Comparing the values of B_1 across Parts A–E of Table 10.5.1, we see that B_1 decreases in value and ultimately becomes *negative* at the highest values of r_{12} (e.g., $B_1 = -1.03$ for $r_{12} = .949$). In contrast, B_2 initially decreases in value, but reaches a minimum following which it rapidly increases[14] at very high levels of r_{12}. The standard errors of B_1 and B_2 initially increase slowly in magnitude as r_{12}

---

[13] Statistical packages typically compare one of the indices of multicollinearity (to be presented later) with a very extreme cutoff value (e.g., tolerance = .0001). This procedure detects cases in which exact collinearity is obscured by computer rounding errors.

[14] The rapid increase of B_2 at high levels of r_{12} is an example of statistical suppression discussed in Section 3.4.

TABLE 10.5.1

Effects of Multicollinearity:
Two-Independent-Variable Example

A. $r_{12} = 0.00; r_{Y1} = .30; r_{Y2} = .40; R^2 = .250$.

Variable	B	SE	pr^2	Tolerance	VIF
Intercept	20.000	0.196			
x_1	0.387	0.114	0.107	1.000	1.000
x_2	0.447	0.098	0.176	1.000	1.000

B. $r_{12} = 0.10; r_{Y1} = .30; r_{Y2} = .40; R^2 = .228$.

Variable	B	SE	pr^2	Tolerance	VIF
Intercept	20.000	0.198			
x_1	0.339	0.116	0.081	0.990	1.010
x_2	0.418	0.100	0.152	0.990	1.010

C. $r_{12} = 0.50; r_{Y1} = .30; r_{Y2} = .40; R^2 = .173$.

Variable	B	SE	pr^2	Tolerance	VIF
Intercept	20.000	0.205			
x_1	0.172	0.138	0.016	0.750	1.333
x_2	0.373	0.119	0.092	0.750	1.333

D. $r_{12} = 0.90; r_{Y1} = .30; r_{Y2} = .40; R^2 = .179$.

Variable	B	SE	pr^2	Tolerance	VIF
Intercept	20.000	0.205			
x_1	−0.407	0.272	0.023	0.190	5.263
x_2	0.765	0.236	0.098	0.190	5.263

E. $r_{12} = 0.949; r_{Y1} = .30; r_{Y2} = .40; R^2 = .224$.

Variable	B	SE	pr^2	Tolerance	VIF
Intercept	20.000	0.199			
x_1	−1.034	0.366	0.076	0.099	10.060
x_2	1.297	0.317	0.147	0.099	10.060

Note: $sd_Y^2 = 5.00; sd_1^2 = 3.00; sd_2^2 = 4.00; M_Y = 20$.

increases in value, but then rise rapidly as r_{12} becomes close to 1. Indeed, when $r_{12} = .949$, the standard errors of B_1 and B_2 are more than 3 times larger than when $r_{12} = 0$. Necessarily, this increase in both SE_{B_1} and SE_{B_2} leads to corresponding increases in the associated CIs: −.95 to +.13 for B_1 and +.30 to 1.23 for B_2. Thus, Table 10.5.1 illustrates both the increased difficulty that can arise in interpreting the regression coefficients and the increase in SEs that occurs as two predictors become highly correlated.

Table 10.5.2A provides a second illustration of the effects of multicollinearity, this time with four centered IVs, x_1, x_2, x_3, and x_4. This example compares the results of two regression analyses. In the first analysis, presented in Table 10.5.2A, the IVs are uncorrelated. In the second analysis, presented in Table 10.5.2B, x_1, x_2 and x_3 are highly intercorrelated ($r_{12} = r_{13} = r_{23} = .933$). Note in the second analysis that x_4 is uncorrelated with x_1, x_2, or x_3. As in our first example presented in Table 10.5.1, the correlations of the IVs with Y were kept at

TABLE 10.5.2
Effects of Multicollinearity: Four-Independent-Variable
Example

A. $r_{12} = r_{13} = r_{23} = 0.00$; $r_{14} = 0$; $R^2 = .495$.

Variable	B	SE	pr^2	Tolerance	VIF
Intercept	20.000	0.162			
x_1	0.387	0.094	0.151	1.000	1.000
x_2	0.391	0.082	0.195	1.000	1.000
x_3	0.400	0.073	0.240	1.000	1.000
x_4	0.391	0.082	0.195	1.000	1.000

B. $r_{12} = r_{13} = r_{23} = 0.933$; $r_{14} = 0$; $R^2 = .325$.

Variable	B	SE	pr^2	Tolerance	VIF
Intercept	20.000	0.187			
x_1	−0.806	0.345	0.054	0.099	10.067
x_2	0.137	0.299	0.002	0.099	10.067
x_3	0.868	0.267	0.100	0.099	10.067
x_4	0.391	0.094	0.154	1.000	1.000

Note: $r_{Y1} = .30$; $r_{Y2} = .40$; $r_{Y3} = .30$; $r_{Y4} = .40$; $sd_Y^2 = 5.00$; $sd_1^2 = 3.00$; $sd_2^2 = 4.00$; $sd_3^2 = 3.00$; $sd_4^2 = 4.00$; $M_Y = 20$.

constant values within the range .30 to .40 and the variances of all variables were also kept constant, within the range 3 to 5.

Table 10.5.2A displays the results of the first analysis when the IVs are uncorrelated. Under these circumstances, the B_1 to B_4 regression coefficients range from .39 to .40 and the SEs range from .07 to .09 (to two decimals). In contrast, Table 10.5.2B shows the results when x_1 to x_3 are highly intercorrelated, but x_4 is uncorrelated with x_1, x_2, or x_3. The same pattern that we observed in the first example emerges for x_1 to x_3. The regression coefficients now range from $-.0.81$ to $+0.86$ and their SEs now range from 0.27 to 0.35, over a three fold increase in SEs relative to the uncorrelated case. In contrast, note that the value of $B_4 = 0.39$, is *exactly* the same value obtained in Table 10.5.2A when all IVs were uncorrelated. The SE of B_4 does increase from .082 to .094, but this increase is very modest relative to the increase in the SEs of the regression coefficients.

Both examples illustrate the increased complexity in interpreting the meaning of the Bs and the increase in SE when there are high correlations among the IVs. However, the Bs of IVs that are unrelated to the other predictors (here, x_4) are not affected and their SEs are only minimally affected, even when there is a high degree of multicollinearity among the other predictors in the regression equation.

10.5.3 Measures of the Degree of Multicollinearity

$r^2_{X_i X_j}$

The squared correlation between each of the pairs of predictor variables provides an index of bivariate multicollinearity. As its value increases toward 1.0, the magnitude of potential problems associated with multicollinearity increases correspondingly. With two IVs, this index is sufficient. As the number of IVs in the regression model increases, this index becomes increasingly likely to miss substantial multicollinearity.

The Variance Inflation Factor

The variance inflation factor (*VIF*) provides an index of the amount that the variance of each regression coefficient is increased relative to a situation in which all of the predictor variables are uncorrelated. To understand the *VIF*, recall from Section 3.6 that the standard error of B_i is

(3.6.1)
$$SE_{B_i} = \frac{sd_Y}{sd_{X_i}} \sqrt{\frac{1 - R^2_{Y.12...k}}{n - k - 1}} \sqrt{\frac{1}{1 - R^2_{i.12...(i)...k}}}.$$

where $R^2_{i.12...(i)...k}$ is the squared multiple correlation between X_i and the other predictor variables in the regression equation. Squaring this equation, we get the variance of B_i, $V(B_i)$:

(10.5.1)
$$V(B_i) = \frac{sd_Y^2}{sd_{X_i}^2} \left(\frac{1 - R^2_{Y.12...k}}{n - k - 1} \right) \left(\frac{1}{R^2_{i.12...(i)...k}} \right).$$

The *VIF* is simply the third term in Eq. (10.5.1), so

(10.5.2)
$$VIF \left(\frac{1}{1 - R^2_{i.12...(i)...k}} \right).$$

A *VIF* is calculated for each term in the regression equation, excluding the intercept. A commonly used rule of thumb is that any *VIF* of 10 or more provides evidence of serious multicollinearity involving the corresponding IV. Given the relationships between Eq. (3.6.1) and (10.5.1), $\sqrt{VIF}$ will represent the amount that the *SE* of B_i will increase relative to the situation in which all of the predictor variables are uncorrelated. Thus, a *VIF* of 10 means that there is a $\sqrt{10} = 3.16$ or slightly more than a threefold increase in SE_{B_i} relative to the situation of no correlation between any of the IVs. Table 10.5.1E and Table 10.5.2B include values of intercorrelations among IVs that produce *VIF*s of about 10. Note that the *SE*s show slightly more than a threefold increase relative to their values when $r_{X_iX_j} = 0$. As illustrated in Table 10.5.1, in the two-predictor case, the *VIF*s for X_1 and X_2 will always be equal. In the three or more predictor case, the VIFs will, in general, not be equal. The *VIF*s for X_1 to X_3 in Table 10.5.2 are equal only because the correlations between predictors are precisely equal, $r_{12} = r_{13} = r_{23}$.

We remind readers that extremely high intercorrelations between predictors were necessary to produce *VIF*s = 10 in Tables 10.5.1 and 10.5.2. We believe that this common rule of thumb guideline is too high (lenient) for most behavioral science applications. We discuss issues in measuring multicollinearity later in this section.

Tolerance

Some statistical packages present the tolerance in addition to or instead of the *VIF*. The tolerance is the reciprocal of the *VIF*,

(10.5.3)
$$\text{tolerance} = \frac{1}{VIF} = 1 - R^2_{X_i.X_1X_2...(i)...p}.$$

and therefore tells us how much of the variance in X_i is independent of other IVs. This relationship can be verified in Tables 10.5.1 and 10.5.2. A commonly used rule of thumb is that tolerance values of .10 or less indicate that there may be serious problems of multicollinearity in the regression equation (and, of course, are equivalent to a *VIF* of 10). Some statistical packages use very low values of tolerance (e.g., .0001) as a means of detecting exact collinearity.

Condition Number

The correlation matrix of the IVs may be decomposed into a set of orthogonal dimensions. Orthogonal dimensions are completely nonoverlapping and share no variance in common. Major statistical programs will perform this decomposition, which is known as principal components analysis. When this analysis is performed on the correlation matrix of the k IVs, a set of k *eigenvalues* or characteristic roots of the matrix is produced. The proportion of the variance in the IVs accounted for by each orthogonal dimension i is λ/k, where λ is the eigenvalue. The eigenvalues are ordered from largest to smallest so that each orthogonal dimension in turn accounts for a smaller proportion of the variance of the IVs. With two independent variables, if the two IVs are uncorrelated, each eigenvalue will equal 1.0, so that each *independent* dimension will account for $\lambda_i/2$, or .50 of the variance in the set of IVs. As the IVs become increasingly correlated, more and more of the variance in the IVs is associated with the first dimension, so that the value of the first eigenvalue will become larger and the value of the second eigenvalue will become correspondingly smaller. When r_{12} reaches its maximum, $r_{12} = 1.0$, $\lambda_1 = 2$ and $\lambda_2 = 0$, so that the first dimension will account for 1.0 of the variance in the IVs, whereas the second dimension will account for no additional variance in the IVs.

The condition number[15] κ (kappa) is defined as the square root of the ratio of the largest eigenvalue ($\lambda_{\max}$) to the smallest eigenvalue ($\lambda_{\min}$).

(10.5.4)
$$\kappa = \sqrt{\frac{\lambda_{\max}}{\lambda_{\min}}}.$$

Traditionally, a rule of thumb has been suggested that values of κ (kappa) that are 30 or larger indicate highly severe problems of multicollinearity. However, no strong statistical rationale exists for this choice of 30 as a threshold value above which serious problems of multicollinearity are indicated.

Some Issues in Measuring Multicollinearity

In discussing the measures of multicollinearity, we noted rule of thumb cutoff values that have been offered above which multicollinearity appear to be problematic in most behavioral science applications. Note that the problems associated with multicollinearity differ in degree; they do not differ in kind. Thus, there is no good statistical rationale for the choice of any of the traditional rule of thumb threshold values for separating acceptable from unacceptable levels of multicollinearity[16]. A review of Table 10.5.1 indicates that the magnitude and direction of the regression coefficients may change appreciably at values of the *VIF* that are substantially less than the typically suggested threshold value of 10. As presented in Section 3.4.1, when *B* increases or changes its sign when one or more other IVs are added to the equation, we have

---

[15]The condition number may be computed from matrices involving uncentered scores on the IVs, centered scores on the IVs, or the correlation matrix of the IVs. This choice can lead to differences in the eigenvalues that are obtained. Consequently the value of the condition number may depend on the specific matrix which the statistical package uses to compute eigenvalues. Typically, the eigenvalues are based on the $(\mathbf{X}_c'\mathbf{X}_c)$ matrix, where $\mathbf{X}_c$ is the $(n \times k)$ matrix of the centered predictor values. Belsley (1984, 1991) and R. D. Cook (1984) discuss this issue and indicate cases under which computations based on each matrix may be preferred.

[16]For example, some authors have proposed values of 6 or 7 as a threshold value for the *VIF* or 15 or 20 as a threshold value for the condition index.

a situation of statistical suppression. Although such findings may sometimes be theoretically anticipated, they are often indicative of a serious problem of multicollinearity. Thus, the values of the multicollinearity indices at which the interpretation of regression coefficients may become problematic will often be considerably smaller than traditional rule of thumb guidelines such as $VIF = 10$.

Multicollinearity indices provide useful information but do not substitute for more basic checks on the data. First, researchers should carefully examine the scatterplot matrix of the predictor variables and the leverages for each case, looking for outlying observations that may affect the relationship between each pair of IVs. As we saw earlier in this chapter, outliers can greatly increase or decrease the magnitude of the relationship between variables, leading to values of multicollinearity indices that may be too high or too low. Second, researchers should compare the results of simple univariate regression analyses in which the outcome is regressed separately on each predictor variable with the results of the full multiple regression analysis in which the outcome is regressed on all of the predictor variables of interest. Probably the easiest way to accomplish this is by comparison of r_{YX} for each IV with its corresponding standardized β in the regression equation. Large, unexpected changes in direction and magnitude of these coefficients suggest a substantial influence of multicollinearity.

Relatively high values of the standard multicollinearity indices may occur in some of the more complex regression analyses we considered in earlier chapters of this book. In these analyses a single substantive IV was represented by more than one term in the regression equation. In Chapter 6 we used several polynomial terms (e.g., X, X^2) to represent a variable's nonlinear relationship with Y. In Chapter 7 we used terms that are products of IVs (e.g., XZ) to represent interactions. In Chapter 8 we introduced coding schemes (e.g., dummy codes C_1, C_2, C_3) that used multiple terms to represent qualitative variables such as religious affiliation or experimental treatment groups. In these circumstances, high values on standard measures of multicollinearity are not necessarily problematic—the degree of multicollinearity depends on the particular scaling of the IVs. For example, we showed in Chapter 7 that in a regression model with an interaction term the correlation between X and XZ can be reduced by centering each of the IVs. Fox and Monette (1992) present a general index of multicollinearity that is not affected by the scaling of the IVs that is appropriate in such applications.

VIF, tolerance, and the condition number implemented in most statistical packages do not take multicollinearity involving the intercept into account. This characteristic is fully appropriate in most applications in the behavioral sciences. However, in some areas of economics and the physical and biological sciences, IVs such as interest rates and body size are measured on ratio level measurement scales (see Chapter 1). With a ratio level of measurement, the value of the intercept estimated when each of the IVs takes on a true value of 0 can be a parameter that is of considerable theoretical interest. In such cases, alternative versions of the VIF, tolerance, or condition number discussed by Belsley (1991) should be calculated.[17]

10.6 REMEDIES FOR MULTICOLLINEARITY

When a researcher is interested solely in the prediction of Y or in the value of R^2, multicollinearity has little effect and no remedial action is needed. However, in research testing a substantive theory in which the researcher is interested in the value of each B_i, high values

---

[17]Belsley (1991, Chapter 5) has also developed a useful extension of the condition number that more precisely pinpoints the sources of multicollinearity. This approach to detecting multicollinearity is of particular value in time series analysis and complex econometric models that include large numbers of IVs.

of multicollinearity present a potentially serious problem. Four general approaches to solving problems of multicollinearity have been proposed.

10.6.1 Model Respecification

In some cases, it may be possible to revise the regression model so that the degree of multi-collinearity is reduced. This remedy is particularly applicable when the analyst has included several highly correlated variables that can be thought of as measuring the same underlying construct. For example, suppose a researcher were interested in the effects of socioeconomic status (SES) and IQ on undergraduate GPA (Y). Suppose the researcher has collected several measures of SES—mother's income (X_1), father's income (X_2), mother's education (X_3), and father's education (X_4), father's occupational status (X_5), and mother's occupational status (X_6)—as well as IQ (X_7)—and has included all seven predictors in a regression equation,

$$\hat{Y} = B_1X_1 + B_2X_2 + B_3X_3 + B_4X_4 + B_5X_5 + B_6X_6 + B_7X_7 + B_0.$$

The IVs X_1 to X_6 are all measures of SES and are likely to be moderately to very highly correlated, leading to high levels of multicollinearity. In such cases, it is often useful to combine the variables measuring the underlying construct, here SES, into a single index. The simplest way to do this is to convert each of the measures to z scores. The z scores are then averaged to produce an overall index of SES for each person in the sample. In cases where theory or prior empirical work point to differential importance of each of the variables assessing the construct, more complex weighting schemes can be used to form the overall index. In either case, a different regression model is now estimated,

$$\hat{Y} = B_1z_{SES} + B_2X_7 + B_0$$

Note that in this equation, B_1 represents the unique contribution of the index of SES over and above IQ to the prediction of GPA, whereas in the previous equation B_1 represented the unique contribution of mother's income over and above the five other measures of socioeconomic status and IQ to the prediction of GPA. Thus, we have respecified the model so that it answers a different question than the one posed by the original analysis, but a question that in many cases may more adequately represent the researcher's question of interest.

An alternative approach to model respecification is to drop one (or more) IVs from the regression equation. Multicollinearity measures provide information about sources of multi-collinearity, but they do not tell the researcher which IVs should be retained in the regression equation. When either theory or prior empirical work exists, it should be used as a strong guide. For example, if a variable has been thrown into the regression equation "to see what happens," it is a prime candidate for deletion. In other situations, choosing a variable or variables to delete among several variables that are contributing to high multicollinearity may be largely an arbitrary decision. Deletion of IVs on the basis of correlation with other IVs always carries a risk. If the IV in question is truly relevant to the theory, the estimates of all other IVs will be biased in its absence.

This caution about dropping variables from the regression equation takes on particular importance in complex regression equations in which multiple terms are used to represent a curvilinear effect (Chapter 6), an interaction (Chapters 7 and 9), or a categorical IV (Chapter 8). Deletion of lower order terms that are included in higher order terms leads to poorly structured regression models with Bs that are not readily interpretable (Peixoto, 1987). For example, in Chapter 7 we presented the interpretation of regression equation specifying a linear XZ interaction, $\hat{Y} = B_1X + B_2Z + B_3XZ + B_0$. If the X term were now dropped from the equation,

$\hat{Y} = B_2Z + B_3XZ + B_0$, the B_3 coefficient for the XZ term no longer represents purely the interaction between X and Z, but confounds the interaction with the first order effect of X. Lower order terms should *not* be dropped (see Chapter 7 and Aiken & West, 1991, Chapter 3).

10.6.2 Collection of Additional Data

The collection of additional data reduces some but not all of the problems associated with multicollinearity. Larger sample sizes will always improve the precision of the estimate of B With small samples, the degree of multicollinearity will typically be overestimated if there are a large number of IVs in the regression model. Large samples will reduce this problem. However, the pattern of correlations among the IVs would not be expected to change as sample size increases. Thus, the use of large samples alone cannot eliminate difficulties that arise in *interpreting* regression coefficients when IVs are highly multicollinear.

An alternative approach is to try to reduce the correlations among the IVs. In some cases, it may be possible to manipulate one or more of the predictors in an experimental setting. For example, suppose a researcher is studying stress (X_1) and coping skills (X_2) as predictors of well being. X_1 and X_2 are very highly correlated in the population. To minimize this correlation, study participants could be randomly assigned in a laboratory experiment to a highly or mildly stressful experience so that $r_{X_1X_2}$ would on average be expected to be 0. Alternatively, if the scores of potential participants on the IVs (but not the DV) were known in the population (e.g., a large school district), the researcher could devise a sampling plan so that the correlation between X_1 and X_2 would be substantially reduced in magnitude (see McClelland & Judd, 1993; Pitts & West, 2001). Such procedures can permit a greater understanding of the independent effects of each of the predictor variables as reflected in the unstandardized regression coefficients (Bs). At the same time, they change the estimates of standardized effect sizes for each predictor variable and R^2 so that these statistics no longer estimate the values in the original population. Pitts and West (2001) discuss these procedures, their strengths, their limitations, and appropriate methods of estimating population effect sizes.

10.6.3 Ridge Regression

As was the case with outliers, alternative estimation techniques exist that can provide "improved" estimates of each regression coefficient and its associated standard error when multicollinearity is present. Ridge regression is an alternative estimation method that may be used when there is an *extremely* high degree of multicollinearity in a data set (Darlington, 1978). In ridge regression a constant is added to the variance of each IV. This procedure leads to a biased estimate of each regression coefficient B_i—the estimate is slightly attenuated (too close to 0) so that it is no longer on average equal to the value of β_i^* in the population. However, the estimate of SE_B may be substantially reduced. When multicollinearity is extremely high, it may be advantageous to trade off a small increase in bias for a substantial increase in the precision of the estimate of the regression coefficient. The regression coefficients will be far less sensitive to small changes in the data set such as adding or deleting a case.

The details of implementing ridge regression are presented in Ryan (1997, Chapter 12). Draper and Smith (1998, Chapter 17) provide a discussion of the strengths and weaknesses of ridge regression and note that ridge regression estimates are not always superior to OLS estimates. Unlike OLS estimates, ridge regression estimates of the regression coefficients are biased; consequently, alternative methods presented in Neter, Kutner, Nachtsheim, and Wasserman (1996, Chapter 10) must be used to construct confidence intervals and conduct significance tests. Although the SAS, SPSS, and SYSTAT regression modules do not presently include ridge regression, software is available in other statistical packages (see Ryan, 1997, for an overview). Box 10.6.1 presents an illustration of ridge regression.

BOX 10.6.1
Illustration of Ridge Regression

To illustrate how ridge regression works, consider a case with two predictors X_1 and X_2. Multicollinearity between two predictor variables can be assessed by r_{12}^2, which can be calculated using Eq. (2.3.5). We have squared and rewritten original Eq. (2.3.5) below for ease of presentation:

(2.3.5)
$$r_{12}^2 = \frac{\left[\sum x_1 x_2 / (n-1)\right]^2}{sd_1^2 sd_2^2}$$

The numerator $\left[\sum x_1 x_2 / (n-1)\right]^2$, is the squared covariance between x_1 and x_2, and the denominator terms are the variances of the two IVs. Suppose the covariance of x_1 and $x_2 = 141, sd_1^2 = 100$, and $sd_2^2 = 200$. Substituting these values into Eq. (2.3.5) gives $r_{12}^2 = .994$. From Eq. (10.5.2), the *VIF* is $1/(1 - .994) = 168.1$, an extremely high value. Now what happens to r_{12}^2 and the *VIF* if we add a constant value of 10 to each variance? r_{12}^2 now equals $(141)^2/((110)(210)) = .861$ so that the *VIF* will be $1/(1 - .861) = 7.19$. Thus, the addition of a relatively small constant to the variance of each predictor decreases the correlation between the IVs and the value of the *VIF*, and hence greatly reduces the standard errors of the tests of the regression coefficients. The central problem in ridge regression is to choose the value of the constant that will provide the maximum benefit in terms of improvement of the precision of the estimate at the minimum cost in terms of bias in the estimates of the regression coefficient. Several methods exist for making this choice; they are discussed in Draper and Smith (1998) and Ryan (1997).

10.6.4 Principal Components Regression

In Section 10.5.3, we briefly noted that a set of independent dimensions can be created that are combinations of the predictor variables. In principal components regression, we regress the dependent variable on these independent dimensions rather than on the original set of predictor variables. To create these independent dimensions, a procedure known as principal components analysis is used (see e.g., Harris, 2001; Tabachnick & Fidell, 2001). These dimensions are termed *components*. Principal components analysis produces a set of k eigenvalues $(\lambda_1, \lambda_2, \ldots, \lambda_k)$, each of which has a corresponding eigenvector. The elements of the eigenvectors are weights, with a different set of weights being produced for each component. These weights allow the researcher to transform the participant's original score on the set of IVs into a score on each component, C_i. The raw scores for each IV are first standardized and then the weights are applied. Thus, with four IVs the participant's score on component i would be

(10.6.1)
$$C_i = w_{i1}z_1 + w_{i2}z_2 + w_{i3}z_3 + w_{i4}z_4,$$

where z_1 to z_4 are the participant's z-scores that correspond to scores on the original IVs, X_1 to X_4, and w_{i1} to w_{i4} are the weights for component i determined by the principal components analysis.

Each principal component represents an orthogonal dimension. The components are ordered from largest to smallest in terms of the variance of the original IVs that is reproduced in the component. Thus, each principal component, in turn, accounts for a smaller and smaller proportion of the variance in the IVs. The last component (or last few components) will often account for little variance in the IVs; small components are sources of multicollinearity in the original data. Thus, we have created a new set of orthogonal variables $C_1, C_2, \ldots, C_k$ that collectively represent all of the information that is contained in the k original IVs, but that reorganize the information into orthogonal sources. Indeed, if we regressed Y on C_1 to C_k, we will obtain the identical R^2 as we would if we regressed Y on X_1 to X_k.

To illustrate principal components regression, suppose we had a regression equation with 4 IVs and that the four components accounted for 61%, 28%, 10.5%, and 0.5% of the variance in the IVs. The unique feature of this procedure is that we may be able to discard the last orthogonal component (which accounts for very little variance) with little loss of information. We then regress Y on the three remaining orthogonal component scores,

$$(10.6.2) \qquad \hat{Y} = \tilde{B}_1 C_1 + \tilde{B}_2 C_2 + \tilde{B}_3 C_3 + \tilde{B}_0,$$

where $\tilde{B}_i$ represents the regression coefficient for the ith component. Since the components are orthogonal, the discarding of small components has no impact on statistical inference about the $\tilde{B}_i$ terms. We simply use the standard significance testing and confidence interval procedures discussed in Chapter 3.

Unfortunately, however, these $\tilde{B}_i$ are only rarely interpretable. The component scores are linear combinations of the original IVs (see Eq. 10.6.1) and will not typically have a clear meaning. Consequently, most sources recommend that researchers transform the regression coefficients for the components back to the regression coefficients for the original scores, B_i. The procedure of discarding small components means that this transformation will not reproduce the results of the regression analysis on the original IVs. On the positive side, dropping components that account for small proportions of variance eliminates major sources of multicollinearity. The result is that the back transformed regression coefficients, B_i, for the original IVs will be biased, but will be more robust to small changes in the data set than are original OLS estimates. Once again, constructing confidence intervals and performing significance tests on the B_is becomes more complex because these estimates are biased and do not follow a t distribution (see Chatterjee & Price, 1991).

Chatterjee and Price (1991) present a good introduction and Jackson (1991), Jolliffe (1986) and Hadi and Ling (1998) present a thorough discussion of the strengths and weaknesses of regression on principal components. In some data sets the small rather than the large components may account for most of the predictable variance in Y so that the small components cannot be discarded without substantially affecting the results of the regression analysis. Regression on principal components is limited to regression equations that are linear in the variables (e.g., no interactions or polynomial terms; see Cronbach, 1987). Software to conduct principal components analysis is available in the SAS PROC Factor, SPSS Factor, and SYSTAT.

10.6.5 Summary of Multicollinearity Considerations

In most areas of the behavioral sciences, severe multicollinearity according to traditional statistical standards does not occur. Cases only rarely occur in which conventional statistical rules of thumb such as a $VIF = 10$ or a condition index $= 30$ are exceeded. Instead, multicollinearity occurs to a lesser degree, but enough to produce regression coefficients that may be difficult to interpret. In these cases of "moderate" multicollinearity, alternative estimation procedures such as ridge regression or principal components regression cannot be counted on to produce better estimates than OLS regression. Instead, the researcher's focus should be on attempting to understand the nature and the source of the multicollinearity problem. In some cases, the regression model may be modified by combining IVs that are measures of the same underlying construct or by dropping variables from the equation. The primary risk here is that important IVs may be inadvertently dropped from the model.[18] In other cases, it may be possible to experimentally manipulate one of the IVs or to systematically sample participants so that the IVs are less correlated. Careful selection of the IVs with regard to their relationship to theoretical constructs will also often help reduce the problem of multicollinearity.

10.7 SUMMARY

We begin this chapter with a consideration of outliers, atypical data points that can affect the results in multiple regression analysis. After an illustration of the potential effects of outliers particularly in small samples (Section 10.2), we consider measures of extremity of a single case on the IVs (leverage, h_{ii}), on the DV (discrepancy, t_i), and on the overall results of the regression equation (global influence, $DFFITS_i$ and Cook's D_i) as well as the individual regression coefficients (specific influence, $DFBETAS_{ij}$). A small number of cases may be identified as outliers if they are extreme relative to the other cases in the data set and exceed minimum rule of thumb cutoff values (Section 10.3). Outliers may be produced by contaminated observations or rare cases. Contaminated observations may be corrected or the case may be removed from the data set; in contrast, the proper procedures to take with rare cases are more difficult, involving both statistical and substantive considerations. Potential remedial actions include deleting the case(s) from the data set (possibly changing to population to which the results may be generalized), respecification of the regression equation, transformation of the variables to account for the case(s), and robust regression approaches that downweight the influence of the outliers in the regression analysis (Section 10.4).

We then consider the problem of multicollinearity in regression analysis which occurs when the IVs become highly correlated. Several measures of the degree of multicollinearity including $r_{X_iX_j}^2$, the variance inflation factor, tolerance, and the condition number are presented. Standard cutoff values for these measures are presented, but they appear to be far too high for many behavioral science applications (Section 10.5). The advantages and disadvantages of several remedies for multicollinearity including model respecification, collection of additional data, ridge regression, and principal components regression are presented. Careful design of studies, selection of conceptually relevant measures, and specification of regression models can often help avoid problems of multicollinearity (Section 10.6).

---

[18] See our presentation of sensitivity analysis in Chapter 5.

11
Missing Data

An all too frequent characteristic of research data is that some of the values called for by the substantive issues being addressed are missing for some subjects. This can occur for many reasons, to varying degrees, and in various patterns. It can be so serious that different investigators analyzing the same data files may come to different conclusions just because they have chosen different methods of coping with missing data. In this chapter we list some of the considerations that enter into decisions about handling missing data and review contemporary methods.

11.1 BASIC ISSUES IN HANDLING MISSING DATA

11.1.1 Minimize Missing Data

It is almost always possible to keep the amount of missing data down by thorough preparation for data collection, careful monitoring of the collection process, and rigorous attention to the data preparation process. It is no exaggeration to say that more than two-thirds of all the time spent analyzing data is spent in data preparation, and much of this time is occupied in managing missing data, so time spent in prevention is likely to pay off handsomely at later stages, as well as improving the quality of the inferences from the data. A few basic rules for keeping missing data rates down are:

1. Know exactly what information you will need for each variable you will use in your data analysis before you begin data collection.
2. Don't ask subjects questions that they will frequently not be able to answer. (Sounds obvious, but this rule is violated all too often.)
3. Time your review of the collected data so that it won't be too late to go back and obtain missing information when it is first detected.

Many other rules apply to special circumstances, such as maximizing retrieval rates in surveys and retaining subjects in longitudinal studies. Although these cannot be reviewed here (but see Stouthammer-Loeber & van Kammens, 1995), they define a critical set of skills and characteristics that need to be acquired by any investigator using these methods. There are, however, circumstances in which an investigator can and should plan to have missing data. The most common is when the data collection for a study is so demanding that it cannot feasibly be completed on any single study participant. Under these circumstances the protocol may be split into units and a scheme for randomly assigning subjects to overlapping sets of units devised. This procedure is feasible only when the sample size is very large, but when appropriate may permit investigation of a substantive area (or a set of substantive areas) with a thoroughness that is not otherwise possible.

11.1.2 Types of Missing Data

There are a host of circumstances that result in missing data. In survey research, for example, some subjects may refuse or simply fail to respond to some items while responding to others. In laboratory experiments, equipment failure, animal mortality, a dropped tray of test tubes, or dropped-out subjects may create some blanks in some columns of the data sheets. In research in school settings, absences or transfer of pupils or teachers may result in incomplete data, and so on. It is only a slight exaggeration to paraphrase Murphy's law for behavior science research to read, "If there are any ways in which data can be missing, they will be." As noted in the previous section, in addition, there are research situations in which it is desirable to design the data collection with planned missing data.

In selecting one's method of coping with missing data there are several factors that need to be taken into consideration:

How much data are missing?   Obviously, if the missing data account for only a tiny fraction (say, 3% or less) of the data it will make much less difference how the problem is handled than if 10, 20, or 30% are missing.

How large is the sample?   Some of the current methods are suitable only for large samples (preferably $n > 200$).

Why are data missing?   Although the investigator may not be able to answer this question definitively, it is important to make every effort to discriminate the following circumstances:

Data on X may be missing because respondents with particular values of X did not wish to reveal some information, or were not able to provide some information, or were not even asked. Formally this may be identified as a case in which missingness on X is (usually partially) dependent on the (unknown) value of X. An example may be when individuals who engage in illicit activities decline to respond to inquiries about whether they do so. Another example may be the absence of a score on a test for a subject whose responses are out of the test's range. Yet a third example is the circumstance in which some questions are contingent on the response to other questions. These circumstances include both some of the easiest and some of the most difficult missing data problems. In the first case, when a refusal to respond may depend on the value of X, the investigator may have to guess at the extent of bias or use proxy variables that may not entirely correct the bias. The other examples, in contrast, may be managed by some of the simplest of techniques.

Data on X may be missing for some kinds of respondents who may be identified by distinctive values on other variables in the data set. For example, less educated respondents may not respond to some questions, or individuals who have somewhat atypical attitudes on one variable may be less likely to respond on some other variable. In longitudinal or multiple informant studies, variables missing at one time point or from one informant may be approximated by other available data. In the very common circumstance in which other measured variables are related to missing X, an important consideration is the magnitude of the relationship of these proxy or predictor variables to X. Another issue to consider is whether the variables that may be used to estimate X are to be included in the theoretical model predicting Y. When consideration of the available variables allows one to remove all bias in X associated with missingness from the analysis the situation is frequently referred to as "missing at random." This means that no cases of missing X are due to unmeasurable influence reflected in the value of X.

Data on X may be "missing *completely* at random," as when a laboratory assistant drops a tray of test tubes or a power failure causes data on the computer to be lost (although in both of these cases if the observations differ systematically over time, such a "random" event will produce systematic biases in the data). Obviously this implies that missingness on X is not correlated either with X or with any other variable in the data set. One circumstance in which this occurs is that noted earlier, in which the study design and random selection of subjects determine the presence or absence of data on X.

Who Will Be Using the Data Set?   Often, multiple researchers will be employing variables in overlapping analyses, or the data set may be made available to other investigators for secondary analyses. Under these circumstances, there are obvious advantages to having made a consistent approach to the problem of missing information for variable X. In some cases, there may be information that should be incorporated into this solution that will not be commonly available to all investigators.

A traditional consideration, the availability of computer programs and data-analytic resources, is generally no longer a realistic concern for anyone with access to the major statistical programs. These programs are gradually incorporating the most sophisticated statistical methods of handling missing data and doing so in increasingly user-friendly ways.

11.1.3 Traditional Approaches to Missing Data

Prior to relatively recently developed methods for imputing (estimating or modeling) scores that are missing, three approaches predominated:

Dropping Variables

When, for one or a few variables, a substantial proportion of cases lack data, the analyst may simply opt to drop the variables. This is obviously no loss when the variable(s) in question do not contribute materially to accounting for Y and they are not essential to the theory being tested. When, however, these conditions are not met (the usual case, else why were they included?), the loss of information through dropping variables is hardly a satisfactory solution to the missing data problem.

Dropping Subjects

When the pattern of missing data is such that they occur exclusively for a proportion of subjects (P_a), the analyst may opt to drop these subjects and perform the analysis on the remainder of the sample, a practice called *listwise deletion* in computer programs. If P_a is small enough and n is large enough there can hardly be a material difference between the results obtained with these subjects dropped and those which would have been obtained from all cases. However, even with small proportions of data missing (say 2 or 3%) on each variable, it is easy for cases with missing data on one or more of several variables used in the analysis to mount up to 10 or 15% of the full sample. Under these circumstances the question of whether the remaining sample is unbiased (still representative of the population from which it was drawn), or in the case of experimental studies whether the sample is still equivalent to a randomly assigned one, becomes important. Even when the investigator shows that the residual sample (the "complete cases") are very similar to the dropped cases on *certain* variables, (for example, on demographic variables), the question of whether they are also equivalent on other unexamined but relevant variables arises. In addition, such comparisons of the missing proportion of the sample with the remainder may often be useless because the confidence interval on the estimates for missing cases is large because of the small n (and the negative result of a test of "statistical significance" is a foregone conclusion because of the minimal resulting statistical power). Of course, the loss of this fraction of the sample and the accompanying df will also affect the precision of the estimated effects of variables on which there is no missing information.

Use of a Missing-Data Correlation Matrix, or Pair-Wise Deletion

Such a matrix is computed by using for each pair of variables (X_i, X_j) as many cases as have values for both variables. Thus, when data are missing for either (or both) variables for a case, it is excluded from the computation of r_{ij}. As a result different correlation coefficients are not necessarily based on the same subjects or the same number of subjects. This correlation matrix yields R^2 and the other correlation results, and when combined with the mean and sd computed from all available observations for each X_i, produces the B_is and B_0 of the regression equation.

This procedure is fully justified if (and only if) the data are missing completely at random. In this case, each statistic is an unbiased estimate of its population parameter for full data, and therefore the analyses are similarly unbiased. This method leaves some awkwardness in inference and confidence limits due to the varying n on which the results are based. They are clearly not as sturdy as if the maximum n had obtained throughout, nor as frail as the minimum n would suggest.

Table 11.1.1 presents a small data set with missing values that may clarify the complexity of the makeup of the statistics that go into the MRC analyses when a pair-wise deleted correlation matrix is used. The correlations with Y (r_{Yi}) are based on nonidentical subsets of subjects $(n_{Y1} = 7, n_{Y2} = 6, n_{Y3} = 7)$. The IV intercorrelations (r_{ij}), too, are based on nonidentical subsets of subjects $(n_{12} = 5, n_{13} = 5,$ and $n_{23} = 4)$. The Ms and sds of X_i entering the r_{ij} differ with the X_j variables being correlated, because whether a given subject's X_i value is included depends on whether it has a value for the given X_j under consideration. Thus, Subject 4's X_1 value of 63 is included in the M and sd of X_1 which enters r_{12}, but not in the M and sd of X_1 which enters r_{13}. Finally, in r_{Yi} and in the raw score regression equation, all available values on each IV are used for the M and sd. Thus, Subject 9's X_3 value of 130 enters into this "official" M and sd of X_3, even though it was not included in the computation of the M and sd entering

TABLE 11.1.1
Illustrative Missing-Data
Score Matrix

Subject	Y	X_1	X_2	X_3
1	72	38	6	92
2	84	52	12	114
3	63	47		108
4	81	63	8	
5	47			
6	62		7	110
7	39	31	9	
8	61	56		93
9	71			130
10	46	44	10	86

either r_{13} or r_{23}. For example, for X_3, the M and sd based on all available values and entering r_{Y3} are 104.7 and 14.2, but those entering r_{13} are 98.6 and 10.6, and those entering r_{23} are 100.5 and 11.8. A veritable mishmash!

Now, if data are missing for reasons related to Y or to other IVs, the pieces put together for the MRC refer to systematically different subsets of the population. Clearly, the MRC results cannot be coherently interpreted with regard to the entire population or to any specifiable subpopulation.

Indeed, under the circumstances of nonrandomly missing data, one can obtain a correlation matrix from pair-wise deletion whose values are mutually inconsistent, that is, a matrix that would be mathematically impossible to obtain were the data complete. For complete data, the correlation between any two variables is constrained by their correlations with a third. Thus, r_{12} may take on any value within the full limits of -1 to $+1$ if and only if X_1 and X_2 correlate 0 with all other variables under the sun. If this condition is not met, then ata the range of possible values for r_{12} is constrained. Specifically, for complete data, the mathematically possible upper and lower limits for r_{12} that take into account one other possible correlate are given by

(11.1.1) $$r_{13}r_{23} \pm \sqrt{(1 - r_{12})(1 - r_{23})}.$$

Values for r_{12} outside these limits are inconsistent with the other correlations.

To illustrate, if $r_{13} = .8$ and $r_{23} = .4$, substitution gives $.32 \pm .55$: r_{12} cannot take on a value less than $-.23$ or more than $+.87$. If $r_{13} = 8$ and $r_{23} = .6$, r_{12} is constrained to fall with the limits $.48 \pm .48$, that is, $.00$ and $.96$—a negative value for r_{12} is inconsistent, that is, mathematically impossible. These constraints have been illustrated for three variables for the sake of simplicity; they obviously obtain for more than three variables.

Now, although inconsistent rs may occur in a pair-wise deleted correlation matrix where the data are *randomly* missing, this possibility is small, at least for reasonably large n with relatively small proportions of missing data. But when the absence of data is nonrandom, that is, related to the other variables in the system, the possibility of inconsistent rs is obviously larger, because the sample values are no longer estimating necessarily consistent population rs. This is not to say that nonrandomly missing data will *probably* result in inconsistent rs and an error message from the computer program. Unfortunately, nonrandomly missing data will more often than not yield consistent missing-data correlation matrices, but that does not make them right, given the absence of a coherent population about which conclusions may be drawn.

11.2 MISSING DATA IN NOMINAL SCALES

Because the consequences of certain options for treating missing data are more readily illustrated for missing data in nominal scales, we will begin with this problem.

11.2.1 Coding Nominal Scale X for Missing Data

Consider a g-level nominal scale to which we can assign n_p of our n subjects but do not know to which of the g levels the remaining n_a $(= n - n_p)$ subjects belong. Then, in fact we have a total of $g + 1$ groups or a g-level nominal scale, the additional level representing no information or absent data in regard to membership in one of the other g groups, plus the information about which subjects have missing data.

Concretely, imagine a survey about attitude toward abortion (ATA) in which religious affiliation (G) is to be used as one of several IVs, with provision for $G_1 = $ Protestant,

G_2 = Catholic, G_3 = Jewish, and G_4 = Other or no religious affiliation. Assume that a subset of the sample declines to respond to this item. We need not drop the item, nor drop these nonresponding subjects completely, nor drop them from correlations involving the set of IVs carrying religious affiliation (pair-wise deletion method). We merely categorize them on this nominal scale as G_5 = absent data or "no response." To an objection that G_5 is not a religious affiliation and is of a different character from G_1 through G_4, we offer the counterargument that there is no structure in a nominal scale other than that we impose by our coding. *All* information about the subjects' responses to this item is included in our categorization into five groups. The meaning of the categorization is expressed in the coding and in the interpretation of the results of the analysis.

Employing this simple device, one proceeds to code the groups of this nominal scale into a set of g IVs, namely $X_1, X_2 \ldots X_j$, each an aspect or function of group membership. Any of the coding methods described in Chapter 8 may be used, because all we are doing is treating G_a, the group with absent data, as just another group.

Dummy-Variable Coding

All the formulas and interpretations of Section 8.3 obtain. G_a (the absent-data group) may be used as the reference group if its comparison with each of the others is of particular interest. Suppose that data are missing because the question was contingent on the response to a previous question. For example in a study looking at family composition the first question is whether the respondent has siblings and the follow-up question inquires about the particular constellation of siblings (e.g., by birth order, gender match, or spacing) that is hypothesized to be an influence on Y in the particular study. In this case it is entirely possible that the "missing" group is the most appropriate reference group (here, the group with no siblings). Or, some other group may serve as the reference group, in which case the partial coefficients reflect the difference between cases with missing data and this reference group. In addition, the correlation of the missing-data dummy variable with the other independent variables as well as Y will inform the investigator about potential bias and meaning that may be attributed to missingness. The investigator should be wary, however, of implicitly assuming that the missing-data group is the appropriate reference by failing to provide it with a variable on which it is coded 1.

Effects Coding

If the substance of our research suggests treating all g groups including the missing data G_a on the same footing, the methods and interpretation of Section 8.4 on effects coding can be used. If another group is selected as the group that is coded by a string of -1s, then X_a will, in the partialed results, carry the distinction in Y between G_a and the unweighted aggregate of all g groups. This differs from the dummy-variable coding in that it compares those with missing data with an average of equally weighted groups, whereas the dummy variable r_{Ya} contrasts missingness with all other responders pooled. Of course, if only a small proportion of the cases are missing the variable, it may be useful to keep in mind that unweighted effects coding will treat this group's mean as equal in importance to the means of the other groups in determining the mean of group means. This will, of course, be true even if the missing-data group is coded as the omitted group with -1.0 throughout.

Contrast Coding

To whatever contrast IVs one may wish to examine among the g groups whose membership is known, one can readily add a missing-data contrast whose coefficients are orthogonal to those of the other contrasts.

Mean Substitution

Another method of coding missing cases is to substitute the mean value for each of the variables reflecting group membership. This method may be used in combination with any of the above methods of coding the missing data and other groups. The consequence of mean substitution is to render missingness orthogonal to, and hence uninvolved in, the contrasts among the groups of known membership.

Because certain properties will be more easily apparent, we will examine the case in which the dependent variable is a dichotomy. Suppose we have the raw data presented as variables X and Y in Table 11.2.1, where $\vdots$ indicates a series of cases with the same response pattern. Of the 90 cases originally included in the investigation, 10 (cases 81 through 90) did not respond to the question we have identified as the independent variable X. We have created a new variable X_{miss} on which cases without data on X are coded 1 and cases with data = 0. Let us examine some of the alternative methods of filling in the blanks on X.

CH11EX01

Coding by dummy variables, we recode $X_{\text{zero}} = 1$ for the cases for whom $X = 1$ and 0 for the remaining cases (including the cases missing X). Now we use X_{zero} and X_{miss} in the equation predicting Y. Note that the $r_{Y\text{zero}}$ (= .104) is smaller than r_{YX} (= .244), in this example. This is because the missing cases have an exceptionally high mean on Y. The bivariate regression of Y on X_{zero} is similarly smaller than that of the complete cases. However, when X_{zero} and X_{miss} (the missing data dichotomy) are entered into the simultaneous equation predicting Y, the resulting coefficients are $\hat{Y} = .167 + .233\,(X_{\text{zero}}) + .533\,(X_{\text{miss}})$. These values are readily interpreted: The estimated score for those cases coded 0 on both X_{zero} and X_{miss} is .167, the mean for the zero cases on the original X. The $B_{Y\text{zero.miss}}$ for X_1 is .233, the difference between the $\hat{Y}$s of the original cases coded 0 and of those coded 1. Note that this is *identically* the value for the complete cases. The B for X_{miss}, the absent data dichotomy, is the difference between the mean of the $X = 0$ cases (.167) and that of the missing X cases (.70), or .533. The multiple correlation for this example = .338 and the standard error of X_1 = .106. (Of course, in this case, given the dichotomous Y, the usual extrapolations from these values cannot be made.)

Suppose that instead of X_{zero} we use X_{mean} where the missing cases are coded at the mean (= $50/80 = .625$) to represent X. Note that X_{mean} correlates less than the complete data sample with Y (= .222). This lower correlation is a necessary consequence of the fact that we have not increased the covariance or numerator of the correlation (since each deviation score on X for the missing cases = 0 and therefore cannot contribute to the covariance) whereas we have increased the denominator (since the full variance of Y now enters the equation). We have also reduced the correlation between X_{mean} and X_{miss} to zero so that when these are combined to predict Y, the resulting estimates are

$$\hat{Y} = .167 + .233\,(X_{\text{mean}}) + .388\,(X_{\text{miss}}),$$

with identical multiple R and standard error for X_{mean}. Note that $B_{YX\text{mean}}$ is the same as B_{YX} for the complete cases, whether or not the missing data dichotomy is included. It can be shown that no matter what single value of X is given to the missing cases (even 3,209!), simultaneous consideration of X and the absent data dichotomy will produce the same multiple R, B_{YX}, and SE_{BX}. Furthermore, even the use of 1-0 coding for X_{miss} is a convention. It can also be shown that any two values for absent and present X will produce the same partialed B_{YX} value, .233, with the same SE and R.

Another way of "filling in" the absent data on X is to use the information about other variables, in this case, Y. We note that of the 20 cases where $Y = 1$, 15 or .75 had X scores of 1. Of the 60 cases where $Y = 0$, 35 or .583 had X scores of 1. In X_e we have substituted these estimated scores for the absent data on X. This way of estimating the missing values on

TABLE 11.2.1

Data for 90 Cases With Some Missing Data on X

Case number	X	Y	X_{miss}	X_{zero}	X_{mean}	X_{est}
1	0	0	0	0	0	0
2	0	0	0	0	0	0
3	0	0	0	0	0	0
4	0	0	0	0	0	0
⋮	⋮	⋮	⋮	⋮	⋮	⋮
25	0	0	0	0	0	0
26	0	1	0	0	0	0
27	0	1	0	0	0	0
28	0	1	0	0	0	0
29	0	1	0	0	0	0
30	0	1	0	0	0	0
31	1	0	0	1	1	1
32	1	0	0	1	1	1
⋮	⋮	⋮	⋮	⋮	⋮	⋮
58	1	0	0	1	1	1
59	1	0	0	1	1	1
60	1	0	0	1	1	1
61	1	1	0	1	1	1
62	1	1	0	1	1	1
63	1	1	0	1	1	1
⋮	⋮	⋮	⋮	⋮	⋮	⋮
78	1	1	0	1	1	1
79	1	1	0	1	1	1
80	1	1	0	1	1	1
81		0	1	0	.625	.583
82		0	1	0	.625	.583
83		0	1	0	.625	.583
84		1	1	0	.625	.75
85		1	1	0	.625	.75
86		1	1	0	.625	.75
87		1	1	0	.625	.75
88		1	1	0	.625	.75
89		1	1	0	.625	.75
90		1	1	0	.625	.75
M	.625	.30	.11	.556	.625	.633
sd	.487	.356	.316	.500	.459	.460
r_Y	.244		.254	.104	.222	.253
B_Y	.233		.450	.100	.233	.264
B_Y (partialing X_a)				.233	.233	.251

X gives us a B_{Ye} of .264, which reduces to .251 if the missing data dichotomy is included. We will discuss this method further below.

Suppose that we had more than one predictor variable? In this case the necessary identity between the complete-data sample regression coefficient B_{YX} and the estimated effect when the missing-data dichotomy is included in the equation would no longer hold. If the correlations among the other variables in the equation were at all different between the cases missing X and those with data on X there would be likely differences on B_{YX} as well. Since even when data are missing completely at random some minor differences would be expected on the basis of sampling variation, at least minor changes in B_{YX} are to be expected. The correlation between the missing-data dichotomy and other independent variables and potential conditionality of relationships among other variables on the missing-data dichotomy may also be used to examine hypotheses about the reasons for missingness and the nature of the population for whom data are not available. In the cases illustrated here it is clear that cases missing data on X are not likely to be a random sample from the same population as the remaining cases. Perhaps they are similar to the $X = 1$ cases, although their mean on Y is even higher.

11.2.2 Missing Data on Two Dichotomies

Thus far we have considered only the case of one variable on which data are missing. What if data are missing for two variables? If both are IVs one may simply include two missing-data dichotomies. However, if one of the variables is Y, the method of coding that includes a missing-data dichotomy is no longer available (given a model with a single dependent variable). Therefore the study conclusions will be limited to those cases that have data on the dependent variable. We may be concerned that this sample may not represent the same population as the full sample, and we may also regret the loss in sample n. What can be done?

Under these circumstances we may turn to a different set of procedures in which we *estimate* the statistics for the full sample by making certain assumptions about the *model*. For example, let us assume that in the problem examined in the last section we also had data on X for 10 cases for whom we had no data on Y. Two (20%) of these cases were $X = 1$ and 8 were $X = 0$. We will change the format of presentation to express the data as a 2 by 2 table, with missing data. These are presented in Table 11.2.2, where we have also multiplied the ns by 10 to emphasize that the method to be illustrated is appropriate for large samples only.

As noted earlier when we considered missing data on X only, one way to estimate values is to assume that the missing data on X are distributed on X the same way as those cases who have data, and that the missing data on Y are distributed on Y the same way as those who have data. This, then, represents our *model* of the data. Our goal is to reduce this table to a 2 by 2 with a total sample of 1000. To estimate the frequency in each cell we use the proportionate distribution for the missing cases. Thus the estimate for the 0, 0 cell is:

250 (the complete cases) $+$
250/300 (the proportion of the observed cases for this value of X that had this value of Y) $\times$ 80 (the number of missing Y cases for this value of $X = 66.67$,
$+250/600$ (the proportion of those missing X attributable to this cell) $\times$ 30
$= 12.5$.

TABLE 11.2.2
Raw Data: 1000 Cases Missing Some Values
of Both X and Y

	$Y = 0$	$Y = 1$	Missing Y	Total n
$X = 0$	250	50	80	380
$X = 1$	350	150	20	520
Missing X	30	70		100
Total	630	270	100	1000

TABLE 11.2.3
Two Dichotomies, Estimation of Cell Frequencies

Complete cases: Cell and marginal proportions

	$Y = 0$	$Y = 1$	Total
$X = 0$	$250/800 = .3125$	$50/800 = .0625$	.375
$X = 1$	$350/800 = .4375$	$150/800 = .1875$	.625
Total	.75	.25	1.00

Estimated cell frequencies assuming complete case distributions

	$Y = 0$	$Y = 1$	Total
$X = 0$	$250 + 80(250/300) + 30(250/600)$ $= 329.17$	$50 + 80(50/300) + 70(50/200)$ $= 80.83$	410
$X = 1$	$350 + 20(350/500) + 30(350/600)$ $= 381.50$	$150 + 20(150/500) + 70(150/200)$ $= 208.5$	590
Total	710.67	289.33	1000

These values sum to $250 + 66.67 + 12.5 = 329.17$. Other cells are estimated by the same procedure, as shown in Table 11.2.3. The resulting table has allotted the missing cases to cells in conformity with our "model," with a change in the fraction of total cases that are in each cell. For example, we can see easily by dividing by 1000 $(= n)$ that the proportion of cases estimated to be in the 0, 0 cell is now .3293 instead of the original .3125, and that the proportion of cases in the second column is .2892 instead of the original .25.

But if these new estimates of cell proportions are better than the original ones, would it not be better to have used them instead of the complete case data in the determination of cell frequencies? In Table 11.2.4 we do just that. As we see, the first re-estimation (iteration) uses the cell proportions from the previous estimate, and the resulting proportions of cases in the cells and marginals are, on the average, a little more discrepant from those of the complete cases than were the previous estimates. Again we argue that if this is the best estimate, then *it* is the estimate that we should have used for the missing cases. So again we iterate (2) and yet again (3). By the time we have completed the third iteration we see that frequencies are hardly changing, so we accept these as the final frequencies.

What has happened to the means of these two variables and to the relationship (phi coefficient) between them? The estimated final means are .585 on X and .294 on Y, in comparison to .625 on X and .25 on Y for the complete data. The correlation of the final estimates is .153, in comparison to .149 on the complete data. The regression coefficients are .171 and .133 respectively.

11.2.3 Estimation Using the EM Algorithm

The procedure just carried out on the above example is mathematically equivalent to a maximum likelihood (ML) estimation, using the EM algorithm, where one alternately estimates and maximizes (Little and Rubin, 1987). Computer programs that employ these procedures are also designed to provide appropriate standard errors for the estimates for studies using appropriately large samples ($n > 200$). In the example we have created large mean differences between the

TABLE 11.2.4

Iterations of Estimated Cell Frequencies for Two Dichotomies

Iteration 1

	$Y = 0$	$Y = 1$	Total
$X = 0$	$250 + 80(329.17/410) + 30(329.17/710.67) = 328.04$	$50 + 80(80.83/410) + 70(80.83/289.33) = 85.32$	413.36
$X = 1$	$350 + 20(381.5/590) + 30(381.5/710.67) = 379.03$	$150 + 20(208.5/59) + 70(208.5/289.33) = 207.51$	586.54
Total	707.07	292.83	1000

Iteration 2

	$Y = 0$	$Y = 1$	Total
$X = 0$	$250 + 80(328.04/413.36) + 30(328.04/707.07) = 327.41$	$50 + 80(85.32/413.36) + 70(85.32/292.83) = 86.91$	414.32
$X = 1$	$350 + 20(379.03/586.54) + 30(379.03/707.07) = 379$	$150 + 20(207.51/586.54) + 70(85.32/292.83) = 206.68$	585.68
Total	706.41	293.59	1000

Iteration 3

	$Y = 0$	$Y = 1$	Total
$X = 0$	$250 + 80(327.41/414.32) + 30(327.41/706.41) = 327.12$	$50 + 80(86.91/414.32) + 70(86.91/293.59) = 87.50$	414.62
$X = 1$	$350 + 20(379/585.68) + 30(379/706.41) = 379.04$	$150 + 20(206.68/585.68) + 70(206.68/293.59) = 206.34$	585.38
Total	706.16	293.84	1000

441

missing values and the original frequencies so as to maximize the differences between the final estimates and the complete data. The model we employed, however, assumes that missing cases are not biased representatives from the same population. Were this assumption true we would expect the final estimates to be much closer to the complete data estimates, unless, of course, the samples were small and a large proportion missing.

How does this procedure differ from the previously discussed method of "plugging" some value for missing values and employing a missing-data dichotomy to adjust for information conveyed by the "missingness"? The model-estimating procedure assumes that the missing information does not convey any new information—that the data are missing at random. When that assumption is true, it will provide the best possible estimates of the population values (the maximum likelihood estimates). As we will see, even if that assumption is not true, providing that relevant missingness is completely accounted for by variables in the model, the estimates are the best possible.

A second relevant difference is that the model-estimating ML procedure "doesn't care" whether the data are missing on X or on Y. As was clear in the preceding example, the procedure estimates cell frequencies (in the dichotomous variable case), which are equivalent to means, variances (or sds), and covariances (or correlations) *without regard to IV or DV status*. This means that when the assumptions are valid, one is not limited in generalization of one's findings to the sample with complete data on Y.

A third relevant difference is that this model-estimating procedure did not estimate values of *individual* cases in the data set. As we saw, the missing-plug plus dichotomy solution does not actually estimate individual observations either, but it does provide a unique score for each. Lest there be some confusion at this point between the estimated values (X_e) used in the previous section to predict Y, there is a critical difference between this *modeling* procedure and any method of estimating values for individual cases.[1] When we used estimated X values in Table 11.2.1 we literally gave each case where $Y = 1$ the score of .75. The EM-ML procedure, in effect, assumes that 75% of the missing X cases who have $Y = 1$ have $X = 1$, and that the other 25% have $X = 0$. This difference has consequences for the sd of X, and thus for the consequent r_{YX} and B_{YX}. Of course, any new user of the data set who uses this EM-ML method of estimation for missing values may find and report different values of, for example, the mean and variance of Y, depending on what IV(s) are used. And this can happen even when Y cases are exactly the same in the old and new analyses if there are new IVs employed.

11.3 MISSING DATA IN QUANTITATIVE SCALES

11.3.1 Available Alternatives

CH11EX02

When data are missing in quantitative scales, we have a similar array of options and issues to be considered. The simplest and historically most frequently used is to code cases with absent data at the mean. To examine this and other options, let us return to our ongoing academic example. Let us assume that the analyses we have done thus far with this fictitious data set (Section 3.5.1) have been based only on the cases with complete data. However, there are another seven cases on whom we have all the information except citations (Table 11.3.1). Suppose we begin by inserting 40.23 (the mean years for cases with data) for each case missing citations, creating the variable we call cit_m. (Ignore for the present the variable labeled cit_1.) Note that although plugging the mean does not change our estimate of the population mean

---

[1] Some computer programs that use this general procedure do, however, permit the imputation of values to individual cases.

TABLE 11.3.1

Academic Salary Example With Cases Missing Citation Data

ID no.	Time since Ph.D.	Sex	No. of publications	cit_m	Cit_1	Salary	ID no.	Time since Ph.D.	Sex	No. of publications	cit_m	Cit_1	Salary
01	3	0	18	50	13	$51,876	36	3	1	11	69	18	$55,579
02	6	0	3	26	0	54,511	37	9	1	31	27	0	54,671
03	3	0	2	50	10	53,425	38	3	1	9	50	0	57,704
04	8	1	17	34	12	61,863	39	4	0	12	32	3	44,045
05	9	0	11	41	9	52,926	40	10	1	32	33	5	51,122
06	6	1	6	37	22	47,034	41	1	1	26	45	15	47,082
07	16	1	38	48	23	66,432	42	11	1	12	54	9	60,009
08	10	1	48	56	10	61,100	43	5	1	9	47	15	58,632
09	2	1	9	19	7	41,934	44	1	1	6	29	0	38,340
10	5	1	22	29	1	47,454	45	21	1	39	69	19	71,219
11	5	0	30	28	6	49,832	46	7	0	16	47	12	53,712
12	6	1	21	31	0	47,047	47	5	0	12	43	15	54,782
13	7	0	10	25	0	39,115	48	16	1	50	55	14	83,503
14	11	1	27	40	11	59,677	49	5	1	18	33	19	47,212
15	18	1	37	61	28	61,458	50	4	0	16	28	2	52,840
16	6	1	8	32	3	54,528	51	5	1	5	42	9	53,650
17	9	0	13	36	14	60,327	52	11	1	20	24	1	50,931
18	7	1	6	69	19	56,600	53	16	0	50	31	8	66,784
19	7	0	12	47	4	52,542	54	3	0	6	27	7	49,751
20	3	0	29	29	6	50,455	55	4	0	19	83	23	74,343
21	7	0	29	35	1	51,647	56	4	0	11	49	5	57,710
22	5	1	7	35	1	62,895	57	5	1	13	14	0	52,676
23	7	1	6	18	2	53,740	58	6	0	3	36	14	41,195
24	13	1	69	90	16	75,822	59	4	0	8	34	11	45,662
25	5	1	11	60	19	56,596	60	8	0	11	70	23	47,606
26	8	0	9	30	0	55,682	61	3	0	25	27	0	44,301
27	8	0	20	27	0	62,091	62	4	0	4	28	0	58,582
28	7	0	41	35	10	42,162	63	4	1	10	—	9	53,725
29	2	0	3	14	0	52,646	64	5	1	10	—	0	63,501
30	13	1	27	56	20	74,199	65	12	1	18	—	7	60,422
31	5	1	14	50	22	50,729	66	8	1	7	—	0	61,600
32	3	1	23	25	11	70,011	67	9	0	15	—	11	55,622
33	1	1	1	35	14	37,939	68	3	0	17	—	9	56,780
34	3	1	7	1	0	39,652	69	8	0	36	—	22	67,133
35	9	1	19	69	31	68,987							

	M_{cit}bar	sd_{cit}	B_{cit}	$SE_{B.cit}$	$B_{cit.t,s,p}$	$SE_{Bcit,t,s,p}$	$r_{sal,cit}$
Complete data (62)	40.23	17.17	310.75	60.95	201.93	57.51	.550
All cases (69)	40.23	16.26	310.75	59.56	202.32	56.13	.538

of cit_m, it lowers the estimated sd, and necessarily also the estimated correlation with salary. These are the same effects that we saw when we considered mean plugging for a dichotomous variable (Section 11.3.1) and can be understood by considering the deviation score equations for sd [Eq. (2.2.1)] and r [Eq. (2.3.5)]. In both we have added cases that cannot contribute to the numerator because their deviation from the mean is zero.

When, however, we examine B_{cit}, the regression of salary on cit_m, we find that the new estimate 310.45 is identical to the value for cases without missing data, as we showed previously for dichotomous variables. On the other hand, the $SE_{B_{cit}}$ is smaller, reflecting the new $n = 69$ as contrasted with the previous $n = 62$. Obviously we have not really added any new information on citations, and so this smaller value may seem to be cheating and is a source of concern whenever the difference between these two SEs is material. This method is not favored by experts in the area partly because of this deflation of the error estimate and partly for other reasons. First, the cases with missing data may differ systematically from the cases with data present, and thus representing them at the mean distorts the mean as well as its sd and correlation with other variables. Second, although the bivariate B equals that of complete cases, other relationships in the matrix are influenced in part by the "complete cases" and in part by the cases with some missing values.

These problems are improved but not entirely solved if one treats missingness as information by including a missing-data dummy variable. The correlation between this dichotomy and other variables will enable one to identify variables with which missingness is correlated. Including it in the regression equation then provides appropriate adjustments so that differences between the average value of X and the estimated value given the other variables are taken into account. For example, in our running academic salary study, if we include the missing-data dichotomy in the equation with the mean-plugged citations we get $B_{miss} = 4514$ ($SE = 2733$), indicating that the cases who are missing data on citations are paid, on average \$4514 more than we would expect if they did in fact have an average number of citations. As noted before, the B_{cit} remains 310.75. When the missing-data dichotomy is included in the full equation with the four other predictors, we find that this discrepancy shrinks slightly to \$4438. In this case the $B_{cit.t,s,p,m}$ is 201.97 ($SE = 55.39$), a value very close to that of the complete data.

Thus, despite its disrepute, mean plugging for modest proportions of missing data in IVs, especially when used with a missing data dichotomy, has several advantages. It is simple, it does not "make up" data (because plugging the mean is a convenience rather than an estimated score), and it is informative about why cases may be missing data. It also has the same meaning and consequences for each of the multiple users of the data set.

There are also disadvantages of employing the missing-data dichotomy. In the common case of a small percentage of data missing on each of a number of variables, it is not likely that the correlations of these dichotomies with other variables will be very informative because their confidence limits will be so large. When each of the variables in a problem has some missing data, it is cumbersome to carry around so many nonsubstantive variables (although not necessarily more cumbersome than alternative analytic solutions to the problem). Under some circumstances these missing-data variables may be multicollinear (again, not an overwhelming problem, as they may be used selectively or consolidated into a general index). In general, missing-data dichotomies have not been widely used.

11.3.2 Imputation of Values for Missing Cases

It is frequently the case that it is possible to estimate missing cases from other data at hand. This is referred to as *imputing* values and can be done in several different ways.

Hot Deck Imputation

In very large data sets like the U.S. census a method called *hot deck* has been used effectively. In this procedure, for each case (e.g., census tract of residence or member of an age-gender group) with missing data, a "substitute" case is randomly selected from those cases that are the same or very similar on one or several variables that are relevant to the missing variable. This case is then used as a proxy for the missing data (essentially appearing twice or more in the final data set). The advantage of this method is that it will not only provide a "match" on the variables of selection but that it also allows the influence of unmeasured variables to operate appropriately. Thus, for example, if there is a "neighborhood" effect on certain unmatched variables, or on the relationship between measured or unmeasured variables, it will be appropriately represented. Because this is a method suitable only for very large data sets, it will not be further described here.

A related method that has been used on moderate sample sizes is called the "twin" method. In this method a set of variables that relate to the missing variable are selected and standardized. Then another case in the data set is identified for which the average of the squared differences on these variables is a minimum (and less than .5). The value of the missing variable for that case is then imputed to the case with missing data.

Multiple Imputation and the Representation of Uncertainty

When an imputation method such as the hot deck has been used, Rubin (1987) has pointed out that the uncertainty of the imputed value is unrepresented, and thus the estimated *SE*s are too small. One way to correct this is to examine multiple imputations for each missing value. When one includes both the mean and the variance of these values in the determination of statistics, including the mean and variance of the entire sample and the covariance matrix with other variables, this source of uncertainty is appropriately represented. This option is gradually being incorporated into standard statistical packages, and, in principal, it represents an additional improvement to other methods of imputation. It can remove bias in missing values of both dependent and independent variables, providing other variables are available that are nontrivially related to that bias. Because certain study designs may intrinsically produce such bias in Y (see, for example, P. Cohen & J. Cohen, 1984), this can be a critical issue. It can substantially improve the statistical power when variables related to Y for missing cases are available. It will produce appropriate standard errors. And, unlike most current ML methods, it does not require that the variables related to missingness or to the variables on which missing data occurs are part of a structural model (Collins, Shafer, & Kam, 2001).

Imputation by Ordinary Least Squares (OLS)

There are two general approaches to using the information about the relationship among the variables to estimate the value of X for cases missing this datum. The first is a straightforward prediction of X using OLS procedures as described in this text, and the second involves the modeling methods described in the next section. In the OLS technique, variables that are known to be strongly related to X are selected and employed in a prediction equation for cases with complete data. Then this empirical regression equation is used to estimate the value for cases missing X. For example, let us return to our problem of missing citations for seven faculty members. Upon further inquiry we find that the reason data are missing for these cases is that they are all foreign scholars who have been recruited into the department. Although other data are available, the citation service that is available does not cover citations in foreign national journals. However, because all of these scholars have been on the faculty for at least three years, we may examine their citations in the past year. If we can show that this variable has a reasonable relationship to lifetime citations (*cit*), we may use the past year as a substitute variable. These data are shown as cit_1 in Table 11.3.1.

The correlation between *cit* and cit_1 is .73, and the regression equation predicting *cit* is $25.92 + 1.5\,cit_1$, based of course on the 62 complete data cases. For each of the seven cases without lifetime citation data we estimate cit_i as $25.92 + 1.5(cit_1)$. Once generated, these individual scores may be used as if they were actual responses to the citation question, regardless of whether variables used to estimate the scores (e.g., in this case cit_1) are or are not also included in the model. When these estimated scores are used for these cases the bivariate B predicting salary is 305.93 (SE_B = 58.18), and r = .54 (in comparison to .55 for the complete cases. When the other variables are added to the regression equation predicting salary, the $B_{cit.t,p,s}$ = 199.48 (SE = 55.12), whereas the 62 complete case value was $B_{cit.Y,p,s}$ = 201.93 (SE = 57.51).

It should be noted that when prediction of the missing values by these "substitute variables" is poor, this solution or any other method of imputation will be only marginally different from mean substitution because all estimated values will be very near the mean. It is, however, also quite possible that estimated scores will have a mean quite different from the complete data sample, if these cases are atypical on the variables used in the estimation; thus all statistics may be biased. One may employ a missing-data dichotomy to identify atypicality of missing cases on estimators or on estimated scores. To the extent that the missing-data dichotomy correlates with the variable that includes the imputed scores, we can identify the kind of cases that are more likely to be missing. If there is any reason to suspect that these cases may be different from those with data, we may also examine interactions between the imputed variable and the missing-data dichotomy in their relationship with any other variable.

In this example, for simplicity, we have used only a single variable in this imputation. However, one may use as many variables as usefully add to the relationship between the estimated and observed scores, that is, that add materially to the multiple R. One simply determines the prediction equation on the basis of complete cases and applies it to the cases with missing data. Some newer statistical package options (e.g., SYSTAT) do provide imputed values for individual cases based on the other variables in the model.

It is useful to remind oneself that there is nothing in this (or any other) method that will take care of the possibility of bias in these estimations not represented by other variables in the analysis. For example, suppose faculty members who were recruited from foreign countries actually had many fewer lifetime citations than would have been expected, because the publication outlets in those countries were fewer. That is, the estimated citations for this sample may be greater than the actual citations, if one could have obtained them.[2]

When the prediction of X is excellent, this appears to be a sound solution. When the prediction is poor, it has the disadvantages of mean substitution, although it retains the advantage of being a "permanent" solution to the problem in any given data set.

In this example we have used an outside variable, annual citations, that we do not intend to use in the prediction model because it may be less stable and thus deemed less appropriate for this analysis than lifetime citations. This method of imputation is particularly attractive when the variables to be used for imputation are not generally or typically expected to be used in the same prediction equations as are the imputed variables. However, it is also possible to use the method when the variables to be used in the imputation are also to be used in the substantive testing of hypotheses. In this case, an alternative ML procedure (discussed later) is also available.

In general this method is not used when the data missing are on the dependent variable, although of course it is equally feasible in this case. Most investigators are less comfortable with the underlying assumption of a consistent model across subpopulations on Y, perhaps because it is the central focus of the investigation and thus misrepresentations of relationships are likely to be more theoretically consequential.

In sum, the imputation of missing scores from other variables in the data set has several advantages. Since it generates a single imputed X score for each case, each user of the data set will be analyzing the same variable. The variables used in the imputation do not need to be

---

[2]Of course that suggests that some variable should also be in the model to indicate that for these individuals citations may have a different meaning, in which case the estimated values may be more "valid" than the actual values.

included (and often or even typically would not be included) in models employing X. In this way both sample sizes and variables will tend to be consistent across users of the data files.

11.3.3 Modeling Solutions to Missing Data in Scaled Variables

As in the illustration of the case of two dichotomies shown earlier, it is possible to obtain analytic ML solutions by starting with a model of the data. The model that is typically assumed is that the data are missing at random. This means that although cases missing data may have atypical values on one or more of the other variables included in the same model, they are not atypical on any other variables (not included in the model) that are (nontrivially) related to Y. Nor are the correlations among the various variables different for these cases (or actually, for cases like these) than for the remainder of the population. Multivariate normality is also assumed (as it is for the OLS and ML prediction models). This means that the variables that would be predictors of missing data (and thus the identifiers of any nonrandomness that can be corrected) must be in the same matrix (model). In practice, this computerized technique begins with the pair-wise deletion matrix and "adjusts" it to resolve inconsistencies. (See the earlier EM illustration of adjustment of the relationship between two dichotomies.)

11.3.4 An Illustrative Comparison of Alternative Methods

Let us return one more time to the ongoing academic salary example. In addition to the 7 cases missing data on citations, suppose we also had another 18 cases missing data on time since Ph.D. or on both number of publications and citations. Table 11.3.2 provides the data set for all 87 individuals in the department. Table 11.3.3 provides the solutions for each of several approaches to the problem. We previously showed the prediction equation for salary based on the 62 faculty members with complete data (given here as the listwise deletion solution). Now let us estimate the solutions for the full set of 87 cases.

The first full-sample solution provides coefficients for the mean-plugged variables, and the next solution uses the same variables plus missing data dichotomies for each of the three predictors that had missing data. Note that for at least two of the predictors the missing cases had salaries quite discrepant from those that would have been expected if they had been typical (average) on the variable that they were missing. Those who were missing time since Ph.D. had salaries that were quite high in comparison with other cases, given their publications, citations, and gender. The explanation of this could come from either of several sources. Either this group was paid more (presumably because of some unmeasured variable), or they actually had higher than average time since Ph.D. (so the higher salaries were "justified"), or the model in some way was different for these individuals (e.g., some unassessed interaction or a difference in the relationships among the variables, may be present).

Similarly, those missing citations also appear to be getting unusually high salaries. As we noted earlier, this discrepancy was present even when we imputed scores, and it may just be that some additional salary was offered these foreign scholars in order to entice them to this academic department.

Moving on to the next regression equation, we examine the EM algorithm solution. In this problem with several scaled variables, the variance-covariance matrix underlying the regression solution is "filled in" with estimates of the effects of the missing values. Although the actual mathematical operations are too complex to demonstrate here, they may be intuited by analogy to the operations examined in the section on the relationship between two dichotomies with missing data on each. This algorithm operates under the assumption that the data model is the same for both present and absent data. By saying that the model is the same we mean that the

TABLE 11.3.2
Academic Salary Example for 87 Faculty Members

ID no.	Time since Ph.D.	Sex	No. of publications	Citations	Salary	ID no.	Time since Ph.D.	Sex	No. of publications	Citations	Salary
01	3	0	18	50	$51,876	45	21	1	39	69	$71,219
02	6	0	3	26	54,511	46	7	0	16	47	53,712
03	3	0	2	50	53,425	47	5	0	12	43	54,782
04	8	1	17	34	61,863	48	16	1	50	55	83,503
05	9	0	11	41	52,926	49	5	1	18	33	47,212
06	6	1	6	37	47,034	50	4	0	16	28	52,840
07	16	1	38	48	66,432	51	5	1	5	42	53,650
08	10	1	48	56	61,100	52	11	1	20	24	50,931
09	2	1	9	19	41,934	53	16	0	50	31	66,784
10	5	1	22	29	47,454	54	3	0	6	27	49,751
11	5	0	30	28	49,832	55	4	0	19	83	74,343
12	6	1	21	31	47,047	56	4	0	11	49	57,710
13	7	0	10	25	39,115	57	5	1	13	14	52,676
14	11	1	27	40	59,677	58	6	0	3	36	41,195
15	18	1	37	61	61,458	59	4	0	8	34	45,662
16	6	1	8	32	54,528	60	8	0	11	70	47,606
17	9	0	13	36	60,327	61	3	0	25	27	44,301
18	7	1	6	69	56,600	62	4	0	4	28	58,582
19	7	0	12	47	52,542	63	4	1	10	.	53,725
20	3	0	29	29	50,455	64	5	1	10	.	63,501
21	7	0	29	35	51,647	65	12	1	18	.	60,422
22	5	1	7	35	62,895	66	8	1	7	.	61,600
23	7	1	6	18	53,740	67	9	0	15	.	55,622
24	13	1	69	90	75,822	68	3	0	17	.	56,780
25	5	1	11	60	56,596	69	8	0	36	.	67,133
26	8	0	9	30	55,682	70	—	1	7	12	54,832
27	8	0	20	27	62,091	71	—	1	11	24	53,981
28	7	0	41	35	42,162	72	—	1	15	15	63,111
29	2	0	3	14	52,646	73	—	1	22	33	61,891
30	13	1	27	56	74,199	74	—	1	21	39	60,989
31	5	1	14	50	50,729	75	—	1	25	30	60,154
32	3	1	23	25	70,011	76	—	0	10	14	57,370
33	1	1	1	35	37,939	77	—	0	16	42	58,647
34	3	1	7	1	39,652	78	5	1	—	—	47,855
35	9	1	19	69	68,987	79	8	1	—	—	50,080
36	3	1	11	69	55,579	80	9	1	—	—	63,602
37	9	1	31	27	54,671	81	6	1	—	—	61,220
38	3	1	9	50	57,704	82	12	1	—	—	84,071
39	4	0	12	32	44,045	83	3	1	—	—	48,879
40	10	1	32	33	51,122	84	4	1	—	—	58,521
41	1	1	26	45	47,082	85	1	1	—	—	47,222
42	11	1	12	54	60,009	86	14	0	—	—	62,290
43	5	1	9	47	58,632	87	3	0	—	—	49,705
44	1	1	6	29	38,340						

Variables means for cases with and without data:

	Time	Sex	Publications	Citations	Salary
Cases with complete data ($n = 62$)	6.79	.56	18.18	40.23	$54,816
Cases missing citations only ($n = 7$)	7.00	.57	16.14		59,255
Cases missing time only ($n = 8$)		.75	15.87	26.12	58,872
Cases missing publications and citations ($n = 10$)	6.50	.80			57,344

TABLE 11.3.3
Academic Salary Example: Estimated Full Data Effects

Method (n) (R^2)	B_0	B_{time} (SE)	B_{sex} (SE)	$B_{publications}$ (SE)	$B_{citations}$ (SE)	Missing time	Missing publications	Missing citations
Listwise deletion	38,670	857	918	93	202			
(62) (.50)		(288)	(1,860)	(86)	(58)			
Plugged means	41,403	769	1,145	128	161			
(87) (.38)		(256)	(1,682)	(83)	(56)			
Plugged means/M_D	39,232	736	502	134	196	7,032	−1708	4,552
(87) (.44)		(250)	(1,663)	(80)	(57)	(2,858)	(3,614)	(2,889)
EM Algorithm		869	1,515	118	154			
(87) (.46)		(241)	(1,548)	(74)	(47)			
Pair-wise deletion		1,055	1,247	51	144			
(72–87) (.47)		(257)	(1,604)	(80)	(50)			
Filled in/imputation	38,387	743	1,143	131	214			
(87) (.58)		(154)	(1,375)	(57)	(38)			

regressions among the variables in the matrix, including the dependent variable, are the same for cases with all data and those with missing data. In estimating the variance-covariance matrix we note again that we are not obtaining estimates for each of the individual observations (although increasingly this option is available on computer programs, which use the same assumptions). The program does not assume that the variable means are the same for the missing cases as for those with data present. As with the case of the dichotomies, depending on values of other variables, estimated means may change. We also note that the program doesn't care whether the data are missing on the independent or dependent variables.

The next solution to the regression equation employs the pair-wise deletion matrix, in which each bivariate relationship is determined by the number of cases on which data are present. As you would expect by the fact that the EM algorithm "starts" with the pair-wise deletion matrix, these solutions tend to be a little more similar to each other, although the coefficients for publications are quite discrepant.

The next solution returns to basics. As indicated in the first section of the chapter, it is always critically important to try to discern the reasons why data may be missing. In this case, we first ask why it may be that we don't know the time since Ph.D., since this would seem to be readily determined from files typically in the personnel record. As it happens in this fictitious department, these eight faculty are "old-timers"—faculty who never completed their Ph.D.s who were incorporated into the department when the department was first created, some 15 years earlier. One possibility that we may decide to act on is substitution of years since first academic appointment for time since Ph.D., since those with Ph.D.s typically obtained their first appointments around the same time as their degrees.

What about those missing both citations and publications? Well, these faculty members are just laggards—those who had failed to respond to the Dean's request for information on publications and citations. Other information on these faculty has been gathered from the Dean's office. We might suspect that at least some of these faculty will be among the poorer "producers" on staff, with somewhat fewer publications and citations than average. Obviously the first thing we should do has nothing to do with analytic solutions: We should go out and get the missing data on these 10 faculty members! Having done this, the filled in solution is the resulting equation.

Finally, we decide to add the imputed citations (Section 11.3.1) to allow analysis of the complete set of 87 faculty members. Just in case we have residual undetected problems with these subgroups we include the three missing data dichotomies. We are reassured that none of these dichotomies shows a large effect relative to its standard error, and note in addition that they are in the expected direction. That is, the old-timers are a little underpaid ceteris paribus, either because of their absent degrees or because there may be a curvilinear relationship between age and salary. Those missing publications and citations are paid a little more than expected; perhaps that is why they were reluctant to turn in their data on publications and citations! And those foreign scholars who were missing citations may apparently have been given a very slight salary incentive.

11.3.5 Rules of Thumb

Which, then, of these estimates is best? Obviously in this fictitious example there is no true answer. It is, however, reassuring that most substantive conclusions would not change very much regardless of which solution we used (that the most important influences were seniority and citations), although the pair-wise deletion solution tends to be most discrepant. In this example we had a large proportion of cases with missing data, 25 of 87 or nearly 30%. Thus these are circumstances in which the differences between the various solutions are likely to be relatively large.

The real bottom line is that the best scientific solution is to keep the missing data to a minimum and to get as much information about the reasons that data are missing as possible. When the missing data are a small proportion of any variable and not attributable to a few cases on whom hardly any data are available, the determination of the solution may depend on the context. When a number of scientists will employ the variables, it may be optimal to find a best estimate for missing data by imputation. If good indicators of the missing values are not available, it will probably do no harm to use plugged means. If there is the slightest reason to suspect that the cases with absent data may be different from other cases, use the missing data dichotomy. When data are missing in small and apparently random fashion, in a study in which the number of uses and users of the variables will be limited, the EM solution is probably best. When the sample is very, very large, go and study methods developed for census data. When the sampling and data-analytic designs are complex, examine the recent literature addressing these problems (e.g., Graham & Hofer, 2000).

11.4 SUMMARY

The chapter begins with an exhortation to minimize missing data and some suggestions for increasing the likelihood of doing so (Section 11.1.1). The best means of handling missing data depends on the extent of the problem, sample size, reasons why data are missing, and the number of users of the data set (Section 11.1.2). The major ways of handling missing data in the past were to drop variables or subjects with missing data, or to employ statistics based on those with complete data for each computed coefficient. Each of these procedures has serious potential drawbacks (Section 11.1.3). When data are missing completely at random (missingness is not correlated with any relevant variable), all methods will yield unbiased estimates, although some will be statistically more powerful than others. When data are missing on a categorical variable, coding options can be adapted from any of the methods for coding described in Chapter 8, without distortion of coefficients for cases with data (Section 11.2.1). The case in which data are missing on more than one categorical variable can also be handled with estimation methods. These methods can be improved by iteration (Section 11.2.2), which is illustrated for a simple case that is one application of the EM algorithm maximum likelihood procedure. Advantages of this method are discussed, including its potential application to the DV.

Methods of coping with missing data in quantitative scales are reviewed and illustrated in Section 11.3, beginning with a review of alternatives such as mean substitution with or without a missing-data dummy variable. Imputation of missing values for individual cases is discussed in Section 11.3.2, including OLS, "hot deck," and EM procedures. Solutions that are based on a model of the data using EM-ML methods are often optimal if data are missing "at random," meaning that data on any variable W are not missing because of the true value of W, or in a way that is not predictable from other available variables (Section 11.3.3). Finally, all of the alternative methods are illustrated and compared for a worked extension of the faculty salary example. Some general rules of thumb are offered, depending on the circumstances discussed at the beginning of the chapter.

12

Multiple Regression/
Correlation and Causal Models

12.1 INTRODUCTION

12.1.1 Limits on the Current Discussion and the Relationship
Between Causal Analysis and Analysis of Covariance

Necessarily, a chapter-length presentation of causal analysis cannot begin to do justice to the subject matter in its entirety. Therefore, this chapter will be limited to these three relatively modest goals: to introduce readers to the concepts and terminology used in causal analyses, to provide some techniques and illustrations for the simpler procedures, and to present a glimpse of the variety of options available to the data analyst whose goal is illumination of a theory by the full extraction of the information contained in an appropriate data set. We begin by examining the models that are implicit in the special case of MRC that is represented by the analysis of covariance.

As originally devised, ANCOVA was a device for increasing the efficiency (statistical power) of randomized experiments by reducing the size of the error term in ANOVA. Figure 12.1.1(A) gives the implicit causal diagram of this classical form. Randomization assures that there is no relationship between the set A covariates and set B treatment groups in the population (i.e., no group mean differences in the covariates), and Y is the criterion by which one assesses whether the treatments represented by B have different effects. Because the covariates are selected so that they do relate causally to Y, one can remove (by partialing) their variance in Y and produce a smaller error term for the significance test $(1 - R^2_{Y.AB})$ than would be the case without them $(1 - R^2_{Y.B})$ and thus increase power. Because much of experimental design is devoted to the reduction of error, ANCOVA, so used, is obviously a valuable tool. Note that the inclusion of set A has no bearing on the size of the treatment effects of set B, only on our ability to detect them. Put differently, effects of $B \cdot A$ do not differ from B, because A and B are not correlated.

As noted earlier, researchers also employ ANCOVA where randomization did not determine set B group membership. In quasi-experimentation, the purpose remains the evaluation of differential treatment, but for practical or sometimes ethical reasons, pre-existing nonrandomized groups are used. The threats to the validity of conclusions about treatment effects in such circumstances have been thoroughly described by Campbell and his collaborators (Campbell & Stanley, 1966; T. D. Cook & Campbell, 1979; Shadish, Cook, & Campbell,

A. Classical experiment   B. Quasi-experimental

C. Organismic   D. Case-control

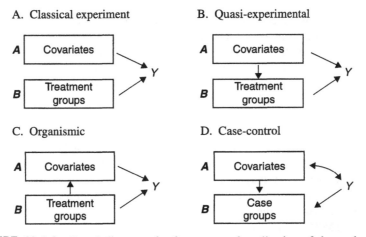

FIGURE 12.1.1 Causal diagrams for four types of application of the analysis of covariance.

2002). The problem is made plain by the causal diagram in Fig. 12.1.1(B): Membership in these pre-existing groups may be caused, in part, by other variables (set A) that, in turn, also have causal influences on Y. Ignoring the causes in A common to set B group membership and Y results in spurious B-Y relationships and inevitably biases our estimates of the effects of treatments per se. In quasi-experimental ANCOVA these common causes are represented in the covariates that make up set A, and the partialing of A from B is the crucial feature: $B \cdot A$ is intended to remove the common causes and leave authentic treatment effects. For this maneuver to be successful, however, there are two basic conditions that set A must satisfy. First, and obviously, the set A covariates must contain all nontrivial common causes of set B and Y. Second, the covariates must be measured reliably, because measurement error in a partialed variable will also bias the group effects. When these conditions are satisfied, ANCOVA is a powerful device for the statistical control of antecedent common causes.

Not infrequently in quasi-experimental research, the nature of the causal relationship between some or all of the set A variables and membership in the groups may be unclear or debatable in that the causal arrow of Fig. 12.1.1(B) may be reversed, or there may be reciprocal causality so that the model may be said to have been misspecified. The complexity of field research is rich in such ambiguities. If we nevertheless partial the effects of A from those of B we may be denying the treatments some of the variance in Y for which they are responsible, this usually conservative analysis being made in the interest of avoiding a false claim of group differences due to the treatments.

Yet another use to which ANCOVA has been put is in research on the effects of some property or properties that define group membership (set B). No experimenter-induced treatment is involved; rather, what is under study is the effect on Y of some "organismic" variable such as sex, diagnosis, age, or ethnicity. The role of the covariates in such cases (if it is clear that set A cannot have caused set B) is to limit our investigation of the effects of set B on Y to *direct effects*, which we will discuss later in this chapter.

Finally, we consider a design popular in epidemiological and clinical research that is typically analyzed by ANCOVA. The case-control study, diagrammed in Fig. 12.1.1(D), is employed in the search for causes of some existing state, usually a pathological condition. A group of cases having this condition, usually constrained by other relevant variables (e.g., age, sex, race, treatment-seeking), is gathered, and one or more comparison (control) groups, similarly constrained, are also constituted. Because the condition is relatively rare in the population, the cases may be gathered over a period of time or in various places in order to have a sufficiently large number for adequate power.[1] The case and control groups constitute set B. Set A is made up of organismic or other antecedent variables that would otherwise provide competing hypotheses. The putative cause (or "risk factor") for the condition, Y, is then related to $B \cdot A$ in the ANCOVA. Note that whereas in the ANCOVA Y is nominally the dependent variable, it appears as a cause in this model. In practice, what is being assessed is the magnitude and significance of the difference in means of the cases and controls when they are adjusted for whatever differences exist in the covariates.

These causal models are the most frequently involved when ANCOVA is applied; they are not exhaustive. For these models B is always group membership but the variables making up set A are unconstrained. They may include variables that code groups, or they may include main effects, interactions, and curvilinearity of scaled variables, or any combination of these variables that makes sense in the particular investigation. As we shall see, when one moves from ANCOVA to MRC, set B (the set of primary investigative interest) may also include data of any of the forms discussed in the earlier chapters.

12.1.2 Theories and Multiple Regression/Correlation Models That Estimate and Test Them

Back in Chapter 2, we noted that the simplest regression equation, $\hat{Y} = B_0 + BX$, may be a prototypical causal model with X the causal variable and B the size of its effect. Regression invites causal thinking because, unlike correlation, it is asymmetrical, just as are a cause and its effect, at least in simple cases.

Both bivariate and multivariate regressions may be used to represent a specific theory. Theories in the behavioral sciences specify what variables need to be in the model to provide adequate tests of causal relationships. A fully adequate theory should also indicate the mechanisms by which an antecedent condition or variable intensity exerts its influence on a change in Y. Ideally the theory also tells us not only the direction but the magnitude of the effects that would be consistent with the theory, as they sometimes do in the physical and biological sciences. Unfortunately most frequently, at present, most behavioral science theories predict only which effects should be nonzero in the population and the hypothesized direction of effect. Thus, when empirical estimates are employed to test a theory, only the consistency of the estimated directions of effects with the theory can be tested. Because of the absence of more specific quantitative predictions, the data that are consistent with one theory are very often consistent with a range of other theories as well. Nevertheless, these theories provide a starting place for building a science. Later in the chapter we will discuss some methods that include tests for differential consistency of the data with (certain) alternative causal models.

Empirical Conditions for Inferring Causality

As introduced in Chapter 3, empirical demonstration that a variable X may be a cause of another variable Y depends on showing that three conditions hold (Bollen, 1989; Kenny, 1979):

1. Relationship: X is correlated with Y;
2. Temporal precedence: X precedes Y in time;

---

[1] We ignore here issues of nonindependence of data as discussed in Section 14.6.

3. Nonspuriousness: The X-Y relationship holds even when the influences of other possible variables on this relationship are eliminated so that the effect can be said to have been isolated.

In addition, there needs to be a theoretically plausible mechanism by which X may exert its influence on Y.

Relationship is established by showing there is a nonzero association between X and Y. Temporal precedence can be established empirically through longitudinal research or on the basis of theory or logic. For example, the finding of a correlation between mother's IQ and child's IQ in a cross-sectional study could not be easily attributed to influences of the child on the mother. Priority of stable IQ in the mother, in addition to research on genetic and environmental factors in IQ, shows clearly that influence proceeds (primarily or overwhelmingly) from the parent to the child. Nonspuriousness is established by removing the influence of variance in other possible extraneous factors that may influence the outcome variable (e.g., level of educational opportunities shared by parent and child). Both genetic and environmental influences make such a relationship plausible.

Alternative Methods of Establishing Isolation of Effects

There are three distinct methods of isolating the effect of a target independent variable: (1) one may examine its effect within constant values of other potential causes, (2) one may create the variable and apply it differentially to groups who are randomly assigned to conditions, or (3) one may measure and statistically control (partial) the effects of potential alternative explanatory variables (Higginbotham, West, & Forsyth, 1988).

First, extraneous factors may be removed or held constant. For example, "nonsense syllables" (e.g., VOLVAP) have been used in verbal learning experiments to minimize extraneous influence on the outcomes due to differential familiarity with the words. Researchers in human evolution study primitive cultures to minimize the influences of modern civilization. A given study may be confined to a single age or ethnic group.

Second, subjects may be randomly assigned to different groups in which the variable of interest is varied by experimental manipulation. In randomization, a chance process (e.g., flipping a coin) is used to assure that each subject has an equal (or proportional) chance of being in a given experimental treatment condition. The random assignment process removes many forms of extraneous influences by assuring that the subjects in all experimental treatment conditions will be equivalent, on average, at the beginning of the experiment.[2]

Finally, extraneous factors representing alternative explanations for the relationship between the putative cause and Y may be statistically controlled, which generally means including them in the statistical equations that estimate the model. This procedure of measurement of and statistical adjustment for (partialing of) known extraneous factors permits isolation of the relationship of interest from any influence of the extraneous variables and is, of course, a central topic of this text.

The three methods of controlling for extraneous variables vary in their strengths and weaknesses and in their areas of application. Philosophers of science and research methodologists also differ in their beliefs about the extent to which the three methods of control can be successful in ruling out extraneous factors (Berk, 1988; Pearl, 2000). Nearly all commentators prefer randomization and experimental manipulation when possible: Random assignment is usually, but not inevitably, better at ruling out the influence of most types of extraneous variables than

---

[2]Given sufficiently large samples and no bias due to participation or drop-out rates.

the other approaches. For this reason, randomized experiments are widely used in such areas as experimental psychology, social psychology, experimental economics, and clinical trials in physical and mental health. Many of these areas have enjoyed rapid scientific progress from the power of randomization and experimental manipulation[3] to rule out extraneous factors. However, randomization has practical limits, particularly when experiments are extended over time or treatments involve nontrivial changes in ongoing behavior or compliance to a strict protocol. Subject attrition may occur; different experimental conditions may be contaminated by communications among subjects or staff, or by access to alternative sources of treatment. Volunteer subjects may be so atypical as to preclude sensible generalization of the results to any population of interest[4] (Shadish, Cook, & Campbell, 2002; West, Biesanz, & Pitts, 2000; West & Sagarin, 2000).

In other areas of the behavioral sciences, the demands of experimental manipulation and random assignment are less feasible, for practical or ethical reasons. In these areas, putative social, cultural, economic, contextual, or organismic causes cannot be manipulated by the investigator. Even when the putative cause can be manipulated, random assignment to treatment conditions may be prohibited by important ethical or legal concerns (e.g., subjects cannot be infected with serious diseases or deprived of efficacious treatment). Potentially possible randomized experiments in natural settings may require financial or administrative support of a magnitude that is not likely to be forthcoming.

As noted earlier, when manipulation of the independent variable is possible but random assignment is not, quasi-experiments can be utilized. Quasi-experiments incorporate features in their design that attempt to eliminate specific classes of extraneous factors, thereby minimizing the number of plausible alternative explanations of the results (e.g., by examining treatments within particular demographic groups). More commonly in the behavioral sciences, control takes the form of measuring these alternatives and partialing their effects. Difficulties arise because potential causes are often many; effects may be subtle, interactive, and delayed; and strong measurement is difficult. Consequently, the process of ruling out the influence of extraneous variables is often lengthy, involving the testing of multiple statistical models in multiple studies.

Drawing on precedents in other sciences (e.g., geology, astronomy) in which randomization and manipulation are not possible, two tacks may be particularly useful in limiting the range of extraneous variables that can explain observed relationships of interest (Shadish, Cook, & Campbell, 2002). The first is to make precise predictions about the direction, form, and strength of relationships, an approach that is widely used in the natural sciences such as astronomy and geology, but to date has been rarely attempted in the behavioral sciences (Meehl, 1967). One example is provided by behavioral genetic theory, which makes precise predictions about heritability differences between fraternal and identical twins for traits determined by single genes.[5]

An approach that reflects the complexity of relationships typically observed in the behavioral sciences is to propose a causal network of relationships among a set of variables (Cochran, 1965). To the degree that the entire hypothesized network of relationships is supported, it may be more difficult to think of parsimonious alternative explanations for the results.

---

[3] We ignore here any issues of problems of external validity in matching experimental manipulations of variables to their "naturally occurring" presumed equivalents (Rosnow & Rosenthal, 1999).

[4] Indeed, specification of the (limitations of the) population for which a given causal system is presumed to operate, although of critical theoretical importance, is probably one of the weakest areas of current causal modeling and analysis.

[5] Although to date these predictions have been used primarily to estimate heritable relationships rather than to test theoretically derived estimates.

12.1.3 Kinds of Variables in Causal Models

The basic strategy of causal analysis is to represent a theory in terms of the network of variables that are involved, explicitly stating the causal direction, sign (+ vs. −), and nature of the relationship, if any, between all pairs of variables that are considered. Path diagrams[6] are typically used to graphically depict the network of relationships. Observational data are then employed to determine whether the model is consistent with them and to estimate the strength of the hypothesized causal relationships. Failure of the model to fit the data results in model falsification, whereas a good fit supports the theoretical arguments that the model is, at least, one of the (potentially many) models that provide adequate goodness-of-fit to the sample data. Repeated failures to falsify the hypothesized model in different studies, particularly when other competing theories are also tested and disproved, adds strength to the investigator's belief in the model. Although no model can be definitively confirmed, the status of a model as "not yet disconfirmed" is often a powerful one in science.

There are a number of distinguishable roles that variables may play in theories. To review, a cause X of some variable (Y) presumably precedes Y in time and has a generative mechanism that accounts for its impact on Y. These mechanisms are often implicit in our theories, residing in some vague if common understanding that such a force may be plausible. Thus, if gender is thought to be a cause of some characteristic, we assume that biological or social mechanisms are present and implicit in the concept of gender (in the given setting or population) that can explain how gender-associated differences arise. Some theories provide, at least partially, for explicit inclusion of some of these mechanisms, they are called *mediators* of the effect of X on Y. Figure 12.1.2(A) provides examples of a mediator Z that totally accounts for the relationship between X and Y, and a mediator W that partially accounts for the relationship between X and Y. Yet another model that is frequently tested is one in which competing variables in the model are alternative potential mediators of an unmeasured cause of Y.

Critical additional variables in a causal model include other variables that may obscure or *confound* the relationship between X and Y, as illustrated by V and W in Fig. 12.1.2(B). In these drawings V is a variable needed in order to correctly estimate the effect of X on Y, and W is a variable that completely accounts for the correlation of X with Y. Thus potential confounders are variables that may have a causal impact on both X and Y. They include common sources of measurement error as well as other influences shared by X and Y. In experimental studies there is a special concern about aspects of the experimental manipulation or setting that may account for the study effects, rather than the motivating theoretical factor (Brewer, 2000). Any of these problems may produce spurious relationships between X and Y *as measured and estimated in their absence*; that is, ignoring them will bias empirical estimates of the causal effect of X, usually, but not always, making them too big.

There is a special class of variables, related to both a cause and an effect, that suppress the relationship between the cause and the effect [Fig. 12.1.2(C)]. *Suppressor* variables such as Z are fairly uncommon in most behavioral science theory, but are extremely common in both biological and economic models. In these models a feedback mechanism exists that tends to promote homeostasis (biological) or equilibrium (economics). Thus, despite a general tendency for an increase in X to cause an increase in Y (e.g., for an increase in income to cause increases in spending) increases in X also cause a change in some other variable Z that causes a decrease in Y (e.g., increases in savings). Suppression variables may be either confounders

---

[6]Path analysis originated independently in genetics (Wright, 1921) and econometrics during the first half of the twentieth century and offers a coherent method for the quantitative analysis and testing of theories based on the natural observation of phenomena. Beginning in the 1960s, these methods grew in sociology, economics, and related fields (Blalock, 1971; O. D. Duncan, 1975; Goldberger & Duncan, 1973), and in the 1970s in education and psychology (Bentler, 1980; Kenny, 1979).

(A) Mediating variables Z and W.

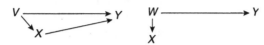

(B) Confounding variables V and W.

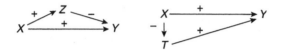

(C) Suppressing mediators Z or confounders T.

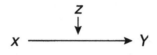

(D) Contingent effects: moderators or augmenters Z.

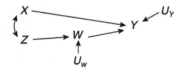

(E) Exogenous variables X and Z, endogenous W and Y, and disturbances or unmeasured residual causes U_W and U_Y.

FIGURE 12.1.2   Types of variables in causal models relating X to Y.

or mediators of the effect of X on Y as shown in Fig. 12.1.2(C), and in general their omission will lead to an underestimate of the effect of X on Y.

Although we will deal with these only slightly in this chapter, other important variables in some causal theories are the *moderators*, variables that modify relationships among other variables [Fig. 12.1.2(D)]. The arrow from Z to another arrow indicates that the estimate of a causal effect of X on Y is conditional on the value of Z, a moderator in the model, as discussed in Chapters 7 and 9.

Three other ways of classifying variables that were introduced in Chapter 3 are useful in discussing empirical causal models [Fig. 12.1.2(E)]. *Exogenous* variables are those that are the starting point for the model because they are assumed *not* to be effects of other variables in the model, except, potentially, other exogenous variables. A convenient characteristic of these variables is that it is not necessary to specify what the reasons may be for correlations among them. Any correlations among them are expressed as curved double-headed arrows, and left uninterpreted. *Endogenous* variables are those for which at least one causal variable is included in the model, and thus are all variables that are not exogenous. Another set of variables are the *residual* causes, usually labeled e_Y (for *error* variance) or U_Y (for *unmeasured* causes), representing the miscellaneous unknown or unmeasured ("random") causes of variables, about which our data, and perhaps our theory as well, are silent [Fig. 12.1.2(E)]. An important set of residual causes of our variables as measured in the behavioral sciences are those collectively referred to as measurement error, and including such things as day to day or moment to moment fluctuation in response probability, unclean test tubes or imperfectly standardized reagents, the impact of temporary illness or fatigue, or that miscellany of item content that is irrelevant to the main thrust of the measures included in the model.

The major analytic tool underlying the structural or path portion of structural equation modeling is MRC, and particularly regression analysis. As the number of variables causing Y increases, we enter the realm of *multiple* regression analysis. As the complexity of the model increases further, we develop systems of interlocking multiple regression analyses in which a variable may be a cause in one regression equation and an effect in another. Further complexity in the form of bidirectional causality ($X \rightarrow Y$ and $Y \rightarrow X$ simultaneously) may require that we change our methods of estimating causal relationships, but our basic tool remains the regression equation.

12.1.4 Regression Models as Causal Models

As noted, excepting models that are strictly designed for predictive purposes, many regression analyses carried out by behavioral scientists are explicitly or implicitly motivated by a causal model. However, to say that a regression equation reflects a causal model is quite different from saying that it reflects a *correct* causal model. For regression coefficients to correctly reflect the causal relationship between X and Y, any sources of spurious relationship between them must be included in the model. For a simple but clear example of the importance of this assumption we may conveniently return yet again to our fictitious academic salary example.

In the Chapter 3 example of 15 faculty members, the correlation of number of publications with salary was .588 and the regression of salary on publications was $336 per publication (see Table 3.2.1). If this value were to be accepted as an estimate of the causal effect of publications on salary (i.e., that each publication resulted on average in an increase in salary of $336), we would be making an invalid assumption, namely, that the two variables had no important causes in common. However, we saw (hardly to our surprise) that time (years) since Ph.D. was substantially correlated with both the number of publications and salary (.657 and .710 respectively). Because there is no mechanism by which either publications or salary can have caused time since Ph.D., whereas there is a plausible mechanism by which time since Ph.D. caused publications (via the academician's cumulative work) and salary (by virtue of seniority, among other mechanisms) we conclude that the causal flow must be in the opposite direction—from time since Ph.D. to publications and salary (but note the later discussion). Therefore, time since Ph.D. is likely to be a source of spurious relationship between salary and publications. Indeed when time was included in the model, the publications effect was reduced to only $122 per publication.[7]

Given the complex subject matter of the behavioral sciences and the fertile imaginations of their practitioners, nonexperimental research for which one can convince one's colleagues that there are no unmeasured common causes, and no alternative mediators of unmeasured causes of the independent variable of interest, may hardly exist. However, the relevant point

---

[7]Actually there is a possible mechanism for a causal effect of publications on years. A faculty member who publishes very little is very unlikely to get tenure. Thus, except for recent graduates, such persons will not appear in the sample, so that only very recent (as yet untenured) faculty members will have few or no publications. This mechanism illustrates how careful it is necessary to be when making generalizations from effects that appear to be chronologically later that may nevertheless have an impact on an earlier variable, especially sample composition. This problem can be eliminated if we assume that the sample, and thus the population to which we wish to generalize, is limited to tenured faculty.

is not whether there are omitted common causes, but whether their probable effect would be sufficiently large to seriously bias the estimated effects of observed variables. Does this representation of our causal models mean that there are no other variables that influence salary? Of course not. We know that politicking with the Dean, communicating offers of employment from other universities, and past and present other services to the university will have influenced the current salary. All this model is saying is that if we had measured them, these variables might be mediators of some of the effects of variables we have explicitly included in the model, or even moderators, but they would not be confounders. Some possibilities for estimating the effects that potential confounders may have on a model are given later (Section 12.4).

The problem of confounders is often referred to as the problem of correlated residuals (correlated disturbances for economists). To understand the reason for this label we return to Fig. 12.1.2(E). Here we have explicitly included causes, U_W and U_Y, that consist of all unmeasured causes of W and Y, respectively. These residual causes are included in complete causal diagrams for each endogenous variable. The effect of the residual or unmeasured causes of Y is estimated as

$$(12.1.1) \qquad U_Y = sd_Y\sqrt{(1 - R_Y^2)} = sd_{Y-\hat{Y}},$$

where the R_Y^2 is computed from all measured causes; this is the standard error of estimate (standard deviation of the residuals $Y_i - \hat{Y}_i$) estimated from measured causes. It is assumed that these unmeasured causes are uncorrelated with the measured causes. Why? Because if they were correlated with any of the measured causes their omission would bias the estimates of the effects on Y of any variable they were correlated with (usually making them larger, because redundancy is more common than suppression).

One must also assume that the remainder of the model is correctly specified (e.g., that X_1 *does* cause Y rather than the other way around).

12.2 MODELS WITHOUT RECIPROCAL CAUSATION

Thus far, the only kinds of causal models we have attempted to estimate have been those in which the variables can be fully sequenced such that no variable that is a cause of a prior variable is an effect of a subsequent variable. These models, often referred to as recursive, can be estimated by ordinary regression equations. In contrast, nonrecursive models are characterized by reciprocal causation or causal feedback loops and require more complex estimation techniques. Because models without reciprocal causation are simpler to understand and to estimate we will begin with these.

12.2.1 Direct and Indirect Effects

In Fig. 12.2.1(A) we have a model in which: V is an exogenous variable; W is caused, in part, by V; X is caused by V and W by means of direct paths, but also by V indirectly by means of its effect on W and W's effect on X. Z is caused by X, W, and V, with potential direct effects of each but also indirect effects of V by way of W, of V by way of W's effect on X, and of W by way of X. Y is caused by $X, W, V,$ and Z. For each of the four endogenous variables we have included an arrow from all unmeasured causes. The direct effect of V on W is estimated by B_{WV} and the effect of unmeasured causes on W is estimated as the standard deviation of the residuals from W predicted from $V(= sd_W\sqrt{1 - r_{WV}^2})$. The direct effects of V and W on X are estimated by $B_{XV \cdot W}$ and $B_{XW \cdot V}$, respectively, and the effect of U_X is given as $sd_X\sqrt{1 - R_{X \cdot VW}^2}$.

(A)

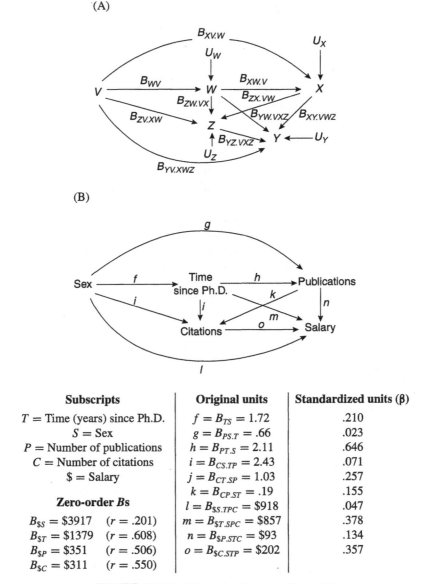

(B)

Subscripts	Original units	Standardized units (β)
T = Time (years) since Ph.D.	$f = B_{TS} = 1.72$	.210
S = Sex	$g = B_{PS.T} = .66$	.023
P = Number of publications	$h = B_{PT.S} = 2.11$	.646
C = Number of citations	$i = B_{CS.TP} = 2.43$	.071
$\$$ = Salary	$j = B_{CT.SP} = 1.03$	.257
	$k = B_{CP.ST} = .19$	.155
Zero-order Bs	$l = B_{\$S.TPC} = \$918$	.047
	$m = B_{\$T.SPC} = \$857$	.378
$B_{\$S} = \$3917 \quad (r = .201)$	$n = B_{\$P.STC} = \$93$	.134
$B_{\$T} = \$1379 \quad (r = .608)$	$o = B_{\$C.STP} = \$202$	.357
$B_{\$P} = \$351 \quad (r = .506)$		
$B_{\$C} = \$311 \quad (r = .550)$		

FIGURE 12.2.1   Illustrative five-variable model.

Similarly, the direct effects of X, W, and V on Z are $B_{ZX.WV}, B_{ZW.VX}$ and $B_{ZV.XW}$, respectively, and the direct effects on Y are estimated by the coefficients of the regression equation in which all four variables are used to estimate Y. Quite simply, then, direct effects are estimated by partial regression coefficients in equations in which all variables with direct effects (i.e., with arrows ending in the dependent variable) are included.

The estimated total effect of any variable on any other may be determined by the tracing rule, in which all single-headed arrows and sets of arrows leading from the potential cause to the effect variable are traced. In this tracing each *causal path* consisting of the *cumulative product* of the coefficients leading from the causal variable of interest (e.g., V), through other causes (e.g., W, X, Z) until the effect variable (Y) is reached constitutes one of the potential several ways in which V influences Y. These paths may be summed to determine the total effect [e.g., V affects Y by means of W ($B_{WV} \times B_{YW \cdot XZV}$), + by means of X ($B_{XV \cdot W} \times B_{YX \cdot VWZ}$), + by means of Z ($B_{ZV \cdot XW} \times B_{YZ \cdot XWV}$), + by means of W via Z ($B_{WV} \times B_{ZW \cdot VX} \times B_{YZ \cdot WVX}$), + by means of X via Z ($B_{XV} \times B_{ZX \cdot WV} \times B_{YZ \cdot WV}$), + by means of W via X via Z ($B_{WV} \times B_{XV} \times B_{ZX \cdot WV} \times B_{YZ \cdot WV}$), + by means of $B_{YV \cdot WXZ}$]. This *total* effect may be further decomposed into a *direct* effect (that is, with all other predictors partialed) and an indirect effect (the sum of all other paths). As we will see subsequently, total effects may be estimated by inclusion in a model in which only potential causes *of the causal variable X* are included, equivalently, no effects of X are included. Such a method makes determination of indirect effects by subtraction practical.

The full model for the academic salaries example, as formulated in Section 3.7, is given as Fig. 12.2.1(B). Note that this model is identical to Fig. 12.2.1(A), except that we have not drawn in the effects of unmeasured causes because they tend to clutter up the diagram and also because their coefficients are not interpreted in the same way as the Bs. (This omission of the explicit symbols representing the unmeasured causes is not strictly standard, although common, and should not be taken as representing a substantive change in the model.)

Going back to the raw data presented in Table 3.3.1 we may calculate the direct effect of sex on time (years) since Ph.D. as $f = B_{YS} = 1.72$ years, the mean sex difference. Sex and time since Ph.D. are the two variables with direct effects on publications, so g and h are estimated as $B_{PS \cdot T} = .66$ publications more for males, and 2.11 publications per year, respectively. The three direct effects on citations are $i = B_{CS \cdot TP} = 2.43$ more citations for males, $j = B_{CT \cdot SP} = 1.03$ citations per year, and $B_{CP \cdot ST} = .19$ citations per publication. Finally, the four direct effects on salary are estimated by the equation with all four IVs, previously found to yield $l = \$918$ higher for males, $m = \$857$ increase per year, $n = \$93$ per publication, and $o = \$202$ per citation. The effects on each variable coming from unmeasured causes [shown in Fig. 12.2.1(A)] are estimated by the standard deviations of the various residuals for the equations that produced the preceding estimates of direct effects.

Using the tracing rule, indirect effects are estimated by products of direct effects. Thus, the indirect effect of sex on publications is estimated by the product of the effects of sex on time (f) and the effect of time on publications (h); $fh = 1.72 (2.11) = 3.63$ or about an average of 3⅔ publications more for male faculty *attributable to their longer time in the field*.

Any other indirect effects may be similarly determined as the product of the sequence of causal estimates from a cause to an effect, that is, of all estimates that form a causal pathway from one variable to another. Thus, one causal path from sex to citations is by means of the direct effect of sex on publications g and the direct effect of publications on citations k (i.e., $gk = .125$). Another indirect effect of sex on citations is by means of the sex effect on time since Ph.D., f, and the direct effect of time on citations, j (i.e., $fj = 1.77$). The third indirect effect of sex on citations is via the indirect effect of time on citations via publications, $fhk = .690$. Indirect effects may be summed to give the total indirect effect. Thus, the total effect of sex on citations attributable to the tendency for women to have had more recent Ph.D.s and fewer publications is $.125 + 1.77 + .690 = 2.585$. We may compare this indirect effect of sex on citations with the direct effect ($l = 2.43$) and note that they are of similar magnitude, thus the mean difference of about five citations more for male faculty members was made up roughly equally of a direct effect and an indirect effect operating mostly through the tendency for women to be more recent Ph.D.s. As noted earlier, these variables through which indirect effects operate are called *mediators*; in this example the primary mediator of the sex difference in citations is time since Ph.D.

The remainder of the indirect effects may be determined in the same manner as the sum of the products of the coefficients for all causal routes from a cause to the endogenous variable in question. It is instructive to determine all indirect effects on salary in our example (see

TABLE 12.2.1
Direct, Indirect, and Spurious Effects on Salary (B and β)

	Zero-order	Spurious	Direct, indirect, and total effects
Sex	$3917 (.210)		$918 (.047)
Via citations ($= io$)		—	$491 (.025)
Via publications ($= gn + gko$)			$86 (.004)
Via time ($= fm + fhn + fjo + fhko$)			$2423 (.134)
Total effect			$= \$3917$ (.210)
Time since Ph.D.	$1379 (.608)	$36 (.016)	$857 (.378)
Via citations ($= jo$)			$209 (.092)
Via publication ($= hn + hko$)			$277 (.122)
Total effect			$= \$1343$ (.592)
Publications	$351 (.506)	$220 (.317)	$93 (.134)
Via citations ($= ko$)			$38 (.055)
Total effect			$= \$131$ (.189)
Citations	$311 (.550)	$109 (.193)	$202 (.357)
Total effect			$= \$202$ (.357)

Table 12.2.1). Sex has three kinds of indirect effects on academic salary. The first is attributable to (mediated by) the sex effect on citations, l, times o, the citation effect on salary, $(2.43)(\$202) = \$491$. Second, the indirect effect of sex via publications is the sum of two products, $gn = (.66)(93) = \$61$ plus $gko = (.66)(.19)(202) = \$25$ for a total of $86. Third, the indirect effect of sex via time is the sum of four products: fm, fhn, fjo, and $fhko$. The indirect effects of time since Ph.D. and publications may also be determined via the products of indirect paths to academic salary. Citations have no indirect effects because the model specifies that no variable except salary is an effect of citations. The various effects of a variable need not have the same sign. In this example all effects happen to be positive; however, it often happens that some direct or indirect effects are positive in sign while others are negative. Lest the details obscure the central issue, we emphasize that each causal variable X_i has a direct effect on Y, which is simply its partial regression coefficient when all other measured causes of Y are partialed: $B_{Yi \cdot 1,2..(i)...k}$ is the ordinary B from a simultaneous analysis of all the measured causes. In general, each X_i has indirect effects, found as products of regression coefficients for all paths from X_i to Y that pass through at least one other variable. The sum of the latter is the total indirect or mediated effect of X_i on Y; let us call it ΣI_i. Thus, the *total* effect of X_i, direct and indirect, is simply the sum:

$$(12.2.1) \qquad T_i = B_{Yi \cdot 1,2..(i)...k} + \sum I_i,$$

where there are k measured causes of Y.

Table 12.2.1 also gives the spurious relationship of each variable with salary. The spurious relationship of a variable can be found as the difference between the zero-order (nothing partialed) B for that variable and the total effect of that variable, thus

$$(12.2.2) \qquad \text{spurious} = B_{yi} - T_i.$$

In the case of sex, there is no spurious relationship, because its zero-order regression coefficient equals its total effect. That is because sex is the only exogenous variable, so that its entire zero-order B is an estimate of its total causal effect on salary T_S. Most of this relationship ($2999 of $3917) is indirect, that is, mediated by other measured variables.

Time since Ph.D. produces a total effect of nearly $1343 per year in increased salary. About two-thirds of this is direct, the remainder being due roughly equally to the effects of the passage of time on the production of publications and on the likelihood of citations. The spurious relationship due to the fact that sex influences both time since Ph.D. and salary is very small, as we would expect from the small (.21) correlation between sex and time (given in Table 3.5.1). As described previously, its zero-order $B_{\$T} = \$1379$ and its total effect is $1343, so its spurious effect is $36 (Table 12.2.1.)

In contrast, number of publications was quite spuriously related to salary, primarily because of its substantial (.651) relationship with time since Ph.D. What causal effect remains is primarily direct.

Finally, citations had a direct effect on salary of $202 per citation (Table 12.2.1). About one-third of its zero-order relationship was spurious, due to common causes.

This model is somewhat atypical because there was only one exogenous variable (sex), all other effects being potentially attributable, in part, to this variable. Suppose another theorist looking at this problem notes that, because the current year (say 2000) is a constant, the variable time since Ph.D. attainment is actually equivalent to the year in which the Ph.D. was obtained. This being so, this theorist prefers to think of gender and year of Ph.D. as exogenous variables, without analyzing the relationships that are dependent on their correlation. Under these circumstances, the total effect of sex would be estimated from $B_{\$S \cdot T}$, and the total effect of time would be as previously described. Indirect effects of sex via time would no longer be part of the model.

12.2.2 Path Analysis and Path Coefficients

The terms *path analysis* and *path coefficients* are among the oldest terms in causal analysis (Wright, 1921). They refer to causal models of the kind we have been describing, except that standardized regression coefficient βs are usually employed as estimates of causal effects rather than the Bs in raw units that we have been using. The use of standardized coefficients has the advantage of simplicity of exposition that ensues when one can ignore the units of measurement (or rather, when the units of measurement are all expressed in terms of the sample standard deviations). There are two circumstances in which βs are particularly useful to index the magnitude of causal effects. The first of these is when the scales on which we measure variables are arbitrary or unfamiliar. A change of one unit on a 25-point attitude scale, a 6-point psychiatric rating scale, or a 15-item neurological exam is not a readily interpretable quantity (but see Section 5.2). However, if only a few variables are arbitrarily scaled, we may wish to standardize only these and leave the remaining units intact. This is readily accomplished, given the simple relationship of Eq. (3.5.2).

The second circumstance for preferring β to B is when we wish to compare the magnitude of effects of different causes. Because unstandardized effects are generally in different units (e.g., dollars per year versus dollars per publication versus citations per publication) one cannot directly compare them. When standardized they are all in standard deviation units and therefore, in at least that sense, comparable. Confidence limits and significance tests for the difference between βs from the same equation are given in Section 3.7.

Standardized estimates of the causal paths (β) for the academic salary example in Fig. 12.2.1 are as follows: $f = .210, g = .023, h = .646, i = .071, j = .257, k = .155, l = .047, m = .378, n = .134, o = .357$. The last four of these coefficients are the direct effects on salary of the four predictors. As noted, we may wish to make direct comparisons, for example, that the effects of time since Ph.D. and citations are very similar in this sample. Note that this comparison is quite different from the $1343 per year and $202 per citation direct effects in the original units. The reason is, of course, that citations are more variable than are years. The reader may imagine what would have happened if we had coded time since Ph.D. in months. Under these conditions the B would have been $1343/12 or $112 per month, about half as large as the citation B. Obviously the underlying relationship has not changed with this change in units. Therefore, standardized units are very widely used when an important goal is comparison of the size of the effects of different variables.

The combination of these paths to determine direct and indirect effects is exactly the same as for the B coefficients, as shown in Table 12.2.1. Thus, for example, the indirect effects via citations for sex, time, and publications, respectively are $io = .025$, $jo = .092$, and $ko = .055$. In this population the direct effects of time since Ph.D. and citations on salary are roughly comparable, whereas effects of publications are estimated to be about one-third as large, and the direct effects of sex are negligible.

Nevertheless, as discussed in Section 5.2, there is good reason to prefer unstandardized estimates whenever the original units of measurement are meaningful: Bs are more stable than βs as one goes from study to study and the variability of the causal variables changes (Blalock, 1964; P. Cohen, J. Cohen, Aiken, & West, 1999; Tukey, 1974). We have already noted that B coefficients have this property of constancy in contrast with rs (Section 2.11.3); βs, like rs, change with changes in variability. It seems to us self-evident that the index of the strength of a cause, operating on any given unit, should depend only on the cause's magnitude and not on the variability of magnitudes of similar causal events with which it is analyzed. For example, the pressure exerted by a gas depends on the temperature (a unit change in temperature produces B_{PT} units change in pressure) and in no way on the variability (range) of the temperatures used in any given experiment. B_{PT} will not change over experiments, whereas β_{PT} will.

A second reason to prefer Bs lies in the very concreteness of familiar units. There is a great communication advantage to being able to speak of numbers of people, gallons, dollars, months, or even IQ points. Any forswearing of this advantage in favor of units understood only by the sophisticated is not easily justified, particularly so in the light of the relative constancy of Bs noted previously (P. Cohen, J. Cohen, Aiken, & West, 1999).

12.2.3 Hierarchical Analysis and Reduced Form Equations

As the reader can see, by this time a great deal of information about the inner workings of these variables has been made available. The analytic yield available for further theory construction and testing is far more than the single equation for all four variables produced in Chapter 3 could provide. If the cost in terms of hand calculations seems a bit high, good news is at hand. There is an easier way! One can obtain all of the detailed partitioning of effects without the necessity of multiplications, and without danger of omitting some paths, by means of a hierarchical analysis procedure. This technique, which produces what the causal analysis literature refers to as *reduced form* equations, proceeds by entering each variable in order of causal priority. The regression coefficient when the variable first enters the hierarchy is its total effect, T_i. The regression coefficient in the final equation is, as always, its direct effect. The difference between the total and direct effects is the (total) indirect effect, ΣT_i. By finding T_i as the B coefficient of X_i when it enters the equation, we can turn Eq. (12.2.1) around, and solve simply for the (total) indirect effect ΣI_i without having to compute products and their sums.

(12.2.3)
$$\sum I_i = T_i - B_{Yi \cdot 1,2..(i)...k}$$

TABLE 12.2.2
Hierarchical Analysis of Academic Salary Example

Variables in equation	$B_\$$	
Equation 1		
Sex	$3917	= total effect of sex
Equation 2		
Sex	$1494	$3917 − $1494 = $2423 = indirect of sex via time
Time since Ph.D.	$1343	= total effect of time since Ph.D.
Equation 3		
Sex	$1408	$1494 − $1408 = $86 = indirect of sex via publications
Time since Ph.D.	$1066	$1343 − $1066 = $277 = indirect of time via publications
Publications	$131	= total effect of publications
Equation 4		
Sex	$918	$1408 − $918 = $312 = indirect of sex via citations
Time since Ph.D.	$857	$1066 − $857 = $209 = indirect of time via citations
Publications	$93	$131 − $93 = $38 = indirect of publication via citations
Citations	$202	= total effect of citations

The indirect effect can be further partitioned in a hierarchical analysis by determining the change in each coefficient as a new variable is added to the equation.

To illustrate this use, in Table 12.2.2 we present the regression coefficients obtained from the hierarchical set of equations for the 62 faculty member sample. The first equation consists of only one IV because sex is the only exogenous variable. Its total effect, as we saw before, is its zero-order $B = 3917, the mean salary difference between female and male faculty. From the second equation we obtain the total effect for the newly added variable, time since Ph.D. (compare with Table 12.2.1). We may also determine the indirect effect of sex via time since Ph.D. as the change in B for sex from the preceding equation, $3917 − $1494 = $2423, as before. The third equation gives the total effect for publications and, by subtraction, the indirect effects of sex and time via publications, $86 and $277 respectively. Finally, the fourth equation yields all direct effects and, by subtraction, the indirect effects via citations. (The reader should check these to see that they do, in fact, match those calculated by the product of effects in Table 12.2.1).

The spurious relationships may be determined by Eq. (12.2.2) and are as presented in Table 12.2.1 (i.e., by finding the difference between the zero-order B and the total effect of each variable). This method works equally well for determining causal paths as β coefficients, as can be seen if the reader carries out the analyses using the correlation matrix as input.

12.2.4 Partial Causal Models and the Hierarchical Analysis of Sets

It is all too frequently the case that our efforts to construct a plausible causal model fall short of complete specification of all relationships among variables. One may be able to assert with some assurance that certain variables (set A) are causally prior to certain other variables (set B), which in turn are causally prior to yet other variables (set C). We may even be reasonably confident that there are no omitted and nontrivial common causes for variables between sets. However, we are not at all confident that there are no omitted common causes of variables within sets, nor are we able to fully specify which variables are likely causes of which others *within* sets. Still, we are extremely reluctant to give up all the analytic yield made possible by our partial knowledge about causal structure, as we would have to do if we treated all variables as exogenous and analyzed the relationships simultaneously in a single equation.

As the reader may have anticipated, it is possible to generalize the causal interpretation of coefficients generated by the hierarchical analysis of single variables to those generated by the hierarchical analysis of sets of variables, as described in Chapter 5. Assuming three sets, the first equation determines the total effect of each variable in set A by entering all of these variables into the prediction equation for Y. The second equation uses both set A and set B in the prediction of Y. The coefficients for the B variables are their total effects, and the differences between the total effects and the coefficients in the second equation for the A variables indicate the portions of these effects that are mediated by B variables. This is a "net" mediation, as it is possible that some of the k_B variables in set B are redundant with a set A variable, whereas one or more other set B variables suppress the relationship of an A variable with Y (see Section 12.1.3). Spurious effects of set B variables are determined as the difference between the k_B partial B coefficients when only set B is in the equation and the $B_{B \cdot A}$ coefficients from the second equation. The third equation, including all A, B, and C variables, provides the direct effects of all variables. Using these estimates along with the earlier equation coefficients again allows the researcher to partial the effects of each variable into total, direct, spurious, and mediated components.

What have we lost by using this not-fully-specified partial causal model? Because variables within sets are treated as exogenous *with regard to each other*, we may have underestimated (or overestimated if there is suppression) the indirect effect of some variables that actually operate via other variables *within the same set*. Nor can we attribute individual indirect effects to specific variables in a subsequent set. All other estimates are equivalent to those from a fully specified model. Because the necessity for specifying within-set relationships is avoided, this procedure may be feasible for many more problems than those that meet the full requirements of specification and identification of effects in causal analysis.

12.2.5 Testing Model Elements

Naturally, having estimated the causal parameters we will wish to determine confidence limits and significance tests against a null hypothesis of zero, or against some other theoretically expected value. These are accomplished by the same means described in Chapter 3 for partial B coefficients (or β for path coefficients.)

12.3 MODELS WITH RECIPROCAL CAUSATION

Many plausible theoretical models involve reciprocal effects of variables on one another over time. For example, pain on movement may cause individuals to cease exercise, which in turn causes the pain to increase. When these processes are present there are frequently problems in using the data to estimate effects. However, in some cases we may obtain an estimate of these effects by means of *instruments*. An instrument is a variable (e.g., W) that is related causally to only one of two variables (e.g., X and Z) that have causal effects on one another. If one has measured one or more instrumental variables for each member of this pair, it is possible to obtain an estimate of the causal effect in each direction. This can be seen in Fig. 12.3.1, where we note that the only reason for W to be correlated with Z is because of the causal effect of X on Z. Similarly, the only reason for V to be correlated with X is because of the causal effect of Z on X. Thus (using standardized estimates or path coefficients), $r_{WZ} = ab$,

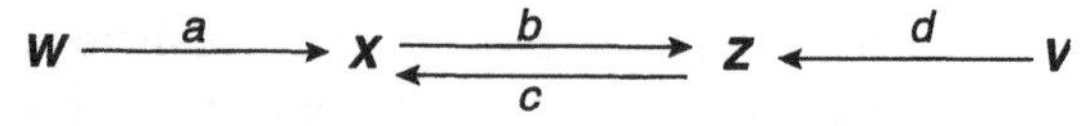

FIGURE 12.3.1   Reciprocal effects in a causal model.

and $r_{VX} = cd$. Further details on this method may be found in Bollen (1989), O. D. Duncan (1975), and Loehlin (1992).

12.4 IDENTIFICATION AND OVERIDENTIFICATION

12.4.1 Just Identified Models

In the causal models we have examined thus far there is just enough information to provide a single unique estimate of each posited causal effect. This is a characteristic of all recursive models in which every earlier cause is hypothesized to have a potential effect on every later endogenous variable. In this kind of model, the number of available correlation or covariance coefficients, $k(k-1)/2$ (where k is the total number of variables), is equal to the number of estimated causal effects between measured variables plus the number of correlations among exogenous variables.

12.4.2 Overidentification

Some of the most interesting models are those in which it is posited that certain variables have no direct effects on other endogenous variables, either because their effects are entirely mediated by other variables in the model or because any relationship between them is entirely accounted for by one or more common causes (confounders). Under these circumstances we would specify certain paths in the model as equal to zero. (However, values that are fixed in models need not necessarily be set to zero but may be set to any theoretically justified value). In the language of structural equation modeling these are called *fixed parameters*, to indicate that we posit these causal estimates to hold in the population. The causal estimates that the statistical analyses produce are called *free parameters*, reflecting the model's assertion that these may be nonzero in the population and that their exact values are unknown so that they are free to be estimated from the sample data. When there are fixed parameters in the model there will be two or more estimates of certain effects, i.e., these estimates will be overidentified. For example, in the simplest case, let us assume that our theory indicates that there is no causal connection between two predictors (IVs). In such a case, the total effect of each IV estimated by the equation in which it is the only predictor should be equal to its total effect when the other predictor is also in the equation. The fact that we have multiple ways of estimating this value allows us to determine whether the model fits the data well or not. If, for example, the estimates in the equation including both IVs as predictors of Y were very different from their zero-order estimates we would have to reconsider our causal model.

When models are overidentified we may use the maximum likelihood (ML) method of estimation rather than least squares. An advantage of the ML method is that it allows us to test the goodness of fit of our observed data to the theoretical model, using a χ^2 test with df equal (approximately) to the number of constraints we have placed on the model. Of course, what we are testing in this goodness-of-fit test is only the consistency of the data with the *fixed* parameters of the model, and the test is not influenced by the free parameters in any way. (A review of the ML method of estimating missing data in Section 11.6 may help the reader with an intuitive grasp of the way that this method "reconciles" the data-based estimates with the assumed model.) In addition to the statistical test of the goodness of fit, there are also a number of indices of goodness of fit that take into account the amount of deviation and the number of estimates being made. These are used to decide the seriousness (as opposed to the statistical significance) of the inconsistencies between the model and the data.

12.4.3 Underidentification

Underidentified models are those in which there is not enough independent information to use to estimate effects uniquely. As a result, many different numerical estimates can be made (usually an infinite number), all of which will fit the empirical data. Underidentification is often a consequence of reciprocal causation or causal feedback loops. To examine the simple case of reciprocal causation, it is clear that if the correlation between two variables X and Z is .5, this relationship is consistent with a wide range of alternative model estimates, even if there are no confounders. All or almost all of the relationship may be due to the effect of X on Z, or of Z on X, or any of the infinite number of combination of effects of each on the other that is consistent with $r = .5$, including combinations in which the sign of one effect is opposite to the sign of the other effect. In our causal model, if confined to these two variables, we must make a commitment to directionality, or to specific values if we think the relationship is reciprocal. In more complex models there can be feedback loops that are not so obvious, so that it can be difficult to determine whether the model estimates are uniquely identified or not.

A model may also be *empirically underidentified*. If relationships in a model are too small, the resulting standard errors will be too large to produce meaningful estimates. For example, in some (overidentified) models a test of whether some path can be omitted involves agreement between two or more estimates of effects. But if both of these estimates are approximately zero in the first place, the test is not informative; that is, there are no material estimates that can disagree. When certain variables are used as instruments in order to estimate nonrecursive models, the relationships of instruments to the variables for which they are instruments must be sufficiently large as to produce estimates of reciprocal causation with reasonably narrow confidence limits.

12.5 LATENT VARIABLE MODELS

One of the most important extensions of regression models over the past quarter century is the development of latent variable (LV) models, in which empirical data are used to estimate the effects of the (unmeasured) theoretical constructs themselves. The advantages of these models, when applicable, include both an estimate of effects of the error-free constructs and an overall test of the fit of the model to the data. These methods are extensions of the factor analytic model, in which the correlations or covariances among measured variables are used to derive a smaller number of dimensions, the inferred meanings of which constitute approximate matches to our theoretical constructs.

12.5.1 An Example of a Latent Variable Model

Structural equation models provide for tests of substantive theories and thus are limited in their utility to the level of development of the relevant theory. For example, thus far in this text we have treated the academic salary example as a proto-theoretical model without embedding the observed variables in a framework of more abstract or general theoretical constructs. But suppose that our interest in this topic is dictated by our theory of society's reward systems. The theory states that social rewards are a function of seniority in the system, status position, productivity, and eminence, and that the relative influence of these components varies in social subsystems. The researcher's goal in studying academic institutions is to establish the relative influence of these theoretical constructs in an academic setting so that they can eventually be compared to other settings, such as business and government. Therefore, each of the variables that we have been examining is representative of one of these theoretical elements. Salary is an aspect of the reward system, time since Ph.D. represents seniority, gender is an aspect of status position, number of publications represents productivity, and citations is our measure of eminence.

When the measured variables are placed in this framework of theoretical constructs, we can readily see that none of them is a perfect representative of its proposed theory component. Whereas time since Ph.D. may be a good indicator of seniority, it fails to take into account the fact that some faculty members may have been active in the field prior to their Ph.D.s, that others may have obtained their Ph.D.s in a part of the field which they subsequently abandoned, so that early work didn't really contribute to their seniority in their current chosen field, and that, in general, this exact measure of time in years is only an approximation to what we mean by seniority. Similarly, although salary is an important part of the reward system, it is not the only aspect of this theoretical construct, which would include "percs" such as office location and quality, deference in disputes and decisions, and rank. Clearly gender is only one aspect of status position, which may include ethnic and cultural background as well as academic subdiscipline. Productivity includes publications; however, it also has other components not measured here, including amount and quality of teaching, research project initiation and participation, academic citizenship activities such as committee and academic government work, consultation, student supervision, etc. Eminence is similarly only imperfectly measured by citations, and we might have included leadership in national organizations, awards, and job offers from other universities.

Thus it is clear that each of the measured variables is far from being a perfectly valid representation of the relevant *theoretical construct*, despite the fact that we may have measurement-error-free measures of some variables we have used in the model. That is, some measures may be perfectly accurate representations of the variable they claim to measure (e.g., sex, salary), but not perfectly accurate with regard to the construct (status position or reward). The entire theoretical model is shown in Fig. 12.5.1.

By convention, the theoretical constructs in the figure are represented as ovals or circles, and are called *latent* (or unobserved) variables. The variables that we may actually measure are represented as rectangles, and are called *manifest* (or observed) variables. Typically, the models that we estimate empirically assume that the latent variables are causes of manifest variables. Thus, the individual's productivity is a cause of the number of publications, teaching load, research activities, and academic citizenship activities. This direction of causality is not always plausible (as in the case of status, where the direction would logically flow in the opposite direction) but is usually the only means of obtaining identified estimates (see MacCallum & Browne, 1993). There are alternative ways of coping with this problem (Bollen, 1989; Bollen & Ting, 2000; P. Cohen, J. Cohen, Teresi, Velez, & Marchi, 1990), but they are beyond this introduction.

We do not mean to suggest that a researcher is likely to start out by measuring these 25 or so variables and then estimating the coefficients for the resulting model. A more likely and probably more successful approach would be to examine a segment at a time, perhaps involving two or three latent variables and three or four manifest measures of each, and then determining the adequacy of the model for these variables before going on to add or explore other segments.

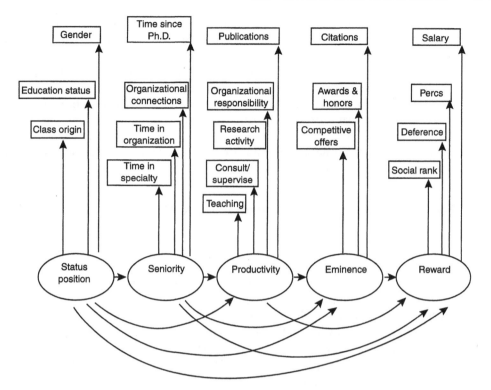

FIGURE 12.5.1   Representation of a theory of society's reward systems.

We have kept the causal sequence of the latent variables consistent with that of the manifest variables that we examined in our earlier models. It is extremely important to remember that the sequencing of these variables is a part of one's theoretical model, and thus, the empirical estimates of effects that are produced in the analyses are totally dependent on this model. Because, in general, the model may fit the observed data no better than a wide range of alternative models (for example, a model in which productivity was an effect rather than a cause of eminence), the justification of the theoretical model itself is a scientifically critical task, and distinctly different from examination of the empirical data. The empirical estimates are provisional to the theoretical framework; that is, they depend on the framework, which must itself be justified by scientific argument and reasoning as a separate operation (Abelson, 1995).

12.5.2 How Latent Variables are Estimated

As noted, latent variables are estimated by factor analytic methods. Factor analysis is a method of determining the number of dimensions, fewer than the number of observed variables, that account (in large part, although usually not entirely) for the correlations or covariance among the observed (manifest) variables. In a successful analysis these latent variables will be representative of the theoretical constructs posed by the investigator. For example, in our reward-system example, we would begin with analyses that tested the validity of the hypothesis that the relationships among the manifest variables were attributable to our theoretical latent constructs (e.g., seniority, productivity, eminence). This part of the analyses is a test of the *measurement model* for the latent variables. Relationships among these latent variables are frequently the major focus of a structural equation model (SEM) analysis. Once the measurement model is shown to be satisfactory, the analyses determine the consistency of the data with the hypothesized causal effects among the latent variables (*the structural model*).[8] Findings of good fit between this hypothesized structure and the sample data would be evidence that the model was consistent with the theory. This information would lead us to efforts to replicate the analyses in a new sample or to move on to investigate how the estimated parameters might vary in a sample from a somewhat different population. For example, support for our theoretical model in one kind of academic department might lead us to focus new studies on the issue of the relative magnitude of performance and eminence effects on reward in different professional fields or universities (as we did in Section 9.3).

12.5.3 Fixed and Free Estimates in Latent Variable Models

Regardless of the statistical program used to estimate LV models, the potential relationship between each pair of variables, whether latent or manifest, needs to be described (a) as to direction of effect, and (b) as to whether, on the basis of the hypothesized model, its value should be constrained (*fixed*, either to zero or to some nonzero value) or *free* (estimated from the empirical data). Some nonzero fixed relationships may be set on the basis of theory, as, for example, when the genetic contribution to a single gene trait is expected to be half as big for dizygotic as for monozygotic twins. In the behavioral sciences thus far, however, most fixed effects are fixed at zero, indicating that there is no (expected) direct causal impact of one variable on the other. One circumstance is when latent variables have ideal manifest variables; the latter may have no causal associations that are not mediated by the latent variable. For example, in our extended faculty reward model, we may posit that there is no relationship between academic citizenship and awards and honors that is not attributable to the relationship between productivity and eminence as more general characteristics. More theoretically informative models are those in which effects among latent variables are posited to be zero (or some other specific value) on the basis of theory. For free effects estimated on the empirical data, computer programs may also provide standard errors or confidence limits, for which the same considerations of utility apply as for models involving only observed variables.[9]

12.5.4 Goodness-of-Fit Tests of Latent Variable Models

Often when there are fixed effects, the model will be somewhat overidentified: that is, there will be more than one means of estimating some effects, or there will be an empirical implication from the observed relationships that may vary from the fixed value, so that it is possible to determine the extent to which these different estimates are consistent.[10] A χ^2 test of the goodness of fit can be made on the overall model. This test compares the model implied by the relationships among the empirical variables with the model specified by the investigator. Here the ideal outcome is a low χ^2, so that the resulting high probability value indicates a good fit between the model and the data. Very low values of χ^2 are fairly rare when the sample is sufficiently large and the model of even moderate complexity. Therefore it is usually more

---

[8]Details on the step-by-step operations used in such an analysis are provided by B. Byrne for computer programs EQS (1994), LISREL (1998), and AMOS (2000).

[9]But there are circumstances in which the program will indicate insufficient information to compute standard errors, and in any case such statistics will be subject to limits on their accuracy in situations of small sample size or failure of distributional assumptions.

[10]Although this is often true, identification in complex models can be very difficult to determine, and different sections of models may be under-, over-, or just identified.

instructive to examine indices of the overall goodness of fit of the data with the model (Byrne, 1998) which are not so influenced by sample size as is χ^2. Of course, because they only reflect the consistency of different estimates (e.g., of fixed effects with the effects implied by the empirical data) neither the χ^2 test nor the goodness-of-fit indices provide a test of the free parameters, which are typically the major interest in the study.

In general, the computer program will provide information regarding which effects have the largest differences between the model and the empirical data, that is, where the more serious sources of misspecification may be present. A researcher may then commonly free previously fixed effects, and thus move from a "confirmatory" analysis, in which a previously specified model is tested, to an "exploratory" analysis, in which the data at hand influence the specification. This practice invalidates both the χ^2 test and the usual implications of the goodness-of-fit indices, and reinforces the need for replication.

It is useful to reflect on how much more theoretically and empirically demanding an SEM with latent variables is likely to be than a regression model of the relationship of a set of observed variables to Y. A regression model is just identified—that is, it uses all the information in the variance-covariance matrix to produce unique estimates of each effect, along with appropriate standard errors or confidence limits (assuming that statistical assumptions have been met). The theorist who includes latent constructs has more potential estimates than can be uniquely provided by the empirical data—it will be underidentified unless some effects are fixed. Furthermore, effects may be fixed because a more parsimonious model is generally to be preferred. As a consequence, very often the first attempts to fit a theoretical LV model onto real data are unsuccessful—because the model is so ill-fitting that it will not converge, or because the overall index of goodness of fit is unacceptably low, or because some of the resulting estimates are grossly implausible (too low or too high, including the possibility of standardized effects greatly exceeding 1.0). These problems necessitate modification of the model, and the investigator will need to consider whether the respecifications are theoretically fatal or only in need of replication. A discussion of these issues can be found in Bollen (1989) and MacCallum (1995). In fact, a model of the complexity of Fig. 12.5.2 is almost certain to be untestable in its entirety, and the theorist must be content with examination of sections including limited numbers of manifest variables in any given analysis, with necessary respecifications being replicated in new samples.

12.5.5 Latent Variable Models and the Correction for Attenuation

What is meant when it is said that LV models provide estimates of effects of error-free variables? Perhaps the easiest way to understand it is to return to the correction for attenuation first presented in Eq. (2.10.5) by drawing a causal diagram. For the sake of simplicity we will assume that we are concerned with two observed variables, X and Y, and that Y is perfectly measured. Let us presume that the reliability of X is .7. As noted earlier, the reliability can be defined as the correlation of X with another equally reliable indicator of the "true" variable

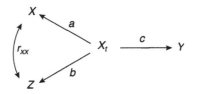

FIGURE 12.5.2 A Latent Variable as a True Score.

(e.g, in this case we have drawn in such a variable as Z). Let us now define the latent variable as X_t. The correlation of X with X_T is equal to the square root of the reliability of X. By the tracing rule we see that the correlation of X with Z, assuming that Z is equally reliable, $r_{XZ} = ab = a^2 = r_{XX}$. We also note, by the tracing rule, that $r_{XY} = ac$. Since we know that $a = \sqrt{r_{XX}}, c = r_{XY}/\sqrt{r_{XX}}$, as given in Section 2.10.2.

In LV models the estimated value of the causal effect (such as a) of the "true" LV on an observed manifest variable is a more complex function of the correlations among the different indicators and other aspects of the model, but the intention is the same, namely to produce a disattenuated estimate. The causal estimate of an LV on its measured indicator is not exactly the same as a reliability, because the indicator may be measuring *something* perfectly, but still be only an imperfect indicator of that particular LV. That is, the causal estimate is really a kind of validity coefficient, especially when the LV is a broader construct than is the measured variable.

12.5.6 Characteristics of Data Sets That Make Latent Variable Analysis the Method of Choice

Not all substantively interesting questions are suitable for LV analysis. The ideal LV model has at least three measured variables for each LV (Cliff, 1983) with intercorrelations among indicators for a given LV of at least about .5 (recalling that this correlation is the product of the two estimated reliability/validity coefficients). Thus two equally valid indicators would each have validity coefficients $\geq.7$. This usually requires that the investigation be planned from the start to include a fair amount of redundancy in measurement. The occasional practice of splitting scales into arbitrary pieces in order to have measures with high intercorrelations has little or nothing to recommend it over the simple use of disattenuated coefficients in OLS analysis, since each segment will be of lower reliability than the sum and the LV will be of no more generality than the original measure. When a latent variable is itself fairly complex, so that theoretically its influences can be seen on a number of different manifest variables, it may be useful to begin with estimating the measurement model and continue by reassigning items from each manifest variable to each of three or more composite measures. The correlations among these composites will then be fairly robust, may reasonably reflect the influence of the latent construct, and will serve the purpose of permitting estimates of effects that are adjusted for unreliability of measurement of the latent construct.

Structural equation models are most readily estimated when there are relatively few LVs—typically no more than three to five. The reasons for this are partly scientific and partly practical. The scientific reasons have to do with the difficulty of specifying all the theoretically plausible connections among the observed and latent variables in a large model, where a story needs to be woven around every pair of variables. As noted, some fixed parameters are required in order to produce an identified model, and additional fixed parameters are desired in order to provide a test of goodness of fit. The practical reasons have to do with the difficulty of generating empirical estimations when the model is complex, a difficulty that will not necessarily be solved by new generations of computer programs.

Ordinary least squares models of observed variables avoid both of these problems, but at the cost of allowing all relationships to be empirically estimated and oriented toward the single outcome variable, without regard to the causal structure and process that presumably generated them. As we have seen, hierarchical entry of predictor variables can provide some additional grist for the inferential mill. Matrices made up of disattenuated correlation coefficients may be used as input for regression models in order to estimate error-free effects. However, such a procedure is virtually never done, perhaps because the confidence limits on the resulting estimates are complex, causing difficulties in the evaluation of the likely precision of the estimated effects. As noted earlier, such a matrix may even be mathematically inconsistent.

Regardless of the method of analysis that leads to causal inference, it is important to keep in mind that other models of the same variables (charmingly referred to as "aliases") may be as consistent with the data as the model actually assessed. This is true even when there is an excellent fit between the model and the data as indicated by a goodness-of-fit index.[11] Necessarily, in these analyses as in all others, there is no substitute for replication for increasing one's confidence in the findings.

12.6 A REVIEW OF CAUSAL MODEL AND STATISTICAL ASSUMPTIONS

12.6.1 Specification Error

The empirical estimates generated in one's analyses will be appropriate estimates of causal effects if:

1. The theoretical model is correctly specified—the sequence is correct and all material sources of spurious relationships among variables have been ruled out by study design or inclusion in the model (statistical control).

2. The causal relationship is well represented by a straight line, unless provision for curvilinearity has been made.

3. Relationships are not conditional on other variables in the model, in which case the model is incomplete unless interaction terms are included.

4. Whatever causal impact prior variables (e.g., X_1 and X_2) have on subsequent variables has already taken place by the time of the assessment. If not, the estimate (e.g., of the effect of X_1 on X_4) may be too low, and other, simultaneously considered, influences may also be affected (e.g., effects of X_3 on X_4).

5. The measured variables included in the model are free of measurement error; otherwise their relationships with other variables will be, in general, too small (although partial relationships may also be too large, see Chapter 4).[12] LV models manage this problem by estimating disattenuated effects that are attributable to imperfect reliability or validity.

6. The variables included in the model are free of correlated bias such as that due to common measurement methods or information sources, or temporary influences on responses. This is really a subcategory of the assumption that all common causes involving endogenous variables are included, which is a part of (1). It is, however, particularly difficult to assess, and all too often any evidence of correlation between variables that are supposed to be related to a given latent variable is taken as indication of the influence of the latent variable, and not of, for example, correlated measurement error.

Failure of any of these assumptions to hold is *specification error*, indicating that we haven't asked quite the right questions of the data.

12.6.2 Identification Error

Specification error nearly always leads to identification error. Identification error is the mis-estimation of the magnitude of some causal parameter. Identification error can also be due

---

[11] Development of methods to determine the set of models that are consistent with both prior knowledge and the data is a very active area of research and development (e.g., Scheines, Spirtes, Glymour, Meek, & Richardson, 1998).

[12] We include this item as specification error although it might equally be thought of as an identification error.

to sampling error or to failure of the data to meet the statistical assumptions required by the estimation. If the model is correctly specified, estimates of causal effects will be unbiased and their standard errors and overall model tests will be valid if the following statistical assumptions have been met:

1. The relationships among the variables are multivariate normal (the residuals from the regressions are homoscedastic in the population), or at least a reasonable approximation thereto.
2. The sample is large enough for the central limit theorem to have ensured that the coefficients will be good estimates of population values.
3. The manifest variables are closely enough related to the latent variables to prevent empirical underidentification.

Failure to meet any of these assumptions will mean that even if we have asked the right questions we may not have the right answers. These statistical assumptions are hardly ever completely reasonable in real data sets of any complexity, and thus the real question is how far can the nonconformity of the data with the statistical model be carried before the estimates lose their meaning. These are matters of current active discussion and testing and are an extension of the same considerations discussed in Chapters 4 and 10.

12.7 COMPARISONS OF CAUSAL MODELS

As MacCallum (1995) has pointed out, all SEMs of any complexity are likely to be only approximations of the more complex and often not-fully-linear processes that operate in the real world, in addition to a variety of minor and not-so-minor violations of distributional assumptions. Thus perfect fits to real data are not to be expected (even aside from issues of sampling error), even when the theory is reasonably veridical. The evaluation of these imperfect models is made more difficult by the fact that other reasonable (or unreasonable) models may fit the data as well or better, even when a satisfactory overall fit has been found. When possible, it is desirable to examine the more theoretically compelling of these alternative models and to present them along with their goodness-of-fit indices.

12.7.1 Nested Models

When models are *nested*, that is, when one model includes all the parameters of the other, plus some additional parameters, it is possible to conduct a statistical test of whether the additional paths in aggregate improve the fit to the data. For example, in our faculty salary model, we may posit that gender has no direct effect on either citations or salary, fixing both i and l in Fig. 12.2.1 at zero. Then we can compare this model to the model in which i and l are left as free parameters, using a χ^2 test with 2 df. In the case of the 62 faculty members, this test yields a χ^2 of 3.085 ($p = .21$, NS), which is not really surprising since both of these coefficients were very small and not statistically significant in the original analysis. The only other coefficient changed in this analysis was the effect of time on citations, which was estimated at 1.03 citations per year, rather than the original 1.09 citations per year (see Fig. 12.2.1), a far from significant difference. Of course, the examination of each single estimated coefficient in a model tells us what the consequences would be of fixing that coefficient at a particular value. For example, if the confidence interval on a coefficient of 5.0 were 2.0 to 8.0, we know that fixing the value at 4 or 6 would not have much effect, but that fixing it at zero would be likely to be wrong.

For other comparisons—for example, if our theoretical model in Fig. 12.5.1 were to be revised so that rewards were considered the cause of productivity and eminence a consequence of both, the resulting models would be equally good fits (given equivalent constraints on correlations among residuals of manifest variables). Thus these observational data may not allow us to choose one theory over the other. The best hope of doing so lies in the use of experimental and longitudinal data, so that temporality may be taken into account.

12.7.2 Longitudinal Data in Causal Models

As noted at the beginning of the chapter, one of the characteristics of a cause is that it precedes the effect. When data are all gathered with regard to the same point in time it is often not possible to know about the ordering in time. Nevertheless, cross-sectional data are commonly used on the assumption that the observed relationships are representative of time-sequenced effects. This assumption may often be reasonable, but it can be particularly inappropriate when variables may have causal effects on each other and there are no available instruments that allow estimation of a nonrecursive model. Unfortunately, it is a frequent characteristic of observationally-based data that a plausible mechanism exists for each of a pair of variables to have an effect on the other. Thus, the social class–intelligence connection, the neurohormone-affect relationship, and the attitude-behavior correlation are all examples of variable pairs for which a causal relationship in either, or both, direction(s) is scientifically plausible.

When longitudinal data are available, direct estimates of each of a pair of reciprocally causal variables on the other are possible. The usual model for such analyses involves estimating the effect of variable V, measured at Time 1, on change in variable W from Time 1 to Time 2, and the effect of variable W, measured at Time 1, on change in variable V from Time 1 to Time 2. In these models the relevant equations would be

$$\hat{W}_2 = B_{W_2 . W_1} W_1 + B_{W_2 . V_1} V_1 + B_{W_2 . X} X + B_{0_{W_2}}$$

and

$$\hat{V}_2 = B_{V_2 . V_1} V_1 + B_{V_2 . W_2} W_2 + B_{V_2 . X} X + B_{0_{V_2}},$$

where subscripts identify the time of measurement and X stands for whatever covariates are appropriately included in the model. In these models, because the Time 1 measure of the dependent variable is included in the equation the effective estimate of the independent variable is on (regressed) change in the dependent variable (see Chapter 15).

These models, although often providing the best available estimates of causal relationships, are also dependent on the validity of an additional assumption, namely that the period from Time 1 to Time 2 provides an appropriate estimate of the time for these causal influences to take effect and reach a state of equilibrium, an assumption that is referred to as the stationarity assumption. This assumption may often be problematic, especially if the effect of one variable on the other takes place in a very different time frame than the effect in the opposite direction. These issues are discussed further in Chapter 15.

12.8 SUMMARY

Section 12.1 introduces the scope of the current presentation and begins with an emphasis on the indispensable role of theory in the development and testing of causal models (Sections 12.1.1 and 12.1.2). In addition to a potential cause (X) of change in some variable Y, other variables may be *confounders* of this relationship, by producing a noncausal relationship between X and Y. Yet other unmeasured variables are collectively reflected as residual causes of Y, including measurement error. Moderators are variables that modify or interact with the relationship between X and Y, and mediators are variables that "carry the influence" or reflect the mechanisms of the effect of X on Y. Suppressors are variables that restrict the influence of X

on Y. Exogenous variables are the variables that are "given" at the start of a causal model and endogenous variables are those that have at least one cause also in the model (Section 12.1.3). Section 12.1.4 discusses the use of regression equations as causal models and the critical importance of isolating the effect of a given X by including potential confounders in the model.

Section 12.2 reviews regression analytic findings as applied to causal models. It is shown that different equations will provide the materials for estimation of direct, indirect, and spurious effects on Y. Such an analysis provides a substantial informational yield on a topic. In addition to raw-unit estimates, standardized units may be employed (Section 12.2.2). Such models are traditionally called path-analytic models, and they have the advantage of a certain kind of comparability of estimates of effects of different variables. When the primary interest is in a single dependent variable, the calculations that are required for the estimation of effects of predictors can be easily carried out by hierarchical regression analysis. Such a series produces the equivalent of "reduced form equations" where the focus is on the direct and indirect effects of each IV (Section 12.2.3). Such a treatment is often useful when theory does not permit an unambiguous ordering of some of the "causes." Estimates in causal models are evaluated by the same confidence limits and significance tests shown elsewhere in the book.

When causal models include variables that have likely reciprocal effects, ordinary regression models will not permit their calculation (Section 12.3). When other variables in the model can be assumed to be causally related to only one of such a pair of variables, it may be possible to estimate the reciprocal effects by two- or three-stage least squares methods (not shown here).

The regression equations we have examined include just enough information to make a unique estimate of every coefficient in the model, they are "just-identified" (Section 12.4.1). With more complex models and multiple endogenous variables it may be that there is enough information to determine the consistency of the data with the model. A model is said to be "overidentified" when there are more covariances or correlations available to estimate the model than are actually needed, so that some are redundant. These come about by a theoretical "fixing" of some effects to a predetermined value—often zero, sometimes equal to some other value or, rarely, to some theoretically determined value. When ML methods are employed, a test of the consistency of the data with one or more models may be carried out (Section 12.4.2). Underidentification is a more serious problem, because it indicates that there is too little information for the model to be uniquely estimated—often because of obvious or not-so-obvious feedback loops in the proposed model (Section 12.4.3).

Latent variable models have been designed to estimate effects of "true" or latent variables that reflect the actual interest of the scientist. Such variables are represented by three or more "manifest" variables that owe some or all of their correlation to the influence of the latent unmeasured construct (Section 12.5). A theoretical model full of such "latent" constructs is illustrated, and fixed and free parameters and goodness-of-fit tests are discussed. It is shown that LV models represent a particular kind of correction for attenuation (Section 12.5.4). Some of the characteristics of data sets that are particularly apt for LV analysis are discussed, as well as the limits of this and alternative methods (Section 12.5.5).

The two problems of causal inference are specification and identification errors (Section 12.6). Relationships with relevant variables that are not included, problems of timing of effects, and failure to include provision for curvilinearity or interactive effects are among the errors of specification. Specification errors as well as statistical assumption failure will cause the causal estimates to be misidentified—identification error.

Often the most theoretically revealing analyses are those for which alternative models can be compared (Section 12.7). This is most easily accomplished when models are "nested" so that one model includes all the causal links of the other plus some additional links. Another interesting set of model comparisons that can be theoretically revealing arises when cross-sectional and longitudinal data address the same model.

13

Alternative Regression Models: Logistic, Poisson Regression, and the Generalized Linear Model

Throughout the text we have used the ordinary least squares regression (OLS) model. For statistical inference, OLS regression assumes that the residuals from our analysis are both normally distributed and exhibit homoscedasticity (see Section 4.3). But we are sometimes confronted with a dependent variable Y that does not result in our meeting these assumptions. For example, Y may be dichotomous, as when someone is diagnosed with a disease or not, referred to in the epidemiological literature as "case" versus "noncase" (e.g., Fleiss, 1981). Or Y may be in the form of counts of rare outcomes, for example, the number of bizarre behaviors exhibited by individuals in a given period of time. When the objects or events counted are rare (e.g., many people exhibit no bizarre behavior), many individuals have zero counts, so that the count variable Y is very positively skewed. By the nature of the dichotomous and count dependent variables, residuals from OLS regression of these dependent variables do not standardly meet OLS assumptions. In such instances the OLS regression model is not efficient and may well lead to i/naccuracies in inference. A class of statistical approaches subsumed under a broad model, the *generalized linear model* (Fahrmier & Tutz, 1994; Long, 1997; McCullagh & Nelder, 1989) has been developed to handle such dependent variables that lead to residuals that violate OLS assumptions.

In this chapter we present two statistical procedures that fall under the generalized linear model: logistic regression and Poisson regression. Having presented these procedures, we integrate them in an overview of the generalized linear model.

13.1 ORDINARY LEAST SQUARES REGRESSION REVISITED

A more formal characterization of the OLS regression model will help to frame the developments in this chapter. To reiterate, throughout the text we have used the OLS regression equation:

(13.1.1) $$\hat{Y} = B_1 X_1 + B_2 X_2 + \cdots + B_k X_k + B_0.$$

A continuous dependent variable Y is written as a linear combination (weighted sum) of a set of predictors. The predictors may be categorical or continuous. Individual predictors may

479

be functions of other predictors, as in Chapter 6 for polynomial regression where we have predictors that are powers of other predictors such as X_i^2, or in Chapter 7 for interactions where we have predictors that are products of other predictors, such as $X_i X_j$. A broader term, the *general linear model*, encompasses OLS regression and other statistical procedures, among them ANOVA.

13.1.1 Three Characteristics of Ordinary Least Squares Regression

There are three important characteristics of OLS regression. The first characteristic is the algebraic form of the model. The model is referred to as a linear model because it is *linear in the parameters*, or, equivalently, *linear in the coefficients*, that is, each predictor is merely multiplied by its regression coefficient, as in Eq. (13.1.1) (see Section 6.1.1).

The second characteristic is the *error structure* or distribution of residuals. As we stated, a critical assumption for OLS regression from the point of view of inference is that the *residuals* $(Y - \hat{Y})$ *be normally distributed*. The normal distribution has the special property that the mean and the variance of the distribution are independent. In regression, we consider the *conditional distribution of Y* for any given value of $\hat{Y}$, that is, the distribution of Y scores associated with a single predicted score, where the predicted score is a linear combination (or weighted sum) of the predictors, $\hat{Y} = B_1 X_1 + B_2 X_2 + \cdots + B_k X_k + B_0$. We assume that all these conditional distributions, one for each value of $\hat{Y}$, are normally distributed. If this is so, then the value of conditional variance of the Y scores given any value of $\hat{Y}$ is independent of the value of $\hat{Y}$. Such independence is required if our data are to exhibit *homoscedasticity*, that the conditional variance of Y at each value of $\hat{Y}$ is constant over all values of $\hat{Y}$ (see Section 4.3.1). Our inferences in OLS regression depend on these assumptions of normality and homoscedasticity, as well as on the assumption that all observations are independent.

The third characteristic is the scale of the predicted score in relation to the scale of the observed Y score. In OLS regression, the scale of the predicted score is the same as the scale of the criterion; put another way, predicted scores are in the *same units* as the observed Y. For example, in familiar OLS regression, if the observed Y is in the units of number of "pounds of weight," then the predicted score will be in those same units of "pounds of weight." It is possible, however, to have forms of a regression equation in which the units of the observed Y differ from the units of the predicted score. For example, in Poisson regression used with count data, the observed Y entered into the regression equation might be the number of aggressive acts a child carries out in a period of time; the predicted score will be in the form of the logarithm of the number of aggressive acts.

In sum, then, OLS regression with which we have worked throughout the text has three characteristics: (1) it is linear in the parameters (i.e., there is a linear equation relating the set of Xs to Y in the form of Eq. 13.2.1), (2) the errors of prediction (residuals) are assumed to be normally distributed and to exhibit homoscedasticity, and (3) the units of the predicted scores are the same as the units of the observed Y scores.

13.1.2 The Generalized Linear Model

A broad class of regression models, collectively known as the *generalized linear model* (McCullagh & Nelder, 1989), has been developed to address multiple regression with a variety of dependent variables Y like dichotomies and counts. OLS regression is one special case of the generalized linear model. Like OLS regression, all these regression models can be expressed in a form that is linear in the parameters (Section 6.1.1). Statistical methods that fall under the generalized linear model include, in addition to OLS regression, other forms of regression analyses for data that do not lead to normally distributed residuals exhibiting homoscedasticity. These methods allow for residuals, the variance of which depends on the predicted value of Y. In addition, in these methods of regression analysis, unlike OLS regression, the form of the predicted score is sometimes different from the form of the observed Y. In this chapter we focus on two examples of the generalized linear model—logistic regression for categorical outcome variables and Poisson regression for count variables that measure frequency of occurrence of rare events. We then characterize the class of generalized linear models, drawing upon logistic and Poisson regression as specific examples. We warn that the conventions for data analysis in the generalized linear model are not so well developed as for OLS regression, for example, measures of overall model fit or regression diagnostics. Where analogs to OLS regression exist, they are described, their limitations noted, and any lack of consensus about their use explained.

13.1.3 Relationship of Dichotomous and Count Dependent Variables Y to a Predictor

For any linear model, we require a dependent variable Y that is linearly related to the set of predictors. Figure 13.1.1 illustrates the relationship of a predictor to Y for three outcomes: (1) Fig. 13.1.1(A) for an ideal continuous Y linearly related to the predictor, as in OLS regression, (2) Fig. 13.1.1(B), for a binary (or dichotomous) Y, and (3) Fig. 13.1.1(C) for a count variable Y.

For a dichotomous dependent variable Y, we consider the score for one individual to be $Y = 1$ if the person exhibits a particular characteristic, $Y = 0$, otherwise; that is, we use 1 and 0 for case versus noncase, respectively. For example, consider whether an assistant professor is promoted to associate professor ($Y = 1$, for case) versus is not promoted ($Y = 0$, for noncase). It is also useful for illustrative purposes to imagine summarizing the dichotomous Y for a set of individuals as the proportion of individuals with $Y = 1$ at each value of some predictor. For example, if we examine a large pool of faculty who were considered for promotion from assistant professor to associate professor, we compute the proportion of those faculty with $Y = 1$ as a function of the number of publications (e.g., the proportion of faculty with seven publications promoted to associate professor). Figure 13.1.1(B) illustrates the likely relationship of the proportion of people classified as a case as a function of a single predictor X. The form of the relationship in Fig. 13.1.1(B), is not linear, but rather S-shaped, suggesting that probability of being a case first increases very slowly as X increases, then increases in a rather linear fashion over the midrange of X, and then reaches asymptote (flattens out) with high values of the predictor. A faculty member would hardly be promoted with none, one, or even several publications, and would very likely be promoted when the number of publications, assuming high quality, exceeds 20. In contrast to a linear model, the impact of adding a single publication on probability of promotion is not constant across the range of predictor X; in our example the effect is much stronger in the middle than at the ends of the distribution of number of publications.

We expect still a different form of the relationship of the predictor to Y if the outcome is in the form of counts (e.g., the number of times a child acts aggressively on the playground), with the predictor being scores on a teacher rating measure of aggressiveness. Figure 13.1.1(C) illustrates a typical form of such count data. There are few, if any, episodes of aggressive behavior when aggressiveness scores are low (there are many zeros on the outcome measure); but the number of aggressive acts accelerates rapidly (i.e., at a faster than linear rate) as the level on the aggressiveness predictor increases.

It is clear from Fig. 13.1.1(B) and (C) that the relationship of the observed outcome to the predictor is not linear when we have dichotomous or count data. Yet, for any linear model, including the generalized linear model, we require a predicted outcome that is linearly related

(A) For a continuous outcome variable Y, the numerical value of Y at each value of X.

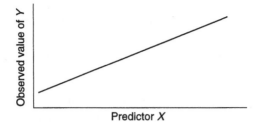

(B) For a binary outcome variable, the proportion of individuals who are "cases" (exhibit a particular outcome property) at each value of X.

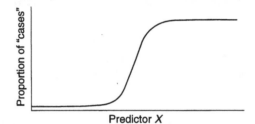

(C) For an outcome in the form of a count variable, the average number of events exhibited at each value of predictor X.

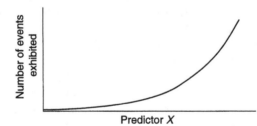

FIGURE 13.1.1 Typical form of relationship of continuous, binary, and count outcome variables to a predictor.

to the predictors. In generalized linear models we generate a predicted outcome that is, in fact, linearly related to the predictors; the linear relationship is achieved by creating a predicted score that is a monotonic but nonlinear transformation of the observed outcome.

13.2 DICHOTOMOUS OUTCOMES AND LOGISTIC REGRESSION

Beyond the continuous dependent variable Y, the most common form of Y is likely the dichotomous (binary, two category) outcome, the analysis of which we will consider in detail. The outcome for each case is dummy coded ($Y = 1$ for case; $Y = 0$ for noncase; see Chapter 8). The probability distribution associated with a dichotomous variable Y is the *binomial distribution*. The proportion P of scores with the characteristic (having values of 1) is the mean of the distribution; the variance of the distribution is a function of (depends on) P, specifically, $\text{var}(Y) = P(1 - P)$. The variance of a binomial distribution is maximum when $P = .5$. That the variance of the distribution depends on the mean of the distribution is different from the familiar normal distribution, in which the mean and variance are independent.

We begin by exploring several statistical approaches to analyzing the dichotomous dependent variable Y as a function of one or more predictors: the linear probability model, discriminant analysis, and probit and logistic regression. Using the example of promotion to associate professor, we then develop a logistic regression model that describes the probability of promotion to associate professor as a function of a single predictor X, the number of publications. In the logistic regression model, the predicted score is not itself dichotomous; we are not predicting whether someone is a case versus a noncase. Rather we are predicting a value on an *underlying variable* that we associate with each individual, the *probability of membership in the case group* (π_i). What we actually observe is the group membership (case/noncase) of each individual, but what we predict is probability of being a case. This is easier to conceptualize for assistant professors who have not yet been considered for promotion—we want to develop a regression equation that predicts the probability that they will be promoted, based on their number of publications.

Throughout the presentation of the prediction of binary outcomes we will need to distinguish three entities. The first is the probability in the population of being a case, which we will note as π_i for person i. The second is the predicted probability of being a case, based on some regression model, which we will note as $\hat{p}_i$ for person i. Third is the proportion of individuals who are cases, which we will note as P, with $Q = (1 - P)$.

13.2.1 Extending Linear Regression: The Linear Probability Model and Discriminant Analysis

First, recall the familiar linear regression model in the one-predictor case, which yields predicted scores associated with a continuous predictor:

$$(13.2.1) \qquad \hat{Y}_i = B_1 X_i + B_0.$$

All the assumptions of OLS regression operate here. In addition, in this equation, predicted scores have a range that is bounded by the actual observed scores; that is, there is no predicted score lower than the lowest observed score and no predicted score higher than the highest observed score.

The Linear Probability Model

One approach to the dichotomous criterion is merely the linear model in Eq. (13.2.1) but with the dichotomous criterion as the dependent variable, that is, OLS regression with a dichotomous criterion. This yields the *linear probability model*, a regression model in which the predicted probability that an individual is a member of the case category $\hat{p}_i$ bears a simple linear relations to the predictor:

$$(13.2.2) \qquad \hat{p}_i = B_1 X_i + B_0.$$

Again, this model is the OLS regression model; thus all the requirements of OLS regression apply.

Since the promotion variable Y is dichotomous, it follows a binomial distribution, described earlier. The arithmetic mean of Y is the proportion P of individuals in the whole sample who are cases (i.e., for whom $Y = 1$). For example, if we have 5 cases with dependent variable scores (1   0   0   1   0), the mean of these scores is .40, the proportion of "cases" in the sample. The variance of the scores in the sample is

$$P(1 - P) = .40(1 - .40) = .24.$$

There are difficulties with this model. First is that the predicted scores, which are supposed to be predicted probabilities of being a case given the value of the predictor, may fall outside the range of the observed criterion scores (i.e., may be less than zero or greater than one). Thus they cannot serve as appropriate estimates of π_i, the population probability of being a case.

Beyond this, there are complications with the residuals that may undermine inference in the linear probability model. An individual can have only one of two scores on Y, that is, $Y = 1$ or $Y = 0$. Thus, only two values of the residual r_i are possible for an individual i, with a given predicted probability $\hat{p}_i$:

Observed score	Predicted score	Residual (r_i)
1	$\hat{p}_i$	$(1 - \hat{p}_i)$
0	$\hat{p}_i$	$(0 - \hat{p}_i)$

In turn, there are two undesirable results of this constraint on the residuals:

1. The residuals exhibit heteroscedasticity. The variance of the residuals, var(r_i), is not constant across the range of the criterion but depends on the value of the predicted score. The variance of the residuals for any value of $\hat{p}_i$ is given as

(13.2.3) $$\text{var}(r_i) = \hat{p}_i(1 - \hat{p}_i).$$

Although the OLS regression coefficients will be unbiased, they will have incorrect standard errors. This problem can be remedied through the use of weighted least squares regression (see Section 4.5.4).

2. The residuals are not normally distributed. This violates a required assumption for statistical tests and the estimation of confidence intervals for individual regression coefficients in OLS regression.

Discriminant Analysis

OLS regression with a dichotomous outcome Y (i.e, the linear probability model) is mathematically equivalent to another statistical procedure called *discriminant analysis* or *discriminant function analysis*. Two-group discriminant analysis was developed by Sir Ronald Fisher in 1936 as a statistical procedure for using a set of predictors to account for the membership of individuals in one of two groups, that is, to classify individuals into groups on the basis of scores on the predictors in a way that best matched their actual classification. (For example, we might have a clinician's diagnoses of a set of psychiatric patients as well as measures on a battery of test scores on these same individuals; we could explore whether we could account for the clinician's diagnosis of each individual based on scores on the test battery.) In discriminant analysis, a set of predictors is used to generate a prediction equation, called the *linear discriminant function*, that best distinguishes between the two groups. Discriminant function analysis yields estimates of coefficients for each predictor in the linear discriminant function, called *discriminant function coefficients*, and predicted scores, which can be used for statistical classification, called *discriminant function scores*. The equivalence of OLS regression predicting a dichotomous criterion reflecting group membership and *two* group discriminant analysis is manifested in several ways. First, the F test for the significance of R^2 (the squared multiple correlation) in OLS regression yields the same value as the F test for the overall discrimination between groups in discriminant analysis. Second, the values of the OLS regression coefficients differ only by a multiplicative constant from the values of the corresponding discriminant function coefficients. Third, the tests of significance of individual regression coefficients in OLS regression are identical to the corresponding tests of significance of the discrimiant function coefficients in the discriminant function. Fourth, the predicted scores in OLS regression are correlated 1.0 with the discriminant function scores in discriminant function analysis. See Tatsuoka (1988) for a classic presentation of discriminant analysis, and Tabachnick and Fidell (2001) for a very accessible introduction.

The question may be raised as to why this chapter presents more recent statistical methods for dealing with dichotomous dependent variables Y, particularly logistic regression, when we have discriminant analysis, which is so closely related to OLS regression. The existence of discriminant analysis versus newer logistic regression reflects the ongoing evolution of statistical procedures over time, with efforts devoted to the development of statistical procedures that make assumptions that are more likely to hold true in observed data.

Discriminant analysis makes *strong* assumptions for inference that are not made in logistic regression, as outlined in a classic paper by Press and Wilson (1978). The assumptions are (a) that for each group on the dependent variable Y, the set of k predictor variables is multivariate normal, and (b) that the within-group covariance matrices are homogeneous across the groups. If these assumptions are met, then newer logistic regression is less powerful than discriminant analysis. However, only rarely are these assumptions met in practice. Violation of these assumptions may lead to a number of difficulties with inference in discriminant analysis. Thus, the current recommendation among statisticians is to use logistic regression rather than discriminant analysis in the two-group case. (As a practical rule of thumb, logistic regression and discriminant analysis will yield similar results when the split between groups is not more extreme than 80% in one group versus 20% in the other group.)

An Alternative Approach: Using a Nonlinear Model

Now consider Fig. 13.1.1(B) once again, which shows the proportion of individuals in the sample who are cases as a function of the predictor. This figure suggests that empirically the proportion of people who are cases is not expected to be linearly related to the value of X, but that the function is S-shaped; thus the linear probability model is not appropriate. Rather, Fig. 13.1.1(B) suggests that we should impose a monotonic but nonlinear function relating the predictor to the observed criterion, where the observed criterion is conceptualized as the proportion of cases at each value of the predictor. The function should be an S-shaped function that follows the form in Fig. 13.1.1(B). That is, we should employ a nonlinear model—a model in which the predicted score $\hat{p}_i$ bears a nonlinear relationship to the value of the predictor. It is this latter option that underlies the regression models that we apply to dichotomous outcomes.

13.2.2 The Nonlinear Transformation From Predictor to Predicted Scores: Probit and Logistic Transformation

To operationalize a regression model for dichotomous outcomes, we require a mathematical function that relates the predictor X to the predicted score $\hat{p}_i$ (i.e., predicted probability of being a case). A number of mathematical functions follow a form that highly resembles the S-shaped curve sketched in Fig. 13.1.1(B). Two commonly used functions are the *probit function* and the *logistic function*. The probit function is one in which the predicted probability of being a case, given a value of X, is generated from the normal curve. The logistic function is developed in detail later. The use of these functions lead to *probit regression* and *logistic regression*, respectively, two special cases of the generalized linear model.

Both the probit and logistic functions are expressions for the relationship between the predictor X and the predicted probability $\hat{p}_i$. The logistic model predominates in use in psychology and sociology, and we will focus on logistic regression. The choice of logistic over probit regression is based on various factors. First is that the logistic regression model has advantages in interpretation of regression coefficients in terms of the *odds*, that is, the ratio of the probability that an individual is a case to the probability that the person is a noncase (odds are a familiar way of expressing probabilities for those who bet on races or other sporting events). A second advantage is the simplicity of interpretation in case-control studies, in which cases are systematically sampled based on their status on the dichotomous outcome; for example, individuals with a particular disease (cases) are matched with those not having the disease (noncases or controls). The proportion of cases in the sample is typically grossly different from that in the population. Nonetheless, with logistic regression strong inferences about the magnitude of effects in the population are appropriate if certain assumptions are made. The most common application of probit regression in psychology is in the context of structural equation modeling with binary variables (see Chapter 12).

Classic sources on the analysis of dichotomous data include Agresti (1990), Fleiss (1981), and Hosmer and Lemeshow (2000). Excellent sources also include Collett (1991) and Long (1997), and the very accessible introductions by Aldrich and Nelson (1984), Menard (2001), and Pampel (2000). We draw on all these sources here. It should be noted that when prediction of dichotomous outcomes is by categorical predictors only, logistic regression is equivalent to a logit model applied to contingency tables (Fox, 1997).

Boxed Material in the Text

We caution the reader at the outset that the form of regression equations, strategies for statistical inference, fit indices, and the like are somewhat more complex in logistic and Poisson regression than in now familiar OLS regression. (The reader may benefit from reviewing Section 6.4.3 on logarithms and exponents before proceeding.) Thus, in this chapter we again adopt a strategy of putting some material into boxes to ease the presentation. The material in the boxes is typically of interest to the more mathematically inclined reader (this same stategy was employed in Chapters 4 and 6). The boxes provide supplementation to the text; the text can be read without the boxes. Boxed material is set apart by bold lines; boxes appear in the section in which the boxed material is relevant. Readers not interested in boxed material should simply skip to the beginning of the next numbered section.

13.2.3 The Logistic Regression Equation

The logistic regression equation for predicting the probability of being a case $\hat{p}_i$ from a single predictor X is given as

$$(13.2.4) \qquad \hat{p}_i = \frac{1}{1 + e^{-(B_1 X_i + B_0)}} = \frac{e^{(B_1 X_i + B_0)}}{1 + e^{(B_1 X_i + B_0)}}.$$

The expression $(B_1 X_i + B_0)$ is what we usually treat as the predicted score in a single-predictor OLS regression (see Chapter 2); it is a straightforward linear function of the value of the predictor. The logistic function given in Eq. (13.2.4) relates this score to the predicted probability of being a case $\hat{p}_i$; this is the first way in which the logistic regression equation is expressed. A plot of $\hat{p}_i$ as a function of X using Eq. (13.2.4) would generate the S-shaped curve of Fig. 13.1.1(B). Equation (13.2.4) gives two equivalent algebraic expressions for the logistic regression equation to predict $\hat{p}_i$. Both of these expressions for $\hat{p}_i$ in Eq. (13.2.4) are unfamiliar forms for a regression equation; we are accustomed to seeing the right-hand side of the regression equation as $(B_1 X_i + B_0)$.

Equation (13.2.4) is actually one of three ways in which the logistic regression equation is expressed. By algebraic manipulation we obtain the second form of the logistic regression:

(13.2.5)
$$\frac{\hat{p}_i}{1 - \hat{p}_i} = e^{(B_1 X_i + B_0)}.$$

Of particular note is that the form of the predicted score in Eq. (13.2.5) differs from that in Eq. (13.2.4). The predicted score in Eq. (13.2.5) is the odds of being a case, explained further later on.

The third form of the logistic regression is actually the natural logarithm of Eq. (13.2.5):

(13.2.6)
$$\ln\left(\frac{\hat{p}_i}{1 - \hat{p}_i}\right) = B_1 X_i + B_0.$$

The right-hand side of the logistic regression equation is now linear in X; that is, it is identical to the predictor side of the one-predictor OLS regression equation presented in Chapter 2 and given as Eq. (13.2.1). Once again, the predicted score has changed form, this time to the *logit*, the logistic probability unit.

(13.2.7)
$$\text{logit} = \ln\left(\frac{\hat{p}_i}{1 - \hat{p}_i}\right).$$

The logit is the function of the predicted probability $\hat{p}_i$ that is linearly related to the predictor X, that is, that lets the predictor side of the regression equation be linear in the parameter estimates. As we will illustrate in detail later, the logit ranges from $-\infty$ to $+\infty$ as $\hat{p}_i$ ranges from 0 to 1. Box 13.2.1 provides the algebraic manipulations to develop the three forms of the logistic regression equation.

13.2.4 Numerical Example: Three Forms of the Logistic Regression Equation

Equations (13.2.4), (13.2.5), and (13.2.6) are the three algebraically equivalent forms of the logistic regression equation. They are illustrated with a fictitious numerical example.

For example, imagine predicting the probability that an assistant professor is promoted to associate professor as a function of the number of publications. The fictitious logistic regression equation of the form of Eq. (13.2.6) predicting the logit of promotion is given as

$$\text{logit(promotion)} = B_1 \text{ (publications)} + B_0$$
$$= .39 \text{ (publications)} - 6.00,$$

where $B_1 = .39$ and $B_0 = -6.00$. Table 13.2.1 gives 31 cases who vary in number of publications from 0 to 30. In addition, the three predicted scores are given: the logit, the odds of being promoted, and the predicted probability of being promoted. The SPSS code to generate these values is provided. One additional entry shows the number of publications that would lead to a $\hat{p} = .50$ predicted probability of promotion, according to the regression equation.

BOX 13.2.1
Development of the Three Forms of the
Logistic Regression Equation

We begin with the logistic function relating some variable z_i to the predicted probability $\hat{p}_i$; this function generates the S-shaped curve of Fig. 13.1.1(B):

$$\hat{p}_i = \frac{1}{1 + e^{-z_i}}.$$

To simplify by getting rid of the negative exponent in the denominator, we multiply numerator and denominator by e^{z_i}.

$$\hat{p}_i = \frac{e^{z_i}}{e^{z_i} + (e^{z_i}e^{-(z_i)})} = \frac{e^{z_i}}{e^{z_i} + 1} = \frac{e^{z_i}}{1 + e^{z_i}}.$$

To generate the equation for a one-predictor logistic regression, we substitute the predictor side of the one-predictor regression equation $(B_1X_i + B_0)$, for z_i, which yields Eq. (13.2.4).

Equation (13.2.4) is actually one of three ways in which the logistic regression equation is expressed. Some relatively simple algebraic manipulations of the left expression of the two in Eq. (13.2.4) will convert Eq. (13.2.4) to a more usual form in which the right-hand side of the regression equation is $(B_1X_i + B_0)$. These algebraic manipulations also lead us to the other two forms besides Eq. (13.2.4) in which the logistic regression may be expressed.

We take the reciprocal of Eq. (13.2.4)

$$\frac{1}{\hat{p}_i} = 1 + e^{-(B_1X_i+B_0)}.$$

Then we move the 1 from the right hand to the left-hand side of the equation:

$$\frac{1}{\hat{p}_i} - 1 = e^{-(B_1X_i+B_0)}.$$

Then we place the expression on the left-hand side over a common denominator:

$$\frac{1 - \hat{p}_i}{\hat{p}_i} = e^{-(B_1X_i+B_0)}.$$

We take the reciprocal of both sides of the equation, yielding Eq. (13.2.5) in the text, the second form of the logistic regression equation. Then, we take the natural logarithm of of Eq. (13.2.5) to yield Eq. (13.2.6), the third form of the logistic regression equation.

In the logistic regression equation, logit(promotion) = .39 (publications) − 6.00, the $B_1 = .39$ indicates that the predicted logit increases by .39 for each increase by one in the number of publications. This can be verified in Table 13.2.1 by examining the two columns Number of publications and Logit. $B_0 = -6.00$ is the value of the predicted logit at $X = 0$ publications, which can again be seen in Table 13.2.1. These interpretations of B_1 and B_0 are identical to the interpretations of the analogous coefficients in OLS regression.

TABLE 13.2.1

Fictitious Logistic Regression Example Predicting Probability of Promotion to Associate Professor as a Function of Number of Publications

The regression equation is

$$\text{logit(promotion)} = .39 \text{ (publications)} - 6.00.$$

Case	Number of publications	Logit	Odds	Probability	
100	0	−6.00	.00	.00	
101	1	−5.61	.00	.00	
102	2	−5.22	.01	.01	
103	3	−4.83	.01	.01	
104	4	−4.44	.01	.01	
105	5	−4.05	.02	.02	
106	6	−3.66	.03	.03	
107	7	−3.27	.04	.04	
108	8	−2.88	.06	.05	
109	9	−2.49	.08	.08	
110	10	−2.10	.12	.11	
111	11	−1.71	.18	.15	
112	12	−1.32	.27	.21	
113	13	−.93	.39	.28	
114	14	−.54	.58	.37	
115	15	−.15	.86	.46	
	15.38	**.00**	**1.00**	**.50**	hypothetical case with 15.38 publications and exactly .50 probability of promotion.
116	16	.24	1.27	.56	
117	17	.63	1.88	.65	
118	18	1.02	2.77	.73	
119	19	1.41	4.10	.80	
120	20	1.80	6.05	.86	
121	21	2.19	8.94	.90	
122	22	2.58	13.20	.93	
123	23	2.97	19.49	.95	
124	24	3.36	28.79	.97	
125	25	3.75	42.52	.98	
126	26	4.14	62.80	.98	
127	27	4.53	92.76	.99	
128	28	4.92	137.00	.99	
129	29	5.31	202.35	1.00	
130	30	5.70	298.87	1.00	

SPSS code

```
compute logit = .39*publications − 6.00.
compute odds = exp(logit).
compute prob = odds/(1 + odds).
```

Equivalently, the logistic regression equation may be written in the form of Eq. (13.2.5), predicting the odds of promotion:

$$\text{odds(promotion)} = e^{(.39 \text{ publications}-6.00)}.$$

Finally, the equation may be written in the form of Eq. (13.2.4), predicting the probability of promotion:

$$\text{probability(promotion)} = \frac{1}{1 + e^{(.39 \text{ publications}-6.00)}}.$$

Three Forms of the Predicted Score

Predicted probability. In Eq. (13.2.4) the predicted score is the predicted probability $\hat{p}_i$ of being a case. In general, the predicted probability ranges from 0.0 to 1.0. In Table 13.2.1, the predicted probability of promotion is zero for assistant professors with 0 publications, and 1.00 for 30 publications. A useful value is $(-B_0/B_1)$, which gives us the value of predictor X for which the predicted probability is .50. For our example, $(-B_0/B_1) = -(-6.00)/.39 = 15.38$ is the number of publications for which the predicted probability of being promoted $= .5$, as illustrated in Table 13.2.1.

Odds. Equation (13.2.5) has the predicted odds $[\hat{p}_i/(1 - \hat{p}_i)]$ of being a case as the predicted score. Odds are defined as the ratio of the predicted probability of being a case $\hat{p}_i$ to the predicted probability of not being a case $(1 - \hat{p}_i)$. Theoretically, the odds range from 0.0 to $+\infty$ as the probability $\hat{p}_i$ ranges from 0.0 to 1.0. If the probability of being a case is exactly .50, the odds of being a case versus not being a case are exactly 1.0. The odds exceed 1.0 when the probability exceeds .5; the odds are less than 1 (but never negative), when the probability is less than .5. In Table 13.2.1, the computed odds range from .00 to 298.87. The odds are 1.00 for $X = 15.38$ publications, when $\hat{p}_i = .50$. Note that for $\hat{p}_i < .50$, the odds are less than one, though never negative; as $\hat{p}_i$ ranges from .50 to 1.00, the odds accelerate rapidly in value.

Logit. Equation (13.2.6) is the expression of the logistic regression in which the predictor side is linear in the parameters, as in OLS regression. The predicted score in this form of regression equation, that is, the logit or natural logarithm of the odds, $\ln/[\hat{p}_i/(1 - \hat{p}_i)]$, is linearly related to the predictor X. The characteristics of the logit and the relationship of the probability $\hat{p}_i$ to the logit are illustrated in Fig. 13.2.1. As the probability of being a case $\hat{p}_i$ ranges from zero to one (on the abscissa of Fig. 13.2.1), the logit theoretically ranges from $-\infty$ to $+\infty$, that is, the logit is a predicted score that potentially ranges without bound, just as in OLS regression. (Note that Fig. 13.2.1 is cast in terms of population probability π). Hence the compression of probabilities close to zero and close to one in Fig. 13.1.1(B) is eliminated in the logit. (Computationally, the logit is well behaved as $\hat{p}_i$ ranges between zero and one, but offers some computational complexities at the boundaries of $\hat{p}_i$ at exactly zero and one). The logit equals zero when $\hat{p}_i = .50$; put another way, the logit is centered at zero. Table 13.2.1 illustrates the behavior of the logit in the numerical example. The logit ranges from -6.00 to $+5.70$ as $\hat{p}_i$ ranges from zero to one. (We do not see the logit go to $-\infty$, because the actual predicted probability for zero publications is .00246, not zero; we do not see the logit go to $+\infty$ for the same reason). Box 13.2.2 explains how the predicted score is transformed from the logit to the odds to the probability.

The behavior of the logit, odds, and probability are well displayed in Table 13.2.1. To summarize, the logit takes on both negative and positive values without bound. The odds range from zero upward without bound. The probabilities naturally range from 0 to 1. When probabilities are less than .50, the odds are less than one, and the logit is negative; for probabilities greater than .5, the logit is positive and the odds greater than one. The logit varies linearly with the value of the predictor (recall the .39 additive increment to the logit for each increase of one

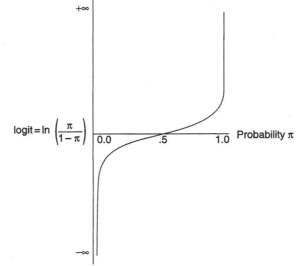

FIGURE 13.2.1 Logit $= \ln\left(\frac{\pi}{1-\pi}\right)$ as a function of the value of probability π. The logit ranges from $-\infty$ to $+\infty$ as probability ranges from 0 to 1. The logit $= 0$ when probability $= .5$.

publication). The probabilities, in contrast, do not. As the number of publications increases from zero to 10, the probability of promotion increases from only .00 to .11. As number of publications increases from 10 to 20, the probability of promotion increases dramatically from .11 to .86. Finally, the diminishing returns of publications above 23 is clearly noted, in that the probability of promotion increases from .95 to 1.00.

BOX 13.2.2
Unwinding the Logit: From Logit to Odds to Probability

The three different logistic regression equations (Eqs. 13.2.4, 13.2.5, and 13.2.6), are merely transformations of one another. Equation (13.2.6) has the most appeal from the predictor side in that it is linear in the coefficients; yet the predicted score is the unfamiliar logit.

Although the form of Eq. (13.2.6) is completely familiar on the predictor side, we might wish to couch the predicted score as the odds or the probability of being a case. We can easily compute the odds and probability from the logit. To find the odds from the logit, we simply exponentiate the logit (equivalently, find the antilog of the logit; see Section 6.4.3). This is straightforward to do. On a calculator, enter the value of the logit and hit the key marked e^x. In SPSS or other statistical packages a statement of the form COMPUTE ODDS = EXP(LOGIT) produces the odds. For example, in Table 13.2.1, with 12 publications, the logit is -1.32; the corresponding odds are $e^{-1.32} = .27$. Finally, to find the probability from the odds, we use the expression

(13.2.8)
$$\hat{p}_i = \frac{\text{odds}_i}{1 + \text{odds}_i}.$$

For example, if the odds are .27, the probability of being promoted are $.27/(1 + .27) = .21$.

13.2.5 Understanding the Coefficients for the Predictor in Logistic Regression

The coefficients for predictors in logistic regression analysis are presented in two forms in most software and in publication. First, they are presented as typical *regression coefficients* from Eq. (13.2.6). In the example of Table 13.2.1, $B_1 = .39$ and $B_0 = -.60$ are the familiar regression coefficient and regression constant. As we have shown, the B_1 coefficient indicates the linear increment in the logit for a one-unit increment in the predictor. Second, coefficients for the predictors are presented as *odds ratios:*

(13.2.9)   odds ratio for predictor $= e^B$, or, equivalently, $\exp(B)$.

An *odds ratio* is the ratio of the odds of being a case for one value of the predictor X divided by the odds of being a case for a value of X one point lower than the value of X in the numerator (see Section 6.4.3 and Box 13.2.4 for e notation). The odds ratio tells us by what amount the odds of being in the case group are *multiplied* when the predictor is incremented by a value of one unit (e.g., by how much the odds of promotion are multiplied for each additional publication). An odds ratio of 1.0 is associated with a regression coefficient $B = 0$, indicating the absence of a relationship with Y; that is, the odds of being a case are equal for subjects with any given score on X and for those with a score one unit higher. Odds ratios greater than 1.0 correspond to positive B (regression) coefficients and reflect the increase in odds of being in the case category associated with each unit increase in X. Thus an odds ratio of 1.80 indicates that the odds of being a case are multiplied by 1.80 each time X is incremented by one unit. Because the relationship is multiplicative in the odds ratio, a two-unit increase in X would be associated with $1.8 \times 1.8 = 3.24$ times the odds of being a case. Odds ratios falling between 0.0 and just below 1.0 correspond to negative B coefficients and signify that the odds of being a case decrease as predictor X increases.

Epidemiologists most often report outcomes in terms of odds ratios for each predictor rather than the value of the regression coefficients themselves. Hence, in epidemiological literature in which the probability of contracting a disease is given as a function of some risk factor, such as exposure to some chemical, the results might be stated as follows: The odds are four times higher of getting a rare form of cancer if one has been exposed versus not exposed to the chemical.

We have rewritten the form of the logistic regression equation for the odds in a slightly different way and substituted in the values of the coefficients from the numerical example in Table 13.2.1 (recall that algebraically, $r^{(s+t)} = r^s r^t = r^t r^s$; see Table 6.4.1):

(13.2.10) $$\frac{\hat{p}_i}{1 - \hat{p}_i} = e^{(B_1 X_i + B_0)} = e^{B_1 X_i} e^{B_0} = e^{B_0} e^{B_1 X_i} = e^{-6.00} e^{.39 X}$$

Suppose we examine the odds of promotion given 3 publications versus 2 publications: for 3 publications,

$$\frac{\hat{p}_i}{1 - \hat{p}_i} = e^{-6.00} e^{.39 \times 3},$$

and for 2 publications,

$$\frac{\hat{p}_i}{1 - \hat{p}_i} = e^{-6.00} e^{.39 \times 2},$$

for an odds ratio of

$$\frac{e^{-6.00} e^{.39 \times 3}}{e^{-6.00} e^{.39 \times 2}} = e^{.39} = 1.48 = \text{odds ratio.}$$

If we repeat this examination for 5 versus 4 publications, or 11 versus 10 publications, we find the value of the odds ratio to be the same. The odds of promotion are multiplied by 1.48 for each increment of 1 publication. In Table 13.2.1, for example, the odds of promotion with 10 publications are .12, and with 11 publications, .12(1.48) = .18. The odds of promotion with 16 publications are 1.27; with 17 publications, 1.27(1.48) = 1.88. In sum, when the logit is incremented by a constant additive amount, here $B_1 = .39$, the odds are multiplied by a constant amount, the odds ratio, here 1.48.

We can also consider increments in the odds when predictor X increases by more than one point. For example, an increase from 10 to 15 publications is associated with an increase in the estimated odds of promotion of $1.48^5 = 7.10$ times. Thus, since the odds of promotions with 10 publications are .12, the odds of promotion with 15 publications are $.12(1.48^5) = .12(7.10) = .85$. Note that increments in the predictor X (here, increasing in the number of publications from 10 to 15) are associated with a corresponding powering of the odds ratio (here, raising the odds ratio to the fifth power).

13.2.6 Multiple Logistic Regression

Multiple logistic regression is the straightforward extension of the univariate case, with the same three forms of the logistic regression equation:

(13.2.11)   for the logit : $\ln\left(\dfrac{\hat{p}}{1-\hat{p}}\right) = (B_1 X_1 + B_2 X_2 + \cdots + B_k X_k + B_0);$

(13.2.12)   for the odds : $\dfrac{\hat{p}}{1-\hat{p}} = e^{(B_1 X_1 + B_2 X_2 + \cdots + B_k X_k + B_0)}.$

In Eq. (13.2.10), we learned that when the logistic regression equation is in the form predicting the odds, the coefficients are multiplicative. Extending this to multiple logistic regression, an alternative expression for the odds that shows the multiplicative nature of the coefficients in predicting the odds is given as

(13.2.13)   for the odds : $\dfrac{\hat{p}}{1-\hat{p}} = e^{B_1 X_1} e^{B_2 X_2} \cdots e^{B_k X_k} e^{B_0}.$

Equations (13.2.11) and (13.2.13) illustrate the two commonly used forms of logistic regression. Equation (13.2.11) is the linear regression, which is expressed in log odds (logits). Just as in OLS regression, each of the regression coefficients in multiple logistic regression is a *partial regression coefficient*; each is interpreted adjusting for other effects in the model. Equation (13.2.13) is the multiplicative equation, in which the coefficients have been transformed to odds ratios (Section 13.2.5) and the predicted scores are odds. This reflects the mathematical relationship between original units and their logs—a relationship that is multiplicative in original units will be additive in their logs. Standard computer programs report both the linear regression coefficients from Eq. (13.2.11) and the odds ratios from Eq. (13.2.13) (equivalently Eq. 13.2.12).

Generalizing from Eq. (13.2.4) for the third form of the logistic regression equation, in which probabilities are predicted, we have the expression

(13.2.14) $\hat{p}_i = \dfrac{1}{1 + e^{-(B_1 X_1 + B_2 X_2 + \cdots + B_k X_k + B_0)}},$

or equivalently,

$$\hat{p}_i = \dfrac{e^{(B_1 X_1 + B_2 X_2 + \cdots + B_k X_k + B_0)}}{1 + e^{(B_1 X_1 + B_2 X_2 + \cdots + B_k X_k + B_0)}}.$$

Interactions and Higher Order Variables

Equation (13.2.11) shows the general form of the linear regression equation to predict the logit. Predictors in logistic regression may take the form of interactions formed as products of other predictors $X_j X_j'$ or powers of other predictors as in polynomial regression X_j^k (Greenland, 1998; Jaccard, 2001). If we consider the multiple logistic regression equation in the form of Eq. (13.2.11), we could characterize the interaction between X_1 and X_2 in predicting the logit as

$$\ln \left(\frac{\hat{p}}{1 - \hat{p}} \right) = (B_1 X_1 + B_2 X_2 + B_3 X_1 X_2 + B_0).$$

In this form, we can think of the interaction as having an impact on the *logit*, as an additive amount over and above the prediction from X_1 and X_2 alone, following the interpretation of interactions in Chapter 7. That is, for a one-unit increase in $X_1 X_2$, from which X_1 and X_2 have been partialed, the logit is increased additively by B_3 units. We can say that the regression of the logit on X_1 depends on the value of X_2 (or the converse), just as in OLS regression.

Our thinking about the interaction is different for the odds and follows our thinking about the meaning of the regression coefficients as amounts by which the odds are multiplied for a one-unit increment in a predictor. In the form of the logistic regression predicting the odds, as in Eq. (13.2.13), the interaction will appear as follows:

$$\frac{\hat{p}}{1 - \hat{p}} = e^{B_1 X_1} e^{B_2 X_2} e^{B_3 X_1 X_2} e^{B_0}.$$

For a one-unit increase in $X_1 X_2$, from which X_1 and X_2 have been partialed, the odds are multiplied by B_3 units. We can again think of the regression of the odds on X_1 as depending on the value of X_2 (or the converse); however, the model is multiplicative in the odds, and this holds for the interaction as well.

If we analyze the same data with a dichotomous outcome in both OLS and logistic regression, and the model contains an interaction, we may not find the same effects for the interaction in the two analyses. We may find an interaction in OLS but not in logistic regression or the converse. The existence of interactions depends on the scale of the dependent variable. Moving from OLS to logistic regression in essence involves changing the scale of the dependent variable as we move from a linear function shown in Fig. 13.1.1(A) to an S-shaped function as shown in Fig. 13.1.1(B). We encourage readers to trust the results of the logistic regression model, which is more suited to the properties and error structure of binary outcome data. It should be noted that discrepancies between OLS and logistic regression are an example of the broader issue of model consistency across linear versus nonlinear models (See Chapter 6). Jaccard (2001) provides an exceptionally clear explanation of the interpretation of interactions in logistic regression.

13.2.7 Numerical Example

In Table 13.2.2 we present a numerical example of the prediction of whether a woman is in compliance with mammography screening recommendations (1 = in compliance, 0 = not in compliance) from four predictors, one reflecting medical input and three reflecting a woman's psychological status with regard to screening: (1) PHYSREC, whether she has received a recommendation for mammography screening from a physician; (2) KNOWLEDG, her knowledge of breast cancer and mammography screening; (3) BENEFITS, her perception of the benefits of mammography screening for her health; and (4) BARRIERS, her perception

TABLE 13.2.2
Multiple Logistic Regression Predicting Compliance
With Mammography Screening Guidelines

I. Logistic Regression

   A. Initial Log Likelihood Function (intercept is included in the model).
       -2 log likelihood   226.473   (D_{null}, the null deviance)

   B. Prediction from four predictors.
       Estimation terminated at iteration number 4 because log likelihood decreased by
       less than .01 percent.

       -2 log likelihood   167.696   (D_k, the model deviance)

	Chi-square	df	significance	
Model chi-square	58.778	4	.001	($D_{null} - D_k$)

   C. Regression equation.

       1. Regression coefficients.

						95% CI	
Variable	B	SE	Wald χ^2	df	Significance	Lower	Upper
PHYSREC	1.842	.488	14.230	1	.001	.88	2.80
KNOWLEDG	−.079	1.074	.001	1	.941	−2.18	2.02
BENEFITS	−.544	.243	5.020	1	.025	.07	1.02
BARRIERS	−.581	.166	12.252	1	.001	−.91	−.26
Constant	−3.051	1.369	4.967	1	.026		

       2. Odds ratios.

		95% CI	
Variable	Exp(B) (odds ratio)	Lower	Upper
PHYSREC	6.311	2.42	16.44
KNOWLEDG	.924	.11	7.54
BENEFITS	1.722	1.07	2.77
BARRIERS	.559	.40	.77
Constant			

II. Discriminant Function Analysis

   A. Prediction from four predictors.
       $F(4, 159) = 16.294, p < .001$

   B. Discriminant function coefficients.

Variable	Discriminant function coefficient	t	Significance
PHYSREC	1.419	4.034	.001
KNOWLEDG	−.312	−.373	.710
BENEFITS	−.295	1.817	.071
BARRIERS	−.416	−3.530	.001
Constant	−1.424	.684	.495

of the barriers to her being screened. The data are a random sample of 175 cases from a larger sample of 615 cases in Aiken, West, Woodward, and Reno (1994); 11 cases were eliminated due to missing data, yielding 164 complete cases for analysis. Of the 164 complete cases, 46% were in compliance with screening guidelines; 69% had received a recommendation for screening from a physician.

We initially considered the relationship of each separate predictor to screening compliance. There is a powerful bivariate relationship between physician recommendation and screening compliance: Of women who had received such a recommendation for screening, 61% were in compliance, as opposed to only 14% of those who had not received such a recommendation, $\chi^2(1) = 31.67, \phi = .44, p < .01$. Both perceived benefits and perceived barriers have strong bivariate correlations with compliance, $r(162) = .36, -.41$, respectively, $p < .01$ in both cases. However, knowledge does not correlate with compliance, $r(162) = -.07$.

CH13EX01

Table 13.2.2, Part I, summarizes the results of the logistic regression. We focus first on the coefficients for the individual variables, presented in two forms, as regression coefficients and odds ratios in Parts I (C1) and I (C2), respectively. In Part I (C1), the variables are listed, with the coefficients in the linear form of the regression analysis:

$$\text{logit(compliance)} = 1.84 \text{ PHYSREC} - .08 \text{ KNOWLEDG}$$
$$+ .54 \text{ BENEFITS} - .58 \text{ BARRIERS} - 3.05.$$

Each regression coefficient is a partial regression coefficient, as in OLS regression. For physician recommendation, holding knowledge, benefits, and barriers constant, the logit increases by $B = 1.84$, when a woman has received a screening recommendation from her physician. As previously explained, the odds ratio for physician recommendation is computed by exponentiating the regression coefficient: $e^{1.842} = 6.31$. Again, partialing out knowledge, benefits, and barriers, the odds of compliance with screening recommendations increase by a factor of over 6, if the women receives a physician recommendation for a mammogram. Perceived benefits are positively related to compliance ($B = .54$), with a corresponding odds ratio greater than one, odds ratio$_{\text{benefits}} = e^{.54} = 1.72$. Perceived barriers are negatively related ($B = -.58$), with a corresponding odds ratio less than one, odds ratio$_{\text{barriers}} = .56$. Finally, knowledge is unrelated to compliance ($B = -.08$), with a corresponding odds ratio very close to one, odds ratio$_{\text{knowledge}} = .92$. Formal significance tests for individual regression coefficients are developed in Section 13.2.12.

Since the split between cases and noncases in this data set is close to equal (i.e., .46/.54 for cases to noncases), we expect very similar results from a discriminant analysis applied to the same data. Results of the discriminant analysis are given in Table 13.2.2, Part II. The discriminant function (analogous to a regression equation) that best distinguished the two groups was as follows:

$$\hat{Y}_{\text{DISCRIMINANT}} = 1.42 \text{ PHYSREC} - .31 \text{ KNOWLEDG} + .30 \text{ BENEFITS}$$
$$- .42 \text{ BARRIERS} - 1.42.$$

Overall, the groups were significantly differentiated by the discriminant function. The discriminant function coefficients for PHYSREC and BARRIERS predictors reached conventional significance levels, and the coefficient for BENEFITS approached significance. As we explore significance testing in logistic regression, we will see that the results of the discriminant analysis and the logistic regression converge. We are not surprised, since the groups are close to evenly divided into cases versus noncases.

13.2.8 Confidence Intervals on Regression Coefficients and Odds Ratios

Regression Coefficients

The estimated regression coefficients in logistic regression are asymptotically normally distributed (more about their estimation is given later). Thus, the structure of the confidence interval for a regression coefficient B_j is the same as for regression coefficients in OLS regression, as given in Chapter 2, Section 2.8.2, and in Chapter 3, Section 3.6.1.

$$(13.2.15) \qquad CI = [B_j - me \le \beta_j^* \le B_j + me],$$

where β_j^* is the population logistic regression coefficient. The margin of error $me = z_{1-\alpha/2}SE_{B_j}$. The value $z_{1-\alpha/2}$ is the familiar critical value from the z distribution, $z = 1.96$ for $\alpha = .05$, two tailed; $z = 2.58$ for $\alpha = .01$, two tailed; SE_{B_j} is the estimate of the standard error of the regression coefficient. This yields a lower limit and an upper limit of an interval within which we are $(1 - \alpha)$ percent confident that the population value β_j^* lies:

$$(13.2.16) \qquad lower = B_j - me; \quad upper = B_j + me.$$

The relationship of the ranges of the confidence intervals to significance of regression coefficients is as in OLS regression. A confidence interval for a nonsignificant coefficient will include zero; the confidence interval for a significant coefficient will not include zero. The 95% confidence intervals are given for the regression coefficients in Table 13.2.2, Part I (C1). For example, for BENEFITS, $me = z_{1-\alpha/2}SE_{B_j} = 1.96 \times .243 = .476$, so that $lower = B_j - me = .544 - .476 = .07$, and $upper = B_j + me = .544 + .476 = 1.02$. The confidence interval does not include zero; just as in OLS regression, a test of the difference of this coefficient from zero would be significant. For KNOWLEDG, $me = z_{1-\alpha/2}SE_{B_j} = 1.96 \times 1.074 = 2.104$ so that $lower = B_j - me = -.0794 - 2.104 = -2.18$, and $upper = B_j + me = -.0794 + 2.104 = 2.02$. This confidence interval includes zero, and, as in OLS regression, is associated with a nonsignificant regression coefficient.

Odds Ratios

The confidence intervals on odds ratios are not symmetric, since the odds ratio has a lower limit of zero. The upper and lower limits of the confidence interval on an odds ratio can be easily computed from the corresponding limits on the confidence interval for the regression coefficient. Each limit for an odds ratio is computed by exponentiating the limits from the confidence interval for the regression coefficient:

$$(13.2.17) \qquad odds\ lower = e^{B_j - me} \quad and \quad odds\ upper = e^{B_j + me}.$$

Again, for BENEFITS, $lower = e^{B_j - me} = e^{.07} = 1.07$, and $e^{B_j + me} = e^{1.02} = 2.77$.

Odds ratios close to 1.0 are associated with regression coefficients close to zero. The confidence interval on an odds ratio for a nonsignificant predictor will include the value of one, when the corresponding confidence interval for the regression coefficient includes the value of zero. For example, in Table 13.2.2, Part I(C2), the confidence interval on the odds ratio for knowledge is $[.11 \le$ odds ratio $\le 7.54]$, corresponding to a confidence interval on the knowledge regression coefficient itself, in Part I(C1), of $[-2.18 \le \beta_j^* \le 2.02]$. The confidence interval on an odds ratio for a negatively predicting variable will range below one when the corresponding confidence interval for the regression coefficient has negative limits. For example, in Table 13.2.2, Part I(C2), the confidence interval on the odds ratio for BARRIERS is $[.40 \le$ odds ratio $\le .77]$, corresponding to a confidence interval on the barriers regression coefficient itself, in Part I(C1), of $[-.91 \leq \beta_j^* \leq -.26]$. Finally, the confidence interval on an odds ratio for a positively predicting variable will range above one when the corresponding confidence interval for the regression coefficient has positive limits. Once again, in Part I(C2) the confidence interval on the odds ratio for BENEFITS is $[1.07 \leq \text{odds ratio} \leq 2.74]$, corresponding to an odds ratio on the benefits regression coefficient itself, in Part I(C1), of $[.07 \leq \beta_j^* \leq 1.02]$.

13.2.9 Estimation of the Regression Model: Maximum Likelihood

In OLS regression, estimated values of regression coefficients are selected that minimize the sum of squared residuals of prediction, the *least squares criterion*. The solution is an *analytic solution*; that is, there is a set of known equations from which the coefficients are calculated, the *normal equations* (see Appendix 1). In logistic regression and in other cases of the generalized linear model (e.g., Poisson regression), there is no analytic solution (i.e., there are not a set of equations from which the coefficients are derived directly). Instead, the solution to the regression coefficient estimates is *iterative*, that is, by trial and error, with each trial informed by the previous trial. A statistical criterion is specified for the coefficients to be chosen, and different values of the coefficients are tried until a set of coefficients is found that makes the solution as close to the statistical criterion as possible. The statistical criterion employed is *maximum likelihood*. We had an earlier encounter with this approach when we estimated a model for a sample for which some cases had missing data (Section 11.2.1). As in the current consideration, the estimation in that case concerned a dichotomous outcome.

The maximum likelihood concept begins with the concept of the *likelihood* of an individual or a sample. A *likelihood* for any person is a measure of how *typical* the person is of some population. The likelihood for a sample is a measure of how typical the sample is of the population. For example, we could quantify the likelihood that a woman $5'3''$ occurs in a population of women, or the likelihood of drawing a sample of women with a mean height of $5'3''$ from a population of women. Extended to regression analysis, the likelihoods under consideration are the likelihoods of individuals having particular scores on the dependent variable Y, given values on the predictors $X_1, \ldots, X_k$, and the *specific values of regression coefficients* chosen as the parameter estimates. The *maximum likelihood estimation* method provides *maximum likelihood estimates* of the regression coefficients (and their standard errors), that is, estimates that make a sample as likely or typical as possible, given values on the predictors and dependent variable Y. The computed likelihood of a sample given the maximum likelihood estimates is termed the *maximum likelihood of the sample*, typically denoted L.

In the course of maximum likelihood estimation, estimates of regression coefficients are tried, the likelihood of the sample, given the estimates, is calculated. Then the estimates are modified slightly according to a search procedure that guides the selection of regression estimates in a manner that increases the likelihood of the sample. This process is repeated, with each attempt referred to as an *iteration*. These iterations continue until the likelihood of the sample, given the set of regression coefficients, ceases to change by more than a small amount termed the *convergence* criterion. A solution has converged when the amount of change from iteration to iteration falls below the convergence criterion. Under some circumstances, convergence fails to be reached. Multicollinearity among predictors and a large number of predictors contribute to nonconvergence. A caution with maximum likelihood estimation is that estimates of the coefficients will not exist if there is *complete separation* on a predictor or set of predictors between the group coded 1 and the group coded 0 (e.g., if all cases in Table 13.2.1 with 15 or fewer publications were not promoted, and all those in with 16 or more publications were promoted).

The iterations in logistic regression (and other generalized linear models like Poisson regression) are accomplished by special mathematical algorithms. Different computer programs use different algorithms and thus may provide (usually slightly) different estimates and statistical test values. This is in contrast to OLS regression, which has a single analytic solution—any discrepancies between computer programs in OLS regression are attributable to differences in accuracy of the programs. Table 13.2.2., Part I(B) shows that the final solution is reached in four iterations for this example.

13.2.10 Deviances: Indices of Overall Fit of the Logistic Regression Model

Measures of model fit and tests of significance for logistic regression are not identical to those in OLS regression, though they are conceptually related. In familiar OLS regression, measures of variation (*sums of squares* or SS) are the building blocks of R^2 (the squared multiple correlation, index of overall fit) as well as of tests of significance of overall prediction and gain in prediction (see Section 3.6.4). For OLS regression, we have the total variation in the DV, that is $SS_Y = \Sigma(Y - M_Y)^2$; this value is a summary number of all the variation in the criterion that can potentially be accounted for by a set of predictors. We also have the predictable variation, the amount of variation in the criterion accounted for by the set of predictors, that is, $SS_{regression} = \Sigma(\hat{Y} - M_{\hat{Y}})^2$. Finally, in OLS regression we have the residual variation, or variation not accounted for by the set of predictors, that is,

$$SS_{residual} = SS_Y - SS_{regression}.$$

In logistic regression, measures of *deviance* replace the sums of squares of OLS regression as the building blocks of measures of fit and statistical tests. These measures can be thought of as analogous to sums of squares, though they do not arise from the same calculations. Each deviance measure in logistic regression is a measure of *lack of fit* of the data to a logistic regression model. Two measures of deviance are particularly useful. The first is the *null deviance*, D_{null}, which is the analog of SS_Y in OLS regression. D_{null} is a summary number of all the deviance that could potentially be accounted for. It can be thought of as a measure of lack of fit of data to a model containing an intercept but no predictors. It provides a baseline against which to compare prediction from other models that contain at least one predictor. The second is the *model deviance* from a model containing k predictors, D_k; it is the analog of $SS_{residual}$ in OLS regression. It is a summary number of all the deviance that remains to be predicted after prediction from a set of k predictors, a measure of lack of fit of the model containing k predictors. In logistic regression, if the model containing k predictors fits better than a model containing no predictors, then the model deviance should be smaller than the null deviance. This is the same idea as in OLS regression; if a set of predictors in OLS regression provides prediction, then $SS_{residual}$ after prediction should be smaller than SS_Y.

We caution here that although these analogies exist between deviance and variation (or variance), deviance is not measured in the same units as variation; thus deviances should not be referred to in writing in terms of variation or variance, a temptation into which we can easily fall when considering goodness of fit indices in logistic regression, presented in Section 13.2.11.

The deviance measures are actually built from maximum likelihoods under various logistic regression models (see Section 13.2.9 for a discussion of likelihoods). As we have said, measures of goodness of fit and test statistics in logistic regression are constructed from the deviance measures. Since the deviance measures are derived from ratios of maximum likelihoods under different models, the statistical tests built on deviances are referred to collectively as *likelihood ratio tests*. A full explanation of the development of deviance measures from maximum likelihoods and likelihood ratios is given in Box 13.2.3. Because of the way in which deviances are structured from likelihoods, standard notation for deviance in many regression texts and computer output is $-2LL$ or -2 *log likelihood*.

An examination of the deviances associated with the mammography screening example in Table 13.2.2 provides some intuition about how we use deviances. In Table 13.2.2, Part I(A), the null deviance, $D_{\text{null}} = 226.47$, from a model containing only the intercept and no predictors. In Table 13.2.2, Part I(B), the model deviance, $D_k = 167.70$ when the four predictors are included in the regression equation. That D_k is smaller than D_{null} tells us that the four predictors collectively contributed to prediction of the DV. Again, model deviance is a measure of lack of fit, or what is left to predict after the inclusion of k predictors.

BOX 13.2.3
Maximum Likelihoods, Likelihood Ratios, and Deviances

Measures of deviance are developed from maximum likelihoods under various regression models. Maximum likelihoods from different models are formed into likelihood ratios. Deviances are then defined as a function of differences between likelihood ratios. The series of steps in the development of deviances is explained here.

Maximum Likelihoods for Varying Models

The likelihood of scores on the dependent variable Y, given scores on the predictors and the set of regression coefficients, varies as a function of the predictors included. For any regression model with a given set of predictors, there is a *maximum likelihood* that can be obtained, given the values of the regression coefficients. Three different maximum likelihoods are used in the development of measures of overall fit and statistical significance of fit in logistic regression.

1. *Maximum likelihood of sample under a perfectly fitting model.* A theoretical model with perfect fit forms the basis of comparison for the fit of other models. Conceptually, such a model has as many predictors as cases. The maximum likelihood under this perfectly fitting model is 1.0, the highest possible.

L_{perfect} = maximum likelihood of sample under a perfectly fitting model = 1.0.

2. *Maximum likelihood of sample under model containing only an intercept.* We define a maximum likelihood under the assumption that the outcomes on Y are randomly related to set of predictors X. We do so by defining a *null* model that contains *only an intercept*. The predicted probability for each individual is the base rate of cases in the sample; the predictors offer no differentiation among cases whatever, the worst possible fit.

L_{null} = maximum likelihood of sample, given null model containing only an intercept, lowest maximum likelihood under any possible model.

3. *Maximum likelihood of sample under model containing intercept plus k predictors.* We compute the maximum likelihood of a sample for any model

containing the intercept plus k predictors.

L_k = maximum likelihood of a sample under a model containing intercept plus k predictors.

We use this likelihood to assess the goodness of prediction from the model containing the intercept plus k predictors.

Likelihood Ratio

A *likelihood ratio* is a ratio of two maximum likelihoods, typically under one model versus under a more complete model (i.e., with more predictors):

(13.2.18) $\text{likelihood ratio} = \dfrac{\text{maximum likelihood under one model}}{\text{maximum likelihood under more complete model}}.$

Deviance

The deviance is a measure of lack of fit of one model compared to another model. The deviance is defined as minus twice the value of the log of the likelihood ratio, and is abbreviated as $-2LL$ in various texts.

(13.2.19) $\text{deviance} = -2LL = -2\ln(\text{likelihood ratio})$

$$= -2\ln\left(\frac{\text{maximum likelihood under one model}}{\text{maximum likelihood under more complete model}}\right).$$

Given that $\ln(a/b) = \ln(a) - \ln(b)$, the expression for deviance can also be written as

(13.2.20) $\text{deviance} = -2LL = -2\ln(\text{likelihood ratio})$

$$= -2[\ln(\text{maximum likelihood under model})$$

$$- \ln(\text{maximum likelihood under more complete model})].$$

Deviances contrast maximum likelihoods under various models. The larger the value of deviance for a particular model, the worse the model; that is, deviances are measures of "badness of fit." The specific deviance calculations we present here have direct analogies to familiar measures of total variation SS_Y and residual variation SS_{residual} in OLS regression.

D_{null}, the Null Deviance

The null deviance D_{null} contrasts the maximum likelihood L_{null} under the model containing only the intercept with the maximum likelihood L_{perfect} under the theoretically perfectly fitting model:

(13.2.21)   null deviance: $D_{\text{null}} = -2[\ln(L_{\text{null}}) - \ln(L_{\text{perfect}})].$

This null deviance is analogous to SS_Y, the total variation in the dependent variable Y, from OLS regression. The null deviance measures the discrepancy from the worst possible to the best possible model, all the discrepancy for which it is possible that a model account.

(Continued)

D_k, the Model Deviance

The model deviance D_k contrasts the maximum likelihood L_k under the model containing a set of k predictors with the maximum likelihood L_{perfect} under the theoretical perfectly fitting model:

(13.2.22)   model deviance: $D_k = -2[\ln(L_k) - \ln(L_{\text{perfect}})]$.

The model deviance is analogous to SS_{residual} from ordinary least squares regression. This deviance measures the amount of the lack of fit that remains after modeling with k predictors, a measure of badness of fit. We expect this value to decrease as we include useful predictors in the regression equation.

13.2.11 Multiple R^2 Analogs in Logistic Regression

In OLS regression we have the squared multiple correlation, R^2 as a single agreed upon measure of goodness of fit of the model, the proportion of total variation in the criterion accounted for by a set of predictors. No single agreed upon index of goodness of fit exists in logistic regression. Instead a number have been defined (see reviews in Estrella, 1998, and Long, 1997; Hosmer and Lemeshow (2000) present a current review). These indices are sometimes referred to as *Pseudo-R^2s*. None of the measures is without limitations, yielding no clear choice for logistic regression. None of these indices is a goodness of fit measure in the sense of having an interpretation as "proportion of variance accounted for," as in OLS regression (more about this later). We present three such indices, the first of which is in common use, the second and third of which will enjoy increasing use now that they are part of standard computer output. Additional information about the relationship of these measures to the likelihoods defined in Box 13.2.3 is given in Box 13.2.4.

R_L^2

A commonly used index in logistic regression (Menard, 2000) follows the form of R^2 from OLS regression, that is, $R^2 = (SS_{\text{total}} - SS_{\text{residual}})/SS_{\text{total}}$, and employs the deviance measures based on measures of likelihood,

(13.2.23) $$R_L^2 = \frac{D_{\text{null}} - D_k}{D_{\text{null}}}$$

R_L^2 ranges between zero and one.[1] The measure is easily calculated from the deviance measures ($-2LL$ measures) from the null model and the model containing k predictors. Simulation work by Estrella (1998) suggests that this measure does not increase monotonically with increases in the odds ratio in the single-predictor case.

Cox and Snell Index

Cox and Snell (1989) offered a second index of overall goodness of model fit that is related to R^2 from OLS regression. The Cox and Snell index is problematic however, in that it does not have a maximum value of one, but rather reaches a maximum value of .75 when the proportion of cases in the sample equals .5.

---

[1] R_L^2 has the same in structure as the normed fit index (NFI) proposed by Bentler and Bonett (1980) in the structural equation modeling context.

Nagelkerke Index

To ameliorate the difficulties with the Cox and Snell index, Nagelkerke (1991) proposed a third measure of overall goodness of fit. The Nagelkerke index corrects the Cox and Snell index by dividing the Cox and Snell index by the maximum possible value that it can attain for a given proportion of cases. Both the Cox and Snell and the Nagelkerke measures are reported in SPSS.

Table 13.2.3 summarizes three R^2 analogs (R_L^2, Cox and Snell, and Nagelkerke) using the example from Table 13.2.2. The null deviance for this model was $D_{\text{null}} = 226.473$. The model deviance for a model containing only the PHYSREC predictor (not given in Table 13.2.2), was $D_{\text{PHYSREC}} = 191.869$, and that containing the four predictors (PHYSREC, KNOWLEDG, BENEFITS, BARRIERS) was $D_4 = 167.696$. R_L^2 for the four predictor model from Eq. (13.2.23) = $(226.473 - 167.696)/226.473 = .26$, or 26% of the null deviance accounted for by the set of predictors (notice that we are careful to avoid referring to this as a "variance accounted for"). We are tempted to think of this as an effect size measure, scaled in the same manner as R^2 from OLS regression, but the two are not directly the same measure. An inspection of Table 13.2.3 shows the substantial differences in the values of the R_L^2, Cox and Snell, and Nagelkerke indices. The R_L^2 and Cox and Snell measures show much closer agreement with one another than either does with the Nagelkerke index. The Nagelkerke index will always be larger than Cox and Snell, because, as explained earlier, the Nagelkerke index corrects for the fact that Cox and Snell does not reach a theoretical maximum of 1.0. Publications employing these measures should clearly indicate which is being used. If the Nagelkerke index is reported, it is important to explain that the index is adjusted so that the maximum value it can attain is 1.00, an appropriate adjustment relative to Cox and Snell.

Why These Aren't "Variance Accounted For" Measures

Again, we caution that all these indices are not goodness of fit indices in the sense of "proportion of variance accounted for," in contrast to R^2 in OLS regression. This seems puzzling, perhaps, but the explanation is straightforward. Reflect for a moment on the OLS regression model, which assumes homoscedasticity—the same error variance for every value of the criterion. Given homoscedasticity, we are able to think of the total proportion of variance that is error variance in a universal sense, across the full range of Y. In contrast, in logistic regression, we have inherent heteroscedasticity, with a different error variance for each different value of the predicted score $\hat{p}_i$ (recall Eq. 13.2.3). For each value of $\hat{p}_i$, then, we would have a different measure of variance accounted for if we were to apply the R^2 analogs to different portions of

TABLE 13.2.3
Measures of Fit for the Example in Table 13.2.2.
Predicting Mammography Compliance

		Measure of fit	
Variables in equation	R_L^2	Cox and Snell	Nagelkerke
PHYSREC alone	.15	.19	.25
PHYSREC, KNOWLEDG	.15	.19	.26
PHYSREC, KNOWLEDG, BENEFITS, BARRIERS	.26	.30	.40

the range of $\hat{p}_i$. Thus, we cannot talk about variance accounted for in a universal sense for logistic regression.

Use of goodness of fit indices in logistic regression is by no means universal as it is in OLS regression, where reporting of R^2 is standard. Traditional users of logistic regression focus on odds ratios for individual predictors. For example, epidemiologists use logistic regression to develop models of specific risk factors for disease. In contrast, psychologists seek overall fit indices based on their grounding in OLS regression. The logistic R^2 analogs are generally not so well behaved statistically as is R^2 in OLS regression. The logistic analogs may fail to reach a maximum of 1; they may fail to track the odds ratios as indices of strength of prediction from individual predictors. According to Hosmer and Lemeshow (2000) the logistic R^2 measures for good logistic regression models are generally smaller than R^2 for good models in OLS regression; this may lead to misperception of logistic regression results as indicating poor models.

13.2.12 Testing Significance of Overall Model Fit: The Likelihood Ratio Test and the Test of Model Deviance

Likelihood Ratio Test of Contribution of the Predictor Set

In OLS regression we have an overall F test for the significance of prediction from the set of k predictors, given in Eq. (3.6.7). The analog to this test in logistic regression is a likelihood ratio χ^2 test for overall model fit.

Recall that in OLS regression, $SS_{regression} = SS_Y - SS_{residual}$, with k degrees of freedom. In logistic regression, we compute a difference between the null and model deviances. This difference is a measure of amount of the null deviance (total deviance that might be accounted for) that is accounted for by a model containing k predictors. The difference is frequently noted as G, for goodness of fit or model prediction:

$$(13.2.24) \qquad G = \text{model } \chi^2 = D_{null} - D_k.$$

BOX 13.2.4
Fit Indices in Terms of Likelihoods

The R_L^2 and Cox and Snell indices of overall model goodness of fit discussed in Section 13.2.11 can be expressed in terms of likelihoods defined in Box 13.2.3. R_L^2 is expressed in terms of likelihoods as follows:

$$(13.2.25) \qquad R_L^2 = \frac{\ln L_k - \ln L_{null}}{\ln L_k - \ln L_{perfect}}$$

This expression is algebraically equivalent to $R_L^2 = (D_{null} - D_k)/D_{null}$ given in Eq. (13.2.23) and is presented in lieu of Eq. (13.2.23) in some texts (e.g., Hosmer and Lemeshow, 2000, which refers to the index as R_{LS}^2).

The Cox and Snell (1989) index of goodness of fit reflects the exact relationship between R^2 and the likelihood ratio statistic in a linear model with normally distributed errors and is given as

$$(13.2.26) \qquad R_{\text{Cox Snell}}^2 = 1 - (L_{null}/L_k)^{2/n}.$$

This measure is distributed as χ^2 with k degrees of freedom, where k is the number of predictors, or, equivalently, the difference in degrees of freedom of the null deviance versus the model deviance. G is a test of the simultaneous contribution of the set of k predictors to the prediction of the dichotomous DV. It can be thought of as a measure of "goodness of contribution from the predictor set." In Table 13.2.2, Part I(B), the model chi square is $G = 226.473 - 167.696 = 58.778$, with $k = 4$ degrees of freedom for the four predictors, and is significant at beyond conventional levels.

As we showed in Box 13.2.3, the null and model deviance are calculated from likelihood ratios. In general, tests that involve likelihood ratios in their calculation are referred to as *likelihood ratio tests* (standardly abbreviated LR); the G statistic in Eq. (13.2.24) is a likelihood ratio test. This test is not the familiar *Pearson* χ^2 test based on contingency tables. Both the likelihood ratio χ^2 test and the Pearson χ^2 test can be computed for logistic regression; both are compared to the same χ^2 critical values for significance. Both are often reported in standard computer output. These two measures depend on different mathematical formulations of the residuals from a logistic regression, as explained in Box 13.2.7. Reporting of the LR tests of model fit in publication is standard practice.[2] Other tests of overall model fit in logistic regression are described in Box 13.2.5.

Is There More Deviance to Be Accounted For:
A Test of Model Deviance

The likelihood ratio test we have just considered assesses the contribution to prediction from a set of k predictors, a test of goodness of fit of the k-predictor model. It leaves open the question of whether there is still more deviance that can be accounted for after the inclusion of the k predictors. In work in model testing—for example, in structural equation modeling, introduced in Chapter 12—there is a focus on testing whether models are adequate or whether they leave significant proportions of deviance unaccounted for. Analogous testing of failure of model fit can be carried out in logistic regression. The G statistic developed earlier tells us whether our model containing a set of predictors is better than the null model; here we learn whether the model provides less than perfect fit.

Model deviance, D_k, is a measure of lack of fit to a model including k predictors. In the numerical example in Table 13.2.2, Part I(B), the model deviance $= 167.696$ with all four predictors in the model. We may test the *null* hypothesis that this model deviance does not differ from that expected by chance alone. The corresponding alternate hypothesis is that the model deviance is systematically larger than expected by chance alone, indicating failure of the predictors to account completely for the criterion (i.e., there is room for improvement in prediction). Here, failure to reject the null hypothesis is the desired outcome to support the adequacy of the regression model. (Note that this is the opposite of classic hypothesis

---

[2]Deviances are labeled "−2 log likelihood" and "−2 log L" in SPSS and SAS, respectively. Deviances carry these labels wherever they appear in output. Both SPSS and SAS begin with a model that contains only the intercept and provide the value of D_{null}, the deviance with the intercept only. Both SPSS and SAS for any particular logistic regression equation containing k predictors provide the value of D_k. For each regression equation, both SPSS and SAS provide a LR χ^2 test of the significance of contribution of the set of predictors to prediction. These tests are labeled "Model chi square" in SPSS and "chi square for covariates" in SAS. SAS also provides the Akaike Information Criterion (labeled AIC) and the Score test (so labeled) as well. SPSS refers to the regression coefficients for predicting the logit from Eq. (13.2.6) as "B"; SAS, as "parameter estimates." SPSS refers to odds ratios as "Exp(B)"; SAS, as "Odds Ratio." There is an important discrepancy between SPSS and SAS. If one codes case $= 1$, noncase $= 0$, then SPSS by default will predict being a case, whereas SAS will predict being a noncase. Hence, all the coefficients will be of opposite sign in the SPSS versus SAS output, and odds ratios will be inverted; the keyword *descending* in SAS causes SAS to predict being the probability of being a case ($Y = 1$), consistent with SPSS.

testing, in which rejection of the null hypothesis supports the research hypothesis.) The actual value of the model deviance value is tested for significance against a χ^2 distribution with $[n - (k + 1)]\ df$, where k is the number of predictors, not including the intercept.

For our numerical example, the critical value for the model deviance has $[n - (k + 1)] = [164 - (4 + 1)] = 159\ df$ and is $\chi^2_{.95}(159) = 189.42$; the model deviance $D_k = 167.696$. We do not reject the null hypothesis, and we interpret this as indicating that the four predictors are adequate to account for mammography screening compliance. There is not a significant amount of unaccounted for deviance remaining after prediction from the four predictors.

Sparseness of Data and Tests of Model Adequacy

There is concern that statistical tests in logistic regression may encounter difficulties if data are sparse. To understand sparseness, conceptualize the data of logistic regression as falling into cells defined by a combination of the dependent variable and values of the predictor. In the mammography screening example PHYSREC takes on two values (1, 0) and BENEFITS takes on six values (0, 5) as predictors. Compliance (1, 0) taking on two values as the DV. Thus we have $2 \times 6 \times 2 = 24$ cells. Sparseness refers to having zero frequencies or very small frequencies in some of these cells. With regard to sparseness of data, likelihood ratio tests like G in Eq. (13.2.6) that are based on differences in deviances are not affected when data are sparse. However, with sparse data, the χ^2 test of model deviance just described is no longer distributed as χ^2 and p values from the χ^2 distribution are no longer accurate. In fact, the test of model deviance for the mammography example is subject to the problem of sparseness and should not be trusted.

BOX 13.2.5
The Wald Test, the Score Test, and the Hosmer-Lemeshow
Index of Fit

In addition to the likelihood ratio test G described in Section 13.2.12 for overall model fit, there are two other tests, the Wald test and the Score test, that may be applied to testing whether a set of predictors contributes to prediction of an outcome. The Score test is also known as the LaGrange multiplier (LM) test. Both the Score and Wald tests are based on the distribution of likelihoods as a function of the values of estimates of the regression coefficients. Long (1997) provides an extended discussion of model testing in generalized linear models.

Hosmer and Lemeshow (2000) provide an additional goodness of fit test that examines whether the S-shaped function of the logistic regression is appropriate for the observed data. It is based on the familiar Pearson χ^2 in which observed frequencies (f_o) are compared to expected frequencies (f_e) qunder a model. The basis of the test is the predicted probabilities $\hat{p}_i$ of being a case. Data are broken into g categories, and the expected frequency of cases versus noncases in each category based on the $\hat{p}_i$s are computed. The Hosmer and Lemeshow goodness of fit statistic is the Pearson χ^2 for the 2 (case, noncase) by g (categories) table, with $g - 2\ df$. Nonsignificance indicates the fit of observed frequencies of cases in the categories compared to those expected based on the logistic regression. The validity of the test of fit depends on there being large expected frequences in all cells; the power of the test is not high for sample sizes less than 400 (Hosmer and Lemeshow, 2000).

13.2.13 χ^2 Test for the Significance of a Single Predictor in a Multiple Logistic Regression Equation

In OLS regression, we test whether each individual predictor contributes to overall prediction. The test of contribution of an individual predictor in OLS regression is actually an F test of the increment in $SS_{regression}$ by the inclusion of that variable, over and above all other variables. This F test (with degrees of freedom $= 1$, $df_{residual}$) is the square of the t test for an individual predictor (with degrees of freedom $= df_{residual}$). The t test is defined as the ratio of the predictor to the estimate of its standard error.

Likelihood Ratio Test

In logistic regression, the direct analogy to the OLS F test of gain of prediction for a single predictor is defined on the basis of the difference in model deviances for the model containing k predictors and one containing $(k - 1)$ predictors, with the predictor in question eliminated. This yields a likelihood ratio χ^2 test with 1 df.

(13.2.27) contribution of individual predictor $= D_{(k-1)} - D_k$, with 1 degree of freedom to multiple logistic regression.

Suppose we wished to compute such measures for each of the four predictors in Table 13.2.2, Part I(C). We would require four further regression analyses, each containing only three predictors. These three predictor equations are compared to the four-predictor equation to test for the increment in prediction from the addition of a single predictor. These three predictor regressions, each eliminating a different predictor, are actually not shown in Table 13.2.2; results of these analyses are reported here. For example, with PHYSREC eliminated, the model deviance from the remaining three predictors (BENEFITS, BARRIERS, KNOWLEDG) was $D_{(k-1)} = 184.368$. With all four predictors including PHYSREC in the model, the model deviance was $D_k = 167.696$, as before, so that $\chi^2(1) = 184.368 - 167.696 = 16.672, p < .01$. The χ^2 values for BENEFITS and BARRIERS are 5.287 ($p < .05$), and 13.770 ($p < .01$), respectively. The test for KNOWLEDG does not reach a conventional significance level, $\chi^2(1) = .005$.

Wald Tests

The likelihood ratio χ^2 test just described is the preferred test for the impact of individual predictors in a set of predictors. However, standard computer programs, among them SPSS and SAS, report Wald tests instead for individual predictors. The Wald statistic reported in SPSS and SAS is the ratio of square of the estimate of the regression coefficient B_j to the square of the estimate of its standard error SE_{B_j}

(13.2.28) $$\text{Wald statistic} = \frac{B_j^2}{SE_{B_j}^2}.$$

The test is distributed as χ^2 with 1 degree of freedom under the null hypothesis. The Wald tests for individual predictors are given in Table 13.2.2, Part I(C), and may be compared to the likelihood ratio tests reported earlier for the individual predictors, since both tests are distributed as χ^2 with 1 degree of freedom. In all cases except the zero value of the test for the KNOWLEDG predictor, the likelihood ratio tests exceed the corresponding Wald tests in value. This is consistent with findings that the Wald test is less powerful than the likelihood ratio test. Wald tests are also biased when data are sparse. Again, the likelihood ratio test is preferred.[3]

13.2.14 Hierarchical Logistic Regression: Likelihood Ratio χ^2 Test for the Significance of a Set of Predictors Above and Beyond Another Set

A common strategy in OLS regression, developed in Section 5.5, is to examine whether a set B of m predictors contributes significant prediction over and above another set A of k predictors. Likelihood ratio (LR) χ^2 tests in logistic regression can be formulated for the same purpose. Hierarchical LR tests of the contribution of a set of m predictors over and above another set of k predictors follow the same structure of differences between deviances. Deviances are computed for the k predictor model, D_k, and the $(m+k)$ predictor model, $D_{(m+k)}$. The difference between these deviances is an LR test for the significance of contribution of the set of m predictors over and above the set of k predictors, with m degrees of freedom.

(13.2.30)   contribution of set of m predictors $= D_k - D_{(m+k)}$, with m degrees of freedom
over and above another k predictor

In the numerical example of Table 13.2.2, we are most interested in whether psychological factors contribute to screening compliance beyond physician recommendation. Thus PHYS-REC constitutes set A with $k = 1$ predictor. The deviance with only PHYSREC as a predictor is 191.869. The second set B consists of $m = 3$ predictors, KNOWLEDG, BENEFITS, and BARRIERS, the psychological factors. The deviance from the four-predictor equation is 167.696. The LR χ^2 test with $m = 3$ degrees of freedom $= 191.869 - 167.696 = 24.173, p < .01$. The psychological factors do add predictability over and above physician recommendation.

Revisiting the Indices of Goodness of Fit

In Section 13.2.11 we reviewed R^2 analogs in logistic regression. We saw (Table 13.2.3) that the indices differed in magnitude from one another for a single model. On the other hand, if we inspect these indices in hierarchical models, they tell a consistent story about the gain in prediction from adding sets of variables. In Table 13.2.3, we present a series of three models: prediction of mammography screening (a) from PHYSREC alone, (b) from PHYSREC plus KNOWLEDG, and (c) from PHYSREC and KNOWLEDG, plus BENEFITS and BARRIERS. All three indices in Table 13.2.3 tell the same story: There is no increment in prediction by the addition of KNOWLEDG to PHYSREC, but the addition of BENEFITS and BARRIERS contributes substantial incremental prediction. Hosmer and Lemeshow (2000) point out the

---

[3]The Wald test for the contribution of an individual predictor is defined in two ways. First is as given in Eq. (13.2.28). Second is as the square root of Eq. (13.2.28) (e.g., Hosmer & Lemeshow, 2000, p. 16):

(13.2.29) $$\text{Wald statistic} = \frac{B_j}{SE_{B_j}}$$

At asymptote, maximum likelihood estimators, including the estimates of the regression coefficients, are normally distributed, meaning that as sample size increases, the distribution of the estimators becomes more and more normal in form. Hence the Wald statistic, as given in Eq. (13.2.29) is distributed as a z test for large samples. The user of statistical software for logistic regression should take care to determine whether the Wald test is given in the χ^2 form of Eq. (13.2.28) or the z test form of Eq. (13.2.29).

utility of the logistic R^2 analogs in the course of model building. Table 13.2.3 illustrates their utility as relative measures for comparison across models.

13.2.15 Akaike's Information Criterion and the Bayesian Information Criterion for Model Comparison

The comparison of models using LR tests described in Section 13.2.14 requires that one model be *nested* within the other. By nested is meant that all the predictors in the smaller model are included among the predictors in the larger model and the identical cases are included in both analysis. Two indices, *Akaike's Information Criterion* (AIC, Akaike, 1973) and the *Bayesian Information Criterion* (*BIC*) provide comparison of model fit in models that are not nested. These two indices also take into account the number of regression coefficients being tested; given equal fit of two models, the more parsimonious model (i.e., having fewer predictors) will have a better AIC fit index. Values of the AIC will be smallest for a model that exhibits good fit with a small number of predictors. (See Box 13.2.6 for computation of the AIC.) The AIC is used by comparing AIC values across estimated models; there is no statistical test of the AIC. The Bayesian Information Criterion (BIC) is a second measure of fit that takes into account the number of predictors. The BIC may be negative or positive in value; the more negative the value of the BIC, the better the fit.

13.2.16 Some Treachery in Variable Scaling and Interpretation of the Odds Ratio

To this point our numerical example has been presented with only unstandardized logistic regression coefficients. The PHYSREC predictor is a dichotomous predictor that ranges from 0 to 1; we now call this $\text{PHYSREC}_{(1,0)}$. The BENEFITS and BARRIERS psychological predictors range from 0 to 5; we call them $\text{BENEFITS}_{(5,0)}$ and $\text{BARRIERS}_{(5,0)}$. Thus, of course, a 1-unit change on $\text{PHYSREC}_{(1,0)}$, which covers the full range of the $\text{PHYSREC}_{(1,0)}$, scale, is not comparable to a 1-unit change on $\text{BENEFITS}_{(5,0)}$, which covers one-fifth of the $\text{BENEFITS}_{(5,0)}$ scale.

Consider the regression equation for predicting mammography screening from PHYSREC and BENEFITS in Table 13.2.4. The same regression equation is shown with four different predictor scalings. Table 13.2.4A gives the analysis of predictors in the original scaling.

BOX 13.2.6
Computation of the Akaike's Information Criterion

Computation of the AIC is based on the likelihood under the model containing $m = k+1$ predictors (including the intercept, L_k)

(13.2.31)
$$\text{AIC} = \frac{-2\ln L_k + 2m}{n}$$

where n is the number of cases. Note the penalty in the numerator for the number of predictors in the model; for two models yielding the same maximum likelihood L_k, the one with the smaller number of predictors will have a smaller AIC.

TABLE 13.2.4
Impact of Predictor Scaling on Regression Coefficients and Odds Ratios

A. Original predictor scaling: physician recommendation (1, 0); benefits (5, 0).

Variable	B	SE	Wald χ^2	df	Significance	Exp(B) (odds ratio)
PHYSREC (1, 0)	1.934	.467	17.164	1	.000	6.920
BENEFITS (5, 0)	.694	.229	9.157	1	.002	2.002
Constant	−4.550	1.053	18.687	1	.001	

B. Revised predictor scaling: physician recommendation (1, −1); benefits (5, 0).

Variable	B	SE	Wald χ^2	df	Significance	Exp(B) (odds ratio)
PHYSREC (1, −1)	.967	.234	17.164	1	.000	2.631
BENEFITS (5, 0)	.694	.229	9.157	1	.002	2.002
Constant	−3.583	1.015	12.454	1	.001	

C. Revised predictor scaling: physician recommendation (1, 0); benefits (1, 0).

Variable	B	SE	Wald χ^2	df	Significance	Exp(B) (odds ratio)
PHYSREC (1, 0)	1.934	.467	17.164	1	.000	6.920
BENEFITS (1, 0)	3.470	1.147	9.157	1	.002	32.129
Constant	−4.550	1.053	18.687	1	.000	

D. Revised predictor scaling: physician recommendation and benefits standardized (z scores), and criterion of compliance unstandardized.

Variable	B	SE	Wald χ^2	df	Significance	Exp(B) (odds ratio)
ZPHYSREC	.898	.2168	17.164	1	.000	2.455
ZBENEFIT	.718	.2373	9.157	1	.002	2.051
Constant	−.327	.1941	2.843	1	.092	

Note: Dependent variable is COMPLY (1, 0).

Scaling a Dichotomous Predictor

For physician recommendation, the dummy-variable coding (see Section 8.2) is 1 = recommendation and 0 = no recommendation, which means that a *1-unit* change in the value of the predictor goes from not having a recommendation to having a recommendation. Note that the regression coefficient for PHYSREC$_{(1,0)}$ is $B_{\text{PHYSREC}(1,0)} = 1.934$ and the odds ratio is $e^{B_{\text{PHYSREC}(1,0)}} = 6.92$. The logit for obtaining a mammogram increases by additive amount of 1.934 when a woman receives a recommmendation for screening from her physician, and the odds of her obtaining a mammogram are multiplied by 6.92. Recall that in general the odds ratio is the amount by which the odds are multiplied for a 1-unit increase in the predictor (here, of receiving a recommendation for a mammogram).

Now we repeat the analysis, but with an unweighted effects code form of the PHYSREC predictor (see Section 8.3), that is, 1 = recommendation, −1 = no recommendation. The change in interpretation of regression coefficients for unweighted effects versus dummy coding is the same as in OLS regression. The results of an analysis with unweighted effects coded $PHYSREC_{(1,-1)}$, that is, $1 =$ yes; $-1 =$ no, are given in Table 13.2.4B. First, as in OLS regression, the regression coefficient for $PHYSREC_{(1,-1)}$ is .967, exactly half of the value of the corresponding coefficient in the first dummy-coded analysis. What value is the odds ratio for $PHYSREC_{(1,-1)}$ relative to that for $PHYSREC_{(1,0)}$?

For $PHYSREC_{(1,0)}, B_{(1/0)} = 1.934$ and $e^B =$ odds ratio $= e^{1.934} = e^{2(.967)} = 6.92$.

For $PHYSREC_{(1,-1)}, B_{(1/-1)} = .967$ and $e^B =$ odds ratio $= e^{.967} = 2.63$.

Note that $2.63 = \sqrt{6.92}$. Halving the regression coefficient corresponds to taking the square root of the odds.

The odds ratio based on effects coding $(1, -1)$ does not inform us directly of odds that a woman will receive a mammogram if she does versus does not receive a physician's recommendation. To get this odds ratio directly we must use the $(1, 0)$ coding of physician recommendation. With the $(1, -1)$ effects codes, a 1-unit increase in the $PHYSREC_{(1,-1)}$ predictor is only half the distance from no recommendation (-1) to recommendation (1). The regression coefficient from the effects coded predictor can be converted to the odds ratio for the impact of recommendation on odds of screening. First, double the regression coefficient from the effects coded analysis (since $B_{(1/-1)} = .967, 2 \times B_{(1/-1)} = 1.934$). Then *exponentiate the doubled coefficient* to get the proper odds ratio for the increase in odds of mammography screening when one has received a physician recommendation ($e^{1.934} = 6.92$).

Treachery in Scaling a Continuous Predictor

We often combine medical or demographic variables that are dichotomous (male, female; African American, Caucasian; family history, no family history; physician recommendation, no physician recommendation) with continuous variables such as psychological variables (e.g., perceived benefits, barriers) that are scaled and cover a range well beyond (0, 1). If we ignore the difference in scaling, we may misinterpret the smaller regression coefficients that result from prediction from the psychological variables with larger ranges as indicating weaker prediction from the psychological variables. The differences in coefficient magnitude are accentuated when we move to odds ratios. To the uninitiated or casual consumer of logistic regression, who quickly scans a column of odds ratios, the binary variables may appear much more powerful than the psychological variables. The benefits predictor $BENEFITS_{(5,0)}$ has a 5-point range, so a 1-unit change in benefits covers only a fifth of the scale. A 1-unit change in $PHYSREC_{(1,0)}$ is from no recommendation to a recommendation. We rescale the benefits scale to have the range from 0 to 1 by dividing each benefits score by 5, yielding $BENEFITS_{(1,0)}$. Having divided the benefits scale by 5, the regression coefficient for $BENEFITS_{(1,0)}$ is multiplied by 5; $B = .694 \times 5 = 3.47$, as shown in Table 13.2.4C. Then we rescale the odds ratio: $e^{B_{rescaled}} = e^{3.4698} = 32.13$. If a woman moves from the lowest to highest score on BENEFITS (perhaps a goal for an intervention to increase screening rates), her odds of being screened increase by a factor of 32; perceived benefit appears to be a very powerful psychological variable.

This example illustrates the importance of addressing predictor scaling when comparing odds ratios. Hosmer and Lemeshow (2000) suggest that when working with a continuous predictor, one should consider the magnitude of change in units on that predictor that would be meaningful and report coefficients and odds ratios associated with that change. For example, if a 2-unit change seemed meaningful for the BENEFITS scale, then one would report the rescaled B coefficient and odds ratio for a 2-unit change. For a 1-unit change on the 5-point BENEFIT scale (Table 13.2.4A), the logit increases by $B_{BENEFITS(5,0)} = .694$. For a w-unit increase in benefits, recall that the amount of change in the logit is simply wB. Here, for a

2-unit increase in BENEFITS$_{(5,0)}$, the increase in the logit is $2 \times .694 = 1.388$. The odds are multiplied by the value e^{wB_j} for a w-unit increase in the predictor. For a 2-point increase in BENEFITS$_{(5,0)}$, the odds ratio is $e^{2 \times .694} = 4.01$, or, equivalently, the odds of compliance are multiplied by 4.01. If one reports coefficients and odds for greater than a 1-unit change on a scale, what is being reported should be clearly explained to the reader.

Standardized Regression Coefficients

The use of standardized regression coefficients is the familiar way in OLS regression to address the issue of differential scaling of predictors. However, standardized regression coefficients are a matter of some complexity in logistic regression. In OLS regression, we compute the standardized regression coefficient β_j from the corresponding unstandardized coefficient B_j as follows (rearranged from Eq. 3.2.5):

(13.2.32)
$$\beta_j = B_j \frac{sd_X}{sd_Y},$$

where sd_X is the standard deviation of the predictor, and sd_Y is the standard deviation of Y. Using this equation in logistic regression poses problems, because in the linear form of logistic regression, the variable being predicted is the logit of the underlying probability of being a case and not the observed Y (case, noncase). Thus, to standardize coefficients, we would require the standard deviation of this underlying logit. Although some software packages do report standardized coefficients, it may be unclear precisely how standardization is accomplished. If the analyst wishes to report a standardized solution, then a simple strategy exists: Standardize the predictors and estimate the unstandardized logistic regression (Pampel, 2000). The resulting coefficients give the change in the logit for a one standard deviation change in the predictors. The coefficients are "semistandardized," that is, standardized only on the predictor side. Use of this approach should be explained in publication, due to the unusual semistandardization. In Table 13.2.4D, the data are reanalyzed with the dependent variable retained as COMPLY (1, 0), and both predictors first converted to standardized scores (z scores, i.e., ZPHYSREC and ZBENEFIT for the z scores associated with PHYSREC and BENEFITS, respectively). The resulting regression coefficients and odds ratios are approximately equal, suggesting relatively equal strength of the predictors. There is a downside to this approach: The coefficients and odds ratios for the dichotomous predictors lose their straightforward interpretation because the values of 0 and 1 in the z score scale metric no longer represent the two categories of the scale. This leads some analysts to object to the approach. Menard (1995) and Pampel (2000) provide clear discussions of standardization in logistic regression, including standardization of predicted logits to come closer to full standardization.

Another way of thinking about the contributions of two predictors, as in OLS regression, is to ask whether each contributes prediction over and above the other. Thus we may ask whether BENEFITS contributes to reduction in deviance over and above PHYSREC and vice versa, according to Eq. (13.2.27).

13.2.17 Regression Diagnostics in Logistic Regression

Section 10.3 provides a full exposition of regression diagnostics and their use in OLS regression. These regression diagnostics are based on the assumption that the residuals in an analysis are normally distributed, according to the general linear model. Regression diagnostic measures of leverage, distance, and influence have been generalized to logistic regression in classic work by Pregibon (1981). The reader is cautioned that the generalizations are not complete, due to the complexity of the logistic regression model. Graphical diagnostics are more difficult to interpret because of the dichotomous distribution of the criterion. Informative discussions of diagnostics in the logistic regression context are found in Collett (1991), Fox (1997), Hosmer and Lemeshow (2000), Long (1997), Menard (1995), and Ryan (1997).

The present section does not give a full explication of diagnostics in logistic regression. Rather, since regression diagnostics are regularly reported in logistic regression software, this section aims to highlight divergences between OLS and logistic regression diagnostics and to caution analysts concerning issues in the use of diagnostics in logistic regression. A review of Section 10.3 is recommended to set this section in context.

Leverage in Logistic Regression

Recall that in OLS regression, the leverage of a point, h_{ii}, is a measure of the potential of a case to influence regression results, (i.e., to change the regression coefficients by its presence in the data set). Leverage in OLS regression is based solely on scores on the predictors. In OLS regression the farther a case is from the centroid of the points on the predictors (the means of all the predictors), the greater is the leverage (see Section 10.3.1, Eq. 10.3.1). In OLS regression the value of the dependent variable (DV) for the case has no effect on the leverage measure. Pregibon (1981) provided a generalization of the measure of leverage to logistic regression. In this generalization, the leverage values h_{ii} depend on the DV scores as well as on the predictors, yielding a discontinuity between the definitions of leverage in OLS and logistic regression. A further discontinuity exists between leverage measures in the two cases. Leverage in OLS regression is greatest for those cases most extreme in the predictor space (i.e., farthest from the centroid of points). However, leverage in logistic regression increases as the extremeness of cases increases up to a point and then diminishes rapidly for the most extreme cases. In other words, a very extreme case can have a lower leverage score than a less extreme case! Hosmer and Lemeshow (2000) recommend that one should examine the predicted probability $\hat{p}_i$ for a case before interpreting leverage measures; only for $\hat{p}_i$ between .10 and .90 are leverages assured to increase with increasing distance of the point from the centroid of the predictor space.

Residuals in Logistic Regression

Residuals play a central role in regression diagnostics. The fact that the residuals in OLS regression are theoretically normally distributed yields great simplification in regression diagnostics. The distribution of residuals in OLS is expected to be independent of the predicted score $\hat{Y}$, so the size of residuals can be interpreted in the same manner across the range of the predictor. Further, if the homoscedasticity assumed in OLS regression holds, the variance of the residuals is constant for all values of the predicted score; residuals associated with different predicted scores may be directly compared. In logistic regression, the size of residuals and their variance is dependent upon the predicted probability, $\hat{p}_i$; the residuals are non-normal and heteroscedastic. This adds a layer of complexity to the analysis of residuals.

Deviance residuals. In OLS regression the squared residual of each case $(Y - \hat{Y})^2$ contributes to $SS_{residual}$, the overall measure of lack of fit of the OLS regression model. The residuals from individual cases form the basis of a number of regression diagnostic measures in OLS regression.

In logistic regression, a *deviance residual* is computed for each case; it measures the numerical contribution of the case to the overall model deviance D_k, the overall measure of lack of fit of a logistic regression model. Adding to the complexity of residual diagnostics is the fact that there is a second type of residual in logistic regression, the *Pearson residual*. Both the deviance and Pearson residuals are used in the computation of diagnostic measures in logistic regression that are analogs of residual diagnostics in OLS regression. There is a preference in the literature for the use of deviance residuals over Pearson residuals for two reasons: (1) deviance residuals are closer to normally distributed, and (2) Pearson residuals are unstable when $\hat{p}_i$ is close to zero or one. Deviance residuals pose problems for interpretation, however, in that the expected value of the deviance residual (the average deviance residual) depends on the value of $\hat{p}$, the overall probability of a case; the value of the residual cannot be considered independent of this overall probability. Details of the computation of the deviance and Pearson residuals are given in Box 13.2.7.

Externally studentized residuals.   In OLS regression externally studentized residuals are useful in identifying outliers. The externally studentized residual for each case is based on a regression analysis in which the case in question has been omitted (see Section 10.3.2). Externally studentized residuals in logistic regression have been defined for both deviance and Pearson residuals. Those based on deviance residuals are asymptotically normally distributed; the difficulty for psychology is that we have small sample sizes—we can hardly assume asymptotic distributions.

In Section 10.3.2 *t* tests were provided for externally studentized residuals (see Eq. 10.3.4). In addition, suggestions were made for cut scores, beyond which a residual is seen as signaling a potentially problematic case. We do not see these same *t* tests and suggestions for cut scores in the logistic regression context. The definition of cut scores for residuals is typically justified by normal theory, based on the number of standard deviations on a normal curve. Recall again that residuals in logistic regression are not normally distributed; in fact, the residuals follow a binomial distribution for each value of $\hat{p}_i$.

Influence in Logistic Regression

Influence diagnostics, that is, measures of the extent to which individual cases affect the regression coefficient estimates (Section 10.3.3) have been extended to logistic regression; these include an analog of Cook's distance for impact of a case on the overall fit of the regression model and *DFBETA* for the impact of a case on individual regression coefficients. *DFBETA*s are useful in logistic regression for identifying cases that may have an undue impact on particular regression coefficients.

Graphical Approaches to Diagnostics

A number of graphical displays, among them index plots of residuals, normal probability plots of residuals (q-q plots) and added variable plots have been suggested for use in diagnostics in logistic regression (for a discussion of the use of these graphs in OLS regression, see Chapter 4). Collett (1991) and Cook and Weisberg (1999) provide an extensive review of graphical displays applied to logistic regression. These plots may also be extended to model checking, that is, to examining whether the fitted model is an adequate representation of the data. As Collett (1991) pointed out, however, since residuals in logistic regression are generally not normally distributed, a correct logistic regression model may yield plots that suggest difficulties with the model. For example, a normal probability plot of deviance residuals may well show residuals deviating from a straight line even with a well-fitting model.

How to Proceed With Diagnostics in Logistic Regression

In light of these caveats, the reader must be cautious in drawing conclusions from diagnostics in logistic regression. One may examine measures of leverage for cases for which $\hat{p}_i$ falls between .10 and .90, remembering that beyond these values leverage no longer reflects distance from the centroid of the X space. Studentized residuals that are very large relative to the rest of the sample may reflect cases that are problematic. Cases that will have the largest residuals are those with extreme predicted probabilities, either close to 0 or close to 1. They will be cases that do not follow the model (e.g., a student who by virtue of exceptionally strong scores on a set of academic ability predictors in a model should succeed in college but who, unlike other students with these same scores, fails miserably). *DFBETA*s may also flag potentially problematic cases, which may well be the same cases that simply do not follow the model. Graphical displays of diagnostics will aid detection of potentially problematic points. The reader should take the view, however, that diagnostics in logistic regression are not so straightforward as in OLS regression. Even greater caution should be applied before cases are deleted based on diagnostic measures in logistic regression than in OLS regression.[4]

BOX 13.2.7
Deviance and Pearson Residuals in Logistic Regression

The Pearson residual for case i is given as (Long, 1997, p. 98)

$$(13.2.33) \qquad r_i = \frac{Y_i - \hat{p}_i}{\sqrt{\hat{p}_i(1 - \hat{p}_i)}}.$$

Since the residuals exhibit heteroscedasticity, the residual $(Y_i - \hat{p}_i)$ is divided by its binomial standard error, which depends upon $\hat{p}_i$.

The *deviance residual* is defined as

$$(13.2.34) \qquad d_i = \text{sign}\,(Y_i - \hat{p}_i)\sqrt{-2[(-\,Y_i \ln(\hat{p}_i) - (1 - Y_i) \ln(1 - \hat{p}_i)]},$$

where sign $(Y_i - \hat{p}_i)$ is the sign of the discrepancy between the observed score Y $(1, 0)$ and the predicted probability. The expression compares the observed Y_i to the predicted $\hat{p}_i$ score.

Neither the Pearson nor the deviance residual given here is standardized; that is, neither has a standard deviation of 1. Both may be standardized by dividing each value by the value $\sqrt{1 - h_{ii}}$, yielding *standardized Pearson and deviance residuals*, respectively.

---

[4]The naming of the diagnostics identified here is inconsistent across software packages. These are the terms used in SPSS and SAS: (a) leverage h_{ii} (LEVER in SPSS, H in SAS); (b) Pearson residual, Eq. (13.2.33), (ZRESID in SPSS, RESCHI in SAS); (c) deviance residual, Eq. (13.2.34), (DEV in SPSS; RESDEV in SAS); (d) externally studentized residual (SRESID in SPSS); (e) *DFBETA* (DFBETA in SPSS; DFBETAS in SAS); (f) analog of Cook's distance (COOK in SPSS; CBAR in SAS).

A final complication in the computation of diagnostics in logistic regression is that they are computed in one of two ways: (1) based on individual cases in the data set, as they are presented here, or, (2) based on aggregated data (see Hosmer and Lemeshow, 2000 for a discussion). For the aggregated measures, data are broken into categories, where a category consists of all those cases that have the same values on the predictors. With continuous predictors, categories will be sparse (i.e., contain few cases). Basic diagnostic building blocks, specifically residuals and leverage values, are defined somewhat differently depending on whether aggregation is or is not used; further, the asymptotic distributions of the measures differ depending on aggregation strategy. Numerical results of diagnostics differ depending on aggregation. It may be unclear what strategy is used for computation in any particular software package, adding a layer of uncertainty to the meaning of specific values of the measures.

13.2.18 Sparseness of Data

We defined sparseness of data in Section 13.2.12 and indicated how sparseness biases tests of model deviance and Wald tests, as well. Sparseness (having numerous cells with zero counts) also decreases the power of statistical tests in logistic regression. In addition, sparseness may cause difficulties in estimation. The analysis may not converge (see Section 13.2.9). Or, estimates of regression coefficients and their standard errors may "blow up" (i.e., become huge), signaling estimation difficulties.

13.2.19 Classification of Cases

Once a logistic regression has been accomplished, the predicted probabilities $\hat{p}_i$ for each individual may be used to generate a predicted case status (i.e., whether the individual is predicted to be a case or a noncase). This is accomplished by choosing a cut score on the $\hat{p}_i$ continuum, above which an individual is classified as a case; otherwise, noncase. Then the predicted status (case, noncase) can be compared with the observed case status to determine how well the logistic regression model recovers case status. The classification of cases is ancillary to logistic regression and is also carried out following other statistical procedures, particularly discriminant analysis, which is described in Section 13.2.1. Classification is useful when statistical models are developed to make decisions among individuals (e.g., hiring decisions based on a battery of test scores). Classification provides another way of characterizing the goodness of fit of a logistic regression model. A description of classification is given in Box 13.2.8, along with a numerical example. The critical issue of selection of a cutoff score for classification is discussed.

BOX 13.2.8
How Accurately Does a Logistic Regression Model Identify Cases?

Suppose we compute for each case the predicted probability of being a case, $\hat{p}_i$. Then we classify each individual as case versus noncase based on whether the $\hat{p}_i$ score exceeds some cutoff. These classifications are *statistical classifications*, based on logistic regression model. We then compare the statistical classifications to the actual classifications in a 2×2 *classification table*, shown in Table 13.2.5. The number of correct statistical classifications is the sum of the *correct rejections* (classifying a noncase as a noncase) plus *hits* (classifying a case as a case) in the parlance of statistical decision theory. In epidemiological terms, one can examine *sensitivity*, the proportion of actual cases who are classified as cases, and *specificity*, the proportion of noncases who are classified as noncases (Fleiss, 1981). Such an analysis may be informative if the goal of the logistic regression analysis is, in fact, classification of cases, as in computerized medical diagnosis, rather than the derivation of a model of "caseness" based on a set of predictors.

A most critical issue in classification is the choice of cutoff on the $\hat{p}_i$ continuum. Neter, Kutner, Nachtsheim, and Wasserman (1996) have suggested three criteria: (1) use a cutoff of .5, such that if the predicted probability of being a case is greater than .5, the individual is classified as a case; (2) select the cutoff that leads to the most accurate classification, through a process of trial and error; and (3) use some a priori information about the proportion of cases versus noncases in the population (e.g. the actual proportion of women who are in compliance with mammography screening guidelines in the population). The choice of cutoff will change the sensitivity versus specificity of the classification scheme (this is analogous to the inverse relationship between Type I and Type II error in hypothesis testing as one changes the critical value of a statistical test).

(Continued)

TABLE 13.2.5
Classification Results From the Mammography Example

A. Classification table.

		Predicted class membership	
		0	1
Observed class membership	0	Correct rejections	False alarms
	1	Misses	Hits

B. Classifications under various cut scores.
1. Cut $= \hat{p}_i = .50$.

Observed class membership	Predicted class membership 0	1	Total	Number correct	R^2_{Count}	$R^2_{AdjCount}$
0	60	28	88			
1	23	53	76	113	.68	.33
	$\overline{83}$	$\overline{81}$	$\overline{164}$			

2. Cut $= \hat{p}_i = .20$.

Observed class membership	Predicted class membership 0	1	Total	Number correct	R^2_{Count}	$R^2_{AdjCount}$
0	40	48	88			
1	4	72	76	112	.68	.32
	$\overline{44}$	$\overline{120}$	$\overline{164}$			

3. Cut $= \hat{p}_i = .80$.

Observed class membership	Predicted class membership 0	1	Total	Number correct	R^2_{Count}	$R^2_{AdjCount}$
0	81	7	88			
1	50	26	76	107	.65	.25
	$\overline{131}$	$\overline{33}$	$\overline{164}$			

Note: R^2_{Count} is the unadjusted proportion of correct classifications, the sum of the main diagonal elements divided by the total $n = 164$.
$R^2_{AdjCount}$ is the adjusted proportion of correct classifications, "the proportion of correct guesses beyond the number that would be correctly guessed by choosing the largest marginal" (Long, 1997, p. 108).

A number of measures of the agreement of two classifications have been developed, among them the phi coefficient, weighted kappa (Cohen, 1968a), and Goodman and Kruskal's λ (Goodman & Kruskal, 1979). Treatments of these measures are given in Fleiss (1981), Kraemer (1985; 1988), and Menard (2001). Kraemer, Kazdin, Offord, Kessler, Jensen, and Kupfer (1999) provide a useful explication of such measures and their interrelationships.

(*Continued*)

Classification accuracy depends on the *base rate* of a phenomenon in the population, that is, the proportion of individuals in the population who are cases. If, for example, a base rate of 80% of the adults in a community suffer from allergies during a particular month, then a physician has an 80% chance of being correct in diagnosing a new patient from that community as having allergies without ever seeing the patient!

Two simple measures of classification accuracy (Long, 1997) are the *proportion of correct classifications* (hits plus correct rejections) and the *proportion of additional classification accuracy* gained by the logistic regression scheme, over and above classification accuracy based on the distribution of the outcome alone (e.g., above the base rate of 80% in the above example). The former measure does not handle the base-rate issue; the latter does. These are given as follows, where n is the total number of cases, and $n$max is the total number of cases in the larger observed category:

$$(13.2.35) \qquad R^2_{\text{Count}} = \frac{\text{hits} + \text{correct rejections}}{n}$$

for the uncorrected proportion correct, and

$$(13.2.36) \qquad R^2_{\text{AdjCount}} = \frac{\text{hits} + \text{correct rejections} - n\text{max}}{n - n\text{max}}$$

for the proportion gain in prediction accuracy over and above that provided by classification based on marginals alone. This is Goodman and Kruskal's λ (Long, 1997).

Computations are given for the mammography data in Table 13.2.5B. Part B1 gives the classification table for a cut score of $\hat{p}_i = .50$. There are 88 cases observed to be noncases, and 76 cases, of the 164 cases in all. In all 60 of the noncases are correctly classified, along with 53 of the cases. The proportion of correct classifications with a .50 criterion is .68, that is, $R^2_{\text{Count}} = (53 + 60)/164$. The adjusted count is $R^2_{\text{AdjCount}} = (53 + 60 - 88)/(164 - 88) = .33$, where 88 is the number of cases in the larger observed class. This .33 indicates that the prediction scheme produces classification accuracy that is 33% higher than by merely guessing that all cases arise from the more frequent category.

Table 13.2.5 shows how insensitive measures of overall classification accuracy are to the choice of cutoff, but how dramatically measures of sensitivity (proportion of actual cases classified as cases) and specificity (proportion of actual noncases classified as noncases) are affected by cutoff choice. Part B2 gives the classification results for a cut score of $\hat{p}_i = .20$; Part B3, for a cut score of $\hat{p}_i = .80$. R^2_{Count} essentially does not change as the cut score is moved from .20 to .80. However, sensitivity and specificity change dramatically as the cutoff is moved. The sensitivity, or proportion of actual cases classified as cases, decreases from sensitivity of $72/76 = .95$ when the cut score is .20 (Part 2) and fully 120 of the 164 individuals are classified as in compliance to sensitivity $= 26/76 = .34$, when the cut score is .80 (Part 3) and only 33 of 164 individuals are classified as in compliance. Conversely, specificity increases from $40/88 = .45$ when the cut score is .20 (Part 2) to 81/88 when the cut score is .80 (Part 3). The issue of cutoff is well illuminated by considering the use of medical diagnostic tests; a change in cutoff may well determine whether an individual is diagnosed or not as having a disease.

Classification results reflect the adequacy of the model in distinguishing cases from noncases (once accuracy that can be achieved from the base rate by just predicting the larger category is taken into account). These results provide a useful adjunct to other meaures of fit in logistic regression. However, sometimes we may have a well-fitting

(Continued)

model in terms of predicted probabilities of being in a category and simultaneously low classification accuracy, above and beyond the base rate. For example, suppose our model is very accurate in predicting that a person with a certain profile has a predicted probability of being a case of $\hat{p}_i = .50$. For this person, we have a 50/50 chance of being wrong in classification based on the model because we can only classify this person as a case versus a noncase. Poor classification results in the face of a well-fitting model may particularly occur when we are predicting rare events. A mathematically based science of classification has been developed in which classification rules take into account prior odds of class membership and the costs of misclassification. Tatsuoka (1988) provides an introduction to misclassification models.

13.3 EXTENSIONS OF LOGISTIC REGRESSION TO MULTIPLE RESPONSE CATEGORIES: POLYTOMOUS LOGISTIC REGRESSION AND ORDINAL LOGISTIC REGRESSION

We may encounter dependent variables for which the outcomes fall into several nonordered categories. For example, we may wish to account for the college (business, engineering, liberal arts) into which a student matriculates as a function of ability and interest scores. Alternatively, the outcome categories may be ordered, as when students express one of three levels of interest in being liberal arts majors (low, moderate, and high). *Polytomous logistic regression* (also refered to as *multinomial logistic regression*) is used to examine an outcome variable consisting of nonordered responses. A second approach is the analysis of *nested categories*, in which contrasts among categories, like familiar contrasts in ANOVA and OLS regression (Chapter 8), are accomplished in a series of dichotomous outcome logistic regressions. Categories may be either ordered or not. Third, *ordinal logistic regression* is used to examine an outcome variable consisting of ordered categories.

13.3.1 Polytomous Logistic Regression

Expositions of polytomous logistic regression of increasing mathematical detail are given in Menard (2001), Hosmer and Lemeshow (2000), who use the term *multinomial logistic regression*, and Fox (1997), along with numerical examples. Assume that as a dependent variable we are comparing a group of college students who are undecided about a major (major = 0) to those who have elected a humanities (major = 1) or a science (major = 2) major. We wish to distinguish these $g = 3$ nonordered groups on the basis of a series of interest test measures $X_1, X_2, \ldots, X_k$. We begin by choosing one group to serve as a baseline group, here those students who are undecided about a major. The data from all three groups are entered into a single polytomous logistic regression analysis. In the course of the analysis, $(g-1)$ distinct logistic regression functions, all with the same k predictors, are computed for the g groups (here, $g-1 = 2$ for the three student groups). The first contrasts the humanities majors with the undecided students; the second contrasts the science majors with the undecided students. The logistic regression functions are combined into one overall polytomous regression equation that includes the intercepts from the $(g-1)$ logistic regression functions plus the $(g-1)k$ regression coefficients for the k predictors in the $(g-1)$ regression functions. Testing of model fit of this combined regression equation proceeds along the lines previously described for likelihood ratio tests (see Section 13.2.12, Eq. 13.2.26). There is one overall likelihood ratio χ^2 test (G test) of fit of the model, with $(g-1)k$ degrees of freedom. Tests for the impact of individual predictors proceed as before. Indices of fit such as R_L^2 in Eq. (13.2.23) can be computed for the full model. Numerical examples of polytomous logistic regression are provided in Menard (2001), Hosmer and Lemeshow (2000), and Fox (1997).[5]

13.3.2 Nested Dichotomies

An alternative to polytomous logistic regressions is a series of dichotomous logistic regressions (Fox, 1997). The particular dichotomous logistic regressions are a series of nested regressions based on a series of *nested partitions* of the multiple categories represented by the dependent variable. The partitions follow the patterns of sets of orthogonal contrasts, described in Section 8.5. For the example of majors (undecided $= 0$; humanities $= 1$; science $= 2$), we might first consider a partition of the undecided versus the other students (0 versus $1 + 2$) and then a second partition in which we contrast the humanities majors versus the science majors. The patterns of nested contrasts of the categories follow from the logic or theory underlying the research. In the case of predicting choice of major from a number of academic interest measures, we might predict that undecided students have a lower overall level of interest in academic subjects than those who have declared any major (contrast 1); we might then predict that differential patterns of interest predict the choice of science versus humanities major (contrast 2). As Fox (1997) shows, a variety of partitions can be generated from a set of categories. Some do not imply an order among the full set of categories (e.g., for four categories, $1 + 3$ versus $2 + 4$, followed by 1 versus 3 and 2 versus 4). Other series imply an underlying order (e.g., for a series, 1 versus $2 + 3 + 4$, followed by 2 versus $3 + 4$, followed by 3 versus 4, referred to as *continuation dichotomies* (Fox, 1997) or as following a *continuation-ratio model* (Greenland, 1998). The individual contrasts are treated in separate dichotomous logistic regressions. For the example of majors, the first logistic regression would be of the group coded 0 versus the group formed by combining the groups coded 1 and 2. The second would contain only the groups coded 1 versus 2. Each analysis yields a likelihood ratio χ^2 test (G test). By virtue of the fact that the contrasts are orthogonal, the likelihood ratio tests from the two analyses may be pooled into an overall fit statistic by adding the likelihood ratio χ^2 values and the corresponding degrees of freedom.

CH13EX02

Table 13.3.1 presents the analysis of an ordinal outcome variable Y, the steps (STEPS) women have taken to obtaining a mammogram following an intervention (versus no-intervention control) to increase mammography screening. Data are a subset of those presented in Aiken, West, Woodward, Reno, and Reynolds (1994). Four ordered categories of the outcome are (1) to do nothing about getting a mammogram, (2) to contact a health professional about mammograms, (3) to make an appointment for a mammogram, (4) to actually obtain a mammogram. The single predictor is whether the woman participated in a psychosocial intervention to increase mammography screening or served as a control subject (INTERVEN), with participants coded 1 and control subjects coded 0. Three continuation dichotomies were created from the STEPS outcome: (a) S123V4, which measures whether women *obtained* a mammogram [category 4] versus not [categories 1, 2, 3]; (b) S12V3, which measures whether a woman made an appointment [category 3] versus did nothing or contacted a health professional [categories 1, 2]; and (c) S1V2, which measures whether a woman contacted a health professional [category 2] versus did nothing [category 1]. Three separate dichotomous logistic regression analyses are presented in Table 13.3.1A, B, and C for S123V4, S12V3, S1V2, respectively. From the analysis of S123V4 (Table 13.3.1A), we see that the odds of obtaining a mammogram were increased by a factor of 4 (odds ratio $= 4.15$) if women participated in

---

[5]SPSS 10.0 has a procedure for polytomous regression. Epidemiologists recommend STATA for handling polytomous data.

TABLE 13.3.1

Three Approaches to Analysis of Ordinal Outcome Variable of STEPS to Compliance as a Function of Intervention (INTERVEN).

A. Dichotomous logistic regression predicting S123V4 from INTERVEN, i.e., obtaining a mammogram (4) versus all other categories (1, 2, 3)

Null deviance	170.326	$R_L^2 = .07$	
Model deviance	159.081		
Model chi square	11.245	1 df $p < .001$	

	Variables in the Equation					
Variable	B	SE	Wald	df	Significance	Exp(B)
INTERVEN	1.423	.461	9.504	1	.002	4.148
Constant	−1.838	.407	20.403	1	.001	

B. Dichotomous logistic regression predicting S12V3 from INTERVEN, i.e., having an appointment for a mammogram (3) versus taking no action or contacting a health professional (1, 2)

Null deviance	39.391	$R_L^2 = .04$	
Model deviance	37.908		
Model chi square	1.483	1 df $p = .223$	

	Variables in the Equation					
Variable	B	SE	Wald	df	Significance	Exp(B)
INTERVEN	1.255	1.137	1.218	1	.270	3.508
Constant	−3.761	1.011	13.829	1	.001	

C. Dichotomous logistic regression predicting S1V2 from INTERVEN, i.e., contacting a health professional concerning mammograms (2) versus doing nothing (1)

Null deviance	120.090	$R_L^2 = .05$	
Model deviance	114.387		
Model chi square	5.704	1 df $p = .017$	

	Variables in the Equation					
Variable	B	SE	Wald	df	Significance	Exp(B)
INTERVEN	1.071	.461	5.408	1	.020	2.919
Constant	−1.194	.361	10.940	1	.001	

D. Ordinal Regression Analysis predicting STEPS continuum from INTERVEN

Null deviance	329.806	$R_L^2 = .05$	
Model deviance	311.406		
Model chi square	17.479	1 df $p < .001$	

521

TABLE 13.3.1
(Continued)

Variable	B	SE	Wald	df	Significance	Exp(B)
			Variables in the Equation			
Threshold-1	−1.872	.324	33.295	1	.001	
Threshold-2	−1.692	.318	28.274	1	.001	
Threshold-3	−.601	.288	4.365	1	.037	
INTERVEN	1.464	.354	17.106	1	.021	4.324

Score Test of Proportional Odds Assumption
Chi-square = .032 with 2 *df* (*p* = .984)

E. OLS Regression, predicting STEPS continuum from INTERVEN
   (1 = intervention, 0 = control)
$R^2 = .12$, $F(1, 137) = 17.899$, $p < .001$

Variable	B	SE	Beta	t	Significance of t
			Variables in the Equation		
INTERVEN	.898	.212	.340	4.231	.001
(Constant)	1.647	.169		9.748	.001

Note: Analyses A, B, and C are continuation category analyses. Analysis D is an ordinal logistic regression. Analysis E is an ordinary least squares regression.

an intervention, model $\chi^2(1) = 11.24, p < .01$. From the analysis of S12V3 (Table 13.3.1B), we see that the odds of making an appointment were increased by a factor of between 3 and 4 (odds ratio = 3.51) if women participated in an intervention, model $\chi^2(1) = 1.48$, *ns*. (Lack of model significance is attributable to the very small group (*n* = 5) who made an appointment for a mammogram but did not actually obtain the mammogram by the time of data collection). Finally, from the analysis of S1V2 (Table 13.3.1C), we see that the odds of contacting a health provider were increased by a factor of 3 (odds ratio = 2.92) if women participated in an intervention, model $\chi^2(1) = 5.70, p < .05$. The model χ^2 values are summed to yield an overall test of the impact of the intervention on the propensity of a woman to obtain a mammogram, $\chi^2 = 11.25 + 1.48 + 5.7046 = 18.43$ with 3 $df, p < .01$. From these analyses, we may conclude that the intervention does have a strong impact on propensity to obtain a mammogram. Further, we may conclude that the odds of moving up the steps toward a mammogram are similarly impacted by the intervention across the continuum, since all three odds ratios were within close range of one another. This last result is clearly not a necessary outcome. It might have been the case, for example, that the intervention was powerful in stimulating women who had already contacted a health professional about a mammogram to make an appointment for a mammogram or to obtain a mammogram (S12V3) and (S123V4), respectively, but that the intervention did nothing to stimulate women to take the first step of contacting a health professional (S1V2).

13.3.3 Ordinal Logistic Regression

Suppose we believe that the steps are, in fact, a logically ordered behavioral progression of movement toward obtaining a mammogram. Conceptually, the four categories that will serve as the DV are thought of as reflecting an *underlying continuum of propensity to obtain a mammogram* (ψ). Movement from step to step indicates that the woman has passed a threshold along the *underlying continuum*. The thresholds need not be equally spaced, since only ordinality is assumed. With four different ordered behaviors, as in the STEPS outcome, there are three hypothesized latent thresholds τ_j. Categories 1 versus 2, 3, and 4 are separated by threshold τ_1; categories 1 and 2 versus 3 and 4, by threshold τ_2; categories 1, 2, and 3 versus 4 by threshold τ_3.

Movement along the latent continuum as a function of predictor(s) can be modeled in a form of ordinal regression model, also referred to as a *proportional odds model* or *parallel regression model*. These names are informative about the assumptions of the model. The structure of the model can be cast in terms of the odds of transition across thresholds, given values on the predictors. In the ordinal logistic regression model, it is assumed that these odds are equal across the continuum, given values of the predictors, hence the term *proportional odds model*. Put another way, we assume that the predictors have the same impact on crossing all the thresholds. For the mammography intervention, this amounts to saying that the intervention has the same impact on moving a woman from doing nothing to contacting a health professional (i.e., crossing the first threshold τ_1) as on moving a woman from contacting a health professional to making an appointment for a mammogram (i.e., crossing the second threshold τ_2) as on moving a woman from making an appointment for a mammogram to obtaining a mammogram (i.e., crossing the third threshold τ_3).

Estimation of an ordinal logistic model involves estimation of a model for the probability of membership in a particular category, given values on the predictors and values of the thresholds. Consider a 3-category scale—disagree (*D*), undecided (*U*), and agree (*A*). Calling p_{ij} the probability that case$_i$ is in category$_j$, we have three predicted probabilities for each case: $\hat{p}_{iD}, \hat{p}_{iU}$, and $\hat{p}_{iA}$. Threshold τ_1 is between *D* and *U*; and threshold τ_2 is between *U* and *A*. Then in ordinal logistic regression the following equations are estimated in the one predictor case:

(13.3.1)
$$\ln\left(\frac{\hat{p}_{iU} + \hat{p}_{iA}}{\hat{p}_{iD}}\right) = t_1 + BX_i;$$

(13.3.2)
$$\ln\left(\frac{\hat{p}_{iA}}{\hat{p}_{iD} + \hat{p}_{iU}}\right) = t_2 + BX_i.$$

where t_1 and t_2 are the sample estimates of the population thresholds τ_1 and τ_2, respectively. Note that the regression coefficient B is constant across equations, following the parallel response assumption. The estimated thresholds t_1 and t_2 differ across equations (for simplicity, an overall regression intercept is omitted).

Operationally, a single analysis is performed in which the dependent variable entered is the ordered step variable in which each individual is assigned the value of the category in which he/she falls. In *ordinal logistic regression*, the logistic regression model is used to predict the probability of membership in a category. A single regression coefficient B_j and corresponding odds ratio for predictor X_j are estimated for the full data set, corresponding to the overall impact of the predictor on the probability of membership in a category. The regression coefficient and odds ratio are assumed to apply equally across the continuum of categories. Estimates of the latent thresholds are also given. The scale of the latent variable is arbitrary; hence the scale of the thresholds τ_j is arbitrary (not in any particular units). The progression of thresholds along a continuum, however, can be seen. Long (1997) provides a discussion of standardization and interpretation of values on the latent continuum.[6]

---

[6]Ordinal logistic regression is implemented in SAS PROC LOGISTIC by simply entering an ordered categorical variable as the DV, and in SPSS PLUM as well.

An ordinal logistic regression of the STEPS variable is given in Table 13.3.1D. Overall, the odds of moving along the STEPS continuum from category to category as a function of the intervention are 4.32, an estimate of the overall impact of the treatment across the continuum.

The critical assumption of the model of proportional odds (or, equivalently, parallel slopes) is tested by a Score test. This test compares the fit of a model in which a single slope is applied to the whole continuum (the ordinal regression model) versus an unconstrained model in which a different slope is permitted for cases below versus above each threshold. The null hypothesis is that the parallel slopes model applies, that is, that the predictors have the same impact on crossing all the thresholds or, equivalently, that the odds ratios for crossing the thresholds, given the predictors, are equal. For the data set in Table 13.3.1D, the model is not rejected, $\chi^2(2) = .03$, *ns*. The assumption of parallel slopes is met. This is consistent with our conclusions from the analysis of the continuation thresholds in Table 13.3.1A, B, and C, that the odds ratios are quite similar across the continuum.

What if this test of proportional odds were significant, signifying that the ordinal regression model is not appropriate? The continuation category approach might be applied to develop separate models of the transition across each of the thresholds. In the ordinal regression model, a single set of predictors with identical regression coefficients must apply across the whole continuum. With the continuation category approach, there is the opportunity to develop different models of each transition, each containing its own set of predictors.

Ordinal Logistic Regression Versus the Nested Dichotomies Approach

If the researcher has reason to believe that a single model describes movement along the full latent propensity continuum across all thresholds, it is useful to begin with ordinal logistic regression. The associated Score test provides useful information about whether the researcher's hunch is correct or not. If the researcher is correct (i.e., the Score test is nonsignificant for an adequate sized sample), then a simple and parsimonious model of movement along the propensity continuum has been established, the overall ordinal logistic regression equation. In addition, the researcher obtains estimates of the thresholds. Should the Score test be rejected for ordinal logistic regression, then the researcher can move to a more complex representation of crossing each threshold, using the nested dichotomies approach for continuation categories.

Ordered Category Methods Versus Ordinary Least Squares Regression

Finally, an alternative approach to the analysis of the STEPS continuum is a usual OLS regression in which we assume that the four steps constitute an *interval scale* of propensity to obtain a mammogram, with the three thresholds *equally* spaced across the continuum. If this is so, then the OLS and ordinal regression results converge. An OLS analysis of the STEPS variable is reported in Table 13.3.1E. Of course, the INTERVEN predictor does predict STEPS, as we would expect from the three dichotomous logistic regressions and the ordinal logistic regression. The use of the OLS model for an ordinal DV that lacks equally spaced scale intervals may result in the same difficulties we saw with OLS regression applied to a dichotomous variable: non-normality of residuals and heteroscedasticity.

The analysis strategies of ordinal logistic regression and nested dichotomous logistic regressions with continuation categories may be useful when the outcome is measured on a Likert scale (e.g., strongly disagree ... strongly agree), as well as with behavioral continua. In psychology, at least, we use Likert scales frequently for attitude measurement, for example. Yet in attitude change experiments, we typically examine arithmetic mean shifts. We do not ask whether our experimental manipulations are equally effective across the attitude continuum, a question that is answered with ordinal logistic regression and the nested dichotomies strategy. Use of OLS regression with Likert scales or other ordered category scales does not inform this question. In OLS, an overall regression coefficient is assumed to apply across the continuum; no test of this assumption like the Score test for parallel slopes in ordinal logistic regression is supplied in the OLS framework. Neither are measures of the odds of crossing thresholds on the Likert scale supplied in OLS regression as they are in both ordinal logistic regression and nested dichotomous logistic regressions with continuation categories. Ordinal logistic regression also offers measures of thresholds; these threshold estimates provide information about category width. We believe that ordinal logistic regression and nested category approaches merit more frequent use than they currently enjoy.

13.4 MODELS FOR COUNT DATA: POISSON REGRESSION AND ALTERNATIVES

Count data in many substantive areas provide an informative dependent variable. As pointed out earlier, counts might include the number of aggressive acts a child commits during a 30-minute playground period, the number of cigarettes an individual smokes in an hour, the number of scholarly articles a faculty member publishes in a year. In all cases, the measure is characterized as the number of events that occur in a particular time period—a count. *Poisson regression analysis* predicts the number of events that occur in a specific time period from one or more independent variables. The assumption is that the number of events generated in a period of time depends on an *underlying rate* parameter. Because both logistic regression and Poisson regression are cases of the generalized linear model, there are direct parallels between logistic regression analysis and Poisson regression analysis. We present the Poisson regression model and then draw parallels to the logistic regression model. Finally, we use the characteristics of logistic regression and Poisson regression as examples of the generalized linear model to provide a more complete characterization of the generalized linear model.

Poisson regression is appropriate when we examine a phenomenon of very rare events, so that if we count the number of events for each of a sample of people, there are numerous people with scores of zero. To return to the example of number of cigarettes smoked, if we count the number of cigarettes smoked in an hour by attendees at a large party, there will many zeros, since many people do not smoke at all. We warn the reader at the outset that there are relatively few examples in behavioral science of the use of Poisson regression. Further, less effort has been devoted to data-analytic conventions (e.g., diagnostics) and interpretation of results than in logistic regression.

13.4.1 Linear Regression Applied to Count Data

The problems that we encounter in applying OLS regression to count data mirror those encountered in applying OLS regression to dichotomous outcomes. The residuals are not normally distributed, and they exhibit heteroscedasticity; therefore inferences about individual predictors and overall prediction may well be biased if OLS regression is applied. Moreover predicted scores can be out of range, specifically, below zero, which is impossible for counts. Further, the regression coefficients from OLS regression applied to count data may be biased and inconsistent, meaning that they do not become more accurate as sample size increases (Long, 1997). Moreover, the standard errors from the OLS regression may underestimate true standard errors, leading to inflated t tests for individual regression coefficients; significance of these coefficients is thus overestimated (Gardner, Mulvey, & Shaw, 1995).

Transforming Y Versus Poisson Regression

In Chapter 6 we discussed transformations that can be applied to dependent (and independent) variables in order to render the data better behaved for us in OLS regression. By better behaved we mean closer to meeting assumptions of normality of residuals and homoscedasticity. For a count dependent variable, the square root is suggested as a potentially useful transformation (see Section 6.4.13). The question may be raised as to whether one need use Poisson regression. Might it not be possible to simply take the square root of each count and apply OLS regression to the square roots of the counts? When we are dealing with rare events for which there are many zero counts, the OLS approach does not handle the excess of very low scores relative to the rates predicted by OLS regression; it also does not handle the heteroscedasticity problem (Gardner, Mulvey, & Shaw, 1995). Poisson regression is preferred. This question of the use of transformations plus OLS regression versus the use of newer methodologies is reflective of the evolution of statistics, a point made in Section 13.2.1 in the discussion of discriminant analysis versus logistic regression. The work on transformations historically precedes some of the developments of numerical methods for the generalized linear model. If one takes the approach of transformation of the count DV followed by OLS regression, it is important to examine residuals for non-normality and heteroscedasticity before accepting conclusions based on the analysis.

13.4.2 Poisson Probability Distribution

An understanding of Poisson regression is facilitated by a consideration of the Poisson distribution. The Poisson distribution is a probability distribution, like the normal, binomial, or t distribution. The Poisson distribution is used to represent the error structure in Poisson regression. Five examples of the Poisson distribution are plotted in Fig. 13.4.1. Each distribution shows the probability that an individual will produce a specific number of events in a given time period. The x axis shows number of events and the y axis, the probability of each number of events. Each of the distributions is generated by the same equation, but a characteristic known as the *rate parameter* differs across the distributions. The *rate parameter* is the *average number of events expected in the time period*. The rate parameter is typically denoted as μ, as in Fig. 13.4.1. The numerical values of the probabilities plotted in each distribution are also given above the graphical representation. Imagine that the probabilities for $\mu = .50$ are probabilities of achieving various numbers of scholarly publications in a year in a work environment that does not emphasize publication for merit and promotion; the probability of no publications is .61; of one publication, .30, of four or more publications, 0.00. Those probabilities for $\mu = 4.00$ might represent probabilities of different numbers of publications in a year for an institution that heavily emphasizes scholarly publication for merit and promotion. Note that the probability of no publications is only .02; of four or more publications, .57. The source of these probabilities in Fig. 13.4.1 is the *Poisson distribution*, given in Box 13.4.1.

The Poisson distribution is the most basic probability distribution applied to regression when the outcomes are count data. The five examples in Fig. 13.4.1 highlight important characteristics of the Poisson distribution. First, the probabilities only apply to counts of events; counts are whole numbers that range from 0 to $+\infty$, as represented on the x axis of Fig. 13.4.1. The rate parameter, however, can have decimal values, because it represents the average or expected number of counts. Second, when the rate parameter or mean (μ) is very small (e.g., when the expected number of events is $\mu = .50$ in Fig. 13.4.1), then many cases with zero events are expected, and the distribution is very positively skewed. As the mean number of events increases, the distribution becomes increasingly symmetrical, approaching a normal distribution. With $\mu = 10$, the distribution is almost normal in form; what we see in Fig. 13.4.1

Expected number of events (μ)

Case	Y	$\mu = .50$	$\mu = 1.25$	$\mu = 2.00$	$\mu = 4.00$	$\mu = 10.00$
100	0	.61	.29	.14	.02	.00
101	1	.30	.36	.27	.07	.00
102	2	.08	.22	.27	.15	.00
103	3	.01	.09	.18	.20	.01
104	4	.00	.03	.09	.20	.02
105	5	.00	.01	.04	.16	.04
106	6	.00	.00	.01	.10	.06
107	7	.00	.00	.00	.06	.09
108	8	.00	.00	.00	.03	.11
109	9	.00	.00	.00	.01	.13
110	10	.00	.00	.00	.01	.13

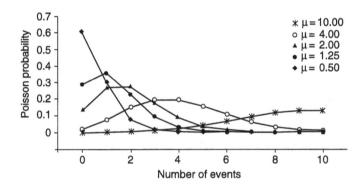

Note: Each curve reflects a different rate parameter (μ). The illustration of the curve for $\mu = 10$ shows only the left half of this distribution. The curve would decline almost symmetrically to the right if the number of events from 11 to 20 were provided.

FIGURE 13.4.1   Probability of Y events according to Poisson distribution as a function of the expected (mean) number of events. The expected number of events (or the rate parameter) is noted as μ.

for $\mu = 10$ is the left half of such a distribution that declines almost symmetrically to zero as the number of events continues to increase from 11 to 20 (the right half of the distribution is not shown in Fig. 13.4.1). Third, as the mean number of events increases, the variance of the number of events across the population also increases. When the mean number of events is $\mu = .50$, the majority of cases have counts of 0, and the highest count is 3. When the mean is $\mu = 4.00$, in contrast, the counts given in Fig. 13.4.1 range from 0 to 10. In fact, for the Poisson probability distribution, the mean and the variance of the distribution are equal:

$$(13.4.1) \qquad\qquad \text{variance } (Y) = \mu.$$

This last property is important; it states that the variance of the Poisson distribution is completely determined by the mean of the distribution.

When the mean count in a distribution is large so that symmetry of the distribution of events is approached, then OLS regression may be tried. Careful checking of residuals for heteroscedasticity and nonnormality is advised, in justifying the appropriateness of OLS regression.

BOX 13.4.1
The Poisson Probability Distribution

The expression for the *Poisson distribution* is as follows:

(13.4.2)
$$P(Y) = \frac{e^{(-\mu)}\mu^Y}{Y!}$$

where Y = the number of events and μ = the expected or mean number of events, and $Y!$ is Y factorial = $Y(Y-1)(Y-2)\ldots 1$.

This expression generates all the curves displayed in Fig. 13.4.1. For example, for $\mu = 4.00$ and $Y = 3$ publications,

$$P(Y) = \frac{e^{(-4.00)}\mu^3}{3!} = \frac{.0183 \times 4^3}{3 \times 2 \times 1} = .20.$$

(As before, to find $e^{-4.00}$, enter -4.00 into a calculator, and press the e^x button; see Box 13.2.2.)

13.4.3 Poisson Regression Analysis

Exactly paralleling logistic regression, we have three forms of the regression equation in Poisson regression. First, we predict the expected number of events ($\hat{\mu}$) from values on a set of predictors $X_1, X_2, \ldots, X_k$.

(13.4.3)
$$\hat{\mu} = e^{(B_1X_1 + B_2X_2 + \cdots + B_kX_k + B_0)}.$$

Equation (13.4.3) is not in a form that is linear in the coefficients. If we take the logarithm of both sides, we have a second regression equation that is linear in the coefficients and in which the logarithm of the predicted expected number of events is the predicted score:

(13.4.4)
$$\ln(\hat{\mu}) = B_1X_1 + B_2X_2 + \cdots + B_kX_k + B_0.$$

Third, we can write an equation in which we predict the probability of each specific number of events, given the expected average number of events $\hat{\mu}$. For the predicted probability of a count of c events ($\hat{p}_c$) we have

(13.4.5)
$$\hat{p}_c = \frac{e^{(-\hat{\mu})}\hat{\mu}^c}{c!}.$$

Let us focus on Eq. (13.4.3). This is a simple exponential equation. The equation represents a curve like that in Fig. 13.1.1(C), which shows the predicted number of events as a function of values of a predictor X. The curve rises faster than a straight line as X increases. Equation (13.4.3) predicts more events when X is high than would be predicted from a linear equation.

A natural question, given the curve in Fig. 13.1.1(C) is, whether a quadratic polynomial regression equation $\hat{Y} = B_1X + B_2X^2$ (a form of OLS regression) would fit the curve. In fact, a quadratic polynomial might closely approximate the curve. However, the increasing variance of Y with increasing X, a characteristic of count data, would still exist in the data and would be ignored in polynomial regression, potentially causing difficulties in inference that are handled in Poisson regression.

Fictitious Example of Poisson Regression and Interpretation of Coefficients

A fictitious example illustrates the form of a Poisson regression for count data. Assume we are predicting the expected number of aggressive acts that a young child will exhibit on a playground during a 30-minute recess period. The single predictor X is a 0–10 rating of each child's aggressiveness by the teacher. We have a one-predictor Poisson regression equation; Eq. (13.4.3) simplifies to

(13.4.6)
$$\hat{\mu} = e^{(B_1 X + B_0)}.$$

Assume that the appropriate Poisson regression equation is $\hat{\mu} = e^{(.35X - 1.68)}$. Figure 13.4.2 provides the aggressiveness ratings for 11 children, one at each value of rated aggressiveness. The expected rate (predicted number of aggressive acts) for each child according to the Poisson regression equation and the predicted number of aggressive acts from a linear regression analysis (OLS) are also presented. The predicted rate ($\hat{\mu}$) from Poisson regression indicates that aggressive acts are rare if the child is rated 5 or lower in aggressiveness (at a rating of 5, only 1.07 acts are expected). Thereafter, as the rating rises from 6 to 10, the number of expected aggressive acts increases rapidly to 6. Poisson predicted rates are noted with dots,

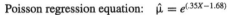

Poisson regression equation: $\hat{\mu} = e^{(.35X - 1.68)}$

Case	Aggressiveness rating	Predicted rate ($\hat{\mu}$) from Poisson regression	Predicted number of acts from linear regression	$\ln(\hat{\mu})$ from Poisson regression
100	0	0.19	−0.79	−1.68
101	1	0.26	−0.26	−1.33
102	2	0.38	0.27	−0.98
103	3	0.53	0.80	−0.63
104	4	0.76	1.33	−0.28
105	5	1.07	1.86	0.07
106	6	1.52	2.39	0.42
107	7	2.16	2.92	0.77
108	8	3.06	3.45	1.12
109	9	4.35	3.98	1.47
110	10	6.17	4.51	1.82

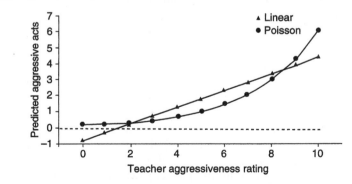

FIGURE 13.4.2 Poisson regression versus linear regression for a fictitious example predicting number of aggressive acts in a 30-minute recess as a function of teacher rating of aggressiveness according to a Poisson regression equation.

linear regression predicted scores with filled triangles. Note that when the rating is either very low or very high, the Poisson regression analysis predicts a higher number of aggressive acts than the linear regression equation, whereas the linear regression equation predicts higher scores in the midrange of the rating scale. The Poisson model accounts for the cases with zero counts and with very high counts, whereas OLS regression misses these aspects of the count data.

The B coefficient in the Poisson equation, $B = .35$, can be interpreted in two ways. First, for a 1-unit increase in X (the aggressiveness rating), the predicted rate ($\hat{\mu}$, expected number of aggressive acts) is *multiplied* by the value e^B. For $B = .35$, $e^{.35} = 1.42$. For example, for a child with a rating of 6, we expect $\hat{\mu} = e^{(.35X-1.68)} = \hat{\mu} = e^{[.35(6)-1.68]} = 1.52$ aggressive acts; for a child with a rating of 7, we expect 2.16 aggressive acts, $(1.52)(1.42) = 2.16$. Second, for a unit-1 increase in X, the predicted score in the linear equation, $\ln(\hat{\mu})$, the natural logarithm of the expected number of aggressive acts, increases by .35. For a rating of 7, $\ln(\hat{\mu}) = .77$; for a rating of 8, $\ln(\hat{\mu}) = .77 + .35 = 1.12$. (Interpreting the meaning of the Poisson regression equation is clear in the e^B form, which yields a predicted count, whereas the value of the logarithm of the expected count cannot be interpreted directly in terms of counts). It should be noted that all the predicted rates from the Poisson regression equation are positive, corresponding to numbers of events, which cannot fall below zero. In contrast, the predicted number of acts from the linear regression equation is negative for aggressiveness scores of 0 and 1, an impossible situation.

Heteroscedasticity of Residuals

Refer again to Fig. 13.4.1, and assume that the values μ represent values of predicted scores from Eq. (13.4.3). For each curve based on a particular value of μ we see a distribution of Y scores (the number of events); each curve is a conditional distribution of Y scores, (i.e., the Y scores of all individuals with a particular value of μ.) There is clear heteroscedasticity of the conditional distributions of Y. As the value of μ increases, the spread of the expected distribution of Y scores becomes broader. For example, for $\mu = .50$, Y scores between 0 and 3 have expected probabilities greater than zero; for $\mu = 4.00$, Y scores between 0 and 10 have expected probabilities greater than zero.

13.4.4 Overdispersion and Alternative Models

The Poisson regression model makes the very restrictive assumption that we have already encountered: The variance $\sigma^2 = \hat{\mu}$, or the variance of the residuals around each predicted rate equals the predicted rate. In order that this assumption be met, all of the systematic variation in rates $\hat{\mu}_i$ across individuals must be accounted for completely by the set of predictors; no other potential predictor could account for additional variance. Put another way, all individuals with the same values on the predictors should have the same observed rate parameter. In the fictitious example, this means that all the systematic variation in the observed number of aggressive acts would be accounted for by scores on the teacher aggressiveness rating scale. If there is systematic variation in rates that is not accounted for by the predictor set, then there will be greater variation in the residuals around each predicted rate than is permitted by the Poisson regression model (i.e., $\sigma^2 > \hat{\mu}$). This condition is termed *overdispersion* (see Gardner, Mulvey & Shaw, 1995, and Land, McCall, and Nagin, 1996 for discussions of overdispersion). Overdispersion is frequently found in count data. Overdispersion leads to inflation of the goodness of fit χ^2 test. In addition, with overdispersion, the standard errors of Poisson regression coefficients are too small, so the significance of predictors is overestimated. The level of dispersion relative to a Poisson distribution is often characterized by a *dispersion parameter* ϕ, which equals 1 if the Poisson variance assumption is met, is greater than 1 for overdispersion, and is less than 1 for *underdispersion.*

There are a number of statistical approaches for analysis of count data that exhibit overdispersion. First, is the *overdispersed Poisson model*, which belongs to a class of models called *quasi-likelihood regression models* (Fahrmier & Tutz, 1994). A second approach to overdispersion is the use of an alternative regression model, the *negative binomial regression model.* Both approaches are described in Box 13.4.2.

BOX 13.4.2
Alternative Models for Count Data With Overdispersion:
The Overdispersed Poisson Model and the Negative
Binomial Regression Model

In the overdispersed Poisson model, the dispersion parameter ϕ is calculated from the data themselves; the standard errors of the regression coefficients for overdispersed data are adjusted by multiplying them by ϕ. If there is overdispersion, and thus $\phi > 1$, the values of the standard errors are increased, thereby decreasing the excess significance in the statistical tests of the regresison coefficients. If $\phi = 1$, the Poisson model holds. No special model is specified of the distribution of the excess variance relative to the Poisson variance. That is, no probability distribution is assumed for how the individual rate parameters μ_i vary around the expected rate parameter μ, given values on the set of predictors. This is the hallmark of quasi-likelihood models, that a portion of the variance is not assumed to follow a particular probability model.

The negative binomial model assumes that for each individual, a Poisson distribution applies, but that the rates for individuals μ_i, given specific values on the predictors, vary across individuals. A new probability distribution known as the negative binomial distribution is used to characterize the variance of the residuals. The variance of the negative binomial distribution is comprised of two components: (1) the expected rate μ (as in Poisson regression) plus (2) a second amount that characterizes the additional variance in the rate parameter across individuals, not accounted for by the Poisson distribution (see Gardner, Mulvey, and Shaw, 1995, p. 399; Land, McCall, and Nagin, 1996, p. 397; Long, 1997, p. 233). As a result, the negative binomial variance for each value of μ_i is greater than μ_i. Put another way, the negative binomial model of the errors allows greater variance than is permitted by Poisson regression, thereby accounting for overdispersion in count data. Negative binomial regression may still result in inflated t values.

The negative binomial regression model is one of a class of *mixed Poisson models* that mix a second source of variance with the Poisson variance to account for overdispersion (Land, McCall, & Nagin, 1996, p. 397). In contrast to quasi-likelihood models, which specify no particular probability distribution for the excess variance, mixture models specify a second probability distribution for the second source of variance, over and above the Poisson distribution, which characterizes the first source of variance. In the negative binomial regression model, the second probability distribution is another discrete probability distribution, the gamma distribution. The combination of the Poisson distribution with the gamma distribution yields the negative binomial distribution. It is this mixture of probability distributions that is the hallmark of mixture models. Newer approaches to overdispersion include the *semiparametric mixed Poisson regression* characterized by Land, McCall, and Nagin (1996).

13.4.5 Independence of Observations

Poisson regression also assumes that the observations are *independent* of one another, just as in OLS regression and logistic regression. However, the basic datum in Poisson regression is an event (a publication, an aggressive act, etc.) exhibited by one individual. Such events emitted by one individual tend to be correlated; that is, the fact that one event has occurred may increase the probability of subsequent events. This correlation between events is referred to in economics as *state dependence*, or in biometric and sociological literature as the *contagion model* (see Land, McCall, & Nagin, 1996, p. 395). Considering our example of number of aggressive acts, it is easy to imagine how a single aggressive act of a child on the playground can lead to still other aggressive acts as a fight ensues. Such nonindependence of events leads to clusters of events, or higher numbers of events in particular individuals than would be expected from the Poisson distribution. In addition, it leads to an excess of zeros, that is, more cases in which there are zero events than would be expected by the Poisson model. In the case of state dependence, the distribution of the counts observed for individuals in the sample does not follow Poisson distributions, and other count models must be employed.

13.4.6 Sources on Poisson Regression

Accessible sources on Poisson regression are less readily available than are sources on logistic regression. Neter, Kutner, Nachtsheim, and Wasserman (1996, pp. 609–614) provide an introduction; Long (1997, pp. 217–249) provides a more extensive treatment. Gardner, Mulvey, and Shaw (1995) and Land, McCall, and Nagin (1996) provide discussions of limitations of Poisson regression and alternative models.

13.5 FULL CIRCLE: PARALLELS BETWEEN LOGISTIC AND POISSON REGRESSION, AND THE GENERALIZED LINEAR MODEL

13.5.1 Parallels Between Poisson and Logistic Regression

There are many parallels between Poisson regression and logistic regression. Having reviewed the presentation of logistic regression in detail, the reader should find these parallels facilitate an understanding of Poisson regression. These parallels will also facilitate a characterization of the generalized linear model, of which logistic regression and Poisson regression are two special cases.

Parallels between logistic and Poisson regression exist in six areas: (1) three forms of regression equation, (2) the interpretation of coefficients, (3) the relationship of the form of observed Y scores to the form of predicted scores, (4) the concept of error structure, (5) nature of the estimates and estimation procedures, and (6) the nature of significance tests.

Three Equations

Three forms of the logistic regression equation predict the odds of a case, the log of the odds (the logit), and the probability of being a case, given in Eqs. (13.2.12), (13.2.11), and (13.2.14), respectively. In Poisson regression, the three forms of the Poisson regression equation predict the expected number of events ($\hat{\mu}$), the log of the expected number of events, $\ln(\hat{\mu})$, and the predicted probability of observing c events ($\hat{p}_c$), in Eqs. (13.4.3), (13.4.4), and (13.4.5), respectively. In logistic regression we move from the predicted score in the form of the logit to the odds by taking the antilog; we then compute the probability from the odds. In Poisson regression, we move from the predicted score in the linear equation form, that is, $\ln(\hat{\mu})$, to the predicted number of events, by taking the antilog of $\ln(\hat{\mu})$, yielding $(\hat{\mu})$. Then we can substitute $(\hat{\mu})$ into Eq. (13.4.5) to obtain predicted probabilities.

Interpretation of Coefficients

Consider the one-predictor logistic regression equation Eq. (13.2.6) and the one-predictor Poisson regression equation, written in linear form as

(13.5.1)
$$\ln(\hat{\mu}) = B_1 X + B_0.$$

In logistic regression, the value of the logit, $\ln[\hat{p}/(1 - \hat{p})]$, increases linearly with the value of B_1, the regression coefficient. In Poisson regression, the value of $\ln(\hat{\mu})$ increases linearly with the value of B_1, the regression coefficient. In logistic regression the odds, $[\hat{p}/(1 - \hat{p})]$, are multiplied by the value e^{B_1} for each one unit increase in X, as in Eq. (13.2.5). In Poisson regression, written as Eq. (13.4.3), the expected rate $(\hat{\mu})$ is multiplied by the value e^{B_1} for each one unit increase in X. For both logistic and Poisson regression, these interpretations generalize to the multiple predictor case.

Form of Observed Y Versus Predicted Score

In both logistic regression and Poisson regression, the predicted score in the linear form of the regression equation is not in the same units as the observed Y score. In logistic regression, the observed Y score indicates group membership ($1 = $ case; $0 = $ noncase). However, in the linear form of the logistic regression equation, the predicted score is in the form of a logit, as shown in Eq. (13.2.11). In Poisson regression, the predicted score in the linear form of the regression equation is again not in the same units as the observed Y score. The observed Y score is a count of the number of events in a specific time period. However, in the linear form of the Poisson regression equation, the predicted score is the logarithm of the count, as shown in Eq. (13.4.4).

Error Structure

Both Poisson regression and logistic regression have non-normally distributed residuals as inherent in the model. In both cases the variance of the errors around the predicted score is determined by the value of the predicted score, leading to heteroscedasticity in both models.

Estimates and Estimation Procedures

Both Poisson and logistic regression employ maximum likelihood estimation, with iterative solutions for the regression coefficients.

Significance Tests

Likelihood ratios, deviances (null and model), and likelihood ratio χ^2 tests proceed in the same fashion for Poisson as for logistic regression for testing overall model fit, contribution of predictor sets and individual predictors. As with all maximum likelihood estimates, the distributions of estimates of the regression coefficients in Poisson regression approach normality as sample size approaches infinity; Wald tests apply to individual coefficients and combinations of coefficients.

13.5.2 The Generalized Linear Model Revisited

The generalized linear model is a highly flexible approach to characterizing the relationship of predictors to a dependent variable Y that subsumes a variety of specific regression models. Logistic and Poisson regression are two such specific instances of the generalized linear model; they serve to illustrate the characteristics of this broad class of models of prediction, which also includes OLS regression. The regression models included in the generalized linear model can all be expressed in a form that is *linear in the parameters*. For OLS regression, logistic regression, and Poisson regression, these forms are given as Eqs. (13.1.1), (13.2.11), and (13.4.4), respectively. All instances of the generalized linear model assume that observations are independent. The varieties of the generalized linear model are characterized in two ways, explained next: the *variance function* and the *link function*.

Variance Function

The generalized linear model gains part of its great flexibility by extending the assumption of the distribution of the residuals from normality to a *family of probability distributions*, the *exponential family*. If the dependent variable is dichotomous, then the residuals follow a binomial distribution (see Section 13.2). If the dependent variable consists of counts of the number of events in a period of time, then the residuals follow a Poisson distribution (see Section 13.4.2). The binomial and Poisson distributions, and other distributions that are members of the exponential family (e.g. gamma, inverse Gaussian) in general have the property that the mean and the variance of the distribution are not independent, that is, the variance depends on the mean. (The Gaussian or normal distribution, which is also a member of the exponential family, is an exception in which the mean and variance are independent). The lack of independence of the mean and variance of the distribution of residuals leads to heteroscedasticity, since the conditional variance of the criterion around a predicted value $\hat{Y}$ depends on the value of $\hat{Y}$. We saw this dependence in Eq. (13.2.3) for the variance of residuals associated with dichotomous Y and Eq. (13.4.1) for the variance of residuals for a count variable Y. When we find residuals that are not normally distributed, we require a model of the *variance function*, that is, a model of how the conditional variance of Y varies as a function of Y. For example, the Poisson distribution, which gives Poisson regression its name, comes into play in the assumed *variance function* for the residuals, a central aspect of the generalized linear model. In Poisson regression, it is assumed that the residuals at each value of $\hat{\mu}$, the predicted rate, are distributed as a Poisson distribution, with variance also equal to $\hat{\mu}$.

Link Function

In each form of regression we have encountered—OLS regression, logistic regression, and Poisson regression—we have considered the relationship of the form of the observed Y score versus the predicted score in the regression equation that is linear in the coefficients. We have noted that in OLS regression, observed Y and predicted scores are in the same units. Once again, in logistic regression we have dichotomous Y versus the predicted logit, in Poisson regression, the count versus the predicted log (count). The *link function* in the generalized linear model is the transformation that relates the predicted outcome to the observed dependent variable Y. A second source of flexibility in generalized linear models is the variety of link functions that are possible. For OLS regression, the link function is the *identity* function, since observed and predicted scores are on the same scale. For logistic regression, the link function is the *logit*; for Poisson regression, the link function is the *logarithm*.

Regression models that are linear in the coefficients, whose residuals are assumed to follow a variance function from the exponential family, with one of a variety of link functions are members of the generalized linear model. McCullagh and Nelder (1989) is the classic reference work on generalized linear models. Fahrmier and Tutz (1994) is a second complete source.

13.6 SUMMARY

Ordinary least squares regression assumes that the dependent variable has normally distributed errors that exhibit homoscedasticity. Categorical dependent variables and count variables do not exhibit these properties. If these conditions are not met, OLS regression may be inefficient and lead to inaccurate conclusions (Section 13.1).

Binary dependent variables traditionally have been examined using two-group discriminant analysis. The logistic regression model for binary dependent variables is presented as an appropriate alternative, first for the single-predictor case, and then for the multiple-predictor case (Section 13.2). Three forms of the logistic regression model—predicting the logit (log odds), the odds, and the probability of being a case—are developed and explained (Sections 13.2.3 and 13.2.4). The characterization of regression coefficients in the form of odds ratios is explained (Section 13.2.5). Confidence intervals for regression coefficients and odds ratios are presented (Section 13.2.8). Maximum likelihood estimates and maximum likelihood estimation are characterized (Section 13.2.9). Likelihood ratios, deviances, and statistical tests for overall model fit based on likelihood ratios and deviances are introduced (Section 13.2.10, 13.2.12). Indices of overall model fit are introduced (Section 13.2.11). Wald and likelihood ratio tests for significance of individual predictors are presented (Section 13.2.13), and likelihood ratio tests of gain in prediction from sets of predictors are explained (Section 13.2.14). Difficulties in predictor scaling are addressed in logistic regression (Section 13.2.16). Issues in the use of regression diagnostics in logistic regression are explained (Section 13.2.17). The application of logistic regression to statistical classification is introduced (Section 13.2.19).

The logistic regression model is extended to multiple response categories with presentation of polytomous logistic regression. The analysis of ordered categories by nested dichotomies and ordinal logistic regression is illustrated (Section 13.3).

Poisson regression is developed for count data, that is, dependent variables that are counts of rare events, such that there are many scores of zero and the count dependent variable is highly positively skewed (Section 13.4).

Logistic regression and Poisson regression are used to illustrate the characteristics of the generalized linear model, with explication of the variance function and the link function (Section 13.5).

14

Random Coefficient Regression and Multilevel Models

OLS regression and the regression approaches subsumed under the generalized linear model, including logistic and Poisson regression, all assume that observations are independent of one another. If observations on two individuals are independent of one another, then knowledge of scores on one individual provides no information whatever about scores on the other individual. Put another way, there is no relationship between the measures on one individual and measures on any other individual. Should there be repeated observations on the same individuals, standard OLS regression analyses assume that these observations are independent across time.

14.1 CLUSTERING WITHIN DATA SETS

Our observations may well not be independent. Sections 4.3.1 and 4.4.5 introduced the issue of dependency among residuals, which may occur when the cases are members of an intact group, (e.g., a family, a community organization). Consider, for example, the IQ scores of children within families. We expect correlation among these IQ scores; the IQ scores of children within a single family may be more similar to one another in value than would be expected in a random sample of children. Measures taken on members of dyads—for example, spouses or twins—are also highly interrelated. Dependency can arise in measures of demographic characteristics of individuals who live in close proximity (e.g., among the incomes or ethnicities of individuals who live in particular neighborhoods of a large metropolitan area). Dependency can also occur in experimental research when we run participants in groups, and the behavior of group members can influence the responses of individuals, for example, in experiments in group processes in social psychology. Under some circumstances dependency can arise in experiments when the presentation of the treatment condition inadvertently varies slightly from session to session in which groups of subjects participate. Correlation or dependency among subsets of cases within a data set, as reflected in all these examples, is referred to as *clustering*.

Dependency in data can also arise when we take repeated measures on single individuals over time. For example, we might measure the anxiety level of each of a set of individuals once a month for a period of months. We would expect that the anxiety measures from any one individual would be more correlated with one another than the anxiety measures across individuals. This is another form of dependency in data, referred to as *serial dependency* (see Section 4.4.5). In this chapter we focus on clustering among individuals within groups, and approaches to handling data that contain such clustering of individuals. Chapter 15 is devoted to the treatment of repeated measures data that may exhibit serial dependency. Much of what is developed here for the treatment of clustering among individuals generalizes directly to serial dependency; Section 15.4 develops this generalization.

When data are clustered, OLS regression may lead to inaccuracies in inference. The *random coefficient regression model*, an alternative to OLS regression, is structured to handle clustered data. The random coefficient (RC) regression model differs from OLS regression in the assumptions made about the nature of the regression coefficients and correlational structure of the individual observations. Further, when individuals are clustered into groups, we may have multiple levels of measurement, at both the individual and the group level. For clients in therapy groups, for example, we may measure characteristics of the clients (individual level) and characteristics of the therapist that impact all members of the group (group level). Measures taken on multiple levels may be treated in *multilevel models* (equivalently termed *hierarchical linear models*), which employ random coefficient regression (Goldstein, 1995; Kreft & de Leeuw, 1998; Raudenbush & Bryk, 2002; Snijders & Bosker, 1999).

14.1.1 Clustering, Alpha Inflation, and the Intraclass Correlation

As indicated, clustering poses difficulties for statistical inference in the general linear model and generalized linear model frameworks. If data are clustered, the standard errors of OLS regression coefficients are typically negatively biased (i.e., too small). Thus the confidence intervals around individual regression coefficients are typically too small. Statistical tests for the significance of individual regression coefficients, which involve division of the coefficients by their standard errors, will in general be too large, leading to overestimation of significance, or *alpha inflation*. As clustering increases (i.e., as scores within clusters become increasingly similar to one another), alpha inflation increases as well; that is, the actual level of Type I error increasingly exceeds the nominal level. This same bias occurs if logistic regression is applied to clustered data.

The degree of clustering, (i.e., the degree of correlation or nonindependence among a set of observations), is measured by the *intraclass correlation* (ICC; Shrout & Fleiss, 1979). The ICC measures the proportion of the total variance of a variable that is accounted for by the clustering (group membership) of the cases. The ICC also can be conceptualized as a measure of the extent to which members of the same category (for example, children within families) are more similar to one another than to members of other categories.[1] Put another way, the ICC measures whether scores from different groups are more discrepant from one another than scores within the same group. The ICC ranges from 0 for complete independence of observations to 1 for complete dependence.[2] An assumption underlying the general linear model and generalized linear model is that ICC = 0.

---

[1] There are multiple definitions of the intraclass correlation (ICC) that arise in the context of varying experimental designs. The ICC is often used as a measure of interjudge reliability in designs in which multiple judges rate multiple targets. Shrout and Fleiss (1979) provide an explication of the multiple definitions of the ICC in the estimation of interjudge reliability.

[2] This presentation of the ICC assumes that clustering produces similarity or positive correlation among cases within a cluster; this is by far the usual situation in clustered data. In rare instances, for a particular research purpose, an experimenter may create clusters in which the individuals are sampled to be highly discrepant from one another, (i.e., more dissimilar from one another than might be expected by chance alone). In this exceptional instance, the ICC can be negative and lead to an actual Type I error rate lower than the nominal Type I error rate (Kenny & Judd, 1986).

14.1.2 Estimating the Intraclass Correlation

We can calculate the ICC for any variable in a data set with a clustered structure, that is, in which individuals are members of groups or clusters. Using common notation, if we let τ represent the amount of variance in a variable that is due to differences among groups in the population, and σ^2 represent the variance among scores within groups, pooled across all groups, then the total variance is given as $\tau + \sigma^2$. The population expression for the ICC is given as follows:[3]

$$(14.1.1) \qquad\qquad\qquad ICC = \frac{\tau}{\tau + \sigma^2}.$$

If groups do not differ from one another, then $\tau = 0$, and the ICC $= 0$.

Data on a common dependent variable taken across a set of groups are required to estimate the ICC (e.g., the educational attainment of children within families, each of which has at least two children). The ICC can be estimated from a fixed effects one-factor nonrepeated measures analysis of variance (ANOVA) in which the factor is the grouping variable (for example, family), and the levels are the particular groups (the particular families). Members of the groups (children within families) serve as the observations. For those familiar with ANOVA, the estimate $\hat{\tau}$ of τ is taken from $MS_{treatment}$ and MS_{error}, where $\hat{\tau} = MS_{treatment} - MS_{error}/n$, where n is the number of cases per cell for equal group sizes. The estimate $\hat{\sigma}^2$ of σ^2 is taken directly from MS_{error} as $\hat{\sigma}^2 = MS_{error}$. Then the estimate of the ICC based on the fixed effects one-factor ANOVA is given as follows:

$$(14.1.2) \qquad\qquad\qquad ICC = \frac{MS_{treatment} - MS_{error}}{MS_{treatment} + (n-1)MS_{error}}.$$

For unequal group sizes, n is replaced by $\tilde{n} = M_n - [sd^2(n_j)/(gM_n)]$, where M_n is the mean number of cases per group, $sd^2(n_j)$ is the variance of the number of cases per group, and g is the number of groups (Snijders & Bosker, 1999).

For those familiar with fixed effects one-factor ANOVA, examination of the ICC in relation to the omnibus F test for the one-factor ANOVA may provide more insight into the ICC. The omnibus F test in one-factor fixed effects ANOVA is given as $F = MS_{treatment}/MS_{error}$. We see that if $MS_{treatment} = MS_{error}$, indicating that there is no effect of the grouping factor, then the ICC $= 0$.

An ICC of .01 or .05 may seem very small; however, the actual alpha level of statistical tests increases dramatically even with such apparently small ICCs. For example, in a one-factor fixed effects ANOVA with $n = 25$ cases per cell and an ICC of only .01, the actual alpha level for the test of the treatment factor is .11 when the nominal alpha level (the alpha level for the tabled critical value) is .05. With $n = 25$ cases per cell and an ICC of .05, the actual alpha level is .19 for nominal alpha of .05. The alpha inflation increases as the ICC and sample size increase (see Barcikowski, 1981, p. 270; Kreft & de Leeuw, 1998, p. 10 for further numerical examples). This same sort of alpha inflation occurs in regression analysis with clustered data.

---

[3]This expression corresponds to ICC(1, 1) of Shrout and Fleiss (1979), one of a number of expressions for the ICC, which vary across designs and data structures.

14.2 ANALYSIS OF CLUSTERED DATA
WITH ORDINARY LEAST SQUARES APPROACHES

Clustered data historically have been the cause of great statistical hand wringing and analytic acrobatics. Clustering has been viewed as a "problem" with data, something that requires handling in order to get on with the study of the relationships of predictor measures on individuals (e.g., the IQ scores of individual children within families) to some DV of interest (e.g., educational attainment, or the level of education achieved by each child). In the OLS regression context, three approaches have been taken to examining the relationship of predictors to a dependent variable when data are clustered (have group structure). The first is to ignore clustering and analyze the individual cases as if there were no group structure in the data, referred to as *disaggregated analysis*. In the IQ example, we might predict educational attainment from the child's IQ, ignoring the fact that there may well be clustering among siblings, who appear in the same data set. Here we expect alpha inflation. The second is to aggregate data at the group level, obtaining a mean on each predictor variable and on the DV for each group; the groups are then treated as the unit of analysis, referred to as *aggregated analysis*. In the IQ example, we might relate the mean IQ of the children in each family to the mean level of schooling achieved by the children of that family. There are conceptual difficulties with this approach. The resulting regression equation describes the relationship of the means of predictors in individual clusters to the mean of the dependent variable in those clusters. We set out to study how the IQ scores of individual children relate to their level of educational attainment. However, the aggregated analysis tells us how mean child IQ in a family relates to mean level of schooling in that family. Generalizing or more correctly particularizing from the group equation to the individual might lead to very inaccurate conclusions; generalization from results at one level of aggregation to another (or unit of analysis to another) is referred to as the *ecological fallacy* (Robinson, 1950).

The disaggregated analysis and the aggregated analysis estimate very different regression coefficients. Using the terminology of analysis of covariance (ANCOVA), the disaggregated analysis estimates the *total regression coefficient* of the criterion on the predictor, B_T, illustrated in Fig. 14.2.1(A). The aggregated analysis estimates the *between-class regression coefficient*, B_B. Again there is a single regression equation; here each group is treated as a single case. The disaggregated versus the aggregated analyses may yield very different results. Kreft and de Leeuw (1998) provided an example in which this is so; they examined the relationship between education (the predictor) and income (the dependent variable) within 12 industries: The total regression coefficient in the disaggregated analysis was positive, with higher education associated with higher income overall. However, the between-class coefficient was negative. Overall the highest paid industries had lower average education levels than did lower paid industries (e.g., there was lower average education and higher average salary in the transportation industry; in the teaching industry, there was higher average education and lower average salary).

The third OLS approach is to analyze the regression of a dependent variable on predictors of interest at the individual case level, but to include as predictors a set of $(g - 1)$ dummy codes for g groups or clusters to identify the group membership of each individual in the data set (see Section 8.2). Consider Fig. 14.2.1(B), which shows a series of regression lines, one for each group. The regression lines all have the same slope; however, all the intercepts differ, indicating that the different groups have different arithmetic mean levels on the dependent variable. Having the $(g - 1)$ dummy codes as predictors takes into account these differences in intercepts of the individual groups. There is only one slope, a constant across all the groups; that is, it is assumed that the slope of the regression of Y on X is constant across all groups.

(A) Total regression of Y on X, ignoring group structure.

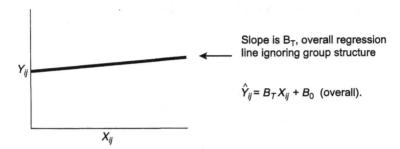

(B) Separate regression lines within each group. All slopes are equal to one another and to B_T. Intercepts differ across groups; intercepts represent overall level on Y within each group at $X = 0$.

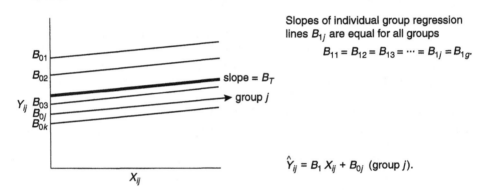

(C) Separate regression lines within each group. Both slopes and intercepts differ across groups.

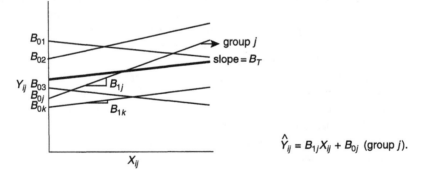

FIGURE 14.2.1 Slopes and intercepts in OLS and random coefficient models.

Once the dummy codes for the groups are included in the analysis, the regression coefficient for the predictor in question (here, child's IQ) is the *pooled within-class regression coefficient*, B_W. The pooled within-class regression coefficient is the weighted average of the regression coefficients in each of the individual groups. This approach is, in fact, the analysis of covariance (ANCOVA) model (see Section 8.7.5). Typically, when we use ANCOVA, the focus is on the effect of groups on the outcome when the individual level predictor (the covariate) is partialed out. In contrast, here the focus is on the relationship of the individual level predictor to the dependent variable when differences among group means are partialed out. This third analysis corrects for any differences in the means of the groups when the predictive utility of particular individual level predictors is assessed (e.g., the regression of educational attainment on IQ with family membership controlled).

It is also possible to model interactions between group membership and predictors; for example, one could include in the regression analysis interaction terms between each dummy code and IQ; the set of interaction terms measures whether the relationship of IQ to educational attainment varies across families. In Fig. 14.2.1(C), each group has a different intercept and a different slope. The differences in intercepts would be captured by the $(g - 1)$ dummy codes discussed earlier. Another $(g - 1)$ interaction codes, the cross product of each dummy code with the predictor in question (here, IQ), would be required to capture the differences in slopes.

The approach to handling clustering with dummy codes to account for group mean differences on the dependent variable is often referred to as the *fixed effects approach to clustering* (see, for example, Snijders & Boskers, 1999). This name arises because OLS regression analysis, on which the approach is based, is also referred to as a *fixed effects* regression analysis, for reasons explained in Section 14.4. As is explained in Section 14.14, under some conditions, (e.g., small numbers of clusters in the data set) this approach is recommended for the analysis of clustered data.

14.2.1 Numerical Example, Analysis of Clustered Data With Ordinary Least Squares Regression

In this section we present a numerical example of the use of OLS approaches to handling clustered data. Here we introduce a simulated numerical example of the prediction of weight loss as a function of motivation to lose weight; we will use this example throughout the chapter. We assume that the data have been collected from intact women's groups that have a focus on diet and weight control; the groups meet regularly to discuss diet and weight control, and have some level of cohesion. We may thus expect some correlation among the women within a group j in both their motivation to lose weight and weight loss success. There are a total of 386 women in all distributed across the 40 groups. Group size ranges from 5 to 15 women. There is substantial clustering in the data, reflected in the fact that the groups differ substantially in mean pounds of weight lost, from a low mean of 9.75 pounds lost to a high mean of 24.43 pounds lost. Using Eq. (14.1.2) we estimate the ICC. Based on a fixed effects one-factor analysis of variance with the 40 groups as levels of the group factor, the ICC is estimated at .22. Specifically, $MS_{treatment} = 60.0225, MS_{error} = 16.0231$, and $\tilde{n} = 9.63$, and the ICC $= (60.0225 - 16.0231)/[60.0225 + (9.63 - 1)(16.0231)] = .22$.

Disaggregated Analysis

Table 14.2.1 provides analyses of these data by three OLS approaches. The disaggregated analysis is given in Table 14.2.1A. Here weight loss in pounds (POUNDS) for each individual woman is predicted from motivation to lose weight (MOTIVATC); MOTIVATC is measured on a six-point scale and is *centered* around the grand mean of the 386 cases. Group membership is completely ignored. This analysis yields the total regression coefficient $B_T = 3.27$ with a standard error of .15. With $n = 386$ cases and a single predictor $(k = 1)$, there are $(n - k - 1)$ degrees of freedom for $MS_{residual}$, and $(1, 384)$ *df* for the F test for overall regression. The total regression coefficient $B_T = 3.27$ indicates that on average, across all cases, with group structure ignored, there is a 3.27-pound predicted weight loss for each one unit increase in motivation.

CH14EX01

TABLE 14.2.1

OLS Regression of Pounds Lost on Motivation With Three Approaches
to Clustering Within the Data

A. Disaggregated analysis of individual cases with clustering ignored

$R^2 = .545$, $F(1, 384) = 459.57$, $p < .001$

Variable	B	$SE\ B$	Beta	t	Significance of t
MOTIVATC	3.270	.153	.738	21.438	.001
(Constant)	15.003	.156		96.409	.001

B. Aggregated analysis using group means of predictor and criterion

$R^2 = .492$, $F(1, 38) = 36.80$, $p < .001$

Variable	B	$SE\ B$	Beta	t	Significance of t
MOTMEANC	4.162	.686	.701	6.067	.001
(Constant)	15.159	.304		49.910	.001

C. Disaggregated analysis with dummy coded groups ($k - 1 = 39$ dummy codes in all)

39 Group Codes:	$R^2 = .297$,	$F(39, 346) = 3.75$, $p < .001$
39 Group Codes plus MOTIVATC:	$R^2 = .704$,	$F(40, 345) = 20.48$, $p < .001$

Variable	B	$SE\ B$	Beta	t	Significance of t
GR1	−1.192	1.098	−.0419	−1.086	.278
GR2	1.254	1.130	.0419	1.110	.268
.	.	.	.	.	.
GR38	2.444	1.285	.067	1.902	.058
GR39	−2.931	1.178	−.092	−2.488	.013
MOTIVATC	3.119	.143	.704	21.765	.001
(Constant)	15.264	.722		21.138	.001

Note: The notation GRXX refers to the dummy code for group XX. For example, GR38 refers to the dummy code in which group 38 is coded "1"; all other groups, "0".

Aggregated Analysis

CH14EX02

The aggregated analysis is given in Table 14.2.1B. The dependent variable is the mean weight loss in the group; the predictor, the mean motivation level in the group. There are 40 groups and hence 40 cases in all. Mean weight loss is predicted from mean motivation level, yielding the between class regression coefficient $B_B = 4.16$; the standard error is .69. With 40 groups and a single predictor, there are 38 degrees of freedom for $MS_{residual}$, and (1, 38) df for the F test for overall regression. Note that the ratio of the regression coefficient for MOTIVATC to its standard error is much larger in the disaggregated analysis, $t(384) = 21.44$, than in the aggregated analysis, $t(38) = 6.07$. The between class coefficient B_B of 4.16 indicates that if we consider only the mean weight loss per group as a function of mean motivation in the group, the mean weight loss increases by 4.16 pounds for each one-unit increase in mean motivation in the group; each group contributes equally to this result, regardless of sample size. This value is larger than the total regression coefficient $B_T = 3.27$. The reason is that a small group with both high mean motivation and high mean weight loss or a small group with both low mean motivation and low mean weight loss can have a strong positive impact on the between class regression coefficient, since there are only 40 pairs of observations (i.e., pairs of group means) in the analysis. In fact, such groups exist in the data set. The few cases within each such extreme group have less influence when treated as individual data points in the large overall sample of $n = 386$ cases in the previous disaggregated analysis.

Disaggregated Analysis With Dummy-Coded Groups

The disaggregated analysis with $(g - 1)$ dummy codes for the g groups is given in Table 14.2.1C. For the 40 groups there are 39 dummy codes. For each dummy code, members of all the groups except one are coded zero (0); the members of the remaining group are coded one (1); the 40th group is coded zero on all 39 dummy codes and serves as the base group. Choice of the base group is arbitrary in this analysis, since the dummy codes are used together to characterize the influence of group structure on the dependent variable. The pooled within-class regression coefficient for MOTIVATC is $B_W = 3.12$ with a standard error of .14. This coefficient is the weighted average of the regression coefficient of pounds lost on motivation within each group. With 39 dummy coded predictors for group membership and the MOTIVATC predictor, there are $k = 40$ predictors in all, and again $n = 386$ for the individual women. There are $(n - k - 1) = (386 - 40 - 1) = 345$ df for $MS_{residual}$, and $(40, 345)$ df for the F test for overall regression. This analysis controls for (partials out) the differences in mean weight loss per group when the impact of motivation on weight loss is estimated. The 39 group dummy codes account for almost 30% of the variance in pounds lost ($R^2_{groups} = .297$). MOTIVATC accounts for another 40% of the variance in pounds lost ($R^2_{groups+MOTIVATC} = .704$). The ratio of the regression coefficient for MOTIVATC to its standard error in this analysis is only very slightly smaller than in the disaggregated analysis, $t(345) = 21.77$. We are comfortable in concluding that there is an impact of motivation, once mean differences in pounds lost across groups are controlled. In this particular data set, the results of this analysis differ very little from those of the disaggregated regression analysis in Table 14.2.1A; this is hardly a necessary result. In fact, it is more usual that the standard error of the predictor in question (here MOTIVATC) is larger when group structure (clustering) is taken into account than when it is not.

This last result makes it appear that clustering has little effect on the estimate of the significance of the relationship of motivation to weight loss. However, there is more to the story. These particular data were simulated to have widely varying slopes of the regression of weight loss on motivation across groups, and the analysis with the 39 dummy codes in Table 14.2.1C does not take into account these slope differences. As previously discussed, we could estimate a model in which slope differences were permitted by forming the cross-product terms between each of the dummy codes and MOTIVATC. This analysis poses complexities due to centering. We would have to change from using dummy codes to represent groups to using weighted effects codes (see Section 8.4) so that all predictors would be centered. With weighted effects codes and centered MOTIVATC, the estimate of the regression of pounds lost on MOTIVATC in the model containing all the interaction terms would be at the mean of all the groups (see West, Aiken, & Krull, 1996).

14.3 THE RANDOM COEFFICIENT REGRESSION MODEL

We now have available a newer regression model than OLS, the *random coefficient (RC) regression model*, which provides a highly flexible approach to the handling of clustered data. The RC regression model is mathematically different from OLS regression, as are the estimation procedures employed. When data are clustered, the RC model provides accurate estimates of relationships of individual level predictors to a dependent variable while at the same time taking into account clustering and providing accurate estimates of the standard errors of regression coefficients so that alpha inflation is avoided. Random coefficient regression also permits the analysis of *multilevel data* within a single regression model. Multilevel data contain predictors measured at more than one level of aggregation, for example, measures of IQ taken on individual children within a multichild family, plus a measure of total family income taken at the level of the family. The term *multilevel model* (or, equivalently, *hierarchical linear model*) is applied to these random coefficient regression applications in which there are predictors at multiple levels of aggregation (Raudenbush & Bryk, 2002). It is in this multilevel framework that the RC regression model has enjoyed extensive use in educational research, for example, in the study of the impact of type of school (public, private) on the relationship of children's socioeconomic status to mathematics achievement (Raudenbush & Bryk, 2002) and in sociology in the study of the impact of individual and contextual (e.g., societal) variables on such outcomes as contraceptive utilization by individual women (e.g., Wong & Mason, 1985). These models have an advantage, explained in Section 14.7.3, that the *cross-level interaction* between variables that occur at different levels of aggregation can be examined (for example, the interaction between family income and child IQ on educational achievement). These models are now enjoying increasing use within psychology. In this chapter we present the random coefficient model for the continuous DV. These models have also been extended to binary, ordered category, and count variables (see Snijders & Bosker, 1999, chapter 14; Wong & Mason, 1985).

14.4 RANDOM COEFFICIENT REGRESSION MODEL AND MULTILEVEL DATA STRUCTURE

A brief review of several aspects of OLS regression sets the stage for the introduction to random coefficient regression.

14.4.1 Ordinary Least Squares (Fixed Effects) Regression Revisited

Recall that in OLS regression we have a single population regression equation, which, in the one-predictor case, is as follows:

$$(14.4.1) \qquad\qquad \underline{Y_i} = \beta_1^* X_i + \beta_0^* + \underline{\epsilon_i}$$

where β_0^* is the population intercept, β_1^* is the population unstandardized regression slope, and ϵ_i is the random error in prediction for case i. (Readers should not confuse the notation β_1^* for population unstandardized regression coefficient with the notation β_1 for the sample standardized regression coefficient.)

14.4.2 Fixed and Random Variables

Following the convention of Kreft and de Leeuw (1998), we underline random variables. By *random variables* are meant variables whose values are selected at random from a probability distribution. Both the error term ϵ_i and the dependent variable $\underline{Y}$ are random variables. Here we assume a normal probability distribution of error in the population with mean $\mu = 0$ and variance σ_ϵ^2. In OLS regression the Xs are assumed to be *fixed*, that is to take on a predetermined set of values (though in many applications of OLS regression, we do not meet this assumption). In addition, β_0^* and β_1^* are the fixed parameters of the unstandardized regression equation for the whole population regression equation. This is the source of the term *fixed effects* regression analysis applied to OLS regression.

In any single OLS regression analysis we draw a random sample of cases from the population and estimate a single regression equation for the sample:

$$(14.4.2) \qquad\qquad \underline{Y_i} = B_1 X_i + B_0 + \underline{e_i}.$$

In OLS regression the sample intercept (regression constant) B_0 and slope (regression coefficient) B_1 are estimates of the fixed intercept β_0^* and slope β_1^* in the population, respectively, and are considered fixed; there is one estimate of the fixed intercept β_0^* and one estimate of the fixed slope β_1^* from the analysis; $\underline{e_i}$ is the random error associated with observation X_i in the sample.

14.4.3 Clustering and Hierarchically Structured Data

In random coefficient regression we retain the notion of a population regression equation with a population intercept and population slope. However, we add complexity in terms of the data structure, that the data are clustered into groups, or *hierarchically structured*. The clustering yields *levels* within the data structure. The lowest level of aggregation, the individual, is referred to as *level 1* or the *micro-level*. The cluster or group level is referred to as *level 2* or the *macro-level*. It is possible to have more than two levels in the data structure (e.g., children within families within neighborhoods); we limit the presentation to two levels. The clusters in any data set are assumed to be a random sample of all possible clusters in the population. For example, the 40 women's diet groups in the numerical example are assumed to be a random sample of the population of all women's diet groups. Although in OLS regression the individual case is the unit that is randomly sampled, in random coefficient regression it is the cluster or group that is randomly sampled.

14.4.4 Structure of the Random Coefficient Regression Model

The notation of random coefficient regression and multilevel modeling is somewhat arcane. In developing the RC regression model and its application to multilevel modeling, we use common notation from leading texts in the multilevel modeling field. We do so in order that the reader may refer to other sources for further information and may follow the terminology of common software for multilevel modeling. Our notation follows that of Raudenbush and Bryk (2002) and Snijders and Bosker (1999), and is very close to that of Kreft and de Leeuw (1998) and Goldstein (1995). It is summarized in Table 14.4.1.

Within a single random coefficient regression analysis, we have g groups in all. We use the subscript j to denote any one of the groups, with the particular group unspecified (i.e., group j). The group membership of each case in the analysis is identified; hence we think of case i in group j.

The RC regression model is more complex than OLS regression because the RC model addresses the group structure inherent in the data as well as both individual level and group level relationships among variables. There are three types of regression equations in the random coefficient regression model. First, there are level 1 (micro-level) regression equations, one for each group in the data set. Second, there are level 2 regression equations that carry the group structure. Third, there is an overall regression equation, the *mixed model equation*, that combines the level 1 and level 2 equations. In addition, there are a set of *variance components* that summarize the differences among the groups. In what follows we develop the RC model and its extension to

TABLE 14.4.1

Notation for Random Coefficient Regression in the Multilevel Framework

---

A. Coefficients in micro-level equation for group j.

B_{0j} = level 1 regression intercept in group j.

B_{1j} = level 1 regression coefficient (slope) in group j.

B. Fixed population regression coefficients: the fixed part of the model.

γ_{00} = the population regression intercept.

γ_{10} = the population regression coefficient for the regression of the dependent variable on the level 1 predictor.

γ_{01} = the population regression coefficient for the regression of the dependent variable on the level 2 predictor.

γ_{11} = the population regression coefficient for the interaction between the level 1 and level 2 variables in predicting the dependent variable.

C. Residuals and variance components: the random part of the model.

1. Residuals.

r_{ij} = level 1 error for subject i in group j (level 1 equation).

u_{0j} = random deviation of the intercept of an individual group j from the overall population intercept (level 2 equation).

u_{1j} = random deviation of the regression coefficient of an individual group j from the overall population regression coefficient (level 2 equation).

2. Variance components.

σ^2 = variance due to random error at level 1 (i.e., variance of the r_{ij}).

τ_{00} = variance of the random intercepts (i.e., variance of u_{0j}).

τ_{11} = variance of the random regression coefficients (i.e., variance of u_{1j}).

τ_{01} = covariance between the errors of the random regression coefficients and the random regression intercepts (i.e., covariance between u_{0j} and u_{1j}).

Note: Notation follows Raudenbush and Bryk (2002) and the HLM software (Raudenbush, Bryk, Cheong, & Congdon, 2001) as well as Snijders and Bosker (1999); the only difference from Kreft and de Leeuw (1998) is their use of ϵ_{ij}, rather than r_{ij}, for the level 1 residual. Goldstein (1995) also uses ϵ_{ij}, rather than r_{ij}; also, the τ notation for variance components is replaced with σ_{u0}^2, etc., as in the MLwiN software (Goldstein et al., 1998).

multilevel modeling with no more than one predictor at each level. We do this for ease of presentation only. Any number of predictors may be entered at each level (micro, macro) of the model.

14.4.5 Level 1 Equations

We have the following level 1 (micro-level) equations, one for each group in the analysis:

level 1 equation in group 1: $y_{i1} = B_{11}x_{i1} + B_{01} + r_{i1}.$

level 2 equation in group 2: $y_{i2} = B_{12}x_{i2} + B_{02} + r_{i2}.$

(14.4.3) $\vdots$

level 1 equation in group j: $y_{ij} = B_{1j}x_{ij} + B_{0j} + r_{ij}.$

level 2 equation in group g: $y_{ig} = B_{1g}x_{ig} + B_{0g} + r_{ig}.$

For each group j, we have made one equation specific to that group by appending the subscript j to every term in the equation: to the dependent variable y_{ij} for case i in group j, to the predictor

x_{ij} for case i in group j, to the level 1 residual or random error r_{ij} for case i in group j. The level 1 regression intercept $\underline{B}_{0j}$ and the level 1 slope $\underline{B}_{1j}$ also carry the subscript j, again showing the specificity to group j. Since we assume that the groups are a random sample from a population of groups, the intercepts and slopes of the level 1 equations for the various groups become random variables in the random coefficient regression model. Hence they are underlined in these level 1 equations. Put another way, in any single random coefficient regression analysis, we conceptually have a whole series of regression analyses, one for each group, each with its own intercept and slope. Within the single random coefficient regression analysis there is a distribution of these intercepts and a distribution of the slopes. The term *random coefficient regression* stems from the assumption that the intercept $\underline{B}_{0j}$ and the slope $\underline{B}_{1j}$ are themselves random variables.

14.4.6 Level 2 Equations

In random coefficient regression analysis, we still retain the notion that there is an overall population regression equation. The level 2 or macro-level equations express how the set of level 1 intercepts for each cluster ($\underline{B}_{0j}$) and the level 1 slopes ($\underline{B}_{1j}$) relate to the intercept and slope from the overall population regression equation. Again, we use common notation from multilevel modeling with γ_{00} (gamma zero zero) for the population regression intercept and γ_{10} for the population regression slope. These are the *fixed parameters* of the population regression equation. We assume that the level 1 (micro-level) intercepts from the various individual groups, $\underline{B}_{01}, \underline{B}_{02}, \ldots, \underline{B}_{0j}, \underline{B}_{0g}$, vary randomly in value around the population intercept γ_{00}.

We specify a level 2 model for how the intercept $\underline{B}_{0j}$ in each group relates to the population intercept γ_{00}. The equation indicates that any $\underline{B}_{0j}$ is comprised of a fixed part γ_{00} and a random part $\underline{u}_{0j}$:

(14.4.4)   level 2 model, regression intercept: $\underline{B}_{0j} = \gamma_{00} + \underline{u}_{0j}.$

Once again, Eq. (14.4.4) indicates that the regression intercept $\underline{B}_{0j}$ in any particular group j is a function of the fixed population intercept γ_{00} plus a random deviation $\underline{u}_{0j} = \underline{B}_{0j} - \gamma_{00}$ of the group intercept from the overall fixed population intercept.

Similarly, we assume that the level 1 regression slopes from the various groups $\underline{B}_{11}, \underline{B}_{12}, \ldots, \underline{B}_{1j}, \underline{B}_{1g}$, vary randomly in value around the fixed population regression coefficient γ_{10}, with random deviation $\underline{u}_{1j}$ of $\underline{B}_{1j}$ from γ_{10}, yielding the following level 2 model for the regression slope:

(14.4.5)   level 2 model, regression slope: $\underline{B}_{1j} = \gamma_{10} + \underline{u}_{1j}.$

The level 2 equations characterize the group structure inherent in the data, as noted in the j subscript for each group. The identity of the groups within the analysis is embodied in the level 2 equations. The clustered nature of the data is captured at level 2. Recall that in OLS regression the group structure is identified with a set of $(g - 1)$ dummy variables for g groups. The level 2 model characterized by only Eq. (14.4.4) in random coefficient regression *replaces* the $(g - 1)$ dummy codes in OLS regression (see Section 14.4.9).

There is a relationship between the random coefficient regression model and the fixed OLS regression model, further explained later. If there is no variation among the intercepts across the groups and no variation among the slopes across the groups, then the random coefficient regression model is equivalent to fixed OLS regression.

14.4.7 Mixed Model Equation for Random Coefficient Regression

The presentation of the RC model thus far makes it appear that the level 1 and level 2 equations are treated separately. In fact, they are combined to form a single RC regression equation, referred to as the *mixed model* because it "mixes" the two levels, in that it contains terms from both the level 1 and level 2 models (the term *mixed model*, extensively used in econometrics, is enjoying increasing use in psychology). If we substitute Eqs. (14.4.4) and (14.4.5) for the intercept and slope, respectively, in group j into the level 1 equation for that group j (Eq. 14.4.3) we obtain the *mixed model* form of the random coefficient model:

$$y_{ij} = (\gamma_{00} + u_{0j}) + (\gamma_{10} + u_{1j}) x_{ij} + r_{ij};$$

$$y_{ij} = \gamma_{00} + u_{0j} + \gamma_{10} x_{ij} + u_{1j} x_{ij} + r_{ij};$$

(14.4.6)
$$y_{ij} = \gamma_{10} x_{ij} + \gamma_{00} + (u_{0j} + u_{1j} x_{ij} + r_{ij}).$$

The final expression (Eq. 14.4.6) is the *mixed model equation*. It gives the regression of the Y on the level 1 predictor in terms of fixed population values, the population intercept γ_{00} and population slope γ_{10}, plus a complex error term that includes the level 1 error r_{ij} plus the level 2 deviations u_{0j} and u_{1j}. The residual r_{ij} has the same interpretation as the residual in OLS regression, the extent to which the DV is not predicted from the level 1 predictor(s). The u_{0j} deviation measures the discrepancy between the specific group intercept and the fixed population intercept. The u_{1j} deviation measures the discrepancy between the specific group slope and the fixed population slope. The mixed model error term is larger than the error term for a corresponding disaggregated OLS total regression equation that ignores group membership and predicts y_{ij} from x_{ij}; the OLS error term in Eq. (14.4.1) only consists of ϵ_i, which is the analog of r_{ij} in the RC model. Equation (14.4.6) characterizes the outcome of RC regression analysis, a single regression equation that takes into account group structure in the estimation of the regression coefficient for the regression of the criterion on the level 1 predictor.

In the example of predicting pounds lost from motivation, Eq. (14.4.6) gives the regression of weight loss on motivation, taking into account the group structure of the data. The regression coefficient and intercept resulting from a single predictor RC regression as in Eq. (14.4.6) may be highly similar to the coefficient and intercept from a total regression disaggregated OLS regression analysis of the whole data set, ignoring group membership. However, the standard error of the intercept $\hat{\gamma}_{00}$ from the RC regression equation is expected to be larger (appropriately so) than in the OLS regression equation, so long as the groups exhibit variation in their individual intercepts, $B_{01}, B_{02}, \ldots, B_{0j}, B_{0g}$. Similarly, the standard error of the slope coefficient $\hat{\gamma}_{10}$ from the multilevel formulation is expected to be larger (appropriately so) than in the OLS regression equation, so long as the groups exhibit variation in their individual slopes $B_{11}, B_{12}, \ldots, B_{1j}, B_{1g}$.

14.4.8 Variance Components—New Parameters in the Multilevel Model

The RC regression model employs a concept not employed in OLS regression, that of *variance components*. The variance components are a hallmark of random coefficient models. In the random coefficient regression model we have three different sources of random errors or deviations : (1) the level 1 random errors, r_{ij}, from random variation in the Y scores in Eq. (14.4.3); (2) the level 2 deviations of the random intercepts around the population intercept, u_{0j} in Eq. (14.4.4), and (3) the level 2 deviations of the random slopes around the population slope, u_{1j} in

Eq. (14.4.5). Each of these sources of random deviation can be summarized as a variance. First we have the level 1 variance σ^2 of the r_{ij}s. The level 1 variance is typically assumed to be constant across groups and thus bears no group subscript here. At level 2, we have the variance of the level 1 random intercepts around the population intercept, (i.e., the variance of the u_{0j}s), noted τ_{00} (tau zero zero). At level 2, we also have the variance of the level 1 random slopes around the population slopes (i.e., the variance of the u_{1j}s) noted τ_{11}. Each of these variances—that is, σ^2, τ_{00}, and τ_{11}—is a *variance component* of the random coefficient regression model.

The variance components τ_{00}, and τ_{11} provide a simple way to capture the impact of group structure on the relationship of predictors to the dependent variable. Consider τ_{00}, the variance of the level 1 random intercepts in the random coefficient regression model; to the extent that individual groups have different random intercepts (B_{0j}), the value of τ_{00} will be large. The parameter τ_{00} is an elegant construction: instead of keeping track of the individual intercepts $\underline{B}_{01}, \underline{B}_{02}, \ldots, \underline{B}_{0j}, \underline{B}_{0g}$ of the g groups, the intercepts of the g groups are replaced in the random coefficient model with a single variance component, the *variance of the intercepts*, τ_{00}. What about the variance of the slopes, τ_{11}? Instead of keeping track of the individual slopes $\underline{B}_{11}, \underline{B}_{12}, \ldots, \underline{B}_{1j}, \underline{B}_{1g}$ of the g groups, the slopes of the g groups are replaced in the random coefficient model with a single *variance of the slopes*, τ_{11}.

We can make a conceptual link between the variance components and the dummy codes for group membership in the third OLS regression analysis, described in Section 14.2.1 and illustrated in Table 14.2.1C. In the OLS framework, we had a much more cumbersome way to model the intercepts of the individual groups: We used ($g - 1$) dummy codes in the regression equation. If the groups had different means on the dependent variable (in our example, if the different groups had different average amounts of weight loss) then the set of ($g - 1$) dummy codes would account for significant variance in the dependent variable, because the set of dummy codes capture differences among the means of the groups on the dependent variable (equivalently, differences in intercepts if we think of estimating a regression equation in each group). Conceptually, we can replace the ($g-1$) dummy codes of OLS regression with the single variance component τ_{00} in random coefficient regression. The random coefficient regression model requires only two variance components, τ_{00} and τ_{11}, to summarize all the between-group differences in intercepts and slopes, respectively. To summarize this same variance in OLS regression, we would need ($g - 1$) dummy codes to capture intercept differences, plus another ($g - 1$) interaction terms of each dummy code with the level 1 predictor to capture the variance of the slopes. Thus two terms in the RC regression model replace $2(g - 1)$ terms in OLS regression to fully characterize the differences in regression equations across the groups.

As a final note, there is actually one more variance component in the RC regression model. The random slopes and intercepts may also covary. Thus a third variance component is estimated: the *covariance* between the level 1 slopes and intercepts across groups, noted τ_{01}. This term provides interesting information from a theoretical perspective. It may be that the intercept and slope are positively related; in the weight example, this would mean that the groups that showed the highest average weight loss also exhibited the strongest relationship between motivation and weight loss.

14.4.9 Variance Components and Random Coefficient versus Ordinary Least Squares (Fixed Effects) Regression

When does the RC regression model simplify to the fixed OLS regression model? In fixed effects regression analysis, we have only one variance component, σ^2, which is estimated by $MS_{residual}$. In RC regression, we have the level 1 variance component σ^2, plus two level 2 variance components, τ_{00} and τ_{11}. If τ_{00} and τ_{11} are equal to zero in a population, then the random coefficient regression model simplifies to fixed OLS regression. Under what circumstance would both τ_{00} and τ_{11} be zero? If the intercepts of all the level 1 regression equations in all the groups were identical, then τ_{00} would equal zero (no variance among the intercepts). If the slopes of all the level 1 regression equations in all the groups were identical, then τ_{11} would equal zero (no variance among the slopes). If both τ_{00} and τ_{11} are zero, then there is no effect of clustering or group membership on the outcome of the regression equation; the random coefficient regression equation is equivalent to an OLS regression that ignores group membership.

The Random Intercept Model

It is possible that either τ_{00} or τ_{11} is equal to zero but the other variance component is not. For example, suppose we estimate an RC regression model with a single level 1 predictor and with both *random intercepts and slopes*, as in Eqs. (14.4.3), (14.4.4), (14.4.5), and find that τ_{00} is greater than zero but τ_{11} equals zero. (Statistical inference for variance components is illustrated and explained later.) Again, that τ_{00} is greater than zero indicates that the intercepts differ across groups. That τ_{11} equals zero signifies that the slopes across groups are all equal to one another and can be considered as fixed (i.e., to take on a constant value across groups). Figure 14.2.1(B) illustrates this data structure. In the weight loss example, we would say that the groups differed in pounds lost (intercept) but reflected a constant relationship of MOTIVATC to pounds lost (slope). We could respecify the model as a *random intercept* model, with Eqs. (14.4.3) and (14.4.4) as before, but Eq. (14.4.5) replaced by the expression $B_{1j} = \gamma_{10}$. The random intercept model is the analog in RC regression to the OLS (fixed effects) regression analysis in which $(g - 1)$ dummy codes represent differences among the means of g groups. We consider the choice between the random intercept and fixed model in Section 14.14.

14.4.10 Parameters of the Random Coefficient Regression Model: Fixed and Random Effects

We can organize all the parameters of the RC regression model into two classes, referred to as the *fixed effects* and the *random effects*. The population regression intercept and slope (regression coefficient), γ_{00}, γ_{10}, respectively, in Eqs. (14.4.4), (14.4.5), and (14.4.6) are referred to as the *fixed effects*. The variance components are referred to as the *random effects*. These two classes of parameters are two distinct foci of hypothesis testing in the random coefficient regression model, as we illustrate later.

14.5 NUMERICAL EXAMPLE: ANALYSIS OF CLUSTERED DATA WITH RANDOM COEFFICIENT REGRESSION

CH14EX03

We now use what we have learned about random coefficient regression. We return to the weight reduction example introduced in Section 14.2.1 and employ RC regression to predict pounds lost from motivation. Random coefficient models were executed in SAS PROC MIXED; Singer (1998) has provided an excellent tutorial on the use of PROC MIXED for analyzing multilevel models and longitudinal growth models. Results are presented in Table 14.5.1, which shows output from SAS PROC MIXED.

TABLE 14.5.1
Analyses of Weight Loss as a Function of Motivation
With Random Coefficient Regression

A. Random coefficient regression: unconditional cell means model to derive
intraclass correlation.

Random Part: Covariance Parameter Estimates (REML)

	Cov Parm	Subject	Estimate	Std Error	Z	Pr > |Z|
$\hat{\tau}_{00}$, variance of intercepts	UN(1, 1)	GROUP	4.906	1.560	3.14	0.002
$\hat{\sigma}^2$, level 1 residual	Residual		16.069	1.225	13.12	0.001

B. Random coefficient regression: prediction of pounds lost from motivation (level 1)
at outset of diet program

Random Part: Covariance Parameter Estimates (REML)

	Cov Parm	Subject	Estimate	Std Error	Z	Pr > |Z|
$\hat{\tau}_{00}$, variance of intercepts	UN(1, 1)	GROUP	2.397	0.741	3.23	0.001
$\hat{\tau}_{01}$, covariance between slope and intercept	UN(2, 1)	GROUP	0.585	0.385	1.52	0.128
$\hat{\tau}_{11}$, variance of slopes	UN(2, 2)	GROUP	0.933	0.376	2.48	0.013
$\hat{\sigma}^2$ level 1 residual	Residual		5.933	0.476	12.47	0.001

Solution for Fixed Effects

	Effect	Estimate	Std Error	DF	t	Pr > |t|
$\hat{\gamma}_{00}$	NTERCEPT	15.138	0.280	39	54.13	0.001
$\hat{\gamma}_{10}$	MOTIVATC	3.118	0.211	345	14.80	0.001

Note: The UN notation is the SAS notation for a variance component. REML stands for restricted maximum likelihood (Section 14.10.1).

14.5.1 Unconditional Cell Means Model and the Intraclass Correlation

We begin with estimation of the ICC in RC regression as an alternative to the approach shown for estimating the ICC in the fixed model (Section 14.1.2). Actually, the RC model used for estimating the ICC is a bit simpler than the one presented in Eqs. (14.4.3), (14.4.4), and (14.4.5). It contains no level 1 predictor X in Eq. (14.4.3), so the level 1 equation corresponding to Eq. (14.4.3) becomes $y_{ij} = B_{0j} + r_{ij}$ for group j. Each group's equation has an intercept B_{0j} but no slope; each individual score is predicted solely from the mean of the group. The hierarchical structure of identifying group membership is retained in the level 2 equation for the intercept, which is identical to Eq. (14.4.4). Since there is no longer a predictor X and thus no longer a random slope B_{1j} in the model, there is no equation Eq. (14.4.5). This model is called an *unconditional cell means model*. It is equivalent to a one-factor *random effects* ANOVA of pounds lost with group as the sole factor;[4] the 40 groups become the 40 levels of the group

---

[4]The analysis of variance (ANOVA) model in common use is the *fixed effects ANOVA* model. Consider a one-factor model. A fixed effects one-factor ANOVA assumes that the levels of the factor included in the data set are a fixed set of levels, in fact, all the levels to which we wish to generalize. This corresponds to the fixed effects OLS regression

factor. This analysis provides estimates of $\hat{\tau}_{00}$, the variance among the 40 group intercepts (or equivalently, the variance among the groups in mean number of pounds lost), and $\hat{\sigma}^2$, the level 1 residual variance. (The $\hat{\tau}_{00}$ here is the same parameter as τ in Section 14.1.2; that is, $\hat{\tau}_{00}$ and τ measure the same thing. What differs here is the estimation approach.) As shown in Table 14.5.1A, the estimates of $\hat{\tau}_{00}$ and $\hat{\sigma}^2$ are 4.906 and 16.069, respectively. They reflect 4.906 units of between class variance in pounds lost (differences between groups in mean pounds lost by the end of the experiment) and 16.069 units of within class variance in pounds lost that might be accounted for by the treatment and motivation predictors. Both these values are significantly greater than zero, according to the z tests reported in Table 14.5.1A (i.e., $z = 3.14, z = 13.12$, for $\hat{\tau}_{00}$ and $\hat{\sigma}^2$, respectively). That the value of $\hat{\tau}_{00}$ is significantly greater than zero tells us that there is random variation among the intercepts of the individual groups— we should not ignore clustering. We will use the values of $\hat{\tau}_{00}$ and $\hat{\sigma}^2$ to track the impact of the level 1 and level 2 predictors in accounting for weight loss. These two values are used to compute the ICC, which is given as ICC $= \hat{\tau}_{00}/(\hat{\tau}_{00} + \hat{\sigma}^2) = 4.906/(4.906 + 16.069) = .24$ (this is the same as the ICC formula in Eq. 14.1.1). The estimated ICC of .24 is very substantial. This estimate is very similar to that derived from the fixed effects ANOVA in Section 14.2.1 (ICC estimate of .22). We expect that if disaggregated OLS regression and RC regression are applied to these data, the standard errors of regression coefficients in OLS will be smaller than in RC regression, leading to overestimates of significance of predictors.

14.5.2 Testing the Fixed and Random Parts of the Random Coefficient Regression Model

In a next step we examine the prediction of pounds lost from motivation in an RC regression model, given in Table 14.5.1B. There are two parts to the analysis: (1) a *random part* that provides the estimates of the variance components, $\hat{\tau}_{00}, \hat{\tau}_{01}, \hat{\tau}_{11}$, and $\hat{\sigma}^2$, and (2) a *fixed part* that provides the estimates $\hat{\gamma}_{00}$ and $\hat{\gamma}_{10}$ of the fixed regression constant and fixed regression slope, γ_{00} and γ_{10}, respectively. We consider first the fixed part, given under Solution for Fixed Effects in Table 14.5.1B. The RC regression equation predicting pounds lost from motivation is $\hat{Y} = 3.12$ MOTIVATC $+ 15.14$, where $\hat{\gamma}_{00} = 15.14$, and $\hat{\gamma}_{10} = 3.12$. For every 1-unit increase in motivation (on a 6-point scale), predicted pounds lost increases by 3.12 pounds, with an average weight loss per group of 15.14 pounds. Note the standard error of the random regression coefficient is .211.

Now we consider the random part. In the model in Table 14.5.1A, which contained no level 1 predictor, there are only two variance components, τ_{00} and σ^2. When motivation is added as a level 1 predictor, the possibility arises that the slope of the regression of pounds lost on motivation may vary across groups; hence the model presented in Table 14.5.1B contains two more variance components, the variance of the slopes across groups, τ_{11}, and the covariance

---

model, which assumes that predictor X takes on a fixed set of values, and that our results pertain only to those values. The *random effects ANOVA model* assumes that the levels of the factor included in the data set are a random sample of all possible levels to which we wish to generalize. Consider the 40 women's groups in the diet example. If we create a fixed factor of Women's Group in a fixed effects ANOVA, with the 40 women's groups as 40 levels of the factor (as we did to estimate the ICC from the one-factor fixed effects ANOVA in Section 14.2.1), we should conceptualize any results as pertaining to only those 40 groups. If we create a random factor of Women's Group in a random effects ANOVA, with the 40 women's groups as a random sample of possible levels of the factor, then we may generalize our results to the "population of women's groups." Historically, in the 1960s and 1970s, much attention was paid to the distinction between fixed and random ANOVA models. This distinction has not been a focus for over 20 years; researchers in psychology, at least, have automatically used fixed effects ANOVA, perhaps without awareness of the distinction from random effects ANOVA (software packages for ANOVA as a default provide fixed effects ANOVA). Now that random coefficient regression models are becoming more popular, there is a new awareness of the distinction between fixed and random models.

between the intercept and slope, τ_{01}. The estimate of the variance of the slopes across groups is $\hat{\tau}_{11} = .933$, and is significantly greater than zero, $z = 2.48$; this tells us that the groups differ in the slopes of pounds lost on motivation, and that once again, the clustering should not be ignored. The covariance between the random slopes and random intercepts of the 40 groups τ_{01} is estimated as $\hat{\tau}_{01} = .585$. The positive covariance tells us that the higher the intercept for a group (the higher the pounds lost), the higher the slope, or the stronger the positive relationship of pounds lost to motivation. However, this covariance does not differ significantly from zero, $z = 1.52$, ns.

What has happened to the estimated within group variance in pounds lost $\hat{\sigma}^2$ with the addition of the level 1 predictor motivation? Recall that $\hat{\sigma}^2 = 16.069$ in the unconditional means model without the motivation predictor in Table 14.5.1A. The addition of motivation as a predictor yields a substantially reduced $\hat{\sigma}^2 = 5.933$ (Table 14.5.1B); in all $[(16.069 - 5.933)/16.069] \times 100 = 63\%$ of the within group variance in pounds lost has been accounted for by the level 1 motivation variable. Similarly, consider $\hat{\tau}_{00} = 4.906$ in the unconditional means model without the motivation predictor (Table 14.5.1A). The addition of motivation as a predictor yields a substantially reduced $\hat{\tau}_{00} = 2.397$ (Table 14.5.1B); in all $[(4.906 - 2.397)/4.906] \times 100 = 51\%$ of the between-group differences in average number of pounds lost has been accounted for by the level 1 motivation variable. The 40 groups fluctuated in mean number of pounds lost; this fluctuation was systematically related to the mean motivation level of individuals within the groups.

14.6 CLUSTERING AS A MEANINGFUL ASPECT OF THE DATA

To this point we have treated clustering or group structure in the data as if it were a nuisance that posed problems when we study the relationship of a level 1 predictor to a dependent variable (here, MOTIVATC to pounds lost). Clustering in data arises for meaningful reasons occasioned by the nature of research questions. For example, what is the effect of a mother's interest in literature on her children's development of reading habits? Or, is the relationship between students' mathematics background and their performance in graduate courses in applied statistics affected by the characteristics of the instructor?

In our study of weight loss, we might consider how level of group cohesiveness (level 2) and women's motivation (level 1) affect the number of pounds lost, a level 1 outcome. We may further ask whether there is a *cross-level interaction* between group cohesion and individual women's motivation in predicting individual women's pounds lost; perhaps cohesiveness in the group enhances the relationship of motivation to weight loss among individual women. Our research questions reflect this multilevel structure.

14.7 MULTILEVEL MODELING WITH A PREDICTOR AT LEVEL 2

To translate the preceding examples into the RC regression model we add predictors at level 2. The term *multilevel modeling* is typically applied here, when we have both level 1 and level 2 predictors. In the weight loss example, we might add a measure of group cohesiveness W as a level 2 predictor.

14.7.1 Level 1 Equations

When we add a level 2 predictor to the regression equations the level 1 equation is unaffected, remaining the same as earlier:

(14.4.3)   level 1 equation in group j: $\underline{y_{ij}} = \underline{B_{1j}}x_{ij} + \underline{B_{0j}} + \underline{r_{ij}}.$

14.7.2 Revised Level 2 Equations

The level 2 equations show the addition of the level 2 predictor W_j. This predictor has one score for each group (e.g., a measure of group cohesion). If we believe that the intercepts of the groups are affected by the level 2 predictor, we add the level 2 predictor to Eq. (14.4.4). For example, if we believe that the average pounds lost per group depended on group cohesion (a source of mutual social support for dieting), we would add the group cohesion predictor W_j to the level 2 equation for the random intercept. Note that there is only one score on group cohesion for each group; that is, cohesion is a characteristic of the group. We might hypothesize that higher group cohesion is associated with greater average weight loss in a group. Average weight loss per group is reflected in the intercept for the group B_{0j}.

(14.7.1)   level 2 equation, intercept: $B_{0j} = \gamma_{01} W_j + \gamma_{00} + u_{0j}.$

Note that we have a new fixed effect, γ_{01}, the regression coefficient of the group intercept B_{0j} on the level 2 predictor.

If we believed that the relationship of the dependent variable Y to the level 1 predictor is affected by the level 2 predictor, we add the level 2 predictor to Eq. (14.4.5). For example, we might hypothesize that high group cohesion would strengthen the relationship of motivation to weight loss, which is reflected in the level 1 regression coefficient B_{1j} for each group. We would then add the group cohesion measure W_j to the level 2 slope equation:

(14.7.2)   level 2 equation, slope: $B_{1j} = \gamma_{11} W_j + \gamma_{10} + u_{1j}.$

Again, we have a new fixed effect, γ_{11}, the regression coefficient of the group random slope B_{1j} on the level 2 predictor.

14.7.3 Mixed Model Equation With Level 1 Predictor and Level 2 Predictor of Intercept and Slope and the Cross-Level Interaction

Once again, we write a mixed model equation that shows the prediction of Y from the level 1 and level 2 predictors. We substitute the level 2 equations (Eqs. 14.7.1 and 14.7.2) into the level 1 equation (Eq. 14.4.3) to obtain a mixed model equation:

$$y_{ij} = (\gamma_{01} W_j + \gamma_{00} + u_{0j}) + (\gamma_{11} W_j + \gamma_{10} + u_{1j}) x_{ij} + r_{ij}$$

$$y_{ij} = \gamma_{01} W_j + \gamma_{00} + u_{0j} + \gamma_{11} W_j x_{ij} + \gamma_{10} x_{ij} + u_{1j} x_{ij} + r_{ij}$$

(14.7.3) $$y_{ij} = \gamma_{01} W_j + \gamma_{10} x_{ij} + \gamma_{11} W_j x_{ij} + \gamma_{00} + (u_{0j} + u_{1j} x_{ij} + r_{ij}).$$

Cross-Level Interaction

The first three terms of Eq. (14.7.3) indicate that the pounds lost criterion is predicted from the level 2 cohesion predictor W_j, the level 1 centered motivation predictor x_{ij}, and the *cross-level interaction* $W_j x_{ij}$ between cohesion W_j and centered motivation x_{ij}. The cross-level interaction in the mixed model expression for the slope (Eq. 14.7.3) results from the level 2 equation for the slope (Eq. 14.7.2), which states that the level 2 predictor predicts the level 1 slope. In causal terms, the level 2 predictor changes (or moderates) the relationship of the level 1 predictor to the dependent variable (see Section 7.3.2 for a discussion of moderation). This *fixed part* of the equation is analogous to the OLS regression equation with a two-predictor interaction in Eq. (7.1.2); there are now four *fixed effects*—$\gamma_{01}, \gamma_{10}, \gamma_{11}, \gamma_{00}$—in the multilevel model. They correspond to the regression coefficients and regression intercept, respectively, in OLS regression equation $\hat{Y} = B_1 W + B_2 X + B_3 WX + B_0$, containing a WX interaction.

Variance Components

The final term in Eq. (14.7.3) contains the random components of the model. It is once again a complex error term, characteristic of RC regression equations. It contains the same components as in the model with no level 2 predictor, in Eq. (14.4.6), the level 1 residual r_{ij} plus level 2 residuals u_{0j} and u_{1j} for the intercept and slope, respectively. The level 1 residual r_{ij} retains the same interpretation as in Eq. (14.4.6). However, the interpretation of the level 2 random error terms u_{0j} and u_{1j} changes when a level 2 predictor is added. The term u_{0j} is now the residual deviation of the level 1 intercept B_{0j} from the population intercept γ_{00} after the level 1 intercept has been predicted from the level 2 predictor. Put another way, u_{0j} measures the part of the discrepancy between the group j intercept B_{0j} and the population intercept γ_{00} that cannot be predicted from the level 2 predictor. If the level 2 predictor W provides prediction of the level 1 intercept, then u_{0j} in Eq. (14.7.1) will be smaller than in Eq. (14.4.4) in a model with no level 2 predictor. In the weight loss example, with group cohesion as the level 2 predictor, u_{0j} represents the part of the level 1 intercept that cannot be accounted for by group cohesion. The same is true for residual u_{1j} in Eq. (14.7.2). If the level 2 predictor explains some of the variance in the level 1 slopes, then the residual in Eq. (14.7.2) will be smaller than in Eq. (14.4.5).

Finally, instead of considering the residuals u_{0j} and u_{1j}, we can think of their variances, τ_{00}, and τ_{11}, the variance components in the model. *A goal of multilevel modeling is to account for these variances of the random intercepts and slopes, respectively, by level 2 predictors (i.e., to explain the differences among the groups in their intercepts and slopes).*

14.8 AN EXPERIMENTAL DESIGN AS A MULTILEVEL DATA STRUCTURE: COMBINING EXPERIMENTAL MANIPULATION WITH INDIVIDUAL DIFFERENCES

We have strong interest in psychology in the effects of experimental manipulations. Moreover, we have interest in how individual differences interact with experimental manipulations. We often examine whether individuals respond to an experimental manipulation or intervention more strongly or weakly as a function of some stable individual difference characteristics. In multilevel analysis the experimental manipulation and individual difference characteristics are readily portrayed, with participation in conditions of an experiment treated as a level 2 variable and individual characteristics that may affect how individuals respond to the conditions as level 1 variables. Note that if there is no clustering in the data set, then a fixed OLS regression approach can be taken instead. The experimental manipulation (e.g., treatment versus control), the individual difference variable, and the manipulation by individual difference interaction serve as predictors. Note that this is not the classic ANCOVA model described in Section 8.7.5, which assumes no interaction between the manipulation and individual difference covariate. Rather it is the aptitude-treatment or experimental personality design considered in West, Aiken, and Krull (1996; see also Section 9.3).

Again consider the diet example. Now assume that the 40 women's groups are entered into a research project to evaluate the impact of a diet program (the "treatment") on the number of pounds lost in a three-month period. Groups are randomly assigned to experimental condition (i.e., the level 2 unit is the unit of random assignment). There are two conditions: (1) baseline condition (control group) of weekly group meetings to discuss dieting triumphs and tragedies, or (2) a multicomponent treatment (experimental group) consisting of diet specification, weigh-in and counseling, exercise, food preparation lessons, plus weekly group meetings to discuss dieting triumphs and tragedies. As before, at the individual level, the motivation of each individual to lose weight at the outset of the intervention is assessed as the level 1 predictor of weight loss. The treatment condition (experimental versus control) is a level 2 predictor called TREATC. Issues of appropriate coding of the treatment variable and centering the motivation variable are considered in Section 14.9.

The mixed model regression equation for the experiment is as follows:

$$\text{(14.8.1)} \qquad \underline{y_{ij}} = \gamma_{01}\,\text{TREATC}_j + \gamma_{10}\,\text{MOTIVATC}_{ij} + \gamma_{11}\,\text{TREATC}_j \times \text{MOTIVATC}_{ij}$$

$$+\, \gamma_{00} + (\underline{u_{0j}} + \underline{u_{1j}}\,x_{ij} + \underline{r_{ij}})$$

In a multilevel analysis we would learn whether the treatment (TREATC) had an effect on weight loss (experimental manipulation), whether motivation (MOTIVATC) predicted weight loss (individual difference), and whether there was a cross-level interaction between treatment and motivation (TREATC × MOTIVATC). We might hypothesize that treatment strengthens the relationship of motivation to pounds lost by giving motivated participants the vehicles for effective dieting. In terms of level 2 Eq. (14.7.2), we are hypothesizing that treatment moderates the relationship of motivation to weight loss, an interaction hypothesis. This example provides a model for analysis of the many experimental studies in which experimental conditions are administered to groups of subjects and in which either group composition or group processes (e.g. increased cohesion), could affect outcomes.

The mixed model framework can accommodate a second interpretation of the cross-level interaction as well. We can conceptualize that the level of motivation moderates the impact of treatment. This conceptualization is consistent with research that asks, "for whom is treatment most effective," under the assumption that characteristics of the individual (e.g., motivation) condition the impact of treatment. This second conception does not fit into the hierarchical structure that the level 2 variable affects the level 1 variable. Nevertheless, the cross-level interaction in the mixed model framework can accommodate this interpretation.

14.9 NUMERICAL EXAMPLE: MULTILEVEL ANALYSIS

We now explore the analysis of the diet treatment, assuming that 60% of the 40 groups, or 24 groups (comprised of $n = 230$ individual cases in all) were randomly assigned to the treatment, the other 16 groups (comprised of $n = 156$ individual cases in all), to control. Treatment is centered around the grand mean at the individual level into a weighted effects coded predictor[5] TREATC, where experimental $= 156/(156 + 230) = .404$, and

---

[5]Coding and centering (scaling) issues become very complex in multilevel models with cross level interactions in which there are unequal sample sizes in each group. Since the regression model contains an interaction, the first order effects of MOTIVATC and TREATC are conditional (i.e., are interpreted at the value of zero on the other predictor), just as in OLS regression with interactions (see Section 7.12). The scaling of the IVs to produce appropriate 0-points on each variable will depend on the sampling plan and the effect(s) of most interest in the study. In the present case, we centered MOTIVATC around the grand mean of all of the individual cases. A weighted effects code based on the number of cases in the treatment and control at the individual level was used to create TREATC. This choice parallels the centering of MOTIVATC and thus facilitates interpretation. The interpretation of each conditional main effect is at the mean of all *individual* cases on the other predictor. This choice also permits the most direct comparison of the present multilevel results with those of the original OLS analysis which ignores group membership.

TABLE 14.9.1

Multilevel Analysis and OLS Regression Analysis of the Weight Experiment
With an Intervention and an Individual Difference Variable

A. Multilevel random coefficient regression: prediction of pounds lost from motivation (level 1),
treatment (level 2) and the cross-level interaction between motivation and treatment

		Random Part: Covariance Parameter Estimates (REML)				
	Cov Parm	Subject	Estimate	Std Error	Z	Pr > |Z|
$\hat{\tau}_{00}$, variance of intercepts	UN(1, 1)	GROUP	1.967	0.657	2.99	0.003
$\hat{\tau}_{01}$, covariance between slope and intercept	UN(2, 1)	GROUP	0.145	0.314	0.46	0.645
$\hat{\tau}_{11}$, variance of slopes	UN(2, 2)	GROUP	0.556	0.301	1.85	0.065
$\hat{\sigma}^2$ level 1 residual	Residual		5.933	0.475	12.48	0.001

		Solution for Fixed Effects				
	Effect	Estimate	Std Error	df	t	Pr > |t|
$\hat{\gamma}_{00}$	INTERCEPT	15.166	0.259	38	58.49	0.001
$\hat{\gamma}_{01}$	TREATC	1.528	0.529	38	2.89	0.006
$\hat{\gamma}_{10}$	MOTIVATC	3.130	0.185	344	16.95	0.001
$\hat{\gamma}_{11}$	TREATC*MOTIVATC	1.245	0.377	344	3.30	0.001

B. OLS regression: prediction of pounds lost from motivation, treatment and the interaction
between motivation and treatment

Effect	Estimate	Std Error	df	t	Sig t
INTERCEPT	15.105	.148			
TREATC	1.578	.301	1	5.239	.000
MOTIVATC	3.330	.145	1	22.968	.000
TREATC*MOTIVATC	1.446	.300	1	4.820	.000

Note: MOTIVATC and TREATC are the motivation and treatment predictors each centered around the grand mean of the variable. SAS reports Sig t as .000; in publication report $p < .001$.

control $= (-230)/(156 + 230) = -.596$. Table 14.9.1A provides the analysis of the multilevel (mixed) model Eq. (14.8.1). The fixed part of the analysis yields the regression equation:

$$\hat{Y} = 1.53 \text{ TREATC} + 3.13 \text{ MOTIVATC} + 1.25 \text{ TREATC} \times \text{MOTIVATC} + 15.17$$

The positive interaction of treatment with motivation indicates a synergy between individual level motivation and treatment. (See Section 9.3, for a treatment of continuous by categorical variable interactions.)

We first take the interpretation of the cross-level interaction that is consistent with the multilevel formulation, that the level 2 predictor (treatment) affects the random intercepts (average pounds lost per group), and that the level 2 predictor also modifies the random slopes (the relationship between motivation and pounds lost).

We form the simple regression equations for the regression of pounds lost on motivation within each treatment condition, just as is done in OLS regression (see Section 7.3). To do so, we rearrange the regression equation to obtain the simple slope of pounds lost on motivation as a function of treatment.

$$\hat{Y} = (3.13 + 1.25 \text{ TREATC}) \text{ MOTIVATC} + 1.53 \text{ TREATC} + 15.17.$$

For the control group, where TREATC $= -.596$, the regression of pounds lost on motivation is as follows:

$$\hat{Y} = [3.13 + 1.25(-.596)]\text{MOTIVATC} + 1.53(-.596) + 15.17$$

$$\hat{Y} = 2.38 \text{ MOTIVATC} + 14.26.$$

For the experimental group, where TREATC $= .404$, the regression of pounds lost on motivation is as follows:

$$\hat{Y} = [3.13 + 1.25(.404)]\text{MOTIVATC} + 1.53(.404) + 15.17$$

$$\hat{Y} = 3.64 \text{ MOTIVATC} + 15.79.$$

The simple regression equations are illustrated in Fig. 14.9.1(A). The treatment raised the average number of pounds lost at the mean motivation level of the 386 cases from 14.26 to 15.79 pounds. Further, it strengthened the relationship of motivation to pounds lost. In the control group, each 1 unit increase in motivation was associated with a predicted 2.38 pounds lost. In the experimental group, each 1 unit increase in motivation was associated with a predicted 3.64 pounds lost.

We now take the second interpretation of the interaction, asking whether the impact of treatment varies at different levels of motivation. We rearrange the regression equation to obtain simple regression equations of pounds lost on treatment at different levels of motivation (see also Aiken & West, 1991, Chapter 7; West, Aiken, & Krull, 1996.)

$$\hat{Y} = (1.53 + 1.25 \text{ MOTIVATC}) \text{ TREATC} + (3.13 \text{ MOTIVATC} + 15.17)$$

Motivation is centered at the grand mean of the 386 cases, so that $M_{\text{MOTIVATC}} = 0.00$; and $sd_{\text{MOTIVATC}} = 1.02$. The regression of pounds lost on treatment is shown next at one standard deviation below the mean of motivation, at the mean of motivation, and one standard deviation above the mean of motivation:

1 *sd* below: $\hat{Y} = [(1.53 + (1.25)(-1.02)]\text{TREATC} + [(3.13)(-1.02) + 15.17]$

$\hat{Y} = .26 \text{ TREATC} + 11.97.$

at the mean: $\hat{Y} = 1.53 \text{ TREATC} + 15.17.$

1 *sd* above: $\hat{Y} = [(1.53 + (1.25)(1.02)]\text{TREATC} + [(3.13)(1.02) + 15.17]$

$\hat{Y} = 2.80 \text{ TREATC} + 18.36.$

These simple regression equations are illustrated in Fig. 14.9.1(B). As individual motivation increases, the impact of treatment on weight loss increases as well. There is essentially no impact of treatment when motivation is low, with an increase to 2.80 pounds of weight loss attributable to treatment when motivation is high.

The variances of the intercepts and slopes are conceptualized as sources of variance to be accounted for by level 2 predictor TREATC. Recall that the intercept from each individual group (with motivation centered) reflects the amount of weight lost in that group; if the intervention has an effect, the variance in intercepts should at least in part be accounted for by the treatment

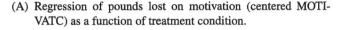

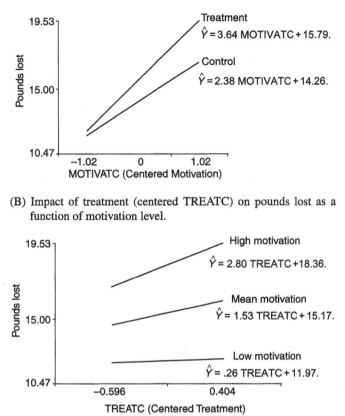

(A) Regression of pounds lost on motivation (centered MOTI-
VATC) as a function of treatment condition.

(B) Impact of treatment (centered TREATC) on pounds lost as a
function of motivation level.

FIGURE 14.9.1   Simple slopes for cross-level interaction between MOTIVATC
(level 1) and TREATC (level 2) predictors.

condition. The random part of the analysis in Table 14.9.1A versus that in Table 14.5.1B
shows that all three level 2 variance components have been reduced by the addition of the
level 2 treatment variable plus the cross-level interaction. The variance of the intercepts is in
part accounted for by the treatment, with $\hat{\tau}_{00}$ dropping from 2.397 to 1.967, or a [(2.397 −
1.967)/.2.397] × 100 = 18% reduction in variance unaccounted for intercept variance. There
is still a significant amount of intercept variance remaining to be accounted for, $z = 2.99$. The
variance of the slopes is well accounted for by treatment, with $\hat{\tau}_{11}$ dropping from .933 to .556,
or a [(.933 − .556)/.933] × 100 = 35% reduction in unaccounted for slope variance; there is,
however, unaccounted for variance remaining in the slopes, $z = 1.85, p = .06$.

Table 14.9.1B gives the disaggregated OLS regression analysis ignoring group membership,
for comparison with the random coefficient regression analysis in Table 14.9.1A. Pounds lost
is again predicted from TREATC, MOTIVATC, and their interaction. The regression equation
is almost identical in the two analyses; for the OLS analysis,

$$\hat{Y} = 1.58 \text{ TREATC} + 3.33 \text{ MOTIVATC} + 1.45 \text{ TREATC} \times \text{MOTIVATC} + 15.10.$$

However, the standard errors are uniformly smaller in OLS than in the random coefficient
model, leading to alpha inflation in significance tests. Of particular note is that the standard

error for the level 2 TREATC variable is .529 in the multilevel model in Table 14.9.1A and only .301 in the disaggregated OLS regression equation in Table 14.9.1B. The multilevel analysis handles the TREATC variable as if it were based on 40 observations (one per group). The OLS analysis handles the TREATC variable as if it were based on 386 independent cases, yielding a negatively biased standard error. Overall, the difference in standard errors between the single-level OLS model and the multilevel model can be attributed to two sources. First is the change in model from one that ignores clustering (single-level OLS regression) to a model that accounts for clustering (multilevel RC regression). Second is the difference in estimation procedures for OLS versus the multilevel model, described in the next section.

14.10 ESTIMATION OF THE MULTILEVEL MODEL PARAMETERS: FIXED EFFECTS, VARIANCE COMPONENTS, AND LEVEL 1 EQUATIONS

14.10.1 Fixed Effects and Variance Components

The approach to estimation is a key difference between OLS regression and RC regression. The parameter estimates in RC regression are obtained by maximum likelihood estimation (ML), described in Section 11.2 and in Section 13.2.9, or alternatively by a related method, restricted maximum likelihood (REML). Chapter 3 of Raudenbush and Bryk (2002) provides detail on estimation of the multilevel model and on hypothesis testing within the multilevel model. The fixed and random parts of the model (i.e., the fixed effects and variance components) are estimated using iterative procedures. The estimation begins with an initial estimate of one set of parameters (say, the fixed effects) and uses these values in the estimation of the other set (the variance components). The new estimates of the second set are used to update those of the first set, and the procedure continues in this manner until the process converges. (Convergence of iterative solutions is explained in Section 13.2.9.) Estimation of variance components involves algorithms that produce maximum likelihood estimates.

Confidence intervals (interval estimates) are available for the fixed effects and for the variance components. The confidence intervals (and statistical tests) for variance components are problematic because the sampling distributions of the variance components are skewed.

14.10.2 An Equation for Each Group: Empirical Bayes Estimates of Level 1 Coefficients

To this point, we have ignored the regression equations within each group. Yet a third class of parameters may be estimated—these are the level 1 *random intercept* B_{0j} and *random slope* B_{1j} for each individual group. These estimators are another important contribution of the RC regression model. We have not heretofore focused on regression equations for the individual groups. In many application of RC regression and the multilevel framework, the focus is on the overall relationships of level 1 and 2 predictors to some outcome, and whether there is evidence of variability in the intercepts and slopes across groups. There is not a focus on the regression estimates B_{0j} and B_{1j} in particular groups. However, there are instances in which the estimates of regression equations for individual groups are of importance, for example, in policy-related research in which decisions are made as to what classes of individuals might receive special treatments or interventions based on evidence of the efficacy of the treatments for those particular classes.

One obvious option for obtaining the estimates is to carry out an OLS regression in each group. If group sizes are large, this is a viable strategy. But what if we have small group sizes? It is possible to have groups so small in RC regression analysis that there are fewer cases in the group than there are level 1 predictors in the RC regression equation. The OLS regression equation cannot even be estimated! Alternatively, we may have groups large enough to estimate the OLS equation, but still so small that we have little, if any, confidence in the resulting estimates. In still other groups, larger in size, the OLS estimates may be quite reliable. An approach to estimation of regression coefficients called *empirical Bayes estimation* allows us to obtain an estimate of the regression coefficients in each group. The approach actually combines estimates of the intercept and slope for each group from two different sources.

Two Estimates of Regression Coefficients for a Single Group

Assume we have a very large sample size in group j to estimate the OLS regression slope and intercept for that group. We compute an OLS regression using only the data from group j and obtain our first set of estimates. The first set of estimates are the OLS estimates, which we will call $B_{0j,\text{OLS}}$ and $B_{1j,\text{OLS}}$ for the estimates of the intercept and slope, respectively, in group j.

Assume now that we have no information about group j. We would use the RC regression equation, generated from all the cases from all the groups, to provide a set of estimates of the coefficients that could be used for the individual group j. This second set of estimates for individual group j is based on the estimates from the full data set of the population fixed effects, $\hat{\gamma}_{00}, \hat{\gamma}_{01}, \hat{\gamma}_{10}$, and $\hat{\gamma}_{11}$. The estimates for group j, which we will call $B_{0j,\text{POP}}$ and $B_{1j,\text{POP}}$ to indicate that they are based on estimates of the population fixed effects, are

(14.10.1) $$B_{0j,\text{POP}} = \hat{\gamma}_{00} + \hat{\gamma}_{01} W_j;$$

(14.10.2) $$B_{1j,\text{POP}} = \hat{\gamma}_{10} + \hat{\gamma}_{11} W_j.$$

where W is the level 2 predictor and W_j is the value of this predictor in group j. Note again that the estimates of the fixed population effects $\hat{\gamma}_{00}, \hat{\gamma}_{01}, \hat{\gamma}_{10}$, and $\hat{\gamma}_{11}$ are based on all the cases in the whole analysis, regardless of group membership.

Empirical Bayes Estimators

In practice we are usually somewhere between the two extreme situations so that both sets of estimates provide useful information. Estimators of the level 1 coefficients for each group j are obtained by taking a weighted average of the two sets of estimates; these estimators are termed *shrinkage estimators* or *empirical Bayes* (*EB*) estimators. We use the notation $B_{0j,\text{EB}}$ and $B_{1j,\text{EB}}$ for the resulting empirical Bayes estimates of the intercept and slope. Whether the estimates from the single group j, $B_{0j,\text{OLS}}$ and $\hat{B}_{1j,\text{OLS}}$, or the estimates from the full data set, $B_{0j,\text{POP}}$ and $B_{1j,\text{POP}}$, are more heavily weighted in forming $B_{0j,\text{EB}}$ and $B_{1j,\text{EB}}$ depends on the precision of the estimates from the individual group estimates, that is, the standard errors of $B_{0j,\text{OLS}}$ and $B_{1j,\text{OLS}}$. The more precise the estimates $B_{0j,\text{OLS}}$ and $B_{1j,\text{OLS}}$, the more we are willing to rely on the coefficients derived for the individual group. Yet, at the same time, it is advantageous to capitalize on the highly precise estimates based on the whole data set, $B_{0j,\text{POP}}$ and $B_{1j,\text{POP}}$. Because the empirical Bayes (EB) estimators use the information taken from the full sample to estimate coefficients for each individual group, the EB estimates for individual groups are said to "borrow strength" from the estimates based on the whole data set. As indicated, the EB estimators are also called *shrinkage estimators*, because the estimates for individual group coefficients are drawn to (shrink toward) the overall population estimates. The term *shrinkage* as used here is completely unrelated to the use of the term *shrinkage* in the context of unbiased estimates of the squared multiple correlation, described in Section 3.5.3.

The relative weighting of the two sets of estimates in deriving the compromise EB estimate depends on the precision of the estimates from the individual group j. The following is an expression for the EB estimator $B_{0j,EB}$ of the level 1 regression intercept in group j:

$$\text{(14.10.3)} \qquad \underline{B_{0j,EB}} = \lambda_{0j} \, \underline{B_{0j,OLS}} + (1 - \lambda_{0j}) \, \underline{B_{0j,POP}}.$$

The weight λ_{0j}, which is the measure of stability of the OLS coefficient B_{0j} for group j, ranges from 0 to 1 and varies inversely as the size of the squared standard error $\overline{SE^2_{0j,OLS}}$ of the OLS coefficient $\underline{B_{0j,OLS}}$ from the sample:

$$\text{(14.10.4)} \qquad \lambda_{0j} = \frac{\tau_{00}}{\tau_{00} + SE^2_{B_{0j,OLS}}}.$$

As can be seen from Eq. (14.10.3), the lower the precision of the estimate of the measure on the group (i.e., the smaller λ_{0j}), the more the EB estimator $B_{0j,EB}$ of the random intercept for that group is drawn to the estimator based on the population fixed effects $B_{0j,POP}$, from Eq. (14.10.1). An analogous shrinkage estimator of the level 1 regression slope in group j is given as follows:

$$\text{(14.10.5)} \qquad \underline{B_{1j,EB}} = \lambda_{1j} \, \underline{B_{1j,OLS}} + (1 - \lambda_{1j}) \, \underline{B_{1j,POP}}.$$

Numerical Example: Empirical Bayes Estimation

A numerical example, based on the analysis in Table 14.9.1A, illustrates the EB estimates. Here the variable W in Eq. (14.10.1) and (14.10.2) is TREATC, the treatment condition. We consider a group assigned to the control condition. In the control condition, the value of the level 2 TREATC predictor is $-.596$. Using Eq. (14.10.1) and (14.10.2), we obtain the estimates from the full data set:

$$\underline{B_{0j,POP}} = \hat{Y}_{00} + \hat{Y}_{01} W_j = 15.166 + 1.528(-.596) = 14.245;$$

$$\underline{B_{1j,POP}} = \hat{Y}_{10} + \hat{Y}_{11} W_j = 3.130 + 1.245(-.596) = 3.130 - .742 = 2.388.$$

In an OLS regression analysis of a single group in the control condition with $n = 9$ cases, we obtain the OLS estimates $\underline{B_{0j,OLS}} = 15.626$ and $\underline{B_{1j,OLS}} = 4.750$. There is quite a discrepancy between the estimate of the relationship between motivation and weight loss in the single sample versus the overall data set. In the overall data set, it is estimated that there is a loss of 2.388 pounds for each 1-unit increase in motivation; in the single sample the estimate of pounds lost as a function of motivation is twice as high at 4.750 pounds. However, the standard error of $\underline{B_{1j,OLS}}$ is quite large, $SE^2_{1j,OLS} = 1.475$. The weight for $\underline{B_{1j,OLS}}$ in the EB estimator is

$$\text{(14.10.6)} \qquad \lambda_{1j} = \frac{\tau_{11}}{\tau_{11} + SE^2_{B_{1j,OLS}}} = \frac{.556}{.556 + 1.475} = .274.$$

Then the EB estimate of the slope in the group is

$$\underline{B_{1j,EB}} = \lambda_{1j} \, \underline{B_{1j,OLS}} + (1 - \lambda_{1j}) \, \underline{B_{1j,POP}} = .274(4.750) + (1 - .274)(2.388) = 2.765.$$

This EB estimate for the slope in the single group has moved much closer to (has "shrunken" to) the overall estimate of the slope from the full data set.

For the intercept, the squared standard error $SE^2_{0j,\text{OLS}} = 1.096$. The value of $\lambda_{0j} = 1.967/(1.967 + 1.096) = .642$. Then the EB estimate of the intercept for the group is

$$\underline{B_{0j,\text{EB}}} = \lambda_{0j}\, B_{0j,\text{OLS}} + (1 - \lambda_{0j})\, B_{0j,\text{POP}} = .642\,(15.626) + (1 - .642)(14.245) = 15.131.$$

Finally, the EB estimate of the regression equation for group j is

$$\hat{Y}_{ij,\text{EB}} = 2.765\,\text{MOTIVATC} + 15.131.$$

This equation is a compromise between the OLS regression equation for the sample, based on only 9 cases and with a large standard error for the sample slope $B_{1j,\text{OLS}}$, and the overall equation from the full data set, $\hat{Y}_{ij,\text{POP}} = 2.388\,\text{MOTIVATC} + 14.245.$

14.11 STATISTICAL TESTS IN MULTILEVEL MODELS

We have examined tests of significance of both fixed and random effects in the numerical example in Tables 14.5.1 and 14.5.2. Here we provide more information about the tests themselves, following expositions by Raudenbush and Bryk (2002) and Singer (1998).

14.11.1 Fixed Effects

Tests of the fixed effects are made against the standard error of the fixed effect, resulting in a z test. Alternatively, a t test is computed, as is given in both SAS PROC MIXED and the specialized multilevel software package HLM (Raudenbush, Bryk, Cheong, & Congdon, 2001). Degrees of freedom for the test depend on whether the predictor is a level 2 predictor or a level 1 predictor. For level 1 predictors, the df depend on the numbers of individual cases, groups, and level 1 predictors. For level 2 predictors, the df depend on number of groups and number of level 2 predictors, and are specifically $(g - S_q - 1)\ df$, where g is the number of contexts (groups) and S_q is the number of level 2 predictors.

14.11.2 Variance Components

Each variance component may be tested for significance of difference from zero in one of several ways. First is a chi square test, based on OLS estimates of within group coefficients, which contrasts within group estimates with the fixed population estimate. Use of this test requires that most or all contexts be of sufficient size to yield OLS estimates. The result is distributed approximately as χ^2, with $(g - S_q - 1)\ df$, where g is the number of contexts (groups) from which OLS estimates can be obtained and S_q is the number of level 2 predictors (this test is reported in HLM output). Second is a z test based on large sample theory, reported in SAS PROC MIXED. Both Raudenbush and Bryk (2002) and Singer (1998) express caution concerning this latter test because of the skew of the sampling distribution of the variance components and because of the dependence on large sample theory (asymptotic normality is assumed but not achieved). There is a third approach to examining variance components, a *model comparison approach*, based on likelihood ratio tests of nested models. This is the same form of test as in the testing of nested models in logistic regression explained in Section 13.2.14. In the RC context we specify a model that allows a particular variance component to be nonzero, for example, the variance of the slopes. We then specify a second, more restrictive, model that forces this variance component to zero. A likelihood ratio χ^2 test is used to test whether the model fit is significantly worse when the variance component is forced to zero. If so, we conclude that the variance component is nonzero.

14.12 SOME MODEL SPECIFICATION ISSUES

There are many issues in the specification and execution of multilevel models. We address two related issues here: (1) the issue of whether there are instances in which the same variable can serve as a level 1 and level 2 predictor in a single equation, and (2) issue of centering variables in multilevel models.

14.12.1 The Same Variable at Two Levels

There is a very interesting but theoretically complex possibility that the same variable can exist at more than one level in a single data set. A classic example from education is the impact on academic achievement of the socioeconomic status (SES) of the child versus the average SES of the children in the child's school (Burstein, 1980; see also Raudenbush & Bryk, 2002). In a group therapy context we might measure the depression level of an individual client at the outset of therapy versus the average depression level among all members in the group; we might hypothesize that being in a group of very depressed individuals would impede the progress of an individual client in overcoming his or her own depression. The conceptual issue in both these examples is whether we can provide a distinct theoretical role for the same variable at the group level and the individual level. For the therapy setting we might argue that the average level of depression in the group reflects the depressed cognitions expressed by group members in response to statements by the individual client in question, whereas the client's own level of depression at therapy outset would reflect the level of individual disturbance. These two aspects of depression might have separate influences or even interact in predicting therapy outcome.

14.12.2 Centering in Multilevel Models

Centering in multilevel models is useful for decreasing multicollinearity among predictors and between random intercepts and slopes, thereby stabilizing the analysis. Centering in multilevel models is more complex than in OLS regression. Kreft and de Leeuw (1998) provide a straight-forward exposition; a more technical exposition is given in Kreft, de Leeuw, and Aiken (1995). Singer (1998) provides advice on centering in contextual models in the multilevel framework.

For level 1 variables there are two common options for centering: (1) centering each score around the grand mean (CGM) of all the cases in the sample, ignoring group membership, and (2) centering each score around the group mean in which the case occurs, referred to as centering within context (CWC) (Kreft, de Leeuw, & Aiken, 1995). We contrast these approaches with retaining data in their raw score (RS) form.

The CGM approach simply involves subtracting a single constant from each score in the whole distribution regardless of group. In a multilevel model containing a cross-level inter-action, the resulting fixed effect parameters change from raw score (RS) to CGM scaling, as does the variance component of the intercept, but there is a straightforward algebraic relation-ship between the CGM and RS results. It is parallel to the algebraic relationship shown in Section 7.2.5 for centering OLS in equations including interactions. Moreover, measures of fit, predicted scores, and residual scores remain the same across RS and CGM.

CWC is a very different matter. CWC eliminates all the information on mean level differences between the groups because the group means are subtracted out. The mean of each group becomes zero. In order to not lose valuable information (in our weight example, information on the mean pounds lost per group), one must build back mean weight loss per group as a level 2 variable. We refer to the use of CWC without building back group means as CWC_1 and CWC with the group means entered at the second level as CWC_2 in Kreft, de Leeuw, and Aiken

(1995). With CWC_1 there is no way to recover the between class information available in the RS analysis. Only if it can be powerfully argued that differences between the group means on a predictor bear no relationship to the outcome would one consider using CWC_1. CWC_2 reinstates the eliminated between class mean differences at level 2. Even if the focus is on the impact of within group variation on a predictor, we recommend CWC_2; then the presence versus absence of effect of a predictor at the group level becomes a matter for exploration, rather than an untested assumption (see Singer, 1998, for an example).

The choice of centering approach depends on the research question. CGM was used in all the multilevel numerical examples reported here. The rationale for this choice was that the level 1 motivation variable was a person variable to be controlled when the impact of the intervention was assessed; there was no theoretical rationale provided for a special role of the mean level of motivation in the group versus the motivation of the individual within the group to which she belonged on dieting outcomes. Had there been such an interest, we would have used the CWC_2 approach for characterizing motivation and then added the treatment variable as a level 2 predictor. We might have hypothesized a level 2 interaction between treatment and mean level of motivation of the group as well as, or instead of, the cross-level interaction between treatment and individual level of motivation.

Level 2 variables may be centered or not. We also centered the level 2 treatment predictor of treatment (experimental, control) around the grand mean, using weighted effect codes (Chapter 8) at the individual level. We did so to avoid multicollinearity and estimation difficulties, and to facilitate interpretation. (See footnote 5.)

Users of specialized software for multilevel modeling (mentioned in Section 14.15) should take caution to understand how data are being centered by the software. A safe approach is to first center (or not) the level 1 and level 2 data in the form assumed appropriate for the particular problem at hand and then enter the data into the software. This assures that one will obtain the centering desired.

14.13 STATISTICAL POWER OF MULTILEVEL MODELS

OLS ignoring group membership has a substantially inflated Type I error rate when group sizes are large and the intraclass correlation increases. Kreft and de Leeuw (1998) discuss the complex issues involved in statistical power for multilevel models and provide a summary of simulation studies on power. Statistical power must be addressed separately for level 1 and level 2 effects. Power for level 2 effects is dependent on number of groups, power for level 1, on number of cases. Simulation studies suggest that large samples are needed for adequate power in multilevel models and that the number of groups is more important than the number of cases per group. Kreft and de Leeuw suggest that at least 20 groups are needed to detect cross-level interactions when group sizes are not too small. The whole issue of statistical power is complicated, because the power differs for fixed effects versus random effects as a function of effect size and intraclass correlation, and both the number of groups and number of cases per group.

14.14 CHOOSING BETWEEN THE FIXED EFFECTS MODEL AND THE RANDOM COEFFICIENT MODEL

We began the discussion of the handling of clustered data with an exposition of OLS approaches, among which was a *fixed effects model* in which the dependent variable Y was predicted from level 1 variables plus a set of $(g - 1)$ dummy codes to account for differences in means of the *g* groups or clusters in the data. The alternative presented was the *random coefficient (RC) regression model* in Eqs. (14.4.3) through Eq. (14.6.6). Snijders and Bosker (1999) provide a clear exposition of the issues in choosing and provide recommendations, several of which are mentioned here. The choice depends on the number of groups, the sample sizes per group, the distribution of the level 1 and level 2 residuals, assumptions about how groups were sampled, the resulting generalizations one wishes to make, and the focus of the analysis. Constraints on the available data may dictate choice. With a small number of groups (fewer than 10 according to Snijders and Bosker, 1999), the fixed effects approach is recommended. Further, if the individual groups have special meaning (e.g., various ethnicities) and one wishes to speak to the model within each of the special groups, then the fixed effects approach is more appropriate. On the other hand, if the groups are merely a random sample from a larger population of groups and one wishes to generalize to the population of groups (e.g., from a sample of families to the population of families), then the RC approach is appropriate. Small numbers of cases per group lead one to the RC model, since shrinkage estimators can borrow strength from the full data set and the fixed effects approach may be very unstable (with large standard errors). On the other hand the RC model as it is typically implemented makes the assumption that the level 2 residuals are normally distributed.

14.15 SOURCES ON MULTILEVEL MODELING

We have barely scratched the surface of the large and complex area of multilevel modeling. As previously pointed out, Kreft and de Leeuw (1998) is an excellent starting point for further studying of multilevel models, followed by Snijders and Bosker (1999), and then by Raudenbush and Bryk (2002) and finally by Goldstein (1995). Singer (1998) provides a highly accessible introduction to the use of SAS PROC MIXED for random coefficient regression. Littell, Milliken, Stroup, and Wolfinger (1996) provide extensive documentation of SAS PROC MIXED. In addition to SAS PROC MIXED, there are several specialized software packages for multilevel modeling, of which the HLM software (Raudenbush, Bryk, Cheong, & Congdon, 2001) is perhaps the easiest to use. MlwiN (Goldstein et al., 1998) is another popular package. Chapter 15 of Snijders and Bosker (1999) is devoted to a review of software that can accomplish multilevel models.

14.16 MULTILEVEL MODELS APPLIED TO REPEATED MEASURES DATA

This section has addressed only clustering of individuals within groups. However, RC regression and multilevel models can also be applied to clustering (or serial dependency) that results from having repeated measurements on individuals. In repeated measures applications, the individual becomes the level 2 unit of aggregation. The repeated observations on each individual become the level 1 units. The interest in such repeated measures applications is on modeling an overall trajectory of how individuals on average change over time (the population fixed effects), of developing a trajectory for each individual, and in modeling the individual differences in the trajectory from both level 1 and level 2 predictors. Repeated measures multilevel analysis is presented in Section 15.4. In addition, Snijders and Bosker (1999) provide an accessible introduction.

14.17 SUMMARY

OLS regression and regression approaches subsumed under the generalized linear model (Chapter 13) all assume that observations are independent. When data are clustered such that individuals within clusters (e.g., children within the same family) are more like one another than are randomly selected individuals, bias is introduced into inference in OLS regression. Standard errors of OLS regression coefficients are negatively biased (too small), leading to alpha inflation (Section 14.1). Degree of clustering is measured with the intraclass correlation (ICC, Section 14.1). Clustering can be handled within the OLS regression framework by adding code predictors that identify the clusters and account for cluster differences (Section 14.2). A newer alternative regression model, the random coefficient (RC) regression analysis, handles clustering in a different way from OLS. RC regression permits the appropriate modeling of the impact of individual level predictors on a DV when data are clustered, yielding proper estimates of standard errors (Section 14.3). The RC regression model is presented, and its components explained: level 1 and level 2 equations, the mixed model equation, the variance components (Section 14.4). Concepts of fixed versus random parts of the model are explained. A numerical example is provided (Section 14.5). Clustering in data can be a meaningful aspect of the data (Section 14.6). Random coefficient regression is used to model multilevel data (Section 14.6), that is, data that contain predictors measured at different levels of aggregation, for example, on individual children within families (level 1) and on the families themselves (level 2). The multilevel RC regression model is developed (Section 14.7) with predictors at two levels of aggregation. The use of the multilevel model for the analysis of experiments in which individual differences may interact with treatment effects is developed (Section 14.8) and illustrated with a numerical example (Section 14.9). Estimation of fixed effects, variance components and empirical Bayes estimators are explained (Section 14.10). Statistical tests of the fixed and random components of RC regression are described (Section 14.11). Issues in model specification, including centering of predictors are addressed (Section 14.12). The choice between OLS regression based approaches and the random coefficient approach to handling clustered data is discussed (Section 14.14).

15

Longitudinal Regression Methods

15.1 INTRODUCTION

15.1.1 Chapter Goals

For the most part, the regression techniques we have reviewed in this book have been equally applicable to data gathered in cross-sectional surveys, laboratory or field experiments and trials, and two-wave longitudinal studies. However, when variable sequencing and changes over time are important aspects of the research, there are new kinds of questions that can be asked and an additional range of data analytic options. This chapter is intended to provide an introductory bridge to the more complex regression-based methods for answering research questions with data characterized by multiple assessments over time.

The analytic methods selected by the researcher will depend on both the structure of the data and the goals of the research. Our goal is to acquaint the reader with the major questions that can be addressed by repeated measure data, with the factors to be considered in choosing among available analytic alternatives, and with some simple illustrations. Section 15.12 at the end of the chapter reviews the essence of these research questions and the corresponding data structure for each of the major models described in this chapter. We will not cover issues of study design (e.g., retrospective or prospective data collection) or data quality (e.g., retention of sample). Our coverage of assumptions required by the methods (e.g., that the model for the subjects lost to follow-up or missing data is equivalent to that for those remaining in the sample) should not be assumed to be comprehensive. Almost all methods designed for scaled variables assume multivariate normality of the random error terms, and the models described here will be more or less sensitive to failure of this assumption. The need to carry out the diagnostic procedures described in Chapter 4 is likely to be more, rather than less, critical as the complexity of the analysis increases.

15.1.2 Purposes of Gathering Data on Multiple Occasions

As a rule there are three overarching reasons for gathering longitudinal data.[1] The first is that the investigators are interested in change over time per se. Such an interest is often the rationale for repeated measure designs in experimental studies. It is also an important focus for developmental researchers who may investigate changes that take place with age. The second reason is that one needs to know what variables may account for individual or group differences in change over time: Much of this chapter is devoted to these topics.

The third major reason for measuring variables at multiple time points is clarification of the sequencing of variables and changes in variables as a way of bolstering causal inferences. Equivalently, we may say that these analyses focus on variables that influence change in other variables. In these analyses, if experimental introduction of change-producing variables is not feasible or not carried out, naturally occurring changes over time are often used as a proxy for controlled changes. As almost any examination of published structural equation models will show, it is extremely common to find that causal effects operating in a direction contrary to that of the interpretation are all too plausible. When data are gathered without reference to the timing of changes in variables, as in cross-sectional data, our inferences about the functional relationships that give rise to the observations are bound to be correspondingly weak.

Another problem with causal inferences from cross-sectional data is that we are forced to use the differences *between* subjects as a proxy for what happens when a variable changes *within* or for each (or for some) of a given set of subjects. Often the propositions we use in our causal theories apply to individual subjects, rather than to differences between individuals. Thus we may say that the occurrence of a particular experience X is expected to have an effect B_X on some outcome, averaged across individuals. However, with cross-sectional data we make this inference by comparing not the individuals before and after event X but different individuals who have and have not experienced X, thus assuming that those who have not experienced X were equivalent collectively to those who have experienced X prior to this experience, or, put differently, would have been equivalent were it not for X. Of course, some of the variables to which we wish to attribute causal effects are relatively fixed characteristics such as blue eyes or gender or social class of birth. Our theories typically do not address the issue of the means by which changes in such variables would come about, or whether these means of change themselves would have differential effects on Y. Therefore we must presume that these variables are a kind of proxy for the mechanisms of other variables that may have more direct active influence on Y.[2]

15.2 ANALYSES OF TWO-TIME-POINT DATA

In the vast majority of published longitudinal studies in psychology and other behavioral sciences, data are collected at two time points. Thus, although there are scientists who will insist that such data may hardly be considered longitudinal, we will begin here.

---

[1] See Baltes and Nesselroade (1979) for a more extended discussion of the uses of longitudinal data.
[2] See Lord (1969) for a discussion of this issue, also Holland and Rubin (1988). Time itself is such a variable, being only a "stand-in" for a potentially large number of change mechanisms.

15.2.1 Change or Regressed Change?

One of the first decisions that arises is whether to use as one's dependent variable the raw change in Y from T_1 to T_2 or to use a regression model with Y_2 as the dependent variable.[3] One issue, introduced in Section 2.10.4, is that the correlations of change scores with postscores and prescores $(r_{(Y_2-Y_1)Y_2})$ and $(r_{(Y_2-Y_1)Y_1})$ are rather like part-whole correlations and may be considered to produce misleading findings when the goal is to remove the influence of the earlier variable. The heart of the problem with simple change scores, therefore, lies squarely in their necessary dependence on prescores. It is possible to write the equation of the correlation of the prescore with change as a function of the correlation between Y_1 and Y_2 and the two sds as

$$(15.2.1) \qquad r_{Y_1(Y_2-Y_1)} = \frac{r_{Y_1 Y_2} sd_{Y_1} - sd_{Y_2}}{\sqrt{sd_{Y_1}^2 + sd_{Y_2}^2 - 2r_{Y_1 Y_2} sd_{Y_1} sd_{Y_2}}}.$$

Note that the numerator subtracts from a fraction $(r_{Y_1 Y_2})$ of sd_{Y_1} *all* of sd_{Y_2}. For example, when $r_{Y_1 Y_2} = .64, sd_{Y_1} = 12$, and $sd_{Y_2} = 10$, Eq. (15.2.1) yields $r_{Y_1(Y_2-Y_1)} = -.24$. If $r_{Y_1 Y_2}$ were smaller (say, .50), $r_{Y_1(Y_2-Y_1)}$ would be even further from zero $(-.36)$. Note that this formula is an identity, that is, an algebraic necessity that makes no special assumptions. In particular, note that it contains no reference whatever to the reliability of Y. Thus, the dependence of change on initial level operates irrespective of unreliability, although, all things equal, unreliability will enhance it. Thus, if it is our intention by subtracting the prescore from the postscore to remove the effect of the initial level of Y and produce a measure that only reflects change in Y, we have obviously failed. This intuitively obvious method produces a measure that contains some variance wholly due to the prescore Y_1. Thus, its relationship to other variables is therefore influenced by their positive or negative relationships to Y_1.

This problem, once identified, is readily solved. As we have seen throughout the book, we may remove the influence of all correlation of Y with any variable by including that variable in the equation. Such a method works as well when the dependent variable is Y_2 and the variable the influence of which we wish to remove is Y_1 as it does for any other pair of variables. The structure of such regressed or partialed change scores helps clarify the nature of the problem with simple change scores. The variable Y_2 partialing Y_1 is literally $Y_2 - B_{Y_2 Y_1} Y_1$. Now $B_{Y_2 Y_1} = r_{Y_1 Y_2} sd_{Y_2}/sd_{Y_1}$, a quantity that will almost certainly be less than one and almost certainly positive. For example, for such representative values as $r_{Y_1 Y_2} = .50, sd_{Y_1} = 10$ and $sd_{Y_2} = 12, B_{Y_2 Y_1} = (.50)(12)/(10) = .60$. This says that for each unit increase in Y_1 we expect a .6-unit increase in Y_2, and that for an uncorrelated-with-Y_1 index of change we must use $Y_2 - .6Y_1$. However, the simple change score is $Y_2 - Y_1$, for which we can write $Y_2 - 1.0 (Y_1)$. The trouble with using the simple change score is that it suggests that the regression of Y_2 on Y_1 has a slope of 1.0 instead of the actual $B_{Y_2 Y_1}$, that is, that there is a unit increase in Y_2 associated with each unit increase in Y_1, instead of what in the example was only a .6-unit increase in Y_2. Regression coefficients of postscore on prescore of 1.00 almost never occur in the behavioral sciences; as noted, they are almost always less than one. For $B_{Y_2 Y_1}$ to equal 1.00 requires that $r_{Y_1 Y_2} = 1.00$ when the sds are equal, and more generally that $r_{Y_1 Y_2} = sd_{Y_1}/sd_{Y_2}$, a most unlikely

---

[3]Numerical subscripts in this chapter refer to the successive time points; thus X_1 and X_2 refer to X measured at the study's first and second time point, respectively. T_1 and T_2 refer to study time points 1 and 2, where it is presumed that T_2 came after T_1.

occurrence. Thus the effect of using change scores is typically one of *over*correction of the postscore by the prescore.[4]

This analysis may illuminate why simple change scores work quite well in the physical sciences. Whereas in the behavioral sciences individual differences in true change and measurement error both operate to reduce $B_{Y_2 Y_1}$, neither of these factors operates so significantly in the physical sciences. Indeed, in the physical sciences $B_{Y_2 Y_1}$ is often equal to 1.00 to a close approximation, so that simple change scores are automatically regressed change scores. This analysis also alerts us to the possibility of encountering in a behavioral science application the circumstance that $B_{Y_2 Y_1}$ approaches 1.00, in which case simple change scores will approximate regressed change scores and may be used interchangeably.

15.2.2 Alternative Regression Models for Effects Over a Single Unit of Time

When regression methods are selected for assessing regressed change and the methods are limited to the single equation regression analyses described in the early chapters of this book, there are still several optional models. If the time period between assessments varies for different subjects, one may include a variable reflecting this period in order to examine possible main effects and more probable interactions (moderating effects) of variations in duration on the effects of earlier predictors. For example, it is generally a reasonable expectation that the longer the time period the weaker the stability in a given variable and often the weaker the expected influence of a variable measured at the earlier time point on a later Y or on change in Y (that is, $Y_{2 \cdot 1}$). The inclusion of a variable T reflecting the period of time may show that the regression of $Y_{2 \cdot 1}$ on X_1 declines as a function of time (T) between observations (tested by the interaction of T with X_1).

This rule of thumb, however, raises the question of what the optimal interval should be for examining causal effects of one variable on another. It takes no more than slight reflection to realize that no generalization can be made and that such decisions are likely to be domain dependent. For example, experimental effects are often expected to have short term actions whereas surveys of cohorts are usually designed to ask questions about relatively slowly changing variables. However, timing effects may differ for subsets of variables even within study designs and domains. This is not to say that the question of plausible timing of effects is not an important one (P. Cohen, 1991; Gollob and Reichardt, 1991). Consideration of timing effects is a central part of the theoretical scientific task of specifying the mechanisms for functional relationships, albeit one that has been infrequently addressed in the social sciences thus far (McArdle and Woodcock, 1997).

There are several different models for examining the relationship between a given X and Y in two-wave longitudinal data. The simplest model is one in which X_1 is used to predict Y_2; this may be thought of as a simple prediction model. In Fig. 15.2.1 Model A, we use earlier assessed symptoms to predict subsequent role performance. This model is not unambiguously relevant to causal inference in any circumstance in which either a causal effect of Y on X is plausible or when common causes of X and Y (potentially including shared measurement error) are likely. The issue with regard to common causes is the same one discussed in Section 12.2. However, in this case, Y_1 (or an earlier version of Y) may also be thought to be a potential common cause of X_1 and Y_2.

---

[4]We will see in later sections, however, that this point of view depends on our theoretical model of change, and that difference scores may be exactly what we need to match our model. Although there has been an historic debate about the reliability of change scores, we will not discuss this issue here.

Model	Regression Equation
(A) Predicting Y	

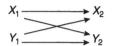

$$\hat{Y}_2 = B_{X_1}X_1 + B_0$$
$$\text{RPerf}_2 = .504\,(\text{Sympt}_1) + 24.529$$

(B) Cross-lagged estimation
    (predicting change)

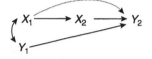

$$\hat{Y}_2 = B_{X_1}X_1 + B_{Y_1}Y_1 + B_0$$
$$\hat{X}_2 = B_{X_1}X_1 + B_{Y_1}Y_1 + B_0$$
$$\text{RPerf}_2 = .138\,(\text{Sympt}_1)$$
$$+ .616\,(\text{RPerf}_1) + 12.542$$

(C) Quick acting effects of X on

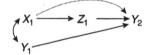

$$\hat{Y}_2 = B_{X_1}X_1 + B_{Y_1}Y_1 + B_{X_2}X_2 + B_0$$
$$\text{RPerf}_2 = -.017\,(\text{Sympt}_1) + .594\,(\text{RPerf}_1)$$
$$+ .417\,(\text{Sympt}_2) + .283$$

(D) Mediation with 2 assessment
    times: mediator measured at T_1

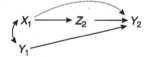

$$\hat{Y}_2 = B_{X_1}X_1 + B_{Y_1}Y_1 + B_{Z_1}Z_1 + B_0$$
$$\text{RPerf}_2 = -.102\,(\text{Sympt}_1) + .580\,(\text{RPerf}_1)$$
$$+ .071\,(\text{Exper}_1) + 12.652$$

(E) Mediation with 2 assessment
    times: mediator measured at T_2

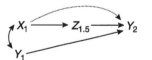

$$\hat{Y}_2 = B_{X_1}X_1 + B_{Y_1}Y_1 + B_{Z_2}Z_2 + B_0$$
$$\text{RPerf}_2 = -.016\,(\text{Sympt}_1) + .550\,(\text{RPerf}_1)$$
$$+ 0.248\,(\text{Exper}_2) + 11.323$$

(F) Mediation with 3 assessment
    times: mediator measured at $T_{1.5}$

$$\hat{Y}_2 = B_{X_1}X_1 + B_{Y_1}Y_1 + B_{Z_{1.5}}Z_{1.5} + B_0$$
$$\text{RPerf}_2 = .061\,(\text{Sympt}_1) + .537\,(\text{RPerf}_1)$$
$$+ .190\,(\text{Exper}_{1.5}) + 10.680$$

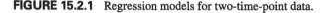

FIGURE 15.2.1   Regression models for two-time-point data.

CH15EX01

The most straightforward way to remove the potential influence of Y_1 is to include it in the equation predicting Y_2 so that the estimated effects of other IVs are independent of it. This is the predominant model for estimating such effects from two wave data in the published literature. In Fig. 15.2.1, Model B, we begin with the familiar model often referred to as "cross-lagged" analyses, in which we focus on the equation predicting Y_2. (Another equation predicting the T_2 value of symptoms would determine whether earlier role impairment effected the change in symptoms.) As can be seen in this example, it is typical that the estimated effect (B_X) in such a cross-lagged model is smaller in absolute magnitude than the effect when the earlier measure of Y is omitted from the equation (Model A). This is because of the typical positive correlation of Y_1 with Y_2 and Y_1 with X_1. In testing such a model we are providing for the potential presence of causal effects in both (or several) directions, including common effects of other variables that would be reflected in the correlation between X_1 and Y_1.

As noted in earlier chapters, these estimates are subject to potential distortion by the effect of measurement error in the covariate (here, Y_1), which typically (but not always) leads to underadjustment and therefore an overestimate of the effects of variables that are correlated with Y_1. Thus, when feasible, many investigators turn to SEM with multiple indicators in order to estimate effects for error-free variables (see Chapter 12).

However, if the effects of X on Y_2 take place over a much shorter period of time than is represented by the interval between study waves, employing X_1 may lead to a serious underestimate of its impact. Under these circumstances, using X_2 in predicting Y_2 may provide an estimate that is closer to the true impact of X than using X_1. Model C in Fig. 15.2.1 illustrates such a circumstance. In these analyses it would be prudent to include both X_1 and Y_1 as predictors as well, and to be cautious in interpreting the direction of the effect. One would need a strong theoretical argument or prior evidence to justify such an analysis. On the other hand, an analysis in which the interval between "cause" and "effect" is too great is not easier to justify, since findings from this analysis may seriously underestimate the effect of X and will have a lowered statistical power to reject the null. Better yet, the researcher should carry out a study in which a more appropriate timing is included.

Another limitation that arises with two-wave data is in the estimation of potential mediating effects of other variables (e.g., Z). Suppose, for example, that our theoretical interest is in estimating the influence of symptoms on role impairment and in determining whether the increase in likelihood of negative experiences associated with higher levels of symptoms may mediate this effect. If Z_1 is the representative of that mediator in the equation, the effects of X_1 on Z may not have been complete by T_1. Therefore the mediating effect of Z may be underestimated by B_{Z_1} (Fig. 15.2.1, Model D). On the other hand, if Z_2 is employed (Model E) there is the possibility that its relationship with Y_2 is in part due to a causal effect of Y on Z. In such a case its mediating effect would be overestimated.

15.2.3 Three- or Four-Time-Point Data

These problems with determining effects of mediators may be mitigated, and in some cases solved, by the availability of three waves of data, so that the mediating effect of Z can be estimated by including its value in the middle wave (Model F). Of course, as implied earlier, no number of data collection points can adequately compensate for grossly inappropriate timing with respect to the influences being studied. Thus a strong theory including the probable intervals or sequences involved in the phenomena under study is of great importance.

Of course, if we have three or four time points of measurement we may specify and test multiwave structural equation models as described in Chapter 12 and as elaborated in later sections of this chapter. Perhaps the simplest of these models are those in which we test whether the effects of certain variables are comparable across time points. Alternatively, we may have more complex hypotheses, examples of which will be taken up in the next sections.

15.3 REPEATED MEASURE ANALYSIS OF VARIANCE

In considering the many choices of extensions of the regression model it may be useful to think about data in terms of a three dimensional structure. One dimension (n) is subjects (e.g., individuals, geographical or political units, biological cells, etc.). The second dimension is variables (X), which, for purposes of this discussion, will include both the dependent variable

TABLE 15.3.1
Repeated Measure Data in Analysis of Variance Format

Group	ID no.	RPerf$_1$	RPerf$_2$	RPerf$_3$	RPerf$_4$	Sum RPerf
1	1	102.93	80.24	61.71	85.84	330.72
1	2	56.34	56.82	56.84	52.98	221.98
1	3	40.92	53.99	60.92	62.54	218.38
0	4	21.29	11.83	00.00	32.77	65.89
1	5	72.53	47.98	54.97	55.70	234.17
0	6	28.03	47.03	46.97	69.97	192.00
0	7	19.73	59.42	47.06	53.60	179.81
1	8	56.80	65.35	50.07	55.76	227.98
	⋮					
1	193	55.14	74.66	40.88	54.97	225.64
0	194	26.05	41.06	54.87	42.75	164.73
1	195	63.84	80.74	94.27	82.32	321.17
1	196	38.01	39.79	45.31	68.90	192.01
0	197	62.00	63.43	99.22	105.35	330.01
1	198	54.86	24.48	28.90	55.62	163.87
1	199	57.17	56.99	61.12	62.44	237.71
0	200	20.76	34.84	60.15	67.43	188.17
Total	M_Y	48.83	51.08	55.67	57.54	213.12
0	M_Y	40.28	44.66	51.28	56.79	193.01
1	M_Y	56.57	56.88	59.63	58.23	231.31

CH15EX02

Y of interest and all potential predictors. The third dimension is time (T), which includes all time points at which there are data.

The traditional method of handling such data has been within the framework of repeated measure ANOVA. In such a design each subject generates a score at each of two or more (fixed) time points, or under two or more different experimental conditions. Subjects are also often divided into groups representing the independent variable(s) of interest. Other variables may also be included as covariates, but their inclusion may be ignored for the present.

Let us consider, for example, data from two groups of subjects arrayed in columns, measured on four occasions, represented as a row of four scores for each subject, as in Table 15.3.1. In the typical case we are interested in both the row and the column means in this data set, and there might have been covariates, other variables characterizing the individual subjects, as well.

15.3.1 Multiple Error Terms in Repeated Measure Analysis of Variance

When data have this three-dimensional structure, we employ different variance components to provide appropriate standard errors and significance tests for the different parameters that are estimated. For parameters involving differences *between* subjects' average scores across the repeated measures (called trials here), an error term generated from the variance of these average scores is required. For parameters involving changes in the mean scores over the repeated trials, the appropriate error term involves variation around the individual subjects' means, that is *within* subjects. Thus, unlike ordinary regression analysis, multiple error terms

TABLE 15.3.2
Significance Tests for Repeated Measure Analysis of Variance

Source	SS	df	MS	F	p
Between subjects					
Groups	18, 283.575	1	18, 283.575	27.225	<.001
Subjects within groups (error)	132, 972.682	198	671.579		
Within subjects					
Trials	10, 434.979	3	3, 478.326	21.574	<.001
Groups by trials	5, 970.968	3	1, 990.323	12.345	<.001
Subjects within trials within groups (error)	95, 767.216	594	161.224		
Polynomial tests					
Linear across trials	10, 184.063	1	10, 184.063	38.459	<.001
Group difference in linear trend	5, 844.542	1	5, 844.542	22.071	<.001
Linear trials residual (error)	42, 430.784	198	264.802		
Quadratic across trials	4.178	1	4.178	0.032	.858
Group difference in quadratic trend	100.631	1	100.631	0.777	.379
Quadratic trials residual (error)	25, 656.498	198	129.578		
Cubic across trials	246.737	1	246.737	2.763	.098
Group difference in cubic trend	25.795	1	25.795	0.289	.592
Cubic trials residual (error)	89.293	198	89.293		

are required. In ordinary regression analyses, as we have seen, the total variance in Y is either associated with the IVs or not associated with them, so that a single error term may be employed in the tests of all statistical estimates in the final equation. However, in all of the models that follow it should be assumed that the computer algorithms that carry out the analyses include operations that separate variation into within subjects and between subjects components.

In Table 15.3.2 we note a significant effect for "groups," which is a test of the difference between the last two values in the final column of Table 15.3.1, 193.01 and 231.31. We also see a significant "trials" effect, which is a comparison of the first four values in the Table 15.3.1 row labeled Total: 48.83, 51.08, 55.67, and 57.54. The "groups by trials" significant effect tells us that the two groups did not show the same pattern across the four trials, as can be seen in the first four values in the last two rows, where, for example, the largest value for the group coded 0 was in the final trial while the largest value for the group coded 1 was in the third trial.[5]

15.3.2 Trend Analysis in Analysis of Variance

As noted, a major purpose of a repeated measure ANOVA is often the investigation of systematic changes in mean Y over time. There will be $t - 1$ degrees of freedom associated with these differences in means, where t is the number of times the measures were observed. When the measures are gathered at least three times, it is often the case that the investigator's major interest is in whether this change follows a straight line (is linear), and sometimes there is also an interest in whether it shows a significant bend in the line representing the means over

---

[5]We address issues of covariance heterogeneity that may occur in sequenced data in the next sections; such heterogeneity formally violates the assumptions of ANOVA models.

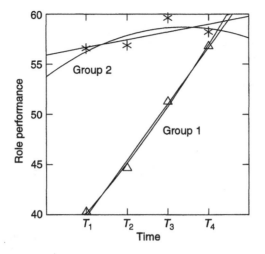

FIGURE 15.3.1 Linear and quadratic slopes for two groups.

time (i.e., is quadratic). As in linear regression, each of these functions has a single degree of freedom. The linear term is the estimate of the systematic increase or decrease of mean scores over the measurement occasions and thus represents the slope over time (where the time units are whatever period separates the repeated measures). To estimate the quadratic (U- or inverted U-shaped) tendency of the means over the repeated measures, the various occasions are coded in a way that is directly comparable to that described for ordinary regression (Chapter 7). A quadratic slope can be estimated and, as for the linear slope, an appropriate standard error provided. In fully balanced designs (no missing data, equal intervals) these two components are statistically independent.

For our illustrative example the means are plotted in Fig. 15.3.1. The presence of a linear slope for the group coded 0 is obvious, as is the lack of such a slope in the group coded 1. On examination of the statistical tests (Table 15.3.2) we find that the 1 df linear slope for the combined group is statistically significant (MS $= 10,184, F_{1,198} = 38.46, p < .001$), as is the difference between the linear slopes of the two groups (MS $= 5,845, F_{1,198} = 22.07$, $p < .001$). As can be seen, neither the quadratic nor the cubic effect is statistically significant for the group as a whole, nor are these effects different for the two groups.

15.3.3 Repeated Measure Analysis of Variance in Which Time Is Not the Issue

Suppose we have the following alternative theoretical predictions to test: Both theories recognize that a certain kind of experience—let us call it here "disappointment"—will lead to an increase in dysphoria. The first theory predicts that repeated exposure will lead to a "steeling" or accommodation effect in which it loses its effect on dysphoria. The second theory predicts that repeated exposure will lead to a cumulative effect. These two predictions are put to the test in a repeated measure experiment in which subjects are each tested for dysphoria three times. Subjects are subjected to four experimental conditions. The first group is simply tested on three occasions without experimental manipulation in order to serve as a control for the repeated assessment of dysphoria. The second group is tested on two occasions and subjected to the disappointment treatment on the third. The third group is tested on one occasion, subjected to the treatment prior to the second assessment, and assessed again on a third occasion. The fourth

TABLE 15.3.3
Tests of Steeling Versus Cumulative Effects

	T_1M_Y	(sd)	T_2M_Y	(sd)	T_3M_Y	(sd)
Total sample	9.93	(0.95)	11.19	(1.60)	11.70	(2.36)
Group 1	10.02	(0.69)	9.80	(0.76)	9.93	(1.28)
Group 2	10.26	(1.05)	10.00	(1.09)	13.01	(0.45)
Group 3	9.46	(0.93)	12.36	(1.18)	10.59	(1.08)
Group 4	9.98	(1.04)	12.58	(0.75)	13.26	(3.42)
	SS	df	MS	F	p	
Between subjects						
Group	62.69	3	20.90	11.81	<.001	
Subjects within groups	63.69	36	1.77			
Within subjects						
Between sessions	66.21	2	33.10	17.78	<.001	
Sessions by group	92.50	6	15.42	8.28	<.01	
Residual	134.03	72	1.86			

CH15EX03

group is tested on one occasion and then twice again, each time receiving the disappointment condition. The critical question is what happens on this last assessment—is there a further increase in dysphoria as predicted by the cumulation model or a decline as predicted by the steeling model? The ANOVA findings are shown in Table 15.3.3.

At first glance it appears that our study has come to a draw—although there was an effect of the disappointment treatment on each group, the effect on group 4 who got it twice was the same the second time as the first time. However, when we look closer we notice that there was a much larger standard deviation in this group (3.42) than in the other groups. Such a finding invalidates the assumptions of the ANOVA, and we decide to look further. Figure 15.3.2 plots the three assessments for the 10 subjects in group 4. In this artificial example it is abundantly clear that this group is heterogeneously composed of some subjects who apparently had a

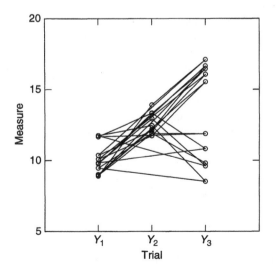

FIGURE 15.3.2   Dysphoria among subjects in group 4.

"cumulative" effect and other subjects who had a "steeling" effect. We are going to have to change our method of analysis to take this problem into account.

15.4 MULTILEVEL REGRESSION OF INDIVIDUAL CHANGES OVER TIME

The ANOVA repeated measure framework assumes constant error (residual) Y variances at the different time points and covariances between time points. This is equivalent to assuming that there are no significant (unaccounted for) individual differences in systematic changes over time (such as linear slopes) and there are equal correlations among all possible pairs of Y values measured at different times. These assumptions may be violated in real data. It is this problem and the opportunities for answering new kinds of questions that the multilevel model (mixed regression, hierarchical linear regression) computer programs are designed to handle for longitudinal data.

In a sense, then, the first question we need to answer when looking at multiple time point data is whether there are "unaccounted for" individual differences in change over time. If there are, there are two implications: first, that these individual differences may be associated with measurable variables, and second, that these individual differences need to be taken into account in order to make the statistical tests of model effects appropriate.

15.4.1 Patterns of Individual Change Over Time

Figure 15.4.1 provides the plots of changes over time for each of six subjects in some illustrative alternative data structures. For YA it appears that the changes over time may be more or less consistent across subjects, but some subjects seem to score higher than others. These data are therefore, on the face of it, consistent with the ANOVA model. In the second plot we see that YB seems to increase at a faster rate for some subjects than for others, giving us a "fan-shaped" distribution over time. In the next plot we see that YC increases over time for some subjects but declines for others. In the final plot it is hard to see what general trend in YG may be present, because some individuals fluctuate wildly in comparison to others.

We have looked thus far at overall differences in means and slopes over time in the framework of the repeated measure ANOVA model. Now we shift our frame to an equation predicting Y *for each subject* from a "fixed" IV consisting of *Time* (e.g., age at each assessment, or any other scale reflecting the time between the assessments). We then can investigate the two coefficients resulting from each individual's equation, B_0 and B_T, as "random" variables only partly reflected in average "fixed" values for the sample as a whole. To accomplish this we employ the same kinds of mixed or multilevel regression techniques that we employed to account for clustering of subjects in Chapter 14.

To review, Chapter 14 introduced the notion of clustered observations, that is, subsets of observations in a data set that are not independent of one another. As described in Section 14.1, there are two broad sources of clustering. First, clustering can arise because there are intact groups of individuals in the data set (e.g., children within families). Second, clustering can arise because the same individual is measured repeatedly and these repeated scores are included in the data analysis. Chapter 14 developed the multilevel model for the analysis of data sets in which individuals are clustered into groups; in this chapter we present the multilevel analysis of observations on individuals from whom data have been gathered at multiple time points. Needless to say, although the multilevel analyses of clustered data and repeated data are very closely related mathematically, some translation in thinking is required to link the two broad classes of application of multilevel analyses.

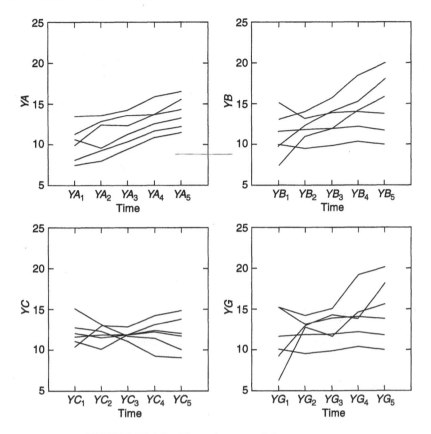

FIGURE 15.4.1 Illustrative sets of change patterns.

In Section 14.4.4 we learned that the full data set, pooled over clusters, yielded a set of fixed regression coeffficients in an overall equation predicting Y from all predictors. Here, with a number of individuals measured over time we can also estimate an overall regression equation that characterizes, on average, how these individuals change over time. The regression coefficients in these overall regression equations are referred to as the "fixed effects" of the multilevel analysis.

The multilevel analysis also allows for measurement of relationships of predictors to Y separately for each individual subject, as it did in the previous chapter for individual clusters of subjects. In longitudinal data this includes the variance due to individual differences in the intercepts of the equations that characterize individual changes over time. There is another variance component associated with the variance across individuals in the slopes in these equations. A third variance component is the covariance between the individual slopes and intercepts across all the individuals. These variance components are the "random effects" in the multilevel model.

In sum, there is a direct translation between multilevel modeling applied to individuals clustered within groups and to repeated measurements on individuals. All the structures of the analysis—fixed effects regression coefficients of an overall equation, regression equations at the level of the cluster or individual, and variance components reflecting differences among clusters or differences among individuals—are the same across applications. The estimation procedures and tests of significance are the same as well.

As in all regression equations, the individual intercepts reflect the estimated value of Y at the zero value of the predictors (e.g., *Time*). If zero is not a meaningful time point the investigator may choose another point (e.g., $Time_1$, or the mean of the *Time* variable, or the final time point) and subtract that value from all the time values (see Section 7.2 for a discussion of centering). If the time point selected as zero is the mean time, so that *Time* is centered, there will be no correlation between the intercept and linear slope across subjects. This may or may not be optimal, depending on the purposes of the analysis (see Kreft, de Leeuw, and Aiken, 1995, for a more complete presentation of this issue in the context of clustering by groups). It has the advantage of separating these elements, which may be desirable, especially if the analysis investigates interactions of the time variable with other predictors. On the other hand, as we will see in the next section, it may fail to reveal certain patterns of particular interest.

CH15EX04

To analyze these data we may use one of the programs for multilevel data. The analysis will indicate how much of the variance in Y is accounted for by these "random" differences between subjects in the intercepts and slopes of their individual equations predicting Y. Table 15.4.1 presents these analyses for our dependent variable, *YA*, in a sample of 60 respondents.[6]

The first model tested will give us an overall reference for the total variance in Y by including as a random IV the individual differences in intercepts of the 60 subjects. Of course, with no other predictors in the model the intercepts are equivalent to subjects' means. The output includes a test of the significance of the variance component attributable to these between-subject differences in Y means. In each of these models it is useful to divide each estimated effect by its standard error (SE), noting that the chance probability of a value of 2 or more is $<.05$. For Model 1, equivalently but depending on the computer analysis program employed, the output may supply a χ^2 test of the improvement of fit between the model in which the only predictor was the fixed mean (intercept) of the total group (so that we have the total Y variance in the "residual" term), and the model in which random variation in means (intercepts) was also included. As we noted in the hierarchical analysis of clustered data (Section 14.11.2) this χ^2 test is based on the difference in the function -2 log likelihood (-2 LL), which in this case is 81.4, with 1 df, clearly statistically significant. Thus, there were clear individual differences over the multiple occasions in these data. Indeed, as in the analysis for clustered subjects we may determine the intraclass correlation associated with subject differences in means on *YA* as $2.46/(2.46 + 3.02) = .45$. In our Model 1 the individual differences in *YA* across the time points are captured in the residual random term.

The next step in the analysis (Model 2) tests whether there is also significant variance in slopes over time (that is, in the B_T of the n subjects that predict *YA* from *Time*) and in the covariance between mean and slope. To test this we add these random effects to the model specification, and test the improvement in fit to the model. If *Time* had been centered, the means and slopes of individuals would generally be uncorrelated. Any other coding of *Time* typically leads to correlation (covariance) between means and slopes across subjects, which is easily pictured if one imagines where a value of zero *Time* would be for those with different slopes. If zero *Time* is the initial measurement or prior to the initial measurement and the general slopes are positive, a negative correlation between slope and intercept may be expected. If zero *Time* corresponds to the final measurement point given the same positive slope, a positive correlation between slope and intercept is the rule. For these data we see in the second row of Table 15.4.1 that there was significant random slope variance as well as negative covariance between means

---

[6]For simplicity, illustrations in this section employ balanced and complete data, and limit analyses to linear changes over time. The accompanying programs provide the algorithms used to create each of these data sets. The reader is encouraged to examine these algorithms in order to concretize the meaning of each of the analyses and findings presented here, and to create additional data sets to check on his/her understanding of the program output. Each of the programs used for these analyses, in this case PROC MIXED of SAS and MixReg in SYSTAT, have different conventions for output, and different options for models, but essentially equivalent estimates for equivalent models.

TABLE 15.4.1
Multilevel Analyses of Longitudinal Data on *YA* and *YB*

Model predictors		Random variance (*SE*)		Fixed effects (*SE*)	$\Delta\chi^2$
YA Model 1:	I[a]	2.46 (0.56)*	I	11.95 (0.23)*	81.4*
random intercept	R	3.02 (0.28)*			
YA Model 2:	I	17.80 (10.84)*	I	12.61 (0.23)*	385.6*
random intercept and slope	S	1.12 (0.21)*			
	I, S	−4.07 (1.63)*			
	R	.228 (.024)*			
YA Model 3:	I	3.22 (0.63)*	I	8.79 (0.24)*	214.8*
fixed *Time*; random	S	.009 (.006)	T	1.05 (0.02)*	
intercept and slope	I, S	−.047 (.046)			
	R	.228 (.024)*			
YB Model 1:	I	2.70 (0.70)*	I	12.96 (0.17)*	45.1*
random intercept	R	5.54 (0.51)*			
YB Model 2:	I	11.91 (2.62)*	I	11.98 (0.22)*	506.3*
random intercept and slope	0	2.12 (0.39)*			
	I, S	−4.39 (0.94)*			
	R	.231 (.024)*			
YB Model 3:	I	7.14 (1.35)*	I	9.80 (0.35)*	43.6*
fixed *Time*; random intercept	S	1.01 (0.19)*	T	1.05 (0.13)*	
and slope	I, S	−2.08 (0.45)*			
	R	.231 (.024)*			
YB Model 4:	I	22.88 (11.66)*	I	7.36 (0.66)	3.8
fixed *Time, Group*; random	S	1.02 (0.19)*	T	1.05 (0.13)	
intercept and slope	I, S	−4.53 (1.50)*	G	4.88 (0.43)	
	R	.230 (.024)*			
YB Model 5:	I	3.11 (0.62)*	I	11.00 (0.34)	209.3*
fixed *Time, Group*,	S	.009 (.006)	T	0.05 (0.03)	
and *Time* × *Group*;	I, S	−.071 (.047)	G	−4.01 (0.47)	
random intercept and slope	R	.230 (.024)*	$G \times T$	2.01 (0.05)	

[a]I = Intercept; S = Slope; I, S = Intercept-slope covariance; R = Residual.
*$p < .01$.

and slopes. In the illustrative data we analyzed here there were five assessment points, and we chose to examine only the linear effect over time, with its single *df*. Other functions of the individual differences over time are captured in the residual "random" effect. We see that, although statistically significant, this effect is much reduced in comparison to Model 1.

Model 3 adds *Time* as a fixed predictor to the model to determine whether there is a significant average (linear) effect of *Time*. In this example we see that there is a significant effect, and thus adding it to the model, necessarily, improved the fit between data and model. For these data we also note that this "fixed" IV accounted for all the significant variance in slopes of *YA* on time—that is, that the differences between the subjects in the slopes (i.e., in the linear change of *YA* over time) were no longer statistically significant (.009/.006 < 2). Individual mean differences (or intercepts) remain a significant source of variance in *YA*, that is, there is still significant variance in the (random) intercepts. In addition there is significant residual variance in the "random" individual differences in means over time.

Turning to the analysis of *YB*, we note that there were significant individual differences (variance) in means (intercepts), Model 1, and in slopes (Model 2), as well as in the covariance between means and slopes. In *YB* Model 3 we see that although there was a significant overall linear effect of time, there remained significant random variance in both intercepts and slopes.

15.4.2 Adding Other Fixed Predictors to the Model

Even where there is significant random variance in a dependent variable associated with the individual differences in slopes and intercepts, it is always possible that we can identify the "fixed" variables that account for these differences. In the case of example *YB*, we have, in fact, created the data to reflect two different subsamples of subjects who differ in their intercepts and slopes. In the usual data-analytic sequence, in Model 4 we add to the model that includes the single fixed IV, *Time*, the dummy variable representing the two groups as a "fixed" IV, and determine whether the fit of the data to this model is improved relative to the previous model. We see that the improvement in fit is marginally significant ($\chi^2 = 3.8, p = .05$), with 1 *df* for the *Group* variable we added as a predictor), indicating that these groups differ with regard to their intercepts. As in OLS, the intercept of the fixed effect portion of the model represents the intercept of the reference group, the group coded 0, and the coefficient attached to the group variable reflects the difference between the intercept of the group coded 1 and the reference group. At this point we also see that the random effects (variances) of individual differences in slope and intercept remain significant. As we move on to Model 5, however, where there is a very significant improvement in model fit as the fixed effects of different slopes for the two groups is added, we no longer have a significant random effect of slope. The average change for the reference group is near zero ($0.05; SE = 0.03$), whereas the average linear slope for the group coded 1 is 2.06 ($= 0.05 + 2.01; SE = 0.05$). Of course, these values reflect the model for the data as created by our algorithm. Thus, what were "random effects" or apparent individual differences in slopes before group membership was considered, now turn out to be effects of the set of fixed IVs, namely group membership.

This model then reduces to (i.e., is equivalent to) the ANOVA model.[7] However, it is important to note that, in contrast to the repeated measure ANOVA model, the variable(s) accounting for the differences in slopes in mixed regression models may be scales rather than categorical (groups), and they may or may not also account for individual differences in intercepts (means on *Y*). In addition, as we saw in the ANOVA model, changes over time that are not linear may also readily be examined as potential fixed or random effects, along the same lines as those examined in Chapter 6. That is, one may add the *Time* × *Time* product to evaluate the quadratic effect of *Time* in either or both the random and fixed predictors, and include it in interactions with *Groups* or other fixed predictors as appropriate to the purposes of the study.

The data illustrated as *YC* in Fig. 15.4.1 include subjects whose scores increase, decrease, or stay approximately constant over time, and may be analyzed by the same methods employed for the *YB* data.

---

[7]The example employed in the previous section is thus in no way structurally different from this analysis, and the reader is invited to analyze the data provided for that example in the same manner.

15.4.3 Individual Differences in Variation Around Individual Slopes

CH15EX05

In Fig. 15.4.1, the data for YG presented a different problem. Here we saw that some subjects had much greater fluctuation over time around their own slopes than did other subjects. In fact, these data were created using the same model as YB. In each data set, half of the subjects have no linear change over time ($Group = 0$) and the other half ($Group = 1$) have a 2-unit average increase at each additional time point. We then created YG, in which the random normal errors added to the change over time of subjects in $Group = 1$ (linear slope, $B_T = 2$) were three times as large as those in the other group ($Group = 0$). As a consequence, in the second data set, YG, the residual random variance was much larger than it had been in YB although the fixed effect estimates were the same.

The purpose of this illustration is to demonstrate an aspect of the algorithm employed in most multilevel regression programs, namely empirical Bayes estimation.[8] According to this algorithm, estimates of statistics (e.g., B_T) of individual subjects are "re-estimated" to be closer to the overall mean B_T as a function of their distance from the overall mean and their standard errors. We illustrate this by examining some particular cases from this data set. In order to accomplish this we need to examine the estimated case-by-case effects employed in the model, which is an optional output from each of the major programs. We then compare these estimates with the actual OLS-calculated slope for each case, based on the $k = 5$ data points for each subject.

Table 15.4.2 presents the estimated slopes for selected subjects along with their OLS slopes based on the five observations. These estimates will vary a little, depending on the error model and what fixed effects are included. Here we will just examine the estimates from a model that includes random slope and intercept and fixed effects of *Time*. In this example, the average slope was 1.05 (a random variation from the model's 1.00) because half of the subject scores were created from a population slope of 0.00 and half with a population slope of 2.00.

Subject 5 and subject 16 each had a similar observed slope over the five assessments. However, the variation around that slope was greater for subject 5. The empirical Bayes procedure moves both estimates of the random component of the slope toward the total sample

TABLE 15.4.2
Comparison of Empirical Bayes Estimates With Ordinary
Least Squares Estimates

Subject	OLS slope (*SE*)	Empirical Bayes slope estimate	Difference
5	−0.1070 (.142)	−0.1010	+.0060
16	−0.1010 (.127)	−0.0956	+.0054
37	2.4810 (.575)	2.3465	−.1315
42	2.4910 (.398)	2.3557	−.1353
32	1.0210 (.452)	0.9653	−.0557

[8]Bayes noted in the eighteenth century that when there is previous information about the value of some parameter, a new estimate of this parameter based on additional statistical information can combine the previous estimate with the new data (Stigler, 1986). In this case the total sample values may be thought of as the previous estimate, and the values of an individual case is "new information." In empirical Bayesian methods such "new information" is "re-estimated" to the extent that its statistics are far from the average values and have large standard errors, either because they are based on fewer data points or because they are based on data with larger residuals or error around an estimated statistic. Section 14.10.2 presents mathematical details on this procedure.

value of 1.05, but moves the less reliable (larger *SE*) subject 5 more. Turning to subjects 37 and 42, we see that each is further from the total sample value than the earlier cases, and each is moved a little more than the earlier cases. Finally, subject 32 is very close to the sample value and is moved very little despite its large *SE* (also note that the average estimated value is no longer the same as the average observed value, which is still reflected in the fixed portion of the model: Because the portion of the sample with the higher slope also had the greater variance around that slope, the estimated value is now less than 1.0). The exact algorithm cannot be inferred from this illustration, but the principles on which it is based remain.

This demonstration of the effects of differential reliability of data-based estimates (larger *SE*s) is probably less crucial in the context of complete and balanced data than it is when the number of data points varies for different subjects, a topic discussed in Section 15.4.6. The moral is the same, however: When you don't learn very much from a given piece or set of data, you don't change your estimate very much from whatever it was before you looked at that information.

15.4.4 Alternative Developmental Models and Error Structures

One of the characteristics of these studies of change over time is that they may find some other model of the change process more theoretically compelling than the between-within subject model for error variance that we have examined thus far. There are a number of such models that have been included as possibilities in one or more computer programs used to analyze repeated measure longitudinal data. This section will examine only a few of these.

One reasonable possibility is an autoregressive or Markov model where each new time point is a combination of the previous time point and some change. This developmental model is theoretically consistent with the presence of influences on Y that create "structural" changes that influence subsequent values. If there is autoregression, the measures at time 3, for example, will reflect the scores at time 2 plus some (random) change. The measures at time 4 will reflect the scores at time 2 plus the change to time 3 plus some additional change. This model may be fit with or without overall individual (random) or group (fixed) differences in means or slopes.

If the data show an autoregressive structure, the correlations among Y values at the different time points will show a "simplex" structure, by which we mean that the correlations between time points gradually decline over time. Thus, we would expect that the correlation between the scores at T_2 and those at T_4 would be smaller than the correlation of either with T_3. In fact, we anticipate that if one partials an intermediate time point set of scores, the correlation between scores at any two time points would be zero (in the population). Such a data structure is consistent with an autoregressive model.

CH15EX06

To illustrate, we have created a data set, *YE*, characterized by first order autoregressive effects (meaning that the data at any point are influenced only by the previous time point and a change). Figure 15.4.2 plots the values for five subjects.

In Table 15.4.3 we show selected output from the PROC MIXED program for this data set. In the first model we see that there are significant effects for the random slope and intercept (and their interaction, because we did not center *Time*). In the next model we added a fixed effect for *Time*, which was not significant, and this model was not an improvement over the previous one. In the third model for *YE*, however, we added a fixed effect of the Lag_1 variable, that is, the value at the previous assessment as a predictor. This model was a substantial improvement of fit, and the fit is entirely due to the fixed effect of the lagged *YE* (consistent with our algorithm for the construction of *YE*). Note that the random effects were no longer statistically significant, except for the residual effect, not included here. Although we created this data set to have no other effects, in real data there may well be other fixed or random effects.

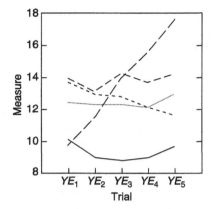

FIGURE 15.4.2   Autoregressive data for five subjects.

It is also possible to have data in which there are differences between subjects in the magnitude of the autocorrelation, so that autocorrelation should be included as a "random" component. From some perspectives these variations over subjects may be viewed as variations in the magnitude of disturbances or autocorrelated error. We have created a data set YF in which there is autocorrelated error as well as fixed effects for slopes and the group by slope interaction. The results of the analyses of these data are also in Table 15.4.3. In the first model we have

TABLE 15.4.3
Autoregressive and Autoregressive Error Analyses

Data and Model		Random effects (*SE*)		Fixed effects (*SE*)	$\Delta\chi^2$
YE autoregressive:	I	.388 (.093)*		9.767 (.048)*	289.6*
random intercept and slope	S	.048 (.011)*			
	I, S	−.054 (.025)*			
Fixed *Time*;	I	.387 (.093)*	I	9.839 (.092)*	0.6
random intercept and slope	S	.048 (.011)*	T	−.024 (.031)	
	I, S	−.053 (.025)*			
Fixed *Time*, lag_1;	I	.180 (.099)	I	3.232 (0.538)*	28.5*
random slope and intercept	S	.012 (.008)	T	0.027 (0.022)	
	I, S	−.030 (.018)	L_1	0.658 (0.053)*	
YF autoregressive error:	I	11.36 (2.45)*	I	11.77 (0.24)*	701.7*
random intercept and slope	S	2.03 (0.37)*			
	I, S	−4.00 (0.87)*			
Random intercept, slope,	I	—	I	11.87 (0.24)*	718.8*
and autoregression	S	2.01 (0.38)*			
	I, S	−3.97 (0.89)*			
	AR	.990 (.002)*			
Random intercept, slope,	I	—	I	12.00 (0.34)*	215.0*
and autoregression; fixed	S	.005 (.012)	T	−.047 (.044)	
Time, *Group*, and	I, S	.093 (.060)	G	−4.21 (0.48)*	
Group × *Time*	AR	.965 (.008)*	$G \times T$	2.05 (0.06)*	

*$p < .01$.

jumped right to the random slope, intercept, and slope by intercept (again, not having centered *Time*). This model is a statistically significant improvement over an intercept-only model (equivalently, these random coefficients account for a significant portion of the total variance in *YF*). In the next model we add autoregression to the *random* portion of the model, and find it to improve the model significantly. We also note that in this model all variance previously associated with individual differences in intercept has gone—that is, it has been shown to be accounted for by random autoregression. In the final model we have added the fixed effects of *Time, Group*, and their interaction. Although there was no main effect for *Time* (no slope for the group coded 0), the three variables added significantly to the model. However, at this point the only significant random terms are the autoregression and the residual term (not shown here).

Theory and this kind of reasoning may lead an investigator to examine the fit of a model with autocorrelated error, or it may even lead to tests of autoregressive moving average models in which one removes the (usually fixed) influence of (usually weighted) averages of (a specified number of) previous values of *Y* in order to investigate change. Such models are often employed when one has time varying IVs, as in time series analyses, or in extensions of the multilevel model we will shortly discuss.[9]

It is beyond the scope of this introductory chapter to discuss all the possible models for error structure in multilevel regression analyses. References and illustrations of alternatives can be found in McArdle and Aber, (1990); Littell, Milliken, Stroup, and Wolfinger (1996); and in the manuals for the computer programs that analyze these data. One method of testing alternative error models is to compare the log likelihoods of alternative models, although they will not necessarily be nested (see Bollen, 1989, and Byrne, 1998, for a discussion of alternative goodness-of-fit measures). In addition, it is always a prudent course to save the residuals from the (final) estimated model to test for homoscedasticity and to determine whether there are changes in the variances and covariances over time. As in all regression analyses, residuals should be normally distributed, with no systematic relationship with the predicted values. Changes in the residual variance over time or a decline in the correlation between measures over longer intervals may suggest that the fit may be improved by inclusion of an autocorrelation structure.

15.4.5 Alternative Link Functions for Predicting *Y* From Time

In addition to alternative methods for defining the error structure of these models, there are also alternative link functions describing the changes in the measures over time. Recall that a model's link function is the function of the dependent variable that is related linearly to the IVs. In Chapter 13 we discussed the logit and probit link functions suitable for dichotomous dependent variables and the Poisson link function as the function of highly skewed count variables that may be linearly related to the IVs. In this discussion we have focused on the linear slope over time, but when the dependent variable has these distributions, these alternative link functions to time (and to other IVs) have the same characteristics and advantages in longitudinal data as in the analyses discussed there. Usually special computer programs are required for these analyses.

With continuous scale values for *Y*, the first thing to do with any data set is to plot the individual curves. As discussed in Chapter 6, it may be that some transform of the data will linearize the changes over time and make the variance around the linear slope more homoscedastic. Alternatively, as noted earlier, one may wish to add quadratic and perhaps even cubic functions of time to the random or fixed predictors. There is, of course, the inconvenience of combining

---

[9] Any effects of constant "fixed" IVs (e.g., sex, group membership, or variables measured at a time prior to the intervals being assessed) will necessarily be removed from both *Y* and the other IVs by this method.

two or more statistics to represent a single curve over time. For some problems one may use a single nonlinear function to represent the theoretically plausible changes over time. For example, if a single bend in the curve over time is expected, one might use some quadratic function instead of a linear function of time. Indeed, in theory, any transform of the time variable that reflects the theoretical model may be produced and used as a random or fixed effect.

Some functions may require that one move away from the OLS models to alternatives available in certain computer programs. For example, an exponential curve, where each increase is proportionate to the earlier value (e.g., so that one expects, for example, greater decline for those with higher scores at the beginning of the study), may be plausible. Another theoretical possibility is that there will be a common time point (a "knot") representing a point following which there is an expected increase or decrease in the average linear slope. So, for example, one might expect one general linear change in "identity" over the first year of high school and a different slope over the remaining years. (And these slopes may reflect significant "random" individual differences as well as potential "fixed" mean differences.) In principle more complex curve functions may be fitted, but in practice there are few empirical examples.[10]

15.4.6 Unbalanced Data: Variable Timing and Missing Data

In the illustrations we have employed thus far, the data have been complete—that is, every subject has an observation at every time point and all time points are the same for all subjects. In real longitudinal data this is very rarely the case, and many of the same issues arise in efforts to cope with missing data that are discussed in Chapter 11. With regard to fixed IVs, the same techniques are potentially available, including imputation of values (Graham, Taylor, & Cumsille, 2001) However, the multilevel regression programs themselves "cope" with other kinds of missing-data problems, and in particular those of missing assessment points or attrition for some subjects, and variable timing of assessment.

When there are a fixed number of assessments at similar intervals for different subjects, the problem of variable timing is the easiest to manage, because we do not need to measure time (or age) as integers, but can use the actual time for each observation or assessment of each subject. In longitudinal data we may plan to assess children at ages 12, 18, and 24 months, for example, but availability, holidays, illness, and other scheduling problems may cause the timing to vary somewhat. To "control" for these variations in OLS analysis we may enter age of observation in a regression equation along with the longitudinal predictors. In doing so, we are acting as if the *average* influence of age of observation is an adequate control for variation in age for each of the subjects. In multilevel longitudinal models, however, the age of assessment for each subject is a part of the individual's prediction equation. Therefore, age effects reflect each individual's own change over the time points.

We will, of course, need to make the assumption that these variations in timing are not related to the functions we are investigating in any way that would distort our model estimates. This assumption can be tested, in part, by examination of the relationship between variations in timing and each of the IVs, and, perhaps even more important, of the interaction between such timing variations (if substantial) and one or more IVs in predicting Y. In general, when there are systematic changes over time the improved precision of measurement associated with exact timing should improve the estimated values from the model.

The problem of missing assessments illustrated in Fig. 15.4.3, and particularly when due to attrition, is a little different. Here, again, we have a choice between two assumptions. The first is that the data are missing "completely at random," that is, that the model of Y for the subjects missing some data points is the same as the model of Y for those with all data points.

---

[10]See Boker (2001) for a discussion of methods to analyze cycling or recurrent phenomena.

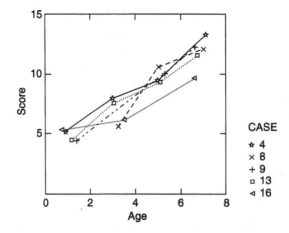

FIGURE 15.4.3   Data with missing and varying measurement points.

The alternative is that the data are missing "at random," meaning that the model of Y for the subjects missing some data points is the same as the model of Y for those with all data points *who are also equivalent on measured covariates*. When either of these assumptions is tenable, the empirical Bayes estimates that are employed may have smaller standard errors and thus tighter confidence limits than those that would be generated by OLS analysis, were it feasible (and certainly than OLS carried out on those with complete data only). As in the case of variations in timing, it is also possible to test for relationships of missingness (coded as a dummy variable) with IVs or Y measured in previous (or subsequent) assessments.

Two particular longitudinal designs may require some special consideration when the focus is on age changes. The first is the cohort sequential design, which is undertaken in order to speed up the coverage of age changes, usually on the assumption that cohort effects (effects of the historical year of birth) are likely to be trivially small over small numbers of years. In such designs the investigator may, for example, begin the study with cohorts born every third year over the age range of interest and follow each cohort for five consecutive years. Thus, for example, the youngest cohort, born in 1990 and first studied in 1995, is seen until 1999, at the ages of 5, 6, 7, 8, and 9. The second cohort, born in 1987 and first studied in 1995, is seen at the ages of 8, 9, 10, 11, and 12. The third cohort, born in 1984 and first studied in 1995, is seen at the ages of 11, 12, 13, 14, and 15. Thus, in a five-year period data have been collected on changes from age 5 to age 15.

Another very common longitudinal design is what is sometimes known as a panel design. In such a case the original sample may vary substantially on age, representing some population heterogeneous with regard to age. Determination of age-associated change from such data is not problematic for the multilevel regression programs, although nonlinear changes and cohort effects are more probable as the age range examined increases.

15.5 LATENT GROWTH MODELS: STRUCTURAL EQUATION MODEL REPRESENTATION OF MULTILEVEL DATA

Whenever there are individual differences in slopes there are also changes in variance and covariances over time. This means that these models may be analyzed not only by multilevel model programs (such as HLM and PROC MIXED), but also by structural equation model (SEM) programs such as LISREL, EQS, and Mx, which work with variance/covariance or sum squares/products matrices. Translations from one kind of program to the other are discussed and illustrated by Willett and Sayer (1994), and emerging practices and programs are clearly bringing these two traditions closer and closer together (e.g., McArdle, 1998). The central features of the SEM representation of the longitudinal models include a more explicit specification of the hypotheses about the causal structure and the potential to estimate subjects' "true" latent variable scores on the change parameters.

15.5.1 Estimation of Changes in True Scores

The first elaboration on repeated measure ANOVA that is available in programs designed to model "growth" is employment of factor structure models to estimate the models for growth in true (error-free) scores rather than observed scores. As we saw in Chapter 12, estimation of relationships among error-free latent variables is a major reason for employing structural equation models. However, in the models examined in Chapter 12 the structure of variable means was generally ignored, with a focus on covariance. Growth models focus instead on both the changes in means over time and covariance, with mean vectors and covariance matrices used to provide information that can be used to generate estimates of change functions in error-free constructs (latent variables).

In longitudinal data the error-free aspects of each individual's scores are usually represented by two latent variables, one representing individual differences in level (mean or intercept) across time and the other representing individual differences in linear slope over time. The "true" portion of each individual's growth trajectory is defined as the (linear or other slope or B_{T_i}) overall trend over time, made up of the individual's "random" variation from the overall average effect weighted by the "fixed" effect at each time point, that is, the effect common to the sample as a whole. The contribution of error at each time point added to this "true" or latent score comprises the observed score (see Aber & McArdle, 1991, for a clear illustration). The errors may have any theoretically relevant and empirically supported structure, autoregressive or other.

Note that variance we include as "error" in the ANOVA sense, that is, residual sources of variation over time, is not necessarily "error" in a measurement sense. In general, it may be prudent to think of it simply as "residual variance." That is, variations in an individual's slope over time may reflect "disturbances" (unmeasured influences) as termed by the econometricians, and may have little or nothing to do with measurement error as such.

15.5.2 Representation of Latent Growth Models in Structural Equation Model Diagrams

One of the most useful features of SEM growth models is the explicitness of the covariance and error structures that can be tested for a fit to the data. Figure 15.5.1 depicts a standard latent growth model (LGM) predicting five repeated observations over time. Model specification for LGM A is "classic" insofar as it assumes that residual scores are all uncorrelated and of equal variance. This model looks a little different from other SEMs because the means and mean changes over time need to be represented as well as the sources of variance and covariance. As always, latent variables are represented in circles or ovals and observed variables are represented in rectangles. The latent variable L represents the individual differences in levels of Y (means over time or intercepts), and this variable has the same impact on the observed variable Y at all time points. The latent variable S represents the individual differences in slopes of Y over time, and it, too, has a constant influence on the observed variable Y at all time points. The triangle K represents all fixed effects estimated in the model (i.e., overall sample mean

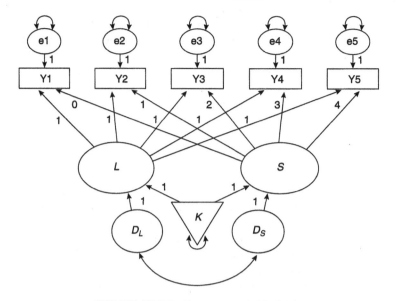

FIGURE 15.5.1   Latent growth Model A.

and average slope), and the "sling" indicates covariance between these constants. Following programming conventions of EQS, disturbance factors are specified for latent variables L and S to account for variance around the sample mean and average slope. In many models we also need to represent the covariance between disturbance factors for L and S. The latent variables e_t are the error terms, and the slings represent their variance.

Using the same data analyzed earlier in multilevel analyses, this classic latent growth model can be specified to predict YA and YB scores and produce essentially the same results. Although illustrations presented here were analyzed with EQS, other SEM programs such as LISREL and Mx also could be used. Before proceeding, the data analyzed with PROC MIXED must be reorganized into a different kind of data file. Instead of placing repeated variables into multiple records for each subject, EQS requires that all repeated data appear in a single record. As depicted in Fig. 15.5.1, the complete model for YA is specified in separate steps and evaluated for improvements in fit in a nested sequence of model comparisons. Based on changes in degrees of freedom with each model respecification, changes in maximum likelihood χ^2 statistics are used to identify significant changes in fits. Overall goodness of fit (i.e., correspondence between estimated and observed covariance matrices) will be evaluated here with the Comparison Fit Index (CFI); (Bentler, 1990). Ranging from zero to 1.00, the CFI indicates an acceptable fit when it reaches scores of .90 or higher.

First, a null model hypothesizing no growth is specified by predicting all five observations of YA based on the overall mean (i.e., the "fixed intercept"). This specification corresponds in Fig. 15.5.1 to the pathway from triangle K to latent variable L and then to all five observed variables. All pathways are equally weighted at 1.00 because, by definition, all variables are equally predicted by the fixed intercept. Also, error variance is specified for each observation of YA. To be consistent with the multilevel analysis presented in Table 15.4.1, all error variances are fixed to be equal.

To assess whether individual variation in intercepts accounts for a significant portion of the data, Model 1 (M1) adds the "random intercept" to the model. In Fig. 15.5.1, this step adds disturbance factor D_L and its pathway to latent variable L to the model. Next, Model 2 (M2) assesses whether individual variability in slope or "random slope" accounts for a significant

TABLE 15.5.1
Structural Equation Model Analysis of *YA* Data

	Model predictors	χ^2	df	CFI	$\Delta\chi^2$	Δdf	p
M0	Intercept and residual	691.46	18	.00	—	—	—
M1	Adds random intercept	609.82	17	.00	81.64	1	<.01
M2	Adds random slope and (Covariance intercept/slope)	233.32	15	.59	376.50	2	<.01
M3	Adds fixed *Slope*	22.98	14	.98	210.34	1	<.01

CFI = Comparison Fit Index.

portion in the data. The random slope is depicted in Fig. 15.5.1 by latent variable S and disturbance factor D_S, which at this stage are identical. (This redundancy disappears once the fixed slope and its pathway from triangle K to latent variable S are added to the model.) The basis coefficients from latent variable S to the five observed measures (0, 1, 2, 3, 4) indicate that linear growth is expected. By beginning these ascending weights with zero, the intercept in the model is set to equal the mean of the first observed variable. Other weights can be used for a variety of purposes, including testing for quadratic or exponential growth. Along with random slope variance, covariance between disturbance factors D_L and D_S (depicted by the curved arrow in Fig. 15.5.1) is added to the model at this stage. Finally, to assess whether there is any "true" change for all subjects, Model 3 (M3) adds the fixed slope to the model. Graphically, the pathway from triangle K to latent variable S is thus added to the model.

Table 15.5.1 presents χ^2 statistics and CFI scores for each successive model fit and contrasts between models. Changes in χ^2 statistics are essentially the same as those in Table 15.4.1. Although each successive model improves overall fit, only the final model produces an acceptable fit as indicated by the CFI score of .98. Table 15.5.2 contrasts parameters estimated by PROC MIXED and EQS for model M3. Aside from the fixed intercept, parameter estimates and standard errors produced by EQS differed little for those calculated by PROC MIXED. Notice that the fixed intercepts estimated by EQS and PROC MIXED differed by 1.053, which exactly equals the fixed slope estimated in both models. When the basis coefficients in the SEM estimation of *YA* are respecified to be consistent with the values used for time in PROC MIXED (1, 2, 3, 4, 5), both models produce essentially the same results, including the same fixed intercept.

Although the classic model also predicts changes in *YB*, additional specifications are necessary to model group effects. First, data from different groups are stored and analyzed in separate data files. The same model comparisons described earlier for *YA* for models M1, M2, and M3 are specified for both groups, and all parameter estimates are constrained to be equal in each sample. To be consistent with PROC MIXED model specifications, the basis coefficients

TABLE 15.5.2
Comparison of Multilevel and Latent Growth Models of *YA* Data

Model predictors	Random Effect (*SE*)		Fixed Effect (*SE*)	
	PROC MIXED	EQS	PROC MIXED	EQS
Intercept	3.222 (.635)	3.191 (.613)	8.790 (.241)	9.843 (.248)
Slope	0.009 (.006)	0.009 (.006)	1.053 (.023)	1.053 (.023)
Covariance intercept/slope	−0.047 (.046)	−0.038 (.044)	— —	— —
Residual	0.228 (.024)	0.232 (.025)	— —	— —

TABLE 15.5.3
Structural Equation Model Analysis of *YB* Data

	Model predictors	χ^2	df	CFI	$\Delta\chi^2$	Δdf	p
M0	Intercept and residual	819.95	38	.00	—	—	—
M1	Adds random intercept	774.52	37	.00	45.43	1	<.01
M2	Adds random slope and Covariance intercept/slope	290.90	35	.50	483.62	1	<.01
M3	Adds fixed *Slope*	248.78	34	.58	42.12	1	<.01
M4	Adds *Group*	245.06	33	.59	3.72	1	<.10
M5	Adds fixed *Slope* × *Group*	44.70	32	.98	200.36	1	<.01

CFI = Comparison Fit Index.

for the slope are specified as 1, 2, 3, 4, and 5. As summarized in Table 15.5.3, Model 4 (M4) tests for group effects by releasing the equality constraint on fixed intercepts, thus allowing separate parameters to be estimated for each group. Then, Model 5 (M5) tests for interactions between groups and slopes by releasing the equality constraint on fixed slopes in the two samples. When comparing nested models, changes in χ^2 statistics in Table 15.5.3 all closely correspond to those in Table 15.4.1. The EQS output indicates that the fixed intercept is 11.81 (*SE* .35) in the group coded 0 and 7.79 (*SE* .35) in the group coded 1. When the fixed intercept in group 0 is subtracted from the same estimate in group 1, the difference (−4.02) is almost identical to the parameter estimate for group effects in Table 13.4.1. When the fixed slopes are subtracted (2.06 − 0.05 = 2.01), we also get the same parameter estimated by PROC MIXED for group by slope interactions.

As illustrated in Fig. 15.5.2, latent growth models can be modified to account for alternative error and covariance structures in longitudinal data. In latent growth Model B, the curved arrows between the error factors represent specifications for autoregressive error. In Model C we see a model that is autoregressive in the observed variables. Although a review of the mathematical estimation of alternative models is beyond the scope of this chapter, it is worth noting that specific techniques may vary depending on the program used. When making nested model comparisons for *YE*, for instance, both PROC MIXED and EQS produced similar results in Models M1, and M2. This is confirmed by comparing changes in χ^2 values in Tables 15.4.3 and 15.5.4. When using the same basis coefficients, both programs also produced essentially the same parameter estimates for Model 2, as summarized in the top section of Table 15.5.5. However, the bottom portion of Table 15.5.5 shows notably different results for Model 3 once autoregressive or "lag" effects between observed variables were added to the model. In EQS autoregressive path specifications between each observation of *YE* were simply added to the model, which means that the first observation of *YE* had no lag effect and was predicted only by latent variables *L* and *S* and its corresponding error factor. To test for autoregressive effects in PROC MIXED, a separate "lag" variable had to be created for all repeated variables, including the first observation of *YE*, and this difference in model specification led to the different results in Table 15.5.5. The specific details are less important here than the overall point that the different modeling techniques are each correct within the context of the corresponding program used. Although multilevel and SEM traditions have indeed come much closer together, there are still certain areas where they do not overlap.

These simple models may be the basis for models to which more fixed or time-varying predictors are added. In addition to the latent growth models of individual variables, newer methods make it possible to examine latent growth models in which multiple indicators are

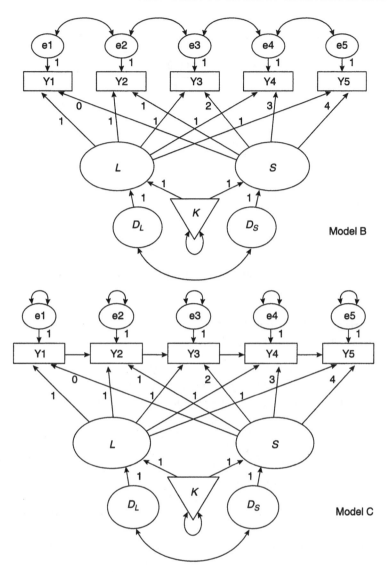

FIGURE 15.5.2 Latent growth Models B and C.

TABLE 15.5.4
Structural Equation Model Analysis of *YE* Data

	Model predictors	χ^2	*df*	CFI	$\Delta\chi^2$	Δdf	*p*
M0	Intercept and residual	313.84	14	.01	—	—	—
M1	Adds random intercept, random slope, and Covariance intercept/slope	36.93	11	.91	276.91	3	<.01
M2	Adds fixed *Slope*	35.07	10	.92	1.86	1	NS
M3	Adds *Lag₁*	30.96	9	.93	4.11	1	<.05

CFI = Comparison Fit Index.

TABLE 15.5.5
Comparison of Multilevel Latent Growth Models of *YE* Data

Model predictors	Random Effect (*SE*)		Fixed Effect (*SE*)	
	PROC MIXED	EQS	PROC MIXED	EQS
Model 2				
Intercept	0.387 (.093)	0.381 (.091)	9.839 (.092)	9.889 (.089)
Slope	0.048 (.011)	0.059 (.013)	−0.024 (.031)	−0.047 (.037)
Covariance intercept/slope	−0.053 (.025)	−0.058 (.027)	— —	— —
Model 3				
Intercept	0.180 (.099)	0.388 (.091)	3.232 (.538)	9.896 (.089)
Slope	0.012 (.008)	0.060 (.013)	0.027 (.022)	−0.017 (.037)
Covariance intercept/slope	−0.030 (.046)	−0.061 (.027)	— —	— —
Lag_1	— —	— —	0.658 (.053)	−0.012 (.006)

employed for the latent variables. Such models also make it possible to explore the constancy of the structure of latent variables over time.

15.5.3 Comparison of Multilevel Regression and Structural Equation Model Analysis of Change

As noted, except for models using some other link or change function, one remains, more or less, in the same framework, and these models can be fitted with either multilevel regression programs or structural equation models. That is, one can do so if the data are at equal intervals and complete (balanced), as in these examples. However, such balanced data are often not available. Some designs, such as staggered longitudinal samples (cohort sequential longitudinal studies) can be analyzed with latent growth models as well as with multilevel regression models (McArdle & Hamagami, 1991). Nonrandom missing data, especially with regard to slope differences, which is an all-too-likely theoretical possibility, is likely to be a serious problem regardless of the analytic approach.[11] If the missing data points are not too many, the full matrix might be estimated by multiple imputation procedures (Section 11.3) and either a multilevel regression or an SEM program employed. Multilevel regression programs can readily cope with unequal intervals and missing data, including data with only a single data point for some individuals. Although perhaps accomplished with a little more difficulty with an SEM program than with a multilevel regression program, panel and staggered cohort designs can be carried out with either approach (see Mehta & West, 2000, for the Mx script for LGM analysis of cohort-sequential or panel data).

In general, the advantages of latent variable SEM models include more flexibility in specification, explicitness of all aspects of the model, and potential latent variable score estimates. However, they are most feasible when there are relatively few data points per subject. The advantages of multilevel model estimation include much more flexibility in the characteristics of the available data and easier employment of all the data. Multilevel regression programs may be more flexible with regard to data that are not "balanced" with regard to the timing and number of measurement points for each subject. In addition the multilevel programs can

---

[11]For example, it is often the case that students with low achievement or potential respondents who are more depressed are more likely to be missing from one or more assessments. If this problem is not taken into account by inclusion of some appropriate indicator, the estimated mean and slope of the population including such individuals may be highly biased by the analysis, and particularly by the empirical Bayesian procedure, which would estimate extreme cases with missing values to be less extreme than they were observed to be.

usually offer more options with regard to link functions and error structures and can handle more time points.

In this chapter we have generated data to illustrate a number of the features and interpretations of the multilevel program output. Analyses of real data, however, are often more ambiguous McArdle and Aber (1990) provide an illuminating example of five different plausible models of change applied to a single data set. This example resulted in "aliases"—multiple models with which the data show approximately equivalent values of the fit indices.

Recent advances in multilevel regression and LGM include clustering subjects by trajectory type (Muthén, 2001; Nagin, 1999) and other elaborations of the model possibilities (Collins & Sayer, 2001). Among the critical issues not discussed here is the question of whether the variables and the relationships among the variables have the same meaning over time. These issues and others are discussed in McArdle and Nesselroade (1994) and in T. E. Duncan, S. C. Duncan, Strycker, Li and Alpert (1999).

15.6 TIME VARYING INDEPENDENT VARIABLES

Often the point of a multilevel analysis of a time-varying DV is estimation of the effect of one or more IVs that change over the course of the longitudinal investigation. As noted in Section 14.2, relationships among the *average* values of variables (as in analyses of variables relating to average income at the county level) can lead to very different conclusions than relating the same variables across the individual units (such as persons) within these aggregates (Robinson, 1950). Similarly, the relationships of the changes in IVs to changes in Y for individual subjects may not be the same as the relationships of differences between subjects in those same IVs with values of Y either cross-sectionally or on the average (Kraemer, Yesavage, Taylor, & Kupfer, 2000). A recent change in health, economic, or marital status will not necessarily show the same change in Y that is observed in cross-sectional comparisons of demographic groups, or the same effects on Y as when they are measured as fixed characteristics throughout the period of study. In the long run it is likely that longitudinal investigations of change in process will be much more informative about short- and long-term effects of variables than cross-sectional studies can ever be.

In addition, there may be substantively and statistically significant differences in the relationship between time-varying IVs and Y for subjects in different subgroups. For example, in clinical randomized tests of differential treatment efficacy, an experience, independent problem, or intervention that takes place early in the trial may not have the same meaning or effect that it would have had later in the trial.

The methods employed by the different multilevel analyses are designed to make tests of these hypotheses appropriate, flexible, and efficient. In doing so, like all model-based techniques, they require specification of one or more hypothesized models that gave rise to the data. Because these models are different from the more familiar ones based on cross-sectional data, we have yet to become fully fluent in the matching of our theoretical reasoning with the implied model. Once specified and tested, such analyses are evaluated in terms of the closeness of the fit of the data to the alternative models. The multilevel regression programs that we discussed earlier provide for such changing IVs and alternative models.

Changes in variance and covariance over time also provide clues as to a likely appropriate structure for the model.[12] For example, suppose that either the observed or the residual covariances (or correlations between scores at different time points) are consistent over time.

---

[12] As Mehta and West (2000) show, differences in the linear slopes for individuals must be reflected in a pattern of decreasing and then increasing variance, although not necessarily the full pattern within the observed age range.

In general, such a circumstance suggests that differences between subjects may be accounted for by "fixed" IVs (stable characteristics of the subjects, such as gender). Random effects that remain may reflect unmeasured but consistent or stable individual differences in traits or contexts. On the other hand, changes in variance and covariance over time not accounted for by simple differences in slopes suggest the existence of important to-be-measured time varying effects that should not be dismissed as "random" error.

15.7 SURVIVAL ANALYSIS

One particular kind of longitudinal question is that of how long it takes to reach some change in dichotomous status (to die, to recover, to get married, or to succeed) and whether there are differences in this time profile associated with sample characteristics or group membership. Special parametric and nonparametric models have been developed for this kind of data.

15.7.1 Regression Analysis of Time Until Outcome and the Problem of Censoring

When the outcome of interest is the time that elapses before some change in state or status such as death or recurrence of a behavior, it may be reasonable to employ that duration as Y in an ordinary regression analysis. For example, suppose the problem was posed as the time to the first gross role failure (represented in our earlier example as role impairment scores of 1.6 or higher). We show some such data as "actual time" in Table 15.7.1. Should the distribution of durations be grossly non-normal, an appropriate transformation may solve the problem (see Section 6.4). However, we note in this example a problem that makes the analyses of durations by ordinary multiple regression problematic. This is the problem that at the end of

CH15EX07

TABLE 15.7.1
Data and t Tests for Time to Role Failure

ID no.	Actual time	Observed time	Group
1	.91	.91	2
2	1.85	1.85	2
3	7.10	7.10	2
4	11.52	—	1
5	1.21	1.21	2
6	9.91	9.91	1
⋮			
193	.81	.81	2
194	10.68	—	1
195	.83	.83	2
196	9.14	9.14	2
197	1.15	1.15	1
198	1.51	1.51	2
Mean Total	5.16	3.88	1.55
Group 1 Mean	6.42	4.84	$n = 92/105$
Group 2 Mean	4.03	3.19	$n = 66/95$
t test (df)	4.69 (198)	3.32 (156)	

the study some subjects had not yet "attained" role failure and therefore there is no clear time to attainment for these subjects. In our example these data are shown as "observed" time in Table 15.7.1. Obviously, if we leave these individuals out of the analysis we may seriously distort the picture.

Among the data we see that of these 12 subjects, 2 took longer to meet the criterion than the follow-up allowed (10 units), namely subjects 4 and 194. We also note that leaving out the subjects who had not met the criterion at follow-up led to a substantial underestimate of the mean time taken by this sample. The mean of those meeting the criterion by follow-up was 3.88 in comparison to 5.16 if the study had continued until all subjects met the criterion, an underestimate of 25% in this sample, in which 42 or 21% of the sample was lost. A similar decline in the estimate of the mean difference between the two groups is apparent. Complete data give a mean difference of 2.39 time units (6.42 − 4.03), whereas incomplete follow-up gives a mean difference of 1.65 time units (4.84 − 3.19).

In order to analyze these data using time to criterion as the dependent variable in a regression equation, one may assign some time beyond the study cutoff date to these subjects, but such an assignment will necessarily be viewed by other scientists as arbitrary. One may treat those who have attained the status in one analysis and examine the correlates of the rate of status attainment in another, but it may be awkward to put these two analyses together.

In some studies the problem is even more serious because the length of follow-up may vary from one subject to another. This can happen when subjects enter the study over a period of time but the study ends at the same time for all subjects. It can also happen when some subjects are lost to follow-up before the end of the study, which may also happen because the individual is no longer in the "at risk" status, as, for example, when a subject dies. This problem is known as the problem of *right censoring*. That is, if each person's time in the original state is viewed as a line that extends to the right to a length representing the time until that state is changed, some lines will be censored (end) before the state is attained, and indeed some participants may never attain the state in question. Figure 15.7.1 illustrates this phenomenon for a (fictitious) study of re-arrest in a group of prison releasees. In general researchers can follow up subjects only for a certain period of time, and some people are lost to follow-up, so that it is not known

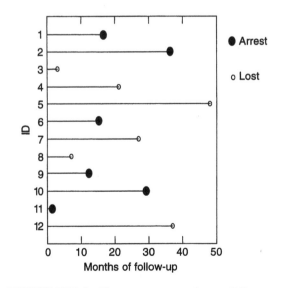

FIGURE 15.7.1 Time to re-arrest or loss to follow-up.

TABLE 15.7.2

Survival Analysis of Time to Role Failure

Stratification by groups; Kaplan-Meier estimation:

Group 1, $n = 66$ of 95 failing:
    Product limit likelihood $= -334.967$.   Mean survival time $= 6.441$.
    Survival Quantiles: 75%, 2.695; 51%, 7.181; 31%, 9.908

Group 2, $n = 92$ of 105 failing:
    Product limit likelihood $= -455.321$.   Mean survival time $= 4.030$
    Survival Quantiles: 75%, 1.272; 50%, 2.300; 25%, 7.100
Log-rank test of group difference: Tarone-Ware : $\chi^2 = 16.212, 1\ df,\ p < .01$.

---

if and when the change of state occurred. As noted, the intake period may extend over time so that some individuals are observed over a longer period than are others, and those who have not yet changed their status when the study ends may include a number with relatively short follow-up periods.

When one can make the assumption that censoring due to loss to follow-up or any other reason is not likely to be related to the timing of the change in status, it is possible to use survival methods to estimate the curves representing the rate of change in status for all members of the sample, or for members of subsamples of interest. This function is called the Kaplan-Meier or *survival function*. It is also possible to focus on the conditional probability of change in status given "survival" in the original state up until that point in time. The logit of this function is called the *hazard function*. The most common statistical approach to estimating this function was devised by Cox (1972; Cox & Oakes, 1984) and is often called Cox regression. This approach begins with data in which the duration of the interval to the event being studied is measured in continuous time, as in our illustrative example. Table 15.7.2 provides a part of the output from a survival analysis of the data presented in Table 15.7.1. We note that the estimated means of the two groups from this analysis, 6.44 and 4.03, are much closer to the complete sample values (6.42 and 4.03) than were the data actually "observed" in the (fictitious) study. The output also provides estimated times at which quartiles (25%, 50%, 75%) of each group had achieved the target status and a significance test on the difference between the curves in the two groups.

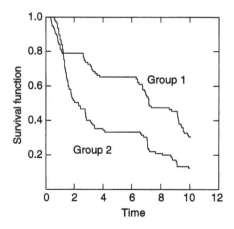

FIGURE 15.7.2 Survival function for two groups.

As a rule survival functions are graphed, and such graphs may be as informative about the data as the formal statistical analyses. Figure 15.7.2 provides the estimated changes over time (survival function or proportion remaining in the original status) for the two groups in the illustrative data. Confidence limits on these lines are usually also available as part of computer program output. The survival function model is nonparametric; however, when a particular model for change over time is appropriate, parametric comparisons of curves are possible.

An alternative common situation is one in which the researcher does not know exactly when the event occurred but knows the interval within which it took place. For example, it may have happened in a given year or in some other unit representing the times between systematic reassessments. Survival methods have been adapted to such data as well, although they will not be reviewed here.

The analysis of data with time in discrete units is easier to link to methods already reviewed in this book, and therefore we will review it here briefly. The analysis of hazard functions over discrete units is mathematically closely related to logistic regression, and indeed may be accomplished by means of a logistic regression program if the data are structured so as to create a record for each subject for each time period up to the point when the change in status occurs (see Singer & Willet, 1991). By such a structure we literally mean that each subject is represented by three variables: ID, time of assessment (e.g., 0 for the beginning of the study), and status (0 at the beginning of the study), as well as any other variables representing group membership or control variables. An additional line of data is entered for the subject with the same variables up to the point at which the status changed to 1 or the subject was lost to follow-up (or not otherwise followed further although still in zero status, because of death, conclusion of the study, etc.). In such a structure the hazards associated with individual subjects are a level 1 variable, as earlier, in a multilevel logistic regression program. The dependent variable is whether the change in status has or has not occurred during the observed time period, and the predictors include the time variable, group membership variables, and controls.

When we include independent variables in the analysis the intercept in the equation for the hazard function (the logit of the conditional probability of changing to the "outcome" state) represents the risk when the values of all IVs are at zero (which suggests the value of centering these variables). The B_i coefficient for each IV represents the (log of the) ratio of odds of moving to the outcome status associated with each increase of one unit in that IV (see Section 12.3). As in the simpler logistic regression model with one line per subject, the analytic programs provide appropriate standard errors or confidence limits for the statistics in the prediction model.

15.7.2 Extension to Time-Varying Independent Variables

A useful elaboration of the survival model is to one in which the values of the IVs may change over time. Again, picture the creation of a file in which subjects are repeatedly entered until the point in time when they enter the status that is the object of the investigation. Since each IV is repeated on each line of data it is possible to enter different values when their values change. The interpretation of the hazard equation is unaltered.

15.7.3 Extension to Multiple Episode Data

There are circumstances in which the "outcome" status may not be final, and individuals may move back into the risk status and potentially re-enter the outcome status. For example, suppose that one is examining relapse from episodes of depression or time to establishment in regular housing among the homeless. The data collection may begin in the former case with recovery from an episode of depression and in the latter case with the loss of housing. Among those who have another episode of depression or who obtain regular housing there may be some subjects who again recover, or who again lose their housing. In the data structure described here, subjects who attain the outcome state (relapse or housing) are not represented in the data until they are once again in the "opening state" (recovered or homeless), at which point they begin as time 1 again. A variable representing the episode number would make it possible to determine whether the hazard associated with a given IV remains constant over multiple episodes. Willet & Singer (1995) provide more detail and examples.

15.7.4 Extension to a Categorical Outcome: Event-History Analysis[13]

As we noted in Chapter 13, it is possible to expand from a two-value dependent variable to a categorical variable with more than two categories. Event-history analysis, a term often used in economics and sociology, may include survival analysis (with two statuses) or elaborations for ordered or unordered categories (Blossfeld & Rohwer, 2002). Such an analysis may often have the goal of determining modal sequences of categorical memberships or states among subjects. Because the statistical treatment and the kinds of questions involving multiple categories go well beyond those readily included in a regression framework, they will not be further discussed here.

15.8 TIME SERIES ANALYSIS

Classical time series analyses examine changes in a variable for a single unit over equally spaced time intervals. Applications may be for the purpose of forecasting future values of Y, or they may be designed to estimate the likely effect on Y of changes in one or more "input" variables (Box, Jenkins, & Reinsel, 1994). In the social sciences they are often used in the analysis of social or economic policy. Thus, in contrast to the techniques discussed earlier, the method and inferences are based on changes seen in a single unit over a number of time periods rather than on contrasts between individual subjects who do or do not change over time. In this design the sample size is not based on the number of subjects (which is one, or one pair, or one set of interacting objects) but on the number of time points. For example, we might study the effect of daily maximum temperature on the number of bottles of drinking water purchased in a city over a series of 90 consecutive summer days. The $n = 90$, the number of bottles is the DV, and maximum temperature is the IV.

Other areas in which studies of single units are employed include certain areas of psychophysics and learning theory (Gregson, 1983) and the interaction of individuals in dyads (e.g., Gottman, 1979, 1994). In some applications coefficients based on time series analyses may be used as variables in between-subjects designs. For example, the extent to which the behavior of one member of a dyad influences the behavior of the other member (the regression of subject B's behavior on the lagged subject A's behavior) may be employed as a descriptor of either the dyad or of one or both members (e.g., Jaffe, Beebe, Feldstein, Crown, & Jasnow, 2001).

---

[13]The term *event-history analysis* is sometimes used exchangeably with *survival analysis*. In this discussion we limit its meaning to situations in which more than two state variables are simultaneously examined.

15.8.1 Units of Observation in Time Series Analyses

Because it would seldom be a behavioral researcher's goal to generate a theory that applied to only one person, and perhaps also because of the very complexity of the potential feedback that may be modeled, such techniques are often applied to aggregated units, as in the testing of economic theory. In such aggregate units, despite the complexity of theory, the causes may be fewer than in the observation of a single individual, where a variety of very short term influences may make the variables unpredictably unstable.

Consider, for example, the investigation of unemployment rates in a large city as compared to unemployment durations for a single individual, both measured over a 30-year period. We may be unlucky and choose an individual who is never unemployed during that time or who is unemployed only once or twice so that inferences about causes would be based on little information. Even if we find an individual who is unemployed several times we would have a range of potential causes—age, past job experience, current economic conditions, opportunity structure in occupations for which she has been trained, the effects of pregnancy and childbearing—that could not reasonably be assessed with regard to so few data points. Many of these causes may change only modestly or not at all for the entire population of a large city, leaving a more feasible number of variables to be included in the theory and tested in the data, which will vary continuously over time. Because of these smaller numbers of operational influences, aggregate data can ordinarily be expected to produce much larger multiple correlations. A useful consequence is that despite the small sample sizes that may characterize the available number of time units on aggregate data, the analyses will have reasonable statistical power because of the small residual variance.

15.8.2 Time Series Analyses Applications

Time series analyses solve the problem of determining priority in changes to bolster causal inferences by measuring both dependent and independent variables over time to trace how changes in one variable are followed by changes in the other. However, the fact that we have moved our focus from differences in changes across subjects to changes over time for a given unit does not mean that we have eliminated the inferential problems caused by potential common causes and causal effects in the opposite direction. Just as in the two-wave study discussed in Section 15.2, we may find that the presumed effect of X_t on $Y_{(t+1)}$ was really due to the effect of Y_t or $Y_{(t-1)}$ on both, or to other common causes (serially correlated errors and omitted variables). Of course, with time series data this is a potential problem with regard to every variable at every time point. One solution is to remove from each variable that proportion of its variance that is attributable to its value in the previous time period. As we noted earlier, this phenomenon is autocorrelation. This may be done by partialing from each variable at each time t the variance attributable to its value at the previous $t - 1$ period. These "lagged" variables (e.g., $X_{t, x_{t-1}}$) then supply the basic data for the analyses.

The time series design makes it possible to consider effects of variables at various lags, that is, over one or more subsequent time periods, and of effects of inertia on the system. Therefore, time series analyses are often suitable for testing more complex models involving direct and indirect feedback or cyclical phenomena. However, unless there is a lot of change in the variables over a large number of time periods, a number of different complex models may fit the data more or less equally well. For this reason, time series analyses may often be more useful in testing theories and estimating magnitudes of theoretically generated parameters than in generating "exploratory" models.

One of the applications of time series analysis in the behavioral sciences is the use of interrupted time series to estimate the effect of an intervention or treatment. The study begins with a thorough model of the relationship between time, changes in other variables, and changes in Y. Then the variable representing the intervention is added to the model to estimate its effect on Y. In such a design it is critical to have an accurate model of what the level of Y would have been in the absence of the intervention (Velicer & Colby, 1997). In our study of temperature and bottles of water, for example, we may have planned this in order to determine the effect of opening a number of city water fountains on the bottles purchased. We could then add a variable coded 0 prior to the fountain opening and 1 thereafter, thus enabling us in our analysis to control for the effects of any unanticipated changes in the weather on our estimate of the fountain effect on water sales.

15.8.3 Time Effects in Time Series

When the effects of previous values of Y are removed, in some sense one may say that the effects of time are not the subject of time series analysis at all. Rather, the focus is on the contingency of change in one variable (Y) on change in other variables (the IVs). If there is a theoretical reason for expecting a longer interval of influence, or for there to be inertia in the system, variables may be lagged for $t - 2$, etc., or the model may provide for autoregressive effects of moving averages (ARIMA models), as deemed appropriate. Time series analyses have many particular features that are integral to the theories being tested. A fuller presentation of these features and options is beyond the purposes of the current brief introduction. Recent developments have linked time series and cross-sectional data (Dielman, 1989).

15.8.4 Extension of Time Series Analyses to Multiple Units or Subjects

Time series analyses of individual subjects may be employed as a prelude to comparisons of models in a sample of individuals (e.g., Zevon & Tellegen, 1982). An examination of our earlier discussion of multilevel analyses with time-varying IVs (Section 15.4.6) reveals a similarity of purpose between these analyses and time series analyses in which the goal is determining an estimate of the *average* timing and magnitude of influence of IVs on Y. Programs for carrying out such analyses with a perspective and functions of variables more like those of traditional time series analyses are under development or available for the matrix-programming data analyst.

15.9 DYNAMIC SYSTEM ANALYSIS

When two or more variables have been measured on several occasions, it may be possible to test mathematical models of theoretically plausible patterns of mutual influence. These models may apply to single subjects (Molenaar, Rovine, & Corneal, 1999; Wood & Brown, 1994) or to groups of subjects (e.g., Boker, Schreiber, Pompe, & Bertenthal,1998; Hamagami, McArdle, & Cohen, 2000). When models are fairly simple, as when the change from one occasion to the next in either or each can be assumed to be reasonably represented as a linear function of the other, it is possible to estimate such models for true or latent variables. With simple additive models, estimation may also be possible using combinations of cross-sectional and longitudinal data.

Although presentation of the method is beyond the scope of this chapter, it is instructive to examine a graphical display of the findings from recent analyses.[14] In this study the topic was

---

[14]Manuscript available from P. Cohen.

Residential/romance vector field

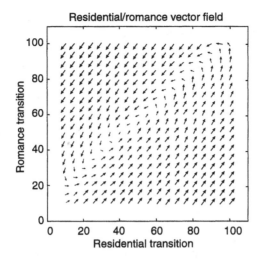

FIGURE 15.9.1 Residential/romance vector field.

the reciprocal influence of residential setting, financial support, and romantic commitment during the transition from adolescence to young adulthood between ages 17 and 27. Each of the three variables was based on structured narrative interviews and rated on a 100-point scale ranging from 0 = a fully childlike state (e.g., residence: living in a residence that was selected, furnished, maintained, and supported entirely by parents) to 99 = a fully adult state (e.g., romance: living with a partner with whom there is a mutual long-term commitment, characterized by efforts to maintain partner satisfaction).

Figure 15.9.1 provides a graphic depiction of the mutual influences between residence and romance and Fig. 15.9.2 between residence and finance.[15] In each figure arrows indicate the predicted direction and magnitude of change in latent variables over the next period (in these

Financial/residential vector field

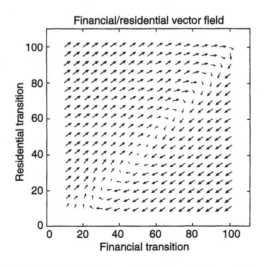

FIGURE 15.9.2 Financial/residential vector field.

---

[15]There is, of course, a third dyad, romance and finance, not depicted here.

data, the following year) for an individual in that segment of the bivariate distribution. The region in which these "arrows" consist of little more than dots indicates the region of stability or no influence on the following year's values of the two variables.

Figure 15.9.1 is interpreted as follows: The region of equilibrium between romance and residence (the region where the "arrows" are minimal or nonexistent) runs from a point of childlike residential status but a score of 20 on the romance variable (casual dating) up through the region of equally adult status on the two variables. When residential transition status was more adult than romantic status, the subsequent changes were predominantly in the more adult direction (arrows upward and to the right) for both romance and residence. When the romantic transition level was more adult than the residential status, both variables tended to move toward a childlike status in the following year.

Looking at the dynamic relationship between financial "adultness" and residence transition level (Fig. 15.9.2) we note that the region of stability occurs when the financial situation is a little more adult than the residential one. When the residential status is more adult than the financial status there is a tendency for both to increase in the following years. When the finances are too much more adult than the residential situation (e.g., mostly self-supporting but still living in a parental home) the outlook in the following year is toward a more childlike status in both variables.

These analyses were carried out by an SEM program and showed all bivariate bidirectional effects to be statistically significant. We will not attempt a full presentation here, these findings being only an illustration of the possibilities when the data are sufficient.

15.10 STATISTICAL INFERENCE AND POWER ANALYSIS IN LONGITUDINAL ANALYSES

Repeated measure ANOVA and ANCOVA use the conventional F tests employed in other OLS procedures, with the required separate error terms for within-subject and between subject effects. Power estimation and analysis methods may be found in J. Cohen (1988); Borenstein, Rothstein, and Cohen (2001); and elsewhere; and will not be elaborated here.

More complex methods employing maximum likelihood and related statistical algorithms ordinarily produce goodness-of-fit measures and indices. As noted in earlier discussions (e.g., Section 12.8) significance tests on these methods employ a different logic. The goal of the analysis is to produce a model that is consistent with the data, and a statistically significant χ^2 in such an analysis indicates that the data are "significantly" unlikely to have been produced by the specified model. The same effect of sample size is seen on these tests, where a statistically significant χ^2 is a sign of *poor* fit, as in traditional tests, where a significant difference from some null hypothetical value is usually the desired goal. Therefore large samples very frequently show "significant" deviation from perfect fit. For this reason, conclusions about the adequacy of the model are usually attentive to both a decline in the χ^2 when additional estimates are added to the model and the goodness-of-fit indices that take both the fit and the number of parameters estimated into account. When models are "nested" so that one model estimates the same parameters as another, plus some additional parameters (so that there are fewer constraints on the model), it is possible to use the difference in χ^2 (with df equal to the difference in number of estimated parameters) to test whether the less constrained model fits the data significantly better. The most constrained model typically assumes that there is no change in means over time, that error variances are equal, that factor loadings on latent variables (if included in the model) are equal, or equivalent "nil" kinds of models. In general investigators will have examined data sufficiently prior to the formal analyses to ascertain that this model is not likely to be optimal.

Perhaps one of the principal problems in longitudinal data is the frequently small number of time intervals covered. The power to test more complex models when there are few time points is sharply limited. As models have more and more parameters there are more and more possible variations that may appear to be similarly compatible with theory and previous research. As noted earlier, McArdle and Aber (1990) provide an explication of a large number of alternatives for a fairly simple multi-occasion data set. Thus, it is extremely critical for the investigator to examine alternatives that are consistent with "principled argument" (Abelson, 1995) before making the case for preferring a particular one based on an empirical estimation.

15.11 SUMMARY

Section 15.1 notes that longitudinal analyses usually have one or more of three goals: (1) They are designed to improve inferences about the direction and magnitude of influences of one variable or set of variables on another by establishing sequence, (2) they are designed to inform about average changes in variables over time/trials/age, or (3) they are designed to inform about individual or group differences in change over time and variables that relate to these differences. The simpler methods in this chapter are usually used with either the first or the second goal in mind. Newer methods may examine two or more of these issues. Almost all of the newer methods are designed to help solve some common data problems as well. The principal problems are measurement error, missing data due to attrition or other problems, different assessment intervals or periods, and sometimes problems due to the sparseness of the number of repeated assessment occasions. This summary describes each section in this chapter with regard to the kind of substantive question being asked and the structure of the data that are being analyzed.

Section 15.2: *Research question*: What are the effects across subjects of prior values of IVs on subsequent values of or change in *Y*? *Data structure*: Multiple subjects measured at each of two occasions on a scaled or dichotomous dependent variable and on the IVs of interest. This section reviews the use of multiple regression with two or more waves of data collection, with an emphasis on bolstering inferences about the direction and magnitude of influences on *Y*. It is shown that the spacing of the assessment interval relative to the timing of effects of independent variables may be critical for estimations of both direct effects and mediation effects.

Section 15.3: *Research questions*: What patterns of change over occasions characterize the average subject, and how do these patterns differ for subjects in different groups? *Data structure*: Multiple (repeated) measures of a scaled dependent variable for each of a number of subjects or other units and one or more variables that divide subjects into groups (often, but not necessarily, of equal size). Intervals between assessments are generally equal. In classical repeated measure ANOVA, the principal goal is determining differences in the average *Y* scores at each measurement point for the sample as a whole or for subgroups. When the data consist of longitudinal assessments, the analyses may also determine whether the pattern of means fit linear or quadratic trends (or higher order shapes if one's theory justifies such an examination), and whether these trends differ for subgroups.

Multilevel regression analyses of longitudinal data (Section 15.4) have goals similar to those of the repeated measure ANOVA but they expand the investigation of effects to include not only the "fixed" variables considered in the ANOVA but also the coefficients of individual subjects' equations predicting *Y* as "random" IVs. *Research questions*: A very wide range of questions may be asked from the straightforward tests of curve components of change to effects of stable or changing individual differences between subjects on levels or rates of change in the dependent variable. *Data structure*: Computer programs now available offer tremendous flexibility with regard to the data requirements, with variations in numbers and timing of assessments for different subjects manageable when certain assumptions are justified or testable. The independent variables in these analyses have the full flexibility of the regression procedures discussed in this book, and in addition they allow analyses to test the fit of the data to models with different error structures and link functions.

Latent growth models (Section 15.5) have a similar goal to that of the polynomial curve tests in repeated measure ANOVA. However, they estimate changes in latent true scores rather than observed scores and include provision for individual differences in levels and slopes. In addition, the explicit SEM specification of observed, true, and error variables enhances the potential informational yield of the analyses. *Research questions*: What is our estimate of average error-free change in means over time or age? What function best characterizes these changes? *Data structure*: A scaled dependent variable measured at multiple time points for a set of subjects.

Section 15.6 addresses analyses with time-varying covariates (IVs). *Research questions*: What are the associations between changes in Y over time and one or more IVs that also change? Do these associations differ for subpopulations? *Data structure*: Scaled dependent and independent variables at multiple (not necessarily the same) time points for multiple subjects who may be further distinguished on variables that are not time dependent. These may be carried out by multilevel regression, SEM, or survival analysis computer programs.

Survival analyses are designed to analyze the time duration to change in a dichotomous dependent variable (Section 15.7). *Research questions*: How much time does it take to attain some change in status? Do the time curves differ for different subgroups of subjects characterized by other variables? *Data structure*: Information on the time to some specified change in state (e.g., death, recovery, marriage, divorce) or, if the change has not occurred, the time until loss to follow-up on each of a number of subjects. Elaborations of this method include time-varying predictors and potential re-entry into the risk status. Event-history analysis is a variation on this technique for multiple category outcomes.

Time series analysis is taken up in Section 15.8. *Research questions*: What can we predict for the future based on current trends in variables? What is the magnitude of the effect of a change in X on a change in Y? Over how long a period do effects operate, and are there cyclical effects or inertia in the system? *Data structure*: Measures of two or more variables at each of a number of consecutive time points or intervals for a single unit (such as an individual or an aggregate such as a city). Time series analyses examine the relationships of earlier IVs to change in Y. Although these analyses provide a very strong case for inferences of effects, they have traditionally been limited to one case or subject at a time. Newer methods may combine time series analyses of multiple units.

Dynamic system analysis is briefly described in Section 15.9. *Research question*: Does one or another particular model of *reciprocal* effect describe the patterns of change in two or more variables over time? *Data structure*: Two or more scaled variables measured on one or more subjects over at least several time points. Current applications focus mainly on the examination of linear reciprocal effects of two variables at a time.

Statistical tests for OLS methods employ standard F tests, for which power analysis techniques are available elsewhere. More complex power and precision analyses are more readily carried out using a special computer program. Most of the newer methods use one or another of the iterative estimation procedures, with likelihood ratio tests for significance of the model improvement and indices of goodness of fit. One limitation of statistical power to test more complex models is the number of data points available for each subject. As the models become increasingly complex they are even more obviously demanding of clearly stated investigator argument and consideration of plausible alternatives than are the OLS methods (Section 15.10).

Data are provided on the accompanying computer disks with appropriate structures for random regression and growth model techniques. Once again we caution the reader that these programs will allow alternative models (assumptions that can be made about the structure of the data) that have substantive implications and should be used with advice and assistance from experienced statisticians. More information on these models may be found in Bryk and Raudenbush (1987); Little, Schnabel, and Baumert (2000); MacCallum, Kim, Malarkey, and Kiecolt-Glaser (1997); Snijders and Bosker (1999); and Wolfinger (1997).

16

Multiple Dependent Variables: Set Correlation

16.1 INTRODUCTION TO ORDINARY LEAST SQUARES TREATMENT OF MULTIPLE DEPENDENT VARIABLES

In Chapter 5 and subsequent sections of this book we have discussed the analytic utility of thinking of independent variables as members of a smaller number of sets. These sets, each of which may have one or more members, may represent a distinct role in the research, such as a set of potential confounders (common causes of independent and dependent variables) or control variables, whose central role is to rule out certain alternative reasons for a relationship between Y and the IVs of interest. Alternatively, they may represent the multiple facets or aspects of a research construct, as, for example demographic factors, or treatment features. Or a set may include the $g - 1$ variables needed to represent the g groups in a categorical variable. Or a set may include curvilinear or interactive aspects of one or more variables.

Now, all this refers to the independent variables, the right-hand side of the equation, which is where the multiplicity of MRC resides. The left-hand side contains the single variable Y. Only when the singular Y is replaced by a plural *set* of variables Y whose interrelationships are taken into account in the analysis does the method properly become multivariate.[1]

16.1.1 Set Correlation Analysis

Consider the benefits that would accrue from a generalization of MRC such that a set Y could be related to a set X, either of them partialed, if and as necessary. The possibility of representing virtually any information, and the use of partialing for control and specification would now extend to the left-hand side, the dependent variables, as well. The resulting method, set correlation (SC), is a realization of the general *multivariate* linear model, and has the following properties:

---

[1] In this chapter as elsewhere in the book we identify *sets* of variables with bold italic letters (e.g., Y) and individual variables within sets by italic letters. In some discussions these sets will be further identified as those of *basic* interest (e.g., Y_B and X_B) and those sets that are *partialed* from the basic sets (e.g., Y_P and X_P).

1. It is generalization of MRC, a truly multivariate MRC, and can employ the structural features of MRC (e.g., hierarchical entry of variables) with dependent research factors of any kind.
2. Set correlation bears the same relationship to the standard OLS multivariate methods that MRC does to the standard OLS univariate methods. Thus, multivariate analysis of variance (MANOVA) and covariance (MANCOVA) are special cases of SC.
3. Its generality frees the analysis from the MANOVA requirement of nominal scale research factors, making possible multivariate analysis of partial variance, multivariate significance tests, and other novel analytic methods.
4. Set correlation provides a single framework of measures of association, parameter estimation, hypothesis testing, and statistical power analysis that encompasses most of the standard data-analytic methods.

16.1.2 Canonical Analysis

The traditional multivariate correlation method is Hotelling's (1936) canonical analysis (CA). Also, the application of CA to variously partialed correlation matrices has been described by Roy (1957), Hooper (1962), Rao (1975), Timm and Carlson (1976), and others. Yet it is not an entirely satisfactory general tool for multivariate analysis.

In CA, the strength of the overall relationship between two sets of variables X and Y is measured by a series of canonical correlations (C), each a product moment correlation between weighted linear combinations of the k_X variables of X and the k_Y variables of Y. These are called x and y canonical factors (cfs), or canonical variates. The weights are such as to maximize the correlations between paired cfs subject to the further condition that each cf correlate zero with all but its paired cf. The number of such cf pairs (and hence of coefficients in C) is the lesser of the number of variables in the two sets, $\min(k_Y, k_X)$, here designated as q. Thus, the X, Y relationship is efficiently summarized by q correlations between as many pairs of weighted combinations of X and Y, each in turn extracting as much (new) between-set covariance as possible.

In a seminal article, Rozeboom (1965) showed that the strength of relationship between two sets can be quantified by the degree of overlap of the spaces they span, and the cfs are covariance-maximizing principal components of the between-set correlations. These are exactly analogous to the familiar variance-maximizing principal components extracted from the correlations among the members of a set in factor analysis.[2]

Two problems arise with the use of CA. First, it provides q Cs where a single measure of the strength of the overall relationship, some generalization of multiple R^2, is desired. The second is the limited utility of the cfs in the understanding of the nature of the X, Y relationship. Efforts to interpret these through the weights of factor loadings of the variables frequently read like laundry lists and are seldom convincing. In light of Rozeboom's demonstrations that they are principal components of the between-set covariances, this is hardly surprising, because we have known in factor analysis for many decades that principal components are not interpretable as functional unities. Thurstone invented rotations to simple structure in order to achieve substantive meaningfulness. Accordingly, the rotation of cfs to simple structure has been advocated (Cliff and Krus, 1976). This may occasionally help, but simple structure

---

[2]Despite our efforts elsewhere in the book to avoid matrix notation and complex mathematical terms, the presentation in this chapter unavoidably assumes some familiarity with matrix operations and more complex mathematics. For readers for whom this material is completely unfamiliar we recommend paying attention to the words and taking the equations more or less on faith. It is also wise to work with these methods under the initial supervision of a more mathematically sophisticated colleague. Of the larger statistical packages, only SYSTAT provides user-friendly means of carrying out these analyses.

in factor analysis is predicated on the employment of many variables so as to provide broad coverage of some behavioral domain; simple structure merely implements the expectation that most of the correlations between many variables and several factors representing the functional unities in a domain will be zero or negligible. However, variables analyzed in CA are, in general, not so selected, and the simple structure rationale does not obtain. Thus, the q pairs of cfs, original or rotated, cannot serve as our primary analytic device. Instead, in SC, we work directly with the original variables, and by means of partialing, we carve out of the overall association the relationships between substantively meaningful components.

16.1.3 Elements of Set Correlation

The technical literature contains the derivations and proofs of the elements of SC: The most important sources are Wilks (1932) and Rozeboom (1965), who first gave the derivation and rationale for whole and partial multivariate R^2. Hooper described trace correlation for whole (1959) and partialed (1962) sets. Roy (1957) and Rao (1975) described the CA of partial correlations, and Timm and Carlson (1976) that of semipartial and bipartial correlations. Van den Burg and Lewis (1988) published comprehensive descriptions and proofs of the properties of multivariate R^2 and trace correlation for whole and partialed sets.

In what follows, Y and X represent basic *sets* of variables. Set Y may be a set of dependent variables Y or a set of dependent variables from which another set Z has been partialed, represented as $Y \cdot Z$. Similarly, set X may be a set of independent variables or a set of independent variables from which another set W has been partialed, $X \cdot W$. All references to sets Y and X in subscripts and in the formulas that follow are to be understood to mean the "left-hand" or dependent variable set and the "right-hand" or independent variable set, whether or not either is a partialed set. Multivariate relationships, such as multivariate R^2, will be indicated by subscripts indicating the set of dependent variables (Y) separated from the set(s) of IVs by a comma, as $R^2_{Y,X}$ or $R^2_{Y,XWZ}$.

16.2 MEASURES OF MULTIVARIATE ASSOCIATION

It is desirable that a measure of association between sets be a natural generalization of multiple R^2, bounded by 0 and 1, invariant over full rank (nonsingular) linear transformation (e.g., rotation) of either or both sets, symmetric (i.e., $R^2_{Y,X} = R^2_{X,Y}$), and not decrease in value when a variable is added to either side. Of the measures of multivariate association that have been proposed (Cramer and Nicewander, 1979), three have been found to be particularly useful for SC; multivariate R^2, and the symmetric (T^2) and asymmetric (P^2) squared trace correlations.

16.2.1 $R^2_{Y,X}$, the Proportion of Generalized Variance

Using determinants of correlation matrices[3]:

(16.2.1)
$$R^2_{Y,X} = 1 - |\mathbf{R}_{Y,X}| / (|\mathbf{R}_Y||\mathbf{R}_X|),$$

where $\mathbf{R}_{Y,X}$ is the full correlation matrix of the variables in the Y and X sets,
$\mathbf{R}_Y$ is the matrix of correlations among the variables of set Y, and
$\mathbf{R}_X$ is the matrix of correlations among the variables of set X.

---

[3]$|\mathbf{R}_{Y,X}|$ stands for the determinant of the correlation marix $\mathbf{R}_{Y,X}$, where there may be multiple variables in either or both sets.

This equation also holds when variance-covariance or sums of squares-products matrices replace the correlation matrices.

$R^2_{Y,X}$ may also be written as a function of the q squared canonical correlations (C^2) where $q = \min(k_Y, k_X)$, the number of variables in the smaller of the two basic sets:

$$(16.2.2) \qquad R^2_{Y,X} = 1 - \left(1 - C^2_1\right)\left(1 - C^2_2\right)(1 - C^2_3) \cdots (1 - C^2_q).$$

$R^2_{Y,X}$ is a generalization of the simple bivariate r^2 and multiple R^2 and is properly interpreted as the proportion of the generalized variance of set Y accounted for by set X (or vice versa, because it is symmetric). Generalized variance (Wilks, 1932) is the generalization of the univariate concept of variance to a set of variables and is defined as the determinant of the variance-covariance matrix of the variables in the set. One may interpret proportions of generalized variance much as one does proportions of variance of a single variable. $R^2_{Y,X}$ may also be interpreted geometrically as the degree of overlap of the spaces defined by the two sets, and is therefore invariant over nonsingular transformations of the two sets, so that, for example, $R^2_{Y,X}$ does not change with changes in the coding (dummy, effects, or contrast) of nominal scales.

$R^2_{Y,X}$ makes possible a multiplicative decomposition in terms of squared (multivariable) partial (but not semipartial) correlations. For example, with set X made up of the subsets A, B, and C, the following relationship holds:

$$(16.2.3) \qquad 1 - R^2_{Y,X} = (1 - R^2_{Y,A})(1 - R^2_{Y \cdot A, B \cdot A})(1 - R^2_{Y \cdot AB, C \cdot AB}).$$

The R^2s on the right (except the first) are squared multivariate *partial* correlations. It is also the case that the multivariate partial R^2 can be written as a function of whole multivariate R^2s:

$$(16.2.4) \qquad R^2_{Y \cdot Z, X \cdot Z} = (R^2_{Y,XZ} - R^2_{Y,Z})/(1 - R^2_{Y,Z}),$$

where $R^2_{Y,XZ}$ is the multivariate R^2 between set Y and the combined sets X and Z.

Both these properties of $R^2_{Y,X}$ are proper generalizations from multiple R^2, that is, they hold when set Y is a single variable, Y. However, the following relationship for the *semipartial* R^2 from multiple R^2, $R^2_{Y(X \cdot Z)} = R^2_{Y(XZ)} - R^2_{YZ}$ (Section 3.3.2) does not generalize to multivariate R^2. Thus, multivariate R^2 affords a multiplicative but not an additive decomposition.

16.2.2 $T^2_{Y,X}$ and $P^2_{Y,X}$, Proportions of Additive Variance

Two other useful measures of multivariate association are based on the trace of the between set variance-covariance matrix of the basic Y and X matrices,

$$(16.2.5) \qquad M_{Y,X} = C^{-1}_{YY} C_{YX} C^{-1}_{XX} C_{XY},$$

The eigenstructure of this matrix is basic to CA, and its trace, $V_{Y,X}$, is used in testing multivariate association (see, e.g., Anderson, 1984, p. 326; Pillai, 1960).

Now, $V_{Y,X}$ is symmetrical $(V_{Y,X} = V_{X,Y})$, invariant over nonsingular linear transformation of either or both sets, and cannot decrease with the addition of variables to either set. But it cannot serve as a measure of association because it increases indefinitely as the number of variables increase. It can be shown that it equals the sum of the q squared canonical correlations. Its maximum, therefore, is q. One way to render a measure of association from $V_{Y,X}$ is to divide it by q. The result,

$$(16.2.6) \qquad T^2_{Y,X} = \frac{V_{Y,X}}{q} = \frac{\sum C^2}{q},$$

the mean of the q squared canonical correlations, is defined as the symmetric squared trace correlation, because $T_{Y,X}^2 = T_{X,Y}^2$. Each canonical factor has unit variance, so the maximum total canonical variance is q, and $T_{Y,X}^2$ is a proportion of variance measure, that is, the proportion of the total canonical variance that the sets account for in each other. Equivalently, and more simply, it is the proportion of the total variance of the smaller set accounted for by the larger. However, unlike $R_{Y,X}^2$, increasing the smaller of the two sets increases q and may result in a drop in $T_{Y,X}^2$.

$T_{Y,X}^2$ offers an interesting identity. Nominal scales (categorical variables) can be coded as sets of variables that can then be employed in correlational analysis (Chapter 8); thus it is possible to analyze contingency tables by means of SC. A two-way frequency table that is routinely subjected to a χ^2 test can instead be represented as two sets of variables and analyzed by SC (with certain advantages, see J. Cohen, 1988). The $T_{Y,X}^2$ from the resulting analysis is demonstrably equal to the Cramĕr ϕ statistic employed as a measure of association for contingency tables (Srikantan, 1970). In a $2 \times k$ table, therefore, the Cramĕr ϕ also equals the multiple R^2 of the dichotomy with the k-level categorical variable and thus has a proportion of variance interpretation.

Another way to derive a measure of association from $V_{Y,X}$ is to divide it by k_Y, the number of dependent variables, which produces

$$(16.2.7) \qquad P_{Y,X}^2 = V_{Y,X}/k_Y,$$

defined as the *asymmetric* squared trace correlation, asymmetric because $P_{Y,X}^2 \neq P_{X,Y}^2$, but rather, when set X is dependent, $P_{X,Y}^2 = V_{Y,X}/k_X$.

In contrast to the multiplicative decomposition in terms of squared multivariate partial correlations made possible by $R_{Y,X}^2$, additive decomposition in terms of squared semipartials can be effected with $P_{Y,X}^2$. It can be shown, for example, that with set X made up of the subsets A, B and C,

$$(16.2.8) \qquad P_{Y,X}^2 = P_{Y,A}^2 + P_{Y,B\cdot A}^2 + P_{Y,C\cdot AB}^2,$$

the P^2s on the right (except the first) being P^2s for X semipartial association (discussed later).

A space may be defined by a set of variables and any nonsingular linear transformation (e.g., rotation) of these variables defines the same space. Consider a nonsingular linear transformation (e.g., a factor-analysis) rotation of the Y variables to any orthogonal position. Find the multiple R^2s of each of the orthogonalized Y variables with the variables in set X. Their sum equals $V_{Y,X}$, so the mean of these multiple R^2s is $P_{Y,X}^2 \cdot P_{Y,X}^2$ also permits a proportion of variance interpretation, but unlike $R_{Y,X}^2$, the definition of variance is additive, the sum of the unit variances of the (standardized) Y variables.

When the number of dependent variables does not exceed the number of independent variables, $R_{Y,X}^2 = T_{Y,X}^2$, but when $k_Y > k_X$, its maximum is not unity but k_X/k_Y. This is reasonable—you cannot expect to be able to account for all the variance in five (nonredundant) Y variables by two X variables, but, at most, two-fifths of it. Thus, implicitly, $R_{Y,X}^2$ defines multivariate association in such a way as to preclude perfect association in these circumstances. In their analysis of the properties of these measures, Van den Burg and Lewis (1988) argued that together with $R_{Y,X}^2$, $P_{Y,X}^2$ rather than $T_{Y,X}^2$ is a direct generalization of multiple R^2.

They are averages of C^2s or multiple R^2s, so there are circumstances where neither $T_{Y,X}^2$ nor $P_{Y,X}^2$ seems appropriate. When SC deals with research factor sets that define unitary entities, for example, religion as a four-category nominal scale or response magnitude (rm) represented polynomially as rm, rm^2, and rm^3, averaging proportions of variance over such elements distorts the magnitude of their collective association with other sets. Only $R^2_{Y,X}$, which cumulates association over the elements of the set, seems appropriate in such circumstances.

In the final analysis, however, analysts must be guided by their substantive and methodological conceptions of the problem at hand in their choice of a measure of association.

16.3 PARTIALING IN SET CORRELATION

16.3.1 Frequent Reasons for Partialing Variable Sets From the Basic Sets

The varied uses of partialing (residualization) made familiar in earlier chapters make possible in SC a functional analysis directly in terms of research factors and their elements. Let the basic X set (X_B) be $X \cdot W$, a set X from which another set W has been partialed. Then $X \cdot W$ may be used in any of the following ways:

The statistical control of the research factor(s) in set **W** *, when relating* **X** *to* **Y**. If the causal model posits a direct effect of X on Y, the $X \cdot W$ "holds W constant"; were W not partialed from X, the effect found for X might be a spurious consequence of the operation of W. Partialing W also has the effect of reducing the error variance, thus increasing the statistical power of the test of X when W is *not* related to X. The analysis of covariance (set X defining group membership) is a special case of this type of use and the analysis of partial variance (set X unconstrained) the more general case.

The representation of interaction of any order between research factors of any kind. For example, the UV interaction set is constructed as a set $UV \cdot U, V$, where the UV set consists of the products of each of the variables in research factor U with each of the variables in research factor V and the partialed set consists of the $k_Y + k_X$ variables of the combined U and V research factors (see Chapters 8 and 9).

The representation of curve components in polynomial (curvilinear) regression. For example, for the cubic component of a variable V, V^3 and the partialed set is made up of V and V^2 (see Chapter 6).

The representation of a specified contrast within a set of means of the categories of a nominal scale. Here set X is made up of a single, suitably coded variable and the partialed set consists of the remaining $g - 2$ variables containing other contrasts (see Chapter 8). For example, for dummy coding for three experimental groups and one control group, one may create three variables, each of which codes one of the experimental groups 1 and the other three groups 0. When one of these variables makes up set X and the other two sets are partialed, the resulting set $X \cdot X_P$ effects a contrast (here a simple difference) between the Y means of one of the experimental groups and the Y means of the control group.

The "purification" of a variable to its "uniqueness". An example is when X is one subtest of a battery of correlated measures and one wishes to determine its effects that are independent of the other subtests. Examples of X are the digit-symbol subtest score of the Wechsler Adult Intelligence Scale or the schizophrenia scale of the Minnesota Multiphasic Personality Inventory, with the partialed set in each case being the remaining subtest or scale scores of the battery. Similarly, one may assign a subset of scores to X and partial another subset X_P.

The incorporation of missing data as positive information (Section 11.3). Here, X (or Y) is a research factor whose missing data have been "plugged" with a constant such as the grand mean and the partialed sets are dichotomies distinguishing subjects with missing data (scored 1) from those with data present (scored 0). This procedure avoids the loss of cases, and, of particular importance when missingness is not random, carries it as a variable whose correlates can be studied.

In SC, these partialing devices may equally be employed for the Y set. Thus, for example, one may control a dependent variable for age, sex, and socioeconomic status, or represent curve components, interactions, missingness, or uniqueness of a dependent variable or set of dependent variables.

16.3.2 The Five Types of Association Between Basic Y and X Sets

Given the option of partialing, there are five types of association possible in SC, shown in Table 16.3.1. These include the association between two sets X and Y, the association between two sets X and Y with a third set partialed from both in their association with a set partialed from either X or Y but not both, and their association with different sets partialed from X and Y. Formulas for the necessary matrices to compute the measures of association for these five types are given in J. Cohen (1982, Table 1). These options have been conveniently presented in a program that is part of the SYSTAT statistical package. Alternatively, they may be programmed by the user who is familiar with computerized matrix operations. Uses of these types of association are described in the examples later in this chapter.

Following an SC analysis, further analytic detail is provided by correlational and regression output for the individual basic X and Y variables, each a single variable in its respective set. Thus, it is for these variables, partialed or whole depending on the type of association, that the following are given:

1. The within-set correlations for each set. If the set has been partialed, these are partial correlations.
2. The rectangular matrix of between set correlations. Depending on the type of association, these are either "whole" (simple, unpartialed) correlations, partial correlations (when the partialed sets are the same for X and Y), Y semipartial, X semipartial, or bipartial correlations (when different sets are partialed from X and Y).
3. A multiple regression analysis for each (partialed) variable in Y on the (partialed) variables in set X: standardized regression coefficients β and their t test values, and the multiple R^2 and its F test value. Correlations among the regression-predicted variables in Y may also be provided.

The information provided by the analysis of these individual basic variables serves to facilitate the interpretation of the SC results of the X and Y sets that they constitute.

TABLE 16.3.1
Types of Association in Set Correlation

	Dependent set		Independent set
Whole	Y	with	X
Partial	$Y \cdot P$	with	$X \cdot P$
Y semipartial	$Y \cdot P$	with	X
X semipartial	Y	with	$X \cdot P$
Bipartial	$Y \cdot P$	with	$X \cdot M$

16.4 TESTS OF STATISTICAL SIGNIFICANCE AND STATISTICAL POWER

16.4.1 Testing the Null Hypothesis

For purposes of testing the hypothesis of no association between sets X_B and Y_B, we treat the basic set Y_B as the dependent variable set, X_B as independent, and employ the fixed model. Wilks's likelihood ratio Λ is the ratio of the determinant of the error covariance matrix $\mathbf{E}$ to the determinant of the sum of the error and hypothesis $\mathbf{H}$ covariance matrices,

$$(16.4.1) \qquad \Lambda = |\mathbf{E}|/|\mathbf{E} + \mathbf{H}|,$$

where $\mathbf{H}$ is the variance-covariance accounted for in the variables in Y by X,

$$(16.4.2) \qquad \mathbf{H} = C_{Y_B X_B} C_{X_B X_B}^{-1} C_{X_B Y_B}.$$

The definition of $\mathbf{E}$ depends on whether the test is to employ Model 1 or Model 2 error. Model 1 error is defined as

$$(16.4.3) \qquad \mathbf{E}_1 = C_{Y_B Y_B} - C_{Y_B X X_P} C_{X X_P}^{-1} C_{X X_P Y_B},$$

that is, the residual Y_B variance-covariance matrix when covariance associated with sets X and Y_P has been removed.

Model 2 error is employed when there exists a set G, made up of variables in neither X nor X_P, that can be used to account for additional variance in $C_{Y_B Y_B}$ and thus reduce $\mathbf{E}$ below $\mathbf{E}_1$ in the interest of unbiasedness and increased statistical power. This occurs when, with multiple research factors, the analyst wishes to use "pure" error, for example, the within cell variance in a factorial design. In this case, the error-reducing set G is made up of the variables comprising the research factors ("main effects") and interactions other than the factor or interaction under test, as is done traditionally in both univariate and multivariate factorial designs.

$$(16.4.4) \qquad \mathbf{E}_2 = C_{Y_B Y_B} - C_{Y_B, X X_P G}^{-1} C_{X X_P G.Y_B}.$$

In whole and Y semipartial association, where X_P does not exist, it is dropped from $\mathbf{E}_1$ and $\mathbf{E}_2$. Formulas for the $\mathbf{H}$ and $\mathbf{E}$ matrices for the five types of association are given in J. Cohen (1982, Table 2). The diagonal values of the error matrix employed in a given analysis are used for the significance tests of the β and multiple R^2s of the supplementary analyses of the individual basic variables.

When Model 1 error (no set G) is used, for the whole and partial types of association, it can be shown that $\Lambda = 1 - R_{Y,X}^2$. Once Λ is determined for a sample, Rao's F test (1973) may be applied to test the null hypothesis. As adapted for SC, the test is quite general, covering all five types of association and both error models. When k_Y or $k_X = 1$, where multivariate $R_{Y,X}^2$ specializes to multiple R^2, the Rao F test specializes to the standard null hypothesis F test for MRC. For this case, and for the case where the smaller set is made up of no more than two variables, the Rao F test is exact; otherwise, it provides a good approximation (J. Cohen and Nee, 1987).

$$(16.4.5) \qquad F = (\Lambda^{-1}/s - 1)(v/u),$$

where $\quad u =$ numerator $df = k_Y k_X,$
$\qquad v =$ denominator $df = ms + 1 - u/2$, where
$\qquad m = n - \max(k_{Y_P}, k_{X_P} + k_G) - (k_Y + k_X + 3)/2$, and
$\qquad s = \sqrt{(k_Y^2 k_X^2 - 4)/(k_Y^2 + k_X^2)},$

except that when $k_Y^2 k_X^2 \leq 4, s = 1$. For partial $R_{Y,X}^2$, set $X_P =$ set Y_P, so k is the number of variables in the set that is being partialed from both Y and X. k_{Y_P}, k_{X_P}, and k_G are zero when the set does not exist for the type of association or error model in question. The standard F tables are used (but note that v need not be an integer and that when $q > 1$, v will be greater than the sample size, n). The test assumes that the variables in X are fixed and those in Y are multivariate normal, but the test is quite robust against assumption failure (J. Cohen and Nee, 1990; Olson, 1976).

As an illustration of the use of the Rao F test, consider the SC analysis of the following MANOVA design of a research in clinical diagnosis. For $n = 97$ cases distributed over four $(= g)$ psychiatric diagnostic groups (set X), scores on five cognitive measures were obtained. To control for possible contamination effects of demographic variables, a covariate set $(X_P = Y_P)$ made up of the variables sex, years of education, age and age^2 was used. The analysis relates the nominal scale of diagnosis $(k_X = g - 1 = 3)$ to the cognitive measures $(k_Y = 5)$, with the covariate set partialed from both $(k_{X_P} = k_{Y_P} = 4)$.

The measures of partial association are found to be $R_{Y,X}^2 = .3016, T_{Y,X}^2 = .1100$, and $P_{Y,X}^2 = .0660$. The Rao F test's ingredients are found as $\Lambda = .6984, s = 2.76$, with df of $u = 15, v = 235.05$. Substituting gives Rao $F = 2.176, p < .05$.

16.4.2 Estimators of the Population $R_{Y,X}^2$, $T_{Y,X}^2$, and $P_{Y,X}^2$

The positive bias (overestimation) of the population multiple R^2 by its sample value is well known and discussed in Section 3.5.3. Bias in R^2 decreases as n increases, and increases with k_X, the numerator df of the F test. In SC, $R_{Y,X}^2$ and the other measures of association are even more strongly positively biased. "Shrunken" values for the three measures of association in SC are given by

$$(16.4.6) \qquad \tilde{R}_{Y,X}^2 = 1 - (1 - R_{Y,X}^2)[(v + u)/v]^s,$$

$$(16.4.7) \qquad \tilde{T}_{Y,X}^2 = 1 - (1 - T_{Y,X}^2)[(w + u)/u],$$

where w is the denominator df of the Pillai (1960) F test for $T_{Y,X}^2, w = q[n - k_Y - k_X - \max(k_{Y_P}, k_{X_P}) - 1]$ (J. Cohen and Nee, 1984), and

$$(16.4.8) \qquad \tilde{P}_{Y,X}^2 = \tilde{T}_{Y,X}^2(k_X/k_Y)$$

When $q = 1$, both $\tilde{R}_{Y,X}^2$ and $\tilde{T}_{Y,X}^2$ specialize to Wherry's (1931) formula for the shrunken multiple R^2, as does $\tilde{P}_{Y,X}^2$ when $k_Y = 1$.

The degree of positive bias in these measures also decreases as n increases and increases with the numerator df of the Rao F test, the *product* of the numbers of variables in the two sets $(u = k_Y k_X)$.

In the previous example, (where $u = 15, v = 235.1$, and $s = 2.76$), the $R_{Y,X}^2$ of .3016 shrinks to .1715, the $T_{Y,X}^2$ of .1100 (for $u = 15$ and $w = 252$) shrinks to .0570, and the $P_{Y,X}^2$ of .0660 shrinks to .0342, which are, respectively, 43%, 48%, and 48% shrinkage. Had there been six diagnostic groups instead of four, u would be 25; v, 309.84; s, 3.72; and w, 410; and the shrunken values are $\tilde{R}_{Y,X}^2 = .0683, \tilde{T}_{Y,X}^2 = .0557$, and $\tilde{P}_{Y,X}^2 = .0334$, shrinkages respectively of 77%, 49%, and 49%.

It is instructive to compare this shrinkage with that of MRC. First note that because MRC is the special case of SC where there is only one dependent variable, $R_{Y,X}^2 = T_{Y,X}^2 = P_{Y,X}^2 =$ multiple R^2, and the previous formulas specialize to the standard Wherry (1931) shrinkage formula. Now for $n = 97$, with one dependent variable, five independent variables and four variables in a covariate set, a multiple R^2 of .3016 shrinks to .2204, with shrinkage of 27%, far less than before.

The very large degree of shrinkage in SC with what would be considered a fairly large n and not very many variables in the two sets is to be expected unless the observed association is quite strong.

16.4.3 Guarding Against Type I Error Inflation

A multivariate significance test treats the variables in a set simultaneously, that is, it takes into account the correlations among the variables. Thus, it provides information different from what is obtained from a series of univariate tests on the individual variables. However, the multivariate test has the virtue of providing a valid test of the null hypothesis that all the population multiple R^2s of the individual Y variables with set X are zero, or, equivalently that all the rs between sets are zero. To provide some protection against the inflation of experiment-wise Type I errors ("probability pyramiding"), it is prudent practice to require that the multivariate test be significant as a precondition for performing tests on individual variables.

In SC, in the interest of full exploitation of a data set, one may find oneself performing many significance tests, both univariate and multivariate (on subsets of variables), with the attendant risk of Type I errors. Considering only univariate tests, with k_Y dependent and k_X independent variables, there are $k_Y k_X$ correlation coefficients and the same number of regression coefficients. Even for such modest set sizes as 3 and 5, that comes to 30 tests, a considerable number.

This problem does not lend itself to any easy mechanical solution, but some general suggestions may, when combined with the scientific judgement of a competent investigator, serve to keep the rate of invalid null hypothesis rejections to a tolerable minimum.

1. Avoid the use of more variables or more sets of variables than are needed to frame the issues—as noted in Chapter 5, "less is more."
2. When possible, combine research factors into (larger) sets and require that the set's contribution be statistically significant as a condition for testing the former. This employs the same logic as the Fisher "protected" (LSD) test on pairs of means discussed in Chapter 5. Set correlation techniques may be particularly useful when the investigator is testing a variety of possible violations of the assumptions of linearity and absence of interactions, as we shall see.
3. Distinguish confirmatory (conclusion-seeking) from exploratory research or aspects of a research problem. Exploratory research, by definition, yields hypotheses to be tested in future research, so error inflation is subject to correction by replication studies.

16.5 STATISTICAL POWER ANALYSIS IN SET CORRELATION

For SC, and therefore for multivariate methods in general, power analysis is complicated by the fact that the effect size is not a simple function of a measure of association, for example, $R^2_{Y,X}$, but rather is inversely related to the sth root of the complement of $R^2_{Y,X}$, where s is itself a complex function of k_Y and k_X, and depends also on the type of association and error model. Thus, power increases as the strength of association increases, but decreases (as shrinkage increases) with $k_Y k_X$ ($= u$, the numerator df of the Rao F test of $R^2_{Y,X}$). As always, power increases with n and α. A comprehensive treatment of power analysis in SC is therefore well beyond the scope

TABLE 16.5.1
Power in Set Correlation as a Function of $R^2_{Y,X}$, n, k_Y, k_X, and α

$R^2_{Y,X}$	n	2, 2	2, 4	2, 8	2, 16	4, 4	4, 8	4, 16	8, 8	8, 16	16, 16
						k_Y, k_X					
						$\alpha = .01$					
.05	50	06	04	03	02	03	02	02	02	01	01
	100	19	12	07	04	07	04	03	03	02	02
	200	50	35	22	12	22	13	07	07	04	03
	500	96	91	79	59	79	60	38	38	21	11
.20	50	52	36	21	09	22	11	05	06	03	02
	100	93	84	67	43	67	45	24	25	12	06
	200	*	*	99	93	99	93	77	78	52	28
	500	*	*	*	*	*	*	*	*	*	96
.40	50	97	90	73	42	74	49	22	26	11	05
	100	*	*	*	97	*	97	83	84	56	29
	200	*	*	*	*	*	*	*	*	99	90
	500	*	*	*	*	*	*	*	*	*	*
						$\alpha = .05$					
.05	50	20	15	11	08	11	09	07	07	06	06
	100	41	30	21	14	21	15	11	11	09	07
	200	73	60	45	31	45	32	21	22	15	11
	500	99	97	92	80	92	80	63	63	44	29
.20	50	76	62	44	27	45	30	18	19	12	09
	100	98	95	86	68	86	70	48	50	32	20
	200	*	*	*	98	*	98	92	92	75	53
	500	*	*	*	*	*	*	*	*	*	99
.40	50	99	97	90	69	90	73	47	51	29	17
	100	*	*	*	99	*	99	95	95	79	54
	200	*	*	*	*	*	*	*	*	*	97
	500	*	*	*	*	*	*	*	*	*	*

*Value > 99.

of this chapter. To actually perform a power analysis, the reader is referred to J. Cohen (1988, Chapter 10), which is replete with formulas, tables, and many worked examples.

Table 16.5.1 may provide the reader with a feel for the relationship to power of the parameters that determine it: the significance criterion, sample size, number of variables in the two sets, and $R^2_{Y,X}$. The power values in the table hold strictly for whole and partial association. In keeping with its modest purpose, this table gives power for only a few selected values of the relevant parameters. The reader is warned not to take the three levels of $R^2_{Y,X}$ as operationally defining small, medium, and large effect sizes (because $R^2_{Y,X}$ is not an effect size parameter), or to interpolate between those or between the values of the other parameters. Another warning must be issues: the $R^2_{Y,X}$ values are population values; the $R^2_{Y,X}$ values found in samples, as we have seen, are positively biased, so the investigator should think in terms of shrunken $\tilde{R}^2_{Y,X}$ in setting estimates for power analysis.

That said, certain implications may be drawn from the table:

1. At the frequently preferred $\alpha = .01$ level, a small degree of association is very unlikely to be detected except for very large n and few variables. Even at $\alpha = .05$, the situation is not much improved.

2. At $R^2_{Y,X} = .20$, a sample of 100 gives satisfactory power at $\alpha = .01$ only for problems with small set sizes; at $\alpha = .05$, somewhat larger sets (say, up to $u = 20$) will yield adequate power.

3. For $R^2_{Y,X} = .40$, at $\alpha = .01$, $n = 50$ will provide adequate power only for small set sizes; at $\alpha = .05$, somewhat larger sets (say, up to $u = 25$) will yield adequate power.

4. The table makes clear the dependence of power on u: Note the close similarity in power values in each row between the entries for 2, 8 and 4, 4 ($u = 16$), and for 2, 16 and 4, 8 ($u = 32$).

Thus, multivariate or otherwise, the same old principle applies—the fewer variables the better—less is more.

16.6 COMPARISON OF SET CORRELATION WITH MULTIVARIATE ANALYSIS OF VARIANCE

Set correlation is both a generalization of the MRC system and a generalization of the other standard multivariate OLS methods, MANOVA and MANCOVA.[4] The latter generalizations may be accomplished in the same way that MRC generalizes the standard univariate methods, that is with a single Y replaced by a set Y, with multiple (semipartial or partial) R^2 replaced by multivariate (semipartial, partial, or bipartial) $R^2_{Y,X}$ (or $T^2_{Y,X}$ or $P^2_{Y,X}$) and tested by Rao's F or one of the other tests (Olson, 1976).

For example, a multivariate analysis of variance (MANOVA) with a single factor ("one-way") calls for the whole association between a set of dependent variables Y ("scores"), and a set X ("groups" or "conditions"), an appropriately coded nominal scale. All the advantages of the MRC system are inherent in this generalization, including measures of strength of association and the availability of different coding methods (dummy, effects, contrast) for X to represent the comparisons of interest. The supplementary multiple regressions of each Y variable on X, which is part of the standard SC output for the overall association, yields the Bs with their t tests for the individual contrast functions of the group means on the Y variables. If one wishes the contrasts' effect sizes expressed as proportions of Y variance accounted for, one can do a series of X semipartial analyses, where X_B is $X_i \cdot X_j$, where X_j signifies the non-i subset of X (see Chapter 8).

For multiple research factors, that is, factorial design MANOVA, the type of SC association is X semipartial, Y versus $X \cdot X_P$. Any research factor ("main effect") is carried by an appropriately coded set X, and (assuming nonorthogonality) the makeup of X_P depends on the causal model. It may contain one or more or all of the other research factors, or it may be empty and thus reduce to whole association. For conditional relationships (interactions among factors), X contains the product set for the factors involved and X_P the factors and lower-order products (if any), exactly as in MRC. It is conventional to use Model 2 ("within cell") error in ANOVA and ANCOVA, so the analysis for each research factor and interaction would include as the error-reducing set G all the other research factors and interactions up to the highest order. Research factors and interactions yielding significant results may be followed up by single df contrasts in the form $X \cdot X_P$ as described earlier. For example, in following up a significant $U \cdot V$ in a two-factor (U by V) design, a single df contrast U_i will have partialed from it not only the research factor V, but also the other variables in the U research factor. Similarly, a single interaction contrast UV_{ij} will have partialed from it both the other product variables in the UV

---

[4]We restrict our attention here to designs with single-error terms, that is, those in which effects are not "multilevel" (see Chapters 14 and 15).

set and also factors U and V. Again, these procedures are exactly those employed for single contrasts in MRC.

Multivariate analysis of covariance versions of any of the aforementioned designs involve only the addition of a set of covariates partialed from both Y and X. For a one-factor design, the type of association is the partial, $Y \cdot Y_P$ with $X \cdot X_P$, where $X_P = Y_P$ is the covariate set. For multifactor covariance designs, where other factors may need to be partialed in defining X_B, the association type is generally bipartial, with the Y_P the covariate set and X_P the covariate set plus whatever other research factors are needed. For example, in testing $U \cdot V$ in a two-factor design with a covariate set C, Y_B is $Y \cdot C$ and X_B is $U \cdot VC$, with VC being the combined V and C sets serving as X_P. We define this as bipartial because X_P does not equal Y_P. Single df contrasts expressed as Bs and their t test values may be obtained from the supplementary regression analyses, or, if a proportion of variance metric is desired, by running new SC analyses with the covariate set included in the partialing of the single variable, that is, $X_B = U_i \cdot U_j, VC$.

As noted in Chapter 14, discriminant function analysis (DFA) is a multivariate procedure that relates membership in g groups to a set of scores. It solves for sets of weights that yield linearly weighted composites of the scores that maximally discriminate (in terms of the F ratio or eta square) among the groups and are mutually orthogonal. Discriminant function analysis is a special case of CA, and can be accomplished by applying the latter to the scores as one set of variables and any form of nominal coding of groups membership as the other. The resulting canonical weights are proportional to (and therefore functionally equivalent with) the discriminant weights. When there are only two groups, DFA reduces to MRC (because there is only one variable in one of the sets, the group dichotomy), as does CA.

DFA is employed for "predicting" group membership much as MRC may be employed in "predicting" a single Y. But it is also frequently used as an aid to understanding group membership, and here it suffers the inadequacies of its parent, CA, as described earlier. SC provides a superior alternative, as was suggested in the discussion of MANOVA. Depending on the investigator's interest or specific hypotheses, a coding method for groups as set X_B may be chosen so as to compare each group with all groups (effects coding), or with a control or reference group (dummy coding), or to effect other contrasts among group means (contrast coding, orthogonal polynomials, see Chapter 8). Single df contrasts can be evaluated as described in the SC approach to MANOVA. Further analytic elaboration of the contrasts may be obtained by assessing unique contributions of subsets of Y variables or single Y variables by analyzing partialed $Y \cdot Y_P$ sets with contrasts represented by $X_i \cdot X_j$, in bipartial analyses (see the illustrative example later).

16.7 NEW ANALYTIC POSSIBILITIES WITH SET CORRELATION

The SC approach to standard multivariate designs enhances their scope and yields additional analytic detail, yet its greatest interest lies in the possibilities it affords for analytic innovations. Prominent among these are analyses that employ Y_B as a partialed set.

One such possibility is the analysis of unique variance components of a single variable or subset of variables in a battery of tests. Many studies employ a group of measures or formal battery of tests as a set of dependent variables that together are designed to cover some domain such as intelligence, personality, values, or psychiatric status. The variables in the battery typically are correlated (sometimes substantially so) with one or more common factors underlying them. The investigator's interest often extends beyond the global construct defined by the battery to the unique variance of single variables or to common variance of subsets of the battery. Thus, an investigator of the correlates of educational intervention and demographic correlates of performance on the subtests of the Wechsler Intelligence Scale for Children may well be interested not only in the subtest aggregate but also in components specific to a single subtest or group of subtests that take the $Y \cdot Y_\mathrm{P}$ form. An example of the former is the Mazes subtest partialing all other subtests and of the latter the perceptual organization subtests (picture arrangement, picture completion, block design, and object assembly) again partialing all the others. Because many such components can be created the reader is reminded of the discussion of Type I error inflation. Other novel analytic forms are illustrated in the following examples.

16.8 ILLUSTRATIVE EXAMPLES

16.8.1 A Simple Whole Association

In this longitudinal study the relationships between potential environmental risks, measured at an average age of 5.5 years, and behavioral disorders measured some 8 years later were assessed.[5] The X set included early childhood poverty (POV), single mother (MONLY), maternal age (MAGE), and maternal employment (MWORK), in addition to age and sex. The Y set included symptom scales for attention deficit/hyperactivity disorder (ADHD), conduct disorder (CD), and oppositional/defiant disorder (ODD). The correlations among the variables are shown in Table 16.8.1, as well as the set correlational and subsequent multiple regression findings.

CH16EX01

TABLE 16.8.1
The Relationship Between Disruptive Behavior Disorder
Symptoms and Earlier Risks in 701 Children

$R_{Y,X}^2 = .199;$ $\tilde{R}_{Y,X}^2 = .178;$ Rao $F = 8.859;$ $(df: u = 18, v = 1957.8);$ $p < .01.$

A. Correlations among basic variables

	Set Y_B			Set X_B				
	ADHD	CD	ODD	Sex	Age	MONLY	MWORK	MAGE
CD	.53							
ODD	.62	.61						
Sex	.19	.23	.03					
Age	−.09	.10	.10	−.02				
MONLY	.08	.18	.12	.02	.05			
MWORK	.02	.02	.03	.00	.06	.22		
MAGE	−.12	−.10	−.06	−.02	.18	−.07	−.01	
Poverty	.08	.15	.12	−.02	.02	.36	−.05	−.03

B. Multiple regression findings

	R^2	Sex	Age	MONLY	MWORK	MAGE	Poverty
ADHD	.062*	.18*	−.07	.05	.02	−.10*	.06
CD	.113*	.23*	.12*	.12*	−.01	−.11*	.10*
ODD	.036*	.03	.11*	.08	.01	−.07	.09*

*$p < .05.$

[5]Data from the Children in the Community study, P. Cohen, P. I. supported by NIMH.

The SC analysis yields $R^2_{Y,X} = .199, T^2_{Y,X} = P^2_{Y,X} = .07$. The shrunken values are given respectively as .178, .046, and .046. The Rao $F = 8.859$ for $u = 18$ and $v = 1957.8\,df$ ($p < .01$; Table 16.8.1).

With the overall association being significant, we can go on to assess the results of the supplementary analysis. The multiple R^2 for ADHD, CD, and ODD with the X set are .062, .113, and .036 respectively, all significant at $\alpha < .01$ on this large sample. Nine of the 18 partial regression coefficients are statistically significant at $\alpha < .05$. Note the risk of experiment-wise Type I error in using the .05 criterion for these tests: Although somewhat protected by the .01 significance level of the overall test, the risk of identifying a true null or trivial effect among the βs is rather greater than .05. For example, if 12 of the 18 population βs were 0, the probability of one or more of these testing significant at the .05 level would be approximately $1 - (.95)^{12} = 46\%$.

16.8.2 A Multivariate Analysis of Partial Variance

Conventional ANCOVA and MANCOVA partial out a covariate set in comparing groups on scores. With MRC this analysis of partial variance (APV) can be generalized to the case where X is not constrained to be group membership, but can be any kind of research factor, including one or more quantitative scales. This idea readily generalizes further to the multivariate analysis of partial variance (MAPV), where the single Y is generalized to the set Y_B.

CH16EX02

In a large-scale study of 755 children at an average age of 13.5,[6] data were obtained on personal qualities the subjects admired and what they thought other children admired (P. Cohen and J. Cohen, 1996). The admired qualities were organized into scales for antisocial, materialistic, and conventional values for the self and also as ascribed to others. In one phase of the investigation, the researchers addressed the relationship between the self and other values. It had been found that several of these scales exhibited sex differences, were nonlinearly (specifically quadratically) related to age, or were differently related to age for girls as compared to boys. For the self-other association to be assessed free of the confounding influence of age, sex, and their interactions, it was necessary to partial these effects from the association. Accordingly, a covariate set was constituted of the variables age, age^2, sex (dummy coded), sex $\times$ age, and sex $\times$ age^2. The type of association is partial, with set X the self scales (Antiso_s, Mater_s, Conven_s), set Y the other scales (Antiso_o, Mater_o, Conven_o) and the covariate set being partialed from both (X_P and Y_P). The main results are given in Table 16.8.2.

The degree of association is substantial, the self scales accounting for 43% of the generalized variance of the other scales ($R^2_{Y,X}$) with the curvilinear (quadratic) effects of age, sex, and their interactions removed. With both these sets partialed by the covariates, all the between- and within-set correlations are partial correlations coefficients, and it is on these partialed variables that the multiple regressions are performed. For example, the significant $\beta = .38$ for Antiso_s in estimating Antiso_o is not only partialed by the covariate set, but Antiso_s is further partialed by Mater_s and Conven_s in the regression equations. Each self scale has a significant β with its paired other scale and, in addition, the Conven_s's β for estimating Mater_o is statistically significant. Each of the other scales has a significant multiple R^2 with the self scales, that for materialism being the largest.

Note that if the X set had been a categorical variable (mother's marital status, religious affiliation), the SC analysis would have exactly the same structure and the design identifiable as a conventional MANOVA. The covariate set employed, however, is hardly of the kind

---

[6]These data are also from the Children in the Community study.

TABLE 16.8.2
Self Versus Other Values in Adolescents, Partialed for
Quadratic Age, Sex, and Their Interactions ($n = 755$)

$R^2_{Y,X} = .429;$ $\tilde{R}^2_{Y,X} = .422;$ Rao $F = 52.007$ ($df: u = 9, v = 1810.9$).

A. (Partial) correlations among basic variables

	Set Y_B			Set X_B		
	Antiso_o	Mater_o	Conven_o	Antiso_s	Mater_s	Conven_s
Antiso_o	1.0					
Mater_o	.20	1.0				
Conven_o	−.42	.11	1.0			
Antiso_s	.39	.08	−.07	1.0		
Mater_s	.14	.46	.05	.21	1.0	
Conven_s	−.26	.13	.35	−.26	.07	1.0

B. βs and multiple R^2s of Y_B variables on set X_B

	Antiso_o	Mater_o	Conven_o
Antiso_s	.38*	.03	.04
Mater_s	.06	.45*	.02
Conven_s	−.02	.10*	.35*
Multiple R^2	.157	.219	.122

*$p < .05$.

encountered in textbook examples and illustrates the flexibility of the method. Not only can one "adjust" for nonlinearly related variables and interactions, but for missing data and categorical variables.

16.8.3 A Hierarchical Analysis of a Quantitative Set and Its Unique Components

Let us return to the set of disruptive behavior indicators examined earlier for relationships with a set of demographic predictors. In that analysis we saw that the set of predictors was associated with the Y set, and in follow-up regression analyses, to each of the Y variables (Table 16.8.1). However, there are several other questions about these data that may usefully be answered by SC analyses. The first is the question of whether any of the Y variables is *uniquely* associated with the X set. Although discriminable, the three scales had intercorrelations of .53, .62, and .61. When treated as a set representing disruptive behavior they largely reflect their substantial common factor. When, however, from each of the three the other two are partialed, the resulting variable is a measure of that which is unique to the scale (including a likely large amount of measurement error).

In addition, we address two new issues on the X side. The first separates age and sex—which may be viewed as "control" variables rather than predictors—from the longitudinal predictors, POV, MAGE, MWORK, and MONLY. The second addresses the question of whether there are curvilinear components of age and whether any of the predictors (including age) may be differently related to Y for boys and girls. In order to answer this question we enter three sets of predictors hierarchically, partialing the previous sets in each analysis. The first set consists of

TABLE 16.8.3
$R^2_{Y,X}$s for the Association of Symptoms of Disruptive Behavior Disorders and Their
Unique Components with Hierarchically Organized Predictors ($n = 701$)

	Any disruptive ADHD, CD, ODD	Unique components of disruptive behavior		
		ADHD · CD, ODD	CD · ADHD, ODD	ODD · ADHD, CD
Age, sex	.150*	.068*	.063*	.058*
Poverty, MAGE, MONLY, MWORK, · (age, sex)	.056*	.004	.023*	.002
Age², age × sex, sex × MAGE, sex × POV, sex × MONLY, SEX × MWORK · (age, sex, Poverty, MAGE, MONLY, MWORK)	.033	.006	.011	.004
All predictors	.225*	.078*	.097*	.063*

*$p < .05$.

age and sex. The second includes the four prospective risks from which age and sex have been partialed. The third consists of six variables: age^2, age × sex, sex × POV, sex × MAGE, sex × MONLY, and sex × MWORK, again partialing both previous sets of predictors.[7] In including as many as six predictors in this third set we are following a strategy in which the hierarchical analysis is used to support a decision—that is, whether these curvilinear or interactive terms are required. If one had more specific hypotheses about one or two of these it would likely be more powerful to treat them as a smaller set and then leave the additional "assumption testing" set as a final set.

A series of SC analysis summarized in Table 16.8.3 addressed the association of the set as a whole and of its unique components with the hierarchical, cumulatively partialed series of predictors. Table 16.8.3 presents the $R^2_{Y,X}$ values for the three-variable set Y (= ADHD, CD, and ODD) in the first column, and for each unique component in the remaining three columns. The first three rows constitute a hierarchical series of research factors with each being partialed by those preceding it in the hierarchy. The final row is for all the predictors combined into a single set. The unique components of the dependent variables are of course single variables, so that the $R^2_{Y,X}$s given in the last three columns specialize to R^2s for single DVs. These DVs, however, are not the observed variables Y but rather the residual for each Y from which the variance associated with the other variables in the Y set have been partialed. Similarly, except for the first and last rows the IVs are not observed variables, but rather variables from which other predictors and other DVs have been partialed.

Examining the first row, we see that age and sex were significantly related to the set and to each of the individual Y variables in a way that is not entirely reflected in their relationship with the general factor. We see in the second row that the prospective risks were significantly related to the set, and also to the unique aspect of conduct disorder symptoms. In the third row we see that the set of curvilinear and interaction terms did not make a significant contribution

---

[7]Note that we do not address the issue here of whether these variables are centered or not—the multivariate tests will be the same either way. Subsequent interpretation of partial relationships, however, is improved by centering, as discussed in earlier chapters.

to the multivariate R^2, and thus the assumption that these terms are not needed may be deemed tenable. The reader is invited to examine the SC analyses in detail, since the $R^2_{Y,X}$ values tell only a small part of the total story. In particular, the reader will note that in the analysis reported in the first column, the interaction (assumption testing) set makes a statistically significant contribution to the *unpartialed* CD. In examining which of these predictors accounts for this contribution, the research may wish to make a different decision than a blanket rejection of the need for these variables.

The first column $R^2_{Y,X}$s in the table are between sets of two or more variables each. The $R^2_{Y,X}$s of the second to fourth columns for unique components specialize to multiple R^2s, because in all these cases one (partialed) Y variable is being related to two or more. Thus, the column for each of the unique components contains the results of a hierarchical multiple R^2, and the entries for the successively partialed research factors are additive; each sum equals the multiple R^2 for that component with all four research factors (within rounding error). However, such is not the case for the three-variable set in the first column, nor in the general case for multiple variable increments to $R^2_{Y,X}$ (X semipartials or bipartials), as noted in the earlier discussion of $R^2_{Y,X}$'s properties: .225 is not the sum of the values above it—they are not cumulative increments to a total $R^2_{Y,X}$.

These findings tell us that the relationship between disruptive behavior symptoms and age and sex differs for the various individual scales. In addition, the risks are related somewhat differently to conduct disorder symptoms than they are to the general factor reflecting the three disruptive measures. (The full SC analysis for the partialed CD measure showed that the risk associated with a single (rather than currently married) mother was greater for CD than it was for the other variables in Y.) The magnitude of the prospective risks for ADHD and ODD were consistent with those for the general disruptive factor. On this evidence neither the interactive nor the curvilinear age terms are needed for these analyses; see, however, the discussion earlier about the evidence based on the relationships with the unpartialed CD measure.

16.8.4 Bipartial Association Among Three Sets

The data for the next example were taken from an experiment on the effects of maternal nutritional supplement during pregnancy on somatic and behavioral characteristics of newborn infants.[8] The subjects were 650 pregnant women coming to a prenatal clinic who were randomly assigned to three groups (high protein supplement, balanced protein/caloric supplement, routine care control), treated, and followed to term. Their newborns were weighed and measured at birth and, within 48 to 99 hours after birth, were subjected to a 19-item behavioral examination assessing degree of neurological development via muscle tone and reflexes. A factor analysis of these items suggested four factors, scores for which were generated by adding the highly loaded items for each factor.

The major issues addressed were the effects of the two forms of dietary supplement on (a) the somatic characteristics of the newborns and (b) their behavior as represented by the four factor scores, and also (c) the relationship between somatic characteristics and behavior. Various maternal attributes with potential effects on their babies served as a covariate (control) set. Concretely, the major analysis used the following research factor sets:

1. Treatment (TRT): two dummy variables with the control group as reference.

---

[8]We are indebted to David Rush (Tufts University) and Mervyn W. Susser and Zena Stein (Columbia University) for permission to use these data.

2. Maternal attribute controls (COV): prepregnant weight, gestation, and weight at time of clinic registration, parity, and number of previous low-birth-weight babies (five variables).
3. Newborn somatic characteristics (SOM): birth weight, length, and head circumference.
4. Newborn behavior (BEH): the four factor-analytically-derived scores.
5. Age at examination (in hours) and baby sex.

The physical maturity of the infant at birth, a matter of considerable medical importance, was assessed by measuring its "age" from conception, using as a reference the date of the onset of the mother's last menstrual period as reported by her at the time of clinic registration (during, on average, the 16th week of pregnancy). The accuracy of this datum (gestation) is suspect, and besides, the theoretical question arises as to whether the "postconceptual age" at birth provides any relevant information beyond that of the observable somatic characteristics, or (more simply) given its size, does it matter how "old" the newborn is? This issue was directly addressed by partialing SOM and sex from gestation and relating it to the suitably partialed BEH set. Its $R^2_{Y,X}$ (a multiple R^2) was .014, which is not significant even at $\alpha = .05$. When each of the other variables was similarly treated, with gestation included among the variables that were partialed, the $R^2_{Y,X}$s for these unique BEH scores were larger and significant at $\alpha = .01$. These results suggest that the postconceptual age at birth as determined from mother's later reported date of last menstruation yields no information relevant to the newborn's behavior beyond what is available from measuring its weight, length, and head circumference.

In the main analysis, the three research factors to be related were treatment, newborn somatic characteristics, and newborn behavior. The maternal attributes were to be statistically controlled as a covariate set; thus they were partialed from each research factor. Furthermore, to control for sex differences, it was partialed from both the somatic and behavior research factors. Because the behavioral examination took place at varying intervals after birth, age at examination was also partialed from the behavior scores. Thus, the following three factors, as partialed, were related to each other in the SC analysis: (a) TRT · COV, (b) SOM · COV, sex, and (c) BEH · COV, sex, age. In addition, preliminary SC were conducted to determine whether two way interactions between COV and sex, between COV and age, or between age and sex contributed to the prediction of any of the sets (TRT, SOM, or BEH) net of main effects.

Table 16.8.4(A) gives the $R^2_{Y,X}$s for each pair. The partialing sets are not exactly the same for the three sets, so the type of association is defined as bipartial. Note that the two $R^2_{Y,X}$s with TRT · COV summarize a MANOVA, but with additional variables partialed from SOM (sex) and BEH (sex and age at examination). Clearly, the results provide no evidence to suggest the existence of treatment effects on either the somatic or behavioral characteristics of the newborn, the $R^2_{Y,X}$ values being both trivial and, despite the large sample size ($n = 650$), nonsignificant by any conventional standard ($p > .15$).

The association of BEH and SOM, as partialed, constitutes another example of the multivariate analysis of partial variance (MAPV). X_B here is a set of three quantitative variables (SOM), but the association is controlled by covariates (COV and sex), with age additionally partialed from BEH. The association is quite substantial ($R^2_{Y,X} = .300$) and highly significant. (The $P^2_{Y,X} = T^2_{Y,X} = .108$, the average of the three canonical R^2s, is also relatively large.) Thus, although the nutritional intervention had no demonstrable effects on either the newborns' physical or behavioral characteristics, there was a material relationship between these two research factors.

TABLE 16.8.4
Nutritional Supplementation During Pregnancy and the Somatic
and Behavioral Characteristics of Newborns ($n = 650$)

A. Association between research factors: bipartial $R_{Y,X}^2$

	TRT · COV	SOM · COV, sex
SOM · COV, sex	.010	
BEH · COV, sex, age	.018	.300*

B. βs and multiple R^2s of BEH · COV, sex, age on SOM · COV, sex

	Partialed BEH scores			
Partialed SOM scores	I	II	III	IV
Birthweight	.08	.29*	.20*	.15
Length	.37*	−.16*	.13	−.02
Head circumference	−.03	−.09	.08	.18*
Multiple R^2	.160*	.039*	.133*	.087*

Note: TRT = 2 dummy-coded nutritional supplementation variables; SOM = 3 somatic characteristics of newborns; COV = 5 maternal attribute variables.
*$p < .001$.

The supplementary analyses provide the multiple R^2s and βs relating the three partialed SOM scores to each of the dependent partialed BEH scores [Table 16.8.4(B)]. It is interesting to note that despite fairly high (partial) correlations among the SOM measures of .60, .70, and .46 (available from the SC printout), they give rise to distinctively different patterns of βs and levels of $R_{Y,X}^2$s in estimating the four partialed BEH scores.

16.9 SUMMARY

The utility of a multivariate method in which dependent variables as well as independent variables can be treated as substantive sets is discussed. Canonical correlation analysis is described and its limitations noted. The elements of set correlation are introduced (Section 16.1).

Measures of multivariate association are reviewed, including the generalization of R^2, the proportion of generalized variance, and proportions of additive variance expressed as the mean of the canonical correlations, $T_{Y,X}^2$, and the multivariate association for the average orthogonalized Y variable, $P_{Y,X}^2$ (Section 16.2).

The rationales for partialing sets of variables from the basic X and Y sets are reviewed, and the five kinds of relationships between these sets are noted to depend on the sets being partialed. These include the relationship between the "whole" unpartialed sets, a partial relationship in which the influence of the same set is removed from both X and Y, semipartial relationships in which a set is partialed from either X or Y but not both, and bipartial relationships in which different sets are partialed from sets X and Y (Section 16.3).

Statistical tests of the null hypothesis of no association are reviewed, including Model 1 error, used in most analyses, and Model 2 error, in which variance from a set G not included in the basic analysis is also removed (as in hierarchial set correlation analysis). Estimators of the population values of the three measures of effect size are reviewed, and the substantial shrinkage that may result is noted. Methods for controlling the error inflation associated with the many significance tests are reviewed (Section 16.4).

Statistical power analysis for set correlation is shown to decline rapidly with increases in the numbers of variables in the X and Y sets, depending on the level of multivariate relationship in the population and, of course, n (Section 16.5).

A comparison with MANOVA is made, with a demonstration of the equivalence under certain conditions shown (Section 16.6).

Set correlation opens up a range of analytic possibilities for sets of DVs comparable to those shown in earlier chapters for a single Y (Section 16.7). These possibilities are reviewed in a series of examples (Section 16.8).

APPENDICES

APPENDIX 1

The Mathematical Basis for Multiple Regression/Correlation and Identification of the Inverse Matrix Elements

The OLS regression model requires the determination of a set of weights for the k independent variables that, when used in the linear regression equation, minimizes the average squared deviation of the estimated $\hat{Y}$ scores from the Y scores. This solution is somewhat simplified by standardizing all variables. Thus the problem is to find a set of β weights such that

$$\sum (z_Y - \beta_1 z_1 - \beta_2 z_2 - \beta_3 z_3 - \cdots - \beta_k z_k)^2$$

is a minimum, as we have seen. By means of the differential calculus, the partial derivative of the function with respect to each unknown β_i is found and set to zero. The β_i weights are then expressed as a system of k normal equations in k unknowns of the form

(A1.1)
$$\beta_1 = r_{Y1} - r_{12}\beta_2 - r_{13}\beta_3 - \cdots - r_{1k}\beta_k$$
$$\beta_2 = r_{Y2} - r_{12}\beta_1 - r_{23}\beta_3 - \cdots - r_{2k}\beta_k$$
$$\vdots$$
$$\beta_k = r_{Yk} - r_{1k}\beta_1 - r_{2k}\beta_2 - \cdots - r_{(k-1)k}\beta_{k-1}.$$

A computer program may be used directly to solve this set of simultaneous equations. For those familiar with matrix algebra the problem may be stated usefully in matrix notation. The set of normal equations may be rearranged as follows:

$$r_{Y1} = \beta_1 + r_{12}\beta_2 + r_{13}\beta_3 + \cdots + r_{1k}\beta_k,$$
$$r_{Y2} = \beta_2 + r_{12}\beta_1 + r_{23}\beta_3 + \cdots + r_{2k}\beta_k.$$

The right-hand side of this set of equations may be recognized as the product the square, symmetric matrix of correlation coefficients between independent variables ($\mathbf{R}_{ij}$) and the vector of β_{Yi}. Thus, the equation set may be restated in matrix form as a single equation,

$$\mathbf{R}_{ij}\beta_{Yi} = \mathbf{r}_{ij}.$$

631

The solution may then be seen to lie in the premultiplication of the vector of correlations of IVs with Y, $\mathbf{r}_{Yi}$, by the inverse of the matrix of correlations among the IVs, $\mathbf{R}_{ij}^{-1}$:

$$\beta_{Yi} = \mathbf{R}_{ij}^{-1} r_{Yi}.$$

The problem, therefore is to invert the correlation matrix, for which many computer programs have been written. Hand calculation of the inverse matrix is practical when there are no more than five or six independent variables. A method for doing so is presented in Appendix 2. Note that once the inverse matrix is determined, it is a relatively easy matter to apply MRC analysis to a new dependent variable W (for the same IVs), because all one needs to do is substitute in this equation for the new dependent variable its $\mathbf{r}_{Wi}$ vector.

Identification of the elements of the inverse matrix will reveal further identities inthe multiple regression/correlation system. Also, because some computer programs provide the inverse matrix as standard or optional output, coefficients not provided by a given program may be readily determined as simple functions of these elements. Concrete illustration of the determination of these coefficients is provided in Appendix 2. The diagonal elements of $\mathbf{R}_{ij}^{-1}$, the inverse of the correlation matrix among the IVs, are

(A1.2)
$$r^{ii} = \frac{1}{1 - R_i^2},$$

where R_i^2 is the squared multiple correlation of the $k - 1$ remaining independent variables with X_i. Thus

(A1.3)
$$R_i^2 = 1 - \frac{1}{r^{ii}}.$$

This quantity is, of course, very useful itself in understanding the system of relationships with Y, especially in cases of high redundancy among some or all IVs because $1 - R_i^2$ equals the tolerance, that part of an IV that is independent of the other IVs and thus available to relate independently to Y. In addition, r^{ii} may be used to determine sr, which may not be provided in the program output, by

(A1.4)
$$sr_i = \frac{\beta_{Yi}}{\sqrt{r^{ii}}}.$$

Finally, we have seen in Eqs. (3.6.1) and (3.6.2) that this quantity is a necessary part of the standard errors of partial regression and standardized partial regression coefficients, which then may be written

(A1.5)
$$SE_{B_i} = \frac{sd_Y}{sd_i} \sqrt{\frac{1 - R_Y^2}{n - k - 1}} \sqrt{r^{ii}}$$

and

(A1.6)
$$SE_{\beta_i} = \sqrt{\frac{1 - R_Y^2}{n - k - 1}} \sqrt{r^{ii}},$$

respectively.

The off-diagonal elements of $\mathbf{R}_{ij}^{-1}$ may be identified as

(A1.7)
$$r^{ij} = \frac{-\beta_{ij}}{1 - R_i^2} = \frac{-\beta_{ji}}{1 - R_j^2} = r^{ji},$$

where β_{ij} is the standardized partial regression coefficient of X_i on X_j, other IVs having been partialed, and β_{ji} is the corresponding coefficient of X_j on X_i. Note that $r^{ij} = r^{ji}$ and thus, like the correlation matrix itself, its inverse is symmetrical about the diagonal. In determining the standard error of a single $\hat{Y}_o$ predicted from a new observed set of values $X_{1o}, X_{2o}, X_{3o}, \ldots, X_{ko}$, as given in Eq. (3.7.1), both diagonal and off-diagonal elements of the inverted matrix are needed. This equation may be restated as

$$(A1.8) \qquad sd_{Y_o - \hat{Y}_o} = \frac{sd_{Y-\hat{Y}}}{\sqrt{n}}\sqrt{n+1+\sum r^{ii}z_{io}^2 + 2\sum r^{ij}z_{io}z_{jo}},$$

where the first summation is over the diagonal elements and the second is over the $k(k-1)/2$ off diagonal elements above (or below, because they are symmetrical) the diagonal.

The inverted matrix is used to determine the β_{Yi} by postmultiplying it by the vector of validity coefficients. Thus

$$(A1.9) \qquad \beta_{Y1} = r^{11}r_{Y1} + r^{12}r_{Y2} + r^{13}r_{Y3} + \cdots + r^{1k}r_{Yk},$$
$$\beta_{Y2} = r^{21}r_{Y1} + r^{22}r_{Y2} + r^{23}r_{Y3} + \cdots + r^{2k}r_{Yk},$$

and so on. Restating the first of these in terms of the equivalents of the inverted matrix elements,

$$\beta_{Y1} = \frac{r_{Y1}}{1-R_1^2} - \frac{r_{Y2}\beta_{12}}{1-R_1^2} - \frac{r_{Y3}\beta_{13}}{1-R_1^2} - \cdots - \frac{r_{Yk}\beta_{1k}}{1-R_1^2}$$
$$= (r_{Y1} - r_{Y2}\beta_{12} - r_{Y3}\beta_{13} - \cdots - r_{Yk}\beta_{1k})/(1-R_1^2).$$

A mathematically equivalent version of the off-diagonal elements is given by

$$(A1.10) \qquad r^{ij} = r^{ji} = \frac{-pr_{ij}}{\sqrt{(1-R_i^2)(1-R_j^2)}}$$

where pr_{ij} is the correlation between X_i and X_j, all other independent variables having been partialed from each. pr_{ij} may be obtained directly by

$$(A1.11) \qquad pr_{ij} = \frac{-r^{ij}}{\sqrt{r^{ii}r^{jj}}},$$

and this matrix of partial correlations among IVs is provided by some MRC programs.

In most MRC studies in which an original set of validity coefficients and a final set of partial relationships with Y are provided in the computer output, a means of sorting out the effects of the independent variables on each other's relationship with Y is needed. It is particularly difficult to surmise these effects from the zero-order correlation matrix when there are more than two or three IVs, especially when their intercorrelations are not trivial. It is often useful to know which of the remaining variables are the source of the redundancy in the relationship between a given X_i and Y. It is also important to be able to detect and to identify sources of suppression among the IVs. A means of determining these effects is the hierarchical procedure for reduced form equations in which one tracks changes in regression coefficients as variables are entered in the model (Section 12.2.3).

A1.1 ALTERNATIVE MATRIX METHODS

Some programs or hand calculation methods choose to invert matrices that express the relationships among the independent variables in raw score form. One such matrix is the variance-covariance matrix $\mathbf{V}_{ij}$, which starts with the sd_i^2 in the diagonal and the cov_{ij} $(= r_{ij}sd_isd_j)$ in the off-diagonal positions. The elements of the inverted matrix $\mathbf{V}_{ij}^{-1}$ are consequently

(A1.12)
$$v^{ii} = \frac{1}{sd_i^2(1 - R_i^2)} = \frac{r^{ii}}{sd_i^2}$$

and

(A1.13)
$$v^{ij} = \frac{-\beta_{ij}}{sd_isd_j(1 - R_i^2)} = \frac{r_{ij}}{sd_isd_j}.$$

When $\mathbf{V}_{ij}$ rather than $\mathbf{R}_{ij}$ is used, the entire matrix equation is

(A1.14)
$$\mathbf{B}_{Yi} = \mathbf{V}_{ij}^{-1}\mathbf{v}_{Yi},$$

where $\mathbf{v}_{Yi}$ is the vector of covariances of the independent variables with Y and $\mathbf{B}_{Yi}$ is the vector of raw-score regression coefficients.

Yet another matrix frequently employed for this purpose, $\mathbf{P}_{ij}$, is made up of the summed (over n) deviation (from mean) squares and cross products, Σx_i^2 and $\Sigma x_i x_j$. This matrix differs from $\mathbf{V}_{ij}$ only in that its elements have not been divided by n. When its inverse is postmultiplied by the vector of summed deviation cross products with Y, $\mathbf{p}_{Yi}$, it also yields the vector of raw-score regression coefficients, $\mathbf{B}_{Yi}$. Similarly, the elements of $\mathbf{P}_{ij}^{-1}$ when divided by n equal the corresponding elements of $\mathbf{V}_{ij}^{-1}$.

One final matrix inversion method may be mentioned. The entire correlation matrix including Y may be inverted and R_Y^2, the pr_{Yi}, and β_{Yi} are then directly determined from the row (or column) corresponding to Y. This method has the disadvantage that the potential analytic uses of the remaining elements of the inverted matrix are lost, because they include the effects of Y on the independent variables.

A1.2 DETERMINANTS

Although an understanding of calculus or matrix algebra is not necessary for the intelligent use of MRC, it is useful to be aware of the characteristics of one numerical value resulting from this system. Every square matrix can be characterized by a unique number, its determinant, which is a complicated function of products of its elements. For the correlation matrix $\mathbf{R}_{ij}$ the determinant $|\mathbf{R}_{ij}|$ may take on any value from zero to one. The size of $|\mathbf{R}_{ij}|$ is a function of the R_i^2 values. When it is zero, at least one variable is a perfect linear function of the others, and the matrix is said to be *singular*. The inverse of a singular matrix does not exist, and the multiple regression problem cannot be solved until the (one or more) offending variables are removed. When $|\mathbf{R}_{ij}| = 1$, the variables all have intercorrelations of zero. As $|\mathbf{R}_{ij}|$ approaches zero, the researcher should be wary for two reasons. The situation is clearly one of high multicollinearity among two or more variables, with all the attendant problems in sorting out the meaning of the results. In addition, there will be a serious decrease in the sampling stability (precision) of coefficients (see Chapter 10).

Because the determinant is often provided in MRC output, one additional equation may prove useful:

(A1.15)
$$R_k^2 = 1 - \frac{|\mathbf{R}_{12\ldots k}|}{|\mathbf{R}_{12\ldots(k-1)}|};$$

that is, the squared multiple correlation of $X_1, X_2, X_3, \ldots, X_{k-1}$ with X_k is equal to one minus the ratio of the determinant of the matrix including X_k to the determinant of the matrix excluding X_k. If we let $X_k = Y$, this gives the standard R_Y^2. If we let X_k be the lastentered variable in a hierarchical sequence, we may determine its R_k^2 with previously entered variables whenever determinants are provided.

APPENDIX 2

Determination of the Inverse Matrix and Applications Thereof

A2.1 HAND CALCULATION OF THE MULTIPLE REGRESSION/CORRELATION PROBLEM

Although most practitioners of MRC analysis are likely to turn over the necessary work to a computer program, it is quite possible to perform these operations with a hand calculator. The major problems in doing so are the many opportunities for error and the amount of time required, both of which increase rapidly as a function of n and k. Several methods for determining the MRC solution are available, of which the best known is the Doolittle solution. We prefer the method that is presented here because it produces the inverse of the correlation matrix among IVs whose elements provide results that are of analytic interest. Using the correlations among IVs given in Table 3.5.1, we shall illustrate the computation of this inverse matrix, and of the various multiple and partial coefficients that its elements yield, and then give the substantive interpretation of the entire set of results.

The method presented here may be generalized to more than, or fewer than, the illustrated four IVs. A mathematical understanding of the purpose of the various operations is not necessary for correct determination of the solution. It is, however, useful to have ways of controlling the error that may creep in. One of these is provided by carrying a sufficient number of decimal places for each of the original correlation coefficients and the subsequent operations. In this example we have used five; with more variables more decimal places would be appropriate. A check against human error is provided by the last column, which, at the points indicated by check marks, should equal the sum of the other numbers in the row, within at most three units in the last decimal.

Table A2.1 illustrates the entire procedure for calculation of the inverse. The first column contains the instructions. The method begins by copying the full correlation matrix among IVs ($\mathbf{R}_{ij}$) and, to its right, a parallel matrix in which the diagonal elements are all 1 and off-diagonal elements are 0 (the identity matrix, $\mathbf{I}$) as shown in the table. Each operation is carried out for every column,[1] with the exception that once a left-hand column contains 1,

---

[1] Thus making the computation particularly easy using a spreadsheet program. Rows have been lettered rather than numbered to facilitate such a means of calculation.

TABLE A2.1

Computing the Inverse of the IV Correlation Matrix for the Salary Example

Operation	Line	R_{ij}				I				Check
		r_1	r_2	r_3	r_4	r^{14}	r^{24}	r^{34}	r^{44}	
	A	1	.65055	.20959	.37290	1	0	0	0	3.23304
	B	.65055	1	.15875	.33339	0	1	0	0	3.14269
	C	.20959	.15875	1	.14915	0	0	1	0	2.51749
	D	.37290	.33339	.14915	1	0	0	0	1	2.85544 ✓✓
Copy A	E	1	.65055	.20959	.37290	1	0	0	0	3.23304
$E \times r_{12}$	F		.42322	.13635	.24259	.65055	0	0	0	2.10325
$B - F$	G		.57678	.02240	.09080	−.65055	1	0	0	1.03944 ✓
$G \div G_2$	H		1	.03884	.15743	−1.12790	1.73376	0	0	1.80214 ✓
$E \times r_{13}$	I			.04393	.07816	.20959	0	0	0	.67761
$G \times H_3$	J			.00087	.00353	−.02527	.03884	0	0	.04037
$C - I - J$	K			.95520	.06747	−.18432	−.03884	1	0	1.79951 ✓
K/K_3	L			1	.07063	−.19297	−.04066	1.04690	0	1.88390 ✓
$E \times r_{14}$	M				.13905	.37290	0	0	0	1.20883
$G \times H_4$	N				.01429	−.10242	.15743	0	0	0.16364
$K \times L_4$	O				.00477	−.01302	−.00274	.07063	0	0.12710
$D - M - N - O$	P				.84189	−.25747	−.15469	−.07063	1	1.35910 ✓
P/P_4	Q				1	−.30582	−.18374	−.08389	1.18780	1.61435 ✓

From Line L:
$r^{33} = 1.0469 - .07063(-.08389) = 1.05283.$
$r^{32} = -.04066 - .07063(-.18374) = -.02768.$
$r^{31} = -.19297 - .07063(-.30582) = -.17137.$

From Line H:
$r^{22} = 1.73376 - .15743(-.18374) - .03884(-.02768) = 1.76376.$
$r^{21} = -1.12790 - .15743(-.30582) - .03884(-.17137) = -1.07310.$

From Line E:
$r^{11} = 1 - .65055(-1.0731) - .20959(-.17137) - .37290(-.30582) = 1.84806.$

no further computations are carried out in that column. Thus, on line F each of the line E numbers is multiplied by the line E, column r_2 value,. On line G these line F values have been subtracted from the line B numbers. Note that the check sum number 1.03944 equals the sum of the row values, as well as $3.14269 - 2.10325$. On line H the line G numbers are divided by the left-hand value in line G, and so on through the table. Note that only some rows provide checks in that the result of the operation performed on the check sum lines equals the row sum, but in all instances it is the result of the operation, not the row sum, that is entered in the check sum column. With a little study, the pattern of computation becomes clear and readily generalized for k IVs. Had there been only three independent variables, column r_4 would be missing. The column headings r^{14}, r^{24}, r^{34}, and r^{44} would be replaced by r^{13}, r^{23}, and r^{33}, and the lines would end with line 12. Five independent variables would require an additional row and column in the $\mathbf{R}_{ij}$ matrix as well as in the $\mathbf{I}$ matrix and six more lines of calculation. Each entry in the next to last line would equal the bottom-row value of the correlation or identity matrix minus the four values in the lines immediately preceding.

Line Q provides the inverse matrix elements for X_4, that is, the r^{i4} values (see Table A2.2). From these numbers and working backward, the elements for X_3 are determined next by subtracting from the right-hand figures in line 12 the product of the left-hand figure and the corresponding r^{i4}. Because $r^{34} = r^{43}$ this element is already provided in row Q. Next, the figures in line H are combined with the previously determined r^{i4} and r^{i3} values to determine r^{22} and r^{21}. Finally, line E and r_{i1} are used to produce r^{11}.

Some insight into the manner in which the method proceeds to systematically remove the proportion of the variance accounted for by each of the variables from the others may be gained by noting some by-products of the method. Looking first at the numbers below the correlation matrix, we see that the r_2 column includes r_{21}, r_{21}^2, and $1 - r_{21}^2$, in lines E, F, and G, respectively. In column r_3 we find $r_{31}^2, sr_{3(2\cdot1)}^2$, and $1 - R_{3\cdot21}^2$ in lines I, J, and K, respectively. Similarly, in the r_4 column we find $r_{41}^2, sr_{4(2\cdot1)}^2, sr_{4(3\cdot21)}^2$, and $1 - R_{4\cdot123}^2$ in lines 13 to 16, respectively. From the numbers under the identity matrix it may be determined that $1.73376 = 1/(1 - r_{12}^2), 1.0469 = 1/(1 - R_{3\cdot12}^2)$, and $1.1878 = 1/(1 - R_{4\cdot123}^2)$. The interested reader may determine more such identities by substitution of the appropriate r_{ij} into the numerical equivalents.

TABLE A2.2
Inverse of IV Correlation Matrix, Validity Coefficients, and βs

| | $\mathbf{R}_{ij}^{-1}$ | | | | |
	Time since Ph.D. X_1	Publications X_2	Sex X_3	Citations X_4	r_{Yi}
X_1	1.84806	−1.07310	−0.17137	−0.30582	.60790
X_2	−1.07310	1.76376	−0.02768	−0.18374	.50615
X_3	−0.17137	−0.02768	1.05283	−0.08780	.20096
X_4	−0.30582	−0.18374	−0.08389	1.18780	.54977

$\beta_1 = (.37771) = 1.12344 - .54315 - .03444 - .16813 = .37772.$

$\beta_2 = (.13382) = -.65234 + .89273 - .00556 - .10101 = .13382.$

$\beta_3 = (.04727) = -.10418 - .01401 + .21158 - .04612 = .04727.$

$\beta_4 = (.35725) = -.18591 - .09300 - .01764 + .65302 = .35726.$

Table A2.2 reproduces the entire inverse matrix, $\mathbf{R}_{ij}^{-1}$, as well as the validity coefficients, r_{Yi}. The β_is are determined by summing the products of the row elements with the corresponding validity coefficients, according to Eq. (A1.9), for example,

(A2.1)
$$\beta_1 = r^{11}r_{Y1} + r^{12}r_{Y2} + r^{13}r_{Y3} + r^{14}r_{Y4}.$$

These products and their sums are given at the bottom of the table.

Finally, it is always useful to have a check against specific accumulated error, or even a computational blunder. The normal equations (A1.1) provide us with such a check, because, for example,

(A2.2)
$$\beta_1 = r_{Y1} - \beta_2 r_{12} - \beta_3 r_{13} - \beta_4 r_{14}.$$

Subtracting β_i from both sides of the equation should yield zero. Checking on the obtained β_1, we find

$$.60790 - .13382(.65055) - .04727(.20959) - .35726(.37290) - .37772 = -.00001$$

well within acceptable limits. The reader may confirm that all the βs check well within acceptable limits.

As we saw in Eq. (A1.3), the proportion of variance in each IV that is shared with the other IVs may be determined by

(A2.3)
$$R_i^2 = 1 - \frac{1}{r^{ii}}.$$

Determining this value for each of our variables we find that

$$R_{1.234}^2 = 1 - \frac{1}{1.84806} = .45889,$$

$$R_{2.134}^2 = 1 - \frac{1}{1.76376} = .43302,$$

$R_{3.124}^2 = .05018$, and $R_{4.123}^2 = .15811$.

In this rather modest example these R^2s may easily be seen to be consistent with the correlation matrix. Thus, the number of years since Ph.D. is fairly substantially associated with two of the other IVs, especially with the number of publications that in turn is modestly correlated with number of citations. Sex is relatively independent of the other IVs. The reader may check the diagonals against the tolerances output by a computer program.

The diagonal elements of the inverse matrix may also be used, together with the β_i, to determine the sr_i, because by Eqs. (A1.4) and (3.5.6),

(A2.4)
$$sr_i = \frac{\beta_i}{\sqrt{r^{ii}}} = \beta_i\sqrt{1 - R_i^2}.$$

For example,

$$sr_1 = \frac{.37771}{\sqrt{1.84806}} = .37771\sqrt{1 - .45889} = .27784.$$

Similarly, $sr_2 = .10076$, $sr_3 = -.04607$, and $sr_4 = .3278$, all of which agree with Table 3.5.2. By including the information on the Ms, sds, and n, all of the other coefficients and their significance tests may be determined by the equations presented in Chapter 3.

If the partial correlations between IVs are desired, they may be determined from the off-diagonal elements of the inverse matrix. The partial correlations are

$$pr_{12 \cdot 34} = \frac{-r^{12}}{\sqrt{r^{11} r^{22}}} = \frac{1.0731}{\sqrt{1.84806(1.76376)}} = .59438,$$

$$pr_{24 \cdot 13} = \frac{-r^{24}}{\sqrt{r^{22} r^{44}}} = \frac{.18374}{\sqrt{1.76376(1.1878)}} = .12694,$$

etc.

The partial correlations among independent variables are often of sufficient interest to warrant significance testing. Because they differ from the off-diagonal elements only by sign and division by a constant, one can test pr_{ij} by testing r^{ij}:

(A2.5)
$$t = \frac{-r^{ij}\sqrt{n-k}}{\sqrt{r^{ii} r^{jj} - r^{ij^2}}}$$

with $df = n - k$. For example, the pr between years since Ph.D. and number of publications, partialing female and number of citations, $pr_{12 \cdot 34}$, assuming $n = 62$, yields

$$t = \frac{-(-1.0731)\sqrt{62 - 4}}{\sqrt{(1.84806)(1.76376) - (-1.0731)^2}} = 5.629,$$

$df = 58$, $(p < .01)$. Clearly, the substantial relationships these variables bear to salary show considerable redundancy.

A2.2 TESTING THE DIFFERENCE BETWEEN PARTIAL βs AND Bs FROM THE SAME SAMPLE

In Section 3.6.3 we described the test for the difference between two independent regression coefficients, that is, those obtained from two independent samples. Now that we have the inverse of the correlation matrix for the IVs (Table A2.2), we can address the case where the two coefficients are for different IVs in the same sample.

The standard error of the difference β_1 and β_2 is given by

(A2.6)
$$SE_{\beta_1 - \beta_2} = \sqrt{\frac{1 - R_Y^2}{n - k - 1}(r^{ii} + r^{jj} + 2r^{ij})}.$$

Dividing the observed difference by Eq. (A2.6) then gives

(A2.7)
$$t = \frac{\beta_i - \beta_j}{SE_{\beta_i - \beta_j}},$$

with $df = n - k - 1$.

For causal analysis with standardized variables (path analysis) β_i is X_i's direct effect on the dependent variable. The comparison of effects of causal effects in the same model (in the absence of otherwise theoretically comparable units) is accomplished via their βs. In the salary example, do the data suggest a population difference in sizes of the direct effects for time since Ph.D. (β_1) and number of publications (β_2)? The standard error of their difference is found by substituting $n = 62, k = 4, R_Y^2 = .5032$, and elements of the inverse matrix as

$$SE_{\beta_1 - \beta_2} = \sqrt{\frac{1 - .5032}{62 - 4 - 1}[1.84806 + 1.76376 - 2(-1.0731)]} = .113029$$

and then finding from Eq. (A2.7)

$$t = \frac{.37772 - .13382}{.11302} = 2.158,$$

for $df = 57, p < .05$.

Similarly, we can test the significance of the difference between raw regression coefficients in a regression equation (i.e., of $B_i - B_j$). The standard error of a partial B_i, already given in Eq. (3.6.1) may also be written as

(A2.8)
$$SE_{B_i} = \frac{sd_Y}{sd_i}\sqrt{\frac{1 - R_Y^2}{n - k - 1}r^{ii}}.$$

Substituting j for i, we have SE_{B_j}. Now, the standard error of their difference is given by

(A2.9)
$$SE_{B_i - B_j} = \sqrt{SE_{B_i}^2 + SE_{B_j}^2 - 2SE_{B_i}SE_{B_j}\left(\frac{r^{ij}}{r^{ii}r^{jj}}\right)},$$

so

(A2.10)
$$t = \frac{B_i - B_j}{SE_{B_i - B_j}},$$

for $df = n - k - 1$.

Equation (A2.9) can be generalized to provide the standard error of any linear contrast function over a set of Bs from the same equation, and beyond that, of any linear function of such a set. Letting a_i be the weight attached to B_i, a linear function is defined as

(A2.11)
$$\text{LF} = \sum a_i B_i$$

where $i = 1.2, \ldots, k$. When the sum of the a_i equals zero, the function is a linear contrast function, as was described for means in Section 8.5. The standard error of such a linear function is

(A2.12)
$$SE_{LF} = \sqrt{\sum a_i^2 SE_{B_i}^2 + 2\sum a_i a_j \text{cov}_{B_i B_j}},$$

where

$$\text{cov}_{B_i B_j} = SE_{B_i}SE_{B_j}\left(\frac{r^{ij}}{\sqrt{r^{ii}r^{jj}}}\right)$$

where $i = 1.2 \ldots k, i < j$. In Eq. (A2.12), the first summation is over ks and the second over all $k(k - 1)/2$ distinct B_i, B_j pairs. The test is an ordinary t test.

An alternative approach to the comparison of correlated Bs or βs is given in Rindskopf (1984). This comparison allows for a wide range of null hypotheses in addition to the preceding test of equality, including tests for the equality of weights of more than two IVs, or the equality of a set of B weights with those specified by a particular theory. The test simply compares the residual from the usual regression estimation with the residual from a regression estimation in which the predictors being examined have been combined (that is, literally added together) according to the null hypothesis. Thus, if one were testing the null hypothesis that the β_is for four IVs were equivalent, one would simply add the four standardized predictors together (or not standardized, depending on one's theory) and uses this combined variable as the predictor of Y. The residual from this equation will necessarily be larger unless the β_is *in this sample* were precisely equal (in which case there wouldn't be much point in the test), since the OLS for the four variable problem is, by definition, optimal. One then tests the difference between the original sum of squares for the regression minus the sum of squares for this combined variable regression, divided by the *df* (in this case 3, since we have reduced the number of estimates from 4 to 1). The error mean square can be taken from the original equation, and the resulting F test will have 3 and $n - 4 - 1$ *df*.

This general method allows for a wide range of tests, including those based on the IVs in their original (rather than standardized) units, when appropriate to the theory.

A2.3 TESTING THE DIFFERENCE BETWEEN βs FOR DIFFERENT DEPENDENT VARIABLES FROM A SINGLE SAMPLE

It is sometimes the case that the research question to be answered is whether a set of predictors have, individually and collectively, a comparable relationship to two or more different DVs in a single sample. A procedure that is basically similar to the comparison of βs for a single DV was devised by P. Cohen, Brook, J. Cohen, Velez, & Garcia (1990). The test begins with the standardization of all variables and the computation of the OLS for one of the DVs of interest, z_{Y1}. From this regression analysis the predicted scores $\hat{z}_{Y1}$ are saved, which, of course, consist of the sum of the β_i weighted z_i scores. This score is then subtracted from another standardized IV of interest (e.g., z_{Y2}). This score, $z_{Y2} - \hat{z}_{Y1}$, is then used as the dependent variable in a regression analysis of the same original standardized IVs. The overall test of the statistical significance of R^2 indicates whether the two DVs have different relationships to the IVs collectively, and the tests of the individual β_is tell which coefficients differ significantly, and in which direction.

Appendix Tables

t Values for $\alpha = .01, .05$ (Two Tailed)[a]

df	α .01	α .05	df	α .01	α .05
6	3.707	2.447	36	2.720	2.028
7	3.499	2.365	37	2.715	2.026
8	3.355	2.306	38	2.712	2.024
9	3.250	2.262	39	2.708	2.023
10	3.169	2.228	40	2.704	2.021
11	3.106	2.201	42	2.698	2.018
12	3.055	2.179	44	2.692	2.015
13	3.012	2.160	46	2.687	2.013
14	2.977	2.145	48	2.682	2.011
15	2.947	2.131	50	2.678	2.009
16	2.921	2.120	52	2.674	2.007
17	2.898	2.110	54	2.670	2.005
18	2.878	2.101	56	2.666	2.003
19	2.861	2.093	58	2.663	2.002
20	2.845	2.086	60	2.660	2.000
21	2.831	2.080	64	2.655	1.998
22	2.819	2.074	68	2.650	1.996
23	2.807	2.069	72	2.646	1.994
24	2.797	2.064	76	2.642	1.992
25	2.787	2.060	80	2.639	1.990
26	2.779	2.056	90	2.632	1.987
27	2.771	2.052	100	2.626	1.984
28	2.763	2.048	120	2.617	1.980
29	2.756	2.045	150	2.609	1.976
30	2.750	2.042	200	2.601	1.972
31	2.744	2.040	300	2.592	1.968
32	2.738	2.037	400	2.588	1.966
33	2.733	2.034	600	2.584	1.964
34	2.728	2.032	1000	2.581	1.962
35	2.724	2.030	∞	2.576	1.960

[a]This table is abridged from Table 2.1 in Owen (1962). (Courtesy of AEC.)

TABLE B
z′ Transformation of r

r	z′	r	z′	r	z′	r	z′
.00	.000	.30	.310	.60	.693	.850	1.256
.01	.010	.31	.321	.61	.709	.855	1.274
.02	.020	.32	.332	.62	.725	.860	1.293
.03	.030	.33	.343	.63	.741	.865	1.313
.04	.040	.34	.354	.64	.758	.870	1.333
.05	.050	.35	.365	.65	.775	.875	1.354
.06	.060	.36	.377	.66	.793	.880	1.376
.07	.070	.37	.388	.67	.811	.885	1.398
.08	.080	.38	.400	.68	.829	.890	1.422
.09	.090	.39	.412	.69	.848	.895	1.447
.10	.100	.40	.424	.70	.867	.900	1.472
.11	.110	.41	.436	.71	.887	.905	1.499
.12	.121	.42	.448	.72	.908	.910	1.528
.13	.131	.43	.460	.73	.929	.915	1.557
.14	.141	.44	.472	.74	.950	.920	1.589
.15	.151	.45	.485	.75	.973	.925	1.623
.16	.161	.46	.497	.76	.996	.930	1.658
.17	.172	.47	.510	.77	1.020	.935	1.697
.18	.182	.48	.523	.78	1.045	.940	1.738
.19	.192	.49	.536	.79	1.071	.945	1.783
.20	.203	.50	.549	.800	1.099	.950	1.832
.21	.213	.51	.563	.805	1.113	.955	1.886
.22	.224	.52	.576	.810	1.127	.960	1.946
.23	.234	.53	.590	.815	1.142	.965	2.014
.24	.245	.54	.604	.820	1.157	.970	2.092
.25	.255	.55	.618	.825	1.172	.975	2.185
.26	.266	.56	.633	.830	1.188	.980	2.298
.27	.277	.57	.648	.835	1.204	.985	2.443
.28	.288	.58	.662	.840	1.221	.990	2.647
.29	.299	.59	.678	.845	1.238	.995	2.994

TABLE C
Normal Distribution[a]

z	P	h	z	P	h	z	P	h
.00	.500	.399	1.25	.106	.183	2.50	.006	.018
.05	.480	.398	1.30	.097	.171	2.55	.005	.015
.10	.460	.397	1.35	.089	.160	2.60	.005	.014
.15	.440	.394	1.40	.081	.150	2.65	.004	.012
.20	.421	.391	1.45	.074	.139	2.70	.003	.010
.25	.401	.387	1.50	.067	.130	2.75	.003	.009
.30	.382	.381	1.55	.061	.120	2.80	.003	.008
.35	.363	.375	1.60	.055	.111	2.85	.002	.007
.40	.345	.368	1.65	.049	.102	2.90	.002	.006
.45	.326	.361	1.70	.045	.094	2.95	.002	.005
.50	.309	.352	1.75	.040	.086	3.00	.0014	.0044
.55	.291	.343	1.80	.036	.079	3.50	.0002	.0009
.60	.274	.333	1.85	.032	.072	4.00	.0000	.0001
.65	.258	.323	1.90	.029	.066	4.50	.0000	.0000
.70	.242	.312	1.95	.026	.060			
						Fractiles		
.75	.227	.301	2.00	.023	.054	.253	.40	.386
.80	.212	.290	2.05	.020	.049	.431	.333	.364
.85	.198	.278	2.10	.018	.044	.524	.30	.348
.90	.184	.266	2.15	.016	.040	.674	.25	.318
.95	.171	.254	2.20	.014	.035	.842	.20	.280
1.00	.159	.242	2.25	.012	.032	1.282	.10	.176
1.05	.147	.230	2.30	.011	.028	1.645	.05	.103
1.10	.136	.218	2.35	.009	.025	1.960	.025	.058
1.15	.125	.206	2.40	.008	.022	2.326	.01	.027
1.20	.115	.194	2.45	.007	.020	2.576	.005	.014

[a]This table is abridged from Tables 1.1, 1.2, and 1.3 in Owen (1962). (Courtesy of AEC.)

TABLE D.1
F Values for $\alpha = .01$[a]

$df_{den.}$	$df_{num.}$												
	1	2	3	4	5	6	7	8	9	10	11	12	13
15	8.68	6.36	5.42	4.89	4.56	4.32	4.14	4.00	3.89	3.80	3.73	3.67	3.61
16	8.53	6.23	5.29	4.77	4.44	4.20	4.03	3.89	3.78	3.69	3.62	3.55	3.50
17	8.40	6.11	5.18	4.67	4.34	4.10	3.93	3.79	3.68	3.59	3.52	3.46	3.40
18	8.29	6.01	5.09	4.58	4.25	4.01	3.84	3.71	3.60	3.51	3.43	3.37	3.32
19	8.18	5.93	5.01	4.50	4.17	3.94	3.77	3.63	3.52	3.43	3.36	3.30	3.24
20	8.10	5.85	4.94	4.43	4.10	3.87	3.70	3.56	3.46	3.37	3.29	3.23	3.18
21	8.02	5.78	4.87	4.37	4.04	3.81	3.64	3.51	3.40	3.31	3.24	3.17	3.12
22	7.95	5.72	4.82	4.31	3.99	3.76	3.59	3.45	3.35	3.26	3.18	3.12	3.07
23	7.88	5.66	4.76	4.26	3.94	3.71	3.54	3.41	3.30	3.21	3.14	3.07	3.02
24	7.82	5.61	4.72	4.22	3.90	3.67	3.50	3.36	3.26	3.17	3.09	3.03	2.98
25	7.77	5.57	4.68	4.18	3.86	3.63	3.46	3.32	3.22	3.13	3.06	2.99	2.94
26	7.72	5.53	4.64	4.14	3.82	3.59	3.42	3.29	3.18	3.09	3.02	2.96	2.90
27	7.68	5.49	4.60	4.11	3.78	3.56	3.39	3.26	3.15	3.06	2.99	2.93	2.87
28	7.64	5.45	4.57	4.07	3.75	3.53	3.36	3.23	3.12	3.03	2.96	2.90	2.84
29	7.60	5.42	4.54	4.04	3.73	3.50	3.33	3.20	3.09	3.00	2.93	2.87	2.81
30	7.56	5.39	4.51	4.02	3.70	3.47	3.30	3.17	3.07	2.98	2.90	2.84	2.79
32	7.50	5.34	4.46	3.97	3.65	3.43	3.26	3.13	3.02	2.93	2.86	2.80	2.74
34	7.45	5.29	4.42	3.93	3.61	3.39	3.22	3.09	2.98	2.90	2.82	2.76	2.70
36	7.40	5.25	4.38	3.89	3.58	3.35	3.18	3.05	2.95	2.86	2.79	2.72	2.67
38	7.35	5.21	4.34	3.86	3.54	3.32	3.15	3.02	2.92	2.83	2.75	2.69	2.64
40	7.31	5.18	4.31	3.83	3.51	3.29	3.12	2.99	2.89	2.80	2.73	2.66	2.61
42	7.28	5.15	4.29	3.80	3.49	3.27	3.10	2.97	2.86	2.78	2.70	2.64	2.59
44	7.25	5.12	4.26	3.78	3.47	3.24	3.08	2.95	2.84	2.75	2.68	2.62	2.56
46	7.22	5.10	4.24	3.76	3.45	3.22	3.06	2.93	2.82	2.73	2.66	2.60	2.54
48	7.20	5.08	4.22	3.74	3.43	3.20	3.04	2.91	2.80	2.72	2.64	2.58	2.53
50	7.17	5.06	4.20	3.72	3.41	3.19	3.02	2.89	2.79	2.70	2.63	2.56	2.51
55	7.12	5.01	4.16	3.68	3.37	3.15	2.98	2.85	2.75	2.66	2.59	2.53	2.47
60	7.08	4.98	4.13	3.65	3.34	3.12	2.95	2.82	2.72	2.63	2.56	2.50	2.44
65	7.04	4.95	4.10	3.62	3.31	3.09	2.93	2.80	2.69	2.61	2.53	2.47	2.42
70	6.98	4.92	4.08	3.60	3.29	3.07	2.91	2.78	2.67	2.59	2.51	2.45	2.40
80	6.96	4.88	4.04	3.56	3.26	3.04	2.87	2.74	2.64	2.55	2.48	2.42	2.36
90	6.93	4.85	4.01	3.54	3.23	3.01	2.85	2.72	2.61	2.53	2.45	2.39	2.33
100	6.90	4.82	3.98	3.51	3.21	2.99	2.82	2.69	2.59	2.50	2.43	2.37	2.31
120	6.85	4.79	3.95	3.48	3.17	2.96	2.79	2.66	2.56	2.47	2.40	2.34	2.28
150	6.81	4.75	3.92	3.45	3.14	2.93	2.76	2.63	2.53	2.44	2.37	2.31	2.25
200	6.76	4.71	3.88	3.42	3.11	2.89	2.73	2.60	2.50	2.41	2.34	2.28	2.22
300	6.72	4.68	3.85	3.38	3.08	2.86	2.70	2.57	2.47	2.38	2.31	2.25	2.19
400	6.70	4.66	3.83	3.37	3.06	2.85	2.69	2.56	2.45	2.37	2.29	2.23	2.17
1000	6.66	4.63	3.80	3.34	3.04	2.82	2.66	2.53	2.43	2.34	2.26	2.20	2.15
∞	6.63	4.61	3.78	3.32	3.02	2.80	2.64	2.51	2.41	2.32	2.25	2.18	2.13

						$df_{num.}$							
14	15	16	18	20	24	30	40	50	60	80	120	∞
3.56	3.52	3.48	3.42	3.37	3.29	3.21	3.13	3.08	3.05	3.00	2.96	2.87
3.45	3.41	3.37	3.31	3.26	3.18	3.10	3.02	2.97	2.93	2.84	2.84	2.75
3.35	3.31	3.27	3.21	3.16	3.08	3.00	2.92	2.87	2.83	2.79	2.75	2.65
3.27	3.23	3.19	3.13	3.08	3.00	2.92	2.84	2.78	2.75	2.70	2.66	2.57
3.19	3.15	3.12	3.05	3.00	2.92	2.84	2.76	2.71	2.67	2.63	2.58	2.49
3.13	3.09	3.05	2.99	2.94	2.86	2.78	2.69	2.64	2.61	2.56	2.52	2.42
3.07	3.03	2.99	2.93	2.88	2.80	2.72	2.64	2.58	2.55	2.50	2.46	2.36
3.02	2.98	2.94	2.88	2.83	2.75	2.67	2.58	2.53	2.50	2.45	2.40	2.31
2.97	2.93	2.89	2.83	2.78	2.70	2.62	2.54	2.48	2.45	2.40	2.35	2.26
2.93	2.89	2.85	2.79	2.74	2.66	2.58	2.49	2.44	2.40	2.36	2.31	2.21
2.89	2.85	2.81	2.75	2.70	2.62	2.54	2.45	2.40	2.36	2.32	2.27	2.17
2.86	2.82	2.78	2.71	2.66	2.58	2.50	2.42	2.36	2.33	2.28	2.23	2.13
2.82	2.78	2.74	2.68	2.63	2.55	2.47	2.38	2.33	2.29	2.25	2.20	2.10
2.79	2.75	2.72	2.65	2.60	2.52	2.44	2.35	2.30	2.26	2.22	2.17	2.06
2.77	2.73	2.69	2.62	2.57	2.49	2.41	2.33	2.27	2.23	2.19	2.14	2.03
2.74	2.70	2.66	2.60	2.55	2.47	2.39	2.30	2.24	2.21	2.16	2.11	2.01
2.70	2.66	2.62	2.55	2.50	2.42	2.34	2.25	2.20	2.16	2.11	2.06	1.96
2.66	2.62	2.58	2.51	2.46	2.38	2.30	2.21	2.16	2.12	2.07	2.02	1.91
2.62	2.58	2.54	2.48	2.43	2.35	2.26	2.18	2.12	2.08	2.03	1.98	1.87
2.59	2.55	2.51	2.45	2.40	2.32	2.23	2.14	2.09	2.05	2.00	1.95	1.84
2.56	2.52	2.48	2.42	2.37	2.29	2.20	2.11	2.06	2.02	1.97	1.92	1.80
2.54	2.50	2.46	2.40	2.34	2.26	2.18	2.09	2.03	1.99	1.94	1.89	1.78
2.52	2.48	2.44	2.37	2.32	2.24	2.16	2.07	2.01	1.97	1.92	1.87	1.75
2.50	2.46	2.42	2.35	2.30	2.22	2.14	2.05	1.99	1.95	1.90	1.84	1.72
2.48	2.44	2.40	2.33	2.28	2.20	2.12	2.03	1.97	1.93	1.87	1.82	1.70
2.46	2.42	2.38	2.32	2.27	2.18	2.10	2.01	1.95	1.91	1.86	1.80	1.68
2.42	2.38	2.34	2.28	2.23	2.15	2.06	1.97	1.91	1.87	1.82	1.76	1.64
2.39	2.35	2.31	2.25	2.20	2.12	2.03	1.94	1.88	1.84	1.78	1.73	1.60
2.37	2.33	2.29	2.22	2.17	2.09	2.00	1.91	1.85	1.81	1.75	1.70	1.57
2.35	2.31	2.27	2.20	2.15	2.07	1.98	1.89	1.83	1.78	1.73	1.67	1.54
2.31	2.27	2.23	2.17	2.12	2.03	1.94	1.85	1.79	1.75	1.69	1.63	1.49
2.29	2.25	2.21	2.14	2.09	2.01	1.92	1.82	1.76	1.72	1.66	1.60	1.45
2.26	2.22	2.18	2.12	2.07	1.98	1.89	1.80	1.73	1.69	1.63	1.57	1.43
2.23	2.19	2.15	2.09	2.03	1.95	1.86	1.76	1.70	1.66	1.59	1.53	1.37
2.20	2.16	2.12	2.06	2.00	1.92	1.83	1.73	1.66	1.62	1.56	1.49	1.33
2.17	2.13	2.09	2.02	1.97	1.89	1.79	1.69	1.63	1.58	1.52	1.45	1.28
2.14	2.10	2.06	1.99	1.94	1.85	1.76	1.66	1.59	1.55	1.48	1.41	1.22
2.13	2.08	2.04	1.98	1.93	1.84	1.75	1.64	1.57	1.53	1.46	1.39	1.19
2.10	2.06	2.02	1.95	1.90	1.81	1.72	1.61	1.54	1.49	1.42	1.35	1.11
2.08	2.04	2.00	1.93	1.88	1.79	1.70	1.59	1.52	1.47	1.40	1.32	1.00

[a]This table is partly abridged from Table 4.1 in Owen (1962), and partly computed by linear interpolations in reciprocals of *df*. (Courtesy of AEC.)

TABLE D.2
F Values for $\alpha = .05^a$

$df_{den.}$	$df_{num.}$ 1	2	3	4	5	6	7	8	9	10	11	12	13
15	4.54	3.68	3.29	3.06	2.90	2.79	2.71	2.64	2.59	2.54	2.51	2.48	2.45
16	4.49	3.63	3.24	3.01	2.85	2.74	2.66	2.59	2.54	2.49	2.46	2.42	2.40
17	4.45	3.59	3.20	2.96	2.81	2.70	2.61	2.55	2.49	2.45	2.41	2.38	2.35
18	4.41	3.55	3.16	2.93	2.77	2.66	2.58	2.51	2.46	2.41	2.37	2.34	2.31
19	4.38	3.52	3.13	2.90	2.74	2.63	2.54	2.48	2.42	2.38	2.34	2.31	2.28
20	4.35	3.49	3.10	2.87	2.71	2.60	2.51	2.45	2.39	2.35	2.31	2.28	2.25
21	4.32	3.47	3.07	2.84	2.68	2.57	2.49	2.42	2.37	2.32	2.28	2.25	2.22
22	4.30	3.44	3.05	2.82	2.66	2.55	2.46	2.40	2.34	2.30	2.26	2.23	2.20
23	4.28	3.42	3.03	2.80	2.64	2.53	2.44	2.38	2.32	2.27	2.24	2.20	2.17
24	4.26	3.40	3.01	2.78	2.62	2.51	2.42	2.36	2.30	2.25	2.22	2.18	2.15
25	4.24	3.39	2.99	2.76	2.60	2.49	2.40	2.34	2.28	2.24	2.20	2.16	2.14
26	4.23	3.37	2.98	2.74	2.59	2.47	2.39	2.32	2.27	2.22	2.18	2.15	2.12
27	4.21	3.35	2.96	2.73	2.57	2.46	2.37	2.31	2.25	2.20	2.16	2.13	2.10
28	4.20	3.34	2.95	2.71	2.56	2.45	2.36	2.29	2.24	2.19	2.15	2.12	2.09
29	4.18	3.33	2.93	2.70	2.55	2.43	2.35	2.28	2.22	2.18	2.14	2.10	2.07
30	4.17	3.32	2.92	2.69	2.53	2.42	2.33	2.27	2.21	2.16	2.13	2.09	2.06
32	4.15	3.30	2.90	2.67	2.51	2.40	2.31	2.24	2.19	2.14	2.10	2.07	2.04
34	4.13	3.28	2.88	2.65	2.49	2.38	2.29	2.23	2.17	2.12	2.08	2.05	2.02
36	4.11	3.26	2.87	2.63	2.48	2.36	2.28	2.21	2.15	2.11	2.07	2.03	2.00
38	4.10	3.24	2.85	2.62	2.46	2.35	2.26	2.19	2.14	2.09	2.05	2.02	1.99
40	4.08	3.23	2.84	2.61	2.45	2.34	2.25	2.18	2.12	2.08	2.04	2.00	1.97
42	4.07	3.22	2.83	2.59	2.44	2.32	2.24	2.17	2.11	2.07	2.02	1.99	1.96
44	4.06	3.21	2.82	2.58	2.43	2.31	2.23	2.16	2.10	2.05	2.01	1.98	1.95
46	4.05	3.20	2.81	2.57	2.42	2.30	2.22	2.15	2.09	2.04	2.00	1.97	1.94
48	4.04	3.19	2.80	2.57	2.41	2.30	2.21	2.14	2.08	2.03	1.99	1.96	1.93
50	4.03	3.18	2.79	2.56	2.40	2.29	2.20	2.13	2.07	2.03	1.99	1.95	1.92
55	4.02	3.17	2.77	2.54	2.38	2.27	2.18	2.11	2.06	2.01	1.97	1.93	1.90
60	4.00	3.15	2.76	2.53	2.37	2.25	2.17	2.10	2.04	1.99	1.95	1.92	1.89
65	3.99	3.14	2.75	2.51	2.36	2.24	2.15	2.08	2.03	1.98	1.94	1.90	1.87
70	3.98	3.13	2.74	2.50	2.35	2.23	2.14	2.07	2.02	1.97	1.93	1.89	1.86
80	3.96	3.11	2.72	2.49	2.33	2.21	2.13	2.06	2.00	1.95	1.91	1.88	1.84
90	3.95	3.10	2.71	2.47	2.32	2.20	2.11	2.04	1.99	1.94	1.90	1.86	1.83
100	3.94	3.09	2.70	2.46	2.31	2.19	2.10	2.03	1.98	1.93	1.89	1.85	1.82
120	3.92	3.07	2.68	2.45	2.29	2.18	2.09	2.02	1.96	1.91	1.87	1.83	1.80
150	3.90	3.06	2.67	2.43	2.27	2.16	2.07	2.00	1.94	1.89	1.85	1.82	1.79
200	3.89	3.04	2.65	2.42	2.26	2.14	2.06	1.99	1.93	1.88	1.84	1.80	1.77
300	3.87	3.03	2.64	2.40	2.24	2.13	2.04	1.97	1.91	1.86	1.82	1.79	1.75
400	3.86	3.02	2.63	2.39	2.23	2.12	2.03	1.96	1.90	1.85	1.81	1.78	1.74
1000	3.85	3.00	2.61	2.38	2.22	2.11	2.02	1.95	1.89	1.84	1.80	1.76	1.73
∞	3.84	3.00	2.60	2.37	2.21	2.10	2.01	1.94	1.88	1.83	1.79	1.75	1.72

TABLE D.2
(*Continued*)

					$df_{\text{num.}}$								
14	15	16	18	20	24	30	40	50	60	80	120	∞
2.42	2.40	2.38	2.35	2.33	2.29	2.25	2.20	2.18	2.16	2.14	2.11	2.07
2.37	2.35	2.33	2.30	2.28	2.24	2.19	2.15	2.12	2.11	2.08	2.06	2.01
2.33	2.31	2.29	2.26	2.23	2.19	2.15	2.10	2.08	2.06	2.03	2.01	1.96
2.29	2.27	2.25	2.22	2.19	2.15	2.11	2.06	2.04	2.02	1.99	1.97	1.92
2.26	2.23	2.21	2.18	2.16	2.11	2.07	2.03	2.00	1.98	1.95	1.93	1.88
2.23	2.20	2.18	2.15	2.12	2.08	2.04	1.99	1.97	1.95	1.92	1.90	1.84
2.20	2.18	2.16	2.12	2.10	2.05	2.01	1.96	1.94	1.92	1.89	1.87	1.81
2.17	2.15	2.13	2.10	2.07	2.03	1.98	1.94	1.91	1.89	1.86	1.84	1.78
2.15	2.13	2.11	2.07	2.05	2.00	1.96	1.91	1.88	1.86	1.84	1.81	1.76
2.13	2.11	2.09	2.05	2.03	1.98	1.94	1.89	1.86	1.84	1.82	1.79	1.73
2.11	2.09	2.07	2.03	2.01	1.96	1.92	1.87	1.84	1.82	1.80	1.77	1.71
2.09	2.07	2.05	2.02	1.99	1.95	1.90	1.85	1.82	1.80	1.78	1.75	1.69
2.08	2.06	2.04	2.00	1.97	1.93	1.88	1.84	1.81	1.79	1.76	1.73	1.67
2.06	2.04	2.02	1.99	1.96	1.91	1.87	1.82	1.79	1.77	1.74	1.71	1.65
2.05	2.03	2.01	1.97	1.94	1.90	1.85	1.81	1.77	1.75	1.73	1.70	1.64
2.04	2.01	1.99	1.96	1.93	1.89	1.84	1.79	1.76	1.74	1.71	1.68	1.62
2.02	1.99	1.97	1.94	1.91	1.86	1.82	1.77	1.74	1.71	1.69	1.66	1.59
2.00	1.97	1.95	1.92	1.89	1.84	1.80	1.75	1.71	1.69	1.66	1.63	1.57
1.98	1.95	1.93	1.90	1.87	1.82	1.78	1.73	1.69	1.67	1.64	1.61	1.55
1.96	1.94	1.92	1.88	1.85	1.81	1.76	1.71	1.68	1.65	1.62	1.59	1.53
1.95	1.92	1.90	1.87	1.84	1.79	1.74	1.69	1.66	1.64	1.61	1.58	1.51
1.93	1.91	1.89	1.85	1.83	1.78	1.73	1.68	1.65	1.62	1.59	1.56	1.49
1.92	1.90	1.88	1.84	1.81	1.77	1.72	1.67	1.63	1.61	1.58	1.55	1.48
1.91	1.89	1.87	1.83	1.80	1.76	1.71	1.65	1.62	1.60	1.57	1.53	1.46
1.90	1.88	1.86	1.82	1.79	1.75	1.70	1.64	1.61	1.59	1.55	1.52	1.45
1.89	1.87	1.85	1.81	1.78	1.74	1.69	1.63	1.60	1.58	1.54	1.51	1.44
1.88	1.85	1.83	1.79	1.76	1.72	1.67	1.61	1.58	1.55	1.52	1.49	1.41
1.86	1.84	1.81	1.78	1.75	1.70	1.65	1.59	1.56	1.53	1.50	1.47	1.39
1.85	1.82	1.80	1.76	1.73	1.69	1.63	1.58	1.54	1.52	1.48	1.45	1.37
1.84	1.81	1.79	1.75	1.72	1.67	1.62	1.56	1.53	1.50	1.47	1.44	1.35
1.82	1.79	1.77	1.73	1.70	1.65	1.60	1.54	1.51	1.48	1.45	1.41	1.32
1.80	1.78	1.76	1.72	1.69	1.64	1.59	1.53	1.49	1.46	1.43	1.39	1.30
1.79	1.77	1.74	1.71	1.68	1.63	1.57	1.52	1.48	1.45	1.41	1.37	1.28
1.77	1.75	1.73	1.69	1.66	1.61	1.55	1.50	1.46	1.43	1.39	1.35	1.25
1.76	1.73	1.71	1.67	1.64	1.59	1.54	1.47	1.43	1.41	1.37	1.33	1.22
1.74	1.72	1.69	1.65	1.62	1.57	1.52	1.45	1.41	1.38	1.34	1.30	1.19
1.73	1.70	1.68	1.64	1.61	1.55	1.50	1.43	1.39	1.36	1.32	1.27	1.15
1.72	1.69	1.67	1.63	1.60	1.54	1.49	1.42	1.38	1.35	1.31	1.26	1.13
1.70	1.68	1.65	1.61	1.58	1.53	1.47	1.41	1.36	1.33	1.28	1.24	1.08
1.69	1.67	1.64	1.60	1.57	1.52	1.46	1.39	1.35	1.32	1.27	1.22	1.00

[a]This table is partly abridged from Table 4.1 in Owen (1962), and partly computed by linear interpolation in reciprocals of *df*. (Courtesy of AEC.)

TABLE E.1
L Values for $\alpha = .01$

| k_B | \multicolumn{11}{c}{Power} |
	.10	.30	.50	.60	.70	.75	.80	.85	.90	.95	.99
1	1.67	4.21	6.64	8.00	9.61	10.57	11.68	13.05	14.88	17.81	24.03
2	2.30	5.37	8.19	9.75	11.57	12.64	13.88	15.40	17.43	20.65	27.42
3	2.76	6.22	9.31	11.01	12.97	14.12	15.46	17.09	19.25	22.67	29.83
4	3.15	6.92	10.23	12.04	14.12	15.34	16.75	18.47	20.74	24.33	31.80
5	3.49	7.52	11.03	12.94	15.12	16.40	17.87	19.66	22.03	25.76	33.50
6	3.79	8.07	11.75	13.74	16.01	17.34	18.87	20.73	23.18	27.04	35.02
7	4.08	8.57	12.41	14.47	16.83	18.20	19.79	21.71	24.24	28.21	36.41
8	4.34	9.03	13.02	15.15	17.59	19.00	20.64	22.61	25.21	29.29	37.69
9	4.58	9.47	13.59	15.79	18.30	19.75	21.43	23.46	26.12	30.31	38.89
10	4.82	9.88	14.13	16.39	18.97	20.46	22.18	24.25	26.98	31.26	40.02
11	5.04	10.27	14.64	16.96	19.60	21.13	22.89	25.01	27.80	32.16	41.09
12	5.25	10.64	15.13	17.51	20.21	21.77	23.56	25.73	28.58	33.02	42.11
13	5.45	11.00	15.59	18.03	20.78	22.38	24.21	26.42	29.32	33.85	43.09
14	5.65	11.35	16.04	18.53	21.34	22.97	24.83	27.09	30.03	34.64	44.03
15	5.84	11.67	16.48	19.01	21.88	23.53	25.43	27.72	30.72	35.40	44.93
16	6.02	12.00	16.90	19.48	22.40	24.08	26.01	28.34	31.39	36.14	45.80
18	6.37	12.61	17.70	20.37	23.39	25.12	27.12	29.52	32.66	37.54	47.46
20	6.70	13.19	18.45	21.21	24.32	26.11	28.16	30.63	33.85	38.87	49.03
22	7.02	13.74	19.17	22.01	25.21	27.05	29.15	31.69	34.99	40.12	50.51
24	7.32	14.27	19.86	22.78	26.06	27.94	30.10	32.69	36.07	41.32	51.93
28	7.89	15.26	21.15	24.21	27.65	29.62	31.88	34.59	38.11	43.58	54.60
32	8.42	16.19	22.35	25.55	29.13	31.19	33.53	36.35	40.01	45.67	57.07
36	8.92	17.06	23.48	26.80	30.52	32.65	35.09	38.00	41.78	47.63	59.39
40	9.39	17.88	24.54	27.99	31.84	34.04	36.55	39.56	43.46	49.49	61.57
50	10.48	19.77	27.00	30.72	34.86	37.23	39.92	43.14	47.31	53.74	66.59
60	11.46	21.48	29.21	33.18	37.59	40.10	42.96	46.38	50.79	57.58	71.12
70	12.37	23.05	31.25	35.45	40.10	42.75	45.76	49.35	53.99	61.11	75.27
80	13.22	24.51	33.15	37.55	42.43	45.21	48.36	52.11	56.96	64.39	79.13
90	14.01	25.89	34.93	39.53	44.62	47.52	50.80	54.71	59.75	67.47	82.76
100	14.76	27.19	36.62	41.41	46.70	49.70	53.11	57.16	62.38	70.37	86.18

TABLE E.2
L Values for $\alpha = .05$

k_B						Power					
	.10	.30	.50	.60	.70	.75	.80	.85	.90	.95	.99
1	.43	2.06	3.84	4.90	6.17	6.94	7.85	8.98	10.51	13.00	18.37
2	.62	2.78	4.96	6.21	7.70	8.59	9.64	10.92	12.65	15.44	21.40
3	.78	3.30	5.76	7.15	8.79	9.77	10.90	12.30	14.17	17.17	23.52
4	.91	3.74	6.42	7.92	9.68	10.72	11.94	13.42	15.41	18.57	25.24
5	1.03	4.12	6.99	8.59	10.45	11.55	12.83	14.39	16.47	19.78	26.73
6	1.13	4.46	7.50	9.19	11.14	12.29	13.62	15.26	17.42	20.86	28.05
7	1.23	4.77	7.97	9.73	11.77	12.96	14.35	16.04	18.28	21.84	29.25
8	1.32	5.06	8.41	10.24	12.35	13.59	15.02	16.77	19.08	22.74	30.36
9	1.40	5.33	8.81	10.71	12.89	14.17	15.65	17.45	19.83	23.59	31.39
10	1.49	5.59	9.19	11.15	13.40	14.72	16.24	18.09	20.53	24.39	32.37
11	1.56	5.83	9.56	11.58	13.89	15.24	16.80	18.70	21.20	25.14	33.29
12	1.64	6.06	9.90	11.98	14.35	15.74	17.34	19.28	21.83	25.86	34.16
13	1.71	6.29	10.24	12.36	14.80	16.21	17.85	19.83	22.44	26.55	35.00
14	1.78	6.50	10.55	12.73	15.22	16.67	18.34	20.36	23.02	27.20	35.11
15	1.84	6.71	10.86	13.09	15.63	17.11	18.81	20.87	23.58	27.84	36.58
16	1.90	6.91	11.16	13.43	16.03	17.53	19.27	21.37	24.13	28.45	37.33
18	2.03	7.29	11.73	14.09	16.78	18.34	20.14	22.31	25.16	29.62	38.76
20	2.14	7.65	12.26	14.71	17.50	19.11	20.96	23.20	26.13	30.72	40.10
22	2.25	8.00	12.77	15.30	18.17	19.83	21.74	24.04	27.06	31.77	41.37
24	2.36	8.33	13.02	15.87	18.82	20.53	22.49	24.85	27.94	32.76	42.59
28	2.56	8.94	14.17	16.93	20.04	21.83	23.89	26.36	29.60	34.64	44.87
32	2.74	9.52	15.02	17.91	21.17	23.04	25.19	27.77	31.14	36.37	46.98
36	2.91	10.06	15.82	18.84	22.23	24.18	26.41	29.09	32.58	38.00	48.96
40	3.08	10.57	16.58	19.71	23.23	25.25	27.56	30.33	33.94	39.54	50.83
50	3.46	11.75	18.31	21.72	25.53	27.71	30.20	33.19	37.07	43.07	55.12
60	3.80	12.81	19.88	23.53	27.61	29.94	32.59	35.77	39.89	46.25	58.98
70	4.12	13.79	21.32	25.20	29.52	31.98	34.79	38.14	42.48	49.17	62.13
80	4.41	14.70	22.67	26.75	31.29	33.88	36.83	40.35	44.89	51.89	65.83
90	4.69	15.56	23.93	28.21	32.96	35.67	38.75	42.14	47.16	54.44	68.92
100	4.95	16.37	25.12	29.59	34.54	37.36	40.56	44.37	49.29	56.85	71.84

TABLE F.1
Power of Significance Test of r at $\alpha = .01$ (Two Tailed)[a]

n	Population r .10	.20	.30	.40	.50	.60	.70	.80	.90	n	Population r .10	.20	.30	.40	.50	.60	.70	.80	.90
15	01	03	06	13	25	44	68	90	*	50	03	12	33	63	89	99	*	*	*
16	01	03	07	14	28	48	73	93		52	03	12	34	66	90	99			
17	01	03	08	16	30	52	77	95		54	03	13	36	68	91	99			
18	01	04	08	17	33	56	80	96		56	03	14	38	70	93	99			
19	02	04	09	19	36	59	83	97		58	03	14	39	72	94	*			
20	02	04	09	20	38	62	85	98		60	03	15	41	74	94				
21	02	04	10	21	41	66	88	98		64	04	16	44	77	96				
22	02	04	11	23	43	68	90	99		68	04	17	47	80	97				
23	02	04	12	25	46	71	91	99		72	04	19	50	83	98				
24	02	05	12	26	49	74	93	99		76	04	20	53	85	98				
25	02	05	13	28	51	76	94	*		80	04	21	56	87	99				
26	02	05	14	30	53	78	95			84	05	23	59	89	99				
27	02	06	14	31	55	80	96			88	05	24	61	91	99				
28	02	06	15	33	57	82	96			92	05	25	64	92	*				
29	02	06	16	34	60	84	97			96	05	27	66	94					
30	02	06	17	36	62	85	98			100	06	29	69	95					
31	02	07	17	37	64	87	98			120	07	35	78	98					
32	02	07	18	39	66	88	98			140	08	42	85	99					
33	02	07	19	40	67	89	99			160	09	49	90	*					
34	02	07	20	42	69	90	99			180	11	55	94						
35	02	08	20	43	71	91	99			200	12	61	96						
36	02	08	21	45	72	92	99			250	16	73	99						
37	02	08	22	47	74	93	99			300	20	82	*						
38	02	08	23	48	76	94	*			350	24	89							
39	02	09	24	49	77	95				400	28	93							
40	02	09	25	50	78	95				500	37	97							
42	03	09	26	53	81	96				600	45	99							
44	03	10	28	56	83	97				700	53	*							
46	03	11	29	58	85	98				800	60								
48	03	11	31	61	87	98				1000	72								

Note: Decimal points omitted in power values.

*Power values at and below this point exceed .995.

[a]Slightly abridged from Table 3.3.4 in Cohen (1977). Reproduced with the permission of the publisher.

TABLE F.2
Power of Significance Test of *r* at α = .05 (Two Tailed)[a]

n	\\ Population *r*									n	\\ Population *r*								
	.10	.20	.30	.40	.50	.60	.70	.80	.90		.10	.20	.30	.40	.50	.60	.70	.80	.90
15	06	11	19	32	50	70	88	98	*	50	11	29	57	83	97	*	*	*	*
16	07	11	21	35	53	73	90	98		52	11	30	59	85	97				
17	07	12	22	37	56	76	92	99		54	11	31	61	86	98				
18	07	12	23	39	59	79	94	99		56	11	32	62	87	98				
19	07	13	24	41	62	81	95	99		58	12	33	64	89	98				
20	07	14	25	43	64	83	96	*		60	12	34	65	90	99				
21	07	14	27	45	66	85	96			64	12	36	68	91	99				
22	07	15	28	47	69	87	97			68	13	38	71	93	99				
23	07	15	29	49	71	89	98			72	13	39	73	94	*				
24	07	16	30	51	73	90	98			76	14	41	76	95					
25	08	16	31	53	75	91	99			80	14	43	78	96					
26	08	17	33	54	76	92	99			84	15	45	80	97					
27	08	17	34	56	78	93	99			88	15	47	82	98					
28	08	18	35	58	80	94	99			92	16	48	83	98					
29	08	18	36	59	81	95	99			96	16	50	85	98					
30	08	19	37	61	83	95	*			100	17	52	86	99					
31	08	19	38	62	84	96				120	19	59	92	*					
32	08	20	39	64	85	97				140	22	66	95						
33	09	20	40	65	86	97				160	24	72	97						
34	09	21	42	67	87	97				180	27	77	98						
35	09	21	43	68	88	98				200	29	81	99						
36	09	22	44	69	89	98				250	35	89	*						
37	09	22	45	70	90	98				300	41	94							
38	09	23	46	72	91	99				350	46	97							
39	09	23	47	73	91	99				400	52	98							
40	09	24	48	74	92	99				500	61	99							
42	10	25	50	76	93	99				600	69	*							
44	10	26	52	78	94	99				700	76								
46	10	27	54	80	95	*				800	81								
48	10	28	55	82	96					1000	89								

Note: Decimal points omitted in power values.

*Power values at and below this point exceed .995.

[a]Slightly abridged from Table 3.3.5 in Cohen (1977). Reproduced with the permission of the publisher.

TABLE G.1

n^* to Detect r by t Test at $\alpha = .01$ (Two Tailed)[a]

Desired power	Population r								
	.10	.20	.30	.40	.50	.60	.70	.80	.90
.25	362	90	40	23	15	11	8	6	5
.50	662	164	71	39	24	16	12	8	6
.60	797	197	86	47	29	19	13	9	7
2/3	901	222	96	53	32	21	15	10	7
.70	957	236	102	56	34	23	15	11	7
.75	1052	259	112	61	37	25	17	11	8
.80	1163	286	124	67	41	27	18	12	8
.85	1299	320	138	75	45	30	20	13	9
.90	1480	364	157	85	51	34	22	15	9
.95	1790	440	190	102	62	40	26	17	11
.99	2390	587	253	136	82	52	34	23	13

[a]Reproduced from Table 3.4.1 in Cohen (1977) with permission of the publisher.

TABLE G.2

n^* to Detect r by t Test at $\alpha = .05$ (Two Tailed)[a]

Desired power	Population r								
	.10	.20	.30	.40	.50	.60	.70	.80	.90
.25	166	42	20	12	8	6	5	4	3
.50	384	95	42	24	15	10	7	6	4
.60	489	121	53	29	18	12	9	6	5
2/3	570	141	62	34	21	14	10	7	5
.70	616	152	66	37	23	15	10	7	5
.75	692	171	74	41	25	17	11	8	6
.80	783	193	84	46	28	18	12	9	6
.85	895	221	96	52	32	21	14	10	6
.90	1046	258	112	61	37	24	16	11	7
.95	1308	322	139	75	46	30	19	13	8
.99	1828	449	194	104	63	40	27	18	11

[a]Reproduced from Table 3.4.1 in Cohen (1977) with permission of the publisher.

References

Abelson, R. P. (1995). *Statistics as principled argument*. Hillsdale, NJ: Erlbaum.

Abelson, R. P. (1997). On the surprising longevity of flogged horses: Why there is a case for significance tests. *Psychological Science, 23,* 12–15.

Abelson, R. P., & Prentice, D. A. (1997). Contrast tests of interaction hypotheses. *Psychological Methods, 2,* 315–328.

Aber, M. S., & McArdle, J. J. (1991). Latent growth curve approaches to modeling the development of competence. In M. Chandler & M. Chapman (Eds.), *Criteria for competence* (pp. 231–258). Hillsdale, NJ: Erlbaum.

Agresti, A. (1990). *Categorical data analysis*. New York: Wiley.

Aiken, L. S., & West, S. G. (1991). *Multiple regression: Testing and interpreting interactions*. Newbury Park, CA: Sage.

Aiken, L. S., & West, S. G. (2000, August). *Probing three-way interactions in multiple regression: Simple interaction tests*. Poster presented at American Psychological Association, Washington, DC.

Aiken, L. S., West, S. G., Woodward, C. K., & Reno, R. R. (1994). Health beliefs and compliance with mammography-screening recommendations in asymptomatic women. *Health Psychology, 13,* 122–129.

Aiken, L. S., West, S. G., Woodward, C. K., Reno, R. R., & Reynolds, K. D. (1994). Increasing screening mammography in asymptomatic women: Evaluation of a second-generation, theory-based program. *Health Psychology, 13,* 526–538.

Akaike, H. (1973). Information theory and an extension of the maximum likelihood principle. In B. N. Petrov & F. Csàki (Eds.), *Proceedings of the Second International Symposium on Information Theory* (pp. 267–281). Budapest: Akadémiai Kiadó.

Alastair, S., & Wild, C. (1991). Transformation and R^2. *American Statistician, 45,* 127–129.

Aldrich, J. H., & Nelson, F. D. (1984). *Linear probability, logit, and probit models*. Newbury Park, CA: Sage.

Anderson, R. L., & Houseman, E. E. (1942). *Tables of orthogonal polynomial values extended to N = 104* (Research Bulletin No. 297). Ames, IA: Agricultural Experiment Station.

Anderson, T. W. (1984). *An introduction to multivariate statistical analysis* (2nd ed.). New York: Wiley.

Anscombe, F. J. (1960). Rejection of outliers. *Technometrics, 2,* 123–147.

Atkinson, A. C. (1985). *Plots, transformations and regression: An introduction to graphical methods of diagnostic regression analysis*. Oxford: Clarendon Press.

Atkinson, A. C., & Donev, A. N. (1992). *Optimal experimental designs*. Oxford: Clarendon Press.

Baker, B., Hardyck, C. D., & Petrinovich, L. F. (1966). Weak measurements vs. strong statistics: An empirical critique of S. S. Steven's proscriptions on statistics. *Educational and Psychological Measurement, 26,* 291–309.

Baltes, P. B., & Nesselroade, J. R. (1979). History and rationale of longitudinal research. In J. R. Nesselroade & P. B. Baltes (Eds.), *Longitudinal research in the study of behavior and development* (pp. 1–39). New York: Academic Press.

Barcikowski, R. S. (1981). Statistical power with group mean as the units of analysis. *Journal of Educational Statistics, 6,* 267–285.

Baron, R. M., & Kenny, D. A. (1986). The moderator-mediator variable distinction in social psychological research: Conceptual, strategic, and statistical considerations. *Journal of Personality and Social Psychology, 51,* 1173–1182.

Beckman, R. J., & Cook, R. D. (1983). Outliers. *Technometrics, 25,* 119–163.

Behnken, D. W., & Draper, N. R. (1972). Residuals and their variance patterns. *Technometrics, 14,* 469–479.

Belsley, D. A. (1984). Demeaning conditioning diagnostics through centering. *American Statistician, 38,* 73–77.

Belsley, D. A. (1991). *Conditioning diagnostics: Collinearity and weak data in regression.* New York: Wiley.

Belsley, D. A., Kuh, E., & Welsch, R. E. (1980). *Regression diagnostics: Identifying influential data and sources of collinearity.* New York: Wiley.

Bentler, P. M. (1980). Multivariate analysis with latent variables: Causal modeling. *Annual Review of Psychology, 31,* 419–456.

Bentler, P. M. (1990). Comparative fit indexes in structural models. *Psychological Bulletin, 107,* 238–246.

Bentler, P. M., & Bonett, D. G. (1980). Significance tests and goodness of fit in the analysis of covariance structures. *Psychological Bulletin, 88,* 588–606.

Berk, R. A. (1988). Causal inference for sociological data. In N. H. Smelser (Ed.), *Handbook of sociology* (pp. 155–172). Newbury Park, CA: Sage.

Berkson, J. (1944). Application of the logistic function to bio-assay. *Journal of the American Statistical Association, 39,* 357–365.

Berkson, J. (1946). Limitations of the application of fourfold table analysis to hospital data. *Biometric Bulletin, 2,* 47–53.

Berry, W. D. (1993). *Understanding regression assumptions.* Newbury Park, CA: Sage.

Blalock, H. M., Jr. (1964). *Causal inferences in nonexperimental research.* Chapel Hill: University of North Carolina Press.

Blalock, H. M., Jr. (Ed.). (1971). *Causal models in the social sciences.* Chicago: Aldine-Atherton.

Blossfeld, H.-P., & Rohwer, G. (2002). *Techniques of event history modeling: New approaches to causal analysis* (2nd ed.). Mahway, NJ: Erlbaum.

Bohrnstedt, G. W., & Marwell, G. (1978). The reliability of products of two random variables. In K. F. Schuessler (Ed.), *Sociological methodology* (pp. 254–273). San Francisco: Jossey-Bass.

Boker, S. M. (2001). Differential structural equation modeling of intraindividual variability. In L. Collins & A. G. Sayer (Eds.), *New methods for the analysis of change* (pp. 5–27). Washington, DC: American Psychological Association Press.

Boker, S. M., Schreiber, T., Pompe, B., & Bertenthal, B. I. (1998). Nonlinear analysis of perceptual motor coupling in the development of postural control. In H. Kantz, J. Kurths, & G. Meyer-Kress (Eds.), *Nonlinear analysis of physiological data* (pp. 251–270). Berlin: Springer.

Bollen, K. A. (1989). *Structural equations with latent variables.* New York: Wiley.

Bollen, K. A., & Jackman, R. W. (1990). Regression diagnostics: An expository treatment of outliers and influential cases. In J. Fox & J. S. Long (Eds.), *Modern methods of data analysis* (pp. 257–291). Newbury Park, CA: Sage.

Bollen, K. A., & Long, J. S. (Eds.). (1993). *Testing structural equation models.* Newbury Park, CA: Sage.

Bollen, K. A., & Ting, K.-F. (2000). A tetrad test for causal indicators. *Psychological Methods, 5,* 3–22.

Borenstein, M., Rothstein, H., & Cohen, J. (2001). *Power and precision.* Englewood, NJ: Biostat.

Box, G. E. P., & Cox, D. R. (1964). An analysis of transformations (with discussion). *Journal of the Royal Statistical Society, B26,* 211–246.

Box, G. E. P., Jenkins, G. M., & Reinsel, G. C. (1994). *Time-series analysis: Forecasting and control* (3rd ed.). Oakland, CA: Holden-Day.

Box, G. E. P., & Tidwell, P. W. (1962). Transformation of the independent variables. *Technometrics, 4,* 531–550.

Breusch, T., & Pagan, A. (1979). A simple test for heteroscedasticity and random coefficient variation. *Econometrica, 47,* 1287–1294.

Brewer, M. (2000). Research design and issues of validity. In H. T. Reis & C. M. Judd (Eds.), *Handbook of research methods in social and personality psychology* (pp. 3–16). New York: Cambridge University Press.

Browne, M., & Cudeck, R. (1993). Alternative ways of assessing model fit. In K. A. Bollen & J. S. Long (Eds.), *Testing structural equation models* (pp. 132–162). Beverly Hills, CA: Sage.

Bryk, A. S., & Raudenbush, S. W. (1987). Application of hierarchical linear models to assessing change. *Psychological Bulletin, 101,* 147–158.

Bryk, A. S., & Raudenbush, S. W. (1992). *Hierarchical linear models: Applications and data analysis methods.* Newbury Park, CA: Sage.

Burstein, L. (1980). The analysis of multilevel data in educational research in evaluation. *Review of Research in Education, 8,* 158–233.

Busemeyer, J. R., & Jones, L. E. (1983). Analysis of multiplicative combination rules when the causal variables are measured with error. *Psychological Bulletin, 93,* 549–562.

Byrne, B. (1994). *Structural equation modeling with EQS and EQS/Windows: Basic concepts, applications, and programming.* Thousand Oaks, CA: Sage.

Byrne, B. (1998). *Structural equation modeling with LISREL, PRELIS, and SIMPLIS: Basic concepts, applications, and programming.* Mahwah, NJ: Erlbaum.

Byrne, B. (2000). *Structural equation modeling with AMOS.* Mahwah, NJ: Erlbaum.

Campbell, D. T., & Erlbacher, A. (1970). How regression artifacts in quasi-experimental evaluations can mistakenly make compensatory education look harmful. In J. Hellmuth (Ed.), *The disadvantaged child: Vol. 3, Compensatory education: A national debate* (pp. 185–210). New York: Brunner/Mazel.

Campbell, D. T., & Kenny, D. A. (1999). *A primer on regression artifacts.* New York: Guilford Press.

Campbell, D. T., & Stanley, J. C. (1966). *Experimental and quasi-experimental designs for research.* Boston: Houghton Mifflin.

Carmer, S. G., & Swanson, M. R. (1973). An evaluation of ten pairwise multiple comparison procedures by Monte Carlo methods. *Journal of the American Statistical Association, 68,* 66–74.

Carroll, R. J., & Ruppert, D. (1988). *Transformation and weighting in regression.* New York: Chapman & Hall.

Champoux, J. E., & Peters, W. S. (1987). Form, effect size, and power in moderated multiple regression. *Journal of Occupational Psychology, 17,* 585–605.

Chaplin W. F. (1991). The next generation of moderator research in personality psychology. *Journal of Personality, 59,* 143–178.

Chatfield, C. (1996). *The analysis of time series: An introduction* (5th ed.). London: Chapman & Hall.

Chatterjee, S., & Hadi, A. S. (1988). *Sensitivity analysis in regression.* New York: Wiley.

Chatterjee, S., & Price, B. (1991). *Regression analysis by example* (2nd ed.). New York: Wiley.

Chatterjee, S., & Wiseman, F. (1983). Use of regression diagnostics in political science research. *American Journal of Political Science, 27,* 601–613.

Cleary, P. D., & Kessler, R. C. (1982). The estimation and interpretation of modifier effects. *Journal of Health and Social Behavior, 23,* 159–169.

Cleveland, W. S. (1979). Robust locally weighted regression and smoothing scatterplots. *Journal of the American Statistical Association, 74,* 829–836.

Cleveland, W. S. (1993). *Visualizing data.* Summit, NJ: Hobart Press.

Cleveland, W. S. (1994). *The elements of graphing data* (2nd ed.). Summit, NJ: Hobart Press.

Cliff, N. (1982). What is and isn't measurement. In G. Keren (Ed.), *Statistical and methodological issues in psychology and social science research* (pp. 3–38). Hillsdale, NJ: Erlbaum.

Cliff, N. (1983). Some cautions regarding the applications of causal modeling methods. *Multivariate Behavioral Research, 18,* 115–126.

Cliff, N. (1996). *Ordinal methods for behavioral data analysis.* Mahwah, NJ: Erlbaum.

Cliff, N., & Krus, D. J. (1976). Interpretation of canonical analysis: Rotated versus unrotated solutions. *Psychometrika, 41,* 35–42.

Cochran, W. G. (1965). The planning of observational studies of human populations (with discussion). *Journal of the Royal Statistical Society,* Series A, *128,* 134–155.

Cohen, J. (1962). The statistical power of abnormal-social psychological research. *Journal of Abnormal and Social Psychology, 65,* 143–153.

Cohen, J. (1965). Some statistical issues in psychological research. In B. B. Wolman (Ed.), *Handbook of clinical psychology* (pp. 95–121). New York: McGraw-Hill.

Cohen, J. (1968a). Multiple regression as a general data-analytic system. *Psychological Bulletin, 70,* 426–443.

Cohen, J. (1968b). Weighted kappa: Nominal scale agreement with provision for scale disagreement or partial credit. *Psychological Bulletin, 70,* 213–220.

Cohen, J. (1978). Partialed products *are* interactions; partialed powers *are* curve components. *Psychological Bulletin, 85,* 858–866.

Cohen, J. (1980). Trend analysis the easy way. *Educational and Psychological Measurement, 40,* 565–568.

Cohen, J. (1983). The cost of dichotomization. *Applied Psychological Measurement, 7,* 249–253.

Cohen, J. (1988). *Statistical power analysis for the behavioral sciences* (2nd ed.). Mahwah, NJ: Erlbaum.

Cohen, J. (1990). Things I have learned (so far). *American Psychologist, 45,* 1304–1312.

Cohen, J. (1993). Set correlation. In G. Keren & C. Lewis (Eds.), *A handbook for data analysis in the behavioral sciences: Statistical issues* (pp. 165–198). Mahwah, NJ: Erlbaum.

Cohen, J. (1994). The earth is round (*p* < .05). *American Psychologist, 49,* 997–1003.

Cohen, J. (1995). The earth is round (*p* < .05): Some comments on the comments. *American Psychologist, 50,* 1103.

Cohen, J., & Cohen, P. (1983). *Applied multiple/regression correlation analysis for the behavioral sciences* (2nd ed.). Hillsdale, NJ: Erlbaum.

Cohen, J., & Nee, J. C. M. (1984). Estimators for two measures of association for set correlation. *Educational and Psychological Measurement, 44,* 907–917.

Cohen, J., & Nee, J. C. M. (1987). A comparison of two noncentral *F* approximations, with applications to power analysis in set correlation. *Multivariate Behavioral Research, 22,* 483–490.

Cohen, J., & Nee, J. C. M. (1990). Robustness of Type I error and power in set correlation analysis of contingency tables. *Multivariate Behavioral Research, 25,* 341–350.

Cohen, P. (1982). To be or not to be: The control and balancing of type I and type II errors in research. *Evaluation and Program Planning, 5,* 247–253.

Cohen, P. (1991). A source of bias in longitudinal investigations of change. In L. Collins & J. Horn (Eds.), *Best methods for the analysis of change* (pp. 18–25). Washington, DC: American Psychological Association.

Cohen, P., Brook, J. S., Cohen, J., Velez, C. N., & Garcia, M. (1990). Common and uncommon pathways to adolescent psychopathology and problem behavior. In L. Robins & M. Rutter (Eds.), *Straight and devious pathways from childhood to adulthood* (pp. 242–258). London: Cambridge University Press.

Cohen, P., Chen, H., Hamagami, F., Gordon, K., & McArdle, J. J. (2000). Multilevel analyses for predicting sequence effects of financial and employment problems on the probability of arrest. *Journal of Quantitative Criminology, 16,* 223–235.

Cohen, P., & Cohen, J. (1984). The clinician's illusion. *Archives of General Psychiatry, 41,* 1178–1182.

Cohen, P., & Cohen, J. (1996). *Life values and adolescent mental health.* Mahwah, NJ: Erlbaum.

Cohen, P., Cohen, J., Aiken, L. S., & West, S. G. (1999). The problem of units and the circumstance for POMP. *Multivariate Behavioral Research, 34,* 315–346.

Cohen, P., Cohen, J., Teresi, J., Velez, C. N., & Marchi, M. (1990). Problems in the measurement of latent variable in structural equation causal models. *Applied Psychological Measurement, 14,* 183–196.

Cohen, S., & Wills, T. A. (1985). Stress, social support, and the buffering hypothesis. *Psychological Bulletin, 98,* 310–357.

Coleman, J. S., Hoffer, T., & Kilgore, S. B. (1982). *High school achievement: Public, Catholic and other schools compared.* New York: Basic Books.

Collett, D. (1991). *Modelling binary data.* London: Chapman & Hall.

Collins, L., & Horn, J. (Eds.) (1993). *Best methods for the analysis of change.* Washington, DC: American Psychological Association.

Collins, L., & Sayer, A. G. (2001). *New methods for the analysis of change.* Washington, DC: American Psychological Association Press.

Collins, L. M., Schafer, J. L., & Kam, C.-M. (2001). A comparison of inclusive and restrictive strategies in modern missing data procedures. *Psychological Methods, 6,* 330–351.

Cook, R. D. (1977). Detection of influential observations in linear regression. *Technometrics, 19,* 15–18.

Cook, R. D. (1984). Comment on Belsley (1984). *American Statistician, 38,* 78–79.

Cook, R. D., Hawkins, D. M., & Weisberg, S. (1992). Comparison of model misspecification diagnostics using residuals from least mean of squares and least median of squares fits. *Journal of the American Statistical Association, 87,* 419–424.

Cook, R. D., & Weisberg, S. (1982). *Residuals and influence in regression.* New York: Chapman & Hall.

Cook, R. D., & Weisberg, S. (1983). Diagnostics for heteroscedasticity in regression. *Biometrika, 70,* 1–10.

Cook, R. D., & Weisberg, S. (1999). *Applied regression including computing and graphics.* New York: Wiley.

Cook, T. D. (1993). A quasi-sampling theory of the generalization of causal relationships. *New Directions for Program Evaluation, 37,* 39–81.

Cook, T. D., & Campbell, D. T. (1979). *Quasi-experimentation: Design and analysis issues for field settings.* Boston: Houghton Mifflin.

Cox, D. R. (1972). Regression models and life tables. *Journal of the Royal Statistical Society, 34,* 187–220.

Cox, D. R., & Oakes, D. (1984). *Analysis of survival data.* New York: Chapman & Hall.

Cox, D. R., & Snell, E. J. (1989). *The analysis of binary data* (2nd ed.). London: Chapman & Hall.

Cramer, E. M., & Nicewander, W. A. (1979). Some symmetric, invariant measures of set association. *Psychometrika, 44,* 43–54.

Crocker, L., & Algina, J. (1986). *Introduction to classical and modern test theory.* Fort Worth, TX: Harcourt, Brace, Jovanovich.

Cronbach, L. J. (1951). Coefficient alpha and the internal structure of tests. *Psychometrika, 16,* 297–334.

Cronbach, L. J. (1987). Statistical tests for moderator variables: Flaws in analyses recently proposed. *Psychological Bulletin, 102,* 414–417.

D'Agostino, R. B. (1986). Tests for the normal distribution. In R. B. D'Agostino & M. D. Stephens (Eds.), *Goodness of fit techniques.* New York: Dekker.

Darlington, R. B. (1978). Reduced-variance regression. *Psychological Bulletin, 85,* 1238–1255.

Darlington, R. B. (1991). *Regression and linear models.* New York: McGraw-Hill.

Darlington, R. B., & Boyce, C. M. (1982). Ridge and other new varieties of regression. In G. Keren (Ed.), *Statistical and methodological issues in psychology and social sciences research* (pp. 71–100). Hillsdale, NJ: Erlbaum.

Davidian, M., & Carroll, R. J. (1987). Variance function estimation. *Journal of the American Statistical Association, 82,* 1079–1091.

Dawes, R. M. (1979). The robust beauty of improper linear models in decision making. *American Psychologist, 34,* 571–582.

Diaconis, P. (1985). Theories of data analysis: From magical thinking through classical statistics. In D. C. Hoaglin, F. Mosteller, & J. W. Tukey (Eds.). *Exploring data tables, trend, and shapes* (pp. 1–36). New York: Wiley.

Dielman, T. E. (1989). *Pooled cross-sectional and times series data analysis.* New York: Dekker.

Diggle, P. J., Liang, K.-Y., & Zeger, S. L. (1994). *Analysis of longitudinal data.* New York, Oxford: Clarendon Press.

Doll, R., & Peto, R. (1981). *Causes of cancer.* Oxford: Oxford Medical Publications.

Draper, N. R., & Smith, H. (1998). *Applied regression analysis* (3rd ed.). New York: Wiley.

Duncan, O. D. (1975). *Introduction to structural equation models*. New York: Academic Press.

Duncan, T. E., Duncan, S. C., Strycker, L. A., Li, F., & Alpert, A. (1999). *An introduction to latent variable growth curve modeling*. Mahwah, NJ: Erlbaum.

Dweck, C. S. (1999). *Self-theories: Their role in motivation, personality, and development*. Philadelphia: Psychology Press/Taylor & Francis.

Eber, H. W., & Cohen, J. (1987). *SETCORAN, a PC program to implement set correlation as a general multivariate data-analytic method*. Atlanta, GA: Psychological Resources.

Edwards, A. E. (1972). *Experimental design in psychological research* (4th ed.). New York: Holt, Rinehart, & Winston.

Ehrenberg, A. S. C. (1977). Rudiments of numeracy. *Journal of the Royal Statistical Society, Series A, 140,* 277–297

Embretson, S. E., & Reise, S. P. (2000). *Item response theory for psychologists*. Mahwah, NJ: Erlbaum.

England, P., Farkas, G., Kilbourne, B. S., & Dou, T. (1988). Explaining occupational sex segregation and wages: Findings from a model with fixed effects. *American Sociological Review, 53,* 544–558.

Estrella, A. (1998). A new measure of fit for equations with dichotomous dependent variables. *Journal of Business and Economic Statistics, 16,* 198–205.

Fahrmier, L., & Tutz, G. (1994). *Multivariate statistical modeling based on generalized linear models*. New York: Springer-Verlag.

Fechner, G. T. (1860). *Elemente der Psychophysik*. Leipzig: Brietkopf und Härtel.

Fisher, R. A. (1971). *The design of experiments* (9th ed.). New York: Hafner.

Fisher, R. A., & Yates, F. (1963). *Statistical tables for biological, agricultural and medical research* (6th ed.). New York: Hafner.

Fleiss, J. L. (1981). *Statistical methods for rates and proportions*. New York: Wiley.

Fox, J. (1990). Describing univariate distributions. In J. Fox & J. S. Long (Eds.), *Modern methods of data analysis* (pp. 58–125). Newbury Park, CA: Sage.

Fox, J. (1997). *Applied regression analysis, linear models, and related methods*. Thousand Oaks, CA: Sage.

Fox, J. (2000a). *Nonparametric simple regression: Smoothing scatterplots*. Thousand Oaks, CA: Sage.

Fox, J. (2000b). *Multiple and generalized nonparametric regression*. Thousand Oaks, CA: Sage.

Fox, J., & Monette, G. (1992). Generalized collinearity diagnostics. *Journal of the American Statistical Association, 87,* 178–183.

Freeman, M. F., & Tukey, J. W. (1950). Transformations related to the angular and the square root. *Annals of Mathematical Statistics, 21,* 607–611.

Friedrich, R. J. (1982). In defense of multiplicative terms in multiple regression equations. *American Journal of Political Science, 26,* 797–833.

Fuller, W. A. (1987). *Measurement error models*. New York: Wiley.

Gaito, J. (1965). Unequal intervals and unequal n in trend analysis. *Psychological Bulletin, 63,* 125–127.

Games, P. A. (1971). Multiple comparisons of means. *American Educational Research Journal, 8,* 531–565.

Ganzach, Y. (1997). Misleading interaction and curvilinear terms. *Psychological Methods, 2,* 235–247.

Gardner, W., Mulvey, E. P., & Shaw, E. C. (1995). Regression analyses of counts and rates: Poisson, overdispersed Poisson, and negative binomial models. *Psychological Bulletin, 118,* 392–404.

Gigerenzer, G. (1993). The superego, the ego, and the id in statistical reasoning. In G. Keren & C. Lewis (Eds.), *A handbook for data analysis in the behavioral sciences: Methodological issues* (pp. 311–339). Hillsdale, NJ: Erlbaum.

Glass, G. V., McGaw, B., & Smith, M. L. (1981). *Meta-analysis in social research*. Beverly Hills, CA: Sage.

Goldberger, A. S. (1998). *Introductory econometrics*. Cambridge, MA: Harvard University Press.

Goldberger, A. S., & Duncan, O. D. (Eds.). (1973). *Structural equation models in the social sciences*. New York: Seminar Press.

Goldstein, H. (1995). *Multilevel statistical models* (2nd ed.). London: Edward Arnold.

Goldstein, H., Rabash, J., Plewis, I., Draper, D., Browne, W., Yang, M., Woodhouse, G., & Healey, M. (1998). *A user's guide to MLwiN*. London: Multi-Level Models Project, Institute of Education, University of London.

Gollob, H. F., & Reichardt, C. S. (1991). Interpreting and estimating indirect effects assuming time lags really matter. In L. Collins & J. Horn (Eds.), *Best methods for the analysis of change* (pp. 243–259). Washington, DC: American Psychological Association.

Goodman, L. A., & Kruskal, W. H. (1979). *Measures of association for cross classifications.* New York: Springer-Verlag.

Gottman, J. M. (1979). *Marital interaction: Experimental investigations.* New York: Academic Press.

Gottman, J. M. (1981). *Time series analysis: A comprehensive introduction for social scientists.* New York: Cambridge University Press.

Gottman, J. M. (1994). *What predicts divorce? The relationship between marital processes and marital outcomes.* Mahwah, NJ: Erlbaum.

Graham, J. W., & Hofer, S. M. (2000). Multiple imputation in multivariate research. In T. D. Little, K. U. Schnabel & J. Baumert (Eds.), *Modeling longitudinal and multilevel data: Practical issues, applied approaches, and specific examples* (pp. 201–218). Mahwah, NJ: Erlbaum.

Graham, J., Taylor, B., & Cumsille, P. (2001). Planned missing data designs in analysis of change. In L. Collins & A. G. Sayer (Eds.), *New methods for the analysis of change* (pp. 335–354). Washington, DC: American Psychological Association Press.

Gray, J. B., & Woodall, W. H. (1994). The maximum size of the standardized and internally studentized residuals in regression analysis. *American Statistician, 48,* 111–113.

Green, B. F., Jr. (1977). Parameter sensitivity in multivariate methods. *Multivariate Behavioral Research, 12,* 263–288.

Greene, W. H. (1997). *Econometric analysis* (3rd ed.). Upper Saddle River, NJ: Prentice Hall.

Greenland, S. (1997). Second-stage least squares versus penalized quasi-likelihood for fitting hierarchical models in epidemiologic analyses. *Statistics in Medicine, 16,* 515–526.

Greenland, S. (1998). Introduction to regression models. In K. J. Rothman & S. Greenland (Eds.), *Modern epidemiology* (2nd ed., pp. 359–399). Philadelphia: Lippincott-Raven.

Granger, C., & Newbold, P. (1986). *Forecasting economic time series.* New York: Academic Press.

Gregson, R. A. M. (1983). *Time series in psychology.* Hillsdale, NJ: Erlbaum.

Hadi, A. S. (1992). Identifying multiple outliers in multivariate data. *Journal of the Royal Statistical Society, Series B, 54,* 761–777.

Hadi, A. S. (1994). A modification of a method for the detection of outliers in multivariate samples. *Journal of the Royal Statistical Society, Series B, 56,* 393–396.

Hadi, A. S., & Ling, R. F. (1998). Some cautionary notes on the use of principal components regression. *American Statistician, 52,* 15–19.

Hadi, A. S., & Simonoff, J. S. (1993). Procedures for the identification of multiple outliers in linear models. *Journal of the American Statistical Association, 88,* 1264–1272.

Hagle, T. M. (1995). *Basic math for social scientists.* Thousand Oaks, CA: Sage.

Hamagami, F., McArdle, J. J., & Cohen, P. (2000). A new approach to modeling bivariate dynamic relationships applied to evaluation of personality disorder symptoms. In V. J. Molfese & D. L. Molfese (Eds.), *Temperament and personality development across the life span* (pp. 253–280). Mahwah, NJ: Erlbaum.

Hamilton, L. C. (1992). *Regression with graphics: A second course in applied statistics.* Pacific Grove, CA: Brooks/Cole.

Hardy, M. A. (1993). *Regression with dummy variables.* Newbury Park, CA: Sage.

Harlow, L. L., Mulaik, S. A., & Steiger, J. H. (Eds.). (1997). *What if there were no significance tests?* Mahwah, NJ: Erlbaum.

Harris, R. J. (2001). *A primer of multivariate statistics* (3rd ed.). Mahwah, NJ: Erlbaum.

Hastie, T., & Tibshirani, R. (1990). *Generalized additive models.* London: Chapman & Hall.

Hays, W. L. (1980). *Statistics* (3rd ed.). New York: Holt, Rinehart, & Winston.

Hays, W. L. (1994). *Statistics* (5th ed.). Forth Worth, TX: Harcourt Brace.

Heath, R. A. (2000). *Nonlinear dynamics: Techniques and applications in psychology.* Mahwah, NJ: Erlbaum.

Heck, R. H., & Thomas, S. L. (2000). *An introduction to multilevel modeling techniques.* Mahwah, NJ: Erlbaum.

Hedeker, D., & Gibbons, R. D. (1996). MIXREG: A computer program for mixed-effects regression analysis with autocorrelated errors. *Computer Methods and Programs in Biomedicine, 49,* 229–252.

Hedges, L. V., & Olkin, I. (1985). *Statistical methods for meta-analysis.* New York: Academic Press.

Higginbotham, H. N., West, S. G., & Forsyth, D. R. (1988). *Psychotherapy and behavior change: Social, cultural, and methodological perspectives.* New York: Pergamon.

Hoaglin, D. C. (1988). Transformations in everyday experience. *Chance: New Directions for Statistics and Computing, 1*(4), 40–45.

Hoaglin, D. C., & Velleman, P. F. (1995). A critical look at some analyses of major-league baseball salaries. *American Statistician, 49,* 277–285.

Holland, P. W., & Rubin, D. B. (1988). Causal inference in retrospective studies. *Evaluation Review, 12,* 203–231.

Hooper, J. W. (1959). Simultaneous equations and cannonical correlation theory. *Econometrica, 27,* 245–256.

Hooper, J. W. (1962). Partial trace correlations. *Econometrica, 30,* 324–331.

Hosmer, D. W., & Lemeshow, S. (2000). *Applied logistic regression* (2nd ed.). New York: Wiley.

Hotelling, H. (1936). Relations between two sets of variables. *Biometrika, 28,* 321–377.

Howell, D. C., & McConaughy, S. H. (1982). Nonorthogonal analysis of variance: Putting the question before the answer. *Educational and Psychological Measurement, 42,* 9–24.

Hoyle, R. H., & Panter, A. T. (1995). Writing about structural equation models. In R. H. Hoyle (Ed.), *Structural equation modeling: Concepts, issues, and applications* (pp. 158–176). Thousand Oaks, CA: Sage.

Huber, P. J. (1981). *Robust statistics.* New York: Wiley.

Hunter, J. E., & Schmidt, F. L. (1990). *Methods of meta-analysis: Correcting error and bias in research findings.* Newbury Park, CA: Sage.

Immer, F. R., Hayes, H. K., & Powers, L. R. (1934). Statistical determination of barley varietal adaption. *Journal of the American Society of Agronomy, 26,* 403–419.

Jaccard, J. (2001). *Interaction effects in logistic regression.* Thousand Oaks, CA: Sage.

Jaccard, J., Turrisi, R., & Wan, C. K. (1990). *Interaction effects in multiple regression.* Newbury Park, CA: Sage.

Jaccard, J., & Wan, C. K. (1995). Measurement error in the analysis of interaction effects between continuous predictors using multiple regression: Multiple indicators and structural equation approaches. *Psychological Bulletin, 117,* 348–357.

Jackson, J. E. (1991). *A user's guide to principal components.* New York: Wiley.

Jaffe, J., Beebe, B., Feldstein, S., Crown, C., & Jasnow, M. (2001). Rhythms of dialogue in infancy. *Monographs of the Society for Research in Child Development, 66*(2), 1–101.

Janis, I. L. (1967). Effects of fear arousal on attitude: Recent developments in theory and research. In L. Berkowitz (Ed.), *Advances in experimental social psychology* (Vol. 3, pp. 167–222). New York: Academic Press.

Joiner, B. L. (1981). Lurking variables: Some examples. *American Statistician, 35,* 227–233.

Jolliffe, I. T. (1986). *Principal component analysis.* New York: Springer-Verlag.

Jones, L. V., & Tukey, J. W. (2000). A sensible formulation of the significance test. *Psychological Methods, 5,* 411–414.

Jones, R. H. (1993). *Longitudinal data with serial correlation: A state-space approach.* London: Chapman & Hall.

Judd, C. M., McClelland, G. H., & Culhane, S. C. (1995). Data analysis: Continuing issues in the everyday analysis of psychological data. *Annual Review of Psychology, 46,* 433–465.

Kenny, D. A. (1979). *Correlation and causality.* New York: Wiley.

Kenny, D. A., & Judd, C. M. (1984). Estimating the nonlinear and interactive effects of latent variables. *Psychological Bulletin, 96,* 201–210.

Kenny, D. A., & Judd, C. M. (1986). Consequences of violating the independence assumption in analysis of variance. *Psychological Bulletin, 99,* 422–431.

Kessler, R. C., & Greenberg, D. F. (1981). *Linear panel analysis: Models of quantitative change.* New York: Academic Press.

Kirk, R. E. (1995). *Experimental design: Procedures for the behavioral sciences* (3rd ed.). Pacific Grove, CA: Brooks/Cole.

Kleinbaum, D. G. (1994). *Logistic regression: A self-learning text*. New York: Springer-Verlag.

Kleinbaum, D. G., Kupper, L. L., & Muller, K. E. (1988). *Applied regression analysis and other multivariable methods*. Belmont, CA: Duxbury Press.

Kraemer, H. C. (1985). The robustness of common measures of 2×2 association to resist bias due to misclassification. *American Statistician, 39,* 286–290.

Kraemer, H. C. (1988). Assessment of 2×2 associations, generalization of signal detection methodology. *American Statistician, 42,* 37–49.

Kraemer, H. C., Kazdin, A. E., Offord, D. R., Kessler, R. C., Jensen, P. S., & Kupfer, D. J. (1999). Measuring the potency of risk factors for clinical or policy significance. *Psychological Methods, 4,* 257–271.

Kraemer, H. C., Yesavage, J. A., Taylor, J. L., & Kupfer, D. (2000). How can we learn about developmental processes from cross-sectional studies, or can we? *American Journal of Psychiatry, 157,* 163–171.

Krantz, D. H. (1999). The null hypothesis testing controversy in psychology. *Journal of the American Statistical Association, 94,* 1372–1381.

Krause, N. (1995). Assessing stress-buffering effects: A cautionary note. *Psychology and Aging, 10,* 518–526.

Kreft, I., & de Leeuw, J. (1998). *Introducing multilevel modeling*. London: Sage.

Kreft, I., de Leeuw, J., & Aiken, L. S. (1995). The effect of different forms of centering in hierarchical linear models. *Multivariate Behavioral Research, 30,* 1–22.

Kruskal, W. H. (1960). Discussion of the papers of Messrs. Anscombe and Daniel. *Technometrics, 2,* 257–258.

Kvålseth, T. O. (1985). Cautionary note about R^2. *American Statistician, 39,* 279–285.

Land, K. C., McCall, P. L., & Nagin, D. S. (1996). A comparison of Poisson, negative binomial, and semiparametric mixed Poisson regression models: With empirical applications to criminal careers data. *Sociological Methods and Research, 24,* 387–442.

Lee, J. J., & Tu, Z. N. (1997). A versatile one-dimensional plot: The BliP plot. *American Statistician, 51,* 353–358.

Lee, V., & Bryk, A. S. (1989). A multilevel model of the social distribution of high school achievement. *Sociology of Education, 62,* 172–192.

Lewis, C., & Keren, G. (1977). You can't have your cake and eat it too: Some considerations of the error term. *Psychological Bulletin, 84,* 1150–1154.

Lindsey, J. K. (1993). *Models for repeated measurements*. New York: Oxford University Press.

Littell, R. C., Milliken, G. A., Stroup, W. W., & Wolfinger, R. D. (1996). *SAS system for mixed models*. Cary, NC: SAS Institute.

Little, R. J. A., & Rubin, D. B. (1987). *Statistical analysis with missing data*. New York: Wiley.

Little, R. J., & Yau, L. H. Y. (1998). Statistical techniques for analyzing data from prevention trials: Treatment of no-shows using Rubin's causal model. *Psychological Methods, 3,* 147–159.

Little, T. D., Schnabel, K. U., & Baumert, J. (Eds.). (2000). *Modeling longitudinal and multilevel data: Practical issues, applied approaches, and specific examples*. Mahwah, NJ: Erlbaum.

Loehlin, J. C. (1992). *Latent variable models: An introduction to factor, path, and structural analysis* (2nd ed.). Mahwah, NJ: Erlbaum.

Long, J. S. (1997). *Regression models for categorical and limited dependent variables*. Thousand Oaks, CA: Sage.

Looney, S. W., & Gulledge, T. R., Jr. (1985). Use of the correlation coefficient with normal probability plots. *American Statistician, 39,* 75–79.

Lord, F. M. (1953). On the statistical treatment of football numbers. *American Psychologist, 8,* 750–751.

Lord, F. M. (1969). Statistical adjustment when comparing preexisting groups. *Psychological Bulletin, 72,* 336–337.

Lubinski, D., & Humphreys, L. G. (1990). Assessing spurious "moderator effects": Illustrated substantively with the hypothesized ("synergistic") relation between spatial and mathematical ability. *Psychological Bulletin, 107,* 385–393.

Lykken, D. T. (1968). Statistical significance in psychological research. *Psychological Bulletin, 70,* 151–159.

MacCallum, R. C. (1995). Model specification: Procedures, strategies, and related issues. In R. H. Hoyle (Ed.), *Structural equation modeling: Concepts, issues, and applications* (pp. 16–36). Thousand Oaks, CA: Sage.

MacCallum, R. C., & Browne, M. W. (1993). The use of causal indicators in covariance structure models: Some practical issues. *Psychological Bulletin, 114,* 533–541.

MacCallum, R. C., Kim, C., Malarkey, W. B., & Kiecolt-Glaser, J. K. (1997). Studying multivariate change using multilevel models and latent curve models. *Multivariate Behavioral Research, 32,* 215–253.

MacCallum, R. C., & Mar, C. M. (1995). Distinguishing between moderator and quadratic effects in multiple regression. *Psychological Bulletin, 118,* 405–421.

Maddala, G. S. (1988). *Introduction to econometrics* (2nd ed.). Englewood Cliffs, NJ: Prentice Hall.

Marks, L. E. (1974). *Sensory processes: The new psychophysics.* New York: Academic Press.

Marquardt, D. W. (1980). You should standardize the predictor variables in your regression models. *Journal of the American Statistical Association, 75,* 87–91.

Marsh, H. W., Balla, J. R., & McDonald, R. P. (1988). Goodness-of-fit indexes in confirmatory factor analysis: The effect of sample size. *Psychological Bulletin, 103,* 391–410.

Mauro, R. (1990). Understanding L.O.V.E. (left out variables error): A method for estimating the effects of omitted variables. *Psychological Bulletin, 108,* 314–329.

Maxwell, S. E. (2000). Sample size and multiple regression analysis. *Psychological Methods, 5,* 434–458.

Maxwell, S. E., & Delaney, H. D. (1990). *Designing experiments and analyzing data: A model comparison perspective.* Pacific Grove, CA: Brooks/Cole.

Maxwell, S. E., & Delaney, H. D. (1993). Bivariate median splits and spurious statistical significance. *Psychological Bulletin, 113,* 181–190.

McArdle, J. J. (1998). Modeling longitudinal data by latent growth curve methods. In G. A. Marcoulides (Ed.), *Modern methods for business research* (pp. 359–406). Mahwah, NJ: Erlbaum.

McArdle, J. J., & Aber, M. S. (1990). Patterns of change within latent variable structural equation models. In A. von Eye (Ed.), *Statistical methods in longitudinal research: Vol. 1. Principles and methods of structuring change* (pp. 151–223). New York: Academic Press.

McArdle, J. J., & Bell, R. Q. (2000). An introduction to latent growth models for developmental data analysis. In T. D. Little, K. U. Schnabel, & J. Baumert (Eds.), *Modeling longitudinal and multi-level data: Practical issues, applied approaches, and specific examples* (pp. 69–107). Mahwah, NJ: Erlbaum.

McArdle, J. J., & Epstein, D. (1987). Latent growth curves within developmental structural equation models. *Child Development, 58,* 110–133.

McArdle, J. J., & Hamagami, F. (1991). Modeling incomplete longitudinal and cross-sectional data using latent growth structural models. In L. Collins & J. Horn (Eds.), *Best methods for the analysis of change* (pp. 276–304). Washington, DC: American Psychological Association.

McArdle, J. J., & Hamagami, F. (1996). Multilevel models from a multiple groups structural equation perspective. In G. Marcoulides & R. Schumacker (Eds.), *Advanced structural equation modeling techniques* (pp. 89–124). Hillsdale, NJ: Erlbaum.

McArdle, J. J., & Nesselroade, J. R. (1994). Structuring data to study development and change. In S. H. Cohen & H. W. Reese (Eds.), *Life-span developmental psychology: Methodological contributions* (pp. 223–267). Hillsdale, NJ: Erlbaum.

McArdle, J. J., & Woodcock, R. W. (1997). Expanding test-retest designs to include developmental time-lag components. *Psychological Methods, 2,* 403–435.

McCleary, R., & Hay, R. A. (1980). *Applied time series analysis.* Beverly Hills, CA: Sage.

McClelland, G. H., & Judd, C. M. (1993). Statistical difficulties of detecting interactions and moderator effects. *Psychological Bulletin, 114,* 376–390.

McCullagh, P., & Nelder, J. A. (1989). *Generalized linear models* (2nd ed.). London: Chapman & Hall.

McDonald, R. P. (1999). *Test theory: A unified treatment.* Mahwah, NJ: Erlbaum.

Meehl, P. E. (1967). Theory testing in psychology and physics: A methodological paradox. *Philosophy of Science, 34,* 103–115.

Meehl, P. E. (1997). The problem is epistemology, not statistics: Replace significance tests by confidence intervals and quantify accuracy of risky numerical predictions. In L. L. Harlow, S. A. Mulaik, & J. H. Steiger (Eds.), *What if there were no significance tests?* (pp. 393–425). Mahwah, NJ: Erlbaum.

Mehta, P. D., & West, S. G. (2000). Putting the individual back into individual growth curves. *Psychological Methods, 5,* 23–43.

Menard, S. (2001). *Applied logistic regression analysis* (2nd ed.). Newbury Park, CA: Sage.

Meng, X.-L., Rosenthal, R., & Rubin, D. B. (1992). Comparing correlated correlation coefficients. *Psychological Bulletin, 111,* 172–175.

Meredith, W., & Tisak, J. (1990). Latent curve analysis. *Psychometrika, 55,* 107–122.

Miller, A. J. (1990). *Subset selection in regression.* New York: Chapman & Hall.

Miller, R. G., Jr. (1966). *Simultaneous statistical inference.* New York: McGraw-Hill.

Molenaar, P. C. M. (1994). Dynamic latent variable models in developmental psychology. In A. von Eye & C. C. Clogg (Eds.), *Latent variable analysis: Applications for developmental research* (pp. 155–180). Thousand Oaks, CA: Sage.

Molenaar, P. C. M., Rovine, M. J., & Corneal, S. E. (1999). Dynamic factor analysis of emotional dispositions of adolescent stepsons towards their stepfathers. In R. K. Silbereisen & A. von Eye (Eds.), *Growing up in times of social change* (pp. 261–286). Berlin: DeGruyter.

Mosteller, F., & Tukey, J. W. (1977). *Data analysis and regression.* Reading, MA: Addison-Wesley.

Murray, D. M., & Wolfinger, R. D. (1994). Analysis issues in the evaluation of community trials: Progress toward solutions in SAS/STAT MIXED. *Journal of Community Psychology,* CSAP Special Issue, 140–154.

Muthén, B. (2001). Second generation SEM growth analysis. In L. Collins & A. G. Sayers (Eds.), *New methods for the analysis of change* (pp. 291–322). Washington, DC: American Psychological Association.

Myers, R. H. (1986). *Classical and modern regression with applications.* Boston: Duxbury Press.

Nagelkerke, N. J. D. (1991). A note on the general definition of the coefficient of determination. *Biometrika, 78,* 691–692.

Nagin, D. S. (1999). Analyzing developmental trajectories: A semi-parametric, group-based approach. *Psychological Methods, 4,* 139–157.

Nagin, D. S., & Tremblay, R. E. (2001). Analyzing developmental trajectories of distinct but related behaviors: A group-based method. *Psychological Methods, 6,* 18–34.

Neale, M. C. (1995). *Mx: Statistical modeling.* Richmond, VA: Department of Human Genetics, Medical College of Virginia.

Neale, M. C. (2000). Individual fit, heterogeneity, and missing data in multigroup structural equation modeling. In T. D. Little, K. U. Schnabel, & J. Baumert (Eds.), *Modeling longitudinal and multilevel data: Practical issues, applied approaches, and specific examples* (pp. 249–281). Mahwah, NJ: Erlbaum.

Nesselroade, J. R., & Baltes, P. B. (Eds.). (1979). *Longitudinal research in the study of behavior and development.* New York: Academic Press.

Neter, J., Kutner, M. H., Nachtsheim, C. J., & Wasserman, W. (1996). *Applied linear regression models* (3rd ed.). Chicago: Irwin.

Neter, J., Wasserman, W., & Kutner, M. H. (1989). *Applied linear regression models* (2nd ed.). Homewood, IL: Irwin.

Nunnally, J., & Bernstein, I. H. (1993). *Psychometric theory* (3rd ed.). New York: McGraw-Hill.

Oakes, M. (1986). *Statistical inference: A commentary for the social and behavioral sciences.* New York: Wiley.

Olkin, I., & Finn, J. D. (1995). Correlations redux. *Psychological Bulletin, 118,* 155–164.

Olson, C. L. (1976). On choosing a test statistical in multivariate analysis of variance. *Psychological Bulletin, 83,* 579–586.

Overall, J. E. (1987). Estimating sample size for longitudinal studies of age-related cognitive decline. *Journal of Gerontology, 42,* 137–141.

Owen, D. B. (1962). *Handbook of statistical tables.* Reading, MA: Addison-Wesley.

Pampel, F. C. (2000). *Logistic regression: A primer.* Thousand Oaks, CA: Sage.

Parmar, M. K. B., & Machin, D. (1995). *Survival analysis: A practical approach.* New York: Wiley.

Pearl, J. (2000). *Causality: Models, reasoning, and inference.* New York: Cambridge University Press.

Pearson, E. S., & Hartley, H. O. (Eds.). (1954). *Biometrika tables for statisticians* (Vol. 1). Cambridge: Cambridge University Press.

Pedhazur, E. J. (1982). *Multiple regression in behavioral research* (2nd ed.). New York: Holt, Rinehart & Winston.

Peixoto, J. L. (1987). Hierarchical variable selection in polynomial regression models. *American Statistician, 41,* 311–313.

Piacentini, J. C., Cohen, P., & Cohen, J. (1992). Combining discrepant diagnostic information from multiple sources. *Journal of Abnormal Child Psychology, 20,* 51–63.

Pillai, K. C. S. (1960). *Statistical tables for tests of multivariate hypotheses.* Manila: Statistical Institute, University of the Philippines.

Pillow, D. R., West, S. G., & Reich, J. W. (1991). Attributional style in relation to self-esteem and depression: Mediational and attributional models. *Journal of Research in Personality, 25,* 57–69.

Pitts, S. C., & West, S. G. (2001). *Alternative sampling designs to detect interactions in multiple regression.* Unpublished manuscript, Department of Psychology, Arizona State University, Tempe, AZ 85287-1104.

Pregibon, D. (1981). Logistic regression diagnostics. *Annals of Statistics, 9,* 705–724.

Press, S. J., & Wilson, S. (1978). Choosing between logistic regression and discriminant analysis. *Journal of the American Statistical Association, 73,* 699–705.

Pruzek, R. M., & Fredericks, B. C. (1978). Weighting predictors in linear models: Alternatives to least squares and limitations of equal weights. *Psychological Bulletin, 85,* 254–266.

Rahe, R. H., Mahan, J. L., & Arthur, R. J. (1970). Prediction of near-future health change from subjects' preceding life changes. *Journal of Psychosomatic Research, 14,* 401–406.

Rao, C. R. (1975). *Linear statistical inference and its applications* (2nd ed.). New York: Wiley.

Ratkowsky, D. A. (1990). *Handbook of nonlinear regression models.* New York: Dekker.

Raudenbush, S. W., & Bryk, A. S. (2002). *Hierarchical linear models: Applications and data analysis methods* (2nd ed.). Thousand Oaks, CA: Sage.

Raudenbush, S. W., Bryk, A. S., Cheong, Y. F., & Congdon, R. (2001). *HLM 5: Hierarchical Linear and Nonlinear Modeling* (2nd ed.). Chicago: Scientific Software International.

Raudenbush, S. W., & Chan, W. (1992). Growth curve analysis in accelerated longitudinal designs. *Journal of Research in Crime and Delinquency, 29,* 387–411.

Raudenbush, S. W., & Chan, W. (1993). Application of a hierarchical linear model to the study of adolescent deviance in an overlapping cohort design. *Journal of Consulting and Clinical Psychology, 61,* 941–951.

Rawlings, J. O. (1988). *Applied regression analysis: A research tool.* Pacific Grove, CA: Wadsworth & Brooks/Cole.

Reichardt, C. S. (1979). The statistical analysis of data from nonequivalent group designs. In T. D. Cook and D. T. Campbell, *Quasi-experimentation: Design and analysis issues for field settings* (pp. 147–205). Boston: Houghton Mifflin.

Rindskopf, D. (1984). Linear equality restrictions in regression and loglinear models. *Psychological Bulletin, 96,* 597–603.

Robinson, W. S. (1950). Ecological correlations and the behavior of individuals. *Sociological Review, 15,* 351–357.

Rogosa, D., & Willett, J. B. (1985). Understanding correlates of change by modeling individual differences in growth. *Psychometrika, 50,* 203–228.

Rosenthal, R. (1991). *Meta-analysis procedures for social research.* Newbury Park, CA: Sage.

Rosenthal, R., & Rosnow, R. L. (1985). *Contrast analysis: Focused comparisons in the analysis of variance.* New York: Cambridge University Press.

Rosnow, R. L., & Rosenthal, R. (1999). *Beginning behavioral research: A conceptual primer* (3rd ed.). Upper Saddle River, NJ: Prentice Hall.

Rousseeuw, P. J. (1998). Robust estimation and identifying outliers. In H. M. Wadsworth (Ed.), *Handbook of statistical methods for engineers and scientists* (2nd ed., pp. 17.1–17.26). New York: McGraw-Hill.

Rousseeuw, P. J., & Leroy, A. (1987). *Robust regression and outlier detection.* New York: Wiley.

Rousseeuw, P. J., Van Aelst, S., & Hubert, M. (1999). Rejoinder to regression depth. *Journal of the American Statistical Association, 94,* 419–445.

Roy, S. N. (1957). *Some aspects of multivariate analysis.* New York: Wiley.

Rozeboom, W. W. (1960). The fallacy of the null-hypothesis significance test. *Psychological Bulletin, 57,* 416–428.

Rozeboom, W. W. (1965). Linear correlations between sets of variables. *Psychometrika, 30,* 57–71.

Rozeboom, W. W. (1979). Sensitivity of linear composites of predictor items to differential item weighting. *Psychometrika, 44,* 289–296.

Rubin, D. B. (1987). *Multiple imputation for nonresponse in surveys.* New York: Wiley.

Rutter, M. (1989). Pathways from childhood to adult life. *Journal of Child Psychology and Psychiatry, 30,* 23–51.

Ryan, T. P. (1997). *Modern regression methods.* New York: Wiley.

Schafer, J. L., & Graham, J. W. (2002). Missing data: Our view of the state of the art. *Psychological Methods, 7,* 147–177.

Schaie, K. W. (1965). General model for the study of developmental problems. *Psychological Bulletin, 64,* 92–107.

Schaie, K. W. (1986). Beyond calendar definitions of age, time, and cohort: The general developmental model revisited. *Developmental Review, 6,* 252–277.

Scheines, R., Spirtes, P., Glymour, C., Meek, C., & Richardson, T. (1998). The TETRAD Project: Constraint based aids to causal model specification. *Multivariate Behavioral Research, 33,* 65–117.

Schmidt, F. (1996). Statistical significance testing and cumulative knowledge in psychology: Implications for the training of researchers. *Psychological Methods, 1,* 115–129.

Seber, G. A. F., & Wild, C. J. (1989). *Nonlinear regression.* New York: Wiley.

Serlin, R. C., & Levin, J. R. (1985). Teaching how to derive directly interpretable coding schemes for multiple regression analysis. *Journal of Educational Statistics, 10,* 223–238.

Shadish, W. R., Cook, T. D., & Campbell, D. T. (2002). *Experimental and quasi-experimental designs for generalized causal inference.* Boston: Houghton-Mifflin.

Shapiro, S. S., & Wilk, M. B. (1965). An analysis of variance test for normality (complete samples). *Biometrika, 52,* 591–611.

Shrout, P. E., & Fleiss, J. L. (1979). Intraclass correlations: Uses in assessing rater reliability. *Psychological Bulletin, 86,* 420–428.

Silverman, B. W. (1986). *Density estimation for statistics and data analysis.* London: Chapman & Hall.

Singer, J. D. (1998). Using SAS PROC MIXED to fit multilevel models, hierarchical models, and individual growth models. *Journal of Educational and Behavioral Statistics, 24*(4), 322–354.

Singer, J. D., & Willett, J. B. (1991). Modeling the days of our lives: Using survival analysis when designing and analyzing longitudinal studies and the timing of events. *Psychological Bulletin, 110,* 268–290.

Snijders, T., & Bosker, R. (1999). *Multilevel analysis: An introduction to basic and advanced multilevel modeling.* London: Sage.

Srikantan, K. S. (1970). Canonical association between nominal measurements. *Journal of the American Statistical Association, 65,* 284–292.

Staudte, R. J., & Sheather, S. J. (1990). *Robust estimation and testing.* New York: Wiley.

Stevens, J. P. (1984). Outliers and influential data points in regression analysis. *Psychological Bulletin, 95,* 334–344.

Stevens, S. S. (1951). Mathematics, measurement, and psychophysics. In S. S. Stevens (Ed.), *Handbook of experimental psychology* (pp. 1–49). New York: Wiley.

Stevens, S. S. (1958). Measurement and man. *Science, 127,* 383–389.

Stevens, S. S. (1961). The psychophysics of sensory function. In W. A. Rosenblith (Ed.), *Sensory communication* (pp. 1–33). New York: Wiley.

Stigler, S. M. (1986). *The history of statistics: The measurement of uncertainty before 1900.* Cambridge, MA: Belnap Press.

Stoolmiller, M. (1995). Using latent growth curve models to study developmental processes. In J. M. Gottman (Ed.), *The analysis of change* (pp. 103–138). Mahwah, NJ: Erlbaum.

Stouthammer-Loeber, M., & van Kammen, W. B. (1995). *Data collection and management: A practical guide*. Thousand Oaks, CA: Sage.

Suits, D. B. (1984). Dummy variables: Mechanics v. interpretation. *Review of Economics and Statistics, 66*, 177–180.

Tabachnick, B. G., & Fidell, L. S. (2001). *Using multivariate statistics* (4th ed.). Boston: Allyn & Bacon.

Tatsuoka, M. M. (1975). *The general linear model: A "new" trend in analysis of variance*. Champaign, IL: Institute for Personality and Ability Testing.

Tatsuoka, M. M. (1988). *Multivariate analysis: Techniques for educational and psychological research*. New York: Macmillan.

Tatsuoka, M. (1993). Elements of the general linear model. In G. Keren & C. Lewis (Eds.), *A handbook for data analysis in the behavioral sciences: Statistical issues* (pp. 3–41). Mahwah, NJ: Erlbaum.

Thompson, B. (1994). The pivotal role of replication in psychological research: Empirically evaluating the replicability of sample results. *Journal of Personality, 62*, 157–176.

Timm, N. H., & Carlson, J. E. (1976). Part and bipartial canonical correlation analysis. *Psychometrika, 41*, 159–176.

Toothaker, L. E. (1991). *Multiple comparisons for researchers*. Newbury Park, CA: Sage.

Tukey, J. W. (1954). Causation, regression, and path analysis. In O. K. Kempthorne, T. A. Bancroft, J. W. Gowen, & J. L. Lush (Eds.), *Statistics and mathematics in biology* (pp. 35–66). Ames, IA: Iowa State College Press.

Tukey, J. W. (1962). The future of data analysis. *Annals of Mathematical Statistics, 33*, 1–67.

Tukey, J. W. (1969). Analyzing data: Sanctification or detective work. *American Psychologist, 24*, 83–91.

Tukey, J. W. (1977). *Exploratory data analysis*. Reading, MA: Addison-Wesley.

Tukey, J. W. (1993). Where should multiple comparisons go next? In F. M. Hoppe (Ed.), *Multiple comparisons: Selection and applications in biometry* (pp. 187–208). New York: Dekker.

Tzelgov, J., & Henik, A. (1991). Suppression situations in psychological research: Definitions, implications, and applications. *Psychological Bulletin, 109*, 524–536.

Van den Burg, W., & Lewis, C. (1988). Some properties of two measures of multivariate aasociation. *Psychometrika, 53*, 109–122.

Van den Burg, W., & Lewis, C. (1990). Testing multivariate partial, semipartial, and bipartial correlation coefficients. *Multivariate Behavioral Research, 25*, 335–340.

Velicer, W. F., & Colby, S. M. (1997). Time series analysis of prevention and treatment research. In K. Bryant, M. Windle, & S. G. West (Eds.), *The science of prevention: Methodological advances from alcohol and substance abuse research* (pp. 211–250). Washington, DC: American Psychological Association.

Wainer, H. (1976). Estimating coefficients in linear models: It don't make no never mind. *Psychological Bulletin, 83*, 213–217.

Wainer, H. (1978). On the sensitivity of regression and regressors. *Psychological Bulletin, 85*, 267–273.

Wainer, H. (2000). The centercept: An estimable and meaningful regression parameter. *Psychological Science, 11*, 434–436.

Wallston, K. A., Wallston, B. S., & DeVellis, R. (1978). Development of the multidimensional health locus of control (MHLC) scale. *Health Education Monographs, 6*, 161–170.

Ware, J. (1985). Linear models for the analysis of longitudinal studies. *American Statistician, 39*, 95–101.

Weisberg, S. (1985). *Applied linear regression* (2nd ed.). New York: Wiley.

Welsch, R. E. (1980). Regression sensitivity analysis and bounded-influence estimation. In J. Kmenta & J. B. Ramsey (Eds.), *Evaluation of econometric models* (pp. 153–167). New York: Academic Press.

West, S. G., Aiken, L. S., & Krull, J. L. (1996). Experimental personality designs: Analyzing categorical by continuous variable interactions. *Journal of Personality, 64*, 1–48.

West, S. G, Biesanz, J., & Pitts, S. C. (2000). Causal inference in field settings: Experimental and quasi-experimental designs. In H. T. Reis & C. M. Judd (Eds.), *Handbook of research methods in social psychology* (pp. 40–84). New York: Cambridge University Press.

West, S. G., Finch, J. F., & Curran, P. J. (1995). Structural equation models with non-normal variables: Problems and remedies. In R. H. Hoyle (Ed.), *Structural equation modeling: Concepts, issues, and applications* (pp. 56–75). Thousand Oaks, CA: Sage.

West, S. G., & Sagarin, B. (2000). Subject selection and loss in randomized experiments. In L. Bickman (Ed.), *Contributions to research design: Donald Campbell's legacy* (Vol. 2, pp. 117–154). Thousand Oaks, CA: Sage.

Wherry, R. J. (1931). The mean and second moment coefficient of the multiple correlation coefficient in samples from a normal population. *Biometrika, 22,* 353–361.

White, H. (1980). A heteroscedasticity-consistent covariance matrix estimator and a direct test for heteroscedasticity. *Econometrica, 48,* 817–838.

Wilcox, R. R. (1997). *Introduction to robust estimation and hypothesis testing.* San Diego, CA: Academic Press.

Wilcox, R. R. (1998). How many discoveries have been lost by ignoring modern statistical methods? *American Psychologist, 53,* 300–314.

Wilkinson, L., & the APA Task Force on Statistical Inference. (1999). Statistical methods in psychology journals: Guidelines and explanations. *American Psychologist, 54,* 594–604.

Wilkinson, L., Blank, G., & Gruber, C. (1996). *Desktop data analysis with SYSTAT.* Upper Saddle River, NJ: Prentice Hall.

Wilks, S. S. (1932). Certain generalizations in the analysis of variance. *Biometrika, 24,* 471–494.

Willett, J. B., & Sayer, A. G. (1994). Using covariance structure analysis to detect correlates and predictors of individual change over time. *Psychological Bulletin, 116,* 363–381.

Willett, J. B., & Sayer, A. G. (1996). Cross-domain analyses of change over time: Combining growth modeling and covariance structure analysis. In G. A. Marcoulides & R. E. Schumacher (Eds.), *Advanced structural equation modeling: Issues and techniques* (pp. 125–157). Mahwah, NJ: Erlbaum.

Willett, J. B., & Singer, J. D. (1995a). It's deja vu all over again: Using multiple-spell discrete-time survival analysis. *Journal of Educational and Behavioral Statistics, 20,* 41–67.

Willett, J. B., & Singer, J. D. (1995b). The times of our lives: Methodological issues when using survival analysis in research. In J. M. Gottman (Ed.), *The analysis of change.* Hillsdale, NJ: Erlbaum.

Winer, B. J. (1971). *Statistical principles in experimental design* (2nd ed.). New York: McGraw-Hill.

Winer, B. J., Brown, D. R., & Michels, K. M. (1991). *Statistical principles in experimental design* (3rd ed.). New York: McGraw-Hill.

Winship, C., & Radbill, L. (1994). Sampling weights and regression analysis. *Sociological Methods and Research, 23,* 230–257.

Wolfinger, R. D. (1997). An example of using mixed models and PROC MIXED for longitudinal data. *Journal of Pharmaceutical Statistics, 7,* 481–500.

Won, E. Y. T. (1982). Incomplete corrections for regressor unreliabilities. *Sociological Methods and Research, 10,* 271–284.

Wong, G. Y., & Mason, W. M. (1985). The hierarchical logistic regression model for multilevel analysis. *Journal of the American Statistical Association, 80,* 513–524.

Wood, P., & Brown, D. (1994). The study of intraindividual differences by means of dynamic factor models: Rationale, implementation, and interpretation. *Psychological Bulletin, 116,* 166–186.

Wright, S. (1921). Correlation and causation. *Journal of Agricultural Research, 20,* 557–585.

Yates, F. (1951). The influence of Statistical Methods for Research Workers on the development of the science of statistics. *Journal of the American Statistical Association, 46,* 19–34.

Yerkes, R. M., & Dodson, J. D. (1908). The relation of strength of stimulus to rapidity of habit formation. *Journal of Comparative Neurology and Psychology, 18,* 459–482.

Yule, G. U. (1911). *An introduction to the theory of statistics.* London: Charles Griffin; Philadelphia: Lippincott.

Zevon, M. A., & Tellegen, A. (1982). The structure of mood change: An idiographic/nomothetic analysis. *Journal of Personality and Social Psychology, 43,* 111–122.

Zwick, R., & Cramer, E. M. (1986). A multivariate perspective on the analysis of categorical data. *Applied Psychological Measurement, 10,* 141–145.

Glossary

In this section we present a brief definition of technical terms as used repeatedly in this text. The intent is to provide a conceptual reminder about the term, rather than a replacement of the more complete presentation or discussion presented in the chapters. For named statistics and for text sections discussing each term consult the subject index.

Additivity Indicating that the regression of Y on X is constant over the values of other predictors.

Augmentation (or synergy) Interactions in which the effect of an IV on Y is larger for high values of another IV.

Autocorrelation In longitudinal data, correlations among observations at adjacent or nearly adjacent time points; also used in time series analysis to refer to correlations among measures on a single variable on a single case over time.

Autoregressive models Analytic models in which values of variables measured at earlier time points are used to predict values of the same variables at later points.

Balanced designs In ANOVA or regression with categorical variables, a design with equal or proportional numbers of cases at each combination of research factors.

Ballantine A diagrammatic representation of the overlap or correlation between variables or sets of variables with respect to a dependent variable Y. It is modeled after the Venn diagram used in set theory, but cannot be taken as mathematically equivalent to it.

Beta coefficient (β) For consistency with the field, this symbol is used in two different ways in this book: To represent Type II error (concluding that the population value is not different from the null hypothesis when it is different) and the standardized regression coefficient.

Binomial distribution In a population in which P is the proportion having some characteristic, the binomial distribution is the distribution of the number of persons with that characteristic across samples of a given size drawn from that population.

Buffering interaction An interaction in which the regression of Y on one IV is lower for high values of another IV than for lower values.

Build-up procedure *See* Stepwise regression and Hierarchical (regression) analysis.

Bulging rule   A method for examining the shape of a relationship between two variables X and Y to suggest an appropriate form from among the power transformations to linearize their relationship.

Canonical analysis (CA)   Analysis in which the relationship between two sets of variables is assessed by means of maximally correlating linear combinations of each set, where each combination is subject to zero correlations with all other linear combinations of the same set.

Case statistics   A statistic that varies for each participant (case) in the sample; case statistics include predicted values, residuals, and regression diagnostics. *See also* Regression diagnostics.

Censored variable   A variable whose value is not observed if it exceeds (or is less than) a specified value. Censored variables commonly occur in survival analysis in which the central interest is in the time until an event occurs (e.g., relapse following treatment) and the event may not occur for all participants by the end of the observation period.

Centering   Subtracting the sample mean on a variable X from each subject's score on X.

Coefficient of alienation, coefficient of noncorrelation   The proportion of sd_Y remaining after the linear influence of the predictor(s) has been removed.

Conditional effect   In a regression equation containing higher order terms such as X^2 or XZ, the value of a regression coefficient is conditional if it holds only at a specific value of other predictors in the regression equation, typically the value zero.

Confidence interval (*CI*)   The interval within which the population value of the statistic is expected to lie with a specified confidence $(1 - \alpha)$. If repeated samples were taken from the population and a confidence interval for the mean were constructed from each sample, $(1 - \alpha)$ of them would contain the population mean.

Confidence limits (*CL*)   The outer boundaries of the confidence interval of a statistic, defined by the statistic $\pm$ the margin of error.

Confirmatory analysis   An analysis in which the fit of the data to a prespecified theoretical model is assessed.

Confounders   Variables that contribute to the variance of both Y and one or more predictors of Y: common causes or correlates of common causes, including correlated measurement error.

Contingent effect   *See* Conditional effect.

Contrast coding   A method of coding a set of g groups that examines $g - 1$ successive contrasts of group means or combinations of means of substantive interest.

Controlling, controlling for   Including certain variables in the equation in order to assess the relationship of other variables to Y independent of the effects of these controlled variables.

Covariance   The average of the products of deviations from the means of two variables expressed in the original units.

Crossed interaction   *See* Disordinal interaction.

Cross-lagged analysis   In longitudinal designs with two measurement periods, the value of each variable at Time 2 is regressed on its value at Time 1 and the value of other variables at Time 1.

Cross-level interaction   In clustered data, the interaction effect of IVs that are measured at different levels of cluster; e.g., a characteristic of schools and a characteristic of individual students such as school size by gender.

Cross-sectional data   Data gathered at a single point in time for each subject.

Cubic function   The effect of an independent variable taken to its third power.

Cumulative R^2   Total R^2 as predictors are added to the equation.

Curvilinear relationship   Any relationship between two variables that is not well described by a straight line.

Dichotomies, dichotomous variables   Variables that can take on only two values, such as Yes or No, Alive or Not alive. Synonymously, binary variables.

Disordinal interaction   In regression analysis with continuous predictors X and Z, an interaction in which the simple regression lines of Y on X at particular values of Z cross within the meaningful range of the variable X. In ANOVA or regression analysis with coded variables for individual groups, interactions in which the order of means of groups on one variable changes as a function of the level of the other variable.

Dummy variables   Representation of a variable consisting of g categories by creating $g - 1$ variables for which each of $g - 1$ categories is coded 1 on a single variable while the remaining categories are coded 0 on these variables.

Effect size (ES)   A measure of the magnitude of a relationship, either in the units of the original measures such as B_{YX} or mean differences, or in standardized units such as $r, r^2, R, \beta,$ or R^2 (as contrasted to measures of the confidence of its exceeding some null value, i.e., its statistical significance).

Effects codes   A method of coding categorical variables in which each group is compared to the (weighted or unweighted) mean of all the groups.

Efficient estimator   A statistic that estimates its population parameter with the smallest possible standard error.

Empirical Bayes estimate (EB)   In general, a parameter estimate that combines information from a sample with information from the population. In mixed models, an estimate of a parameter for a meaningful subset of data in a larger data set that is a combination of the estimate derived from only that subset of data and another estimate derived from the full complement of cases.

Endogenous variables   Variables in a structural (causal) model that are posited to depend, in part, on other variables in the model. *See also* Exogenous variables.

Essential multicollinearity   The correlation between a predictor and a higher order function of the predictor (e.g., X and X^2) that is due to the asymmetry of the distribution of the predictor and that cannot be eliminated by centering the predictor.

Exact collinearity   The circumstance in which one variable is a perfect function of (is perfectly predicted by) one or more other variables.

Exogenous variables   Variables in a structural equation model that are posited *not* to be caused by any other variables in the model. *See also* Endogenous variables.

Exploratory analysis   Any analysis in which a fully specified a priori model is *not* tested. The emphasis is on discovering relationships that may exist in the data. The results of such analyses should ideally be replicated.

Exponential growth, exponential relationships   Change in Y over the X scale that is an exponential function of the X values.

First differences   In time-sequenced data, the differences in values of a variable between adjacent time points for each of the subjects.

First-order effects versus higher order effects   First-order effects refer to the effects of individual variables in a regression equation such as the effects of predictor X or predictor Z, while higher order effects refer to effects of functions of the original variables such as the effects of $X^2, XZ,$ or X^2Z with all lower order terms partialed out.

Fit index (goodness-of-fit index)   Measure of the goodness of fit of a model to the observed data, including R^2, the squared multiple correlation in multiple regression, analogs to R^2 in other regression models, and indices of fit in structural equation modeling.

Fixed linear regression model   The assumption that the values of the IVs to which the investigator wishes to generalize have been specified, selected, or created in advance. This assumption is required in the derivation of the statistical tests that characterize most of the regression models in this text.

F ratio   The ratio of two variance estimates, the numerator representing variance due to the effect under investigation and the denominator representing only random error variance, used to test the statistical significance of the effect.

General linear model   The special case of the generalized linear model in which the link function is the identity function (untransformed Y), of which OLS regression is an example.

Generalized linear model   A class of regression models that relates a transformation of the dependent variable Y linearly to the IVs. The function that transforms Y is the link function. The generalized linear model subsumes logistic and Poisson regression.

Goodness-of-fit test   In structural equation modeling, a statistical test that provides a test of the null hypothesis that the model accounts for all of the systematic relationships in the data. Such tests can only be performed for overidentified models. In structural equation models the goodness-of-fit test is often supplemented by fit indices that provide information about the degree of fit of the model to data. *See also* Fit index.

Growth models   In longitudinal data, models that represent individual trajectories over age or time. A common form of growth trajectory (e.g., linear) is specified for all individuals, but individuals may vary in the parameters that characterize the growth (e.g., slope and intercept for linear growth).

Hierarchical analysis   A regression analysis in which variables or sets of variables are entered into the equation sequentially in an order designed to answer empirical or theoretical questions.

Hierarchical linear models (multilevel models)   Regression analysis models that contain predictors measured at more than one level of aggregation of the data (e.g., measures on individuals within a group and measures on the whole group) and that take into account the clustering in the data in the estimation of error variance.

Hierarchically structured data   Data in which sampling occurs at multiple levels: e.g., groups and then individuals in those groups, or individuals and then multiple time points for those individuals, or combinations thereof.

Homoscedasticity   The circumstance in which the distribution of the residuals or errors of prediction have equal variance for all predicted values of Y in the population.

Identification   The condition in which there are sufficient constraints in the model to permit estimates of parameters. *See also* Just-identified models, Overidentification, and Underidentification.

Identification error   Bias in the estimate of a population parameter attributable to specification error, sampling error, or because certain relationships are too small to be the basis of such estimates.

Imputation   The estimation of one or more values for missing raw data points based on other information or measures on other variables.

Index plot   A variable plotted against the ID or other indicator of the sequence or setting in which data were gathered.

Influence   An index of the effect of a single case on the estimate of B, on the regression equation as a whole, or on the predicted value of Y.

Interaction   The circumstance in which the impact of one variable on Y is conditional on (varies across) the values of another predictor.

Intraclass correlation   A measure of the within-class or group resemblance as a fraction of the total variance.

Intrinsic nonlinearity   Nonlinearity of a regression model that cannot be eliminated by transformation of the model to a form that can be analyzed with linear regression.

Jittering   Adding small random variation to a case's scores on one or more of the variables so that points having the same value are not plotted on top of each other on the graph.

Just-identified models   A model, such as a single regression equation, in which there is just enough information to produce a single estimate of each effect (e.g., B_{YX}).

Lagged variable   In longitudinal data, the values of a predictor at one or more previous time points used to predict later values of Y.

Latent variable models   In structural equation modeling, models in which each theoretical construct is assessed by several different indicators. The latent variable underlies the indicators and represents what they have in common. Latent variables are theoretically free of measurement error. The model specifies relationships among the latent variables.

Level of measurement   The properties of the scale: categorical (without general meaning of the numerical values assigned), ordinal (increases in numbers represent ordered but not necessarily equal increases in the property being assessed), interval (increases in numbers represent equal increases in the property being assessed), and ratio (interval scales for which zero means none of the property).

Leverage   An index of a case's extremity on the IVs.

Likelihood   The probability that a score or set of scores (sample) could occur, given the values of a set of parameters in a specific model; the highest probability possible is the maximum likelihood.

Likelihood ratio   The ratio of the maximum likelihood under one model to the maximum likelihood under a more complete model; used in testing the goodness fit of a model relative to models with fewer or more parameters. *See also* Likelihood and Maximum likelihood.

Likert-type scales   A variable for which responses are made on an ordered multiple-option scale such as " never, occasionally, often" or "1 (completely false), 2, 3, 4, 5 (completely true)." Such scales are used to make finer distinctions than can be made on a 2-point Yes/No or True/False item.

Linear by linear interaction   An interaction XZ between two predictors that is linear in both predictors; that is, the regression of Y on X is linear at all values of Z and the regression of Y on Z is linear at all values of X.

Linear in the coefficients, linear in the parameters   A regression model in which the predicted score is the sum of the products of each predictor multiplied by its corresponding regression coefficient, as in the standard form of OLS regression employed throughout most of this book.

Linear in the variables   Indicating that a straight line well describes the relationship between variables; no additional variables are required to represent nonlinearity.

Linear transformations   Transformations in which the relationships among differences between observations are not altered (e.g., the difference between Subject 2 and Subject 3 remains twice the difference between Subject 1 and Subject 4). These are created by adding or subtracting the same value from every observation and/or multiplying or dividing every observation by the same value.

Link function   In the generalized linear model, the transformation that relates the predicted outcome to the observed Y. In OLS, the link function is the identity function; in logistic regression, the logit; in Poisson regression, the logarithm.

Listwise deletion   A data-analytic option in which only those cases having no missing values are included.

Logistic regression model   A regression model in which the observed dependent variable is binary or comprised of ordered categories (ordinal logistic regression); a form of the generalized linear model in which the link function is the logit, and the regression parameters are expressed as log odds associated with unit increases in the predictors.

Lowess (or Loess) Curve Acronym for *lo*cally *we*ighted *s*catterplot *s*moother. A nonparametric method that produces a smooth regression line or curve that describes the trend of the X-Y relationship in a scatterplot. No assumptions are made about the form of the relationship.

Main effect Arising from ANOVA terminology, the effect of an independent variable on Y averaged across the (main or interaction) effects of other independent variables.

Margin of error (*me*) The potential error in an estimated statistic as compared to the population value, expressed in the units of the statistic under investigation.

Maximum likelihood (ML) A method for the estimation of population parameters and their standard errors based on the principle of maximizing the likelihood of the sample, given the estimates of the population parameters; an alternative to OLS estimation. *See also* Likelihood ratio.

Mean substitution Using the mean of a variable as an estimate of the value of missing data.

Measurement error Error in the employed values of variables due to the presence of distorting influences on the assessment, such as momentary distractions, errors in recording or understanding, influences of other variables on responses to particular items. These are uncorrelated with the " true scores" by definition and treated as " random."

Mediators Variables that stand causally between a predictor and some variable on which it has an effect, and that account, in whole or in part, for that effect.

Missing at random (MAR) Any bias due to missing data is accounted for by the values of other measured variables in the model.

Missing completely at random (MCAR) Missing data on one or more variables are unbiased and do not depend on measured or unmeasured variables.

Mixed model equation In hierarchical linear modeling, a random coefficient regression equation that contains predictors measured at different levels of aggregation (e.g., characteristics of individuals in a group and characteristics of the whole group), referred to as the *mixed model* because it "mixes" the levels of aggregation in analysis. *See also* Hierarchical linear model.

Model 2 error A regression model in which the error term is taken from a model with additional predictors (usually the final model in a hierarchical sequence).

Moderation, moderator An IV that interacts with another IV in predicting Y. The effect of each can be said to be conditional on the other.

Monotonic relationship, monotonic transform A rescaling in which the rank order of variable values is retained without necessarily retaining the relative spacing of the scores: thus, $1, 5, 6, 11, 28$ is a monotonic transform of $1, 2, 3, 4, 5$, and so is $20, 21, 22, 23, 24$.

Moving average A weighted or unweighted average value of Y that corresponds to a fixed range on X in cross-sectional data or a fixed number of adjacent locations in data collected over time. For example, in data measured over time, the moving average of three adjacent time points would be the average of Y_1, Y_2, and Y_3 for Time 2; the average of Y_2, Y_3, and Y_4 for Time 3, and the average of Y_3, Y_4, and Y_5 for Time 4.

Multicollinearity Very high multiple correlations among some or all of the predictors in an equation.

Multilevel models *See* Hierarchical linear models.

Multiple correlation (R and R^2) The correlation between observed Y and the value of Y estimated from a set of predictors ($=R$); the proportion of Y variance associated with a set of predictors ($=R^2$).

Multiple episode data In survival analysis, inclusion of re-entry into the at-risk status.

Multiplicative error   Error in a regression model such that Y is a multiplicative function of the regression model and the error.

Multivariate R^2   The analog to R^2 in analyses with multiple dependent variables as well as independent variables.

Nested models   In ANOVA, models with a hierarchical structure in which only a limited number of possible combinations of the levels of each of the factors occur. In contrast, crossed designs include all possible combinations of the levels of the factors. In multiple regression and structural equation analysis, two models in which one is a more restricted version of the other. The most common restriction is to set one or more of the parameters (e.g., regression coefficients) equal to 0.

Nil hypothesis   The null hypothesis that the value of some population parameter is zero.

Nonessential multicollinearity   Multicollinearity between a variable and a higher order function of the same variable (e.g., X and X^2) that can be eliminated by centering the original variable X.

Nonlinear transformations   Rescaling of a variable in which the order of the values may be changed (nonmonotonic) or remain the same (monotonic) but in which the spacing among the scores is changed.

Nonparametric   Not requiring assumptions about the shape of the population distribution, such as normality, or the shape of the relationship between variables, such as linearity.

Nonparametric regression   An approach to discerning the pattern of relationship of a predictor X (or set of predictors) to Y through the use of data-driven smoothing functions (e.g., lowess) rather than through a regression model.

Nonrecursive model   A structural equation model including reciprocal causation or feedback.

Normal equations   The set of simultaneous equations that are solved to determine the estimated regression coefficients in OLS analysis.

Normality   Having a distribution of values that follows the "bell shaped" curve in the population. The formula for the normal curve itself is fairly complex, and its particular utility lies in the fact that the distribution of various sample statistics tends to be normal if the samples are large.

Null hypothesis significance tests (NHST)   Tests of the significance of the difference between the observed value of a statistic and some value that has been a priori specified, typically zero (the "nil" hypothesis).

Odds, odds ratio   The odds of some event is the probability of the event divided by 1 minus its probability. The odds ratio is the odds of the outcome for a particular value of the IV, divided by the odds for the IV value that is one unit lower.

Omitted variable   A variable that distorts the relationship between Y and some other variable when it is not included in the equation.

Ordinal logistic regression   Logistic regression in which Y has more than two ordered values.

Ordinary least squares (OLS)   Statistical methods based on the minimization of the squared differences between the observed and predicted values of Y.

Orthogonal   When describing variables or sets of variables orthogonal means uncorrelated. When describing code systems for categorical or group variables orthogonal indicates that the codes used to produce the IVs are not linearly correlated, although the variables resulting from their application to the data will be correlated if the numbers of cases in categories are not equal or proportional.

Orthogonal polynomials   A set of orthogonally coded variables that assess linear, quadratic, cubic, etc., relationships with Y for an X consisting of equally spaced ordered categories.

Outliers   Atypical data points that do not fit with the rest of the data and appear to come from another population.

Overcontrol   Employing IVs in a regression model that includes not only appropriate potential predictors and confounders but also variables that may be mediators, or correlates of mediators of the predictors of primary interest or alternative measures of Y.

Overidentification   A structural equation model estimate that may be determined uniquely by each of two or more equations in the same model.

Pairwise deletion   The management of missing data by estimation of correlations or other coefficients based on all sample members who have the data needed for that particular coefficient.

Partial correlation coefficients   The correlation between two variables when each has had the variance attributable to the same set of one or more other variables subtracted from it.

Partial redundancy   Variables whose prediction of Y partly overlaps, so that the sum of their individual predictions is greater than their combined prediction.

Partial regression coefficients   Regression coefficients when there are other predictors in the equation.

Path coefficients   Regression coefficients in path models, typically standardized.

Path model, path analysis   A structural equation model involving only measured variables, typically standardized. Path analysis is the statistical procedure of estimating a path model.

Pearson product moment correlation (r)   The least squares correlation coefficient presented in this book, devised by Karl Pearson; a function of the products of the first moments (the means and the variances) of the two variables.

Percent of maximum possible score (POMP)   A linear transformation of an otherwise arbitrarily scaled score in which the lowest possible score is zero and the maximum possible score is 100.

Phi coefficient   The product moment correlation between two dichotomous variables.

Point biserial   The product moment correlation between a dichotomous variable and a scaled (continuous) variable.

Point of inflection   A point where the rate of acceleration of a curve changes from positive to negative or negative to positive.

Poisson distribution   A probability distribution associated with counts of the number of rare events that occur in a particular time; the distribution of residuals expected in Poisson regression.

Poisson regression   A regression model suitable when Y consists of counts of rare phenomena.

Polynomial regression   Employing power functions of predictors (x, x^2, x^3, etc.) in a regression equation to model curvilinear relationships.

Power, power analysis   The probability of rejecting a null hypothesis that is false to a specified degree for a given sample size, Type I error rate, and effect size. Power analysis is the process of estimating the power of a proposed or completed study.

Power polynomials   *See* Polynomial regression.

Precision (of estimates)   The area within the confidence limits: upper and lower boundaries for a statistic based on sample data.

Product moment r   *See* Pearson product moment correlation.

Protected tests   The requirement that an overall omnibus test (e.g., an F test) be statistically significant prior to conducting subsequent tests of individual parameters (e.g., regression coefficients) or pairs of means (multiple comparisons) included in the omnibus test.

Quadratic function   The effect of X on Y that is represented by the contribution of x^2.

Random effects   In hierarchically structured data (mixed regression), variance associated with differences in parameter estimates between aggregated units, such as differences in regression coefficients and regression constants between groups of cases within a clustered data set, or individual changes over time in longitudinal data.

Random error In OLS regression, random error is that portion of the dependent variable Y that is unrelated to the set of IVs.

Rectilinear *See* Linear in the variables.

Recursive Models without causal reciprocal effects or loops.

Reduced model A regression model developed from a more extensive regression model from which IVs, interactions, or power terms that did not contribute significantly were removed from the equation to yield a reduced regression equation containing fewer predictors.

Regression diagnostics Specialized statistics that help identify cases that are extreme on the IVs, that are discrepant from the value predicted by the model, or that substantially change the results of the regression analysis.

Regression toward the mean The mathematical necessity that the predicted value of z_Y must be closer to zero than is z_X unless $r_{XY} = 1.0$.

Reliability Defined in most psychometric approaches as the squared correlation of the true score with the observed (measured) score.

Respecification A change in the variables, direction of effects, or form of effects in a structural equation model as a consequence of data-based findings.

Ridge regression An estimation method, used when there is substantial multicollinearity, for obtaining slightly biased estimates of regression coefficients with smaller standard errors than OLS regression.

"Rise over the run" The linear regression B. *See also* Slope.

Robustness The extent to which a statistical estimate and its significance test are likely to be relatively unbiased by failure of the statistical model's assumptions.

Scatterplot matrix (SPLOM) The array of all the bivariate scatterplots.

Semipartial correlation coefficients Also called part correlations, the unique relationship of a variable with Y: the square root of its unique contribution to R^2.

Sensitivity analysis Determination of the expected changes in statistical estimates associated with plausible alternative models or assumptions.

Serial dependency *See* Autocorrelation.

Set correlation analysis (SC) Analysis in the OLS framework with sets of dependent variables rather than a single dependent variable.

Shrunken R^2 The estimate of R^2 in the population.

Simple slope, simple regression The regression of Y on X at a particular value of X (in curvilinear regression) or at a particular value of another predictor with which X interacts; analogous to a simple effect in ANOVA.

Simplex structure A pattern of correlations or covariance in which values systematically decrease as a function of the separation of the variables in time or space.

Slope The regression coefficient, the increase in Y per unit increase in X.

Smoothing Using a function of some or all of the data to describe the XY relationship, especially in a scatterplot.

Spearman rank order correlation (r_s) The product moment correlation between the rankings within two sets of ranked observations.

Specification error Fitting an incorrect model to the data. This problem may occur because (a) the form of one or more X-Y relationships is not correct, (b) interactions of IVs are not included, (c) IVs are omitted from the model that should have been included, (d) IVs are mistakenly included in the model, or (e) the IVs are unreliable.

Standard deviation (sd) In a sample, the square root of the average squared deviations from the mean. As a population estimate, the sum of the squared deviations is divided by $n-1$; this estimate is routinely provided by most computer programs.

Standardized scores   Scores linearly transformed by subtracting the mean and dividing by the standard deviation for each observation, z scores.

Stem and leaf displays   A univariate plot closely related to the histogram that also includes the specific numerical values of each score.

Stepwise regression   A sequence of regression analyses in which variables are entered automatically in order of magnitude of contribution to R^2, with or without other constraints. An alternative (step-down or tear-down) is to start with all possible predictors and have them automatically removed sequentially as they fail to contribute to R^2.

Structural equation modeling (SEM)   SEM is a set of statistical procedures for estimating the relationship between underlying constructs (latent variables) and measured variables (the measurement model), and among both measured variables and latent variables themselves (the structural model). Path analysis is a special case of the structural model that includes only measured variables. Specialized computer programs (e.g., AMOS, EQS, LISREL, M-Plus) simultaneously estimate the measurement and structural models.

Structural sets   Sets of IVs grouped because they represent aspects of nominal scales or of the shape of a variable's relationship to Y rather than a common substantive or theoretical role.

Suppression   In regression, the circumstance that adding a predictor to the equation increases or changes the sign of the B of another predictor, or causes the standardized regression coefficient for another predictor to become larger than the correlation of that predictor with the criterion.

Synergistic interactions   *See* Augmentation.

Tear-down procedure   *See* Stepwise regression.

Tetrachoric correlation (r_t)   An estimate of r between two normally distributed variables from data in which the two variables were measured as artificial dichotomies.

Time series data   Longitudinal data in which the variables are collected at equally spaced points in time. Typical applications include the effect of one series on another (concomitant time series) or the effect of an intervention that occurs during the series. The typical focus is on a single unit (e.g., an individual) so that $n =$ the number of time points.

Tolerance   One minus the squared multiple correlation of a given IV from other IVs in the equation.

Tracing rule   In path models, determination of the effects of a predictor by summing the products of coefficients along paths from the IV to the DV.

Type I error   Believing that some zero population effect is nonzero on the basis of a test of statistical significance.

Type II error   Believing that some nonzero population effect is zero on the basis of a test of statistical significance.

Uncrossed interaction   In regression analysis with continuous predictors X and Z, an interaction in which the simple regression lines of Y on X at particular values of Z do not cross within the observed range of X. In ANOVA with interacting factors, the rank order of means of one factor is constant across all levels of the other factor. *See also* Disordinal interaction.

Underidentification   Having too little information (variance, covariance, or predictors) to produce a unique estimate of some statistic.

Unweighted effects, unweighted codes   Codes of categorical independent variables in which the groups contribute equally to the estimates, regardless of their ns.

Variance   The squared standard deviation.

Variance function   The form of the expected distribution of residuals in the generalized linear model (e.g., normal in OLS, binomial in logistic regression, Poisson in Poisson regression).

Variance-stabilizing transformations   Transformations of a variable in a regression equation that serve to decrease the heteroscedasticity of residuals (i.e., to decrease or eliminate the relationship between values of the predicted scores and the variance of the residuals associated with that predicted score).

Weighted effects   Methods of effects coding categorical (group) independent variables in which the groups contribute to estimates proportionately to their numbers. *See also* Unweighted effects.

z scores, z transformation   *See* Standardized scores.

Zero-order correlation   The bivariate product moment correlation.

Statistical Symbols and Abbreviations

A	Set of IVs *A*: Capital letters in bold italic type generally indicate sets of variables.
A	Arcsine transformation
Adj.	Adjusted
AIC	Akaike information criterion
ANCOVA	Analysis of covariance
ANOVA	Analysis of variance
B_0	Regression intercept
B	Regression coefficient of Y on an IV in measured or "raw" units
BG	Between groups
BIC	Bayesian information criterion
c	Number of cells in a multiple categorical IV analysis
C	Matrix of sums of squares and cross products among the IVs: Capital letters in bold roman type generally indicate matrices.
C	Code variable
C_i	Component i (principal components)
CA	Canonical analysis
cf	Canonical factor
CI	Confidence interval
CL	Confidence limit
COV	Variance-covariance matrix of the IVs
Cov	Covariance
D	Deviance, lack of model fit (logistic regression); Durbin-Watson statistic; difference score
D_i	Cook's distance (global influence of a single case i)
d	Bandwidth distance (kernel density estimation)
d_i	Deviance residual for case i (logistic regression); deleted residual for case i, which is the difference between the observed Y for case i and its predicted value with case i deleted from the data set (regression diagnostics)

df	Degrees of freedom
DFBETAS$_{ij}$	Standardized change in regression coefficient B_j when case i is included in versus deleted from the regression analysis
DFFITS$_i$	Standardized change in the predicted score for case i when case i is included in versus deleted from the regression analysis
DV	Dependent variable, Y
e	Regression residual or error in prediction
EM	Expectation-maximization algorithm
ES	Effect size
f	Frequency
F	Statistic used for multiple *df* numerator and denominator significance tests
G	Amount of total deviance accounted for by IVs in logistic regression
g	Number of groups or categories in a nominal scale
GLS	Generalized least squares
GM	Generalized M-estimators
h	Number of variable sets
H	Hat matrix (leverage values and diagonal)
h_{ii}	Leverage for case i, in regression diagnostics
h_{ii}^*	Centered leverage for case i, in regression diagnostics
ICC	Intraclass correlation
IV	Independent variable
k	Number of variables or number of independent variables
L	Logit transformation
L$_1$	Least absolute deviation
LAD	Least absolute deviation
ln	Natural logarithm, to the base e
log	Logarithm
LTS	Least trimmed squares
M	Mean
M_U	Unweighted mean
M_W	Weighted mean
$M_{Y|X}$	Conditional mean of Y at a specified value of X
Max	Maximum
Mdn	Median
me	Margin of error
M-estimation	A robust estimation procedure in which more extreme observations are given lower or 0 weight
Min	Minimum
ML	Maximum likelihood
MLE	Maximum likelihood estimation
MR	Multiple regression
MRC	Multiple regression/correlation
MS	Mean square
n	Number of subjects (cases)
n*	Number of cases required to produce the desired statistical power
OLS	Ordinary least squares
p	Probability
P	Proportion of sample or subsample (usually of cases coded 1)

$\hat{P}_i$	Predicted probability of membership in the "case" group for a binary outcome
$pr_{Y1\cdot23}$	Partial correlation (of Y with X_1, partialing X_2 and X_3)
PR	Probit transformation
q	Lesser number of variables in the DV and IV sets in set correlation
Q	1 minus the proportion
Q_1	First quartile: the score corresponding to the n/4th case from the bottom value
Q_3	Third quartile
q-q	Quantile-quantile plots
r	Pearson product moment correlation coefficient
r_b	Biserial correlation coefficient
r_i	Residual for case i; Pearson residual for case i (logistic regression); level 1 residual in random coefficient regression
r^{ii}, r^{ij}	Elements of the inverted correlation matrix of IVs
r_{pb}	Point biserial correlation coefficient
r_s	Spearman's rank order correlation coefficient
r_t	Tetrachoric correlation coefficient
r_{xx}	Sample estimate of the reliability of variable X
$r_{X_t Y_t}$	Correlation between true scores of X and Y
$\tilde{r}$	Estimated value of r under some change in sample values or in a new sample
$R_{Y\cdot123}$	Multiple correlation of a single DV, Y, estimated from IVs X_1, X_2, and X_3
$\mathbf{R}_{Y,AB}^2$	Multivariate squared correlation of IV set Y estimated from DV sets A and B
$\tilde{R}^2$	Shrunken R^2; unbiased population estimate of R^2
R_L^2	Index of fit in logistic regression
$R_{Y\cdot AB}^2$	Squared multiple correlation from sets A plus B of predictors
$R_{YB\cdot A}^2$	Squared partial correlation of set B with Y with set A held constant (partialed)
$\mathbf{R}_{ij}$	Matrix of correlations among the IVs
RC	Random coefficient regression
$\mathbf{S}_B$	Covariance matrix of the regression coefficients
sd	Standard deviation (generally the sample-based population estimate using $n - 1$ in the denominator)
$sd_{Y0-\hat{Y}0}$	Standard error of the prediction of Y from IVs in a newly observed case
SE	Standard error (subscript indicates for which statistic)
$SE_{Y-\hat{Y}}$	Standard error of estimate
$SIQR$	Semi-interquartile range
sr	Semipartial (or part) correlation (implicitly with all other variables partialed); $sr_{1\cdot23}$ indicates sr of Y with X_1, partialing X_2 and X_3
SS	Sum of squares
t	Student's t test statistic; time
T	Number of equally spaced observations
t_i	Externally studentized residual for case i
u	Number of categories of a categorical variable
u_{ij}	Level 2 residual in random coefficient regression
VIF	Variance inflation factor
$\mathbf{V}$	Matrix of variances and covariances among the IVs

W	An IV in its original units; or a weight for a variable in an equation
W_M	Value of W at the minimum or maximum of a polynomial function
WG	Within groups
WLS	Weighted least squares
x	A centered (mean subtracted from each score) IV
X	An IV in its original units, various italicized letters or numerically subscripted X are used for different IVs
$\mathbf{X}$	A raw data matrix of predictors
X_{cross}	Value of X at which two simple regression lines cross
X_M	Value of X at the minimum or maximum of a polynomial function
X^*	Transformed value of X
XZ	Cross product of two predictors X and Z
Y	Dependent variable
$\hat{Y}_{123}$	Regression-estimated DV, Y, predicted from variables X_1, X_2, and X_3
$\hat{Y}_M$	Maximum or minimum value of predicted score in a polynomial equation
z'	Fisher transformation of r
z	Standardized variable: variable from which the sample mean has been subtracted and the result divided by the sample sd
Z_{cross}	Value of Z at which two simple regression lines cross

Greek Letters

α	Alpha: Type I error rate; Also used to refer to internal consistency reliability of a variable (Cronbach's α); also, smoothing parameter in lowess.
β	Beta: Type II error rate; also, standardized regression coefficient.
β^*	Unstandardized regression coefficient in population, corresponding to B in sample
γ	Gamma: fixed effects parameter in random coefficient regression
ε_i	Epsilon: random error in prediction for case i in the population
ε^2	Epsilon squared: adjusted proportion of variation accounted for
η^2	Eta squared: proportion of variation accounted for
κ	Kappa: condition number
λ	Lambda: eigenvalue; exponent in power transformation
μ	Mu: population mean; rate parameter in Poisson regression
$\mu_{Y|X}$	Mu: conditional population mean of Y at a specified value of X
π_i	Pi: probability of membership in the "case" group for a binary outcome variable
ρ	Rho: correlation in the population; population multiple correlation
ρ_{XX}	Rho: reliability of X in the population
$\rho_{XZ,XZ}$	Rho: reliability of cross-product term XZ in the population
σ	Sigma: standard deviation in the population
$\sigma^2_{Y|\hat{Y}}$	Sigma: conditional population variance of the residuals, given $\hat{Y}$
τ	Tau: variance component in random coefficient regression
ϕ	Phi coefficient (product moment correlation between two dichotomies)
χ^2	Chi-square distribution; statistic used for goodness-of-fit testing

Author Index

A

Abelson, R. P., 50, 183, 333, 335, 388,
    471, 605
Aber, M. S., 586, 589, 595
Agresti, A., 486
Aiken, L. S., 2, 155, 206, 207, 264, 273,
    280, 290, 291, 295, 297, 300,
    317, 331, 373, 381, 427, 465,
    496, 520, 543, 555, 558, 564–565
Akaike, H., 509
Alastair, S., 248
Aldrich, J. H., 486
Algina, J., 130
Alpert, A., 595
Anderson, R.L., 215
Anderson, T. W., 611
Anscombe, F. J., 417
Arthur, R. J., 2
Atkinson, A. C., 137, 213, 237, 238, 239,
    251

B

Baker, B., 23
Baltes, P. B., 569
Barcikowski, R. S., 134, 538
Baron, R. M., 269, 351
Baumert, J., 607
Beckman, R. J., 401
Beebe, B., 600
Behnken, D. W., 398
Belsley, D. A., 397, 402, 424, 425
Bentler, P. M., 457, 502, 590
Berk, R. A., 455
Berkson, J., 50
Bernstein, I. H., 55
Berry, W. D.
Bertenthal, B. I., 602
Biesanz, J., 4, 456
Blalock, H. M., Jr., 457, 465
Blank, G.
Blossfeld, H.-P., 600
Bohrnstedt, G. W., 297
Boker, S. M., 587, 602

Bollen, K. A., 68, 145, 411, 454, 468,
    470, 473, 586
Borenstein, M., 15, 91, 604
Bosker, R., 148, 537, 538, 541, 544, 545,
    546
Box, G. E. P., 149, 236, 239, 600
Boyce, C. M., 14
Breusch, T., 133
Brewer, M.
Brgk, A. S., 537, 544, 545, 546, 560,
    563, 564
Brook, J. S., 642
Brown, D., 602
Brown, D. R., 272, 291
Browne, M. W., 470
Browne, W., 546, 566
Bryk, A. S., 2, 148, 546, 566, 607
Burstein, L., 564
Busemeyer, J. R., 297, 299
Byrne, B., 145, 472–473, 586

C

Campbell, D. T., 4, 36, 37, 123,
    452–453, 456
Carlson, J. E., 609, 610
Carmer, S. G., 184, 188
Carroll, R. J., 147, 251
Champoux, J. E., 275
Chaplin, W. F., 275
Chatfield, C., 149
Chatterjee, S., 398, 411, 415, 429
Cheong, Y. F., 546
Cleary, P. D., 285
Cleveland, W. S., 111, 114, 116, 313, 391
Cliff, N., 154, 247, 474, 609
Cochran, W. G., 456
Cohen, J., 5, 15, 48, 50, 52, 92, 155, 179,
    180, 181, 182, 205, 209, 212,
    220, 256, 284, 297, 298, 362,
    445, 465, 470, 517, 604, 614,
    615, 616, 618, 622, 642, 652,
    653, 654

Cohen, P., 155, 445, 465, 470, 571, 602,
    622, 642
Cohen, S., 285
Colby, S. M., 602
Coleman, J. S., 2
Collett, D., 486, 513, 514
Collins, L., 60, 595
Collins, L. M., 445
Congdon, R., 546
Cook, R. D., 116, 133, 235, 238, 245,
    251, 401, 402, 418, 424, 514
Cook, T. D., 4, 452–453, 456
Corrieal, S. E., 602
Cox, D. R., 236, 502, 504, 598
Cramer, E. M., 610
Crocker, L., 130
Cronbach, L. J., 129, 429
Crown, C., 600
Culhane, S. C., 333
Cumsille, P., 587

D

D'Agostino, R. B., 140
Darlington, R. B., 14, 97, 213, 427
Davidian, M., 147
Dawes, R. M., 97
De Leeuw, J., 148, 537, 538, 539, 544,
    545, 546, 564–565
Delaney, H. D., 256, 363
DeVellis, R., 213
Diaconis, P., 144, 373
Dielman, T. E., 602
Dodson, J. D., 2
Doll, R., 54
Donev, A. N., 213
Dou, T., 2
Draper, D., 546, 566
Draper, N. R., 226, 235, 237, 238, 246,
    251, 252, 398, 419, 427, 428
Duncan, O. D., 123, 124, 457, 468
Duncan, S. C., 595
Duncan, T. E., 595
Dweck, C. S., 367

E

Edwards, A. E., 184
Ehrenberg, A. S. C., 15
Embretson, S. E., 130
England, P., 2
Erlbacher, A.
Estrella, A, 502

F

Fahrmier, L., 479, 531, 535
Farkas, G., 2
Fechner, G. T., 227
Feldstein, S., 600
Fidell, L. S., 428, 485
Finn, J. D., 47
Fisher, R. A., 243, 391
Fleiss, J. L., 479, 486, 516, 517, 537, 538
Forsyth, D. R., 455
Fox, J., 103, 104, 114, 237, 238, 239,
    251, 252, 425, 486, 513, 519, 520
Fredericks, B. C., 98
Freeman, M. F., 245
Friedrich, R. J., 283
Fuller, W. A., 145

G

Gaito, J., 216
Games, P. A., 184
Ganzach, Y., 299, 300
Garcia, M., 642
Gardner, W., 525, 526, 530, 531, 532
Gibbons, R. D.
Gigerenzer, G., 5, 15
Glass, G. V.
Glymour, C., 474
Goldberger, A. S., 155, 457
Goldstein, H., 537, 545, 546, 566
Gollob, H. F., 571
Goodman, L. A., 517
Gottman, J. M., 600
Graham, J., 587
Graham, J. W., 339, 450
Granger, C.
Gray, J. B., 399
Green, B. F., Jr., 97
Greenberg, D. F.
Greene, W. H., 133, 149
Greenland, S., 494, 520
Gregson, R. A. M., 600
Gulledge, T. R., Jr., 140

H

Hadi, A. S., 398, 416, 429
Hagle, T. M., 224
Hamagami, F., 594, 602
Hamilton, L. C., 224
Hardy, M. A., 303
Hardyck, C. D., 23
Harlow, L. L., 5, 15, 50, 183
Harris, R. J., 428
Hartley, H. O., 15, 215
Hastie, T., 195, 253
Hawkins, D. M., 418
Hay, R. A., 149
Hayes, H. K., 391
Healey, M., 546, 566
Henik, A., 78

Higginbotham, H. N., 455
Hoaglin, D. C., 221, 391
Hofer, S. M., 450
Hoffer, T., 2
Holland, P. W., 569
Hooper, J. W., 609, 610
Horn, J., 60
Hosmer, D. W., 486, 502, 504, 506, 508,
    511, 513, 515, 519, 520
Houseman, E. E., 215
Howell, D. C., 363
Huber, P. J., 413, 414, 418
Hubert, M., 418
Humphreys, L. G., 299

I

Immer, F. R., 391

J

Jaccard, J., 275, 283, 494
Jackman, R. W., 411
Jackson, J. E., 429
Jaffe, J., 600
Janis, I. L., 194, 213, 292
Jasnow, M., 600
Jenkins, G. M., 149, 600
Jensen, P. S., 517
Joiner, B. L., 134
Jolliffe, I. T., 429
Jones, L. E., 297
Judd, C. M., 212, 213, 333, 537

K

Kam, C.-M., 445
Kazdin, A. E., 517
Kazdin, A. E. O, 517
Kenny, D. A., 36, 37, 123, 269, 454, 457,
    537
Kessler, R. C., 285, 517
Kiecolt-Glaser, J. K., 607
Kilbourne, B. S., 2
Kilgore, S. B., 2
Kim, C., 607
Kirk, R. E., 216, 272, 291, 296, 316,
    327, 333, 363
Kleinbaum, D. G., 215
Kraemer, H. C., 517, 595
Krause, N., 285, 295
Kreft, I., 148, 537, 538, 539, 544, 545,
    546, 564–565, 566, 580
Krull, J. L., 331, 543, 555, 558
Krus, D. J., 609
Kruskal, W. H., 415, 517
Kuh, E., 397, 402
Kupfer, D., 595
Kupfer, D. J., 517
Kupper, L. L., 215
Kutner, M. H., 197, 206, 427, 516, 532
Kvålseth, T. O., 248

L

Land, K. C., 530, 531, 532
Lee, J. J., 103
Lee, V., 2
Lemeshow, S., 486
Leroy, A., 419
Levin, J. R., 304

Lewis, C., 610, 612
Li, F., 595
Ling, R. F., 429
Littell, R. C., 566, 586
Little, R. J. A., 339, 440
Little, T. D., 607
Loehlin, J. C., 468
Long, J. S., 479, 486, 502, 506, 513, 515,
    517, 518, 523, 525, 531, 532
Looney, S. W., 140
Lord, F. M., 569
Lubinski, D., 299
Lykken, D. T., 50

M

MacCallum, R. C., 299, 300, 470, 473,
    476, 607
Maddala, G. S., 144
Mahan, J. L., 2
Malarkey, W. B., 607
Mar, C. M., 299, 300
Marks, L. E., 228
Marquardt, D. W., 202–203, 264
Marwell, G., 297
Mason, W. M., 544
Mauro, R., 144
Maxwell, S. E., 256, 363, 410
McArdle, J. J., 571, 586, 589, 594, 595,
    602, 605
McCall, P. L., 530, 531, 532
McCleary, R., 149
McClelland, G. H., 212, 213, 298, 299,
    333, 427
McConaughy, S. H., 363
McCullagh, P., 479, 480, 535
McDonald, R. P., 55
Meehl, P. E., 5, 50, 456
Meek, C., 474
Mehta, P. D., 594, 595
Menard, S., 486, 512, 513, 517, 519, 520
Meng, X.-L., 152
Michaels, K. M., 291
Michels, K. M., 272
Miller, A. J., 3
Miller, R. G., Jr., 184, 185
Milliken, G. A., 566
Molenaar, P. C. M., 602
Monette, G., 425
Mosteller, F., 97, 225, 233, 234, 235,
    247, 251, 252
Mulaik, S. A., 5, 15
Muller, K. E., 215
Mulvey, E. P., 525, 526, 530, 531, 532
Muthén, B., 595
Myers, R. H., 231

N

Nachtsheim, C. J., 197, 427, 516, 532
Nagelkerke, N. J. D., 503
Nagin, D. S., 530, 531, 532, 595
Nee, J. C. M., 616
Nelder, J. A., 479, 480
Nesselroade, J. R., 569, 595
Neter, J., 197, 206, 231, 234, 252, 286,
    427, 516, 532
Nicewander, W. A., 610
Nunnally, J., 55, 130

O

Oakes, D., 598
Offord, D. R., 517
Olkin, I., 47, 88, 153, 174, 312
Olson, C. L., 616, 619
Owen, D. B., 15, 215, 241, 243, 643, 645, 647, 649

P

Pagan, A., 133
Pampel, F. C., 486, 512
Pearl, J., 455
Pearson, E. S., 15, 215
Pedhazur, E. J.
Peixoto, J. L., 366, 426
Peters, W. S., 275
Peto, R., 54
Petrinovich, L. F., 23
Piacentini, J. C.
Pillai, K. C. S., 611, 616
Pillow, D. R., 411
Pitts, S. C., 4, 212, 213, 220, 288, 298, 299, 309, 427, 456
Plewis, I., 546, 566
Pompe, B., 602
Powers, L. R., 391
Pregibon, D., 512, 513
Prentice, D. A., 335
Press, S. J., 485
Price, B., 429
Pruzek, R. M., 98

R

Rabash, J., 546, 566
Radbill, L., 309
Rahe, R. H., 2
Rao, C. R., 609, 610, 615
Ratkowsky, D. A., 251
Raudenbush, S. W., 148, 537, 544, 545, 546, 560, 563, 564, 566, 607
Rawlings, 252
Reich, J. W., 411
Reichardt, C. S., 351, 571
Reinsel, G. C., 149, 600
Reise, S. P., 130
Reno, R. R., 2
Richardson, T., 474
Rindskopf, D., 641
Robinson, W. S., 539, 595
Rohwer, G., 600
Rosenthal, R., 5, 152, 333, 456
Rosnow, R. L., 333, 456
Rothstein, H., 15, 604
Rousseeuw, P. J., 418, 419
Rovine, M. J., 602
Roy, S. N., 609, 610
Rozeboom, W. W., 50, 98, 609, 610
Rubin, D. B., 152, 339, 440, 445, 569

Ruppert, D., 251
Ryan, T. P., 237, 239, 248, 249, 252, 419, 427, 428, 513

S

Sagarin, B., 456
Sayer, A. G., 595
Schafer, J. L., 339
Scheines, R., 474
Schnabel, K. U., 607
Schreiber, T., 602
Seber, G. A., 252
Serlin, R. C., 304, 338
Shadish, W. R., 4, 351, 452–453, 456
Shafer, J. L., 445
Shapiro, S. S., 140
Shaw, E. C., 525, 526, 530, 531, 532
Sheather, S. J., 418
Shrout, P. E., 537, 538
Silverman, B. W., 114
Simonoff, J. S., 416
Singer, A. G., 600
Singer, J. D., 550, 563, 564, 565, 566, 599
Smith, H., 226
Snell, E. J., 502, 504
Snijders, T., 148, 537, 538, 541, 544, 545, 546, 566, 607
Spirtes, P., 474
Srikantan, K. S., 612
Stanley, J. C., 452
Staudte, R. J., 418, 419
Steiger, J. H., 5, 15
Stevens, J. P., 398, 415
Stevens, S. S., 7, 228
Stigler, S. M., 583
Stouthammer-Loeber, M., 431
Stroup, W. W., 566
Strycker, L. A., 595
Suits, D. B., 320
Swanson, M. R., 184, 188

T

Tabachnick, B. G., 428, 485
Tatsuoka, M. M., 4, 317, 485, 519
Taylor, B., 587
Taylor, J. L., 595
Tellegen, A., 602
Teresi, J., 470
Tibshirani, R., 195, 253
Tidwell, P. W., 239
Timm, N. H., 609, 610
Ting, K.-F., 470
Toothaker, L. E., 316, 327
Trembley, R. E.
Tu, Z. N., 103
Tukey, J. W., 12, 50, 97, 101, 102, 225, 245, 465
Turrisi, R., 283

Tutz, G., 479
Tzelgov, J., 78

V

Van Aelst, S., 418
Van den Burg, W., 610, 612
Van Kamen, W. B., 431
Velez, C. N., 470, 642
Velez, C. N. G., 642
Velicer, W. F., 602
Velleman, P. F., 391

W

Wainer, H., 34, 97
Wallston, B. S., 213
Wallston, K. A., 213
Wan, C. K., 275, 283
Wasserman, W., 197, 206, 516, 532
Weisberg, S., 116, 133, 398, 402, 418, 514
Welsch, R. E., 397, 402, 418
West, S. G., 2, 4, 155, 206, 207, 212, 213, 220, 291, 331, 351, 382, 411, 455, 456, 465, 543, 555, 558, 594, 595
Wherry, R. J., 616
White, H., 133
Wilcox, R. R., 102, 419
Wild, C., 248
Wild, C. J., 252
Wilk, M. B., 140
Wilkinson, L., 50, 91
Wilks, S. S., 610, 611
Willett, J. B., 599, 600
Wills, T. A., 285
Wilson, S., 485
Winer, B. J., 183, 184, 272, 291, 333
Winship, C., 309
Wiseman, F., 415
Wolfinger, R. D., 566, 607
Won, E. Y. T., 145
Wong, G. Y., 544
Wood, P., 602
Woodall, W. H., 399
Woodcock, R. W., 571
Woodhouse, G., 546, 566
Woodward, C. K., 2
Wright, S., 65, 457, 464

Y

Yang, M., 546, 566
Yates, F., 50, 243
Yerkes, R. M., 2
Yesavage, J. A., 595
Yule, G. E., 4

Z

Zevon, M. A., 602

Subject Index

A

Abbreviations, 683–686
Added variable plot (AVP), 127–129
Additive effects
  in hierarchical analysis, 167–168
  in set correlation, 611–613, 616–617
  vs interactive effects, 258–260
Additive variance, proportions of
  $(T_{Y.X}^2 P_{Y.X}^2)$, 611–613, 616–617
Additivity, 260
Adjusted means, calculating
  for combined nominal and quantitative
    independent variables, 344–348
  for more than two groups, 348–350
  for nominal independent variables,
    343–344
Aggregated analysis, of clustered data,
  539, 542–543
Akaike's Information Criterion (AIC),
  509
Alpha inflation, 537
Alternative regression models
  dichotomous outcomes and, 483–484
  generalized linear *See* Generalized
    linear model
  logistic regression (*See* Logistic
    regression)
  ordinary least squares *See* Ordinary
    least squares regression
  Poisson regression (*See* Poisson
    regression)
Analysis of covariance (ANCOVA)
  assumptions, 350–351
  causal analysis and, 452–454
  effect sizes, 5
  historical background, 1, 4
  multivariate, 609
  multiple regression and, 350–351
Analysis of variance (ANOVA)
  effect sizes, 5
  fixed, 551*n*
  historical background, 1, 4

interpreting interactions in, 272
multivariate, *vs.* set correlation
  analysis, 609, 619–620
one-way, dummy-variable, 317–319
random effects, 552*n*
repeated measure, 573–578
  multiple error terms in, 574–575
  trend analysis, 575–576
  in which time is not the issue,
    576–578
  trend analysis, orthogonal polynomial
    regression and, 219
  Type I error rate, 296
ANCOVA. *See* Analysis of covariance
ANOVA. *See* Analysis of variance
  (ANOVA)
Antagonistic, interference interactions,
  286
ARC, 116*n*
Arcine transformations, 240, 241
Association
  bipartial, between three sets, 625–627
  measures of
    multivariate, 610–613
    with two independent variables,
      69–75
  patterns, between one dependent and
    two independent variables, 75–79
  in set correlation analysis, 614
  strength of, 37–40
Assumptions
  of regression model (OLS), 41–42,
    117–124
  of generalized linear model, 480–481,
    534
  violations of, detection, 125–141
Attenuation
  correction for, 56, 144–145
  due to measurement error, 55–56,
    121–124
  due to range restriction, 57–59
  latent variable models and 473–474

Augmentation (synergy), 10, 257, 285
Autocorrelation, 136–137, 149
Average effect (main effect)
  in 2 by 2 design, 355–356
  with three nominal scales, 367–371
Average regression, 261–262
AVP (added variable plot), 127–129

B

β. *See* Beta coefficient
B_0 (regression intercept)
  confidence interval, 44
  definition of, 34, 41
  estimation, precision of, 51
  null hypothesis test, 49
Ballantine
  semipartial correlation and, 72
  with one IV, 38–39
  with two IVs, 72–74
  with sets of IVs, 166–170, 192
Bandwidth distance, 106, 108
Base group, 321–322, 328–330
Bayesian Information Criterion (BIC),
  509
B_B (between class regression
  coefficient), 539
B coefficient (regression coefficient)
  for one IV, 33–34
  for two IVs, 66–69
  for k IVs, 79–82
  for variables in sets, 169–170
Behavioral science
  complexity, 6–10
    conditional relationships and,
      9–10
    correlation among research factors,
      6–7
    form of information and, 7–8
    general relationships and, 9–10
    multiplicity of influences and, 6
    partialing, 7
    shape of relationship and, 8–9

Behavioral science (Cont.)
  MRC applications, 3
  spectrum of, 16
Best linear unbiased estimator (BLUE),
  124–125
Beta coefficient (β) (standardized
    regression coefficient) *See also B*
    coefficient
  confidence intervals, 86–87
  nominal scale interaction variables
    and, 374
  standard errors, 86–87
  for variables in sets, 169–170
Between-class regression coefficient
  (B_B), 539
Bias
  definition of, 117, 124
  potential, omission of independent
    variables and, 143–144
BIC (Bayesian Information Criterion),
  509
Binary variables. *See* Dichotomous
    outcomes, Discriminant analysis,
    Logistic Regression
  coding as independent variable,
    302–331
    dummy codes, 305
    unweighted effects codes, 322
    weighted effects codes, 329
Binomial distribution, 482
Bipartial association, between three sets,
  625–627
Biserial *r*, 55–56
Bisquare weight function, 107, 114
Bivariate relationships
  asymmetric correlation
    regression coefficient for estimating
      Y from *X*, 32–36
    regression toward the mean, 36–37
  symmetric correlation
    graphical representations, 19–23
    index of linear correlation, 23–28
    perfect negative, 27
    perfect positive, 26–27
    product moment correlation
      coefficient, 28–32
    regression coefficients, 32–36
    tabular representations, 19–23
BLUE (best linear unbiased estimator),
  124–125
Bounded influence estimators, 418
"Box and whiskers" plot, 108
Box–Cox transformation of *Y*, 236–238,
  246, 249
Boxplot, 108
Box-Tidwell transformation of *X*,
  239–240
Breusch Pagan test (homoscedasticity),
  133
Bulging rule, 234–235, 251
B_{YX}. *See* Regression coefficients, of *Y*
  on *X*

C

Canonical analysis, 609–610
Case statistics, 394
Casewise plots (index plots), 134–136

Categorical variable interactions
  group differences
    with one nominal scale, 383–386
    with two or more nominal scales,
      386–388
  nominal scale, 388–389
    by continuous variable, 375–388
    group differences, 383–388
    by nominal scale, 354–366
    with two or more scales, 366–375
  with nonlinear effects of scaled
    independent variables, 383–386
Categorical variables *See also* Nominal
    variables
  coding schemes, 351–353
    comparison of, 352
    in context of other continuous IVs,
      342–351
    contrast coding (*See* Contrast
      coding scheme)
    dummy-variable coding (*See*
      Dummy-variable coding)
    nonsense coding, 341–342
    unweighted effects coding (*See*
      Unweighted effects coding)
    weighted effects coding, 328–332
  interactions (*See* Categorical variable
    interactions)
  representation of, 302–303
  as sets, 302
Causal effects
  indicated by regression coefficients,
    154
  inferring, empirical conditions for,
    454–455
  priority, removal of confounding
    variables and, 158–160
Causal models, 477–478
  analysis of covariance and, 452–454
  assumptions, 475–476
  comparisons of, 476–477
  diagrammatic representation of, 65
  identification, 468
  identification error, 475–476
  latent variable, 469–474
  longitudinal data in, 476–477
  nested, 476
  overidentification, 468–469
  partial, without reciprocal causation,
    466–467
  with reciprocal causation, 467–468
  regression models as, 459–460
  requirements, 64–65
  specification error, 475
  underidentification, 469
  variables in, 457–459
  without reciprocal causation, 460–467
    direct effects, 460–464
    hierarchical analysis, 465–466
    indirect effects, 460–464
    path analysis, 464–465
    path coefficients, 464–465
    reduced form equations, 465–466
    testing model elements, 467
Censoring, 596–599
Centering of predictors
  definition, 34, 201

  in multilevel modeling, 564–565
    around grand mean, 564, 565
    within context, 564–565
  in multiple regression
    interactions between continuous
      variables, 261–267
    in polynominal equations, 201–204
    nominal by continuous variable
      interactions, 375
  of regression equations
    highest order interactions in, 266
    with interactions, 261–267
    with no interaction, 262–267
    recomendations, 266–267
    simple slopes from, 271
Centering of *Y*, 266
  Y, uncentered, 266
Centroid, 261, 396, 403
Change and change (difference) scores,
  59–60
  and regressed change, 31, 570–571
  in survival analysis, 596–600
  in true scores, 589
CI. *See* Confidence intervals
Classification of cases, 516–519
  accuracy measures, 518
Clustering
  alpha inflation and, 537
  correction of, 148
  and OLS regression, 539
    aggregated analysis, 539, 541, 543
    disaggregated analysis, 539, 542
    difficulties with, 539
  in data sets, 536–538
  fixed effects approach, 541
  illustration of, 134
  intraclass correlation and, 537
  multilevel data and, 545
Coding schemes. *See also* specific
    coding schemes
  alternative, for more than two groups,
    348–350
  for missing datas in nominal scales,
    434–439
  in nominal scale interactions, 358–359
    confidence interval and, 359
    significance tests and, 359
  selection, 363
  for three nominal scales, 367–371
Coefficient alpha, 129
Cohen's Kappa, 517
Coefficient of alienation, 39, 41, 71
College GPA prediction, 3
Collinearity, exact, 419–420
Combination conditional relationships,
  10
Computation time, 14
Computer
  for computation, 14
  output, in statistical significance
    determination, 174
Conditional distribution of *Y*, 480
Conditional effects, 255, 259–260
Conditional mean of *Y*, 117–118
Conditional relationships, in behavioral
    science, 9–10
  interactions, 255

Condition number, 424

Confidence intervals (Cl)

for B, 43, 86–87

for B_0, 44

for bivariate r, 310–311

for B_{YX}, 42–44

for difference between correlations, 47

for difference between regression
    coefficients, 46–47

for difference between independent
    R^2s, 88

for estimated Y_i, value, 44–45

for logistic regression coefficients,
    497–498

for odds ratios, 497–498

for R^2, 88

for simple slopes, 279

margin of error, 42, 87, 278

in nominal scale interactions, coding
    scheme and, 359

in orthogonal polynomials, 216–218

in polynomial regression, 199

in stepwise regression, 161

for regression coefficients of dummy
    variables, 314–316

for r_{XY}, 45–46

for $r_{XYV} - r_{XYW}$, 47

for simple slopes, 274, 278

significance testing and, 15

Confidence limits, 43, 50. *See*
    Confidence intervals

Confounders

in causal models, 457, 477

in epidemiology, 78–79

removal, causal priority and, 158–160

Consistency, 124

Constant variance of residuals, 119–120

Contagion model, 532

Continuation-ratio model, 520

Continuous independent variables,
    coding with nominal variables,
    342–343

Continuous variable interactions,
    255–301

in centered equations, 264–266

conditional first-order effects and,
    259–260

crossover, 286–287

curvilinear by linear, 292–295

dichotomization strategy, 256

distinguishing, versus curvilinear
    effects, 299–300

with dummy-variable coded groups,
    375–378

equations with, 261

centered, 262–264

regression coefficients, 262

regression with centered predictors,
    261–262

highest order, in centered equations,
    266

interpreting

in ANOVA, 272

in multiple regression, 272

as joint effects, 257–259

multicollinearity, essential *vs.*
    nonessential, 264

nominal scale, 375–388

with nominal scales, 388–389

categorical with nonlinear effects of
    scaled independent variables,
    383–386

centering and, 375

contrast coding and, 379–380

dummy-variable coding and,
    375–378

of groups, simple slope estimates
    of, 380–383

unweighted effects codes and,
    378–379

weighted effects codes and,
    378–379

numerical example, 275–280

ordinal *vs.* disordinal, 286–290

as partialed effects, 284–285

patterns

buffering, 285–286

interference or antagonism, 286

synergistic or enhancing, 285

plotting, 269

post hoc probing, 272–282

confidence intervals around simple
    slopes, 274

equation dependence of simple
    slopes, 273

first-order coefficients, 281–282

interpretation, 282

numerical example, 275–280

range of data, 282

significance testing, 273

standard error of simple slopes,
    272–273

uncentered equation, 281

power to detect, 297

regression coefficient, 270–271

regression equations, simple, 267–272

of sets, 295–296

simple, 291

simple slopes (*See* Simple slopes, with
    continuous variable interactions)

standardized estimates, 282–284

three-predictor, 290–291

variable reliability, 297

vs. additive effects, 256–259

vs. curvilinear effects, 299–300

Contrast coding, 332–341, 353

B_i

confidence intervals, 339

significance tests, 339

choice of codes, power and,
    340–341

construction of, 333–337

for missing data in nominal scales, 436

nominal scale interactions and, 358,
    359, 379–380

Orthogonal polynomials, 214

partial correlations, 339

partial regression coefficients,
    337–339

R^2 and $\bar{R}^2$, 337

selection considerations, 332–333

semipartial correlations, 339

statistical power, 340–341

vs. other coding schemes, 352–353

Cook's D_i, 402–404, 409, 410

Cook-Weisberg test (homoscedasticity),
    133

Correct rejections (classification), 516

Correlation coefficients

multiple, for two independent
    variables, 69–71

partial, 74–75, 85

product moment (*See* Pearson product
    moment correlation coefficient)

statistical inference with, 41–50

assumptions, 41–42

confidence interval estimations,
    42–47

Correlation matrix, 115–116

Counts, 240, 245

Count dependent variables, 481–482,
    525–532

relation to predictors, 481–482

regression models for, 525–532

Covariance, 29, 549. *See also* Analysis
    of covariance

Cox and Snell index, 502, 504

Crossed interaction, 286, 355

Crossing points, of simple regression
    lines, 288–290

Cross-level interaction, 544, 553,
    554–555

interpreting, 558

simple slopes, 558–559

Cross-product, of z-scores, 282–284

Cross-validation, of prediction, 97–98

Cubic equation, 207–210

Cubic relationship, 197

Curvilinear by linear interactions,
    292–295

Curvilinear effects, *vs.* interactions,
    299–300

Curvilinear regression, 613

Curvilinear relationships, 194

detecting through graphical displays,
    198

examining, approaches for, 195–196

monotonic nonlinear
    transformations, 195

nonlinear regression, 195, 251–252,
    254

nonlinear transformations (*See*
    Nonlinear transformations)

nonparametric regression, 195,
    252–253, 254

polynomial regression (*See*
    Polynomial regression)

negative, 21–22

plots of, 205

positive, 21–22

prediction, 194

size of r and, 61

D

Data. *See also* Data analysis

clustered

analysis with ordinary least squares,
    539–543

analysis with random coefficient
    regression model, 550–553

Data (Cont.)
  level 1 or micro-level, 545
  level 2 or macro-level, 545
  meaningful aspect of, 553
  counted
    linear regression, 525–526
    models for (*See* Poisson regression)
  four-time-point, 573
  hierarchically structured, 545
  longitudinal, in causal models,
    476–477
  missing, 450–451
    incorporation as positive
      information, 613–614
    minimizing, 431–432
    in nominal scales, 434–442
    in quantitative scales, 440–450
    traditional approaches for, 433–435
    types of, 432–433
    variable timing and, 587–588
  multilevel
    experimental design as, 555–556
    random coefficient regression
      model and, 544–550
    structural equation model
      representation of (*See* Latent
      growth models)
  multiple episode, 599–600
  observed, within the range of,
    287–288
  repeated measures, multilevel
    modeling for, 566
  sets (*See* Sets)
  sparseness, 506, 516
  three-time-point, 573
  two-time-point
    analyses of, 569–573
    purposes in gathering, 569
  unbalanced, 587–588
Data analysis
  of data sets (*See* Sets)
  hierarchical (*See* Hierarchical
    analysis)
  statistical inference strategy, 182–190,
    192
    adaptation of Fisher's protected *t*
      test, 187–190
    controlling/balancing type I and II
      errors, 182–185
    "least is last" principle, 186–187
    "less is more" principle,
      185–186
  vs. statistical analysis, 12–13
Dependence of residuals
  characteristics of, 134–137
  correction of, 147–149
Dependent variables
  continuous, 19–477, 536–627
  counts, 481–482, 525–532
  dichotomous, 482–516
  ordered categories, 519–525
  multiple (*See* set correlation)
  nature of, 1
  patterns of association with two IVs,
    75–79
Deviance measures, 499–502
  model deviance, 502

null deviance, 501
  test of model deviance, 505
Deviance residuals, in logistic
  regression, 513–514, 515
Deviation scores, 29
$DFBETAS_{ij}$, 404–406
  guidelines for identifying outliers,
    405–406
$DFFIT_i$, 402
$DFFITS_i$, 402–404, 409–410
  guidelines for identifying outliers, 404
Dichotomous outcomes, 482–519
  (*See also* Logistic Regression, Profit
    Regression) relation to predictor,
    481–482
Dichotomy
  Phi coefficient and, 30–31
  z scores, 29–30
Difference score. *See* Change
Direct effects, between *Y* and two
    independent variables, 75–77
  causal models without reciprocal
    causation, 460–464
Disaggregated analysis, of clustered
    data, 539–543
Discrepancy (residuals), 398–402
  high values, guidelines for identifying
    outliers, 401–402
  residuals
    externally studentized, 399–401,
      402, 410
    test of largest residual, 401–402
    internally studentized, 398–399,
      402, 410
Discriminant analysis, 484–485
  assumptions 485
  discriminant function coefficients, 484
  discriminant function scores, 484
  linear discriminant function 484
Disordinal interactions, 286–290
Dispersion parameter, 530–531
Distance. *See* Discrepancy
Distribution of variables, bivariate,
    53–54
D_k (model deviance), 502
D_{null} (null deviance), 501
Dummy-variable coding. *See also*
    Dummy variables
  for disaggregated analysis of clustered
    data, 539–540, 543
  in groups, 303–307, 353
    continuous variable interactions
      and, 375–378
    without mutual exclusiveness, 320
  for missing data in nominal scales, 436
  nominal scale interactions and,
    358–359
  Pearson correlations with *Y*, 308–311
  vs. other coding schemes, 352
  reference group, choice of, 303–304
Dummy-variable-like coding systems,
    319
Dummy variables, 303–320
  clustering and, 148
  correlations among, 311
  multiple regression/correlation,
    317–319

one-way analysis of variance, 317–319
  partial correlation, 316
  regression coefficients, 312–316
    confidence intervals, 314–316
    graphical displays, 313–314
    significance tests, 314–316
    standardized, 316
  semipartial correlation, 316–317
  sets, multiple correlations with *Y*,
    311–312
Duncan test, Type I error risks, 183
Durbin-Watson test, 136–137
Dynamic system analysis, 602–604

E

Ecological fallacy, 539
Educational policy, hypothesis testing,
    2–3
Effects coding, 298, 320–332, 436
  interactions with, 378
  Unweighted effects coding, 320–328
  Weighted effects, 328–332 (*See also*
    Unweighted effects coding;
    Weighted effects coding)
Effect size (ES), 5, 182. *See also* Power
Efficiency, 124
Effort attribution, 368
Elasticity, 155–156
EM algorithm, for estimating missing
    datas, 440–442
Empirical Bayes estimates, 560–563,
    583, 588
Endogenous variables, 458–459
Epsilon squared (ϵ^2), 319
Error. *See* Measurement error
  causing outliers, 411–415
  identification, in causal models,
    475–476
  margin of, 43–44, 87, 274
  measurement, correction in
    independent variables, 144–145
  model 2 estimate of, 174–176
  multiple terms in repeated measure
    analysis of variance, 574–575
  standard (*See* Standard error)
    of estimate, 45
  structure
    for multilevel regression of
      individual changes over time,
      584–586
    of ordinary least squares regression,
      480
  Poisson regression analysis, 533
  type I, 182–185, 617
  type II, 182–185
  variance, of estimate, 39
ES (effect size), 5, 182
Essential multicollinearity, 202–203, 264
Estimation. *See also* Maximum
    Likelihood Estimation
  Ordinary least squares estimation, 124
Eta squared (η^2), 319
Event-history analysis, 600
Experimental design, as multilevel data
    structure, 555–556
Experimental psychology, hypothesis
    testing, 2–3

Experiments, orthogonal polynomial usage for, 220
Exponential decay, 230
Exponential growth model relationships, 229–231
Exponentiate the doubled coefficient, 511
Exponents, for nonlinear transformations, 223–225
Externally studentized residuals, 399–401

F

Factorial design
  2 by 2, 354–361
  4 by 3, 365–366
First-order effects
  conditional, continuous variable interactions and, 259–260
  patterns, 285–290
    buffering, 285–286
    in equations with interactions, 281
    interference or antagonistic, 286
    synergist or enhancing, 285
  vs. higher order effects, 259–260
Fisher's protected *t* test, 90, 184, 187–190
Fisher ζ transformation of *r*, 49–50, 240, 310, 644
Fit indices
  likelihoods and, 504
  significance testing, 504–519
Fixed effects
  multilevel data and, 544
  in multilevel modeling, 560
    statistical tests, 563
  regression analysis, 541
  variance components, 549–550
  vs. random coefficient model, 565–566
Fixed effects regression, 41–42, 544–545. *See* Ordinary least squares regression
Fixed linear regression model, 41–42, 544–545. *See* Ordinary least squares regression
Fixed parameters, 468
Fixed variables, multilevel data and, 544–545
Form of the relationship
  between independent and dependent variables, 117–119
  nonlinear, 142–143
  of IV and DV, 142
  between IV and DV and heteroscedasticity, 143
  between IV and DV and homoscedasticity, 142
  between IVs, 142
  theoretical predicted, 142
  violations
    remedial actions, 141–143
    detection of, 125–126
Free parameters, 468
Frequency histograms, 103–104
F test
  alternative, 174–176
  in hierarchial analysis, 172–173

for linear probability model, 484–485
on multiple and partial coefficients, 88–90
power analysis, 176–179
for sets, 171
in simultaneous analysis, 173–174
Functional sets, 163–164
F values, 646–649

G

Generalized linear model, 4, 479–481, 532–535
  link function, 534–535
  logistic regression, 479, 532–533
  Poisson regression, 479, 532–533
  relationship of dichotomous and count dependent variables *Y* to a predictor, 481–482
  variance function, 534
  for variance stabilization, 244
Generalized M-estimation, 418
Generalized variance, proportion of $(R^2_{Y.X})$, 610–611, 616–617
General relationships, in behavioral science, 9–10
Global measures of influence
  $DFBETAS_{ij}$, 404–406, 409, 410
  $DFFITS_i$ or Cook's D_i, 402–404, 409, 410
Goodman and Kruskal's λ, 518
Goodness-of-fit tests
  hierarchical logistic regression and, 508–509
  for latent variable models, 472–473
Graphical displays
  bivariate, 110–116
  correlation matrix, 115–116
  curvilinear relationship detection, 198
  of misspecification of form of relationship, 125–126
  of regression coefficients for dummy variables, 313–314
  of regression diagnostics in logistic regression, 514
  of relationships, 19–23, 101, 102
  scatterplot matrix, 115–116
  univariate, 103–110
    boxplot, 108
    comparison with normal distribution, 110
    frequency histograms, 103–104
    smoothing, 105–108
    stem and leaf display, 104–105
Greek letters, 686
Groups
  dummy-variable coding in, 303–307
  simple slopes of, interactions coded to estimate, 380–383

H

h_{ii} (leverage), 394–394
h^*_{ii} (centered leverage), 396–397
Hand calculation, of multiple regression/correlation problem, 636–642
Hazard function, 598
Health sciences, hypothesis testing, 2–3

Heteroscedasticity
  correction, 145–147
    weighted least-squares for, 146–147
  definition of, 120
  elimination, nonlinear transformations for, 221
  nonlinear relationship between IV and DV and, 143
  in Poisson regression analysis, 530
  of residuals, 130–132, 530
  treatment alternatives, 244–247
Hierarchical analysis
  causal models without reciprocal causation, 465–466
  of quantitative set, 623–625
  of sets
    characteristics of, 164–166, 191, 466–467
    F tests, 172–173
  variables, 158–162
    advantages, 158–159
Hierarchical linear models, 148, 158, 537, 544
Hierarchical regression, 158
Hierarchically structured data, 545
  micro-level, 545
  macro-level, 545
Higher order effects, *vs.* first-order effects, 259–260
Higher order variables, 494
Highest order term, 195, 204, 266
Hits (in classification), 516
Homoscedasticity. *See also* Heteroscedasticity
  definition of, 119–120
  detection, 130–132, 145–147
  nonlinear relationship between IV and DV and, 142
  ordinary least squares regression and, 480
  transformation to achieve, 221–223, 244–246
  weighted least squares and, 140–147
Hosmer and Lemeshow goodness of fit statistic, 506
Hot deck imputation, 444–445
Hyperbolic relationship, 231
Hypothesis testing
  ANOVA/ANCOVA and, 5
  examples, 2–3
  MRCA and, 5

I

ICC. *See* Intraclass correlation
Identification error, causal models, 475–476
Imputation
  hot deck, 444–445
  multiple, 445
  by ordinary least squares, 445–447
Increment in prediction (*See* Semipartial R^2)
Independence of residuals, 120
Independent variables (IVs)
  categorical or nominal, 302–303
  correct specification in regression model, 119, 143–149

Independent variables (IVs) (Cont.)
  dummy-variable coding (*See*
    Dummy-variable coding)
  exogenous, 65
  k, number of predictors, 79
    multiple regression/correlation
      with, 79–86
    statistical inference with, 86–90
  measurement error in, correction of,
    144–145
  nature of, 1
  no measurement error in, 119
  omitted, 127–129, 143–144
  relevant, inclusion of, 143–144
  sets (*See* Sets)
  time-varying, 595–596, 599
  two
    measures of association, 69–75
    patterns of association with one
      dependent variable, 75–79
    regression with, 66–69
Index of linear correlation, between two
  variables, 23–28
Index plots (casewise plots), of residuals,
  134–136
Index variables, size of *r* and, 60–61
Indirect effects, between *Y* and two
  independent variables, 75–79
  causal models without reciprocal
    causation, 460–464
Influence (*See* Outliers)
  in multiple regression, 402–406
  in logistic regression, 514
Interactions
  among continuous variables (*See*
    Continuous variable interactions)
  among sets of variables, 295–296
  with categorical variables (*See*
    Categorical variable interactions)
  definition of, 10, 255, 257
  logistic regression and, 494
  patterns of interactions, 285
  versus additive effects, 256
  between nominal variables, 388–389
    beta coefficient and, 374
    in multiple sets, 361–366
    mutual exclusiveness and, 373–374
    pr and, 374
    recommendations for, 374–375
    with three nominal scales, 366–372
    2 by 2 design, 354–361
    variance proportions and, 374
    in which not all combinations are
      considered, 372–373
Interference, continuous variable
  interactions and, 286
Internally studentized residuals, 398–399
Interrater reliability, 129–130
Interval scales, 8
Intraclass correlation (ICC)
  clustering and, 537
  estimating, 538
  unconditional cell means model and,
    551–552
Intraclass correlation coefficient, 134
Intrinsically linearizable, 226
Intrinsically nonlinear, 226

Inverse polynomial model, 231
Isolation of effects, establishing,
  alternative methods for, 455–456
Item response alternatives, as scale, 156
Iteration, 498
Iterative solutions, 251
IV. *See* Independent variables

J

Jittering, 111
Joint effect, 355–357

K

Kaplan-Meier function, 598
  Kappa, measure of agreement, 517
Kernel density estimate, 106–108, 111

L

LAD (least absolute deviation), 417
Ladder of re-expression, 233–234, 251
LaGrange multiplier test, 506
Latent growth models, 588–595
  estimation of changes in true scores,
    589
  representation in structural equation
    model diagrams, 589–594
Latent variable models. *See also*
    Structural equation models
  correction for attenuation, 473–474
  data sets, 474
  estimation
    fixed, 472
    free, 472
    methods for, 471–472
  example of, 469–471
  goodness-of-fit tests for, 472–473
Latent variables, 473–474
Least absolute deviation (LAD), 417
"Least is last" principle, 186–187
Least square criterion, 498
Least trimmed squares (LTS), 417–418
"Less is more" principle, 185–186, 190
Levene's *t** test, 133
Leverage
  in data checking, 398
  in detecting outliers, 394–398, 410
  high values, guidelines for identifying
    outliers, 397–398
  in logistic regression, 513
  Mahalanobis distance and, 398
  centered values, 396–397
Likelihood, 498, 500
Likelihood ratio, 501
Likelihood ratio test, 500, 501, 504–505,
    507
  individual predictor in logistic
    regression, 507
  set of predictors in logistic regression,
    508
0-line, 126
Linear by linear interaction, 271–272
Linear combination of predictors, 193
Linear conversion rule, 33
Linear discriminant function, 484
Linear in the coefficients, 480

Linear in the parameters, 193, 195, 480,
    534
Linear in the variables, 118, 194–195
Linearization of relationships, 225–244
  with correlations, 240
  for counts and proportions, 240–244
  intrinsically linear versus nonlinear
    relationships, 226
  nonlinear transformations for, 222
Linear probability model, 483–484
Linear regression
  characteristics, 117–124, 193–195
  for counted data, 525–526
  formula, 193–194
Linear relationships, 8–9, 193, 194
  negative, 20–21, 62
  positive, 19–20, 62
  weak positive, 22–23
Linear transformations, 25, 222
Link functions
  for generalized linear model, 534–535
  for predicting *Y* from time, 586–587
Listwise deletion, 433
LL, log likelihood, 500
Logarithmic transformation, 227–228,
    232, 245
Logarithms
  linearizing relationships based on,
    227–228, 232
  for nonlinear transformations,
    223–225
Logistic function, 485
Logistic regression, 244, 486, 535
  classification of cases, 516–519
  confidence intervals, 497–498
  data sparseness, 516
  dichotomous, 520–522
  equation, 486–491
  equation forms, 487–488, 532
  estimation procedures, 533
  form of observed *Y* vs. predicted
    score, 533
  hierarchical, 508–509
  higher order variables, 494
  indices of overall fit, 499–502
  influence in, 514
  interactions and, 494
  interpretation of coefficients, 533
  leverage in, 513
  logit, 490–491
  multiple, 493–494
    numerical example, 494–496
    significance testing of single
      predictor, 507–508
  multiple *R²* analogs, 502–504
  nested dichotomous, 520–522
  vs. ordinal logistic regression, 524
  odds 490
    odds ratio, 492–493, 497–498
  ordinal, 522–525
  parallels with Poisson regression,
    532–533
  polytomous, 519–520
  predicted score, 490–491
    logit, 490
    odds, 490
    probability, 490

predictor, coefficients, for, 492–493
regression coefficients, 497
regression diagnostics in, 512–513
residuals in, 513–514, 515
scaling predictors, 510–512
significance tests, 504–508, 533
individual predictors, 507
model fit, 504
sets of predictors, 508
standardized coefficients, 512
Logistic transformation, 485–486
Logit transformations, 240, 243–244, 650–651
Longitudinal regression analysis methods, 605–607
power analysis in, 604–605
research questions, 605–607
Lower order term, 195, 217
Lowess lines, 111–114, 198, 207
and nonparametric regression, 252
LTS (least trimmed squares), 417–418
"Lurking variables," 134

M

Mahalanobis distance, 398
Main effect
in 2 by 2 design, 355–356
with three nominal scales, 367–371
MANCOVA (multivariate analysis of covariance), 609
Manifest variables, 470
MANOVA (multivariate analysis of variance), 609
MAPV (multivariate analysis of partial variance), 622–623
Margin of error (*me*), 43–44, 87, 274. *See* Confidence intervals
Mathematical basis, for multiple regression/correlation, 631–635
Mathematical procedures, 11
Maximum Likelihood, 500
Maximum likelihood estimation, 468–469, 498–499, 500–501
of λ, 238
linearization and, 238
method, 468–469, 498–499
of regression model, 498–499
Means
simple comparisons between, 183–184
unweighted vs weighted, 320–321
Mean substitution, for missing data in nominal scales, 437–439
Measurement
error, 129–130
correction, in independent variables, 144–145
effects in two-predictor regression, 121–124
model, for latent variables, 471–472
scores with zero and maximum defined, 156
units, comparable, standard scoring and, 23–26
Measurement units, with conventionally shared meaning, 155
Measures of association
multivariate, 610–613
with two independent variables, 69–75

Mediators, 457
M-estimation, 418
Missed-data correlation matrix, 433–434
Misspecification, 119–120, 125–130. *See also* Specification error
Mixed model equation, 545, 548
Mixed model regression, 555–556
Mixed Poisson models, 531
Model adequacy tests, 506
Model deviance (D_k), 502
Model deviance test, 505–506
Model 2 error estimate, in significance testing, 174–176
Model fit
assessment of, 231
measuring and comparing, nonlinear transformation for, 248
Moderators, 269, 458
Modified Levene test, 133
Monotonic nonlinear transformations, 195
MRC. *See* Multiple regression/correlation analysis
Multicollinearity
definition of, 390–391
measures of, 422–425
essential *vs.* nonessential, 202–203
continuous variable interactions and, 264
exact collinearity and, 419–420
interpretation, 98–99, 420–422
numerical illustration, 420–422
remedies for, 425–430
collection of additional data, 427
model respecification, 426–427
principal components regression, 428–429
ridge regression, 427–428
sampling stability and, 99, 420–422
Multilevel data, 544
Multilevel models for clustered data, 148, 537, 544
centering, 564–565
empirical Bayes estimates, 560–563
level 1 equation, 546
level 2 equation, 547
intercept, 547
slope, 547
mixed model equation, 548
numerical example, 556–560
parameters of model, 550
parameter estimation, 560–563
with predictor at level 2, 553–555
random effects, 560
random intercept model, 550
for repeated measures data, 566
same variable at two levels, 564
sources on, 566
specification issues, 564–565
statistical power of, 565
statistical tests, 552–553, 560
unconditional cell means model, 551
variance components, 548–549, 555, 560, 563
Multilevel models of individual changes over time, 578–588
centering, 580

Empirical Bayes estimates, 583
adding other fixed predictors in, 582
alternative developmental models, 584–586
alternative link functions for predicting *Y* from time, 586–587
error structures, 584–586
individual differences in variation around individual slopes, 583–584
patterns in, 578–582
unbalanced data and, 587–588
vs. structural equation model analysis of change, 594–595
Multinomial logistic regression, 519
Multiple analysis of variance (MANOVA), set correlation analysis, 619–620
Multiple correlation coefficients, for two independent variables, 69–71
Multiple imputation, 445
Multiple linear regression, assumptions, 149–150
correction of violations, 141–149
description of, 117–124
detection of violations, 125–141
Multiple logistic regression, 493–496
Multiple *R*, 69–71, 82–83
Multiple regression/correlation analysis (MRC). *See also* Specific applications
dummy-variable, 317–319
hierarchical analysis variables, 158–162
historical background, 4–5
with *k* independent variables, 79–86
models, theories and, 454–456
with nominal independent variables, 350–351
overview, 1–2
statistical inference strategy, 182–190
with two or more independent variables, causal analysis, 64–65
vs. analysis of variance approaches, 4–5
Multivariate analysis of covariance (MANCOVA), 609
Multivariate analysis of partial variance (MAPV), 622–623
Multivariate analysis of variance (MANOVA), 609
Multivariate association measures, 610–613

N

n*
determination for *F* test, 177–179
different, reconciliation of, 180–181
setting power for, 180
n (number of subjects), power as function of, 181
Nagelkerke index, 503
Natural logarithms, 224
Natural polynomials, 216
Negative binomial regression model, 531

Nested dichotomies
  logistic regression, 520–522
  versus ordinal logistic regression, 524
  versus OLS regression, 524
Net regression method, 157
Newman-Keuls test, Type I error risks, 183
NHSTs. *See* Null hypothesis significance tests
Nominal scales, 8, 302–303
  categories, representation of specified contrast in, 613
  by continuous variable interactions, 375–388
  interactions (*See* Interactions, between nominal variables)
    with continuous variables (*See* Continuous variable interactions, with nominal scales)
  missing data in, 434–442
    coding for, 434–439
    estimation using EM algorithm, 440–442
    on two dichotomies, 439–440
  three, coded by alternative methods, 367–371
Nominal variables. *See also* Categorical variables
  coding schemes, 351–353
    comparison of, 352
    in context of other continuous variables, 342–351
    contrast (*See* Contrast coding)
    dummy-variable (*See* Dummy-variable coding)
    unweighted effects (*See* Unweighted effects coding)
    weighted effects (*See* Weighted effects coding)
  groups, dummy-variable coding in, 303–307
  independent
    ANCOVA, 350–351
    calculating adjusted means for, 343–344
    multiple regression/correlation, 350–351
    with quantitative variables, calculating adjusted means for, 344–348
  interactions, 354–366
  nonsense coding, 341–342
  2 by 2 design, 354–361
  unweighted effects coding (*See* Unweighted effects coding)
  weighted effects coding, 328–332
Nonconstant variance, statistical tests of, 133, 145–147 (*See also* Homoscedasticity, Heteroscedasticity)
Nonessential multicollinearity, 202–203
  continuous variable interactions and, 264
Nonindependence of residuals
  characteristics, 134–137
  correction of, 147–149
Nonlinear probability model, 485

Nonlinear regression, 195, 226, 251, 254
Nonlinear relationships, multiple regression approaches, 8–9, 193, 195–196
  detection of, 125–127
  monotonic nonlinear transformations, 195, 222
  nonlinear regression, 195
  nonparametric regression, 195
  polynomial regression, 195
Nonlinear transformations, 195, 253
  arcine, 240, 241
  Box-Cox procedure, 236–238
  Box-Tidwell procedure, 239
  choice of, 249–251
  conceptual basis, 223
  diagnostics, 247
  empirically driven
    in absence of strong or weak models, 233
    for linearization, 233–240
  exponents, 223–225
  indications for, 249–251
  for correlations, 240
  for linearizing relationships, 225, 244
    based on strong theoretical models, 227–231
    based on weak theoretical models, 231
    intrinsically linearizable relationship, 225–227
  logarithms, 223–225
  logit, 240, 243–244
  model checking, 223
  model fit, measuring and comparing, 231, 248
  monotonic, 195, 222
  nature of, 221–223
  to normalize variables, 246–247
  one-bend, linearizing, 234, 235
  power, 235
  from predictor to predicted scores, 485–486
  probit, 240, 241–243
  for proportions, 240–244
  proportional relationships, 223–225
  purposes of, 221–223
  in regression, sources on, 251
  two-bend, 240
  variable range, 235
  for variance stabilization, 244–246
  when to transform, 223, 249
Nonorthogonal comparisons, 184–185
Nonparametric regression, 195, 252–253, 254
Nonsense coding, 341–342, 352, 353
Normal distribution, 46, 110, 645
Normality of residuals, 120, 137–141, 222
  tests of 137–141
Normalization, of ranks, 247
Normalizing transformations of proportions (probit transformations), 240, 241–243
Notation, 17
Null deviance (D_{null}), 501

Null hypothesis significance tests (NHSTs), 5, 15, 47–50
  for B_0, 49
  for B_{YX}, 48
  confidence limits and, 50
  for difference between two correlations with Y, 49–50
  parameters, 52
  power of, 51–53
  research goals and, 90–91
  for r_{XY}, 49
  in set correlation analysis, 615–616
  for sets, 171
Number of cases required to produce the desired statistic, 654
Number of subjects (n)
  power as function of, 181
  unequal, orthogonal polynomials and, 220–221
Numerical results, 14–15

O

Observations, independence of, 532
Odds, 486, 490
Odds ratio, 492–493
  interpretation, 509–512
  logistic regression, 497–498
OLS. *See* Ordinary least squares regression
Omitted independent variable, 127–129
  remedies 143–144
One-bend transformations, 234, 235
Optimal design, power to detect interactions and, 298–299
Ordered category methods, *vs.* ordinary least squares regression, 524–525
Ordered variance partitioning procedure, 158–159
Ordinal interactions, 286–290, 355
Ordinal logistic regression, 522–525
Ordinal scales, 8
Ordinary least squares regression (OLS), 37, 40, 124–125, 474, 479, 535, 567
  analysis of clustered data, 539–543
  assumptions, 117
  characteristics of, 479–480
  data clustering in, 537
  estimation, 124
  imputation by, 445–447
  link function, 534
  multilevel data and, 544
  variance components, 549–550
  vs. ordered category methods, 524–525
  vs. set correlation analysis, 609
Orthogonal comparisons, 184
Orthogonal polynomials, 214–222, 253
  applications, 215–216, 220–221
  approaches, selection of, 219
  characteristics, 214–215
  cubic example, 216–219
    confidence intervals, 216–218
    tests of significance, 216–218
  intervals, unequal, 219–220
  power, 218
  residual variance, 218

trend analysis in ANOVA, 219
unequal n, 219–220
Outliers, 102, 110, 391–419, 430
  contaminated observations, 411–412
  definition of, 390
  detection, 394–411, 409–411,
    415–417
    by diagnostic statistics, 406–409,
      411
    in interaction or polynomial terms,
      410–411
    of clumps of outliers, 415–417
    of extremity on dependent variable,
      398
    of extremity on independent
      variable, 394–398
    by global measures of influence,
      402–406, 409, 410
  illustration of measures, 212, 391, 394
  measures
    discrepancy (distance), 398
    Influence, 402
    leverage, 394
  rare cases, 412–413
  remedial actions for, 415–419
    respecification and transformation,
      417
    robust approaches, 417–419
  sources, 411–415
  suggestions for detecting, 409–411
Overdispersion, 530–531
  dispersion parameter, 530
  overdispersed Poisson model, 531
  negative binomial regression, 531
Overdispersed Poisson model, 531
Overplotting, 108

P

Pair-wise deletion, 433–434
Parallel regression, 523
Parameters, 42
  dispersion, 530–531
  fixed, 468
  free, 468
  linearity in, 195
  of random coefficient regression
    model, 550
Partial coefficients
  correlation, 74–75, 85, 153, 316
  regression, 66–69, 80–82, 169
  regression with interactions, 284–285
  R^2, 168–169
Partial correlation, 153, 316
Partial correlation coefficients, 74–75, 85
Partialing, in set correlation, 613–614
Partial R^2, 168–169
Partial regression coefficients, 66–69,
  493
  causal effects indicated by, 154
  for highest order predictor in full
    polynomial equation, 203
  for k independent variables, 80–82
  standardized, 82
Partial regression leverage plot (added
  variable plot), 127–129
Partial relationships, in behavioral
  science, 7

Partialing
  meaning of, 7, 85–86, 154
  in hierarchical regression analysis,
    158–160
  in polynomial regression, 200
  of main effects for interaction terms,
    284–285
  in set correlation, 613–614
Part-whole correlations, size of r and,
  59–60
Path analysis, causal models without
  reciprocal causation, 464–465
Path coefficients, causal models without
  reciprocal causation, 464–465
Patterns of association, between one
  dependent and two independent
  variables
  direct effects, 75–76
  indirect effects, 75–76, 78–79
  partial redundancy, 76–77
  spurious effects, 78–79
  suppression in regression models,
    77–78
Pearson product moment correlation
  coefficient (r)
  formulas
    as average product of z scores, 28,
      62
    as function of differences between z
      scores, 28
    Phi coefficient, 30–31
    point biserial, 29–30
    rank correlation, 31–32
    for raw score, 29
  properties of, 28
  size, factors affecting, 53–62, 63
    curvilinear relationships, 61
    distribution of X and Y, 53–55
    part-whole correlations, 59–60
    ratio or index variables, 60–61
    reliability of variables, 55–57
    restriction of range, 57–59
Pearson residuals, in logistic regression,
  515
Pearson χ^2, 506
Percent of maximum possible scores
  (POMP scores), 156
Phi coefficient (ϕ), 30–31
Point biserial r formulas, 29–30
Point estimate, 50
Poisson probability distribution, 526–528
  rate parameter, 526
Poisson regression analysis, 244,
  528–530, 535
  error structure, 533
  estimation procedures, 533
  form of observed Y vs. predicted
    score, 533
  interpretation of coefficients, 533
  overdispersed, 531
  parallels with logistic regression,
    532–533
  significance tests, 533
  sources on, 532
  vs. transformed Y, 526
Polynomial regression, 194, 195
  equations, 195, 198

  build-up procedure, 210–211
  centering predictors in, 201–204
  change in $\bar{R}^2$, 211–212
  complex, 213–214
  conditional effects, 200–201
  instability, 212–213
  optimal design, 213
  outlier impact on stability, 212–213
  predictors, centering of, 204
  quadratic (*See* Quadratic equations)
  sampling impact on stability,
    212–213
  simple slopes, 206–207, 210
  statistical significance
  structuring, 200, 210
  tear-down procedure, 210–211
  examples
    cubic fit, 207–209
    quadratic fit, 198–201
  extrapolation, 207
  interpretation of results, 205–207
    warnings about, 207
  limitations, 209–213
  maximum
    for cubic equation, 210
    for quadratic equation, 205–206
  minimum
    for cubic equation, 210
    for quadratic equation, 205–206
  order, 209–213
  orthogonal (*See* Orthogonal
    polynomials)
  power polynomials, 195–214, 253
    method, 195–198
    order of, 197–198
    quadratic fit, 198–199
    second-order, 248–249
    strategy, 209–213
Polytomous logistic regression, 519–520
Pooled within-class regression
  coefficient, 540–541
Populations R^2 values, estimating,
  179–180
Post hoc comparisons, 184–185
Power
  analysis, 15
    in longitudinal analysis, 604–605
    partial coefficients, 94–95
    R^2, 92–93
    in set correlation analysis, 617–619
    for sets, 176–182
    of significance test, 652–653
    tactics of, 182
  of contrast coding scheme, 340–341
  to detect interactions, 297
    optimal design and, 298–299
  as function of n, 181
  linearizing relationships based on,
    228–229
  of multilevel modeling, 565
  of orthogonal polynomials, 218
Power functions, 234
Power polynomials, 196–214
Power relationships, 228
Power transformations, 233–240,
  245–246

pr, nominal scale interaction variables and, 374
pr^2, for k independent variables, 85
Precision, 91. *See also* Confidence internal, Power.
of estimation, 50–51
partial coefficients, 93–94
R^2, 91–92
Predicted probability, 486
Predicted score, forms of, 490–491
Prediction
cross-validation of, 97–98
equation, 79–80
models, 3
multicollinearity, 98–99, 425
net contributions, 152
using multiple regression equations in, 95–99
utility, comparisons of, 152–153
values, correlation with individual variables, 96
weighted composites in, 97–98
of Y for new observation, 95–96
Predictors
centering in polynomial regression equations, 201–204
continuous, scaling, treachery in, 511–512
dichotomous, scaling of, 510–511
Principal components regression, 428–429
Probability, 15
Probit function, 485
Probit regression, 486
Probit transformations, 240, 241–243, 485–486
Product moment correlation, 26–28. *See also* Pearson product moment correlation coefficient
Proportional odds model, 523
Proportions, 240
for nonlinear transformations, 223–225
variance stabilization of, 246
Protected t test. *See* Fisher's protected t test
Protective factors, 285
Pseudo-R^2's, 502
$P^2_{Y.X}$ (proportion of additive variance), 611–613, 616–617

Q

q-q plot, normal, 137–141, 314
Quadratic equations
centered, 204
maximum for, 205–206
minimum for, 205–206
Quantitative independent variables. *See* Categorical variables, Nominal variables.
Quantitative independent variables with nominal variables, calculating adjusted means for, 344–348
Quantitative scales, 163, 193
linear (*See* Linear relationships)
missing data in, 440–450

alternative methods, illustration of, 447–450
available alternatives, 440–444
imputation of values for missing cases, 444–447
modeling solutions for, 447
rules of thumb for, 450
nonlinear (*See* Nonlinear relationships)
types, 7–8
Quasi-likelihood models, 531

R

r. *See* Pearson product moment correlation coefficient
R^2, 69–71
confidence intervals, 88
increments to, 72–74
for k independent variables, 82–83
partial, 168–169
power analysis, 92–93
precision, 91–92
semipartial, 167–168
Random coefficient regression model, 148, 537, 543–544
analysis of clustered data, 550–553
fixed effects, 550
fixed part, testing of, 552–553
level 1 equations, 546–547
level 2 equations, 547
mixed equations, 548
multilevel data structure and, 544–550
random effects, 550
random part, testing of, 552–553
variance components, 548–549
vs. fixed effects model, 565–566
Random effects, 550
Random intercept model, 550
Random variables, multilevel data and, 544–545
Range restriction, size of r and, 57–59
Rank correlation, product moment correlation formula, 31–32
Ranks, normalization of, 247
Rate variables
size of r and, 57–59
reciprocal transformation and rates, 232
Ratio scales, 7–8
Ratio variables, size of r and, 60–61
Raw score formulas, for r, 29
Reciprocal effects, 157
Reciprocal transformation, 245
linearizing relationships and, 232
Rectilinear relationships. *See* Linear relationships
Redundancy
complete, 79
two-variable, 76–77
Re-expression. *See* Linear transformations, Nonlinear transformations
Regressed change, *vs.* change, 570–571
Regression coefficients
causal effects indicated by, 154, 459
in centered equations, 262

in centered *vs.* uncentered polynomial regressions, 204
continuous variable interactions, 270–271
difference between $B_{ry_v} - B_{xy_w}$, confidence interval for, 46–47
for dummy variables, 312–316
confidence intervals, 314–316
graphical displays, 313–314
significance tests, 314–316
standardized, 316
logistic regression, 497
standardized, 512
statistical inference with, 41–50
assumptions, 41–42
confidence interval estimations, 42–47
in uncentered equations, 262
in unweighted effects coding, 325–327
of Y on independent variable. *See B* coefficient
of Y on X, 32–36, 41, 63
alternative approaches in making sustantively meaningful, 154–157
confidence interval, 42–44, 48
estimation, precision of, 51
null hypothesis test, 48
sampling distribution, 42
standard error, 42
Regression diagnostics. *See* Outliers
in logistic regression, 512–515
in multiple regression, 394–410
leverage, 394
discrepancy (distance), 398
influence, 402
location of outliers and, 406–409
suggestions for interpretation, 409–411
Regression equations
centered (*See* Centering, of regression equations)
with interactions
building, 284–285
standardized solution for, 282–284
simple, with continuous variable interactions, 267–272
Regression intercept. *See* B_0
Regression lines, crossing points of, 288–290
Regression models
alternative
for four-time-point data, 573
for three-time-point data, 573
for two-time-point data, 571–573
as causal models, 459–460
correct specification of independent variables in, 119
estimation, by maximum likelihood, 498–499
suppression in, 77–78
Regression plane, 118, 257–259
Regression residuals, 40
Regression toward the mean, 36–37
Relationships. *See also* Specific relationships
linearization of
with correlations, 240

for counts and proportions, 240–244
  nonlinear transformations for, 222
simplifying, nonlinear transformations
  for, 221
Reliability. *See* Measurement error
  measure of, 129–130
  of variables (r_{xx}), 55–57
Repeated measure analysis of variance,
  573–578
  multiple error terms in, 574–575
  trend analysis, 575–576
  in which time is not the issue, 576–578
Reporting, 14–15
Representation of uncertainty, 445
Research
  factors, 162–163
    correlation among, 6–7
    interactions, 613
    significance tests, 362–363
    statistical control of, 613
  goals, null hypothesis and, 90–91
  questions
    answered by B or β, 154–157, 191
    answered by correlations and their
      squares, 151–154, 191
    for longitudinal regression analysis,
      605–607
    relevance, 160
Residual Scatterplot, 126–127, 130–132
Residuals, 45
  with one independent variable, 39–40
  with k independent variables, 79
  casewise plots, 134–136
  constant variance of, 119–120
  dependence
    characteristics of, 134–137
    correction of, 147–149
  deviance residuals, 513–515
  externally studentized, 399–401, 402,
    410, 514
  heteroscedasticity of, 130–132
  homoscedasticity of, 130–132
  independence of, 120
  index plots of, 134–136
  internally studentized, 398–399, 402,
    410
  in logistic regression, 513–514, 515
  nonconstant variance
    correction of, 145–147
    magnitude, determination of, 146
  normality of, 120, 137–141, 222–223
  normalizing, nonlinear
    transformations for, 221–222
  Pearson residuals, 513–515
  scatterplots of, 198
Residual variance, 39, 218
Ridge regression, 427–428
Right censoring, 597–598
Risk factors, 285
Robust regression methods, 417–418
  recommendations, 418–419
Robustness, 41
Rounding, 14–15
R^2s, two independent, differences
  between, confidence intervals for,
  88
r_s (Spearman rank correlation), 31–32

Running average, 105–106
$r^2_{x_i x_i}$, 422–423
r_{xx} (reliability of variables), 55–57
r_{xy}, 41
  confidence interval, 45–46
  null hypothesis test, 49
$R^2_{Y,X}$ (proportion of generalized
  variance), 610–611, 616–617

S

Sampling
  from continuum, orthogonal
    polynomial usage for, 220
  designs, to enhance power to detect
    interaction, 298–299
  distribution, 42
  stability, multicollinearity and, 99
Scaled variable, correlation with
  dichotomous variable, 29–30
Scales
  interval, 8
  nominal (See Nominal scales)
  quantitative (See Quantitative scales)
  with true zero, 155–156
  using item response alternatives as,
    156
  using sample's standard deviation as,
    156–157
Scaling IVs, 154–157. *See also*
  Transformations, Centering
Scatterplot matrix, 96, 115–116
Scatterplots, 19–21, 110–114, 125–126,
  198
  of residuals, 125–126, 198
  detecting heteroscedasticity, 130–132
Scheffé test, 184–185
Score test, 506
  of parallel slopes, 524
  of proportional odds, 524
Scores
  true, estimation of changes in, 589
  with zero and maximum defined, 156
Semi-inter quartile range (SIQR), 108
Semi-parametric mixed Poisson
  regression, 531
Semipartial coefficients, interpretation,
  example of, 85–86
Semipartial correlation, for dummy
  variables, 316–317
Semipartial correlation coefficient (*sr*),
  for k independent variables,
  84–85
Semipartial correlation coefficients,
  72–74
Semipartial R^2, 167–168, 205
Sensitivity, 516
Sensitivity analysis, 144
Serial data without replication,
  orthogonal polynomial usage for,
  221
Serial dependency, 134, 148, 537
Set correlation analysis, 627–628
  canonical analysis and, 609–610
  elements of, 610
  illustrative examples, 621–627
    bipartial association between three
      sets, 625–627

hierarchical analysis of quantitative
  set, 623–625
multivariate analysis of partial
  variance, 622–623
whole association, 621–622
new analytical possibilities with,
  620–621
partialing in, 613–614
power analysis in, 617–619
properties, 608–609
statistical significance tests
  estimators of population $R^2_{Y,X}$, $T^2_{Y,X}$,
    and $P^2_{y,x}$, 616–617
  guarding against type I error
    inflation, 617
  null hypothesis, 615–616
types of associations in, 614
vs. multiple analysis of variance,
  619–620
Sets, 101
  alternative hierarchical sequences, 160
  ballantine for, 166, 192
  clustering in, 536–538
  difference of effects on two different
    outcomes, 157
  graphical displays, 101, 102–116
  hierarchical analysis of, 164–166, 192,
    466–467
  interactions of, 295–296
  of multiple nominal variables with
    more than two categories,
    regression analyses of, 361–366
  power analysis, 176–182
  significance testing for, 171–176, 192
  simultaneous analysis of, 164–166,
    192
  types of, 162–164
  unweighted, regression coefficients in,
    325–327
  variables in, B and β coefficients for,
    169–170
  variance proportions, 166–169
Shape of relationship, 8–9
Shrinkage estimates, 561 (*See* empirical
  Bayes, estimates)
Shrunken or adjusted R^2, for k
  independent variables, 83–84,
  312
Significance tests, 5, 15. *See also*
  Specific significance tests
  for bivariate r, 310–311
  of highest order coefficient and gain in
    prediction, 204–205
  logistic regression, 533
  in nominal scale interactions, coding
    scheme and, 359
  of polynomial terms, 204–205
  for orthogonal polynomials, 216–218
  of overall model fit, 504–519
  Poisson regression, 533
  for regression coefficients of dummy
    variables, 314–316
  of research factors, 362–363
  sample size, 176
  for semipartial R^2, 171–173, 211
  for sets, 171–176, 192, 508

Significance tests (Cont.)
  for simple slopes in simple regression equations, 267–272
  of single predictor, in multiple logistic regression, 507–508
Simple interactions, 291
Simple regression line, 268
Simple slopes, 206–207, 270–271, 380–383
  confidence interval, 279
  with continuous variable interactions, 270–271
    equation dependence of, 273
    significance testing, 273–277
    standard errors, 272–273, 277
  with cross-level interactions in multilevel models, 587–588
  cubic equation, 210
  of groups, interactions coded to estimate, 380–383
  polynomial equation, 206–207, 210
  quadratic equation, 206
Simultaneous analysis of sets
  F tests, 173–174
  method, 164–166, 191
Skew
  changes in, 234
  elimination, transformations for, 246–247
Slope of regression line, 34
Smoothing, 105–108
Smoothing window, 106, 108
Sociology, hypothesis testing, 2–3
Sparseness of data, 506, 516
Spearman rank correlation (r_s), 31–32, 62
Specification error, 13, 475. See also Misspecification
  and non-normality, 119
  and measurement error, 119
  and residual non-normality, 120
  and systematic residual variation, 125–126
Specification of Models. See also Misspecification
  of models with interactions, 257, 284–285, 290–295
    linear by linear interactions, 271–272
    three-way interactions, 291–292
    curvilinear by linear interactions, 295–298
  of polynomial regression models, 197, 200, 209–214
  of models with nominal variable interactions, 354–361, 363–366
  of models with nominal by continuous variable interactions, 375–382
Specificity, 516
Spurious relationship, of variable, 463
Squared correlations, 154
Square root transformation, 245
sr^2, for k independent variables, 84–85
Standard deviation, 24–25, 26, 156–157
Standard error. See also Confidence interval
  of B, univariate regression, 42

of B_0, univariate regression, 44
of B, multiple regression, 86
of estimate, 37–41, 45, 63
of r, 45
of R^2, 88
of simple slopes
of simple slopes (linear by linear interaction), 272–273
of difference between Bs, 46
of difference between rs, 47
of difference between independent R^2, 88
Standard scores. See z-scores
Started logs, 235
Started powers, 235
State dependence, 532
Statistic, 42
Statistical classification, of cases, in logistic regression, 516–519
Statistical inference, 604–605
  with k independent variables, 86–90
  with regression and correlation coefficients, 41–50, 63
    assumptions, 41–42
    confidence interval estimations, 42–47
    null hypothesis significance tests, 47–50
  stage of scientific investigation and, 190
  strategy, 182–190, 192
    adaptation of Fisher's protected t test, 187–190
    controlling/balancing type I and II errors, 182–185
    "least is last" principle, 186–187
    "less is more" principle, 185–186
Statistical power. See Power
Statistical precision. See Precision
Statistical significance, 52, 174
Statistical software, 14
Statistical tables, 15, 643–654
Statistical tests
  on multiple and partial coefficients, with k independent variables, 88–90
  of nonconstant variance, 133
Stem and leaf display, 104–105
Stepwise regression, 161–162
Strength of association, measures of, 37–40
Structural equation model analysis
  of change, vs. multilevel regression, 594–595
  diagrams, of latent growth models, 589–594
Structural equation models
  of causal effects, 474
  of latent growth, 589–595
  with latent variables, 471–474
Structural sets, 162–163
Student's t test statistic, 90, 643
  for bivariate f, 310
Sturgis' rule, 104n
Subjects
  dropping, 433–434
  multiple, time series analysis of, 602

Sums of squares
  type I, 362–363
  type II, 362–363
  type III, 362–363
Suppression, in regression models, 77–78, 457–458
Survival analysis, 596–600
Survival function, 598
Symbols, 683–686
Synergy (augmentation), 10, 255, 257, 285

T

Tabular representations of relationships, 19–23
Test-retest reliability, 129
Tetrachoric r, 56
Three-predictor interactions, 290–291
Time
  dependence of residuals and, 134
  effects, in time series analysis, 602
  individual changes in See Multilevel regression, of individual changes over time
  regression analysis, until outcome, 596–599
Time series analysis, 149, 321, 600–602
  applications, 601–602
  extension to multiple units or subjects, 602
  time effects in, 602
  units of observation, 601
Time-varying independent variables, 595–596, 599
Tolerance, 423–424
Total regression coefficient, 539
Trait attribution, 368
Transformations, 25–26, 141–143, 149, 221–251, 417 (See Linear transformations, nonlinear transformations)
  to linearize relationships 233–240
  to produce normal residuals 246–247
  to stabilize variances 244–246
Trend analysis and polynomial regression, 219
Transformed Y, vs. Poisson regression, 526
Trend analysis, in repeated measure analysis of variance, 575–576
Two-bend transformations, 240
2 by 2 design, 354–361
Type I errors of inference, 387
  and protected t tests, 90
  and shrunken R^2, 84
  balancing, controlling, 182–185
  in stepwise regression, 161
  in clustered data, 537
  in set correlation, 617
  rate of, 296, 537
Type II errors of inference. See also Power
  balancing, controlling, 182–185
$T_{Y,X}^2$ (proportion of additive variance), 611–613, 616–617

U

Uncentered regression equations, 281
  highest order interactions in, 266
  simple slopes from, 271
Unconditional cell means model,
  551–552
Unconditional relationships, in
  behavioral science, 9–10
Unequal *ns* and polynomial regression,
  219
  weighted versus unweighted effects
  coded, 321, 378
Unit weighting, 97–98
Unweighted effects coding, 320–328,
  353
  B_i
    confidence intervals for, 326–327
    significance tests for, 326–327
  construction of, 321–324
  for nominal scale interactions with
    continuous variables, 378–379
  partial correlations, 328
  Pearson correlations, 325
  R^2 and $\bar{R}^2$, 324–325
  regression coefficients, 325–327
  semipartial correlations, 328
  vs. other coding schemes, 352
  vs. weighted effects coding, 320–321,
    328

V

Validity, 55, 152
Variables. *See also* Dependent variables;
  Independent variables
  confounding (*See* Confounders)
  continuous, 54 *See also* Continuous
    variable interactions
  controlling statistical or partialing, 13
  dependent *See* Dependent variables
  dichotomous, correlation with scaled
    variable, 29–30
  dropping, 433
  dummy, 148

endogenous, 458–459
exogenous, 458
linearity in, 194–195
manifest, 470
mediators, 457
moderator, 269, 458
normalizing, nonlinear
  transformations for, 246–247
number of
  "least is last" principle, 186–187
  "less is more" principle, 185–186,
    190
  "purification" to its "uniqueness," 613
  quantitative or scaled, 54
  reliability of, 55–57
  scaled, correlation with dichotomous
    variable, 29–30
  sets of (*See* Sets)
  spurious relationship of, 463
  suppressor, 457–458
  third, attribution, in *XY* relationship,
    153
  two, reciprocal effects of, 157
Variable scaling, treachery in, 509–512
Variance components, 545, 555
  in multilevel modeling, 560
    statistical tests, 563
  in ordinary least squares regression,
    549–550
  in random coefficient regression
    model, 545, 548–549
Variance error of estimate, 39
Variance function, for generalized linear
  model, 534
Variance inflation factor, 423
Variance proportions
  for independent variable sets, 166–169
  nominal scale interaction variables
    and, 374
Variance stabilization
  Box-Cox transformation and, 246
    λ estimation, 245–246
  of proportions, 246
  transformation for, 244–245

weighted least squares regression for,
  246
Venn diagrams, 38

W

Wald tests, 506, 507–508
Weighted effects coding, 328–332, 353
  B_i
    confidence intervals, 331–332
    significance tests for, 331–332
  construction of, 328–330
  for nominal scale interactions with
    continuous variables,
    378–379
  R^2 and $\bar{R}^2$, 330
  regression coefficient, 331
  selection considerations, 328
  vs. other coding schemes, 352
  vs. unweighted effects coding,
    320–321
Weighted least-squares regression (WLS)
  for heteroscedasticity, 146–147
  for variance stabilization, 244, 246
  to adjust for group size, 309n
  in lowess, 114
"Within the range of the observed data,"
  287–288
WLS. *See* Weighted least-squares
  regression

X–Y

XY relationship
  third variable attribution, 153
  variables, variance proportions of, 153

Z

Zero-order coefficients, 66, 68
z prime (ζ) transformation of *r*, 45–47
z-scores, 23–26, 156–157
  average product of, 28
  cross-product, 282–284
  differences between, 26–28
z transformation of scores, 25